GIRLS
3

child development

ELIZABETH B. HURLOCK, PH.D.
Graduate School of Education
University of Pennsylvania

child
development

FOURTH EDITION

McGRAW-HILL BOOK COMPANY
New York, San Francisco, Toronto, London

child development

Library of Congress Catalog Card Number:
64–16846

31420

3 4 5 6 7 8 9 -JE- 11 10 9 8 7 6

*Cover and title-page photos, Standard Oil
Company (N.J.); half-title page photo, Lucia
Barooshian.*

To my daughters Daryl and Gail

Preface

The only justification for revising a textbook is to improve it as a teaching aid. In this, the fourth edition of a text which first appeared in 1942, it is hoped that the changes made have accomplished this aim. The changes fall into three major categories, each intended to increase the value of the text for the students who will learn from it and for those who are teaching the course.

The *first* and most obvious innovation is the updating of subject matter and illustrations. Since *Child Development* appeared in its first edition, there has been research in many areas which at that time were in their infancy or did not even exist. This revision includes much new research material, particularly in the areas of child-training methods, family relationships, emotional deprivation, levels of aspiration, under- and overachievement in school, social class differences in attitudes and values, and the effects of social mobility on personal and social adjustments. The updating of the text has not been limited to subject matter alone: Curves and graphs indicating important new statistics have been introduced to replace many which were outdated. Functional line drawings take the place of many photographs that appeared in the earlier editions.

The *second* major change has been in the method used to document the sources of the material used throughout the text. In order to avoid distractions and maintain reading continuity, I have used numbers enclosed in parentheses to refer the reader to the appropriate citation in the bibliography sections which follow each chapter. The inclusion of a complete bibliography for each chapter, rather than a general bibliography for the entire text, is also an innovation in this revision. In many cases, the bibliographic references are provided not so much to document statements based on widely accepted facts but more to tell the reader specifically where this material is available should he wish to pursue any particular subject further. Some of the books and articles listed in the bibliographies are not directly referred to in the text. Nevertheless, they have all been used either directly or indirectly as sources for material in the book.

The *third* major change in this edition has been the use of brief sections in each chapter, headed by such phrases as "Seriousness of," "Advantages of," "Disadvantages of," etc., in order to focus the reader's attention on the question: What does this section of material mean in terms of understanding the child and his development? It is hoped that this approach will prove helpful in directing the reader's attention to the application of research findings to the practical problems of the child's developmental pattern. In some cases, the interpretations given in these sections may not be totally acceptable to the reader. If, however, these sections serve as a challenge to independent thought and interpretation, their value will be increased all the more.

I am greatly indebted to my many professional colleagues, especially those who are members of the Division on Developmental Psychology of the American Psychological Association, for their suggestions and criticisms. I also extend my appreciation to those who have provided suggestions and criticisms based on their classroom experience with the earlier editions of this book. These suggestions and criticisms have been most helpful in planning this revision. Finally, I am greatly indebted to all who have graciously given their consent for the use of their material in this book.

Elizabeth B. Hurlock

Contents

Contents

child development

Until recently, the study of child development began at the time of the child's birth. Today, however, it is recognized that many things of great significance to postnatal development occur before birth. Limiting our study to the years after birth would be like coming into a play in the middle of the first act; we would not know what happened earlier to make the characters on the stage behave as they do.

So it is with the child. We must know what happens to a child before he is born to have a full appreciation of the pattern of his development after birth. Consequently, the study of child development now encompasses that span of time which begins with conception and extends to the period of adolescence.

1

PRINCIPLES OF DEVELOPMENT

MEANING OF DEVELOPMENT

Many people use the terms "growth" and "development" interchangeably. In reality they are different, though they are inseparable; neither takes place alone. Growth refers to *quantitative* changes—increase in size and structure. Not only does the child become larger physically, but there is also an increase in the size and structure of the internal organs and of the brain. As a result of the growth of the brain, the child has a greater capacity for learning, for remembering, and for reasoning. He grows mentally as well as physically.

Development, by contrast, refers to those changes which are *qualitative* in nature. It may be defined as a progressive series of orderly, coherent changes leading toward the goal of maturity. The term "progressive" as it is used here signifies that the changes are directional, that they lead forward rather than backward. The terms "orderly" and "coherent" suggest that there is a definite relationship between a given stage and the stages which have preceded or followed it. As Anderson has emphasized, "Nor is development merely a matter of adding inches to stature, or ability to ability; instead, it is a complex process of integrating many struc-

1

tures and functions" (7).* Because of this integration, each change is dependent upon what preceded it, and it, in turn, affects what will come after.

"Maturity" marks the end of growth and development. It is characterized by completion of structural changes and attainment of the capacity to function physically and mentally in a manner characteristic of the normal adult. While each change brings the child closer to the ultimate goal of maturity, it also serves as an indicator of what progress he is making along the way. The first permanent tooth, for example, may be regarded as a maturity indicator because it shows that the child is on the way to dental maturity. In some aspects of development, maturity of structure and function comes at a fairly early age, whereas in others it comes later. The sense organs, for example, are ready to function at the time of birth, but the sex organs do not reach maturity until adolescence.

Types of Change. The human being is never static. From the moment he is conceived to the time of his death, he is undergoing constant changes. At every age, some of these changes are just beginning, some are at their peak, and some are in the process of decline (111).

Different kinds of changes influence development in different ways. As Anderson has pointed out:

Growth and development are not merely changes in physical size or body proportions. Changes occur in almost every relation within and without the human being. For our present purpose, we may call attention to the increased range of objects and experiences to

* The numbers found throughout the text refer to the bibliography at the end of each chapter. In some instances, the references are to a specific study or statement made by another author; in others, they are given as a source of further information. When several numbers are given together, it means that several authors have reported similar results from their individual research studies. A number of studies are listed in the bibliography which are not directly referred to in the chapter but which have influenced the thinking of the author.

which the growing person responds; to his increased strength, speed and motor skill; to his growing intellectual and problem-solving capacity; to his greater ease in using language and communicating with others; to his enriched social life with its web of interrelations; and to his changed interests, activities, and values. From the dependence of infancy, the person moves to the maturity and responsibility of adult life (7).

Changes may be divided into four major categories:

1. Changes in Size. Each year, as the child grows older, his height, weight, and circumference measurements normally increase. Likewise, internal organs and structures grow larger to take care of the increasing needs of the body. Mental development shows similar changes in magnitude. The child's vocabulary increases annually, and normally his ability to reason, remember, perceive, and use creative imagination expands during the growth years.

2. Changes in Proportion. The child is not merely a "miniature adult," as was formerly believed. His bodily proportions are quite different from those of an adult. This is illustrated in Figure 1-1, where the body of a newborn infant is magnified to adult size. Not until the child reaches puberty will his proportions begin to approximate those of the adult.

Changes in proportion are also apparent in mental development. In early childhood, imagination is predominantly fantastic, with little reference to reality. Gradually, the fantastic element gives way to a very realistic, matter-of-fact, commonsense sort of imagination, so harnessed and controlled as to be useful in planning and in creative work. A change also occurs in the interests of the child. At first, his interests are concentrated on himself and his toys. Gradually, they shift to other children and the activities of the neighborhood gang. Then, in adolescence, interests are focused on members of the opposite sex, clothes, and all that is closely bound up with courtship.

3. Disappearance of Old Features. The most important physical features to disappear gradually or to atrophy are the thymus gland, often called the "gland of babyhood," located in the chest; the pineal gland, at the base of the brain; the Babinski and Darwinian reflexes; baby hair; and the first set of teeth. Among the mental traits which gradually outlive their usefulness and then disappear are babbling and all other forms of baby speech, and childish impulses to act before thinking. Babyish forms of locomotion, such as creeping and crawling, also disappear, as does sensory keenness, especially in regard to taste and smell.

4. Acquisition of New Features. Some new physical and mental features are acquired through learning, but many result from the unfolding of native traits not fully developed at birth. Among the physical features are first and second teeth and primary and secondary sex characteristics, the latter making their appearance during late childhood and early adolescence. Among the new mental traits are curiosity, the sex urge, knowledge, moral standards, religious beliefs, different forms of language, and all types of neurotic tendencies.

Thus there are two essentially different and often antagonistic processes in development which occur simultaneously at all ages: *evolution,* or the development of new traits, and *involution,* or the atrophy of old traits. In the early years of life, evolution predominates, but atrophic changes, such as the deterioration of the gill clefts in the mammalian embryo, occur even before birth. In the latter part of life, atrophy predominates, but development continues, as in the growth of hair and cellular replacements (35, 143).

While some of the changes that occur in development are antagonistic, others are interrelated. This may be seen in the changes in size and proportions. Increase in body size is accompanied by modifications of the composition of the body. Gain in weight in babyhood, for example, comes not from increase in fat tissue alone but also

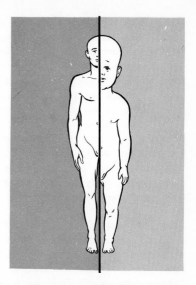

Figure 1–1. The body proportions of the newborn infant and adult. (After Stratz, from K. Bühler, *Mental development of the child,* Harcourt, Brace & World, 1930. Used by permission.)

from increase in neural, bone, glandular, and muscle tissue; in childhood, the gain comes principally from bone and muscle tissue; in adulthood, by contrast, the gain is from an accumulation of fat tissue (116).

Interrelated changes in size and proportions are apparent also in the mental characteristics of the child. The young child's emotions, for example, lack gradations; violent temper outbursts may have no relation to the intensity of the frustrating situation. With increased intelligence and experience, the child is able to control his anger responses to meet the approved standards of the social group (15, 91).

Rate of Development. Development, whether physical or mental, is not a uniform process. It is most rapid during the 9 months before birth, when the individual grows from a microscopically small germ cell to an infant of approximately 7 pounds in weight and 20 inches in length.

Development is extremely rapid throughout babyhood to the age of three years. To realize how rapidly the changes occur, all one has to do is to compare a three-year-old with a newborn infant. During this period, one can almost see the baby grow. Moreover, physical development is closely paralleled by rapid mental development (14). From three to six, the child continues to grow rapidly, though not so fast as in the preceding 3 years. From about the age of six until just before adolescence, he slows down somewhat. Then he has a spurt of rapid growth, only to slow down again in 2 or 3 years as he approaches maturity.

Attitudes toward Development. The young child may not realize that he is growing and changing unless someone comments on his size. Older children, however, become "change-conscious." They know that they outgrow their clothes and pass them down to a younger sibling; they look forward to shedding their baby teeth and getting new ones. When changes are rapid—especially in the latter part of childhood—the child must constantly revise his patterns of motor coordination.

Typically, the adult dreads every change, whether it is failing eyesight that necessitates the constant wearing of glasses or the accumulation of middle-age fat. These changes proclaim to the world that he is "growing old." By contrast, the child welcomes each change because it brings him closer to the privileges and freedom of adulthood. Social attitudes toward change affect the child, just as they do the adult. Most parents encourage their children to "grow up" as soon as possible. When the child lives up to the parents' expectations, he is praised; when he falls below their expectations, he is reproved for not "acting his age" (140, 144).

Davis and Havighurst have explained the child's desire to grow up as follows:

Age is the ladder by which the young child hopes to climb to his Arcadia. . . . Very early he discovers that other children, whether in his family or his nursery school, measure his prestige by his age. On the ladder of age, each step will lead him to higher privileges at home and at school, to sweeter triumphs over more and more "small fry," and to more dazzling signs of prestige. . . . Everything good, he is told by his parents, comes with age. More than anything else, therefore, the child yearns to become bigger and older. . . . To the young child . . . age seems to be the key which unlocks all the forbidden doors of life. It is the magic gift of adults, which brings power and social acceptance. It lifts the barriers to the most inviting and mysterious roads, opening toward freedom and adventure. . . . As long as he is young, he must be the underdog, he must yield, he must obey. It is not easy for a child to be always inferior, simply because he is inferior in size (42).

That children's attitudes toward development are, for the most part, favorable is also apparent in studies of happiness. Retrospective reports, in which adults looked back over the span of their lives and tried to recall how they felt about their life experiences at different ages, have revealed that they were happiest when they were young, though they naturally had some memories of unhappy experiences. Their outstanding memories were related to their first new experiences, each of which was a symbol of their progress toward maturity (12, 152, 162).

STUDIES OF CHILDREN'S DEVELOPMENT

The fundamental purpose of studying the development of children is to discover the normal pattern of the normal child and to determine, when deviations occur in this pattern, what has been responsible for them. Because change is a function of age, the developmental psychologist attempts to find out what the changes are from one age to another, what causes them, and how they affect the child's behavior. Despite this aim, there are gaps in our knowledge of different developmental processes. In some instances, only the beginnings of the processes have been carefully explored; in others, only the terminal states have been. In very few is the picture complete (8).

Even more serious than the gaps themselves has been the tendency to fill them in with material drawn from studies of adults or adolescents. There have, for example, been many studies of adolescent gangs but very few of children's gangs. Consequently, it has been assumed that since adolescent gangs are delinquent, children's gangs are also delinquent. A few studies of children's gangs show very definitely that this assumption is false; children's gangs do not conform to the adolescent pattern but to a pattern of their own (40).

In time, as research progresses, these gaps will be filled in. The developmental psychologist has already, to some extent, drawn on the research findings of related fields of study, mainly medicine, education, sociology, anthropology, and gerontology. From anthropological studies, for example, we have important evidence of the effects of child-training methods on personality development. From the sociologists, we have learned much about the effects of family size and sibling relationships on social behavior and personality development. Because behavioral changes are closely related to physical changes, it is possible to draw on the research findings of medicine and then correlate them with behavioral changes. Although gerontology is concerned with the study of the aging process, this field has contributed valuable information to our understanding of the importance of the foundation years of childhood, especially in personality development (8, 121, 152).

Values of Knowing the Developmental Pattern. Knowledge of the patterns of human development enables us, first, to know *what to expect* of a child, when to expect it, and at what ages different patterns of behavior will normally emerge into more mature forms. If too much is expected of a child at a given age, he is likely to develop feelings of inadequacy because he does not measure up to the standards his parents and teachers set. If too little is expected, a child is deprived of an incentive to develop his capacities. Equally serious, he builds up resentments toward those who underestimate his capacity.

Second, knowing what to expect enables us to *set up standards,* or "measuring rods," in the form of height-weight scales, age-weight scales, age-height scales, mental-age scales, and social- or emotional-development scales. Since these standards represent what can be expected from the average child, child training and education are now on a firmer foundation than in the past.

One of the most comprehensive and practical standards for judging a child's development has been outlined by Havighurst in his series of "developmental tasks." A developmental task is a "task which arises at or about a certain period in the life of an individual, successful achievement of which leads to his happiness and success with later tasks, while failure leads to unhappiness in the individual, disapproval by society, and difficulty with later tasks." Some developmental tasks arise mainly as a result of physical maturation (learning to walk); others are developed mainly from the cultural pressures of society (learning to read or learning appropriate sex roles); still others grow out of the personal values and aspirations of the individual (choosing and preparing for a vocation). Most developmental tasks arise from all three of these forces working together.

The major developmental tasks for childhood are as follows:

INFANCY AND EARLY CHILDHOOD (BIRTH TO 6 YEARS)

Learning to walk
Learning to take solid foods
Learning to talk
Learning to control the elimination of body wastes
Learning sex differences and sexual modesty
Achieving physiological stability
Forming simple concepts of social and physical reality
Learning to relate oneself emotionally to parents, siblings, and other people
Learning to distinguish right and wrong and developing a conscience

MIDDLE CHILDHOOD (6 TO 12 YEARS)

Learning physical skills necessary for ordinary games

Building wholesome attitudes toward oneself
as a growing organism
Learning to get along with age-mates
Learning an appropriate masculine or femi-
nine sex role
Developing fundamental skills in reading,
writing, and calculating
Developing concepts necessary for everyday
living
Developing conscience, morality, and a scale
of values
Achieving personal independence
Developing attitudes toward social groups
and institutions (76)

Because the pattern of development for
all normal children is approximately the
same, we can judge each child in terms of
the norm for his age. If his development is
typical for his age, he is making normal
adjustments to social expectations. If his development deviates from the norm, it may
be a signal of poor social, emotional, or
personal adjustment, and immediate steps
should be taken to discover why his development is deviating and what should be
done about it. For example, if deviation is
due to mental deficiency, there may be
little that can be done to overcome it, but
the child can be placed in an environment
where he will not develop feelings of inadequacy from constant comparison with children whose development is normal (68).
Should the deviation be the result of lack
of opportunities to learn, the child must be
given learning opportunities and encouragement. Corey and Herrick have stressed this
point:

Each of the developmental tasks . . . represents a lesson that must be learned at least
to some degree of mastery. There is no
choice if the individual is to make a relatively
normal, wholesome, and acceptable adjustment to his culture. The boy or girl who fails
to learn one of these developmental lessons
in ways that conform, at least approximately,
to the standards of his cultural group, is
punished in various ways. The punishment
may be calculated and overt, as in the case
of persons who engage in unorthodox sex
practices, or it may be subjective, like the
anxiety of the chronic coward (38).

All development requires guidance. The
third advantage of knowing the developmental pattern is that it enables teachers
and parents to *guide the child into new
channels at the most appropriate time.*
When a baby is ready to learn to walk, for
example, he must be given opportunities to
practice walking in a safe place so that falls
will not intimidate him. In addition, he must
be given the encouragement to try as often
as necessary until he succeeds in walking
without adult help. Lack of opportunity to
walk and lack of encouragement may delay
the child's normal development. Similarly,
when a child shows an interest in learning
to read, that is the "teachable moment" to
begin formal instruction. Incorrect timing of
instruction may lead to reading difficulties
later on (62, 94).

Fourth, knowing what the normal developmental pattern is makes it possible for
parents and teachers to *prepare the child*
ahead of time for the changes that will take
place in his body, his interests, or his behavior. For example, the child can be prepared for what will be expected of him
when he enters school (25). While this psychological preparation will not eliminate all
tensions, it will go a long way toward
minimizing them.

OBSTACLES TO STUDYING DEVELOPMENT

Scientific study of the child's developmental
pattern has been beset with many obstacles.
Some of these have been partially overcome,
and some are still formidable. In the following paragraphs we shall discuss the four
biggest stumbling blocks.

FOCUS OF INTEREST IN CHILDREN

Early interest in the study of children came
not from an interest in the child himself or
in his development but rather from an interest in the best method of educating him to
be a useful citizen. One of the earliest educational reformers to study children as indi-

viduals was Johann Amos Comenius, the famous Slavic educational reformer of the seventeenth century. Comenius strongly felt that the child should be studied not as an embryonic adult but in his essential child nature so as to understand his capacities and know how to deal with them.

Comenius wrote two books explaining his philosophy of education: the *School of Infancy,* published in 1628, in which he described the type of education he considered suitable for the first six years of a child's life, and *Orbis Pictus,* or the *World in Pictures,* published in 1657, in which the reading matter was illustrated with pictures to make it more understandable to the child. This was the first practical recognition of the child's ability to comprehend objective facts before he can understand abstract terms.

Following the pioneer work of Comenius, two definite trends appeared in the study of children. The first was characterized by philosophical treatises on education in which the child was studied only indirectly, and the second was characterized by the direct study of the child through daily observation. The influence of the philosophical treatises was great, as far as educational reform was concerned. Among the educational reformers who indirectly contributed information about children and their capacities were Locke, of England; Rousseau, of France; Pestalozzi, of Switzerland; and Herbart and Froebal, of Germany.

Observations of children, on the other hand, proved to be far more fruitful because they focused attention on the child rather than on how to educate him. Educational and pediatric literature of the sixteenth and seventeenth centuries referred to problems common today, such as breastfeeding, feeding problems, and the emotional care of the child during illness (31). The first scientific record of the development of a young child, published in 1774, was based on the observational notes Pestalozzi made of his 3½-year-old son. Several years later, Tiedemann, of Germany, kept biographical records of the development of his children during the early years of their lives. The best-known and most thorough of the early American observational records was Millicent Shinn's *Biography of a Baby,* based on her observations of her niece from birth through the first year of life. This appeared in 1900 and was modeled along the lines of the German baby biographies (146).

Interest in scientific studies of children was given great impetus by the work of G. Stanley Hall, of Clark University. Beginning with his study of children's concepts, reported in 1891 in his *Contents of Children's Minds on Entering School,* Hall emphasized that children are not miniature adults (73). Hall's students also adopted this point of view, and soon an interest in studying the child himself, without reference to education, became the focus of scientific investigation by many psychologists and educators. Because of the interest Hall stimulated, he is often referred to as the "father of the child-study movement."

Since Hall's original study, literally thousands of studies of almost every phase of child life have made their appearance. Most of the early studies were poorly controlled, and few employed a scientific methodology. Their attention was focused primarily on some psychological pattern of behavior— emotions, memory, concepts, or personality —and they contributed little to our knowledge of how children develop or how they change from one age to another. Dennis has stated: "Psychologic studies of children have been conducted for a number of decades. These studies might reasonably be expected to provide information of great value to those concerned with child care. Yet the cautious child psychologist will be the first to indicate that, as yet, his field possesses only a modest amount of scientific data" (44).

As has already been pointed out, interest in studying children was first motivated by a desire to improve educational practices. Later, preschool children were studied in the hope of throwing light on problems related to child-training practices. Still later, the newborn infant was studied for the purpose of discovering what behavioral capacities are a part of his hereditary endowment and how much he must be taught.

The study of children has also been motivated by a desire to refute or substantiate prevailing theories. Watson's theory of the "three primary emotions" and his emphasis on conditioning as the principal force in emotional development have led to many studies of emotions at different age levels (171). Similarly, the theory of the constancy of the IQ has motivated long-term studies of the development of intelligence to determine just how constant the IQ is and under what conditions constancy gives way to variability (14).

DIFFICULTIES IN SECURING CHILDREN FOR SCIENTIFIC STUDIES

Securing large and unselected groups of children for scientific research was long a troublesome and often insurmountable problem. In recent years, this problem has become less serious. Today most babies are born in hospitals and are available to the scientist. Furthermore, there is no longer a widespread feeling that babies are "too delicate" to be studied. Nursery schools, kindergartens, and health and mental-health clinics give the psychologist of today excellent opportunities to study children of the preschool age. Parents bring their children to these centers for free medical care and for advice on behavior problems. In return they permit the children to be studied and tested at regular intervals.

There are still some serious obstacles to studying school-age children. Although many school people today willingly cooperate with the scientist, whereas in the past they disliked having their school routine interrupted, this has not solved the problem completely. School children themselves are often reluctant to cooperate. They feel that "their affairs are being pried into," that they are being "treated like guinea pigs," or that testing is a "waste of their time." Even more serious is the limitation placed on what can be studied. School authorities often will not permit research on a "touchy" subject, such as sex, religion, or parent-child or sibling

relationships, because it might "put ideas into the children's heads" or the parents "would object."

Finally, there is the obstacle of parental and societal antagonism. The main objection to using babies and young children for scientific research is that it might cause permanent damage to them (112). Parents of school-age children often feel that the time spent on research should be used for classroom teaching; others dislike having their children subjected to experimental regimes which might conflict with home teachings. Dennis, in discussing parental objections, has pointed out that:

Medical research on child health meets little objection because the medical researcher wants to discover ways of making children well, not ways to make them ill. Likewise, the psychologist is interested in reducing the incidence of school failures, of delinquency and of parent-child conflict—not in increasing them. A wider understanding of the purposes of research, and of the ethical standards under which the investigator conducts his studies, should insure public approval (44).

TRADITIONAL BELIEFS ABOUT CHILDREN

Many traditional beliefs about children— known in the scientific world as "old wives' tales"—have been passed down from generation to generation. Because they are accepted uncritically by each subsequent generation, they develop a halo of infallibility; people believe they *must* be true because they have been believed for so many generations. While not all old wives' tales are completely false, most of them cannot bear up under the scrutiny of scientific investigation.

The stereotype of the "child genius," for example, is widely known. "Such children," as Mead has remarked, "have proportionally large heads, are somewhat obese, often myopic. They combine extraordinary intellectual abilities with a kind of frightening ruthless clarity, and while their mental performance equals and often surpasses that of superior adults, there is a childlike quality about their human relationships" (122). Studies of very bright children and adolescents have shown that they are, on the whole, above average in physical attractiveness, that they have fewer sensory defects than the average, and that they are above average in social acceptance, often playing leadership roles (57, 83).

Another example of an old wives' tale is the widespread belief that leniency is ruinous to a child—that if parents "spare the rod, they will spoil the child." Studies of the effects of corporal punishment on children have revealed that it more often results in lying, stealing, cheating, and resentment toward all people in authority than in a wish to be law-abiding (41, 79). From the parent's point of view, acceptance of this traditional belief has two advantages: First, the parent does not have to make a decision about how to handle his child's misbehavior; he merely spanks him. Second, a parent need have no feeling of guilt about behaving primitively toward his child (32).

The seriousness of traditional beliefs is that they are held to, even in the face of contradictory evidence. Many scientists, unfortunately, assume that traditional beliefs are true. Only when contradictory evidence appears, often indirectly in connection with some other line of research, does the falsity of the traditional belief become obvious. Knowledge about the effects of punishment on the child's attitudes and personality, for example, came from research in the area of juvenile delinquency; the old wives' tale was not attacked directly at first.

In commenting on the setback this unscientific attitude toward old wives' tales has given to scientific research in the area of prenatal influences, Pasamanick and Knobloch have said:

Towards the end of the last century quite reliable journals and textbooks published reports by reputable observers of congenital effects consequent to emotional stress. We all remember and smile condescendingly at the grandmother's story of the rat-faced boy whose mother was frightened by the appropriate rodent during her pregnancy. We must not forget that while these beliefs arose in folklore, they were accepted and given clinical support by the writings of physicians (132).

The effect of traditional beliefs on those whose responsibility it is to guide the child's development is even more serious. Several examples will help to emphasize this. Mothers who reported food refusals on the part of their children were advised to try permissive feeding. Out of a group of 57 mothers, only 8 were willing to adopt permissive feeding as a customary procedure. A few tried the permissive method but soon rejected it as a "newfangled idea" and reverted to their former authoritarian practices (29).

Most parents and many teachers cling to the belief that the "slow learner is the slow forgetter, and the quick learner is the quick forgetter." As a result, they often insist that a child spend more time drilling and studying than he actually needs. Research on learning and forgetting has shown that people who learn quickly do so because they are bright and have developed efficient study habits. Insisting that a child spend more time on his lessons than he needs not only encourages dawdling but also develops in the child an attitude of boredom toward studying in general (93, 129).

METHODS OF STUDYING CHILDREN

The problem of methodology in the study of children has always been a thorny one. To find a method that is applicable to children and at the same time has the necessary accuracy to give validity to the results obtained is not easy. Many approaches have been abandoned because they proved to be too complicated or because they lacked reliability as measuring instruments. For example, baby biographies and questionnaires are seldom used today unless they can be sufficiently controlled to achieve an accuracy which the early biographies and questionnaires lacked.

John B. Watson, of The Johns Hopkins University, in the early years of this century, felt that he had found *the* way to study young children whose speech development has not yet reached the point where they could answer questions or verbalize their thoughts, feelings, and emotions. He would find out what went on in their minds by watching their behavior and then draw conclusions about their thoughts and emotions. This "behavioristic" approach, he had found, worked successfully in the study of animals. Therefore he believed that it would work equally well in the study of children (171).

It soon became apparent, however, that there were three major limitations to this method. In the *first* place, children quickly learn that society expects certain reactions from them. If they behave as the social group expects, they are rewarded; if not, they are punished. Boys, long before they enter school, for example, discover that they are expected to be brave and not show fear. Consequently, a little boy will stand his ground and hold back his tears, even though he may be "quaking in his boots." Observing him, one might conclude that he was brave, but this conclusion would not be justified by reality. Observations of babies and young children may give accurate information about their true thoughts and feelings, but observations of older children are more likely to give information about how well they have learned to conform to social expectations.

Even little babies will respond in different ways when they are in the presence of others and when they are alone. Preschool children are very conscious of the watchful eyes of parents and teachers; they know that they must act as parents and teachers expect or they will be punished. Consequently, observations may not reveal their true behavior patterns. Young children, for example, tend to be more aggressive when there is an adult present than when they are alone with other children (148). Gesell, many years ago, suggested a way of eliminating this methodological obstacle: By the use of a one-way-vision screen, scientists could observe a child without his realizing it (58). Children beyond the three-year age level, however, find ways to explore the area behind the screen and soon discover that it is a device for watching them. Thus its usefulness is limited.

The *second* difficulty of the behavioristic approach is that it is sometimes necessary to use the observations of people not trained in the methods of scientific research. In order to collect data relating to home behavior, scientists often have to rely on reports of parents. Generally, parents are given some preliminary training to help increase the accuracy of their reports and to focus their attention on what they are to observe. In a study of preschool children's temper tantrums, for example, Goodenough trained the parents who took part in the experiment (67). Macfarlane and her associates used a similar approach in collecting data about common forms of problem behavior in children ranging from twenty-one months to fourteen years of age (115).

Such training *does not guarantee* effective control. The observer's attitudes toward the behavior of children—whether it will be considered "normal" or "problem"—are influenced by his own personality, his professional skills, his experience, and his attitude toward children. Even when a systematic topical framework is laid out for the reporting of observations, the giving or withholding of material will be influenced by the observer's attitudes regarding the significance of certain material to the problem being studied. Furthermore, the perceptiveness of the observer is an important factor in determining what will be reported and what will be withheld (133).

A simple incident, for example, such as a child's pout when a sibling gets more attention than he, may not be perceived as a sign of jealousy by the observer; consequently, it will not be reported. In the study of problem behavior in the home, parental expectations play an important role in determining what parents will observe and how they will report it. Because mothers, as a rule, have higher expectations of good behavior in their daughters than in their sons, they tend to be more critical of their daughters' behavior. Likewise, fathers expect their sons to be more aggressive than their daughters. Similar behavior in sons and daughters will, as a result, be differently interpreted by fathers (75, 121).

Biased attitudes which affect the accuracy of observations also exist among observers in the schools. What constitutes problem behavior in the school, for example, depends upon the teacher's frame of reference. To teachers, anything that disrupts the efficiency of teaching or the quiet needed for study is problem behavior. Giggling, passing notes, or talking to another pupil all belong in this category. A clinician, whose frame of reference relates to the effects different forms of behavior have on a child's adjustments now and as he grows older, regards such behavior as of minor importance. Withdrawal and other forms of behavior which lead to maladjustment are labeled "problem behavior" by the clinician. Under such conditions, it is obvious that the observations of teachers and clinicians of the same children in the same situation differ markedly (18, 161).

To avoid the effect of biased attitudes on observations, clinicians sometimes use retrospections of earlier experiences for observational studies. By seeing a situation in the perspective of time, the observer will be less likely to distort his observations. This is especially applicable in parent-child relationships, where annoyances of the moment can readily color the parents' reports (173). While bias may be avoided, other factors that impair the accuracy of the report, such as forgetting, attitude change over a period of time, the desire to say the "right thing" when questioned, or the desire to justify an act which might be unfavorably judged, may make the retrospections no more reliable than observations made when the acts occur (19, 142).

The *third* but by no means the least important limitation of the behavioristic approach concerns accuracy. Even trained observers find it difficult to watch all parts of a child's body simultaneously or to observe every action he makes (158). When the child is walking, for example, it is diffi-

cult to observe everything he does with his hands, feet, arms, legs, head, and trunk. If several observers are assigned to watch different specific areas of the child's body, they can later pool their observations and get a composite picture.

To increase the accuracy of observation, Gesell introduced the use of the moving-picture camera in his studies at Yale University in 1926 (59). By photographing the child in action and studying the pictures in slow motion, the observer can see all parts of the body in movement. Furthermore, the film can be rerun if any movement is missed in one observation. An equally important advantage of this method is that it eliminates the temptation on the part of the observer to interpret what he is observing. In a rerun, he sees the child's activity in a more objective manner than he might while he is actually watching the child (133). Figure 1–2 shows how this technique is used to study movements of newborn infants.

Accuracy of observation is an especially serious problem in the area of speech research. To understand speech development, one must know what prespeech forms of language the baby used. Few studies in this area have been made because of the difficulty of analyzing the sound by ear and because auditory memory is unreliable. As Lynip pointed out:

It is totally impractical to try to express in adult sounds an utterance of an infant prior to his speech maturation. Infant utterances are not *like* any of the well-defined values of adult language. They are produced differently and they are shaped differently, their relationships with adult sounds are at first only fortuitous. Infant sounds cannot be described except in terms of themselves (114).

To overcome this observational handicap, Lynip used a magnetic recorder and a sound spectrograph, which provides a pictorial analysis of the sound samplings secured by the recorder. From these records, accurate in both auditory and visual forms, it is possible to determine how prespeech sounds

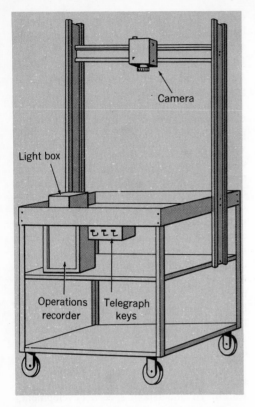

Figure 1–2. Observation cart for photographing newborn infants. (Adapted from W. Kessen, L. S. Hendry, and A. M. Leutzendorff, Measurement of movement in the human newborn: a new technique, *Child Develpm.*, 1961, 32, 95–105. Used by permission.)

change over a period of time until they become recognizable as speech (114).

Need for Different Methods. One of the major obstacles to a satisfactory study of child development is that *no one method of study is suitable for all age levels or for all forms of behavior.* Entirely different methods must be used for studying children who cannot verbalize their thoughts and for those whose speech is well developed (6, 163). Similarly, different measuring techniques must be used for children who cannot read and write and for those who can. Sociometric techniques, borrowed from the sociologists, are valuable in studies of the social

development of the child, but they are completely inadequate and inappropriate for studies of language or motor development.

Devising appropriate methods for studying different age levels and different psychological phenomena has been one of the biggest obstacles to the scientific study of children. As a result, our accumulation of information about children's development has been slow as well as spotty. The difficulty has been met, in part, by borrowing methods used in related fields of research—mainly medicine, sociology, and experimental psychology. Since many of these methods were devised for use with adult subjects or adolescents of high-school or college age, however, they had to be modified before they could be applied to the study of children.

Cross-sectional versus Longitudinal Approach. Information from questionnaires, observations, retrospective reports, and other sources can be combined with data from other studies to give a composite picture of the course of child development. This is known as the *normative cross-sectional approach* because the norms for different areas of development are obtained not from studying the development of any one group of children over an extended period of time but rather from studying many groups over a short period of time. When the groups are made up of representative samplings of the population, environmental influences are, to a large extent, ruled out, and the normative pattern of development can then be observed (6).

In spite of the practical and methodological advantages of the cross-sectional approach, it has some serious disadvantages. Because of these disadvantages, the results obtained by this approach give approximations rather than accurate representations of the developmental process. A cross-sectional study of fourteen-year-olds, for example, would include boys and girls in many different stages of sexual maturity, with the accompanying typical variations in psychological maturity. There would not, as a result, be a true norm for a fourteen-year-old. Furthermore, cross-sectional studies do not take into consideration cultural or environmental changes that occur during the life-span of a single person. In a study of changes of recreational interests over the childhood years, for example, differences found might be due to the cultural and environmental backgrounds of the groups studied, not to developmental changes in the child (6).

Child development has also been studied using the *longitudinal approach*. This consists of the reexamination of the same children at certain intervals of time throughout the childhood and adolescent years. As Dennis has pointed out, "Child psychology has been almost alone in undertaking longitudinal studies." He further emphasizes that one of the reasons for the gaps in our knowledge of children is that "longitudinal studies are inherently slow" (44). They are also expensive in time and money and are cumbersome to handle (19). Furthermore, it is difficult to maintain the original sample. Vocational mobility takes children away from the community in which the study is made, and lack of cooperation on the part of the children or their parents causes them to be withdrawn from the sample before the study is completed.

A longitudinal study has three very important advantages over the cross-sectional approach: (*1*) It permits an analysis of the development and growth of each individual child; (*2*) it permits a study of growth increments, both for the individual child and for the group; and (*3*) it provides an opportunity to analyze the interrelations between growth processes, both maturational and experiential, since all data are obtained from the study of the same children (6).

Longitudinal studies have literally transformed our knowledge of both childhood and adolescence by bringing out facts impossible to see in a cross-sectional approach, where individual variations are cloaked by "averages." Some of the most important longitudinal studies to date have been those of intellectual growth by Bayley, Owens, and Terman (14, 131, 164); studies of the long-term effects of age of sexual maturity on social behavior and personality by Jones and Mussen (97, 99); and studies of the persistence of personality characteristics from childhood into adulthood and old age by Smith (152).

Human versus Animal Subjects. A methodological obstacle of great seriousness in the study of children is the possible psychological damage of methods which have proved, in the case of animals, to be highly reliable and yet harmless. From a scientific as well as from a practical angle, for example, it is important to know how much of a child's development will occur of its own accord and how much will depend on the child's experiences. In studies of the hereditary endowment of animals, the animals can be deprived of learning opportunities; they can be isolated from other members of their species or kept in cages so that they have no opportunities to practice acts characteristically found in their species. Then, should the behavior characteristic of their species appear, it could logically be concluded that this was a hereditary trait.

The *method of isolation* has been used with human subjects but has always been quickly abandoned. Not only is there the practical difficulty of gaining parental consent for using babies for such studies, but there are also strong objections, raised by parents and others, that isolation is unfair to a child and might damage him so seriously psychologically that he would never again be "normal" (6, 43).

A second method of discovering how much nature does for the child and how much he must do for himself is the *co-twin control method*. On the assumption that identical twins are alike both physically and psychologically, clinicians give one twin, Twin *T* (or "trained twin") practice in learning different functions, while Twin *C* (or "control twin") is given no training. After a certain length of time, the results of training for Twin *T* are compared with the achievements of Twin *C*. As in the isolation method, there is a practical difficulty of getting an adequate number of identical twins whose parents will allow them to participate in an experiment in which one might be psychologically damaged by being deprived of learning opportunities and the other damaged by being made to feel superior to his twin (6, 65).

Genetic studies of large groups have, for the most part, proved to be much more practical for widespread use than the isolation and co-twin control methods. The fundamental principle of the genetic study is that when environmental factors are controlled by having many different racial, socioeconomic, religious, intellectual, and physical factors represented in the group, environmental influences are ruled out; any similarity in the developmental patterns of children in the group may then be regarded as "nature's work." If children who have been subjected to different child-training methods and different opportunities for learning show behavior that is similar in its fundamentals even though it differs in specific details, clinicians assume that this behavior has not been learned entirely but is partially the result of the unfolding of hereditary traits (6, 44).

The seriousness of the methodological obstacles in the study of development is highlighted in a quotation from Anderson's summary of his report on methods of child psychology:

In child psychology scientific problems are being attacked in a variety of ways by workers who are becoming more and more concerned with methodology. Child psychology, which at first accepted uncritically almost any observations or results obtained from the study of children, has become more mature. It now critically examines its methods and results and deliberately goes about designing experiments. In many areas the study of the child has moved from the exploratory phase to the comprehensive investigation carried on over a long period. . . . From today's studies, however inadequate, come the highly developed techniques of tomorrow. . . . The scientist of today has a great advantage over the one of yesterday, not in his interest or ability but in the better tools that have been forged in the intervening period. . . . To understand growth and development, which

appear ever more complex as we learn more about them, we need not one but many competent investigators, not one but many and varied investigations (6).

CHARACTERISTICS OF DEVELOPMENT

In spite of the many obstacles to the study of human development, we do have enough information to enable us to see what its pattern is and to know that certain factors influence it. Although we cannot evaluate these factors in such a way as to list them in the order of their importance, we shall list first those which, on the basis of evidence now available, *seem* to be the most influential.

DEVELOPMENT COMES FROM MATURATION AND LEARNING

Development of physical and mental traits comes partly from an intrinsic maturing of those traits and partly from exercise and experience on the part of the individual. Intrinsic maturing—*maturation*—is the unfolding of traits potentially present in the individual resulting from his hereditary endowment. It is, as Gesell has pointed out, the "net sum of the gene effects operating in a self-limited life cycle." He further adds, "Here lies an important key to his [the individual's] constitutional individuality" (61). Traits that are potentially present develop into predictable characteristics for all members of the species. Some of these are relatively immune to environmental influences, while others not only are influenced by environmental factors but may appear only under particular environmental conditions.

In *phylogenetic* functions—functions common to the race—such as crawling, creeping, sitting, and walking, training is of little advantage and may even be a retarding influence. Control of the environment to prevent the baby from having opportunities to practice reaching, sitting, and standing, on the other hand, has little influence on the development of these functions. By contrast, in *ontogenetic functions*—functions specific to the individual—such as swimming, roller skating, tricycle riding, or scaling inclines, training is essential; without it, development will not take place. No hereditary tendency can mature fully, however, without proper environmental support. Children living in environments where educational opportunities are limited will not develop their hereditary potentials to the same extent as children whose environments offer better educational opportunities. Individual differences in intelligence are, in part, attributable to such environmental differences (5, 43).

The sudden appearance of traits that develop through maturation is quite common. For example, a baby may start to walk literally overnight, even though he had seemed to be behind the norm in developing this particular skill (62). Behavioral changes at the time of puberty occur suddenly, without any apparent reason. Because many of the behavioral characteristics of puberty are antisocial, their development is usually discouraged; yet they appear almost universally just before sexual maturity is achieved and with a suddenness similar to that of the baby's walking (54, 160).

Learning is development that comes from exercise and effort on the part of the individual. Through learning the child brings about changes in his physical structure and behavior and acquires competence in using his hereditary resources. Unless he has opportunities for learning, many of his hereditary potentials will never reach their optimum development. A child may, for example, have a high aptitude for musical performance because of his superior neuromuscular organization, but if he is deprived of opportunities for practice and systematic training, he will not reach his hereditary potential.

Some learning comes from practice or the mere repetition of an act which, in time, brings about a change in the person's behavior. It may consist of *imitation,* in which the child consciously copies what he sees others do, or of *identification,* in which he attempts to adopt as his own the values, attitudes, motives, and behavior of persons for whom he has a strong admiration or an emotional tie (129, 159).

Learning may take the form of *training,* which is a selective, directed, and purposive type of activity. The child is directed in his behavior by adults or older children who attempt to mold his behavior into patterns that will contribute to his welfare and be acceptable to the social group with which he is identified. In the home, parents make sure that the child will learn what society expects him to learn by rewarding him when his behavior is acceptable and punishing him when his behavior falls below social standards.

In the school, teachers use the same technique. They reward or punish the child according to his success in meeting their expectations. The child's training in school is not limited to academic subjects. He is also trained to behave as the school thinks he should behave so that the teacher can carry on her work efficiently. When he gives his teacher minimum trouble, he is rewarded with high grades for conduct; when he is troublesome, he is punished by receiving low grades for conduct (64).

Interaction of Maturation and Learning. Development during the prenatal period comes mainly from maturation and is very little dependent upon exercise, although there is evidence that fetal activity is related to the development of certain motor performances in early postnatal life (62, 155). Infants who are most active as fetuses, for example, acquire skills postnatally at an earlier age than those who are less active. Postnatal maturation and learning are closely interrelated; one influences the other (174). The high correlation between growth and skills indicates that gross physical development is accompanied by the ability to manipulate the parts of the body that have grown (69).

Development thus depends not on hereditary endowment alone but rather on the interaction of this endowment and the social and cultural forces of the environment. There is, however, evidence of a "ground plan for development governed by an inherent dynamic morphology, imposed by a combination of racial and familial inheritance. For this reason a child of a given stock in a given culture tends to exhibit at advancing age levels maturity traits which are more or less typical for the group as well as representative of his constitutional self" (61). Thus maturation provides the raw material for learning and determines to a large extent the more general patterns and sequences of the child's behavior. As Kelly has pointed out:

Beginning with the complex structures and functions provided by its unique genetic constitution, each organism, while maintaining its organic integrity and a considerable residue of its original nature, moves through its maturational cycle adapting to and permitting itself to be modified by selected aspects of its immediate environment. These adaptive changes, occurring most rapidly in the years of infancy and childhood, are so appropriately timed that they do not threaten the organism either physiologically or psychologically (106).

Significance of Interrelationship. An important consequence of the learning-maturation interrelationship is that children display "extraordinary" *variations* in their patterns of development. Were development due to maturation alone, as in many animal species, there would be no such thing as individuality (137). Maturation, however, *sets limits* beyond which development cannot go even when learning is encouraged. As Gesell has said, "This intrinsic growth is a gift of nature. It can be guided, but it cannot be created: nor can it be transcended by an educational agency" (60). This means that all learning and adjustment, both physical and mental, is "limited by inherent properties of the organism." In education and guidance, this limitation must be taken into consideration because psychological damage usually results when a child is pushed to learn more than he is inherently capable of learning.

In the early days of child psychology, there was a tendency to accept the popular belief that a person can do or become whatever he wants, as long as he is willing to work hard and is given the opportunity. J. B. Watson, for example, maintained that he could train any normal infant to become any kind of specialist he wished—doctor, lawyer, artist, or even beggar and thief—regardless of the child's talents, abilities, tendencies, and racial origin (171). If this could be done, it would certainly "put an awesome degree of power into the hands of parents and other 'teachers' " (32).

This early overemphasis on the influence of learning has gradually been abandoned as studies of intelligence, aptitudes, and physical growth have revealed differences in ability which are, to a large extent, immune to environmental influences. The inability to educate mentally defective children as normal children are educated, for example, is a practical illustration of the limiting effects of heredity.

In spite of the fact that there are maturational limits, there is evidence that *few people ever reach their limits.* This is especially apparent in very bright children. Those who do not develop their innate capacities to the limit never realize how great their capacities are. When they reach a plateau in learning and show little improvement over a period of time, they often conclude that no further improvement is possible. Studies of learning, however, have revealed that changed methods of learning or the introduction of new incentives often enables the learners to forge ahead (129).

Therefore, *innate capacities must be stimulated* by environmental factors (74). Good seeds, planted in poor soil, will result in stunted plants. So it is with children. If they grow up in an environment devoid of educational and cultural opportunities, their physical and mental development will likewise be stunted. Children who have been institutionalized during the first three or more years of life—when speech development progresses rapidly—do not develop the communication skills they are potentially capable of because of lack of opportunities to learn (72).

Differences in parental attitudes toward education and in the types of schooling given to children of the Negro and white races also illustrate the importance of stimulation. Because Negro children are subjected to prejudice by classmates and even by teachers; because they are frequently in schools where educational and cultural advantages are limited; because they know that many vocational opportunities will be closed to them on account of their race; and because their parents sometimes put little value on education, there is a tendency for them to develop into underachievers. They receive little encouragement either at home or outside the home to make the most of their native abilities. By contrast, white children are subjected to more pressures at home to achieve academic success, and their environment offers more educational and cultural opportunities. As a result, they show better achievement than Negro children (101, 132, 175).

Stimulation to the development of innate abilities usually comes from the environment, but it may also come from the child himself. When a child sets a goal for himself, he will try to reach it. He will often have to draw upon all his resources and use them to the maximum, especially when the goal is beyond his capacities. Self-direction can be as important a stimulant to development as outer-direction, though the former is less common in the early years of childhood than the latter. Only after a child has learned how important achievement is to social recognition has he the motivation to aspire to high goals (139).

Perhaps the most significant point about the interrelationship of maturation and learning is that *the effectiveness of learning depends upon proper timing.* A child cannot learn until he is ready to learn. This means that the necessary physical and mental foundations must be present before new abilities can be built on them. While structure and function parallel each other in childhood, structure actually precedes function. This is true in the case of motor skills, mental skills, and sexual behavior (76). In babies, for example, learning a conditioned-reflex action is impossible, even with excessive drill, until maturation has laid the foundations. Similarly, until an adequate neuromuscular pattern has developed, grasping cannot be mastered even when environmental opportunities are given (62).

It has been reported that children subjected to a regular program of reading from the time they were thirteen months old showed little improvement in their spontaneous vocalizations until they reached seventeen months of age. From that age on, however, they improved greatly in comparison with children not given this learning opportunity. The early lack of improvement shown by the babies who received special training can, unquestionably, be traced to their lack of readiness to learn (88). Similar results have been found in studies of toilet training. Such training is ineffectual until the baby is maturationally ready for it (127).

Maturational readiness has a practical bearing on the education of the child. It suggests at what age training should begin and in what sequence the training should occur. As Blum has pointed out, "Learning, whether in the intellectual, social, or motor sphere, is best achieved when what is offered educationally is timed to the child's state of readiness or maturity" (22). If the child is not mature enough to profit by the teaching, it can be regarded as wasted time and effort, and it may lead to resistant behavior, which militates against successful learning. If, on the other hand, the necessary maturation has been attained and the child is not permitted to learn, his interest may reach such a low ebb that he will be unwilling to put forth effort needed later for successful learning. Also, as Harris has stressed, "It is possible, indeed likely, that a person who comes late to his training will never realize the full measure of his potential" (74).

Havighurst has referred to maturational readiness as the "teachable moment." According to him, "When the body is ripe, and society requires it, and the self is ready to achieve a certain task, the teachable moment has come. Efforts at teaching which would have been largely wasted if they had come earlier give gratifying results when they come at the *teachable moment,* when the task should be learned" (76).

There are two reasons why education is often not related to the maturational level of the child. In the first place, the age at which the maturation of different mental and physical functions occurs is not fully established. Because of individual variations, it would be impossible to set a specific age that was correct for all children. Then, second, there are misconceptions and biases which have led to an established pattern for educating a child. For example, it has been assumed for generations that all children are ready to begin reading when they enter school; in reality, some are ready before they enter school, and others are not ready for some time afterward.

In schools, standard tests are used to measure the child's readiness to study various school subjects, such as reading, arithmetic, or a foreign language. In everyday life, however, tests are not usually available to answer the question, "Is the child ready to learn?" Three practical and easily applied criteria are generally used by psychologists to indicate the child's state of readiness: (*1*) the child's interest in learning, as shown by his desire to be taught or to try to teach himself, (*2*) how long his interest is sustained, and (*3*) what progress he makes with practice.

To ensure an accurate picture of the child's readiness, all three of these criteria should be applied. An interest, for example, may be merely transitory—a whim—resulting from a desire to imitate an older sibling or playmate. If a general interest is sustained over a period of time, this is a better indication of readiness than a strong interest that is transitory. Parental or peer pressures may cause the child to sustain his interest in learning over a long enough period of time to justify the conclusion that he has reached the teachable moment. Application of the third criterion—progress with practice—may show, however, that his developmental readiness has not yet reached the point

where he can benefit from learning opportunities. When the child's interest wanes quickly or when he seems to make no appreciable improvement, in spite of continued practice, there is reason to question whether the teachable moment has arrived.

DEVELOPMENT FOLLOWS A PREDICTABLE PATTERN

Every species, whether animal or human, follows a pattern of development peculiar to that species. In prenatal development, there is a genetic sequence, with certain traits appearing each month. The same orderly pattern is evident in postnatal development, though the individual rate of development may vary more in the postnatal period than in the prenatal.

Genetic studies of children over a period of years have demonstrated that behavioral development, too, follows a pattern and that this pattern is relatively little influenced by experience. Gesell has concluded from these studies that, "although no two individuals are exactly alike, all normal children tend to follow a general sequence of growth characteristic of the species and of a cultural group. Every child has a unique pattern of growth but that pattern is a variant of a basic ground plan. The species sequences are part of an established order of nature" (60).

Characteristics of Pattern. There are certain predictable characteristics of this "basic ground plan":

1. Development is similar for all. All children follow a similar pattern of development, with one stage leading into the next. The baby stands before he walks, for example, and draws a circle before a square. In no instance is this order normally reversed. Furthermore, the general pattern is not altered by individual variations in speed of development. The child who is born prematurely may lag behind in development for about a year, but after that he catches up to the norm for full-term babies and follows the same pattern as they and at about the same rate (62). Only when the prematurely born baby is damaged before or during birth is the normal sequence of development likely to be altered (2). The very bright child and the very dull child likewise follow the same developmental sequence as the average; the very bright child develops at a more rapid rate, however, and the very dull at a slower rate (68).

2. Development proceeds from general to specific responses. In mental as well as motor responses, general activity always precedes specific activity. Before birth, the fetus moves his whole body but is incapable of making specific responses. So it is in early postnatal life. The baby waves his arms in general movements before he is capable of as specific a response as reaching.

Studies of speech have revealed that the young child learns general words before specific ones (117). He uses the word "toy," for example, before he learns to call each toy by its name. All dogs are "doggie" before they are designated as "Rowdy," "Penny," or "Scottie." In emotional behavior, the baby first responds to strange or unusual objects with a general fear; later his fears become more specific and are characterized by different types of behavior, such as crying, running away and hiding, or standing his ground and pretending that he is not afraid (91).

3. Development is continuous. From a superficial study of the growth of one feature, such as height, it might seem that the child grows by "fits and starts." Likewise, the use of such terms as "babyhood" and "adolescence" suggests that there are definite periods when development takes place and others when it ceases. This, however, is not true. On the contrary, development is continuous from the moment of conception to death, but it occurs at different rates—sometimes slowly and sometimes rapidly.

The appearance of baby teeth, often overnight, for example, may lead one to conclude that they developed suddenly. They did not. As early as the fifth fetal month, teeth begin to develop in the jaw, but they are not ready to cut through the gums much before the baby is five months old. Similarly, speech does not develop overnight. Instead,

it gradually evolves from the coos, gurgles, and babbling sounds made by the baby from the time of birth.

Because development is continuous, what happens at one stage has an influence on the following stage. Emotional tension in the home will affect the young child's developing personality and will be reflected in certain personality scars, even though his later home environment may be relatively free from stress and tension. This has been demonstrated in many cases where the child's parents were divorced. Unhealthy attitudes about self or about relationships with others during the early years are rarely eliminated completely. They are reflected in the individual's outlook on life even in middle and old age (152).

4. Development proceeds at different rates. While the development of different physical and mental traits is continuous, it is never uniform for the entire organism (174). If the body is to attain its adult proportions, inequalities in rate must occur. The feet, hands, and nose, for example, reach their maximum developmental level early in adolescence, while the lower parts of the face and shoulders are slower in reaching theirs. Refer to Figure 1-1, page 3, for a graphic illustration of the differences in body proportions of a newborn infant and an adult. Different internal organs likewise reach their mature level at different times. The heart, liver, and digestive system, for example, grow slowly in childhood but rapidly during the early years of adolescence.

Measurements of different intellectual capacities have revealed that they, like the physical traits, develop at different rates and reach maturity at different ages (96). As Bayley has stressed, longitudinal studies of the same group of children over a long period of time have resulted in many changes in accepted ideas and theories about intelligence. Earlier studies, carried on over a short period, led to the conclusion that the IQ was constant and that "intelligence is a basic entity which changes only by accretions and decrements in quantity with childhood growth, adult stability, and senescent decline" (14). Retests of the same children over a period of years, however, have shown that "intelligence is a dynamic succession of developing functions, with the more advanced and complex functions in the hierarchy depending on the prior maturing of earlier simpler ones (given, of course, normal conditions of care)" (14).

As children grow older, there is increasing independence in the development of their mental abilities. Each develops at its own rate and reaches its mature level at its own age. Creative imagination, for example, develops rapidly in childhood and reaches its peak early in adolescence. Reasoning, on the other hand, proceeds at a relatively slow rate. Rote memory and memory for concrete objects and facts develop more quickly than memory for abstract, theoretical material (96).

Variations in the rate of development of different physical and mental traits, especially when pronounced, lead to many adjustment problems. The "superior-immature" child, whose intellectual development outpaces his physical, social, or emotional development, will be out of step with both his contemporaries and older children. Similarly, the fact that some parts of the body reach their mature size earlier than others accounts in part at least for the awkwardness and self-consciousness of the young adolescent (34, 64).

5. *There is correlation in development.* The stage of maturity in one trait affects that in others. Gesell stressed the importance of correlation when he said, "The products of growth are envisaged as a fabric in which threads and designs are visible" (62). Correlation between physical and mental development is especially marked. Body configuration—the relationship of the different areas of the body to one another as well as to the total form—is related to school readiness because of the correlation of mental and physical development (151). There is also a marked relationship between sexual maturing and patterns of interest and behavior. As a result, early maturers differ not only in physical but in mental and behavioral development from children of the same age who are late maturers (98). Studies of symbolic behavior have shown that the pattern of development in this area follows the pattern of biologic growth (81).

There is a popular belief that nature compensates for inadequacies in one area by greater development in other areas. The girl who is "beautiful but dumb" and the boy who is "brainy but a physical weakling" are stereotypes of this belief. This belief has not been borne out by experimental studies. It is not true that a child who is above average in one trait will be below average in other traits (68, 164). From genetic studies of gifted children up to middle age, Terman came to the conclusion that "desirable traits tend to go together. No negative correlations were found between intelligence and size, strength, physical well-being, or emotional stability" (165).

Some Predictable Patterns. From the many evidences of an orderly, predictable pattern in *physical development,* in both prenatal and postnatal life, have come two laws of the directional sequence of development: the *cephalocaudal law* and the *proximodistal law.* According to the cephalocaudal law, development spreads over the body from head to foot. This means that improvements in structure and function come first in the head region, then in the trunk, and last in the leg region. The top-heavy body of the baby shows that much more development has occurred in the head than in the leg region. This is true of motor functions also. When a baby is placed in a prone position, he can raise his head by lifting his neck before he can do so by lifting his chest. At the age of twenty weeks, the baby has control over the muscles of his eyes, head, and shoulders, but his trunk is still so flaccid that he must be propped or strapped in a chair to be able to maintain a sitting position (62).

According to the proximodistal law, development proceeds from near to far—outward from the central axis of the body toward the extremities. In prenatal development, the head and trunk are fairly well developed when the rudimentary limb buds appear. Gradually, the arm buds lengthen and then develop into the hands and fingers. Functionally, the baby can use his arms before his hands and can use his hands as a unit before he can control the movements of his fingers (62). The laws of developmental direction are illustrated in Figure 1–3.

The teeth provide another example of the predictable pattern of physical development. The lower teeth erupt before the upper, and the incisors, or biting teeth, before the molars, which are used for chewing. The pattern for shedding and replacing the baby teeth is likewise predictable. Normally, the first of the baby teeth to erupt are the first to be replaced by permanent teeth (166). Studies of the physical changes at the time of puberty have shown that development of the sex organs and the appearance of the secondary sex characteristics also follow a patterned sequence (160).

Longitudinal studies of *intelligence* have revealed that the pattern of mental development is as predictable as the pattern of physical development. From Figure 1–4, which comprises the results of several longitudinal studies covering different segments of the life-span from birth to fifty years, it is apparent that the major part of mental growth comes when the body is developing most rapidly, during the first sixteen to eighteen years of life. Following this, the curve rises slowly up to fifty years. What happens after that is still undecided because there have been too few longitudinal studies, to date, to be certain when mental decline begins or how it progresses (14). There is also a predictable pattern for development of the different intellectual functions, such as memory and reasoning, that constitute general intelligence (131).

Genetic studies of babies from birth to five years have shown that there is a general *behavioral* pattern that all babies follow. This pattern, which is illustrated in Figure 1–5, is as follows:

From 4 to 16 weeks, the baby gains control of his 12 oculomotor muscles.
From 16 to 28 weeks, he gains command of

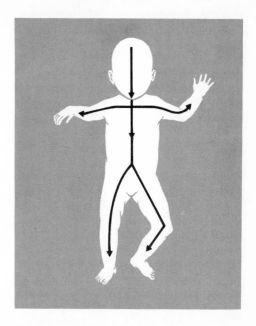

Figure 1–3. The laws of developmental direction. (Adapted from E. L. Vincent and P. C. Martin, *Human psychological development,* Ronald, 1961. Used by permission.)

the muscles which support his head and move his arms. He then begins to reach out for things.
From 28 to 40 weeks, he gains control of his trunk and hands. This enables him to sit and to grasp, transfer, and manipulate objects.
From 40 to 52 weeks, he extends control to his legs and feet, to his forefinger and thumb. He can now stand upright, poke, and pluck.
During the second year, he walks and runs; articulates words and phrases; achieves bowel and bladder control; and acquires a rudimentary sense of personal identity and of personal possession.
During the third year, he speaks in sentences and uses words as tools of thought. He displays a propensity to understand his environment and to comply with cultural demands.
During the fourth year, he asks innumerable questions, perceives analogies, and displays a tendency to generalize and conceptualize. In the routines of home life, he is nearly self-dependent.

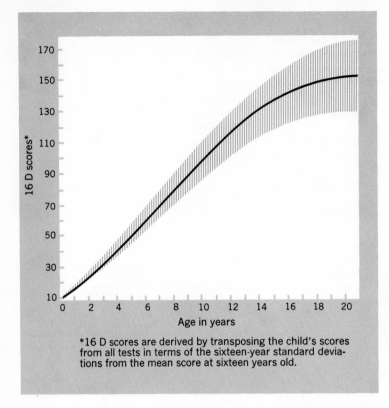

Figure 1–4. The pattern of intellectual development. (Adapted from N. Bayley, On the growth of intelligence, *Amer. Psychologist*, 1955, 10, 805–818. Used by permission.)

*16 D scores are derived by transposing the child's scores from all tests in terms of the sixteen-year standard deviations from the mean score at sixteen years old.

At the age of five years, the child is well matured in motor control. He can hop and skip. He talks without infantile articulation and can narrate a long tale. He prefers associative play and feels socialized pride in clothes and accomplishments. He is now a self-assured, conforming citizen in his small world (62).

Specific areas of development likewise follow predictable patterns. Patterns in different aspects of motor development, emotional behavior, speech, social behavior, and academic learning have been found. Concept development follows patterns in the areas of time, of self, of moral and religious beliefs, of the comic, and of the beautiful. Characteristic patterns in the child's identification with another person and in goals and interests have also been reported. All these patterns will be discussed in subsequent chapters.

Deviant Development. Because development is influenced by environment as well as by hereditary potentials, unfavorable environmental conditions can alter the predictable pattern either temporarily or permanently. When there are deviations from the normal pattern of physical development, there are generally deviations in psychological development. Alterations in the pattern of development may be in the rate of development or, less commonly, in the actual pattern itself. While the time needed to complete the developmental pattern differs from child to child, it will be completed by all at approximately twenty-one years of age.

Poor health, inadequate nutrition, emotional deprivation, lack of incentive to learn, and many other factors may retard the normal rate. Unless these factors persist over a long period of time, their influence is generally only temporary. Some factors, however, such as level of intelligence, may have a permanent influence. In the case of walking, for example, bright children start to walk at an average age of thirteen months; average children, at fourteen months; morons, at twenty-two months; and high-grade idiots, at thirty months. Very bright children talk first at an average age of eleven months; children of average intelligence, at sixteen months; morons, at thirty-four months; and high-grade idiots, at fifty-one months. Low-grade idiots never learn to walk or talk (165).

The pattern of development may also be altered permanently by unfavorable environmental conditions before or after birth (4). Deficiency of thyroid activity during the prenatal period stunts physical and mental growth, thus producing a "cretin," or deformed idiot. Calcium deficiency during the

prenatal and early postnatal months results in rickets—a disease in which the bones do not harden normally, thus resulting in carious teeth, flat chests, crooked backs, or deformed pelvises. Emotional deprivation and overprotection, as well as other restrictions on normal development, may result in personality distortions. All these alterations in both the rate and pattern of development will be discussed more fully in later chapters.

Importance of Predicting Development. Because the rate and pattern of physical development are predictable, it is possible to anticipate at a fairly early age the range within which the child will fall at maturity, barring unfavorable environmental conditions during the time when development is taking place. This may be quite important in the case of a child whose size deviates so

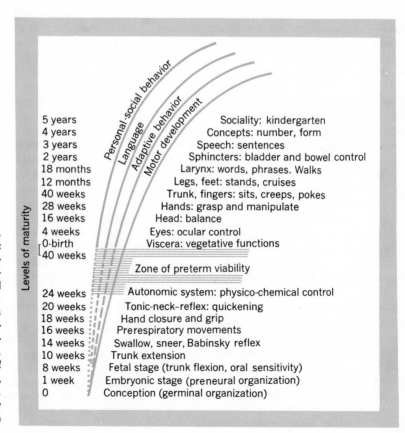

Figure 1–5. Ontogenetic trends and sequences of behavior. (Adapted from A. Gesell, The ontogenesis of infant behavior, in L. Carmichael (Ed.), *Manual of child psychology,* 2d ed., Wiley, 1954. Used by permission.)

markedly from that of his agemates that he feels "abnormal." Similarly, the predictable pattern of intellectual development enables parents to plan a child's education and to train him for the type of work he is best fitted to do. It has also proved to be helpful in the selection of babies for adoption.

Knowing that different mental abilities develop in unique ways makes it possible to plan an educational curriculum which will further the development of children's mental capacities and to prepare them for the next step in the educational ladder.

THERE ARE INDIVIDUAL DIFFERENCES IN THE DEVELOPMENTAL PATTERN

Although the pattern of development is similar for all children, each child follows the predictable pattern in his own way and at his own rate. All children do not, therefore, reach the same point of development at the same age. Frank has described the individuality of development thus: "The life career is a broad highway along which every individual must travel. Each individual, with his unique heredity and nurture (including prenatal) will travel along that highway at his or her own rate of progress and will attain the size, shape, capacity, and developmental status which are uniquely his or her own at each stage in the life career" (51).

There are many reasons for individual differences in the rate and pattern of development; both can be changed by conditions either within or without the body (4). *Physical development,* for example, depends partly on hereditary potentials and partly on such environmental factors as food, general health conditions, sunlight, fresh air, climatic conditions, absence or presence of prolonged emotional strain, and pressures or absence of pressures from hard physical work. The *intellectual development* of a child is the result of varied and complex factors, such as inherent capacity for growth, the emotional climate, whether he is encouraged or discouraged in intellectual activities, whether his drive is strong in intellectual processes or directed into other channels, and whether he has opportunities

for experiences and learning. *Personality development* is influenced by attitudes and social relationships.

Even though the rate of development may vary for different children, it is consistent for the same child. Children who are tall at one age, for example, are tall at other ages, while those who are short remain short (87). The same principle holds true in behavioral patterns. Individual movements, whether of simple or advanced patterns, remain remarkably constant over a period of time. Similarly, growth curves for mental age for bright, average, and dull children have shown a constancy that is also found in curves for physical growth. Accelerated mental growth continues to be accelerated, while children who are mentally deficient do not, except in unusual cases, "catch up" to the normal child. What is more likely to happen is that they will become more and more retarded as they grow older (68, 131).

From retests of the intelligence of children from birth to maturity, it has become apparent that for each child there is a strong underlying consistency. Figure 1–6 shows curves for five boys and five girls, from one month to twenty-five years of age. As may be seen in these curves, there is similarity for all at first, but then, around six years of age, individual differences begin to appear. This similarity in the earlier years may not be as great as it appears: Tests for the early years may not be as diagnostic of differences as those for the older age levels are (14).

Consistency means that the child will progress at the rate at which he started and will follow a pattern of development that is characteristically his, controlled by his unique combination of heredity and environment. Commenting on this consistency, Bayley stated:

We were amazed at the precocity of some of the babies whose mothers seemed not very bright, and embarrassed at the poor records of other babies who, by the laws of inheritance, should have done better. But we soon found that our embarrassments and amazements were alleviated with time: a slow baby would forge ahead and redeem his inheritance, a precocious infant often seemed

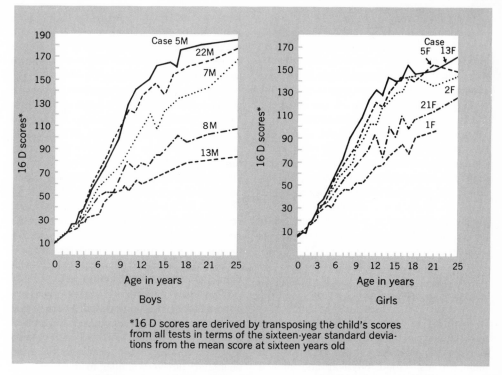

Figure 1–6. Individual differences in intellectual development. (Adapted from N. Bayley, On the growth of intelligence, *Amer. Psychologist*, 1955, 10, 805–818. Used by permission.)

to rest on his laurels, while the others caught up with him (14).

In childhood, variations in the pattern of intellectual development may be altered by such conditions as emotional climate, cultural milieu, emotional deprivation, and developmental changes in the behaviors tested. But these variations are slight: The child remains true to his own pattern of development (14).

Practical Significance of Individual Differences. Because each child has his own characteristic rate of development, we cannot expect the same behavior from all children of the same age. We cannot, for example, fairly compare babies who were born prematurely with those who were born at full term. Similarly, because of the marked individual differences in the time and rate

of sexual maturing, we must expect differences in the interests, attitudes, and behavior patterns of boys and girls of the same chronological age who are early, late, or average maturers.

Mental development, too, is influenced by both hereditary endowment and environment. Therefore, we cannot expect *all* children of the same chronological or mental age to be ready for the same learning experiences at the same time (105). A child with normal intelligence who has not been encouraged to use his mental capacities will not be as ready for the learning experiences of first grade, especially reading, as children whose parents put a high value on education and encourage mental activity in their children (124).

Finally, because the pattern of development is influenced by deviant physical or mental development, and by sex, race, and many other factors, these must be taken into consideration in judging and comparing children. For example, it is recognized that in girls the pattern of speech development is more rapid than in boys. Consequently, one cannot expect boys to measure as favorably in language skills as girls of the same age (117). Similarly, children of different racial groups should be judged by the norms for their group, not by norms for other racial groups. Negro and white babies of approximately equal socioeconomic status, for example, develop differently. Negro babies show a slightly lower developmental trend during the second year of life than white babies; after that, the developmental trends become even more divergent (132).

EARLY DEVELOPMENT IS MORE IMPORTANT THAN LATER DEVELOPMENT

In building a house, the foundations are more important than the superstructure; so it is in the development of physical and mental traits. Good physical and mental potentials can be seriously damaged by unfavorable environmental conditions during prenatal and early postnatal life. Later, such conditions are less damaging. Furthermore, if the patterns of attitudes, interests, skills, and emotional behavior are well laid, further development will result in behavior that will lead to good life adjustments, and vice versa. Carlson and Stieglitz said, "We are what we are today, to a great degree, because of what happened to us in our yesterday, and no two people have had identical sequences of yesterdays. Furthermore, the effect of all these experiences increases with age, because they accumulate" (35).

The plasticity of the human physical and nervous structures makes it possible for a child to be molded into patterns that would be impossible in animals, where such structures are nearly ready to function at birth. Because of this plasticity, the child can learn varied types of adjustment and, as a result, can make greater progress and rise to a higher level of development (132). This great plasticity is not always an advantage. Like clay that can be transformed into a

work of art or a monstrosity, the young child can be molded into a person who will make good adjustments to life or one who is so seriously maladjusted that his usefulness to society is nil.

The first important scientific clue of the significance of the early years came from Freud's studies of personality maladjustments. These maladjustments, Freud found, could be traced to unfavorable experiences during childhood years (32, 56). More recent studies of maladjustments have substantiated Freud's contentions (30). A study of children in a mental hospital, for example, revealed that 80 per cent of them were so poorly adjusted that they had never belonged to any group and had few friends. In addition, many of them had speech, academic, and enuretic difficulties (9).

That early patterns of behavior are persistent has been demonstrated by studies in different areas of development. Clinical records of adult mental patients have revealed that, as children, they displayed behavior characteristics very similar to those of their adult years, only in milder forms. By contrast, it has been found that well-adjusted children generally develop into well-adjusted adults (55, 152). In attitudes and values and in preferred leisure activities, people change little as life progresses, even when there are marked cultural changes taking place (78). As a result of this constancy, many adults who are approaching middle age seem "set in their ways" or "rigid." Studies of this phenomenon lead one to conclude that the "foundations and most of the framework of the human action system are laid down in the first decade" (64).

Importance of Early Foundations.   There are two implications to be drawn from our knowledge of the importance of early foundations to later development. First, because learning plays an increasingly dominant role as the child grows older, the pattern of his *development can be controlled and directed* into channels that will result in good adjustment. Allowing a child to "grow up like Topsy," doing what he wishes when he wishes, is obviously unfair to him. A child is too inexperienced to know when he is on the right or on the wrong track. How, for example, can a child know that developing right-handed skills will be more useful to him than developing left-handed skills, that mispronunciation of words and grammatical errors will create the impression that he is an ignorant person, or that aggressive attacks on playmates will win more enemies than friends?

Indirectly, a child receives some guidance in establishing patterns of behavior from the social group. In a genetic study of striving for achievement and social recognition, the persistence of behavior patterns from early childhood into adulthood was explained by the reinforcement that came from social approval, with its accompaniment of personal satisfaction. Behavior that is not rewarded by social approval gives little satisfaction to the child, and he abandons it. This is well illustrated by dependency. Dependency is not considered sex-appropriate for boys, and it is met with parental disapproval. The opposite occurs in the case of girls. Were dependency discouraged among girls, it would be extinguished and replaced by independence as it is in boys (126).

Guidance is most needed in the early stages of learning, when the foundations are being laid. If the child is put on the right track at first and encouraged to remain there until he becomes accustomed to it or realizes why it is best, he will be less likely to get on the wrong track later. He will need less guidance as he grows older, although guidance can never be completely relaxed.

The second important implication is that, since early foundations are so important, it is sometimes desirable to *make changes in what has been learned*. The sooner the change is made, the easier it is for the child, and consequently, the more likely he will be to cooperate in making the change. Once a pattern of behavior has been thoroughly learned, it must be unlearned before it can be replaced by a new pattern. This is hard and time-consuming. Once a child learns to use his left hand efficiently, for example, he will rebel against learning to shift to the right hand (80).

DEVELOPMENT PROCEEDS BY STAGES

As Feldman has pointed out, "Human life proceeds by stages. The life periods of the human individual are no less real and significant than the geological ages of the earth or the evolutionary stages of life. . . . Each stage is distinguished by a dominant feature, a leading characteristic, which gives the period its coherence, its unity, and its uniqueness" (48). At different ages certain traits stand out more conspicuously than others.

It is possible, therefore, to mark off major periods, each characterized by a specific form of development which overshadows in importance other forms of development taking place. Owing to individual variations, the age limits for these periods can be only roughly predicted. Apropos of this, English has commented, "Let us frankly admit that all the distinctions are arbitrary. There is not one of the life periods which could not perfectly well have its limits shifted forward or backward" (47).

The five major developmental periods, with their characteristic forms of development and *approximate* ages, are as follows:

1. **Prenatal Period.** This period extends from conception, when the female ovum is fertilized by the male spermatozoon, to the time of birth, roughly 9 calendar months, or 280 days. While the prenatal period is a short one, it is nevertheless one of extremely rapid development. The primary development taking place at this time is physiological and consists of the growth of all the bodily structures.

2. **Infancy.** Infancy begins at birth and extends to the age of ten to fourteen days. This is the period of the *newborn,* or the *neonate* (derived from the Greek word *neos,* meaning "new," and the Latin verb *nascor,* meaning "to be born"), and is a plateau, or resting stage, in human development. It is at this time that adjustment to a totally new environment outside the mother's body must be made. During this time, growth almost

comes to a standstill and is not resumed until the infant is able to cope successfully with his new environment.

3. Babyhood. The third developmental age in the child's life is babyhood, a period extending from the age of two weeks to approximately two years. At first the baby is helpless. He must depend on others for his every need. Gradually he becomes more self-reliant, learning to control his muscles so that he can feed himself, walk, dress himself, talk, and play. He develops an attitude of independence and resents being "babied."

4. Childhood. The childhood years include the years from age two to adolescence, though the entire period of immaturity is often included. The child, who as a baby learned to control his body, now seeks to gain control over his environment. In addition, he learns to make social adjustments. From approximately the sixth year, socialization is of paramount importance. This period is often called the "gang age" because group activities play so important a role in the child's life.

As this is a relatively long period, and as the dominant form of development in early childhood differs from that in later childhood, it is common to subdivide childhood into two stages, "early" and "late," with the dividing line at the age of school entrance, six years.

5. Adolescence. The adolescent years extend from the time the child becomes sexually mature—about age thirteen for girls and fourteen for boys—to legal maturity, at twenty-one years of age. It is customary to divide adolescence into two periods, "early" and "late" adolescence, with the dividing line coming around the seventeenth year.

The major developmental task of adolescence is preparation for adulthood. In early adolescence, emphasis is on learning to be independent of adult guidance and control; in late adolescence, emphasis is on learning the specific skills needed to be an adult. Late adolescence may be looked upon as the last

step in the long period of development which begins at conception.

Practical Significance of Developmental Stages. Because all children normally pass through the different stages of development at approximately the same ages, child training and provisions for learning are planned to fit into the pattern characteristic of children of a given cultural group. Furthermore, the cultural group expects each child to master the developmental tasks it sets for these stages. There are individual variations, however, as has been stressed before. A slight variation from the norm can generally be compensated for with help from parents and teachers.

When deviations are great, either above or below the norm, special provisions must be made. Otherwise, the child will be too out of step to profit by the learning experiences provided for his agemates. This has long been recognized in education, and, as a result, classes with specialized instruction are provided for very bright and very dull children or for those who suffer from a physical handicap, such as blindness, deafness, or lameness. Unfortunately, the necessity of special learning opportunities for those who deviate from the norm is not always recognized in the home. As a result, far too many children are expected to adjust to an environment unsuited to their individual levels of development.

When the developmental pattern is normal, one stage prepares the child for, and leads him successfully into, the next. In social development, for example, the preschool child is expected to learn to make social adjustments to his agemates. If he is deprived of the necessary learning opportunities, he will be unready for the next higher stage, the gang age, when there is little or no adult supervision.

Even though the child's development in other areas may have followed the normal pattern, retardation in an area that is dominant at a given age is likely to interfere with development in related areas. It has been found, for example, that children who are unpopular are deprived of opportunities to become socialized. Being cut off from social contacts with agemates, such children are likewise deprived of opportunities to develop motor skills, communications skills, and emotional control. As a result, the whole developmental pattern is affected.

EACH STAGE HAS CHARACTERISTIC TRAITS

The behavior of any given child at any given age is colored partly by his own basic individuality and partly by the pattern of his age level. The pattern is not affected so much by what the child can accomplish as by the way in which he behaves (85). There is a consistency in each child which stems from the way he attacks the problems that arise at each stage. This consistency results in individual differences. Lawton has explained these differences in the following way:

Our life span is divided into periods, each with its own problems of adjustment. These age periods are not related in surface story since the problems change; it is the method of attacking these problems which is likely to remain the same. Throughout the life span, people develop techniques of handling each of their difficulties. Some of these techniques are suitable and efficient, others are inappropriate and wasteful, or a method may be suitable for one age period and not another (110).

Phases of Equilibrium and Disequilibrium. In the developmental pattern, some phases are characterized by "equilibrium," and others by "disequilibrium." These phases alternate in accordance with the principle of neuromotor interweaving. In the former, the child is making good adjustments and is easy to live with. In the latter, his adjustments appear to be disrupted by conditions within himself or by environmental factors; there are tensions, indecisions, insecurities, and similar behavior problems. As a result, the child is difficult to live with. His behavior difficulties are not individual aberrations but are characteristic of his age level and, hence, predictable (62).

Genetic studies of children have revealed the predictable ages of equilibrium and disequilibrium in the childhood years. Periods of disequilibrium occur at the ages of 15 months, 2½ years, 3½ years, and 5½ years and again as childhood is drawing to a close. At these times, the child seems to be "loosening up" and "snapping old bonds." Between the periods of disequilibrium are periods of equilibrium, when the child is "in focus" and when his behavior shows signs of better adjustment. After a child enters school, his behavior generally improves, and he remains in equilibrium until the physical changes accompanying puberty begin. After the "storm and stress" of puberty, the child, now sexually mature, normally reverts to a state of equilibrium (157, 160).

The ages given above are only averages. Since boys and girls develop at different rates, their periods of equilibrium and disequilibrium can be expected to occur at different ages. Within each sex group there are also marked differences between early and late maturers (64, 160).

Cautions in Judging Children's Behavior. Every stage of development is characterized by certain forms of age-appropriate behavior which might be labeled "problem behavior" if it were judged by adult standards.

Parents and teachers often describe behavior that interferes with the efficient running of the home or school as problem behavior. The child is called "immature" or is accused of "not acting his age." A child who refuses to take a nap or who calls out for a drink of water as soon as he is put to bed is likely to be considered a "problem child" because his behavior is annoying. Studies of young children have shown, however, that such behavior is common during the first three years of life (86).

Minor pilfering is very common during the first and second grades, while lying is almost universal just before the child enters school (84, 115). Similarly, carelessness about work and appearance, destructiveness, shouting, name calling, indifference to school work, and daydreaming are perfectly normal in the early grades of school (104).

Annoying as such behavior may be, it is unfair to consider it problem behavior or to punish the child for it.

Lack of understanding of the normal behavior of children at different ages is responsible for much of the friction between parents and children and between teachers and pupils. When adults treat normal behavior as problem behavior, they are likely to develop in the child unfavorable attitudes toward them and toward the situation in which the behavior occurs. The result is that many children then develop real problem behavior, such as lying, sneakiness, or destructiveness, as a way of getting their revenge.

Most forms of real problem behavior are normal for a younger age. Often a child clings to immature behavior because he has not yet learned how to meet his needs in a more mature manner or because he derives less satisfaction from mature than from immature behavior. For example, a child often reverts to infantile behavior when he is jealous. He derives satisfaction from the attention his helplessness brings. If a child clings to these patterns of behavior as he grows older or reverts to them after he has learned more mature patterns, it is symptomatic of some disturbance in his social relationships and may be regarded as true problem behavior. Children who behave in a manner characteristic of younger ages not only make poor adjustments to life but are punished by society by social rejection. Stealing, for example, will be tolerated in preschool children, but in an older child or adolescent it will be regarded as "delinquent" behavior (104, 115).

Just because certain forms of behavior are normal for the ages at which they occur does not make them acceptable, nor does it mean that they should be tolerated without any effort to make them more acceptable. If a child is capable of learning to say "No," he is also capable of learning to say "Thank you." Similarly, if he has enough muscle coordination to grab another child's toys, he has enough muscle coordination to offer the child whose toys he grabs one of his in exchange. Only when he has direction will he learn that certain forms of behavior are socially acceptable and others unacceptable. Naturally, one cannot expect a child to behave like an adult, but one can expect a child to learn more and more adult-approved behavior patterns with each passing year. If this is done, the unacceptable behavior will gradually be replaced by acceptable behavior.

No form of problem behavior should be overlooked on the grounds that it is "typical" and that the child will "outgrow" it in time. He may, but the chances are just as great that he will not. Furthermore, if it is overlooked, the child is likely to assume that it is acceptable. *Behavior that is not typically found at the child's age or maturity level is a danger signal of possible future trouble.* As such, it should be remedied before it has developed into a habitual method of adjustment.

BIBLIOGRAPHY

(1) ABERLE, D. F., and K. D. NAEGELE: Middle-class fathers' occupational roles and attitudes toward children. *Amer. J. Orthopsychiat.,* 1952, **22,** 366–378.

(2) ALM, I.: The long-term prognosis for prematurely born children. *Acta paediat., Stockh.,* 1953, **42,** 591–594.

(3) AMEN, E. W., and N. RENISON: A study of the relationship between play patterns and anxiety in young children. *Genet. Psychol. Monogr.,* 1954, **50,** 3–41.

(4) ANASTASI, A.: Heredity, environment, and the question "how?" *Psychol. Rev.,* 1958, **65,** 197–208.

(5) ANASTASI, A., and J. P. FOLEY: A proposed reorientation in the heredity-environment controversy. *Psychol. Rev.,* 1948, **55,** 239–249.

(6) ANDERSON, J. E.: Methods of child psychology. In L. Carmichael (Ed.), *Manual of child psychology,* 2d ed. New York: Wiley, 1954. Pp. 1–59.

(7) ANDERSON, J. E.: Behavior and personality. In E. Ginzberg, *The nation's children*. Vol. 2. *Development and education*. New York: Columbia, 1960. Pp. 43–69.

(8) ANDERSON, J. E.: Child development research: the next 25 years. *Child Develpm.*, 1960, **31**, 191–199.

(9) BAKER, J. W., and A. HOLGWORTH: Social histories of successful and unsuccessful children. *Child Develpm.*, 1961, **32**, 135–149.

(10) BAKWIN, H.: Juvenile delinquency. *J. Pediat.*, 1953, **42**, 387–391; 1954, **44**, 338–342.

(11) BANHAM, K. M.: Senescence and the emotions: a genetic theory, *J. genet. Psychol.*, 1951, **78**, 175–183.

(12) BARSCHAK, E.: Happiness and unhappiness in the childhood and adolescence of a group of women students: a comparative study of English and American girls. *Brit. J. Psychol.*, 1952, **43**, 129–140.

(13) BAYLEY, N.: Some increasing parent-child similarities during the growth of children. *J. educ. Psychol.*, 1954, **45**, 1–21.

(14) BAYLEY, N.: On the growth of intelligence. *Amer. Psychologist*, 1955, **10**, 805–818.

(15) BAYLEY, N.: Individual patterns of development. *Child Develpm.*, 1956, **27**, 45–74.

(16) BAYLEY, N., and M. H. ODEN: The maintenance of intellectual ability in gifted adults. *J. Gerontol.*, 1955, **10**, 91–107.

(17) BAYLEY, N., and S. R. PINNAU: Tables for predicting adult height from skeletal age: revised for use with the Greulich-Pyle Hand Standards. *J. Pediat.*, 1952, **40**, 423–441.

(18) BEILIN, H.: Teachers' and clinicians' attitudes toward the behavior problems of children. *Child Develpm.*, 1959, **30**, 9–25.

(19) BELL, R. Q.: Retrospective attitude studies of parent-child relations. *Child Develpm.*, 1958, **29**, 323–338.

(20) BLEGEN, S. D.: The primitive child. *Acta paediat., Stockh.*, 1953, **42**, Suppl. 88.

(21) BLOOMERS, P., L. M. KNIEF, and J. B. STROUD: The organismic age concept. *J. educ. Psychol.*, 1955, **46**, 142–150.

(22) BLUM, L. H.: Pediatric practice and the science of child development. *Nerv. Child*, 1952, **9**, 233–241.

(23) BOBROFF, A.: The stages of maturation in socialized thinking and in the ego development of two groups of children. *Child Develpm.*, 1960, **31**, 321–338.

(24) BOLL, E. S.: The role of preschool playmates: a situational approach. *Child Develpm.*, 1957, **28**, 327–342.

(25) BONNEY, M. E., and E. L. NICHOLSON. Comparative social adjustments of elementary school pupils with and without preschool training. *Child Develpm.*, 1958, **29**, 125–133.

(26) BOSSARD, J. H. S.: *Parent and child*. Philadelphia: University Pennsylvania Press, 1953.

(27) BOSSARD, J. H. S., and E. S. BOLL: *The sociology of child development*, 3d ed. New York: Harper & Row, 1960.

(28) BRECKENRIDGE, M. E., and E. L. VINCENT: *Child development*, 4th ed. Philadelphia: Saunders, 1960.

(29) BRIM, O. G.: The acceptance of new behavior in child rearing. *Hum. Relat.*, 1954, **7**, 473–491.

(30) BROWN, F.: Depression and childhood bereavement. *J. ment. Sci.*, 1961, **107**, 754–777.

(31) BURLINGHAM, D. T.: Precursors of some psychoanalytic ideas about children in the sixteenth and seventeenth centuries. In R. S. Eissler, *The psychoanalytic study of the child*. New York: International Universities Press, 1951. Pp. 244–254.

(32) CALDWELL, B. M., and J. B. RICHMOND: The impact of theories of child development. *Children*, 1962, **9**, 73–78.

(33) CANADY, H. G.: The contributions of cultural anthropology to the study of human behavior. *Sch. Soc.*, 1948, **68**, 267–270.

(34) CAPLAN, H.: The role of deviant maturation in the pathogenesis of anxiety. *Amer. J. Orthopsychiat.*, 1956, **26**, 94–107.

(35) CARLSON, A. J., and E. J. STIEGLITZ: Physiological changes in aging. *Ann. Amer. Acad. Pol. Soc. Sci.*, 1952, **279**, 18–31.

(36) CATTELL, R. B., G. J. STICE, and N. F. KRISTY: A first approximation to nature-nurture ratios for eleven primary personality factors in objective tests. *J. abnorm. soc. Psychol.*, 1957, **54**, 143–159.

(37) CHRISTENSEN, C. M.: Relationships between pupil achievement, pupil affect-need, teacher warmth, and teacher permissiveness. *J. educ. Psychol.*, 1960, **51**, 169–174.

(38) COREY, S. M., and V. E. HERRICK: The developmental tasks of children and young people. In J. M. Seidman (Ed.), *The child, a book of readings*. New York: Holt, 1958. Pp. 31–41.

(39) CRANE, A. R.: Stereotypes of the adult held by early adolescents. *J. educ. Res.*, 1956, **50**, 227–230.

(40) CRANE, A. R.: The development of moral values in children. IV. Preadolescent gangs and the moral development of children. *Brit. J. educ. Psychol.*, 1958, **28**, 201–208.

(41) DAMERON, L. E.: Mother-child interaction in the development of self-restraint. *J. genet. Psychol.*, 1955, **86**, 289–308.

(42) DAVIS, A., and R. J. HAVIGHURST: *Father of the man*. Boston: Houghton Mifflin, 1947.

(43) DENNIS, W.: Infant development under conditions of restricted practice and minimum social stimulation. *Genet. Psychol. Monogr.*, 1941, **23**, 143–189.

(44) DENNIS, W.: Scientific models for the investigation of child development. In P. H. Hoch and J. Zubin, *Psychopathology of*

childhood. New York: Grune & Stratton, 1955. Pp. 15–24.

(45) DESMOND, T. C.: America's unknown middle-agers. *The New York Times,* July 29, 1956.

(46) ENGEL, C. E., and P. HANSELL: Use and abuse of the film in recording the behavior and reactions of the newborn infant. *Cerebral Palsy Bull.,* 1961, **3**, 472–480.

(47) ENGLISH, H. B.: Chronological divisions of the life span. *J. educ. Psychol.,* 1957, **48**, 437–439.

(48) FELDMAN, S.: Origins of behavior and man's life career. *Amer. J. Psychol.,* 1941, **54**, 53–63.

(49) FISH, B.: Longitudinal observations of biological deviations in a schizophrenic infant. *Amer. J. Psychiat.,* 1959, **116**, 25–31.

(50) FOLKMAN, J. D.: Stressful and supportive interaction. *Marriage fam. Liv.,* 1956, **18**, 102–106.

(51) FRANK, L. K.: The concept of maturity. *Child Develpm.,* 1950, **21**, 21–24.

(52) FRANK, L. K.: Genetic psychology and its prospects. *Amer. J. Orthopsychiat.,* 1951, **21**, 506–522.

(53) FRANK, L. K., and M. H. FRANK: Teachers' attitudes affect children's relationships. *Education,* 1954, **75**, 6–12.

(54) FRANK, L. K., and M. H. FRANK: *Your adolescent, at home and in school.* New York: Viking, 1956.

(55) FRAZEE, H. E.: Children who later became schizophrenic. *Smith Coll. Stud. soc. Wk,* 1953, **23**, 125–149.

(56) FREUD, S.: *The standard edition of the complete works of Sigmund Freud.* London: Hogarth, 1953–1962.

(57) GALLAGHER, J. J.: Peer acceptance of highly gifted children in elementary school. *Elem. Sch. J.,* 1958, **58**, 465–470.

(58) GESELL, A.: *Infancy and human growth.* New York: Macmillan, 1928.

(59) GESELL, A.: How science studies the child. *Sci. Mon., N. Y.,* 1932, **34**, 265–267.

(60) GESELL, A.: Growth potentials of the human infant. *Sci. Mon., N. Y.,* 1949, **68**, 252–256.

(61) GESELL, A.: Developmental pediatrics. *Nerv. Child,* 1952, **9**, 225–227.

(62) GESELL, A.: The ontogenesis of infant behavior. In L. Carmichael (Ed.), *Manual of child psychology,* 2d ed. New York: Wiley, 1954. Pp. 335–373.

(63) GESELL, A., and F. L. ILG: *Child development.* New York: Harper & Row, 1949.

(64) GESELL, A., F. L. ILG, and L. B. AMES: *Youth: the years from ten to sixteen.* New York: Harper & Row, 1956.

(65) GESELL, A., and H. THOMPSON: Twins T and C from infancy to adolescence: a biogenetic study of individual differences by the method of co-twin control. *Genet. Psychol. Monogr.,* 1941, **24**, 3–121.

(66) GLUECK, S., and E. T. GLUECK: *Unravelling juvenile delinquency.* New York: Commonwealth Fund, 1950.

(67) GOODENOUGH, F. L.: *Anger in young children.* Minneapolis: University of Minnesota Press, 1931.

(68) GOODENOUGH, F. L.: The measurement of mental growth in childhood. In L. Carmichael (Ed.), *Manual of child psychology,* 2d ed. New York: Wiley, 1954. Pp. 459–491.

(69) GOVATOS, L. A.: Relationships and age differences in growth measures and motor skills. *Child Develpm.,* 1959, **30**, 333–340.

(70) GRANT, D. A.: Statistical theory and research design. *Annu. Rev. Psychol.,* 1950, **1**, 277–296.

(71) GUTTERIDGE, M. V.: A study of motor achievements of young children. *Arch. Psychol., N. Y.,* 1939, No. 244.

(72) HAGGERTY, A. D.: The effects of long-term hospitalization or institutionalization upon the language development of children. *J. genet. Psychol.,* 1959, **94**, 205–229.

(73) HALL, G. S.: The contents of children's minds on entering school. *Ped. Sem.,* 1891, **1**, 139–173.

(74) HARRIS, D. B.: The development of potentiality. *Teachers Coll. Rec.,* 1960, **61**, 423–428.

(75) HAVIGHURST, R. J.: Social class and basic personality structure. *Sociol. soc. Res.,* 1952, **36**, 355–363.

(76) HAVIGHURST, R. J.: *Human development and education.* New York: Longmans, 1953.

(77) HAVIGHURST, R. J.: The social competence of middle-aged people. *Genet. Psychol. Monogr.,* 1957, **56**, 297–375.

(78) HAVIGHURST, R. J., and K. FEIGENBAUM: Leisure and life-style. *Amer. J. Sociol.,* 1959, **64**, 396–404.

(79) HAWKES, G. R., L. G. BURCHINAL, and B. GARDNER: Measurement of pre-adolescents' views of family control of behavior. *Child Develpm.,* 1957, **28**, 388–392.

(80) HILDRETH, G.: The development and training of hand dominance. *J. genet. Psychol.,* 1950, **76**, 39–144.

(81) HODGES, A.: A developmental study of symbolic behavior. *Child Develpm.,* 1954, **25**, 277–280.

(82) HOFSTATTER, P. R.: The rate of maturation and the cephalization coefficient: a hypothesis. *J. Psychol.,* 1951, **31**, 271–280.

(83) HOLLINGSWORTH, L. S.: *Children above 180 I.Q.: origin and development.* New York: Harcourt, Brace & World, 1950.

(84) ILG, F. L., and L. B. AMES: *Child behavior.* New York: Harper & Row, 1955.

(85) ILG, F. L., J. LEARNED, A. LOCKWOOD, and

L. B. AMES: The three-and-a-half-year-old. *J. genet. Psychol.,* 1949, **75,** 21–31.

(86) ILLINGWORTH, R. S.: Sleep problems in the first three years. *Brit. med. J.,* 1951, **1,** 722–728.

(87) ILLINGWORTH, R. S., C. C. HARVEY, and S-Y GIN: Relation of birth weight to physical development in childhood. *Lancet,* 1949, **247,** 598–602.

(88) IRWIN, O. G.: Infant speech: effect of systematic reading of stories. *J. speech hear. Res.,* 1960, **3,** 187–190.

(89) JERSILD, A. T.: Training and growth in the development of children. *Child Develpm. Monogr.,* 1932, **10,** 1–73.

(90) JERSILD, A. T.: *In search of self.* New York: Teachers College, Columbia University, 1952.

(91) JERSILD, A. T.: Emotional development. In L. Carmichael (Ed.), *Manual of child psychology,* 2d ed. New York: Wiley, 1954. Pp. 833–917.

(92) JERSILD, A. T.: *Child psychology,* 5th ed. Englewood Cliffs, N.J.: Prentice-Hall, 1960.

(93) JERSILD, A. T., and R. J. TASCH: *Children's interests and what they suggest for education.* New York: Teachers College, Columbia University, 1949.

(94) JOHNSON, M. S.: Factors related to disability in reading. *J. exp. Educ.,* 1957, **26,** 1–26.

(95) JONES, H. E.: The adolescent growth study: principles and methods. II. Procedures. *J. consult. Psychol.,* 1939, **3,** 157–159, 177–180.

(96) JONES, H. E.: The environment and mental development. In L. Carmichael (Ed.), *Manual of child psychology,* 2d ed. New York: Wiley, 1954. Pp. 631–696.

(97) JONES, M. C.: The later careers of boys who were early- and later-maturers. *Child Develpm.,* 1957, **28,** 113–128.

(98) JONES, M. C., and N. BAYLEY: Physical maturing among boys as related to behavior. *J. educ. Psychol.,* 1950, **41,** 129–148.

(99) JONES, M. C., and P. H. MUSSEN: Self-conceptions, motivations, and interpersonal attitudes of early- and later-maturing girls. *Child Develpm.,* 1958, **29,** 491–501.

(100) JONES, V.: Character development in children: an objective approach. In L. Carmichael (Ed.), *Manual of child psychology,* 2d ed. New York: Wiley, 1954. Pp. 781–832.

(101) KAGAN, J., and H. A. MOSS: Parental correlates of child's IQ and height: a cross-validation of the Berkeley Growth Study results. *Child Develpm.,* 1959, **30,** 325–332.

(102) KAHN, E., and L. W. SIMMONS: Problems of middle age. *Yale Rev.,* 1940, **29,** 349–363.

(103) KALLMAN, F. J., and G. SANDER: Twin studies in senescence. *Amer. J. Psychiat.,* 1949, **106,** 29–36.

(104) KAPLAN, L.: The annoyances of elementary school teachers. *J. educ. Res.,* 1952, **45,** 649–665.

(105) KARLIN, M. S.: Mother's management of atypical children. *Smith Coll. Stud. soc. Wk,* 1961, **31,** 120–151.

(106) KELLY, E. L.: Consistency of the adult personality. *Amer. Psychologist,* 1955, **10,** 659–681.

(107) KESSEN, W., L. S. HENDRY, and A. M. LEUZENDORFF. Measurement of movement in the human newborn: a new technique. *Child Develpm.,* 1961, **32,** 95–105.

(108) KLATSKIN, E. H., E. B. JACKSON, and L. C. WILKIN: The influence of degree of flexibility in maternal child care practices on early child behavior. *Amer. J. Orthopsychiat.,* 1956, **26,** 79–93.

(109) KUHLEN, R. G.: Social change: a neglected factor in psychological studies of the life span. *Sch. Soc.,* 1940, **52,** 14–16.

(110) LAWTON, G.: *New goals for old age.* New York: Columbia, 1943.

(111) LINDEN, M. E., and D. COURTNEY: The human life cycle and its interruptions. *Amer. J. Psychiat.,* 1953, **109,** 905–915.

(112) LINDZEY, G., D. T. LYKKEN, and H. H. WINSTON: Infantile trauma, genetic factors, and adult temperament. *J. abnorm. soc. Psychol.,* 1960, **61,** 7–14.

(113) LOMBARD, O. M.: Breadth of bone and muscle by age and sex in childhood. *Child Develpm.,* 1950, **21,** 229–239.

(114) LYNIP, A. W.: The use of magnetic devices in the collection and analysis of preverbal utterances of an infant. *Genet. Psychol. Monogr.,* 1951, **44,** 221–262.

(115) MACFARLANE, J., L. ALLEN, and M. P. HONZIK: *A developmental study of the behavior problems of normal children between twenty-one months and fourteen years.* Berkeley, Calif.: University of California Press, 1954.

(116) MACY, I. G., and H. J. KELLY: Body composition in childhood. *Hum. Biol.,* 1956, **28,** 289–308.

(117) MC CARTHY, D.: Language development. In L. Carmichael (Ed.), *Manual of child psychology,* 2d ed. New York: Wiley, 1954. Pp. 492–630.

(118) MC CLUSKY, H. Y., and G. JENSEN: The psychology of adults. *Rev. educ. Res.,* 1959, **29,** 246–255.

(119) MC GRAW, M. B.: Neural maturation as exemplified in achievement of bladder control. *J. Pediat.,* 1940, **17,** 747–771.

(120) MC KEE, J. P., and D. H. EICHORN: The relation between metabolism and height and weight during adolescence. *Child Develpm.,* 1955, **26,** 205–212.

(121) MEAD, M.: *Male and female.* New York: Morrow, 1952.

(122) MEAD, M.: Book review of "The child buyer." *Science,* 1961, **133**, 573.

(123) MICHAEL, D. N.: Scientists through adolescent eyes: what we need to know, why we need to know it. *Sci. Mon., N.Y.,* 1957, **85**, 135–140.

(124) MILNER, E. A.: A study of the relationships between reading readiness in grade one school children and patterns of parent-child interaction. *Child Develpm.,* 1951, **22**, 95–112.

(125) MORENO, J. L.: *Who shall survive? A new approach to the problems of human interrelations.* Washington: Nervous and Mental Disease Publishing Co., 1934.

(126) MOSS, H. A., and J. KAGAN: Stability of achievement and recognition seeking behaviors from early childhood through adulthood. *J. abnorm. soc. Psychol.,* 1961, **62**, 504–513.

(127) MUELLER, S. R.: Development of urinary control in children. *J. Amer. Med. Ass.,* 1960, **172**, 1256–1261.

(128) MUHSAM, F. V.: Correlation in growth. *Hum. Biol.,* 1947, **19**, 260–269.

(129) MUNN, N. L.: Learning in children. In L. Carmichael (Ed.), *Manual of child psychology,* 2d ed. New York: Wiley, 1954. Pp. 374–458.

(130) MUSSEN, P. H., and L. DISTLER: Masculinity, identification and father-son relationships. *J. abnorm. soc. Psychol.,* 1959, **59**, 350–356.

(131) OWENS, W. A.: Age and mental abilities: a longitudinal study. *Genet. Psychol. Monogr.,* 1953, **48**, 3–54.

(132) PASAMANICK, B., and H. KNOBLOCH: The contribution of some organic factors to school retardation in Negro children. *J. Negro Educ.,* 1958, **27**, 4–9.

(133) PEASE, D., and G. R. HAWKES: Direct study of child-parent interactions. 2. Observation of parent-child interaction. *Amer. J. Orthopsychiat.,* 1960, **30**, 453–459.

(134) PODOLSKY, E.: The first six years. *Understanding the Child,* 1953, **22**, 71–72.

(135) POFFENBERGER, T., and D. NORTON: Factors in the formation of attitudes toward mathematics. *J. educ. Res.,* 1959, **52**, 171–176.

(136) PRESSEY, S. L., and A. W. JONES: 1923–1953 and 20–60 age changes in moral codes, anxieties, and interests, as shown by the "X-O Tests." *J. Psychol.,* 1955, **39**, 485–502.

(137) PUNKE, H. H.: Neglected social values of prolonged human infancy. *Sch. Soc.,* 1950, **71**, 369–372.

(138) RAINWATER, L.: A study of personality differences between middle and lower class adolescents: the Szondi Test in culture-personality research. *Genet. Psychol. Monogr.,* 1956, **54**, 3–86.

(139) ROSE, A. M.: The role of self-direction in child development. *Sociol. soc. Res.,* 1950, **34**, 424–430.

(140) ROSEN, B. C., and R. D'ANDRADE: The psychosocial origins of achievement motivation. *Sociometry,* 1959, **22**, 185–218.

(141) ROYCE, J. R.: Factor theory and genetics. *Educ. psychol. Measmt,* 1957, **17**, 361–376.

(142) SCHAEFER, E. S., and R. G. BELL: Development of a parental attitude research instrument. *Child Develpm.,* 1958, **29**, 339–361.

(143) SCHEINFELD, A.: *The human heredity handbook.* Philadelphia: Lippincott, 1956.

(144) SEARS, R. R., E. E. MACCOBY, and H. LEVIN: *Patterns in child rearing.* New York: Harper & Row, 1957.

(145) SHAW, M. C., and J. T. MC CUEN: The onset of academic underachievement in bright children. *J. educ. Psychol.,* 1960, **51**, 103–108.

(146) SHINN, M. W.: *The biography of a baby.* New York: Macmillan, 1900.

(147) SHOCK, N. W.: Gerontology (later maturity). *Annu. Rev. Psychol.,* 1951, **2**, 353–366.

(148) SIEGAL, A. E.: Aggressive behavior of young children in the absence of an adult. *Child Develpm.,* 1957, **28**, 371–378.

(149) SIEGAL, A. E., and L. G. KOHN: Permissiveness, permission and aggression: the effect of adult presence or absence on aggression in children's play. *Child Develpm.,* 1959, **30**, 131–141.

(150) SILVERMAN, J. S., M. W. FITE, and M. M. MOSHER: Clinical findings in reading disability children: special cases of intellectual inhibition. *Amer. J. Orthopsychiat.,* 1959, **29**, 298–314.

(151) SIMON, M. D.: Body configuration and school readiness. *Child Develpm.,* 1959, **30**, 493–512.

(152) SMITH, M. E.: A comparison of certain personality traits as rated in the same individuals in childhood and fifty years later. *Child Develpm.,* 1952, **23**, 159–180.

(153) SMITH, M. E.: Childhood memories compared with those of adult life. *J. genet. Psychol.,* 1952, **80**, 151–182.

(154) SMITH, M. E.: Mental test ability in a family of four generations. *J. genet. Psychol.,* 1954, **85**, 321–335.

(155) SONTAG, L. W.: Some psychosomatic aspects of childhood. *Nerv. Child,* 1946, **5**, 296–304.

(156) SPITZ, R. A.: Purposive grasping. *Personality,* 1951, **1**, 141–148.

(157) STENDLER, C. B., and N. YOUNG: The impact of beginning first grade upon socialization as reported by mothers. *Child Develpm.,* 1950, **21**, 241–260.

(158) STEVENSON, H. W., and N. G. STEVENSON: A method for simultaneous observation and analysis of children's behavior. *J. genet. Psychol.,* 1961, **99,** 253–260.

(159) STOKE, S. M.: An inquiry into the concept of identification. In W. E. Martin and C. B. Stendler (Eds.), *Readings in child Development.* New York: Harcourt, Brace, & World, 1954. Pp. 227–239.

(160) STOLZ, H. R., and L. M. STOLZ: *Somatic development of adolescent boys.* New York: Macmillan, 1951.

(161) STOUFFER, G. A. W., and J. OWENS: Behavior problems identified by today's teachers and compared with those reported by E. K. Wickman. *J. educ. Res.,* 1955, **48,** 321–331.

(162) STRANG, R.: *The adolescent views himself.* New York: McGraw-Hill, 1957.

(163) SUTTON-SMITH, B., B. G. ROSENBERG, and E. F. MORGAN: Historical changes in the freedom with which children express themselves on personality inventories. *J. genet. Psychol.,* 1961, **99,** 309–315.

(164) TERMAN, L. M., and M. H. ODEN: *The gifted child grows up.* Stanford, Calif.: Stanford, 1947.

(165) TERMAN, L. M., and M. H. ODEN: *Genetic studies of genius. V. The gifted group at mid-life.* Stanford, Calif.: Stanford, 1959.

(166) THOMPSON, H.: Physical growth. In L. Carmichael (Ed.), *Manual of child psychology,* 2d ed. New York: Wiley, 1954. Pp. 292–334.

(167) TOPP, R. F.: Behavior difficulties in childhood as portents of future emotional disorders. *Elem. Sch. J.,* 1950, **51,** 196–200.

(168) TUCKMAN, J., and I. LORGE: Attitudes toward old people. *J. soc. Psychol.,* 1953, **37,** 249–260.

(169) TUCKMAN, J., and I. LORGE: Old people's appraisal of adjustment over the life span. *J. Pers.,* 1954, **22,** 417–422.

(170) VINACKE, W. E.: Stereotypes as social concepts. *J. soc. Psychol.,* 1957, **46,** 229–243.

(171) WATSON, J. B.: *Behaviorism.* New York: People's Institute Publishing Co., 1925.

(172) WECHSLER, D.: Intellectual development and psychological maturity. *Child Develpm.,* 1950, **21,** 45–50.

(173) WENAR, C.: The reliability of mothers' histories. *Child Develpm.,* 1961, **32,** 491–500.

(174) WISHIK, S. M.: The importance of "timing" in child health supervision. *Child Develpm.,* 1950, **21,** 51–60.

(175) WOODS, W. A., and R. TOAL: Subtest disparity of Negro and white groups matched for IQs on the Revised Beta Test. *J. consult. Psychol.,* 1957, **21,** 136–138.

(176) YARROW, L. J.: Infancy. *Children,* 1960, **7,** 110–111.

There are two important reasons for studying the prenatal period. First, this is the foundation age. What a child will ultimately be is largely determined by what happens to him before he is born. At this time, hereditary endowment is fixed, once and for all. Favorable prenatal environmental conditions can foster the development of hereditary potentials just as unfavorable conditions can stunt their development. In addition, this is the time when attitudes toward the child are beginning to take form in the minds of significant people in his life. These attitudes will affect the treatment he receives—a factor of major importance in his later development (18).

Second, knowing what happens to a child before he is born is essential to a complete understanding of the pattern of human development. In spite of the fact that growth and development are very rapid during the short time before the baby is born, his development at birth is only in its beginning stage. To be able to guide and foster his future development, we must know just where the newborn infant is in his journey toward maturity.

INTEREST IN PRENATAL DEVELOPMENT

Early interest in prenatal development centered around the origin of life rather than on the development of the unborn child. In ancient times, among both primitive and civilized peoples, there was a great deal of speculation about how a new human being comes into existence. Because primitive peoples did not associate intercourse between the sexes with the birth of the child, many theories of a mystical sort grew up to explain birth. Greek philosophers, on the other hand, knew that sexual intercourse *always preceded* the birth of a baby. With this knowledge, they evolved a theory which maintained that the woman was the receptive soil in which the seed from the male was planted.

This theory held that the role of the mother was to supply nourishment for the

2

FOUNDATIONS OF THE DEVELOPMENTAL PATTERN

developing baby. The source of this nourishment was believed to be the menstrual blood which ceased flowing during the period preceding the child's birth. Never, in ancient times, was there any recognition that the mother produced a seed which united with the male seed to give rise to a new individual.

It was not until the seventeenth century that the woman's contribution to fertilization was recognized. During that era, de Graaf, a Dutch physician, suggested that the woman supplied an egg. A few years later, a Dutch spectaclemaker, van Leeuwenhoek, reported that "little animals," or what are now known as *sperm cells,* were found in the male semen. These, he contended, were the male contribution to the new human being.

During the nineteenth century, scientists discovered that the union of the egg and the male cell was essential to the creation of a new organism. Since this discovery, the study of embryology has produced a wealth of information about the pattern of prenatal development.

Interest in Heredity. Early scientific interest was concentrated on the hereditary endowment of the baby: *How* does he inherit his potentials from his parents and other ancestors, and *what* does he inherit from them? These questions have not yet been answered to the satisfaction of all scientists. Figure 2–1 illustrates one of the theories that grew up to answer them.

One of the most controversial aspects of the study of development deals with the relative importance of heredity and environment. Although there is little chance that a complete and satisfactory solution to this controversy will be found in the near future, study of the problem has led to an interest in the pattern of prenatal development (5). It is now known that development before birth is as predictable as development after birth.

Interest in Environment. Throughout history, there have been many superstitious beliefs about the influence of the mother's

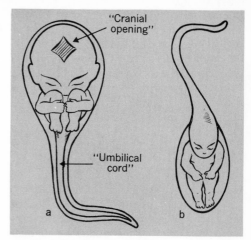

Figure 2–1. The homunculus (or manikin), which early scientists believed was contained in the sperm. After drawings by (*a***) Hartsoeker, 1694 and (***b***) Dalempatius, 1699. (Adapted from A. Scheinfeld,** *The new you and heredity,* **Lippincott, 1961. Used by permission.)**

experiences on the development of her unborn child. Physical and mental abnormalities in children have often been attributed to "bad blood" inherited from one of the parents. Today, medical science is turning its attention to the study of *prenatal influences.* After scientists discovered that the mother's blood and that of her unborn child do not mingle, they found that oxygen, water, and nutrients are absorbed into the fetal bloodstream through a sievelike structure—the *placenta*—attached to the wall of the mother's uterus and connected to the baby's body by the *umbilical cord.*

Should the mother's bloodstream contain harmful substances, they are likely to find their way into the unborn baby's bloodstream. What effects they have on the development of the unborn child is engaging the attention of many scientists today. In general, studies are showing that the prenatal environment is as important as the postnatal environment. Furthermore, scientists are finding that the pattern of the child's postnatal environment is greatly influenced by the type of prenatal environment he had (26, 118, 125).

Interest in Attitudes of Significant People.
The latest focal point of scientific interest in
prenatal development has been the effects of
the attitudes of significant people toward the
child during the early years of his life. These
attitudes—primarily of parents and siblings
—are actually formed before the child is
born. Attitudes toward parenthood, toward
the sex of the child, and toward his capacities often originate in childhood experiences
of the parents and are colored by misconceptions about the relative influences of
heredity and environment. Once established,
they tend to be persistent and to influence
the parents' treatment of the child. Furthermore, they influence the mother's emotional
reactions during pregnancy. These, in turn,
affect the chemical content of her bloodstream, thus affecting her unborn child
(54). Recent studies indicate that the indirect influence of unfavorable parental and
sibling attitudes has a far greater force in
both postnatal and prenatal development
than had ever been suspected. True, these
attitudes may change as time goes on, but
the chances are that they will not improve
but will become even more unfavorable
(122).

METHODS OF STUDYING PRENATAL DEVELOPMENT

Study of prenatal development is extremely
difficult and, in some cases, almost impossible in human subjects. To date, no em-
bryologist has been able to devise a technique for observing the progress of the fertilized human ovum down the Fallopian
tube or the process by which it becomes
embedded in the maternal uterine wall (26).

Information about the living fetus comes
from four sources: (*1*) the mother's report
of fetal movements, (*2*) sounds of fetal
heartbeats and movements detected by instruments used on the mother's abdominal
wall, (*3*) direct observations of fetuses operatively removed from the mother's body,
and (*4*) studies of animals.

Reports given by mothers in regard to
fetal movements are, like all introspective

reports, subject to error. How accurately the
mother will be able to report will depend,
in large measure, on her interest in the subject and on her training in scientific techniques. For the most part, the only information of importance to be derived from this
technique is the fact that prenatal activity is
so pronounced that the mother is able to
feel it and localize it.

Technical aids and special apparatus, such
as the stethoscope, cardiograph, string gal-
vanometer, and X ray, have been used to
study fetal heartbeat, fetal activity, position
of the fetus, and whether or not there will
be twins. Fetal movements have been measured by placing a tambour on the mother's
abdomen, through which fetal movements
may be recorded. Direct observations of
operatively removed fetuses are of limited
value because the fetuses are rarely normal;
this was the reason for their removal. Furthermore, because these fetuses are cut
off from normal oxygen supply, their
movements are those of an increasingly
asphyxiated organism (97). Most information available at the present time regarding
developmental irregularities comes from the
abnormal development of the fetus itself or
from experimentally induced structural
changes in lower animals. It is impossible to
study the normal human fetus experimentally, but experiments with animals have
thrown light on certain problems.

By varying the amount of oxygen available to the animal fetus and by using cold
water, chemicals, or ultraviolet rays to
change the environmental conditions of animal fetuses, scientists have experimentally
produced *monsters,* or individuals departing
greatly in form or structure from the usual
type of the species (104).

Two-headed monsters among tadpoles
can, for example, be produced through the
use of chemical or mechanical stimuli. The
addition of magnesium chloride to water
will displace the eyes of minnows. Changed
environmental conditions disturb the rate of
development, thus altering the balance of
growth among the different parts of the
organism. In an experiment on mice, Ingalls
induced specific physical defects in the

young by a systematic reduction of oxygen at different periods in pregnancy. The nature of the deformity in the offspring was determined by the intensity, duration, and timing of oxygen deficiency. Deprivation of oxygen on the eighth day of pregnancy, for example, resulted in incompletely formed skulls, while deprivation of oxygen on the twelfth day resulted in harelips (67). By depriving pregnant rats of vitamin A, scientists have produced deformities in the eyes of the young. Riboflavin-deficient mothers had offspring with skeletal deformities. A vitamin D-deficient diet of the mother also produced certain kinds of skeletal deformities in the offspring. To date, about six hundred kinds of congenital malformation have been produced by experiments on animals (152).

Though far from conclusive, the evidence certainly seems to indicate that environment rather than heredity is the major cause of congenital malformations. If further evidence substantiates the present findings, it will be possible, by controlling environmental factors, to eliminate many of the malformations which distort the pattern of a child's development both before and after birth (118).

FERTILIZATION

After *fertilization,* or conception, the fertilized egg—unless some abnormal condition interferes—will develop into a child within a period of approximately 280 days. The male and female cells develop in the reproductive organs, the *gonads.* The male gonads —the testes—produce the male germ cells, the *spermatozoa,* while the female gonads —the ovaries—produce the female germ cells, the *ova.* While normally only one ovum is produced every menstrual cycle, spermatozoa are very numerous, with as many as 200,000,000 found in 3 cubic centimeters of seminal fluid in one ejaculation. Several hundred million spermatozoa develop every 4 or 5 days, as compared with one ovum every 28 days (37, 149). Before these cells can produce a new individual, they must go through a process known as

maturation. Maturation consists of chromosome reduction through cell division.

Within each sex cell, whether ovum or spermatozoon, there are 23 pairs of *chromosomes* before the maturational process takes place.* Chromosomes are threadlike particles within each of which are strings of microscopically small particles, the *genes.* The genes are the physical substances passed on from parent to offspring; they are the true carriers of hereditary traits (37, 94).

During the maturational process, the chromosomes of each cell arrange themselves into pairs on opposite sides of the cell's nucleus, with each pair containing one chromosome from the mother and one from the father. When the pairs separate, one chromosome goes to one of the newly formed cells, and its mate goes to the other. The two cells thus formed split again, but this time lengthwise, so that one-half of the original number of chromosomes is retained. This means that after the maturational process has been completed, there are four mature cells of each sex; each mature sex cell contains 23 chromosomes (84, 98). In the case of the sperm cells, each one of the four mature cells that came from the original cell is capable of fertilizing an ovum. In the ovum, on the other hand, only one—the part that retains most of the yolk—is capable of being fertilized; the other three cells, the *polar bodies,* are absorbed and secreted. In normal fertilization, the ovum (plural— "ova") is in the Fallopian tube on its way from the ovary to the uterus. As a result of coitus, spermatozoa (singular—"spermatozoon") from the male are deposited at the mouth of the uterus and make their way toward the Fallopian tubes. They are attracted to the ovum by a strong hormonal force which draws them into the tube. After one sperm cell enters the ovum, the surface of the ovum is so changed that no other sperm can enter it. Thus fertilization is completed when union with one sperm has

* It was formerly believed that sex cells contained 24 pairs of chromosomes. Now it has been established that there are only 23 pairs, though many books and articles published before 1960 refer to 24 pairs.

occurred. When the sperm cell penetrates the wall of the ovum, the nuclei from the two cells approach each other. There is a breakdown in the membrane surrounding each, and the two nuclei merge. The new cell thus formed has 23 pairs of chromosomes, one-half of which have come from the male and one-half from the female cell.

From his two parents, the child receives a *new* combination of parental genes. This combination is made up of the genes the parents themselves received from their parents, and they, in turn, from their parents. Some of the chromosomes which the child receives from each parent may come from either or both grandparents on that parent's side of the family. As a result, a child may have many traits in common with one or both of his parents; he may also resemble one of his grandparents or great-grandparents (116).

Some characteristics are associated with the sex of the individual. These "sex-linked" characteristics are produced by genes carried by the chromosomes responsible for determining sex. Traits known to be sex-linked are, for example, color blindness, hereditary baldness, and hemophilia. Sex-linked traits rarely appear in both father and son. They generally skip a generation and are transmitted from a man, through his daughter or daughters, to one or more of his grandsons (138).

Because there is no specific scientific knowledge of how the pairs of chromosomes of either the ovum or the spermatozoon divide during the maturational process, it must be concluded that division is largely a matter of chance. In one cell, for example, after division has occurred, there may be 20 chromosomes from the female and 3 from the male, or 8 from the female and 15 from the male, or any other combination. For that reason, when one cell combines with another in fertilization it is possible and probable that more traits will be inherited from one side of the family than from the other. This explains the "skipping of a generation" in a given trait.

It has been estimated that there are 16,777,216 possible arrangements of chromosome combination (125). Under such conditions, it is understandable why children of the same family are often so different. Only in the case of identical twins do children of the same family have the same genetic makeup. Because the combination of chromosomes is a matter of chance, one cannot predict with any degree of accuracy what the physical and mental characteristics of an unborn child will be.

At the moment of fertilization, three things are determined: *hereditary endowment, sex,* and whether the birth will be *single or multiple.* Each of these will be discussed separately, and its significance, both direct and indirect, to later development will be emphasized.

HEREDITARY ENDOWMENT

When the sperm unites with the ovum, everything the newly conceived individual will ever inherit from his parents, grandparents, and other more remote ancestors is set. As Kuhlen and Thompson have stressed, "Every individual's supply of genes, the bearers of hereditary factors, is given him once for all and inalterably at conception" (84). There are between 40,000 and 60,000 genes in the chromosomes in the male cell after it has matured and a similar number in a mature ovum. This means that the newly created baby's hereditary endowment contains between 80,000 and 120,000 genes, each of which carries potentials for physical and mental traits (125). The transmission of genetic inheritance is illustrated in Figure 2–2.

Because every adult, whether male or female, produces many more germ cells than will ever be used; because in each of these cells there are genes from both parents in varying numbers; and because members of each pair of chromosomes may "cross over" or exchange with each other during the maturational process, chance plays an important role in the hereditary endowment of a child by determining which of a vast number of possible combinations of characteristics he will inherit. As is true of chromosome combinations from parents, it

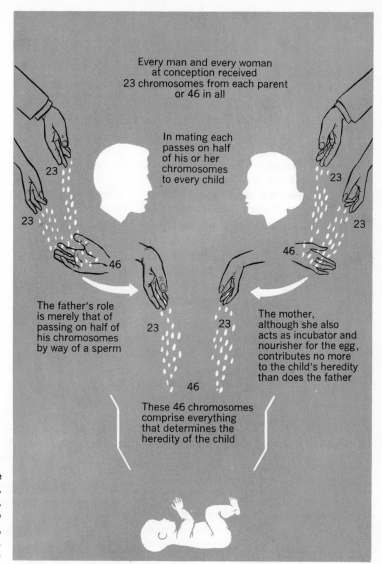

Every man and every woman
at conception received
23 chromosomes from each parent
or 46 in all

In mating each
passes on half
of his or her
chromosomes
to every child

23

23

23

23

46

46

The father's role
is merely that of
passing on half of
his chromosomes
by way of a sperm

The mother,
although she also
acts as incubator and
nourisher for the egg,
contributes no more
to the child's heredity
than does the father

23

23

46

These 46 chromosomes
comprise everything
that determines the
heredity of the child

Figure 2–2. The
hereditary process.
(Adapted from A.
Scheinfeld, *The new
you and heredity*,
Lippincott, 1961.
Used by permission.)

is entirely a matter of chance how many chromosomes from different ancestors on the maternal or paternal side will be passed down to a child. To produce a given kind of person involves the union of a particular ovum with a particular sperm. It has been estimated that the probability that this particular union will occur is but 1 in 300,000,-000,000,000 (125).

After conception, nothing can be done to add to, or subtract from, the individual's hereditary endowment. The traditional belief that a mother can endow her unborn child with musical talent if she spends the months of her pregnancy concentrating on music or that she can make him brilliant by devoting her time to intellectual pursuits simply is not true. If she establishes a favorable prenatal environment for him through good physical health and health attitudes, however, the chances of a favorable development of the genes her unborn child *already has* will be greatly increased. As Montagu has pointed out, "Where we control the environment, we to some extent control heredity. Heredity, it has been said, determines what we *can* do, and environment what we *do* do" (98).

As was stressed in Chapter 1, most people do not develop their hereditary potentials to the maximum. As a result, they reach their limits sooner than their hereditary endowment would justify. Some inherited characteristics, such as eye color and hair texture, are relatively immune to environmental influences. Most inherited characteristics, however, are markedly influenced by environment. A growing child may, for example, have his height potentials stunted if he is deprived of adequate nutrition and sunlight, if he is forced to do work too heavy for his undeveloped body, or if he suffers from a long, wasting illness.

Similarly, the constitutional qualities of energy, vitality, or "pep"—potentialities for leadership—may, under unfavorable conditions develop into destructiveness and restlessness, characteristics which predispose the child to delinquent behavior (2). In speaking of intellectual potentials, Stone and Church have pointed out that "a potential genius may find inspiration for immense achievement, but if not given proper stimulation he may end up in intellectual mediocrity" (143).

If the environment is to stimulate the hereditary potentials, it must be of the right kind at the time when development normally occurs. As Montagu has said, "Genes do not work their effect in a vacuum." He then goes on to say, "The limits of what we can do are determined by the genes, but it is the environment that determines the extent to which the potentialities within these limits are realized. We do not, therefore, stand helpless and impotent before the implacable fate which heredity is misconceived to be. On the other hand, through the intelligent management of the environment there is a great deal we can do about it" (98). These problems were discussed in more detail in Chapter 1 (pages 16 to 17).

Because genes are assorted by chance and there is no way of controlling the assortment, each child will be different from everyone else. *Individuality* is readily apparent at birth, even among identical twins, and it becomes more pronounced after birth as influences in the postnatal environment react differently on hereditary potentials. Continued development of individuality is essential not only to a healthy personality but also to progress (4, 125). Figure 2–3 shows the role that chance plays in individuality.

Indirect Effects of Hereditary Endowment. Failure to recognize the limits set by heredity causes far too many parents to try to mold their child into a pattern. They believe that they can produce in their child the traits they want him to have if they give him an opportunity to develop them. Often these are traits which the parents themselves do not possess and whose lack they believe has been a handicap to their adjustment in life (62).

A father who is short and wants his son to be tall, for example, will bribe and coax the child to eat what he believes to be "growth food"; he will insist upon the child's exercising to "stretch" his body; and he will promise his son that if he will just follow advice and do his share, he will grow into a tall man. Similarly, a mother who wants her child to be a successful musician will make personal sacrifices in time and money to give him the best possible musical education. Then she will prod him constantly to take advantage of the opportunities she has given him. While all parents, to some extent, set up standards for their children and try to force them to come up to these standards, middle-class parents are generally the worst offenders (1). Because women tend, on the whole, to be more idealistic and less realistic than men and because mothers spend more time with children during the early, formative years, mothers have a greater influence on children than fathers.

Studies of parent-child relationships have revealed that children tend to resemble their parents, both physically and mentally, more than they differ from them. The resem-

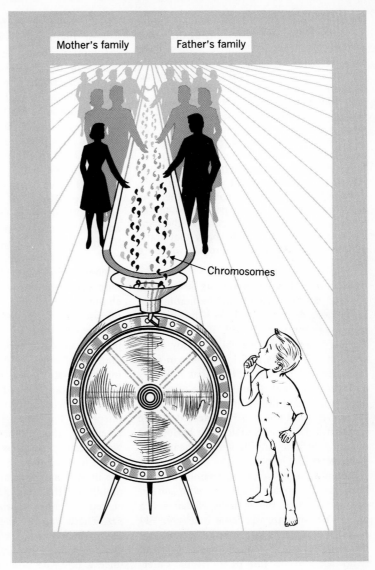

Mother's family

Father's family

Chromosomes

Figure 2–3. Individuality: the "big gamble."

blance increases as children grow older (9, 134). Parents often interpret this growing resemblance to mean that their children have failed to take advantage of the opportunities they have provided. In time, this affects the parent-child relationship adversely. Of even greater significance is the fact that when parents aspire beyond a child's capacity, the child is discouraged when he finds himself falling below their expectations. This often stifles any motivation he may have had to

develop his potentials to the maximum (145).

SEX DETERMINATION

For centuries, people have tried in various ways to *predict* the sex of the unborn child. As Parker has commented:

Prediction of the sex of the unborn has always been an intriguing problem to prospective parents, and their ingenuity in finding a solution has been limited only by the extent of their imagination. Primitive people, living close to nature, sought their answer in the elements and came up with many solutions. Babies conceived in the full of the moon reflect the majestic splendor of that august body and therefore would be males. A waning moon could do no better than produce a girl. When man moved indoors, the elements became less important, and early folklore transferred the responsibility to the parents themselves. If the mother most wanted the baby, it would be a girl, but if it was the father who was most eager for an offspring, it would be a boy. . . . If the mother "carries" the baby low it will be a boy. Or, the baby that starts moving early and kicks vigorously will be a boy (111).

Other methods of predicting sex among civilized peoples are equally ludicrous and inaccurate. A coin tossed over the shoulder of a pregnant woman will, if it comes up "heads," foretell the arrival of a boy baby, while "tails" means a girl. In German folklore there is the superstition that if barley and wheat are soaked in the urine of a pregnant woman and then planted in the ground, the sex of the fetus can be detected by the one that grows first. Should it be barley, the offspring will be a girl, while wheat forecasts the arrival of a boy.

Recently, more scientific techniques have been used to predict sex. The *heartbeat test* maintains that if the fetal heartbeat is 125 or less per minute, the fetus is a boy; 144 or more heartbeats per minute means that the fetus is a girl. Unfortunately, this test is not accurate because of individual differences in the rate of the heartbeat. Attempts have been made to use X ray in the *ossification-of-bones test*. This is based on the knowledge that comparable bones ossify earlier in girls than in boys. But, once again, individual variations make this test far from accurate.

Based on evidence that the maternal hormone levels change in accordance with the fetal sex, a *smear test* has been developed to determine the amount of the estrogenic and androgenic hormones present. This, however, has not proved to be too successful (103). Another method of predicting the sex of the unborn child is based on the assumption that a certain chemical substance in the *maternal saliva*—the precise nature of which is not yet known—is related to the male sex hormone. The presence of this substance has been found to be associated with the birth of a boy, while its absence has been related to the birth of a girl. In a preliminary sampling of this test, accuracy in the predicting of boys was reported in 98.6 per cent of the cases, and in the predicting of girls in 95 per cent (117). To date, no test with 100 per cent accuracy has been devised.

There have likewise been countless theories about how sex can be *controlled*. Among primitive peoples, it has been a common practice for pregnant women to wear charms, to drink magic potions, and to make offerings to their gods to ensure that the unborn child will be male. Among civilized peoples, an early superstition was that if a man went to bed on his wedding night wearing his boots, a boy would be conceived. Some theories stressed that fertilization just after menstruation would result in a female offspring. Others claimed that the food eaten by the mother during pregnancy would determine the sex of the child. A girl child, it was believed, could be produced if the mother ate large amounts of sugar. The month of the year when conception occurred was likewise supposed to determine sex. There was also the belief that if a pregnant woman drank certain potions regularly, she could influence her child's sex. To produce a boy, the potion had to be alkaline, while to produce a girl, it had to be acid. Recent investigations have disproved the old theories and have, at last, given accurate scientific data regarding sex determination (40, 138).

X and Y Chromosomes. Discovery of sex chromosomes has shown that the factors that actually determine sex are internal and that the sex of the child is fixed at the time of fertilization. Of the chromosomes provided by the mature spermatozoon, one differs in character and structure from the others; this is true also of the chromosomes provided by the mature ovum. These different chromosomes are the *sex chromosomes*. They are of two kinds: The larger is the X chromosome, and the smaller—about one-third the size of the X chromosome—is the Y chromosome. One-half of all mature spermatozoa carry the X chromosome, and the other half carry the Y chromosome. By contrast, all mature ova carry the X chromosome.

Thus, in any fertilized ovum, there is always an X chromosome from the ovum and either an X or a Y chromosome from the spermatozoon. If the spermatozoon that unites with the ovum is of the Y-bearing type, the result will be an XY sex chromosome combination; this always results in a male offspring. Should an X-bearing spermatozoon unite with the ovum, the result will be an XX sex chromosome combination; this always produces a female offspring. Figure 2–4 shows how male and female offspring are determined. No one can tell ahead of time whether the ovum will be fertilized by a spermatozoon bearing an X or a Y sex chromosome, and no one can influence the combination in any way. *Sex determination, therefore, is a matter of chance* (37, 98).

Sex Ratio. According to the law of chance, there should be an approximately equal number of children of both sexes conceived. As a matter of fact, medical science reports that there are between 120 and 150 males conceived for every 100 females. The reason for this difference is unknown, although a number of suggestions have been advanced to explain it. Of these, the most credible though still unproven possibility is that since the spermatozoon bearing the Y sex chromosome (the one that produces the male offspring) is slightly lighter and hence swifter in movement than the spermatozoon bearing the X sex chromosome (the type that produces a female offspring), the Y-bearing type has a better chance of reaching the ovum sooner and fertilizing it.

Another reason that has been suggested for this difference in sex ratio is that a

"canny Nature starts the sexes off with a surplus of males to partly provide for the greater drain upon their number later" (125). It has been reported that during the prenatal period, 50 per cent more male fetuses die than female. By the time of birth, there are approximately 105 to 106 male babies, as compared with 100 female. This means that of the males conceived, between 15 and 45 die before birth, as compared with a relatively small number of females (98).

During the first four weeks of postnatal life, 40 per cent more male babies die than female, while among the prematurely born, 50 per cent more males than females die. In the first year of life, 33 per cent more male babies die than female; between five and nine years of age, 44 per cent more boys than girls; between ten and fourteen years, 70 per cent more boys than girls; and between fifteen and nineteen years, 145 per cent more boys than girls (126). The result is that by the time a male child reaches adulthood, his sex is literally the "minority" sex.

In commenting on this, Montagu has said:

Whatever the physical reasons may be which result in more eggs being fertilized by Y-bearing spermatozoa the evolutionary "reason" would appear to be that *since the male is the constitutionally weaker organism he must be conceived in greater numbers than the female if a relatively harmonious numerical balance is to be achieved between the sexes during the reproductive life of the female* (98).

According to traditional belief, more boys are born in wartime than the normal 105 or 106 boys for every 100 girls. Data from the United States, Great Britain, Canada, Australia, and New Zealand, however, showed that the ratio did not change appreciably during the war years. Thus there is no evidence to support this belief (101). Neither has the traditional belief that young fathers produce more male offspring than older fathers stood up under scientific study. Evidence seems to indicate that there is no relationship whatever between the sex of the

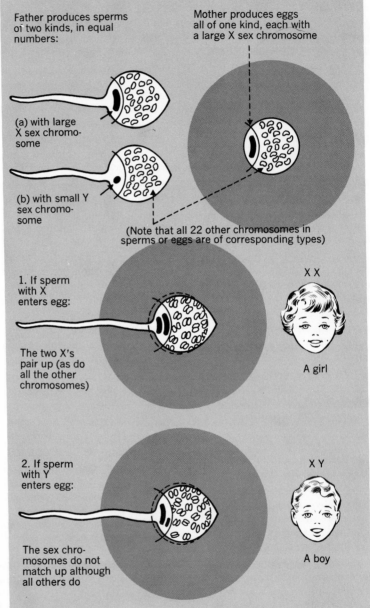

Father produces sperms of two kinds, in equal numbers:

Mother produces eggs all of one kind, each with a large X sex chromosome

(a) with large X sex chromosome

(b) with small Y sex chromosome

(Note that all 22 other chromosomes in sperms or eggs are of corresponding types)

1. If sperm with X enters egg:

The two X's pair up (as do all the other chromosomes)

X X

A girl

2. If sperm with Y enters egg:

The sex chromosomes do not match up although all others do

X Y

A boy

Figure 2–4. How sex is determined. (Adapted from A. Scheinfeld, *The new you and heredity,* Lippincott, 1961. Used by permission.)

offspring and the age of *either* the mother or the father (14).

Another tradition is that boys (or girls) "run in some families." As Spencer has pointed out, "Of course the sex distribution among the children of a given family will be subject to the usual chance fluctuations observed when small samples are used. Even in large families, a certain small proportion of these will be expected to be all of one sex purely by chance" (138). Studies of sex distribution in families have shown that there is an excess of unisexual sibship in two-child and three-child families (13, 100).

In the upper socioeconomic groups, there is some evidence that there is a sex ratio of 120 to 125 males born for every 100 females, but the groups studied have, to date, been too small to warrant much confidence in the results (15). While reports have indicated that men in the "masculine" occupations have a higher percentage of male offspring than men in "feminine" occupations, there is no conclusive evidence that this is true (39, 98).

Effects of Sex on Development. From the moment of conception, the pattern of a child's development is influenced by his sex. Throughout the childhood years, the sex organs of boys and girls produce sex hormones in small quantities. These sex hormones differ in quantity but not in type. Both sexes produce *androgen,* the male hormone, and *estrogen,* the female hormone. Males produce more androgen, and females more estrogen. It is the predominance of the sex hormone appropriate for their sex that is responsible for the differences in physical and psychological development of boys and girls (125, 147). If this balance is upset, variations result. Boys who are castrated, for example, become "feminine" in appearance and behavior, while girls whose ovaries are removed because of a diseased condition become "masculine" (98, 111).

Indirectly, sex is an important determinant of development also. From the time the child is born, strong cultural pressures demand that he conform to the culturally approved pattern for his sex. Even before his babyhood days are over, he is dressed like members of his sex and is expected to act like them. Throughout the childhood years, both boys and girls are molded—first by the family, later by the school and peer group, and still later by the community group—into a pattern the group considers appropriate for the child's sex.

In the molding process, children are denied opportunities to learn sexually inappropriate patterns of behavior. Little boys, for example, are discouraged from playing with dolls and other "girls' toys," while girls are given few opportunities to learn to play the typically "masculine" games of baseball and football. Should the child rebel and prefer the role of members of the opposite sex, he is likely to be rejected not only by children of his own sex but also by members of the opposite sex, whose behavior he imitates. At no age is a sex-inappropriate person admired or accepted by the group (50, 81, 130).

Perhaps the most important influence comes from the attitudes and treatment of significant people—parents, siblings, and teachers. Studies of sex preferences for offspring have revealed that the traditional preference for male offspring persists, especially in the case of the first-born child. For second-born children, parents generally prefer a child whose sex is opposite to that of the first-born. If all children have to be of the same sex, however, the preference is definitely in favor of boys (34, 38).

Most parents would like to have a family composed of an equal number of boys and girls. One of the reasons for wanting more children in an all-girl or all-boy family is to have at least one child of the other sex. In one-child families, the husband generally prefers a boy, while the wife prefers a girl. Sex preferences have been found to be more important to Protestant than to Catholic or Jewish parents (29, 42).

Most parents have reasons for wanting children of a given sex; it is not just a whim on their part. This is important because a rational wish is far more persistent than a momentary desire. Studies of sex preferences have shown that men generally prefer a son for the first-born child because he will perpetuate the family name. They also feel that they understand boys and can participate in their activities better than in girls'. Many men feel that producing a son is a sign of virility. Many do not want to be the only male in an all-female household.

Women, knowing how men feel about sons, often want a son to please their husbands. Others want the first-born to be a son in case they will be unable to have other children. After having a son, most women want at least one daughter. Like their husbands, they want a child whose interests coincide with theirs. Should the child not be of the desired sex, most parents claim that the "next one" surely will be. This is an indication of how strong their preference is (42, 49).

Sex preferences have a strong influence on parents' attitudes. Their attitudes, in turn, affect their treatment of the child. If the child is of the desired sex, parents tend to show their satisfaction by being indulgent. Should the child not be of the desired sex, many parents feel guilty and try to compensate by being overindulgent. Others show their disappointment by favoring a sibling of the desired sex. Still others try to mold the child into a pattern appropriate for a child of the sex they wanted.

Many "tomboys" are products of a father's compensation for the son he wanted, and many "sissies" are a mother's compensation for the daughter she never had (81, 96). Even though mothers claim that they want at least one daughter, they show their preference for sons by being more lenient with them. Similarly, fathers who say they want sons are often more indulgent with their daughters (129).

A child's siblings and relatives react to his sex much as his parents do. If an older sibling is promised that the new baby will be of a certain sex, he will naturally be disappointed if the baby is not what he wanted. Furthermore, when he reaches school age, he will discover that his classmates have definite ideas about members of the other sex and that these ideas are far from favorable. He soon accepts the ideas of his peers and carries them home, expressing them in his treatment of his siblings (82, 130). The preferences shown by grandparents and other relatives will be discussed in the chapter on family relationships.

Most teachers, whether men or women, prefer boys to girls during the early school years. They claim that boys are more "interesting" to teach than girls and have more originality. Teachers are also more tolerant of misbehavior on the part of boys than of girls, on the grounds that "boys will be boys." In the upper grades and in high school, however, many teachers prefer girls.

They find boys harder to handle and less interested in school. Their changed preferences are reflected in their treatment of the pupils. Boys, having been the favorites earlier, resent this shift and claim that the teachers "play favorites"—an attitude that contributes to their increasing dislike for school (59).

NUMBER OF OFFSPRING

Whether the birth will be single or multiple is the third important thing that is determined at the time of conception. The term "multiple birth" refers to the birth of two or more babies within a few hours or days; twins, triplets, quadruplets, and quintuplets all belong in this category. A *singleton* is a child who is born alone. He may have siblings—brothers and sisters—but a period of 9 months or more separates their births from his. It has been estimated that twins occur once in every 87 births; triplets, once in every 7,000; quadruplets, once in every 550,000; and quintuplets, once in every 57,000,000 births. Sextuplets are extremely rare; only six cases have been recorded to date (125, 142).

Multiple births occur more frequently among Negroes than among whites and among whites more often than among members of the yellow race. Maternal age has been found to have no effect on multiple births coming from the division of one egg. Up to the age of thirty-eight years, however, women show a definite tendency to have twins from two eggs, after which age there is a rapid decline in the tendency (98). The probability of later multiple maternity is ten times greater for a woman who has produced children of multiple birth than for a woman who has not. Contrary to popular belief, there is no evidence that twins "run in families," nor is there any evidence of weather or seasonal effects on multiple birth (125).

Superstitions about Multiple Births. Among some primitive people, twins are regarded as a good omen; they are given special honors and privileges. Among others, multiple births are regarded as such bad omens that the babies are destroyed at birth. Most tribes in the Congo consider twins the innocent victims of a wicked mother. The children are not harmed or scorned, but the village witch doctor puts a curse on the unfortunate mother and orders her to advertise her "crime" by smearing her face with ashes whenever she appears in public. In Kenya, on the East African Coast, a mother considers it detrimental to her health to feed two infants at one time. As a result, one is allowed to die of starvation. In the case of mixed twins, the girl is generally spared because she will bring a "bride price" when she is old enough to marry (106).

Some civilized people regard multiple births as "animallike," while others believe that twins and other multiply born children have special hereditary endowments. Still others consider them "scientific curiosities" (125). In cultures where boys are held in higher esteem than girls, the boy is generally given the advantage of survival—if a choice must be made—in the case of mixed twins. Because the Koran teaches that girls are inferior to boys, a twin boy born to a Moslem mother has a better chance of survival than his twin sister (106).

Twins. There are two distinctly different types of twins. *Identical,* or uniovular, twins come from a single ovum fertilized by a single sperm; *nonidentical*—biovular, or fraternal—twins are the product of two ova fertilized simultaneously. Though no precise statistics are available, it is estimated that one-fourth of all twins are of the one-egg type. Figure 2–5 illustrates the two types of twins.

Identical Twins. When one ovum is fertilized by one spermatozoon, it occasionally happens that at the time of the first division of the cell the new cells separate instead of remaining together. Why this separation takes place no one knows for certain, but there is some evidence that it is the result of hormonal disturbances. There is also the belief—as yet unproved—that the egg has an inherent tendency to divide. Whatever

its cause, if a separation occurs before the reduction division, during the maturational process, two separate eggs will be formed. Twins thus formed are called "identical"; they have exactly the same assortment of genes (35). Because of their identical hereditary endowment, identical twins resemble each other very closely in all their hereditary traits. They have the closest degree of kinship possible for two distinctly separated individuals. They are always of the same sex, and they have only one placenta. When the division of the fertilized ovum is incomplete, the result is *siamese twins.* They are always of the same sex and, like other identical twins, closely alike in physical and mental traits. Whether they can be separated depends upon where the joining of their bodies occurs.

Nonidentical Twins. Occasionally, two ova develop simultaneously and are fertilized at the same time. The individuals who develop from these two ova are nonidentical twins. The name "nonidentical" suggests lack of similarity in the physical and mental makeup of the twins. When the chromosomes of the two ova divide, the grouping is not likely to be the same for both. One ovum may receive a preponderance of chromosomes from the maternal grandfather, and the other from the maternal grandmother. In addition, the ova are fertilized by individual spermatozoa, each with its own assortment of chromosomes. Nonidentical twins may be of the same sex or of opposite sexes. During the prenatal period, two distinct placentas are formed, and each ovum thus has its own prenatal environment. Nonidentical twins are not really twins; rather, they are the result of simultaneous pregnancies.

Characteristics of Twins. Many studies have been made of twins to determine how similar they are in physical and mental makeup, how they differ from ordinary siblings, and how long their similarities persist. In general, these studies have revealed that twins are more likely to miscarry, to be born ahead of schedule, to suffer from birth in-

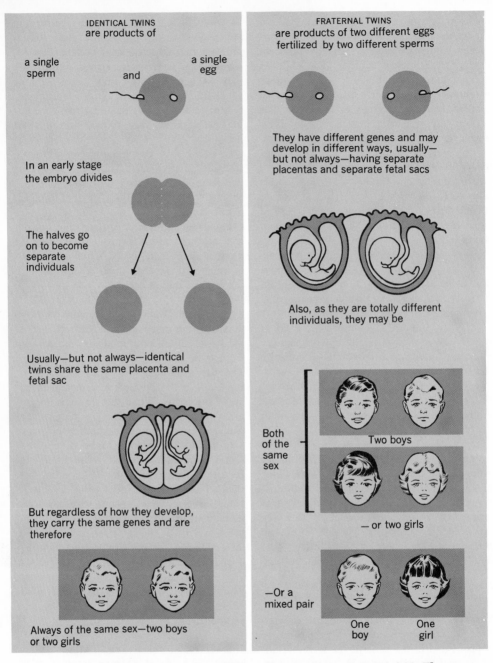

Figure 2–5. Two types of twins. (Adapted from A. Scheinfeld, *The new you and heredity*, Lippincott, 1961. Used by permission.)

juries, or to be stillborn than singletons (3, 47). Those who do survive are, on the average, slightly inferior, both physically and mentally, to singletons.

In *physical characteristics,* identical twins are much more alike than nonidentical twins, who often show no greater resemblance to one another than ordinary siblings (74). Even in senescence, and in spite of marked differences in environment over a period of years, identical twins show a similarity in graying and thinning of the hair, senile wrinkle formation, and teeth deficiencies (75).

Mental similarities, as revealed by intelligence tests and educational achievement, are much more striking in identical twins than in nonidentical twins. On the whole, however, twins are slightly below the average level of siblings in intelligence-test scores. Mental similarities in identical twins have been reported to persist beyond the age of sixty years. In *special abilities,* such as musical or athletic ability, similarities between identical twins are great; in *mechanical ability,* where environmental influences are strong, similarities are less pronounced (156). In all aspects of *language ability,* twins are markedly retarded as compared with singletons. This retardation is not due so much to intellectual differences as to the fact that twins develop a private language of deformed words which are often unintelligible even to members of their own families (74, 95, 156).

The effects of twinship on *social development* have been subjected to intensive study. As identical twins spend more time together, have more interests in common, and are more self-sufficient as far as outside companionship is concerned than nonidentical twins or regular siblings, it is not surprising that they enjoy similar reputations among their peers and show a marked similarity in social competence as measured by a scale of social maturity. Even during the preschool years, twins are competitive for attention. They copy each other and show similar feelings toward others (24).

The closeness and mutual dependence of twins affect their *personality development.*

It is difficult for an identical twin, especially, to distinguish between himself and his twin. This does not help to develop individual personalities. Rivalries and antagonisms, however, leave their mark, and one twin is likely to become dominant. The dominant twin will develop a personality pattern that differs from that of the dominated twin. In personality traits, identical twins are not much more alike than nonidentical twins (74, 90, 99). The reason for this is that personality traits are more subject to environmental influences than physical traits and intelligence are.

In a study of pairs of identical twins sixty years of age and older, it was found that their marital histories differed markedly from those of nonidentical twins and of ordinary siblings. Many more of the identical twins, for example, were celibate than the nonidentical twins, and fewer of them had children. Marital disharmony is particularly common among identical twins, owing to their twin relationship. Senile twins have been reported to develop similar senile psychoses. The life-span of identical twins has been found to differ by an average of 36.9 months, as compared with a difference of 78.3 months for nonidentical twins (75).

Triplets. Triplets may be of three types: (*1*) identical, in that all three have come from the same fertilized ovum; (*2*) two identical and one sibling; and (*3*) three siblings, each having come from a separate fertilized ovum. A few sets of triplets have been studied extensively to determine what their physical and mental characteristics are (65, 125).

Physically, there is a lag in tempo of development as compared with twins and singletons. The eruption of the first tooth, for example, comes a month later than for twins. In *developmental traits,* such as sitting alone, standing alone, and walking, there is also a lag. Triplets are slower in saying their *first words* and in *forming sentences* than twins and singletons (95).

Mental development, as measured by intelligence tests, likewise shows a lag. Among older triplets, however, the lag is less pronounced, suggesting that it may affect only the early development. Tests of *emotional* and *personality development* indicated that triplets behaved socially and temperamentally like single-born children of the same age and had interests and attitudes normal for their sex (65, 98).

Quintuplets. One of the most authoritative reports of the famous Dionne quintuplets is that of Blatz. According to Blatz, the quintuplets did not begin to walk until they were about fifteen months old. They used gesture language, as is true of twins, and did not catch up to single children until about the fifth year. At the age of three years, they had a vocabulary of 110 words, which is retarded for that age.

Annette, who was the most advanced of the five in language, began to use words at the nineteenth month, while all the others were using a few words by the time they were twenty-one months old (20). McCarthy maintains that it is difficult to explain their language retardation entirely in terms of the social situation since they had much individual attention from adults during this time. Intelligence tests were given only until the quintuplets were about 3½ years old. These tests showed them to be backward as compared with norms for single children (95).

Developmental Differences of Singletons and Multiple Births. Whether the child is a singleton or one of multiple birth will have a marked influence on his development both before and after birth. Identical children of multiple birth have similar physical and mental potentials. Consequently, it is inevitable that they will have less individuality —even if they have markedly different postnatal environments—than children of nonidentical multiple birth or singletons.

The prenatal environment of children of multiple birth differs in important respects from that of singletons. Children of multiple birth are crowded into a space nature intended for only one. As a result, one child in the set may be in a less favorable position than the others. The significance of this

crowding will be discussed later, in the section on fetal activity. Of equal seriousness is the fact that children of multiple birth are often born prematurely because the uterus is incapable of further expansion as the fetuses grow larger. Of course, not all children of multiple birth are subjected to the physical or psychological hazards of unfavorable prenatal environment or prematurity. There are such marked individual differences that it would be unfair to make such a generalization. Physical or psychological handicaps have, however, been found to be more common among children of multiple birth than among singletons (3, 66, 73, 108).

The postnatal environment of children of multiple birth is also quite different from that of singletons. Children of multiple birth must share parental time and attention. If one is weaker than his sibling, he is likely to get the lion's share; thus, this sibling may feel that the parents are playing favorites. In addition, the weaker child of a multiple birth normally plays the role of follower, giving in to the stronger sibling both at home and in the outside social group. He develops a "follower" personality pattern, while the stronger learns to play the role of leader (24, 99).

Furthermore, sibling rivalries and competition, animosities, and resentments are heightened if a child feels that his parents are showing favoritism. The weaker child may develop feelings of inadequacy and martyrdom. The stronger child may feel that his parents discriminate against him (77).

Because tradition holds that children who shared the same prenatal environment should share the same postnatal environment, children of multiple birth are thrown together constantly. They are expected to play together, share the same toys and friends, and dress alike, whether or not they are of the same sex. As a result, they fail to develop a sense of individuality; they feel that they are parts of a whole, not individuals in their own right. Those who are identical and, hence, of the same sex are more often subjected to such influences than those who are nonidentical (74, 99).

On the other hand, nonidentical twins of the same sex are subjected to more similar treatment than those of opposite sexes. In commenting on the various effects of similar treatment for twins, Barclay has written:

Nothing is cuter than a pair of pretty— and identical—youngsters, identically dressed, answering to names like Pammy and Patty, playing together in idyllic peace, each one's welfare the other's prime thought. What this discloses of possible overdependence and overidentification, however, may take some of the "cuteness" out of the picture. Although nobody condemns all dress-alike, play-alike occasions, many a twin exposed to nothing else from birth has had extreme difficulty later on recognizing himself, within himself, as a separate entity. It becomes almost impossible in such a situation for either to stand alone (8).

Parental attitudes toward multiple births, reflected in parental behavior, *indirectly* affect the children's development. Multiple births are seldom regarded as a disgrace today; they are, in fact, often a source of pride. Many parents, however, find that they mean heavy expense and greatly increased work loads. If the babies are born prematurely, there will be larger hospital bills than the family budget had allowed for. The extra work needed to care for two or three helpless babies simultaneously and the difficulties in interpersonal relationships among children of the same age during the early years of life affect many parents unfavorably (8). This is certain to be reflected in parent-child relationships.

Interviews with mothers of twins have revealed some interesting facts about parental attitudes. Many mothers report anxiety and feelings of inadequacy at the thought of caring for two small babies. The early pride of being mothers of twins, some mothers have reported, is soon overshadowed by practical child-care problems. The mothers may feel exhausted from overwork. Feeding difficulties may arise when babies must be given bottles simultaneously or when one twin eats the other's food. When children share the same room, overstimulation may cause sleep difficulties—too little sleep or nightmares. So often both children want the mother's attention or want to participate in her activities simultaneously. Especially when one twin is bright and the other dull or one dominating and the other submissive, a mother has great difficulty accepting the differences she sees in her children. Having to cope with all these problems often makes the mother feel "victimized," an attitude that does not lead to good parent-child relationships (115).

One of the most common and difficult problems parents of children of multiple birth must face is their children's *developmental lag*. Parental attitudes may be unfavorable when children of multiple birth fall below the norms for motor, speech, mental, or physical development and appear to be less bright than their agemates. Some parents react to a child who is "backward" by trying to force him to come up to the standards for his age; others feel ashamed of having a child who is "not normal" and reject him. This may be done directly, by showing little understanding and love, or indirectly, by favoring another child of the family who is more normal. Other parents become overly sympathetic and protective, thus depriving the child of opportunities and motivation to develop his potentials. Whatever form parental reaction to the child's developmental lag may take, it is likely to be reflected in unhealthy relationships with the child and unfavorable treatment of him (8, 65, 99).

TIMETABLE OF PRENATAL DEVELOPMENT

As soon as an ovum is fertilized by a spermatozoon, development begins. Growth from a single cell, microscopically small, to a baby composed of about two hundred billion cells of different types is phenomenal in the short period of 9 calendar months. Equally phenomenal is the change from a single cell with no power of its own to a child composed of bones, muscles, skin, internal organs, and a nervous system ready to function at birth or even before birth (125).

From scientific studies of animals and human beings, it has been found that development follows a pattern not only in the development of the different parts of the body but in their functioning as well. At no time during the prenatal period is the developing organism a miniature adult, as may readily be seen from Figure 2–6, which shows the different body proportions in the early stages of prenatal development. Because development is orderly and predictable, it is possible to give a "timetable" of the development of structures and functions. As Parker has explained:

To accomplish such a tremendous task in such a short period, nature has a perfect plan—a timetable that specifies just how far along she must be with each minute detail each succeeding day. She is exceedingly proficient in adhering to this. Her timing is perfect, her accomplishments rapid, accurate, and purposefully correlated. We cannot follow

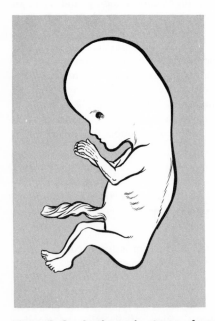

Figure 2–6. In the early stages of prenatal development, the head develops first. (Adapted from Heredity and Prenatal Development, a McGraw-Hill Text-Film.)

her day by day as she accomplishes this but will have to content ourselves with spot checking at regular intervals (111).

Subdivisions of Prenatal Period. The prenatal period is divided into 10 *lunar* months of 28 days each. The 10 lunar months are marked off into three subdivisions, each of which is characterized by development peculiar to it. These are regarded as the "stops in nature's timetable" and are known as the *period of the ovum*, the *period of the embryo*, and the *period of the fetus*.

The *period of the ovum* extends from the moment of fertilization to the end of the second week of life. During this time, the fertilized egg remains practically unchanged in size because it receives little or no external nourishment; it must live off the yolk in the ovum itself. As it passes down the Fallopian tube in which fertilization occurred, it divides and subdivides many times until a globular cluster of many cells is formed. By the time it reaches the uterus, it is about the size of a pinhead.

During the first week of life, the fertilized ovum is unattached and free-moving. On about the tenth day after fertilization, *implantation occurs*. The ovum finds a place in the wall of the uterus and shoots out feelers which push their way through the blood vessels in the uterine wall. By tapping a new source of nourishment, it then becomes a parasite, deriving its nourishment from the mother. If the ovum remains unattached for too long, it will die when it uses up all its yolk (116).

During the *period of the embryo*, which extends from the second week to the end of the second lunar month, rapid development and rapid growth in size take place. By the end of this period, the embryo has all the important external and internal features of a human being. All the facial features are present, the fingers and toes are well formed, and the beginnings of the external genitalia are apparent. The heart begins to function by the end of the third week, the liver secretes bile, and peristaltic movements begin as early as the seventh week. By the end of the period of the embryo, the body is approximately 1½ to 2 inches long and weighs about 2 grams, or ⅔ ounce. This is an increase of approximately 2,000,000 per cent since fertilization (26).

In addition to the development of the embryo itself, special structures—known as "accessory apparatus"—form to provide nourishment and protection until the baby is born. Where the fertilized ovum embedded itself in the uterine wall and sent out threadlike structures to tap a source of nourishment, the *placenta* develops. As the villi, or threadlike structures, become more and more branched and intertwine, they form a fairly solid-looking mass, somewhat pie-shaped. This mass is the placenta.

The *umbilical cord,* which is the connecting link between the embryo and the placenta, is attached to the embryo's abdominal wall at one end and the placenta at the other. It is composed of blood vessels united in a single ropelike structure. There are no nerves in the cord; therefore, transfer of thoughts from the mother to the embryo is impossible. In time, the cord grows to the thickness of a man's thumb and measures 10 to 20 inches in length. This length makes fetal activity possible.

A third structure which develops during the period of the embryo and which serves a useful purpose until birth is the *amniotic sac.* This is a water jacket, or bag, which protects the delicate tissues of the embryo from possible injury. The sac is attached to the placenta and contains a watery fluid, the *amniotic fluid,* in which the embryo develops. As the baby grows during the period of the fetus, the sac enlarges to adjust to the changing size of the fetus. Once the cord, placenta, and sac have been established, the embryo is protected and nourished so it can grow and develop. The maternal blood flows into the placenta from arteries in the uterine wall, and oxygen, water, and food materials in the mother's bloodstream are thus transported through the umbilical cord to the embryo. *There is no direct connection between maternal and embryonic bloodstreams.* The only connection is in the placenta, where certain ele-

ments from the mother's blood are sucked into the cord and carried to the embryo.

Through this same cord, embryonic waste products are filtered back through the placenta into the maternal blood and are removed from her blood through the organs of excretion. The embryo develops its own circulatory system but must rely upon the placenta, which acts as a filter, for its source of nourishment and elimination of waste products (26, 47, 94).

The third period in the timetable for prenatal development is the *period of the fetus,* which extends from the end of the second lunar month to birth. This is by far the longest of the three subdivisions but, in most respects, the least important. While there is growth and development during this period, no new features appear. Growth in size follows the laws of developmental direction (see Figure 1–3, page 21). The head, for example, is nearly one-third the total body length at the third fetal month, one-fourth at the sixth month, and slightly less than one-fourth at birth. By contrast, the body-length increase is sevenfold between the third month and birth.

By the fifth fetal month, the internal organs are well developed; they assume positions nearly like those in an adult body and are already functioning. By the sixth or seventh month, the fetus has reached the *age of viability.* This means that it has a chance of survival if born then; the nervous system is now adequately developed to function independently. Usually, however, 180 or 181 days is considered the average lower limit below which viability cannot be maintained (26). The timetable for the development of the human body in the prenatal period is shown in Figure 2–7.

FETAL ACTIVITY

Studies of fetal activity have revealed that movements in different parts of the body occur at predictable times. Between the second and third prenatal months, the umbilical cord shows regular spiral twists, which are due, it is believed, to the turning of the

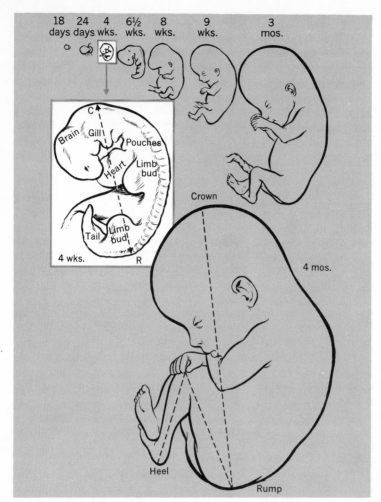

18   24   4   6½   8   9   3
days days wks. wks. wks.   wks.   mos.

Brain Gill
Pouches
Heart Limb
bud
Tail Limb
bud
4 wks.   R
C

Crown

4 mos.

Heel

Rump

Figure 2–7. The development of body form during the prenatal period. (Adapted from P. C. Martin and E. L. Vincent, *Human development*, Ronald, 1960. Used by permission.)

fetus in the uterus. In operatively removed fetuses, spontaneous movements can be observed at this time. These movements are wormlike contractions of the arms, legs, and thorax; they are ideomuscular—not evoked by external stimulation. Peristaltic movements may begin as early as the seventh week, at the end of the period of the embryo (26).

Fetal activities are of two types: specific *reflexes* and mass activity, or *generalized movements,* involving a large part of the body. Most of the basic reflexes, such as swallowing and the palmar, plantar, flexion, and Babinski reflexes, are established between the fourth and fifth prenatal months.

By birth, all the others are present. Owing to the maturation of the nerves and muscles, generalized activity in response to external stimuli occurs as early as the third month. This appears first in the head region. Later, generalized movement becomes spontaneous and does not have to be externally stimulated. Between the fourth and fifth months, this activity becomes more differentiated, allowing the head to move independently of the trunk, or the arms and legs to move without movements of the head (47).

Newberry recorded three types of generalized movements in fetal activity: (*1*) slow squirming, stretching, pushing, and turning movements; (*2*) quick kicks, jerks, and thrusts of the extremities; and (3) hiccups, or rhythmic series of quick convulsive movements. Kicking activity is the largest component of the total, and hiccuping is the smallest (107).

Variations in Fetal Activity. Some fetuses are active as much as 75 per cent of the time, and others as little as 5 per cent. There are also individual differences in the type of fetal activity. Some fetuses constantly turn and squirm, while others keep the same position but kick and thrust with their hands and feet. Some have hiccups almost every day, and others not at all. In the first month of perceived motility, there is the greatest increase in strength and number of fetal movements. From then until the ninth lunar month, there is a regular increase in movements, though large variations in the amount of movement occur from day to day (64). During the last lunar month before birth, lack of increase in movement may be explained by the fact that there is increased pressure on the fetal head, thus inhibiting bodily movement, or there is crowding of the entire fetal body in the amniotic sac, thus decreasing the space available for movement (107).

In the early part of the fetal period, there is more activity in the head than in the leg region. Gradually, as the fetal period draws to a close, the amount of activity in the leg region almost equals that in the head region. This shows the operation of the laws of developmental direction (57, 64). With increase in fetal age, the number of periods of fetal activity tends to decrease, but the periods increase in length (107).

A number of factors are associated with variations in fetal activity. Following maternal activity, the number of fetal movements is smallest during the first five minutes, gradually increasing until, after 30 minutes, there are approximately as many movements as after sleep. The explanation given for decrease in fetal activity after maternal exercise is that there is an increase in the supply of oxygen available to the fetus at that time.

Maternal fatigue seems to increase fetal activity. The fetus is usually most active at the close of the day. More frequent and more violent fetal movements occur when the mother is severely fatigued. Fetal activity is not differently affected by different kinds of maternal activity except that the fetus is significantly less active when the mother is eating. Sudden feelings of fear or anger on the mother's part produce immediate and marked increases in the number and violence of fetal movements (12, 57).

Excessive activity of fetuses may cause them to be considerably underweight for their body length because energy-producing foods are used up rather than stored as fat (135). Infants who were most active as fetuses acquire certain motor skills earlier than the average, and those who were least active as fetuses acquire them later. The less active, however, generally have less difficulty in adjusting to their postnatal environment than the more active (43, 136).

DEVELOPMENTAL IRREGULARITIES

The environment in which the child lives before birth—the mother's uterus—determines whether or not the fetus will follow nature's timetable. Normally, conditions within the uterus are ideal for the development of a healthy child. Should there be *marked* variations, nature's timetable is likely to be upset. Any injurious agent introduced through the placental bloodstream can distort the normal balance of the uterine environment. If it is introduced at a critical time in the developmental timetable, it can temporarily or permanently change the pattern. In discussing the importance of the prenatal environment, Montagu has pointed out:

Genes will respond to the environment only in the manner which the environment enables them to do so. What a given set of genes will produce, therefore, depends not upon themselves but upon their interaction with the environment. Under different environmental conditions the same genes will produce different results. It is therefore not true that because an individual has inherited a given set of genes, he is thereby destined to develop certain characters and no others. The kind of characters he will develop will depend upon the kind of environments in which the building blocks of these characters undergo development (98).

Traditional Beliefs. Traditional explanations for children's deviant development, especially when the parents are normal and healthy, may be divided into two categories: those which emphasize heredity and those which emphasize the role of maternal impressions. The latter are more numerous. In the past, deformities were believed to be due to a *hereditary weakness.* Such deviations as cleft palate, clubfoot, or idiocy, for example, were attributed to heredity and, in most instances, to bad heredity from the mother's side of the family.

Later, tales about the way a mother's thoughts, emotions, or cravings could *mark* her unborn child became popular. Marking was believed to be the result of "thought transference" or some mystical relationship between mother and fetus. Accounts of terrors due to black cats or burglars or overindulgence in certain favorite foods have been offered as conclusive proof of the cause of birthmarks or other disfigurations on the infant's body (138). A mother frightened by a hare when she was pregnant, for example, would attribute her child's harelip to this fright. But as Fasten has remarked, "If the body of the developing child were strongly influenced by all the cravings, desires, worries, and frights of the pregnant mother, it would bear hardly any resemblance to a normal human being" (40).

Present knowledge of the relationship between the body of the fetus and that of the mother disproves these traditional beliefs about maternal markings. There are two lines of evidence. The first is that the same types of abnormalities are found in most of the lower animals, where, because of the low level of development of the nervous system, maternal impressions do not exist. The second comes from knowledge of the fact that there is no direct connection between the mother and the fetus. There is

only an indirect connection through the umbilical cord and placenta—where there are no nerves, only blood vessels—and hence the mental, emotional, or nervous condition of the mother can have no direct effect whatever on the fetus (125).

Science has revealed a new kind of maternal influence, however, which comes not through the mother's thoughts, emotions, or cravings but through harmful substances in the mother's bloodstream that pass through the placental barrier into the bloodstream of the unborn child. Thus it is apparent that deviations come from an *environmental disturbance* more often than from hereditary weakness or from a conscious or unconscious act on the mother's part. As was pointed out earlier in the chapter, it is now known that the form of different animals can be experimentally changed by altering the conditions of the prenatal environment. There is growing evidence that this is also true of man.

Scientific Facts. Two important facts have been revealed by scientific studies of developmental irregularities. The *first* is:

Developmental irregularities may be due to defective genes, but they are far more likely to result from environmental disturbances in the uterus.

Irregularities may be the result "either of a good egg in a bad environment or of a bad egg in a good environment" (32). When there are defective genes, the chances are that nature will eliminate the unfit by a miscarriage during the early part of pregnancy, by a spontaneous abortion during the latter part of pregnancy, or by a stillbirth. While not all miscarriages, spontaneous abortions, or stillbirths result from developmental irregularities, more than a chance percentage of them do. A miscarriage due to a defective fertilized ovum generally occurs early in the prenatal period. When the fertilized ovum is normal but the environment in which it is developing is abnormal, the miscarriage usually comes later (53, 116).

In discussing the important role of the

intra-uterine environment, Ingalls has concluded that "mongolism and other congenital defects can no longer be shrugged off as mysterious acts of God or allowed to go to the geneticist by default" (68). Instead, there is evidence that variations in diet, health, glandular secretions, emotional states, and many other factors which influence the chemical condition of the mother's blood play dominant roles in producing these irregularities. While it is difficult to tell whether an irregularity is actually produced by one factor or another, it is widely agreed that the following factors have the most influence:

1. Maternal Nutrition. Because the unborn child's nourishment comes from the maternal bloodstream through the placenta, it is essential that the mother's diet contain the necessary food elements. These consist of *proteins* for tissue building and repair; *fats* to form fat tissue, to provide fuel for the body, and to store in the body as a reserve; and *carbohydrates* for strength and energy.

Mild quantitative or qualitative hunger is not serious; severe hunger of either type, especially when prolonged, is. Malnutrition —*qualitative* hunger—is more serious than insufficient food—*quantitative* hunger. The reason for this is that malnutrition generally results in vitamin deficiency, while insufficient food, provided it contains the necessary elements, rarely does. The unborn baby usually gets his due share from the mother's body, even if it is at her expense.

Serious malnutrition of the mother leads to mental deficiency or to some physical abnormality, such as rickets, nervous instability, general physical weakness, epilepsy, cerebral palsy, and neuropsychiatric disabilities in the child (60, 80). A deficiency of vitamin B in expectant mothers' diets has been found to affect the intelligence of their children during the early years of life. Whether this effect will ever be compensated for has not yet been determined. It has been found, however, that many children who have difficulties in school have had poor prenatal environments resulting from maternal malnutrition (56, 112). That poor ma-

ternal nutrition is, in part, responsible for children's learning difficulties has been demonstrated by an experiment in which a group of expectant mothers of low-income status was given dietary supplements during pregnancy and lactation, while a control group was given none. Children born to mothers of the experimental group had, in early childhood, significantly higher IQ's than those born to mothers in the control group (56).

Prolonged malnutrition, due to poverty, war conditions, ignorance of proper food values, or the mother's desire to maintain a slim figure, has been reported to be a serious hazard to unborn children. How serious prolonged malnutrition is was demonstrated during the Second World War. During the siege of Leningrad by the Germans, the stillborn rate doubled, and the rate of premature births was abnormally high. Generally lowered vitality of the babies who lived and congenital softening of the skull bones were also common (6).

Much the same situation was reported during the German occupation of Holland. When the maternal food supply was increased after the occupation ended, there was a decrease in stillbirths, premature births, and congenital abnormalities (133). Today, it is recognized that prolonged malnutrition of the expectant mother is one of the most common causes of fetal and neonatal death and of incurably damaged infants (140). It has also been found that the weight and length of fetuses are less when maternal diets are poor (23).

Although malnutrition may occur in any mother, it is most likely to be present in mothers of the lower socioeconomic groups. At the present time, malnutrition is more common among Negro than among white mothers. It has been suggested that the poor academic work of many Negro children is due, in part, to the fact that the poor nutritional status of their mothers during pregnancy prevented the full development of their mental potentials (112). In all social classes in America today, adolescent girls have the poorest diets, in most cases because of the girls' desire to be slender. This fact is especially serious in early marriages because it means that many young mothers-to-be are suffering from malnutrition when their pregnancies begin (140).

2. Maternal Health. Any diseased condition of the mother that affects her general metabolism will influence to a certain extent the development of her unborn child. The conditions believed to be most serious are:

a. *Endocrine disorders,* especially in the case of thyroid deficiency. Pronounced thyroid deficiency results in *cretinism*—the bones and cartilage fail to develop, the abdomen protrudes and becomes large and flabby, the skin is rough and coarse, the hair is shaggy, and the intellectual development is subnormal. Endocrine imbalance may result in *microcephaly*—mental deficiency accompanied by a small pointed skull—or *Mongolianism*—mental deficiency accompanied by slanting eyelids (11, 116).

b. *Infectious diseases,* such as syphilis, gonorrhea, poliomyelitis, and rubella (or German measles). If these diseases are acquired by the mother during the early months of pregnancy, they are especially damaging to the unborn child. They may cause stillbirths, miscarriages, blindness, deafness, mental deficiency, microcephaly, motor disorders, or deaf-mutism (98).

c. *Prolonged or wasting diseases,* such as tuberculosis and diabetes. These diseases have effects on the unborn child similar to those of malnutrition. In the case of diabetes, there is a higher incidence of mortality at birth or shortly afterward. There is, however, little evidence of greater numbers of malformations than in babies whose mothers are nondiabetic. Many defects are not discovered before the baby is six months old (120).

d. *The Rh blood factors*—incompatibility between the maternal and paternal blood types. These have been found to cause miscarriages, spontaneous abortions, stillbirths, and low-grade intelligence (46, 116).

e. The use of *drugs* by the mother during pregnancy. Many drugs, of course, are harmless, but others are dangerous for the unborn child. Quinine for malaria, especially when the doses are large, often causes deafness because of its effects on the fetal inner ear. The use of barbiturates and other pain-killing drugs prior to delivery may affect the oxygen supply to the fetal brain and lead to brain damage of minor or major importance (98). It has now been established that thalidomide, a drug used for morning sickness during the early stages of pregnancy, has been responsible for malformations of the limbs—phocomelia—in which the long bones of the arms fail to grow, with the result that the hands extend almost directly from the shoulders. The legs, while less affected, show similar distortion of growth (146). See Figure 2–8.

f. *X ray and radium.* When these are used early in pregnancy for therapeutic purposes, they are generally of great strength and are likely to have severe effects on the fetus, the most common of which is microcephaly with accompanying mental deficiency. When used lightly at the end of pregnancy for diagnostic purposes, they have no effect on the fetus (98). A preliminary report of the effects of exposure to radioactive materials of the atomic bomb has indicated that stillbirths, abortions, malformations, and decrease in birth weight were common (102).

3. Alcohol. There are many theories but little scientific evidence regarding the effect of the mother's use of alcohol on the fetus. Even if alcohol is not used by the mother, the male germ cell may be weakened by alcohol before fertilization occurs. Owing to the fact that the fetus obtains nourishment from the maternal bloodstream, the constant introduction into the bloodstream of chemical substances which impose a burden of accommodation on the physiological mechanism of the mother must, in one way or another, impose a burden on the fetus. When the limits of accommodation are exceeded, there are certain "danger signals," such as nervousness, wakefulness, or irregular heart action, and as the mother is affected detrimentally, the fetus is likewise affected. Even a moderate intake of alcohol is apparent in minimal quantities in the milk secretion of the mother (98).

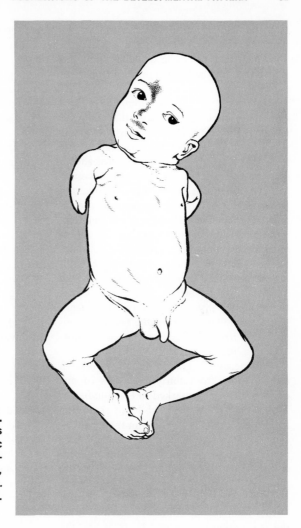

Figure 2–8. Effects of thalidomide. Deformity of infant is typical: useless short arms and hands, characteristic strawberry marks on face and forehead. (Adapted from H. B. Taussig, The thalidomide syndrome, *Scient. American*, 1962, 207, No. 2, 29–35. Used by permission.)

4. Tobacco. Tobacco contains nicotine, a powerful narcotic poison. It is most injurious when inhaled. General resistance to infections is lowered, especially in the mouth and throat. During the last 6 months of pregnancy, cigarette smoking by the mother is followed by an increase in fetal heart rate. The maximum effect appears from 8 to 12 minutes after the cigarette was begun (137).

In commenting on the long-term effects of maternal smoking on the unborn child, Montagu has pointed out that "it is quite possible that the products of tobacco entering the embryonic and fetal circulation adversely affect not only the heart and circulatory system, but also many other organs. The increase in cardiac and circulatory disorders in recent years may not be unconnected, in part at least, with the smoking of pregnant mothers" (98).

There is evidence that smoking is related to the frequency of premature births. Women who are heavy smokers (smoking more than 10 cigarettes a day) have the highest prematurity rate; light smokers (smoking 1 to 10 cigarettes a day) have a lower rate; and nonsmokers have the lowest rate of all. The prematurity rate for smokers is approximately twice as high as for nonsmokers (131). In animals, such as the cow and the cat, nicotine lessens milk secretion. At this time, there are indications, but no definite scientific evidence, that this is also true for the human mother (98).

5. Maternal Age. Older parents have, as a rule, more intelligent children than younger parents. This may, however, be due to the socioeconomic level of the parents and not to age. Studies of maternal age have shown that the best age, on the whole, for women to have children is between twenty-one and twenty-eight. Before age twenty-one, the female reproductive apparatus is not yet fully mature, or the hormones needed for reproduction have not yet reached their optimum levels. There are more miscarriages, stillbirths, and fetal malformations when the maternal age is below twenty-one. From twenty-nine years of age until the menopause, in the latter part of the forties, developmental irregularities increase, as do miscarriages and stillbirths (63, 148).

This increase is gradual at first; it takes a sudden jump from thirty-five years of age on. It is especially marked in the number of Mongoloid idiots and children suffering from hydrocephaly—"water on the brain"— a condition accompanied by mental and motor deficiency. The reason for the increase in defective children with advancing maternal age is that there is a change in the mother's endocrine balance. This change affects the unborn child by slowing down the maturation of ova and by retarding the development of the fetus. As has already been pointed out, endocrine imbalance always has an unfavorable effect on the unborn child. The closer the woman is to the menopause, the greater the likelihood that she will experience endocrine imbalance and, with it, the production of a damaged child (11, 78, 98).

6. Maternal Emotions. If the emotional experiences of the mother influence her developing baby in any way, it is through the glandular changes caused by her emotions (153). Women who are not happy about their pregnancies, because pregnancy interferes with the pattern of their lives or brings economic hardship, often experience continued emotional tension. This is reflected in more nausea and vomiting than occurs among women who are happy about their pregnancies. Should a woman who resents the coming of her baby try unsuccessfully to bring on an abortion, the emotional tension will be increased by feelings of guilt and shame, thus increasing the chances of damage to the unborn child. How serious the effect of emotional tension will be depends mainly on when the tension occurs. If it occurs early in pregnancy and is severe and prolonged enough to cause endocrine imbalance, it will have a more damaging effect than if it occurs in the latter part of pregnancy (45, 151).

Severe and prolonged emotional tension during the period of the fetus is unlikely to cause malformations, either physical or mental. It leads to increased fetal activity, however, with the result that, at birth, the baby is leaner than the average newborn infant. A more active fetus also has greater than normal postnatal adjustment difficulties (41, 52, 144, 151). Sontag has described the effects of maternal emotions as "blood-borne" anxieties. According to him, blood-borne anxieties not only affect the fetus but may also carry over and affect the postnatal adjustment of the newborn infant. Poor postnatal adjustment may, in turn, result in behavioral upset or deviant behavior (136).

7. Uterine Crowding. In multiple births crowding is inevitable. When the uterus reaches its limit of expansion, the fetuses are expelled, even though they are not ready to be born. The damaging effects of crowding are not limited to premature births and neonatal deaths—a common accompaniment of prematurity; they are seen also in developmental irregularities. Crowding is especially serious in identical multiple births because the fetuses share the same sac. As a result, one is likely to get a more favored position, while the other, whose position is cramped, is unable to assimilate the substances from the placenta needed for normal development (108, 125).

One way in which a fetus may accommodate itself to this cramped position is to relax its body. As a result, the hip bones may fail to ossify; this leads to a congenital dislocation of the hip (27). In the case of the Dionne quintuplets, two were so cramped in their prenatal environment that they were smaller at birth than the other three, and their physical and mental development was damaged. After birth, they frequently turned blue from respiratory difficulties, and as they grew older they showed a developmental lag in their motor and mental abilities (20). It has been suggested that the epileptic seizures which plagued one of them, Emilie, throughout her life and which finally caused her death were related to her fetal handicap (58).

The *second* important fact which has come from scientific studies of the abnormal development of human and animal fetuses is:

Developmental irregularities result from environmental disturbances which occur at the same time as the formation of a particular organ.

This means that the *time* when the agent is introduced, rather than the agent itself, is the determining influence in the production of abnormalities. As has already been pointed out, there is a special time in the timetable of prenatal development for the formation of each organ. If something interferes to prevent the organ from forming at that time, the course of growth in the different parts of the body will be altered, and abnormalities will result (121, 141).

Montagu has stressed the importance of timing of environmental influences thus:

This follows a general law of embryological development, namely, the younger the developing organism the more likely it is to be seriously affected in development by disturbing conditions. There are periods in the development of the organism which are known as critical developmental periods, so called because during these periods fundamental developmental changes are occurring which depend on perfect timing and the correlation of many different processes. Any disturbing factor that is introduced into the developmental process at such a time is likely to produce structural and functional disorders in varying degrees and of various kinds (98).

The first 3 months of prenatal life are the "critical developmental periods." During the period of the embryo, all the structures of the body are being formed. From the eighth week on—the period of the fetus—the major development consists in the completion of the structures whose foundations were laid during the period of the embryo. Some develop more in the period of the fetus than others; their foundations are, however, well laid by the end of the third lunar month—the first month of the period of the fetus.

The embryo is extremely sensitive to all sorts of changes in the uterine environment. This has led Landreth to say that "by the end of the second month of prenatal life, chance and environmental circumstances have already played a part in the destiny of the human being, determining some of the congenital characteristics which will help or hinder him in his interactions with his environment" (86). Norris, even more emphatic about the importance of this period, has said that the "first trimester may be the most significant period of our lives" (109).

Even though the first trimester is the most critical period in prenatal life, this does not mean that all possibility of damage from an unfavorable prenatal environment ends then. As Garn has pointed out:

From the sixth through the ninth month of pregnancy, hazards are fewer and the completion of major stages of development makes the fetus less vulnerable to injury. Yet it is in this time period when mental growth may be set back by environmental insults too mild to yield gross anatomical defects. Nutritional deficiencies during later pregnancy may lead to unsound teeth, jaw and face defects, and disturbances of behavior and personality observable in later life (44).

Unfavorable conditions in the prenatal

environment rarely produce developmental irregularities when they occur *before* a certain part of the body has started to develop or *after* it has formed (69, 116). German measles, for example, contracted after the fifth month of pregnancy, have no effect on the unborn child because the parts of the body affected by this disease are already formed. Similarly, thalidomide, taken for morning sickness or nervous tension has no damaging effect on the unborn child if used after the first trimester of pregnancy (146). Only those parts of the body which develop and those processes which take place during the period of the fetus, such as the mineralization of the skeleton, will be markedly influenced by unfavorable conditions then. Once the damage has been done, however, nothing can correct it.

Many of the studies of developmental irregularities have, of necessity, been made on animals. Ingalls' experiments on rats, referred to earlier, not only showed that certain conditions in the prenatal environment produced developmental irregularities but also showed that *particular defects* are caused by disturbances at *particular moments* of pregnancy and *at those moments only* (69). Studies of human subjects are somewhat limited, but they are numerous enough to emphasize the importance of the timetable of abnormalities.

Rubella, or German measles, which in childhood is a mild disease, has serious effects on an unborn child if the mother contracts the disease *during the first 3 or 4 months of pregnancy.* It causes neonatal deaths and stillbirths and produces such defects as cataracts, deafness, anomalies in the structure of the heart, defective teeth, microcephaly, and mental deficiency. Of these defects, deafness is most frequent. Rubella occurring at a critical period in the development of the end organs of the ear produces vascular changes in the fetus. The vessels are the first to suffer. Lack of nutrition is then followed by developmental arrest in the ear, causing deafness (17, 51, 69, 92, 124). Severe *malnutrition* during the early months of pregnancy not only causes a wide variety of developmental irregularities but often leads to neonatal deaths and stillbirths (60, 80). In America today, as was stressed earlier, malnutrition is not limited to mothers in the lower socioeconomic groups; it is found among very young mothers in *all* social groups. In discussing the role of malnutrition, Peckos has emphasized that it is "futile to correct the maternal diet after the first trimester of pregnancy in an attempt to prevent congenital anomalies" (113).

Rickets, a disease which is common in prematurely born children, does not result from dietary deficiencies in postnatal life as is commonly believed. Instead, there is evidence that children who do not spend the last months of their prenatal development *in utero,* when mineralization of the skeleton is most active, are likely to suffer from rickets. In *Mongolian idiocy,* the parts of the body usually deformed are those which are just "budding" around the eighth week of pregnancy. An abnormal condition of the prenatal environment at this time is now known to produce these deformities (11, 69).

Prolonged emotional stress of the mother during the early part of pregnancy is now believed to be partially or totally responsible for *cleft palates* and *harelips.* The bones of the palate are in the process of forming between the seventh and tenth weeks of prenatal life. Emotional stress at this time causes hyperactivity of the mother's adrenal glands, thus releasing an increased supply of the hormone *hydrocortisone.* There is evidence that this interferes with the normal development of the palate, and as a result it is cleft instead of normal. This endocrine disturbance likewise interferes with the normal development of the upper jawbone, and this produces a harelip. There is also evidence that severe emotional stress during the first 3 months of pregnancy leads to *mental retardation,* for it is at this time that the brain is developing (105, 109).

Importance of Prenatal Environment. It is apparent that a child's prenatal environment affects the whole course of his life. A child who is born with a physical defect, such as blindness or deafness, will be forced to live a life that is different from what it would have been had these defects not developed. As a result, he may "then be subject to a miserable life" (127). Furthermore, physical defects are reflected in the child's concept of himself as a person and thus influence the developing pattern of his personality. Whether a child will grow up to be a socially and emotionally well-adjusted person or not will depend, to some extent, upon whether he comes into the world prepared to make good adjustments.

Family relationships—not only parent-child relationships but also relationships between husband and wife and between siblings—are influenced by the type of child born into a family and by what parents *believe* to be the cause of any irregularities in the child. Even though science has gone far to clear up the superstitions about maternal marking, many women even today are still influenced by them and fail to get proper medical care during pregnancy and at the time of birth.

Of even greater seriousness, the belief that the mother is primarily responsible for any developmental irregularity that may appear in her baby, whether it is a small birthmark or a more serious developmental irregularity such as mental deficiency, blindness, or deafness, often leads to feelings of guilt on her part and an unhealthy overprotective or overindulgent attitude toward the baby. Such an attitude will affect the child's whole future. The belief that the mother is responsible may also lead to friction between the parents (98, 138). The effect of a handicapped child on family relationships will be discussed in more detail later.

Practical Implications. Knowing that the critical time for developmental irregularities comes during the early part of pregnancy has a practical aspect. It suggests that a mother-to-be must be in good physical and mental condition *before* her pregnancy begins. It also suggests that superstitions about the "best times" to be born may have some merit not always recognized today. Babies conceived during the winter months reach the critical age for malformations at the time when children's diseases most often occur—during the spring months (80). If the mother-to-be has never had rubella, and should there be an epidemic in her community, the chances of her contracting this disease are great, especially if there are children in the family. Because of this risk, Ingalls has advocated that every girl make it her business to have rubella before she begins her pregnancy, preferably before she marries. This will guarantee her an immunity if she is exposed to the disease during pregnancy (69).

The critical early months of a baby conceived during the spring occur when the mother's diet tends to be poorest. During the hot months of summer the mother's diet may be especially deficient in proteins. Because proteins are a vitally important source of nutrition when the different organs of the unborn child's body are being formed, a dietary deficiency at this time can lead to developmental irregularities. Regardless of when the baby is conceived, a mother who tries to maintain her slender figure by fad diets before her pregnancy and during its early months can bring serious harm to her child (80, 140).

It is a widespread belief that childbearing is a natural function of the female body and that a mother does not need medical care unless there is evidence that pregnancy is not progressing normally. Furthermore, there are many "remedies" for such normal accompaniments of pregnancy as morning sickness or unusual fatigue. Should a mother-to-be take these remedies without consulting her doctor, she may, unwittingly, injure her unborn child.

Thalidomide, for example, was marketed as freely as aspirin under the trade name "Contergan" in West Germany from 1959 to 1961. Many German mothers, as well as some Americans whose husbands were located in Germany, used this medicine for the discomforts of early pregnancy. As a result, there was a wave of deformed newborn babies whose defects were later traced to this drug. Had it been possible to buy thalidomide in America without a doctor's prescription, we could easily have had a similar experience (146).

Some of the ill effects of an unfavorable prenatal environment may not become apparent until many months after birth. As there are no adequate tests for measuring mental retardation in the newborn infant or the very young child, mental retardation caused by unfavorable prenatal environmental conditions may not become apparent for several years. Furthermore, some of the ill effects, such as failure to recover from the shock of birth and gain weight, may, at first, be attributed to other factors—to feeding difficulties, for example. In time, early ill health, failure to gain weight, and other physiological symptoms may lead to the suspicion that the child suffered prenatal damage (144).

Because of the seriousness of unfavorable conditions in the prenatal environment and because of the widespread publicity given to them today, there is a tendency to conclude that more children are damaged before birth than is actually the case. In this connection, Parker has said:

Only one baby in two hundred, as an average, has some apparent abnormality at birth. Even this incidence is not as bad as it might seem at first, for it includes minor defects that will not mar the child's appearance or interfere with its normal life. It also includes defects that, while serious in nature, can be corrected surgically so that the baby need not be handicapped for life. Only a few will be hopelessly defective. Truly, nature has conducted well these journeys of the unborn. One of the reasons for nature's success in producing normal babies in such a high percentage of births is that she rejects a seriously faulty product long before it has reached completion (111).

ATTITUDES OF SIGNIFICANT PEOPLE

While maternal health, nutrition, age, and the other factors discussed above are, unquestionably, the major influences in determining how the fertilized ovum will develop, *indirect* influences in the form of attitudes of significant people in the unborn child's life are too important to be ignored. As has already been stressed, a woman cannot influence her unborn child directly by her thoughts or feelings, except when they are accompanied by strong and prolonged emotions. The attitudes formed at this time are important, however, because they serve as the bases for maternal attitudes toward the child after he is born, toward the role of parent, and toward the child-training methods used during the early, formative years of his life. What is true of maternal attitudes is likewise true of the father's attitudes and, to a lesser extent, of the attitudes of siblings and other family members (22, 123, 138).

Most attitudes toward children and toward parenthood originate in the childhood experiences of the parents-to-be and crystallize when pregnancy is confirmed. Most women, from the time when they played with dolls, have looked forward to having children of their own, and they have *well-formed* concepts of what they want their children to be like. Men are generally too concerned about their vocations to give much thought to parenthood during their childhood and youth. They do, however, have *general* ideas of what parenthood will mean to them (22).

Once formed, attitudes are unlikely to change radically, especially when they are emotionally toned. In a study of maternal attitudes during pregnancy and after the birth of the child, it was found that mothers who had a rejective attitude toward their unborn children became more acceptant after the children's birth. This shift may have been due primarily to a *repression* of their feelings of rejection, resulting from feelings of guilt, rather than to an actual change in attitudes (18, 85, 158).

Similarly, while attitudes toward the role of parenthood may and often do change after the child is born, the fundamental elements of these attitudes persist. Attitudes that have been favorable during pregnancy, for example, may change to less favorable after the child is born or when the helplessness of the baby gives way to the growing independence of a toddler. This is especially likely to happen if attitudes have been unrealistic and romanticized before the child's birth or if there is more work and personal privation than the parent had anticipated, as in the case of twins (115). Unfavorable attitudes may likewise give way to favorable attitudes when the parent experiences the satisfactions of parenthood (61, 72, 87, 88, 154).

Parental Concepts. Parental attitudes are markedly influenced by the parents' concept of the child as a person and by their concept of the parental role.

Concepts of "Their" Child. Parental concepts of the child as a person tend to be less realistic and more highly romanticized than concepts of the role of parenthood. This is more applicable to mothers than to fathers. Mothers-to-be, it has been found, want not just a child but a *particular type* of child. The physical and mental characteristics, the sex, and the personality of this "dream child" become sharply defined in the mother's mind as pregnancy progresses. In a study of college girls, it was reported that their concepts of a baby included facial features like those of baby-card pictures, features that are "ideal and are probably

far from typical" (62). Figure 2–9 shows the discrepancy between the mother's "dream child" and her real child.

Should the real child, especially with regard to sex, match the parental concept, postnatal treatment of the child will be more favorable than if the child falls short of the parents' concept. His appearance and his achievements, as he grows older, will also assure him of more favorable treatment if they come up to parental expectations (1, 31). In a study of "planned-for" children, it was found that mothers often could not reconcile their children with the concept they had built up of what *their* children would be (132).

Many forms of so-called "problem behavior" in children are merely discrepancies between the behavior of real children and parental concepts of ideal behavior (132). The intolerance of a father toward his son frequently traces its origin to the fact that the son falls short of what the father thinks *his* son should be (1). Similarly, parental intolerance of childish dawdling may come from a parent's concept of the importance of efficiency and his belief that the child must be quick-moving to attain success in life (93).

Concepts of the Role of Parents. Concepts of parenthood are formed during the preg-

Figure 2–9. "Dream child" versus real child.

nancy period, too, though they have their roots in the childhood experiences of the parents. A parent brought up in an authoritarian home, for example, may have decided during his childhood days that when he became a parent "things would be different" for his children. On the other hand, he may have decided that his parents did "a pretty good job on him" and that, by following the pattern of training they used, he will do an equally good job on his children (70).

There are marked *variations* in concepts of the role of the parent and of parenthood. These concepts range from highly romanticized to highly realistic and from favorable to unfavorable; they have emotional accompaniments ranging from joy to fear, anger, or disgust. The variations may be due to early experiences in the lives of the parents-to-be, or they may come from experiences during pregnancy. Because no two parents-to-be have similar childhood experiences or similar experiences during pregnancy, it is understandable that these variations will be extremely wide.

Some of the many factors responsible for the variations are almost universally operative. The *physical* and *emotional states* of the mother-to-be during the months of pregnancy have a profound influence on how she feels about her new role. If she suffers from nausea, vomiting, and periodic discomforts or pain, her attitude will be colored by her health condition. Doubts about her adequacy for parenthood or resentments about having to change a pattern of life she has enjoyed will also influence her (7, 54, 151).

For all women, "pregnancy involves a stirring up of certain psychological conflicts and a marked readjustment of their relationships with their husbands and of the expectations they had of their husbands and of themselves" (91). Women of the lower social classes, women of status occupations, and women who are upwardly or downwardly mobile tend to regard themselves as more sick during pregnancy than they actually are. Whether they use their "sickness" to escape their normal social roles and responsibilities or to win sympathy and atten-

tion is of minor concern. The important thing is that it colors their concept of the role of parenthood unfavorably (119). In commenting on how the mother-to-be's physical and emotional states influence her attitude toward parenthood, Stone and Church have pointed out that "some mothers feel physically ill during most of the pregnancy but are cheered by the thought of the baby to come; others are in robust health but live in dread of motherhood. For most women, pregnancy, like the rest of life, is a mixed bag of discomforts and rewards, hopes and fears, pain and elation" (143).

Concepts of parenthood are markedly influenced by the *age of the parents*. Young parents tend, on the whole, to accept their parenthood lightly, not allowing it to interfere with their pleasures or future plans. Should impending parenthood interfere with the father-to-be's vocational aspirations, it is likely to lead to resentments. Older parents, on the whole, welcome their parental role more wholeheartedly than younger parents (21).

Mothers with *professional training* and *experience* frequently have unfavorable attitudes toward parenthood—at least at first. They resent anything that interferes with the careers they have worked hard to achieve and which they have enjoyed. Later they may derive enough satisfaction from their new role to accept it without resentments. Far too often, however, they find the parental role less interesting and challenging than their former careers. This increases their resentments at having to sacrifice a role they enjoyed for one they find less satisfying (88).

The *social class* with which parents are identified has a marked influence on their concepts. Adults from the lower social classes look upon parenthood as the "inevitable payment for sex relations"—an unfavorable attitude as far as future treatment of the child is concerned. Those from the middle and upper classes regard parenthood as the "fulfillment of marriage" and look upon their children with possessive pride and hope. Lower-class men tend to look upon their parental role as that of provider;

they resent having to assume any responsibility for the child's care. Middle- and upper-class men, by contrast, take pride in being "family men"; they are willing to make personal sacrifices in time, energy, money, or even vocational advancement for their children (21, 55).

Closely related to differences in concepts resulting from social class are those resulting from the *economic status* of the family. If financial conditions are strained because of pregnancy shortly after marriage; if the young couple are just getting on their feet financially; or if the wife planned to work to further her husband's vocational aims, parental attitudes toward the arrival of a child are adversely affected. One of the common reasons for attempted abortion is that the financial resources of the family can face no further strain (45, 157).

Concepts vary according to the strength of parental *desire for children*. Some parents want many children, and others want a few or none; some feel that marriage is incomplete without children, and others feel that children interfere with parental pleasures or place a barrier in the way of vocational success and upward social mobility; some have an egocentric interest in children, and others have little or no interest in them; some want children because it is the "thing to do," and others do not want them because their friends are childless (79, 155, 157).

Certain conditions predispose married women *not* to want children. The most important of these are poor marital adjustments and an engrossing career which would be interrupted or terminated by pregnancy (25, 45, 150). Desire for children is generally strongest among women who have no children. The romanticized concept of parenthood, after the arrival of the first child, often gives way to a more realistic one (31, 88).

Finally, but by no means the least important factor contributing to variations in concepts of parenthood and of the child as a person, is the role played by *mass media*. Books, magazines, movies, television, and radio far too often present a romanticized version of families and family life. Because girls, on the whole, prefer romantic stories and films, while boys prefer realistic stories, the sex differences in attitudes toward parenthood referred to earlier may be at least partially attributed to the influences of mass media.

Types of Parental Attitudes. While any unfavorable parental attitude can result in unhealthy parent-child relationships, those which have the most damaging and far-reaching effects are of three types. The first is the attitude based on the *concept of a "dream child."* Many cases of emotional instability stem from the child's feeling that he is rejected by his parents or is not as well accepted as a sibling because he does not conform to the parents' ideal. Attitudes based on a "dream child" concept are prevalent among siblings as well as among parents. Sibling rivalries and jealousies are common when an older child has an unrealistic concept of what having a baby in the family will mean to him (88, 93, 123).

The tendency to *romanticize the parental role* also has a damaging effect on parent-child relationships. Shortly after the baby is born, most parents begin to realize that parenthood is not what they had believed it to be. A study of male and female college students showed that a majority believed the major tasks of parenthood consisted of reading to the child, playing with him, and buying him clothes. The realistic tasks of child care—changing diapers, toilet training, and giving the baby his 2 A.M. bottle—were little understood (31).

Another study of young mothers and fathers showed how markedly their romanticized concepts of parenthood had to be revised and how they reacted to the adjustments they had to make. According to mothers, parenthood means loss of sleep, chronic tiredness, extensive confinement to the home, added duties, long hours of work, worry about changes in their appearance, giving up the satisfactions and income derived from an interesting job, and decline in housekeeping standards. Fathers found the parental role entailed decline in sexual responsiveness on the part of their wives, economic pressure, interference with their social lives, worry about a second pregnancy, and the feeling of being an "isolate" when the original two-member group expanded into a three-member group. Both mothers and fathers gave a definite suggestion of "disenchantment" with the parental role. When this is added to disenchantment with the child as a person, parental attitudes toward the child can hardly be expected to be entirely favorable (88).

The third, and by far the most serious and long-lasting, parental attitude is that of *not wanting a child*. True, sometimes this attitude changes after the baby is born, even when the child is illegitimate. But it is more likely to persist than to disappear or change. The mother's reason for not wanting a child is based on something that is important to her, and she feels justified in her attitudes. She may feel that she and her husband cannot afford another child; she may feel overworked with the children she already has; she may want to continue to work outside the home because of the satisfaction she derives from the work or the material possessions she can buy with her salary; or, if the child is illegitimate, she may be afraid of the consequences of bringing an illegitimate child into the world.

Because these reasons for not wanting a child are important to the mother-to-be, the attitudes stemming from them will be persistent. Furthermore, the strong emotions—resentment, anger, or fear—that usually accompany these attitudes increase their persistency. If the mother failed in an attempt to bring on an abortion, her resentment toward the child will probably persist, even though cloaked, and will be reflected in the way she treats the child (19, 25). Studies of child beatings, for example, have revealed that the children are often the products of unwanted pregnancies (76). If an unmarried mother does not marry her child's father, she is constantly afraid that the child's illegitimacy will be discovered, that she will be criticized and ostracized by her family and friends, and that her child will be rejected and mistreated by his agemates.

These fears only reinforce her original rejection of the child (71, 91).

Should the parents of an illegitimate child marry before the child's birth, the stigma of illegitimacy will be lessened. There is no guarantee, however, that the parents, forced into a "shotgun" marriage, will be acceptant of the child or that they will provide a happy home atmosphere for him. Because premarital pregnancy tends to intensify the normal conflicts of marriage and because it leads to resentments when marriage is forced, the home atmosphere is likely to be unhealthy. This is especially true when the conflicts lead to divorce—a common ending of "shotgun" marriages (28, 30, 45).

Sibling Attitudes. Attitudes of siblings are usually formed during the prenatal period of the new baby and are well established by the time he is born. How a child feels about a new baby will depend largely upon his age and his other interests. If he is still young, he may resent having to share his parents' time and attention. The older child has friends and interests outside the home. As long as the new baby does not interfere with the pattern of his life, his attitude will be favorable. He may even find the baby more fun to play with than his toys.

Adolescents, especially girls, often have an unfavorable attitude toward a new baby in the family. They are embarrassed about their mothers' pregnancies and are often called on to help take care of the baby. Their social lives may be curtailed somewhat, and, as a result, jealousy and resentment quickly develop (21, 48).

How the child is told about the expected birth of a sibling and by whom he is told likewise influence his attitude. If he has been promised a new playmate, with emphasis on the sex of this playmate, he is likely to build up a romanticized concept of the baby, which will have to be radically revised after the baby's arrival. Even if the baby is of the desired sex, he will not be a real playmate for a long time. To make matters worse, the baby will usurp much of the mother's time and attention, so the older child will be deprived not only of her com-

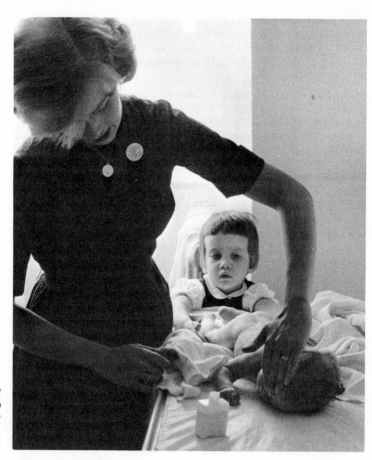

The young child may find it is more fun to play with the new baby than with his toys. (Elizabeth Wilcox.)

panionship but of the expected playmate as well. Should he hear from an outsider that he has a new sibling—after the mother has mysteriously disappeared and a stranger has come to take care of him—he is likely to build up a deep resentment which will be reflected in his behavior toward the sibling, perhaps for years to come (21, 88).

Far-reaching Effects of Attitudes. Maternal health affects the child *before* he is born, while maternal attitudes affect him *after* he is born. When a child is damaged by poor conditions in the prenatal environment, parental attitudes have a marked influence on the way he adjusts to life (33).

When the father-to-be or older siblings look upon the new baby with antagonism, he is not likely to receive a warm welcome.

Added responsibilities and personal deprivations are apt to intensify their already existing resentments. As the child grows older, he will become aware of the fact that he is not wholly accepted, even though he may not be actually rejected (72, 87, 93).

Many forms of problem behavior result from a child's feeling that he is not accepted in the home. Young children whose mothers had a stressful pregnancy and had attempted abortion are more poorly adjusted than children whose mothers wanted them (7). In the area of feeding, poor adjustment is especially pronounced and is displayed in such problems as excessive regurgitation and gastrointestinal disorders by the infant and in food refusals, finicky appetites, and dawdling over food by the older child. The explanation given for this poor adjustment is that "when infants and young children are brought into close contact with an adult, they perceive the emotional status of the adult and respond to it in a consistent manner" (114).

Similarly, unfavorable attitudes of outsiders due to a child's illegitimacy are formed before the child's birth and tend to persist. The child understands these attitudes

better as he grows older. He becomes increasingly aware of his socially unfavorable status both in the home and outside. This is bound to leave serious psychological scars on his developing personality. Many forms of problem behavior in the child may result from his unhealthy relationships with family members or with people outside the home (71, 93).

BIBLIOGRAPHY

(1) ABERLE, D. F., and K. D. NAEGELE: Middle-class fathers' occupational roles and attitudes toward children. *Amer. J. Orthopsychiat.*, 1952, **22**, 366–378.

(2) ALLPORT, G. W.: *Personality.* New York: Holt, 1937.

(3) ALM, I.: The long-term prognosis for prematurely born children: a follow-up study of 999 premature boys born in wedlock and of 1,002 controls. *Acta paediat., Stockh.,* 1953, **42**, Suppl. 94.

(4) AMES, L. B.: The sense of self of nursery school children as manifested by their verbal behavior. *J. genet. Psychol.,* 1952, **81**, 193–232.

(5) ANASTASI, A.: Heredity, environment, and the question "how?" *Psychol. Rev.,* 1958, **65**, 197–208.

(6) ANTONOV, A. N.: Children born during the siege of Leningrad in 1942. *J. Pediat.,* 1947, **30**, 250–259.

(7) BAKER, J. W., and A. HOLZWORTH: Social histories of successful and unsuccessful children. *Child Develpm.,* 1961, **32**, 135–149.

(8) BARCLAY, D.: Twins: not all "togetherness." *The New York Times,* Feb. 15, 1959.

(9) BAYLEY, N.: Some increasing parent-child similarities during the growth of children. *J. educ. Psychol.,* 1954, **45**, 1–21.

(10) BENDA, C. E.: Psychopathology of childhood. In L. Carmichael (Ed.), *Manual of child psychology,* 2d ed. New York: Wiley, 1954. Pp. 1115–1161.

(11) BENDA, C. E.: Mongolism: a comprehensive review. *Arch. Pediat.,* 1956, **73**, 391–407.

(12) BERNARD, J., and L. W. SONTAG: Fetal reactivity to tonal stimulation: a preliminary report. *J. genet. Psychol.,* 1947, **70**, 205–210.

(13) BERNSTEIN, M. E.: Studies in the human sex ratio. II. The proportion of unisexual siblings. *Hum. Biol.,* 1952, **24**, 35–43.

(14) BERNSTEIN, M. E.: Parental age and sex ratio. *Science,* 1953, **118**, 448–449.

(15) BERNSTEIN, M. E.: Studies on the human sex ratio. Evidence of genetic variation of the primary sex ratio in man. *J. Hered.,* 1954, **44**, 59–64.

(16) BESCH, O. F., W. LENZ, and J. MAXWELL: The correlation between mental and physical growth in twins. *Brit. J. educ. Psychol.,* 1961, **31**, 265–267.

(17) BESWICK, R. C., R. WARNER, and J. WARKANY: Congenital anomalies following maternal rubella. *Amer. J. Dis. Children,* 1949, **78**, 334–338.

(18) BIBRING, G. L.: Some considerations of the psychological processes in pregnancy. *Psychoanal. Stud. Child.,* 1959, **14**, 113–121.

(19) BIBRING, G. L., T. F. DWYER, D. S. HUNTINGTON, and A. F. VALENSTEIN: A study of the psychological processes in pregnancy and of the earliest mother-child relationship. *Psychoanal. Stud. Child.,* 1961, **16**, 9–72.

(20) BLATZ, W. E.: *The five sisters.* New York: Morrow, 1938.

(21) BOSSARD, J. H. S.: *Parent and child.* Philadelphia: University of Pennsylvania Press, 1953.

(22) BRIM, O. G.: The sources of parent behavior. *Children,* 1958, **5**, 217–222.

(23) BURKE, B. S., S. S. STEVENSON, J. WORCESTER, and H. G. STUART: Nutrition studies during pregnancy. V. Relation of maternal nutrition to condition of infant at birth. *J. Nutrit.,* 1949, **38**, 453–467.

(24) BURLINGHAM, D. T.: *Twins.* New York: International Universities Press, Inc., 1952.

(25) CAPLAN, G.: The disturbance of the mother-child relationship by unsuccessful attempts at abortion. *Ment. Hyg., N.Y.,* 1954, **38**, 67–80.

(26) CARMICHAEL, L.: The onset and early development of behavior. In L. Carmichael

(Ed.), *Manual of child psychology*, 2d ed. New York: Wiley, 1954. Pp. 60–187.

(27) CHAPPLE, C. C.: Abnormalities of infants resulting from non-genetic factors. *Postgrad. Med.*, 1950, **7**, 323–329.

(28) CHRISTENSEN, H. T., and B. B. RUBINSTEIN: Premarital pregnancy and divorce: a follow-up study by the interview method. *Marriage fam. Liv.*, 1956, **18**, 114–123.

(29) CLARE, J. E., and C. V. KISER: Social and psychological factors affecting fertility. XIV. Preference for children of a given sex in relation to fertility. *Milbank Memorial Fund Quart.*, 1951, **29**, 421–473.

(30) CLIFFORD, E.: Expressed attitudes in pregnancy of unwed women and married primigravida and multigravida. *Child Develpm.*, 1962, **33**, 945–951.

(31) COOPER, L.: Predisposition toward parenthood: a comparison of male and female students. *Sociol. soc. Res.*, 1957, **42**, 31–36.

(32) CORNER, G. W.: *Ourselves unborn.* New Haven: Yale University Press, 1944.

(33) CRUICKSHANK, W. M.: *Psychology of exceptional children and youth.* Englewood Cliffs, N.J.: Prentice-Hall, 1955.

(34) DAHLBERG, G.: Do parents want boys or girls? *Acta Genet. et Statist. Medica.*, 1948, **1**, 163–167.

(35) DAHLBERG, G.: Die Tendenz zu Zwillingsgeburten. *Acta Genet. med. Gemellolog.* 1952, **1**, 80–88.

(36) DAVIS, A., and R. J. HAVIGHURST: *Father of the man.* Boston: Houghton Mifflin, 1947.

(37) DAVIS, M. E.: Ovulation and fertility. In M. Fishbein and R. J. R. Kennedy (Eds.), *Modern marriage and family living.* Fair Lawn, N.J.: Oxford University Press, 1957. Pp. 357–367.

(38) DIMITZ, S., R. R. DYNES, and A. C. CLARKE: Preferences for male or female children: traditional or affectional? *Marriage fam. Liv.*, 1954, **16**, 128–134.

(39) FRANCHER, H. L.: The relationship between the occupational status of individuals and the sex ratio of their offspring. *Hum. Biol.*, 1956, **28**, 316–322.

(40) FASTEN, N.: The myth of prenatal influences. *Today's Hlth*, 1950, **27**, 42–43.

(41) FERREIRA, A. J.: The pregnant woman's emotional attitude and its reflection on the newborn. *Amer. J. Orthopsychiat.*, 1960, **30**, 553–561.

(42) FREEDMAN, D. S., R. FREEDMAN, and P. R. WHELPTON: Size of family and preference for children of each sex. *Amer. J. Sociol.*, 1960, **66**, 141–146.

(43) FRIES, M. E.: Psychosomatic relationship between mother and infant. *Psychosom. Med.*, 1944, **6**, 159–162.

(44) GARN, S. M.: Growth and development. In E. Ginzberg, *The nation's children.* Vol. 2.

Development and education. New York: Columbia, 1960. Pp. 24–42.

(45) GEBHARD, P. H., W. B. POMEROY, C. E. MARTIN, and C. V. CHRISTENSON: *Pregnancy, birth, and abortion.* New York: Harper & Row, 1958.

(46) GERVER, J. M., and R. DAY: Intelligence quotients of children who have recovered from erythroblastosis fetalis. *J. Pediat.*, 1950, **36**, 342–349.

(47) GESELL, A.: The ontogenesis of infant behavior. In L. Carmichael (Ed.), *Manual of child psychology*, 2d ed. New York: Wiley, 1954. Pp. 335–373.

(48) GESELL, A., F. L. ILG, and L. B. AMES: *Youth: the years from ten to sixteen.* New York: Harper & Row, 1956.

(49) GOODENOUGH, E. W.: Interest in persons as an aspect of sex differences in the early years. *Genet. Psychol. Monogr.*, 1957, **55**, 287–323.

(50) GOUGH, H. G.: Identifying psychological femininity. *Educ. psychol. Measmt*, 1952, **12**, 427–439.

(51) GREENBERG, M., O. PELLITTERI, and J. BARTON: Frequency of defects in infants whose mothers had rubella during pregnancy. *J. Amer. Med. Ass.*, 1957, **165**, 675–678.

(52) GRIMM, E. R.: Psychological tension in pregnancy. *Psychosom. Med.*, 1961, **23**, 520–527.

(53) GUTTMACHER, A. F.: Abortions. In M. Fishbein and R. J. R. Kennedy (Eds.), *Modern marriage and family living.* Fair Lawn, N.J.: Oxford University Press, 1957. Pp. 401–414.

(54) HAMILTON, E.: Emotional aspects of pregnancy: an intensive study of fourteen normal primiparae. Ph.D. dissertation. New York: Teachers College, Columbia University, 1955.

(55) HANDEL, C., and R. D. HESS: The family as an emotional organization. *Marriage fam. Liv.*, 1956, **18**, 99–101.

(56) HARRELL, R. F., E. WOODYARD, and A. I. GATES: *The effect of mothers' diets on the intelligence of the offspring.* New York: Teachers College, Columbia University, 1955.

(57) HARRIS, D. B., and E. S. HARRIS: A study of fetal movements in relation to mother's activity. *Hum. Biol.*, 1946, **18**, 221–237.

(58) HARSCH, C. M., and H. C. SCHRICKEL: *Personality development and assessment*, 2d ed. New York: Ronald, 1959.

(59) HENRY, J.: Attitude organization in elementary classrooms. *Amer. J. Orthopsychiat.*, 1957, **27**, 117–133.

(60) HEPNER, R.: Maternal nutrition and the fetus. *J. Amer. Med. Ass.*, 1958, **168**, 1774–1777.

(61) HIGHBERGER, R.: Maternal behavior and attitudes related to behavior of the preschool child. *J. home Econ.*, 1956, **48**, 260–264.

(62) HOCHBERG, J., and W. LAMBERT: Baby scale to measure cuteness. *The New York Times,* Nov. 20, 1958.

(63) HOLLINGWORTH, L. S.: *Children above 180 IQ: origin and development.* New York: Harcourt, Brace & World, 1950.

(64) HOOKER, D.: The development of behavior in the human fetus. In W. Dennis (Ed.), *Readings in child psychology,* 2d ed. Englewood Cliffs, N.J.: Prentice-Hall, 1963. Pp. 1–10.

(65) HOWARD, R. W.: The developmental history of a group of triplets. *J. genet. Psychol.,* 1947, 70, 191–204.

(66) HUSÉN, T.: The abilities of twins. *Beitr. Psychol.,* 1953, 1, 137–145.

(67) INGALLS, T. H.: Congenital deformities not inherited. *The New York Times,* Dec. 20, 1950.

(68) INGALLS, T. H.: Intrauterine stress is key to inborn defects. *Med. News,* Jan. 2, 1956.

(69) INGALLS, T. H.: Congenital deformities. *Scient. American,* 1957, 197, 109–114.

(70) ITKIN, W.: Some relationships between intra-family attitude and pre-parental attitudes toward children. *J. genet. Psychol.,* 1952, 80, 221–252.

(71) JENKINS, W. W.: An experimental study of the relationship of legitimate and illegitimate birth status to school and personal and social adjustment of Negro children. *Amer. J. Sociol.,* 1958, 64, 169–173.

(72) JERSILD, A. T., E. S. WOODYARD, and C. F. DEL SOLAR: *Joys and problems of child rearing.* New York: Teachers College, Columbia University, 1949.

(73) JONES, H. E.: The environment and mental development. In L. Carmichael (Ed.), *Manual of child psychology,* 2d ed. New York: Wiley, 1954. Pp. 631–696.

(74) JONES, H. E.: Perceived differences among twins. *Eugen. Quart.,* 1955, 2, 98–102.

(75) KALLMAN, F. J., and G. SANDER: Twin studies in senescence. *Amer. J. Psychiat.,* 1949, 106, 29–36.

(76) KEMP, C. H., F. N. SILVERMAN, B. F. STEELE, W. DROEGEMÜLLER, and H. K. SILVER: The battered-child syndrome. *J. Amer. Med. Ass.,* 1962, 181, 17–24.

(77) KENT, E.: A study of maladjusted twins. *Smith Coll. Stud. soc. Wk,* 1949, 19, 63–77.

(78) KINSEY, A. C., W. B. POMEROY, C. E. MARTIN, and P. H. GEBHARD: *Sexual behavior in the human female.* Philadelphia: Saunders, 1953.

(79) KISER, C. V., and P. K. WHELPTON: Social and psychological factors affecting fertility. *Millbank Memorial Fund Quart.,* 1958, 36, 282–329.

(80) KNOBLOCH, H., and B. PASAMANICK: Seasonal variations in the births of the mentally deficient. *Amer. J. publ. Hlth,* 1958, 48, 1201–1208.

(81) KOCH, H. L.: Sissiness and tomboyishness in relation to sibling characteristics. *J. genet. Psychol.,* 1956, 88, 231–244.

(82) KOCH, H. L.: The relation in young children between characteristics of their playmates and certain attributes of their siblings. *Child Develpm.,* 1957, 28, 175–202.

(83) KOCH, H. L.: Twins and others. Presidential address to the Division on Developmental Psychology, Amer. Psychological Ass., St. Louis, Mo., Aug. 31, 1962.

(84) KUHLEN, R. G., and G. G. THOMPSON: *Psychological studies of human development,* 2d ed. New York: Appleton-Century-Crofts, 1963.

(85) LAGEY, J. C.: Does teaching change students' attitudes? *J. educ. Res.,* 1956, 50, 307–311.

(86) LANDRETH, C.: *The psychology of early childhood.* New York: Knopf, 1958.

(87) LASKO, J. K.: Parent behavior toward first and second children. *Genet. Psychol. Monogr.,* 1954, 49, 97–137.

(88) LE MASTERS, E. E.: Parenthood as a crisis. *Marriage fam. Liv.,* 1957, 19, 352–355.

(89) LEVY, D. M., and A. HESS: Problems in determining maternal attitudes toward newborn infants. *Psychiatry,* 1952, 15, 273–286.

(90) LÉZINE, I.: Researches on the stages of taking consciousness of self in young twins. *Enfance,* 1951, 4, 35–49.

(91) LOESCH, J. G., and N. H. GREENBERG: Some specific areas of conflict observed during pregnancy: a comparative study of married and unmarried pregnant women. *Amer. J. Orthopsychiat.,* 1962, 32, 624–636.

(92) LUNDSTRÖM, R.: Rubella during pregnancy: its effect on prenatal mortality, the incidence of congenital abnormalities and immaturity. *Acta paediat., Stockh.,* 1952, 41, 583–594.

(93) MACFARLANE, J. W., L. ALLEN, and M. P. HONZIK: *A developmental study of the behavior problems of normal children between twenty-one months and fourteen years.* Berkeley, Calif.: University of California Press, 1954.

(94) MARTIN, P. C., and E. L. VINCENT: *Human development.* New York: Ronald, 1960.

(95) MC CARTHY, D.: Language development. In L. Carmichael (Ed.), *Manual of child psychology,* 2d ed. New York: Wiley, 1954. Pp. 492–630.

(96) MEAD, M.: *Male and female.* New York: Morrow, 1952.

(97) MINKOWSKI, M.: Über die elektrische Erregbarkeit der fötalen Muskulatur-Schweig. *Arch. Neurol. Psychiat.,* 1928, 22, 64–71.

(98) MONTAGU, A.: *Human heredity.* New York: Harcourt, Brace & World, 1959.

(99) MOWRER, E. R.: Some factors in the affectional adjustment of twins. *Amer. sociol. Rev.,* 1954, 19, 468–471.

(100) MYERS, R. G.: Same sexed families. *J. Hered.*, 1949, **40**, 260–270.

(101) MYERS, R. G.: War and post-war experience in regard to the sex ratios at birth in various countries. *Hum. Biol.*, 1949, **21**, 257–259.

(102) NEEL, J. V.: The effect of exposure to the atomic bombs on pregnancy termination in Hiroshima and Nagasaki: preliminary report. *Science*, 1953, **118**, 537–541.

(103) NEIBURGS, H. E., and R. B. GREENBLATT: Specific estrogenic and androgenic smears in relation to the fetal sex during pregnancy. *Amer. J. Obstet. Gynaec.*, 1949, **57**, 356–363.

(104) NELSON, M. M., C. W. ASLING, and H. M. EVANS: Production of multiple congenital abnormalities in young by pteroylglutamic acid deficiency during gestation. *J. Nutrit.*, 1952, **48**, 61–80.

(105) New York Times Report: Studies give clue to cleft palate. *The New York Times*, Sept. 8, 1956.

(106) New York Times Report: Twins bad luck sign in Africa, mideast. *The New York Times*, Aug. 4, 1961.

(107) NEWBERRY, H.: The measurement of three types of fetal activity. *J. comp. Psychol.*, 1941, **32**, 521–530.

(108) NEWMAN, H. H.: *Multiple births: twins, triplets, quadruplets and quintuplets.* New York: Doubleday, 1940.

(109) NORRIS, A. S.: Prenatal factors in intellectual and emotional development. *J. Amer. Med. Ass.*, 1960, **172**, 413–416.

(110) OFFNER, V. S.: A study of mothers of twins. *Smith Coll. Stud. soc. Wk*, 1960, **31**, 45–46.

(111) PARKER, E.: *The seven ages of woman.* Baltimore: Johns Hopkins, 1960.

(112) PASAMANICK, B., and H. KNOBLOCH: The contribution of some organic factors to school retardation in Negro children. *J. Negro Educ.*, 1958, **27**, 4–9.

(113) PECKOS, P. S.: Nutrition during growth and development. *Child Develpm.*, 1957, **28**, 273–285.

(114) PINNEAU, S. R., and H. E. HOPPER: The relationship between incidence of specific gastrointestinal reactions of the infant and psychological characteristics of the mother. *J. genet. Psychol.*, 1958, **93**, 3–13.

(115) PLANK, E. N.: Reactions of mothers of twins in a child study group. *Amer. J. Orthopsychiat.*, 1958, **28**, 196–208.

(116) POTTER, E. L.: Pregnancy. In M. Fishbein and R. J. R. Kennedy (Eds.), *Modern marriage and family living.* Fair Lawn, N.J.: Oxford University Press, 1957. Pp. 378–386.

(117) RAPP, G. W., and G. C. RICHARDSON: A saliva test for prenatal sex determination. *Science*, 1952, **115**, 265.

(118) RIVERS, T. M.: Birth defects to be research target. *J. home Econ.*, 1960, **52**, 27–28.

(119) ROSENGREN, W. R.: Social sources of pregnancy as illness or normality. *Soc. Forces*, 1961, **39**, 260–267.

(120) RUBIN, A., and D. P. MURPHY: The frequency of congenital malformations in the offspring of nondiabetic and diabetic individuals. *J. Pediat.*, 1958, **53**, 579–585.

(121) RUSK, H. A.: "Is the baby normal?" *The New York Times*, May 1, 1955.

(122) SCHAEFER, E. S., and N. BAYLEY: Consistency of maternal behavior from infancy to preadolescence. *J. abnorm. soc. Psychol.*, 1960, **61**, 1–6.

(123) SCHAEFER, E. S., and R. Q. BELL: Patterns of attitudes toward child rearing and the family. *J. abnorm. soc. Psychol.*, 1957, **54**, 391–395.

(124) SCHALL, L., H. H. LURIE, and G. KELEMAN: Embryonic hearing organs after maternal rubella. *Laryngoscope*, 1951, **61**, 99–112.

(125) SCHEINFELD, A.: *The human heredity handbook.* Philadelphia: Lippincott, 1956.

(126) SCHEINFELD, A.: The mortality of men and women. *Scient. American*, 1958, **198**, 22–27.

(127) SCHWARTZ, P.: Birth injuries of the newborn. *Arch. Pediat.*, 1956, **73**, 429–450.

(128) SCOTT, E. M.: Psychological examination of quadruplets. *Psychol. Rep.*, 1960, **6**, 281–282.

(129) SEARS, R. R., E. E. MACCOBY, and H. LEVIN: *Patterns of child rearing.* New York: Harper & Row, 1957.

(130) SHERRIFFS, A. C., and R. F. JARRETT: Sex differences in attitudes about sex differences. *J. Psychol.*, 1953, **35**, 161–168.

(131) SIMPSON, G. G.: *The meaning of evolution.* New Haven: Yale, 1949.

(132) SLOMAN, S. S.: Emotional problems in "planned for" children. *Amer. J. Orthopsychiat.*, 1948, **18**, 523–528.

(133) SMITH, C. A.: Effects of maternal undernutrition upon the newborn infant in Holland (1944–1945). *J. Pediat.*, 1947, **30**, 229–243.

(134) SMITH, M. E.: Mental test ability in a family of four generations. *J. genet. Psychol.*, 1954, **85**, 321–335.

(135) SONTAG, L. W.: Differences in modifiability of fetal behavior and physiology. *Psychosom. Med.*, 1944, **6**, 151–154.

(136) SONTAG, L. W.: Some psychosomatic aspects of childhood. *Nerv. Child*, 1946, **5**, 296–304.

(137) SONTAG, L. W., and T. W. RICHARD: Studies in fetal behavior. I. Fetal heart rate as a behavioral indicator. *Monogr. Soc. Res. Child Develpm.*, 1938, **3**, No. 4.

(138) SPENCER, W. P.: Heredity: facts and fallacies. In M. Fishbein and R. J. R. Kennedy (Eds.), *Modern marriage and family living.*

Fair Lawn, N.J.: Oxford University Press, 1957. Pp. 341–356.

(139) STAINS, K. B.: Developing independence in children. *Understanding the Child*, 1951, **20**, 49.

(140) STEARNS, G.: Nutritional state of the mother prior to conception. *J. Amer. Med. Ass.*, 1958, **168**, 1655–1659.

(141) STOCKARD, C. R.: *The physical basis of personality*. New York: Norton, 1931.

(142) STOCKS, P.: Recent statistics of multiple births in England and Wales. *Acta Genet. med. Gemellolog.*, 1952, **1**, 8–12.

(143) STONE, L. J., and J. CHURCH: *Childhood and adolescence*. New York: Random House, 1957.

(144) STOTT, D. H.: Physical and mental handicaps following a disturbed pregnancy. *Lancet*, 1957, **272**, 1006–1011.

(145) STRYKER, S.: Relationships of married offspring and parents. *Amer. J. Sociol.*, 1956, **62**, 308–319.

(146) TAUSSIG, H. B.: The thalidomide syndrome. *Sci. Amer.*, 1962, **207**, 29–35.

(147) TERMAN, L. M., and C. C. MILES: *Sex and personality*. New York: McGraw-Hill, 1936.

(148) TERMAN, L. M., and M. H. ODEN: *The gifted child grows up*. Stanford, Calif.: Stanford, 1947.

(149) THOMS, H.: New wonders of conception. *Woman's Home Companion*, Nov. 1954, 7–8, 100–103.

(150) VON MERING, F. H.: Professional and nonprofessional women as mothers. *J. soc. Psychol.*, 1955, **42**, 21–34.

(151) WALLIN, P., and R. P. RILEY: Reactions of mothers to pregnancy and adjustment of offspring in infancy. *Amer. J. Orthopsychiat.*, 1950, **20**, 616–622.

(152) WARKANY, J.: Congenital malformations induced by maternal nutritional deficiency. *J. Pediat.*, 1944, **25**, 476–480.

(153) WASMAN, H. S.: Psychological factors involved in normal pregnancy. *Univer. Toronto med. J.*, 1947, **25**, 51–61.

(154) WESTOFF, C. F., E. G. MISHLER, and E. L. KELLY: Preferences in size of family and eventual fertility twenty years after. *Amer. J. Sociol.*, 1957, **62**, 491–497.

(155) WESTOFF, C. F., P. C. SAGI, and E. L. KELLY: Fertility through twenty years of marriage: a study in predictive possibilities. *Amer. sociol. Rev.*, 1958, **23**, 549–556.

(156) WRIGHT, L.: A study of special abilities in identical twins. *J. genet. Psychol.*, 1961, **99**, 245–251.

(157) YERACARIS, C. A.: Differentials in ideal family size. *Sociol. soc. Res.*, 1958, **44**, 8–11.

(158) ZEMBLICK, M. J., and R. I. WATSON: Maternal attitudes of acceptance and rejection during and after pregnancy. *Amer. J. Orthopsychiat.*, 1953, **23**, 570–584.

Legally, life begins at birth; biologically, it begins at conception. That is why birth is merely an *interruption* of the developmental pattern, not the beginning of the pattern. This interruption is characterized by a graduation from the internal to the external environment. For the baby who is about to emerge from the environment in which he has lived since his life began, it is a graduation which may be easy and pleasant or fraught with so many hazards that he will fail to complete it. "In all the rest of his life there will never be such a sudden and complete change in locale. No other journey will ever start from such profound seclusion. Even in his deepest sleep, he will not be so thoroughly hidden as he is at birth" (78).

TIME NEEDED FOR ADJUSTMENT

Although the time needed to bring about the change in locale from the mother's body to the world outside is relatively short—seldom more than 48 hours even in a difficult birth—the time needed to adjust to the change is relatively long. Most babies require at least 2 weeks, and those whose birth has been difficult or premature require proportionally more time. During this period of adjustment to the postnatal environment, no marked changes in development occur (42).

The period of infancy is subdivided into two periods: the *period of the partunate,* which consists of the first fifteen to thirty minutes of life immediately after parturition, or birth, and the *period of the neonate,* which covers the remainder of the infancy period. During the period of the partunate, the infant ceases to be a parasite; with the cutting of the umbilical cord he becomes for the first time a separate, distinct, and independent individual. During the period of the neonate, the infant makes the adjustments essential to a life free from the protection of the intra-uterine environment.

There are two indications of the difficulties the newborn infant faces in his adjustment to postnatal life. First, he *loses weight* —normally for approximately a week. As he becomes adjusted to his new environment, he begins to regain the lost weight and by

3

ADJUSTMENTS TO BIRTH

the end of the second week of life is probably back at his birth weight. There are individual differences in this pattern of weight loss, however. Heavy infants lose more and for a longer time than light infants. First-born infants generally lose less than those born later. Infants born in the summer and autumn regain their birth weight slightly sooner than those born in the winter and spring. Finally, there is a relationship between the loss of weight and the time of the first feeding. Infants fed for the first time less than 6 hours after birth lose more than infants fed somewhat later. This does not always hold true, however; second- or later-born infants can be fed sooner than first-born, and boys sooner than girls, without the corresponding increase in weight loss (102).

The second indication of the difficulties a newborn infant faces in his adjustment is *disorganization of behavior.* All infants experience a state of relative disorganization for 24 to 48 hours following birth (13). Their behavior suggests that they have been stunned by the ordeal they have just experienced. How long it will take for them to recover varies; some infants require much more time than others. On the average, about a week is needed, approximately the time needed to regain lost birth weight. Infants who lose much weight and regain it slowly are likely to take longer to achieve organized behavior.

TYPES OF ADJUSTMENT

There are four major types of adjustment the newborn infant must make as soon as he is born; if he does not make them, and make them quickly, his life will be threatened.

1. Adjustment to Temperature Changes. In the sac in the mother's uterus, the temperature is constantly around 100°F. In the postnatal environment, it will be between 68 and 70°F. and will vary, especially after the infant leaves the hospital nursery.

2. Adjustment to Breathing. In the amniotic sac in the uterus, the fetus is surrounded by a fluid environment; all oxygen comes from the placenta through the umbilical cord. When the cord is cut, after birth, the infant must inhale and exhale air. The birth cry normally comes when breathing begins and thus serves to inflate the lungs. At first, breathing is imperfect and irregular. The infant yawns, gasps, sneezes, and coughs in his efforts to regulate the amount of air he needs.

3. Adjustment to the Taking of Nourishment. Since the reflex activities of sucking and swallowing are often imperfectly developed at birth, the infant is frequently unable to get the nourishment he needs and thus loses weight. This is in direct contrast to the situation in his former environment, where he received a constant supply of nourishment through the umbilical cord.

4. Adjustment to Elimination. Within a few minutes or hours after birth, the excretory organs begin to function, eliminating waste products from the body which formerly were eliminated through the umbilical cord and the maternal placenta.

VARIATIONS IN ADJUSTMENT

How quickly and how successfully the newborn infant will make these four major types of adjustment will depend, first, upon his birth experience and, second, upon the kind of prenatal environment he had, especially during the last months. Because these vary greatly, no two babies make the adjustments in exactly the same time. Furthermore, postnatal environments also contribute to the variations in adjustment that are normal and universally found.

Birth Experience. In general, there are four types of birth. The most common is normal, or *spontaneous,* birth, in which the position of the fetus in the mother's uterus and the size of the fetus in relation to the size of the mother's reproductive organs make it possible for the baby to emerge in a head-first position. After the head has emerged, one shoulder and then the other appear as the fetal body rotates slowly in the birth canal. Next the arms emerge—one at a time—then the trunk, and finally the legs (42). Figure 3–1 shows the position of the fetal body in normal childbirth.

Should the fetus be too large for the mother's organs; should its position be such that a *breech birth* would occur (a birth in which the infant's buttocks appear first, followed by the legs and finally the head); or should the fetus be crosswise in the mother's uterus (*transverse presentation*), then either the position of the fetus must be changed before the birth process begins or instruments must be used to aid the delivery. Figure 3–2 shows the characteristic position of the fetus during a breech birth. Compare this with the position in normal childbirth, Figure 3–1.

By the use of the X ray several weeks before the anticipated birth, doctors today can usually determine whether there will be any difficulties in delivery. If so, they usually deliver the fetus surgically by *caesarean section,* in which the fetus emerges through a slit in the maternal abdominal wall instead of through the birth canal (23, 42, 91).

Infants born spontaneously usually adjust more quickly and more successfully to their

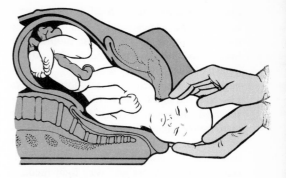

Figure 3–1.   In normal childbirth, the baby emerges from the mother's body headfirst. (Adapted from Heredity and Prenatal Development, a McGraw-Hill Text-Film.)

new environments than those who experience long and difficult labor where instruments have to be used or those born by caesarean section (42, 79). Even in normal childbirth, however, emotional tension on the mother's part, resulting from fear of childbirth or from not wanting the child she is about to have, will complicate the birth process and make the adjustment to postnatal life more difficult for the newborn infant (21, 32, 43, 100).

Heavy dosages of drugs given to the

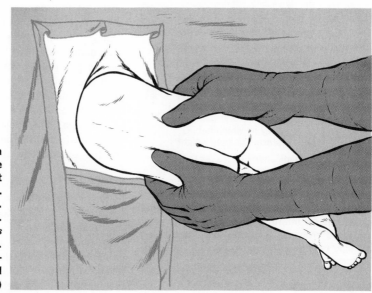

Figure 3–2.   In a breech birth, the buttocks appear first and the head last. (Adapted from N. J. Eastman and L. M. Hellman, *Williams obstetrics,* 12th ed. Appleton-Century-Crofts, 1963. Used by permission.)

mother to ease the pain of birth likewise influence early postnatal adjustment. The more anesthesia given to the mother, the longer and the more difficult the adjustments of the newborn infant (5). A comparison of newborn infants whose mothers had received anesthesia in different amounts revealed that for infants whose mothers were heavily medicated, the disorganization of behavior immediately after birth lasted 3 to 4 days, as compared with 1 to 2 days for those whose mothers had very light medication or none at all. The effects on the infant, however, varied according to the type, amount, and timing of medication. An inhalant anesthesia, for example, had a more transient effect than premedication, such as barbiturates.

The medication likewise affected breastfeeding, though no significant effect was found after the first five days of life, except that infants whose mothers had heavy medication lost more weight and took a longer time to regain it than those whose mothers had less (13). This difference is shown in

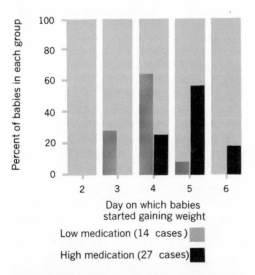

Figure 3–3, which reveals that infants whose mothers had low medication started to regain their lost weight after 3 days, as compared with 6 days for those whose mothers were given high medication.

Prenatal Environment.   Intense and prolonged nervous and emotional disturbances of the mother during the last months of pregnancy cause a hyperactive state in the fetus. (See page 62.) The effects of prenatal disturbances persist after birth and manifest themselves in various body functions as feeding difficulties, gastrointestinal dysfunction, sleep problems, hyperactivity, and general irritability (109). In discussing the effects of an unfavorable prenatal environment on postnatal adjustments, Sontag has pointed out that a newborn infant with such a background is "to all intents and purposes a neurotic infant when he is born—the result of an unsatisfactory fetal environment. In this instance, he has not had to wait until childhood for a bad home situation or other cause to make him neurotic. It was done for him before he even saw the light of day" (108).

FAILURE TO MAKE ADJUSTMENTS

Some infants are unable to adjust to their postnatal environments. As a result, they die at birth or shortly afterward. While the percentages of stillbirths—deaths at birth or immediately following birth—and deaths during the period of postnatal adjustment have been declining in recent years owing to improved medical techniques of prenatal care, childbirth, and postnatal care, the death toll is still high. The most critical time is the day of birth, and the next most critical times are the second and third days after birth (105).

The most common causes of death at birth or immediately afterward are prematurity, congenital debility, malformation, injury at birth, pneumonia, influenza, diarrhea, and deficiency of oxygen resulting either from the excessive use of drugs to relieve the pains of childbirth or from having the umbilical cord tighten around the fetal

Figure 3–3. Effect of medication during childbirth on infant's postnatal weight gain. (Adapted from T. B. Brazelton, Psychophysiologic reactions in the neonate. II. Effect of maternal medication on the neonate and his behavior, *J. Pediat.*, 1961, 58, 513–518. Used by permission.)

neck during the birth process (9, 72). In one study of deaths at birth or within the first few days after birth, 36 per cent of the infants were born prematurely, 21.6 per cent were born in breech position, and 14.7 per cent were born in a posterior position. There are more deaths among infants delivered by caesarean section than among those born spontaneously (25).

A number of factors influence the mortality rate during the neonatal period. *Sex differences* exist, with more boys dying than girls, even when they have the same birth weight (35, 79). *Racial differences* are marked, with nonwhites showing a higher mortality rate than whites (72). In neighborhoods which are predominantly Negro, for example, the mortality rate is greater than in predominantly white neighborhoods. Mortality rates increase as the number of Negroes in the neighborhood increases (62). Women who experience *stressful pregnancies* have more difficulties in childbirth than women whose pregnancies are less emotional, and their babies are more likely to be born dead, to die shortly after birth, or to have some congenital malformation (43).

The *economic level* of the family is likewise a factor of importance, with the highest mortality rate occurring in families of the lowest economic levels (72). The poor prenatal diet of mothers in the low economic groups contributes to the high neonatal mortality rate (14, 119). The greater the *birth weight* of the infant and the longer the *gestation period,* the lower the mortality rate in the neonatal period (105). Finally, neonatal mortality has been reported to increase with increasing *birth order* (35, 86).

TRADITIONS ABOUT BIRTH EFFECTS

Because birth was a mystery until the days of modern medicine, many superstitious beliefs grew up to explain it. One group of beliefs held that there is an auspicious and an inauspicious *time to be born.* In the past, being born under certain stars was supposed to bring good fortune throughout life, while being born under other stars was considered a bad omen. In more recent times, beliefs about certain days of the week and certain seasons of the year have been popular. The old rhyme

Monday's child is fair of face,
Tuesday's child is full of grace,
Wednesday's child is full of woe,
Thursday's child has far to go,
Friday's child is loving and giving,
Saturday's child works hard for a living,
But the child that is born on the Sabbath Day
Is fair and wise and good and gay.

illustrates the widespread traditional belief that a child's personality is influenced by the day of his birth. Figure 3–4 illustrates this traditional belief.

Children born during the "cheerful seasons" of the year, spring and summer, are likewise, according to tradition, destined to have the personalities of extroverts—to be gay, cheerful, and outgoing. Those born in the "gloomy months," the fall and winter months, are destined, by contrast, to be introverted—to be dour and gloomy. While few scientific investigations have been made to determine whether these traditional beliefs are true, there is some evidence that children born in the spring, summer, and autumn months are decidedly more sociable than those born in the winter months (77, 87).

When houses lacked central heating, the cold seasons of the year were hazardous for the newborn infant. Therefore, it is not surprising that traditional beliefs stressed the idea that children born during the spring and summer months were favored in many ways—in intelligence and in the possibility of achieving fame. Scattered studies of eminent men, however, fail to support these beliefs. Some studies have shown that more outstanding men are born in the fall than in the spring, while others claim other "best seasons" (66, 89).

As has already been pointed out, babies conceived in the winter reach the critical period in their physical and mental development during the spring months, when there are usually epidemics of German measles

Monday's child is fair of face

Tuesday's child is full of grace

Wednesday's child is full of woe

Thursday's child has far to go

Friday's child is loving and giving

Saturday's child works hard for a living

But the child that is born on the Sabbath Day Is fair and wise and good and gay

Figure 3–4. Traditional characteristics associated with day of the week on which a child is born.

and other damaging diseases which their mothers may contract. Babies conceived in the spring and born in the winter months are likewise subject to prenatal damage because they reach the critical period in their development during the summer months, when their mothers' diets are the poorest, especially in proteins (62). (Refer to pages 59 to 60 for a discussion of studies on this subject.) Actually, there is no such thing as a "best season" for birth. *Any* season may be good or bad, depending on the hereditary endowment, the prenatal environment, and the birth experience of the child.

Despite the scattered studies that have been made, there is certainly no clear-cut, uncontradictable evidence that time of birth,

per se, has any influence on the physical, intellectual, or personality development of the child. What variations there are among children born at different times may come from health factors or from the fact that parents of the higher intellectual levels, who generally produce children with the best physiques, intelligence, and personalities, plan for their children to be born during the seasons most favorable for postnatal adjustments (52). The general conclusion about the studies reported to date could be the same as that which Gordon and Novack drew from their study of the relationship between IQ and month of birth: "There is nothing in the data reported above that denies a slight IQ advantage for cold-weather conceptions; on the other hand, there is nothing that would warrant long vacations for the country's obstetricians for the first half of each year" (37).

There are also traditional beliefs about the *effect of birth* on the child, both in infancy and as he grows older. One of the oldest recorded beliefs of this type is an ancient Chinese saying, "Difficult birth, difficult child" (12). Since childbirth is an ordeal for the mother, it is logical that people would conclude that birth was an equally great ordeal for the child and, as such, would be certain to have some influence on him. The birth cry has been interpreted through the centuries as an infant's expression of rage at being dislodged from the safety and comfort of the womb and suddenly thrown out into a cold and unfriendly world. Kant, for example, referred to the birth cry as a "cry of wrath at the catastrophe of birth."

BIRTH TRAUMA

In recent years, members of the psychoanalytical school have suggested that there is a psychic *trauma* resulting from the rupture of the fetal relations with the mother. Adler referred to the birth cry as an indication of the infant's sudden and overwhelming feeling of inferiority at being placed in so new and complex an environment. These early suggestions were formulated into a theory of the effects of birth on the personality development of the child —Otto Rank's theory of the birth trauma.

According to this theory, the shock of birth creates a reservoir of anxiety which is the foundation for anxiety throughout life. Because birth is the first danger the child experiences, it provides the model for all later anxieties. As Rank pointed out, "The pleasurable primal state is interrupted through the act of birth." Owing to the anxieties resulting from the shock of birth, the child will have, as long as he lives, an unconscious yearning to return to the safety and security of the womb (95).

While there is inadequate evidence to prove or disprove Rank's theory of the birth trauma, it is questionable whether the newborn infant can experience anxiety or have any memory of the birth shock. His brain, at the time of birth, is at such a low level of development that it is doubtful that memory or reasoning is present at all. It is known that brain cells cannot function in the low-oxygen environment of the uterus. Only after air breathing has supplied the brain with more highly oxygenated blood is there any evidence of consciousness (7). As air breathing normally does not begin until the cry has inflated the lungs—and this occurs after birth—one could then logically conclude that the infant could have no memory of what happened during or before birth.

One could further conclude that a newborn infant or even a young baby could not compare his present status with that which existed before he was born. *Only* if such a comparison could be made could there be anxieties and a longing—even though this longing were only unconscious—to return to the safety and security of the womb. Thus, it should be obvious that it is questionable whether the infant can understand the change that takes place in the pattern of his life with birth. Furthermore, considering the undeveloped state of the fetal brain and autonomic nervous system, it is equally questionable whether an infant can experience any emotion—fear, anger, or anxiety—in a well enough developed form for it to have a lasting influence on his personality (3, 92).

On the other hand, there is no question that birth is a shock to the newborn infant, but it is probably a physical rather than a psychological shock. As Schwartz has pointed out, "Birth is, almost without exception, a brutal process which endangers the life and health of the child" (106). Records of fetal heartbeats obtained from highly sensitive electrodes placed on the mother's abdomen in the vicinity of the fetal heart have shown that in approximately the middle of labor, the fetal heart displays wide swings of beat rate. In the last part of labor, the heartbeat slows down to approximately one-half the normal rate. Uterine contractions in childbirth generally slow the fetal heart; only occasionally do they accelerate it (80).

Evidence from other studies of the state of development of the sense organs at birth shows that the skin sensitivities are not sufficiently developed for the fetus to experience pain from the intense pressure of the muscular contractions of the birth canal (92). As was pointed out earlier in the chapter, however, there are four major adjustments the infant must make, and make very quickly, if he is to survive. Like all major adjustments, those which the infant must make—breathing, taking nourishment through the mouth, eliminating waste products from the body, and reacting quickly and successfully to variations in temperature —result in shock, even though it is only temporary.

DIRECT EFFECTS OF BIRTH

The effects of birth on the infant, as Pratt has pointed out, "may be inconsequential and transitory or they may greatly affect the course of subsequent development" (92). What the effects of birth will be depends largely upon the birth experience and, to a lesser extent, on the prenatal environment. Most infants adjust successfully. A few, unfortunately, do not; in such cases, the child's life pattern is altered because of something that happened to him during the birth process.

While many things *might* happen during the birth process that could temporarily or permanently affect the course of the child's subsequent development, there are two "great killers" at the time of birth. These are *injuries to the brain or nervous system* and damage to the brain cells resulting from *anoxia.* The term "killer" does not necessarily mean that the infant will die. It means, in the broader sense, that his chances for a normal development have been "killed." Even those infants who do not die as a result of damage to their brains at birth may be temporarily or permanently so harmed that their hereditary potentials will

never be reached. This may not be apparent for months or even years after birth (4, 114).

Injuries to the Brain or Nervous System. When babies are born with poorly shaped heads or with marks where forceps have been applied during birth, parents often fear that the brain has been damaged. Ordinarily, this fear is short-lived because the head gradually assumes a normal shape and the marks disappear. As the fetal body passes down the birth canal, there is certain to be some compression of the brain, especially if the fetal head is large. Under normal conditions, nature provides for this by adequately covering the brain tissue with a partially formed skull; however, "almost every baby born normally suffers some disturbance of the cranial and even the cerebral circulation" (106).

The pressure generally has no permanent effect on the brain tissue, though most newborn infants are stunned for a day or two. When birth is long and difficult, the pressure on the brain is increased. This may be severe enough to cause hemorrhages in and around the brain. The effects of these hemorrhages may be temporary or permanent, depending mainly on their severity (9).

Prematurely born infants are especially subject to brain injury during birth. The skull of the premature infant is not so well formed, and consequently the delicate tissue of the brain is not so well protected as it would be if birth were at full term. In addition to injury to the brain tissue itself, injury may be done to some other part of the nervous system. Pressure during birth may cause the fracture of a bone. Should this occur near nerve centers, there may be temporary or permanent damage to some of them or to the sense organs, especially the eyes and ears (92).

Anoxia. Anoxia—interruption of the oxygen supply to the brain—is now regarded by doctors as a more common cause of brain damage than pressure. The average person, however, usually interprets brain damage in terms of pressure on the delicate tissues of the brain; few are aware of the damage that can come when the brain cells are deprived of the necessary supply of oxygen (4). Also, few are aware that a very brief period of deprivation may cause damage.

A total lack of oxygen will kill the brain cells in 18 seconds. Temporary or permanent damage can be done in even a shorter period, depending on the severity of the deprivation. When the time of the deprivation is longer, it can kill the infant. While most cases of anoxia occur during the birth process, difficulties may arise before birth, either because of the premature separation of the placenta, which cuts off the oxygen supply to the fetal bloodstream, or because of abnormalities in circulation which interfere with the fetal supply of nutritional substances and oxygen (4, 9, 29, 39).

Variations in Effects. Studies of different types of birth have revealed that even a natural, spontaneous birth is not without hazards. Records made of the brain waves of newborn infants have revealed that the ordinary birth process produces a minimum of disturbance, suggesting only temporary brain damage (30). Difficult births, on the other hand, many of which necessitate the use of instruments to aid delivery, produce more disturbance and more severe and lasting damage.

In a breech birth, for example, there is always the possibility of anoxia—the possibility that before the head emerges, the fetus will be cut off from the oxygen supply and that this will either damage or kill the brain cells. Since epilepsy is more common among children delivered in breech birth than among those born spontaneously or by caesarean section, this disorder is now believed to be the result of damage to brain cells caused by oxygen deprivation. A transverse presentation inevitably necessitates the use of instruments, and these may, if applied to the fetal head, cause brain injury (18, 29).

The infant delivered by caesarean section is less likely to suffer brain injury at birth than one delivered by a long, difficult birth which necessitates the use of instruments

(12). He often has difficulty in establishing respiration, however, and his brain cells may suffer from oxygen deprivation. The development of a hyaline membrane in the lungs, shortly after birth, is common among infants who have been delivered by caesarean section. When this occurs, it leads to oxygen deprivation which may be damaging—or even fatal—though the infant was healthy at birth (29).

The effects of birth vary also according to the *duration* and *difficulty* of birth. Infants born with minimum difficulty and requiring the average time of 6 to 14 hours for birth are least likely to have any serious or permanent effects (4, 36). Nervousness and anxiety are more common among children born with difficulty. It is impossible to say whether these conditions are the result of brain damage at birth, the mother's attitude and methods of handling the child, or both (12).

Precipitate labor—labor of less than 2 hours' duration—has deleterious effects on later intellectual development. The reason for this is that precipitate labor is likely to introduce the infant to oxygen too suddenly, with the result that he may suffer from anoxia (122). An abnormal birth, however, in terms of either difficulty or duration, *does not necessarily mean an abnormal child.*

Early Indications of Birth Effects. How the newborn infant adjusts to his new environment during the first few days of life will give a clue to whether the effects of birth have been unfavorable and, if so, how unfavorable they have been (4, 114). Other clues may be found in hyperactivity or hypoactivity, the duration of the period of confused and disorganized activity, the type of cry the infant uses in response to internal stimuli, and the degree of maturity in such behavior as holding the head, grasping, or muscle tension (99).

Normally, the pain threshold declines during the first four days of life. This means that, with each passing day, the infant responds to weaker and weaker pain stimuli. For babies who have suffered from anoxia at birth, the pain threshold not only is higher than normal at birth but does not follow the normal pattern of decline. Increased sensitivity to pain or lack of it may thus be used as a clue to how birth has affected the infant (67).

The cry of the damaged infant differs from that of the normal infant. Instead of the loud and lusty cry of the normal infant, the cries of damaged infants may be weak and intermittent; they may be high-pitched; or they may be low-pitched and persistent, often creating the impression that the infant is fussy and whimpering. However, fussing and whimpering may be due to other causes. Infants who receive little attention and "mothering" cry significantly more, when there is no external instigation, than other infants (38, 39, 84, 99). Furthermore, it must be emphasized that early indications of brain damage are not necessarily shown in one set pattern of behavior. Some infants who have been injured during birth are hyperactive, irritable, and sensitive to any kind of mild stimulation and give generalized rather than specific responses; others show diminished general activity and are flaccid and apathetic. On the other hand, if the infant makes satisfactory adjustments to his new life, the chances of later ill effects are slim.

The behavior of the newborn infant is not, per se, foolproof evidence of what effect birth has had on him. An unusual circumstance connected with birth may be responsible for deviation from the normal pattern of behavior. For example, caesarean babies cry the least of all newborn infants, but this does not mean, necessarily, that their apparent apathy is a sign of birth damage. On the contrary, except when they have been damaged by oxygen deprivation due to difficulties in establishing respiration, caesarean babies make better adjustments to their postnatal environments than instrument-delivered babies. Thus, the intensity and frequency of their crying, falling as it does below the norm, cannot be interpreted as an indication of birth damage (101).

Similarly, the use of drugs during childbirth may retard the infant's adjustment to postnatal life or cause deviant behavior. A comparison of the electroencephalograms of infants whose mothers had received sodium seconal to ease childbirth pains with those of infants whose mothers had not received this pain-killer showed that the depressed cortical activity of the former persisted in many instances after the normal postnatal drowsiness of the latter had disappeared (50). While drowsiness and disorganized behavior persisting beyond the normal time could be interpreted as an indication of birth damage, they should not be so interpreted when it is known that special circumstances associated with birth have been responsible.

Later Indications of Birth Effects. The low level of physical and mental development present at birth ordinarily makes it impossible to detect symptoms of birth damage immediately. Motor disabilities, cerebral palsy, epilepsy, low-grade intelligence, and sensory defects, for example, may not be apparent until the child is old enough to be tested or until the baby fails to develop according to the normal pattern (106, 113). Normally all children show some fears and anxieties. It is therefore understandable that these would not be regarded as symptomatic of trouble. When the young child shows more fears and anxieties than are usual for his age, however, it is suggestive of trouble. Frequently, intense anxiety is the first symptom of the aftereffects of brain damage during a long and difficult birth (12). On the other hand, it may be the result of unfavorable environmental conditions.

The long-term effects of anoxia have been reported to be greater in conceptual ability than in vocabulary skill or in perceptual or motor functions. Only a slight reduction in intelligence, as measured by tests, has been found. (See Figure 3–5.) In speaking of the effects of anoxia, Graham and his associates have emphasized that "the prognosis for an individual child is not alarmingly worsened if he has suffered the degree of anoxia or other complications, represented by the ma-

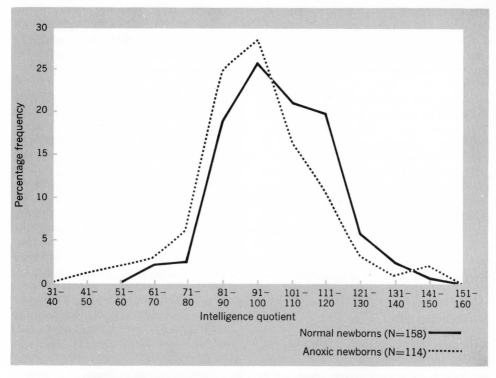

Figure 3–5. Distributions of IQ scores for normal and anoxic newborns 3 years after birth. (Adapted from F. K. Graham, C. B. Ernhart, D. Thurston, and M. Craft, Development three years after perinatal anoxia and other potentially damaging newborn experiences, *Psychol. Monogr.*, 1962, 76, No. 3. Used by permission.)

jority of children in the present study. . . . Anoxia does not appear to have an all-or-none effect" (39).

It has been found that *some* school children who have difficulties in learning to read had complications during birth. The greater the birth complications, the greater the chance of retardation in reading (57). But it must be emphasized that there are many causes of reading difficulties, and brain damage is *only one* of them. How common or uncommon a cause it is has not been determined. Studies of older children and adolescents who were born with the aid of instruments have shown that "instrumental delivery has not had a devastating effect upon the mentality of children who survive" (118). Many of them, however, have more

unfavorable personality characteristics than those born spontaneously. Among the traits reported as more common among those born with the aid of instruments are general hyperactivity, restlessness, speech defects, and poor concentration (11). Whether these were directly caused by the birth experience, by the attitudes of parents, or by some other factor is still undetermined.

A study of the long-term effects of precipitate labor on intellectual development has revealed that more children with low IQ's in late childhood were born in precipitate birth than in normal birth. Whether there will be brain damage from precipitate labor, however, will depend largely on how quickly the infant can establish respiration. If he has difficulty in doing so, he will suffer from anoxia, with its damaging effects on the brain cells. In commenting on the results of a study of precipitate birth, Yacorzynski and Tucker have emphasized that "at the minimum our data indicate that parents of children born under unusual conditions of anoxia or precipitate birth need not necessarily harbor anxieties. It may be true that the sequelae may be deleterious, but it may also happen that such children may be of potentially above average ability" (122).

This statement may be applied to all cases of difficult birth. While the chances are greater that complications during the birth process will have some unfavorable effect, there is no evidence that they will lead to permanent brain damage. It is true, on the other hand, that complications at birth will color parental attitudes and therefore will leave their marks on the pattern of the child's development. This will be discussed later in this chapter.

Prevalence of Birth Effects. Because of the widespread publicity given to defects resulting from brain damage before or at birth, most people assume that many more children are damaged than is actually the case. Parents-to-be become apprehensive as the time for their child's birth approaches, and after his birth they are concerned if his appearance or behavior deviates in any way from what they had anticipated. While there are no medical statistics showing exactly how many babies are damaged at birth, it has been *estimated* that, of all infants who survive birth, only approximately 7.5 per cent suffer from any kind of malformation. The most common results of birth damage are mental deficiency, motor disabilities, paralysis, cerebral palsy, birthmarks, and sensory defects, mainly in vision and hearing. Malformations of the muscularskeletal system and of the skin are especially common (9, 75, 99).

There are more malformations resulting from brain damage among male than among female infants and more among nonwhites than among whites (92). In the former case, the usual explanation is that the head of the male fetus is larger than that of the female

and is thus subject to greater pressure during the birth process. Malformations are more common among nonwhites than among whites because, as a group, the mothers of nonwhite babies receive less medical attention during pregnancy. As a result, complications in childbirth, which may lead to damage to the infant, are more common among the nonwhites. When socioeconomic status is held constant—that is, when infants of the nonwhite group are compared with infants of the white group of the same socioeconomic status—these differences disappear (9, 42).

Furthermore, there are more children with defects due to brain damage now than in the past. This is not because more fetuses are damaged at birth; in fact, modern techniques of delivery have reduced the number of cases of brain damage. However, at the same time, modern techniques and improved postnatal care keep many birth-injured infants alive today who, in the past, would have died. As a result, more children with such handicaps as cerebral palsy, mental deficiency, blindness, deafness, or congenital heart deficiencies survive today (75, 99).

INDIRECT EFFECTS OF BIRTH

Important as the direct effects of birth are on the child's development, indirect effects, in the form of parental attitudes resulting from the way the child was born and what birth did to him, are too important to be ignored. In fact, they may be more lasting in their influence than the effects of birth itself. A mother's attitude toward her role as a parent has a marked influence on her attitude toward childbirth and the adjustment she makes to it. Anxiety during pregnancy causes tension which usually carries over to the delivery room. Furthermore, the realization that "what once had been only fantasy would soon be reality" is likely to increase the anxiety of the mother-to-be. The greater the childbirth anxiety, the greater the likelihood that what might otherwise have been a normal birth will become a difficult one (123).

The emotional reactions of parents toward a birth which has given the mother a minimum of discomfort will be quite different from those aroused by a prolonged and difficult labor, especially when this labor results in damage to the baby. A difficult birth is likely to make the mother overprotective of the child, and this is even more likely if she has been warned by the doctor of the danger of future pregnancies. If the mother blames herself, she will feel guilty about not having more children, particularly if her husband's concept of an "ideal family" includes many children (24, 43, 81).

The father's attitude, under such conditions, is likely to be colored by resentments and antagonism toward the child, partly because he feels this child has endangered his wife's life, partly because he feels it has deprived him of the number of children he wanted, and partly because he does not wish to be thought of as a man who lacks the virility to produce a large family (17, 48).

The woman who gives birth to her child easily, quickly, and with relatively little pain is likely to have a relaxed attitude toward the child. Her attitude will be reflected in her husband's attitude, with the result that the home will provide a healthier emotional climate for the child. There will be less tendency to overprotect the child or to overindulge him than there would be if he were the only child the mother could have (81).

By contrast, the parents of a baby who is damaged at birth or whose life hangs in the balance for days or weeks after birth will have an apprehensive attitude, and this will be reflected in their treatment of him long after the danger has passed. This has been illustrated in a study of "blue babies" —babies born with a congenital malformation of the heart which can be corrected by surgery. Even though these babies usually develop into healthy, normal children, the apprehensive attitudes of their parents, developed at the time of the children's births, tend to persist and have a marked influence on the type of social and emotional adjustments the children make (107).

Should birth damage result in the child's total disability, an element of hopelessness serves to frighten and embitter the parents. Because of the necessity of special care for the brain-damaged child, the mother is likely to become overpossessive and overprotective, thus retarding even further the child's development. Such parental behavior is often the mother's method of compensating for, or her attempt to deny, guilt about having such a child (60). Catholic mothers, it has been reported, are more acceptant in their attitudes toward retarded children than non-Catholic mothers. This comes mainly from their feelings of guilt about being responsible for the retardation of their children. Their more acceptant attitudes are stronger, however, when the children are under three years of age than when they are older (124).

A woman who is not happy about the prospects of motherhood or who is disappointed when her newborn child does not conform to her concept of a "dream child" is likely to reflect her feelings in her methods of handling the infant. As a result, he has difficulty in adjusting to his postnatal environment and becomes fussy, irritable, and prone to excessive crying. This makes him seem even less desirable to his parents (65, 88, 116). In addition, the attitudes of a new mother are often confused and unstable, and this further complicates the infant's adjustment problems. Should the mother suspect that there is something the matter with her baby, her reactions will be even more unstable and confused, adding to the adjustment problems already present. The younger and more inexperienced the parents are, the greater the likelihood that they will increase the infant's adjustment problems. Their own attitudes toward the infant will then tend to worsen (16, 81).

Unfavorable as this may sound, it is important to recognize that birth and the adjustment period after birth can hold psychological hazards for parents just as they can hold physical hazards for the child. While it is true that the great majority of babies are only temporarily affected by the physical hazards of birth, there is less evidence that the psychological effects on the parents pass as quickly. Parental attitudes are often quite resistant to change (see pages 66 to 67). Consequently, they are likely to have greater and more persisting effects on the child's development than the physical hazards of birth are. Parental attitudes affect the type of relationship the child has with his parents, and this, in turn, has a profound influence on his pattern of development (104).

When parental attitudes change, the direction of the change will be influenced by what the parent had anticipated before the baby's birth, how the baby adjusts to his new environment, and whether his adjustment compares favorably with what the parent had expected. If the parent's attitude toward parenthood is already favorable, a difficult birth or a temporarily poor adjustment on the infant's part will do little to change this attitude. Similarly, if the parent's attitude is unfavorable, an easy birth and the infant's quick adjustment to postnatal life are not likely to make the parent more acceptant of the parental role.

A traumatic experience, such as evidence of injury to the infant at birth or brain damage reflected in deviant adjustive behavior, may have a greater effect on parental attitudes. The parent who did not want the child is likely to feel guilty or to regard this as "God's punishment." An already favorable attitude, on the other hand, is not likely to change just because the child gives signs of not being normal. Instead, there will be a desire to compensate for the child's handicap by doing everything possible to lessen his burden and a desire to have another child as quickly as possible in the hope that it will fulfill parental expectations (65).

Jersild, in discussing change in parental attitudes following the child's birth, stressed the fact that persistence is more characteristic than radical change. He emphasizes, however, that the *type* of person the parent is will be the determining factor in this matter:

A woman who vowed that she could never become "crazy" about a baby may find when the baby comes that he has completely taken her over. A father who was secretly convinced that he could never love a second child as much as the first may discover that it is quite a different story when the new youngster nestles in his arms. The tide may, of course, run in the other direction if the parents have nurtured a glorified image of a baby-to-be and then find that the real baby is quite somebody else; if they fear the responsibilities which the child places upon them; or if they are rather mechanical and detached people who shrink from him not just because he is so small but because they have never learned to come into close emotional contact with any other human being (54).

THE NEWBORN INFANT

To understand postnatal development, one must know what the status of the child is when he begins life outside the mother's body. A brief and concise picture of the child at the starting point of his postnatal development can be given by describing the characteristics of the neonate. These will be divided into three categories: *appearance, helplessness,* and *individuality*. It must be remembered that all newborn infants are different and that their differences tend to become greater as they adjust to postnatal life (8). Consequently, the description given will be of a typical or "average" newborn infant, not of any specific infant. Furthermore, because the premature infant differs markedly in all three categories, the following description relates only to the normal full-term infant whose development before birth has covered approximately 280 days.

APPEARANCE

The average weight of the newborn infant is 7.5 pounds, and the average length is 19.5 inches. Weight ranges from 3 to 16 pounds; length ranges from approximately 17 to 21 inches. Male infants are generally slightly larger than female infants, but the differences are not so great between the sexes as within the sex group. Variability in birth size is dependent upon many factors, the most important of which are the following: (*1*)

Maternal diet, especially during the last months of pregnancy. There is a significant relationship between the protein content of the mother's diet and the size of the infant at birth. The poorer the mother's diet, the smaller the infant will be (14). *(2) Economic status.* The family's economic status affects the quantity and quality of the maternal diet, and this, in turn, affects the infant's size. In poor districts, the average size of infants is slightly but significantly smaller than in better districts (35). *(3) Ordinal position.* On the average, first-born infants weigh less than later-born infants (76). *(4) Fetal activity.* Especially when excessive, fetal activity may cause the infant to be considerably underweight for his body length (108).

The *physical proportions* of the infant differ greatly from those of the adult (refer to Figure 1–1, page 3). In the infant, the head is about one-fourth the entire body length, while in the adult, it is one-seventh. The part of the head where the greatest disproportion exists is in the area above the eyes, the cranial region. In the infant, the ratio between the cranium and face is 8:1, while in the adult it is 1:2. The infant's face appears to be broad and short because of lack of teeth, the undeveloped condition of the jaws, and the flatness of the nose. The arms, legs, and trunk are small in relation to the head. The abdominal region of the trunk is large and bulging, while the shoulders are narrow, just the opposite of adult proportions.

Typical *infantile features* include bluish-gray eyes, which gradually change to whatever the permanent color will be. Though almost mature in size, they are uncontrolled in motion and roll in a meaningless, unrelated fashion. The tear glands are inactive, and therefore crying is not accompanied by a flow of tears. The neck is so short that it scarcely exists, and the skin covering it lies in deep folds or creases. A heavy growth of fine-textured hair often covers the head.

The muscles of the newborn are small, soft, and uncontrolled, with those of the legs and neck less developed than those of the arms and hands. The bones are composed chiefly of cartilage, or gristle, and consequently are soft and flexible. The flesh is firm and elastic, while the skin is soft, deep pink in color, and often blotchy, especially in the head region. Sometimes a soft, downy growth of hair is found on the body, mostly on the back, but this soon disappears. Approximately once in every 2,000 births, an infant is born with a tooth or even two teeth (71).

Effects of the Infant's Appearance. From this brief description, it is apparent that the typical or "average" infant is not a thing of beauty; in fact, most newborn infants range from homely to ugly. The ugliest have generally experienced difficult births, having their skin blotched from bruises, their heads misshapen, and their noses flattened by pressure as they pass down the birth canal. Infants born slightly ahead of time tend to be even less attractive than those born on schedule or a trifle late because their body fat has not had time to develop, though the fat pads that fill out the cheeks may have. Consequently, they tend to have a wizened, "old man" look. Those who are extremely premature look "remarkably senile," with the "withered look of a toothless old person" because the fat pads in their cheeks have not yet filled out the area around the mouth (112). By far the best-looking infants are those who arrive in the world by caesarean section and who, as a result, are spared the ordeal of birth with its tendency to bruise and misshape the body.

For parents who have a romanticized concept of a "dream child," the first sight of their newborn baby can be a disappointment if not a traumatic experience. While parents are not likely to verbalize their feelings, the anxious question of a mother, "Isn't he adorable?" or the father's statement that he "looks just like his grandfather, who was the handsomest man in town," gives clues to what their real feelings are. Parents of first children are far more likely to experience this disappointment than parents who have learned from experience that it is unusual for the newborn baby to look like a

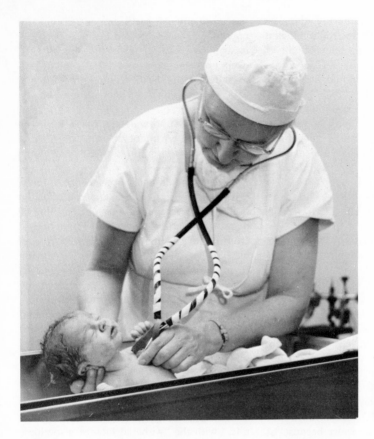

The newborn infant is not a creature of beauty. (Columbia Presbyterian Hospital, by Elizabeth Wilcox.)

"cherub." In commenting on parental reactions to the newborn infant's appearance, Stone and Church have remarked:

Many people, whose ideas . . . of what a newborn baby looks like are based on pictures that appear in advertising addressed to new parents, are surprised by their first actual view of a neonate. The idealized "newborn" babies shown in such advertising are probably two or three months old. Truth to tell, exciting though his newness may be, many a neonate begins on the unattractive side. Even for eager parents, there is often a discrepancy between the tiny, wet, sticky, often red and wizened creature of the first few days and the images formed in the months of hopeful, anxious waiting (112).

Most infants begin to look better even before they leave the hospital. By the end of the period of the neonate, if they have made satisfactory adjustments to postnatal life, their appearance is vastly improved. Before the end of the second week of life, for example, the blotchy redness of their skin begins to disappear, their heads are less misshapen, their noses are less flat. Although the infant improves in appearance within a relatively short time, the effect of his birth appearance on unprepared parents can be long-lasting. This emphasizes how unfortunate it is for parents-to-be to develop romanticized concepts of a child.

HELPLESSNESS

Because his capacities for independent living are so poorly developed at birth, the human infant is the most helpless of all neonates. His helplessness, which is at first all-pervading, is in the long run an advantage. It enables the human infant to develop along lines that would be impossible in animals, for whom nature has a more rigid pattern of development. In time, he will be able to make more varied responses than are possible among animals and, as a result, he can rise to a higher level (94).

All helplessness originates either in an undeveloped condition of the body and nervous system, which makes learning impossible, or in a lack of opportunity to learn when a state of readiness is present. Both these causes of helplessness are operative in the newborn infant. He is maturationally unready to learn and he has been in the world too short a time to be able to take advantage of any learning opportunities that might be available. Consequently, because of these conditions, he would be unable to survive were it not for the constant attention and care he receives from others.

Causes of Helplessness. A survey of the most important areas of maturational unreadiness to learn will indicate the complete helplessness of the newborn infant.

1. Maintenance of Homeostasis. Because of the undeveloped state of the autonomic nervous system at birth, the infant is unable to maintain homeostasis—the tendency of an organism to maintain within itself relatively stable conditions of temperature, chemical composition, or the like by means of its own regulatory mechanism. In the prenatal environment, homeostasis was maintained for the fetus by the mother's homeostasis. Now that he is on his own, his body must take over this responsibility.

Studies of the physiological functions of the newborn infant have shown how unstable they are. The *basal pulse rate* at birth ranges from 130 to 150 beats per minute and then drops to an average of 117 beats several days later. This compares with the average adult basal rate of 70 beats per minute. Even within the same infant, however, there are marked variations in the

pulse rate, ranging from a mean rate of 123.5 beats per minute in profound sleep to 218.2 during crying (44, 45, 92).

The *respiration rate* during the first week of life is 35 breathing movements per minute, compared with 18 at adulthood. Breathing is rapid, irregular, and abdominal in the newborn infant. There are, however, marked variations in both the rate and type of breathing from infant to infant and in the same infant under different conditions. Just before the infant awakes, for example, the mean rate has been found to be 32.3, as compared with 133.3 respirations per minute during crying (73). The heart is small in comparison with the arteries, and so it must beat more rapidly to maintain normal *blood pressure*. The *body temperature* is higher and more variable in a healthy infant than in an adult (92).

Because the stomach and intestines have different rates of emptying and because the infant has difficulty in sucking and swallowing, he has frequent *defecations, wheezing, colic,* and *regurgitations. Voidings* are also variable in time and amount (44, 83). As motor activity uses up energy and as this tends to interfere with homeostasis, restriction of motor activity by swaddling increases the stability of the heart rate and produces a pacification of the general physiologic state (68).

Perhaps in no area of body function is lack of homeostasis more marked than in *sleep.* Typically, the infant's sleep is broken by short waking periods caused by pain, hunger, and internal sources of discomfort. He sleeps lightly, can be wakened easily, and then falls to sleep easily (92, 96). Lack of stability in sleep patterns is illustrated in Figure 3–6.

Among newborn infants, two distinct patterns of sleep are common: *regular,* during which the breathing rhythm is smooth and regular, and *irregular,* during which breathing is irregular or alternates between rapid, shallow excursions and slow, deep excursions. In regular sleep, there are frequent spontaneous startles; otherwise the infant moves little. In irregular sleep, there are few

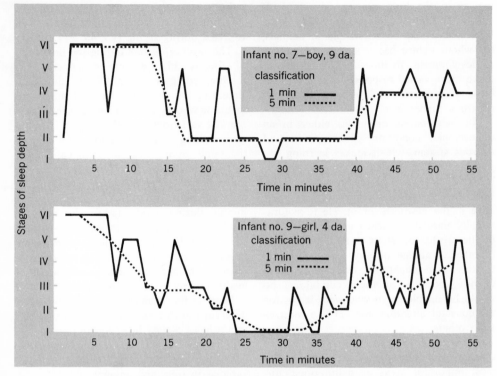

Figure 3–6. Typical sleep curves for infants with records of 50 minutes or more. (Adapted from M. C. Reynard and F. C. Dockeray, The comparison of temporal intervals in judging depth of sleep in newborn infants, *J. genet. Psychol.*, 1939, 55, 103–120. Used by permission.)

spontaneous startles but many other movements ranging from simple limb movements to "voluptuous writhing of the whole body" (120). Swaddling causes infants to sleep more and to sleep more quietly (68).

2. Voluntary Activity. To be independent, a person must be capable of voluntary activity—activity controlled by conscious desire. No infant is capable of this. His responses can only tenuously and with difficulty be related to the events in his environment. Since he behaves randomly, without goals, he is helpless. He is not inert, however; he is a moving, acting creature. The motor activities of the newborn infant can be categorized roughly as either mass activity or specific activities.

Mass activity includes general movements of the whole body. When one part of the body is stimulated, the whole body responds, though most profoundly in the area stimulated. Because of the neurological immaturity of the infant, mass activity is highly uncoordinated and diffuse and results in a great expenditure of energy. Not all parts of the infant's body are equally active. The greatest amount of activity is in the trunk and legs, and the least is in the head. While mass activity appears at birth, it normally increases in frequency as the infant adjusts to his new environment (58, 59).

As has been pointed out before, those infants who were most active before birth are also most active after birth (109). There are wide and stable differences from one infant to another not only in general bodily movements but also in some specific movements, such as hand-mouth contacting. These trace their origin, in part, to differences in tension resulting from the types of treatment newborn infants receive (59). Furthermore, there are variations in activity at different times in the day, with the peak coming in the early morning and the least at noon (see Figure 3–7).

The bodily condition of the infant likewise influences his activity. Activity is greatest during crying, hunger, pain, and general bodily discomfort and is least when the infant is asleep or has just been fed. Environmental conditions also influence activity. Light and auditory stimuli, for example, increase the amount of activity, as do clothing and covers (92).

Specific activities, which involve certain limited areas of the body, are in reality outgrowths of mass activity. They are of two types: reflexes and general responses. The first reflexes to make their appearance are those which have distinct survival value—heart action, sneezing, breathing, and the patellar, pupillary, and digestive reflexes; the other reflexes in the human repertoire can be aroused within a few hours or days after birth. General responses involve larger portions of the body than reflexes do. Like reflexes, they are direct responses to either internal or external stimuli.

Visual fixation on light; spontaneous eye movements; yawning; rhythmic mouthing movements; turning and lifting the head; random arm and hand movement; prancing, kicking, and stretching movements with the legs and feet; turning movements; and body jerks, are just a few of the general responses which have been observed in the newborn infant. All these movements are so random and uncoordinated that they make the newborn infant completely helpless, but they are important because they are the basis from which the highly coordinated movements of the young child will later develop (59, 92, 115).

3. Ability to Communicate. Lack of ability to communicate his needs and wants to others is the third important cause of the newborn infant's helplessness. Owing to the

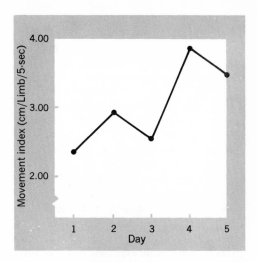

Figure 3–7. **Changes in neonatal movement during the first five days of life. (Adapted from W. Kessen, E. J. Williams, and J. P. Williams, Selection and test of response measures in the study of the human newborn,** *Child Develpm.,* **1961, 32, 7–24. Used by permission.)**

uncoordinated state of his body, he cannot speak or point or use other gestures. The best he can do is cry. The *birth cry* is purely reflex. It is caused by air being drawn rapidly over the vocal cords, thus setting up vibrations in them.

The birth cry serves two purposes: to supply the blood with sufficient oxygen and to inflate the lungs, thus making breathing possible. The birth cry is not a true precursor of speech. Once the lungs are inflated, crying comes from internal or external stimulation and is part of the pattern of generalized behavior characteristic of the newborn infant. Most crying during infancy occurs when the infant is hungry, in pain, or in a state of discomfort. Occasionally he cries from fatigue, from lack of exercise, or for unknown reasons (1, 74, 92).

During the first 24 hours after birth, the infant's cry may have different meanings, which can be determined from the pitch, intensity, and continuity of the cry. In general discomfort, the cry at first is monotonous in pitch, staccato-like, and intermittent;

then gradually, unless some relief is given, the cry becomes more insistent. *Pain* is characterized by a cry which rises in pitch. If pain is accompanied by increasing physical weakness, piercing tones give way to low moans. In *rage,* the cry is longer, the breath is held, and the infant's face often becomes purplish. Gulping sounds, which generally accompany the rage cry, result from the opening of the infant's mouth, with the resultant closing of the air passages of the throat. Intermittent sobs usually continue even after rage has subsided. While variations in the tonal quality and intensity of crying increase its value as a form of communication, only persons familiar with infant's cries can be expected to know what they mean.

Bodily activity of some sort generally begins when crying begins. In vigorous crying, every part of the body is thrown into action. (See Figure 3–8.) The infant squirms, kicks, rolls his body, turns his head from side to side, and flexes and extends his arms, legs, fingers, and toes. The kicking is usually fairly rhythmic but varies somewhat according to the conditions which aroused the crying. In anger, for example, the kicking is more vigorous and abrupt than during other emotional states, and the feet are generally thrust out simultaneously instead of alter-

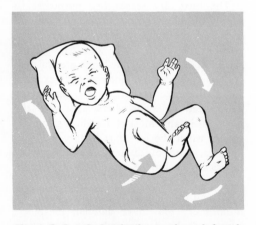

Figure 3–8.   Crying in the newborn infant is accompanied by mass activity. (Adapted from Heredity and Prenatal Development, a McGraw-Hill Text-Film.)

nately. This activity is a signal that the infant needs attention, and it thus serves as a form of language (74).

The infant is capable of another type of vocalization, *explosive sounds,* which are not unlike heavy breathing. They are uttered without intent and without meaning and occur purely by chance whenever there is a contraction of the vocal muscles. Since these sounds are low in pitch and weak, compared with cries, they are often regarded as unimportant.

From the long-term point of view, however, explosive sounds are far more important than cries. The explosive sounds are gradually strengthened and develop, during the second half of the first year, into babbling, which in turn develops into speech. When one realizes that the explosive sounds are in reality the fundamentals of speech, their true significance becomes apparent.

4. Sense-organ Development.   Helplessness is an inevitable accompaniment of sense-organ deficiency. At birth, the sense organs are ready to function, but some of them are more highly developed than others. Smell, taste, skin sensitivities (touch, pressure, pain, and temperature), and the organic sensitivities (hunger and thirst), for example, are well developed at birth or shortly thereafter, while vision and hearing are poorly developed (92).

Pain sensitivity increases rapidly after birth but at different rates for different parts of the body. The pain threshold is lower for the head than for the extremities. Since every normal infant experiences some anoxia, owing to the immaturity of his respiratory system during the early hours or days following birth, he is less sensitive to pain than he will be when his respiration improves.

Infants whose mothers receive anesthesia to ease the pains of childbirth require slightly longer to recover from the effects, and, as a result, their pain thresholds drop more slowly than those of infants whose mothers did not receive anesthesia. Because infants recover at different rates from these respiratory traumas, there are individual differences in the pain threshold during the early postnatal days (67). This is illustrated in Figure 3–9. Those infants who suffer most from anoxia at birth have the highest pain thresholds and require the longest time to experience a drop in these thresholds (41).

At birth, the retina of the eye has not reached its mature development. The cones (which are responsible for color vision) are short and ill defined. This would suggest that the infant can see black and white but not color. The infant does, however, respond to light by turning his head and closing his eyelids when the light is bright. In addition, optic nystagmus—the ability to follow moving objects and then move the eyes back in the opposite direction—comes several hours after birth. Ocular pursuit of a moving object is likewise possible but is poor unless the object moves very slowly. In order to see objects clearly, both eyes must focus on the same object at the same time and in the right position. Otherwise, each eye gets a different picture, and this results in a blur. Until the baby can control the muscles of his eyes—and this will not be possible much before he is two or three months old—nothing will be seen distinctly (34, 92).

Although the infant's ears are so fully formed at birth that one might logically conclude that his hearing was well developed, such is not the case. The areas of the ears which contain the sense organs for hearing are undeveloped, and consequently the functioning of the ears as receptors for sound stimuli is greatly hampered. At birth, hearing *appears* to be at the lowest stage of development of all the sensitivities. Most infants are totally deaf for several hours or days after birth, owing primarily to the stoppage of the middle ear with amniotic fluid. Until this drains out, sounds will be unable to penetrate and the infant will literally be "deaf." Even loud noises near the ear of a newborn infant produce little or no reaction. As is true of all sensitivities, however, there are individual differences in sensitivity to sound (92).

5. Capacity for Learning. The helplessness of the newborn infant could be reduced if

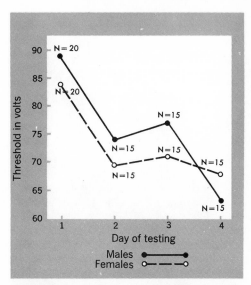

Figure 3–9. Individual differences in pain thresholds for male and female infants during the first four days of postnatal life. (Adapted from L. P. Lipsitt and N. Levy, Electrotactual threshold in the neonate, *Child Develpm.*, 1959, 30, 547–554. Used by permission.)

he were capable of learning. Studies of learning among neonates, however, have revealed that even the simplest form of learning—conditioning or learning by association—is too complex for an infant. A number of attempts have been made to see whether conditioning can be achieved during the first few days of life. For the most part, these studies have shown that, with the possible exception of conditioning in feeding situations, conditioned responses are difficult to elicit and, when they do appear, are unstable and of little permanent value. On the whole, it appears that many infants cannot be conditioned because of their cortical immaturity (69, 92).

Effects of Helplessness on Parental Attitudes. The survival of the newborn infant depends upon the attention and care he receives from others, particularly his mother. Most infants are well taken care of. Having their wishes and needs met promptly and to their satisfaction, they are relaxed and

The newborn infant's helplessness and dependency are appealing, and normally elicit an attitude of love and protectiveness. (Elizabeth Wilcox.)

happy babies and follow the normal pattern in their physical and mental development. Not all infants, however, are fortunate enough to have the right kind of care. If an infant is deprived of the attention of his mother or a mother substitute who is responsible for his day-in, day-out care, his personal, emotional, and social development will be adversely affected. Studies of institutionalized babies deprived of the care of a stable person have revealed that they become listless and backward in their de-

velopment. By contrast, those who have a stable person to care for them, even though they are institutionalized, make improved adjustments and follow developmental patterns more closely, approximating the norm for their ages (82, 97).

Because a newborn infant's helplessness and dependency are appealing and because he is easier to manage when he is helpless than when he becomes independent, some parents get into the habit of waiting on the child hand and foot. This habit, once established, tends to persist long after the helplessness of infancy has passed and long after the child either needs or wants help. The parents either cannot or will not adjust their concept of a child's abilities—a concept formed when the child was a helpless infant—to keep pace with his rapid development.

Few parents of first babies realize that 1 year hence the infant will be starting to walk and talk; will make repeated attempts to feed, dress, and bathe himself; and will be able to manipulate toys. Sometimes a mother continues to wait upon her child simply because of selfishness or because she thinks that is what a "good mother" should do. It may give her personal satisfaction to feel that she is indispensable to him.

Whatever the reason for clinging to the concept of infantile helplessness long after infancy has passed, it is damaging to a child's development. It deprives the child of opportunities to learn the things that other children his age are learning. This makes him backward and can bring embarrassment and shame to the parents and feelings of inadequacy to the child. Furthermore, because society expects children to master certain "developmental tasks" at certain ages, the child who fails to do so makes poor social adjustments, and this leads to poor personal adjustments (47). (See pages 5 to 6 for a more complete discussion of developmental tasks and their significance.)

A serious consequence of this parental habit is that a child resents being frustrated in his attempts to learn when he is ready to do so. The more a child is frustrated, the more angry, resistant, and negativistic he becomes toward those who frustrate him. This makes him less appealing to his parents, and as the situation grows worse, there is a deterioration in parent-child relationships.

INDIVIDUALITY

No two newborn infants, even those of identical birth, are exactly alike in appearance or behavior (8). Each starts life with an individuality that will continue to manifest itself as his hereditary potentials unfold. Individuality results partly from hereditary differences, but different prenatal environments and birth experiences also contribute to it. In *appearance,* the only thing that all newborn infants have in common is their smallness and top-heaviness. Some are chubby and cherubic in appearance, while others look wizened and senile. Not all newborn infants feel the same when they are held. Some are "compactly and comfortably curled, like a kitten, others sprawl like a bundle of loosely joined sticks, still others hold themselves tense and stiff" (112).

Newborn infants vary markedly in *maintaining homeostasis,* especially in the rate of respiration and pulse. Some show far better physiological balance at birth than others, and some who begin life with poor homeostasis gain it earlier than others. This difference in homeostasis contributes to individuality in adjustment, especially in response to food, patterns of sleep, crying, motor activities, and need for attention (44).

Some infants, for example, are able to *take nourishment* and keep it down from the very beginning, with the result that they lose little of their birth weight. Others have difficulty adjusting to sucking and swallowing and, consequently, may lose a frightening amount of weight (102). While all newborn infants follow a similar *sleep* pattern, characterized by brief waking periods every 2 or 3 hours, some infants sleep longer between the waking periods, some are more restless during sleep, and some

have more difficulty falling asleep after feedings than others (92, 96). Individuality in sleep patterns was illustrated in Figure 3–6, page 94.

Individuality is even more strikingly illustrated in *motor activity.* Some infants show slow, poorly developed reflex responses, while others have reflexes similar in form —though slower in rate—to those of older children (92). A particular infant's general responses, as shown in mouthing movements and hand-mouth contacting, follow a consistent pattern during the first five days of life, but for different infants the patterns differ (59). Marked variations occur in mass activity, with some infants in constant motion, even in sleep. These variations depend partly on the general physical condition of the infant, partly on whether he is full-term or premature, and partly on how active he was during fetal life (109).

There is no area in which individuality expresses itself as forcibly as in *crying.* The birth cry is influenced by the type of birth as well as by the infant's physical condition. In the quick, explosive delivery, for example, the cry is sharp and deep; in premature births or when the infant is in poor condition, the cry is like a little moan. Prolonged labor, resulting in the exhaustion of the infant, generally causes a weak, short, intermittent cry. Infants damaged prenatally or at birth have cries that differ in pitch, volume, rhythm, and accentual character from those of normal infants (85). Individuality in the tonal quality of cries persists throughout the neonatal period. It is possible, in a hospital nursery, to identify different infants by their cries.

There is individuality in the amount of crying as well as in the tonal quality. Some infants are "good as gold," crying only infrequently and for short intervals. Others seem to be angry or frustrated all the time, crying incessantly and at the top of their lungs. Nothing seems to satisfy them. Some infants appear to have a greater need for attention and affectional gratification than others and cry when they are denied these (110).

In a study of the amount of crying of different infants during the first eight days of life, it was found that the infant who cried the least cried a total of 386 minutes, or an average of 48.2 minutes a day, as compared with a total of 1,947 minutes by the infant who cried the most (1). As a general rule, infants brought into the world by caesarean section cry less than those born spontaneously or by the use of instruments. There is little evidence, however, that the amount of crying is influenced by the length of labor (101).

Effects of Individuality on Parental Attitudes. Because all newborn infants are different, one cannot logically expect the same behavior from them. Most parents do, however, and are concerned if their expectations are not realized. If it is a second-, third-, or later-born child, parents are likely to judge its behavior according to their *memories* of how their other children behaved. Even when there has been no older sibling to use as a standard, many a mother has steeped herself in "baby-care" information from books, magazines, and newspapers and has learned what the "norms" are. These she uses as a measuring rod for her own newborn infant. If he conforms to these norms, she feels that all is well; if he is ahead of them, she is smugly satisfied that he is superior; but if he falls below the norms, she becomes panicky and is convinced that all is not well.

A baby's crying is, to most parents, a signal that something is wrong. They compare their infant's cries with their memories of the cries of earlier-born children or of other infants in the hospital nursery and inevitably conclude that something is the matter if he cries more or more loudly than others or if he sounds weak and worn out.

When he refuses to nurse or when he regurgitates what nourishment he takes, the mother wonders if her milk or the formula given him in a bottle is "right" for him. Little does she suspect that her own tenseness and nervousness may be interfering with the quality of her milk or upsetting her baby. Furthermore, it does not ease her concern to be told by other mothers how easily and quickly their babies have adjusted.

Unless a mother is seriously ill, she will want to look at her baby in his bassinet in the maternity nursery. This often proves to be a traumatic experience. After seeing her baby in the privacy of her room and convincing herself that "all babies look that way," she may discover that other babies in the nursery are much prettier than hers. In fact, he may be the ugliest. The scars of birth, which still stand out on him, may have already disappeared from those who were born earlier. The father's pride may likewise be dimmed when he peers through the glass window of the nursery to spot his child and, in the process of doing so, looks at the other babies. He may overhear the comment of another parent about the baby who "looks like a little ape," only to discover that the comment was made about his child.

Experiences of this type cannot fail to color parental attitudes, and they, in turn, affect parental behavior. Concern because a newborn infant is different in appearance, in the way he is adjusting to his new environment, and in the amount of crying he does far too often leads to the suspicion that he is not normal. Back of this concern is the belief held by many parents that *similarity and normalcy go hand in hand, just as individuality and abnormality do.* Even when a doctor assures the anxious parent that all is well, parental concern may be intensified by an increase in crying and adjustment difficulties when the infant is taken home from the hospital. As a result of this concern, oversolicitousness and overprotectiveness develop—patterns of parental behavior which may become habitual.

PREMATURITY

Birth is a hazard at any time. It is more hazardous if it occurs ahead of the schedule that nature has planned. All the risks associated with normal childbirth are present but in a more pronounced form. The more premature the birth, the greater the hazards.

Prematurity means a condition in which the newborn infant is relatively unfit for extra-uterine life because of a lack of development or a retardation in development caused by a shortening of the fetal period. Two criteria are generally used in determining whether or not a newborn infant is premature. The first is the *length of the gestation period.* When the gestation period is estimated to have been between 28 and 38 weeks long, the infant is considered premature. The second criterion is *birth size,* either in terms of weight or in terms of relation of weight to length. This criterion is more commonly used than the length of the gestation period, which cannot always be estimated accurately. When the infant at birth weighs 2,500 grams (5 pounds 8 ounces) or less, he is considered premature. Should the head circumference be less than 33 centimeters and the crown-rump length less than 32 centimeters, this is taken as additional proof of prematurity (31).

Seriousness of Prematurity.   Survival is relatively rare when birth weight is 1,000 grams (2 pounds 3 ounces) or less. For those infants whose weight is above this, the chances of survival vary according to birth weight (19, 29). If the infant weighs more than 1,500 grams (3 pounds 5 ounces), its chances of survival are estimated to be four times as great as if its weight were 1,500 grams or less (29).

Separate norms must, however, be used for infants of different races and for the two sexes. Infants whose gestation age is 29 weeks or less have a mortality rate of 63.3 per cent, as compared with 21.5 per cent for those whose gestation age is 34 to 37 weeks. When weights are the same, those with a younger gestation age have as good a chance of survival as those who are older, which emphasizes the fact that weight is more important than age (111).

The ratio of male to female deaths in the postnatal period among prematurely born infants is 2:1 (19). Prematurity is more common among first-born than among later-born children, and this accounts partially for the higher mortality rate among the first-born (55). It is also more common among infants of the lower socioeconomic classes and among nonwhites. Small women give birth prematurely more often than larger women (98). Prematurity occurs more often in cases of multiple birth than in singletons. The larger the number of premature births, the greater the chances of prematurity and the greater the prematurity. Twins and triplets, for example, are more often premature than singletons (29).

In recent years, medical science has found ways of preventing miscarriages but not of preventing the fetus from arriving in the world ahead of schedule. As a result, there has been an increase in the number of premature births. It has been reported that 7 out of every 100 babies born in the United States today are premature (29). In spite of medical progress in caring for prematurely born infants, the mortality rate is still very high. One-third of the deaths in the first year of life are among babies whose birth weight is less than 5½ pounds. It has been estimated that a premature infant has only one-ninth the chance for life that a full-term infant has. Furthermore, congenital malformations and injuries resulting from birth itself are far greater among the prematurely born than among those born at full term (2, 12, 28, 53, 79).

There are reasons for the higher incidence of malformations and deaths among the prematures. In the latter part of pregnancy, the bones of the fetal body develop rapidly. This includes the bony covering of the brain, the skull. Even in a full-term infant, however, the bones are composed chiefly of cartilage, or gristle, and as a result are soft. The skull is not yet completely formed, and there are six soft spots, or *fontanels*—openings in the skull covered by a tough, resilient membrane. Of these, the largest and best-known to parents is the fontanel on the top of the infant's head.

Should the fetus be born prematurely, the skull is unready for the pressures of birth, and the chances of brain damage are greatly increased. Furthermore, because the prematurely born infant often has difficulty establishing respiration, the brain may be deprived of the necessary supply of oxygen, with consequent damage to the brain cells. As premature births are often difficult and prolonged, the possibility of brain damage from oxygen deprivation is great (28, 29, 53).

For a child born prematurely, adjustment to postnatal life is especially hard (12). His most difficult adjustment problems are due to the undeveloped state of his brain. While the frontal lobes are better developed than the other areas, this development alone is not adequate to enable him to cope with the problems of breathing, eating, eliminating, and other functions vital to survival (121).

As a result of neurological immaturity, the premature infant breathes in jerks and gasps and requires almost three times as much oxygen as a full-term baby. He is often anemic and requires blood transfusions. Because the sucking and swallowing reflexes are weak, the premature infant must usually be fed artificially, through a tube or intravenously. His ability to withstand changes in temperature is poor, and this necessitates keeping him in an incubator, where the temperature can be kept constant as it was in the prenatal environment. Also, because he is extremely susceptible to infection, he must have careful medical attention to avoid developing an illness that might prove fatal (10, 29, 46).

Traditional Beliefs about Prematurity. It has been believed for centuries, and it is still believed by many today, that prematurity is caused by an imprudent act on the part of the mother. Her "imprudence" may be that she engages in too strenuous physical activity, especially if she swims, plays tennis, or rides horseback, or it may be that she allows herself to become emotionally disturbed. In recent years, drinking and smoking have been added to the list of imprudent acts that are blamed for the prematurity of a child.

Because science does not yet know what actually causes prematurity, it is difficult to contradict these traditional beliefs. In the absence of scientific knowledge, mothers blame themselves—and their husbands blame them—for not taking their maternal obligations more seriously and thus preventing what might be, and often are, lifetime handicaps to their children.

From the beginnings of history, among both primitive and civilized peoples, traditional beliefs have stressed the adverse effects of prematurity. These beliefs center around the assumption that because the individual has been deprived of normal development before birth, he will be physically and mentally weak throughout life and will become a social dependent. Among many primitive peoples and among civilized peoples in ancient times, before the dawn of Christianity, it was a common practice to put prematurely born infants to death at birth or to put them on a mountainside, with other defectives, and allow them to perish—for the good of the rest of the population. Even today, many of the traditional beliefs about the ultimate outcome of the prematurely born individual have a marked influence on the treatment the child receives (49).

Effects of Prematurity. Recent scientific studies of the effects of prematurity have, for the most part, shown that prematurity, per se, is not so serious as tradition claims. Furthermore, they have indicated that many of the ill effects are the result of unfavorable parental attitudes, colored by the acceptance of the traditional belief that premature children are destined to be handicapped.

While most of the studies of prematurely born infants have been limited to an investigation of the effects of prematurity during the first few years of life, some have attempted to discover the long-range effects. Follow-up studies of prematurely born infants into childhood and late adolescence have revealed two important sets of facts: *the effects prematurity has* and *how long the effects will persist.* Gesell has pointed out that the "healthy premature infant does not acquire any unnatural precocity from his head start. Neither does he suffer any setback" (33). If the prematurely born infant is not healthy, however, or if he suffers injury at birth, the long-term effects will be serious in proportion to the unfavorable birth conditions (28).

The *developmental status* of babies born prematurely is generally below normal for the first five or six months of life. After that, the retardation becomes increasingly less until the age of two years, when the gap between full-term and prematurely born children usually closes. When the starting point for measuring development is taken from conception, rather than from birth, less difference is noted between full-term and premature babies, even in the early months of life. A specific example will serve to illustrate this point. A baby born 2 months prematurely will, when he is two months old, be more mature than a full-term baby who has just been born. Both have had 9 months of development since the time of conception. For the former, 7 months have been *in utero* and 2 outside; for the latter, 9 months have been *in utero*. When the premature baby is judged by norms for a two-month-old full-term baby, he is at a decided disadvantage because the latter has had 11 months for development since conception, as compared with his 9 months. On the other hand, if his *age from conception* is considered, he will compare favorably with the full-term baby (33).

Studies of the effects of prematurity in different areas of development have revealed that the behavior patterns of the prematurely born infant are similar to those of the full-term infant, though the former lags behind for a while. How much lag there is depends largely upon birth weight, *unless* the baby was injured in birth. Babies who weigh under 4 pounds at birth will be retarded by a month or more during the first eighteen months of their lives; those weighing 4 to 5 pounds at birth will catch up to the norm for their ages by the time they are nine or ten months old (2, 26, 61).

In *physical development*, prematurely born babies are slower to reach the growth spurt characteristic of the early months of life, but by the end of the first year they have almost caught up to the norm for full-term babies (121). This is illustrated in Figure 3–10. How quickly they will catch up is influenced to some extent by the socio-economic status of their families. Those who come from better homes catch up sooner than those from poorer backgrounds. There is a tendency, however, for the prematurely born, regardless of socioeconomic background, to be slightly smaller at maturity than persons who were born at full term (2, 27, 53, 111).

Differences have been reported in the *health status* of premature and full-term children. In the first year of life, premature babies have more illnesses, especially respiratory and nasopharyngeal disturbances. As they grow older, they suffer slightly more from such physical defects as malnutrition, dwarfism, and obesity. The most serious defect associated with prematurity is poor vision. Because of the difficulty in establishing respiration at birth, many prematurely born infants must be given oxygen. The use of oxygen, if extensive and prolonged, may result in *retrolenthal fibroplasia*—the formation of scar tissue in the eye which leaves damage ranging from mild impairment of vision to blindness (20, 53). Developmental retardation is especially apparent in *motor control*. Prematurely born babies are retarded in the use of the index finger for pointing, in the pincer grasp, in postural and motor control, and in locomotion. Prematures sit, stand, and walk at a much later age than full-term babies, with the greatest retardation in those who were smallest at birth. As young children, they are less graceful in their movements. Some prematures, as they grow older, are very active, whereas others are slow and sluggish (20, 26).

If the amount of prematurity is taken into consideration, premature children as a group are not *intellectually* inferior to full-term children. There are, however, more cases of serious mental defects among the prematures than in the general population. For the most part, these defects are found among those

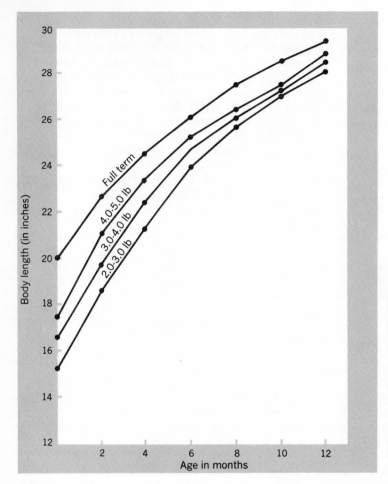

Figure 3–10. Comparison of the physical development of prematurely born babies with those born at full term during the first year of life. (Adapted from P. V. Wooley and L. Q. Valdecanas, Growth of premature infants, *Amer. J. Dis. Children,* 1960, 90, 642–647. Used by permission.)

who suffered from cerebral hemorrhages at birth or immediately after birth. The smallest prematures contribute more than their share to the ranks of the mental defectives (20, 61, 103).

Retardation in *speech* development is common among young children who were born prematurely. They persist longer in using baby talk, and they have more speech defects—especially stuttering—than full-term children. Prematurely born infants are highly *sensitive* to sounds and noises. As babies, they are not only more keenly aware of sounds but also more interested in their meanings than full-term children are. They are, however, easily distracted by voices, traffic noises, and sounds made by other babies. They are likewise very sensitive to moving objects and colors (22, 26, 103).

Conflicting reports about the *emotional behavior* of prematurely born babies have been given. Some are described as "gentle babies," but most are described as shy, petulent, irascible, and negativistic. *Nervous traits* and *behavior disorders,* such as thumb and finger sucking, nail biting, masturbation, excessive shyness, dogged determination not to comply with instructions, peculiar hand gestures, temper outbursts, poor concentration, and a tendency to cry frequently, are more common among the prematures than among full-term children. Even among older adolescents, nail biting, habit spasms, and chronic masturbation are more commonly found among those born prematurely (28, 49, 63).

How prematurely born children react to people and social situations and what sort of *social adjustments* they make have been extensively investigated. In general, prematurely born children make better adjustments in the early years of life than later. As babies, they tend to be shy, closely attached to their mothers, and more dependent than full-term babies of the same age. In the preschool years, they show more forms of problem behavior, especially feeding problems, and this is true likewise in the early elementary-school years. By late adolescence, some prematurely born children —boys especially—are making good social adjustments, but comparisons of groups of prematurely born boys and girls with those born at full term have indicated that the former, as a whole, make inferior social adjustments, tending to be either submissive and passive or aggressive (2, 63, 103).

Effects of Parental Attitudes. The indirect effects of prematurity—parental attitudes and associated behavior—can be as serious as the direct effects. It is often impossible to separate the physical influences from the psychological, but there is ample evidence that many of the traits found among prematurely born children—the "prematurity syndrome," as it is often called—are psychological in origin. There is no question that a mother's concern about her premature child increases the adjustment difficulties he must overcome. Likewise, there is no question that unless parental concern is controlled or eliminated, its influence will persist and affect the type of adjustment to life the child makes as he grows older.

Prevention of Prematurity. Because the potential hazards of premature birth, whether they are physical or psychological, are so great, medical science is trying to find ways to *prevent* prematurity. As there is no known way of hastening the ripening of the brain cells which are essential to survival or of hastening the hardening of the skull to prevent damage to the brain during the birth process, prevention of prematurity will eliminate some of the neonatal deaths and congenital malformations caused by premature birth.

But to prevent prematurity, medical science must first know what causes it. There is evidence that uterine crowding, in the case of multiple births, leads to prematurity, and there is evidence that prematurity and neonatal death are more common when the prenatal environment is unfavorable owing to the mother's malnutrition, prolonged emotional stress, illness at critical times in pregnancy, and excessive drinking and smoking (10, 29, 79). Today there is medical hope that the missing link between these conditions and prematurity has been found. Scientists now know that when there is a deficiency of *releasin,* a hormone produced by the female reproductive glands, uterine contractions begin too soon and bring on premature labor. It is hoped that by increasing the amount of releasin in the mother's blood during the latter part of pregnancy, premature births can be prevented (56). If this can be done on a wide scale, one of the serious causes of deviant development will be eliminated.

Controlling the psychological effects of prematurity is a far more difficult problem. Until medical science can *prove* what causes prematurity, parents will continue to believe that it resulted from an imprudent act on the mother's part.

Furthermore, there is little hope that parents can be persuaded to treat their prematurely born child like a normal full-term infant as long as doctors use elaborate precautions in the hospital to ensure the baby's survival. Often these precautions serve merely to reinforce the traditional belief that prematurely born children are different from full-term children and that this difference means that they are inferior.

Mothers who have accepted the traditional belief that some imprudent act on their part was responsible for bringing their children into the world ahead of nature's schedule suffer from anxiety and feelings of guilt. These feelings, intensified in inverse ratio to the size of the baby at birth, lie at the basis of much of the mother's oversolicitude (93). Because a prematurely born child must spend extra days, weeks, or even months in the hospital with special care by trained nurses, it is not surprising that a mother would feel inadequate to assume the responsibility for the care of such a delicate baby when he is released from the hospital (21). A study of babies under 4 pounds in weight at the time of birth showed that all parents experienced a "crisis" when the babies were finally large and healthy enough to be brought home. After facing this crisis, some parents made good adjustments to their parental roles. Others made poor adjustments, having negative feelings about their parental roles and scapegoating in order to free themselves from responsibility for the crisis. All, however, showed concern about the financial problem prematurity brought them (15).

Fear of harming a prematurely born baby causes many parents to *understimulate* him, often even until he reaches school age. Furthermore, parental anxiety tends to make the young child nervous and afraid of himself. Not only is the child deprived of opportunities to develop his potential capacities, but he feels inadequate to use what

opportunities are given. Some of the developmental lag of premature children can, unquestionably, be traced to this (22, 49, 63).

When prematurely born babies make good adjustments, parents often start to push them in an attempt to try to close the gap between them and their contemporaries. At the same time, parents continue to be overprotective. This merely prolongs the unfavorable environmental conditions that do so much psychological damage. Being pushed always makes a child nervous. In addition, the child feels that the parents are unfair; one minute they are doing things for him, and the next minute they are criticizing him for not doing things for himself. Feelings of inadequacy, lack of self-confidence, resentments, and antagonisms are the inevitable results (26, 49).

Until there is foolproof evidence that the age-old beliefs about prematurity are incorrect, there is little possibility that prematurely born children can escape the psychological damage that stems from unfavorable parental attitudes. That is the true significance—and misfortune—of the widely held belief that a prematurely born child is at a disadvantage from the very start of his life.

BIBLIOGRAPHY

(1) ALDRICH, C. A., C. SUNG, and C. KNOP: The crying of newly born babies. *J. Pediat.,* 1945, **26,** 313–326; **27,** 89–96, 429–435.

(2) ALM, I.: The long-term prognosis for prematurely born children: a follow-up study of 999 premature boys born in wedlock and 1,002 controls. *Acta paediat., Stockh.,* 1953, **42,** Suppl. 94.

(3) ANDERSON, J. E.: Personality organization in children. *Amer. Psychologist,* 1948, **3,** 409–416.

(4) APGAR, V., B. R. GIRDANY, R. MC INTOSH, and H. C. TAYLOR: Neonatal anoxia. *Pediatrics,* 1955, **15,** 653–662.

(5) APGAR, V., D. A. HOLADAY, L. S. JAMES, I. M. WEISBROT, and C. BERRIEN: Evaluation of the newborn infant: second report. *J. Amer. Med. Ass.,* 1958, **168,** 1985–1988.

(6) BAIRD, D., and E. M. SCOTT: Intelligence and child-bearing. *Eugen. Rev.,* 1953, **45,** 139–154.

(7) BARCROFT, J.: *The brain and its environment.* New Haven: Yale University Press, 1938.

(8) BELL, R. Q.: Relations between behavior manifestations in the human neonate. *Child Develpm.,* 1960, **31,** 463–477.

(9) BENDA, C. E.: Psychopathology of childhood. In L. Carmichael (Ed.), *Manual of child psychology,* 2d ed. New York: Wiley, 1954. Pp. 1115–1161.

(10) BLEGEN, S. D.: The premature child. *Acta paediat., Stockh.,* 1953, **42,** Suppl. 88.

(11) BOLAND, J. L.: Type of birth as related to stuttering. *J. speech hear. Dis.,* 1951, **16,** 40–43.

(12) BOLIN, B. J.: An investigation of the relationship between birth-duration, and childhood anxieties. *J. ment. Sci.,* 1959, **105,** 1045–1052.

(13) BRAZELTON, T. B.: Psychophysiologic reactions in the neonate. II. Effect of maternal medication on the neonate and his behavior. *J. Pediat.,* 1961, **58,** 513–518.

(14) BURKE, B. S., S. S. STEVENSON, J. WORCESTER, and H. G. STUART: Nutrition studies during pregnancy. V. Relations of maternal nutrition to condition of infant at birth. *J. Nutrit.,* 1949, **38,** 453–467.

(15) CAPLAN, G.: Patterns of parental response to the crisis of premature birth. *Psychiatry,* 1960, **23,** 365–374.

(16) CARITHERS, H. A.: Mother-pediatrician relationship in the neonatal period. *J. Pediat.,* 1951, **38,** 654–660.

(17) CHRISTENSEN, H. T., and R. E. PHILBRICK: Family size as a factor in the marital adjustments of college couples. *Amer. sociol. Rev.,* 1952, **17,** 306–310.

(18) CHURCHILL, J. A.: The relationship of epilepsy to breech delivery. *Neurophysiology,* 1959, **11,** 1–12.

(19) CRUMP, E. B., C. WILSON-WEBB, and M. P. POINTER: Prematurity in the Negro infant. *Amer. J. Dis. Children,* 1952, **83,** 463–474.

(20) DANN, M., S. Z. LEVINE, and E. V. NEW: The development of prematurely born children with birth weights or minimal postnatal weights of 1,000 grams or less. *Pediatrics,* 1958, **22,** 1037–1052.

(21) DAVIDS, A., S. DE VAULT, and M. TALMADGE: Anxiety, pregnancy, and childbirth abnormalities. *J. consult. Psychol.,* 1961, **25,** 74–77.

(22) DAVIS, D. C.: Comparative studies of the growth and development of premature and full-term children with special reference to oral communication. *Speech Monogr.,* 1952, **19,** 114–115.

(23) DAVIS, M. E.: Progress in the management of labor and delivery. *J. Amer. Med. Ass.,* 1960, **172,** 409–413.

(24) DENHOFF, E.: The impact of parents on the growth of exceptional children. *Except. Children,* 1960, **26,** 271–274.

(25) DE GIULIO, V. S., and R. A. MC CALLEN: Neonatal deaths. *Obstet. Gynaec.,* 1958, **11,** 170–175.

(26) DRILLIEN, C. M.: Studies in prematurity. IV. Development and progress of the prematurely born child in the preschool period. *Arch. Dis. Childh.,* 1948, **23,** 69–83.

(27) DRILLIEN, C. M.: A longitudinal study of the growth and development of prematurely and maturely born children. *Arch. Dis. Childh.,* 1958, **33,** 417–422, 423–431.

(28) DRILLIEN, C. M.: Growth and development in a group of children of very low birth weight. *Arch. Dis. Childh.,* 1958, **33,** 10–18.

(29) EICHENLAUB, J. E.: The premature. *Today's Hlth,* Dec. 1956, 38–39, 46.

(30) ELLINGSON, R. J., and D. B. LINDSLEY: Brain waves and cortical development in newborn and young infants. *Amer. Psychologist,* 1949, **4,** 248–249.

(31) ELLIS, R. W. B.: Assessment of prematurity by birth weight, crown-rump length, and head circumference. *Arch. Dis. Childh.,* 1951, **26,** 411–422.

(32) EYSENCK, S. B. G.: Personality, and pain assessment in childbirth of married and unmarried mothers. *J. ment. Sci.,* 1961, **107,** 417–430.

(33) GESELL, A.: Behavior aspects of the care of the premature infant. *J. Pediat.,* 1946, **29,** 210–212.

(34) GESELL, A.: The developmental aspect of child vision. *J. Pediat.,* 1949, **35,** 310–317.

(35) GIBSON, J. R., and T. MC KEOWN: Observations on all births (23,970) in Birmingham, 1947. VII. Effect of changing family size on infant mortality. *Brit. J. soc. Med.,* 1952, **6,** 183–187.

(36) GLASER, K., A. H. PARMELEE, and E. P. PLATTNER: Growth patterns of prematurely born infants. *Pediatrics (Springfield),* 1950, **5,** 130–144.

(37) GORDON, H. C., and B. J. NOVACK: I.Q. and month of birth. *Science,* 1950, **112,** 62–63.

(38) GRAHAM, F. K.: Behavioral differences between normal and traumatized newborns. I. The test procedure. *Psychol. Monogr.,* 1956, **70,** No. 20.

(39) GRAHAM, F. K., C. B. ERNHART, D. THURSTON, and M. CRAFT: Development three years after perinatal anoxia and other potentially damaging newborn experiences. *Psychol. Monogr.,* 1962, **76,** No. 3.

(40) GRAHAM, F. K., R. G. MATARAZZO, and B. M. CALDWELL: Behavioral differences between normal and traumatized newborns. II. Standardization, reliability, and validity. *Psychol. Monogr.,* 1956, **70,** No. 21.

(41) GRAHAM, F. K., M. M. PENNOYER, B. M. CALDWELL, M. GREENMAN, and A. F. HARHMAN: Relationship between clinical status and behavior test performance in a newborn group with a history suggesting anoxia. *J. Pediat.,* 1957, **50,** 177–183.

(42) GREENHILL, J. P.: The birth of the baby. In M. Fishbein and R. J. R. Kennedy (Eds.), *Modern marriage and family living.* Fair Lawn, N.J.: Oxford University Press, 1957. Pp. 387–400.

(43) GRIMM, E. R.: Psychological tension in pregnancy. *Psychosom. Med.,* 1961, **23,** 520–527.

(44) GROSSMAN, H. J., and N. H. GREENBERG: Psychosomatic differentiation in infancy. *Psychosom. Med.,* 1957, **19,** 293–306.

(45) HALVERSON, H. M.: Variations in pulse and respiration during different phases of infant behavior. *J. genet. Psychol.*, 1941, **59**, 259–330.

(46) HARDY, J. B., and E. O. GOLDSTEIN: The feeding of premature infants. *J. Pediat.*, 1951, **38**, 154–157.

(47) HAVIGHURST, R. J.: *Human development and education.* New York: Longmans, 1953.

(48) HEATH, C. W.: Physique, temperament, and sex ratio. *Hum. Biol.*, 1954, **26**, 335–342.

(49) HOWARD, P. J., and C. H. MORRELL: Premature infants in later life: study of intelligence and personality of 22 premature infants at ages 8 to 19 years. *Pediatrics*, 1952, **9**, 577–584.

(50) HUGHES, J. G., B. EHEMANN, and W. A. BROWN: Electroencephalography of the newborn, *Amer. J. Dis. Children*, 1948, **76**, 503–512, 626–633.

(51) HUGHES, J. G., B. C. DAVIS, and M. L. BRENNAN: Electroencephalography of the newborn infant. VI. Studies on premature infants. *Pediatrics (Springfield)*, 1951, **7**, 707.

(52) HUNTINGTON, E.: Season of birth and fame. *J. genet. Psychol.*, 1944, **64**, 323–328.

(53) INGALLS, T. H.: Congenital deformities. *Scient. American*, 1957, **197**, 109–114.

(54) JERSILD, A. T.: *Child psychology*, 5th ed. Englewood Cliffs, N.J.: Prentice-Hall, 1960.

(55) JONES, H. E.: The environment and mental development. In L. Carmichael (Ed.), *Manual of child psychology*, 2d ed. New York: Wiley, 1954. Pp. 631–696.

(56) KAEMPFFERT, W.: Discovery is expected to save the lives of many thousands unborn infants. *The New York Times*, July 15, 1956.

(57) KAWI, A. A., and B. PASAMANICK: Prenatal and paranatal factors in the development of childhood reading disorders. *Monogr. Soc. Res. Child Develpm.*, 1959, **24**, No. 4.

(58) KESSEN, W., L. S. HENDRY, and A. M. LEUTZENDORFF: Measurement of movement in the human newborn: a new technique. *Child Develpm.*, 1961, **32**, 95–105.

(59) KESSEN, W., E. J. WILLIAMS, and J. P. WILLIAMS: Selection and test of response measures in the study of the human newborn. *Child Develpm.*, 1961, **32**, 7–24.

(60) KLEBANOFF, L. B.: Parental attitudes of mothers of schizophrenic, brain-injured and retarded, and normal children. *Amer. J. Orthopsychiat.*, 1959, **29**, 445–454.

(61) KNEHR, C. A., and A. SOBEL: Mental ability of prematurely born children at early school age. *J. Psychol.*, 1949, **27**, 355–361.

(62) KNOBLOCH, H., and B. PASAMANICK: Seasonal variations in the births of the mentally deficient. *Amer. J. publ. Hlth*, 1958, **48**, 1201–1208.

(63) KNOBLOCH, H., R. V. RIDER, P. HARPER, and B. PASAMANICK: Neuropsychiatric sequelae of prematurity: a longitudinal study. *J. Amer. Med. Ass.*, 1956, **161**, 581–585.

(64) LAKIN, M.: Personality factors in mothers of excessively crying (colicky) infants. *Monogr. Soc. Res. Child Develpm.*, 1957, **22**, No. 1.

(65) LEVY, D. M., and A. HESS: Problems in determining maternal attitudes toward newborn infants. *Psychiatry*, 1952, **15**, 273–286.

(66) LEWINSKI, R. J.: Variations in mental ability according to month, season, and period of birth. *J. genet. Psychol.*, 1954, **85**, 281–288.

(67) LIPSITT, L. P., and N. LEVY: Electrotactual threshold in the neonate. *Child Develpm.*, 1959, **30**, 547–554.

(68) LIPTON, E. L., A. STEINSCHNEIDER, and J. B. RICHMOND: Autonomic function in the neonate. *Psychosom. Med.*, 1960, **22**, 57–67.

(69) MARQUIS, D. P.: Learning in the neonate: the modification of behavior under three feeding schedules. *J. exp. Psychol.*, 1941, **29**, 263–282.

(70) MARTIN, P. C., and E. L. VINCENT: *Human development.* New York: Ronald, 1960.

(71) MASSLER, M., and B. S. SAVARA: Natal and neonatal teeth. *J. Pediat.*, 1950, **36**, 349–359.

(72) MAYER, A. J., and R. V. MARKS: Differentials in infant mortality by race, economic level, and cause of death for Detroit: 1940 to 1950. *Hum. Biol.*, 1954, **26**, 145–155.

(73) MC CARTHY, D.: Organismic interpretation of infant vocalization. *Child Develpm.*, 1952, **23**, 273–280.

(74) MC CARTHY, D.: Language development. In L. Carmichael (Ed.), *Manual of child psychology*, 2d ed. New York: Wiley, 1954. Pp. 492–630.

(75) MC INTOSH, R., K. K. MERRITT, M. B. RICHARDS, M. H. SAMUELS, and M. T. BELLOWS. The incidence of congenital malformations: a study of 5,964 pregnancies. *Pediatrics*, 1954, **14**, 505–522.

(76) MEREDITH, H. V.: Birth order and body size. II. Neonatal and childhood materials. *Amer. J. phys. Anthrop.*, 1950, **8**, 196–225.

(77) MIDDLETON, C. E., and F. C. SUMNER: Season of birth as related to seasonal preference and personality traits. *J. Psychol.*, 1953, **36**, 423–425.

(78) MILLER, V. L.: *The miracle of growth.* Urbana, Ill.: The University of Illinois Press, 1950.

(79) MONTAGU, A.: *Human heredity handbook.* New York: Harcourt, Brace & World, 1959.

(80) New York Times Report: Device monitors fetal heartbeat. *The New York Times*, Feb. 20, 1961.

(81) NEWTON, N.: *Maternal emotions.* New York: Hoeber-Harper, 1955.

(82) O'CONNOR, N.: The evidence for the permanently disturbing effects of mother-child separation. *Acta psychol.*, 1956, **12**, 174–197.

(83) OLMSTEAD, R. W., and E. B. JACKSON: Self-demand feeding in the first week of life. *Pediatrics*, 1950, **6**, 396–401.

(84) OURTH, L., and K. B. BROWN: Inadequate mothering and disturbances in the neonatal period. *Child Develpm.*, 1961, **32**, 287–295.

(85) PALMER, M. F.: The speech development of normal children. *J. speech Dis.*, 1940, **5**, 185–188.

(86) PECKOS, P. S.: Nutrition during growth and development. *Child Develpm.*, 1957, **28**, 273–285.

(87) PILE, W. J.: A study of the correlation between dementia praecox and the month of birth. *Virginia med. Monthly*, 1951, **78**, 438–440.

(88) PINNEAU, S. R., and H. E. HOPPER: The relationship between the incidence of specific gastro-intestinal reactions of the infant and psychological characteristics of the mother. *J. genet. Psychol.*, 1958, **93**, 3–13.

(89) PINTNER, R., and G. FORLANO: The birth month of eminent men. *J. appl. Psychol.*, 1934, **18**, 178–188.

(90) POLANI, P. E.: Prematurity and "cerebral palsy." *Brit. med. J.*, 1958, **2**, 1497–1499.

(91) POTTER, E. L.: Pregnancy. In M. Fishbein and R. J. R. Kennedy (Eds.), *Modern marriage and family living*. Fair Lawn, N.J.: Oxford University Press, 1957. Pp. 378–386.

(92) PRATT, K. C.: The neonate. In L. Carmichael (Ed.), *Manual of child psychology*, 2d ed. New York: Wiley, 1954. Pp. 215–291.

(93) PRUGH, D. G.: Emotional problems of the premature infant's parents. *Nurs. Outlook*, 1953, **1**, 461–464.

(94) PUNKE, H. H.: Neglected social values of prolonged human infancy. *Sch. Soc.*, 1950, **71**, 369–372.

(95) RANK, O.: *The trauma of birth*. New York: Harcourt, Brace & World, 1929.

(96) REYNARD, M. C., and F. C. DOCKERAY: The comparison of temporal intervals in judging depth of sleep in newborn infants. *J. genet. Psychol.*, 1939, **55**, 103–120.

(97) RHEINGOLD, H. L.: The modification of social responsiveness in institutional babies. *Monogr. Soc. Res. Child Develpm.*, 1956, **21**, No. 2.

(98) RIDER, R. V., M. TABACK, and H. KNOBLOCH: Associations between premature birth and sociometric status. *Amer. J. publ. Hlth*, 1955, **45**, 1022–1028.

(99) ROGERS, M. E., A. M. LILIENFELD, and B. PASAMANICK: Prenatal and paranatal factors in the development of childhood behavior disorders. *Acta Psychiat. Neurol., Scand.*, 1955, Suppl. 102.

(100) ROSENGREN, W. R.: Some social psychological aspects of delivery room difficulties. *J. nerv. ment. Dis.*, 1961, **132**, 515–521.

(101) RUJA, H.: The relation between neonate crying and the length of labor. *J. genet. Psychol.*, 1948, **73**, 53–55.

(102) SALBER, E. J., and E. S. BRADSHAW: The effect of birth weight and time of first feed on the weight of Bantu babies in the first 10 days of life. *Hum. Biol.*, 1954, **26**, 156–171.

(103) SCHACTER, M., and S. COTTE: A study of the mental development of premature infants. *Pediatrics*, 1951, **8**, 955.

(104) SCHAEFER, E. S., and N. BAYLEY: Consistency of maternal behavior from infancy to preadolescence. *J. abnorm. soc. Psychol.*, 1960, **61**, 1–6.

(105) SCHLESINGER, E. R., and N. C. ALLAWAY: The combined effect of birth weight and length of gestation on neonatal mortality among single premature births. *Pediatrics*, 1955, **15**, 698–704.

(106) SCHWARTZ, P.: Birth injuries of the newborn. *Arch. Pediat.*, 1956, **73**, 429–450.

(107) SOLOMON, W. W.: Postoperative adjustment of "blue babies." *Smith Coll. Stud. soc. Wk*, 1949, **19**, 139–140.

(108) SONTAG, L. W.: War and fetal maternal relationship. *Marriage fam. Liv.*, 1944, **6**, 1–5.

(109) SONTAG, L. W.: Some psychosomatic aspects of childhood. *Nerv. Child*, 1946, **5**, 296–304.

(110) SQUIER, R., and F. DUNBAR: Emotional factors in the course of pregnancy. *Psychosom. Med.*, 1946, **8**, 996–1003.

(111) STEINER, M., and W. POMERANCE: Studies in prematurity. IV. Influence of fetal maturity on weight lag period. *Pediatrics*, 1951, **8**, 513–517.

(112) STONE, L. J., and J. CHURCH: *Childhood and adolescence*. New York: Random House, 1957.

(113) STOTT, D. H.: Physical and mental handicaps following a disturbed pregnancy. *Lancet*, 1957, **272**, 1006–1011.

(114) USDIN, G. L., and M. L. WEIL: Effect of apnea neonatorum on intellectual development. *Pediatrics*, 1952, **9**, 387–394.

(115) WAGNER, I. F.: The body jerk of the neonate. *J. genet. Psychol.*, 1938, **52**, 65–77.

(116) WALLIN, P., and R. P. RILEY: Reactions of mothers to pregnancy and adjustment of offspring in infancy. *Amer. J. Orthopsychiat.*, 1950, **20**, 616–622.

(117) WERTHEIMER, M.: Psychomotor coordination of auditory and visual space at birth. *Science*, 1961, **134**, 1692.

(118) WILE, S., and R. DAVIS: The relation of birth to behavior. *Amer. J. Orthopsychiat.*, 1941, **11**, 320–334.

(119) WILLIE, C. V., and W. B. ROTHNEY: Racial, ethnic, and income factors in the epidemiology of neonatal mortality. *Amer. sociol. Rev.*, 1962, **27**, 522–526.

(120) WOLFF, P. H.: Observations on newborn infants. *Psychosom. Med.,* 1959, **21,** 110–118.

(121) WOOLEY, P. V., and L. Q. VALDECANAS: Growth of premature infants. *Amer. J. Dis. Children,* 1960, **90,** 642–647.

(122) YACORZYNSKI, J. K., and B. E. TUCKER: What price intelligence? *Amer. Psychologist,* 1960, **15,** 201–203.

(123) ZEMLICH, M. J., and R. I. WATSON: Maternal attitudes of acceptance and rejection during and after pregnancy. *Amer. J. Orthopsychiat.,* 1953, **23,** 570–584.

(124) ZUK, G. H.: The religious factor and the role of guilt in parental acceptance of the retarded child. *Amer. J. ment. Def.,* 1959, **64,** 139–147.

4

PHYSICAL DEVELOPMENT

The child's physical development has a marked influence on the quality and quantity of his behavior. This influence may be direct or indirect. *Directly,* a child's physical development at a given age determines what he can do. If he is well developed for his age, he will be able to compete on equal terms with his peers in games and sports; if not, he will be handicapped in competition with them and may be excluded from their games. How he feels at the moment—whether he is well or tired or ill—likewise has a direct effect on the way he reacts to people and situations.

Indirectly, a child's physical development influences his attitudes toward himself and others. These in turn are reflected in the type of adjustments he makes. A child who is markedly overweight, for example, soon discovers that he cannot keep up the pace set by his thinner agemates, and this often leads to a feeling of personal inadequacy. If his agemates refuse to play with him because he is too slow, feelings of martyrdom will be added to feelings of inadequacy (31).

Realization of how others feel about his size and appearance has a marked influence on his concept of self. As Thompson has pointed out, "Children may suffer emotionally from being a 'Shrimp,' 'Tubby,' 'Redhead,' or 'Bucktooth.' The taunt, 'Brown eyes turn around and tell a lie' can leave permanent personality scars" (200). At no time do the indirect influences of physical development have more serious or more lasting effects on behavior than at the end of childhood, when the body is being transformed from that of a child into that of an adult (118).

In order to understand the interaction between physical development and behavior, one must know what the normal pattern of physical development is and what effects this has on the behavior characteristically found at different ages in childhood. Such knowledge will help one to understand the differences *among* children as well as the changes that take place in the *same* child at different ages and under different circumstances (134). Because of his size, for example, a little child feels shy in the presence of adults and inferior in the presence of bigger children. By contrast, he feels at ease and behaves in a relaxed, natural way in the presence of children his own size or slightly smaller. Similarly, with increasing strength a child will react more confidently to a bully than he does when he is small and recognizes that his lack of strength puts him at a disadvantage.

It is also important to know what causes deviant physical development. Not only does any deviation from the normal pattern of development have a direct effect on a child's behavior, but it also has a profound indirect effect on his attitude toward himself and the attitudes of others toward him. A physically handicapped child, for example, can engage only in those play activities in which his physical handicap will not be an obstacle. Furthermore, how his agemates react to his handicap will have a pronounced influence on his behavior. Their favorable reaction will go a long way toward developing in him attitudes which will contribute to good social and personal adjustment, and vice versa (41).

NORMAL AND DEVIANT PHYSICAL DEVELOPMENT

There are five major areas in which the relationship between *normal* physical development and the child's behavior may be seen. With the development of the *nervous system,* an increase in intelligence brings about new patterns of behavior. The emotional behavior of the child is directly related to his ability to perceive meanings in situations, just as the degree of social acceptance he enjoys is related to his ability to understand the thoughts, feelings, and emotions of others. Growth of the *muscles* brings changes in motor capacities and strength and in the number and type of activities enjoyed, especially games and sports.

Changes in the functioning of the *endocrine glands* result in new patterns of behavior. At puberty, for example, there is a shift from dislike for members of the opposite sex to a liking for them, from activities with others of one's own sex to activities with members of the opposite sex, and from lack of interest in personal appearance to preoccupation with looks and dress. Changes in a child's gross physical structure—his *physique*—in terms of height, weight, body proportions, and general appearance affect behavior.

As Thompson has pointed out, "The toddler whose eyes are at the level of an adult's knees sees a far different world from that envisioned by an adult; a child whose center of gravity is relatively low will have less difficulty in balance than one whose center of gravity is high. The mechanics of picking up an inch cube present a different problem to the tiny hand of the 1-year-old from the one presented to the hand of the 5-year-old" (200). Finally, behavior is influenced by the child's *physical condition,* which is dependent upon a balanced functioning of the different parts of the body. This balanced functioning results in homeostasis—normal blood sugar, water balance, rate of oxygen utilization, and so forth. This is achieved by the regulatory action of the central and autonomic nervous systems and by the endocrine system. The glands of the endocrine system, for example, normally work in harmony and produce chemical secretions or "hormones" in just the right amount to maintain a steady state of the internal environment of the body. The most important regulatory glands of the endocrine system are the pituitary gland, at the base of the brain; the thyroid glands, in the throat; the adrenal glands, located near the kidneys; and the gonads, attached to the sex organs (47, 196).

The interrelationship between *deviant* physical development and behavior is strikingly apparent. Body size and shape influence the child's physical performances. Thin boys of average height, for example, perform better than boys of medium physique or above-average height. Those who are tall and obese are the poorest performers of all (25). Marked deviations in size also affect the child's social behavior and acceptance by his peers. The obese child loses out in active play and, as a result, misses many opportunities to learn the skills essential to social success (31).

The malfunctioning of an organ upsets the body's *homeostasis* and results in behavioral changes. The greater the disturbance to body balance, the more deviant the behavior. Reduction in the amount of oxygen in the inspired air, as in an attack of asthma, for example, leads to emotional outbursts, loss of critical ability, lack of concentration, and reduction in the speed and quality of mental work. A drop in blood-sugar level affects mental activities and leads to alterations in mood, irritability, and vague feelings of apprehension. A rise in the blood-sugar level above normal results in depressive mental states (47, 196). An acute deficiency of vitamin B complex brings about serious behavioral changes, as shown in depression, hysteria, and increased emotionality. Wide fluctuations of autonomic functioning lead to emotional instability, nervousness, anxiety, and distractibility (29, 213).

Disturbances in homeostasis may be temporary or permanent. The longer the duration or the more frequent the temporary disturbance, the greater the effect on the child's behavior. A common form of temporary upset in body balance in children comes from high fever. This is reflected in mental and emotional confusion accompanied by irrational and irascible behavior and a tendency to resist aggressively any suggestions from others. As the fever subsides, so do the behavioral changes that accompanied it (196). In pubescent girls, balance is temporarily disrupted by the menstrual period. For several days preceding and during the beginning of the period, hormonal imbalance causes changes in blood pressure, body temperature, basal metabolism, and water accumulation which may press on nerve centers. These lead to tension, irritability, and general nervousness (2, 97).

A more permanent disturbance of homeostasis comes from malnutrition and endocrine disorders. Prolonged *malnutrition* makes the child apathetic, depressed, irritable, undependable, and nervous. Nutritional anemia in children, resulting more often from emotional and social problems than from improper diet, causes heightened emotional tension (124, 179). Excess or gross deficiency of one or more of the hormones produced by the *glands of the endocrine system* is usually associated with characteristic behavior patterns. Furthermore, should the excess or deficiency occur during the growth years, it is likely to lead to physical deviations and to changes in intelligence and personality. Personality changes may be due to glandular changes, to social attitudes toward the physical malformations caused by hormonal imbalance, or to both.

In *pituitary dwarfism,* for example, there is a deficiency of the growth hormone from the pituitary gland. The individual is a perfectly formed and proportioned miniature adult. The mental development is normal because only the growth-promoting factor is absent. Any psychological effect will be indirect, as it affects the individual's attitude toward his dwarfism. In *hypothyroid dwarfism,* on the other hand, the whole development of the child is affected. In severe cases, this is known as *cretinism.*

Since the thyroid hormone is responsible for cell development, all the cells of the body are affected unfavorably by a deficiency of this hormone. The bones grow slowly, and their ossification is retarded. The brain cells develop inadequately, and this causes mental deficiency. How thyroid deficiency will influence the child's development depends partly upon the seriousness of the deficiency and partly upon the period in the growth cycle when it occurs. The most serious time is the period of prenatal development, when growth and development are most rapid (152).

Mild thyroid deficiency will cause lethargy, lack of vitality, and general fatigue accompanied by a tendency to be irascible, depressed, distrustful, and melancholy. An excess of thyroxin—the hormone from the thyroid glands—leads to an increase in the tempo of the bodily processes and to restlessness, excitability, anxiety, distractibility, marked nervous tension, and wide mood swings (196). Increase in the sex hormone at puberty not only is responsible for the physical changes that occur but also has a marked influence on the changes in body proportions. If the sex hormone is introduced too early, as in early-maturing children, growth of the body ceases before the legs have attained their full growth; the result is a short, stocky-legged person. If there is a hypogonadal condition resulting from a delay in the introduction of the sex hormone, physical growth will continue beyond the normal time, the lower measurements of the body will exceed the upper, and at maturity the child will have long, slender legs (84, 152).

GROWTH CYCLES

Growth is rhythmic, not regular. A child does not gain a given number of pounds annually or grow a given number of inches. Growth comes, on the contrary, in cycles or waves—"periods," or "phases" (53, 200). It is orderly and predictable. As Parker has pointed out in describing the cycles of normal physical growth, "Sometimes the tempo is slow, sometimes fast but always in complete harmony" (176).

Studies of growth have revealed that there are four distinct periods, two characterized by slow growth and two by rapid growth. From birth to two years, there is rapid growth. This is followed by a period of slow growth up to the time of puberty, or sexual maturing, beginning usually between the eighth and eleventh years. From then until fifteen or sixteen years, there is rapid growth, and this is followed by a period of fairly abrupt tapering off of growth to the time of maturity. Until the "settling process" characteristic of old age, there is a maintenance of the height attained in the fourth growth cycle, although there may be an increase in weight (154).

These growth cycles are so universal that clothing for children is sized accordingly. The rapid growth in the first year necessi-

tates two sets of clothing, the *infant* size for the first 6 months and the *first* size for the last 6 months. The next larger size is adequate for the child up to his second birthday, while the next serves for 2 years, from the second to the fourth birthday. Sizes for older children and adolescents likewise take into consideration the growth and the resting periods.

Variations in Growth Cycles. There are variations in the normal pattern of growth cycles, but as Krogman has stressed:

With few exceptions, the variation follows an orderly progress; there is a range which we have learned to expect. Growth is not a narrow path; it is, rather, a broad highway. We do not so much stray from the path of growth as we meander along the highway of growth. Variation is in and of itself an unequal factor, for some children are more variable than others, and variability, in general, increases with age. The excessive variability of some children may be explained in part by their hereditary background, and in part by their food and health habits, as well as their health vicissitudes. As a rule, a markedly erratic growth progress in a child is a signal for more intensive investigation, for health problems seem to be correlated with extreme deviates. A growth item, i.e., length of a limb segment, which is less variable than, say, weight, will be more significant in its deviation (132).

Most children are fairly consistent in their pattern of growth, showing a constant tendency toward earliness or lateness in reaching critical points. Furthermore, there is no known way of speeding up or retarding the pattern of changes (18, 78, 165).

A number of factors determine whether the child will grow at a rapid rate or in a more leisurely fashion. The influence of *family* and *ethnic background* on height, bone development, age of sexual maturing, and eruption and decaying of teeth has been reported (15). There are *sex differences,* with boys growing faster than girls at certain ages and girls faster than boys at others. From about nine or ten to thirteen or fourteen years of age, for example, girls are taller and heavier than boys because of their earlier pubertal development. After that, boys become taller and heavier than girls and remain taller for the rest of their lives, though they may not be heavier. Variability within the sex group is usually greater among boys than among girls, though variability in growth rates for both sexes increases with age (18, 154). Characteristic patterns of growth for the two sexes are shown in Figure 4–1.

Body size and *body type* influence the rate of growth and are responsible for some of the variations that occur. A small child, for example, grows over a longer period of time than a large child who has a greater period of initial growth, though he may not catch up with the large child even at maturity. The child with the tall, slender, fragile build—the *ectomorph*—grows in height over a longer period of time than the child with a heavyset, blocky structure. However, the latter—the *mesomorph*—grows faster at each age level, especially in weight. Placid children tend to grow faster than those who experience *emotional tension,* though tension has a greater effect on weight than on height (56, 176).

July to mid-December is the *season* most favorable for increase in weight, with the most rapid gains occurring from September to December. At this time, the average gain is four times that from February to June. The least growth comes from the beginning of May to early July. Growth in height, on the other hand, follows an entirely different cycle. The greatest increase comes from April to the middle of August, paralleling the slow period of increase in weight, while the least increase comes from August to the end of November, the period of greatest increase in weight. Because seasonal variations are most marked in weight, they may indicate merely seasonal differences in water content of the body rather than true growth trends. Day-to-day variations in weight may reflect differences in water content at different times of the day (42, 53, 176).

Growth Cycles for Different Organs. The different parts of the body have their own periods of rapid and slow growth, and

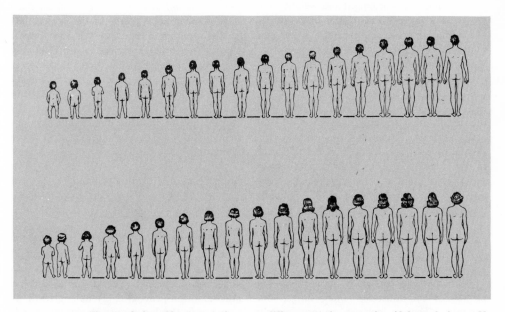

Figure 4–1. Characteristic sex differences in growth. (Adapted from N. Bayley, Individual patterns of development, *Child Develpm.*, 1956, 27, 45–74. Used by permission.)

each reaches its mature size at its own time. This is known as *asynchronous growth,* or "split growth" (197, 203). All phases of growth are continuous, however, and take place concurrently. A child's brain, for example, does not stop growing while his muscles, lungs, and bones are growing. Instead, there is some growth taking place in *all* parts of the body at *all* times during the growth years.

Although there is an interrelationship or correlation among the growth patterns for different organs or bones, the different areas of a child's body will be at widely disparate points of maturity at any given age. At no time is this more apparent than at puberty. Then, with little or no regard for overall proportions, the arms, legs, nose, and chin seem suddenly to "sprout" individually, each growing rapidly at its own time and rate. Even the two sides of the body may grow at different rates then, though by the time physical maturity is reached, there is generally an approximate balance (197). Thus, there are not only interindividual differences in physical growth but also marked *intraindividual* differences (197, 203).

Growth curves for height and weight have shown that, except during the first year of life, children grow more rapidly in height than in weight. To express this relationship, Krogman has suggested a simple rule: "Children grow tall before they grow heavy" (134). In the latter part of childhood, the extremities grow faster than the trunk, with the result that the child seems to be "all arms and legs," like a little colt (176). Asynchronous growth is likewise apparent in the face, where the lower part grows more rapidly than the upper, especially from ages five through eight years (7). Studies of changes in head hair from birth to maturity have shown that the hair shaft increases in size at a rapid and uniform rate during the first three years of life and then less uniformly and at a slower rate (54).

Asynchrony is especially apparent in the growth of the muscles, bones, lungs, and genitals. These increase approximately twenty times in size during the growth years, while the eyes, brain, and some other organs which are relatively more developed at birth increase much less. The eyeball, for example, completes most of its growth during the first five years of postnatal life and the brain during the first ten, whereas the heart and some other internal organs require more than 20 years (77).

The pattern for muscular growth is characterized by a rapidly decelerating rate during the second year, a slowly decelerating rate until the onset of puberty, an accelerating rate during puberty, and a decelerating rate thereafter until growth ceases (34, 142). Because muscle growth is relatively slow, strength is relatively late in developing. The spurt in growth of strength, for example, comes later in puberty than weight increase. This asynchrony is illustrated in Figure 4–2. Finally, there are changes in the weights of body tissues at different ages. The greatest increase in bone and muscle tissue, for example, comes during the childhood and adolescent years, whereas the greatest increase in fat tissue comes during adulthood (148).

In spite of asynchronous growth, the development of the body follows the *laws of developmental direction.* For the most part, development occurs first in the upper part of the body and later in the lower part. Changes in body proportions are relatively slight during the first half year of postnatal life. From then until puberty, however, head growth is slow, limb growth rapid, and trunk growth intermediate. The brain and facial features attain maturity in size and development before the organs and features of the trunk and limbs (200).

Importance of Growth Cycles. The six most important effects of irregular growth on the child's behavior are:

1. Adjustment Difficulties. During periods of rapid growth, the child must constantly make new adjustments. This necessity to adapt and adjust is likely to be disturbing and emotion-provoking. When growth is slow, as in the latter part of childhood, adjustments are much easier. As Stone and Church have pointed out, "Both physically

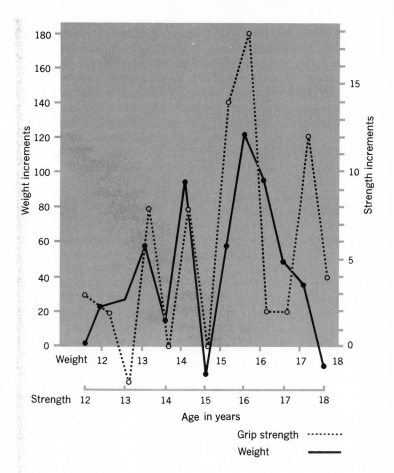

Figure 4–2. Relation between spurts in growth, in weight, and in muscular strength at puberty for one boy. Note that the spurt in strength comes later than the spurt in weight. (Adapted from F. T. Tyler, Organismic growth: some relationships within the individual among cycles of growth in physical characteristics, *Child Develpm.*, 1957, 28, 55–63. Used by permission.)

and psychologically, the school years are a relatively quiet interlude between two periods of turbulence. They are the 'halcyon days of childhood,' the era to which so many adults look back with a nostalgic, and perhaps misdirected, sense of longing" (197).

2. Energy Level. Rapid growth is much more energy-consuming than slow growth. During the first two years of life, rapid growth would leave the baby exhausted were he not given plenty of time for rest and sleep and also proper food to provide energy for growth. Little is expected of him, so he can sleep whenever he becomes tired. Only when his schedule is interrupted and he is deprived of the rest he needs or is given

food when he is too tired to eat will his disposition be affected (78, 110).

The second period of rapid growth in childhood is at the onset of puberty. Because the pubescent child is beginning to look like an adult, more and more is expected of him at home and in school. Furthermore, he is given less time to sleep and rest than before. His energy is consumed in growth; he is tired and listless and tends to procrastinate. He becomes moody, irritable, irascible, and generally difficult to live with. He enters what is commonly referred to as the "negative phase"—a time when he behaves both physically and psychologically as if he were "dead on his feet" (198).

Between these two periods of rapid growth is a time of slow growth, a time when energy is used primarily for play or work. From two or three years of age until the puberty changes begin to appear, the normal, healthy child seems to have a boundless supply of energy. He wants to be on the go all the time and finds sitting still in school very difficult. He becomes restless if he cannot move around and do things during his waking hours, claiming that he is not tired, does not need a rest period during the day, or is "not sleepy" at bedtime. When free to play, he runs, climbs, and jumps constantly, shouting and laughing to let off extra energy. Although he is sometimes angry, cranky, or generally disagreeable, this is mainly because he feels that he has not been fairly treated, rarely because he is tired (197).

3. Nutritional Needs. Growth comes partly from inherent drives, but it is also dependent on nourishment of the right kind and in the right amounts. Nutritional requirements are greatest during periods of rapid growth —during the first two or three months of life and during the growth spurt of puberty. It has been estimated that the pubescent child needs 2,500 to 3,000 calories a day. Even this is often not sufficient, as is shown by the fact that pubescent children eat almost all the time.

When the child's nutritional needs are not met, either quantitatively or qualitatively, there are likely to be disturbances in many parts of the body, just as there are when the fetal environment is poor because of the mother's malnutrition. Malnutrition keeps the child from attaining his expected height. Furthermore, it causes a lag in skeletal development and a delay in the fusion of the epiphyses in the hand (52, 166, 177). Pronounced disturbances resulting from nutritional deficiencies manifest themselves in scurvy, rickets, and beriberi. Less pronounced manifestations include extreme fat, circles under the eyes, scaliness of the skin on the arms and legs, crusted eyelids, and lesions at the corners of the mouth.

Accompanying the physical disturbances are behavioral disturbances. The child who is not getting enough nourishment for his growth needs is tired, fretful, and irritable. He is careless about his duties and his school work. He shows little interest in active play and generally makes poor social adjustments. Poor nutrition is also at the basis of some of the stresses and strains of puberty (146).

Commenting on the importance of nutrition to growth, Peckos has said:

> It is not enough to prevent a child from having rickets, scurvy, and any other disease. It is important that his body be ready to do what the will commands and do it without undue conscious effort. There are too many children today who live in that "twilight zone" between the absence of actual disease and the level of buoyant health which liberates the body and makes enjoying of life possible, who are victims of a "hidden hunger" almost as devastating as "stomach hunger" (177).

4. Maintenance of Homeostasis. During periods of slow growth, as in the early school years, the body normally can maintain homeostasis. But as Dunbar has pointed out, "The maintenance of homeostasis . . . is particularly difficult during a period of developmental change" (55). Whenever there is a disturbance in homeostasis, it is reflected in behavioral changes. Studies have revealed that there is increased physiological instability during the early part of puberty, especially in body temperature and blood pressure.

The more rapid the puberty growth spurt, the greater the upset in homeostasis and the more pronounced the effects on the child's behavior. Few children, even those whose pubertal growth is slow, escape a "negative" period of "disequilibrium," characterized by restlessness, moodiness, fits of depression, withdrawal from family and friends, touchiness, irritability, rebelliousness, and critical attacks on others (58, 67).

That these behavioral changes result in part at least from an upset in homeostasis may be seen by the fact that they are accompanied by such physical manifestations as headaches, backaches, digestive upsets, finicky appetites, and a general feeling of fatigue. Because girls mature, on the whole, more rapidly than boys, they are more likely to experience these behavioral disturbances. Even a temporary upset in homeostasis, however, will throw a child of any age out of focus and make him difficult to live with. The longer the upset, the more out of focus the child is and the more unsocial his behavior (11, 78). See pages 29 to 30 for a more complete discussion of the characteristic behavior of children during periods of equilibrium and disequilibrium.

5. Awkwardness. One of the most apparent behavioral changes accompanying rapid growth is awkwardness. Owing to his neurological immaturity, the young baby is characteristically awkward. As nerves and muscles develop, however, and as the young child has opportunities to learn skills, this incoordination gives way to coordination. During the childhood period of relatively slow growth, there is little to disturb this coordination, and as a result, the older child can do most of the things an adult can and can do them equally well (26, 176).

Then, often very suddenly, there seems to be a complete change. Because the child's hands and feet enlarge quickly, he loses his former control over them; he becomes "all thumbs" and seems to "fall over his own feet." Not recognizing the reason for this sudden awkwardness, many parents accuse the rapidly growing pubescent child of being "careless" when he bumps into furniture, trips over rugs, or drops objects. Scoldings and ridicule not only embarrass the child but make him feel inadequate and wonder whether he is normal (67, 68).

6. Concern about Body Disproportions. Because of asynchronous growth, every child has some features which seem to be out of proper proportion. As long as other children have the same appearance, this does not concern the child. For example, the young child is not bothered by his top-heavy, dwarflike appearance. But when growth begins to speed up at the time of puberty, the child who is out of step with his contemporaries because he has reached this spurt either earlier or later than they becomes acutely aware of his body disproportions. A nose too large for a small chin, hands and feet too big for small arms and legs, or hips too big for small shoulders then become a source of great concern. An early-maturing child who is the "first" of his agemates to experience these body disproportions may feel, miserably, that he is the focal point of attention (9, 60, 165).

BODY SIZE

Body size is determined by measurements of height and weight. While these measurements follow patterns of development that are markedly similar—with slow gains in weight being paralleled by slow gains in height, and vice versa—the total growth in height from birth to maturity is less than the total growth in weight. It has been estimated that the total increase in height is $3\frac{1}{2}$-fold and that the total increase in weight is twentyfold (134). Increases in body size for boys and girls at different ages are shown in Figure 4–1, page 115.

Growth in body size is controlled by the *growth hormone,* secreted by the anterior lobe of the pituitary gland—a small gland located at the base of the brain. If growth is to proceed in a normal, orderly fashion, the growth hormone must be produced in the right amounts and at the right times. If the pituitary does not produce enough of the growth hormone, growth ceases earlier than normal, and the child does not reach the size his hereditary endowment provided. If too much growth hormone is produced, on the other hand, overgrowth results. Whether or not the growth hormone will be produced in the right amounts and at the right times depends not upon the pituitary gland alone but also upon the thyroid glands and gonads.

At puberty, for example, the hormones produced by the gonads—*estrogen* in the female and *androgen* in the male—increase in amount; they act as retarding influences on the growth hormone, stimulating the deposition of calcium, which causes the bones to ossify, and bringing about the closure of the epiphyses of the bones. Thus growth is gradually brought to a halt, and body size is then stationary (126, 176).

Height.   While marked variations exist in the height of children of the same age, there is a pattern of growth which is similar for all children. Expressed in terms of averages, the pattern gives a picture of the typical growth of the typical child. The baby at birth measures between 19 and 20 inches. During the first two years of life, there are rapid increases in height. At four months of age, his height is, on the average, 23 to 24 inches; at eight months, 26 to 28 inches; and at one year, 28 to 30 inches. At two years, he is 32 to 34 inches tall, and by five years, his birth height should have doubled. From then until the onset of puberty, there is a slow gain of approximately 3 inches annually. Then, at the onset of puberty, increase in height is accelerated. At eleven years of age, when the average American girl of today begins her puberty growth spurt, she is 58 inches tall. By the time she is sexually mature, at thirteen years, she is 63 inches tall, and at eighteen years, when her growth in height is complete, she measures 66 inches (134).

Because boys begin their puberty growth spurt approximately a year later than girls, the average American boy is from ½ to 1 inch shorter than the average girl at thirteen years of age. From then on, however, boys increase in height at a more rapid rate than girls and continue the increase approximately a year longer, so that at maturity they are taller than girls. At thirteen years of age, for example, the average boy measures 62 inches. A year later, when he becomes sexually mature, he measures 65 inches; at eighteen years, he measures 69.5 inches. Between eighteen and twenty, he may add another half inch or even an inch (134). The difference in height between the sexes after the puberty growth spurt is shown in Figure 4–1, page 115.

Adult height can be predicted with *relative* accuracy today because it has been found that there is a high correlation between the skeletal age of a child, as determined by X rays of the bones of the hand and wrist, and the proportion of adult stature achieved at the time of the X rays (19). Furthermore, because a child's height shows a general tendency to increase in correlation with the height of his parents, their height may likewise be used as a basis for prediction. The relationship between the height of parents and their children is greater as the children get older, and this adds to the accuracy of prediction in late childhood (15, 57).

It is never possible to know exactly how tall a child will ultimately be until it is known when the puberty growth spurt occurs. The early maturer is generally shorter, as an adult, than his height as a child might have indicated. The late maturer is generally taller, as an adult, than one would have anticipated. Since there is a close relationship between the age at which a child matures and the age at which the parent of the same sex matured, knowledge of the parent's growth history will increase the accuracy of prediction (17, 73, 151).

Weight.   While the average baby may weigh between 6 and 8 pounds at birth, some weigh only 3 or 4 pounds, and others weigh nearly 16. The pattern of increase, however, is much the same for all. By the end of the first month of life, the average baby not only has regained the weight lost after birth but has begun to show a weight increase. At four months, he should have doubled his birth weight and, at the end of the first year, trebled it. During the second and third years, he gains from 3 to 5 pounds annually.

After the third year, gains in weight are at a slower rate until the onset of puberty. At five years, the child should be approximately five times his birth weight and at the onset of puberty should weigh between 80 and 90 pounds. The average girl of eleven, when the puberty growth spurt begins, weighs 88.5 pounds, while boys of the same age weigh 85.5 pounds. By the time the average girl is fifteen years old, her weight will have increased to 126.5 pounds, after which the increase will be relatively small. The average weight for boys when they begin their puberty growth spurt at twelve years is 96 pounds and, at sixteen years, when the spurt is nearly complete, 142 pounds (134, 198).

The "normal" weight of the child at every age is dependent to a certain extent upon his *body build*. Roughly, body builds fall into three major categories: the *endomorph,* characterized by a tendency toward an excessively fat body; the *mesomorph,* characterized by a heavy, hard, and rectangularly outlined body; and the *ectomorph,* characterized by a long, slender body; slender muscles; and long, thin bones. A mesomorph would be expected to weigh more for his height than an ectomorph (157, 189). The relation of weight to body build is illustrated in Figure 4–3.

Increase in weight during the growth years is dependent not on increase in fat tissue alone but also on increase in bone and muscle tissue. In babyhood, increase in weight comes mainly from an increase in fat tissue owing to the high content of fat in milk, the chief component of the baby's diet. As childhood progresses, body weight comes more from bone and muscle tissue than from fat tissue. In the latter part of childhood, for example, fat tissue is responsible

for only 21 to 29 per cent of total weight (72, 148).

During puberty, with the growth spurt in height, there is an increase in the length of the bones of the body. Shortly afterward, the bones begin to harden, or ossify, and the muscle tissue begins to increase, both adding to the child's weight. During the latter part of childhood, the muscles make up approximately one-fourth of the total body weight. When the body is sexually mature, they make up approximately 45 per cent of total weight (78, 198).

Relation between Height and Weight. In obese children, weight is proportionally too great for height; in thin or "skinny" children, weight is proportionally not great enough for height. *Obesity* and *excessive thinness* are more often psychosomatic than physical in origin; very rarely are they due to a glandular condition (31). Some excessively thin children may be in poor health or suffering from starvation or malnutrition; more often they are suffering from nervous tension, which leads to lack of appetite and digestive disorders.

Nervous tension is generally the result of parental anxiety about the child's well-being. The anxious parent attempts to make the child eat more than he wants or needs by

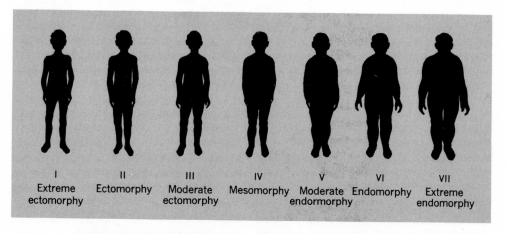

I	II	III	IV	V	VI	VII
Extreme	Ectomorphy	Moderate	Mesomorphy	Moderate	Endomorphy	Extreme
ectomorphy		ectomorphy		endormorphy		endomorphy

Figure 4–3. Body types in childhood. (Adapted from M. Massler and T. Suher, Calculation of "normal" weight in children, *Child Develpm.,* 1951, 22, 75–94. Used by permission.)

punishing him for not eating everything on his plate, by making derogatory comparisons with his siblings, or by using threats and bribes. All these make the child anxious and tense, a condition that militates against his wanting to eat (85, 155).

While faulty eating habits, encouraged by parental pressures to overeat, may be partially responsible for obesity, obesity more often stems from unfavorable psychological factors, such as overdependency, feelings of inadequacy, or feelings of rejection. Obesity is more likely to occur when the child comes from a small family or is the "baby of the family." There is some evidence that people who inherit genes leading to heavy body builds are especially sensitive to stressful situations, and this precipitates overeating with its accompaniment of obesity (30, 69, 201). That psychological factors are more likely to be responsible for obesity than physical factors is shown by the fact that among persons wanting to lose weight, those who have good emotional adjustments are four times as successful in limiting their food intake as those who suffer from emotional disturbances (31).

Obesity is not an overnight development in children; in fact, most obese children have been fat from early babyhood. Growing up in an environment where parents tend to overeat or where parents are anxious that the child be well nourished encourages the child to overeat; as he becomes fat, he has little interest in exercise and so increases his obesity. In time, obesity serves as an alibi for avoiding threatening or unacceptable social demands. Also, when an obese child cannot participate in the activities of his more slender peers, he may find that food provides a substitute satisfaction which temporarily soothes his feelings of inadequacy (30, 144).

Because of the changes which normally occur in body tissues as children grow older, a child may actually weigh more but *look* scrawny and lanky. The distribution of fat is largely responsible for making a person look "thin" or "fat." Where the fat is located on the body depends partly on the stage of development of the individual, partly on his heredity, and partly on how much exercise he has. Some people seem to gain weight mostly in their faces, others around the abdomen, and still others in the arms and legs. The more active the person, the less likely he is to have fat accumulations in any one area of the body.

During the puberty growth spurt, most boys and girls experience a "puberty fat period"—a time when they *look* fatter than they actually are. At this time, many boys and girls have a marked increase of fat over the abdomen, around the nipples, in the hips and thighs, and in their faces, especially in the cheeks and around the chin. This fat comes partly from the hormonal dislocation that accompanies sexual maturing and partly from the ravenous appetites that result from rapid growth. Generally, this "fat look" disappears as balance in hormonal functioning is regained at sexual maturity and as the pubescent learns to cut down on his caloric intake (17, 214).

VARIATIONS IN BODY SIZE

Variations in body size are present at birth and become more pronounced as children grow older. They are especially great in late childhood because of individual differences in the time of the pubertal growth spurt. Variations in weight are greater at all ages than variations in height because weight is more susceptible to environmental influences. Since each child has his own growth pattern, influenced by his body build, any variation from averages for his age group should take into consideration his "type" (17).

Variations in birth weight are maintained through the growth years and remain constant. For example, in girls at the age of seven years, a mean difference of 11.2 pounds was found between those whose birth weight was 9 pounds 9 ounces or more and those whose birth weight was 5 pounds 8 ounces or less. At eleven years, the difference was 12.8 pounds. This was true of boys also. Variations in birth length likewise remain relatively constant throughout the childhood years. While some change in relative heights may occur at the time of the puberty growth spurt, tall children remain tall, and short children remain relatively short (106).

Causes of Variations.   Throughout the childhood years, *family influences* play an important role in determining what the child's body size is. These influences become more and more apparent as growth progresses. In the case of weight, for example, the genes of some children cause a greater accumulation of fat from ingested food than the genes of other children. Environment helps to determine whether or not hereditary growth potentials will be reached. Weight is influenced by environment at every age more than height (141, 154).

Children who are *well nourished*—fat but not excessively fat or obese—are taller and reach puberty sooner than children who are poorly nourished. As Garn and Haskell have pointed out, "Calories are growth-promoting. With more food, children of the same racial stock are taller in the United States than in their homelands" (74). Growth curves for the fattest and leanest in a sample of boys and girls at 9.5 and 8.5 years of age, respectively, have shown that height is correlated with weight (see Figure 4–4). A well-nourished child has enough energy to engage in the strenuous activities of childhood and still have a reserve supply for growth.

After a child reaches the age of twelve, weight is less related to growth in height than earlier. Also, in extreme cases of obesity, the relationship between height and time of sexual maturity breaks down. There is no evidence that the more obese the child, the taller he will be or the earlier he will reach puberty (74). To achieve his hereditary potential in height, the child must have a diet that provides him with the "building materials" for growth. How important these building materials are has been demonstrated by the effects of poor nutrition. During periods of war, when nutritional

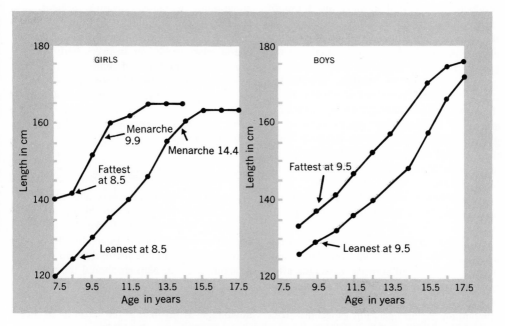

Figure 4–4.   Comparative growth curves of boys and girls who were leanest and fattest respectively at 8.5 and 9.5 years of age. (Adapted from S. M. Garn and J. A. Haskell, Fat thickness and developmental status in childhood and adolescence, *Amer. J. Dis. Children*, 1960, 99, 746–751. Used by permission.)

standards are lowered for the civilian population, children show less increase in height and weight during the growth years and are smaller in stature at maturity than children from the same socioeconomic groups during peacetime (37).

In the early part of puberty, many boys and girls, anxious to avoid the common tendency to "look fat," may refuse to eat enough to enable them to grow as nature had planned. As a result, the spurt in growth is less pronounced than it would have been had food intake been adequate. Because growth in height comes to an end shortly after the child becomes sexually mature, his chances of achieving his hereditary potentials will be lost if he is not well nourished during puberty (173, 194).

Even when there is adequate nutrition for growth, it is possible that tension, anxiety, and other forms of persistent *emotional disturbance* may interfere with normal growth. Just how emotional disturbance affects growth is still uncertain. It is believed, however, that chronic anxiety causes an overproduction of adrenal steroids, and these, in turn, inhibit growth by acting to antagonize the growth hormone from the pituitary gland. A diminished production of the growth hormone may also result from an inadequate intake of calories. Should the supply of growth hormone be inadequate in the latter part of childhood, owing to chronic emotional tension or malnutrition, the growth spurt is likely to be delayed. This, then, causes the child to be shorter as an adult than his hereditary potential would justify (154).

In both height and weight, *sex differences* tend to favor boys from birth until eleven or twelve years of age. Girls surpass boys from about twelve to fifteen years, and then boys again, on the average, are the taller and heavier sex. Sex differences in weight after maturity are due to the heavier bones and muscles of the boy rather than to fat accumulation. At all ages, but especially from puberty on, girls tend to accumulate more fat than boys; this is apparent in the female curves and bulges (154, 200).

Variations due to *racial* stock have been reported for children of all ages. While Negro babies during the first year of life do not differ in size significantly from white babies of comparable socioeconomic levels, differences become greater with age. There are two reasons for this: First, Negroes as a group have less favorable environments in which to grow; and second, the Negro child is typically of a more slender build than the white child. At all ages, children of Finnish ancestry are larger than those of Italian or Mexican ancestry. Children from Okinawa are smaller in both height and weight than French, South African, or American Indian children. Japanese children are smaller, age for age, than white children (132, 163).

Size varies with level of *intelligence*. In general, children of high intelligence are taller and heavier for their ages than children of low intelligence (123). Variations in size, especially in weight, are related to the *socioeconomic* status of the family. These variations, due to differences in diet (particularly during the early years of life), housing conditions, health practices, and occupational demands, become greater as children become older. Children whose fathers belong to the professional or managerial class are larger in every body measurement than children of skilled or unskilled workers. Children from impoverished homes are smaller, and their rate of growth is retarded as compared with children of the same age whose economic status is better (51, 83, 163).

SIGNIFICANCE OF BODY SIZE

Although parents often worry about the size of the child's body, size and health are not necessarily correlated. As Parker has pointed out, "The parents of the large child have no reason to congratulate themselves on having a healthier child. Neither should the parents of the small child be concerned that their child is retarded. The child derives no health advantage from being the largest in her group, and the small child is not at a disadvantage" (176).

How important body size is psychologically to a child will depend on how others, especially peers, react to his size. Most children are not body-size-conscious except when there is a marked deviation from the norm. In a study of children in grades 3 to 5, it was found that the child's height was unrelated to his status in the social group. Being slightly taller or shorter than the other children did not affect a child's popularity (96).

Variations in weight, however, are far more common than variations in height.

Furthermore, deviations in weight are most often on the plus side; there are relatively few skinny children in our overnourished society. The majority of obese children become aware, even before they enter school, of how others feel about their fatness. They know that adults feel sorry for them and that their peers feel that their fat interferes with their capacity to participate in active play. They are exposed to severe social condemnation and are regarded as greedy, self-

Body size and shape have a definite influence on the child's appearance, his physical performance, his play, his self-concept, and his relations with his peers. (Standard Oil Co., N.J.)

indulgent, and lacking in willpower. Usually they are exposed to humiliating rejection and social isolation, with the result that they are deprived of opportunities to learn how to get along in social situations and, consequently, are poorly equipped to meet the demands of life as they grow older (30, 31).

Naturally, obese children develop severe feelings of personal inadequacy, and they often compensate by eating even more than before, thus becoming fatter and less acceptable to their peers (133). How markedly deviations in body size can influence peer attitudes toward a child has been pointed out by Sontag, who said, "The unconscious cruelty of children toward anyone of them whose body does not conform to theirs in size, form, and function may be an important factor in the emotional adjustment of children lacking this conformity" (195).

PHYSICAL PROPORTIONS

At birth, the proportions of the body are quite different from those of the adult (see Figure 1–1, page 3). The child's growth therefore results not only in an increase in size but, of equal importance, in a marked change in the proportions of the different parts of the body. Not all parts of the body attain mature proportions at the same time, but they have, for the most part, assumed their mature proportions by the time the adolescent is sixteen or seventeen years old. Changes in proportions from birth to adulthood are shown in Figure 4–5. The head of the adult is twice the size of the infant's; the trunk is three times its birth size; and the arms and legs are, respectively, four and five times their birth length.

In general, changes in proportions follow the laws of developmental direction (pages 20 to 21). Throughout childhood, there are no marked sex differences in body proportions (154).

Proportions of the Head. The *head* grows proportionately less after birth than most other parts of the body. At birth, the length of the head is 22 per cent of the total body length. If these proportions remained constant, a mature man of 6 feet would have a head about 16 inches in length instead of the average 8 or 9 inches. It would extend to the level of his armpits and nipples. From birth to maturity, the length of the head doubles, but the total stature more than trebles. The surface area of the head is 21 per cent of the total surface area of the body at birth, 13 per cent at five years, 10 per cent at twelve years, and 8 per cent at eighteen years. At ten years, the head is 95 per cent of its adult size, and at fifteen years, 98 per cent (154, 200).

The cranial part of the head is large and the facial area small at birth. The child's head is broader in relation to length than the adult's head. The head has practically finished its growth in width by the time the child is three years old, but it continues to increase in length until he is seventeen or eighteen. Short and narrow heads show somewhat greater increase than long and broad heads. The growth pattern in length and width is much the same for boys and girls, though boys' heads are slightly larger at every age (26).

Proportions of the Face. Because the cranium completes its growth so early, the top of the head appears to be too large for the face. The lower part of the head throughout babyhood and early childhood is small and undeveloped, owing primarily to the smallness of the baby teeth. The facial skeleton becomes larger in proportion to the cranium from birth to eight years, thereby eliminating the "babyish" look. There is greater growth between the ages of five and eight years, especially among boys, than at any other time. If there were not this radical change in facial proportions, the adult eyes would be in approximately the middle of the face (7, 154). Changes in facial proportions from birth to adulthood are shown in Figure 4–5, page 127.

During the transition from baby to permanent teeth, there are changes in occlusion —the fitting together of the upper and lower teeth—which affect the shape of the lower part of the child's face. Malocclusion may be caused or aggravated by irregularities in the growth of the two jaws; variations in the size of the upper and lower teeth; thumb sucking, especially before the child is five years of age; mouth breathing; pressure on the chin, as in stomach sleeping during the babyhood years; or tongue biting.

Not only will malocclusion result in a poorly shaped mouth and chin, but it will also interfere with chewing and thus affect digestion. While malocclusions may correct themselves as development progresses, corrective work (orthodontics) is often necessary for the child to develop a well-shaped face with teeth and chin in correct proportions and lines (26, 75).

There are changes in the features of the face as well as in its shape. At first, the *forehead* is large, rounded, and prominent. It starts to flatten and to decrease in size, relative to the rest of the face, when the child is about five years old. The *eyes* reach their mature size as the child approaches puberty and become set farther apart as the face broadens. The narrow, slitlike *lips* of the little child gradually fill out, but they do not acquire their adult size and shape until the child has become sexually mature.

The *nose* is one of the most disproportionate of the facial features in childhood. For the first few years of the child's life, it is small and rather flat on the face. Then, from five to ten years, it grows faster than any of the other facial features. The result is that the nose is the first of the facial features to reach mature size, generally around the age of fourteen years. During this growth spurt, the cartilage framework of the nose develops, and the nose becomes larger and assumes a more definite shape (162). As the different facial features mature, the "blank look" of the young child is gradually replaced by a more "critical" expression. Individuality in facial expression increases as the features assume new shapes and proportions (192).

Proportions of the Trunk. The top-heavy development of the baby militates against good balance and must be partially corrected before he can sit, stand, or walk. As

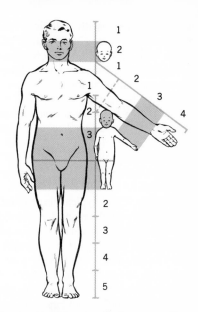

Figure 4–5. Changes in body proportion from birth to adulthood. (Adapted from P. C. Martin and E. L. Vincent, *Human development*, Ronald, 1960. Used by permission.)

the child grows older, the change in proportions essential to good balance comes about through a gradual lengthening of the trunk, legs, and neck. By the age of six years, the trunk is twice as long and twice as wide as it was at birth. From then until adolescence, body length increases approximately 50 per cent. By maturity, birth dimensions are trebled (163, 200). A baby's head literally sits on top of his shoulders; the infant has no neck. Gradually, in early childhood, he develops a short, stocky neck which blends into the sloping shoulders. Around the fifth year, the neck begins to lengthen and becomes more slender, while the shoulders become broader and more firmly molded. As the shoulders drop, with the lengthening of the neck, the weight of the child's body is more evenly distributed (192, 193).

The shape of the trunk also undergoes rapid changes. In the first year, the baby's body is thickset because of the greater increase in the girths and transverse diameters than in the length. Up to four or five years, the trunk is sacklike, with no apparent waistline and with sloping shoulders, rounded chest, and protruding abdomen. From then until the end of childhood, there is a gradual decrease in the stockiness of the trunk and a tendency toward a cone-shaped body. In this cone-shaped body, the shoulder line becomes square, the abdomen flattens, the chest broadens and flattens, the waistline is clearly indicated, and the pelvis broadens and is less vertical (26, 192).

The shape of the adult trunk is greatly influenced by the age at which sexual maturing occurs. The typical masculine figure, with broad shoulders and narrow hips, is characteristic of boys who mature later than the average. By contrast, a somewhat effeminate build, with broad hips and narrow shoulders, is more characteristic of boys who mature early. Late-maturing girls tend to have broader shoulders and hips than early-maturing girls. Regardless of the age of maturing, girls tend to have a greater enlargement in the area of the hips than boys because of the broadening of the pelvic arch (17, 163).

Proportions of Arms and Legs. Changes in proportions cause the body to become less apelike and more characteristically human. This is due to the relative increase in leg length. At birth, the legs of the infant are proportionally too short, the arms too long, and the hands and feet too small. If the adult had legs proportionate to those of the newbo n infant, for example, his hips would be just above the knee level (154). This is illustrated in Figure 4–5, page 127. Growth at different rates must, therefore, occur before mature proportions are attained.

The length of the *arms* increases between 60 and 75 per cent from birth to two years. When the child is eight years old, the arms are nearly 50 per cent longer than they were at two years. Because the arms are very thin, with no marked development in the musculature, the child has a spindly, "all arms" look. From eight until sixteen or eighteen years, growth in the length of the arms is slow, while development in shape, due to increased musculature, is taking place. The early-maturing child generally has shorter arms at maturity than the late maturer (17, 198).

The *legs* of the newborn infant are short and flexed so that the soles of the feet point toward each other. As the legs grow in length, they straighten. By the time the child is six years old, his legs and knees should be straight. During the first two years of life, the legs grow 40 per cent; at eight years, they are 50 per cent longer than at two years. Thus the legs grow at a slower rate at first than the arms. By adolescence, the legs are four times as long as at birth, and at maturity, five times as long. As is true of the arms, the legs are thin and spindly until puberty. Then, as the increase in length slows, there is a growth in the muscular development which results in a marked change in their shape. Early maturers tend to have short, stocky legs at maturity, while late maturers characteristically have long, slender legs (163).

The *hands* and *feet* of the newborn infant must increase in size as well as in muscular development before they can be used. Throughout early and middle childhood, the fingers are short and stubby because of the slow growth of the bones. The hands grow rapidly early in puberty and attain their mature size and shape by the fourteenth or fifteenth year.

The feet also have a growth spurt early in puberty, reaching their adult size at approximately the same time as the hands. There are marked individual variations in the size and shape of the feet in childhood. Boys, at every age, have larger feet than girls, and their feet reach mature size later. There is some correlation between the size of the foot and the height of the individual (198, 200).

IMPORTANCE OF CHANGES IN PROPORTIONS

There are three important consequences of the changes in body proportions that take place as the child develops. In the first place, when proportions change rapidly, there is a temporary *loss of control* over the body. The child who has mastered skills involving the use of his hands, for example, finds these skills upset when at puberty his hands start to grow larger and his short, stubby fingers become long and tapering. It is not easy for a child to revise his skills, but unless he does he will appear to be awkward and clumsy in comparison with his age-mates, and this will handicap him in his social relationships.

The second important consequence of bodily disproportions is the effect they have on *appearance*. Because beauty is judged by conformity to adult proportions, the child creates the impression that he is homely, especially in late childhood and early puberty. In the transition from baby to permanent teeth, for example, the child's mouth seems too large for the rest of the face and for the small, childish lips. When the arms and legs become long and spindly, the child has a coltlike appearance, and the hands and feet seem proportionally much too big.

In the transition from the fine-textured hair of the small child to the coarser hair of the adolescent, the hair is unmanageable and often looks shaggy. The child's contempt for grooming makes him even more homely than his disproportions otherwise would (54, 78). To boys, interest in appearance is a sign of a "sissy." As a result, they take delight in being as slovenly as parents will permit. Girls, on the other hand, begin to take an interest in their appearance as they approach puberty. Because children are little concerned about their appearance, homeliness does not bother them unless they are so homely that others comment on it (9, 202).

A child's appearance is of great concern to parents, especially to the mother. If he is not physically attractive she worries about him and seeks ways of improving his appearance—most of which the child resists or ignores. The child's appearance is likewise important to adults outside the family. It influences their treatment of him, and this,

in turn, affects the child's attitude toward other people in general and toward himself.

Children who are attractive elicit more favorable responses from adults than those who are homely. The more favorably a child is treated, the more conditioned he is to like people and to seek repetition of this favorable treatment by behaving in a manner that will guarantee it. By contrast, the unattractive child senses that he is not creating a favorable impression, and this leads to social withdrawal or socially unacceptable behavior (39).

A third consequence of asynchronous growth is that body proportions at different ages serve as important cues to the *maturational status* of the child. There is evidence that body configuration—the relationship of the different parts of the body to one another—is closely associated with maturity level. This, in turn, is an indication of readiness for school. In early childhood, when body proportions are characterized by top-heaviness, the child is too immature to be ready for what school expects of him. Should the child continue to have a top-heavy body when he reaches school age, he is likely to fail in the first grade, even though his IQ falls within the normal range. The more slender, lanky build of the older child—the characteristic body build of middle childhood—is found among those who are ready for school (192). The typical body configuration of the child who is ready for school and that of the child who is still unready are shown in Figure 4–6.

As Simon has stressed, in discussing the relationship between body configuration and level of maturity, "Physical maturity is more than skin-deep: it is reflected not only in superficial body features but in the maturational status of the central nervous system which in turn underlies such behavior as readiness to submit to restrictions and the application to tasks." The child who is overweight creates the impression that he is less mature than he actually is, while the lean, long-legged child may look unduly mature. Furthermore, there is a tendency for people to associate infantilism with a chubby build

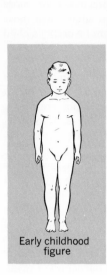
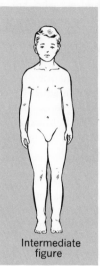
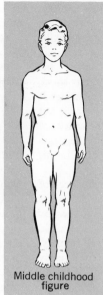

Early childhood
figure

Intermediate
figure

Middle childhood
figure

Figure 4–6. The three main body configurations in children of school age. (Adapted from M. D. Simon, Body configuration and school readiness, *Child Develpm.*, 1959, 30, 493–512. Used by permission.)

and maturity with a lean build and to treat the child in accordance with his appearance (192).

BONES

Bone development consists of growth in bone size, change in the number of bones, and change in their composition. It follows the same general trend as growth in size; that is, it is most rapid during the first year of life, then relatively slow up to the time of puberty, and then once again more rapid (92, 200).

In the early months of postnatal life, the bone tissue is soft and spongy. There is cartilage or membrane in some places where there will later be bone. The child's bones have more water and proteinlike substances and less mineral content than adult bones. They are more vascular, and more blood flows through them to supply materials for growth. The outcovering, or *periosteum,* is thick, and this prevents complicated fractures. The child's bones are not firmly knit together. Instead, there is much space between the ends of the bones. The ligaments

at the joints are longer and less firmly attached than in the adult.

Bones grow in length at the ends, the *epiphyses,* where a strip of cartilage separates the bone shaft, or *diaphysis,* from other bony masses. The original cartilage at the epiphyses is gradually converted into bone, and as long as the epiphysis and the diaphysis do not fuse, the bone will continue to grow. Stimulation by the sex hormone, at puberty, is responsible for the fusion of the two portions and, ultimately, the limitation of growth. Bones grow in width by adding new bone tissue at their outer edges (152).

OSSIFICATION

Ossification, or hardening of the bones, is entirely postnatal, beginning in the early part of the first year and ending during puberty. Ossification takes place gradually and is due to the introduction of calcium, phosphorus, and other mineral salts into the bone structure. The process of ossification begins at the "ossification center" in the cartilage and gradually spreads throughout the bone. A bone may have more than one ossification center. It is estimated that there are over eight hundred such centers in the human body, half of which do not appear until after birth. New centers continue to appear until skeletal maturity has been attained. When the process of ossification is finished, each bone has its characteristic shape (200).

Ossification proceeds at different rates for different parts of the body. The fontanels, for example, are closed in over 50 per cent of all babies by the age of eighteen months and in nearly all by two years. Ossification of the long bones of the legs, on the other hand, does not occur until puberty. There are likewise marked sex differences in rates of ossification, with girls ahead of boys at every age level. By means of X rays of the hand and wrist, it is possible to tell at what rate a child is progressing in his osseous development and to predict the approximate ages at which he will reach puberty and the maturity of his skeletal development (18, 92).

Importance of Ossification. Because the bones are soft at first, the baby's body is pliable; he can, without difficulty, get into strange positions. For example, he can put his toes in his mouth when lying on his back. In addition, the bones are liable to be deformed, through pressure, unless care is taken. The shape of the head can be flattened if the baby always sleeps on his back, or the chest can be flattened if he spends most of his sleep time on his stomach. Even in the elementary-school years, bone deformities can result from short shoes or from sitting in a cramped posture at a school desk.

Ossification is dependent largely upon the secretion of a hormone from the thyroid glands. If there is a deficiency of this hormone, the process of ossification will be delayed. There is also a close relationship between ossification and nutrition. Children from superior socioeconomic groups are accelerated in their anatomical development. If ossification is retarded because of inadequate mineralization resulting from a thyroid deficiency or a dietary deficiency, the child will have bowed legs and other skeletal deformities because the bones will not be sufficiently hard to withstand the pressure from the weight of his body (52, 152).

MUSCLES AND FAT

In addition to the weight contributed by the bones, increase in body weight comes mainly from *muscle* and *adipose,* or fatty, *tissue.* In the early years of childhood, adipose tissue develops more rapidly than muscle. From the ages of twelve to fifteen in girls and fifteen to sixteen in boys, there is a marked increase in muscle tissue. What proportion of the child's body weight will come from muscle and what from adipose tissue will depend largely upon his body type.

Children who tend toward *endomorphy* have more soft adipose tissue than muscular tissue. The tendency toward *mesomorphy,* on the other hand, means a predominance of muscle and connective tissue. In the *ectomorph,* there is not a predominance of either; the muscles are slender, and there is little adipose tissue (189). Different body types in childhood are illustrated in Figure 4–3, page 121.

Muscles. The muscles play a major role in regulating the vital organs of the body, such as the heart, the organs of the digestive system, and the glands. They are also responsible for strength and coordination of activity. At birth, muscle fibers are present in an undeveloped state. That is why the newborn infant is so helpless and his activities so weak and uncoordinated. While no new muscle fibers develop after birth, the ones that are present change in size, shape, and composition. Muscles increase in size by growth in the length, breadth, and thickness of the fibers. With growth comes an increase in weight.

For the average person, muscle weight increases fortyfold from birth to maturity. Up to five years of age, the muscles grow in proportion to the increase in body weight. Then, from five to six years, there is a rapid spurt in muscle growth, at which time the child's weight gain is approximately 75 per cent muscle weight. After this time, the growth of the muscles is relatively slow but is followed by a marked spurt at puberty.

In early childhood, the muscles contain more water and less solids and proteins than adult muscles. In addition, they are more delicate and less firmly attached to the bones. At maturity, the muscles are five or more times as thick as at birth. Their composition changes from 72 per cent water and 28 per cent solid matter to 66 per cent water and 34 per cent solid matter. Consequently, the muscles become firmer and stronger. As the muscles become stronger, the child has a strong drive for muscular activity. He is constantly on the go, is restless when forced to be inactive, and frequently overtaxes his strength.

As is true of other physical features, there are marked individual differences in the muscular equipment of children. Those who have broad, thick muscles have superior physical strength; those with smaller muscles are usually more agile and show better coordination in skilled activities. Some children have muscles that fatigue easily; others have muscles that show great endurance.

The condition of a child's muscles depends partly upon his hereditary endowment and partly upon his general health condition and the use he makes of his muscles. Even within the same child, there are temporary variations. After an illness, for example, the child's muscle tone is lowered, and he becomes fatigued easily. While differences in the muscular development of boys and girls are not marked in childhood, these differences become pronounced at puberty, when boys' muscles grow larger and stronger.

Girls, however, are superior to boys at all ages in flexibility and use of their muscles, while boys are superior in muscular strength (127).

Fat. The amount of adipose tissue a child has depends not only upon his heredity and body build but also upon his eating habits. Certain changes are related to age. From birth to nine months, there is a rapid increase in adipose tissue in all children; this is followed by an abrupt and rapid decrease up to 2½ years. The decrease slows down until approximately 5½ years and remains practically unchanged to eleven years. Then the amount of adipose tissue increases rapidly between eleven and thirteen years, the "puberty fat period." Normally, there is a decrease in the latter part of adolescence, with the result that the adolescent body becomes slender. There may, however, be an increase in body weight due to an increase in muscular tissue (198).

At every age, there are *individual differences* in the relative amounts of muscle and adipose tissue in the body. Studies of the distribution of different tissues in the leg have shown that the relation of breadth of fat to breadth of bone tends to decrease with age in males and to increase in females. In the male leg, there is more muscle, and in the female leg, more fat. Among children over thirteen years of age, sex differences become increasingly great. Differences are also associated with socioeconomic status. Because children from the superior socioeconomic groups have greater amounts of muscle mass and subcutaneous fat, they tend to be heavier from eight through eleven years of age than children from inferior socioeconomic groups. Among girls, this socioeconomic difference is especially pronounced between the ages of six and eight years (83).

EFFECTS OF AMOUNT OF FAT AND MUSCLES

The relative amounts of adipose tissue and muscles are important both directly and indirectly to the child. *Directly,* they are important because they influence the type and quality of his behavior. A child with a predominance of muscular tissue, for example, has the physique to excel in sports and games which lead to prestige in the eyes of his peers. By contrast, the "fatty," whose muscular development is overshadowed by adipose tissue, is so poor in sports and games that he fails to gain social acceptance with his peers and generally finds himself rejected or ridiculed by them.

The energy level of a child is likewise influenced by his body build. The boy with a mesomorphic build tends to be more athletic, assertive, and dominant than boys with endomorphic or ectomorphic builds (14, 89). The ectomorphic child is generally submissive either because he is easygoing or because he is too speculative to reach a decision on his own; there is a relative absence of thrust in his constitutional makeup. The endomorphic child likewise tends to be rather unassertive and easygoing (14, 89). He has a low energy level, and this is reflected in his casual and carefree behavior. As Davidson et al. have pointed out, "The anxious mother of an endomorphic child may possibly derive some consolation from realizing that her failure to make the child as careful as she would like arises, not from her own shortcoming, but from the fact that the child is just not built that way" (46).

Indirectly, the relative amounts of adipose tissue and muscles are important because of their effect on the developing personality pattern of the child. Sheldon and his associates have correlated the three basic components of physique—endomorphy, ectomorphy, and mesomorphy—with temperament components. Endomorphy, characterized by a relative predominance of digestive viscera over bone, muscle, and connective tissue, is correlated with *viscerotonia*—love of comfort, sociability, conviviality, and gluttony for food, people, and affection. Ectomorphy, characterized by poorly developed visceral and somatic (bodily) structure and slender, long, and poorly muscled extremities, is correlated with *cerebrotonia*—withdrawal from social contacts and general inhibition of somatic and visceral expression. *Somatotonia,* characterized by bodily assertiveness, love of power and risk, and a craving for muscular activity, is correlated with mesomorphy—the "athletic physique," in which bone, muscle, and connective tissue are relatively predominant (189).

While Sheldon's theory has been subjected to severe criticism, there is some evidence that body build, in its *more extreme forms,* does affect a person's characteristic method of adjusting to life. Children with endo-morphic builds, it has been reported, tend to form and borrow their attitudes in close association with their friends and acquaintances because of their indiscriminate amiability; they are "other-directed" people. By contrast, the child with an ectomorphic build works out his beliefs and life philosophy intellectually and is not influenced greatly by others; he is "inner-directed" and hence more consistent in his attitudes (210). Mesomorphic children tend to have high standards and to be meticulous in whatever they do. Like the ectomorphs, they are submissive, not because they do not care—as is characteristic of ectomorphs—but rather because they simply cannot make up their minds and, consequently, allow others to make their decisions for them. A child who rates low in mesomorphy is not likely to be made into an athlete because he has neither the necessary body build nor the temperament (46). Even among preschool children, some relationship has been found to exist between the body build of the child and his personality pattern (207).

TEETH

The child has two sets of teeth—the baby, or temporary, teeth and the permanent teeth. They differ in several important respects: (*1*) There are 20 temporary teeth and 32 permanent ones; (*2*) the temporary teeth are smaller than the permanent ones; and (*3*) the permanent teeth are of better quality and are therefore more durable. The growth of teeth is a continuous process from the third prenatal month, when the teeth begin to form in the jaw, until the wisdom teeth reach their full size, between the ages of twenty-one and twenty-five years. The eruption of the temporary teeth is accompanied by discomfort or actual pain, often causing the baby to lose his appetite and become irritable and nervous. Permanent teeth, for the most part, cut through the gums without any appreciable discomfort.

Temporary Teeth.   Ordinarily, the first of the temporary teeth makes its appearance between the sixth and eighth months, but the time of eruption is variable and depends upon health, hereditary trends, nutrition before and after birth, race, sex, and other factors. Approximately once in every 2,000 births, an infant is born with one or more teeth, usually lower central incisors. It has been estimated that only 1 per cent of white infants erupt their first tooth before they are four months old, and approximately 1 per cent not until after the first birthday. By six months, one baby out of three has at least one tooth, and by nine months, the average baby has three teeth (156, 200). Girls, as a rule, erupt their first tooth slightly before boys, but between the ages of nine months and two years, boys are generally ahead of girls.

The *sequence* of eruption of the temporary teeth is more important than the age of eruption. The lower teeth, as a rule, erupt before the upper. When there is irregularity in the sequence of eruption, it is likely to throw the jaws out of position and result in malocclusion, or poor alignment of the teeth. This may affect permanently the shape of the lower part of the face and cause even the permanent teeth to be out of line. In the fetal period, and at ten months, 2½ years, and five years of age, the temporary teeth are especially susceptible to metabolic and cellular disturbances (134).

Permanent Teeth.   Even after the temporary teeth have erupted, much activity goes on inside the gums as the permanent teeth begin to calcify. The order of calcifying is the same as the later order of eruption. On the average, the child at six years of age has one or two permanent teeth; at eight years, 10 or 11; at ten years, 14 or 16; at twelve years, 24 or 26; and at thirteen, 27 or 28. The last four of the permanent teeth, the wisdom teeth, erupt between the ages of seventeen and twenty-five years, if they appear at all.

Girls are more precocious in shedding their temporary teeth than boys. They are also more precocious in getting their permanent teeth, except the wisdom teeth. Children of subnormal intelligence get their permanent teeth more slowly than those of normal intelligence, while those of superior intelligence are slightly precocious in this area (134, 200).

Even before all the permanent teeth have erupted, most children begin to suffer from dental caries. Between the ages of six and fifteen years, the average child acquires one or two caries a year. Dental caries most often develop at times of rapid growth, when nutritional demands are greatest and when nutrition is likely to be unbalanced. During the puberty growth spurt, for example, dental caries are especially common (177).

PSYCHOLOGICAL IMPORTANCE OF TEETH

Teeth are psychologically important to a child, just as they are physiologically important. The physical discomfort accompanying the eruption of the temporary teeth is partially responsible for the heightened emotionality that begins in the latter part of the first year of life and persists into the third. While teething alone is not responsible for the disequilibrium of this age, there is no question that teething makes the baby uncomfortable and interferes with his normal patterns of eating and sleeping.

The last of the baby teeth to cut through the gums—the large molars—are most likely to make the young child uncomfortable. Their eruption occurs late in the second and early in the third years of life, at the time when the young child has gained enough control over his body to want to be independent of adult help and supervision. Being uncomfortable or in pain predisposes him to react to thwartings with greater emotional intensity than he normally would. As a result, the "good-as-gold baby" often turns into a "problem child." When parents attempt to discipline him, they frequently make him even more rebellious and more "out of focus."

While the cutting of permanent teeth is, for the most part, far less painful than the cutting of baby teeth—because most of the permanent teeth come through holes in the gums where baby teeth have been—permanent teeth are psychologically important both as an *indication of the child's maturity level* and as an insignia to others that he is growing up. As Church and Stone have pointed out, "As the child loses his baby teeth, his physical appearance alters in ways that quite accurately mirror the inner changes taking place" (35). Furthermore, with the appearance of each new permanent tooth, the child feels that he is leaving babyhood farther and farther behind and achieving a more mature status.

Because of this, many children like to hasten nature's work. When a baby tooth starts to loosen in the gum, the child will wiggle it back and forth to try to get it out. Chewing or biting with a tooth that is loose can be painful; this adds to the child's desire to get the tooth out of the gum as soon as possible. In many homes, parents help the child to shed his baby teeth by tying a string to the loose tooth and giving it a quick jerk. If it is customary for the "good fairy" to leave money under the child's pillow in place of the baby tooth that was put there before the child went to sleep, the child has an added incentive to pull out his baby teeth as soon as possible.

In spite of the satisfaction the shedding of baby teeth gives the child, hastening their shedding is a bad practice. Nature's timetable will not be speeded up just because the child wants it to be. Normally there is a relatively short time interval between the shedding of a baby tooth and the eruption of the permanent tooth that replaces it; this time interval is lengthened when the baby tooth is pulled out prematurely. As a result, there is a tendency for the jaw to shrink where there is no tooth close enough to the surface to stretch the gum. When the permanent tooth is finally ready to erupt, the space for it may be too small. This often causes the permanent tooth to come in crooked and to overlap the tooth adjacent to it. Crooked teeth may not bother the child when he is young, but it will disturb him when he reaches the *appearance-conscious stage of adolescence*. Studies of physical features which cause concern to adolescents have revealed that crooked teeth rank high on the list. Many adolescents whose teeth are unattractive because they have not come in straight try to avoid smiling; they thus create the impression that they are unfriendly or have "unpleasant personalities." Furthermore, because smiling adds to facial attractiveness, the person who consciously represses a smile to hide his crooked teeth is depriving himself of both an aid to natural beauty and an aid to social acceptance (9, 76, 187).

An even more serious consequence of premature shedding of baby teeth is the effect on *speech*. During the transitional stage from baby to permanent teeth, there is normally a gap in the front of the jaws, and few children escape *lisping*. Because the front teeth are prominent and are the ones the child is most anxious to replace with large, permanent teeth, they are the ones he is most likely to try to pull out as soon as they become loose. The longer the interval between baby and permanent teeth, the longer the period of lisping, and the less likely the habit is to disappear when permanent teeth finally erupt. Unless remedial steps are taken to correct lisping, it may become a permanent speech defect (160).

DEVELOPMENT OF THE NERVOUS SYSTEM

The growth of the nervous system is very rapid before birth and in the first 3 to 4 years after birth. Growth during the prenatal period, as was pointed out in the chapter on prenatal development, consists primarily of increase in the number and size of *nerve cells,* whereas later growth consists primarily of the development of immature cells present at birth. After the age of three or four years, growth of the nervous system proceeds at a relatively slow rate.

Brain growth cannot be studied directly but must be estimated from studying the brains of the dead or from external measurements of the cranial development of living children. These measurements show that brain growth is very rapid from birth to four years, slowing down between the ages of four and eight years and then progressing very slowly until approximately the age of sixteen years, when the mature size of the brain has been attained. Since the bones of the skull are loosely connected by membranes during the first few months of life, there is ample space for growth.

At birth, brain weight averages 350 grams, as contrasted with adult weight, which ranges from 1,260 to 1,400 grams. One-fourth of the adult brain weight is attained by birth, one-half by the age of nine months, three-fourths by the end of the second year, four-fifths by the fourth year, and 90 per cent by the age of six years. At birth, brain weight is one-eighth of body weight; at ten years, one-eighteenth; at fifteen years, one-thirtieth; and at maturity, one-fortieth. This pattern is characteristic of the growth of both the *cerebrum* and the *cerebellum.* The rate of gain in weight of both is greatest during the first two years of life. The cerebellum, which plays an important role in body balance and postural control, gains approximately 300 per cent in weight during the first year of postnatal life (200, 206).

Even though the increase in the size of the brain is very slight during adolescence, there is nevertheless continuation of development in the cortical tissues. By the eighth year, the brain is nearly its mature size, but the development of intercerebral association tracts and the building up of gray matter are far from complete. Development is thus internal and cannot be measured in terms of size or weight.

Effects of Brain Growth. The rapid growth in the size of the brain during the early years of life is one of the causes of the top-heavy look of the young child. Unless his head covering fits tightly, it tends to accentuate the disproportions of the upper part of the head and to increase his dwarf-like appearance. Manufacturers of head coverings for children today are taking this into consideration, with the result that the broadbrimmed hats, in style for children during former generations, are rarely used. Instead, the child's head is protected against cold by closely fitted caps, which do not make the head appear larger and which may, if well styled, actually make it appear smaller.

Because the cerebrum is responsible for control of mental functions, just as the cerebellum is responsible for postural control and balance, rapid growth in both these areas of the brain during the early years of life makes it possible for the baby to shift from a state of complete helplessness to relative independence within the first two years of postnatal life. This matter will be discussed in detail in the chapter on motor development. With rapid growth in size and development of the cortical tissues of the cerebrum comes rapid increase in mental abilities. While it is difficult to measure accurately the growth of intelligence with the "baby tests" now available, there is ample evidence from observations of the baby's behavior that at an early age he is capable of remembering, of associating meanings with people and objects, and of simple forms of reasoning. Each year, there is a marked increase in intellectual capacities (16).

PUBERTY CHANGES

Before childhood comes to an end, the physical changes that transform a child into a sexually mature adult begin. The time when these changes occur is known as *puberty*—from the Latin word *pubertas,* meaning "age of manhood." Contrary to popular belief, the transformation from child to adult is not a quick metamorphosis. It takes, on the average, from 2 to 4 years. Approximately one-half of puberty overlaps the last part of childhood, and approximately one-half overlaps the early part of adolescence. These two parts of puberty are usually called "preadolescence" and "early adolescence." In preadolescence, the child is not, strictly speaking, a child, nor is he an adolescent. He is often referred to as a

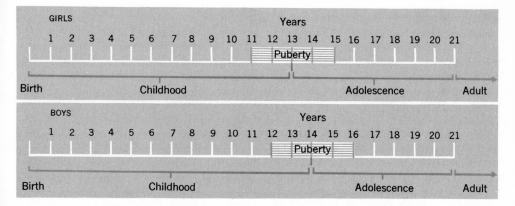

Figure 4–7. Overlap of childhood, puberty, and adolescence.

"pubescent child." Figure 4–7 shows the overlap of puberty, childhood, and adolescence.

Girls, on the average, become sexually mature at thirteen years, when the first menstruation—the *menarche*—occurs. From eleven to thirteen years, many physical changes take place. After the menarche, other changes occur, and those begun earlier are completed. Boys reach sexual maturity —as indicated by the first "nocturnal emission"—at an average age of fourteen years. Puberty changes begin to take place in boys between the ages of twelve and fourteen and are not completed until sixteen or seventeen (151, 180).

CAUSES OF PUBERTY

Until the turn of the present century, the cause or causes of puberty changes were unknown. It was known that puberty occurred at a predictable time and that the body changes of puberty followed a predictable pattern. Today it is known that the puberty changes are caused by an increase in the activity of two glands of the endocrine system, the pituitary gland and the gonads. The *pituitary* gland, located at the base of the brain, produces two hormones closely associated with these changes: the *growth hormone,* which is responsible for growth in body size, and the *gonadotropic—*

or "gonad-stimulating"—*hormone,* which stimulates the gonads to greater activity. Shortly before puberty begins, there is a gradual increase in the release of these two hormones; the increase becomes greater as puberty progresses (176).

The *gonads* are the sex glands of the human reproductive system. In the female they are the *ovaries,* and in the males, the *testes.* While these glands are present and active from the time of birth, their activity is increased at puberty by the gonadotropic hormone from the pituitary gland. This results in marked physical as well as psychological and behavioral changes in the child. Shortly after the child becomes sexually mature, hormones from the gonads stop the activity of the growth hormone; this ends physical growth. If there is a normal balance in the interrelationship between the pituitary gland and the gonads, there will be a normal physical development in the child (120, 126).

Individual Differences.   Owing to variations in the functioning of the endocrine glands, there are differences *between the sexes* and between members of the same sex in age of sexual maturing and in the time needed for it. Girls not only begin puberty earlier than boys but, in general, require less time to complete the puberty changes. As a result, there are differences in the size and appearance of boys and girls at the end of childhood, especially between the ages of twelve and fourteen years, with girls larger and more mature in appearance and behavior (17).

Girls, on the average, require approximately 3 years to complete the puberty changes and are less variable than boys, who require, on the average, from 2 to 4 years. Furthermore, girls are more nearly their adult size when they become sexually mature than boys. As they grow older and approach physical maturity, boys tend to be mesomorphic in physique, while girls tend to be endomorphic. Girls who mature earlier than the average are more endomorphic in body build in adolescence than girls who mature at the average age or slightly later than the average (3, 134, 216).

Within each sex group, heredity, intelligence, physical condition, and many other factors play important roles in determining when sexual maturing will begin. Children from the temperate zones, for example, mature earlier than those from tropical or arctic zones. Urban children tend to mature earlier than rural children. A superior socioeconomic status, with its accompaniments of better medical care and better nutrition during the growth years, favors early maturing (64, 130).

Age of maturing is markedly influenced by the body build of the child. The child with an endomorphic build—a feminine-type body, with broad hips and short legs—is likely to mature earlier than the average, while the child with an ectomorphic build—slender body, broad shoulders, and long legs—usually begins his puberty changes later than the average. Like the endomorphic child, the one whose build is muscular and compact—the mesomorph—is slightly earlier than the average in reaching puberty. Obese children generally reach puberty about a year earlier than those whose weight is more nearly normal. No significant differences have been found in age of sexual maturing in Negro and white children (98, 103, 130, 214).

The time needed to complete the puberty changes varies according to the age at which puberty begins and according to the body build of the child. The late-maturing child, once he starts to mature, generally completes the puberty changes more rapidly than the child who begins puberty at the average age and often even more rapidly than the early maturer (108, 180). Children with endomorphic builds take longer to complete puberty than those of ectomorphic or mesomorphic builds. Among boys, it has been found that the fatter the boy, the slower the rate of maturing (103). *Variations in the pattern* of maturing likewise occur as a result of rate and age of maturing. The late-maturing child who matures rapidly has rather abrupt spurts of growth, whereas slow-maturing and early-maturing children grow at a more even rate and have less organic imbalance. In the late maturer, growth tends to be irregular and asymmetrical, with growth of the body dimensions and the internal organs lagging behind growth in stature (18).

TYPES OF CHANGE

During puberty, the entire body goes through a metamorphosis, both externally and internally, in structure as well as in function. Because the changes follow, for the most part, a predictable timetable, one knows what to expect at different stages. The changes are most rapid and most pronounced during the early part of puberty. In the latter part, there is a tapering off of the speed and a completion of the changes begun earlier. Accompanying and paralleling the speed of the physical changes are changes in attitudes and behavior.

The physical changes taking place during puberty may be grouped into four categories: (*1*) changes in body size, (*2*) changes in body proportions, (*3*) changes in the primary sex characteristics, and (*4*) the development of secondary sex characteristics.

1. Changes in Body Size. After the slow and even growth of the major part of childhood, there is a sudden increase in the tempo of growth about 2 years before the child becomes sexually mature. This tempo speeds up in the year preceding sexual maturity—the "apex" of the pubescent growth spurt. It is not unusual for a child to grow 4 to 6 inches during this year and to gain between 10 and 20 pounds. Once sexual maturity has been attained, the growth spurt begins to slow down (198).

Boys, however, continue to grow at a more rapid tempo than girls, with the result that, for the first time in their lives, they are taller and heavier than girls. If the child matures at approximately the average age, growth will be complete or nearly complete for girls at eighteen years and, for boys, at nineteen or twenty years. During the puberty growth spurt, there is an average increase in height of 25 per cent and a doubling of weight (18, 134).

Because there are marked individual differences in the age at which puberty begins, in the rate of development of the puberty changes, and in the time when adult size is achieved, there will be marked individual differences in the heights and weights of children from approximately twelve to fourteen years of age (140). Children who mature early or whose sexual maturation occurs at a more rapid rate than the average appear to be much larger in comparison with their agemates than they will later be. Their growth slows down as the growth of their agemates accelerates, however, and by the time all have completed their sexual maturation, variations in size are less conspicuous than they were at the end of childhood.

2. Changes in Body Proportions. The disproportions characteristic of the child's body increase in certain areas and decrease in others as the different parts of the body gradually attain their mature size and shape. Not until the puberty changes have been completed will all parts of the body be at their mature levels and, hence, in the right proportions. In the face, for example, the nose reaches its mature size and shape before the mouth and jaws. Thus, in the child's profile, the upper part of the face protrudes, and the chin recedes. Similarly, the hands and feet become mature in size and shape before the arms and legs, giving the child the appearance of being "all hands and feet" until the growth of his arms and legs catches up (198).

Changes in proportions occur in the interior of the body as well as on the surface. In childhood, for example, the heart is small, while the veins and arteries are large. After the puberty changes have taken place, the reverse is true. Furthermore, the veins are smaller in relation to the arteries in childhood than in adolescence. The young child's tubular-shaped stomach, which lies transversely in the body, becomes baglike in shape and more vertical in position at puberty. As a result, it can hold more food and does not empty as quickly as in childhood (105, 206).

3. Primary Sex Characteristics. The sex organs, or "primary sex characteristics," are small and functionally immature in childhood. Shortly before or at the time the growth spurt begins, they start to enlarge in both boys and girls. Because the girl's sex organs are within her body, the only indication of their growth is that her abdomen seems to protrude. In boys, on the other hand, the sex organs are mainly on the exterior of the body, and their growth is readily apparent to the child.

As is true of the other parts of the body, nature has a timetable for the development of the sex organs. The *testes,* or male sex glands, grow in size rapidly at the beginning of puberty and are ready to function a year or two later—at an average age of fourteen years. Shortly after the testes start their growth spurt, the penis, which has been small throughout the early years of childhood, begins to grow first in length and then in circumference (66). At the beginning of puberty, the female sex glands—the *ovaries* —also begin a growth spurt. Proof of their functional maturity is the menarche, which occurs at an average age of thirteen and which marks the end of childhood and the beginning of adolescence. Shortly after the spurt in growth of the ovaries begins, there is also a period of rapid growth of the uterus and other parts of the female reproductive apparatus. Because their development lags behind that of the ovaries, however, the reproductive apparatus is not ready for childbearing for several months or even a year or more after the menarche. This interval is known as the period of "adolescent sterility" (166).

4. Secondary Sex Characteristics.   The secondary sex characteristics are the physical features which distinguish the male from the female body. They are called "secondary" because, unlike the sex organs, they have no direct relationship to reproduction. They, too, follow a predictable pattern of development. At the beginning of puberty, when the primary sex characteristics begin their growth spurt, the secondary sex characteristics likewise begin to develop. They complete their development during the first 2 or 3 years of adolescence. The girl who is mature at the average age of thirteen years has the body of a young woman when she is fifteen or sixteen years old; the average boy has the body of a young man between the ages of sixteen and seventeen years.

Of the many secondary sex characteristics to develop at puberty, the most important are the growth of hair on the body and face, the development of the female breasts and hips, the change in voice from the high pitch of the child to the low pitch of the adult, the development of muscles—especially in the shoulders, arms, and legs—and the change from the thin, transparent skin of the child to the thicker and less transparent skin of the adult. Even though these physical changes are incomplete when childhood draws to a close, they are so well advanced that boys are easily distinguished from girls in appearance; the entire contour of their bodies is different (176, 183).

Effects of Puberty Changes.   Physical changes are always accompanied by changes in behavior and attitudes. When the changes are widespread and rapid, as in puberty, the effects are so pronounced that the established pattern of the child's life is disturbed.

The child feels uncertain, insecure, and confused. This leads to behavior that is unpredictable and often unsocial. For that reason, puberty is often called the "negative phase." The term "phase" suggests that this behavior is of only short duration. As the tempo of growth slows down and as the body changes near completion, there is a gradual improvement in behavior. The child is adjusting to his new body and his new feelings (67, 78, 176).

Because the most rapid growth and development occur before the child is sexually mature, the most difficult part of the negative phase comes at the end of childhood. While some of the effects persist into the early part of adolescence, they wane rapidly. In girls, for example, the worst part of the negative phase is over by the time of the menarche. Furthermore, the behavioral and attitudinal changes accompanying puberty often *seem* worse than they actually are because they follow so closely a period of good social and emotional adjustment (45, 78).

Physical and Social Causes.   The changes in behavior and attitudes during puberty come from social as well as from physical causes. Which is more important is still a matter of conjecture, although it seems likely that the physical factors are more important in bringing about behavioral changes, while the social factors are mainly responsible for bringing about changes in attitudes. Exactly what role each set of factors plays in determining the form and severity of changes is still unknown.

On the *physical* side, it is known that there is a temporary upset in body homeostasis—as shown in rise in blood pressure, basal metabolic rate, and pulse rate—in the early part of puberty. This upset is especially pronounced in both sexes during the year before sexual maturity, though it is more dramatically shown in the girl just before the menarche. The more rapid the growth and development in the early part of puberty, the greater the upset in homeostasis (55, 58). There is evidence that some of the stresses and strains occurring at puberty are traceable to poor eating habits, which affect nutritional status (172). Changes in the endocrine balance, resulting from the increased activity of the pituitary gland and the gonads, contribute to the upset in homeostasis (2, 55, 58, 176). Furthermore, there is evidence that the heterosexual drive —directing the pubescent child's interests, thoughts, and actions to exploratory behavior toward members of the opposite sex —is an endocrine-motivated force. What form the interests, thoughts, and actions will take is largely a matter of learning; this is affected by social pressures (182).

Social influences are sometimes even more important than physical factors. As the child grows bigger and increasingly resembles an adult, there will be changes in his status in the group—in what the social group in the home, the school, and the community expect of him—and in his relationship with members of the opposite sex. Concern about his changing body and how others feel about his body; concern about his relationship with peers of both sexes; and concern about his ability to behave in an approved adult way are largely the result of social expectations and social pressures. In no instance is this more apparent than in the pubescent girl's attitude toward menstruation. What the social group with which she is identified thinks about menstruation will determine, to a large extent, what her own attitude will be (2, 174). That much of the changed behavior and attitudes comes from social rather than physical causes may be seen in the fact that *they persist* even after the body changes of puberty have been completed and homeostasis has been restored (55, 67).

Common Effects on Behavior and Attitudes. While puberty affects all children differently, certain behavioral and attitudinal changes at this time are almost universal. Some of these are physical in origin, and others come from cultural pressures. Typically, the pubescent child's behavior shows outward expressions of tension in the form of restlessness, moodiness, fits of depression, withdrawal from family and friends, a desire for solitude,

irritability, rebellion against authority, assertion of independence, touchiness, critical attacks on others, disinclination to work at home or in school, and a generalized state of unhappiness (89, 118).

As a result of glandular changes and changes in the size and position of the internal organs, the pubescent child suffers at times from such physical disturbances as digestive upsets, finicky appetite, headaches, backache, and a general feeling of wretchedness. On the whole, these disturbances are more common in girls than in boys, though few boys escape them completely. These physical disturbances do not predispose the pubescent child to behave in a socially acceptable way. Furthermore, he is often anemic, owing more to poor eating habits than to marked changes in blood chemistry. This leads to listlessness and predisposition to emotional tension (177, 182).

Most children look forward to the time when they will be grown up and have the freedom adulthood brings, but they usually find that growing up is a difficult and tension-producing process. This comes, in part, from the fact that they are not feeling up to par physically and, in part, from the concerns that growing up brings. These concerns are largely caused by an ignorance of the normal pattern of puberty and of the time needed to mature. They are often intensified by the gap between what children had hoped to be and what they see happening to their bodies in the transformation process. Furthermore, if they deviate in any way from their agemates, they wonder if they are "normal." They become excessively modest and attempt to keep their bodies so completely covered that their friends will not see how well or how poorly developed they are (9, 167).

Having a rather definite concept of what is sex-appropriate in appearance—based on the movies, comics, television programs, or examples set by people they yearn to be like—children are concerned when they see how far below their ideals of sex-appropriateness they fall. Not realizing that they are still unfinished products of a slow maturational process, they fear that they will be sex-inappropriate in appearance for the rest of their lives (170, 176). Furthermore, they are greatly concerned about the conspicuous disproportions of certain features, such as the nose, the hands, and the feet. As long as disproportions exist, children realize that they cannot hope to measure up to their anticipated attractiveness. Improvement in the self-concept normally occurs as the body becomes more adult and attractive, but the pubescent child is likely to be dissatisfied with himself because he is dissatisfied with his appearance (99, 117).

Some of the *sex differences* in negative-phase behavior may be traced to the fact that girls, as a whole, are less satisfied with their appearances and with the role society expects them to play as they grow up than boys are. Girls become very much concerned about their developing bodies, and as they develop into women, they begin to feel that the days of equality between the sexes ended with childhood. The girls' gripes and fears about accepting the feminine role and their resentments against boys whose roles they consider more favorable tend to lead to menstrual discomforts not found among women of primitive cultures, where acceptance of the feminine role is accompanied by a more favorable attitude (95, 161, 176).

Long-term Effects.   If the unfavorable effects of puberty on behavior and attitudes were merely temporary and could be counted on to disappear when homeostasis was restored, they would not be serious, although this would still be an unhappy period for the child and a difficult time for all who had to live and work with him. The child does not automatically "outgrow" the undesirable personality traits or behavior patterns, however. Studies have revealed that these traits are persistent and that they often grow worse with the passage of time (116). This subject will be discussed in Chapter 9 in connection with the patterns of social behavior characteristically found among pubescent children.

The most serious and the most persistent of the unfavorable effects of puberty come from deviant age of sexual maturing. On the whole, the late maturer is more likely to be psychologically damaged than the early maturer, though neither will necessarily escape without some damage. This, likewise, will be discussed in detail in Chapter 9. Furthermore, deviant sexual development affects boys and girls differently, both at puberty and afterward. For boys, early maturing is socially advantageous, while for girls, it is not. Superior height, weight, and strength add to a boy's athletic ability and give him prestige in the eyes of peers of both sexes. By comparison, the early-maturing girl often acquires the reputation of being "fast." This affects her social adjustments then as well as later. The late-maturing girl escapes these social problems, while the late-maturing boy is deprived of the sources of recognition and prestige that come from being a good athlete (62, 170). Figure 4–8 shows the effects of early and late maturing on boys and girls.

HEALTH CONDITIONS

Good health is essential to normal growth. The child whose health is poor—even though he may not be actually ill—is handicapped in both his mental and physical development. Illness that has a damaging effect on the child's body likewise leaves scars on his personality. His personality, in turn, may predispose him to illness or intensify or prolong an already existing illness. There is evidence that serious and prolonged illness influences the child's attitude toward himself and affects the quality of his behavior in all areas of life. Furthermore, poor health always upsets homeostasis; this is reflected in the quality of the child's behavior and in his attitudes (41, 154).

Health conditions in childhood are closely associated with the *socioeconomic status* of the family. Poor general health conditions are common among children from the lower-income classes because their diets are often poor during the growth years. A comparison of elementary-school children whose diets were rated as either good or poor showed that the group with good diets was superior

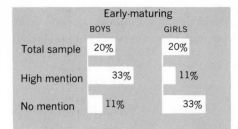
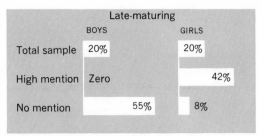

Figure 4–8.   Social recognition among boys and girls who are early and late maturers. (Adapted from M. C. Jones, A study of socialization patterns at the high school level, *J. genet. Psychol.*, 1958, 93, 87–111. Used by permission.)

in physical status, dental status, days absent because of illness, and educational ratings and was outstandingly superior in social adjustments (176, 177).

Good and Poor Health. The child's general health condition is shown in his appearance as well as in the quality and quantity of his behavior. In a *healthy* child, the mucous membranes (especially of the lips) are definitely pink; the facial expression is happy, often radiant; smiling is frequent; the eyes are bright and responsive; the skin is smooth and elastic; the limbs are rounded because of a sufficient layer of subcutaneous fat; the muscles are well formed, and their tonus is good; the stance is well balanced, erect, and graceful; the limb muscles are almost straight; the spine is straight; the shoulder girdles do not droop; the arches of the feet are well formed; and the movements of the limbs and body in walking and running are characterized by elasticity, vigor, and poise.

By contrast, the child whose health is *poor* is either underweight or soft and flabby; his posture is poor, his shoulders are rounded, his legs tend to be bowed, and his teeth are carious. The healthy child is full of energy and anxious to be on the go; he shows an alertness that is rarely seen in the child whose health is poor. When given a choice of play activities, the healthy child will choose those which require bodily activity. The child in poor health will select sedentary activities, such as watching television or going to the movies (26, 200).

At certain times during the growing-up years, children are characteristically healthy, and at others they are characteristically unhealthy. During babyhood, diseases are frequent and sometimes fatal. Susceptibility to disease is marked from three to six or eight years of age. Most boys and girls at this age are subject to a series of quarantines for different childhood diseases, such as mumps, measles, or chicken pox. Normally, the period from six or eight years to the onset of puberty is a very healthy age, when physical strength and endurance are adequate to permit the boy or girl to engage in active play for hours at a time without noticeable fatigue.

According to Bayer and Snyder, "Every period of childhood has its special health hazards, none of them . . . too serious when ordinary care is given. Only a small percentage of children become afflicted with permanent ill health" (13). Although modern medical methods, immunization, and new drugs have resulted in a marked decrease in infant and child mortality, the mortality rates are still high during the first year of life, especially toward the end of that year.

Respiratory illnesses cause most deaths during the first year, though there are seasonal fluctuations in the incidence of these illnesses. The next most common causes of death in the first year of life are gastrointestinal disturbances. Among children of school age, cardiovascular diseases and cancer cause more deaths than all the infectious and parasitic diseases—whooping cough,

measles, influenza, diphtheria, or poliomyelitis (121, 154).

Variations in Health. Just as there are certain children who are more "accident-prone"
than others, so are there those who are more
"illness-prone." They seem to have more
than their due share of illness and to be
sicker, when they are ill, than other children. Studies of illness-prone children have
revealed that the cause may be physical or
psychological. Children who had a poor prenatal environment or whose birth was difficult have the most trouble adjusting to postnatal life (158). Children whose nutrition is
good, before and after birth, tend to be
healthier and less illness-prone than those
whose nutrition is poor. Birth order has
been found to contribute to illness-proneness,
with first-born children less subject to illness
than those born later (154, 177).

That psychological factors are important
in predisposing a child to illness is apparent
from the fact that young babies who are
nervous and high-strung have great difficulty adjusting to postnatal life; they experience more feeding difficulties and digestive
disturbances than less nervous babies (195).
Young children brought up by authoritarian
child-training methods tend to be more nervous and sickly than those brought up by
more democratic methods (128). If the
child is deprived of "mothering" during the
early years of life, he is likely to have more
illness then and as he grows older than the
child whose home life has been emotionally
more normal (175, 184). That emotional
and social problems contribute to illness-
proneness has been shown by a study of
adults in which it was found that those who
had difficulties in their interpersonal relationships and were preoccupied with their
own problems were more vulnerable to illness than those who made better social adjustments, finding their lives interesting,
satisfying, and varied (100).

Common Childhood Illnesses. While children may and do contract almost every kind
of illness, certain illnesses may be regarded
as "typical" of given ages. Figure 4–9 shows
graphically the most common illnesses at
different times during the growth years.
Colds and upper-respiratory infections are
most common at all ages. Communicable
diseases, such as measles and chicken pox,
are most common in the elementary-school
years, while gastrointestinal disturbances
and allergies are especially frequent in
babyhood and adolescence. Allergic reactions, such as milk rash, hives, and asthma,
are found at every age, and few children
escape them. Tuberculosis, heart diseases,
rheumatic fever, and cancer are less common than other diseases but are more prevalent than is popularly realized (13, 204).
Diseased tonsils and adenoids are less frequent in adolescence than in childhood
owing to the fact that these conditions are
generally cared for in childhood. Girls show
a higher average incidence of most diseases
than boys, especially as they approach adolescence, when they have less interest in
various body-building activities than boys.
Girls also suffer more from gastrointestinal
disturbances and endocrine symptoms. While
first-born children do not have more illnesses than later-born children, they do
suffer more from gastrointestinal upsets,
feeding disorders, constipation, stomach disorders, allergies, and asthma. It has been
suggested that this may be due to the tensions of overanxious "new" parents (13,
125).

Imaginary Illnesses. All children at some
time or other complain of "not feeling well"
in order to escape an unpleasant duty or
avoid punishment. How well developed
imaginary invalidism is in childhood has not
yet been determined. It unquestionably occurs more frequently during adolescence
than during childhood. In an analysis of
physical complaints without organic basis,
it was found that pains were rarely simulated for gaining attention. In most cases,
complaints of illness were used to ameliorate
distressing or intolerable situations. A wide
range of physical disturbances, such as
anorexia nervosa, enuresis, diabetes, asthma,
allergy reactions, and ulcerative colitis, are
a reflection of the relationship between the

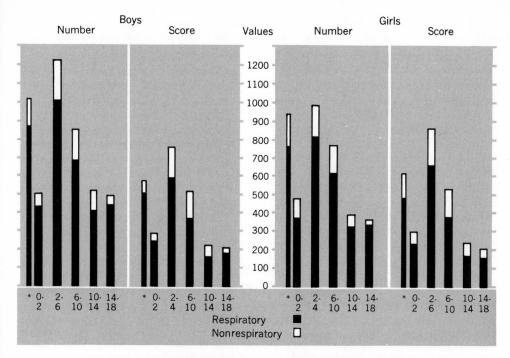

Figure 4–9.   Common illnesses at different ages in childhood. (Adapted from I. Valadian, H. C. Stuart, and R. B. Reed, Studies of illness of children followed from birth to eighteen years, *Monogr. Soc. Res. Child Develpm.*, 1961, 26, No. 1. Used by permission.)

child and his parents or of the child's interpretation of this relationship (26, 119).

Effects of Illness.   Regardless of whether an illness is physical or psychological in origin, chronic or transitory, mild or intense and prolonged by unfavorable attitudes stemming from the illness itself or from the attitudes of significant people in the child's life, it brings changes in development, behavior, attitudes, and personality. How severe and how lasting the influence of the illness will be is dependent largely on the child's attitude. His attitude, in turn, is markedly affected by the attitudes of parents. When parental attitudes toward a child's illness are wholesome and when family life is carried on in a regular fashion, the child's attitude toward his illness will be far more normal than when his parents regard his illness as a family calamity or

blame him for the inconvenience he has caused (115).

It has been found, for example, that the severity of asthma is influenced more by the overprotective attitude of mothers than by the presence of house dust or other allergy-producing stimuli. When a disease is known to be fatal—as in the case of leukemia and other cancerous diseases—parental attitudes are understandably pessimistic. This affects the child's adjustment to his illness. When there is hope of recovery, on the other hand, parents tend to take a more favorable attitude toward the child's illness (143, 169).

Studies have revealed many specific effects of illness. *Physical growth* and *development* may be affected, depending upon the severity, length, and nature of the illness. Any illness, no matter how slight, usually causes a temporary loss in weight. A long and severe illness may adversely affect the child's

ultimate height, especially if the illness coincides with a period of relatively rapid
growth. Ordinary illnesses, on the other
hand, have no permanent measurable effect
upon the growth of the older child and little
if any on the preschool child (88, 200).

The growth of the bones and the maturity of the skeleton may be affected by a
severe and prolonged illness. Certain illnesses may cause scars to appear on the
bones, and others, such as rickets and poliomyelitis, generally cause bone deformities.
Because of inactivity during illness, the
muscles lose some of their tone, become
flabby, and are easily fatigued. Anemia is a
common aftermath of illness, especially
when the illness has been severe. While most
of the physical effects of illness are temporary, certain illnesses have permanent
effects, such as a damaged heart following
rheumatic fever or damage to the brain
from encephalitis (26, 154).

Illness always causes an upset in homeostasis and is normally accompanied by
heightened *emotionality.* The sick child is
fretful, irritable, and subject to anxieties and
temper tantrums not ordinarily experienced
when he is well. Should the illness be serious
enough to necessitate hospitalization, his
anxieties and fretfulness will be heightened.
A long hospitalization results in emotional
deprivation for the child. Not having the
love and affection he has been accustomed
to at home, he withdraws into himself and
develops a hostility toward what he considers a cold and unaccepting environment.
These attitudes persist and affect the child's
personality and socialization even after he
returns to his normal environment (88,
181).

There is no doubt that prolonged illness
will affect the child's status in the social
group. The child who is segregated from the
social group fails to learn patterns of *social
behavior* at the time his peers are learning
them. Because he is likely to be pampered at
home during his illness, he may have unhealthy attitudes about his own importance
when he returns to the social group. Furthermore, because social contacts in childhood are mainly in play, the child who has

been ill has not had the opportunity to learn
new play skills or to practice old ones. Consequently, when he returns to the social
group, he discovers that he cannot keep up
with the standards the group has acquired
during his illness and that he is not considered an acceptable playmate any longer.
Prolonged or frequent illness during childhood can play havoc with a child's socialization (24, 86).

Even though a sick child may receive special help from his parents or teachers, his
school work generally suffers. The longer he
remains ill and the more severe the illness is,
the greater its effect is likely to be. Furthermore, the child whose illness has resulted in
a decrease in social acceptance or actual rejection by his former playmates will have
less interest in school and less desire to do
well in his school work than formerly. Even
an illness too minor to keep the child away
from school—diseased tonsils and adenoids
or malnutrition—will have a profound effect
on the quality of his school work. Not feeling up to par physically, he will not do the
work he is capable of doing (63, 112, 199).

Illness of any kind *limits the child's activities.* He is not permitted to join in the play
of his peers, to go to the movies with them,
or even to go to school or Sunday school.
While he is recovering from an illness, he
may be permitted to engage in some of his
former activities but is restricted in others.
This is frustrating to children of all ages. It
is especially so for older children, for whom
play with their peers is important. Even the
opportunity to miss school and the special
attention they receive at home will not compensate for what they are missing at school.
The child who is unsure of his status in the
group becomes apprehensive and anxious
about being away and fears that his absence
may cause the loss of what status he now
has (137).

Illness may be the starting point for *behavior difficulties,* especially eating and
social-adjustment problems. Having had
their eating likes and dislikes catered to
during illness, many children want this to
continue after they are well. Because parents
often coax or bribe a convalescent child to

eat—in the belief that this will speed up his recovery—it is not surprising that the child will wait to be coaxed or bribed even after he has recovered from the illness. Many children, especially when they are young, become accustomed to special attention during illness. The result is that they become aggressive and demanding (146). Furthermore, the routine of the child's life and the responsibilities he has had to assume are, of necessity, interrupted during illness. Should the illness last for several months, the child will be thoroughly "spoiled" unless precautions are taken to avoid it. If he is spoiled, his unfavorable social attitude and behavior patterns will bring social neglect or social rejection from his former playmates.

Illness during the childhood years frequently leads to *personality disturbances,* especially if the illness is prolonged or if it interferes with the child's social adjustments. Prolonged illness frequently impairs motivation and affects the child's self-confidence in new situations. The child becomes "mousy," shy, and retiring when he is with other children. The personality changes accompanying a prolonged illness may also intensify and prolong the illness. A study of the breathing difficulties of patients with spinobulbar or bulbar poliomyelitis, for example, has revealed that all experienced some emotional disturbances stemming from the illness, but those who were emotionally unstable before the illness showed greater emotional reaction to their breathing difficulties than those who were more stable (93, 199).

Some illnesses affect personality more seriously than others, especially if they occur during childhood, when the personality pattern is in the formative stage. Studies have revealed that children who suffer from severe asthma attacks have personality disorders, the most serious of which are emotional and dependency problems. When young children suffer from asthma, they become overly dependent and show fears of separation from their mothers. In older children, dependency problems are manifested in an unwillingness to be alone and an intense need to cling to someone. Because

these dependency needs are rarely met successfully, asthmatic children are likely to be depressed and anxious (94, 129).

In order to determine whether the personality syndrome associated with asthma—overanxiety, lack of self-confidence, deep-seated dependency, and a high incidence of psychoneurotic difficulties and behavior problems—is due to psychological or physiological causes, asthmatics have been compared with cardiacs, whose illness is physical in origin. Much the same personality syndrome was found in the two groups. This led to the conclusion that children suffering from *any* chronic illness, whether physical or psychological in origin, "display an emotional pattern that deviates from the normal" (172).

Allergies, like asthma, are chronic and have much the same effect on personality. Allergic children frequently block their outgoing hostilities and turn them toward themselves. When allergies that cause a child to be fretful, irritable, and quarrelsome are controlled, much nervous tension is removed, parental attitudes become more favorable, and there is a marked improvement in the child's personality (36).

Children suffering from diabetes experience tension and anxiety which leads to frustrations when they try to conform to the demands of their social environment. As a result of these frustrations, they become aggressive and often turn their frustrations outward rather than on themselves. Instead of glossing over or denying a frustration, they are apt to emphasize it. Severely diabetic children show a precocious maturity of behavior because they must assume considerable responsibility for taking their medication and for controlling their impulses to eat (20, 114).

PHYSICAL DEFECTS

Physical defects, even when slight, place limitations on the child. Because of this, "any kind of physical defect is a definite mental hazard" (178). Among the most common physical defects of children are

The attitudes of other people toward a child's defect color the child's attitude. (Standard Oil Co., N.J.)

dental caries, visual and auditory impairments, orthopedic disabilities, central-nervous-system disorders, heart disturbances, speech defects, harelips, cleft palates, facial or bodily birthmarks, abnormalities of physique (such as webbed fingers, cross-eyes, hunchbacks, obesity, or excessive thinness), and scars or contractures resulting from burns (200).

Some of these defects the child is born with. They may be hereditary, or they may come from an unfavorable prenatal environment or an injury during birth itself. Others are acquired as a result of illness or accident. While most defects are physical in origin, a few, such as stuttering and slurring, are psychosomatic in that they are mental

or emotional in origin. This subject will be discussed in detail in Chapter 6, Speech Development (138, 166, 186).

Few people at any age are completely free from physical defects. Some defects can be cured or minimized, some can be covered up so that other people do not know about them, and some become progressively worse with time. More children are crippled before six or seven years of age than later; boys are more often disabled than girls; and more children of the poorer socioeconomic groups are crippled than those of other groups. Some ailments, such as teeth defects, diseased tonsils and adenoids, speech and hearing defects, and defects resulting from malnutrition, show a decline with age. Others, such as visual defects, heart conditions, hormonal defects, and orthopedic defects, including defects of the feet and posture, increase with age (12).

EFFECTS OF PHYSICAL DEFECTS

Throughout the ages, people with physical defects have realized that they were different and have been beset with feelings of inferiority or inadequacy. Scientific attention was first directed to this problem by Alfred Adler. According to his theory of "organ inferiority," neurosis and other manifestations of maladjustment are compensations for organ inferiority. Adler further claimed that feelings of inferiority, stemming from organ inferiority, lead to a desire to excel. This gives rise to the "will to power," a common form of compensation for an inferiority complex. Stated in another way, a child who suffers from a physical defect develops an inferiority complex; because such a complex gives the child little happiness or satisfaction, he compensates for it by trying to achieve prestige, superiority, or fame—all of which will give him the satisfaction denied by his physical handicap (4).

While it is unquestionably true that *some* children do try to compensate for a physical defect by intellectual success or by gaining prestige in the eyes of the peer group in some other way, this is certainly not universally true. On the contrary, *most* children who suffer from feelings of inadequacy develop unhealthy personality patterns which lead to poor personal and social adjustment. They are more likely to develop neuroses and other manifestations of maladjustment than to achieve success. Furthermore, studies of children, adolescents, and adults have shown that the effects of physical defects will depend on how much the defects limit activities, on how other people react to the defects, and on how the defects affect the self-concepts of the disabled people themselves.

Variations in Effects. All children are psychologically damaged by a physical defect, but the extent of the damage varies markedly. As Lemkau has pointed out, "Every handicapped child is a child deprived of certain experiences. The range of the deprivation goes from that experienced by a bed-fast, blind, and deaf idiot—about the maximum deprivation compatible with life —to that experienced by a child with a slight limp deprived only perhaps of being able to win a foot race" (139).

Of the many factors that influence the effect of physical defects on children, the following are most significant.

Type of Defect. The type of defect the child has, as well as its severity, will influence the child's reaction to it. His reaction, in turn, will determine how serious the effects will be. A child who has rheumatic fever, for example, and is left with a heart condition that requires a long convalescence and makes it impossible for him to engage in activities with other children will be more affected psychologically than a child whose only defect is poor eyesight that can be corrected by wearing glasses.

The better the defect can be camouflaged, the less revision the child will have to make in his body-image and the less serious, in turn, its effect will be (208). An analysis of figure drawings made both before and after corrective surgery by people suffering from facial disfigurements revealed dramatic changes in some and less change in others. In general, however, there was an improvement in the individual's attitude toward himself as a result of improvement in his appearance (1).

Timing of Defect. If crippling occurs early in life, the child can adjust to the dependence necessitated by the crippling better than he can if it occurs after he has learned to be independent (41). A study of the psychological concomitants of amputation in children has revealed that children under eight years of age are less sensitive to the social appraisal of their defect than older children. Children with congenital amputations are the least affected because they do not have to change and reconstruct their self-concepts. The more recent the amputation, the more traumatic its effect will be on the child (41, 190). If a person has always had a facial disfigurement, it "occupies a central role in the development of his self-concept" (1). Should the disfigurement be acquired at an age when appearance is very important, however—as in adolescence—it will have a more damaging effect than if acquired when appearance is less important— as in the preschool years (147).

Limitations Caused by Defect.   The degree of restriction of activity will greatly influence the child's attitude toward his defect. His attitude, in turn, will influence the effect it has on him. The child who is blind or crippled, for example, will be more restricted than the child who is deaf or suffers from a facial disfigurement. When a physical defect magnifies the child's difficulties in gaining social acceptance, its psychological damage is greater (41, 65).

That restrictions on the child's activities —especially activities with other children— have a serious effect may be seen by the fact that when a group of adults were asked to recall their school experiences, some who suffered from physical handicaps during their school days reported that they felt lonely and excluded, others said that they suffered from the contempt of stronger children, while still others felt that their school work and social relationships in school had compensated for many of the things they had missed, such as sports and parties. Those who were least handicapped by their defects had the most favorable memories of their school experiences (32).

Attitudes of Others toward the Defect.   The attitudes of other people toward the defect are important because they will color the child's attitude. If other people feel sorry for him, he will pity himself and develop feelings of martyrdom. If they reject him, he will reject himself. Facial deformities, unless accompanied by a functional impairment, such as a harelip or cleft palate, would not affect the child's attitude toward

himself were it not for the unfavorable attitudes of other people (147). Similarly, children who have experienced amputations are sensitive to the negative feelings of others, and this affects their own attitudes (102, 147, 190, 208).

Of all the people whose attitudes are important in determining what the child's attitude toward his handicap will be, *parents* come first. Mothers of children with hearing handicaps, it has been found, tend to overprotect their children. As a result, the children feel inferior because they need more help than other children. They are also deprived of an incentive to learn to be as independent as their handicap will permit. Because a handicapped child requires more attention and care than other children of the same age, the lives of his parents are profoundly affected (81, 159, 164).

The *mother* must, of necessity, become socially withdrawn. This, combined with the time she must devote to the handicapped child, often leads to friction with her husband and other children. As the handicapped child grows older, parents become more acutely aware of the difference between their child and other children. Furthermore, with the passage of time, the mother is more and more aware of the difference between her life and that of other mothers. Should the mother believe that the child's handicap is partially her fault, she is likely to develop feelings of guilt; she will try to compensate by devoting more time and effort to the handicapped child, even though the rest of the family may be neglected. The *father* of a handicapped child often feels frustrated because the child is a liability to him and because he does not have a child of whom he can be proud (23).

The attitudes of *siblings* toward the handicapped child are generally a reflection of their parents' attitudes, combined with their own resentments at having a sibling they must help to care for and who may be embarrassing to them or who deprives them of their parents' time and attention.

When the child's defect is readily apparent, *teachers, peers,* and other people outside the home are generally sympathetic in their treatment of him. When the defect is not readily apparent, however, as in the case of hearing difficulties, they often misunderstand the child, interpreting his actions as an indication of stupidity; or they reject or neglect him because he seems to be withdrawn and uninterested in other people. He is often accused of being rude or impolite when he does not answer a question, or of being "stupid" when he answers incorrectly (26, 185). See illustration on page 148.

Child's Attitude toward the Defect. Unquestionably, one of the most important single factors influencing the effect of physical handicaps is the child's own attitude toward it—an attitude which is markedly influenced by the attitudes of significant people in his life. Different children react differently to their handicaps. Some succumb to their obstacles and accept non-expression as their lot; some develop a compensatory abundance of overexpression to satisfy their injured egos; still others find alternative modes of self-expression. Many children feel guilty about a disability, especially if it resulted from engaging in a forbidden activity or one they were warned against (40, 178, 209). Their guilt is increased when they realize the effects their disabilities have on their parents and siblings.

Some children recognize and accept their defects. Most disabled children, however, deny or try to ignore the fact that they are different from other children (23, 208). A study of the figure drawings of children suffering from orthopedic disabilities following poliomyelitis, for example, revealed that the children projected their impairment by omitting legs from their drawings, by showing a size discrepancy in the drawings of legs, or by including some external support for the body in their drawings (191). This is illustrated in Figure 4–10.

Figure 4–10. Self-figures drawn by children with lower-extremity disability following poliomyelitis. (Adapted from A. B. Silverstein and H. A. Robinson, The representation of orthopedic disability in children's figure drawings, J. consult. Psychol., 1956, 20, 333–341. Used by permission.)

Recognition of Being Different. Whether the child's attitude toward his handicap will be favorable or unfavorable will depend to some extent upon how clearly he recognizes that he is *different* from other children of his age and how they feel about his being different. As long as a physically handicapped child has children who are not handicapped in his environment, he will constantly compare himself with them. The more he recognizes that he is different, the more psychologically damaging his defect will be. For example, it has been found that children who are deaf or blind or suffer from cerebral palsy have less favorable attitudes toward their defects and develop more personality disturbances when they are with children who do not suffer from these disabilities than when they are in special schools for those with similar handicaps (22, 27, 82, 171).

Areas of Influence. A number of studies have revealed that physical defects have serious effects on the child's personality, his development, and his adjustment to life. The *developmental status* of a child suffering from a physical defect is usually below that of the normal child (80). Blind children, for example, are slower in walking, feeding, dressing, or bathing themselves than are children with normal vision. This is partly because they must substitute ear-hand for eye-hand coordinations and partly because they are hindered by parental desires to do things for them or to shield them from possible injury (27). What is true of blind children is true, to a greater or lesser extent, of all handicapped children. Because they are overprotected, they are deprived of learning opportunities and are not motivated to do things for themselves. Even when parents provide their normal children with learning opportunities and encourage them to be independent, they tend to overprotect handicapped children (81, 139).

The physically handicapped child is often an *underachiever* in school work. This may be a direct or indirect result of his defect. The child who is hard of hearing, for example, may not hear what the teacher says; he may give an incorrect answer or say he "doesn't know" rather than admit that he was unable to hear the question. Similarly, a child with poor vision may not be able to see the blackboard well enough to follow the teacher's instructions; consequently he may do his work incorrectly (10, 38, 49). A physical handicap affects a child's school achievement indirectly by making him feel lonely and excluded, thus leading to a dislike for school and to a lack of motivation to do well. While teachers may be tolerant of poor school achievement when the handicapped child is young, they are less likely to be tolerant as the child grows older. This is especially apparent in the case of children with speech defects or with multiple handicaps that interfere with their school work (21, 59).

Because physical defects often prevent a child from acquiring the *skills* needed for play, he is deprived of social contacts with his peers and feels that others scorn him because of his awkwardness and backwardness. As a result, he is forced to play alone when he wants to play with others. This makes him feel lonely and rejected. Since he has few opportunities to learn how to get along with others, he usually makes poorer *social adjustments* and behaves in a less acceptable way than the normal child (171, 190). Being forced out of certain social activities because of his handicap leads to a *constriction in interests,* boredom, and envy of those who can engage in many activities freely. Social deprivations of this sort result in frustration, anxiety, and rage—often expressed in offensive forms of aggression. Even though the children may feel guilty afterward, they still cannot win the social acceptance they crave (21, 65, 209).

Because most children with physical defects do not have enough positive assets to offset the negative effects of such behavior, they are usually doomed to *social isolation* (65). They are apt to be ignored rather than actively disliked. Those who have very serious handicaps or very mild handicaps are more easily accepted than those with in-between handicaps. A child who is so hard of hearing that he must wear a hearing aid, for example, is less likely to be accepted than one whose deafness is so slight that few children notice it (59). A seriously handicapped child, on the other hand, arouses the pity and sympathy of his peers, and this leads to their acceptance of him. Blindness, it has been found, does not prevent a child from being accepted by his nonblind peers, but the partially blind child is more likely to be ignored or rejected because he does not arouse their sympathy. Furthermore, he often behaves in an aggressive way to compensate for his feelings of inadequacy (215).

It is not uncommon for physically handicapped children to develop undesirable *personality* patterns. They tend to be withdrawn and unsocial and to have more fears and feelings of guilt than other children. In addition, they usually feel that they are "different," unloved, and unwanted. These characteristics are apparent even in the preschool years. At every age, handicapped children tend to be immature because of overprotection and egocentric because of social isolation (171).

Recognition that they are different from other children often leads handicapped children to feel that they are "inferior." Consequently, they accept many of the negative social attitudes toward the handicapped. As a result, they tend to be depressed, to develop feelings of self-hate, and to acquire inferiority complexes. Their unfavorable attitudes predispose them to make poor social adjustments, and this further increases the unfavorable effects on their personalities (164, 190, 209). Should the physical defect be serious enough to necessitate putting the child in a special school, he may become more neurotic and less self-confident or self-sufficient than handicapped children who attend regular schools (82). In such cases, one must assume that the special school is not meeting the child's needs.

The physically handicapped child is faced with the *adjustment problems* characteristic of his age and level of development in addition to those arising from his handicap. Thus he tends to be less well adjusted than children of his age who do not have a physical handicap to cope with. To be well adjusted, the child must recognize and accept his disability. This means that he must not resent the extra help he needs from others; he must adjust his level of aspiration to the level of his capacity and realize that he cannot go as far as he could if he were not handicapped; he must try to learn to be independent but recognize that he is limited to some degree; and he must understand that he will have a small number of friends, not extensive social contacts (41, 171).

That few children learn to accept and adjust successfully to their disabilities is shown by the fact that many handicapped adults—most of whom have been handicapped from childhood—fail to make good adjustments. In studies of adults with physical handicaps who seek employment or rehabilitation, it has been found that a large number have emotional problems that may interfere with occupational success. In many instances, these emotional problems trace back to childhood years (136).

How physical handicaps affect the adjustments to life in adult years is illustrated by a follow-up of graduates of a school for crippled children. Those who had been socially active in school were very inactive after they left school, spending their time reading, going to movies, watching television, and playing cards—generally with members of the family. When questioned about their failure to participate in community activities, many of them claimed that they were unable to do so because of the difficulties involved in getting out to see people or in going to centers of social activity. Even though they had enjoyed social participation in school, they felt that they were forced to give it up as adults. This led to unhappiness and dissatisfaction with their present lives. The more seriously they were handicapped, the greater their dissatisfaction, the poorer their adjustments to their handicaps, and the greater their maladjustments to life (33).

ACCIDENTS

Of the many types of accidents that injure children, falls, burns, dislocations, sprains, dog bites, fractures, cuts, bruises, and poisonings are the most common. In the childhood years, accidents are the leading cause of death. *Deaths* most often result from motor-vehicle accidents, drownings, fires and explosives, obstructions, and suffocations. In addition, many children survive the effects of accidents but are crippled, maimed, or disfigured for life. Accidents that *injure* the child temporarily or permanently consist mainly of falls, cuts, piercings with instruments, blows from objects, animal bites, and injuries from motor vehicles (48, 80, 107).

Variations in Accidents.   Certain types of accidents occur more frequently at certain

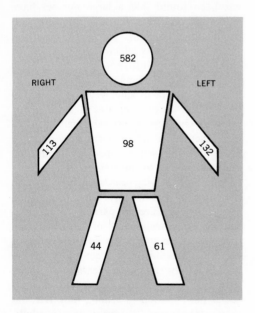

Figure 4–11. Parts of the body most often injured in 1,000 nonfatal childhood accidents reported to the Bureau of Child Health, New York City. (Adapted from H. Jacobziner, Accidents—a major child health problem, *J. Pediat.*, 1955, 46, 419–436. Used by permission.)

ages, and certain age groups seem to be more accident-prone than others. Approximately two-thirds of all childhood accidents occur before the child is nine years old, with ages two and three years the most vulnerable and five and six next. Accident incidence varies also according to sex. Boys at all ages have more accidents than girls. Four out of every ten boys under fifteen years of age suffer some sort of accidental injury, as compared with two out of every ten girls. In the prepubescent age group, ten to fourteen years, boys have nearly three times as many accidents as girls (80, 91).

While *home* accidents predominate among younger children, older children have more accidents outside the home—on the playgrounds or in the streets. Among all children, but especially among older ones, accidents occur more frequently in the *afternoon* and *evening* hours than in the morning, with a peak between seven and eight o'clock in the evening. The *part of the body* most often injured by accident is the head. Under one year of age, six out of every ten accidents affect the head (13, 107). Figure 4–11 shows the most common areas of the body injured by nonfatal accidents during the childhood years.

Causes of Accidents.   Accidents are not necessarily caused by the child's carelessness. *Curiosity* leads young children to explore, and since their curiosity is not checked by fear, they do not realize the potential dangers in new objects and situations. With experience and increased insight, they learn to be more cautious. Then fear or timidity holds curiosity in check, and accidents are less frequent. Accidents in the home are most likely to occur when the child is unsupervised. A busy mother cannot keep her eye on a young child constantly. When her back is turned, the child may hurt himself in his zest to satisfy his curiosity (80).

Lack of supervision on playgrounds and in streets is the cause of many of the accidents of older children. In the absence of a parent or teacher to warn them of danger, they do many things on the *impulse of the moment* and are hurt. To prove to themselves and to others how brave and how "masculine" they are, many older boys do foolhardy things, often on a *dare from a peer,* and are injured when they fail to use reasonable caution or common sense. Because the cultural stereotype of sex-appropriate behavior for girls does not include such traits as bravery and daring, a girl does not feel the need to prove her femininity by taking chances or accepting dares to do dangerous things. As a result, she is far less likely to have accidents than boys (78, 211).

ACCIDENT-PRONENESS

Some children, as well as some adults, have more accidents than others. They are *accident-prone.* Recently, a number of studies have been made to determine what makes a person accident-prone. They have revealed that certain personality characteristics and environmental influences predispose an individual to behavior that leads to accidents. They have also revealed that many accidents involving temporary or permanent damage to the individual, either physically or psychologically, might be avoided (150).

Though old wives' tales about accident-proneness are contradictory to the findings of scientific research, they are widely accepted and have a profound influence on many people. Some people, it is said, are born under "unlucky stars" and will inevitably have more than their share of accidents, while other people are born with good-luck "horseshoes around their necks." Certain physical features are also blamed for accident-proneness. People with red hair traditionally act impulsively, and since accidents are frequently caused by impulsive acts, the redhead is regarded as an accident-prone person.

When parents accept these impossible and even ludicrous old wives' tales, they tend to believe that a child with given traits or a certain background is *naturally* doomed to misfortune and that nothing can be done about it. Under such conditions, there is little motivation for the parents to try to discover *why* the child has accidents, and there is even less motivation for the child to try to control the factors that lead to accidents. As a result, he will continue to have more accidents than is reasonable or normal.

Causes of Accident-proneness. Scientific studies have revealed many causes of accident-proneness. The following two have been most frequently reported:

1. Personality Patterns. In their personality patterns, accident-prone children differ from those who have fewer accidents in three major respects. *First,* accident-prone children frequently suffer from repeated and severe frustrations. Some of these children turn their aggressions inward and feel guilty or suffer from fear of possible punishment. Because they lack inhibitions over their frustration-induced aggressive drives, they often react with temper outbursts out of all proportion to the stimulus that has given rise to them, directing their reactions to frustrating adults or peers. This often leads to an accident that hurts them or the person they have attacked.

Other children who suffer from frustrations turn their aggressions outward; they become overactive, impulsive, hostile, restless, resentful of supervision and desirous of independence, adventuresome, and anxious for attention and approval, and they take chances that may lead to accidents (107, 131, 150). In discussing the effects of frustrations in predisposing a child to more than his share of accidents, Dunbar has pointed out that "children who feel hopeless about making themselves understood tend to do something to get attention, smash things or hurt themselves, until, if no one comes to the rescue, they get the habit" (55).

Second, accident-prone children often have feelings of insecurity. These feelings usually, though not always, originate in the home; they are carried out into the school and peer group, where they are intensified by the poor adjustments the child makes. The child who is not sure of his status in

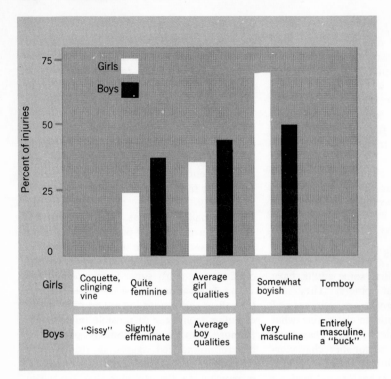

Figure 4–12. Relation between sex-appropriateness and accident-proneness in boys and girls. (Adapted from E. M. Fuller, Injury-prone children, *Amer. J. Orthopsychiat.*, 1948, 18, 708–723. Used by permission.)

the group or who is neglected or actively rejected by the group frequently becomes aggressive in an attempt to establish his status. Many accidents occur because of conflicts with other children; this is more characteristic of unpopular than of popular children. Accident-prone children tend to be unusually high-strung, nervous, impudent, rude, insulting, insolent, saucy, unmannerly, bold, and insensitive to the feelings of others—all of which lead to social neglect and rejection and create feelings of insecurity (71, 150).

A *third* personality pattern characteristically found among accident-prone children is lack of sex-appropriateness in appearance and in behavior. The quiet, feminine boy, for example, tends to have more accidents than the "regular boy," just as the "tomboy" girl tends to have more accidents than the feminine girl (70). This is illustrated in Figure 4–12. It is not lack of sex-appropriateness per se that makes a child accident-prone; rather, it is his attempt

to compensate for the social disapproval and rejection that sex-inappropriateness arouses. The child takes chances to prove to himself and to others that he is brave and that he is not sex-inappropriate. Much of the "stunting" of the older child springs from his desire for attention and approval. Many children are hurt when they accept a dare. Should they be successful in carrying out the dare, they will win great prestige and counteract any impression of sex-inappropriateness. Refusal to accept a dare, on the other hand, gives an impression of cowardice. For boys, this means sex-inappropriateness (78, 211).

Children who have few accidents are characteristically timid, shy, quiet, and submissive and have good control over their emotions. While they may suffer less from feelings of insecurity in social relationships than the accident-prone child, they rarely enjoy a high level of popularity, and even more rarely do they fill leadership roles. They seldom complain about not being permitted to do the things they want to do, and, as a result, they get along well with parents and teachers. They lack, however, the personality traits that lead to real popularity or leadership (71, 131).

By contrast, the accident-prone child has many of the traits that contribute to social acceptance and leadership—traits "usually considered desirable in children but which operate against them in combinations under certain circumstances to produce the accident-prone child" (70). For example, hostility toward adult authority is highly rated in boys and leads to social acceptance and leadership, but it also leads to accident-proneness (131, 202).

2. Backgrounds.
It has been reported that the backgrounds of accident-prone children are different from those of children who have fewer accidents. The *home* atmosphere of accident-prone children is more authoritarian. There are more commands, threats, and prohibitions. In addition, they often come from large families where they have less parental supervision and more sibling supervision. Many times, they are later in birth order than their less accident-prone siblings, suggesting that they may have been less welcome or actually rejected. Recognition of their lack of status in the home leads to feelings of insecurity—feelings common in accident-prone children.

Furthermore, many accident-prone children come from homes broken by death or divorce; they lack supervision because of the social disorganization of the home environment. This, likewise, contributes to feelings of insecurity, rejection, and hostility and militates against close relationships with the parents or feelings of affection for the family members (61, 131).

The *school* histories of accident-prone children are also unfavorable. Many have transferred from school to school, with the resultant feeling of insecurity that comes from the necessity of making repeated academic and social adjustments. Because of this feeling of insecurity and of not belonging, many do poorer work than their intel-

lectual capacities would justify. Moreover, it is not uncommon for accident-prone children to be "school problems" and to be known to the school counselors because of their poor academic and social adjustments (131).

Persistence of Accident-proneness.
Although there are no genetic studies of accident-prone individuals from childhood into adulthood, there is evidence that those who, as adults, are accident-prone were accident-prone when they were children. Apparently, the personality characteristics which predispose the individual to accident-proneness are persistent. They may even be intensified with advancing age. Revolt against authority, for example, is common in childhood and stems from feelings of frustration. As the child grows older, if the frustrations from his home or school environment persist, the tendency to revolt will increase. This is very common at the time of puberty.

When an adolescent feels that he is misunderstood or mistreated by parents or teachers, he rebels. This leads to impetuous or reckless behavior which may result in an accident. The more frequently he feels frustrated, the more impetuous and reckless his behavior is likely to be. As Dunbar has pointed out, the child's tendency to smash things or to hurt himself to get attention or win his independence may "disappear, but it is likely to revive at puberty and continue throughout teenage and even longer if satisfactory communication has not been established" (55).

At any time of stress, whether it is in adolescence or adulthood, the habit of revolting against authority—a habit which often traces its origin to early childhood—is likely to lead to behavior that predisposes the individual to accidents. This suggests that accident-proneness is closely correlated with a particular personality syndrome (61, 70). Studies of industrial workers, for example, have revealed that if their attitudes toward their work and coworkers were unfavorable and if they suffered from feelings of frustration engendered either by their work or by situations in the home or in their social lives, they had more accidents than those whose attitudes were favorable (44).

EFFECTS OF ACCIDENTS

Even a minor accident may leave a *physical scar*. A small cut on the face, for example, may leave a scar in a conspicuous place which will make the child very self-conscious when he reaches the appearance-conscious years of adolescence. A fall may be too minor to break a bone but may chip a corner off a front tooth, thus marring an otherwise attractive smile. Should the effect make the child self-conscious, his parents may have to spend money they can ill afford for expensive dental work to remove the psychological hazard of the disfigurement to the child's social adjustment. More serious accidents may maim the child for life or bring about his death. The physical effects of an accident may be only temporary, forgotten by those who witnessed the accident almost at once as the child dries his tears and resumes his play, or they may leave the child so disabled that his entire life pattern will have to be changed to adjust to his disability. He and all who are closely related to him in home, school, business, or social activities will be constantly reminded of the accident and the scars it has left.

While some accidents leave no physical scars, there is no accident that does not leave a *psychological scar*. When accidents are serious or when a child has frequent accidents, the psychological damage is intensified and may bring about serious changes in his personality. Even the most minor accident is a source of embarrassment to the child. He is afraid that people will think him clumsy, awkward, or careless, and he dreads their teasings or scoldings. Furthermore, he dreads the possibility of a repetition of the accident. All this intimidates him, and he feels insecure and wonders if there is something wrong with him, especially if he has more accidents than his siblings or friends. His insecurity may make

him overcautious and afraid to take chances. He may "lose his nerve" when he must face a new situation. Even worse, he may develop a generalized anxiety which will make him timid, retiring, and self-effacing in *any* situation where new tasks or new people must be coped with.

Many children who have been intimidated by an accident or a number of accidents try to conceal their timidity; they may boast of their bravery, accept a dare to show that they have not lost their nerve, or insist that a fall or cut "doesn't hurt" and they "can't even feel it." In spite of their apparent bravery, however, they generally live in dread of any situation which will force them to act to retain their prestige in the eyes of their family or peers. Many times they avoid situations where they will be forced to show their bravery, thus limiting their social contacts to children who are younger or weaker than they and who, as a result, are less likely to "call their bluffs."

Effects of Attitudes of Others. The attitudes of significant people in the child's life —especially his parents and peers—will have a marked influence on the effects accidents have on his personality. They will also determine the extent of the psychological damage. If, for example, parents are sympathetic; if they try to convince the child that he was not at fault; or if they project the blame on something, on someone, or on "bad luck," the child will be spared the humiliation of feeling that there is something the matter with him.

If the accident occurs when the child does something he has been warned repeatedly not to do or has been forbidden to do, feelings of guilt, along with other psychological scars, are certain to disquiet him. The more his parents emphasize his naughtiness and thoughtlessness and the inconvenience, expense, and disruption to family plans the accident has caused, the more guilty and ashamed he will feel (40, 209).

Few children have enough understanding to realize that a child who has had even a minor accident may be suffering physical pain and embarrassment. Unless there is evidence that he is in real pain, he is likely to seem comic to other children. Consequently, they will laugh at him. This increases the child's embarrassment and humiliation and leads to feelings of personal inadequacy. Should he have accidents so frequently that he wins the nickname "Big Feet" or "Clumsy," he will feel insecure about his status in the peer group. This will motivate him to take more and more dangerous chances to prove to his peers that he is brave, not clumsy, and skilled, not awkward (212).

When an accident results in an injury serious enough to cause bleeding, swelling of the skin, or cries of pain, the peer group will usually react with sympathy. If the child is incapacitated by the accident—with a leg or arm in a cast or a bandage in a conspicuous area of the body—he will become a "wounded hero" in the eyes of the group. For any child, this role brings enjoyable attention and sympathy (146, 168). However, for a child who has previously enjoyed little attention and prestige in the group, this new-found attention more than compensates for the pain or physical discomfort of the accident. Should this enviable status persist after the injury has healed, living up to peer expectations will put a heavy burden on his shoulders. This will lead to constant anxiety and dread of another accident and will increase his psychological problems.

It is apparent that psychological damage from accidents can be more far-reaching and persistent than physical damage. Physical damage from accidents may be temporary, but psychological damage is permanent. In no other area of physical development are the psychological implications more dramatically shown than in accidents. For that reason, concluding a chapter on physical development with a discussion of childhood accidents serves to highlight the relationship between physical and psychological development.

BIBLIOGRAPHY

(1) ABEL, T. M.: Figure drawings and facial disfigurement. *Amer. J. Orthopsychiat.*, 1953, **23**, 253–264.

(2) ABEL, T. M., and N. F. JOFFEE: Cultural backgrounds of female puberty. *Amer. J. Psychother.*, 1950, **4**, 90–113.

(3) ACHESON, R. M., and C. W. DUPERTUIS: The relationship between physique and rate of skeletal maturation in boys. *Hum. Biol.*, 1959, **29**, 167–193.

(4) ADLER, A.: *Individual psychology.* New York: Harcourt, Brace & World, 1924.

(5) ALBERT, R. S.: The role of mass media and the effect of aggressive film content upon children's aggressive responses and identification choices. *Genet. Psychol. Monogr.*, 1957, **55**, 221–285.

(6) ALDOUS, J., and L. KELL: Child-rearing values of mothers in relation to their children's perceptions of their mothers' control: an exploratory study. *Marriage fam. Liv.*, 1956, **18**, 72–74.

(7) ALLEN, I.: Facial growth in children five to eight years of age. *Hum. Biol.*, 1948, **20**, 109–145.

(8) AMES, L. B.: The sense of self in nursery school children as manifested by their verbal behavior. *J. genet. Psychol.*, 1952, **81**, 193–232.

(9) ANGELINO, H., and E. V. MECH: "Fears and worries" concerning physical changes: a preliminary survey of 32 females. *J. Psychol.*, 1955, **39**, 195–198.

(10) ASHCROFT, S. C.: The blind and partially seeing. *Rev. educ. Res.*, 1959, **29**, 519–528.

(11) BANHAM, K. M.: Obstinate children are adaptable. *Ment. Hyg., N.Y.*, 1952, **36**, 84–89.

(12) BARKER, L. S., M. SCHOGGEN, P. SCHOGGEN, and R. G. BARKER: The frequency of physical disability in children: a comparison of sources of information. *Child Develpm.*, 1952, **23**, 215–226.

(13) BAYER, L. M., and M. M. SNYDER: Illness experience of a group of normal children. *Child Develpm.*, 1950, **21**, 93–120.

(14) BAYLEY, N.: Some psychological correlates of somatic androgyny. *Child Develpm.*, 1951, **22**, 47–60.

(15) BAYLEY, N.: Some increasing parent-child similarities during the growth of children. *J. educ. Psychol.*, 1954, **45**, 1–21.

(16) BAYLEY, N.: On the growth of intelligence. *Amer. Psychologist*, 1955, **10**, 805–818.

(17) BAYLEY, N.: Growth curves of height and weight by age for boys and girls scaled according to physical maturity. *J. Pediat.*, 1956, **48**, 187–194.

(18) BAYLEY, N.: Individual patterns of development. *Child Develpm.*, 1956, **27**, 45–74.

(19) BAYLEY, N., and S. R. PINNEAU: Tables for predicting adult height from skeletal age: revised for use with the Greulich-Pyle Hand Standards. *J. Pediat.*, 1952, **40**, 423–441.

(20) BENNETT, E. M., and D. E. JOHANNSON: Psychodynamics of the diabetic child. *Psychol. Monogr.*, 1954, **68**, No. 1.

(21) BERNABEU, E. P.: The effects of severe crippling on the development of a group of children. *Psychiatry*, 1958, **21**, 169–194.

(22) BICE, H. V.: Some factors that contribute to the concept of self in the child with cerebral palsy. *Ment. Hyg.*, N.Y., 1954, **38**, 120–131.

(23) BOLES, G.: Personality factors in mothers of cerebral palsied children. *Genet. Psychol. Monogr.*, 1959, **59**, 159–218.

(24) BONNEY, M. E.: Social behavior differences between second grade children of high and low sociometric status. *J. educ. Res.*, 1955, **48**, 481–495.

(25) BOOKWALTER, K. W.: The relationship of body size and shape to physical performance. *Res. Quart. Amer. Ass. Hlth Phys. Educ. Recr.*, 1952, **23**, 271–279.

(26) BRECKENRIDGE, M. E., and E. L. VINCENT: *Child development*, 4th ed. Philadelphia: Saunders, 1960.

(27) BRIELAND, D.: Personality problems of the blind and visually handicapped as revealed by a projective technique. *Amer. Psychologist*, 1950, **5**, 340.

(28) BROWN, D. B.: Masculinity-femininity development in children. *J. consult. Psychol.*, 1957, **21**, 197–202.

(29) BROZEK, J., H. GUETZKOW, and A. KEYS: A study of personality of normal young men maintained on restricted intakes of vitamins of the B complex. *Psychosom. Med.*, 1946, **8**, 98–109.

(30) BRUCH, H.: Developmental obesity and schizophrenia. *Psychiatry*, 1958, **21**, 65–70.

(31) BRUCH, H.: Psychological aspects of obesity in adolescence. *Amer. J. publ. Hlth*, 1958, **48**, 1349–1353.

(32) BÜHLER, C.: School as a phase of human life. *Education*, 1952, **73**, 219–222.

(33) CARLSEN, A. H.: Vocational and social adjustment of physically handicapped students. *Except. Children*, 1957, **23**, 364–367, 398.

(34) CARLSON, A. J., and E. J. STIEGLITZ: Physiological changes in aging. *Ann. Amer. Acad. Pol. Soc. Sci.*, 1952, **279**, 18–31.

(35) CHURCH, J., and L. J. STONE: The early school years. *Children*, 1960, **7**, 113–114.

(36) CLARKE, T. W.: Allergy and the "problem child." *Nerv. Child*, 1952, **9**, 278–281.

(37) CLEMENTS, E. M. B.: Changes in the mean stature and weight of British children over the past seventy years. *Brit. med. J.*, Oct. 17, 1953, 892–902.

(38) CONNOR, F. P., and I. I. GOLDBERG: Children with crippling conditions and special health problems. *Rev. educ. Res.*, 1959, **29**, 471–496.

(39) CORSINI, R. J.: Appearance and criminality. *Amer. J. Sociol.*, 1959, **65**, 49–51.

(40) CRUICKSHANK, W. M.: The relation of physical disability to fear and guilt feelings. *Child Develpm.*, 1951, **22**, 291–298.

(41) CRUICKSHANK, W. M., and G. O. JOHNSON: *Education of exceptional children and youth.* Englewood Cliffs, N.J.: Prentice-Hall, 1958.

(42) DALE, J.: Seasonal variations in growth of the composite preschool child. *Med. J. Australia*, 1950, **2**, 281–285.

(43) DALE, R. J.: A method for measuring developmental tasks: scales for selected tasks at the beginning of adolescence. *Child Develpm.* 1955, **26**, 111–122.

(44) DAVIDS, A., and J. T. MAHONEY: Personality dynamics and accident proneness in an industrial setting. *J. appl. Psychol.*, 1957, **41**, 303–306.

(45) DAVIDSON, H. L., and L. S. GOTTLIEB: The emotional maturity of pre- and post-menarcheal girls. *J. genet. Psychol.*, 1955, **86**, 261–266.

(46) DAVIDSON, M. A., R. G. MC INNES, and R. W. PARNELL: The distribution of personality traits in seven-year-old children: a combined psychological, psychiatric, and somatotype study. *Brit. J. educ. Psychol.*, 1957, **27**, 48–61.

(47) DEMPSEY, E. W.: Homeostasis. In S. S. Stevens (Ed.), *Handbook of experimental psychology*, N.Y.: Wiley, 1951. Pp. 209–235.

(48) DENNIS, J. M., and A. D. KAISER: Are home accidents in children preventable? *Pediatrics*, 1954, **13**, 568–575.

(49) DI CARLO, L. M.: The deaf and hard-of-hearing. *Rev. educ. Res.*, 1959, **29**, 497–518.

(50) DINGWALL, M.: Maintenance of mental health. III. Going to school the first five years. *Ment. Hlth, Lond.*, 1949, **9**, 31–33.

(51) DREIZEN, S., C. CURRIE, J. GILLEY, and T. D. SPIES: The effect of nutritive failure on the growth patterns of white children in Alabama. *Child Develpm.*, 1953, **24**, 189–202.

(52) DREIZEN, S., R. M. SNODGRASSE, H. WEBB-PEPLOE, and T. D. SPIES: The retarding effect of protracted undernutrition on the appearance of the postnatal ossification in the hand and wrist. *Hum. Biol.*, 1958, **30**, 253–264.

(53) DU BOIS, F. S.: Rhythms, cycles, and periods in health and disease. *Amer. J. Psychiat.*, 1959, **116**, 114–119.

(54) DUGGINS, O. H., and M. TROTTER: Age

changes in head hair from birth to maturity. II. Medulation in hair of children. *Amer. J. phys. Anthrop.*, 1950, **8**, 399–415.

(55) DUNBAR, F.: Homeostatis during puberty. *Amer. J. Psychiat.*, 1958, **114**, 673–682.

(56) DUPERTUIS, C. W., and N. B. MICHAEL: Comparison of growth in height and weight between ectomorphic and mesomorphic boys. *Child Develpm.*, 1953, **24**, 203–214.

(57) EICHORN, D. H.: *Two-generation similarities in weight, height, and weight/height during the first five years.* 25th Annual Meeting, Society for Research in Child Development, National Institutes of Health, Bethesda, Md., March, 1959.

(58) EICHORN, D. H., and J. P. MC KEE: Physiological instability during adolescence. *Child Develpm.*, 1958, **29**, 255–268.

(59) ELSER, R. P.: The social position of hearing handicapped children in the regular grades. *Except. Children*, 1959, **25**, 305–309.

(60) ERIKSON, E. H.: On the sense of inner identity. In R. P. Knight, *Psychoanalytic psychiatry and psychology.* New York: International Universities Press, Inc., 1954.

(61) FABIAN, A. A., and L. BENDER: Head injury in childhood: predisposing factors. *Amer. J. Orthopsychiat.*, 1947, **17**, 68–79.

(62) FAUST, M. S.: Developmental maturity as a determinant in prestige of adolescent girls. *Child Develpm.*, 1960, **31**, 173–184.

(63) FITT, A. B.: An experimental study of children's attitudes toward school in Auckland, N.Z. *Brit. J. educ. Psychol.*, 1956, **26**, 25–30.

(64) FOLL, C. A.: Physical development of school girls in upper Burma. *Arch. Dis. Childh.*, 1958, **33**, 452–454.

(65) FORCE, D. G.: Social status of physically handicapped children. *Except. Children*, 1956, **23**, 104–107, 132.

(66) FORD, C. S., and F. A. BEACH: *Patterns of sexual development.* New York: Harper & Row, 1951.

(67) FRANK, L. K., and M. H. FRANK: *Your adolescent, at home and in school.* New York: Viking, 1956.

(68) FRAZIER, A., and L. K. LISONBEE: Adolescent concerns with physique. *Sch. Rev.*, 1950, **58**, 397–405.

(69) FRY, P. C.: A comparative study of "obese" children selected on the basis of fat pads. *J. clin. Nutrit.*, 1953, **1**, 453–468.

(70) FULLER, E. M.: Injury-prone children. *Amer. J. Orthopsychiat.*, 1948, **18**, 708–723.

(71) FULLER, E. M., and H. B. BAUNE: Injury-proneness and adjustment in a second grade. *Sociometry*, 1951, **14**, 210–225.

(72) GARN, S. M.: Fat thickness and growth process during infancy. *Hum. Biol.*, 1956, **28**, 232–250.

(73) GARN, S. M., A. CLARK, L. LANDKOF, and L. NEWELL: Parental body build and develop-mental progress in the offspring. *Science*, 1960, **132**, 1555–1556.

(74) GARN, S. M., and J. A. HASKELL: Fat and growth during childhood. *Science*, 1959, **130**, 1711–1712.

(75) GARRISON, K. C.: *Growth and development*, 2d ed. New York: Longmans, 1959.

(76) GARRISON, K. C., and B. V. CUNNINGHAM: Personal problems of ninth grade pupils. *Sch. Rev.*, 1952, **60**, 30–33.

(77) GESELL, A.: Developmental pediatrics. *Nerv. Child*, 1952, **9**, 225–227.

(78) GESELL, A., F. L. ILG, and L. B. AMES: *Youth: the years from ten to sixteen.* New York: Harper & Row, 1956.

(79) GLASER, H. H., D. B. LYNN, and G. S. HARRISON: Patterns of anxiety in mothers of children with rheumatic fever. *Amer. J. Dis. Children*, 1961, **102**, 344–354.

(80) GODDARD, J. L.: Childhood accidents. *Children*, 1959, **6**, 83–85.

(81) GORDON, J. E.: Relationships among mothers' achievement, independence training, attitudes, and handicapped children's performance. *J. consult. Psychol.*, 1959, **23**, 207–212.

(82) GREENBERG, H. M., L. ALLISON, M. FEWELL, and C. RICH: The personality of junior high and high school students attending a residential school for the blind. *J. educ. Psychol.*, 1957, **48**, 406–410.

(83) GREENBERG, R. G., and A. H. BRYAN: Methodology in the study of physical measurements of school children. *Hum. Biol.*, 1951, **23**, 160–179.

(84) GREULICH, W. W.: The rationale of assessing the developmental status of children from roentgenograms of the hand and wrist. *Child Develpm.*, 1950, **21**, 33–44.

(85) GRIFFITHS, W.: Changing family health patterns: a review of recent research. *J. home Econ.*, 1954, **46**, 13–16.

(86) GRONLUND, N. E.: Generality of sociometric status over criteria in measurement of social acceptability. *Elem. Sch. J.*, 1955, **55**, 173–176.

(87) GUTTERIDGE, M. V.: A study of motor achievements of young children. *Arch. Psychol., N.Y.*, 1939, No. 244.

(88) HAGGERTY, A. D.: The effect of long-term hospitalization or institutionalization upon the language development of children. *J. genet. Psychol.*, 1959, **94**, 205–209.

(89) HALE, C. J.: Physiological maturity of Little League baseball players. *Res. Quart. Amer. Ass. Hlth Phys. Educ. Recr.*, 1956, **27**, 276–284.

(90) HANLEY, C.: Physique and reputation of junior high school boys. *Child Develpm.*, 1951, **22**, 247–260.

(91) HANLON, C. R., J. B. BUTCHART, and P. R. KEMPF: Injuries in childhood. *J. Pediat.*, 1949, **34**, 688–698.

(92) HARDING, V. S. V.: A method of evaluating osseous development from birth to 14 years. *Child Develpm.*, 1952, **23**, 247–271.

(93) HARRIS, D. B.: Behavior ratings of post-polio cases. *J. consult. Psychol.*, 1950, **14**, 381–385.

(94) HARRIS, I. D., L. RAPOPORT, and M. A. RYNERSON: Observations on asthmatic children. *Amer. J. Orthopsychiat.*, 1950, **20**, 490–505.

(95) HEALD, F. P., R. P. MASLAND, S. H. STURGIS, and J. R. GALLAGHER: Dysmenorrhea in adolescence. *Pediatrics,* 1957, **20**, 121–127.

(96) HEBER, R. F.: The relation of intelligence and physical maturity to social status of children. *J. educ. Psychol.*, 1956, **47**, 158–162.

(97) HENDRIKSEN, E.: Medical report, *Today's Hlth,* Jan. 1957, 15.

(98) HEUTON, C. L.: A comparative study of the onset of menarche among Negro and white children. *J. Psychol.*, 1958, **46**, 65–73.

(99) HILL, T. J.: Attitudes toward self: an experimental study. *J. educ. Sociol.*, 1957, **30**, 395–397.

(100) HINKLE, L. E., W. N. CHRISTENSEN, F. D. KANE, A. OSTFELD, W. N. THETFORD, and H. G. WOLFF: An investigation of the relation between life experience, personality characteristics, and general susceptibility to illness. *Psychosom. Med.*, 1958, **20**, 278–295.

(101) HOLLINGWORTH, L. S.: *Children above 180 IQ: origin and development.* New York: Harcourt, Brace & World, 1950.

(102) HOLLINSHEAD, M. T.: The social psychology of exceptional children. *Except. Children,* 1959, **26**, 137–140.

(103) HUNT, E., E. G. COOKE, and J. R. GALLAGHER: Somatotype and sexual maturation in boys: a method of developmental analysis. *Hum. Biol.*, 1958, **30**, 73–91.

(104) ILG, F. L., J. LEARNED, A. LOCKWOOD, and L. B. AMES: The three-and-a-half-year-old. *J. genet. Psychol.*, 1949, **75**, 21–31.

(105) ILIFF, A., and V. A. LEE: Pulse rate, respiration rate, and body temperature of children between two months and eighteen years. *Child Develpm.*, 1952, **23**, 237–245.

(106) ILLINGWORTH, R. S., C. C. HARVEY, and G. H. JAWETT: The relation of birth weight to physical growth: a statistical study. *Arch. Dis. Childh.*, 1950, **25**, 380–388.

(107) JACOBZINER, H.: Accidents—a major child health problem. *J. Pediat.*, 1955, **46**, 419–436.

(108) JENSEN, K.: Physical growth and physiological aspects of development. *Rev. educ. Res.*, 1950, **20**, 390–410.

(109) JERSILD, A. T.: *In search of self.* New York: Teachers College, Columbia University, 1952.

(110) JERSILD, A. T.: Emotional development. In L. Carmichael (Ed.), *Manual of child psychology,* 2d ed. New York: Wiley, 1954. Pp. 833–917.

(111) JERSILD, A. T.: *Child psychology,* 5th ed. Englewood Cliffs, N.J.: Prentice-Hall, 1960.

(112) JERSILD, A. T., and R. J. TASCH: *Children's interests and what they suggest for education.* New York: Teachers College, Columbia University, 1949.

(113) JERSILD, A. T., E. S. WOODYARD, and C. F. DEL SOLAR: *Joys and problems of child rearing.* New York: Teachers College, Columbia University, 1949.

(114) JOHANNSEN, D. E., and E. M. BENNETT: The personality of diabetic children. *J. genet. Psychol.*, 1955, **87**, 175–185.

(115) JOHNSON, R.: How parents' attitudes affect children's illnesses. Toronto: *Institute of Child Study Bull.*, 1955, **27**, 5–8.

(116) JONES, M. C.: The later careers of boys who were early- or late-maturers. *Child Develpm.*, 1957, **28**, 113–128.

(117) JONES, M. C.: A study of socialization patterns at the high school level. *J. genet. Psychol.*, 1958, **93**, 87–111.

(118) JONES, M. C., and P. H. MUSSEN: Self-conceptions, motivations, and interpersonal attitudes of early- and late-maturing girls. *Child Develpm.*, 1958, **29**, 491–501.

(119) JOURARD, S. M.: *Personal adjustment.* New York: Macmillan, 1958.

(120) JUNGCK, E. C., N. H. BROWN, and N. CARMONA: Constitutional precocious puberty in the male. *Amer. J. Dis. Children,* 1956, **91**, 138–143.

(121) KAHN, H. A.: Changing causes of death in childhood. *Pub. Hlth Rep.*, 1951, **66**, 1246–1247.

(122) KERR, W. A.: Accident proneness of factory departments. *J. appl. Psychol.*, 1950, **34**, 167–170.

(123) KETCHAM, W. A.: Relationship of physical traits and mental traits in intellectually gifted and mentally retarded boys. *Merrill-Palmer Quart.,* 1960, **6**, 171–177.

(124) KEYS, A., J. BROZEK, A. HENSCHEL, O. NICKELSEN, and H. L. TAYLOR: *The biology of human starvation.* Minneapolis: The University of Minnesota Press, 1950.

(125) KINGSLEY, A., and E. L. REYNOLDS: The relation of illness patterns in children to ordinal position in the family. *J. Pediat.*, 1949, **35**, 17–23.

(126) KINSEY, A. C., W. B. POMEROY, C. E. MARTIN, and P. H. GEBHARD: *Sexual behavior in the human female.* Philadelphia: Saunders, 1953.

(127) KIRCHNER, G., and D. GLINES: Comparative analysis of Eugene, Oregon, elementary school children using the Kraus-Weber Test of minimum muscular fitness. *Res. Quart. Amer. Ass. Hlth Phys. Educ. Recr.*, 1957, **28**, 16–25.

(128) KLATSKIN, E. H., E. B. JACKSON, and L. C. WILKIN: The influence of degree of flexibility in maternal child care practices on early child behavior. *Amer. J. Orthopsychiat.*, 1956, **26**, 79–93.

(129) KNAPP, P. H., and S. J. NEMETZ: Personality variations in bronchial asthma. *Psychosom. Med.*, 1957, **19**, 445–465.

(130) KRALJ-CERCEK, L.: The influence of food, body build, and social origin on the age at menarche. *Hum. Biol.*, 1956, **28**, 393–406.

(131) KRALL, V.: Personality characteristics of accident-repeating children. *J. abnorm. soc. Psychol.*, 1953, **48**, 99–107.

(132) KROGMAN, W. M.: A handbook of the measurement and interpretation of height and weight in the growing child. *Monogr. Soc. Res. Child Develpm.*, 1948, **13**, No. 3.

(133) KROGMAN, W. M.: Biological growth as it may affect pupils' success. *Merrill-Palmer Quart.*, 1953, **1**, 90–98.

(134) KROGMAN, W. M.: The physical growth of the child. In M. Fishbein and R. J. R. Kennedy (Eds.), *Modern marriage and family living.* Fair Lawn, N.J.: Oxford University Press, 1957. Pp. 417–425.

(135) KUHLEN, R. G., and G. G. THOMPSON: *Psychological studies of human development*, 2d ed. New York: Appleton-Century-Crofts, 1963.

(136) LAIRD, J. T.: Emotional disturbances among the physically handicapped. *Personnel Guid. J.*, 1957, **36**, 190–191.

(137) LEDERER, H. D.: How the sick view their world. *Pastoral Psychol.*, 1957, **8**, 41–49.

(138) LEHRHOFF, I.: Speech problems in children. *J. Pediat.*, 1958, **52**, 91–95.

(139) LEMKAU, P. V.: The influence of handicapping conditions on child development. *Children*, 1961, **8**, 43–47.

(140) LIVSON, N., and D. MC NEILL: Variability in male stature as function of adolescent maturation rate. *Science*, 1961, **133**, 708–709.

(141) LIVSON, N., D. MC NEILL, and K. THOMAS: Pooled estimates of parent-child correlations in stature from birth to maturity. *Science*, 1962, **138**, 818–820.

(142) LOMBARD, O. M.: Breadth of bone and muscle by age and sex in childhood. *Child Develpm.*, 1950, **21**, 229–239.

(143) LONG, R. T.: A psychosomatic study of allergic and emotional factors in children with asthma. *Amer. J. Psychiat.*, 1958, **114**, 890–899.

(144) LOWREY, G. H.: Obesity in the adolescent. *Amer. J. publ. Hlth*, 1958, **48**, 1354–1358.

(145) LUCHINS, A. S.: On the theories and problems of adolescence. *J. genet. Psychol.*, 1954, **85**, 47–63.

(146) MACFARLANE, J., L. ALLEN, and M. P. HONZIK: *A developmental study of the behavior problems of normal children between twenty-one months and fourteen years.* Berkeley, Calif.: University of California Press, 1954.

(147) MAC GREGOR, F. C.: Some psycho-social problems associated with facial deformities. *Amer. sociol. Rev.*, 1951, **16**, 629–638.

(148) MACY, I. G., and H. J. KELLY: Body composition in childhood. *Hum. Biol.*, 1956, **28**, 289–308.

(149) MANDELBAUM, A., and M. E. WHEELER: The meaning of a defective child to parents. *Soc. Casewk*, 1960, **41**, 360–367.

(150) MARCUS, I. M., W. WILSON, I. KRAFT, D. SWANDER, F. SUTHERLAND, and E. SCHULHOFER: An interdisciplinary approach to accident patterns in children. *Monogr. Soc. Res. Child Develpm.*, 1960, **25**, No. 2.

(151) MARESH, M. M.: Linear growth of long bones of extremities from infancy through adolescence. *Amer. J. Dis. Children*, 1955, **89**, 725–742.

(152) MARGOLESE, M. S.: Mental disorders in childhood due to endocrine disorders. *Nerv. Child*, 1948, **7**, 55–77.

(153) MARGOLIS, M.: The mother-child relationship in bronchial asthma. *J. abnorm. soc. Psychol.*, 1961, **63**, 360–367.

(154) MARTIN, P. C., and E. L. VINCENT: *Human development.* New York: Ronald, 1960.

(155) MASLANSKY, E., and N. JOLLIFFE: Factors related to underweight in a selected group of 100 children in New York City. *Amer. J. publ. Hlth*, 1955, **45**, 1054–1061.

(156) MASSLER, M., and B. S. SAVARA: Natal and neonatal teeth. *J. Pediat.*, 1950, **36**, 349–359.

(157) MASSLER, M., and T. SUHER: Calculation of "normal" weight in children. *Child Develpm.*, 1951, **22**, 75–94.

(158) MAYER, A. J., and R. V. MARKS: Differentials in infant mortality by race, economic level, and cause of death for Detroit: 1940 to 1950. *Hum. Biol.*, 1954, **26**, 145–155.

(159) MC ANDREW, M. C.: Rigidity and isolation: a study of the deaf and the blind. *J. abnorm. soc. Psychol.*, 1948, **43**, 476–494.

(160) MC CARTHY, D.: Language development. In L. Carmichael (Ed.), *Manual of child psychology*, 2d ed. New York: Wiley, 1954. Pp. 492–630.

(161) MC HUGH, G., and J. K. WASSER: Application of the Thurstone-Chave Attitude Rating technique to attitudes toward menstruation. *Psychol. Rep.*, 1959, **5**, 677–682.

(162) MEREDITH, H. V.: A time series analysis of growth in nose height during childhood. *Child Develpm.*, 1958, **29**, 19–34.

(163) MEREDITH, H. V., and E. M. MEREDITH: The body size and form of present-day white elementary children residing in West-Central Oregon. *Child Develpm.*, 1953, **24**, 83–102.

(164) MEYERSON, L.: Special disabilities. *Annu. Rev. Psychol.*, 1957, **8**, 437–456.

(165) MILLICHAMP, D. A.: The child does his own growing up. Toronto: *Bull. Instit. Child Study*, 1953, **15**, 9–12.

(166) MONTAGU, A.: *Human heredity*. New York: Harcourt, Brace & World, 1959.

(167) MORE, D. M.: Developmental concordance and discordance during puberty and early adolescence. *Monogr. Soc. Res. Child Develpm.*, 1953, **18**, 1–128.

(168) MURPHY, L. B.: *Personality in young children*. New York: Basic Books, Inc., Publishers, 1957.

(169) MURSTEIN, B. I.: The effect of long-term illness of children on the emotional adjustment of parents. *Child Develpm.*, 1960, **31**, 157–171.

(170) MUSSEN, P. H., and M. C. JONES: The behavior-inferred motivations of late- and early-maturing boys. *Child Develpm.*, 1958, **29**, 61–67.

(171) MUSSEN, P. H., and D. K. NEWMAN: Acceptance of handicap, motivation, and adjustment in physically disabled children. *Except. Children*, 1958, **24**, 225–260, 277–278.

(172) NEUHAUS, E. C.: A personality study of asthmatic and cardiac children. *Psychosom. Med.*, 1958, **20**, 181–186.

(173) New York Times Report: Youths suffering from poor diets. *The New York Times*, Mar. 27, 1960.

(174) NEWTON, N.: *Maternal emotions*. New York: Hoeber-Harper, 1955.

(175) O'CONNOR, N.: The evidence for the permanently disturbing effects of mother-child separation. *Acta psychol.*, 1956, **12**, 174–197.

(176) PARKER, E.: *The seven ages of woman*. Baltimore: Johns Hopkins, 1960.

(177) PECKOS, P. S.: Nutrition during growth and development. *Child Develpm.*, 1957, **28**, 273–285.

(178) PODOLSKY, E.: How the child reacts to his physical defects. *Ment. Hyg., N.Y.*, 1953, **37**, 581–584.

(179) POLLOCK, G. H., and J. B. RICHMOND: Nutritional anemia in children. *Psychosom. Med.*, 1953, **15**, 477–484.

(180) PROVIS, H. S., and R. W. B. ELLIS: An anthropometric study of Edinburgh school children. *Arch. Dis. Childh.*, 1955, **30**, 328–337.

(181) PRUGH, D. G., E. M. STAUB, H. H. SANDS, R. M. KIRSCHBAUM, and A. E. LONIHAN: A study of the emotional reactions of children and families to hospitalization and illness. *Amer. J. Orthopsychiat.*, 1953, **23**, 70–106.

(182) RAFFERTY, F. T., and E. S. STEIN: A study of the relationship of early menarche and ego development. *Amer. J. Orthopsychiat.*, 1958, **28**, 170–179.

(183) REYNOLDS, E. L., and J. V. WINES: Physical changes associated with adolescence in boys. *Amer. J. Dis. Children*, 1951, **82**, 529–547.

(184) RHEINGOLD, H. L.: The modification of social responsiveness in institutional babies. *Monogr. Soc. Res. Child Develpm.*, 1956, **21**, No. 2.

(185) RICHARDSON, S. A., N. GOODMAN, A. H. HASTORF, and S. M. DORNBUSCH: Cultural uniformity in reaction to physical disabilities. *Amer. sociol. Rev.*, 1961, **21**, 241–247.

(186) SCHEINFELD, A.: *The human heredity handbook*. Philadelphia: Lippincott, 1956.

(187) SCHIFF, H.: Judgmental response sets in the perception of sociometric status. *Sociometry*, 1954, **17**, 207–227.

(188) SCHUTZ, R. E.: Patterns of personal problems of adolescent girls. *J. educ. Psychol.*, 1958, **49**, 1–5.

(189) SHELDON, W. H., C. W. DUPERTUIS, and E. MC DERMOTT: *Atlas of man: a guide for somatotyping the adult male at all ages*. New York: Harper & Row, 1954.

(190) SILLER, J.: Psychological concomitants of amputation in children. *Child Develpm.*, 1960, **31**, 109–120.

(191) SILVERSTEIN, A. B., and H. A. ROBINSON: The representation of orthopedic disability in children's figure drawings. *J. consult. Psychol.*, 1956, **20**, 333–341.

(192) SIMON, M. D.: Body configuration and school readiness. *Child Develpm.*, 1959, **30**, 493–512.

(193) SMILLIE, D.: Familial resemblance in physique changes in infancy. *Merrill-Palmer Quart.*, 1962, **8**, 27–31.

(194) SMITH, W. I., E. K. POWELL, and S. ROSS: Food aversions: some additional personality correlates. *J. consult. Psychol.*, 1955, **19**, 145–149.

(195) SONTAG, L. W.: Some psychosomatic aspects of childhood. *Nerv. Child*, 1946, **5**, 296–304.

(196) STAGNER, R.: Homeostasis as a unifying concept in personality theory. *Psychol. Rev.*, 1951, **58**, 5–17.

(197) STONE, L. J., and J. CHURCH: *Childhood and adolescence*. New York: Random House, 1957.

(198) STOLZ, H. R., and L. M. STOLZ: *Somatic development of adolescent boys*. New York: Macmillan, 1951.

(199) STOTT, D. H.: Infantile illness and subsequent mental and emotional development. *J. genet. Psychol.*, 1959, **94**, 233–251.

(200) THOMPSON, H.: Physical growth. In L. Carmichael (Ed.), *Manual of child psychology*, 2d ed. New York: Wiley, 1954. Pp. 292–334.

(201) TOLSTRUP, K.: On psychologenic obesity in childhood. *Acta paediat., Stockh.*, 1953, **42**, 289–304.

(202) TUDDENHAM, R. D.: Studies in reputation. I. Sex and grade differences in school children's evaluations of their peers. II. The diagnosis of social adjustment. *Psychol. Monogr.*, 1952, **66,** No. 1.

(203) TYLER, F. T.: Organismic growth: some relationships within the individual among cycles of growth in physical characteristics. *Child Develpm.*, 1957, **28,** 55–63.

(204) VALADIAN, I., H. C. STUART, and R. B. REED: Studies of illness of children followed from birth to eighteen years. *Monogr. Soc. Res. Child Develpm.*, 1961, **26,** No. 3.

(205) VEZNEDAROGLU, K. N.: A study of mothers' discipline and control of asthmatic children. *Smith Coll. Stud. soc. Wk,* 1961, **32,** 69–70.

(206) VINCENT, E. L., and P. C. MARTIN: *Human psychological development.* New York: Ronald, 1961.

(207) WALKER, R. N.: Body build and behavior in young children: 1. Body build and nursery school teachers' ratings. *Monogr. Soc. Res. Child Develpm.*, 1962, **27,** No. 3.

(208) WATSON, E. J., and A. M. JOHNSON: The emotional significance of acquired physical disfigurement in children. *Amer. J. Orthopsychiat.,* 1958, **28,** 85–97.

(209) WENAR, C.: The effects of a motor handicap on personality. III. The effects on certain fantasies and adjustive techniques. *Child Develpm.*, 1956, **27,** 9–15.

(210) WINTHROP, H.: The consistency of attitude patterns as a function of body type. *J. Pers.,* 1957, **25,** 372–382.

(211) WITRYOL, S. L., and J. E. CALKINS: Marginal social values of rural school children. *J. genet. Psychol.,* 1958, **92,** 81–93.

(212) WOLFENSTEIN, M.: Children's understanding of jokes. *Psychoanal. Stud. Child.,* 1954, **8,** 162–176.

(213) WOLFF, E., and L. M. BAYER: Psychosomatic disorders of childhood and adolescence. *Amer. J. Orthopsychiat.,* 1952, **22,** 510–521.

(214) WOLFF, O. H.: Obesity in childhood: a study of the birth weight, the height, and the onset of puberty. *Quart. J. Med.,* 1955, **24,** 109–123.

(215) WOLMAN, M. J.: Preschool and kindergarten child attitudes toward the blind in an integrated program. *New Outlook Blind,* 1958, **52,** 128–133.

(216) ZUK, G. H.: The plasticity of the physique from early adolescence through adulthood. *J. genet. Psychol.,* 1958, **92,** 205–214.

5

MOTOR DEVELOPMENT

One of the most important and rapid areas of development during the early years of life is motor development, the development of control over the different muscles of the body. From a helpless infant who cannot move his body from the place where he has been laid or who cannot reach out and grasp an object offered to him, the young child emerges, reaching in the period of a few short years a phase during which he is relatively independent of others. As Pressey and Kuhlen have pointed out, "The newborn infant is a strangely incoordinated, helpless mite of humanity. Its very first years are devoted to the fascinating but difficult problem of getting control of its own body" (98).

Motor development begins before birth. During the third month of prenatal life, the fetal muscles are well enough developed to enable the fetus to move its arms and legs spontaneously. From the end of the fourth lunar month, the mother can feel the fetal movements and can detect variations in their frequency and intensity at different times (126). Fetal activity is especially pronounced between the sixth and ninth lunar months. Activity decreases, in most fetuses, during the last month before birth, owing in part to the increased pressure on the fetal head and in part to the crowding of the fetal body in the amniotic sac.

For the first few weeks after birth, motor development progresses at a rapid rate. Because of the neurological immaturity of the infant, most of his movements are random and uncoordinated and involve large areas of the body. In a short time, however, his mass activity develops into coordinated voluntary movements (97). Gradually, as he gains control over his muscular mechanism, he makes specific responses. Instead of moving his entire body, he is able to call only certain muscles or teams of muscles into action.

During the first four or five years of life, the child gains control over *gross movements*. These movements involve the large areas of the body used in walking, running, swimming, and bicycling. After five years of age, major development takes place in the control of *finer coordinations,* which involve the smaller muscle groups used in grasping, throwing and catching balls, writing, or using tools.

After the foundation skills, such as self-feeding, dressing, walking, and running, have been established, more complicated skills, such as writing, playing the piano, skating, and dancing, are built up. At first, these skills are crude. With practice, however, they become refined and require the expenditure of much less energy than formerly (54).

Unless environmental obstacles or physical or mental handicaps interfere with normal motor development, the six-year-old will be ready to adjust to the demands of school and to participate in the play activities of his peers. Society expects this of the child. Some of the most important developmental tasks of the preschool and early school years consist of the development of motor skills based on the coordinated use of different teams of muscles (54). (See pages 5 to 6 for a list of the developmental tasks of early childhood.) The child who measures up to social expectations makes good adjustments unless some personality obstacle stands in his way. The child who falls below social expectations develops feelings of personal inadequacy which weaken his motivation to try to learn what his agemates have already learned.

IMPORTANCE OF MOTOR DEVELOPMENT

Being able to control his body as well as, if not better than, his peers is important to a child for a number of reasons. First, good *health,* which is vital to the child's development and happiness, is partially dependent on exercise. If his motor coordination is so poor that he performs below the standards of the peer group, the child will derive little satisfaction from participating in physical activities. Consequently, he will have little motivation to take part. He does not want to be accused of being awkward and clumsy,

and as a result, he will deprive his body of the exercise needed for good health. As Martin and Vincent have stated:

The contribution to physical health comes in part from the fact that physical play and other activities stimulate respiration and circulation so that the cells are better nourished and their wastes are more effectively removed. It comes in part from the use and, hence, the strengthening of the bones and muscles. Considering the amount of energy that is translated into productive work and happiness through human bodies, or is wasted by human beings in tensions and other destructive ways, the importance of effective use of the body becomes evident (84).

The second value of good motor control is that it motivates the child to engage in physical activities that will serve as an emotional catharsis and thus promote good *mental health* (67). Through strenuous play, the child frees his body from the tensions of anxiety and frustration; he gets rid of the pent-up energy nature supplies to meet the dangers or annoyances of daily life. Once the body has been cleared of the physical preparation for action—caused by the arousal of strong emotions such as fear, anger, or jealousy—the child will relax psychologically as well as physically. His outlook on life will be healthier than that of the child, subjected to similar emotion-provoking situations, who shuns motor activities because he feels inadequate. Such a child frequently expends his pent-up energy in fighting mental battles or in pitying himself because he feels that people have treated him unfairly (67). This topic will be discussed in more detail in Chapter 7, Emotional Development.

The third advantage of good motor control is that it enables the child to *entertain himself.* In the preschool years, opportunities for group play are limited. The young child whose motor development is too poor to enable him to amuse himself with his toys becomes bored, fretful, and demanding of attention. Among older children, too, areas of interest are limited if children are not physically able to explore and control the environment (44, 69).

The fourth advantage of motor development is that it provides the child opportunities for *socialization*. The child who cannot throw a ball, roller-skate, ride a bicycle, or swim with a skill equal to that of the members of the peer group becomes a group liability and is doomed to social neglect or rejection (84). He is forced to play alone or with younger children whose play skills are similar to his. As younger children generally do not want to play with an older child for fear that he will "boss" them, the child spends his time alone, watching television, reading the comics, or going to the movies (93).

Social isolation, for a child who craves companionship, militates against happiness and leads to poor personal and social adjustments. Many children who develop into shy, retiring introverts with little interest and limited competence in social activities are victims of inferior motor development. Unfavorable attitudes toward social activities, developed because of unfavorable childhood play experiences, tend to persist into adult life and even into old age (55). By contrast, superior motor development contributes to social acceptance. It is also one of the essential qualities of leadership in childhood. The child whose play skills contribute to his social acceptance learns how to get along with people and how to adjust to different types of social situations (84).

In all social classes in our culture, boys are expected to learn more play skills than girls and to be more proficient in them. Boys who rank high in athletic achievement have been found to make better personal and social adjustments than boys who rank low. When motor skill is backed up by daring and good sportsmanship, the boy not only fits in well with the group but also possesses the components of leadership. Boys who do poorly in games are considered "sissies" by their peers. They lose status. They not only are socially unacceptable and thus neglected, but they are often rejected (14, 21).

Certain skills have prestige value for girls and are just as important to their social acceptance as athletic skills are to boys. A "typical" girl, for example, is expected to be graceful and ladylike in her movements. With the approach of sexual maturity, the importance of gracefulness and skill in social activities increases (18, 35, 121).

Each year, the child becomes increasingly resentful of adult domination and assistance. The fifth important contribution of motor development, therefore, is that it enables the child to achieve *independence*. The more he can do for himself, the greater his self-confidence and happiness will be. Unless he has the motor skills to become self-reliant, he must depend on others to help him to do the things his peers can do for themselves. In time, this dependency leads to feelings of resentment and personal inadequacy which affect his personality unfavorably. Figure 5–1 shows how motor skills contribute to the child's development.

Finally, motor development is important to the child's *self-concept*. When the young child acquires motor skills, he develops a feeling of physical security which is soon translated into psychological security. If he can walk without too many falls, for example, ride a tricycle, run, jump, and skip, he can explore his environment without feeling that every step leads to potential danger. As his confidence increases, he is willing to tackle many problems where motor coordinations are not needed. Self-confidence thus becomes *generalized*. By contrast, the child whose motor development is inferior to that of his agemates hesitates to tackle a new problem or enter into a new situation (64). As Havighurst has emphasized,

To an increasing extent, a child's conception of himself is tied up with the skills he has. It is as though his acceptance of himself comes in part from his ability to master different forms of the world outside himself. . . . As a child becomes part of an activity group . . . he contributes certain skills, certain knowledge. He has an opportunity to test his skills against those of his peers. He adds to his conception of himself as his peers react to his skills (54).

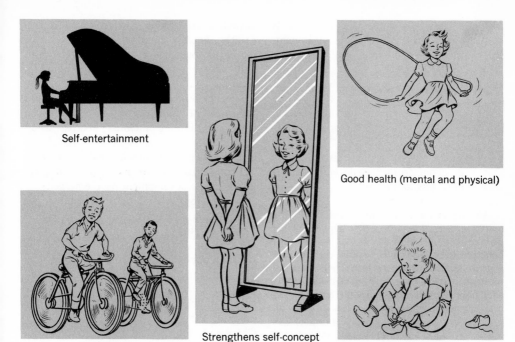

Self-entertainment

Good health (mental and physical)

Socialization

Strengthens self-concept

Independence

Figure 5–1.   Motor skills contribute to the child's development.

That motor skills make an important contribution to the child's personality has been well illustrated in a study of third-grade children. Among these children, those who showed proficiency in motor tests were better adjusted and more active, popular, calm, resourceful, attentive, and cooperative than those who lacked such proficiency. Because of their superior motor coordinations, they were better accepted, and this was reflected in a favorable concept of self (100). Group approval determines what the child's status in the group will be. When approval depends largely on the child's proficiency in motor skills, it means that a healthy self-concept hinges upon how well the child's motor coordinations conform to the social expectations for his age level (106).

Not only does the child's motor development affect his self-concept and hence his personality, but his personality affects his motor development. It thus becomes a circular reaction. The child who is timid, for example, will be hesitant to try to learn new motor skills, and this will delay his motor development. An uninhibited child, on the other hand, will plunge into a new learning experience and will show a higher level of development in this area than the timid child of equal ability who has had equal learning opportunities but has not taken advantage of them. Similarly, an aggressive, competitive child will try to develop more skills than the less aggressive, competitive child, but the former's skills will be on a lower level of proficiency because of his impetuous approach to the learning situation. The less aggressive or less competitive child, who approaches the learning situation more cautiously, will develop better skills, even though his ability and his opportunities for learning are no greater than those of the aggressive child (66, 69).

Disadvantages of Motor Skills.   While motor skills are important to a child, they are sometimes handicaps. The child who is able to walk, to explore his environment, and to manipulate different mechanical devices may be harmed if he has not developed enough caution to control his desire to try out his newly acquired skills. When anxious parents attempt to curb his actions, the child resents their interference, and this leads to parent-child friction (70, 81). In discussing the advantages and disadvantages that may come from the development of motor skills, Jersild has said:

> Walking is an important milestone in the child's life. It affects all other aspects of his development. He is able now to increase his contacts with other people and with things. But while able to walk into new areas of interest, exploration, and adventure, he is also able to walk into mischief and danger. It is harder now for his parents to keep an eye on him. . . . The child's ability to get about and to get into things far exceeds his judgment and awareness of danger (69).

Furthermore, the child's acquisition of skills often leads to friction with his siblings. As long as a child is helpless, he waits for others to initiate play with him, but when he has enough control over his muscles to be able to manipulate toys, he will no longer be content to sit and wait. If his siblings are older than he, they may resent his interference; if younger, they are likely to resent his attempts to take away their toys and then not include them in his play (78).

CHARACTERISTICS OF MOTOR DEVELOPMENT

Numerous longitudinal studies have been made of groups of babies and young children, testing and observing them over a period of time to see when certain forms of motor behavior appear and to discover whether these forms are similar for other children of approximately the same age. Extensive studies of the ages at which various motor performances involving the arms, wrists, and fingers develop, as in reaching, grasping, and thumb opposition, have re-

vealed a predictable pattern of sequences (102). There are also many studies of motor performance involving the feet, legs, and whole body, as in walking, jumping, running, and hopping. In addition, a few studies have been made of the ages and sequences of development of specific skills, such as climbing inclined boards, using wheel toys—doll carriages and tricycles—and throwing and catching balls (51, 71).

From these studies, five important facts about motor development have emerged:

1. Development of muscle control depends upon the *maturation* of the neural structures, bones, and muscles and upon changes in body proportions, as well as upon an opportunity to *learn* how to use the different muscle teams in a coordinated fashion. Development of control over the body parallels the development of the motor areas of the brain. As was pointed out in Chapter 4, the cerebellum, or lower brain, which controls balance, develops rapidly during the early years of life and practically reaches its mature size by the time the child is five years old. The period of most rapid growth comes during the last half of the first year and the first half of the second year—the time when the baby is developing the ability to walk. Development in the upper brain, or cerebrum, especially in the frontal lobes, which control skilled movements, likewise occurs in the early years of childhood. This is paralleled by development of skilled movements involving different parts of the body (41).

Before skilled movements can be learned, a state of maturity in the muscular mechanism of the child must also exist. The smooth muscles, which control involuntary action, are fairly well developed at birth, but the striped or striated muscles, which control voluntary movements, develop at a slower rate. Until they have matured sufficiently to be controlled by the nerves and nerve center, coordinated action of a voluntary type will be impossible. This occurs gradually throughout the childhood years (84). They reach maturity at the time of puberty, when they increase rapidly in both length and weight.

2. Learning cannot occur until maturation has laid the groundwork for it. It is impossible to teach the child skilled movements until his nervous system and muscles are well enough developed for him to profit from the teaching. This is equally true of practice he, himself, may initiate. While training before the child is ready to learn may produce some *temporary* improvement, the long-term effects are insignificant (46). This has been well illustrated in a study of identical twins where one received training and the other did not. The trained twin, at first, progressed in his motor development more rapidly than the twin used as a control, but after training was given to the control twin, he soon caught up (45, 86).

The *damaging effects* of forcing learning before the child is maturationally ready have been demonstrated in the case of toilet training. Many parents believe that they should toilet-train the child as soon as possible. If he is trained earlier than the average age or earlier than the babies of their friends, many parents regard this as a feather in the parental cap. It proclaims to the world that they are "good parents" and suggests that their baby is above average in intelligence.

To control the organs of elimination, the child must inhibit processes which are completely involuntary at birth and for many months afterward. The baby is too immature in his neurological and muscular development to be ready to be trained until after his first or second birthday (94). As Spock has pointed out, "Generally speaking, babies gradually gain control of their bowels and bladders as they grow older. The most that a mother needs to do is to watch her child— to see what stage of readiness he is in—and give him some positive encouragement" (114).

Unfortunately, mothers are not usually willing to take this "watch-and-see" approach, especially those from middle-class backgrounds who are anxious to be considered "good mothers" and whose desire for social status makes them vulnerable to the opinions of others. As a result, they begin toilet training when their friends start to

train their babies or at the time when they trained an older sibling (81). The baby may or may not be ready for it. If he is, he will make steady improvement as the training progresses, with only an occasional "accident." If he is not ready, there will be little improvement and many lapses. Instead of taking these lapses as a cue that the baby is not yet ready, many mothers interpret it to mean that the baby is being balky and rebellious. If the mother is insistent in her efforts, the child builds up an unfavorable attitude and may fail to cooperate even when he becomes maturationally ready for the training (94).

The effects of forced training are long-lasting. It has been found that excessively early and severe training frequently causes the child to be nervous. This, in turn, is expressed in such behavior problems as enuresis, nail biting, thumb sucking, speech defects, or fussiness about neatness and cleanliness (81). If the child has been made to feel guilty about his "accidents," he may develop into the kind of person who is "afraid to enjoy himself or try anything new, the kind who is unhappy unless everything is just so" (114). Jersild has said:

To regard a child under the age of two as a "problem" if he wets or soils himself when he is still too immature to control his elimination is much the same as viewing a child in the creeping or babbling stage as a "problem" because he is still too immature to walk or talk. When parents thus regard a child as a problem and try to "train" him out of it, the youngster is bound to feel the pressure. If the pressure is severe he will feel that his parents disapprove of him and, in his own way, he may feel that *he* has failed and should disapprove of himself. A child who feels disapproved of by others and then disapproves of himself *for not achieving something which he does not have the power to achieve* is measuring himself *as he is* (one who is unable to control his bladder at times) against an ideal of *what he should be* (one who *ought* always to be able to control his bladder) (69).

3. Motor development follows a predictable pattern. The *cephalocaudal* sequence of

development occurs before birth just as it does after birth (see pages 21 and 55). Early fetal movements, as was stressed earlier, are greater in the head than in the leg region. Not until close to the end of the prenatal period does the amount of activity in the leg region become as great as that in the head region (61). Early in babyhood, there is greater movement in the head region than in the rest of the body. As the baby's neuromuscular mechanisms mature, there is more and better controlled movement in the trunk and later in the leg regions (97).

A description of the way in which babies are held can be used to illustrate the direction of the developmental pattern. At birth and shortly afterward, the baby rests his head upon the shoulder or the bosom of the person holding him. If he is held away from the body, his head must be supported because the muscles of his neck are not yet strong enough to support the weight of his head. As the muscles of the neck and head strengthen and come under his control, support is needed only at the nape of the neck. Gradually, the support can be shifted downward, to the shoulders, then to the back, and finally under the buttocks.

Motor development also proceeds in the *proximodistal* direction. The structures lying nearest to the main axis develop earlier than those in more remote areas. In reaching for an object, for example, the infant uses his shoulders and elbows before using the wrist and fingers. Similarly, in locomotion—whether prone or erect—the child controls the upper arm and upper leg earlier than the forearm, foreleg, hands, and feet (41). The pattern of motor development, showing the cephalocaudal and proximodistal directions, is illustrated in Figure 1–3, page 21, where the arrows indicate the direction of control.

The predictable pattern of motor development is also evident in the change from *mass* to *specific* activities. With the maturation of the neuromuscular mechanisms of the body, mass activity is replaced by specific activities, and gross random movements give way to refined movements which involve only the appropriate muscles and limbs (41, 97).

4. There are predictable stages within the pattern of motor development. Numerous studies of the sequence of stages in the motor development of different areas of the body tend to confirm the belief that maturation rather than learning is largely responsible for motor development. There is not, however, perfect agreement about how many stages there are. Ames, for example, distinguished 14 stages in crawling and creeping alone (2). Shirley and McGraw agree that there are 16 stages in the development that leads up to, and includes, the assumption of an erect posture (86, 108). The stages identified by McGraw are illustrated in Figure 5–2. Halverson's study led him to the conclusion that there are 10 stages in the development of prehension, each distinct from the other but each dependent on the stage preceding it and influencing the stage following it (52). Four stages of this sequence are illustrated in Figure 5–3.

5. There are individual differences in the rate of motor development. Even though motor development follows a pattern that is inflexible in its broader aspects, individual differences occur in the detail of the pattern, especially in the ages at which different individuals reach different stages (50). Owing to lack of opportunity for practice, for example, a child may be behind schedule in developing control over his hands, and, as a result of encouragement or aid, he may be ahead of schedule in walking; or he may spend so little time in one stage leading up to locomotion—in hitching, for example—that he seems to skip that stage, while another baby spends twice or three times as long in the hitching stage and does little crawling (9, 41).

Insofar as readiness to learn is influenced by the maturation of muscle coordinations, motor development is influenced by intelligence. However, the relationship between intelligence and skills is much lower because the acquisition of skills depends upon opportunities for learning and motivation to learn in addition to readiness to learn. A study of such motor skills as running, jumping, throwing, and kicking, for example, revealed that there was little relationship between

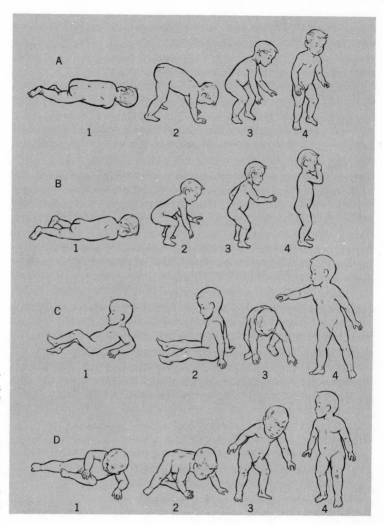

Figure 5–2. Developmental phases in the assumption of an erect posture. (Adapted from M. B. McGraw, *Growth: a study of Johnny and Jimmy*, Appleton-Century-Crofts, 1935. Used by permission.)

them and the mental development of the child or between them and the child's reading ability (46).

The role played by motivation and environmental influences in producing individual differences in motor development is well illustrated by a study in which the motor development of babies in Uganda, Africa, was compared with that of babies in the United States and in different European countries. This comparison revealed that the babies in Uganda show an all-around superiority in motor development during the first year of life. For example, at one day of age,

they can draw themselves up to a sitting position and can keep their heads from falling back; at four months, they can sit alone; at eight months, they can stand without support; and at ten months, they can walk. The explanation given for their precociousness in motor development is that before weaning, they are constantly with the mother; she plays with them and encourages them to do things. After weaning, however, they are expected to be independent and are given less stimulation and encouragement. As a result, there are marked changes in their rate of motor development (38).

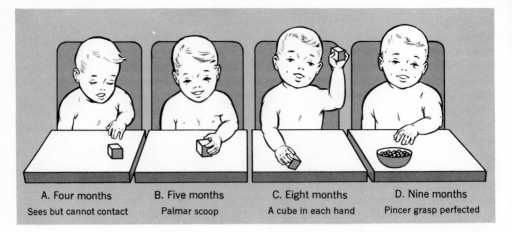

A. Four months   B. Five months   C. Eight months   D. Nine months

Sees but cannot contact   Palmar scoop   A cube in each hand   Pincer grasp perfected

Figure 5–3. Pattern of development of hand skills. (Adapted from E. L. Vincent and P. C. Martin, *Human psychological development,* **Ronald, 1961. Used by permission.)**

SEQUENCE OF MOTOR DEVELOPMENT

Experimental studies of motor development not only have pointed out the normal pattern of stages in achieving muscle control but also have given us the ages at which the average child is able to control different parts of his body. This material is presented according to the laws of developmental direction and is divided into four major areas of motor development: (*1*) the head region, (*2*) the trunk, (*3*) the arms and hands, and (*4*) the legs and feet. In each stage, *norms,* or *average ages,* for the attainment of a particular type of motor control will be given. As has already been stressed, there are marked individual differences in the ages at which children achieve muscle control in a given area of the body. These differences are by no means the result of differences in intelligence alone; very often, they are the result of differences in opportunities for learning, in training methods, and in motivation.

MOTOR DEVELOPMENT IN THE HEAD REGION

Eye coordination, which is very poor during the first few hours after birth, improves so

rapidly that by the end of the fourth month, every normal baby is capable of the most difficult type of eye movement. By the end of the second month, the baby can focus his eyes on a stationary object, and by the third month, he is capable of the three types of eye coordination necessary to follow a moving object: horizontal (present in the second month), vertical, and circular. Optic *nystagmus*—the response of the eyes to a succession of moving objects, as when one looks from the window of a fast-moving train—occurs within a few hours after birth. Ocular *pursuit* movements appear during the third or fourth week after birth. Eye coordination is not developed enough for reading without eyestrain much before the child is six years old. Voluntary *blinking* is present in most babies by the end of the fourth month (41, 54).

Reflex smiles, in response to tactual, organic, or kinesthetic stimulus, appear as early as the first week of life. "Social" smiling, or smiling in response to a smile from another person, does not occur until the third month (72). This response has been used by many writers as a criterion for the beginning of social behavior.

Most newborn infants have the ability to *hold up their heads* momentarily. If a baby of one month of age is supported in a prone position at chest and abdomen, he can hold his head erect in a horizontal plane. At the age of two months, he can, for a few seconds, hold his head above the horizontal plane at an angle of as much as 30 degrees. A month or two later, he can hold up his head and chest by pushing with his hands and arms. Not until the fifth or sixth month can he hold up his head when lying on his back—and then for only a few seconds at a time (17, 108). When seated with suitable support on a person's lap, most babies can hold up their heads at the age of four months. A month or two later, they can turn their heads when seated by turning the shoulders and using the muscles in the upper part of the trunk. The ability to maintain the head momentarily in an upright position while sitting without support appears about the time the baby is six months old. Several months later, with the strengthening of the neck and trunk muscles, he can hold up his head for periods of time varying from a few minutes to half an hour (43, 124).

MOTOR DEVELOPMENT IN THE TRUNK

The ability to *turn the body* from side to side, or from back to stomach, is not present at birth. By the second month, the baby should be able to turn from side to back, and by the fourth month, from back to side. By the age of six months, he should be able to make a complete turn from stomach to stomach. This complete turn is not necessarily made at one time at first, but rather in several partial turns. In turning, the body moves first in the head region and last in the legs. The baby turns his head, then his shoulders, then his pelvis; finally, with a pushing, kicking movement of his legs, he manages to turn his entire body (103).

Before he can *sit alone,* the baby must have his whole trunk under control. At the age of sixteen weeks, a baby can pull himself to a sitting position. At twenty weeks, he can sit alone, when supported, with his body erect. If unsupported, he will lean forward passively, though his head is kept erect. Between the ninth and tenth months, the average baby should be able to sit alone,

without support, for 10 or more minutes. Girls usually sit alone slightly earlier than boys (17, 43).

In attaining a sitting position, the baby goes from a dorsal to a sitting position by turning his whole body to a ventral position, then squats on all fours, and finally pushes himself upright. By the second or third year, the young child no longer turns the whole body axis but leaves the pelvis in contact with the floor on one side, supporting himself with his arm on that side. By the fourth or fifth year, the child can sit like an adult; the body is rolled up symmetrically, with the aid of the arms on both sides. At first, when the baby sits down, he falls or topples over by giving way in the lower part of his trunk. Gradually, he learns by trial and error, combined with demonstrations, how to bend his knees and slide down instead of keeping his knees stiff and falling over. This ability is achieved by the time the average baby is one year old (103).

When the baby first sits alone, he often leans forward to keep his balance. His arms are generally outstretched at the side of his body, and his legs are bowed, with the soles of his feet turned toward each other to give him a wider base for balance. When seated in this way, the baby cannot raise himself to a standing position. If he tries to move, he generally topples over.

Of all the muscles in the trunk region, those which control the *organs of elimination* are the slowest to come under voluntary control. This is understandable because the finer muscles are involved. As has been pointed out, control of elimination means the inhibiting of processes which are, at first, completely involuntary. Because the baby must hold back waste products that are trying to emerge from his body, his muscles must be strong enough and sufficiently coordinated to make this possible. To refrain from doing something that is voluntary requires great control over the muscles.

While there are marked individual differences in the ages at which babies can develop control over their organs of elimination, it has been found that *bowel control* begins, on the average, at six months, and

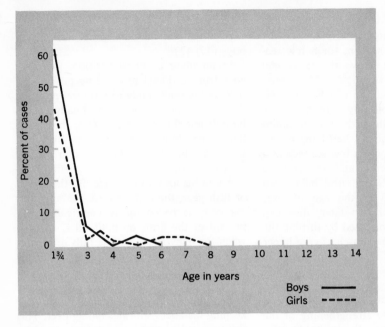

Figure 5–4. Pattern of development of the "dry habit." (Adapted from J. Macfarlane, L. Allen, and M. P. Honzik, *A developmental study of the behavior problems of normal children between twenty-one months and fourteen years,* University of California Press, 1954. Used by permission.)

bladder control, between the ages of fifteen and sixteen months. By the time a baby is two years old, he should have achieved control over his bowels, though temporary lapses are to be expected when the baby is tired, ill, or emotionally excited. Most babies acquire the "dry habit" during the day between the ages of 2 and 2½ years, though they have frequent lapses when they are tired or excited. It is another year before the "dry habit" develops at night, and this, too, is subject to many lapses. By the time the child is ready to enter school, bladder control should be so complete that fatigue and emotional tension will not interfere with it (88, 114, 118). Figure 5–4 shows the pattern of development of the "dry habit."

MOTOR DEVELOPMENT IN THE ARMS AND HANDS

One of the earliest forms of coordinated movements of the arms consists of defensive movements. These appear during the first few days of life. At first they are poorly coordinated, but by the end of the second week of life, there is marked improvement in coordination. Reaching and grasping, ex-

cept where the hand accidentally touches the stimulus, require eye-hand coordination—the working together of the eyes and hands so that the former direct the movements of the latter. In the early period of eye coordination, the baby looks at an object but does not grasp for it. As his eye coordination improves, he begins to reach for the object. During the fourth month, grasping is slow and awkward, but by the sixth month, it is developed; several months later, the baby can reach for an object, grasp it, and then carry it to his mouth (17, 113).

Studies of reaching for a cube have shown that the approach to the cube takes three different forms: the *backhand sweep,* the *circuitous sweep,* and the *direct approach.* From sixteen to twenty-eight weeks, either the backhand or the circuitous sweep is used; from thirty-two to thirty-six weeks, a less circuitous form of approach predominates, and by forty to fifty-two weeks, the direct approach is the usual one. Up to the age of twenty-eight weeks, the baby lifts his hands high in reaching for the cube; from then until the fifty-second week, the height of the approach gradually decreases. By the age of one year, most babies have acquired a fairly mature pattern of reaching, but adult performance may not be achieved until the child is four or five years old (17, 124).

In the grasping reflex, which appears at birth or shortly afterward, the thumb and fingers act together as a hook. Before the hand can become useful for purposes other than grasping, however, the thumb must work in opposition to the fingers and thus function as a separate unit. *Thumb opposition* occurs in grasping normally between the third and fourth months, and in picking up objects, between the eighth and ninth months. The ability to *grasp* and *hold* more than one object appears somewhat later. The average baby of five months should be able to accept one object handed to him, while the average baby of seven months should be able to accept two objects, and the average baby of ten months, three (52, 113).

MOTOR DEVELOPMENT IN THE LEGS AND FEET

Walking movements begin at birth or perhaps even before. The newborn infant makes alternate kicking movements that closely resemble stepping. As a result of stretching and kicking, the baby learns to coordinate the muscles of his legs and trunk. Later, he develops balance and equilibrium. All this is essential to walking and cannot be accomplished in a brief space of time. Most babies are biologically ready to walk between the ages of nine and fifteen months. The bones, muscles, and nerves of the legs and trunk are ready, but the baby must have varying amounts of stimulation and assistance from others before he can master the task (41, 54).

When prone on his stomach or lying on his back, the young baby kicks and squirms, often moving his body a few inches. By the time he is two weeks old, he can push against a hard surface, such as the end of the crib, with enough force to be able to move himself forward slightly. When held in an upright position, he at first prances and dances; later, as his muscles strengthen, he plants his feet firmly and makes definite stepping movements (84, 97).

The earliest form of locomotion is *rolling*. In this, the baby moves his body by means of crude leg and arm movements. Rolling is usually followed in the sixth month by *hitching*—backward locomotion in a sitting position. The baby uses one leg to push himself along and keeps the other doubled under him or extended to help maintain his balance. The arms and hands are also used to aid the movement of the body (23). Figure 5–5 shows the characteristic hitching position.

Crawling follows hitching in the normal sequence of development. It appears as early as the fourth month and reaches its peak between the seventh and ninth. The body is prone, with the abdomen in contact with the floor. The head and shoulders are raised by supporting the weight in the upper part of the body on the elbows. The body is pulled along by the use of the arms, while the legs drag or make kicking movements. If only

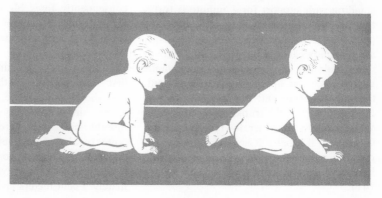

Figure 5–5. Hitching. (Adapted from L. H. Burnside, Coordination in the locomotion of infants, *Genet. Psychol. Monogr.*, 1927, No. 2. Used by permission.)

one leg is used to push the body forward, the other is used in an extended position to propel the body. Generally, the leg movements approximate swimming, in that the legs are drawn up to the body and kicked out suddenly in a froglike manner.

By the age of nine months, the normal baby can *creep*. In this form of locomotion, the trunk is carried free from the floor but parallel to it, and movement comes from the use of the hands and knees. With practice, rhythm improves, and cross-coordination is perfected to the point where only one limb moves at a time. As the baby acquires greater strength, he raises his knees from the floor, stiffens his legs, and walks "on all fours." There are marked individual differences in crawling and creeping. Some babies crawl mostly in a prone position, and others hitch or crawl while sitting. Some babies may skip either creeping or crawling or may remain in one stage for a very short time and then pass on to the next (88).

In the early stages of locomotion preceding walking, there is a marked overproduction of movement in the entire body. With practice, coordination spreads from the head to the leg region. While the action of the legs remains arhythmic during the crawling stages, the arms are flexed and used in alternate fashion. By the time the baby is creeping, nearly perfect coordination appears, and a gradual increase in speed of movement is apparent.

Standing is the next step in the developmental sequence leading up to walking. Normally, standing with support overlaps creeping and crawling. The median age for standing with support for 1 minute is forty-two weeks and for pulling to a standing position, forty-seven weeks. Girls, as a rule, stand slightly earlier than boys (40, 88).

To maintain his balance, the baby stands with the feet far apart, the toes turned out, the knees locked, and the head, as well as the upper part of the trunk, carried forward. When he falls he generally falls backward. Gradually, the baby lessens the amount of pressure placed upon the object supporting him and finally stands completely alone (41).

Walking. Some babies start to walk almost as soon as they stand, whereas others require time to gain enough confidence to take the first step. *Walking with support* comes when the baby is learning to stand alone—at about one year. In a study of one baby it was found that a period of 25 days elapsed between standing alone and taking the first steps independently. Once this hurdle is crossed, walking generally develops rapidly (107). Figure 5–6 shows the pattern of development. Note the rapid increase after self-balance is achieved.

To predict the age of first walking alone, a fairly safe rule is to double the age of sitting alone; or, if the baby creeps, the age of walking will be approximately 1½ times the age of creeping. If the baby is precocious in sitting alone, it is safe to predict that he will be precocious in walking, and vice versa (17).

In all forms of locomotion, the baby holds his head erect in order to see where he is going. In walking, the body is erect, and motion comes from the use of the legs alone. As an aid to maintaining equilibrium, the baby's arms are held outright, much like those of a tightrope walker, or are pulled up to the body. The feet are turned outward, and the legs are stiff. There is a rhythmic alternation of the two legs. The head is held slightly forward, and the baby looks straight ahead of him instead of at the floor. This is necessary if balance is to be maintained, though it usually results in many falls. Falls are caused also by poor general coordination and the fact that the baby raises his feet far from the floor and consequently loses his balance. Figure 5–7 illustrates the characteristic body posture of the baby in the early stages of walking.

Foot Positions in Walking. When the baby first starts to walk with support, his steps are short and erratic. They increase in length until the baby is about eighteen months old, and thereafter they become quite regular. Noticeable changes are also apparent in the width of step. In early stepping, the toes of the two feet are approximately 5 centimeters apart, and the heels do

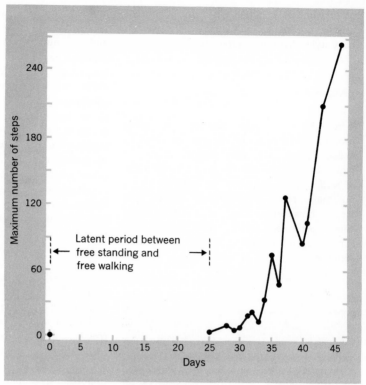

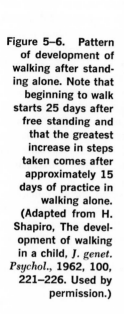

Figure 5–6.   Pattern of development of walking after standing alone. Note that beginning to walk starts 25 days after free standing and that the greatest increase in steps taken comes after approximately 15 days of practice in walking alone. (Adapted from H. Shapiro, The development of walking in a child, *J. genet. Psychol.*, 1962, 100, 221–226. Used by permission.)

not touch the floor. When the baby begins to walk with support, the width of the step increases sharply. It continues to increase until the end of the second year. Also, as he begins to walk, the whole sole of his foot is placed in contact with the floor. At first, the toes turn outward, but with improvements in walking, the feet become parallel (23, 90, 108). Analysis of cinema records of baby footprints has indicated that the type of stepping movement is a more important index of progress than the number of steps taken. In the early stages of walking, the baby places one foot firmly before he starts to move the other. As his skill improves, however, he starts to raise the second foot before he has completely placed the first (90).

As the baby grows older, two major changes take place in walking: The height of the center of gravity of the legs decreases, and the path becomes smoother. The baby just learning to walk expends a large amount

of energy and puts forth a tremendous effort for the distance covered. He lifts his leg higher than he will later and wastes motion in the irregular path the leg takes through space. "Efficiency of locomotion," as determined by the ratio between the horizontal distance covered and the length of the path of the center of gravity of the lower leg, is achieved at two or three years of age (89).

Stability of gait is usually attained toward the end of the second or the early part of the third year. In a well-developed gait, about 70 per cent of the time in stepping is consumed in the ground stroke of the foot, and about 30 per cent is consumed in the moving-through-space stroke. In a faulty or unstable gait, the length of time spent in making these two strokes is different for each foot, so the gait becomes asymmetrical (89). Marked individual variations appear in the style of walking of different children. Too tight or too stiff shoes; overweight; fear of taking a long, striding step because of repeated falls in the past; and other factors have a marked influence on the permanent style of the individual's gait.

SKILLS

After the baby gains control over gross motor movements, he begins to develop skills. These are fine coordinations in which the smaller muscles play a major role. A *skill* can be described "in such words as automatic, rapid, accurate, and smooth. It is wrong, however, to think of a skill as some single perfected action. Any skilled performance, even writing the letter *a,* is a series of hundreds of nerve-muscle coordi-

nations. A skilled movement is a very complex process involving differentiation of cues and continual correction of errors" (26).

Motor skills can be divided, roughly, into two major categories: the *gross* muscular skills, such as running, jumping, lifting, and climbing; and the *finer* muscular skills, such as writing, playing musical instruments, or doing skilled manipulative work. A well-learned skill develops into a *habit,* "any sort of smooth-running repetitive activity, composed of recognizable movement patterns. . . . A person commonly pays little attention to the details of his habitual performances. . . . Habits . . . are relatively automatic, repeated movement patterns, especially as they are revealed in skilled movements" (59).

Skills will not develop through maturation, though the foundations for them come from the maturation of the nerves, muscles, and brain centers connected with the control of coordinated voluntary activities. Skills must be learned, but there is ample evidence that *when* they are learned is as important as *how* they are learned. Learning must be *properly timed.* In running, jumping, throwing, and catching, for example, children who receive training that is correlated with their maturational readiness are distinctly superior to those who receive no training (17, 105). In a study of the effects of training on ball throwing, it was found that in the three- to four-year-old group neither those who received training nor those who acted as a control group improved as much as children in the five- to six-year-old group. In the latter age group, the children who received training made a distinct gain over those who received little or no training. This result indicates that the five- to six-year-olds were ready to profit by training (34). (See Figure 5–8.)

ESSENTIALS IN DEVELOPMENT OF SKILLS

There are three essentials to the development of skills: practice, guidance, and motivation. The neglect of any of these will result in a development below the child's capacity.

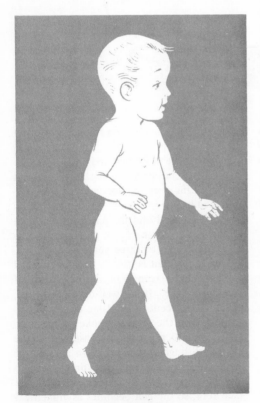

Figure 5–7. Walking. (Adapted from L. H. Burnside, Coordination in the locomotion of infants, *Genet. Psychol. Monogr.,* 1927, No. 2. Used by permission.)

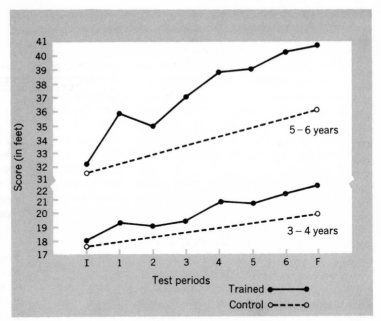

Figure 5–8. Effects of training in distance throws among preschool boys. (Adapted from L. Dusenberry. A study of the effects of training in ball throwing by children ages three to seven, *Res. Quart. Amer. Ass. Hlth Phys. Educ. Recr.*, 1952, 23, 9–14. Used by permission.)

1. Practice. According to tradition, "practice makes perfect," but the *quality* of the practice is far more important than the quantity. Practice without direction or practice without the child's knowledge of what the end result should be will not lead to a "perfect" skill or even to an efficient one. Should the child continue to practice in a blind, hit-or-miss fashion, he will develop an inefficient skill that is so well learned that it will be automatic. Should he discover, in time, that this skill is below his capacities, he may have the motivation to change the skill into a more efficient one. Wanting to change and being able to do so are different things. Once a skill is well learned, it becomes so automatic that changing it is a major task.

Young children, as a rule, enjoy repetition. Furthermore, their time is occupied so little with duties and responsibilities that they have time for repetition and can practice fine motor coordinations until they develop into skills. For this reason, early childhood is the ideal age for mastering skills.

In most cultures, the *developmental tasks of early childhood include the mastery of skills that will be useful to the child in that* culture (54). As the child grows older, he has less free time for practice and is more likely to find repetition boring. If he has been deprived of learning opportunities earlier, when many of the skills necessary for adjustment to life should have been learned, the chances are that he will never expend enough time in practice to master them. As a result, he will be awkward in comparison with his peers.

2. Guidance. While practice is essential to the development of skills, it must be directed if it is to be effective. True, the child can learn skills through trial and error, but this is inefficient, not only in terms of time and energy, but also in terms of end result. Many children learn skills by imitating a model set by an older child, a parent, or a teacher. Imitative learning unquestionably requires less time and effort than the trial-and-error method, but it is limited by faults in the model. The better the model, the better the skill the child will learn, and the less time and effort he will expend in the learning process. Imitative learning is further limited by faulty observation on the part of the child.

The child needs guidance if he is to imitate the model correctly. Through guidance by a good teacher, the child comes to *understand* the characteristics of a good performance—the end that he is striving to reach—and the errors that he must be on the alert to avoid. With training in the correct method of throwing a ball, for example, children improve their skill, as shown by increased distance of the throw (34, 59, 99).

One of the most important things about directed practice is that it gives the child greater satisfaction because the end results are better. This satisfaction, in turn, is a source of motivation for the child to continue the practice until the skill is mastered. Motivation is especially important for older children, who often find continued practice boring. In stressing the importance of guidance in the development of skills, Hilgard has pointed out that "*mere* practice is not enough: what is wanted is *good* practice, which means practice with understanding" (59).

That guidance leads to better and more satisfactory results for the child may be seen by the degree of proficiency he develops in *different types of skills.* Many of the *play* skills are learned by trial and error or by imitation of another child. Consequently, they are often so poor that they give the child little satisfaction. As a result, he devotes his free time to amusements in which his participation is reduced to a minimum. Even when he receives guidance from playmates and older siblings, his play skills are often poorly developed.

Skills connected with *household chores* are generally learned by imitating the mother. Because many mothers of today have laborsaving devices which eliminate the need for the child's help and which are too complicated and too costly to put into the hands of an unskilled child, many American children learn the skills involved in homemaking duties only by trial and error or by imitation without guidance. As a consequence, the end results are often far from satisfactory, and motivation to practice the skills lags. In the large family, where each child must assume some responsibility, children are more likely to receive training in household skills and to achieve more proficiency in them.

The skills most likely to develop under guidance are those learned in *school,* in *play groups,* or in *summer camps.* Common skills of this type are writing, drawing, painting, clay modeling, dancing, and those related to sports, which range from such simple forms as throwing a ball to such complicated activities as diving or synchronized swimming. Because these skills are learned under the careful supervision of teachers who know how to direct the child's efforts into the best channels from the start, who are alert to possible errors, and who are ready to correct errors before repeated practice makes them habitual, it is not surprising that the child shows greater proficiency in such skills, that he derives more pleasure from them, and that he is more anxious to practice them until he reaches a proficiency that closely approaches his level of aspiration (26, 34, 37).

3. Motivation. For a child to be willing to invest time and effort in the practice essential to the development of a skill, there must be some source of satisfaction to provide the motivation. Without this driving force, the child's interest will lag and, with it, his efforts. Common sources of motivation for the child's development of skills are the *personal satisfaction* he obtains from the activity itself, from the *independence* it gives him, or from the *approval* he wins from significant people in his life, especially his parents and teachers. Other sources of motivation are the *value of the skill* to him, whether it is a means of gaining independence or of getting high grades in school, and the *prestige* it gives him in the eyes of the peer group. Some children use skills as a *compensation* for feelings of inadequacy in other areas, especially in intellectual activities in school (26, 34, 37).

In the early stages of learning a skill, progress is generally fairly rapid, and the effort needed is far less than it will be later. This situation soon changes, and the child

begins to hit snags which are far more difficult to cope with than anything he faced
earlier. He becomes discouraged when he
sees little improvement day after day, in
spite of conscientious practice, or when he
experiences a temporary setback. Unless he
is given encouragement, his motivation is
likely to ebb. His flagging interest can be
revived if he is provided with equipment he
can use, if he is shown how to use it effectively, if he receives help in overcoming obstacles that arise in his practice, and, most
important of all, if he is praised for his
efforts, even though the end results fall far
short of adult expectations. Only under such
conditions can the child's motivation be
kept up to the level needed to be a driving
force to continued practice. In young children this is especially important because
they frequently are frustrated and exhausted
by their efforts to achieve the fine controls
needed in the development of skills (65).

Perhaps the most serious threat to motivation is the tendency of children to set their
levels of aspiration too high. Children base
their levels of aspiration partly on curiosity
—they want to find out if they can do what
they observe others doing—and partly on
past successful experiences. Even the most
complicated skill "looks easy" to a child as
he watches a competent person perform it.
He has no appreciation of how complex the
skill is or of how long it took the person to
acquire the skill that he performs so quickly
and easily and with both grace and accuracy. When the child tries to duplicate what
he has observed, it becomes apparent to him
that the skill is far more complicated and
difficult than he realized. He sets his goals
lower and still finds the skill too complicated. After several lowerings of his goals,
he is likely to become discouraged and want
to give up further attempts to learn. At this
point, encouragement is essential if motivation is to be kept alive. Had the learning
been properly guided, he would not have set
levels of aspiration too high for his present
ability; he would have been given a model
which was within his capacity to imitate.
When a child succeeds in his efforts to imitate a model, he sets his future level of
aspiration higher; his success increases his
motivation (104). Figure 5–9 shows the
three essentials in the development of skills.

IMPROVEMENT IN SKILLS

In the early stages of development of skills,
movements are clumsy, awkward, and uncoordinated. Bodily movements are not inte-

Figure 5–9. Three essentials in the development of a skill.

As a result of cultural pressures, sex differences in motor skills become marked as children grow older. (Standard Oil Co., N.J.)

grated, and many unnecessary movements are made. When a child is learning to throw a ball, for example, he literally throws it with his whole body (34). He makes unusual facial expressions, his trunk and legs play too prominent a part in the activity, and his arms and hands work piecemeal. With continued practice, he improves his skills, and his movements become graceful, rhythmic, and coordinated. The individual movements become fused into a pattern of action. As Breckenridge and Vincent have pointed out:

The clumsiness of the eighteen-month-old child in walking passes into the awkward, flat-footed run of the two-year-old; and this passes into the increasing skill and balance of the three- and four-year-old; but one seldom sees the flow and ease of movement which are referred to as grace in walking or running until the child is five. So it is with roller skating or bicycle riding (17).

As skills develop, speed, accuracy, and economy of movement are increased, much to the satisfaction of the child. Accompanying this satisfaction is greater self-assurance and a strong motivation to make further improvements through continued practice (53, 132). *Speed* increases at a fairly uniform rate throughout childhood and up to the sixteenth or eighteenth year; the increase is greatest in the early childhood years and then slows down as the child approaches puberty (3, 91). *Accuracy,* as measured by laboratory tests of tracing and aiming at a target, improves up to thirteen or fourteen years and then comes to a standstill. The greatest increase in accuracy comes early in childhood. The six-year-old child, for example, is nearly twice as accurate in his movements as the three-year-old. *Steadiness,* as measured by how little movement occurs when the finger, hand, arm, or whole body is held as nearly motionless as possible, improves with age. When the greatest improvement occurs has not yet been determined. *Strength* increases with physical development, but not markedly until puberty, when there is a rapid growth in the size of the muscles (73, 115).

Stunting. Once a child learns a skill well enough to be able to enjoy it, he usually begins to "stunt." The young child, after mastering the ability to walk, starts to walk on low fences or to walk backward or sideways. No sooner has he learned to ride a tricycle than he tries riding while standing up or sitting backward. The older child engages in stunts also, but for him the pleasure of the activity itself is not so important as the attention it draws. The successful accomplishment of a dare has great prestige value for the child (131).

The ability to stunt shows that the child has motor abilities far greater than is usually recognized. It further indicates that the child could use his energy and practice time to perfect skills which would be of greater use to him if he were only given the encouragement and necessary equipment. In a study of nursery-school and kindergarten children, it was found that after the children had mastered the skills related to the equipment provided for them, they either repeated the old performances or attempted to elaborate on them for lack of anything else to do (44, 51). Much the same is true of older children.

SEX DIFFERENCES

No significant sex differences have been found during the early years of life in motor performances in which boys and girls are given equal training, encouragement, equipment, and opportunities for practice. As children grow older, however, certain skills are considered more appropriate for boys than for girls, and vice versa. As a result of cultural pressures, sex differences in motor skills begin to appear around the kindergarten age and become more marked as children grow older (44, 46). Cultural pressures influence sex differences in skills mainly by limiting learning opportunities. Among elementary-school children, boys are generally superior to girls in skills requiring strength and endurance—skills which are considered more sex-appropriate for boys than for girls (46). In ball throwing, boys show greater gains than girls primarily because boys receive more encouragement to become proficient in this skill (34).

The role of cultural pressures is especially strong in children's play skills. Girls, for example, are not encouraged to participate in games and sports which require speed and strength. They are encouraged to concentrate on activities such as doll play, crayoning, and sewing which will develop the smaller muscles. As a result of differences in training, girls usually surpass boys in skills that emphasize precision, while boys surpass girls in skills that emphasize speed and strength. Sex differences in motor performance are accentuated by the differences in muscular strength which come at puberty. Because boys' muscles grow larger and are heavier than girls' at this time, boys show a definite superiority in motor performances where speed and strength play dominant roles (46, 84, 115).

HANDEDNESS

For many of the practical performances of the child's life, motor development in the hands and arms is more important than motor development in the legs and feet. A majority of hand skills, however, require the use of only one hand or of one hand aided by the other. As a result, the child develops one *dominant* hand, and if the act requires help, the other hand—the *auxiliary* hand—is called into action. In writing, for example, the dominant hand holds the pencil or pen and does the writing. The auxiliary hand is needed only to hold the paper firmly in place.

Handedness means the predominant use of one hand. The person is said to be right-handed if he uses the right hand as the dominant hand *most* of the time, and left-handed if he favors the left. Few people are so dominantly right- or left-handed that they *always* use the preferred hand. At all ages, shifts in hand usage are common, though they tend to decrease as the child approaches adolescence. Left-handed people are less consistent in the use of their dominant hand than right-handed people. They

favor the left hand for certain spontaneous acts, such as throwing a ball or picking up an object, but in situations where training and social influences dominate, they often use the right hand (19, 41).

A person is *ambidextrous* if he uses both hands equally well and approximately an equal amount of the time. A child who is ambidextrous can feed himself or bat a ball equally well with both hands. Fewer people are ambidextrous than are right- or left-handed. Left-handed people tend to be more ambidextrous than right-handed people. Children who show a preference for the use of their left hands, for example, are often taught to perform certain formal skills, such as writing or painting, with their right hands. In time, they build up a repertoire of skills carried out by both their right and left hands. Those skills carried out by the right hand are done equally well as those by the left hand. By contrast, when a right-hander shifts to the use of his left hand for a certain act, he generally shows less skill than he does when using his right hand (58, 63).

The type of skill the child acquires and his proficiency in this skill will be greatly influenced by whether he is right- or left-handed or ambidextrous. Furthermore, the ease or difficulty of learning a skill will be influenced by whether he learns it with his preferred hand or is expected to use the less preferred hand. A left-handed child, for example, has more difficulty in learning to write with his right hand than with his left hand. Because all learning is influenced by motivation, the strength of a child's desire to favor the culturally approved hand (the right hand, ordinarily) will influence the speed and proficiency of his learning. It thus becomes apparent that handedness is a problem of practical importance in the motor development of the child as well as one of theoretical significance.

THEORIES ABOUT HANDEDNESS

Whether handedness is a hereditary trait or the result of training and social conditioning has been a matter of dispute for generations. The popular belief is that handedness is hereditary and that any attempt to interfere with it will lead to serious nervous disorders, apparent most often in speech defects (83).

One explanation given for preferential use of the right hand is that the left side of the cerebrum is functionally superior to the right and thus determines right-hand preference. Another is that the right hand is structurally superior to the left, owing to the position of the fetus in the uterus. Still another is that handedness is a product of "sidedness," or lateral dominance, with one side functioning spontaneously in preference to the other in involuntary acts, such as focusing one eye (8).

Experimental evidence has not borne out the theories that handedness is hereditary or that it is closely related to eyedness. In fact, evidence indicates that there is a greater relationship between handedness and footedness than between handedness and eyedness. When dominance occurs, it is general and affects the entire side of the body (41). Hildreth remarks that "hand dominance is commonly believed to be hereditary because it is difficult to explain in any other way" (56). She stresses that there is no such thing as "natural handedness." Evidence from genetic studies of children and from studies of cultural differences in child-rearing practices points to the fact that "acquiring handedness follows the laws of learning and habit formation just as any other behavior that results from practice and exercise" (56). Furthermore, experience has proved that both children and older people can acquire new skills with either hand, regardless of the accustomed hand usage, without experiencing any emotional upset.

PREVALENCE OF RIGHT-HANDEDNESS

In most cultures, for reasons that we do not know, there are more right-handed people than left-handed. What percentage of the population of a country or a community will be right-handed will depend to some extent upon the social attitudes toward left-handedness. At the present time, approximately 95 per cent of Americans are right-handed. More males than females are left-handed (8, 56).

Owing primarily to the popular belief that handedness is hereditary and that any attempt to interfere with left-handedness will result in stuttering and other indications of nervous tension, more children are permitted to develop left-handed skills today than in the past. Furthermore, owing to the permissive methods of teaching writing in the elementary school, there are more left-handed boys and girls in the junior and senior high schools than there previously were (54, 83, 110).

In many Oriental countries, such as China, left-handedness is far less common than here. Chinese parents are far stricter in correcting left-handed traits than American parents. To them, left-handedness is a departure from convention, which is strictly frowned upon. If not corrected, it is likely to be interpreted as an indication of laxity on the part of the parents (56). Among the American Indians, left-handedness was practically eradicated in the past. This was done by deliberately releasing the right arm of the baby while he was still bound to the cradleboard on the mother's back. With the disappearance of the cradleboard, there has been a marked increase in left-handedness among Indian babies (95).

It has been noted that left-handedness increases in the United States during years of stress, notably during periods of depression or war. In a study of a sampling of college graduates born before 1918, only 2.6 per cent were left-handed; among those born during and immediately after the war years —1918 to 1921—the percentage rose to 8.3. Between the First World War and the Depression—1929 to 1931—the percentage of left-handed students in the sample was 5.7, as compared with 9.2 in the Depression years. In 1932, when the Depression was at its peak, the percentage soared to 17.64, one of the highest percentages of left-handedness recorded anywhere in the world at any time. The explanation given for the rise in left-handedness during periods of stress is that the preoccupation of parents with other problems results in laxity in the training of children. During the war years, for example, when many fathers were in the service and many mothers worked outside the home, it was possible to give far less attention to child training than in peacetime (95).

ADVANTAGES OF HAND DOMINANCE

During the first two years of life, the child shifts from one hand to the other, though he generally shows a slight preference for one. The period from three to five years is the "critical period" in establishing handedness. At this time, the child shows more and more preference for the use of one hand. Left to chance, he may develop habits of right-hand dominance, of left-hand dominance, or of ambidexterity, using the right hand for certain activities and the left for others (19). Hildreth has stated that "handedness should be trained, not left to chance, since manual dexterity can affect an individual's educational and vocational success" (57). In a similar vein, Wiley has pointed out that because the human infant has no definite sidedness, either right or left, "it is wrong to let a child choose for himself as there is a 50–50 chance he may select the wrong side" (95). Many parents of today, however, protest against guidance in handedness on the grounds that it "interferes with nature."

Dominant handedness is advantageous. With the establishment of hand dominance come not only feelings of stability and security but also opportunities to develop levels of skill that would be impossible if attempts were made to use both hands with equal or nearly equal frequency. If a child learns to perform the majority of skills with one hand, the auxiliary hand is then trained to work with the dominant hand, and as a team the two can operate with great efficiency. As Hildreth has emphasized, "Only a genius would have the ability to attain equal mastery of the two hands in a lifetime so as to be able to use them alternately in the same role" (57). Most children who lack hand dominance or who are slow in acquiring it are somewhat deficient in the use of both hands. They usually have less strength, speed, and accuracy in movements than the child who is either right- or left-handed (22, 83).

RIGHT- VERSUS LEFT-HANDEDNESS

The next important question is, "Which hand should be the dominant one, the right or the left?" The only answer in our culture is that a child should become right-handed unless it is difficult or impossible for him to do so. There is no reason to believe that the right hand is superior to the left or that a nation of right-handed people is superior to a nation of left-handers. It has become traditional, however, to regard the right hand as the preferred hand, and much in our culture has been built on this traditional preference. As Hildreth explains, "Right-handedness is a cultural and social convention to which most people are trained and find it expedient to conform. . . . In an unbiased world, left-handedness would be as common as right-handedness, for the play of chance factors would be equal for the two sides" (57). But this is not an unbiased world. Instead, as Dayhaw has emphasized, "Our modern world is dextral-minded" (30). Machines, home appliances, sporting equipment, desk chairs, desk drawers, illumination, and the tools of our modern machine age are all designed and made for the right-handers. Methods of teaching are also geared to the right-handed (95).

Disadvantages of Left-handedness. In a right-handed world, it is certainly easier and less confusing for an individual to be right-handed than left-handed. There are many practical learning difficulties associated with left-handedness. For example, all systems of teaching writing are based on the assumption that the writer will use his right hand. Unless the teacher is able to demonstrate how to write with the left hand, left-handed pupils must adapt the right-handed model to fit their left-hand imitations (110).

What does this mean for the child? While the left-handed child normally would write from right to left, he tries to imitate the right-handed model—writing from left to right. This means that he must resort to awkward and inefficient movements. It means, also, that he must push his pencil or pen across the page and must incline his paper toward the diagonal—top right, bottom left—just the opposite of what a right-handed child does. If he uses a pen, he runs the risk of smudging the first letters with his writing hand (110). When he writes in this "crablike fashion," he becomes fatigued more quickly than the right-handed child because he must flex his arm rather than extending it as he writes. In addition, his school papers generally have an untidy appearance from the smudging of his writing as he writes across the page from left to right in imitation of the right-handed model (101). Figure 5–10 shows the characteristic positions of the writing hand, the auxiliary hand, and the paper for right- and left-handed writers.

While *speed* of writing varies from child to child regardless of the hand used, children who write with their left hands write, on the average, at about four-fifths the speed of the average right-hander. Furthermore, the tension in the flexed muscles of the hand and arm of the left-hander not only increases his fatigue but tends to slow down the rate of his writing. The handwriting itself has a cramped appearance. If left-handed children are given a left-handed model instead of having to adapt to a right-handed model, this difference in speed disappears, as does much of the tension (101, 110).

Learning difficulties for the left-hander extend to every motor skill. These difficulties spring from two sources: the equipment and the demonstration of the method of using the equipment. Baseball gloves, for example, are made for right-handers. Machines of all kinds are "right-handed"; a left-hander must adapt to them (69, 95).

Demonstrations of how to use equipment are generally given for the benefit of people who are right-handed. This is true outside of school as well as in school. It is confusing and frustrating to a left-handed child to have to adapt for his own use the play models meant for the right-hander in addition to having to adjust to the right-handed equipment. Furthermore, it is difficult for a right-handed person to instruct a left-hander in such simple performances as tying a bow, drawing, or throwing a ball. The more complicated the performance, the greater the difficulty in demonstrating it. When a teacher tries to adapt the model to meet the needs of the left-hander, the result may be as confusing to the child as his own trial-and-error attempts.

The practical difficulties associated with left-handedness often increase as the individual grows older. In adolescence, boys and girls become "manners-conscious" in their

 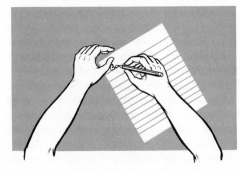

Figure 5–10.   Positions of right and left hands in writing. (Adapted from G. Hildreth, The development and training of hand dominance. 1. Characteristics of handedness, J. genet. Psychol., 1949, 75, 197–220. Used by permission.)

desire to increase their social acceptance. *Manners,* too, are designed for the right-handed person. In our culture, one is expected to shake hands with the right hand, to serve oneself from a platter passed on the left side, and to cut with the knife held in the right hand while the left hand acts as the auxiliary, holding the food in place with a fork. The adolescent will become embarrassed and self-conscious if he automatically holds out his left hand to greet someone, if he nudges the person seated next to him when he is cutting his food, or if he finds it difficult to serve himself from a platter held at his left side.

When he applies for work that requires the manipulation of complicated machinery, the left-handed person finds that even if he can adapt the training methods to his left-handed needs, he still cannot make as great speed as the right-handers do. Many employers do not like to hire left-handed applicants; they believe that left-handers are harder to train, are slower workers, and are "safety hazards" (95).

In addition to the practical difficulties associated with left-handedness is the effect it has upon the child's *personality,* upon his attitudes toward self, and upon his social adjustments. Because the prejudice against left-handedness has persisted since earliest times, many left-handed children are made to feel inadequate and ashamed when they are constantly reminded to use their right hands (8). This may cause the child to try to avoid social situations in which he might be awkward. Any factor that curtails a child's spontaneity and sense of freedom or that causes him to withdraw into his shell so that it hinders his communication with others leaves a mark on his personality.

Frustrations in learning or in social situations often lead to lack of interest and motivation, discouragement, and antisocial behavior (63). The extent to which left-handedness causes frustrations will influence the extent to which it affects the child's personality. Commenting on the problems of the left-handed child and the effect of these problems on his personality, Jersild maintains that "the hardship a child must bear

because of being left-handed may be very light, yet there is bound to be at least some hardship connected with being a left-hander. A person cannot differ from most other people without having to pay at least a small price for such a difference." How big a price this will be varies. As Jersild has stressed, "Handedness *as such* is likely to have a very small impact on the child's personality and his view of himself if other circumstances in his life and in his relationship with others are favorable." The inconveniences and frustrations caused by being left-handed in a right-handed world, he adds, may be compensated for, in part, by the greater degree of ambidexterity many left-handed children develop in their attempts to adjust to the equipment and methods of teaching designed for those who are right-handed (69).

Changing Left-handedness. As evidence today seems to point to the fact that in most cases left-handedness results from learning, a child should learn to use his right hand from the time he is capable of doing things with one hand alone. If he has learned to do things with his left hand, can he change and become right-handed? Experience has shown that he can, but the longer he waits to make the shift, the more difficult it will be.

Whenever changes must be made and new adjustments learned, there will be nervous tension. This may lead to resistance, especially if the child is *forced* to make the change instead of being encouraged to do so. Should resistance develop, it will increase the confusion and tension for the child. It is not true, however, that corrective measures will, per se, cause serious psychological difficulties, especially if the change is made before left-hand habits have been strongly established (58). It is true that the tension aroused when there is interference with partially established habits *may* lead to stuttering and other forms of nervous behavior, such as nail biting and thumb sucking. These are more likely to be *symptoms* of the tension resulting from the child's attempts to break an old habit and establish a new one than of the change of handedness. This point of view was well summarized by Jersild:

That children who have been compelled to change from the left to the right hand may show a tendency to stutter, at least for some time, has been observed in some cases, but the cause-and-effect relationship here is not entirely clear. It is difficult to determine whether the stuttering is directly due to the change in handedness or whether it is due primarily to the methods that are used and the atmosphere that prevails when the child is being forced into using his right hand. The stuttering, in other words, may be a symptom of the tension and confusion produced by the pressures that are brought to bear rather than a direct result of the change itself. Furthermore, while stuttering sometimes occurs, it by no means occurs in all cases in which a child is prevailed upon to change to the right hand; in addition, stuttering appears in cases in which there is no clear evidence of difficulty with regard to hand preference. To sum up, a change in hand preference as the result of pressure from others may, in individual cases, have unwholesome consequences. Risking such consequences is certainly not worthwhile (69).

Normally, the tension caused by attempts to change handedness will subside when the change has been made unless there is too long a delay in making the change and unless the stuttering or other nervous mannerisms have become fixed habits. It is also possible that the child's resistance to change may be so great that attempts to break down his resistance may do permanent damage to his personality and establish habits of stuttering or other nervous forms of behavior that will persist throughout life (8, 30, 58).

The extent and duration of psychological damage resulting from attempts to change the child from a left- to a right-hander will vary according to the personality makeup of the child. A high-strung, nervous child, for example, will suffer greater and longer-lasting damage than a child who is placid and easygoing. Under certain conditions, the risk of psychological damage is reduced to a minimum. Hildreth has suggested the following conditions as favorable prognostic indications for changing handedness:

The child is under six years of age.
The child uses both hands interchangeably.
The handedness index is bilateral.
A trial period shows no permanent difficulty.
The child is agreeable to the change.
The child is above average in intelligence (58).

In conclusion, then, it becomes apparent that parents and teachers must make a choice between two alternatives: (1) trying to change the child's handedness from left to right and running the risk of damaging his personality, and (2) allowing the child to persist in the use of his left hand and running the risk of his feeling embarrassed and inferior because he is "different." While being left-handed in a right-handed world has disadvantages, it is sometimes questionable whether they are not preferable to the damage that may result from trying to change left-handed habits that have been permitted to become firmly established (69).

COMMON SKILLS IN CHILDHOOD

The repertoire of skills acquired after the basic coordinations have been attained depends to a large extent upon the child's environment, his opportunities to learn, and his motivation to do so. Children in rural districts, for example, acquire more skills in climbing than children in urban communities, where opportunities for climbing are distinctly limited. Similarly, a child may have little motivation to acquire a skill that has no prestige in the eyes of the peer group, even though he has ample opportunities for learning. The skills needed to play the piano may not be acquired by a boy whose parents give him music lessons and time free from home duties for practice because, in the eyes of the peer group, "only sissies" play the piano.

Furthermore, the development of skills depends not on an all-around motor ability but on many relatively independent motor abilities. Children differ in motor abilities, as they do in other abilities that have their roots in the hereditary endowment of the individual. Because no two children are exactly alike in their specific motor abilities, it is obvious that the repertoire of skills they acquire will also vary. A child who stands high in motor abilities related to speed, for example, will develop skill in more activities requiring speed than the child who rates low in speed but high in coordination or flexibility (50).

Some skills are commonly found among all children in a given culture because of common learning experiences and common adult expectations. In our culture, every child is expected to learn to feed and dress himself, to write, and to play the games in common usage in the social group with which he is identified. Furthermore, he is expected to learn these skills at approximately the same age at which other children learn them; they are among the "developmental tasks" of childhood (54). A brief summary of the most important common skills of childhood will illustrate the approximate ages at which the skills will be acquired and the pattern of development they follow. The norms have been established on the basis of tests of intelligence and motor development.

Norms for Hand Skills. At twelve months, the baby can hold a pencil or crayon; he can remove a paper cap from his head. At the age of two years, he can open boxes; unscrew lids from bottles or jars; turn the leaves of a book; build a tower of four or five blocks; insert a circle, square, or triangle in a form board; scribble with pencil or crayon; string beads; smear paint; roll clay; drive a nail into soap or soft wood; and cut a gash in paper with scissors. By the third year, the child can take care of many of his bodily needs, such as undressing himself, feeding himself, going to the toilet, and washing himself; he can dry dishes, dust, carry a tray, string four beads in 2 minutes, build a bridge of three blocks in imitation of a model, copy a circle in

imitation of a model, and cover a picture with paint.

At the age of five years, the average child can fold a triangle from a paper 6 inches square in imitation of a model; copy a square when given a model to imitate; trace around a diamond drawn on paper; draw a triangle, a diagonal, and a recognizable picture of a man; cut with scissors; put toys away neatly in a box; wash himself without getting his clothes very wet; and tie a single knot around a pencil with a shoelace after looking at a model of a knot. The six-year-old can use his skills in carpentry to make a table, wagon, or boat; he can model with clay, make cookies, sew, copy a diamond, and help with simple household tasks such as carrying glasses and pitchers of milk without spilling (37, 84, 117).

After six years of age, skilled movements with the hands may be acquired quickly and easily if the child is given guidance and an opportunity to learn the most effective methods to use. Control of the muscles of the arms, shoulders, and wrists improves rapidly and reaches almost the adult level of perfection by the time the child is twelve years old. Control of the fine muscles of the fingers, by contrast, develops at a slower rate, as shown by the fact that the control necessary for speedy writing or the playing of musical instruments is not attained by most children until they are twelve years old or older (17). In copying geometric figures, which requires fine coordinations of the finger muscles, children show rapid improvement up to the age of seven years. After that age, the improvement is slow and irregular, with the greatest improvement shown by children with high IQs (120).

A number of studies of the pattern of development of different skills reveal that most children pass through similar stages in their mastery of *specific hand skills*. Of the skills that have received the greatest attention, the following are the most important:

1. Self-feeding. The baby shows his interest in self-feeding during the latter part of the first year of life, when he tries to hold

his bottle or cup and reaches for the spoon with which he is being fed. By the age of eight months, the baby can hold his bottle after it has been placed in his mouth; one month later, he can remove the bottle as well as put it back. By the end of the first year, he can hold his cup momentarily, and he tries to feed himself with a spoon, though he usually spills most of the food as he carries it to his mouth. With practice, this skill improves, and he spills less and less. While mastering the skill of using his spoon, he is also learning to hold his cup. At first, he holds on with both hands, but gradually, with practice, he can hold it with only one hand (17, 43).

By the end of the second year, the young child spills less food and uses his fork in addition to his spoon. During the third year, he can spread butter or jam on his bread with a knife. A year later, he may have mastered the complicated skill of using his knife to cut with. Because self-feeding requires concentration, the young child becomes fatigued, and this leads to dawdling. The peak of dawdling comes usually between the third and fourth years. As the skills improve, the child can eat and talk simultaneously. By ten years of age, the child should have good control of his eating utensils, his table manners should be almost mature, and he should require only occasional help (91).

2. Self-dressing. It is easier for a little child to pull off his socks and shoes than to put them on; the motor skill involved in the former is much less than in the latter. The period of most rapid improvement in dressing is between 1½ and 3½ years (75). Some garments are more difficult to put on than others, and some require more adjusting and fastening. Girls, as a rule, dress themselves earlier and more efficiently than boys, primarily because girls have more flexibility of the wrist, better general motor coordination, and simpler clothing. By the time the child is five years old, he should be able to dress himself completely, with the exception of tying the bowknot on his shoes.

This he generally learns to do by the time he is six (91).

Eye-hand coordination is necessary until the child learns to dress himself so automatically that he can do so by "feel" alone. While learning to dress himself, the child must be able to see the button, hook, or fastener before he can manipulate it. By three or four years of age, most children can deal with fasteners in difficult positions if they look in the mirror. Only after the skilled movements involved in dressing are well developed, around the sixth year, can the child's hands manipulate fasteners without the aid of the eyes to guide the hands (125).

Skills connected with *grooming* develop along with dressing skills. The baby will take a hairbrush and try to brush his hair even before he can walk. Not before two or three years of age, however, can he brush his hair without rumpling it. By the time he reaches kindergarten age, he should be able to brush and comb his hair successfully, though he will doubtless need help in getting a straight part for a year or so longer. Because girls have more complicated hair styles, they are likely to be slower in developing the skills needed in grooming their hair than are boys (17).

During the bath, a baby will try to bathe himself, using the soap, sponge, or washcloth to run down the center of his face and body. Most of his early attempts at self-bathing, however, are limited to splashing the water and playing with the equipment used for bathing. Toward the end of the second year, the young child settles down to the business of bathing himself; he covers most of the front of his body but will be unable to wash his own back until he is six or seven years old. Brushing the teeth, especially when he likes the taste of the toothpaste, is a game for a young child. By the time he acquires all his baby teeth, during the middle of the third year of life, he is able to brush them successfully with little or no help (43, 64).

3. Writing. Studies of writing have revealed that the development of this skill follows a

fairly definite pattern, in which there is a clear-cut gradient in the age changes. Up to one year, the baby bangs and scribbles with his pencil. By eighteen months, he will scribble in the middle of the page, and by three years, he will attempt to make simple symbol units, though these are scarcely recognizable as letters. On the average, the body is not biologically ready for handwriting before the child is approximately six years old. Up until that age, the nerves and muscles of the fingers, hand, wrist, and arm are not developed enough to make the fine coordinations needed in writing. In his early attempts at writing, the child moves his hand from the lower right-hand corner of the paper to the center, then to the top center, and finally to the top left. This final position comes between the seventh and eighth years. He will then transfer the habit of starting to write at the top left position on the page to drawing and will begin his drawings there (4, 32).

The pattern of development in the forming of letters is as follows:

3½ years	Prints a few capital letters, large, single letters, anywhere on the page.
4 years	Prints a few capitals, large and irregular, usually the initial capital of his first name.
5 years	Prints first name in large and irregular letters, getting larger toward the middle or end of the name. Frequently reverses letters, especially *S*. Prints numbers 1 to 5, uneven and medium-sized.
6 years	Prints entire alphabet in large, irregular letters with many reversals. Copies words, using all capitals with some reversal of letters and in the wrong order. Prints numbers 1 to 20, with frequent reversals in the numbers 3, 7, and 9.
7 years	Most children can write, though some still print in capitals. Writing is large, straight, labored, and irregular in size and shape. Numbers are smaller, but there are many errors.
8 years	Most children write by now, in

large, square, and quite black letters. Capitals and looped letters are disproportionately tall. Numbers are smaller, and there are fewer errors.

9 years	Children no longer print. The writing is smaller, neater, more even, slanted, and shows the beginning of an individual style. Letters are in good proportions. Beginnings of an individual style are shown in the writing of the child's name. Girls' writing is smaller, neater, and more evenly slanted than boys' (6).

4. Copying.   Copying even the simplest geometric figures from a model is very difficult for a young child because it requires not only control over the finer muscles of the hand and arm but also the ability to perceive relationships. Thus it is a skill that cannot be developed until the muscles, nerves, and brain have reached the developmental status needed for such an intricate act. Because there is a relationship between neuromuscular development and intelligence, copying is used as a measure of intelligence in some of the intelligence tests for the early age levels (27). In the Stanford Revision of the Binet Scale, tests include copying a square at five years of age, a diamond at seven, and reproducing a simple geometric figure from memory at ten (119). According to the Gesell norms, the average five-year-old can copy a triangle, but not until he is seven years old can a child copy a diamond—in spite of the fact that a diamond is two triangles put together. He must be able to see this relationship before he can reproduce it in his drawing (39).

Between the ages of 2½ and 5 years, most children show consistent improvement in their ability to copy simple geometric figures. They make many errors, however, not only in the forms of their drawings but also in size, tending to underestimate or overestimate the size of the model. In a study of young children, it has been found that copying improves with chronological and mental age, but *more* with mental than with chronological age. The reason for the closer relationship between the development of this skill and mental age is that form perception plays an important role in copying. Copying is not merely a manual skill which can be developed without an understanding of the meaning of the activity involved (47, 120).

5. **Ball Throwing and Catching.** The ability to throw and catch balls requires well-coordinated movements, not only of the arms and hands, but of the entire body. As Gesell has pointed out, "Skill in throwing a ball requires a fine sense of static and dynamic balance, accurate timing of delivery and release, good eye-hand coordination, and appropriate functioning of the fingers, as well as the arms, trunk, head, and legs, in controlling the trajectory of the ball" (39). While some babies roll and may even attempt to throw balls before they are two years old, none is able to do so well. Even at four years, few can throw or catch well. By six years, most children are proficient, though there are marked variations in the skill at every age.

The size of the ball influences the method of throwing and the distance thrown. At first, both hands are used, and there is mass movement of the body. Gradually, the movements become more specialized, and only one hand is used. The norm for throwing a 9½-inch ball 12 to 13 feet is fifty-seven months, and for a 16½-inch ball, seventy-two months (51, 128).

Ball catching is likewise difficult. At four years, few children are proficient, while at six years, approximately two-thirds are. Girls, on the whole, are more proficient in ball catching than boys. At first, the child uses his whole body to clasp the ball and then uses his arms, with less movement. Later, he perfects a coordinated movement of the hand, or hands, to catch the ball between the palms. A five-year-old catches best a ball 5 inches in diameter, whereas a six-year-old catches well with a ball of 12 inches (51).

6. **Block Building.** The child first carries blocks from place to place and manipulates them in irregular masses. By the age of three, he places them in regular piles or rows to build simple structures or enclosures. Gradually, his constructions become more complex and are often used as part of dramatic play. The more difficult structures tend to be built obliquely at the edge of a table, while the more familiar structures are symmetrically centered (4).

Skills Following Walking. After the child reaches eighteen months of age, motor development in the legs consists primarily of the perfection of walking and the acquisition of related skills. Running, hopping, skipping, jumping, climbing, and other skills soon follow walking. Before a child is two years old, he can walk sideways and backward; he can walk upstairs and downstairs with help; and he can stand on one foot and then the other with help. By the time he is three years old, he can walk upstairs and downstairs alone, stand on one foot without help, and walk on tiptoe.

By his fourth birthday, the child can jump from a height of about 12 inches and make a standing jump of about 23 to 33 inches. Between the fifth and sixth years, he can jump rope; he can balance on a narrow plank elevated at one end or on a chalk mark on the floor; and he can roller-skate on four wheels but cannot ice-skate if the skates have a single runner. By the time he is six years old, he can ride a bicycle and keep time to music by walking and skipping. During the first 3 years of school, the child can dance imaginative rhythms and skip to music, skate on a single runner, and participate in a wide number of games requiring skills related to walking (50, 84, 117).

A number of studies have been made of the patterns of development of *specific leg skills*. The most important of these are as follows:

1. **Running.** At first, running is little more than fast walking with crude, uneven steps and a general clumsiness of the entire body that leads to many falls. By the age of five or six years, the young child can not only run with relatively few falls but can play

games at the same time. When the young child first starts to run, he does so, not because he wants to get to a given place quickly, but because he derives satisfaction from the activity itself. Later, when the ability to run is well developed, he reserves this activity for occasions requiring speed (91).

2. Jumping.   Jumping is at first an exaggerated stepping with one foot and then the other; or the child may drop himself from the place of support, lifting both feet simultaneously and stepping with both at once. The body is not propelled forward, and, as a result, the child generally lands in a sprawl and has trouble getting up. This is the characteristic method of jumping of the two-year-old. By the age of four, the child can jump well. He propels his body upward and forward, bends his knees, swings from higher to lower levels, and lands in a standing position. Jumping over an obstacle is difficult even for a four-year-old, and few children attempt long jumps much before they are five (51, 91).

3. Skipping and Hopping.   Skipping and hopping are modifications of jumping. While children attempt to hop before they are three years old, they are not skillful until they are six or seven. Hopping on two feet precedes hopping on one. After achieving skillful hopping, the child adds variations by hopping backward or by turning around while hopping. Because skipping is more difficult than hopping, few children are proficient in skipping by the time they are six years old. In learning to skip, the child first introduces a hop or jump into his running. Then he skips with one foot, using a running step with the other. Later, he skips with both feet and, as he becomes proficient, introduces variations, such as crossing his feet, twirling, or skipping sideways (51, 91).

4. Galloping.   Galloping, which is another modification of jumping, develops later than skipping. Not until the child is 6½ or 7 years old can he gallop well. The child first introduces a galloping step into his running,

or he pounds on the strong beat of music. Later, he learns the basic movement of galloping, which is to throw the weight on the forward foot. After skill in galloping is achieved, many variations are introduced, such as galloping sideways or backward (51, 91).

5. Climbing.   Climbing steps is accomplished first by crawling and creeping, even before the baby can walk. In going down steps, the baby generally goes backward. After he can walk alone, he goes upstairs and downstairs in an upright position, holding the railing of the stairs or the hand of a person. At first, one foot is placed on the step, and the other is drawn up to it. The same foot is used each time to make the advance. A similar method is used for going downstairs. Gradually, with practice, the child lets go of the railing and uses his legs alternately, as in walking. This adult manner of step climbing is attained by four years of age, provided the child has had ample opportunity to learn. Girls are generally slower than boys in acquiring skill in climbing. After gaining sufficient skill to climb well, children start to do stunts, such as racing, competing, and climbing in dramatic projects (51, 91).

Stair climbing has a pattern almost identical to that observed in creeping. Typically, the left foot moves first; then the left hand and the right foot almost simultaneously; then, after a pause, the right hand and the left foot. The pattern is closely similar to that used for progression on level surfaces. A child who creeps on hands and knees, for example, climbs stairs on hands and knees; the child who creeps on hands, knee, and one foot climbs stairs in that fashion. Much the same pattern of behavior is found in ladder climbing (64, 65). Figure 5–11 shows the characteristic stages in learning to climb.

6. Swimming.   How soon a child will acquire swimming skills will depend to a large extent upon the opportunities he has to learn. Few children acquire these skills much before the age of four years, and many do not acquire them until several

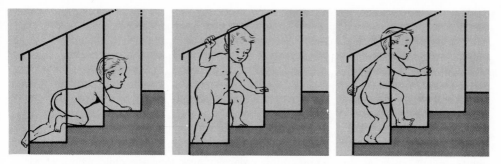

Figure 5–11.   Stages in climbing.

years later. Because swimming is such a highly coordinated type of skill, it requires more practice than many of the other skills of childhood. When submerged in water in a prone position, a baby a few weeks old will make rhythmical, coordinated reflex movements of the upper and lower extremities which resemble swimming. Several months later, he makes disorganized struggling movements, tending to rotate the body from a prone to a supine position. These movements are accompanied by difficulties in respiration. Toward the end of the second year, the baby makes deliberate swimming movements, especially in the lower extremities, and shows a tendency to remain in a prone position (87, 88).

7. Tricycling.   By the age of two years, a few children can ride tricycles. Between three and four, any child who has an opportunity to learn can do so. After achieving a skilled performance, children use their tricycles for stunting, such as riding backward, turning corners, riding while standing up, and avoiding obstacles (51, 91).

AWKWARDNESS

Not all children progress through the stages of motor development outlined above at the average ages. There are many instances of accelerated development and even more of retarded development. Where motor development is appreciably delayed, it is usually apparent at an early age. If remedial treat-

ment is given as soon as the delay is recognized, retardation can, in most instances, be eliminated or minimized. Because skills are built upon the foundations laid by the maturation of the basic motor coordinations, delay in maturation of muscle control will automatically result in delay in the development of skills. As a result, the child will be regarded as awkward, clumsy, or careless because he falls below the norms for his age.

Not all children who are judged so are, in reality, awkward. They may *seem* to be awkward because they are judged by standards inappropriate for them. Naturally, as skills take years to develop, one cannot, in fairness to a child, expect adult behavior in this area any more than one can expect adult behavior in other areas. A child who is mentally precocious enough to be in a grade above that of his agemates is very likely to be judged in terms of his *apparent age,* not his real age. Hilgard has called this the "size-age confusion," which creates the false impression that the child is awkward when, in reality, he may have better motor coordination than most children of his chronological age. A two-year-old who is so large for his age that he looks like a three-year-old is likely to be judged awkward when standards of motor development for the three-year-old are applied to him. Similarly, as childhood draws to a close, the early-maturing child is bigger and behaves more like an older child than his late-maturing agemates. Under such conditions, it is unfair to judge him by standards for older children (59).

Variations in Awkwardness. There are not only interindividual differences in awkwardness but also intraindividual differences. A child who is temporarily nervous, tense, and emotionally disturbed, for example, will be more awkward than he normally is. A well-coordinated child may be so clumsy and awkward when he is in a fit of temper or is fatigued that he seems to be all thumbs. During periods of rapid growth, as in the puberty growth spurt at the end of childhood, established patterns of muscular coordination are upset. Children who mature rapidly are more awkward at this time than slow maturers who have time to adjust to their newly enlarged hands and feet. Although this awkwardness is likely to be only temporary—as is that caused by fatigue or emotional tension—it is serious because of the psychological effect it has on the child (12, 115).

Children differ in the degree of motor control they have in different situations. As a result of differences in learning opportunities, in the time spent in acquiring skills, and in motivation, children are well coordinated in some activities and awkward in others. A child who has plenty of opportunity to practice ice skating but little opportunity to play ball or ride a bicycle, for example, will be a proficient skater but will be below the norm for his age in ball playing and bicycling. The high prestige associated with athletic skills motivates boys to practice these skills until they become proficient in them. Social skills, on the other hand, are often regarded as "sissy," and boys have little motivation to practice them (121).

Causes of Awkwardness. Some causes of awkwardness are controllable, and others are not. A child may be awkward for several reasons or for only one. The most common causes of awkwardness are the following:

1. Poor Physical Condition. Popular opinion holds that there is a close relationship between the physical condition of the child and his motor development. This would mean that children who were in the best physical condition would be more precocious in their motor development than children of the same age who were in poor physical condition. This hypothesis is not necessarily true because it fails to take into consideration factors other than health which contribute to the child's motor development. There is evidence, however, that, other factors being equal, the child of superior health is more precocious in motor development than the child whose physical condition is poor (80).

A child whose health is poor has little motivation to exercise and, as a consequence, does not get the practice needed to develop skills. As Martin and Vincent have pointed out, when the child's health is poor, "the body does not have the energy or the vitality to move, to seek new experiences, to practice new learnings. . . . *Exercise* of the body as a whole is important to the development and strengthening of muscles. Without it muscles are not used and, hence, are not 'educated' to increasing ease and accuracy of movement" (84).

In the prenatal environment, a healthy condition predisposes the fetus to greater activity; this is reflected in advanced motor development during the first postnatal year. Should the baby be in poor health, the age at which he sits, stands, and walks will most likely be delayed. Sensory defects, especially early blindness, are likely to retard the motor development of the child owing mainly to timidity on the child's part and lack of stimulation on the part of his parents (28, 38).

2. Body Build. The body build of the child will determine to some degree the ease or difficulty with which he can handle his body. The child with a stocky build, for example, is better adapted to activities requiring strength than those requiring speed. If he tries to move quickly, he may do so at the expense of grace. In the early years of life, however, all children are characteristically "top-heavy" and more awkward in their movements than they will be later. There must be an increase in the ratio of leg to trunk length and a decrease in the ratio of weight to height before the child can maintain his balance gracefully.

Small-boned, thin, or muscular babies, in general, walk sooner than short, rotund, or exceedingly heavy babies. When weight is held constant, an increase of 1 inch in length at birth has been found to be associated with a mean decrease of 22 days in walking age. When, on the other hand, length at birth is held constant, an increase of 1 pound in weight is associated with a mean increase of 8 days in age of walking alone (96, 117).

Once the muscular and skeletal equipment for sitting, standing, and walking has been developed, the course of the child's motor development will be influenced by factors other than body build. Among older children, body build is of little importance in determining motor coordinations. Excessive weight alone, for example, does not delay motor development seriously. If weight gain occurs rapidly, however, motor skills develop more slowly than when weight gain is gradual. The reason for this is that rapid changes in body proportions necessitate more relearning than gradual changes (84, 127).

At every age, excessive deviation from the norm in body build is a handicap to the performance of motor skills. Extremely thin or extremely stocky children, for example, show less agility than those who are more nearly average in build. The very thin child, like the one who is obese, tends to be inactive. Consequently, his motor skills are inferior to those of his agemates, not because of his body build, per se, but because his body build motivates him *not* to practice enough to acquire skills (20).

3. Intelligence. The relationship between intelligence and motor development, especially during the first years of life, is so marked that motor items figure largely in tests of general intelligence for children under two years of age. Babies who are slow in sitting, standing, or walking generally prove, as time goes on, to be backward in intellectual development (82). On the other hand, those who are precocious in motor development prove to be, for the most part, intellectually precocious. In the age of walking, there has been found to be a mean difference of an appreciable amount between babies of high- and low-grade intelligence. Unusually high intelligence, however, is not always accompanied by early walking; other factors may be responsible for delaying the walking (28, 31).

Among older children and adolescents, there is practically no relationship between normal intelligence and motor performance (48, 71). In a study of elementary-school children, it was found that mental growth and reading ability were not correlated with motor skills. When the child is mentally deficient, however, he is likely to be below the norm for his age in motor development; the more deficient he is mentally, the more awkward and clumsy he will be (46, 82). Furthermore, the difference between mentally retarded and normal children in motor performances increases with age. As Francis and Rarick have said, "The great [motor] differences . . . between the normal and the mentally retarded . . . clearly show that the degree of mental retardation of these [retarded] children is perhaps greater than had been previously supposed" (36). If given special training, mentally retarded children *might* improve their motor skills, but probably not enough to bring them up to the level of children with normal intelligence (62).

A high level of intelligence in older children would, by contrast, logically be associated with superior motor coordinations. This usually is not the case. In fact, very bright children are often awkward and clumsy in activities in which skills are involved—in games and sports of all types, in dancing, and in manual skills, such as painting, drawing, sewing, or clay modeling. The explanation for this is not that they cannot develop skills, as is true of mentally deficient children, but rather that they *do not want* to. Having little interest in activities in which skills play a major role, they have little motivation to practice, and, as a result, they fail to develop these skills. In comparison with children of their own age, they appear to be awkward, and in comparison with children a year or two older, with whom they are often associated in their school classes and, consequently, in their play, they appear to be even more awkward (28, 60).

4. Lack of Opportunity to Develop Muscle Control.

In many instances, motor development is delayed because of lack of opportunity for practice. The baby whose environment is restricted to crib, coach, or playpen or who, if given a wider environment, finds that the floors are so slippery that he falls and that everything he leans on for support slides under his weight is hampered in developing muscle control. The environment of an adult is, in almost every respect, unsuited to the needs of a young baby and thus offers him little opportunity for the practice needed to acquire motor control.

A study of institutional children in Iran revealed that the children were retarded in sitting, creeping, and walking. An analysis of the possible causes for the retardation showed that, as babies, the children were not propped up in sitting positions, nor were they placed in varied prone positions. Furthermore, they were kept in very small cribs. Clearly, their retardation in motor development stemmed from lack of opportunity to learn. This explanation was substantiated by the fact that by the time the children were four years old, they had caught up to the norm for children of that age (33).

The advanced motor development of Negro babies from the lower social classes is due mainly to the permissive child-training methods used with these children. Among middle- and upper-class Negro families, as among white families, there is a tendency to restrict the babies' environment by cribs, tenders, and high chairs; as a result, they lag behind Negro babies of the lower social classes (130).

Children who get a poor start in the development of motor control often continue to lag behind their agemates as they grow older. Even those who are not handicapped by a poor start are often limited in their opportunities to learn by the environment in which they live, by lack of materials—especially play equipment—or by lack of someone to teach them skills. A city child from a poor neighborhood, for example, may have insufficient play space or play equipment. When he enters school, his play skills will be inferior to those of children from better neighborhoods who have had opportunities to develop such skills, and he will seem awkward and clumsy in comparison (48, 66, 129). His environment will also encourage him to develop substitute play activities where skills are less important. When this happens, the motivation to learn skills is weakened. Consequently, he will not be interested in taking advantage of opportunities which may come to him later. As a result, he will continue to lag behind his contemporaries. His awkwardness will become more and more apparent, and he will withdraw further and further from activities in which skills play an important role (55, 84).

5. Lack of Incentive to Develop Muscle Control.

Even if the young child is given an environment suited to his needs, he may be slow in developing muscle control because of lack of incentive to do so. If he is pampered and waited on, and if his every wish is satisfied, he becomes lazy. In walking, dressing, and self-feeding, this is especially obvious. Permissive methods of child training lead to better motor control than authoritarian methods, which emphasize pushing the baby to come up to standards set by overzealous parents. Under such proddings, the baby usually becomes balky and resistant; any motivation he might otherwise have had to develop his capacities is thus stifled (130).

A comparison of young children from homes of high and low economic status revealed that while those from the more favored environments ranked above those from the poorer environments in verbal, practical, and emotional abilities, the former were inferior in skills involved in self-care, such as washing the face and hands and combing the hair. The difference was found to be due largely to the greater motivation children from the poorer environments had to do things for themselves; they had no one to do them for them. This is likewise true of children from large families as compared with those from small families (16).

Children who are very bright, children who have some special talent that interests them more than activities involving motor skills, and children who are unpopular and have few playmates often lack motivation to take advantage of opportunities to develop motor skills. This lack of a desire to learn is also common among older children. Many school-age children today develop "antiwork" attitudes; they scorn anything that suggests "manual labor" (123). To them, being "helpless" and awkward is a status symbol. It shows that they are above work. They are encouraged in this attitude by group pressures and group approval. Evidence of the role such pressures play is

. . . found in the rewarding and indulging of sedentary behavior by television programs and automobile rides. To many children, physical inactivity is made to appear the ultimate juvenile virtue. Gadget manipulation of fine-muscle push-button type is also rewarded by a variety of ingenious toys. Many young Americans are thus given considerable encouragement toward the life of sedentary onlookers controlling mechanical activity by the push of a button or the twist of a wrist (80).

6. Emphasis on "Perfection." Some adults —parents and occasionally teachers—expect a child's motor skills to approach the level of perfection characteristic of adult skills (1). They push the child into a learning situation before he is ready, and they expect him to learn specific movements before the gross movements have been perfected. For example, in writing or dancing, the child is expected to coordinate the smaller muscle teams before coordinating the larger ones. Because this is too complicated for him, he becomes discouraged and rebellious. Later, when he is physically and neurologically ready, he resists learning. As a result, he lags behind other children of his age and soon begins to think of himself as inferior to them. Thus, two factors—lack of practice

in developing motor coordinations and an unfavorable attitude toward his abilities— contribute to his awkwardness. When he is scolded or punished for his clumsiness or accused of "not trying," he becomes tense and thus more awkward.

7. Emotional Tension.   Any strong emotion, whether it is fear, anger, jealousy, or hatred, is accompanied by bodily preparation for action. This preparation consists, among other things, of tensing the muscles so that they are alert and ready for instantaneous action. Under such conditions, even the well-coordinated individual has less control over his muscles than he has during periods of emotional calm, and he will appear to be clumsy and awkward.

Children who tend to be nervous and high-strung inevitably have less control over their movements than those who are more relaxed. When given equal abilities to begin with, equal motivation to learn, equal opportunities for practice under guidance, and equal practice time, those who are emotionally calm are likely to be superior in skills of all types to those who are emotionally disturbed. The more disturbed emotionally the child is, the less well coordinated he will be (67, 81).

Fear often causes an inhibition that makes the child hesitant to repeat the act associated with the fear. When, for example, a child is forced to walk before he is ready to do so, to climb stairs when he is not sure of himself, or to dive before he can swim with ease and confidence, fear is the usual outcome. Parental concern about the child's safety or his ability to measure up to the standards of his age group often intimidates the child and makes him nervous and tense when he tries to carry out the skill. The inevitable result is that he performs below his capacity (104).

Obesity in childhood and awkwardness have been reported to go hand in hand; the more obese the child, the more awkward he is. Parents of obese children are usually apprehensive about the dangers of physical activities. They discourage their children from engaging in such activities. Therefore, it is not surprising that the child turns to reading comics or watching television, where activity is at a minimum and potential dangers do not exist but where the muscles are being deprived of the exercise needed for strength and coordination. When he does attempt to play with other children, he is so awkward and clumsy in comparison with them that they refuse to admit him to the play group. To compensate, he eats and grows fatter and more awkward. Only when the fear that he has accepted uncritically from his parents has been removed will he be able to exercise and to overcome his awkwardness and his desire to eat more than he needs (16, 20).

Children brought up by authoritarian child-training methods are subjected to nagging, scolding, and ridicule when they fail to measure up to parental expectations. Such treatment leads to fear and resentment, to tension, and thus to awkwardness. Children brought up by more democratic methods—where praise, approval, and encouragement are more often used—suffer far less from emotional tension and thus have better motor coordination. This encourages them to engage further in the practice needed to improve (13, 76, 116).

The far-reaching effect of tension, caused by fear, has been emphasized by Breckenridge and Vincent. According to them, "Ridicule, sarcasm, scolding, or laughing at a child's clumsiness in the early learning stages, or at the inevitable slips which cause dropping of objects, stumbling, or falling, may cause an emotional blocking which can result in tense movement and awkwardness throughout the child's life" (17).

Psychological Damage of Awkwardness. Just as good motor coordination contributes to good physical and mental health, so awkwardness contributes to poor physical and mental health. The psychological damage of awkwardness is, in many respects, even greater than the physical. This damage comes mainly from the development of feelings of personal inadequacy and inferiority. These feelings are generally accompanied by resentments against children who are more

successful in motor performances and against the adults who, the child believes, are responsible for his inferiority.

A child rarely blames himself for his awkwardness; instead, he generally finds a scapegoat to blame. Furthermore, believing that he is guiltless, he doubts his ability to overcome his awkwardness. This stifles his motivation to try to come up to the norm of his agemates. Feelings of inadequacy or of inferiority always undermine self-confidence. The awkward child's lack of self-confidence is apparent in everything he undertakes, even in his manner of speech, his gait, or his attack on a new problem.

When the child learns to think of himself as an inferior person, he continues to do so even after the cause of the attitude has been removed. As a result, his adjustment to life —not his adjustment in childhood alone—is adversely affected. Studies of awkward children have revealed that they often become "almost apologetic" in their posture and gait, in the way they shake hands, and even in the manner in which they enter a room (68). This "almost apologetic" behavior is a direct reflection of lack of self-confidence and feelings of inadequacy.

The individual who lacks self-confidence and has feelings of inadequacy does not try to do his best; he is dependent on others, makes poor social adjustments, and compares himself unfavorably with persons who have better coordinations in prestigeful activities. The awkward child lacks confidence in his ability to do things because, in the past, he has been accused of being awkward and clumsy or has been laughed at by his less awkward peers. Physical timidity, or timidity in situations where physical activity is involved, is a natural outcome of awkwardness. The child suffering from such timidity is afraid to engage in activities where skills are involved because he is afraid he will not have enough control over his body to perform successfully. Even when a minimum of motor activity is involved, he will hesitate to tackle a new activity for fear of failing. Figure 5–12 shows the characteristic pattern of physical timidity for boys and girls up to adolescence. Boys show less

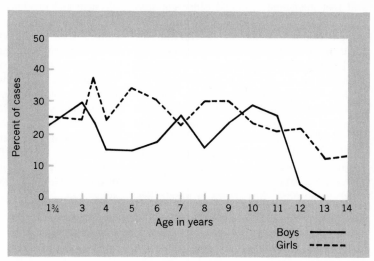

Figure 5–12. Pattern of physical timidity for boys and girls throughout childhood. (Adapted from J. Macfarlane, L. Allen, and M. P. Honzik, *A developmental study of the behavior problems of normal children between twenty-one months and fourteen years*, University of California Press, 1954. Used by permission.)

physical timidity, on the whole, than girls. Boys also learn to control or hide their timidity more than girls as they approach adolescence because it is considered sex-inappropriate. There is evidence, nevertheless, that physical timidity is a common characteristic of children of both sexes (81).

Physical timidity is not an isolated behavior pattern; it is closely related to other expressions of lack of self-confidence and feelings of inadequacy, such as demands for excessive attention, negativism, and specific fears. The child suffering from physical timidity will, as time goes on, become timid in *any* situation where something new or different is involved. As a result, he will "hide his light behind a bushel basket," working at a level far below his capacity and often experiencing failures when he should be experiencing successes (81, 111).

Awkwardness prevents the child from reaching the stage of independent action when he normally should. Because of this, he must *depend on others* to do the things for him which he wants to do for himself. Not only is this a constant source of frustration and irritation to him, but it makes him shy and self-conscious in the presence of children whose independent action enables them to take care of themselves and their needs without help. With the accumulation

of such experiences, a generalized feeling of inferiority and inadequacy develops (7).

Feelings of inadequacy, from whatever source they develop, interfere with *social adjustments*. When awkwardness is the basis of these feelings, the child's difficulties are accentuated because so many of his contacts with the peer group are in play where awkwardness is a serious handicap. The awkward child discovers that he cannot keep up with the other children of his age and join in the play activities of the group. If he is not rejected by the group, he is likely to withdraw voluntarily because of the constant embarrassment and shame his awkwardness causes. This lays the foundations for unsocial attitudes and behavior (79, 92).

As soon as a child begins to associate with other children of his age, he begins to *compare his activities and achievements with theirs*. In school, he will compare his handwriting and drawing with the writing and drawing of his classmates; on the playground, he will compare his ability to jump, climb, ride a bicycle, roller-skate, or throw a ball with similar play skills in his contemporaries. If he does as well as, or slightly better than, they do, he will be happy and confident that he can hold his own in the group; if he falls below them in these skills, he will be upset emotionally and will feel inadequate. Should other children comment on his clumsiness or give that as a reason for not wanting to play with him, his feelings of inadequacy will be intensified. Falling below the achievement level of his agemates in *any* activity is ego-deflating for a child; falling below in activities that are important to them and are used as the basis of social acceptance is a very serious blow to the child's self-concept. The further the child falls below his contemporaries in prestigeful activities, the more inadequate he feels (14, 92).

In conclusion, then, there is ample evidence that awkwardness is a threat to good physical and mental health. There is further evidence that the psychological damage resulting from childhood awkwardness may leave a permanent scar on the child's personality, never to be completely eradicated even though the awkwardness is overcome. Because motor development is controllable in most cases, it justifies serious attention on the part of everyone responsible for guiding the child's development. Furthermore, it is essential to the child's happiness that his motor abilities be at least equivalent to those of other children with whom he is constantly associated.

BIBLIOGRAPHY

(1) ABERLE, D. F., and K. D. NAEGELE: Middle-class fathers' occupational roles and attitudes toward children. *Amer. J. Orthopsychiat.*, 1952, **22**, 366–378.

(2) AMES, L. B.: The sequential patterning of prone progression in the human infant. *Genet. Psychol. Monogr.*, 1937, **19**, 409–460.

(3) AMES, L. B.: The constancy of psycho-motor tempo in individual infants. *J. genet. Psychol.*, 1940, **57**, 445–450.

(4) AMES, L. B.: Postural and placement orientation in writing and block behavior: developmental trends from infancy to age ten. *J. genet. Psychol.*, 1948, **73**, 45–52.

(5) AMES, L. B.: Bilaterality. *J. genet. Psychol.*, 1949, **75**, 45–50.

(6) AMES, L. B., and F. L. ILG: Developmental trends in writing behavior. *J. genet. Psychol.*, 1951, **79**, 28–46.

(7) AUSUBEL, D. P.: Relationships between shame and guilt in the socialization process. *Psychol. Rev.*, 1955, **62**, 378–390.

(8) BAKWIN, H.: Lateral dominance. *J. Pediat.*, 1950, **36**, 385–391.

(9) BAYLEY, N.: The development of motor abilities during the first three years. *Monogr. Soc. Res. Child Develpm.*, 1935, **1**, 1–26.

(10) BAYLEY, N.: *Studies in the development of young children.* Berkeley, Calif.: The University of California Press, 1940.

(11) BAYLEY, N.: Some increasing parent-child similarities during the growth of children. *J. educ. Psychol.*, 1954, **45**, 1–21.

(12) BAYLEY, N.: Individual patterns of development. *Child Develpm.*, 1956, **27**, 805–818.

(13) BEHERS, M. L.: Child rearing and the character structure of the mother. *Child Develpm.*, 1954, **25**, 225–238.

(14) BIDDULPH, L. G.: Athletic achievement and the personal and social adjustment of high school boys. *Res. Quart. Amer. Ass. Hlth Phys. Educ. Recr.*, 1954, **25**, 1–7.

(15) BONNEY, M. E.: Social behavior differences between second grade children of high and low sociometric status. *J. educ. Res.*, 1955, **48**, 481–495.

(16) BOSSARD, J. H. S.: *Parent and child.* Philadelphia: University of Pennsylvania Press, 1953.

(17) BRECKENRIDGE, M. E., and E. L. VINCENT: *Child development*, 4th ed. Philadelphia: Saunders, 1960.

(18) BRETSCH, H. S.: Social skills and activities of socially accepted and unaccepted adolescents. *J. educ. Psychol.*, 1952, **43**, 449–458.

(19) BROWN, J. L.: Differential hand usage in three-year-old children. *J. genet. Psychol.*, 1962, **100**, 167–175.

(20) BRUCH, H.: Developmental obesity and schizophrenia. *Psychiatry*, 1958, **21**, 65–70.

(21) BULL, K. R.: An investigation into the relationship between physique, motor capacity, and certain temperamental traits. *Brit. J. educ. Psychol.*, 1958, **28**, 149–154.

(22) BURGE, I. C.: Some aspects of handedness in primary school children. *Brit. J. educ. Psychol.*, 1952, **22**, 45–51.

(23) BURNSIDE, L. H.: Coordination in the locomotion of infants. *Genet. Psychol. Monogr.*, 1927, No. 2.

(24) CARROTHERS, J. E.: Left-handedness among

school pupils. *Amer. School Board J.*, 1947, **114,** 17–19.

(25) COOKE, R. E.: The behavioral response of infants to heat stress. *Yale J. Biol. Med.*, 1952, **24,** 334–340.

(26) CRONBACH, L. J.: *Educational psychology*, 2d ed. New York: Harcourt, Brace & World, 1963.

(27) CRONBACH, L. J.: *Essentials of psychological testing*, 2d ed. New York: Harper & Row, 1960.

(28) CRUICKSHANK, W. M., and G. O. JOHNSON: *Education of exceptional children and youth*. Englewood Cliffs, N.J.: Prentice-Hall, 1958.

(29) DAMANN, V. T.: Developmental changes in attitude as one factor determining energy output in a motor performance. *Child Develpm.*, 1941, **12,** 241–246.

(30) DAYHAW, L. T.: Guiding handedness in the development of the child. *Education*, 1953, **74,** 196–199.

(31) DENNIS, W.: On the possibility of advancing and retarding the motor development of infants. *Psychol. Rev.*, 1943, **50,** 203–218.

(32) DENNIS, W.: Handwriting conventions as determinants of human figure drawings. *J. consult. Psychol.*, 1958, **22,** 293–295.

(33) DENNIS, W.: Causes of retardation among institutional children: Iran. *J. genet. Psychol.*, 1960, **96,** 47–59.

(34) DUSENBERRY, L.: A study of the effects of training in ball throwing by children ages three to seven. *Res. Quart. Amer. Ass. Hlth Phys. Educ. Recr.*, 1952, **23,** 9–14.

(35) FEINBERG, M. R.: Relation of background experience to social acceptance. *J. abnorm. soc. Psychol.*, 1953, **48,** 206–214.

(36) FRANCIS, R. J., and G. L. RARICK: Motor characteristics of the mentally retarded. *Amer. J. ment. Def.*, 1959, **63,** 792–811.

(37) FRANSDEN, A. N.: *Educational psychology*. New York: McGraw-Hill, 1961.

(38) GEBER, M.: The psycho-motor development of African children in the first year, and the influence of maternal behavior. *J. soc. Psychol.*, 1958, **47,** 185–195.

(39) GESELL, A.: *The child from five to ten*. New York: Harper & Row, 1946.

(40) GESELL, A.: Developmental pediatrics. *Nerv. Child*, 1952, **9,** 225–227.

(41) GESELL, A.: The ontogenesis of infant behavior. In L. Carmichael (Ed.), *Manual of child psychology*, 2d ed. New York: Wiley, 1954. Pp. 335–373.

(42) GESELL, A., and L. B. AMES: The infant's reaction to his mirror image. *J. genet. Psychol.*, 1947, **70,** 141–154.

(43) GESELL, A., and F. L. ILG: *Child development*. New York: Harper & Row, 1949.

(44) GESELL, A., F. L. ILG, and L. B. AMES: *Youth: the years from ten to sixteen*. New York: Harper & Row, 1956.

(45) GESELL, A., and H. THOMPSON: Learning and growth in identical twins: an experimental study by the method of co-twin control. *Genet. Psychol. Monogr.*, 1929, **6,** 1–123.

(46) GOVATOS, L. A.: Relationships and age differences in growth measures and motor skills. *Child Develpm.*, 1959, **30,** 333–340.

(47) GRAHAM, F. K., P. W. BERMAN, and C. B. ERNHART: Development in preschool children of the ability to copy forms. *Child Develpm.*, 1960, **31,** 339–359.

(48) GREEN, C., and E. ZIGLER: Social deprivation and the performance of retarded and normal children on a satiation type task. *Child Develpm.*, 1962, **33,** 499–508.

(49) GRONLUND, N. E.: Generality of sociometric status over criteria in measurement of social acceptability. *Elem. Sch. J.*, 1955, **55,** 173–176.

(50) GUILFORD, J. P.: A system of psychomotor abilities. *Amer. J. Psychol.*, 1958, **71,** 164–174.

(51) GUTTERIDGE, M. V.: A study of motor achievements of young children. *Arch. Psychol., N.Y.*, 1939, No. 244.

(52) HALVERSON, H. M.: An experimental study of prehension in infants by means of systematic cinema records. *Genet. Psychol. Monogr.*, 1931, **10,** 107–286.

(53) HARMON, J. M., and A. MILLER: Time patterns in motor learning. *Res. Quart. Amer. Ass. Hlth Phys. Educ. Recr.*, 1950, **21,** 182–186.

(54) HAVIGHURST, R. J.: *Human development and education*. New York: Longmans, 1953.

(55) HAVIGHURST, R. J.: The social competence of middle-aged people. *Genet. Psychol. Monogr.*, 1957, **56,** 297–375.

(56) HILDRETH, G.: Manual dominance in nursery school children. *J. genet. Psychol.*, 1948, **72,** 29–45.

(57) HILDRETH, G.: The development and training of hand dominance. *J. genet. Psychol.*, 1949, **75,** 197–220.

(58) HILDRETH, G.: The development and training of hand dominance. *J. genet. Psychol.*, 1950, **76,** 39–100, 101–144.

(59) HILGARD, E. R.: *Introduction to psychology*, 3d ed. New York: Harcourt, Brace & World, 1962.

(60) HOLLINGWORTH, L. S.: *Children above 180 IQ: origin and development*. New York: Harcourt, Brace & World, 1950.

(61) HOOKER, D.: The development of behavior in the human fetus. In W. Dennis (Ed.), *Readings in child psychology*, 2d ed. Englewood Cliffs, N.J.: Prentice-Hall, 1963. Pp. 1–10.

(62) HOWE, C. E.: A comparison of motor skills of mentally retarded and normal children. *Except. Children*, 1959, **25,** 352–354.

(63) HUMPHREY, M. E.: Consistency of hand usage. *Brit. J. educ. Psychol.*, 1951, **21**, 214–225.

(64) HUTT, M. L., and R. G. GIBBY: *The child: development and adjustment.* Boston: Allyn and Bacon, 1959.

(65) ILG, F. L., J. LEARNED, A. LOCKWOOD, and L. B. AMES: The three-and-a-half-year-old. *J. genet. Psychol.*, 1949, **75**, 21–31.

(66) ISMAIL, A. H., and C. C. COWELL: Factor analysis of motor aptitude of preadolescent boys. *Res. Quart. Amer. Ass. Hlth Phys. Educ. Recr.*, 1961, **32**, 507–513.

(67) JERSILD, A. T.: Emotional development. In L. Carmichael (Ed.), *Manual of child psychology*, 2d ed. New York: Wiley, 1954. Pp. 833–917.

(68) JERSILD, A. T.: *The psychology of adolescence.* New York: Macmillan, 1957.

(69) JERSILD, A. T.: *Child psychology*, 5th ed. Englewood Cliffs, N.J.: Prentice-Hall, 1960.

(70) JERSILD, A. T., E. S. WOODYARD, and C. F. DEL SOLAR: *Joys and problems of child rearing.* New York: Teachers College, Columbia University, 1949.

(71) JONES, H. E.: *Motor performance and growth.* Berkeley, Calif.: The University of California Press, 1949.

(72) JONES, M. C.: The development of early behavior patterns in young children. *J. genet. Psychol.*, 1926, **33**, 537–585.

(73) JONES, M. C.: The later careers of boys who were early- or late-maturers. *Child Develpm.*, 1957, **28**, 113–128.

(74) JONES, T. D.: The development of certain motor skills and play activities in young children, *Child Develpm. Monogr.*, 1939, No. 26.

(75) KEY, C. B., M. R. WHITE, W. P. HONZIK, A. B. HEINEY, and D. ERWIN: The process of learning to dress among nursery-school children. *Genet. Psychol. Monogr.*, 1936, **18**, 67–163.

(76) KLATSKIN, E. H., E. B. JACKSON, and L. C. WILKIN: The influence of degree of flexibility in maternal child care practices in early child behavior. *Amer. J. Orthopsychiat.*, 1956, **26**, 79–93.

(77) KNAPP, C. G., W. R. DIXON, and M. LAZIER: Learning to juggle: III. A study of performance by two different age groups. *Res. Quart. Amer. Ass. Hlth Phys. Educ. Recr.*, 1958, **29**, 32–36.

(78) KOCH, H. L.: The relation of certain formal attributes of siblings to attitudes held toward each other and toward their parents. *Monogr. Soc. Res. Child Develpm.*, 1960, **25**, No. 4.

(79) KUBIE, L. S.: Competitive sports and the awkward child. *Child Study*, 1954, **31**, 10–15.

(80) LANDRETH, C.: *The psychology of early childhood.* New York: Knopf, 1958.

(81) MACFARLANE, J., L. ALLEN, and M. P. HONZIK: *A developmental study of the behavior problems of normal children between twenty-one months and fourteen years.* Berkeley, Calif.: The University of California Press, 1954.

(82) MALPASS, L. F.: Motor proficiency in institutionalized and non-institutionalized retarded and normal children. *Amer. J. ment. Def.*, 1960, **64**, 1012–1015.

(83) MARTIN, K. L.: Handedness: a review of the literature on the history, development, and research of laterality preference. *J. educ. Res.*, 1952, **45**, 527–533.

(84) MARTIN, P. C., and E. L. VINCENT: *Human development.* New York: Ronald, 1960.

(85) MARTIN, W. E., and C. B. STENDLER: *Child development*, 2d ed. New York: Harcourt, Brace & World, 1959.

(86) MC GRAW, M. B.: *Growth: a study of Johnny and Jimmy.* New York: Appleton-Century-Crofts, 1935.

(87) MC GRAW, M. B.: Swimming behavior of the human infant. *J. Pediat.*, 1939, **15**, 485–490.

(88) MC GRAW, M. B.: Neuromuscular development of the human infant as exemplified in the achievement of erect locomotion. *J. Pediat.*, 1940, **17**, 744–771.

(89) MC GRAW, M. B., and K. W. BREEZE: Quantitative studies in the development of erect locomotion. *Child Develpm.*, 1941, **12**, 267–303.

(90) MC GRAW, M. B., and A. P. WEINBACH: Quantitative measures in studying development of behavior patterns (locomotion). *Bull. Neurol. Inst., N.Y.*, 1936, **4**, 563–572.

(91) MERRY, F. K., and R. V. MERRY: *The first two decades of life*, 2d ed. New York: Harper & Row, 1958.

(92) MOODY, C. B.: Physical education and neurotic behavior disorders. *Understanding the Child*, 1952, **27**, 20–24.

(93) MORRISON, I. E., and I. F. PERRY: Acceptance of overage children by their classmates. *Elem. Sch. J.*, 1956, **56**, 217–220.

(94) MUELLNER, S. R.: Development of urinary control in children. *J. Amer. Med. Ass.*, 1960, **172**, 1256–1261.

(95) New York Times Report: Left-handed find handicap grows. *The New York Times*, Aug. 2, 1959.

(96) NORVAL, M. A.: Relationship of weight and length of infants at birth to the age at which they begin to walk. *J. Pediat.*, 1947, **30**, 676–679.

(97) PRATT, K. C.: The neonate. In L. Carmichael (Ed.), *Manual of child psychology*, 2d ed. New York: Wiley, 1954, Pp. 215–291.

(98) PRESSEY, S. L., and R. G. KUHLEN: *Psychological development through the life span.* New York: Harper & Row, 1957.

(99) RAGSDALE, C. E.: How children learn the

motor types of behavior. *49th Yearb. Nat. Soc. Stud. Educ.*, 1950, Pt. 1, 69–91.

(100) RARICK, G. L., and R. MC KEE: A study of twenty third-grade children exhibiting extreme levels of achievement on tests of motor proficiency. *Res. Quart. Amer. Ass. Hlth Phys. Educ. Recr.*, 1949, **20**, 142–152.

(101) REED, G. F., and A. C. SMITH: A further experimental investigation of the relative speeds of left- and right-handed writers. *J. genet. Psychol.*, 1962, **100**, 275–288.

(102) RHEINGOLD, H. L., W. C. STANLEY, and J. A. COOLEY: Method for studying exploratory behavior in infants. *Science*, 1962, **136**, 1054–1055.

(103) SCHALTENBRAND, C.: The development of human motility and motor disturbances. *Arch. Neur. Psychiat.*, 1928, **20**, 720–730.

(104) SEARS, P. S., and H. LEVIN: Levels of aspiration in preschool children. *Child Develpm.*, 1957, **28**, 317–326.

(105) SEILS, L. G.: The relationship between measures of physical growth and gross motor performance of primary-grade school children. *Res. Quart. Amer. Ass. Hlth Phys. Educ. Recr.*, 1951, **22**, 244–260.

(106) SEWELL, W. H., and A. O. HALLER: Social status and the personality adjustment of the child. *Sociometry*, 1956, **19**, 114–125.

(107) SHAPIRO, H.: The development of walking in a child. *J. genet. Psychol.*, 1962, **100**, 221–226.

(108) SHIRLEY, M. M.: *The first two years of life.* Minneapolis: The University of Minnesota Press, vol. 1, 1931; vol. 2, 1933.

(109) SIMON, M. D.: Body configuration and school readiness. *Child Develpm.*, 1959, **30**, 493–512.

(110) SMITH, A. C., and G. F. REED: An experimental investigation of the relative speeds of left- and right-handed writers. *J. genet. Psychol.*, 1959, **94**, 67–76.

(111) SOLLEY, W. H.: Ratio of physical development as a factor in motor coordination of boys ages 10–14. *Res. Quart. Amer. Ass. Hlth Phys. Educ. Recr.*, 1957, **28**, 295–304.

(112) SONTAG, L. W.: The significance of fetal environmental differences. *Amer. J. Obstet. Gynaec.*, 1941, **42**, 996–1003.

(113) SPITZ, R. A.: Purposive grasping. *Personality*, 1951, **1**, 141–148.

(114) SPOCK, B.: *Baby and child care.* New York: Pocket Books, 1957.

(115) STOLZ, H. R., and L. M. STOLZ: *Somatic development of adolescent boys.* New York: Macmillan, 1951.

(116) STOUT, I. W., and G. LANGDON: A study of the home life of well-adjusted children. *J. educ. Sociol.*, 1950, **23**, 442–460.

(117) STRANG, R.: *An introduction to child study*, 4th ed. New York: Macmillan, 1959.

(118) SWEET, C.: Enuresis: a psychologic problem of childhood. *J. Amer. Med. Ass.*, 1946, **32**, 279–281.

(119) TERMAN, L. M., and M. A. MERRILL: *Stanford-Binet Intelligence Scale*, 3d Rev. Boston: Houghton Mifflin, 1960.

(120) TOWNSEND, E. A.: A study of copying ability in children. *Genet. Psychol. Monogr.*, 1951, **43**, 3–51.

(121) TUDDENHAM, R. D.: Studies in reputation. I. Sex and grade differences in school children's evaluation of their peers. II. The diagnosis of social adjustment. *Psychol. Monogr.*, 1952, **66**, No. 1.

(122) TWINING, W. E.: Mental practice and physical practice in learning a motor skill. *Res. Quart. Amer. Ass. Hlth Phys. Educ. Recr.*, 1949, **20**, 432–435.

(123) TYLER, L. E.: The development of "vocational interests": 1. The organization of likes and dislikes in ten-year-old children. *J. genet. Psychol.*, 1955, **86**, 33–34.

(124) VINCENT, E. L., and P. C. MARTIN: *Human psychological development.* New York: Ronald, 1961.

(125) WAGONER, L. C., and E. M. ARMSTRONG: The motor control of children as involved in the dressing process. *J. genet. Psychol.*, 1928, **35**, 84–97.

(126) WATSON, E. H., and G. H. LOWREY: *Growth and development of children.* Chicago: The Year Book Medical Publishers, Inc., 1954.

(127) WELCH, A. A., and R. V. CAMPBELL: The relation between the development of behavior and the pattern of physical growth. *Child Develpm.*, 1941, **12**, 237–240.

(128) WELLMAN, B. L.: Motor achievement of preschool children. *Childh. Educ.*, 1937, **13**, 311–316.

(129) WHIPPLE, H. D.: Effects of elementary-school physical education upon aspects of physical, motor, and personality development. *Res. Quart. Amer. Ass. Hlth Phys. Educ. Recr.*, 1961, **32**, 249–260.

(130) WILLIAMS, J. R., and R. B. SCOTT: Growth and development of Negro infants. II. Motor development and its relationship to child rearing practices in two groups of Negro infants. *Child Develpm.*, 1953, **24**, 103–121.

(131) WITRYOL, S. L., and J. E. CALKINS: Marginal social values of rural school children. *J. genet. Psychol.*, 1958, **92**, 81–93.

(132) WOODWORTH, R. S.: *Dynamics of behavior.* New York: Holt, 1958.

6

SPEECH
DEVELOPMENT

Language is the basis of communication with others. It encompasses every means of communication in which thoughts and feelings are symbolized so as to convey meaning, including such widely differing forms of communication as writing, speaking, sign language, facial expression, gesture, pantomime, and art. It is one of the main things that differentiates human beings from the lower forms of animals. *Speech* is a form of language in which articulate sounds or words are used to convey meanings. Speech development is "sound-shaping development, a growth process proceeding from the vague, indistinct, and fortuitously shaped to the clear, distinct, and controlled" (99).

All sounds made by a child are not necessarily "speech." The *first criterion* of speech is that the child must know the meaning of the words he uses and must associate them with the objects they represent. Vocalization does not become speech until meaning is associated with sounds. Even when the baby says recognizable words, such as "da-da" or "ball," he is not using real speech unless he associates the words with the objects they represent. "Da-da," for example, must refer to one person only, not to all men; "ball" must refer to balls only, not to toys in general.

The *second criterion* of speech is that the child must pronounce his words so that they are readily understandable by others in the society. Words that are comprehensible only to those who, because of constant contact with the child, have learned to understand him or to guess at what he is trying to say do not meet this criterion. "Baby talk" may satisfy the first criterion of speech, since words are identified with objects, but it does not satisfy the second.

It is often difficult to know when real speech begins for a child. Some of his words may satisfy both criteria; others may satisfy only one. He may, for example, use the word "milk" to refer to anything he drinks, and he may say it so correctly that his parents *assume* he knows its real meaning. On the other hand, he may associate "mil" with milk, not with any other drink, but it cannot be considered real speech because it does not satisfy the criterion of correct and understandable pronunciation. The marked variations reported in size of vocabulary of different children during the preschool years are unquestionably due in part to the fact that most parents do not apply *both criteria* of speech when listing the words their children use; they apply only the criterion of correct and understandable pronunciation and assume that, because the child says the word, he automatically knows what it means (103).

IMPORTANCE OF SPEECH

Speech serves many purposes. It is more than a means of communicating thoughts, feelings, and emotions. As Baldridge has pointed out:

Speech is a kind of behavior which helps to form the world of the child; to transform him from an egocentric to a social being; to make assumptions for him; to set up conventions to guide and control him; to inform him; to instill in him thoughts, feelings, and attitudes; to make him feel secure and insecure—all these effects and many more may be brought about in the child through the use of words (12).

That speech is important to a child's personal and social adjustment is clearly seen in children who are cut off from others by deafness or by inability to communicate. The deaf child is socially isolated. Even though his playmates recognize his inability to hear them, they fail to take this into consideration when they talk to one another. They do not mean to leave him out, but he feels that he does not belong to the group because he cannot hear what they are saying, and he hesitates to speak to them for fear that he will say the wrong thing and cause them to laugh at him (44).

Bilingual children likewise run into social difficulties. When they are just beginning to learn the language of their playmates, they feel insecure in its use and handicapped by small vocabularies. They fail to understand much of what their contemporaries say, and their contemporaries fail to understand much of what they say. As a result, they say little, remain on the sidelines, and feel left out of things (103, 148).

Children who are able to communicate well with others make better social adjustments than children who lack the ability or who have it but fail to use it for fear of making mistakes. Studies of popularity show that among children of all ages, those who express themselves in words as well as in actions are more popular, other factors being equal, than those who are quiet and reserved. Furthermore, those who talk more about other people or things are more popular than those who are so self-bound that their conversations center around themselves (22, 51).

Similarly, children who become leaders must have the ability to communicate and to influence the actions of others through speech. The child who has acquired the ability to put his thoughts and feelings into words and who is not held back from doing so by fear of how others will react is in line for a leadership role. The quiet, introverted child is likely to be overlooked, even though he may have other qualities that are superior to those of the extroverted child who makes himself the center of group attention by expressing himself frankly, freely, and with confidence (16).

PRESPEECH COMMUNICATIONS

Learning to speak is a long and complicated process. Most reports indicate that a baby does not say his first word until sometime between the ages of twelve and fifteen months. This means that for the first twelve or fifteen months of life, his communications must be in forms preliminary to speech. The communication needs of the baby are expressed by gesture and by vocalization in the form of cries, explosive sounds, or "babbling." When meaning is associated with the sounds, the baby can communicate with those who know him well enough to understand what he is attempting to say, even though the sounds may be meaningless to strangers.

Prespeech Forms. During the first few months of life, babies use three preliminary forms of communication: *crying;* "explosive sounds," which soon develop into *babbling;* and *gestures.* Of the three, the second is the most important from the long-range point of view because it becomes the basis for real speech. As is true of all stopgap measures, prespeech forms of communication should be abandoned when their usefulness ends and when the child learns to communicate in words.

CRYING

In the early days of life, most vocalization takes the form of crying. This early crying is, in effect, "emergency respiration"; it is irregular and uncontrolled (99). During the first two weeks of life, crying appears at irregular intervals, often from a state of sleep. The infant, without any apparent reason, begins to cry intensely. This is accompanied by reddening or mottling of the skin, clenching of the fists, alternate extension and flexion of the extremities, increased activity of the entire body, irregular breathing, prolonged expiration, and increased pulse rate (141).

While all newborn infants cry, individual differences in the amount of crying appear at the end of the second week of life. Beginning with the third week, there is normally less crying, and by the third or fourth month, night waking, accompanied by crying, decreases. No tears are shed in crying until the child is about one month old (103, 141).

Causes of Crying. Among babies less than seven weeks of age, hunger is the most common cause of crying; noise and light are the least likely causes. Unknown causes are next in frequency to hunger. Colic is a common cause of crying during the first three months of life. Older babies cry because of pain, bright lights, sharp noises, uncomfortable positions, strong disturbances during sleep,

fatigue, hunger, inability to move due to restrictive clothes or covers, loss or removal of a plaything, fear, and withdrawal of contact with others. Crying is most frequent before feeding and before the baby goes to sleep for the night (1, 141).

Before he is three months old, the normal baby has learned that crying is a sure method of getting attention. He learns to use crying as a means to an end. At four months, a baby will cry when an adult ceases to play with him; at five months, he will increase his crying if an adult enters the room but pays no attention to him; and at nine months, he will cry if an adult approaches another child. Crying is also caused in the latter part of the first year of life by fear of strange situations and by unusual handling (99, 103).

The young child cries when he is hungry, tired, or frightened or when an activity is interrupted. Among nursery-school children, crying is predominantly social, thus indicating a more mature type of adjustment. There is relatively little crying in routine situations, such as dressing, eating, or toileting. A comparison of crying in the home and in the nursery school revealed that young children cry at home mostly because of conflicts with adults or with siblings; they cry at meals or when they are injured. In the nursery school, the most common causes of crying were found to be attacks on the child's person, attacks on his property, frustrations by another child, and accidental injury (92). (See Figure 6–1.)

Variations in Crying. From the second month of life, the baby's cry varies in intensity, tonal quality, and rhythm. Pain cries, for example, are shrill, loud, and interrupted by whimpering and groaning, or they are short, sharp, and piercing. The cry of discomfort is low and whimpering, while that of hunger is loud and interrupted by sucking movements. Variations of crying, such as groaning, "fussing," whimpering, and sighing, appear by the end of the second month. Every baby has a fairly large repertoire of cries, and each child's repertoire is different (103).

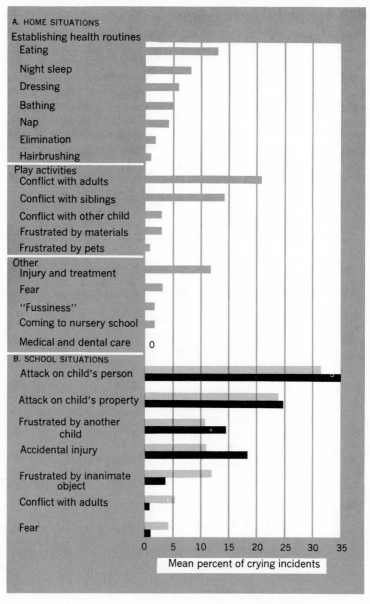

A. HOME SITUATIONS

Establishing health routines
  Eating
  Night sleep
  Dressing
  Bathing
  Nap
  Elimination
  Hairbrushing

Play activities
  Conflict with adults
  Conflict with siblings
  Conflict with other child
  Frustrated by materials
  Frustrated by pets

Other
  Injury and treatment
  Fear
  "Fussiness"
  Coming to nursery school
  Medical and dental care

0

B. SCHOOL SITUATIONS

  Attack on child's person
  Attack on child's property
  Frustrated by another child
  Accidental injury
  Frustrated by inanimate object
  Conflict with adults
  Fear

0   5   10   15   20   25   30   35

Mean percent of crying incidents

Boys and girls
Boys
Girls

Figure 6–1. Causes of crying in young children at home and in nursery school. (Adapted from C. Landreth, *The psychology of early childhood,* Knopf, 1958. Used by permission.)

Cries are differentiated more by intensity than by meaning. The stress of excitement, hunger, and pain causes greater tension of the muscles, flattens the sound, and makes it more shrill. There is, therefore, no "vocabulary" of crying. Crying is not differentiated according to changing wants but, rather, by the *intensity* of wants. Recent experimental studies have suggested that it is possible to identify the age of an infant by his cry and also to identify the cretin, the mongol, and the baby suffering from infantile amaurotic idiocy by their cries (99, 103).

Analyses of the elements of crying have revealed that an overwhelming majority of the sounds in the cries of newborn infants are front vowels, with the *ae* sound predominating. Consonant sounds during the first ten days of life are very infrequent. Of these, the glottal sound *h* is the most frequent. *K* is heard occasionally, while *b, p,* and *m* are not heard at all. As babies grow older, front vowels are heard less frequently, and middle and back vowels more often. During the second quarter of the first year, more of the consonant sounds are heard, especially *h, g, m, n, b, d, k, w, l, j,* and *c* (78).

Motor Accompaniment of Crying. Crying in young babies is always accompanied by bodily action. The entire body is active, and fatigue sets in if the crying continues over a prolonged period of time. Crying caused by fatigue is often accompanied by yawning, drooping, and rubbing the eyes, while crying caused by strange places or people is accompanied by clinging to the mother and turning away from the frightening situation. Each baby has its own individual type of hand reaction in crying. There is also a marked difference in general body activity in crying and in noncrying. In general, crying is accompanied by vigorous limb activity, strong flexor tendencies, and the disorganizing of postures prevailing at the onset of crying. Noncrying behavior, on the other hand, is characterized by limb extension, bilateral postures, greater arm than leg activity, and the holding of set postures (4). As the baby grows older, less and less activity accompanies crying. The crying of the two- or three-year-old is accompanied by no more activity than any other emotional outburst.

Reactions to Crying. How children and adults react to a child's crying will depend partly upon the age of the child and partly upon their own beliefs regarding the function of crying. It is a commonly accepted belief that the only means of communication a young baby has is crying. Parents, therefore, *expect* the baby to cry. This belief, in turn, affects the baby's behavior; he learns that he must cry if his wants and needs are to receive any attention. He is thus *conditioned* to cry because his other modes of expression have failed to bring him what he wants. The baby learns to cry instead of learning to use noncrying modes of communication (124).

A small baby can communicate his simple wants by noncrying methods, such as smacking the lips or ejecting the tongue when hungry, squirming and trembling when cold, or sneezing when wet. If these signals are understood, the baby will then cry only in pain and genuine distress. Some babies continue to cry excessively after the first two weeks of life. It has been found that the mothers of these babies allowed a long time to elapse before heeding their cries, were inconsistent about responding to the babies' cries, or were insecure, anxious, tense, and unable to gain satisfaction from contacts with their babies (90).

Excessive crying without a physical cause is especially common in babies from nervous family backgrounds where neurotic instability and parental apprehension are evident. When the mother suffers from feelings of frustration about vocational or other ambitions, has a poor concept of herself, has a poor relationship with her husband, has general feelings of insecurity or specific feelings of insecurity about her role as a mother, and thus engages in less "mothering" than normal, she is likely to have a baby who cries excessively (90, 152).

Lack of security in interpersonal relationships thus predisposes babies to excessive crying. Feelings of security can be greatly enhanced if babies receive prompt attention to their needs. As Gesell has stressed, "Punctual attention to crying in the early weeks reduces the total amount of crying" (59). In hospital nurseries, the infant's needs cannot always be met promptly; therefore, there are more periods of prolonged crying in nurseries than at home or in hospitals where the baby "rooms in" with the mother (1). Even in the home, a mother cannot always drop what she is doing to heed the baby's cries; or she may intentionally ignore his cries, fearing that she will "spoil" him. That this fear is unwarranted has been shown by the fact that by the age of six weeks, babies whose needs are met promptly cry relatively little in comparison with those whose needs are not met promptly or are met inconsistently (90, 124, 141).

People react to the crying of a young child who has learned to talk and to that of a baby quite differently. Instead of coming to the young child's rescue, even if somewhat belatedly, parents often regard his crying as a signal that he is "spoiled." They may scold or punish him. Later, the child discovers that other children look upon crying as "babyish" and scorn him for it. In a study of crying at home and in the nursery school, it was found that adults responded very differently to crying in these two situations. In the nursery school, crying was most frequently met by consoling the child, by censuring the child who caused the crying, by suggesting arbitration in property disputes, and by distracting the crying child. At home, crying was most often responded to by ignoring the child, reasoning with him, spanking him, or removing him from the social group (92). Among older children, crying is so scorned that the child who cries is likely to become a social isolate. This will be discussed further in the chapter on social adjustments.

Effects of Crying. Excessive crying is *physically* and *psychologically damaging*. In cases of distress, however, some crying is normal even among school-age children. A short period of crying leaves the child tense and tired; a prolonged period relaxes him but also exhausts him. Babies, especially, become exhausted because they literally "cry all over." In the newborn infant and the very young baby, the mass activity that accompanies crying depletes the energy reserve and interferes with normal physical growth.

Depletion of energy, serious as it is, is not the only physical consequence of crying; the normal functioning of the entire body is also upset. The results are variability in gastrointestinal functions, regurgitations, night waking, enuresis, and general nervous tension that is expressed in such mannerisms as thumb sucking and nail biting (141). The older child who cries more often and more violently than is normal for his age is affected in much the same way, though a short cry may serve to relax nervous tension caused by bottled-up emotions.

The psychological damage from crying is likewise serious. As has already been pointed out, most adults expect a young baby to cry. When he cries more than they consider normal, however, they respond in one of two ways. They worry about him and become overprotective, or they consider him ornery and overdemanding and try to ignore his cries.

By ignoring his cries, parents expect to teach the child that he cannot get what he wants by crying. Unfortunately, a young baby, or even an older one, does not have the reasoning capacity to figure this out for himself. Instead, he develops feelings of insecurity and helplessness. Furthermore, because crying is physically exhausting, a baby who is ignored when he cries is likely to become somewhat hysterical; as a result, he is unable to stop crying even when his needs are attended to. Many parents, not realizing this to be true, react to him as if he were intentionally trying to make life difficult for them. Their attitude further increases his feelings of insecurity and helplessness (90).

There is no question that the less crying a baby does, the better his relationships with his parents and other members of the family will be, and the better he will adjust to his environment. Parents and other family members react more favorably to a "good baby" than to a fretful one. Rosenzweig has commented that a "quieter atmosphere in the nursery is pleasanter for all members of the family" (124).

Just as the baby's social adjustments within the home are influenced by the amount and severity of his cries, so are the older child's adjustments outside the home affected. Young children—and even older children—are unable to recognize distress unless they see some tangible evidence of it. When a child is hurt, they will not sympathize with him when he cries unless they can *see* the flow of blood from a cut or the swelling of the flesh from a sprain or a broken bone. Instead, they are likely to regard him as a "crybaby" (22). Because social rejection is damaging to a child's self-concept and leads to feelings of inadequacy, the psychological damage from excessive crying is even more serious than the physical. This is especially true in older children, for whom social acceptance is important and for whom the degree of acceptance they enjoy is the measuring rod by which they judge themselves.

Decrease in Crying. Because of its long-lasting damage, excessive and prolonged crying should be eliminated as early as possible. Any act that brings satisfaction will be repeated; the more often it is repeated, the more likely it is to develop into a firmly rooted habit. Learning not to cry is a long and laborious task. The habit of crying will not be "outgrown," nor will it disappear of its own accord. Instead, it will have to be "unlearned" and replaced by methods of communication that are more mature and more socially acceptable. The sooner the child abandons crying and learns more mature methods of communication, the easier it will be for him and the more satisfying the end results will be.

It must be understood, however, that even when a young baby can say a few words, his need for crying as a form of communication has not come to an end. Not until he has an adequate vocabulary to express his needs, wants, thoughts, and feelings has he reached the point where crying is no longer necessary. When he will reach this point will depend upon his learning opportunities, his ability, and his motivation. The young child who has learned that crying is a tried and trusted method of coping with his wants and needs will not readily give it up without assurance that a substitute method will work equally effectively.

For every child, the *curve for crying should go down as the curve for speech rises*. If the speech curve rises slowly, the crying curve will have to descend slowly. The interrelationship of the curves for speech and crying is shown in Figure 6–2.

Even when the child has an adequate vocabulary, he will not automatically and immediately abandon crying in favor of speech. He will do so more quickly and more effectively, however, if he is *taught* how to get what he wants by speaking. With guidance and encouragement, a child should be almost ready to abandon crying by the time he reaches kindergarten age. Children who have been allowed to cry excessively will take more time, more guidance, and more encouragement. Unfortunately, the type of home environment that encourages excessive crying in babies is likely to persist. It will not provide the guidance and encouragement necessary for the development of more mature forms of expression. While few genetic studies have been made of chil-

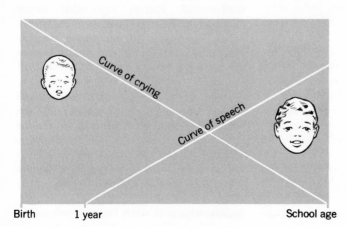

Birth   1 year   School age

Figure 6–2. Curve of crying diminishes as curve of speech rises.

dren who, as babies, cried excessively, reports from mothers indicate that children who are "problems" as they grow older were "problems" when they were babies because of their excessive crying and the accompanying adjustment difficulties (100).

EXPLOSIVE SOUNDS AND BABBLING

In addition to cries, babies make many simple sounds during the first months of life. There are grunts of pain or disgust, squeals of delight, yawns, sneezes, sighs, belching, coughing, guttural barking sounds, growls, and simulated animal cries, sounding like the whine of a young pig or the bleat of a goat (99, 103).

Cooing. Early sounds are explosive in character and are caused by chance movements of the vocal mechanism. The sounds themselves depend largely on the shape of the oral cavity and the way it modifies the stream of air expelled from the lungs and passing over the vocal cords. They are unlearned and are universally found, even among the deaf. There is no deliberate attempt on the baby's part to produce these sounds; they are called forth as responses to physical needs and as accompaniments of general bodily activity. Some of them accompany states of comfort, while others accompany states of discomfort. Because they have no significance for the baby and are not used as a form of communication, they may be regarded as a *playful activity* which gives enjoyment to the baby. This type of vocalization is usually referred to as "cooing" (98, 103).

Many of these early sounds will disappear as the baby's vocal mechanism develops. Some will develop into babbling and, still later, into words. As Lynip has emphasized:

The infant's vocalizations have no more relation to an adult's words than his leg kickings have to a grown-up's genuflections. It therefore follows that the beginnings and changes of vocalization must be considered as a gradually unfolding process from the simple to the complex shrouded in the mysterious veils that conceal the miracle of growth of all organisms—not to be crudely analyzed in measurements applicable only to a restricted variety of adult sound productions (99).

Babbling. Gradually, the number of sounds the baby can produce increases. There is, as well, an increasing definiteness of utterance of various sounds. At first, vowels are combined with consonants, for example, "da," "ma," "ugh," or "na." Later, with practice, vocal control makes it possible for the child to repeat these sounds by stringing them together, as in "ma-ma-ma-ma" or "ugh-ugh-ugh." This is real babbling, or "lalling." Owing to the baby's growing ability to control the flow of air over the vocal cords, he can pronounce sounds at will. Babbling is, therefore, a form of vocal gymnastics, voluntarily produced, but with no real meaning or association for the baby.

The age of babbling is between the third and twelfth months, with a peak around the eighth month. How soon the baby will begin to babble and when he will abandon babbling in favor of a more mature form of communication will depend largely upon the development of his vocal mechanism and his incentive to use it for speaking. Some babies continue to babble into the second year (98, 99, 103).

Babbling is a form of "play speech," in that sounds are "uttered for the mere delight of uttering them" (103). It occurs mostly in periods of contentment, more frequently when the baby is alone than when he is with others who can amuse him. That the baby derives enjoyment from listening to his own voice is shown by the fact that he often smiles and laughs at the sounds he is making and by the fact that deaf babies, who begin to babble at the usual age, soon lose interest in it. Further evidence of the playful element of babbling is found in the fact that babies vocalize more when adults talk to them than when adults are silent. It is a part of the total response they give to the adult—a form of social reaction rather than an attempt at communication (103).

At no time is babbling linked with specific

objects, people, or situations. Therefore it is not real speech. It is engaged in only so long as the baby enjoys it or until an opportunity arises for another form of play of a more enjoyable type. It is seldom related to adult sounds, though the sounds made with the mouth open more closely resemble adult sounds than those made with the mouth partially closed (99). Thus there is little evidence that babbling will turn into real speech when the baby has more control over his vocal mechanism. As Carroll has pointed out, "It is as if the child starts learning afresh when he begins to utter meaningful speech." His explanation of this is that "the particular sound-types uttered by the babbling child have little relevance for later learning, for the types appear in more or less random sequences which bear little relation to the sequences observed after true language learning starts" (36). This point of view is likewise held by Miller, who maintains that it "is not clear just how important early babbling is for the development of words," and by Simon, who states that "the most frequently used language sounds are not those that babies babble earliest and most often. . . . The child must tediously relearn his babbled sounds as words and parts of words" (130).

Value of Babbling.   The value of both crying and gestures is *immediate;* they serve as temporary measures to bridge the gap between the time when the baby is unable to learn to speak and the time when he has learned to speak well enough to dispense with stopgap measures. The reverse is true of babbling; it has no immediate value other than the enjoyment it gives to the baby— an enjoyment he could derive from other forms of play were he unable to babble. On the other hand, it has great long-term value. It is *verbal practice that lays the foundation for developing the skilled movements required in speech.* True, without babbling the baby would, eventually, learn to speak. But babbling hastens the learning process by providing the foundation skills needed to control the vocal mechanism for the more highly complicated skills of speech.

With practice in babbling, the baby increases the number and variety of sound combinations that he can produce. In addition, he acquires variations in pitch and inflection; his babbling takes on a conversational tone. In a social situation, he may try to join in the conversation of adults. If his parents are accustomed to the sounds he is making, they may fail to distinguish them from real speech and treat the baby as though he were actually taking part in the conversation. Thus, in addition to the practice he is getting in learning to control the muscles of the vocal mechanism, he is also learning to participate in a social group. In this way, he is laying social as well as speech foundations. Furthermore, he is spared the feelings of social isolation which come when an individual at any age is unable to communicate with those around him. The baby who babbles while others speak actually *feels* that he belongs to the group; he is not an outsider with the feelings of loneliness that social isolation normally brings.

The socializing value of babbling is great enough to justify its encouragement. Even though babies derive enjoyment from listening to their own voices, a time comes when their interest lags. Then they want to communicate. Studies of institutionalized babies have shown that lack of communication with others results, in time, in withdrawal. When this happens, the babies cut themselves off from practice which will lay the foundations for speech skills, and they develop negative attitudes toward further attempts to establish communication with others. As a result, they will have little motivation to learn to speak when they are maturationally ready to do so. Prolonged withdrawal is believed to be one of the important contributing factors in the development of schizophrenia (103, 149).

GESTURES

The third preliminary form of communication consists of gestures—movements of the limbs or the body which serve as *substitutes* for, or *supplements* to, speech. As a substitute for speech, gestures take the place of words; the idea is conveyed to others by meaningful movements of the limbs or some part of the body. As a supplement to speech, gestures emphasize the meaning of spoken words. Studies of young babies have revealed that, at first, gestures often accompany unintelligible vocalizations. This suggests that the babies are trying to make others understand them by supplementing sounds with movements. This is called "whole-body language" (103).

In time, the baby discovers that he can make himself understood by gestures alone; he therefore substitutes gestures for speech. If his gestures are not understood, however, or if they do not bring the desired results, it is likely that he will revert to crying—a form of communication he has found to be useful (124). In young babies, gestures play a role similar to that of crying; they are substitutes for, not supplements to, speech. Unlike babbling, which is fundamentally a form of play, gestures have the serious purpose of communication, just as crying has.

Commonly observed gestures during early babyhood include pushing the nipple from the mouth with the tongue, turning the head away from the nipple, or allowing food to run out of the mouth, which shows that the baby is not hungry; smiling and holding out the arms, which indicate that the baby wants to be picked up; squirming, wiggling, and crying during dressing and bathing, which show that the baby resents the restrictions to his activities; pouting when displeased; and reaching movements, which indicate efforts to accept, reject, or avert. Most gestures made by babies are easy to understand if parents will take the time and make the effort to do so (103).

The need for gestures as a substitute for speech does not end when the baby says his first words. It takes a long time to build a vocabulary that will adequately replace crying and gestures. In addition, the child has the problem of putting his words into sentences, and for a long time he will use gestures as substitutes for parts of speech needed to make his sentences meaningful. The early sentences of a young child are,

therefore, a combination of words and gestures (92, 103). As speech improves, however, the need for gestures decreases. Before the child enters school, his vocabulary should be large enough to enable him to abandon the use of gestures entirely.

Because many children find that their ability to express their feelings and emotions through words alone is inadequate, they continue to use gestures as a supplement to speech. They may discover this use of gestures by chance, or they may learn it by imitating an adult or an older child. A simple "No," for example, may not convey much meaning to a listener, but the child soon discovers that if he stamps his foot when he says "No," he commands attention. When a child is with parents or others who use gestures to make their words more meaningful and effective, he assumes that this is the correct thing to do, and he imitates them. In any event, every child sooner or later learns the value of gestures in emphasizing the meanings of words.

Value of Gestures. Gestures enable the baby to communicate with others and to feel that he is part of the social group. Without this form of communication, many of his needs would remain unsatisfied, and many of his wants would be frustrated. Like crying, however, many gestures are socially unacceptable forms of behavior. Members of the lower socioeconomic groups use gestures more—both as substitutes for, and supplements to, their speech—than members of the middle and upper groups, for whom "talking with one's hands" is considered "bad taste" (26).

Gestures can become habitual methods of communication if they are permitted to persist after the need for them no longer exists. Many parents, unfortunately, believe that a child will "outgrow" gestures when he is able to communicate by speech; as a result, they do little or nothing to encourage him to abandon them. Intelligent children, who learn to speak at an early age, need gestures for a shorter period of time than the average child. In many cases, too, their parents come from the upper socioeconomic groups, where the use of gestures is regarded as socially inappropriate. Consequently, they are encouraged to abandon the use of gestures as soon as possible, and by so doing, they do not develop a strongly rooted habit.

Even where parents do nothing to break the gesture-using habit, children often discover, as they go out into the neighborhood, that gestures are regarded as "bad form"; they then try to break the habit themselves. In a neighborhood or community where gestures are not disapproved, however, the child has little motivation to abandon them. As a result, the habit becomes so strongly rooted that when he reaches adolescence or adulthood, he may discover—if his associations bring him in contact with members of higher socioeconomic groups—that it is a distinct social handicap for him. When acceptance is greatly influenced by social "know-how," using gestures in a group that regards them as gauche will be a stumbling block to social acceptance and will make the individual feel socially inadequate and inferior (28).

HOW CHILDREN LEARN TO SPEAK

Speech is a skill. Like all skills, it must be learned. Because it involves so many complicated activities, it develops more slowly than the motor skills described in the preceding chapter. As has already been stressed, speech consists of, first, the ability to produce certain sounds in combinations that are recognizable as words—the *motor* aspect of speech—and, second, the ability to associate meanings with these words—the *mental* aspect of speech. The muscle coordinations needed to produce sound combinations that are recognizable as words are certainly as complicated as the most intricate motor skills and require as much time and practice to learn. Furthermore, the necessity of associating meanings with words and of learning grammatical forms adds further to the complicated activities associated with speech skills.

Readiness to Speak. Speech development is built upon the foundations established by the maturation of the various parts of the *speech mechanism* and of the *brain*—especially the association areas of the brain. At birth, both the speech mechanisms and the brain are so immature that neither is ready for the development of speech. Speech is produced by the coordinated activity of the lip, tongue, and throat muscles as well as by the larynx and tongue. It takes time for these to mature, and it takes time and practice to perfect the coordinated actions of these organs.

At birth, the oral cavity is small, with a short anterior to posterior measurement. The palate is flat and lacks the arch characteristically found in older persons. The infant's tongue is proportionally too large, filling much of the oral cavity and even protruding much of the time. As the baby grows older, changes in size and shape of the different parts of the vocal mechanism occur. Throughout the early months of life, the infant lies down most of the time. The uvula and soft palate are pulled downward by the force of gravity, with the result that the nasal passage, which is very small, is virtually blocked off, making the pronunciation of nasal sounds impossible. Consonant sounds, which are produced through the coordination of the lips and teeth, must wait upon the development of the front teeth. At birth, the nerves and muscles of the vocal apparatus are fairly well developed, but their use must wait upon the development of the other parts of the vocal mechanism (70, 103).

Mental readiness to speak comes somewhat later than motor readiness. That is why, during the prespeech stage, the baby can babble sounds that approximate words and can even say isolated words in "parrot fashion." In explaining the transition from "parrot speech" to the use of sounds with associated meanings, McCarthy has pointed out that "this change is undoubtedly related to the relatively late development of Broca's area reported by deCrinis at about 17 months of age. He says this area which we know to be related to the speech function does not attain the degree of anatomical differentiation shown by other motor centers some six months earlier" (103).

Association of meanings is also dependent upon memory and reasoning. Until the brain is well enough developed to permit a young child to remember past experiences and to see the relationship between a new experience similar to an old one that is associated with a specific word, he will be mentally unready to learn to speak.

There is evidence that a period of "speech readiness" occurs between the ages of twelve and eighteen months in most babies. This period may be regarded as the "teachable moment" in speech development. If the baby is not encouraged to make use of this period of readiness or if he is deprived of opportunities to do so by obstacles in his environment or within himself—as in the case of deafness, which deprives the child of an opportunity to hear others speak and, consequently, of a model to imitate—he is likely to become emotionally disturbed. This is especially likely to occur when the young child cannot make others understand what he is trying to tell them or when he is unable to express his feelings because of inadequate speech. Inadequate speech is only rarely traceable to delay in the physical or mental development of the child. It can generally be traced to a lack of either opportunity or motivation to learn (70).

Methods of Learning. The child can learn to speak by *trial and error,* though it is questionable whether he would speak a language other people could understand. This is characteristic of twins. While they literally "make up" their own speech and can understand each other, few people know what they are trying to communicate; even their parents often guess incorrectly (103). *Imitation of a model* is a more effective way of learning how to pronounce words, though imitation without guidance produces less effective results than imitation with guidance. Learning to associate meanings with words follows the process of *conditioning and re-*

inforcement, though insight resulting from reasoning plays an important role. As McCarthy has stressed:

Children learn to speak not only by imitation and gradual approximation of the sounds they hear others make, but much of the meaning that words acquire for them must occur by the so-called Insight or Contiguity principle, as when Helen Keller first realized that everything has a name when she experienced the manual spelling of the word for "water" and felt the cool stream from the pump wash over her hand. The discovery that everything has a name and that *this* is the name for *that* obviously occurs by insight and contiguity. Perhaps we might postulate that the insight aspect of learning operates on the receptive or listening and understanding side of language and that the conditioning and reinforcing aspect operates on the productive, outgoing motor side of the process (104).

Fulfilling the Two Criteria of Speech. In learning to speak, the child must pronounce words intelligibly and associate meanings with the words spoken (see pages 208 to 209 for a more complete discussion of these criteria). To understand how the child learns to speak, we must know how and when he learns to fulfill these criteria.

Learning to Pronounce Words. The ability to reproduce heard sounds is too complicated for a young baby. During the first six months of life, babies make many meaningless sounds in their cooing and babbling. In the presence of other people, the baby will sometimes imitate them by "talking back," but he does not imitate the sounds they are making. He is merely imitating *sound making in general.* This is called the "echoreaction stage" of imitation. Even before he can imitate specific sounds, the baby acquires the ability to imitate the intonations and inflections of the voices of others. There will be some elemental imitation of sounds, such as "re-re-re," by the age of six months, and of simple syllables, such as "ma-ma" and "da-da," by eleven months (99, 103, 140).

"Readiness to imitate" occurs toward the

end of the first year of life. At that time, the baby attempts to imitate specific sounds which had not previously appeared in his babbling. The child's attempts to imitate, as well as the number of words attempted, increase with age. Increase in correctness of imitation proceeds slowly, however. Many of the young child's imitations bear little resemblance to the original model (105). With practice comes improvement, and in time the child learns to pronounce new words quickly and easily. This ability is used for the rest of his life in learning new words, whether in his own language or in a foreign language. While it is true that all standard dictionaries show the reader how to pronounce words—by the use of certain symbols to indicate where emphasis should be placed or whether to make a given sound hard or soft—most people learn to pronounce words by imitating the pronunciation of others. Children literally "pick up" the pronunciation of words from the people with whom they associate.

Association of Meanings. No child naturally associates any meaning with any word; he must learn that certain words have certain meanings. And because some words have more than one meaning—often meanings that are contradictory—it is a far more difficult learning task for the child than most adults realize. In fact, learning to pronounce words is, by comparison, relatively easy. Furthermore, there is a greater chance for error in learning correct associations; unless a child has guidance, he is likely to make mistakes which will result in incorrect usage. Why and how this happens will be discussed in more detail in the section of the chapter dealing with defective speech.

Association of meaning with different sounds follows the technique of the *conditioned reflex.* From the many sounds the baby uses, people around him select certain ones to repeat, and these he eventually learns to associate with certain objects, people, and situations. If, for example, the mother says a word when she gives an object to the baby, he learns, after several repetitions, that that particular combination

of sounds stands for the object presented. The more often he sees an object when the name of that object is given, the more quickly he will progress from the "parrot" stage, in which he merely imitates words, into a phase of speech development that may be called "true speech." Figure 6–3 shows the ways a child learns to associate meanings with words.

A child associates meanings with words in two ways. The first is the *direct,* or explicit, way, in which the adult names a thing or defines a word for the child; the second is the *indirect,* or implicit, way, in which the child makes associations through experience with concrete and/or verbal context (153). What meaning is associated with different words depends largely upon the environment in which the child lives, especially the environment of the home. The ability to associate meanings with words develops slightly later than the ability to imitate heard sounds. By the time the baby is a year old, he first indicates that he recognizes the sounds that he has heard an adult use in association with a specific person or object. Not until several months later, however, is there any real indication that he is attempting to associate, in his own usage, a specific sound or group of sounds with a specific person or object.

All meanings are first learned in connection with a specific object, person, or situation. Young children do not generalize. Instead, they emphasize the particular or isolated aspect of the word. For example, when a young child learns to call his father "daddy," he is likely to call all men "daddy." Only gradually does he learn to generalize and to apply general meanings to general categories and specific words to specific objects or situations. This learning, as has already been pointed out, comes from insight. As McCarthy has explained, the child not only discovers that everything has a name but he also discovers that *"this* is the name for *that"* (104).

As the child grows older, he is able to stress the abstract, or "class," features of certain words; as a result, he can associate certain class names with certain objects (12,

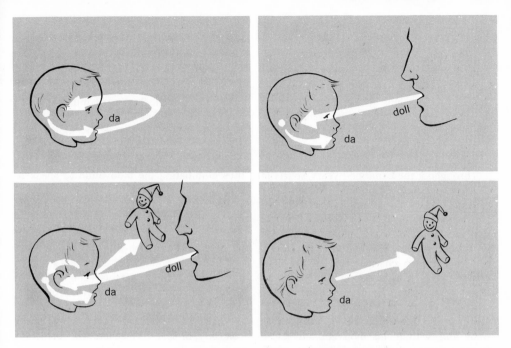

Figure 6–3.   Development of language habits in the young child. (Adapted from F. H. Allport, *Social psychology,* Houghton Mifflin, 1924. Used by permission.)

53). Children tend, however, to make word associations that are different from those made by adults. In a word-association test, it was found that the stimulus word "table" suggests "eat" to children and "chair" to adults. Similarly, the stimulus word "man" mainly suggests "work" to children, while to adults, it usually suggests "woman" (31).

Pattern of Development.   The pattern of speech development, regardless of the language learned, is much the same for all children. Rates of learning vary with the native endowment of children and the environmental stimulation they receive. An accelerated rate is usually accompanied by rapid development along other lines. In general, the age of learning to talk is approximately the same in all cultures, though it may be slightly later in primitive than in civilized cultures. In our culture, children from the lower classes learn slightly later than those from the higher classes (70, 99, 103).

The pattern of learning to speak closely parallels the pattern of development of postural control (103, 114). Cooing and vocalizing in response to social stimulation come just about the time the baby is able to hold his head erect, between the second and third months. Babbling begins between the sixth and seventh months, just after the baby has mastered the skill of sitting alone. The baby says his first words at the end of the first year, at approximately the time when he is standing alone. Between the fifteenth and eighteenth months, when the baby is walking alone, his independence is "also revealed in the realm of language, for it is at this same period that he begins to enlarge his vocabulary and to combine two and three words into rudimentary sentences" (117).

The pattern of speech development is marked by spurts and resting periods, or *plateaus*—times when no apparent improvement occurs. Whenever a new motor act is being established, whether it is reaching and grasping, sitting alone, standing, or walking, there will be a temporary plateau in the pattern of speech development. Between the ages of nine and eighteen months, when the baby is mastering the skill of walking, the urge to walk seems to be more powerful than the urge to talk. After walking becomes habitual, the baby's attention is again directed to talking, and a spurt in learning to talk follows.

Throughout the childhood years, spurts in development are commonly followed by plateaus. When, for example, the child begins school, he is likely to acquire a whole new vocabulary of words in connection with his school studies. Furthermore, his eagerness to learn—a characteristic of the first-grader—gives him a strong motivation to learn new words. By the middle of the second grade or the beginning of the third, however, his interest in school will start to wane and, with it, his motivation to learn. Because the curriculum areas remain much the same though on a higher level, he is introduced to fewer new words, and it is not surprising that his speech development reaches a plateau (70, 92, 104).

Essentials in Learning to Speak. As in learning motor skills, the three essentials in learning to speak are opportunities for practice, motivation to learn, and guidance in learning. Most children are provided with the first two; they are given plenty of *opportunities to practice* talking, and they are *encouraged* to do so. Many parents regard early speaking as an indication of their child's intelligence. Like early toilet training (see pages 171 and 175), early speaking is a feather in the parental cap. Because of the personal satisfaction parents derive from having their children learn to talk as soon as possible, many parents are willing to spend time and effort in helping them to do so.

Some parents do not provide *adequate motivation*, even though they provide adequate learning opportunities. The young child learns to speak according to his needs. If he can get what he wants without asking for it, and if substitutes for speech, such as crying or gestures, serve his purpose, his incentive to learn to speak is weakened. Baby talk, for example, is likely to continue until the child starts to play with other children. When he discovers that they do not understand him, he will be motivated to improve his speech. Studies of multiple births have revealed that twins and triplets are generally delayed in speech development because they associate mainly with one another and learn to understand their own jargons, thus eliminating the motivation to speak so they can be understood by others (103).

Far too many parents fall short in supplying the third essential—*guidance in learning.* This is sometimes due to laziness on the part of parents, but more often it comes from not knowing how to guide a child's speech development. Some parents believe that the child will "outgrow" incorrect pronunciation, that he will automatically realize his mistakes when he hears other people speak correctly, or that his teachers will correct his speech.

The most valuable ways to guide speech development are, first, by providing a good model and, second, by providing help in following this model correctly. Because much of the imitation of a model is unconscious, and because the child learns good or bungled speech equally easily, it is obvious that the better the model, the better his speech will be. As Bluemel has pointed out, "Most children catch their speech in much the same way as they catch measles—by being exposed to it" (20). Even when the model is good, as judged by adult standards, it may not be good for the child. To be a good model for a child, the speaker must say each word slowly enough to be heard clearly and distinctly. The child must have enough time to comprehend the correct pronunciation of each word and the correct relationships of each word to every other word.

Having a good model does not ensure correct imitation; the child may imitate the words as he hears them—a jumble of sounds or words shortened by dropping the last syllable as one word runs into the word following it. The child must be helped to imitate the model correctly. Specific training in pronunciation and in association of meaning of words results in better pronunciation and in learning of more words with their correct meanings (20, 31).

Twins speak poorly mainly because they listen to each other and imitate a poor model with little or no guidance. Similarly, when a child is closely associated with someone who stutters, he is likely to imitate this speech defect. Studies of only children have revealed that, in most cases, their speech is superior for their age level because they listen primarily to the mature speech of their parents. In addition, parents of only children have more time to guide their children's speech development than parents of larger families (26, 103, 104).

MAJOR TASKS IN SPEECH DEVELOPMENT

Real communication involves the ability to combine words into sentences that are meaningful to others and, in addition, the ability to understand what others say. In learning to speak, the child has four major developmental tasks. These are so interrelated that successful achievement in one is essential to success in the others. The tasks are (1) comprehending the speech of others, (2) pronouncing words, (3) building a vocabulary, and (4) combining words into sentences.

COMPREHENSION

At every age, the passive, or "comprehension," vocabulary is larger than the active, or "speech," vocabulary. A somewhat analogous situation exists when an adolescent or adult learns a foreign language; he understands words spoken by others and can follow a conversation before he himself can talk intelligibly in that language (103).

The baby's understanding of the behavior of others begins with his understanding of their actions, voice intonations, and gestures, not with his understanding of their words. A baby becomes quiet when he is talked to; he distinguishes between friendly and angry

talking; and he is, in general, responsive to the affective intonations of the voice even before he shows evidence of understanding gestures or of making differential responses to words. It would be impossible for him to comprehend the meaning of what was said to him if he had to rely entirely upon the interpretation of the sounds he heard (98).

In the development of comprehension, the baby responds affectively to *both* the intonational pattern of what he hears and the situation in which he hears it. A baby can understand his mother through "emotional contagion" because he can understand nonverbal signs, such as her smile or the tone of her voice (33). As early as the third month of life, pleasure, anger, and fear can be understood. Later, when the baby hears a word alone, he is able to respond to it without the situation in which its meaning was learned. There are, thus, three distinct forms of communication between the baby and another person: speech, facial expressions, and actions (26, 98). It is often difficult to tell how much of a young child's comprehension is due to any one of these. Very young children learn to comprehend the meaning of commands, such as "No-no," "Stop," "Come here," or "Lie down," partly by associating the sounds with an act which accompanies them, such as associating "No-no" with the lifting of the hand, and partly through an interpretation of the tone of voice used by the individual who gives the commands. Up to the age of eighteen months, words must be reinforced with gestures if the speaker wants to be sure that the child will comprehend what he hears. Even simple directions, such as "Put the cup on the table," need to be supplemented by a gesture of pointing to the table and to the cup.

From standard tests of intelligence and from normative summaries, we know approximately what level of comprehension can be expected of a child of a given age. At sixteen weeks, a baby will turn his head to the sound of a human voice and will show that he recognizes his mother by smiling. Between six and eight months, he responds to words, and at twelve months, to simple commands (78). According to the Terman-Merrill Scale of Intelligence Tests, by the time the average baby is two years old he should comprehend well enough to respond correctly to two out of six simple commands, such as "Give me the kitty" or "Put the spoon in the cup," when the objects are placed on a table before him (146).

Before the child enters school, he normally has a large enough passive vocabulary to understand instructions given by unfamiliar people, to understand the meaning of the stories read to him, and to distinguish the similarities and differences in simple words (27, 58, 99). Listening to the radio and watching television are proving to be assets to the development of the comprehension vocabularies of today's young children (104).

PRONUNCIATION

The pronunciation of words, as has already been pointed out, is learned by imitation. In early childhood, the ability to imitate sounds is so flexible that a child's entire pronunciation can readily change in a short period of time if he is placed in a new environment where those with whom he associates pronounce words differently from those with whom he formerly associated. Because of this flexibility—due to the plasticity of the vocal mechanism and the absence of well-developed habits of pronunciation—many parents and educators contend that the proper time to begin learning a foreign language is during the early years of childhood. If the child learns to pronounce words in the foreign language at that time, they maintain, he will "speak like a native," but if he waits until he reaches the junior or senior high-school age, he will always speak with an American accent. Certainly, pronunciation has settled into a habit by adolescence and is hard to change.

Studies of pronunciation have shown that between the ages of twelve and eighteen months, much of what the baby says is incomprehensible to people outside his immediate family. Between eighteen months and three years, he attempts to say many words but makes little improvement in pronunciation. This leads to many misunderstandings of what he wants and proves to be quite frustrating to him (103, 105, 125). After three, he makes rapid strides toward correct pronunciation.

As in other aspects of speech development, there are marked *individual differences* in pronunciation. These variations depend partly upon the rate of development of the vocal mechanism but mostly upon the guidance and help the young child receives in mastering the difficult skill of combining sounds into meaningful words. The ability to pronounce words so they can be understood by others frequently lags behind the development of a rather large vocabulary. Most young children know the meanings of many words that they cannot pronounce in a comprehensible manner.

Studies of the sounds and the sound combinations the young child has the greatest difficulty in pronouncing correctly reveal that consonants and consonant blends are more difficult to pronounce than vowels and diphthongs. Some of the easiest consonants for a child to pronounce are *t, p, b, m,* and *n.* Easy vowels are *i, a, e,* and *u.* Among the consonants difficult to pronounce are *z, w, d, s,* and *g.* Difficult consonant blends consist of *st, str, sk, dr,* and *fl.* Little consistency has been found in the misarticulations of young children. Articulatory defects are due more often to auditory confusions than to muscular incoordination (108, 138).

Tonal Qualities. Typically, the baby's voice is high-pitched. Nasal sounds, which are absent at first, begin to appear as changes take place in the development of the vocal mechanism. Gradually, the tone of voice changes, so that by the time the child is three years old, the voice is less high-pitched than previously. At this time, there are often voice tremors, and many young children develop a nasal quality in their voice if their adenoids become enlarged. The voice becomes stronger and louder, and by the time the child is four years old, his normal speech tone very often has a strained, raucous quality. Frequently, he expresses himself in "high, full-volumed" yells (108).

One of the most characteristic and unfortunate aspects of speech during the school years is the coarsening of the tonal qualities of the voice. This is not the result of maturation but comes from screaming and shouting, which so invariably accompany play activities. This strain on the immature vocal mechanism generally results in a coarsening of the tonal qualities that can never be overcome completely. This coarseness is of little importance to children, especially to boys, who feel that talking in a pleasant voice is a sign of a "sissy" (142).

In the latter part of childhood, new changes appear in the tonal quality of the voice. With growth in the vocal mechanism comes a lengthening of the vocal cords; this, in turn, causes the voice to become lower-pitched. During the voice changes of puberty, boys' voices frequently have a husky sound, suggesting that they are suffering from sore throats. The huskiness gradually disappears as the tonal quality becomes deeper. Girls' voices likewise change to a lower pitch at puberty, but they do not become husky (45, 60).

BUILDING A VOCABULARY

The child learns to use the words he needs. In building a vocabulary, he learns first the words for which he has the greatest need, but he also uses substitutes, such as crying and gesturing, when he lacks adequate words to convey his meanings. As he grows older and abandons prespeech forms, he frequently uses slang terms as substitutes when no adequate word is readily available in his vocabulary. The child's vocabulary comes partly from direct teaching of words and their meanings and partly from his own curiosity, which leads him to ask people about word meanings. In the development of vocabulary, the child, in effect, learns (1) a general vocabulary, consisting of words such as "man," "beautiful," and "go," which can be used in a variety of different situations, and (2) special vocabularies, consisting of words with specific meanings which can be used only in certain situations. Because words of the general vocabulary are more useful, they are learned first. At every age, the general vocabulary is larger than the special vocabularies.

General Vocabulary. The first words used by the child are *nouns,* generally monosyllables, taken from favorite sounds the child has babbled. Later, these are doubled or trebled. The words are used to designate persons or objects in the child's environment, such as "mamma," "dada," "choo-choo," or "baby." After the child has learned enough nouns to apply names to the people and objects in his environment, he begins to learn *verbs,* especially those which designate action, such as "give," "take," "hold," and so on.

Adjectives and *adverbs* appear in a baby's vocabulary from the age of 1½ years, while *prepositions* and *pronouns* appear last. The adjectives most commonly used at first are "good," "bad," "nice," "naughty," "hot," and "cold"; these are applied principally to people, food, and toys. The earliest adverbs to appear in the child's vocabulary are generally "here" and "where." The difficulty the young child experiences in trying to discover when to use "me," "my," "mine," or "I" to refer to himself causes no small amount of confusion, and he avoids their use as long as possible (103, 148).

Size of Vocabulary. The child increases his vocabulary not only by learning new words but also by learning *new meanings for old words* (53, 125, 153). For example, the word "orange" may be known only as a type of fruit at first. Later, the child discovers that this word also refers to a color and, still later, that it is a complex color, made up of a combination of red and yellow.

It has been estimated from studies of large numbers of babies that the mean number of different words used by babies at eighteen months is 10, and at twenty-four months, 29.1. In these early months, girls surpass boys in size of vocabulary. It has been reported that the average vocabulary of a two-year-old contains 272 words and, again, that girls surpass boys in vocabulary size. After the child enters school, the rapid increase in vocabulary size comes partly from direct teaching of words and their usages by teachers, partly from interesting associations with objects and experiences, and partly from the child's reading for pleasure, listening to the radio, and watching television. Estimates of the size of vocabulary have revealed that the average first-grader knows between 20,000 and 24,000 words, or 5 to 6 per cent of the words in a standard dictionary. The sixth-grader knows approximately 50,000 words, and the child entering high school, about 80,000 words, or 22 per cent of the words in a standard dictionary (35, 103).

There are, of course, marked *individual differences* in size of vocabulary at every age. While some of the differences that have been reported are, without question, due to the fact that the studies were made on different-sized groups and with different techniques, they are not due to this alone. They are *real differences*. Differences in size of vocabulary appear as early as eighteen months of age and become increasingly greater as children grow older. While differences in intelligence are partially responsible for differences in size of vocabulary, environmental influences, opportunities to learn, and motivation to learn are also factors that play roles of major importance. Girls, as a general rule, have larger vocabularies at every age than boys (60, 103).

Importance of Vocabulary Size.   Size of vocabulary is very important to a child's social and emotional development. In order to become an active participant in the social group, a child must be able to communicate with other children in terms they can understand. The child whose vocabulary is inadequate is forced into the role of an outsider. This is well illustrated in the case of bilingual children. They may know more words in the two languages than mono-lingual children know, but they may not know enough words in the language of their peers to be able to communicate. As a result, they feel inadequate and fail to communicate even when they can (91).

Children of all ages feel frustrated when they want to say something but cannot do so either because they lack the necessary words or because they cannot make themselves understood in the words they can use. When their vocabularies are inadequate to meet their communication needs, they become angry at the person who does not understand them. Frequent experiences of this sort lead, in time, to a generalized frustration. This frustration is accompanied by feelings of martyrdom resulting from the belief that people *do not want* to understand.

The child's *writing* is affected by the size of his vocabulary, just as his speech is. While some children can express themselves better verbally than in writing, this difference is largely a matter of training in writing, not size of vocabulary. Studies of the relationship of oral and written vocabularies have revealed that the number and variety of words used in writing are directly related to the child's oral vocabulary. Success in writing is thus dependent upon the child's achievement in oral language. Furthermore, success in school work is greatly influenced by how well the child can express himself in writing and how well he writes on examinations. In turn, how well the child does academically has a marked influence on how he feels about school, about studying, and about the importance of education (60, 139).

The significance of vocabulary size has been stressed by Garrison:

The number of words a child knows determines in large measure his school progress, and failure to progress normally has far-reaching significance. Words are the means by which the child learns about his world. If his knowledge of words is grossly inadequate, the interpretation of his environment will be correspondingly so. In an age of radio, television, films, rapid transportation, and world relationships, the child needs to know many words and to be able to use them. Failure tends to result in impaired social adjustment (58).

Special Vocabularies. Early in childhood, when attention is concentrated on the development of a usable vocabulary, the child has little time to build up special vocabularies. Once he has a usable general vocabulary, however, he discovers that words of special usage are often essential as a means of expression. Some of the most important special vocabularies and the ages at which they normally develop are outlined below:

1. The "Trick" Vocabulary. This consists of words pronounced correctly by the child in response to the request of another. The little child is asked to say long and complicated words, such as "Mississippi" and "esophagus," for the delight of the adults encouraging him. As the child rarely knows the meaning of the words, their use is merely a form of "showing off." The age at which the trick vocabulary is most used is between one and two years.

2. The "Etiquette" Vocabulary. This type of special vocabulary consists of such words as "please," "thank you," and "I'm sorry." Children can learn to use these words as soon as they can speak coherently. Many children, however, do not want to use them. Boys, especially, pretend to be "tough" and regard etiquette words as a sign of a "sissy" (27). Some children, particularly those of the lower social classes, do not have an opportunity to learn etiquette words until they enter school; their parents do not feel that such words are necessary, and they are not in common use in the home and neighborhood. How large the etiquette vocabulary will be and when it will be learned will depend upon the training the child receives (70).

3. The Color Vocabulary. Because of the young child's interest in color, names of different colors are learned at an early age. Most children know the names of the primary colors by the time they are four years old (146). How soon they will learn other color names will depend partly upon their interest in colors and partly upon their opportunities to learn.

4. The Number Vocabulary. While many young children of 2½ or 3 years of age can count up to 10 or more, it is questionable whether they understand the meanings of the words they use. Their number vocabularies therefore fall into the category of "parrot speech." Through play or direct teaching, the child gradually learns the meanings of many numbers. In the Stanford-Binet Intelligence Scale, the five-year-old child is expected to be able to count three objects; the six-year-old is expected to know the meanings of the words "three," "nine," "five," "ten," and "seven" well enough to count out the number of blocks requested from the 12 that are placed before him (146).

5. The Time Vocabulary. Because of the diversity of activities characteristic of the different parts of the day, the child comes to know the meanings of words related to them. By the age of six or seven years, the child should know the meanings of such simple words as "morning," "afternoon," "night," "summer," and "winter." When he enters school, he soon learns the names of the different days of the week and months of the year (146).

6. The Money Vocabulary. While to the very young child, all coins are "money" or "pennies," to the child of four or five years, the different coins begin to have specific names, according to their size and color. How large the child's money vocabulary is depends upon the environment. Children of poorer environments have, as a rule, larger money vocabularies than children from the better neighborhoods because they are often entrusted with money for errands (103).

7. The Slang Vocabulary. Slang is a form of unauthorized speech. This means that slang words are not to be found in a dictionary or that their use is not sanctioned

by authorities on correct speech. Offensive slang is generally referred to as "swearing." The dividing line between slang and swearing depends primarily upon *personal reactions* of the hearer.

During early childhood, the use of slang or swear vocabularies is purely imitative. Slang is thus a form of "parrot speech." The slang vocabularies of young children are, on the whole, larger in poorer neighborhoods than in better neighborhoods (42).

From the age of seven or eight years, the use of slang is no longer imitative or "show-off"; instead, it serves as a means of expressing feelings and emotions for which the child has no adequate form of vocal expression. While the child may invent some of the swear or slang words he uses, this vocabulary is, for the most part, an imitation of the words used by others. Elementary-school children pick up their slang and swear words from junior and senior high-school students, while they, in turn, pick them up from college students or from men in the armed services. Children from the upper social classes often get their slang vocabularies, especially obscene expressions that adults consider "swearing," from children of the lower social classes with whom they are associated at school or in play (42). Thus, not only does the child have the satisfaction of a readily usable vocabulary for emotional expression, but, of even greater importance, he has the added feeling of self-importance which comes from identifying himself with older people. Both boys and girls use slang freely after they enter school; the words they use are the ones in vogue at the time. Boys, as a rule, use more slang than girls. Furthermore, boys show a greater preference for slang that resembles swearing.

To most adults, the use of slang and swearing by children is objectionable. Even today, when the *value of slang* is widely recognized, many parents believe that they should put a stop to its use by washing the child's mouth out with strong-tasting soap— to "get rid of the dirty words." These parents are motivated partly by the belief that slang and swearing will reflect badly on

the child and partly by the belief that it will reflect badly on them as parents. Washing out the child's mouth with soap may, however—like any form of corporal punishment —only drive the objectionable behavior under cover. In the presence of parents and relatives, the child will use only the words they expect him to use, but when he is out of earshot, he will probably use any words he likes. Furthermore, it is questionable whether he should feel constrained to use only those words that his parents approve.

In our culture, it is characteristic for children to "go tough" between the ages of four and eight years. At this time, they are trying to identify themselves with the peer group and to cut the ties of dependency on their parents. In their attempts to assert their independence, children use many bombastic phrases, "dirty words" referring to sex and elimination, and tabooed words, especially those relating to religion. Such terms serve to inflate the child's developing ego, and, of far greater importance, they help to create the impression among members of the peer group that he is a good sport. Speaking the language of the group helps him to identify himself with it and makes the members of the group feel that he is one of them. Slang is thus a *socializing agent;* as such, it plays an important role in the social development of the child (27, 60, 86).

Swearing is often used by little boys to compensate for feelings of inadequacy and inferiority; it makes them feel big and important. By using the language of the "big boys," they hope to increase their social acceptance, especially among the "big boys." As boys grow older, swearing adds to their feelings of superiority over the younger boys and over girls, whom they now regard as the "weaker sex." In addition, they regard it as a symbol of masculinity—a sign that they are "regular boys," not "sissies." Depriving them of this prop to their developing egos is of questionable value.

While swearing is generally associated with members of the lower social classes and may be interpreted as an indication of poor child training, it is a common way of "cutting parental apron strings" in our culture. As such, it is just a phase of growing up (42). A child who is deprived of doing what his peers do may find himself deprived of their acceptance. In the long run, this can do far more damage to his personality than the use of profanity can do to his reputation. Furthermore, the use of profanity is generally curbed by social pressures as the child grows older.

8. Secret Language. A common accompaniment of the "gang" behavior of late childhood is the development of a "secret language" which the child uses in communicating with his intimate friends—the members of his gang. Secret language may take any one of three common forms: *verbal,* generally known as "pig Latin" or "pidgin English" because it is a distortion of the child's own language; *written,* consisting of codes formed by symbols or crude drawings to express words or complete thoughts; and *kinetic,* consisting of gestures and the formation of words by use of the fingers, as in the language of the deaf and dumb. The purpose of secret language—to communicate with members of the gang without making the secrets of the gang known to outsiders—is generally served best by the verbal and written forms because they can be camouflaged better than the kinetic (27, 34).

Most children start to use secret language by the time they enter third grade, with the peak period of usage coming between ten and thirteen years. It is seldom used after fifteen years of age. If it is, it generally consists of a code for passing notes in school or for writing letters to intimate friends. Both boys and girls use secret language, but it is more popular among girls than boys. Girls delight in spending hours trying to develop words, signs, or symbols that cannot be understood by the uninitiated (60, 107). Figure 6–4 illustrates three forms of verbal secret language.

Many parents and teachers have an unsympathetic or even intolerant attitude toward secret language. They accuse the child of being "silly" and of "wasting time" which, they claim, could be better spent in learning words in the English language. Secret language plays important roles, however, in the *social* and *personality development* of a child—roles that cannot be played by words in a general vocabulary.

The socializing value of secret language comes from the fact that it welds children together into closely knit friendship groups. It gives a child a feeling of security to know that he can have secrets with his friends that

Opish   Pig Latin   Tut-A-Hash

Figure 6–4. Secret language. (Adapted from C. Brownstone, Why children's secret language? *Parents' Magazine,* May, 1940. Used by permission.)

others cannot pry into. Even more important, it gives him a feeling of belonging—a status symbol in the eyes of others. While the child who uses secret language may not win the admiration of his parents and teachers, he wins the admiration of his peers and, often, their envy. Not only does he "belong," but his status in the group is so secure that he is entrusted with knowledge of their secret forms of communication.

Secret language is also important for a child because it stimulates an *interest in language* and a *motivation to learn* it. Secret languages require an ingenuity and alertness that are not necessary in the more conventional forms of communication. The child who wants to be able to communicate secretly is motivated to study words, to go through a dictionary, and to discover word meanings which, otherwise, he would have little interest in learning. This interest in learning words will not necessarily end when the child no longer uses secret language. In attempting to find ingenious ways of outwitting others, many children discover the fascination of words.

FORMING SENTENCES

In the earliest sentences, one word alone is used—a noun or verb that, when combined with a gesture, expresses a complete thought. For example, "give," when accompanied by pointing to a toy, means "give me the toy." The word "ball," when accompanied by the holding out of the arms in the direction of the ball, means "give me the ball." The child uses this "single-word" type of sentence from approximately twelve to eighteen months of age.

By the time the child is two years old, he combines words into short sentences, most of which are incomplete. These sentences contain one or more nouns, a verb, and occasionally adjectives and adverbs. Prepositions, pronouns, and conjunctions are omitted. Typical sentences of this type are "Hold doll," "Go bed," "Go bye-bye," and "Want drink." By the time the child is four years old, his sentences are nearly complete; a year later, they are complete in that all

parts of speech are used. The child usually continues to supplement what he says with gestures until the latter part of childhood, when he discovers that gestures are not a socially approved form of behavior (103).

An analysis of various types of sentences used up to the age of eight years has revealed a decline in incomplete as well as in structurally complete but functionally incomplete sentences. There is a slight but steady increase in the use of simple sentences with phrases, compound and complex sentences, and elaborated sentences. These are illustrated in Figure 6–5. The use of clauses of all types increases markedly between three and six years of age (104).

Sentence *length* increases up to the age of 9½ years, after which there is a tendency for the length to remain static or decrease slightly. Sentences of two or three words are used as early as two years of age, though they are much more common at three. After three, sentences of six to eight words frequently appear. Young children often increase the length of their sentences by combining two or more simple sentences with the conjunction "and." As a result, their sentences tend to be rambling and loosely knit. Older children, by contrast, increase the length and complexity of their sentences by using clauses (104, 148).

Studies of the length of sentences used by children of different ages have revealed that there is a tendency for children of today to use longer sentences, age for age, than children did 20 years ago (145). In explanation of this tendency, McCarthy has stated:

Several possibilities account for this. Among those I would list are the advent of radio and television, fewer foreign-born and bilingual children, the rise of nursery schools affording more opportunities for language stimulation outside the home for the formerly underprivileged groups of children, more leisure time for parents to spend with their children, reduced amount of time that children are cared for by nursemaids of limited verbal ability, better economic conditions allowing parents even in lower income brackets to provide more stimulating environments for their children, and finally the somewhat

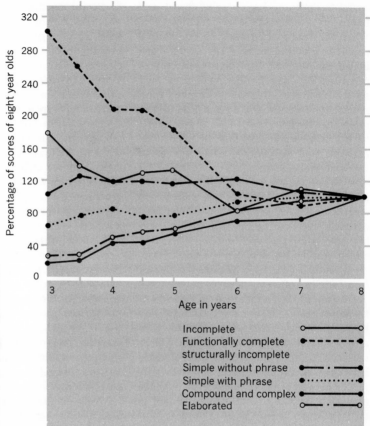

Figure 6–5. Common types of sentences used at different ages in childhood. (Adapted from D. McCarthy, Research in language development: retrospect and prospect, *Child Develpm. Monogr.*, 1959, 25, No. 5. Used by permission.)

greater tendency for children to be treated more permissively and to find greater acceptance in the modern home (104).

At every age, there are marked *individual differences* in both the length and the pattern of the sentence. Bright children and those from the higher socioeconomic groups usually use longer and more complex sentences than the average. Girls are superior to boys in their sentence usage at every age. Variations in sentence length and structure among white and Negro children are likely to reflect socioeconomic differences rather than racial differences (7, 104).

Perhaps the greatest variations reflect differences in the speaking situation. When playing with their contemporaries, children are likely to converse in phrases rather than in complete sentences. When with adults,

they lengthen their sentences somewhat, but in a classroom situation, where there are both children and a teacher, they lengthen them even further (68, 101).

VARIATIONS IN SPEECH DEVELOPMENT

While the pattern of speech development is much the same for all children, there are marked variations in the rate of development, the size and quality of the vocabulary, and the correctness of pronunciation at every age level. A number of factors are responsible for these variations, the most important of which are the following:

1. Health. Severe and prolonged illness during the first two years of life has been

found to delay the beginning of speech and the use of sentences by 1 to 2 months (99). When the young child must be hospitalized for 3 or more years or when a prolonged illness cuts him off from play contacts, the effect on his speech development is very serious. Owing to isolation and limited communication with others, he has little opportunity to learn to talk (67). Furthermore, he has little incentive to talk; he is not feeling well, and his every need is anticipated for him.

2. Intelligence.   There is an increase in correlation between speech sounds and level of intelligence during the first two years of life, and after the age of two, there is a strong relationship between speech development and IQ (129). It has been suggested from studies of early speech sounds that consonant types and the consonant-vowel-frequency ratio in a baby's babbling are better predictors of later intelligence than any of the present measures of infant intelligence (38). A child who is precocious in his early speech development is usually normal or above normal in intelligence. A delay of several or many months in beginning to talk, however, is not at all a sure sign of dullness (78).

Studies of mentally deficient children have shown that the lower the intellectual rating, the poorer the speech. Children of intellectual superiority, on the other hand, have been found to show marked linguistic superiority, both in size of vocabulary and in length and correctness of sentence structure (44). In addition to their maturity of expression, they show maturity in the content of their speech. Before their elementary school days are over, they can learn several languages with little or no confusion, they are able to speak before groups, and they enjoy dramatization. Among elementary-school children, there is a high correlation between knowledge of word meanings and overall school achievement. By contrast, children with articulation defects often have reading disabilities and do poor school work (44, 73, 157).

3. Socioeconomic Status.   In forms of vocalization which are purely "instinctive," such as crying, no differences are found between babies of different socioeconomic classes. Differences in speech development, in size of vocabulary, in sentence forms and correctness, and in pronunciation become increasingly great as children grow older. Children of the upper socioeconomic groups talk sooner, talk better, and talk more than those of the lower groups. At every age, the articulation of children of the upper groups is superior to that of children of the lower groups (18, 42, 92). Comparisons of the mastery of speech sounds of babies from business, clerical, and professional families with those from laboring-class families revealed no significant difference between the two groups during the first 1½ years of the babies' lives. After that, more speech sounds appeared in the vocalizations of babies from the former groups (78, 103). (See Figure 6–6.) There is clear-cut evidence of a marked relationship between the child's speech and the occupational status of the father. This relationship is well established even among five-year-olds (126).

While intelligence may play some role in determining variations in speech development, differences in environmental influences cannot be overlooked. Environmental factors that are closely correlated with the young child's speech development include the number of children's books he sees, the opportunities he has for constructive play, the number of hours he is read to or told stories, the number of adults in daily contact with him, and the number of playmates he has (104).

Children who associate primarily with adults are more precocious in their speech development than children who associate mainly with other children. Children from the higher socioeconomic groups are likely to have more associations with their parents than children from poorer groups, where mothers may work away from home or have too many home duties to be able to devote much time to them (81, 103). Furthermore, parents from the upper socioeconomic

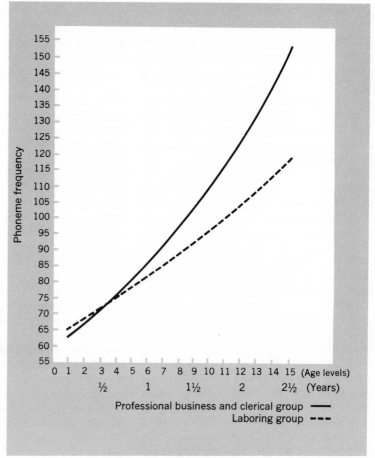

Figure 6–6. Social-class differences in speech development in the early years of life. (Adapted from O. C. Irwin, Infant speech: the effect of family occupational status and of age on sound frequencies, *J. speech hear. Disord.*, 1948, 13, 320–323. Used by permission.)

groups usually provide a better model of speech for their children to imitate; they give their children more encouragement to learn word meanings and pronunciation; and they are more likely to correct faulty sentence structure than parents from the lower socioeconomic groups are. Parents from the upper groups generally feel that speech is very important. As a result, they pressure their children to learn to speak early and correctly. By contrast, the linguistic environment for lower-class children is one of "relative deprivation" (18, 70).

4. Sex. Boys lag behind girls in learning to talk; boys' sentences are shorter and less correct grammatically, their use and com-

prehension vocabularies are smaller, and their pronunciation of words is less accurate at every age. Differences between the sexes become more pronounced with every passing year and are greater among children of the lower socioeconomic groups than among those of the higher groups (7, 126).

There is no completely satisfactory explanation of the sex difference in speech development, nor do we know whether this difference is universal or characteristic of our culture alone. McCarthy has offered an explanation in terms of family relationships. According to her, during the first year of life, when no real sex differences in quantity or quality of vocalization have been found, the baby babbles back to the mother approximations of the sounds made by her. This is the "echo-reaction" stage of babbling; at this time, babies of both sexes show similar feelings toward the mother. Soon after babyhood is over, girls begin to identify with their mothers, while boys try to identify with their fathers. Because, in our culture, the father is away from home more than the mother, boys have fewer and less intimate contacts with the father than girls have with the mother. The closeness of the mother-daughter relationship throughout childhood helps the girl to learn to speak sooner and better than the boy. Furthermore, because there is a greater difference in tonal quality between the boy's voice and the adult male voice than between the girl's voice and the adult female voice, the echo reaction is less satisfactory for the boy and less favorable to learning (103).

5. Family Relationships. Babies in institutions cry more but babble less and make fewer different sounds than family babies, whatever the socioeconomic group (2). They are slow in learning to talk and are, throughout their lives, retarded in language development (67, 98, 120, 122). These facts show that close personal relationships are a significant factor in speech development, but the quality of the relationships is also extremely important.

A *healthy* relationship between the child and other family members, especially the mother, facilitates speech development. Wyatt has stressed this point:

Satisfactory interpersonal relations, in particular the relationship between mother and child, on the prelinguistic as well as on the linguistic level, are the prerequisites for the development of symbol formation and for the successful acquisition of language. The vicissitudes of the mother-child relationship have a determining effect upon the nature and outcome of the process of language learning (155).

By contrast, an *unhealthy* family relationship—in which the young child is babied and pampered—may not only result in speech retardation but may also lead to such speech disorders as lisping, stuttering, and slurring. Many of the most serious cases of stuttering, for example, have been found in children whose family relationships were characterized by emotional tensions (111).

Size of family is also important. Speech-sound development progresses in the same pattern for all children, but as they grow older, those who are only children are definitely superior in every phase of linguistic skill. The only child is the center of the mother's attention for longer periods of time than the child with older siblings. Furthermore, an only child is spared sibling rivalry, which sometimes manifests itself in speech disorders, especially stuttering (103).

6. Encouragement to Speak. In an experiment in which the experimenter leaned over the baby's crib and vocalized to him, with the accompaniments of smiling and clucking, the baby "vocalized as part of the total response" he gave the adult. When the experimenter leaned over the crib with an expressionless face and without vocalizing, the baby responded with very much less vocalization (121). As has already been pointed out, babies babble more when someone talks to them than when they are alone. The more attention they get, the greater their motivation to try to join in the adult conversation.

In a study of children between the ages of thirteen and thirty months, those who were read to regularly were compared with those who were not read to. Up to the age of seventeen months, there was little difference between the two groups in spontaneous vocalizations; after that age, the experimental group had consistently higher scores in vocalization frequency (79).

There are many ways in which children can be motivated to develop their speech. Mothers have reported that they stimulated speech in preschoolers by encouraging family conversations, by reading to the children, by letting them watch television, and by providing play opportunities and outings. Older children were encouraged to talk about what they had seen or done, to discuss television programs, and to point to different objects in pictures and to discuss them. Answering children's questions also motivates them to speak more freely. With practice in speaking, children increase their vocabularies, improve their pronunciations, and become more fluent (64).

Significance of Variations. It is apparent from the above discussion that most of the factors responsible for variations in speech are controllable. Even in the lower socioeconomic groups, parents who want their children to learn to speak correctly and fluently can encourage them to do good work in school, to read good books, and to watch the better programs on television. Parents can improve their own speech through reading, radio listening, and television watching so that they can provide better models for their children to imitate.

It is widely agreed by educators and psychologists that most children fall below their capacities in speech development. Far too many parents, however, tend to accept the traditional belief that children will "outgrow" poor speech. They often discourage children from speaking, partly because they find their questioning a source of annoyance and embarrassment and partly because they believe that children should not monopolize the conversation. Encouragement is even more important for children who tend to lag behind their peers. It is especially important for boys because good speech and confidence in one's ability to speak are assets in the business world.

DEFECTIVE SPEECH

When a child speaks correctly or nearly correctly but on a level below that of the norm for his age, he has a *quantitative* speech lag. His vocabulary, for example, is smaller than that of other children of his age, and his pronunciation is on a more infantile level. This condition is generally called *delayed speech*. By contrast, *defective speech* is inaccurate speech; it varies *qualitatively* from the norm for the child's age and contains more than the usual number of errors.

Defective speech is more difficult to control than delayed speech. This is due, in part, to the fact that the causes of defective speech are more serious and, in part, to the failure of parents to recognize the necessity of taking remedial action before the defects have become habitual. In many cases, defective speech can be traced to inferior models which the child has imitated or to lack of guidance in following a good model correctly. In serious cases, however, a defect in the speech mechanism or emotional tension is often responsible.

During the first few years of life, every child has difficulty in controlling his speech mechanism. The result is that defects in pronunciation are almost universal. The child's limited understanding makes it difficult for him to associate correct meanings with the words he uses. In addition, he has trouble combining words into sentences correctly. How much difficulty a child will have in these areas will depend on the level of his intelligence, the opportunities he has to learn, the guidance and help he receives in his learning, and the motivation he has. Up to four years of age, children show many speech defects; after that, they normally speak more correctly.

TYPES OF SPEECH DEFECTS

The term "defect" is generally applied only to defects in pronunciation, but in its broader sense it can be applied to *any* form of speech that is incorrect. The term "disorder," on the other hand, refers to a serious defect in pronunciation. A speech disorder is thus a kind of speech defect. The common forms of defective speech in childhood may be divided into three major categories: defects in word meanings, defects in pronunciation, and defects in sentence structure.

DEFECTS IN WORD MEANINGS

Since in every language a number of meanings are associated with words that *sound alike*, it is not surprising that in the process of learning meanings, the child makes many wrong associations. Such errors in word meanings affect the child's comprehension of what others say and of what he himself says. Many disciplinary problems arise not from the child's willful breaking of rules but from misinterpretation of the words used in the rules. Because understanding and misunderstanding are so important, Chapter 11 is devoted to the subject of development of understanding. Misunderstanding of rules is discussed in connection with discipline in the chapter, Moral Development.

Errors in word associations are at the basis of many of the frustrations of childhood. The child uses words which mean one thing to him but another to his hearer, and he becomes annoyed or even exasperated when he finds himself misunderstood. In addition, he becomes annoyed when people laugh at something "funny" he has said. To him, it is not funny but meaningful; to others, it is funny because he has used a word in the wrong way (151).

Ordinarily, errors of association are quickly checked by parents or teachers. The result is that the child learns to use words more correctly as he grows older. Furthermore, he learns to avoid using words whose meanings he is unsure of. Unless he verbalizes his interpretation of a word or behaves in a manner to suggest that he misunderstands it, however, adults cannot know what the word means to him and cannot correct wrong associations. When the child says that a "butterfly" is a "fly made out of butter," it is obvious that his association is incorrect, and his error can be corrected. If he turns to the left when he is told to go to the right, it may mean that he has the words "left" and "right" confused. He may, on the other hand, know the correct meaning of the words but may intentionally do the opposite of what he is told in order to demonstrate his independence of adult authority. Only by questioning him will it be possible to know why he acted as he did.

DEFECTS IN PRONUNCIATION

Because learning to pronounce words is a complicated skill, all young children mispronounce some of the words they use.

Even older children, adolescents, and adults mispronounce words occasionally. There should, however, be a gradual decrease in mispronunciations with each passing year. In general, adults give children more guidance and help in pronunciation than in word associations. If mispronunciations continue, and often they do, the sources of the errors should be uncovered. When defective pronunciation is due primarily to faulty learning, it can be corrected relatively easily and quickly. When it is due to malformation of the speech mechanism or to emotional tension, it is more persistent, and correction is far more difficult.

Occasionally a defect in pronunciation can be traced to a tongue-tied condition or to deformed teeth, palate, lips, or jaws. However, the majority of mispronunciations are due to environmental causes—faulty learning, imitation of a poor model, or attempts to speak too quickly because of emotional excitement. Imperfect hearing and muscular weakness or partial paralysis of the tongue and lips, as in some cases of cerebral palsy, may also lead to mispronunciations. The more serious the cause of the mispronunciations, the more persistent they will be.

Defects in pronunciation may be roughly divided into two categories: *speech errors* and *speech disorders*. The difference between the two is largely arbitrary and is based primarily on the severity and persistence of the defect. In speech disorders, there are sometimes organic causes which must be corrected; in speech errors, the cause is generally less serious.

Speech Errors. From eighteen months to three or four years of age, most children make many mistakes in pronunciation. The errors which characterize baby talk generally come from faulty learning which has not been corrected. In fact, some parents encourage baby talk because they think it is "cute." The faulty learning that gives rise to baby talk is more often the result of the child's crude perception of the words he hears than of his inability to pronounce the elemental sounds. Furthermore, in his zeal to say everything he hears, he often makes only sketchy efforts, omitting the harder details. In his attempt to say "cream," for example, he is likely to omit the letter *r* because it takes considerable effort to pronounce two consecutive consonants.

The most common errors in pronunciation are as follows: the omission of one or more syllables, usually in the middle of a word, such as "buttfly" for "butterfly"; substitutions of letters or syllables, or even words, such as "tolly" for "dolly" or "handakerchief" for "handkerchief"; interchanges of letters or syllables in the longer and less frequently used words, such as "tautomobile" for "automobile"; and substitutions of words for names of objects, such as "choo-choo" for "train" or "tick-tock" for "clock."

Consonants and consonant blends are more difficult for the young child to pronounce than vowels and diphthongs. Of the consonants, the most difficult are *z, w, s, d,* and *g;* the most difficult blends are *st, str, sk, dr,* and *fl.* The young child more often omits the final than the initial consonant of a word. Of the vowels, *o* is the most difficult for the young child to pronounce correctly (138). Baby talk, of course, varies from child to child not only in quantity but also in quality. It is greatly influenced by the order in which the child learns to pronounce the different letters or combinations of letters as well as by how much help, guidance, and encouragement he has in pronouncing his words correctly (70).

Speech Disorders. While some speech disorders are due to organic causes—such as nasal obstructions; malformations of the teeth, jaws, lips, or palate; or a tongue-tied condition—they are far more often the result of emotional disturbances. As such, they are only one symptom of maladjustment. It has been found that many children who suffer from speech disorders had abnormal birth conditions or were subjected to forced feeding and early weaning and toilet training. They often make poor social adjustments and have difficulty with school adjustments, and they frequently have poor relationships with their families (56).

Speech disorders are especially common in families where neuroticism of one or both parents exists, where the quality of parent-child relationships is poor, where there is a dominant mother and submissive father, or where the mother ignores the child, is exceptionally possessive or demanding of him, or has excessively high levels of aspiration for him. This suggests that speech disorders are a part of the *syndrome of poor adjustment* (56, 104). They are often correlated with excessive dependency, soiling, destructiveness, restlessness in sleep, temper tantrums, negativism, excessive timidity, and food finickiness (100, 126).

Each speech disorder has its own cause or causes, and each has serious effects on the child's personal and social adjustments. There is little likelihood that a speech disorder will disappear of its own accord. Unless the underlying cause or causes of the disorder are eliminated—whether they are organic or psychological—the disorder not only will persist but will become more pronounced with the passage of time.

Of the different speech disorders, the following are the most common:

1. Lisping. Lisping consists of letter-sound substitutions. The most common of these are the substitution of *th* for *s* or *z,* as in "Thimple Thimon" for "Simple Simon," and of *w* for *r,* as in "wed wose" for "red rose." Other common forms of letter-sound substitution are *s* for *th* or *sh; sh* for voiceless *l; r* for *u;* and *u* or *y* for *r.* The two most common causes of lisping are deformation of the jaw, teeth, or lips and a tendency to cling to infantile speech. When the lower jaw protrudes beyond the upper; when there is a space between the two front upper teeth; or when one of the upper teeth is missing—during the transitional stage from baby to permanent teeth—there is apt to be a slight lisp.

During the kindergarten and first-grade years, the child is normally in the process of losing his teeth. With his front teeth missing, he has no "sounding board" for the production of the harsher sounds, and he usually lisps. Unless there is a malformation of the jaw, teeth, or lips, he will overcome his lisp soon after his front permanent teeth cut through. He does not "outgrow" his lisp; rather, he makes a conscious effort to correct it. Boys are even more anxious than girls to overcome a lisp because they know their peers regard it as a "sissy" way of talking. When lisping persists into the adolescent years, it is usually caused by a physical condition—generally a space between the upper front teeth.

2. Slurring, or Indistinctness of Speech.

Slurring is due to inactivity of the lips, tongue, or jaw. It is sometimes caused by paralysis of the vocal organs or lack of development of the musculature of the tongue, which often is an accompaniment of rickets. In other cases, an emotional attitude of timidity may be responsible. The child frightened by the presence of other people keeps his lips partially closed and mumbles his words. Finally, slurring may be due to rapid speech caused by excitement in which the child, in his haste to say all that he wants to say, rushes through the words without pronouncing each one carefully and distinctly.

Most children experience this disorder at some time or other. It is most common during the preschool years because speech has not yet become habitual, and it is markedly influenced by emotional tension. In his haste to tell something that has interested, frightened, or angered him, the child will run his words together to such an extent that it is almost impossible to know what he is saying. As the ability to speak becomes better developed, the child can speak quickly *and* distinctly at the same time. Occasionally a child will develop a distinct slur after starting school. This is generally accompanied by other manifestations of nervous tension suggestive of difficulties in the child's adjustment to school.

Because slurring is met with social disapproval and criticism, most children try to correct it. Often a child needs guidance to know that slurring can best be corrected if he opens his lips when he speaks so that

"the sounds can come out." Even though children have a strong motivation to control their slurring, they frequently revert to it when they are excited. When they are with the peer group and are anxious to dominate the conversation, they often speak quickly so that no one else can "get a word in edgewise."

3. Stuttering.

Stuttering is hesitant, repetitious speech accompanied by spasms of the muscles of the throat and diaphragm. It comes from a disturbance of the normal rhythm of breathing due to partial or total failure of the speech muscles to coordinate. In form, it resembles a case of stage fright in that the person seems at a loss to know what to say. Stuttering is usually accompanied by a deadlocking of speech, often called *stammering;* the speaker is temporarily unable to produce any sound. Then, as the muscular tension is released, there is a flood of words, which will soon be checked by another spasm (19, 20).

Not only do children differ from one another in the amount of stuttering they do, but they also show intraindividual differences. The child who stutters when he gets up to read before the class, for example, may not stutter when he sings, talks over the telephone, recites lines in a play, or talks to members of the immediate family. He may stutter more as the day progresses and as he becomes tired (19, 44).

Stuttering is frequently accompanied by facial grimaces, blowing of the cheeks, blinking of the eyes, wrinkling of the forehead, protruding of the lips, and reddening of the skin. Often, as he stutters, the child seems to be choking for breath. This helps to call attention to the stuttering and is likely to lead to ridicule, mimicking, and laughter from other children. Most children do not realize that the stutterer is embarrassed. They think he is trying to be funny, and they laugh at him because he *is* "funny" (19).

Studies of the onset of stuttering have revealed that approximately 85 per cent of American children today begin to stutter between the ages of 2½ and 3½ years. At this age, stuttering is due mainly to a time discrepancy between thought and speech, especially when the child is excited (19, 108). The young child, whose vocabulary is still limited and who is just mastering the skill of combining words into sentences, is trying to say more than he is equal to saying. As a result, he encounters a "sort of roadblock in word thinking." As Bluemel has pointed out, stuttering at this early age is nothing more than "speech in the making. It is immature speech: it is trial-and-error speech. It is speech that is not yet organized into a pattern that the child can use and control" (20).

The amount of stuttering the preschool child does is affected by his speech fluency and by the emotional climate in the home and the type of child training he has been subjected to. The preschooler is trying to be independent; he has a negativistic attitude toward adult authority. The stricter the home discipline, the more negativistic he is likely to become, and the more he will stutter (56). This is also the age when the young child is anxious to make new social contacts. If he can communicate successfully, he is likely to be better accepted, and this adds to his self-confidence. As a result, he is less excitable and stutters less. Difficulties in communication cause frustration, which in turn increases the child's tendency to stutter. When speech is not securely organized, it breaks down under stress, and this leads to stuttering (20).

Normally, stuttering decreases as the child makes better social and home adjustments, only to flare up again when he changes from the narrow environment of the home to the broader environment of the school (19). It is more common during the first three grades of elementary school than in the upper grades or in high school. The onset of stuttering after the child is nine years old is unusual. Only 1 or 2 per cent of the adult population stutters (19, 103).

Studies have revealed that primitive peoples do not stutter (19). Whether there are conditions in civilized life that are responsible for stuttering and why it persists in some children longer than in others are questions that have been only partially answered. Most studies emphasize that stuttering is a learned reaction and is not hereditary; that it is psychological rather than organic in origin; and that it comes from environmental pressures that lead to poor adjustment (103, 113).

It has also been found that stuttering is part of a syndrome of behavior patterns characteristic of maladjustment. The emotional stress in the child's environment that leads to stuttering also gives rise to digestive disturbances, enuresis, sleep problems—such as nightmares and night terrors—temper outbursts, negativism, "fussy" eating habits, a need for frequent discipline, and a host of other forms of behavior indicative of poor adjustment (20, 113). A comparison of a group of stutterers with a group of nonstutterers has revealed that the stutterers showed more and severer symptoms of maladjustment than the nonstutterers (111). This difference is illustrated in Figure 6–7.

Stuttering children often have parents who are perfectionistic, overprotective, dominating, and overanxious about the child's welfare, especially his speech. Frequently, stutterers have been pressured to learn two languages simultaneously. Prematurely born children or children whose birth has been difficult are often the victims of overprotective parents. These environmental factors cause children to be nervous, easily upset, overanxious, and tortured by feelings of rejection. Such psychological conditions lead to stuttering and cause it to persist (21, 41, 113).

4. Cluttering.   Cluttering is a rapid, confused, and jumbled type of speech which is often mistaken for stuttering. It is usually accompanied by motor awkwardness and is found mainly in children whose speech development has been delayed. It represents an exaggeration of the errors of speech made by normal people. Unlike the stutterer, the clutterer can improve his speech when he is careful and pays attention to

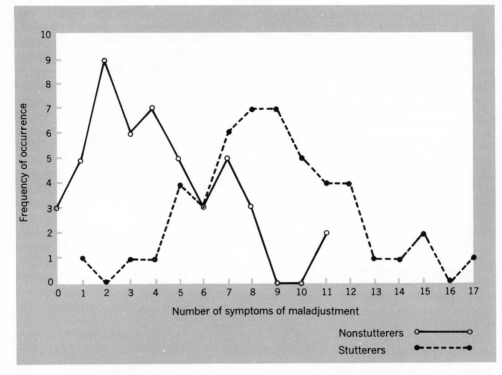

Figure 6–7.   Symptoms of maladjustment among stutterers and nonstutterers. (Adapted from J. F. Moncur, Symptoms of maladjustment differentiating young stutterers from non-stutterers, *Child Develpm.*, 1955, 26, 91–96. Used by permission.)

what he wants to say. The more the stutterer pays attention to his speech, the worse it tends to be (11).

Sex Differences in Defective Pronunciation. Speech defects and speech disorders, with the exception of lisping, are much more common among boys than among girls. Estimates indicate that various defects are from two to eight times more common in boys and that the ratio becomes larger as children grow older (100, 103).

There are a number of explanations for this sex difference, all emphasizing to a greater or lesser extent differences in adjustment and emotional stability. McCarthy explains the sex difference on the grounds that boys are more emotionally insecure than girls; they have more troubles and are punished more harshly than girls. Furthermore, with the father away from home so much of the time, the boy cannot identify himself with the father as the girl can with the mother and thus derive that feeling of security which is essential to emotional stability (103).

Seriousness of Defective Pronunciation. Each year that a speech defect is allowed to continue, it becomes increasingly difficult to correct. Even mild defects, such as baby talk, are handicaps to personal and social adjustments, and the more pronounced the defect, the more serious the handicap. Mispronunciations make the school child feel conspicuous and embarrassed. As a result, he suffers from profound feelings of anxiety, fearing that he will be called on to speak before his classmates or that they will laugh at him (74).

Many maladjustive forms of behavior stem from feelings of inadequacy which have been caused or intensified by a speech defect. Defective speech thus becomes a part of the syndrome of maladjustive behavior (19, 136, 154). In commenting on the relationship between speech defects and maladjustive behavior, McCarthy states: "The recent literature is replete with descriptions of language disorder syndromes which enable us to scan the entire range of children's behavior disorders. Rarely does one find a child in need of clinical services who does not have some symptoms of difficulty with one or more aspects of language" (104).

The effects of maladjustive behavior are far-reaching; they influence all phases of a child's life. Many of the problems of adjustment are influenced, either directly or indirectly, by a speech defect, and these problems then tend to intensify the defect. Thus a vicious circle is set into motion. The child is likely to suffer from an impaired relationship with parents and siblings, resulting from feelings of insecurity in the home or from resentment at the treatment he receives from siblings because of his speech defect. The child with a speech defect frequently fails to take advantage of educational opportunities and often becomes an underachiever. In isolated cases, however, by becoming an overachiever, he may compensate for feelings of inadequacy (9, 57).

When a speech defect is serious enough to necessitate placing the child in a speech-correction class, the child may seem to be so "out of line" or "different" that he is socially isolated from children of normal speech. Only when a defect gives rise to maladjustive behavior, however, will it have a pronounced effect. There is evidence that stutterers are better accepted than children with other forms of speech defects because their peers "feel sorry" for them (113, 145). A child with a speech defect does not usu-

ally become a leader, nor does he usually rise to the top of his class scholastically (19, 57, 118, 155).

DEFECTS IN SENTENCE STRUCTURE

Up to the age of three or four years, young children, even those who hear good speech models in the home, make many grammatical errors. While all word combinations are difficult for the young child, his major problems are in the use of pronouns and verb tenses. Few two-year-olds use pronouns correctly; among three-year-olds, about 75 per cent do. Typical examples of errors made by young children are, in *verbs,* confusion of "can" and "may" and of "lay" and "lie"; in *nouns,* use of "mans" instead of "men" and of "tooths" instead of "teeth"; in *articles,* confusion of "a" and "an"; in *agreement of subject and verb,* "it don't"; and in *confused parts of speech,* "I am going to the low (bottom of page)" and "Give me the rub (eraser)" (70).

From the age of three years, children tighten their hold on grammar, though they continue to make grammatical mistakes throughout the elementary-school years and into high school and college. Errors occur in their written compositions in approximately the same form and proportion as in their speech. Children from the lower socioeconomic groups who hear patterns of incorrect speech generally make more grammatical errors at every age than those from more privileged homes. There is a high correlation between the grammatical errors made by the child and those made by his parents (106, 115). There is also a sex difference in grammatical mistakes, with boys at every age making more mistakes than girls (103).

Grammatical mistakes persist in spite of efforts made in the schools to correct them. In an attempt to explain this, Havighurst has pointed out that, while a child may show remarkable reasoning ability, the English language has "little reason to its structure." Even though the child reasons, he still makes mistakes. For example, to show an act is past, he is told to add "ed" to the verb. He then says, "I rided the streetcar." He is corrected and told he should say, "I rode the streetcar." Reasoning on this basis, he later says, "I gode to the store," but he is told that this is incorrect and that he should say, "I went to the store." Then he tries logic once more and says, "I wented to the store" (70).

Seriousness of Grammatical Mistakes. In the first place, defects in sentence structure cause a child to *think incorrectly*. Changes in sentence structure, for example, can give a totally different meaning to a sentence. This affects the child's understanding of what others say as well as their understanding of what he is trying to communicate to them. Should the child say "I ate my lunch" instead of "I eat my lunch," he will create the impression that he has already eaten when, in reality, he means that he is now eating. Similarly, if his mother tells him it is dangerous to play in the street, he may readily interpret this to mean that it is dangerous *now;* tomorrow, he may be found playing in the street. When reprimanded, he will probably say, "But you said it was dangerous yesterday; you didn't say it is dangerous today."

The second serious consequence of grammatical mistakes is that they create an *unfavorable impression* on others. This can prove to be a handicap to social adjustment and, later, to vocational success. Judgments are often made on the basis of first impressions. The child whose speech is erroneous will create a less favorable first impression than the child whose speech is correct. Furthermore, speech becomes a "status symbol" as the child grows older. Because incorrect speech is more commonly found among children and adults of the lower socio-economic groups than among those of the upper groups, the child who makes grammatical mistakes is likely to be pigeonholed as having a lower-class background (42).

The third important implication of grammatical mistakes is that they will become *habitual* with repeated use. The child's ear becomes accustomed to hearing words in certain combinations, and any change in these combinations "sounds funny" to him. A child who has become accustomed to saying "It's me" will claim that it sounds funny to say "It's I." He will be self-conscious about making the change and will resist it.

On the positive side, it has been reported that children of today use longer sentences and make fewer grammatical mistakes than children of a generation ago. With the widespread use of radio and television in the home, most young children hear good models of speech every day as they listen to the programs specially designed for them (104). While this does not entirely counteract the influence of a poor model set by parents, siblings, and relatives, it tends to offset some of the effects. As long as a child hears grammatical mistakes in the speech of his parents, he is likely to continue to make errors. Furthermore, parents who speak incorrectly are not likely to correct their children's grammatical mistakes; they usually do not recognize them as mistakes. As a result, even though children of today may use longer sentences, the correctness of their sentences has not kept pace with the increase in length (115).

BILINGUALISM

Bilingualism is the ability to *use* two languages. It involves not only speaking and writing in two different languages but also the ability to comprehend the meaning of what others attempt to communicate either orally or in writing. A truly bilingual child is as much at home in a foreign language as in his mother tongue; he is able to speak, write, and read both languages with facility and accuracy (133).

Few children are truly bilingual. Most are more adept in the use of one language than of the other. As Jersild has pointed out, "There are many interesting combinations of bilinguality: a child may be able to understand and use both languages: he may be able to speak both, but able to write only one; he may be able to understand both, but able to speak only one" (81).

Bilingual Dominance versus Bilingual Balance. Bilingual *dominance* means that in spite of the fact that a person uses two languages, he uses one better than the other. In bilingual *balance,* by contrast, both languages are used equally well. This holds true for reading and writing as well as for speaking. Whether there is dominance or balance in bilingualism can be determined by the speed and accuracy in the use of the two languages. When speech is well learned, it becomes automatic; its chief characteristic is speed. The speaker does not have to attend to the language process itself but can give his attention to the organization of what he wants to say and its appropriateness. When a child has learned a language well, he speaks fluently; that is, he speaks with little or no hesitation, thus increasing his *speed.* Fluency is generally, though not always, accompanied by a minimum of errors in grammatical structure; the fluent speaker shows greater *accuracy* of speech than the less fluent speaker (133, 134).

Which of the two languages a child speaks will be the dominant language will depend largely upon the circumstances under which he became bilingual. In America today, most bilingual children have foreign-born parents. In the home and neighborhood, the language of the country from which the parents and neighbors have come is used. Only after the child is old enough to enter school has he enough contacts with English-speaking people to find it essential to learn English. Because he spends more of his time in the home and neighborhood than in the school or the areas of the community where English is spoken, he becomes far more proficient in the language of his parents than in English. For him, the mother tongue of his parents is the dominant language (135).

Few American-born children have experiences similar to those of children with foreign-born parents. Should an American family live in a foreign country, for business or pleasure, the child will usually learn the language of the country in which he lives as the dominant language. He will, without doubt, learn some English, but his use of English will be limited mainly to communication with his family or friends of the family.

In the upper socioeconomic groups, parents sometimes employ a foreign-born nurse or governess to teach the child a foreign language from the time he begins to talk, in the belief that this is the only way to make sure that he will learn to "speak like a native." This will be the "language of the nursery." When he goes out of the nursery, he will have to use English if he wants to communicate with those around him. Whether there will be a dominance or a balance in his bilingualism will depend on how much time he spends in the nursery and how much outside. In some schools— mainly private schools—children study a foreign language, generally French, from the time they enter school. Such children become bilingual, with English the dominant language (80).

From this brief account, it can be seen that the effects bilingualism has on a child will depend largely on (*1*) the conditions under which he became bilingual and (*2*) the relationship of the child's dominant language to the dominant language of the neighborhood, school, and peer group. The latter, in particular, determines how much influence bilingualism has on the child's speech, emotional, social, and personality development. That is to say, the *type* of bilingualism, not bilingualism per se, determines the effect it has on the child (133, 134).

Learning Tasks in Bilingualism. Every language has its own vocabulary, its own grammatical structures, its own word meanings, and its own pronunciation of different letters or letter combinations. The child who is expected to learn two languages *simultaneously* must learn two different words for every object he names or for every thought he wishes to express. He must learn two sets of grammatical forms—one often in direct conflict with the other.

Furthermore, he must learn how to pronounce the same letters or letter combinations differently; the letter *r,* for example, is pronounced quite differently in French and in English, though it is the same letter on the printed page. These learning tasks are very difficult for the student in junior or senior high school; they are even more difficult for a young child who has not yet mastered one language well enough to feel at ease when using it. As a result, the child is likely to combine the two languages and be unable to keep them separated into two distinct language systems (46, 80).

When the second language is begun after the first has progressed to the point where it can be used automatically or nearly automatically, the tasks involved in learning the second are still far from easy. Conflicts in pronunciation, in grammatical structures, and in word associations will prove to be confusing to the child (91). In addition, the speech mechanism is not so easy to control as it was when the child was younger. Having become accustomed through repeated use to pronounce different letters or letter combinations in one way, he finds it hard to pronounce them in a different way for the new language. He can, of course, eventually master the pronunciation of the new language, but unless he has a strong motivation to do so, he may not be willing to give the time and effort required. As a result, he will speak the second language with an English accent, not "like a native."

Effects of Bilingualism.   As has already been stressed, the effects of bilingualism do not depend so much upon bilingualism, per se, as upon the conditions surrounding bilingualism. Four of these conditions have a marked effect on the child:

1. Type of Bilingualism.   Most so-called "bilingual" children have a dominant language. When the child's dominant language is different from the one used by the children with whom he associates at school or in play, he finds it difficult to communicate. Difficulties in communication increase his social-adjustment problems. The least harm comes when the child is in a school or neighborhood where there are a number of other children of his national origin who,

likewise, have to meet the problem of bilingualism (54, 134).

Studies of bilingualism where the dominant language is a foreign language have revealed that the child acquires an accent, when speaking English, that is very often never completely lost (89). In addition, he makes more grammatical mistakes in English than the child of his age and level of intelligence who is monolingual. Because the child feels insecure in his use of English, he is self-conscious when he must use it (80, 135). If he is nervous and emotionally tense, he is likely to begin stuttering, and this intensifies his speech problem as well as his social-adjustment problems (20). When he tries to express his thoughts in words, he is aware of the tittering, laughter, annoyance, or boredom of other children. He may become so self-conscious that he refuses to engage in oral communication and becomes a "quiet child."

"Quiet" children, who make little or no contribution to the group, are generally neglected or rejected. The bilingual child, consequently, has the burden of social neglect or rejection added to his communication problem. This is likely to leave a serious scar on his developing personality (72, 89). Even in college, students with a bilingual background in which a foreign language has been dominant make poorer social and emotional adjustments than monolinguals or bilinguals whose dominant language is English.

A bilingual child whose dominant language is different from that of the social group with which he is associated has serious academic problems to cope with. Because he is not linguistically ready for school, his feelings of insecurity are greater than those most children normally experience when they first enter school. As a result, he is handicapped in his adjustment to school from the very start (72, 134).

A study of Puerto Rican children showed that when they are suddenly required to cope with an all-English school situation, they "insulate" themselves by becoming passive and apathetic. They do poorer work in school and make poorer social adjustments than they would if they were not handicapped by having a dominant language which is of little use to them in the school situation. Achievement on intelligence tests, especially those which use language, likewise reflects the handicap of bilingualism (6, 87, 96).

2. Time When Bilingualism Is Acquired.

Learning two languages *simultaneously* is very likely to delay speech development in both languages. Size of vocabulary, sentence length and construction, and articulation are retarded. Furthermore, the bilingual child is apt to be confused in his thinking; as a result, he is self-conscious about talking (20, 46, 132).

In a study of third-grade children's achievement in language skills, as measured by standardized tests of intelligence, reading comprehension, etc., it was found that monolingual children were superior to bilingual children in oral reading accuracy and comprehension, hearing vocabulary, and arithmetic reasoning. The monolingual children were significantly better in speaking— not only in the number of different words spoken but also in the correctness of pronunciation and in grammatical forms. A comparison of the monolingual children with the bilinguals in different tests of linguistic achievement is illustrated in Figure 6–8. There was less difference in reading between the two groups than in speaking because both had had the same amount of formal classroom instruction in reading (37). While the effects of learning two languages simultaneously seem to be especially serious during the early years of schooling, it is questionable whether a child with such a poor start would ever catch up to his age group completely, either academically or socially.

3. Prestige of Dominant Language.

A third condition that influences the seriousness of the effect of bilingualism on the child's development is the prestige of the dominant language. By the time children are four or five years old, they can distinguish racial differences by skin color, facial features, and speech (40). As a child learns

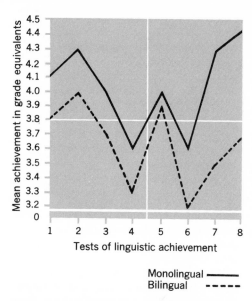

Figure 6–8. Comparison of bilingual with monolingual children in different tests of linguistic achievement. (Adapted from Sister M. A. Carrow, Linguistic functioning of bilingual and monolingual children, *J. speech hear. Disord.*, 1957, 22, 371–380. Used by permission.)

to distinguish racial differences, he also learns that some racial groups are looked down upon as "inferior." In time, he develops stereotyped opinions of different races, judging all members of a particular group favorably or unfavorably.

As a result of these stereotypes, a person who uses the language identified with the group that is regarded favorably will be less damaged by bilingualism than the person who uses the language of a group against whom there is prejudice. A child who can speak French in addition to English, for example, is more likely to be regarded favorably by his peers than a child who speaks Russian, Polish, or Yiddish. If he speaks English with an accent, however, this marks him as "different" and proves to be a handicap to his adjustments, both socially and academically (46, 54, 158).

4. Degree of "Differentness."

The fourth important condition influencing the effects

of bilingualism on the adjustments of the child is the degree of "differentness" associated with bilingualism. The bilingual child whose dominant language is a foreign language and whose parents live and act like foreigners will be different from other children in many ways. His home and his manner of dressing and eating will often be different, and he will be subjected to child-training methods different in many respects from those used in the homes of his schoolmates. This syndrome of "differentness," constantly apparent in his speech, is likely to be a serious handicap to social adjustment; his poor adjustment, in turn, leads to feelings of inferiority and inadequacy (48, 60).

When the child speaks with a foreign accent, it proclaims to all that he is "different." Teasing and ridicule only increase his speech problem; in addition, he suffers from the effects of being considered an "outsider"—a "foreigner"—by other children. How successfully the child can overcome his foreign accent will have a marked influence on how lasting the effects of bilingualism will be. The bilingual child whose dominant language is that of the group with which he is identified is likely to have a background similar to that of the group; the problems stemming from "differentness" in areas other than speech are thus eliminated. If he can speak another language and still be like the group, his bilingualism may add to his prestige; it will not harm his social acceptance (89, 103).

Handicaps of Bilingualism. From what has been said, it is logical to conclude that bilingualism is more of a handicap than an asset to a child, especially during the preschool years. This is the opinion widely held by psychologists and educators today. Thompson expressed this opinion when he said, "There can be no doubt that the child reared in a bilingual atmosphere is handicapped in his language growth. One can debate the issue as to whether speech facility in two languages is worth the consequent retardation in the common language of the realm" (148).

There are, however, as in every area of life, exceptions to the rule. As Carrow has pointed out, there is a difference between language difficulties arising from bilingualism, per se, and those stemming from a bilingual environment. Thus bilingualism need not be "detrimental to all bilingual children, at all ages, at all periods during their lives. In homes where there is a language atmosphere favorable to wide experiences in both languages and where good speech models are present, the bilingual child may not experience any problem in either language" (37).

Foreign-language Study. Studies of the effects of bilingualism show that the present-day interest in introducing foreign-language study into the elementary-school curriculum must take into consideration the readiness of children of that age to master a second language without doing harm to their mastery of English. Some educators favor introducing foreign-language study in the kindergarten or first grade; others favor waiting until the second, third, or even fourth grade; still others maintain that the child will master the foreign language more quickly and with less damage to his mastery of English if he waits until he reaches junior high school.

It is impossible to lay down a hard-and-fast rule to apply to all children; as in other areas of their development, children differ so widely in their speech development that some may be ready for the learning of a foreign language several years before others. As it is impossible to give individualized instruction in a large class, however, we may conclude that it *might* be wise to defer the study of a foreign language at least until the third grade for the majority of children. By that time, the study of a new language will probably not add any new adjustment burdens to those already existing. Furthermore, by that time children from linguistically poor home environments should have had an opportunity to correct some of their most serious pronunciation and grammatical mistakes, under the guidance of their teachers. They should therefore be ready to learn the rudiments of a new language without too much confusion in their mastery of the English language.

Bright children from a linguistically superior home environment could begin the study of a foreign language much earlier. As Smith has pointed out, "It would seem unwise to start any but children of superior linguistic ability at a second language unnecessarily during the preschool years" (132). While the preschooler or even a first- or second-grader could doubtless master the task of pronouncing words in a foreign language as easily as a third- or fourth-grader—or perhaps more easily—there is more to learning a foreign language than pronouncing words; it is in the other areas of learning that confusion and difficulty are likely to occur.

AMOUNT OF TALKING

After a child begins to talk, he talks almost incessantly. While he prefers to talk to people, he will also talk when he is alone, playing with his toys. He will even talk to people who pay little or no attention to what he is saying or who do not bother to answer his questions. The older child resents such treatment, but the young child enjoys the sense of power and independence his new skill gives him; talking is thus a source of tremendous personal satisfaction to him. It has been estimated that three- and four-year-olds say, on the average, 15,000 words a day, or approximately 5,500,000 words a year. This gives them much practice in oral language and a facility in speaking that is a strong support to their self-confidence (103).

A child whose speech is delayed gets less practice than the child who begins to talk at the usual time. A delay of 6 months to 1 year in starting to talk means, in many cases, that the child is not ready, linguistically, to begin school at the age of six years. Once he begins to talk, he may catch up to the speech level of his agemates, but lack of practice is likely to deprive him of the self-confidence essential to fluent speech. As a result, he hesitates to express himself orally; this handicaps him in his academic and social adjustments (104).

The "quiet" child, who talks less than his peers, develops feelings of inadequacy which often persist long after he has caught up with them in ability to speak. As children grow older, they talk with one another more and more; this helps them to play together in a more social and more enjoyable way. The quiet child finds himself left out of things. He may not be rejected by his playmates, but he is neglected because he has little to contribute. It has been reported that there is a close association between speech and social acceptance throughout childhood; children who talk most are, other things being equal, the most popular, and vice versa (102).

CONTENT OF SPEECH

What the child talks about is as important as the amount of talking he does. Studies of the content of children's speech at different ages give information about the size and correctness of vocabulary, ability to combine words into sentences, dominant interests, and concept of self (104). From what the child says, it is possible to know how he feels about himself and about his relationships with others and how he compares himself with his peers. In early childhood, "the pattern of personality is clearly woven in the fabric of speech" (129). Furthermore, the child's speech tells us something about his emotional states—whether he is happy, frightened, angry, jealous, or curious. It is a "thermometer of emotional reactions" because it tells how emotionally calm or disturbed the child is (15).

Individual differences in the need for speech influence the amount and the content of children's speech. A child who is deprived of affection, for example, will talk more when he is with adults and will make more demands on them than the child who feels secure in the affection of parents and peers. Figure 6–9 shows that young children seek the attention and approval of adults through comments and questions and

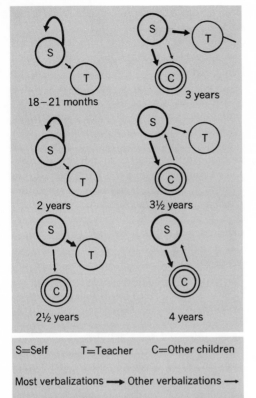

S=Self   T=Teacher   C=Other children

Most verbalizations ⟶   Other verbalizations ⟶

Figure 6–9. Early forms of interpersonal verbalization. (Adapted from L. B. Ames, The sense of self of nursery school children as manifested by their verbal behavior, *J. genet. Psychol.*, 1952, 81, 193–232. Used by permission.)

in other ways. The child whose need for affection is adequately met will use speech, not for attention-getting, but to satisfy his desire for power over his environment or merely for the satisfaction he derives from hearing himself talk. What a child talks about and his manner of expression are, in general, compatible with his personality traits. Therefore, listening to a child's speech gives one an excellent clue to his personality (129).

At first, the young child's speech generally accompanies *motor activity*. Running, playing, eating, and bathing all have some vocal accompaniment, whether it takes the form of shouts, grunts, squeaks, or words. All these have a definite relationship to what the child is doing and are, in reality, a form of "thinking out loud." The little girl playing with her doll will say, "I cover dolly," as she puts a cover over the doll. Very little of the young child's speech is conversational; instead, it is more of a monologue, a running commentary on his own actions (108, 119).

Types of Speech. The speech of children has been classified into two major categories: *egocentric speech* and *socialized speech*. In the former, the child talks either for his own pleasure or for the pleasure of associating with anyone who happens to be present. There is no attempt to exchange ideas or to consider the other person's point of view. Egocentric speech is thus "pseudo conversation," a form of "collective monologue," which springs from the child's intellectual limitations and his inability to analyze his own thought processes and check on the conclusions he draws (119).

Socialized speech occurs when social contacts are established between the child and his social environment. It is subdivided into (1) *adapted information*, in which thoughts or ideas may be exchanged or a common aim pursued; (2) criticism, involving the child's remarks about the work or behavior of others, specified in relation to an audience; (3) *commands, requests,* and *threats;* (4) *questions;* and (5) *answers* made to real questions. While egocentric speech may be an aid to the development of the child's thinking, socialized speech is an aid to his social adjustments (107, 119).

Most of the young child's speech is egocentric. Gradually, as his desire to be one of a social group grows stronger, he uses speech as a social tool. Just when there will be a marked shift from egocentric to socialized speech is difficult to tell. Various experimenters have reported different ages, ranging from two to seven or eight years. During these years, children talk more to members of the peer group than to adults if members of the peer group are available (5). This is illustrated in Figure 6–9.

The shift from egocentric to socialized speech will depend not so much upon chronological age as upon other factors. The child's personality is an important determinant. Children whose self-concept is egocentric will continue to talk about themselves and show little interest in talking to others for a longer time than children who are able to assess themselves more realistically. Experiences with others enable the child to acquire a degree of social maturity which will be reflected in the extent to which he can understand and share the points of view of others. As the group with which the child associates grows larger, his speech becomes more socialized and less egocentric.

Socialized speech is most pronounced when children are with their own agemates. Adults encourage children to talk about themselves. They ask questions about what the child is doing, how he likes school, or what he plans to be when he grows up (33). With other children, this encouragement to egocentric speech is lacking. Consequently, the child steers his conversation with them into channels that will hold their attention and win their approval, thus strengthening his acceptance by them (22, 60, 65).

Children use both statements and questions. Questions, the young child soon discovers, have far greater attention value than statements. As a result, much of his early speech takes the form of *general* questioning. He asks questions about everything. Later, questions are more specific; they are used to test partially formed hypotheses and to fill gaps in his information. Still later, they are definitive; they are used to confirm his conclusions. Figure 6–10 shows the types of questions children ask at different ages. As may be seen, "why" questions reach a peak between the second and third grades and then decrease in frequency as

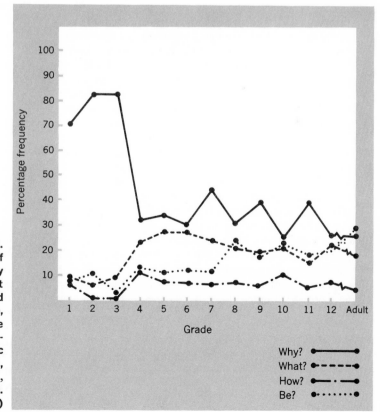

Figure 6–10. Common types of questions asked by children at different age levels. (Adapted from K. Yamamato, Development of the ability to ask questions under specific testing conditions, *J. genet. Psychol.,* 1962, 101, 83–90. Used by permission.)

the other types, especially the "what" questions, increase (156).

Conversational Topics. What children talk about when they are together or with an adult will be influenced by their ages, the breadth of their experiences, and their personality patterns. For the most part, young children talk about the most commonplace, simple subjects in a homely situation. They concentrate mainly on themselves and their activities, bringing into their conversations their families and their relationships with different members of the family. Many topics that are characteristic of adult conversation in our society appear in a rudimentary form in the conversations of preschool children. Topics such as clothes, likes and dislikes, where one lives, and matters of everyday routine predominate (51, 88).

Among older children, there is a wider variety of topics, owing to the broadening of their experiences. Much of their conversation centers around school, its activities, the teachers, and their lessons; their own accomplishments; their families, including their siblings, their relatives, and the family pet; games and sports; trips and excursions; clothes; shows, television programs, comics, and other forms of entertainment; personal experiences of all types; and tabooed subjects, especially sex and sex organs. The child feels freer to discuss these topics with his contemporaries than with adults (26, 60).

The conversational importance of broad experiences has been shown in a comparison of orphanage and nonorphanage children. Orphanage children were found to talk more about the parts of the body, play materials, activities and routines, and buildings and furnishings than the nonorphanage children. Nonorphanage children, on the other hand, talked more about other children, activities, clothing, and nature than the orphanage children did. They also mentioned a greater variety of topics (112). Children who have been institutionalized or hospitalized for a long time have so few interests and so few things to talk about that they withdraw into themselves and speak very little, even when they are free from the restrictions placed on their speech by the isolation of an institution (67).

Methods of Presentation. The child's method of presenting what he says often has more influence on the reactions of others than the content of what he says. Young children tend to use matter-of-fact statements or questions; older children use a wider range of methods of presentation. Some of the methods of presentation the child uses are learned by trial and error; others are learned by imitation. Of the many methods of presentation, the following are those most commonly and widely used by American children today:

1. Exaggerations. From the ages of five to seven years in particular, when imagination develops more rapidly than reasoning, the child tends to exaggerate what he says because his imagination has filled in gaps in reality. He soon discovers, mainly through trial and error, that these exaggerated statements—statements which *seem* true to him —are interpreted as "white lies" by adults and win more attention than matter-of-fact statements. As a result, he either consciously or unconsciously begins to exaggerate what he says whenever he wants to win the attention or approval of others.

2. Boasting. Boasting is a form of exaggeration. The child "embroiders" statements of fact to make them more colorful and to increase their attention value. There is an element of truth in all boasting, but the favorable aspects of the truth are given proportionally more emphasis than the unfavorable. At some time or other, every child engages in boasting as a means of gaining the attention of his listener. While he may discover that this method, like other forms of exaggeration, wins attention of an unfavorable type from adults, he generally finds that it wins favorable attention from the peer group.

The greatest amount of boasting generally comes between the ages of eight and twelve years—the time when both boys and girls are especially anxious to win favor from their contemporaries and ensure their status in the group. Boasting is not limited to these years, however. Most children who discover the attention value of exaggeration find boasting a good way to inflate their egos; they use it whenever they feel inadequate to a situation or inferior to those with whom they are associated (60, 84).

What children boast about is determined largely by the values of the peer group. Because toys and material possessions are important to a young child, he boasts about such things as the family house or car, his clothes and toys, or even the family pets. Skills are more important than material possessions to an older child; therefore, older children boast mainly about their strength and their skill in games. Sex differences in boasting appear only after the interests and values of the sexes change—about the time children enter elementary school. At that time, boys boast mainly about their athletic abilities, and girls boast mainly about material possessions, especially clothes (88, 142).

3. Name Calling. Among older children, name calling is a form of boasting. When a child calls another by a derogatory name, the name caller is indirectly saying that he is superior to the other child. If, for example, he calls someone a "dumbbell," an "idiot," or a "shrimp," the child is inflating his own ego by implying that he is superior. Furthermore, name calling has great attention value. The child who does the name calling is the focus of attention, not the one who is the butt of the ridicule. Consequently, the child who wants attention and wants to impress others with his superiority often finds name calling a more satisfactory way of boasting than making a direct statement about his superior possessions or abilities (81).

4. Criticism. Not only do young children criticize other people, but also they make critical comments about animals and inanimate objects. They are likely to call a toy that will not work a "dumb toy" or to refer to a train that is late as a "stupid train." A pet that will not do what the child wants him to do is "my mean old cat."

While some children make favorable criticisms of others, most of their criticisms are unfavorable. Critical comments serve to inflate the ego of the child who feels inadequate; they also, he soon discovers, have great attention value. For the most part, the young child will criticize another person behind his back. Not only does this enable the child to say things he might hesitate to say in the person's presence, but also it removes any competition for attention from his listener; when he is criticizing another, he is in the spotlight of attention.

Older children often address their criticisms to the person being criticized. They use criticism mainly to comment on the conduct and personality of another child, for example, the other's lack of knowledge, his clumsiness, his failure to do what he was expected to do, or his clothing and personal appearance. Sometimes these criticisms are made in the hope of correcting the shortcomings of the other child, but usually they are for the satisfaction of demonstrating the speaker's superiority. Most children, especially boys, are brutally frank in their criticisms of even their best friends. With those whom they dislike or to whom they feel superior, they do not hesitate to add ridicule to criticism. This is characteristic of boys' criticisms of girls and of minority-group children against whom there is prejudice (60, 69).

5. Tattling. Tattling is a form of criticism. A child tattles about another behind his back, to a person whose assistance he hopes to gain. Typically, a young child will go to a parent or teacher with such complaints as "He took my ball" or "He broke my skate." If he feels that the teacher has been unfair to him, he criticizes her behind her back, tattling to his parents about her "unfairness" or her "having favorites." By doing this, he hopes to focus favorable attention upon himself or to gain parental sympathy for his poor grades. In such instances, he is projecting the blame for his shortcomings on another (81, 84).

In spite of the personal satisfaction a child derives from tattling, it is one of the quickest and surest ways of winning social disapproval. As Barclay has pointed out, "In all the hierarchy of childhood crimes, 'tattling' is regarded as one of the worst" (14). Many generations of children have been brought up on the old rhyme:

Tattle tale tit,
Your tongue shall be slit,
And all the dogs in town
Shall have a little bit.

From this, they learn how the social group feels about tattling and how likely it is to lead to social rejection. As a result, most children abandon tattling when the desire for social acceptance becomes strong.

6. Derogatory Comments.   Many children inflate their egos by making derogatory comments about others. Beginning around the age of three years, children use this method of presentation partly to relieve injured feelings and partly to let other children know how they feel about them. Typical examples of these childish comments are "You're a crazy cat," "You're a lazybones," "You're silly," and "You're nuts." As children grow older, they tend to increase their usage of derogatory comments and to use a wider range of adjectives. Elementary-school children, even those from good home environments where such language is rarely heard, "go tough" in their dealings with other children. They seem to feel that they must use fairly obvious means to make their point (26, 27).

The older child does not reserve his derogatory comments for his playmates, schoolmates, and siblings. When he starts to play with a peer group, he discovers that it is the "thing to do" to talk about *all* adults in a derogatory manner. His parents are described as "mean," his grandparents as "a little coo-coo," or the President of the United States as "so dumb he doesn't know what it's all about." The child is indirectly telling his friends that he is independent, that he is not "tied to anyone's apron strings," and that he is a "regular guy" who uses words not approved by the adult group.

Effects of Socially Unacceptable Speech. If judged by adult standards, what a child says and how he says it are not always socially acceptable. Because people at all ages are judged by their speech, a child whose speech is socially unacceptable makes an unfavorable impression and often acquires an unfavorable reputation. The effect on his personal and social adjustments may be severe. Furthermore, talking in a socially unacceptable manner can become habitual and will be an increasingly serious handicap each year.

A quick survey of some of the far-reaching effects of socially unacceptable speech will highlight its significance. The child who talks mostly about himself thinks more about himself than about others. *Egocentric speech* is thus not an isolated pattern of behavior; instead, it is part of the syndrome of egocentricity. Studies of social acceptance have revealed that children who are egocentric are less popular than those who think of others and consider their welfare. Furthermore, children whose speech is mainly egocentric have little of interest to offer to others; they soon acquire the reputation of being "bores."

As was stressed earlier, a child normally shifts from egocentric to socialized speech as he grows older and as his social interests broaden. Just because he talks about other people and other things, however, is no guarantee that he will talk about them in a manner that will lead to good social adjustments. For example, a child may talk to another child about that child's activities; but if what he says is critical or derogatory, it can have an unfavorable effect. Similarly, how serious an effect egocentric speech will have on the child's adjustments will be influenced by his method of presentation. Talking about himself in a matter-of-fact way may be merely boring; talking about himself in a boastful way may be so antagonizing that other children will reject him.

Socially unacceptable methods of presentation have serious effects on the child's adjustments. The child who is constantly *boasting* about himself, his possessions, and his achievements makes other children feel inferior; they resent his implications that he is superior and do not want to be friends with him. The boaster is likely to acquire the reputation of having a "swelled head" or of being "stuck-up"—a reputation that militates against social acceptance. Furthermore, the peer group realizes, in time, that the boaster is exaggerating; this does not add to their respect or liking for him.

Boasting also affects the child's personal adjustments. While he may derive temporary ego-satisfaction from boasting, he will in time build up an unrealistic concept of himself and of his abilities. As his capacity for reasoning increases, he will recognize that there is a gap between what he says he is and what he actually is—a gap that will lead to self-dissatisfaction and discontent. To close this gap, he will look for scapegoats upon whom he can project the blame for his not being, in reality, what he said he was.

Criticism in its many related forms— tattling, name calling, and derogatory comments—may be ego-inflating for the child, but it is ego-deflating for the person who is the butt of the criticism. Furthermore, it irritates a person to have someone sit in judgment on him and imply that he is inferior. A friendship based on irritations and resentments cannot survive for long. Criticism within the family is one of the causes of deterioration in family relationships as children grow older. Parents and older relatives regard the child's critical comments as indications of "impertinence" or "lack of respect" and reprove him for them. A warm, loving parent-child relationship is difficult to maintain under such conditions. Siblings, too, resent the name calling, the tattling, and the "talking down their noses" comments of critical children, and they generally retaliate in kind. If parents try to stop the quarreling that ensues, they are generally accused of "playing favorites," and parent-child relationships deteriorate still further.

Criticism damages both the child who criticizes and those who are subjected to his criticisms. Not only is the child building up habits of speech which will lead to social rejection with its accompanying psychological damage, but he is also building up a distorted concept of his superiority and his right to treat others as he wishes. The people who bear the brunt of the child's comments cannot escape wondering whether they are as inadequate and inferior as the child's criticism suggests.

Children can be very seriously damaged by repeated criticism. The "female inferiority complex," for example, is largely the result of the critical and derogatory comments girls are subjected to by brothers and male classmates. The more important a critical person is to a child, the more the child will be influenced by what he says. Thus there is little evidence of the truth of the old saying, "Sticks and stones will hurt my bones, but words will never harm me"; critical and derogatory words certainly *will harm* a child.

Constructive Suggestions for Improving a Child's Speech. Because what a child says and how he says it have such far-reaching effects, it should be readily apparent that this area of his speech development should not be left to chance. *Family and school discussions about topics unrelated to the child* go a long way toward encouraging him to engage in socialized rather than egocentric speech. It is always easier to keep a conversation on an impersonal level when the topic under discussion is impersonal. If an impersonal topic is presented in an interesting way, the child can derive as much satisfaction from it as he can from talking about himself. In addition, he will be spared the resentments which come when criticisms and derogatory comments are made about him, as so often happens when he is the focal point of the conversation.

That adult direction of conversations can go a long way toward encouraging children to shift from egocentric to socialized speech has been demonstrated by experiments with preschool children. The results showed that girls who were encouraged to express themselves freely at home on adult-approved topics were more popular than girls whose parents gave less direction to what they said. Boys whose parents placed some restraint on the methods of expression the boys used achieved greater popularity than boys who were allowed to say whatever they pleased.

In stressing the importance of adult direction of the child's conversation as a means of increasing the child's social acceptance, Marshall has commented thus:

When parents and adults talk with the preschool child about more of the topics the child can use in play with other children, the child talks about and plays these topics with peers, and has a better chance of social acceptance in the preschool group. These relations suggest "positive" ways to induce socially accepted and, hence, "desired" behavior in children (102).

Just as it is important that the child be directed into channels of socialized speech, so should he be directed in *how to express himself*. No child has enough experience or enough social insight to realize how harmful certain methods of self-expression can be. If he can make another child angry by a derogatory comment; if he can hurt the feelings of a person who has angered him; or if he can feel superior because he boasts of his accomplishments, he will naturally want to repeat the experience that has given him such great personal satisfaction. Parents and teachers, however, should have enough foresight to realize that there may be a heavy penalty for this temporary satisfaction. It is their responsibility to see that the child does not have to pay this penalty. One aspect of child training should include guidance in self-expression to make sure that the temporary effects of undesirable speech are not pleasurable to the child. At the same time, it should include rewards for socially acceptable forms of speech to encourage the child to repeat such forms.

Guidance in learning to speak in a socially acceptable manner has two aspects: *rules* and a *good model* to imitate. Rules should serve as guideposts to tell the child what is socially acceptable and what is unacceptable. In the home or school, for example, there should be a rule that boys are not permitted to criticize a girl just because she is a girl or to make derogatory comments about all members of the female sex. There should be rules about criticism of family members and name calling. A child, in a democratic home, should be encouraged to express his opinion about people. He should be taught, however, that an opinion can be expressed tactfully; it does not have to take the form of criticism or ridicule. Similarly, a child should feel free to come to the parent for help if he is attacked by a sibling or a playmate. Getting help and tattling are different things.

If rules are to serve their purpose as guides to behavior, there should be punishment for willful breaking of the rules and reward for obeying them. Only in this way will the child have the motivation necessary to use the rules as a guide in learning socially acceptable forms. If he is sent from the table or deprived of seeing his favorite television show when he calls a younger sibling by an uncomplimentary name or tells his mother she is "too fat," he will think twice the next time he is tempted to make such comments. On the other hand, if he is praised for a pleasant comment and rewarded with a smile, a pat on the shoulder, or a special treat when he tells a younger sibling he did a "swell job" in his crayoning or tells his mother that she is "the prettiest mother in his class," he will find it to his personal advantage to substitute positive for negative comments, compliments for criticisms, and helpful suggestions for derogatory comments or name calling.

Guidance also includes giving the child a good model to copy. Just as no child can be expected to speak correctly if he constantly hears grammatical errors in the home, so no child can be expected to talk in a socially approved manner if he is surrounded by people who criticize, ridicule, tattle, or call names. If parents and teachers express their feelings about the child and what he does in a critical way or by making derogatory comparisons with another child, it is not surprising if he assumes that this is the way to handle an unsatisfactory situation.

Blind imitation—imitation without understanding—rarely produces satisfactory results. Imitation should be based on reason and understanding. Three simple homespun maxims can be used to increase the child's understanding and, with it, his motivation to imitate a model of socially acceptable speech: (*1*) "If you can't say something pleasant, don't say anything"; (*2*) "That is not the way to win friends and influence people"; and (*3*) "You can catch more flies with sugar than with vinegar."

While it is true that one cannot expect a child to know just what these maxims mean, he will understand, first, that there is a reason for his using speech that will not hurt others and, second, that it will benefit him to do so.

If these maxims are repeated often enough, the child will be conditioned to associate pleasant remarks with social acceptance. He will be strongly motivated to see that his speech is of the type that will win friends for him.

BIBLIOGRAPHY

(1) ALDRICH, C. A., C. SUNG, and C. KNOP: The crying of newly born babies. *J. Pediat.,* 1945, **26**, 313–326; **27**, 89–96, 429–435.
(2) ALDRICH, C. A., M. A. NORVAL, C. KNOP, and F. VENEGAS: The crying of newly born babies. IV. A follow-up study after additional nursing care had been provided. *J. Pediat.,* 1946, **28**, 665–670.
(3) ALLEN, D. A.: Antifemininity in men. *Amer. sociol. Rev.,* 1954, **19**, 591–593.
(4) AMES, L. B.: Motor correlates of infant crying. *J. genet. Psychol.,* 1941, **59**, 239–247.
(5) AMES, L. B.: The sense of self of nursery school children as manifested by their verbal behavior. *J. genet. Psychol.,* 1952, **81**, 193–232.
(6) ANASTASI, A., and F. A. CORDOVA: Some effects of bilingualism upon the intelligence test performance of Puerto Rican children in New York City. *J. educ. Psychol.,* 1953, **44**, 1–19.
(7) ANASTASI, A., and R. D'ANGELO: A comparison of Negro and white preschool children in language development and Goodenough draw-a-man I.Q. *J. genet. Psychol.,* 1952, **81**, 147–165.
(8) ANASTASI, A., and C. DE JÉSUS: Language development and non-verbal I.Q. of Puerto Rican preschool children in New York City. *J. abnorm. soc. Psychol.,* 1953, **48**, 357–366.
(9) A.S.H.A. Committee on the Midcentury White House Conference: Speech disorders and speech correction. *J. speech hear. Disord.,* 1952, **17**, 129–137.
(10) AUSUBEL, D. P., E. E. BALTHAZAR, I. ROSENTHAL, L. S. BLACKMAN, S. H. SCHPOONT, and J. WELKOWITZ: Perceived parent attitudes as determinants of children's ego structure. *Child Develpm.,* 1954, **25**, 173–183.

(11) BAKWIN, R. M., and H. BAKWIN: Cluttering. *J. Pediat.,* 1952, **40**, 393–396.
(12) BALDRIDGE, M.: Three decades of language study. *Childh. Educ.,* 1949, **26**, 117–124.
(13) BALDWIN, A. L.: Differences in parent behavior toward three- and nine-year-old children. *J. Pers.,* 1945, **15**, 143–165.
(14) BARCLAY, D.: What tattling really tells. *The New York Times,* Aug. 12, 1962.
(15) BAYLEY, N.: *Studies in the development of young children.* Berkeley, Calif.: The University of California Press, 1940.
(16) BELL, G. B., and H. E. HALL: The relationship between leadership and latency. *J. abnorm. soc. Psychol.,* 1954, **49**, 156–157.
(17) BEREITER, C.: Fluency abilities in preschool children. *J. genet. Psychol.,* 1961, **98**, 47–48.
(18) BERNSTEIN, B.: Language and social class. *Brit. J. Sociol.,* 1960, **11**, 271–276.
(19) BLOODSTEIN, O.: The development of stuttering. *J. speech hear. Disord.,* 1960, **25**, 219–237, 366–376; 1961, **26**, 67–82.
(20) BLUEMEL, C. S.: If a child stammers. *Ment. Hyg., N.Y.,* 1959, **43**, 390–393.
(21) BOLAND, J. C.: Type of birth as related to stuttering. *J. speech hear. Disord.,* 1951, **16**, 40–43.
(22) BONNEY, M. E.: Social behavior differences between second grade children of high and low sociometric status. *J. educ. Res.,* 1955, **48**, 481–495.
(23) BORING, E. G.: The woman problem. *Amer. Psychologist,* 1951, **6**, 679–692.
(24) BOSSARD, J. H. S.: *Parent and child.* Philadelphia: University of Pennsylvania Press, 1953.
(25) BOSSARD, J. H. S., and E. S. BOLL: Marital unhappiness in the life cycle. *Marriage fam. Liv.,* 1955, **17**, 10–14.

(26) BOSSARD, J. H. S., and E. S. BOLL: *The sociology of child development*, 3d ed. New York: Harper & Row, 1960.

(27) BRECKENRIDGE, M. E., and E. L. VINCENT: *Child development*, 4th ed. Philadelphia: Saunders, 1960.

(28) BRETSCH, H. S.: Social skills and activities of socially accepted and unaccepted adolescents. *J. educ. Psychol.*, 1952, **43**, 449–458.

(29) BRODBECK, A. J., and O. C. IRWIN: The speech behavior of infants without families. *Child Developm.*, 1946, **17**, 145–146.

(30) BROWN, D. G.: Masculinity-femininity development in children. *J. consult. Psychol.*, 1957, **21**, 197–202.

(31) BROWN, R., and J. BERKO: Word association and the acquisition of grammar. *Child Develpm.*, 1960, **31**, 1–14.

(32) BROWN, W. H., and V. C. MORRIS: Social acceptance among "Texas" children. *Understanding the Child*, 1954, **23**, 56–60.

(33) BROWNFIELD, E. D.: Communication—key to dynamics of family interaction. *Marriage fam. Liv.*, 1953, **15**, 316–319.

(34) BROWNSTONE, C.: Why children's secret language. *Parents' Mag.*, May 1940, 30–31.

(35) BRYAN, F. E.: How large are children's vocabularies? *Elem. Sch. J.*, 1953, **54**, 210–216.

(36) CARROLL, J. B.: Language development. In *Encyclopedia of educational research*, 3d ed. New York: Macmillan, 1960. Pp. 744–752.

(37) CARROW, SISTER M. A.: Linguistic functioning of bilingual and monolingual children. *J. speech hear. Disord.*, 1957, **22**, 371–380.

(38) CATALANO, F. L., and D. MC CARTHY: Infant speech as possible predictor of later intelligence. *J. Psychol.*, 1954, **38**, 203–209.

(39) CATTELL, P.: *The measurement of intelligence of infants and young children*. New York: The Psychological Corporation, 1940.

(40) CENTERS, R.: Social-class identification of American youth. *J. Pers.*, 1950, **18**, 290–302.

(41) CHRISTENSEN, A. H.: A quantitative study of personality dynamics in stuttering and nonstuttering siblings. *Speech Monogr.*, 1952, **19**, 144–145.

(42) COHN, W.: On the language of lower-class children. *Sch. Rev.*, 1959, **67**, 435–440.

(43) CRANE, A. R.: Pre-adolescent gangs: a socio-psychological interpretation. *J. genet. Psychol.*, 1955, **86**, 275–279.

(44) CRUICKSHANK, W. M., and G. O. JOHNSON: *Education of exceptional children and youth.* Englewood Cliffs, N.J.: Prentice-Hall, 1958.

(45) CURRY, E. T.: Hoarseness and voice change in male adolescents. *J. speech hear. Disord.*, 1949, **14**, 23–25.

(46) DARCY, N. T.: A review of the literature on the effects of bilingualism upon the measurement of intelligence. *J. genet. Psychol.*, 1953, **82**, 21–57.

(47) DAVIS, A., and R. J. HAVIGHURST: *Father of the man*. Boston: Houghton Mifflin, 1947.

(48) DAVITZ, J. R.: Social perception and sociometric choice of children. *J. abnorm. soc. Psychol.*, 1955, **50**, 173–176.

(49) DAWSON, M. A.: Children's preferences for conversational topics. *Elem. Sch. J.*, 1937, **37**, 429–437.

(50) DOUGLASS, R. L.: Basic feelings and speech defects. *Except. Children*, 1959, **25**, 319–324.

(51) DREGER, R. M.: Spontaneous conversation and story-telling of children in a naturalistic setting. *J. Psychol.*, 1955, **40**, 163–180.

(52) FEA, H. R.: Interrelationships among materials read, written, and spoken by pupils of the fifth and sixth grades. *J. educ. Psychol.*, 1953, **44**, 159–174.

(53) FEIFEL, H., and I. LORGE: Quantitative differences in the vocabulary responses of children. *J. educ. Psychol.*, 1950, **41**, 1–18.

(54) FISHMAN, J. A.: Negative stereotypes concerning Americans among American-born children receiving various types of minority group education. *Genet. Psychol. Monogr.*, 1955, **51**, 107–182.

(55) FITT, A. B.: An experimental study of children's attitudes toward school in Auckland, N.Z. *Brit. J. educ. Psychol.*, 1956, **26**, 25–30.

(56) FITZSIMONS, R.: Developmental, psychosocial, and educational factors in children with nonorganic articulation problems. *Child Develpm.*, 1958, **29**, 481–489.

(57) FREEMAN, G. G., and J. A. SONNEGA: Peer evaluation of children in speech correction class. *J. speech hear. Disord.*, 1956, **21**, 179–182.

(58) GARRISON, K. C.: *Growth and development*, 2d ed. New York: Longmans, 1959.

(59) GESELL, A.: The ontogenesis of infant behavior. In L. Carmichael (Ed.), *Manual of child psychology*, 2d ed. New York: Wiley, 1954. Pp. 335–373.

(60) GESELL, A., F. L. ILG, and L. B. AMES: *Youth: the years from ten to sixteen*. New York: Harper & Row, 1956.

(61) GEWIRTZ, J. L.: Three determinants of attention-seeking in young children. *Monogr. Soc. Res. Child Develpm.*, 1954, **19**, No. 2.

(62) GLASNER, P. J.: Personality characteristics and emotional problems in stutterers under the age of five. *J. speech hear. Disord.*, 1949, **14**, 135–138.

(63) GLICK, P. C.: The life cycle of the family. *Marriage fam. Liv.*, 1955, **17**, 3–9.

(64) GOYA, S., and K. SMITH: Speech stimulation practices among mothers of preschool children. *J. speech hear. Disord.*, 1959, **24**, 150–153.

(65) GRONLUND, N. E.: Generality of sociometric status over criteria in measurement of social acceptability. *Elem. Sch. J.*, 1955, **55**, 173–176.

(66) HACKER, H. M.: Women as a minority group. *Soc. Forces*, 1951, **30**, 60–69.

(67) HAGGERTY, A. D.: The effects of long-term hospitalization and institutionalization upon the language development of children. *J. genet. Psychol.*, 1959, **94**, 205–209.

(68) HAHN, E.: Analysis of the content and form of speech of first grade children. *Quart. J. Speech*, 1948, **34**, 361–366.

(69) HARRIS, D. B., and S. C. TSENG: Children's attitudes toward peers and parents as revealed by sentence completions. *Child Develpm.*, 1957, **28**, 401–411.

(70) HAVIGHURST, R. J.: *Human development and education*. New York: Longmans, 1953.

(71) HILDRETH, G.: The development and training of hand dominance. IV. Developmental problems associated with handedness. *J. genet. Psychol.*, 1950, **76**, 39–100.

(72) HOLLAND, W. R.: Language barrier as an educational problem of Spanish-speaking children. *Except. Children*, 1956, **27**, 42-50.

(73) HOLLINGWORTH, L. S.: *Children above 180 IQ: origin and development*. New York: Harcourt, Brace & World, 1950.

(74) HOROWITZ, L. S.: Attitudes of speech defectives toward humor based on speech defects. *Speech Monogr.*, 1957, **24**, 46–55.

(75) HORROCKS, J. E., and M. E. BUKER: A study of the friendship fluctuations of preadolescents. *J. genet. Psychol.*, 1951, **78**, 131–144.

(76) HOWARD, R. W.: The developmental history of a group of triplets. *J. genet. Psychol.*, 1947, **70**, 191–204.

(77) ILG, F. L., J. LEARNED, A. LOCKWOOD, and L. B. AMES: The three-and-a-half-year-old. *J. genet. Psychol.*, 1949, **75**, 21–31.

(78) IRWIN, O. C.: Research on speech sounds for the first six months of life. *Psychol. Bull.*, 1941, **38**, 277–285.

(79) IRWIN, O. C.: Infant speech: effect of systematic reading of stories. *J. speech hear. Res.*, 1960, **3**, 187–190.

(80) JENSEN, J. V.: Effects of childhood bilingualism. *Elem. Eng.*, 1962, **39**, 132–143, 358–366.

(81) JERSILD, A. T.: *Child psychology*, 5th ed. Englewood Cliffs, N.J.: Prentice-Hall, 1960.

(82) JERSILD, A. T., and R. J. TASCH: *Children's interests and what they suggest for education*. New York: Teachers College, Columbia University, 1949.

(83) JONES, H. E.: Perceived differences among twins. *Eugen. Quart.*, 1955, **1**, 98–102.

(84) JOURARD, S. M.: *Personal adjustment*. New York: Macmillan, 1958.

(85) KAPOS, E., and N. A. FATTU: Behavioral rigidity in speech-handicapped children. *J. speech hear. Disord.*, 1957, **22**, 707–713.

(86) KASSER, E.: The growth and decline of a child's slang vocabulary at Mooseheart: a self-contained community. *J. genet. Psychol.*, 1945, **66**, 129–137.

(87) KITTELL, J. E.: Bilingualism and language —non-language intelligence scores of third-grade children. *J. educ. Res.*, 1959, **52**, 263–268.

(88) KOCH, H. L.: The relation of certain formal attributes of siblings to attitudes held toward each other and toward their parents. *Monogr. Soc. Res. Child. Develpm.*, 1960, **25**, No. 4.

(89) KOENIG, F. G.: Improving the language abilities of bilingual children. *Except. Children*, 1953, **14**, 183–186.

(90) LAKIN, M.: Personality factors in mothers of excessively crying (colicky) infants. *Monogr. Soc. Res. Child Develpm.*, 1957, **22**, No. 1.

(91) LAMBERT, W. E., J. HAVELKA, and R. C. GARDNER: Linguistic manifestations of bilingualism. *Amer. J. Psychol.*, 1959, **72**, 77–82.

(92) LANDRETH, C.: *The psychology of early childhood*. New York: Knopf, 1958.

(93) LASKO, J. K.: Parent behavior toward first and second children. *Genet. Psychol. Monogr.*, 1954, **49**, 97–137.

(94) LATIF, I.: The physiological basis of linguistic development and the ontogeny of meaning. *Psychol. Rev.*, 1934, **41**, 55–85, 153–156.

(95) LEHRHOF, I.: Speech problems in children. *J. Pediat.*, 1958, **52**, 91–95.

(96) LEWIS, D. G.: Bilingualism and non-verbal intelligence: a further study of test results. *Brit. J. educ. Psychol.*, 1959, **29**, 17–22.

(97) LEWIS, E.: The function of group play during middle childhood in developing the ego complex. *Brit. J. med. Psychol.*, 1954, **27**, 15–29.

(98) LEWIS, M. M.: *Infant speech: a study of the beginnings of language*. New York: Humanities Press, 1951.

(99) LYNIP, A. W.: The use of magnetic devices in the collection and analysis of the preverbal utterances of an infant. *Genet. Psychol. Monogr.*, 1951, **44**, 221–262.

(100) MACFARLANE, J., L. ALLEN, and M. P. HONZIK: *A developmental study of the behavior problems of normal children between twenty-one months and fourteen years*. Berkeley, Calif.: The University of California Press, 1954.

(101) MADDOCK, E.: A collection and analysis of conversational patterns of children. *Speech Monogr.*, 1947, **14**, 214–215.

(102) MARSHALL, H. R.: Relations between home experiences and children's use of language in play interactions with peers. *Psychol. Monogr.*, 1961, **75**, No. 5.

(103) MC CARTHY, D.: Language development. In L. Carmichael (Ed.), *Manual of child psychology*, 2d ed. New York: Wiley, 1954. Pp. 492–630.

(104) MC CARTHY, D.: Language development.

Monogr. Soc. Res. Child Develpm., 1960, **25**, No. 3, 5–14.

(105) MC CURRY, W. H., and O. C. IRWIN: A study of word approximations in the spontaneous speech of infants. *J. speech hear. Disord.*, 1953, **18**, 133–139.

(106) MC QUOWN, N. A.: Language-learning from an anthropological point of view. *Elem. Sch. J.*, 1954, **54**, 402–408.

(107) MERRY, F. K., and R. V. MERRY: *The first two decades of life*, 2d ed. New York: Harper & Row, 1958.

(108) MÉTRAUX, R. W.: Speech profile of the preschool child. *J. speech hear. Disord.*, 1950, **15**, 37–53.

(109) MISSILDINE, W. H., and P. J. GLASNER: Stuttering: a reorientation. *J. Pediat.*, 1947, **31**, 200–305.

(110) MOLL, K. L., and F. L. DARLEY: Attitudes of mothers of articulatory-impaired and speech-retarded children. *J. speech hear. Disord.*, 1960, **25**, 377–384.

(111) MONCUR, J. P.: Symptoms of maladjustment differentiating young stutterers from non-stutterers. *Child Develpm.*, 1955, **26**, 91–96.

(112) MOORE, J. K.: Speech content of selected groups of orphanage and nonorphanage preschool children. *J. exp. Educ.*, 1948, **16**, 122–133.

(113) MORGENSTERN, J. J.: Socioeconomic factors in stuttering. *J. speech hear. Disord.*, 1956, **21**, 25–33.

(114) MYSAK, E. D.: Organismic development of oral language. *J. speech hear. Disord.*, 1961, **26**, 377–384.

(115) NOEL, D. I.: A comparative study of the relationship between the quality of the child's language usage and the quality and types of language used in the home. *J. educ. Res.*, 1953, **47**, 161–167.

(116) OSBORN, S. S.: Concepts of speech development. *J. speech hear. Disord.*, 1961, **26**, 391–392.

(117) PARMELEE, A. A.: Infant speech development: a report of the study of one child by magnetic tape recordings. *J. Pediat.*, 1955, **46**, 447–450.

(118) PERRIN, E. H.: The social position of the speech defective child. *J. speech hear. Disord.*, 1954, **19**, 250–252.

(119) PIAGET, J., and B. INHELDER: *The growth of logical thinking from childhood to adolescence. An essay on the construction of formal operations.* New York: Basic Books, Inc., Publishers, 1958.

(120) RHEINGOLD, H. L., and N. BAYLEY: The later effects of an experimental modification of mothering. *Child Develpm.*, 1959, **30**, 363–372.

(121) RHEINGOLD, H. L., and J. L. GEWIRTZ: *The conditioning of vocalization in infants using*

an adult's social response as reinforcer. Bethesda, Md.: Nat. Instit. Ment. Hlth Lab. Psychol., 1957.

(122) RIBBLE, M. A.: *The personality of the young child.* New York: Columbia University Press, 1955.

(123) ROSEN, S.: Effects of emotional disturbances on social skills. *Counseling*, 1952, **10**, 6–7.

(124) ROSENZWEIG, S.: Babies are taught to cry: an hypothesis. *Ment. Hyg., N.Y.*, 1954, **38**, 81–84.

(125) RUSSELL, D. H., and I. Q. SAADEH: Qualitative levels in children's vocabularies. *J. educ. Psychol.*, 1962, **53**, 170–174.

(126) SAMPSON, O. C.: The speech and language development of five-year-old children. *Brit. J. educ. Psychol.*, 1959, **29**, 217–222.

(127) SEEGERS, J. C., and H. R. SEASHORE: How large are children's vocabularies? A discussion. *Elem. Sch. J.*, 1949, **26**, 181–194.

(128) SHELTON, R. L., W. B. ARNDT, and J. B. MILLER: Learning principles and teaching of speech language. *J. speech hear. Disord.*, 1961, **26**, 368–370.

(129) SHIRLEY, M. M.: *The first two years.* Vol. 3. *Personality manifestations.* Minneapolis: The University of Minnesota Press, 1933.

(130) SIMON, C. T.: The development of speech. In L. E. Travis (Ed.), *Handbook of speech pathology.* New York: Appleton-Century-Crofts, 1957.

(131) SMITH, M. E.: The preschool child's use of criticism. *Child Develpm.*, 1932, **3**, 137–141.

(132) SMITH, M. E.: A study of the speech of eight bilingual children of the same family. *Child Develpm.*, 1935, **6**, 19–25.

(133) SMITH, M. E.: Word variety as a measure of bilingualism in preschool children. *J. genet. Psychol.*, 1957, **90**, 143–150.

(134) SMITH, M. E., and L. M. KASDON: Progress in the use of English after twenty years by children of Filipino and Japanese ancestry in Hawaii. *J. genet. Psychol.*, 1961, **99**, 129–138.

(135) SOFFIETTI, J. P.: Bilingualism and biculturalism. *J. educ. Psychol.*, 1955, **46**, 222–227.

(136) SOLOMON, A. L.: Personality and behavior patterns of children with functional defects of articulation. *Child Develpm.*, 1961, **32**, 731–737.

(137) SPIKER, C. C., and O. C. IRWIN: The relationship between I.Q. and indices of infant speech sound development. *J. speech hear. Disord.*, 1949, **14**, 335–343.

(138) SPRIESTERBACH, D. C., and J. F. CURTIS: Misarticulation and discrimination of speech sounds. *Quart. J. Speech*, 1951, **37**, 483–491.

(139) STAATS, A. W., and C. K. STAATS: A comparison of the development of speech and reading behavior with implications for research. *Child Develpm.*, 1962, **33**, 831–846.

(140) STENGEL, E.: A critical and psychological study of echo reactions. *J. ment. Sci.*, 1947, **93**, 598–612.

(141) STEWART, A. H., I. H. WEILAND, A. R. LEIDER, C. A. MANGHAM, T. H. HOLMES, and H. S. RIPLEY: Excessive infant crying (colic) in relation to parent behavior. *Amer. J. Psychiat.*, 1954, **110**, 687–694.

(142) STOLTZ, H. R., and L. M. STOLTZ: *Somatic development of adolescent boys.* New York: Macmillan, 1951.

(143) STRANG, R.: Students' perceptions of factors affecting their studying. *Ment. Hyg., N.Y.*, 1957, **41**, 97–102.

(144) STRICKLAND, R. G.: *The language arts in the elementary school.* Boston: Heath, 1951.

(145) TEMPLIN, M.: Certain language skills in children, their development and interrelationships. *Univer. Minnesota Instit. Child Welf. Monogr.*, 1957, No. 26.

(146) TERMAN, L. M., and M. A. MERRILL: *Stanford-Binet Intelligence Scale,* 3d rev. Boston: Houghton Mifflin, 1960.

(147) THEVAOS, D. G.: *The influence of sematic variation on word difficulty with consequent effects on vocabulary estimates and frequency-difficulty variations.* Ed. D. thesis, Teachers College, Columbia University, 1951.

(148) THOMPSON, G. G.: *Child psychology,* rev. ed. Boston: Houghton Mifflin, 1962.

(149) TRAVIS, L. E.: *Handbook of speech pathology.* New York: Appleton-Century-Crofts, 1957.

(150) TYLER, L. E.: The relationship of interests to abilities and reputation among first grade children. *Educ. psychol. Measmt,* 1951, **11**, 255–264.

(151) VINACKE, W. E.: Concept formation in children of school age. *Education,* 1954, **74**, 527–534.

(152) WEILAND, I. H., A. R. LEIDER, and C. A. MAUGHAN: A psychiatric study of the mothers of excessively crying infants. *Psychiat. Quart.*, 1957, **31**, 508–520.

(153) WERNER, A., and E. KAPLAN: Development of word meaning through verbal context: an experimental study. *J. Psychol.*, 1950, **29**, 251–257.

(154) WOODS, SISTER F. J., and SISTER M. A. CARROW: The choice-rejection status of speech defective children. *Except. Children,* 1959, **25**, 279–283.

(155) WYATT, G. L.: *Speech and interpersonal relations.* New York: Free Press, 1959.

(156) YAMAMATO, K.: Development of ability to ask questions under specific testing conditions. *J. genet. Psychol.*, 1962, **101**, 83–90.

(157) YEDINACK, J. G.: A study of the linguistic functioning of children with articulation and reading disabilities. *J. genet. Psychol.*, 1949, **74**, 23–59.

(158) ZELIGS, R.: Races and nationalities most and least liked by children. *J. educ. Res.*, 1954, **48**, 1–14.

EMOTIONAL
DEVELOPMENT

The emotions play a role of major importance in the child's life. They add pleasure to his everyday experiences, they serve as a motivation to action, and they color the form that action will take. In addition, they influence his perception of people and of his environment and determine what his characteristic pattern of adjustment to life will be. As is true of all patterns of behavior, the emotional reactions the child most often experiences develop into habits. As such, they become important driving forces in his life.

Every child enters the world with the potentialities for both pleasant and unpleasant emotions—those which give him pleasure and personal satisfaction and those which make him unhappy and dissatisfied. Which will become dominant will be determined mainly by the environment in which he grows up and the relationship he has with the people in his environment. Childhood is the critical age in the development of the emotions. If they are to be powerful forces for *good* in the child's life, they must be *good* emotions.

As emotional patterns settle into habits and become driving forces for good or poor adjustment, the child's fate will be sealed. That emotions color the way the individual views life and his role in the social group is readily apparent from the type of memories he carries into adulthood. People who have predominantly happy memories of childhood are, for the most part, better adjusted as adolescents and adults than those whose memories center around unhappy experiences. Children who grow up in a home devoid of emotional warmth find it difficult to establish affectional relationships with others or to get the pleasure out of experiences which others whose memories of childhood are happier find ego-satisfying (43, 105).

Most parents know this, and consequently they want to guarantee their children a happy childhood. They recognize that "a healthy child is a happy child"; therefore, they try to keep their children healthy. They believe that satisfying the child's desires for material possessions will make him happy;

therefore, they give him the material possessions he asks for, even at great personal sacrifice.

Parents often fail to recognize, however, that happiness cannot exist if the pleasant emotions are dominated by the unpleasant —if frustrations, anxieties, jealousies, and envies are stronger and more persistent than the happy experiences they have provided for their child. They also fail to recognize that a child cannot know that his parents love and respect him as an individual unless they demonstrate their love and respect by words and actions. His reasoning capacity is too limited to allow him to see that behind their critical comments and punishment is a parental love that is overshadowed by their desire to be "good parents."

EMOTIONAL DEPRIVATION

Emotional deprivation does *not* mean that the child is deprived of all emotional experiences; this would be impossible and certainly undesirable. Instead, it means that he is deprived of opportunities to experience reasonable amounts of the pleasant emotions, especially curiosity, joy, happiness, love, and affection. In its narrowest sense, it is generally limited to the deprivation of affection, though this in turn deprives the child of opportunities to experience joy and happiness also. Most children grow up in environments that tend to stimulate the development of the unpleasant emotions, especially anger, fear, hatred, jealousy, and envy, though they may be curbed in the way they express these emotions. A few children grow up in environments where they have almost no opportunities to experience any of the pleasant emotions that normal children experience: They are "emotionally starved."

Studies of the effects of "emotional starvation" on children have served to highlight the role the emotions play in the normal pattern of physical and mental development and in the child's personal and social adjustments. From studies of this type, one can best appreciate the role the emotions play.

The seriousness of the effects will be influenced by when the deprivation occurs, how long it persists, the type of emotion of which the child is deprived, and many other factors (45, 213). For example, a child who is frustrated in every attempt to satisfy his curiosity or who is deprived of stimuli which normally call forth curiosity, because of an intellectually sterile environment or an environment planned for persons of greater or lesser intellectual capacities than his, will not attain the level of mental development he is capable of, nor will his achievements come up to his potentials. He will become apathetic and bored; he will develop a mental rigidity that interferes with creativity; and he will become frustrated because he is not permitted to do what he is capable of doing (155, 204).

Similarly, lack of opportunity to experience reasonable amounts of happiness from a sense of achievement is likely to warp a child's personality. A child who is brought up in a home where parents believe that praise makes a child lazy will be deprived of the pleasure that comes from recognition of his achievements; he will develop feelings of inadequacy, with the emotional accompaniments of unhappiness and resentment toward those who criticize his accomplishments. These resentments often express themselves in underachievement, not only in school but in all areas of life. Underachievement is the child's way of "getting even" with those who have deprived him of the happiness he seeks (118, 204).

Deprivation of Affection. The most serious and damaging effects of emotional deprivation come when the child is deprived of opportunities to experience affection. Being loved by others is an ego-satisfying experience. There is a practical angle to the experience also. Love determines the intensity of attraction toward or away from intimate relations with others; as a result, it influences the individual's decisions and actions (86). For every child, the "initial love responses . . . are made . . . to the mother or some mother surrogate. From this intimate attachment of the child to the mother, multiple learned and generalized affectional responses are formed" (91).

Because the mother's warm and loving behavior provides protection for the child, his behavior during the early years of life is directed largely toward gaining the warmth and affection he craves. Consequently, he learns behavior patterns which will bring him parental approval. Later, when he comes in contact with other people, he learns effective means of gratifying his own needs, thus freeing him from some of the vulnerability that emotional dependence on the mother or mother surrogate is likely to bring (82).

Deprivation of emotional warmth results in a deficiency of both emotional nourishment and intellectual stimulation. If intellectual stimulation alone is present, however, *autism,* or a state of "emotional refrigeration," will result, in which the child has no interest in people. The quality and quantity of affection, its appropriateness for the child's age and level of development, and its continuity or discontinuity all play important roles in determining the effects it will have on the child's behavior and personality (194).

Causes of Deprivation of Affection. There are many causes of deprivation of affection and many conditions under which it occurs. It may come from the institutionalization of a baby or young child or from the death of one or both of the parents. Even when a child lives with one or both parents, he may be deprived of affection because of their rejection or neglect or because they believe that showing affection will "spoil" him (19, 45).

This is well illustrated in a study of Sinhalese children, who show a pattern of behavior characteristic of a "burnt child." Their basic insecurity and anxiety cause them to avoid affectionate responsiveness, to be excessively cautious, and to lack creativeness. This pattern stems from the cultural tendency of parents to withdraw overt signs of affection for their children (199). Deprivation of affection, on the other hand, may result from a child's rejection of his parents because they do not meet his needs or because he is ashamed of them. Under such conditions, the parent cannot influence the child or supply him with the affection he craves. Children who are unpopular with their peers and whose parents do not find them "satisfactory" are deprived of the two most important sources of emotional satisfaction and security (65, 162).

Effects of Deprivation of Affection. Whatever the cause of deprivation of affection, it is damaging to the child. Babies deprived of affection suffer a delay in normal *physical development,* accompanied by such specific effects as listlessness, emaciation, quietness, general apathy, loss of appetite, and psychosomatic illnesses. When the young child's health is poor, he often becomes highly nervous, developing nervous mannerisms and speech disorders. Accompanying the delay in physical development is a delay in *mental development.* The child lacks the ability to concentrate and is distractible, and his speech development is delayed (45, 213).

Socially, children who have been deprived of love are handicapped in learning how to get along with people; they lack responsiveness to the advances of others and tend to be uncooperative and hostile. They suffer from feelings of inadequacy and show their resentments in aggressiveness, disobedience, and other forms of asocial behavior. In spite of their asocial behavior, children deprived of affection more often become dependent rather than independent in their behavior (35, 82, 210).

The effect on the child's *emotional development* is especially serious. The baby brought up in an emotionally sterile environment becomes listless, quiet, and unresponsive to the smiles and coos of others; he shows patterns of temper tantrums, with violent kicks and screams, as if seeking attention; and he gives the general appearance of being unhappy. An older child, hungry for food or affection, becomes irritable, cantankerous, and unreasonable (13, 118). All these unfavorable social and emotional reactions affect the child's developing *personality* unfavorably. Rejection may generate hate, hostility, or vengefulness, and these emotions may be manifested in neurotic, psychotic, or psychosomatic symptoms or in behavior which may, in time, lead to juvenile delinquency. The child may push himself in intellectual or scholarly pursuits and become an overachiever in the hope of winning parental or teacher approval, or he may work far below his capacity, becoming an underachiever (19, 120, 194).

Variations in Effects. The *degree* of deprivation varies from child to child. A slight frustration of the child's desire for affection has been found to whet his desire for it. Young children who must compete with siblings for the mother's attention become friendly and eager to please. Pronounced deprivation of affection, on the other hand, has many of the serious effects reported above (95, 119).

When the deprivation occurs is equally as serious as how great it is. During the first year of life, deprivation of affection produces a state of general depression and a retardation in physical growth. Should it occur between one and five years, a psychopathic personality pattern, lacking in emotionality, develops, and the child becomes maladjusted. Deprivation after five years of age has minor effects because the child can seek and find substitute relations. It is thus apparent that the "critical period" for separation from the mother or mother substitute is from six months to five years of age (35, 82, 195).

During the critical period, babies and young children need a stable environment. Those who are separated from their mothers at birth or shortly after birth do not suffer from loss of an emotional attachment to one person because such an attachment was never firmly established (57). A study of babies taken from unmarried mothers shortly after birth and those removed from a normal home environment showed that, at one month, they were comparable in developmental status (13). As they grow older, the retardation in developmental status of institutionalized babies suffering from deprivation of affection is marked. This may, however, be more the result of limited learning opportunities in an institutional environment than of feelings of insecurity engendered by deprivation (57).

Separation from the father during the critical period is not likely to have a serious effect because few babies or young children develop a deep emotional attachment to their fathers. In the case of the mother, it is different. After becoming accustomed to the care and love of the mother or a mother surrogate, a baby or young child cannot comprehend the sudden withdrawal—even temporarily—of this source of emotional security. As a result, he feels unwanted, unloved, and rejected (99, 120).

A study of two-year-olds, some of whom were living temporarily in a nursery residence during the mother's illness or absence from home and some of whom were there only during the day while the mother worked, showed how serious the separation was at this early age. Those who were separated completely from the mother were affected more severely. They reacted to the separation by a constant seeking of the parent, accompanied by crying and shrieking; their relations with the members of the residential staff were very hostile and demanding; and they indulged in more autoerotic practices, showed more regression in sphincter control, and had more illnesses. This is illustrated in Figure 7–1. Furthermore, they were more anxious to identify with adults than the day-nursery children were, who seemed satisfied just to be near the nurses or other adults (99).

Deprivation of affection for any *length of time* is far more serious during the critical period than before or after it. If the deprivation lasts for less than 3 months, reestablishment of emotional interchange and resumption of close personal contacts with the original source of emotional satisfaction will lead to a resumption of normal physical and mental development, accompanied by a waning of the emotional disturbance. If the deprivation lasts for 5 months or longer, however, reestablishment of close personal

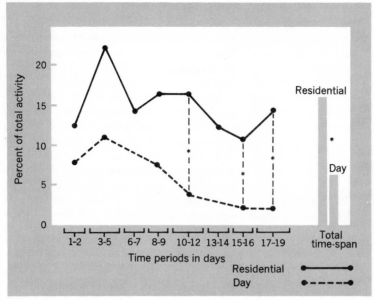

Figure 7–1. Effects of different degrees of emotional deprivation on babies and young children. (Adapted from C. H. Heinicke, Some effects of separating two-year-old children from their parents, *Hum. Relat.*, 1956, 9, 105–176. Used by permission.)

contacts with the loved one will not necessarily produce an improvement, although the developmental decline will continue at a slower rate (82). When the two-year-olds in the study reported above were reunited with their parents, they displayed little affection at first, even for the mother, and often showed hostility. A separation of only 19 days proved to have an unfavorable effect on their personalities; they continued to be more aggressive and demanding than they were before the separations, showing patterns of behavior acquired during the separation. In addition, they tended to feel ambivalent toward the mother and hostile toward the father and siblings for a long time (99, 120). Among older children, deprivation of love over a long period of time has devastating effects on behavior and on developing personalities (58).

Much of the psychological damage can be avoided if there is a *satisfactory substitute* for the child's original source of emotional satisfaction (56). Harlow has demonstrated this point in an experiment in which he constructed a surrogate mother for infant monkeys deprived of their mothers. The surrogate mother was constructed of wood, covered with rubber sponge, sheathed in tan cotton terry cloth, and heated with a light bulb. She was "soft, warm, and tender, a mother with infinite patience, a mother available twenty-four hours a day, a mother that never scolded her infant and never struck or bit her baby in anger" (91). A comparison of baby monkeys raised by their own mothers with an experimental monkey for whom the cloth substitute was provided revealed that the substitute gave the love and security the monkey needed for normal development (92).

Human babies, provided with a substitute source of emotional satisfaction, react in a similar manner. When institutional babies are cared for by one person, they show none of the detrimental effects characteristically found among institutional babies. Instead, their speech and motor development progress faster than that of babies cared for by several people. Their physical development progresses normally, they show no evidence of lack of emotional responsiveness to the substitute mother, and they show no fear of strangers (176).

If the mother works away from home during the day, however, and leaves the baby or young child in the care of a person who is not a satisfactory substitute—who uses different child-care techniques and who does not give the child the affection he has become accustomed to—the arrangement may not prove to be satisfactory. If there is a stable source of affection and child care, as in the case of adoption, young children soon adapt themselves to the substitute parents and make good adjustments (140, 167, 175).

When a child remains in an institution and lacks a stable source of emotional interchange, the retardation in his development is not necessarily the result of emotional deprivation. If the child has never had the care of one person, there is no indication, as he grows older, of personality distortion because of emotional deprivation. Any distortion that occurs is more likely the result of lack of learning opportunities in the institutional environment (57, 111).

Long-term Effects. Whether the effects of deprivation of affection will be minor or major, temporary or permanent, will depend largely upon the factors discussed above. A satisfactory substitute for the source of affection the child has come to rely upon is especially important. While it was formerly believed that deprivation of sources of emotional satisfaction during the early years of life would lay the foundations for adult personality disorders, there is evidence that this may not be so (175, 177). The tendency to develop "affectionless or psychopathic characters" is often offset by favorable experiences later in childhood (36, 84). When institutionalized children, for example, are adopted and given a stable substitute source of emotional satisfaction, the unfavorable effects of early deprivation may be offset (76, 175). If the substitute proves to be unsatisfactory to the child, however, the effects of deprivation of affection may, and often do, persist. While deprivation of affection is not the only cause of maladjustments in adolescence and adulthood, it certainly is an important contributing factor (64, 163).

Maladjustments resulting directly or indirectly from emotional deprivation range from general unhappiness to antisocial behavior, psychopathic personality, psychoneuroses, or even certain forms of psychosis, such as schizophrenia. Although emotional deprivation alone may not cause maladjustive forms of behavior, it is likely to increase the tendency toward maladjustment when it occurs with other unfavorable conditions (88). Rebellion against authority in adolescence, for example, may be increased if the adolescent feels that he has never received the affection he craves.

Teen-age marriages are often a means of satisfying a longing for affection and emotional security never completely satisfied by love from parents, siblings, or peers (146). Poor adjustments to marriage and work and poor attitudes toward the law in adult life are likewise increased by the feelings of insecurity engendered by emotional deprivation during the early years of childhood (63). While there are many causes of juvenile delinquency and adult criminality, certainly one of them is emotional insecurity stemming from feelings of being unwanted and unloved. In many instances, this is a carryover of feelings engendered during the early years of life. Boys are more likely to experience long-term effects of emotional deprivation than girls because boys have less chance to identify with the people who substitute for their parents (64, 84).

HOW THE EMOTIONS DEVELOP

As Bakwin has pointed out, "The ability to respond emotionally is present in the newborn as part of the developmental process and does not have to be learned" (13). That prematurely born infants are capable of emotional reactions suggests that such behavior is possible several months before birth normally occurs. The first sign of emotional behavior in the newborn infant is general excitement due to strong stimulation. This diffuse excitement is part of the mass activity present at birth. There are no indications of clear-cut, definite emotional patterns that can be recognized and identified as specific emotional states.

Often before the period of the newborn

is over, the general excitement becomes differentiated into simple reactions that suggest pleasure and displeasure. The *unpleasant responses* are elicited by changing the baby's position abruptly, by making sudden loud noises, by hampering the baby's movements, by the baby's wearing wet diapers, and by applying cold objects to the baby's skin. Such stimuli cause crying and mass activity. *Pleasant responses,* on the other hand, are apparent when the baby sucks. They can also be elicited by rocking, patting, providing warmth, and snug holding. The baby shows his pleasure by a general relaxation of the entire body, not, as he will later, by smiling, cooing, or laughing (33).

Even before the baby is one year old, emotional expressions are recognizably similar to emotional states in adults. As the child becomes older, he displays an increasing repertoire of emotional responses—*joy, anger, fear, jealousy, happiness, curiosity, envy,* and *hate.* These forms of emotional behavior can be aroused by a wide range of stimuli, including people, objects, and situations which were originally ineffective (14). As Gesell has pointed out, the emotions are "not fixed entities. They change with age throughout infancy, childhood, and youth" (80).

Not only does the general state of excitement present at birth develop into specific emotional patterns, but the emotional responses become less diffuse, random, and undifferentiated. At first, the baby shows displeasure merely by screaming and crying. Later, his reactions include resisting, throwing things, stiffening his body, throwing back his body, running away, hiding, and verbalizing his displeasure. With increasing age, there is an increase in linguistic responses and a decrease in motor responses. This is especially apparent in responses to fear- and anger-provoking stimuli.

How children's emotional behavior becomes increasingly directed and, therefore, less irrelevant and chaotic is well illustrated in a study of anger responses of children two to seven years of age. Verbal manifestations, mainly crying, are characteristic of younger children; physical aggression against self and others, such as pulling hair, tearing clothes, and kicking, is usually found among older children. Still later come verbal aggressions, especially name calling and tattling, as the child discovers that physical aggression against others will not be tolerated (29, 104).

Variations in Development. While the regularity of the pattern of emotional development suggests that emotions are largely a product of heredity, differences in health and environment produce individual variations in the frequency, intensity, and duration of the different emotions. Patterns of emotional behavior established early in life tend to persist as the child grows older unless there are radical changes in his health, his environment, or his personal-social relationships. For example, a baby who is kept in a quiet environment and whose needs are met promptly and consistently is less likely to suffer from nervous tension as he grows older than the one who lives in a noisy and exciting environment and who must cry persistently before anyone bothers to come to him (124).

When parental expectations are high, the environment is likely to produce many emotional tensions for the child. Similarly, the sex and ordinal position of the child influence the treatment he receives during the early, formative years. First-born children, for example, have a status to defend, and they are in constant competition with their siblings. It has been found that a child with a brother becomes less sensitive than the child with a sister; in addition, he learns better control over his emotional expressions (119). Early experiences such as these lay the foundations for the emotional patterns that develop from the hereditary patterns present at birth.

CAUSES OF DEVELOPMENT

Although emotions are present at birth, emotional development is due to *maturation* and *learning,* not to either one alone. The fact that a certain emotional reaction does not appear early in life is no proof that it is not innate. It may develop later with the maturing of intelligence or with the development of the endocrine system. Learning and maturation are so closely interwoven in the development of emotions that at times it is difficult to determine the relative effects of the two.

ROLE OF MATURATION

The ability to respond emotionally is dependent upon neural and endocrine development. Establishment of cortical control, especially in the frontal lobes, is not achieved until adulthood. How this affects the pattern of emotional development has been demonstrated by studies of animals in which removal of the cortex caused them to be extremely placid. When the frontal lobes are removed in human beings, emotional behavior is lacking in depth; they are inhibited, and transition from one emotional state to another occurs rapidly. This explains the typical emotional behavior of children and shows that mature emotional reactions must wait upon the development of the cortical centers, especially of the frontal lobes (33).

Intellectual development in children results in an ability to perceive meanings not previously perceived, to attend for a longer time to one stimulus, and to concentrate emotional tension on one object. With the growth of imagination and understanding, things affect the child differently. Increase in ability to remember and anticipate likewise affects his emotional reactions. Thus he becomes responsive to stimuli to which he was impervious at an earlier age (104, 106).

Young children, for example, prefer stories about animals to those about people because those about people have more anxiety-arousing content and more ego-involvement (37). Children's emotional reactions to death are closely related to their understanding of death. Until they are eight or nine years old, few children show fear of death, even though they may know the biological facts about it. Not until they reach adolescence do they associate death with themselves and members of their families or appreciate the significance of death to them personally; then they react emotionally to it (3).

Similarly, the emotional effect of movies or other mass media of communication will depend largely upon the child's ability to understand what he sees and hears, to realize that it is fiction rather than reality, and to evaluate the meaning of what is said by the different characters. For example, many young children have learned to fear policemen because of the stereotype of policemen they have seen in the movies or comics or on the television screen (187).

Development of the endocrine glands is likewise essential to the development of a mature level of emotional behavior. The baby is relatively lacking in the endocrine products that sustain some of the physiological response to stress. In the case of the adrenal glands, which play a dominant role in the emotions, it has been found that there is a rapid decrease in size after birth. Then they gain rapidly up to five years, slowly from five to eleven years, and more rapidly up to sixteen years, at which time they have regained their birth weight. Until the growth in size has increased, there will be less adrenalin produced and secreted. This has a marked influence on the emotional states in childhood (33).

Studies have shown the close relationship of fear to intellectual and endocrine maturation. At first, fear is general—like a state of panic. As the child grows older, his fear responses become more and more specific. He avoids situations which frighten him, holds himself aloof, or withdraws partially or totally from the situation. There is likewise a change in the causes of fear. Not until the child is four years old, for example, does he appreciate the potential danger of snakes and, as a result, show fear of snakes. Fear of strange people and strange situations comes only when the baby or young child appreciates the fact that they are strange. A child who is precocious in his mental development will be afraid of things which other children of his age will not fear until a year or two later (33, 106).

ROLE OF LEARNING

The newborn baby is incapable of expressing his anger except by crying. Maturation of the nervous system and muscles provides the potentials for differentiated reactions, while learning determines the manner in which anger will be expressed. The form of expression the child uses will depend on what he has learned is socially approved in his cultural group, what he has learned will bring him the greatest satisfaction, and what he has learned is the quickest and most expedient way of getting what he wants. As the child learns that crying is regarded as infantile, for example, he substitutes other forms of expression which he has discovered are more socially acceptable (80).

In general, two forms of learning, *conditioning* and *imitation,* are responsible for the development of emotional patterns in childhood.

Conditioning. Objects and situations which at first failed to call forth emotional responses later come to do so as a result of *conditioning,* or learning by association. The famous experiment on "Albert" by Watson and Raynor demonstrated how a baby learns to be afraid. Albert, at nine months of age, was shown a large number of objects, including a sealskin coat, a rabbit, a dog, a monkey, a white rat, and some cotton wool. In no instance did he display fear. Later, he was conditioned to fear the white rat in the following manner: The rat was presented to him, and at the moment that he reached for it a loud noise was sounded behind his head. This resulted in a startled response on Albert's part, and he fell forward on his face. The next time the loud noise accompanied the presentation of the white rat, he whimpered. After five more presentations of the rat and the noise, the rat was presented alone. Albert cried, withdrew, and showed a typical fear response (209). How conditioning occurs is illustrated in Figure 7–2.

Children acquire many irrational fears in this way, and because they are often acquired without conscious realization, the child does not appreciate how irrational they are. Some objects and situations are more fear-provoking than others, and the child can be conditioned to fear them more easily. It is easier, for example, to condition children to fear animals and people than to condition them to fear inanimate objects, such as blocks, curtains, or opera glasses (154). Conditioning occurs easily and quickly during the early years of life because the young child lacks both the reasoning ability and the experience to assess a situation critically and to recognize how irrational many of his emotional experiences are. Furthermore, because imagination develops more rapidly than reasoning, the child often exaggerates the meaning of a situation, imagining it to be more danger-provoking than it actually is (21).

Conditioned emotions do not remain static: They *spread* to people, objects, and situations similar to those with which they have become associated. Watson and Raynor, carrying their experiment with Albert further, found that Albert's fear of the rat had spread to the rabbit, the dog, the seal-skin coat, and the cotton wool, all of which had been shown to Albert before the conditioning experiment was started and for which he had shown no fear whatsoever (209). In the same way, it has been found that when conditioned fear of inoculation spreads to white coats, it may become general and spread to *anyone* in a white coat, such as a barber; in turn, it spreads to haircuts (133). It is thus apparent that the spreading of emotional reactions to other stimuli may be quite direct, specific, and related, or it may involve indirect or intermediate steps as when the child dreams about the thing that frightened him and thus becomes afraid of the dark (209).

After a particularly frightening experience, a child is likely to show a heightened tendency to be afraid of the thing that frightened him and of other things as well. The aftereffects of frightening experiences will be greater when the child has had a past history of being anxious and easily disturbed. Experiences in the home or in the school which threaten the child's self-esteem,

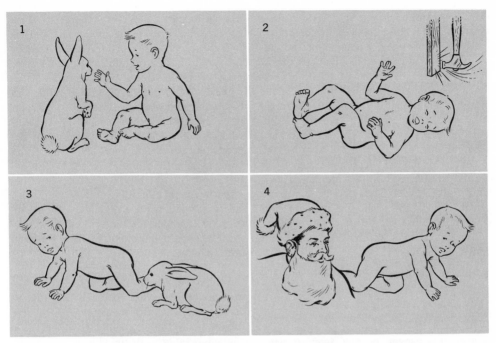

Figure 7–2. How emotions can be conditioned. (*1*) Infant's response to a rabbit before conditioning; (*2*) the unconditioned stimulus which was presented simultaneously with the rabbit on several occasions; (*3*) the infant's response to the rabbit after conditioning; and (*4*) the generalization of conditioning to a Santa Claus beard. (Adapted from G. G. Thompson, *Child psychology*, rev. ed., Houghton Mifflin, 1962. Used by permission.)

and thus his self-confidence, tend to increase his predisposition to be anxious and easily frightened (106).

Conditioning is not limited to fear, nor is its spread found only in fear. Many children are conditioned to like people who are kind to them, even though they are unrelated, and to dislike relatives. Whether the child will have affection or hatred for a person will be determined largely by how that person treats him. A child's preference for the mother rather than the father is often due to the fact that the mother is more warm and understanding of the child and punishes him less than the father does. Similarly, the child's greater affection for one sibling is generally the result of the way that sibling has treated him. He may actually dislike a sibling who teases or ignores him (31, 119,

198). Like fear, affection spreads to other people and things. A child who has an affectional relationship with his parents is better able to develop affection for others than the child whose family relationships are unsatisfactory (106).

Preferences, or likes and dislikes, are generalized emotional responses that have spread from specific people, objects, or situations by conditioning. A dislike for milk, for example, may develop if a child is punished by an overzealous babysitter for refusing to drink his milk. When dislikes become highly charged with emotion and resistant to change, they are known as *prejudices.* A child's prejudice against *all* members of a particular racial or religious group may be the result of an unhappy experience with one member of that group.

Imitation.   Emotional reactions to specific situations can be learned by observing them in others. The child imitates the emotional behavior he observes in others and responds in an emotional manner to situations that at one time were incapable of eliciting emotional responses from him. The effect of the mother's emotional attitude on the child comes from the mother's "emotional tension." Babies less than four weeks old have been found to refuse the breast if the mother was tense. Older babies sometimes violently resist food from a mother who is tense but eat well when fed by a relaxed person. Thus babies who are in close contact with a tense person perceive the emotional state of that person and respond in a consistent manner (194).

Emotions are "contagious" in that they

Because the child's imagination develops more rapidly than reasoning, he often exaggerates the danger of any fear-provoking situation. (Elizabeth Wilcox.)

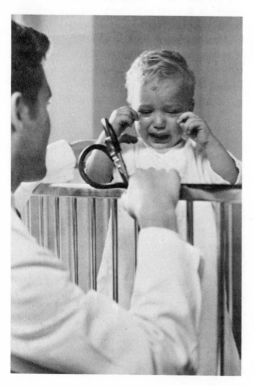

spread from person to person. One child may be angry at a teacher or parent because of some imagined mistreatment. Soon all his friends are likewise angry. A cross teacher is likely to have a roomful of cross children, most of whom will go home cross and disagreeable. On the other hand, a child who is anxious and fearful may learn to be calm if he associates with a teacher or a friend who is calm. The degree of contagion depends not so much upon the age of the child as upon the emotion itself.

Importance of Learning.   Knowing that emotional patterns are mainly a product of learning is important for a number of reasons. The most important of these patterns are discussed below.

Development of Temperament.   The kind of emotion the child learns to experience determines what his *temperament* will be. Predominance of emotional reactions of a characteristic type, or the child's "prevailing mood," reflects his temperament. A child who is temperamentally apprehensive, for example, experiences more fear than other children, though he also experiences joy, happiness, anger, and other emotions. Similarly, the child with a cheerful temperament is more often cheerful than sad, angry, or frightened.

Temperament differs from *mood* in that a mood is a temporary emotional pattern, while temperament is persistent and colors the child's characteristic method of adjusting to life. A child who has a "cheerful disposition," or who is temperamentally cheerful, will react in a predictable way. When he encounters minor obstacles, he will "take them in stride" and show little or no annoyance. The child who has a "bad disposition" can also be counted on to react in a predictable way. His anger will be out of all proportion to the stimulus that produced it. While moods predispose a child to react in a certain way, his moody behavior is not necessarily characteristic of his usual manner of adjusting.

At one time it was believed that temperament was the product of heredity—that it was determined by "body humors," glands, and even body build. Today, there is evidence that the child's temperament is largely a product of learning. Health and endocrine balance do play some role, however, in determining what the child's temperament will be. The predominant emotional stimuli of the early, formative years of childhood and the way the child learns to respond to them will eventually determine his temperament. Temperament is reflected not only in the child's characteristic method of adjusting to life but also in his facial expression. Even when the child is in repose, it is possible to judge whether he has a happy, sad, or irritable disposition. His face tells the story often more eloquently than his actions (87).

Because temperament is largely a product of learning, the child can develop a temperament that will lead to good or bad personal and social adjustments. If he is brought up in a restrictive home environment where little emotional warmth prevails, where parental expectations are beyond the child's capacities, and where he is constantly reproved or punished because he falls below parental expectations, he is likely to experience predominantly unpleasant emotions. This will lead to unhappiness, feelings of insecurity, poor adjustment, and a tendency to respond to future situations with unpleasant emotions. In time, this pattern will become habitual. The emotionally disturbed child is one in whom the unpleasant emotions predominate, though he does, at times, experience pleasant emotions (51, 157).

A predominance of the pleasant emotions, such as affection, love, joy, happiness, and curiosity, is essential to normal development. These emotions lead to feelings of security, which help the child to approach his problems with self-confidence and assurance, to react to minor obstacles with a minimum of emotional tension, and to maintain his emotional balance, even when he encounters major obstacles. The child whose emotions are predominantly pleasant is happy and well liked; he generally makes a success of whatever he undertakes. Because of his cheerful disposition, people like to have him around. Furthermore, he has a good chance

of being selected for leadership roles (65, 89).

Children brought up in lower-class homes, where strict authoritarian child-training methods are commonly used, are subjected to severe punishment or threat of punishment by parents. This encourages the development of fear and resentment. Children from middle-class homes, by contrast, often develop strong feelings of guilt and anxiety because democratic child training puts emphasis on pleasing the parent and showing gratitude for the sacrifices the parents make. Children brought up in such environments tend to become anxious because they never know when their parents will be disappointed with them or will withhold their love (12, 117).

In a cultural group that places high value on social acceptance, the child is encouraged to worry excessively about what others will think of him and about whether he will be popular (10). Because emotions are "contagious," a child brought up in a home where he is surrounded by worriers will become a worrier too. If he is surrounded by people who are anxious, he will imitate their anxiety, even though he has no personal reason to be anxious. If, on the other hand, the home atmosphere is characterized by emotional warmth and affection, he will learn to be a "warm" person (184).

Every child is subjected to both pleasant and unpleasant emotional experiences. Which type of experience is dominant is a factor of major importance in determining what his temperament will be, but this alone does not determine whether the child will be well adjusted or badly adjusted. How the child learns to express his negative emotions is equally as important as how frequent they are. In a well-adjusted child, the unpleasant emotions, especially anxiety and hostility, are expressed less often, with less intensity, and with more focus and direction than in the poorly adjusted child. The well-adjusted child experiences unpleasant emotions, but he handles them in such a way that they damage his adjustments only minimally. The poorly adjusted child allows these emotions to develop into generalized patterns of response; such patterns are apparent in prejudice and in other forms of neurotic, maladjustive behavior (67, 154).

Emotional Balance.   Every child needs an opportunity to experience both pleasant and unpleasant emotions, with the pleasant preferably showing a slight dominance over the unpleasant. That pleasant emotions lead to good personal and social adjustments, however, does not mean that the more pleasant and the fewer unpleasant emotions the child experiences, the better adjusted he will be. Too much affection, for example, is generally expressed in overprotection of the child. This, in turn, leads to heightened emotionality on the child's part, which is shown in excitability, anxiety, worry, oversensitivity, and a tendency to have his feelings easily hurt and to show little affection for others (184).

The child who is pampered or shielded from unpleasant experiences may have a happy, carefree childhood, but he is ill prepared to meet the disappointments, frustrations, and other unpleasant experiences he will confront when his parents can no longer protect him from them. Every child needs a *reasonable* number of unhappy experiences and frustrations to build up *frustration tolerance*—to be "able to take it"—without going to pieces emotionally in the face of trouble. The child who is overprotected and deprived of opportunities to learn how to cope with unpleasant experiences develops feelings of vulnerability, which lead to anxiety (194).

Having an opportunity to experience all kinds of emotions and learning how to cope with them provide "mental-health insurance" —a psychological protection against life's hazards (197). Stagner has emphasized the importance of having an opportunity to experience both pleasant and unpleasant emotions when he said

A boy or girl who has no fear or suspicion whatever of other people is not too well prepared for life in our competitive culture. Furthermore, we can sympathize with others only if we have had experiences in some degree similar to theirs. A person who has never encountered any misfortune cannot truly appreciate the position of those who suffer. An ideal child-rearing program, therefore, would give the growing personality a sufficient breadth of emotional experiences, but not an excess (196).

Control of Learning.   Because emotional patterns are so greatly influenced by learning, the direction of their development can be controlled. If undesirable emotional patterns become dominant, it is possible to change them. Changes in the environment, for example, may have a profound influence on the dominant pattern of the child's emotional expression. A child who has been accustomed to having the mother's undivided attention may bitterly resent her preoccupation with the new baby and express this resentment in frequent and intense outbursts of anger and jealousy. This will cause him to change from a happy, calm child to a tense, anxious, and irascible one (119). The happy, carefree child may develop into an anxious, guilt-ridden one when parental pressures are placed on him to achieve academic success. As Cole has pointed out, "It may suddenly strike a third-grade child that school work is competitive, and this new idea may generate in him a feeling of shame because he has thus far puttered happily about at the bottom of the class" (50).

CHARACTERISTICS OF CHILDREN'S EMOTIONS

The emotions of young children differ markedly from those of adolescents and adults. They even differ from those of older children. Unless these differences are recognized, adults will tend to regard the child's emotional reactions as "immature." Even more serious is the tendency to reprove or punish a child whose emotional reaction is normal for his age and level of development on the grounds that he is not "acting his age." Since learning plays such an important role in emotional development, it is illogical to expect all children of a given age to have similar emotional patterns. Individual differences are inevitable because of differences in maturational levels and learning opportunities.

Regardless of individual differences, however, there are certain characteristic features of children's emotions which make them different from those of adults or even of adolescents. These characteristics are as follows:

1. Children's emotions are brief. Typically, the young child's emotions last only a few minutes and then end abruptly. Because the child expresses his emotions in overt actions, he "clears his system" quickly. As he grows older, social restraints on overt responses lead to "moods," which are expressed in long, drawn-out responses rather than in short, abrupt outbursts (154).

2. Children's emotions are intense. The young child's emotional outbursts are characterized by an intensity seldom observed in an adult. His emotional responses lack gradations of intensity, and his response to a trivial situation will call forth an emotional reaction of great intensity. The intense emotional reactions of a little child to a petty annoyance are the source of great surprise and wonder to many adults. Fear, anger, and joy are all expressed in pronounced overt responses. Even the preadolescent child reacts with intense emotions to what appear, to an adult, to be trivial frustrations or matters of minor concern (80, 157).

3. Children's emotions are transitory. The young child's rapid shifts from laughter to tears, from anger to smiles, or from jealousy to affection are incomprehensible to many adults. These rapid shifts are attributable to three factors: (*a*) The young child expresses his emotions in an unreserved manner, thereby clearing his system of pent-up emotions; (*b*) he lacks complete understanding of the situation because of his immature intellectual development and limited experiences; and (*c*) he has a short attention span, which makes it possible for him to be diverted easily (33).

4. Children's emotions appear frequently. Children display their emotions more frequently, on the average, than the typical adult. As the child grows older, he learns that social disapproval or punishment often follows an emotional outburst. He therefore learns to adjust to emotion-arousing situations and to react to them in more acceptable ways.

5. Children's emotional responses are different. Observations of children of different ages show that there is wide variability in their emotional responses. Among all newborn infants, the patterns of response are similar. Gradually, however, as the influences of learning and environment are felt, the behavior accompanying the different emotions is individualized. For example, one child will run out of the room when he is frightened, another will hide behind his mother's skirt, while still another will stand his ground and cry.

6. Emotions can be detected by symptoms of behavior. An adult is generally able to hide his feelings and emotions so well that it is difficult for others to know just how he feels. Not so with children. Even though they may not show their emotional reactions directly in behavior related to the way they feel, their emotionality can be detected by tension, restlessness, fidgeting, daydreaming, frequency of micturition, nervous mannerisms—such as nail biting, thumb sucking, eye blinking, and rubbing the genitals—speech difficulties, lack of appetite, babyish behavior, frequent crying, obstinacy, and hysterical outbursts. Boys generally show more symptoms of emotionality than girls (106, 143).

7. Emotions change in strength. Emotions that are very strong at certain ages wane in strength as the child grows older. Others, formerly weak, become strong. For example, little children show marked timidity in the presence of strangers. Later, when they realize there is nothing to be afraid of, their timidity wanes. Similarly, temper tantrums are frequent before the child enters school; afterward, they decrease not only in frequency but also in intensity. Figure 7–3 shows changes in four emotional patterns. This apparent instability in emotional strength is due partly to changes in the strength of drives, partly to the development

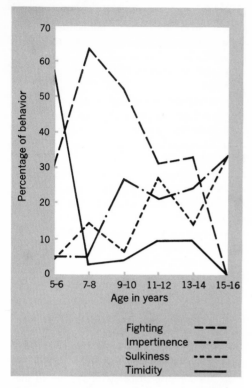

Figure 7–3.   Changes in emotional behavior with age. (Adapted from K. C. Garrison, *Growth and development*, 2d ed., Longmans, 1959. Used by permission.)

of the child's intellectual capacities, and partly to changes in interests and values.

8. Patterns of emotional expression change. The little child wants what he wants when he wants it. He does not stop to consider whether this will be harmful to him or to others, nor does he consider whether getting what he wants is worth the price he will have to pay. Unless he gets what he wants, he will become angry and fly into a fit of temper. Similarly, when frightened, he does not hesitate to run away and hide or to show his fear by crying. When happy, he does not wait to express it. He smiles or laughs when he feels like it, even though others may think he is gloating.

Parents try to teach their young children to control their emotional expressions. Later, similar pressures come from the social group outside the home. By the time the childhood days are over, the individual knows that social approval is dependent upon the degree of control he is able to exert over the expression of his emotions (106).

COMMON EMOTIONAL PATTERNS OF CHILDHOOD

After the early months of babyhood have passed, a number of differentiated emotional patterns, each with its own specific form of behavior, may be observed. The most common of the emotional patterns characteristically found in childhood, the stimuli which arouse them, and the form of response made are discussed in the following sections.

FEAR

A baby is protected as much as possible from fear-provoking stimuli, but before the end of the first year of life, fear-provoking stimuli begin to affect him, and with each passing year, more and more things that are likely to frighten him appear in his ever-enlarging environment. Furthermore, as his intellectual development progresses, he recognizes threats in objects, situations, or even people which formerly he was incapable of perceiving. As a result, his fears not only are more numerous but are likely to be more intense.

Whether fears are rational or irrational, they have their foundations in the child's experiences. Most fears are learned, but they are not all learned in the same way. Some come from direct association of experiences with stimuli that naturally arouse fear, such as loud, harsh noises. Others are acquired through imitation; fear of thunderstorms for example, is often learned by imitating the fear behavior of a parent, sibling, or playmate. A third type of fear comes as an aftermath of an unpleasant experience; fears of doctors, dentists, hospitals, large animals, and certain people originate in this way.

Finally, fears may develop from frightening experiences depicted on the movie screen, in comic books, on the radio or television, or in fairy tales. Even though the child never experiences such fears directly, he does so vicariously through his ability to imagine himself having the experiences of others (1).

Variations in Fear. What frightens a child depends upon many factors, especially his age, sex, and past experiences; the level of his intellectual development; the social and cultural values he has learned from parents and peers; and the degree of personal security he enjoys. The number and severity of fears reach a peak at three years of age and, again, at eleven years. During the early peak period, fears are mainly *situationally* determined; they arise mainly from people, objects, or animals in the child's environment, for example, fear of dogs and of the dark. During the preadolescent peak, on the other hand, fears become more *generalized,* taking the form of anxiety or worry (141).

While fears change with age, there is no sudden shift from one type of fear to another; instead, there is a gradual shift from specific to general fears (9). Figure 7–4 shows variations in the frequency of different fears from early babyhood to six years of age. At every age, but especially as children grow older, there are *sex* differences in fears. It is socially acceptable for girls to fear certain things, such as snakes and bugs, but for boys, such fears are regarded as a sign of a "sissy" (126).

Because fears are greatly influenced by learning, what a child fears will vary according to the *socioeconomic* status of his family. Lower-class boys, for example, are more concerned about violence from robbers, killers, guns, whippings, and their parents, whereas upper-class boys are more afraid of car accidents, storms, and school accidents. As the child approaches adolescence, social-class values play an increasingly important role in his life. This is well illustrated in the case of school fears. Lower-class boys, it has been found, are more afraid of the teacher and are more

susceptible to stage fright in class, while upper-class boys are more concerned about getting good grades, finishing school, and getting into college (9). Social-class differences in fears about economic problems are illustrated in Figure 7–5.

The child's *physical* and *psychological condition* at the time the fear stimulus is presented will determine to a large extent how he will respond. If he is tired, hungry, or emotionally disturbed, he will respond with greater fear. Should he remember *similar experiences* which were unpleasant or even terrifying, he will react with fear to a new situation which, in and of itself, would normally not arouse fear. *Bright* children are aware of the possibilities of danger in situations in which their less bright contemporaries see no danger. As a result, the bright child is likely to show more fears (106).

The *personality pattern* of the child plays an important role in determining his susceptibility to fear. Children who are insecure show a greater tendency to be easily frightened than children who are emotionally secure (40). Being with others who are frightened makes a child more susceptible to fear, while being with persons who are calm decreases this susceptibility. As the number of individuals in a group increases, fears are shared, and the total number of different fears for each child increases (171).

Thus it becomes apparent that it is difficult to predict when a child will be frightened and what will give rise to his fear. Fear is not dependent on a given stimulus alone, but on the surrounding circumstances, the manner in which the stimulus is presented, the child's past experiences, the child's present physiological and psychological condition, and many related circumstances. One child will show fear, and another will show no fear, in identical situations. Whether or not a child will be frightened in a particular situation and how intense his fear will be are predictable only if we know the child's present physiological and psychological condition and the history of his fear reactions.

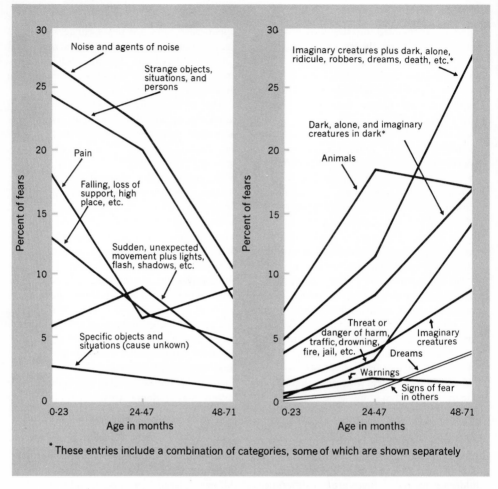

Figure 7–4.   Relative frequency of different fear situations among young children. (Adapted from A. T. Jersild, Emotional development, in L. Carmichael,
Manual of child psychology, 2d ed., Wiley, 1954, pp. 833–917. Used by
permission.)

What Children Fear. In spite of the fact
that fears vary from child to child, there is
evidence that certain fears are characteristically found at different ages. These might
be called the "typical fears" for various age
levels. There will be exceptions because of
individual experiences and because of variations in physical and mental development.
Precocious children will have fears more
characteristic of an older group, while retarded children will have fears characteristic
of younger children.

In general, the most common fears of
babyhood are of loud noises; animals;
strange persons, places, and objects; dark
rooms; high places; sudden displacement;
being alone; and pain. Young children are
afraid of more things than either the baby
or the older child. This is the peak period of
specific fear in the normal pattern of development. The young child is capable of
recognizing dangers which formerly he was
unable to recognize, but his lack of experience prevents him from realizing that they

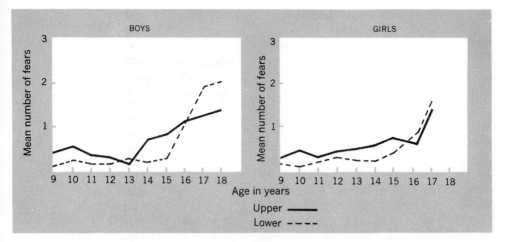

Figure 7–5. Fears and worries about economic problems among boys and girls of high and low socioeconomic groups. (Adapted from H. Angelino, J. Dollins, and E. V. Mech, Trends in the "fears and worries" of school children as related to socioeconomic status and age, *J. genet. Psychol.*, 1956, 89, 263–276. Used by permission.)

may not be personal threats (106, 125). For example, fear of snakes usually appears between the ages of 3½ and 4 years and then wanes when the child is capable of realizing that a snake in a zoo is not a threat. Likewise, growth of memory makes it possible for the young child to remember many unpleasant or terrifying past experiences, such as visits to a doctor or dentist. Development of imagination, without an accompanying increase in reasoning ability, encourages the young child to develop many fears related to experiences, animals, or people he has heard or read about (98).

Many fears of young children are carried over from babyhood, and many of the new fears they acquire are *imaginary;* they fear ghosts, robbers, skeletons, bogeymen, and characters and places they have heard about in the stories read to them or have seen in movies and on television. Their fears of animals are more related to strange and unusual animals than to those they come in contact with in daily life, such as dogs, cats, and horses (106).

In the preschool period, marked changes take place, not only in the type of object or situation which arouses fear, but also in the number and severity of fears. Fear of animals is progressively more frequent up to four years and then declines. Fears of the dark; of being alone; and of the imaginary, fanciful, and supernatural, by contrast, increase with age. This is especially true of fears associated with death and with characters recalled from stories and pictures. There is a definite and consistent decrease in number and severity of fears after the preschool period. For three-year-olds, for example, the average number of fears has been reported to be 5.5, as contrasted with an average of 3.2 for six-year-olds (106, 141).

After children enter school, their fears are concentrated on imaginary, fanciful, supernatural, or remote dangers; on the dark and imaginary creatures associated with the dark; on death or being injured; on the elements, especially thunder, lightning, and storms; and on characters recalled from stories, movies, comics, and television. There is a marked increase in fears related to self or status; older children are afraid of failing, of being ridiculed, and of being "different." *Sex differences* in things feared are also noted. In the case of animals, for example, boys are more afraid of wild animals, while girls are more afraid of insects and spiders. Boys are more troubled about school work, especially tests and exams, while girls are more troubled about disease, illness, darkness, and night (9, 126). On the whole, girls show more fears than boys.

Characteristics of Fear Stimuli. An important characteristic of all fear stimuli is that they occur *suddenly* and *unexpectedly;* the child has little opportunity to adjust himself to them. Fear of strangers, which most babies show, is due in part to the fact that the baby is adjusted to seeing a familiar face and is unable to adjust himself at first to the sudden appearance of a stranger. As the child grows older and becomes more mature intellectually, he can adjust himself more quickly to sudden and unexpected circumstances.

Closely related to the qualities of suddenness and unexpectedness is that of *novelty,* or *strangeness.* Stimuli that embody the element of novelty are apt to arouse fear, while the same stimuli, after the element of novelty has disappeared, will not arouse fear. Many instances of fear in the presence of familiar people can be traced to the fact that they are dressed in an unfamiliar way, as when the child's mother wears her street clothes in place of the accustomed housedress. As soon as the child recognizes the mother and the element of novelty in her appearance disappears, the fear itself disappears (33, 106).

Fear-response Patterns. In a child under three years of age, the response occurring in fear is typically one of helplessness. The cry is the baby's call for help. He hides his face and gets as far away from the feared object as he can, by creeping or walking. He hides behind a person or a piece of furniture and remains there until the fear subsides or until he feels that it is safe to emerge.

As the child grows older, the overt responses in fear are checked as a result of social pressure. The crying reactions cease, though the characteristic facial expressions remain, and the child withdraws from the feared object. The 3½-year-old, for example, protects himself from fear stimuli by saying, "No," or, "I can't do it," or by avoiding the things that arouse his fear (103).

Not only do older children inhibit the impulse to show fear, but they try to keep away from a situation if they have reason to believe it might prove to be frightening. If confronted with a fear stimulus, they may express their fear indirectly in a general motor discharge that is more like a temper outburst than a fear reaction. Shyness, which is a type of fear reaction, consists of nervous mannerisms, such as pulling at the ears or clothing and bending the head to one side and then coyly raising it to look at others (40, 141). Figure 7–6 shows some typical ways of exhibiting fear in childhood.

Value of Fear. Fear is valuable to a child only as long as it is kept from becoming too intense; it serves as a warning of danger. Unfortunately, most children learn to fear things that are not dangerous. Fear then acts as a block to action that might prove to be useful or enjoyable. Of even greater seriousness, many children develop so many and such intense fears that their physical and mental well-being is affected. Unless satisfactory outlets are provided for this emotional tension, the child's health will be adversely affected, his outlook on life will be warped, and his adjustments to people will be unfavorable. Fear thus becomes a handicap to a child instead of a warning of potential dangers. This is especially true of needless fears, many of which are irrational (106).

Because fear, except as a restraint on action in the presence of danger, is more harmful than helpful to a child, its appearance should be prevented as much as possible. Diverting a child's attention from something he might fear is only a temporary measure; it fails to be of any value when the child must meet a situation alone. Since fear is almost inevitable when a child is suddenly and unexpectedly confronted with a new and different stimulus, forewarnings may be effective in warding off fear.

Parents and teachers, however, cannot always anticipate what a child will fear. As a result, they cannot always forewarn him. Then, too, as Jersild has pointed out, "The very fact that his elders go out of their way to forewarn him may, under some conditions, endow an event with terrifying qualities and thus aggravate rather than forestall a child's fear" (107).

WORRY

Worry is an imaginary form of fear. Unlike real fear, it is not aroused directly by a stimulus in the environment. It may come from imagining situations which could arise and which might, in turn, be dangerous. It may also come from books, movies, comics, radio, television, or other popular recreations. Because worries are caused by imaginary rather than real stimuli, they are not found among very young children. The child must reach a stage of intellectual development in which it is possible for him to imagine things not immediately present before he is capable of worrying.

That many of the so-called "fears" of older children are, in reality, worries has been shown by studies of what children say they are afraid of and what they say are the "worst happenings" they have experienced. For example, 14 per cent of a group of children questioned said they were afraid of animals, but only 2 per cent of the group had ever been attacked by animals. Nineteen per cent claimed to be afraid of ghosts, but none had, of course, ever seen a ghost (106). Worries about school work and not being promoted are very common. In one group of elementary-school children, 53 per cent said they worried about not being promoted, while the promotion policy of the school was to promote all but about 1 per cent of each class (106). Thus it is apparent that worries are usually illogical exaggerations of what is likely to happen. They are normal in childhood, however, and are found in even the best-adjusted children.

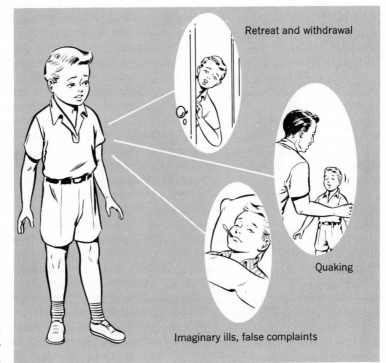

Figure 7–6.
Some typical ways
of showing fear
in childhood.

Retreat and withdrawal

Quaking

Imaginary ills, false complaints

When children get together and talk about their fears, there is a tendency for each child in the group to imagine that such experiences *could* happen to him. As a result, he develops new worries, many of which have no relationship to his own experiences. This is common in puberty when the child begins to worry because his appearance, owing to early or late maturing, is different from that of his agemates. If his agemates call attention to the fact he is "different," his tendency to worry will increase, and he will soon convince himself that there is "something wrong" with him (10, 152). The pubescent child's concern about his changing body and behavior is intensified by parental concern, especially when parents verbalize their concern in the child's presence (181).

Common Worries.   Although there are marked individual differences in what children of different ages worry about, certain trends are commonly found among American children at different ages. The most common worries center around home, family relationships, and school problems, with the latter becoming more common as children progress in school. Typical family worries relate to the health and safety of members of the family and to being scolded or punished by the father or the mother. School worries center around being late for school, failing tests, being scolded or punished by the teacher, doing school reports, and being left behind in school.

In addition to home and school worries, children are concerned about their health, about dying or being killed, about their personal and social adequacy, about economic problems, and about their clothes. School worries, on the whole, are more common than out-of-school worries. Girls worry more than boys, especially about school and safety (10, 106).

Worries, like fears, are greatly influenced by the values of the child; these, in turn, vary from one age to another and according to the socioeconomic group with which the child is identified. Lower-class children, as they approach adolescence, worry more about money problems than children of

higher socioeconomic groups (see Figure 7–5). There is also a difference in worries about social relationships among children of different socioeconomic groups. Girls of the lower groups are more concerned about their popularity and reputations, while girls of the upper groups are more concerned about dates and getting boyfriends (9). Worries are also influenced by social pressures, especially as children grow older and become more anxious to be socially acceptable (173).

ANXIETY

Worries, when frequent and intense, may lead to *anxiety*—a "painful uneasiness of mind concerning impending or anticipated ill" (106). Anxiety is characterized by apprehension, uneasiness, and foreboding from which the individual cannot escape; it is accompanied by a feeling of helplessness because the anxious person feels blocked and unable to find a solution for his problem (151, 185). Though anxiety develops from fear and worry, it is distinguished from them in several important respects. It is more vague than fear. Unlike fear, it does not come from a present situation, which the individual can perceive, but from an *anticipated* one. The anxious child is often unaware of the cause of his anxiety. He does not realize that it comes from feelings of insecurity within himself, not from an external situation to which he projects his fear.

Like worry, anxiety is due to imaginary rather than real causes. The causes are often irrational. Anxiety differs from worry, however, in two important respects. First, worry is related to *specific* situations, such as parties, examinations, or money problems, whereas anxiety is a *generalized* emotional state. Second, worry comes from an *objective* problem, whereas anxiety comes from a *subjective* problem (106, 185). The child who worries more than is usual for his age is likely to develop a state of anxiety which will interfere with his adjustments.

Because anxiety depends upon the ability to imagine something not present, it develops later than fear, just as worry does. It frequently develops after a period of intense worry. Too many and too frequent worries tend to undermine the child's self-confidence and to predispose him to a generalized feeling of inadequacy which often leads to anxiety. Anxiety tends to increase during childhood, especially from the fourth to the sixth grades (46). It is more commonly associated with child-child relationships than with adult-child relationships or with routine activities, such as going to bed alone.

Anxiety varies from one child to another, both in quantity and in quality, and within the same child from one time to another. Girls, on the whole, tend to experience greater anxiety than boys, and Negro children more than white children (165, 180). Children who are unpopular experience greater anxiety than do popular children (150). The less successful the child is in whatever he undertakes, the more likely he is to be anxious (179). The less secure the child feels of his abilities to cope with the problems that face him, the more likely it is that specific worries will lead to a generalized state of anxiety, which predisposes the child to be anxious in *any* situation in which there is a threat to his security (40, 136, 173).

Characteristic Responses. The behavior characteristically associated with anxiety is very similar to that connected with worry. On the surface, it is almost impossible to tell whether the child's behavior is a response to one or the other. The child who is worried or anxious may keep his concerns to himself, brooding over them and often intensifying them; he may turn outward, verbalizing his concerns, and thus bid for attention and sympathy; or he may thrust the blame for his troubles on others, thus freeing himself from some of his feelings of inadequacy or insecurity.

In its milder forms, anxiety may be expressed in readily recognizable behavior, such as depression, unaccountable nervousness and edginess, irritability, mood swings, restless sleep, quick anger, and extraordinary sensitivity. In its stronger forms, it may be cloaked so that it is not so easily recogniz-

able (80, 141). The highly anxious child, for example, may be a boisterous child and a show-off; he may appear to be bored, or he may be restless and ill at ease when with people or when alone. In addition, he often suffers from strong feelings of guilt because he has not lived up to his expectations (5). Perhaps the most cloaked and least easily recognized expression of anxiety is the avoidance or warding off of experiences that might lead to anxiety; the child seeks to "blunt the sharp edge of anxiety" if it is aroused. These cloaks may take many forms. The child may go to sleep, even though he is not tired; he may keep himself too busy to think; or he may withdraw into a fantasy world, overeat, or revert to infantile forms of behavior (40). Figure 7–7 shows some of the common ways of expressing anxiety.

The actions of a highly anxious child and his concern over apparently trivial matters may seem irrational, and the child himself may be at a loss to understand his behavior. As Jersild has said, "One of the marks of an anxious person is that he tends to overdo or to underdo. A slight affront or criticism may send him into a rage, or he may have what seems like an excess of calm when there really is something to get emotional about, as though he were under duress to put a tight lid on his feelings" (107). The anxious child often behaves in a manner completely "out of character." An otherwise friendly child might show curious streaks of cruelty, or "the best boy in town" may commit a brutal act that no one can understand (107).

Shaffer and Shoben have explained this seemingly irrational behavior thus: "There is no specific effective adjustment to anxiety. When you are anxious, you are merely stirred up, unhappy, and driven to do something when there is really little to do. Anxiety is therefore primary evidence of a lack of adjustment" (185).

Sex differences in the responses characteristically made to anxiety have been reported. Girls generally react by daydreaming or by developing feelings of inadequacy which are expressed in withdrawal behavior. Boys, on the other hand, find that anxiety is not

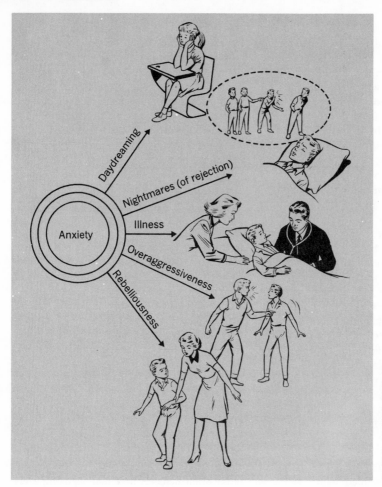

Figure 7–7. Anxiety affects children in different ways. (Adapted from M. E. Breckenridge and E. L. Vincent, *Child development*, 4th ed., Saunders, 1960. Used by permission.)

considered "masculine," and they may try to compensate by being rebellious or by committing acts which have a "nuisance value" (122, 200).

ANGER

Anger is a more frequent emotional response in childhood than fear in its different forms because there are more anger-provoking stimuli in the child's environment and because many children discover at an early age that anger is a good way to get attention or to satisfy their desires. Each year, there is an increase in the number of situations that arouse anger. The result is

that the child displays more angry reactions, of one form or another, with increased age. Fear reactions decrease because the child comes to realize that in most instances there is no real need for fear (104).

There is, nonetheless, a close relationship between fear and anger. Sometimes the child vacillates between the two. At other times, both are aroused simultaneously and by the same stimulus. In a well-protected environment, where a child can be shielded from fears more than from anger-producing stimuli, anger is likely to be more common than fear. This difference may be more apparent than real, however, because there are greater social pressures on the child to conceal fears. Furthermore, the child frequently finds means of avoiding situations that might call forth a display of fear (106).

Variations in Anger. People of all ages vary in "frustration tolerance"—the "level of tension below which the person can think rationally and behave effectively" (185). Some children can withstand anger-provoking stimuli better than others. In a particular child, the ability to withstand such stimuli varies according to the need that is being blocked, the child's physical and emotional condition at the time, and the situation in which the anger-provoking stimuli occur. One child may react with petty annoyance to a situation, while another may react with an angry outburst, and still another with withdrawal, showing intense disappointment and feelings of inadequacy. There are, however, certain predictable variations in children's anger—differences not only in what gives rise to anger but also in the form their responses will take.

The *environment* of the home and of the school plays an important role in determining the intensity and frequency of a child's anger. Among young children, for example, temper tantrums are more frequent when there are guests or when there are more than two adults present (31). The child with siblings has more temper outbursts than the only child. Boys, at every age, experience more anger than girls, though there are variations within each *sex group* (164). The child who is *identified* with a person who is easily aroused to anger will experience more angry outbursts than the child who is identified with a calm person (130).

The type of *discipline* and the *child-training methods* used likewise influence the frequency and intensity of the child's angry outbursts. Children who are punished most tend, on the whole, to experience the most anger. Furthermore, the more the parents try to transform the child's behavior into a pattern they consider socially acceptable, the more angry outbursts the child will have (130, 161). Children from the lower *socio-economic groups,* who are usually subjected to more authoritarian discipline and who have more of their needs and wants thwarted than children of the middle and upper socioeconomic groups, experience more frequent and more intense anger than those of the higher groups (85).

Variations in anger responses are well illustrated in the thwarting of the *child's need* for power and dominance and in his need for affection. When a child wants to make a success of what he is doing and fails to do so; when he wants to be socially accepted and is rejected; or when he craves love and receives less than he wants, he will become angry and resentful. Feelings of hostility are especially strong in children with authoritarian *personalities.* Such children perceive people and things as hostile and react with anger to them as threats to their security (186). Finally, the frequency and intensity of a child's anger vary according to whether he feels "at home" in a situation or is *shy* and *frightened.* For example, young school children who have attended preschool display their anger overtly more than newcomers who, while experiencing anger, tend to control it (164, 189).

Stimuli to Anger. In general, the situations that give rise to angry responses are those involving body restraint; interference with movements the child wishes to make, either caused by others or due to his own inabilities; blocking of activities already in progress; thwarting of wishes, plans, and purposes the child wants to carry out; and a number of cumulative irritations. As Jersild has stated, "The occasions that elicit anger parallel the course of development. A child's susceptibility to anger at any given maturity level is influenced by the *limitations* and by the *urges, strivings,* and *activity tendencies* that are characteristic of that level" (106).

Babies respond with angry outbursts to minor physical discomforts, interference with physical activities, and activities connected with physical care, such as bathing and dressing. The baby's growing independence makes him want to do some of these things for himself. Then, when he is given an opportunity to do more for himself, he often becomes angry at his own ineptitude. If he cannot put a garment on or get food to his mouth with a spoon or fork, he becomes angry. His inability to make himself understood through his babblings or his early attempts at speech likewise irritates him. Then, too, he becomes angry if people do not give him as much attention as he craves or if his possessions are interfered with (104).

Preschool children are angered by many of the same conditions that anger babies. They especially resent interference with their possessions, they object to having to do what they are told to do, and they fight continually with other children who grab their toys or interfere with their play. Their feelings are easily hurt by comments from others or by punishments, and they are angry when the toys or objects they try to handle do not work as they want them to or if they make mistakes in what they are attempting to do (106).

In an older child, thwarting of desires, interruption of activities in progress, constant faultfinding, teasing, "lecturing," or making unfavorable comparisons with other children will lead to anger. The older child likewise becomes angry when he makes mistakes or is inept; when he feels that he or his friends are unjustly reprimanded or punished; or when he is slighted, neglected, or ridiculed by other children. As his interests outside the home increase, there are more sources of annoyance and anger outside the home than in the home (80, 104).

A study of older children showed that the most common social annoyances included being blamed for something they had not done and reports of other people cheating, doing unfair things, or bullying. At home they were annoyed when whipped or scolded, especially for something they had not done. School annoyances included getting low marks, being with teachers who have pets, having the mother come to school, and having certain teachers. Personal-conduct annoyances most frequently re-

ported included cursing, telling lies, biting fingernails, having bad habits, and being accused of lying. The older child frequently sets goals beyond his abilities. When he fails to reach these goals, he becomes angry at himself or tries to find a scapegoat to blame for his failures (217).

Anger Responses. Certain anger responses are typical of different age levels. In babies, these responses are, at first, random and diffuse. The baby cries, screams, kicks, arches his back, struggles, and twists his whole body.

Violent outbursts of anger, or *temper tantrums,* are typical in young children. A temper tantrum may last only a few minutes; rarely does it last more than 5 minutes. While it lasts, it is violent and directed against a person or thing that the child believes was responsible for the thwarting of his desire. The child is more destructive than the baby in his attacks; he does not hesitate to hurt others by any method he can, whether it is hitting, kicking, biting, spitting, punching, poking, or pulling. If he is thwarted in his efforts to reach the person or thing that angered him, he is likely to do anything he has discovered from past experience will earn attention and perhaps remove the obstacle that stood in his way. Little children soon add new responses to the typical temper-tantrum pattern. At the age of four years, language is added to the repertoire of responses; this gradually replaces much of the typical temper-tantrum behavior (106, 206).

Temper tantrums are not a monopoly of children, though they are most common between the ages of two and four years. As may be seen in Figure 7–8, the peak generally comes at three years for both boys and girls. After a peak has been reached, the decline in frequency and intensity is slower for boys than for girls. There are two possible reasons for this: First, boys have greater energy than girls, and consequently they let off "emotional steam" by having temper tantrums more than girls do; and second, the cultural acceptance of aggression is greater for boys than for girls (141).

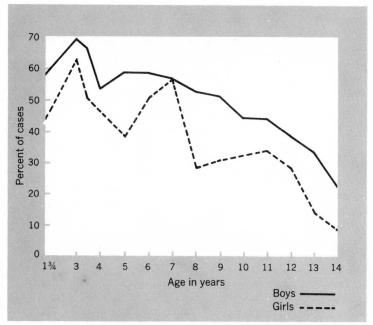

Figure 7–8. Temper tantrums normally decrease with age. (Adapted from J. Macfarlane, L. Allen, and M. P. Honzik, *A developmental study of behavior problems of normal children between twenty-one months and fourteen years,* University of California Press, 1954. Used by permission.)

In all children, one of the outstanding characteristics of tantrums is that they are usually out of all proportion to the stimulus which gave rise to them. As temper tantrums seem to occur among all children at approximately the same ages, however, there is reason to believe that they are a normal phenomenon of growth. Owing partly to social pressure and partly to increased ability to do the things they want to do, combined with an understanding of why they are not permitted to do certain things, children have fewer tantrums and less violent outbursts as they grow older (103, 184).

Older children continue to fight, kick, push, tease, poke, throw stones, and bully, but they gradually substitute other anger responses which meet with less social disapproval. Verbal attacks, in the form of name calling, ridicule, sarcastic comments, swearing, boasting, threats, rudeness, and sauciness, gradually replace bodily attacks. When an older child is angry at a classmate, he excludes him from the group activities and often refuses to speak to him. He may take out his anger on animals, smaller children, children against whom there is some

prejudice, or even his parents and relatives. He may refuse to do things he is expected to do, or he may do them as badly as possible, out of spite. Some children show their anger by displaying hurt feelings, acting sullen, feeling abused, being sorry for themselves, threatening to run away, or even inflicting physical pain on themselves (80, 106).

Variations in Anger Responses. The above description of typical anger responses shows that there are variations in anger responses at every age. The variations increase as children grow older because older children have learned how people react to their anger and have discovered, from past experiences, the *best* way to express their anger and still win minimum social disapproval. In spite of the large range of expressions of anger children use at every age, most expressions fall into two major categories: *impulsive* and *inhibited* (110, 218).

Impulsive Expressions. Impulsive expressions—usually called *aggression*—consist of responses directed outward against a person or object that has angered the child. They may take the form of a physical or a verbal attack, and they occur in varying degrees of intensity. Impulsive expressions of anger are more common than inhibited expressions. They appear earlier, are more annoying to others, and are more socially unacceptable (128, 218). While most impulsive expressions of anger are *extrapunitive,* in that they are directed against others, sometimes they are *intrapunitive,* in the sense that the child directs the anger against himself, blaming himself rather than others for his anger (110, 164).

Inhibited Expressions.   Inhibited responses are kept under control or "bottled up" within the child. The child may withdraw into himself, thus fleeing from the offending person or object. He then becomes apathetic, suggesting that he is indifferent, that he is not disturbed enough to bother about the frustration, or that he is lacking in "guts," for he is willing to "take it lying down." Such a response is labeled *impunitive,* as contrasted with *extrapunitive* and *intrapunitive.* The apathetic child, however, is not so indifferent to anger-provoking situations as he may seem; he may simply feel that resistance is futile, that it is to his best interests to accept the frustration, or that it is better for him to conceal his anger than to express it and run the risk of punishment or social disapproval (110, 218).

Factors Influencing Variations.   It is never possible to predict whether a given child will express his anger impulsively or inhibitedly in a given anger-producing situation. Even though a child may habitually express his anger impulsively, there may be times when he will inhibit the expression. Similarly, a child who characteristically inhibits the expression of his anger at home, for fear of punishment or less parental love, may express it in aggressive forms in the nursery school or on the playground, where his parents are not present (131, 164). If he feels inadequate to cope with the situation alone, he may inhibit his aggressiveness in a play situation when an adult is not present to protect him. When a child is with comparative strangers, he is likely to be on his "good behavior." When he gets to know the peer group better, he may be less inhibited (188).

Characteristically, there are *sex differences* in the form of expression anger takes. Girls, on the whole, learn to express their anger in inhibited forms, such as daydreaming, crying, or criticizing a scapegoat, while boys tend to use impulsive forms, especially rough, violent, or physically harmful attacks on others. When girls express their anger impulsively, they generally make a mental rather than a physical attack; the girl will ridicule, scold, or make trouble for the person who has angered her (182, 183). This sex difference is illustrated in Figure 7–9.

Home *child-training* methods influence the form of expression the child's anger takes. Angry outbursts and aggressive behavior are stronger when adult authority and discipline are absent than when fear of punishment or adult disapproval curbs the child's behavior (164, 218). The very nature of child training creates frustrations which are likely to lead to aggressive behavior: The child becomes angry when he is kept from doing what he wants to do and is forced to do what he does not want to do. This results in a vicious circle. The mother who is attempting to socialize her child instigates—by her very training—the angry behavior she is trying to eliminate (131).

How successful the child is in learning to inhibit the overt expressions of his anger will be greatly influenced by how the parent applies the training method and what *example* of emotional behavior she provides. Impulsive responses in older children are found mostly among those whose parents are inconsistent in their child-training methods, who are immature in their own behavior, and who do not, as a result, give their children either the motivation to control their aggressive responses or a good model to imitate (22).

The severity of the punishment used in child training has a greater influence on the type of angry responses the child makes than the form of punishment. Mild punishment tends to increase the child's aggressiveness; severe punishment reduces it. The child learns to inhibit his angry reactions in order to avoid more severe punishment. Punishment *does not eradicate* the anger but merely drives it underground. Severely punished children usually displace their anger by attacks on others, and their aggressiveness therefore increases. Figure 7–9 shows how aggressiveness is increased in doll play by the severe punishment the child receives at home.

The effect of punishment on the child's expression of anger is also influenced by the strength of the drive that is being thwarted. If the punishment is stronger than the urge to be aggressive, the child will inhibit the expression of his anger, often displacing it by turning his wrath on an innocent victim. Should the punishment be milder than the drive to be aggressive, he will be aggressive, even though he must suffer the penalty for his actions (131).

Parental attitudes toward expressions of anger are important in determining what form the child's anger will take. These attitudes often differ according to the object of the child's aggression. Mothers, for example, are intolerant of attacks on themselves, but they tend to be more tolerant of attacks on siblings and most tolerant of attacks on playmates. The child, as a result, learns under what conditions impulsive expressions of anger will be permitted or even encouraged (184). Knowing that attacks in doll play will not lead to punishment or reproof, the child will not try to inhibit his aggressive behavior toward a doll, even when the mother is present (131). In a family where the mother does most of the disciplining, the child learns that the mother expects him to inhibit his anger responses; as a result, he learns to turn his anger inward. The father, by contrast, may ignore anger responses or even encourage them because they are "manly" (100).

The *status of the child in the family* is an important factor in determining how the child will express his anger. Boys with girl siblings, only children, and "babies" of large families tend to use impulsive forms more than inhibited forms. Children who show

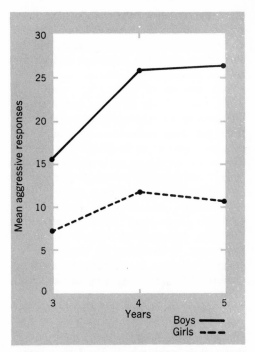

Figure 7–9. **Sex differences in aggressive behavior during the early years of childhood. (Adapted from P. S. Sears, Doll play aggression in normal young children: influence of sex, age, sibling status, father's absence,** *Psychol. Monogr.,* **1951, 65, No. 6. Used by permission.)**

the greatest need for affection, attention, and love—a condition that usually stems from their status in the family group—more often use inhibited expressions of their anger (130).

The child's *personality,* which is greatly influenced by his status in the family, the attitudes of parents and siblings toward him, and the child-training methods used in the family, plays an important role in influencing his characteristic expressions of anger. The child who has been subjected to authoritarian child training, for example, often develops a hostile attitude toward all people in authority. As a result, he frequently displaces his anger by wanting to attack, dominate, or humiliate those he perceives as powerless. He generally finds scapegoats to whom he projects his inhibited anger and derives great satisfaction from hurting them. By contrast, the child who is better adjusted expresses his anger more directly, but he also learns to inhibit expressions which are socially unacceptable (189).

The attitude of the *social group* with which the child is identified has a strong influence on his expression of anger. Boys from the lower socioeconomic groups, for example, learn at an early age that aggressive attacks on others are considered "masculine" and that inhibited anger is regarded as a sign of a coward or a "sissy" (41). Even when children from lower socioeconomic groups learn to inhibit their angry responses, they generally displace their anger by teasing, by bullying, by being cruel to younger children or animals, by resisting authority, or by stealing, lying, or vandalism (184).

Indirectly, the social group influences the child's expressions of anger through the *mass media* produced by the cultural group. While it is popularly believed that mass-communication media that emphasize aggressive behavior—especially comics, movies, and television—tend to make children more aggressive in their reactions to frustrating experiences than they would otherwise be, there is little evidence that *all* children are affected in this way. There is evidence that the effect varies with the child and depends, to a large extent, on whether he is already aggressive. There is evidence, too, that younger children are more influenced by aggression in mass media than older children and that those with lower IQs are influenced more than those with higher IQs (1).

Finally, the form of expression of anger varies with the *age* of the child. As children grow older, they generally discover that impulsive forms are regarded as "babyish"; as a result, they try to inhibit these expressions. Even in the home, they try to inhibit their anger against their parents out of a sense of loyalty and respect. At every age, however, the child's expression of anger varies according to the situation giving rise to the anger, how the child perceives this situation, and what form of expression he has previously found to be satisfactory in coping with anger-producing situations (161).

JEALOUSY

Jealousy is a normal response to actual, supposed, or threatened loss of affection. It is an outgrowth of anger, giving rise to an attitude of resentment directed toward people, while anger may be directed toward people, toward oneself, or toward things. Jealousy may be expressed in an outburst closely resembling a temper tantrum or in behavior which obscures or hides the resentment the individual feels. Often there is some fear combined with anger in the jealousy pattern. The jealous person feels insecure in his relationship with a loved one and is afraid of losing status in that person's affection. What causes jealousy and what form it takes are greatly influenced by training and the treatment the individual receives from others. Whatever its form, it leads to unhappiness. Of even greater seriousness, it often leads to maladjustments of a minor or major degree. Attitudes of jealousy in childhood may affect the individual's attitudes toward people and toward the world, not only in childhood but throughout his entire life (106).

Stimuli to Jealousy. The situation that calls forth jealousy is always a *social* one, involving people, especially those for whom the child has a feeling of affection. In the young child, jealousy involves the parents or other adults who have taken care of him. Because of the child's craving for attention and affection, he often finds himself in competition with another child. In young children, jealousy is a very common emotional experience, originating, generally, with the birth of a sibling when the child is from two to five years old. *This does not necessarily occur.* It is characteristic, however, especially when the older child is the first-born and has been accustomed to having the *full attention* of his parents.

Because the new baby takes much of the time and attention the older child has become accustomed to receiving, the older child feels "neglected." He becomes resentful toward both the mother *and* the new baby. Davis and Havighurst have commented on this as follows:

To the older child, this neglect comes suddenly and stingingly. No longer is he the most important and the most attended. In the normal middle-class family, where mothers devote themselves to infant-care as if it were a ritual, it is almost inevitable that the older child should feel wronged by his mother, and jealous of the baby. . . . To make affairs worse, the mother, of course, can never tell him that she is sorry, never say he has been wronged! But the child, himself, who has been "overloved" and overstimulated by his parents, usually feels deeply that he has been "wronged" (54).

Preparation for the arrival of a new baby —telling the child that he is to have a new brother or sister and that this will give him someone to play with—does not always eliminate jealousy but sometimes intensifies it. The amount of jealousy the child experiences depends mainly on the *type* of preparation he receives. Painting a rosy picture of what it will mean to have a little brother or a little sister as a new playmate is certain to increase the child's jealousy. On the other hand, showing him in a realistic way what having a new baby will mean, by teaching him to play alone and by teaching him how he can help take care of the new baby, will go a long way toward reducing jealousy. Rarely can jealousy be completely eliminated. A young child is too immature and too inexperienced to comprehend all the implications of this event and the inevitable changes it will bring in his life.

Jealousy sometimes occurs as a result of *age differences* of siblings. The younger child resents the privileges given to the older child, while the older child, in turn, resents the affection and attention given to the younger child.

There is also the matter of *parental favoritism*. Without realizing it, many parents show a disproportionate share of interest in children who happen to be especially attractive, affectionate, or gifted (119). Perhaps most parental favoritism, however, is based on sex preferences. Fathers generally claim they want sons, but they are usually more lenient and affectionate in their relationships with their daughters. Mothers generally prefer sons and are more lenient with them. (See pages 47 to 48 for a more complete discussion of this matter.) Children quickly perceive this preferential treatment and resent it (31, 80, 184).

If parents use an older or younger sibling as a model for comparison, in the hope of motivating the child to do better work or to "act his age," they unwittingly increase the child's jealousy by the implication that they prefer the sibling to him. As Jersild has stated, such competitive attitudes on the part of parents "probably contribute more to the development of jealous attitudes in children than the more spontaneous expressions of affection, enthusiasm, admiration, or sympathy which a parent now displays toward one child, now toward another" (107).

Many children show jealousy toward one parent, especially the father. Because of the child's constant association with the mother, he develops a *proprietary attitude* toward her; as a result, he resents her display of affection for the father. When there is friction between parents, the child who resembles one parent in appearance, temperament, or interests may be used as a scapegoat in the hostile struggle between the parents. Because it is impossible for the child to gain satisfaction from his resentment against the parent who rejects him, he is likely to project his resentment to the sibling who is favored by the parent and thus show jealousy toward him (31, 119).

Even when a child begins school and develops interests outside the home, jealousy toward a family member will not necessarily decrease. He may worry about whether the stay-at-home younger sibling is getting the inside track to the mother's affection during his absence. This makes him angry and resentful, especially if he does not like school. He feels that being sent off to school puts him at a disadvantage in his competition with the younger sibling, and he resents being forced to go against his will. This resentment intensifies his jealousy of the sibling whom he regards as the parent's favorite.

Jealousy engendered in this way in the home often carries over to the school and makes the child regard everyone there— teachers as well as classmates—as threats to his security. To safeguard his security, the child then develops a proprietary attitude toward his teacher and the classmates he selects as friends, becoming angry if they show an interest in someone else (107).

While jealousy normally wanes when the child makes good adjustments to school, it will flare up if the teacher compares him unfavorably with classmates or with an older sibling who "was so good in arithmetic when I taught him that I can't understand why you don't do better work." When the child feels that the teacher favors children who are better students than he, he resents those children just as he resents siblings whom he regards as his parents' "pets." In addition, he is often jealous of classmates who excel in athletics, who are more popular than he, or who are selected for a leadership role he craved. Girls are often jealous of the boys in their classes; they feel that the teachers show favoritism toward the boys by permitting them to do things the girls are not permitted to do or by being more lenient when the boys cause disturbances in the classroom or do not do their work (69, 108).

Jealousy may come from *envy*—an emotional state of anger and resentment directed toward another because of the material possessions he has. Envy is a form of covetousness. Most children, even young children, are jealous of persons who have more or bigger material possessions than they. The child whose playmates have toys he does not have wants similar toys and feels abused if he cannot have them. Among siblings, "two of everything" does not necessarily solve the problem. The older child feels that he should have more than the younger by virtue of the fact that he is the older. As the child grows older, he is jealous of children who live in a larger house than his, whose families have more cars than his, who have color television sets when he doesn't, who have more clothes than he has, or who go away on trips oftener and to more "exciting" places than he does (80, 141).

Jealous Responses. Jealousy is charged with tension. It is displayed in responses varying from mild annoyance and anxiety to hostility so intense that the child harms anyone in his way. The child who is jealous will show different forms of behavior at different times and in different situations. His behavior toward the same person will likewise vary from time to time, ranging from attacks to attempts to win favor. Most of his behavior, however, shows an underlying feeling of uncertainty and insecurity; it suggests that he is trying to vindicate or prove himself, even when he has no visible rival. The repertoire of jealous responses used by a child is similar to that of a troubled person who tries out many techniques in the hope of meeting his problem (106).

A study of the reactions of a four-year-old child to the arrival of a sibling revealed the wide variety of adaptive behavior patterns the child used in trying to adjust to this important change in her life. Her reactions included actively seeking attention from the parents, finger sucking, frank verbal aggression toward the baby, and aggression toward the parents (11). In time, most children discover—mainly through trial and error—the response patterns that relieve them of the anxiety engendered by jealousy; they repeat these responses until they develop into a habitual pattern of jealous behavior. Sometimes the jealous responses become an obsession that takes complete possession of the child's thoughts: He is "eaten up with jealousy." At other times, the responses are sporadic and appear only when the child is directly confronted by the conditions that produce jealousy (202).

Among young children, jealous reactions may be direct or indirect. *Direct* reactions are aggressive and include hitting, kicking, biting, pushing, punching, or scratching either the person the child regards as a rival or the person whose attention he craves. Sometimes the attacks are so intense as to constitute a real danger. *Indirect* and more subtle techniques include reversion to infantile forms of behavior, such as bed wetting and thumb sucking; bids for attention in the form of fears never before experienced or food idiosyncrasies; general naughtiness; destructiveness; verbal expressions, such as tattling and name calling; unwonted displays of affection and helpfulness; venting of feelings on toys or animals; and subdued behavior, as in grieving (106, 107).

Because jealousy involves competition for the attention and affection of the loved one, it often motivates a child to try to outdo his rival. In a study of two-child families, it was found that when the child's sibling was a competitor for the mother's affection, the child made a great effort to win the attention and affection of *all* adults (119).

If a young child is anxious to win attention and affection from any adult who is available, it is generally an indication that a strong jealousy has motivated him to try to win back what he feels he has lost to a rival (31). If the child discovers that he is unable to compete with the rival, however, he is likely to withdraw from the competition and seek an indirect way of venting his jealousy. He may feel sorry for himself, fight imaginary battles in which he comes out the victor, displace his hostility by teasing and bullying younger children or animals, or blame a sibling for some imaginary part that sibling has played in causing him to lose the parents' affection (80, 106).

Among older children, jealous responses are more varied and more indirect than among younger children. Some aggressiveness does occur, more often at school and on the playground than at home. Older children, however, concentrate more on teasing and bullying younger children and animals; instigating quarrels; being destructive; being sulky, surly, and disagreeable; assuming a martyr's role and brooding or complaining; daydreaming, especially about being a martyr; swaggering, strutting, and assuming an attitude of nonchalance; conspicuously ignoring others; becoming overcompetitive or undercompetitive in school or in play; tattling; making disparaging comments; lying and cheating; and using "dirty words" or gossiping about others. As Garrison has commented, the jealous child "may become a loud-mouthed show-off or a very 'good' child" (78).

When jealousy springs from envy of what others have, the child becomes rivalrous; he wants to have bigger and better possessions than they. If competition does not lead to success, however, he may be motivated to engage in socially disapproved acts, such as cheating in school or stealing. If his envy is kept in check by moral standards, he is likely to express his jealousy of those whose possessions he envies by verbal reactions. He may complain about his lot or make disparaging comments about his possessions and envious comments about the other person's possessions in the hope that these will be given to him, or he may rationalize his lack of material possessions on the grounds that he has "all the bad luck" while others "get all the breaks." Some children relieve the emotional tension stemming from envy by the "sour-grapes mechanism"—making disparaging comments about the very things they crave; others displace their reactions—blaming the father, as the breadwinner of the family, for their inability to have the things others have (110).

Variations in Jealousy. Children vary greatly in the amount and intensity of the jealousy they experience. Furthermore, each child has his own method of showing jealousy, developed on the basis of what he has discovered through trial and error gives him the greatest satisfaction. Definite *sex differences* in jealousy exist: Two out of three jealous children are girls. There are also *age differences* in jealousy, with two peaks occurring during the childhood years, the first at three years and the second just before puberty, at eleven years. More girls show jealousy at the early age, and more boys at

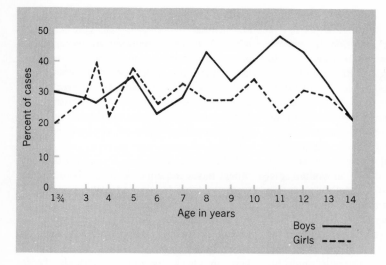

Figure 7–10. Age and sex differences in jealousy in childhood. (Adapted from J. Macfarlane, L. Allen, and M. P. Honzik, *A developmental study of behavior problems of normal children between twenty-one months and fourteen years,* University of California Press, 1954. Used by permission.)

the later age (141). (See Figure 7–10.) Jealousy is associated with *differences in age*. It is most common between children whose ages differ by eighteen to forty-two months. Sixty-seven per cent of children of that age difference show jealousy, as compared with 33 per cent of those whose age differences are greater or less. There is more jealousy in children of the higher *intellectual* levels than of the lower (119).

The *oldest child* in the family is more often jealous than later-born children because the oldest child hates to share the parents' love with younger children. Jealousy occurs more often in girl-girl combinations than in boy-boy or boy-girl combinations. In *small families,* of two or three children, jealousy is a more common experience than in large families or in families where there is an only child (202).

Jealousy is often a product of the home situation, especially of the *attitude of the mother* and the *method of discipline* used. The jealousy of the child is in direct proportion to the strength of the maternal bond. This is because the closer a child is to his mother, the more he has to lose when she turns away from him (31). The less attention the mother pays to her children, the less likely they are to be jealous. Inconsistency in the application of discipline tends to increase jealousy.

CURIOSITY

Interest in the environment is limited during the first two or three months of life unless a strong stimulus is directed toward the baby. Poor eye coordination makes it difficult for the baby to distinguish objects, and the undeveloped state of his hearing makes it impossible for him to hear all sounds. After the baby reaches three months of age, anything *new* or *unusual* which is recognized as such by the baby is certain to arouse his curiosity. New or unusual objects, people, or situations lead to fear in the young child, but as he approaches the object, person, or situation, his fear is often overshadowed by curiosity. For a time, he may alternate between fear and curiosity, first approaching, then withdrawing (148, 193).

Unless the stimulus is more fear-provoking than curiosity-provoking, however, curiosity usually dominates in the end. The child is thus motivated to explore the object, cautiously at first but then in a more daring manner. In describing a curious child, Maw and Maw have said that he

. . . reacts positively to new, strange, incongruous, or mysterious elements in his environment by moving toward them, by exploring them or by manipulating them. He exhibits a need or a desire to know more about himself and/or his environment, he scans his surroundings seeking new experiences, and he persists in examining and exploring stimuli in order to know more about them (148).

Stimuli to Curiosity. The child's curiosity is almost unlimited; he is interested in, and curious about, everything in his environment, including himself. He is curious about his body, why different parts of his body exist, what they do, and why they have the form they have. He wants to know about the inside of his body as well as about the outside—what is in his head, his stomach, his arms, and his legs. He wants to know why his body differs from that of members of the other sex and why children's bodies differ from those of adolescents and adults (153).

He is curious about people: why they dress, act, and speak as they do; why older people differ in looks and behavior from younger people and what their clothes or ornaments are made of, how they feel, and why they wear them. He is as curious about familiar objects such as a cake of soap or a vase of flowers as about those which are used only occasionally or seasonally, such as a mechanical rug shampooer or the storm windows that are put up in the fall. Long before he enters school, his curiosity is aroused by such mechanical devices as electric-light switches, gas burners, vacuum sweepers, radios, television sets, and automobiles (193).

As his environment expands, so does his curiosity. Some of the mysteries of life which have never been explained to his complete satisfaction become a part of his formal education, as do many new things, unheard of during his earlier years. At home or in the immediate neighborhood, his attention is occupied by things he was not permitted to explore when he was younger: how matches and gas burners work; what is stored away in the cellar or attic; where a stream behind his home leads. Many new sources of curiosity open up to him as he learns to read and as his school work brings him in contact with history, geography, and science (26, 148).

Sudden changes usually arouse the curi-

osity of an older child. When mother has a new hair style, father starts to wear glasses, or new draperies appear in the living room, he notices the change at once and is curious to explore it. Changes in his body likewise arouse his curiosity. When a second tooth begins to cut through where the baby tooth has formerly been, he will spend endless time watching its progress in the mirror and will feel it every few hours to see if it is getting bigger. When the puberty changes bring new physical characteristics to his childish body, he will not only watch these changes but examine them closely. In addition, he will ask what they mean; he will compare what is happening to his body with what is happening to the bodies of his friends; and he will compare his body with pictures of adults of his sex to see how his body is developing in relation to the cultural ideal (10, 159).

Responses in Curiosity. In young babies, curiosity is expressed by tensing the face

The child is normally curious, not only about his environment but also about himself. (Standard Oil Co., N.J.)

muscles, opening the mouth, stretching out the tongue, and wrinkling the forehead. At first, a slight startle may accompany curiosity, suggesting that the baby is frightened by new and unfamiliar objects. Soon, however, as he explores the object, the startled expression gives way to pleasure and laughter. By the second half of the first year, bodily expressions of interest occur; the baby stretches his body, leans toward the object, and grasps for it. As soon as he gets hold of the object, he begins a more thorough exploration by handling, pulling, sucking, shaking, and rattling it.

Social pressures—admonitions and punishment—act as a check on the satisfaction of curiosity through direct exploration. Therefore, as soon as the child is old enough to put words together in sentences, he asks *questions* about the things that arouse his curiosity. The "questioning age" begins around the third year and reaches its peak at approximately the sixth year. How important a role questioning plays depends to a large extent upon the satisfaction the child receives from those whom he questions. When the child is old enough to read without giving too much attention to the mechanics of reading, he discovers that he can satisfy much of his curiosity through reading (147, 149).

Variations in Curiosity.   Children vary in the intensity of their curiosity and in the way in which they express it. Each individual child, as well, shows variations at different ages and in different situations. There are *sex differences,* with boys showing greater variability in curiosity than girls. Some boys are more curious than girls, and some are distinctly less curious than girls (148). This difference may be due, in part, to the fact that boys are given more freedom to explore than girls. In some cases, however, this very freedom leads boys into situations that frighten them; their fear may, in turn, serve to dampen their curiosity.

Curiosity varies according to the *personality pattern* of the child and the kind of adjustment he experiences. It is negatively related to psychological maladjustment and positively related to adequate adjustment. The self-bound child, who makes poor personal and social adjustments, is far less curious than the outer-directed child. The latter's curiosity is expressed in a willingness to move out from the family and other secure positions in order to establish contacts with an environment that is new and different (148, 153).

Variations in expression of curiosity are likewise common, especially as children grow older. Many children discover that attempts to satisfy their curiosity can get them into trouble and that the satisfaction they derive from exploring is not worth the price they have to pay. If their curiosity is too strong to be held in check by fear, they may drive the expressions underground, becoming sneaky and exploring when no one is looking. Many a child who fears punishment if he opens a letter or bureau drawer, for example, will wait until the family is out of the house or occupied elsewhere before he ventures to explore. The child whose questions are not answered may likewise redirect his expressions of curiosity. He may turn to adults or peers who are more tolerant of his questions than his parents; he may ask a younger sibling to ask the parents the question for him; or he may satisfy his curiosity by his own efforts, through exploration or reading. Just because a child asks many questions, however, we cannot assume that he is more curious than the child who asks few questions. As Jersild has pointed out, "Children's questions may spring from motives more pressing than intellectual curiosity. There may be fear, worry, or uneasiness" (107). The child who has been frightened by an animal may ask questions about any new or strange thing he sees, wondering if it, like the animal, is an object to be feared.

JOY, PLEASURE, DELIGHT

Joy, which in its milder forms is known as "pleasure," "delight," or "happiness," is a *positive* emotion. It gives satisfaction to the person who experiences it. While joy may arise from situations in the environment, it often comes from the satisfactory expression of drives within the child. When a child wants to build a block tower, is able to do so to his satisfaction, and receives praise from others for his achievement, he is happy.

Unlike fear, jealousy, curiosity, and the other specific emotions discussed above, joy is generalized and undifferentiated. It is, however, readily recognizable because it is accompanied by smiling or laughing and other overt responses. Even in its mildest form, there is an expression of satisfaction on the child's face which tells how he feels about himself and what he is doing.

Individual Differences. There are definite and predictable age trends in the *amount* of joy children experience as well as in the *stimuli* that give rise to joy and elicit smiling and laughing (6). Children whose home, school, and neighborhood environments are pleasant have many more happy experiences than those who must live, work, and play in unpleasant environments. How the child feels physically and emotionally likewise affects his reactions. In a situation that usually calls forth happiness, a child may be glum if he is tired, or supercilious if he is angry (106).

Children who expect to achieve more than they are capable of have less to be happy about than children whose levels of aspiration are realistic. Very bright children, for example, are often less happy than those who are not so bright; more is expected of bright children, and they feel under constant pressure to live up to expectations (155, 204). Children of average ability are likewise often expected to do more than they are capable of, and as a result they have more disappointments than satisfactions.

Children *express* their joy in many ways, ranging from a quiet, calm, and self-satisfied contentment to a bubbling-over exuberance. Boys, on the whole, tend to be more overtly expressive of their happiness than girls, but within both sex groups, there are marked individual differences. There are likewise social-class differences. In the middle and upper socioeconomic groups, the child is expected to maintain control over the expression of *all* emotions, whereas in the lower socioeconomic groups, overt expression of the emotions is not only tolerated but approved.

As children grow older, they learn how to express their joy in the socially approved pattern for the group with which they are identified. Boys, for example, learn that gloating over a person they have defeated is considered poor sportsmanship; they therefore learn not to show their joy, even though inwardly they may be glowing with pleasure (80).

Stimuli to Joy. In spite of what has been said about individual differences in the stimuli that give rise to joy, there is a predictable pattern of these stimuli. Among babies, the pleasant emotions of joy, happiness, and delight come from physical wellbeing. They are also associated with the baby's activities, such as cooing, babbling, creeping, standing up, walking, and running. As Jersild has commented, "Like the healthy puppy who frisks playfully even though no fleas are biting him, the child draws satisfaction from being active on his own accord" (107). His pleasure is greatly increased when the activity is difficult or when an obstacle must be overcome. Babies derive keen enjoyment from being played with, whether it is tickling or simple little games such as "peek-a-boo," clapping hands in unison, or the sudden appearance of the other person from behind a door. A gay approach by another is enough to give rise to a smile or a laugh (154).

The preschool child responds to more stimuli than the baby. His pleasure comes mainly from activities in which others are involved, primarily children, and is particularly strong when his achievements surpass those of other children. He is pleased by new discoveries, especially when obstacles have had to be overcome. He likes to initiate games and take the lead in introducing humorous elements into them. Teasing others, playing pranks, and putting animals or other children in a predicament give him a feeling of superiority which leads to pleasurable emotions. He can see incongruities in real situations as well as in comics, on the television screen, or in the movies. Because he can understand slapstick comedy better than more subtle forms of humor, he enjoys humor of that type best of all (7, 31).

As children grow older, the stimuli that aroused pleasant emotions at the younger ages continue to please them. Physical well-being, incongruous situations, play on words, slight calamities, and sudden or unexpected noises never fail to call forth a smile or a laugh. In addition to these, the older child responds with laughter to situations in which he feels superior, especially those which offer him an opportunity to achieve success. Release from the strain of pent-up emotions, such as anger and fear, and general physical well-being serve to call forth the pleasant emotions. These emotions are, for the most part, more pronounced when the individual is with the group than when he is alone.

The older child derives keen pleasure from mild dangers, especially when he is successful in doing something he has been told not to do. The pleasure comes mainly from the feeling of superiority his success gives him. Similarly, while he enjoys all jokes relating to people in predicaments or to incongruities, he gets special satisfaction from jokes and comics relating to such forbidden subjects as sex and elimination. Practical jokes, especially when older children or adults are the victims, please him because they give him a feeling of superiority. The satisfaction he gets from eating foods that are usually forbidden or from taking a taste of liquor or a puff of a cigarette comes mainly from the feeling of superiority he has when he is not caught in the act (80, 107).

Responses in Joy. The joyful emotions are always accompanied by smiling or laughing and a generally relaxed state of the entire body. This contrasts markedly with the tenseness that occurs in the unpleasant emotions. Not only do little children smile and laugh when they are happy, but they express

their happiness also with their entire bodies. They jump up and down; roll on the floor; crow with glee; clap their hands; hug the person, animal, or object that has given rise to their joy; and laugh so uproariously that they can be heard in all parts of the house. Because of social pressures, the older child controls his expressions of joy in order to avoid being considered infantile; he is less noisy and rambunctious than the younger child. He does, however, laugh in a loud, raucous manner. A boy will slap a friend or anyone nearby on the back or head when he is particularly happy. Girls learn that such behavior is considered sex-inappropriate. They are more likely to throw their arms around a friend and hug and kiss her. Boys slap whoever happens to be nearest when they are happy, but girls transfer their strongest expressions of joy to a pet animal or to an inanimate object, such as a doll or pillow, if no friend is immediately available.

AFFECTION

Affection is an emotional reaction directed toward a person, an animal, or a thing. It indicates warm regard, friendliness, sympathy, or helpfulness, and it may take a physical or a verbal form. A young child's affection for others appears spontaneously and is aroused by a minimum of social stimulation. Learning plays an important role, however, in determining the *particular* persons or objects to which the child's affection becomes attached. The child tends to like most those who like him and are "friendly" in their relationships with him (113, 206). In such a reciprocal relationship —the *empathic complex*—there is an emotional linkage between the child and significant people in his environment (32).

Because affection is conditioned by pleasant experiences with a particular person, the little child learns to have affection for those who take care of his bodily needs, who play with him, and who are responsible for giving him pleasure and satisfaction. The child's affection is concentrated on those who give him an opportunity to express his love for them. Thus his affection for different members of the family as well as for those who have no blood tie with him will depend on the way they treat him, whether his associations with them are pleasurable, and whether they meet his needs. The child's affections develop primarily in relation to people and only secondarily in relation to animals and inanimate objects. Animals and inanimate "love objects" are used as substitutes for a human object of affection (14).

Stimuli to Affection. Studies of babies and young children have revealed that there is a pattern in the types of stimuli that call forth affection. A baby under five months of age expresses affection indiscriminately for all who approach him in a friendly manner. As early as six months, however, he shows affection for a particular person or persons within the family circle (83). During the second half of the first year, he behaves affectionately toward familiar people but with fear toward strangers. During the second year, he includes himself, his toys, and other possessions in his affection. He discriminates little between inanimate and animate stimuli. In fact, the young child's affection for a family pet or even some inanimate object, such as a toy, a blanket, a spoon, or an old sweater, may be as great as his affection for a family member (14, 106).

Around the fourth year, the child's emotional dependence on the family gives way, in part, to emotional dependence on children and adults outside the home. He shows affection for those who recognize him as an individual; who show interest in, or affection for, him; and who make his contacts with them pleasant. These people he regards as his "friends." Even before childhood is over, the child may become romantically attached to a member of the opposite sex in his peer group, though his affection is generally concentrated on members of his own sex. Throughout childhood, affectionate behavior develops along with the child's social contacts. The more people he comes in contact with and the more pleasurable these contacts are, the more people he has affection for (93, 98).

Since the child's affection for others is conditioned by the type of relationships he has with them, his affection for different family members will vary. Most young children have greater affection for their mothers than for their fathers because the mother is a more constant companion to the child and is, as a rule, a less strict disciplinarian (31, 198). To a young child, a father may seem cold and forbidding, even though he is a "good father" by adult standards. As the father does not meet the needs of the young child as completely as the mother, the child is likely to be conditioned toward greater affection for the mother (32). After the child is six, the father usually plays with him less, punishes him more, and gives him fewer gifts than the mother. Children claim that they like best the parent who caters to their material wants, who expresses affection for them, who plays most with them, and who punishes them least (97, 201).

The affection the child has for his siblings depends largely upon the way they treat him. He shows greater affection for siblings who show affection for him and do not ignore, criticize, tease, or bully him. If an older child in a large family "adopts" one of the younger children as his special pet, a strong affection will exist between them. Similarly, two children in a family who are close enough together in age to be companionable and to share common interests will have a strong affection for each other. Girls frequently look up to, admire, and have great affection for an older brother who pays attention to them or treats them in a kindly fashion (31, 119).

Studies of children's reactions to grandparents have revealed that most children have a greater affection for their grandmothers than for their grandfathers. Grandmothers spend more time with the children, do more for them, and show them more affection than grandfathers do. Even though grandfathers may love their grandchildren dearly, they regard child care as "woman's work." As a result, they have few close, personal contacts with their grandchildren (32).

Outside the home, the same principle holds true: The child shows the greatest affection for peers, teachers, or other adults who like him and give evidence of it in their speech and behavior. A lonely child, for example, may develop a strong affectionate attachment for a vigorous, impressive-looking man who shows an interest in him, even though other people may regard the man as a bombastic show-off (32). Similarly, a teacher who shows an interest in the child and a willingness to help him will quickly win the child's affection (80, 108). Within the peer group, the child selects as his friends those who like him and who show affection for him. Because boys tend to regard girls as their inferiors during the latter part of childhood, girls show little affection for boys, and vice versa (93, 206).

Affectionate Responses. Just as the stimulus that gives rise to affection follows a predictable pattern, so does the form of affectionate responses. Affection is first shown in an outgoing, striving, approaching kind of behavior. Babies under five months of age fix their gaze on a person's face, kick, hold out and wave their arms, try to raise their bodies, smile, and turn their trunks. By the sixth month, the baby has enough control over his arm movements to reach the loved one. At this age he begins to respond reciprocally to cuddling by reaching for the loved one's face and by mouth fondling (14, 105).

After the first year, the young child shows his affection for others in much the same uncontrolled manner as he expresses other emotions; he hugs, pats, strokes, and kisses the loved person or object. Kissing is a less frequent expression of affection in young children than hugging or patting, though young children like to be kissed by others. Affectionate responses in sisters include patting, hugging, and kissing; verbal expressions, such as love names and endearing statements; and attempts on the part of older sisters to protect and help the younger ones.

In addition to these responses, young children show their affection by wanting to be with the loved person constantly and by trying to assist him in whatever he is doing. The young child follows much the same pat-

tern of behavior in relation to pets or toys. Favorite toys are hugged and patted until they are literally loved to pieces. A pet animal is hugged and stroked until it is almost choked to death. Typically, the young child takes with him, wherever he goes, the toys for which he has a deep affection; typically, he wants to play constantly with a pet animal (106).

After the child enters school, he is likely to feel that demonstrations of affection are "childish" and to be embarrassed by them. He then shows his affection for members of the family and friends by wanting to be with them and by exchanging confidences with them. As long as his parents show a genuine interest in him, his interests, and his activities, he is satisfied that they love him. He, in turn, shows his affection for them by wanting to be with them, to do things with them, and to come to them with his problems (119).

Spontaneous expressions of affection, however, do occur occasionally even in older children, at home or with their playmates. These generally occur in "bursts" and at unexpected times, as when an older child is happy because he has been given a gift he especially wanted or permission to do something he had not expected to be able to do (80). His affection for his special friends—his "pals"—is not usually shown by physical or verbal demonstrations of affection but by a desire to be with them constantly, by confiding his innermost secrets to them, and by trying to keep in constant touch with them by telephone calls or letters.

Individual Differences. How much affection a child has for others and how he shows it will depend on many factors, but most importantly on how much affection he receives from others and how it is shown. As Garrison has emphasized:

Love seems to be a two-way affair and grows best when it is both given and received. A constant rejection in the home may leave the child's capacity for giving forth affection undeveloped, or may cause him to seek affection from individuals outside the home. Overaffection and indulgence may have as undesirable effects as lack of affection or rejection. . . . There is, therefore, the danger that overaffection for one or both parents will tend to exclude affection for children of the child's own age level (78).

Throughout the child's first year, love for others predominates over love for self. During the second year, however, whether the baby will turn his love outward or toward himself will depend largely upon how he is treated. Should the mother or other familiar person neglect him, or should he interpret her preoccupation with a new baby to mean neglect of him, he will respond by withdrawal behavior and by turning his affection on himself. If he is subjected to this kind of experience frequently, his withdrawn behavior and overconcern with himself may become habitual. Children who show little affection for others generally display such characteristics as devaluation of self, dependency, anxiety, and conflict. These consume the child's energy, make him self-bound, and interfere with emotional exchange with others (4, 14).

At the other extreme are babies and children who are smothered with affection. Parents who are oversolicitous and overdemonstrative do not encourage the child to express his affections; rather, they encourage him to focus his affection on himself (14). Much the same effect comes when he receives affection sporadically. For example, should parents bestow their love on the child when he does the right thing and withhold it when he does something that displeases them, he will develop feelings of guilt and anxiety and a tendency to be self-bound (2, 120). By contrast, children who demonstrate affection for others show little dependency on others and experience little anxiety or conflict. They are able to form close and intimate relationships with others. Because they have received love from others, they want to love others in return (4, 29).

Girls, on the whole, are more affectionate than boys and show their affection more overtly. This is not because boys are more self-bound than girls, but because affectionate behavior is considered sex-inappropriate for boys (206). Children from the lower *socioeconomic groups* have been found to be more affectionate than those from the middle or upper groups. The reason for this has never been fully explained, though it is probably due to the fact that social pressures to control overt expressions of affection are less stringent in the lower groups. Regardless of individual differences, due to sex, socioeconomic status, or early experiences, *all* children tend to be less affectionate as they grow older. While they may experience as deep affection for people as when they were younger, older children extend their affection to more people instead of concentrating it on a few. As a result, they *seem* to be less affectionate than formerly (120).

Just as children want other people to show affection for them in a *developmentally appropriate manner,* so they want to show their affection for others in what they regard as the socially approved pattern for their age. They shun "babyish" and embarrassing overt physical demonstrations of affection, preferring instead verbal responses (206).

Even so, they avoid using words that might be interpreted as sentimental. A boy's closest friends, for example, are "good guys"; family members are "good sports," "good eggs," or "OK." Girls show their affection for others by wanting to be with them, by doing things for and with them, and by expressing a desire to "grow up just like" them. In addition, they seek the attention and approval of those they love, even though they may not verbalize their affection or show it overtly as they did when they were younger (2, 98, 206).

IMPORTANCE OF CHILDREN'S EMOTIONS

From the preceding detailed description of the common emotional patterns of childhood, it is evident that *all emotions play an important role in the child's life.* Anger, for example, can be harnessed into competitiveness and, as such, serve as an important driving force to success. Fear can lead to caution and the avoidance of behavior that might otherwise harm the child physically or psychologically. Even jealousy and envy, generally regarded as "poisonous emotions" because of the way they distort the individual's outlook on life, have their good qualities. They may lead to competitiveness if properly directed; they also help the child to gain social insight and understanding of people and situations which have disturbed him.

The more obvious good effects of the emotions can be seen in the emotions of joy, happiness, affection, and curiosity. The child whose environment in the home, school, or community provides him with opportunities to satisfy his curiosity will be happier, more alert, more interested, and better adjusted than the child in whom this drive has been repressed. Curiosity will encourage him to develop his intellectual capacities; it will encourage him to be creative and inventive; and it will help him to be prepared for the unexpected (27, 147). Becoming accustomed to exploring curiosity-arousing situations soon convinces a child that newness or differentness, per se, holds no cause for fear. By contrast, the child who is discouraged from showing his curiosity learns to be timid in new and unexpected situations or to feel inadequate to meet them successfully.

The emotion of joy provides another example of the good effects of the pleasant emotions. Physically, joy is one of nature's best medicines. The happy person experiences far fewer disturbances to body homeostasis than the unhappy person. Furthermore, because of its relaxing influence on the body, joy helps to dispel the tensions produced by such emotions as anger, fear, or jealousy. Even more important, joy contributes to a favorable self-concept, which, in turn, contributes to good personal and social adjustment. Whatever form it takes, joy is a good emotion because it is good for the child (62, 106).

Since it is known that certain emotions contribute more to successful adjustments to life than others, *emotions that are good for the child should be encouraged in their development.* The good aspects of the emotions that are less favorable should also be developed. Because curiosity is so important to the child's intellectual development, it should be especially encouraged. Similarly, the good effects of fear—a cautious approach to things new and different until it is apparent that they are not harmful—should be encouraged to develop. The development of harmful and less desirable effects, on the other hand, should be discouraged.

A third important implication to be drawn from our knowledge of the common emotional patterns of childhood is that *there should be guidance to help the child develop the forms of emotional expression that can be most valuable to him.* For example, the child can be guided to use his curiosity in creative and intellectual pursuits. Left to chance, curiosity can lead to trouble. Just removing restraints from the expressions of curiosity is a negative approach to the problem. A positive approach consists in introducing the child to situations where there are new and different elements to stimulate his curiosity and then in showing him how to explore in a constructive manner.

Directed anger can also be valuable. The child must learn how to direct his anger into socially acceptable channels rather than having to restrain it and allowing it to become a source of future trouble. In this guidance, training at home and at school must avoid too many and too frequent frustrations of the child's needs and drives. If the child's drives are to be transformed into socially acceptable behavior patterns, some frustrations are essential. They should not be so frequent, however, that the child will develop the habit of regarding everyone in authority as hostile and threatening. When frustrations are necessary, attempts should be made to help the child to understand *why* they are necessary and why it is to his personal advantage to accept them (72, 132).

Every child must learn "frustration tolerance"—the ability to accept frustrations imposed by the social group—because too many or too frequent frustrations result in psychological damage. On the surface, the child may appear to have good emotional control and to be "sensible" about accepting thwartings; under the surface, he may be fighting imaginary battles with the people who have frustrated him—battles in which he emerges the victor. He may develop stereotyped patterns of behavior that seem totally unrelated to anger, such as nail biting, thumb sucking, stuttering, or reading difficulties. These are symptomatic of inhibited anger which could have been prevented had proper guidance been given.

The final important fact about children's emotions is that *any emotion, stimulated often enough, will become a habitual method of adjusting to life.* In addition, the method of expressing the emotion, if repeated often enough, will settle into a habit. Because the stimulation of most emotions comes from the environment, the environment should be controlled to ensure that desirable emotions will be stimulated more often than undesirable. Praising the child for his efforts in the home or the school, combined with constructive guides to improvement, will guarantee more frequent expressions of happiness than of anger. Furthermore, the association of happiness with a specific achievement rarely remains static. It spreads to similar situations and provides a strong source of motivation for the child to put forth effort in a new task in the hope of repeating the happiness that praise brings (108).

Because jealousy can develop into a habit quickly when there is a new baby to usurp the time and attention of the mother, allowing the older child to become part of a team to take care of the new baby will go a long way toward forestalling the jealous habit. Similarly, when discipline requires frustrations, a habit of resenting all in authority or of feeling martyred can be prevented if the child knows why the frustrations are essential and if every frustration is compensated for by experiences that

provide sources of happiness. Praise for good sportsmanship in accepting the frustrations may be such an experience.

HEIGHTENED EMOTIONALITY

Heightened emotionality means increased frequency and intensity of emotional experiences in relation to what is normal. In judging heightened emotionality in a child, one must consider the normal pattern of emotionality for *that particular child.*

Any emotion may be experienced more frequently or more intensely at some times than at others. There are days, for example, when everything seems to "break right"; consequently, the person experiences more happiness and more intense forms of happiness on those days. Heightened emotionality when the happy emotions predominate may be called *euphoria*—a sense of well-being and buoyancy. When the most frequent and intense emotions are unpleasant, whether they are anger, fear, jealousy, or envy, the person is said to be in a *state of disequilibrium;* he feels grumpy, disagreeable, and out of sorts. There are times when there is no heightened emotionality—times when the individual is emotionally calm. These Gesell has described as *states of equilibrium* (80).

All children experience euphoria, equilibrium, and disequilibrium. What proportion of their time will be characterized by each will vary from child to child and, in the same child, from time to time. Many children, unfortunately, experience more disequilibrium than euphoria during periods of heightened emotionality, though no child at any age experiences only one of these states. Refer to pages 29 to 30 for an earlier discussion of states of equilibrium and disequilibrium.

Accompaniments of Heightened Emotionality.
Heightened emotionality is readily recognized by the behavior that characteristically accompanies it. If it stems from one of the unpleasant emotions, it is marked by moods and rages which come and go with

greater or lesser violence, often outside the range of conscious control or even awareness (62). Which form it will take will depend not so much upon the intensity of the emotional state as upon what the child has learned from past experience is socially most acceptable or will bring the least disapproval or punishment.

If heightened emotionality is expressed in moodiness, the child is likely to be grouchy, disagreeable, glum, surly, rude, or "snappy." Should pleasant emotions predominate, he will be so happy and cheerful that he will be "walking on the clouds," singing, offering to help people, saying pleasant things to everyone, slapping or hugging his friends or pet animal, and even skipping and dancing around instead of walking. If curiosity is raised to a high pitch, he will be nervous and edgy, asking innumerable questions and trying to find out what he wants to know in every possible way.

There is always some nervous tension accompanying heightened emotionality. It may be expressed by thumb sucking in young children, nail biting in older children, scratching the head, giggling, or bursting into tears (143, 214). When the emotion is strong, it is likely to lead to temporary stuttering or slurring. The extremely happy child, like the very angry or anxious child, will stumble over his words, repeat syllables, choke in the middle of a word, or speak so rapidly that he runs one word into another. Furthermore, at times of heightened emotionality the child is predisposed to react emotionally more readily and more intensely than he normally does. In cases of strong unpleasant emotions, for example, he is ready to fly off the handle and go into a temper tantrum at the slightest provocation.

Should the emotional state be happy, the child is predisposed to laugh uproariously at a joke which, under other circumstances, he might find "stupid"; he will be overpleased by a gift or a complimentary remark; or he will be more demonstrative in his display of affection than usual. Whatever the stimulus, he will *overreact* to it because he is already in a state of readiness to react. His reactions will tend to be less focused and directed, however, than when he is more calm. When the heightened emotionality is that of anxiety or frustration, for example, the child will "blow his top," letting off emotional steam in an undirected and uncontrolled manner (157).

Causes of Heightened Emotionality. Heightened emotionality may result from physical, psychological, or environmental causes. Frequently more than one cause is operative. Should the child become upset because his work at school has fallen below his expectations, for example, he is likely to become nervous. His nervousness will interfere with his eating and sleeping, and the more hungry and tired he is, the more likely he is to react emotionally to any situation, even those which normally call forth little or no emotional reaction. Thus a vicious circle is set into motion, with both physical and psychological causes, often stemming from environmental causes, making their contributions.

Physical Causes. Whenever *homeostasis* is upset, owing to fatigue, poor health, or developmental changes in the body, the child experiences heightened emotionality. The tired child is predisposed to irritability and angry outbursts. Whether fatigue comes from too little food, too little rest, poor health, or too much excitement, the effect is the same (44). Fatigue is especially serious in younger children, who do not recognize their tiredness and continue to play actively. It has been shown that when nursery-school children are given time out to rest and a drink of fruit juice to supply extra energy and ward off fatigue, they have fewer emotional outbursts (114).

When the child is in *poor health,* owing to malnutrition, digestive disturbances, diseased tonsils and adenoids, decayed teeth, poor eyesight, or colds, he is predisposed to emotionality just as he is when tired. A low energy level resulting from malnutrition, for example, makes a child irritable, depressed, unsocial, and reserved (23). Children who have a history of illness are more emotionally unstable than those whose health is better. An irritating physical condition, such as hives or eczema, causes nervousness and a predisposition to emotional tension. Any chronic disturbance, such as asthma or diabetes, produces more or less constant emotional tension (24, 48). Children suffering from asthma have been reported to show emotional instability in which the ups and downs come with almost incredible swiftness and intensity. Healthy children, by contrast, have fewer emotional swings (59).

Glandular changes, which are especially pronounced at puberty, are generally accompanied by heightened emotionality. As Dunbar has pointed out, "The maintenance of homeostasis . . . is particularly difficult during a period of developmental change. Next to infancy . . . puberty is probably the period of the most rapid psychosomatic change" (62). The more rapid the glandular changes, the greater the tendency toward heightened emotionality. That is why rapid maturers experience more characteristics of the negative phase than slow maturers (see pages 140 to 142). Temporary upsets in endocrine balance before and during the menarche lead to greater nervousness and irritability than will be experienced later, when the menstrual function becomes better regulated (53).

Emotional stress itself causes a temporary upset in the endocrine balance, and this accentuates the child's heightened emotionality. Because of the important role the thyroid glands play in emotionality, a hyperactive condition of these glands predisposes the child to more or less constant emotional tension, with the result that he overreacts to all emotion-provoking situations (145).

Psychological Causes. Among the psychological causes, intelligence and level of aspiration play the most important roles. How a child perceives environmental situations and how he reacts to failure to reach the goals he has set for himself will determine how frequent and how intense his emotions will be. Studies have shown that there is less emotional control, on the average, among children of the lower intellectual levels than among bright children of the same age. Children with greater intellect

have greater emotional scope, however. They are more able to perceive the tragic and comic, to sense and to fear omens of future calamity, to anticipate in their feelings and thoughts the future consummation of their hopes, and to acquire a wider range of interests which may be blocked or fulfilled by their experiences. Even among young children, those who are bright are more sensitive to things that might endanger them than the less bright (33, 132).

While many emotional problems arise because parental expectations are beyond the child's potentialities, some emotional instability is directly traceable to the child's own *level of aspiration.* If a child lacks the abilities and the skills to achieve the goals he has set for himself, he feels inadequate. Repeated failures result in emotional tension —an accompaniment of all feelings of inadequacy. Anything that tends to lower the child's self-confidence, "anything that threatens his self-regard or threatens the role he wishes or pretends to play or threatens to block goals which he regards as important, may increase his tendency to be anxious and afraid" (107).

While the child's aspirations may be of his own making, they are, nevertheless, influenced by what he knows or thinks others expect of him. Because of cultural pressures to achieve success, boys tend to set their levels of aspiration higher than girls. The result is that they experience more threats of failure, with the accompaniment of heightened emotionality (152, 205). Middle-class children experience more heightened emotionality from this cause than lower-class children. A comparison of English and American children has revealed that heightened emotionality from unrealistic levels of aspiration is more common in the latter because American middle-class families are more mobile than the stable, self-satisfied, "backbone-of-the-nation" English middle-class group (156).

Environmental Causes. The environment in which the child grows up plays an important role in his emotional experiences. An environment in which there is constant tension from bickering and quarreling, an overcrowded schedule, and too many exciting experiences for which the child is ill prepared, such as radio and television programs, family entertaining, or trips, tends to stimulate the child's emotions unduly.

How the child is handled by adults, the number of restraints placed on his activities, the type of discipline used to control his behavior, and the ease with which he can get what he wants from others all contribute to his emotionality. Furthermore, the child can develop habits of emotionality from being with others, whether adults or children, who are themselves highly emotional (31). *Parental attitudes* are often responsible for a child's emotionality. Emotional symptoms are most commonly found among children whose parents neglect them, who are away at work for a large part of the day, who are overanxious about their children, who constantly talk about their children's ailments or behavior, who make babies out of them by helping them too much, who "spoil" them by giving way to them too much, or who make them the center of homelife (51). Conflicts between parents and child, arising mainly from the child's desire to conform to his peer culture, tend to increase the child's emotionality. If parents refuse to adjust to the child's changing interpersonal relationships, there will be constant friction and an atmosphere of tension in the home (34).

The *cultural milieu* in which the child finds himself contributes greatly to the frequency and intensity of his emotional experiences. If this milieu is not suited to him and yet he is forced to remain in it, he will feel inadequate. As a result, he will experience many resentments and frustrations which predispose him to heightened emotionality (71). This is well illustrated in the school environment. Authoritarian treatment in school antagonizes pupils and sends them home in a "bad humor." The very bright child, forced to remain in a class with his agemates, feels angry and frustrated in addition to being bored and resentful. Much of the misbehavior of bright children is actually an angry protest against their grade place-

ment. Children who are markedly underage or overage for their grades tend to be emotionally unstable, owing mainly to frustrations resulting from lack of social acceptance by their classmates. In addition to lacking social acceptance, they often become the targets of other children's teasing. Such a situation leads to constant feelings of insecurity and anger (73, 90, 204).

Adjustment to a new situation or experience is likely to be stressful for the child. Adjustment means "loosening up" and "snapping old bonds"; it means learning a new pattern of behavior to replace the habitual pattern (80). How much preparation the child has for the adjustment will influence the degree of emotional tension he will experience. The child who feels unprepared for school, for example, experiences greater emotionality than children whose preparation makes them feel more at home in the school situation. The more difficult the adjustment, the longer and the more severe the emotional tension (43).

The older child, experiencing the physical and psychological changes that accompany puberty, must adjust to his new body, his new interests, and his new attitudes. Because these psychological changes occur at the same time as the developmental changes in his body, his emotionality is intensified (62). This is true also of adjustment to death. The child who is experiencing the developmental changes of puberty reacts with greater emotional intensity to the death of a friend or loved one than the child who is in a period of "equilibrium." Every child, however, will react emotionally to a death which upsets his home and necessitates an adjustment in his life (3).

Critical Periods. Although heightened emotionality may occur at any time, there are certain times when it is almost universal among children and is, consequently, predictable. Because the child becomes more fatigued at certain *times of the day* than at others, these times are accompanied by pronounced emotional disturbances. In babies and young children, emotionality is apt to be at its height during the periods preceding the scheduled times for eating and sleeping. If the child's schedule is upset, he is likely to be fussy and irritable. This holds true for older children also.

Studies of discipline have shown that up to the age of eight years, children need discipline most between twelve and one o'clock and in the late afternoon. Nine-year-olds need discipline most around 8 P.M., just before their usual bedtime. For many children, Monday is "blue Monday" because fatigue, resulting from disruptions to their usual routines over the weekend, makes them cranky and irritable (49).

Genetic studies of children have shown that there are predictable times of "disequilibrium," characterized by tensions, insecurities, and other forms of maladjustive behavior stemming from heightened emotionality. In the preschool period, disequilibrium is common at 2½, 3½, and 5½ years of age. The two- to three-year-old is constantly thwarted in what he wants to do either by restrictions imposed upon him by others or by his own ineptitude. His inability to make others understand him, because of his limited speech, adds to his frustrations. When frustrated, the child flies into a rage and becomes stubborn and negativistic.

While the peak age for temper tantrums is generally three years, such outbursts are common between the ages of two and four years. This is also the peak period for thumb sucking, another indication of heightened emotionality. Just before the child enters school, between his fifth and sixth birthdays, he experiences many outbursts of temper and shows feelings of anxiety, partly because he cannot do what his playmates do—because of either parental restrictions or his own ineptitude—and partly because he is uncertain of social acceptance by his peers (80, 104, 141).

Entry into school necessitates many adjustments, and school rules impose many frustrations. The period of disequilibrium, started before the child enters school, is thus prolonged into the sixth year or even later. With the beginning of formal education, the child "emerges from the family cocoon" and meets many difficult changing demands. This is a time of upheaval in his life, and until he can adjust satisfactorily to the new demands, he is likely to experience serious and prolonged stress (104, 115).

Once adjustment to school has been made, the child normally experiences a period of equilibrium—a "rather benign age" psychologically—before the "storm and stress" of the adolescent years. There are several reasons for this emotional calm: The roles of the older child are well defined, and he knows how to play them; aggressive outlets —games and strenuous play activities—are sanctioned by the cultural group; and complex skills have now been developed, so that the child no longer experiences the ineptitude which formerly gave rise to temper outbursts. As Alexander and Adlerstein have stated, "In short, no great new demands calling for marked change in response patterns are introduced. It is, as life goes, a 'Golden Age' " (3).

With the onset of the physical and psychological changes of puberty, however, there is emotional turmoil. In fact, of all the periods in the developmental span, puberty is the most disturbing. In addition to the upset in body homeostasis that comes with rapid physical changes, there are, at the time of puberty, a particular group of adjustment problems which typically produce anxiety and stress.

Early in puberty, for example, parent-child conflicts reach their peak; these conflicts further exaggerate the physical causes of heightened emotionality. Mood swings are greatest at this time, and the intensity and volume of worry increase (141, 152). Sulkiness and a tendency to burst into tears are especially common at the peak of the growth spurt. Typically, nothing pleases the pubescent child; he is constantly picking on family members—mainly siblings—and engaging in verbal fights. He develops irrational and intense worries about personal and social adequacy, his changing body, his school work, and everything that plays a part in his life. This is such a change from the emotional calm of the preceding years that parents and teachers are likely to criticize the pubescent child for the "way he acts," thus intensifying his belief that "no-body loves me" (73, 80).

Effects of Heightened Emotionality. Because heightened emotionality is far more often characterized by the presence of the unpleasant emotions than of the pleasant, it generally produces a state of disequilibrium. Furthermore, because disequilibrium causes more problems for those who live and work with children than euphoria does, most of the studies of the effects of heightened emotionality have been concentrated on the former rather than on the latter.

The effects of the emotions on the *physical well-being* of the child may be very harmful if they are strong, frequent, or persistent. They can upset the homeostatic balance of the body and prevent it from functioning in its normal way (215). Even among newborn infants and very young babies, emotional disturbances lead to regurgitation and other digestive upsets which interfere with adjustment to postnatal life (102). When body homeostasis is upset by the emotions, all the major functional systems—circulatory, respiratory, reproductive, and glandular—as well as the digestive system may be involved. If the emotional states are prolonged, both the structure and the functioning of the internal organs may be temporarily or permanently impaired (62).

Even mild emotions, resulting in a disturbance of digestion and sleep, can interfere with the maturation of the physical potentials of the child. When emotions are intense and prolonged, the child may suffer from chronic exhaustion, anemia resulting from digestive disturbances, insomnia, headaches, high blood pressure, allergic reactions, skin disturbances, and a host of other physical conditions which are related, either directly or indirectly, to emotional upsets (62). Many of the psychosomatic disorders in childhood discussed earlier (see pages 144 to 145) are caused or aggravated by emotional tension.

When normal body homeostasis is upset by the emotions, the child's *behavior* is less well organized than one would expect. It is more like the behavior of a younger person. His play, for example, is less constructive when he is frustrated because he cannot concentrate on what he is doing. Any activity requiring coordinated movements is likewise affected adversely. Not only does the child work below his capacity, but he makes more mistakes, thus decreasing the quality as well as the quantity of his output. The child's performance is more variable during emotional upset, though the effect of emotions on performance varies according to the skill of the performer. The less skilled he is, the more affected he is by emotions (55, 74).

Emotions also predispose a child to accidents. Children who are accident-prone, as discussed earlier (see pages 155 to 157), tend to suffer excessively from moodiness. If the child has accidents because of emotional disturbances, his self-confidence is undermined, he becomes more tense, and he thus has more accidents. Disturbances in the endocrine balance and in the blood-sugar level, due to emotional tension, often cause mental blocks which lead not only to accidents but also to disturbances of motor coordinations. Speech disorders, especially stuttering, are common in children who suffer from emotional tension. Studies have shown that emotional tension affects skills of athletes. While some may show better skills, most react unfavorably under the influence of emotions (62, 70, 109).

Upsets in body balance are also reflected in decreased *mental efficiency*, especially in the areas of memory, concentration, and reasoning. During a period of emotional tension, the child is unpredictable and unstable. As a result, his performance, particularly when reasoning is involved, is inconsistent. Emotions frequently prove to be a mental block to recall—even of well-learned material. This may be seen in the case of a child who has stage fright when he gets up to recite or to perform in a school play (169).

Emotional tension results in rigidity, which is reflected in a narrowing of the perceptual field and a decreased ability to respond to environmental clues, thus causing the child to act on the basis of minimal information. As a result, he is less capable of improvising in a new problem situation. The child who experiences "free-floating anxiety" may be able to perform his daily routine, but he loses much in his ability to remember and to reason to the level of his full capacity. Anxiety is especially detrimental to mental activities when preparation is impossible, when there is a new learning task, or when the new learning comes at once, giving the child no opportunity to dissipate his anxiety before beginning the new task. As a result, there is an increase in the time needed for learning and in the errors made (75, 165, 179). How anxiety affects the child is illustrated in Figure 7–7, page 282.

Learning of different kinds is affected differently by anxiety. The learning of complicated skills, such as reading and arithmetic, for example, suffers more from the effects of anxiety than does the learning of simpler skills, such as spelling (150). Anxiety is very damaging to learning which involves verbal performance; the detrimental effect increases as the difficulty of the learning task increases (46). In digit-recall tests, anxious children have difficulties in concentrating on what they are trying to learn; this interferes with their ability to recall the digits. When reasoning as well as memory is involved, as in a digit-symbol substitution test, the effects of anxiety on learning are even greater (144). Anxiety affects different learners differently, however, depending on how anxious they already are when the anxiety-provoking situation occurs. Those who are low in anxiety have a motivation to do better, while those high in anxiety are hampered in their learning. This finding suggests that comparable amounts of anxiety can improve or hamper learning, depending on the anxiety-proneness of the learner (168).

The child's *school work* suffers when emotional tension is present. Reading problems, especially, are more common among children predisposed to emotional tension.

High anxiety is shown in a greater need for achievement and more persistent attention to the tasks at hand. As a result, anxious children are strongly motivated to do good work in their classes (180). Furthermore, they tend to blame themselves for failure, and as a result they develop marked feelings of guilt when their school work falls below their expectations (60).

One of the common worries of school children is test failure. Because tests are anxiety-provoking situations, most children do less well on tests than their abilities and knowledge would justify. The more the child feels that he is in a threat situation, the more anxious he becomes, and the poorer the quality of his work. High anxiety may even produce a distortion of the subject matter, causing the child to answer questions incorrectly. It is thus apparent that grades may not be a true indication of the child's mental abilities; they may be merely indications of his anxiety tolerance (144, 151, 180).

The child's emotions affect his *social adjustments,* directly because others judge him by the pattern of his behavior and indirectly because emotions affect his attitudes toward, and behavior with, other people. Frequent and intense emotional outbursts, especially when there is no apparent reason for them, give the impression that the child is "immature," that he is "acting like a baby." On the other hand, if the child tries to control the expression of his emotion by bottling up the energy it gave rise to, the emotion may smolder for hours or days, causing him to be moody and in a bad humor.

Just as people judge a person more favorably when he keeps his emotions under control than when he "blows his top," so would they rather be with a person who is cheerful and happy than with one who is sad, depressed, in a bad humor, constantly talking about his worries, or going around with a chip on his shoulder. It is just as true of children as of adults that "if you laugh, the world will laugh with you; if you weep, you will weep alone." A cheerful expression on a child's face will go a long way toward winning favorable social judgments for him; a scowling, surly, disagreeable expression will lead to unfavorable social judgments, with the accompaniment of social rejection (87, 89).

Indirectly, emotions are important to social adjustments because of the effect they have on the child's attitudes toward other people and the way he treats them. Frequent and intense emotional disturbances result in preoccupation with self and with personal problems and feelings. As a result, the child who experiences too much emotionality becomes self-bound and unable to establish affectional relationships with others. He experiences an "apartness" which has a marked influence on his relationships with others (86).

To be happy and satisfied in his social relationships, not only must the child be loved by others, but he must be able to express his love for them. The child who can do this is more popular and better accepted socially than the child who is self-bound (4, 32). When anxiety leads to feelings of personal inadequacy, the child is susceptible to group persuasion. This is especially true of *socially oriented anxiety,* characterized by shyness, fear of being criticized, and low self-confidence. The stronger the socially oriented anxiety, the more readily the child will be influenced by the group (127, 207).

Because of the close relationship between the social adjustments the child makes and his concept of self, the damaging effects of heightened emotionality on *personality* are very serious. Children who are anxious tend to be dissatisfied with themselves and others. This leads them to use defense mechanisms to cover up their feelings of dissatisfaction or to project the blame on others for causing them to fall below their expectations (168).

Seriousness of Heightened Emotionality. Heightened emotionality is especially serious when it occurs before the child is old enough to have the understanding and insight necessary to cope with the situations that give rise to it. The worry and anxiety caused by

death or divorce in the family, for example, are more intense and more prolonged in young children than in adolescents.

Heightened emotionality may be temporary and limited in its effects if it comes from physical causes alone or from the need to adjust to a new situation, but if it comes from psychological and environmental causes, it may develop into a habit and have persistent and far-reaching effects. For example, a child who becomes nervous, tense, and anxious in his attempts to achieve goals that are beyond his reach is not likely to lower his aspirations to match his capacities. Instead of being encouraged to do so, he is constantly told he must only try harder. Environmental causes of heightened emotionality usually become worse as the child grows older. Parents who believe in strict authoritarian discipline for young children usually become stricter and impose even more frustrations on their adolescent children.

As a result, the child develops a habitual pattern of heightened emotional response. In time, this will become a *generalized* emotional state in which there is a tendency to respond with heightened emotions to any stimulus which resembles the stimuli that gave rise to it. The child who is angry with his parents because of their restrictions on him will develop a "chip-on-the-shoulder" attitude toward all people in authority. Similarly, when daily indications of the parents' preference for one child give rise to jealousy, the child who feels neglected will be predisposed to be jealous of any child or any adult who seems to be more favored than he.

EMOTIONAL CONTROL

In the newborn infant and young baby, emotions are characterized by "wholeheartedness"—a complete lack of gradations of response to stimuli of varying degrees of intensity. When a baby is angry, he is "angry all over" and shows it in random, diffuse, and seemingly meaningless behavior. Because his emotions are expressed in overt acts, he satisfies the drive that gave rise to the emotion, and the emotional state passes quickly and is forgotten. Even a young child often responds to a trivial situation with as intense an emotional reaction as he would have to a more serious situation. He tends to direct the response toward the stimulus which gave rise to it, however, instead of "blowing off emotional steam" in random movements of the whole body.

Adults usually consider the emotional outbursts of the young child unreasonable and unnecessary (33, 106). Although they may be indulgent when he is very young, they disapprove of such reactions when he grows older, and the child soon discovers that unbridled expression of his emotions will not be tolerated.

Outside the home, the child's social acceptance hinges upon his willingness and ability to restrain his emotions. He learns that one does not act out one's feelings, no matter what they may be, though some forms of expression are more acceptable than others (104, 137). He discovers that he is regarded as a "fraidycat" if he shows fears or a "poor sport" if he shows jealousy. He is taught that "overt expressions of hostile feelings are usually kept out of sight by well-mannered people" and that he must learn "to take it" when confronted with frustrations and obstacles (197, 216). Laughter, like other emotional expressions, is regulated by the social group; it is expected to remain under control. Should the child laugh when he is alone, people are likely to wonder whether he is "crazy" (52).

Thus, no sooner has the child learned to express his emotions in a manner that will be comprehended by others, than he discovers that he is expected to inhibit their expression. Long before childhood ends, the child knows that if his emotional expressions do not take a socially approved form, he will be regarded as "babyish" and that this will militate against his social acceptance. Therefore, should he explode when he is tired or has reached his limit of control, he will be ashamed of his "childishness" and will worry about the effect his outburst will have on the judgments of others.

Learning Emotional Control. The attitudes of significant people in the child's life provide the necessary *motivation* for him to develop emotional control. It is then up to him to put forth the effort needed to do so. Through trial and error, for example, the young child discovers which forms of hostile expression will be tolerated by others and which will lead to punishment or social disapproval. Those which give him the greatest satisfaction will be repeated and will eventually become habitual. Also, in threat situations, the form of expression that gives the child the greatest satisfaction, whether it is a defensive or an aggressive form, will become his habitual manner of responding to threats (56, 112, 186).

Imitation plays an important role in determining how the child will react to emotion-provoking situations. If his age-mates fight when they are angry, he will do so too, knowing that he will have their approval, if not the approval of adults. Similarly, if his friends are worried about their school work, he will feel free to verbalize his worries on the grounds that "everyone" feels the same way (9).

Direct teaching of which emotions to express, of how to express them, and of how much emotional expression will be tolerated is part of the training the child receives at home and, later, at school. If this training is to be effective, however, it must be specific, not general. It has been found, for example, that when parents train their children to respond to general stress situations, such training has no significant effect on the child's reaction to a specific situation, such as going to the hospital to have tonsils removed. When children are trained specifically how to respond to hospitalization, however, they experience less fear and are more comfortable in their hospital experience (134).

Variations in Emotional Expression. There is no universally approved method of expressing the emotions and no universally approved standard of control. Different *cultural groups* have different values regarding the expression of emotions. The American Indian, for example, seems unemotional in comparison with a Frenchman because the former is trained not to express his emotions, while the latter not only is encouraged to do so but is trained in appropriate methods of expression. Sinhalese children overcontrol their emotions and fail to show even affective responses because that is the culturally approved pattern for them (199).

Within a cultural group, there are likewise marked individual differences in attitudes toward emotional expression. Some people consider *all* expression of emotion bad, immature, or in poor taste; others are more tolerant and regard emotional expression as justified under certain conditions. Mothers who are intolerant of aggressive behavior directed toward themselves, for example, may be tolerant of fighting among siblings and more tolerant still when their children fight their playmates (112, 184).

The *religious background* of the family will have a marked influence on the amount of control the child exerts over his emotions. If he has been taught to "turn his cheek" when someone fights him, he will avoid expressing his anger or will feel guilty if he does. Another child, with a different kind of training, may allow himself free expression of anger when someone attacks him and will have no feeling of guilt about it (20). The *sex* of the child also influences social expectation regarding emotional expression. Boys are expected to control expressions of fear, anxiety, and disappointment because these emotions are regarded as signs of a "sissy," but they are expected to fight when others show aggression toward them. Girls, by contrast, are expected to control the expression of *all* emotions (180, 200).

The various *socioeconomic* classes have definite ideas about the proper expression of emotions. Members of the lower social classes encourage boys to be aggressive because they believe it is a sign of "manliness." Girls, on the other hand, are expected to be nonaggressive. Both boys and girls of the middle class are taught to inhibit all expressions of aggression (129, 137). *Rural* children, as a result of stricter child training, restrain their expressions of anger more than urban children do. *Dependent* children control their aggressiveness because they fear loss of parental approval if they are aggressive (112). The better *prepared* the child is for a stress situation, the better he can control his emotional reactions to it (66).

Effects of Emotional Control. All emotional states are accompanied by preparation for action, brought about by physical and glandular changes. Controlling the action that normally would occur means that the energy that has been aroused must either be kept bottled up within the child or be channeled into other forms of activity. Furthermore, the chances are that the mental state that accompanies the emotion will persist, even though the overt expression is inhibited.

Release of the physical and mental preparation for action generated whenever an emotion is aroused can be achieved in a number of ways. The child's usual way of responding will depend largely on what he has discovered gives him the greatest satisfaction, wins social approval, or avoids the disapproval of significant people in his life. Of the many ways children release pent-up energy, the following are the most common:

1. Moodiness.   An emotionally aroused child may bottle up the emotional energy and let it smolder for hours or days. This results in moodiness—a drawn-out state of the emotions. Because the unpleasant emotions are the ones most likely to be controlled, the child will be gloomy, morbid, sullen, and reticent; he will be in a bad humor. In general, he will be listless and will work far below his capacity; his interest in people and things will wane, and he will be preoccupied with himself and his feelings (106, 211). Should a pleasant emotion, such as joy, be controlled, his mood will be pleasant; he will glow with an inner satisfaction and will be eager and enthusiastic about whatever he does. In all moodiness, there

is a tendency to *overreact*—to react to a stimulus with greater intensity than the stimulus justifies. (See pages 273 to 274 for an earlier discussion of moods.)

2. Substitute Responses.

Emotional energy can be released by substituting a response that is more socially acceptable than the response normally associated with the emotion. When angry, for example, the child may substitute name calling for hitting or kicking if he finds that the former brings less social disapproval or less threat of punishment, or he may learn to express his anger in a constructive manner by doing something useful or socially approved. For example, he may play vigorously, fight for his team within the rules of the game, or do something creative, such as pounding nails into wood when he is making a table or pressing down hard on his crayon when he is drawing. Syphoning repressed emotions off into socially acceptable patterns of behavior is known as *sublimation*.

3. Displacement.

In displacement, the individual expresses his emotion by directing his response toward a person, object, or situation unrelated to the origin of the emotion. Happiness, for example, may come from successful achievement. The happy child can express his happiness directly by "crowing over his successes," but if he discovers that this is socially unacceptable, he may displace his happiness by showering praise or gifts or other forms of attention on his classmates or even on people he barely knows. An outburst of generosity may be merely displaced happiness on the part of the giver.

Most commonly, displacement occurs when angry reactions are controlled. Instead of hitting and kicking, the angry child will "take it out" on an innocent victim by a verbal or physical attack (94, 218). The child who teases or bullies children smaller and younger than he, who torments animals, who blames his parents or siblings when things go wrong at school, or who picks on members of minority groups is making them scapegoats for his inhibited anger (85, 131).

Studies of young children's behavior in doll play have revealed that when children are angry, they displace their anger by "taking it out" on the dolls who represent the parents or siblings who have made them angry. The more frustrations the child has experienced from a certain family member, the more aggressive his reactions will be toward the doll that represents that person (25, 67, 129).

Older children suffering from frustrations caused by overprotective or dominating parents may hold back their negative feelings toward the parents because of fear or a sense of loyalty. Instead of attacking the parents directly, they may displace their bottled-up anger by being hypercritical of others; by being hostile toward all adults in authority, especially teachers and law-enforcement officers; by engaging in hostile fantasies in which they fight against the parents; or by seeking the "protective coloration" of the peer group in attacking, either physically or verbally, some innocent victim (128, 161).

4. Regression.

Another common way of dealing with controlled emotions is to express them indirectly in behavior which apparently has little or no relationship to the emotion that gives rise to it. The most common indirect form of expression of thwarted emotions is *regression*—going back to earlier forms of behavior which satisfy the child's needs (128). The jealous child, for example, may revert to infantile behavior—wetting his bed or claiming that he needs help in dressing or feeding. He may bid for attention by pretending to be ill or by developing fears for objects which he never before feared (125, 141).

5. Emotional Explosions.

When the child tries to inhibit the expression of an emotion too long or when the emotion is too strong to be inhibited more than momentarily, the child may *explode emotionally*, reacting violently to a seemingly trivial stimulus. When angry, for example, he will have a temper tantrum reminiscent of a three- or four-year-old. Because he is expected to

develop frustration tolerance as he grows older, giving way to the emotions in an explosive manner leads to strong feelings of guilt and inadequacy (211). Figure 7–11 shows three of the common ways in which children react to anger-provoking situations: by rebelling openly, by repressing the angry response (momentarily at least), and by constructive work which releases emotional tension in a socially acceptable manner.

Significant Facts about Emotional Control. From what has been said about emotional control, it is possible to draw several important conclusions:

1. There is no one best way to express a controlled emotion. The form used will depend on what meets the needs of the child best. Unless it is adequate to use up all the energy generated by the emotion, however, there will be unfavorable aftereffects on the child's physical and mental well-being. Even the most favorable indirect expression of anger, for example, such as some form of constructive activity, will not be adequate unless the system is cleared of the energy produced by the anger.

An emotional explosion, on the other hand, clears the system but fails to win the approval of the group; as a result, it does

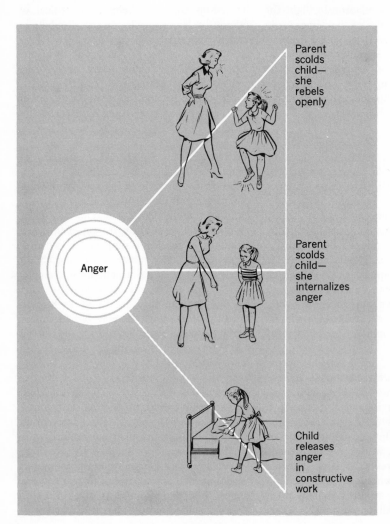

Anger

Parent scolds child— she rebels openly

Parent scolds child— she internalizes anger

Child releases anger in constructive work

Figure 7–11. Three common ways of reacting to anger. (Adapted from M. E. Breckenridge and E. L. Vincent, *Child development,* 4th ed., Saunders, 1960. Used by permission.)

not give satisfaction to the child. Studies of young children have shown that those who most openly revealed their fears at the beginning of kindergarten made better adjustments to school, as time went on, than those who controlled their fears and were outwardly calm (120). As long as the child can avoid winning an unfavorable reputation and developing feelings of guilt, he will be better off in the long run if he expresses his emotions and clears his system of emotional energy.

2. The mental aspects of an emotion must be given as much attention and consideration as the physical. Expressing the emotional response in a socially acceptable form is not enough. The mental aspect of the emotion needs guidance too, lest it keep the emotional state alive and predispose the child to react emotionally to later stimuli which, of their own accord, would be incapable of arousing emotional responses. Just finding a socially acceptable way to react to anger does not guarantee that the child will stop being angry. In fact, the more he thinks about the cause of the anger, the angrier he is likely to become, and the more convinced he will be that his anger is justified. When the anger-evoking situation is repeated, the child will be emotionally more disturbed than previously.

It should be obvious, therefore, that the child must learn how to handle the stimuli that give rise to his emotions as well as the responses that normally accompany the emotions. The child must be capable of assessing the stimulus and deciding whether an emotional reaction is justified or not. If he responds emotionally *before* doing this, he should be helped to assess the situation after the emotional outburst. In the case of anger, for example, a child may "fly off the handle" in a temper outburst, or he may drive the emotional energy underground and become moody. If he is to be prepared to control his emotions in the future, he must learn to assess the situation that led up to the anger and decide whether he could solve his problem better by some other method and whether he should feel guilty and ashamed if he allows himself to become

angry. If he fails to do this, no amount of willpower on his part will be adequate to control temper outbursts to his satisfaction.

3. Once a pattern of emotional expression has been thoroughly learned, it is difficult to eliminate or control it. Conditioned responses do not extinguish themselves. They require an experimental process of extinction, even if the circumstances under which the learning took place have been forgotten. This has been found to be true in the case of fears in which the child is conscious of only certain aspects of the experiences that have conditioned him to react with fear in a new situation. Once the fear response is well learned, getting rid of it or modifying it into a more socially approved form is exceedingly difficult (133).

Of the many techniques used in trying to eliminate fears, those which have produced the best results include giving the child an opportunity to become acquainted with the feared stimulus of his own accord; leading him gradually into contact with the thing he fears; encouraging him to acquire skills that will be of specific aid in dealing with the feared situation; building up pleasant associations with the feared object; verbal explanations and reassurance, combined with a practical demonstration of the harmlessness of the feared object; social imitation in which the child is given an adult model of fearlessness; and an opportunity for self-expression which will lead to self-scrutiny and personal reorientation, thus resulting in a changed concept of self (106, 154).

In summary, it is evident that the only effective way to control the expressions of emotions is to learn to control the mental states accompanying them *in addition* to learning to control the characteristic responses associated with those emotions. This means that if the child is to develop frustration tolerance, he must learn to assess the situation that has blocked a drive and must understand why he could not do what he wanted to do. Similarly, if he is to avoid becoming an anxious person, he must learn to examine critically the objects or situations that give rise to fear and not to let his

imagination run wild (139). When, in addition, he learns to control his impulses to act
out his feelings, he will achieve *emotional
maturity*. As Kirkpatrick has pointed out,
"The achievement of such control is the
hallmark of adult behavior" (116).

EMOTIONAL CATHARSIS

A child cannot be expected to achieve maturity in emotional behavior any more than
he can be expected to achieve maturity in
other areas of development. If he shows
progress toward the goal of maturity, that is
all one can hope for. If a child bottles up his
emotions in order to conform to adult demands, he may *seem* to be growing up, but
how he controls his emotions is far more
important than the fact that he merely controls them.

Unless the *physical* energy released in
preparation for action is used up in activity,
it can upset body homeostasis. In the same
way, unless the *mental* states that accompany the emotions are handled properly,
they can lead to such unfavorable attitudes
that the child will make poor personal and
social adjustments. When the body is in a
stirred-up state, ready to be triggered into
action at any moment, the mentally stirred-
up state—whether it takes the form of anxiety, jealousy, or hostility—is likely to prolong the physical state; it, in turn, will
prolong the mental state. As a result, there
is a circular cause-and-effect relationship
which is likely to continue until something is
done to end it. The needs that have been
thwarted must be met either directly or indirectly. If the child cannot use up the
energy in direct expressions of the emotion,
he must get rid of it in an indirect way.
Clearing the body of pent-up energy is
known as *emotional catharsis*.

Common Forms of Emotional Catharsis.
The need to clear the system of pent-up
emotional energy has been recognized as far
back as the time of Hippocrates, in ancient
Greece, during the fourth century B.C.

People use many different forms of emotional catharsis, the most common of which
are strenuous physical exercise, laughing,
and crying. These activities drain off the
pent-up energy and restore the homeostatic
state of the body which was disrupted when
the emotion was aroused.

Strenuous play activities, such as hammer-
ing, pounding nails, smearing finger paints,
running, jumping, climbing, skating, and
swimming, help the child to let off pent-up
emotional steam. In competitive sports, the
child has an opportunity to focus his emotional energy on his play in the hope of
defeating the competing team. Doll-play
therapy has proved to be a good catharsis
for young children because it permits them
to express their aggressions against a family
member, represented by a doll, who has
been responsible for their frustrations and
consequent hostilities (94, 182, 212).

A good *cry* will, likewise, go a long way
toward using up dammed-up emotional energy. The child soon discovers, however,
that only if he can cry in private will he get
the satisfaction of emotional release without
the accompaniment of social disapproval.
Much the same problem arises when the
child uses *laughter* as an emotional release.
Only if he laughs when others laugh, at a
joke or at a comic scene in the movies or
on the television screen, can he laugh loudly
enough to get the emotional catharsis he
needs without incurring social disapproval
(52).

Essentials of Emotional Catharsis. Just
letting off emotional steam may clear the
system of pent-up physical energy temporarily, but it will not necessarily change the
child's point of view or remove the source
of emotional distress. A parallel may be
found in the treatment of digestive disorders. When the body is being poisoned by
failure to get rid of waste products, a laxa-
tive will purge the body of the accumulated
waste, and the individual will then feel
better temporarily. Unless he gets at the
cause of the trouble, however, he will soon
experience accumulated waste products

again and will be forced to resort to the use of laxatives again.

So it is with an emotional catharsis. The child will feel better after getting rid of his pent-up energy, but the stress will return unless he does something to change his point of view and develop more favorable attitudes. The fundamental principle of psychotherapy gives a clue as to how this can be done. By bringing to the surface the repressed causes of emotional disturbance, by analyzing them, by subjecting them to reality testing to see how justified they are, and then by finding satisfactory ways to give expression to the drives which have been thwarted, the child will change his attitudes and develop a more wholesome point of view.

In babies, this is usually not necessary. Because the baby's memory is short and his attention span brief, he is easily distracted from what upsets him and quickly forgets it (133). The young child, however, begins to associate certain people and certain situations with frustrations and develops an unfavorable attitude toward them. If, for example, the father is a strict disciplinarian, the child begins to fear and resent him, turning his affection toward his mother.

With the rapid development of imagination comes a tendency to exaggerate the causes of emotional reactions and to react more violently to them than the stimuli justify. It becomes necessary, therefore, to use release therapy for unfavorable attitudes as well as for pent-up energy: The child must clear his mind of *hostilities* and *anxieties,* just as he must clear his body of pent-up energy if he is to handle his emotions in such a way as to do minimum damage to his physical and mental well-being. As Worchel has pointed out, how effective "blowing off emotional steam" will prove to be will depend on whether it reduces threat to need-satisfaction patterns (212).

Because young children often have difficulties in recognizing and communicating to others their feelings about people and situations, doll-play therapy is a valuable means of discovering the source of their frustrations and the cause of their anger. Knowing the cause of the emotional trouble will give one a clue as to how to cope with it (182).

As children grow older, not only do they know what makes them angry, frightened, jealous, or envious, but they often *verbalize* their feelings through name calling, ridiculing, and making disparaging or sympathy-provoking comments. This gives a clue to the source of emotional trouble and shows how the emotions have affected the child's attitudes toward himself and others. The jealous child, for example, who complains that "Mommie likes Junior better than she likes me," is verbalizing an attitude that must be corrected if the jealousy is not to flare up again in a new situation that likewise will be interpreted as parental favoritism.

Merely verbalizing attitudes that accompany emotional states is not enough to purge the mind of these emotions. If the catharsis is to be successful, verbalization must lead to *insight* on the child's part (67, 138). If the child shows his hostility toward another through what he says, he may feel better because he has gotten the trouble off his chest, temporarily at least. Unless verbalization enables him to change his attitude toward the person for whom he has a hostile feeling, however, the hostility will return when the person does or says something in the future to annoy him. If, for example, a child feels frustrated by family rules and feels that his parents do not like him as much as they like an older sibling who is given more privileges than he, he will get rid of the hostility toward his parents *only* when he can understand and accept their reasons for the rules and realize that the privileges will be his too when he is older. If he merely expresses his annoyances in gripes, he will not gain insight. Even worse, the more he talks about how "mean" his parents are, the more convinced he will be that they are "mean." This will intensify rather than reduce his hostility.

Talking things over with others, especially those with more mature judgment, is the best form of catharsis for the mental aspects of controlled emotions. Expressing his thoughts and feelings in words helps the child to get rid of emotional steam, but, more importantly, it enables him to look at them objectively and see them through the eyes of another person.

When he talks about his gripes to his parents, his teachers, or his friends, he will get their point of view; this will give him a better insight into his own problem. Similarly, the mere expression of anxiety about anticipated failure may not eliminate the underlying threat unless through this expression the child receives reassurance that he is not likely to experience failure (212). By discussing his gripes with his friends, the child often learns that they have similar gripes. This knowledge helps him to get a better perspective on his own problem.

Sources of Emotional Catharsis.   Most children who learn to control their emotions need an emotional catharsis to help them satisfy their needs (15). Through play, through laughing and crying, and through chores that require physical activity, they can find a source of catharsis for their pent-up *physical* energy.

Some children, however, are deprived of even these sources. An unpopular child may have no one to play with. He then spends his playtime reading, daydreaming, or watching television. A child with a physical handicap or overprotective parents will likewise be cut off from a ready source of catharsis. True, he could use laughing and crying as means of clearing his system of pent-up energy, but children who lack playmates find little to laugh about, and although they may want to cry, they refrain from doing so because they know it will only add to their lack of social acceptance.

Sources of catharsis for the unwholesome *mental* states that develop when negative emotions are controlled are also difficult to find. The child who can talk over his problems with a parent, teacher, or intimate friend, realizing that this person will react sympathetically and help him to solve his problems, has a ready source of mental

catharsis for his unfavorable attitudes. Some children, however, do not have intimate friends in whom they feel free to confide, and some children have such an authoritarian home or school environment that they are afraid to communicate their problems to parents or teachers.

As childhood draws to a close, child-parent relationships often deteriorate because the child's association with the peer group gives rise to friction with his parents. As a result, the channels of communication between child and parent are cut off, and the child is deprived of this source of emotional catharsis (62). Even though he may belong to a peer group and have a number of playmates, he may not have a close enough personal relationship with any one member of the group to want to turn to that child for help. Similarly, in the school he may hesitate to discuss his problems with a teacher because he is afraid that his classmates will accuse him of trying to win the teacher's favor or because he senses that the teacher does not like him or have enough interest in him to make her a good person to confide in.

Whether the child will be willing to confide in a parent, a teacher, or an agemate will be influenced by how he feels about that person and how he thinks that person feels about him. It has been found that there is a close relationship between how much a person is willing to confide in another and the affection he has for that person: The greater the affection, the more he will disclose (110).

How important it is for a person to be able to discuss his problems with others and get their points of view has been further shown in a study of college students, some of whom lived at home and some of whom lived in the college residence halls. The students who lived at home suffered more psychological breakdowns and experienced greater anxiety than those who lived in the residence halls and were able to drain off their anxieties by talking to their pals. Those who lived at home were deprived of this source of close personal contact. Many of them felt that their parents either would not understand their problems or would put pressure on them for greater achievement because of the sacrifices they had made to send them to college (61).

"Mental-health Insurance." Even though a child's environment is such that he experiences few demands to control his emotions, it is essential that he learn to do so with minimum physical and psychological harm. Sooner or later, a time will come when emotional control will be essential; the better prepared he is to deal with the potentially harmful effects of this control, the better off he will be. This may be regarded as "mental-health insurance." Like all insurance, it may not be needed, but if it *is* needed, the child who has it has a safeguard against possible mental illness.

In this "mental-health insurance," the following items should appear. All are not essential for every child, but since no child knows what the future holds in store for him, the wider the coverage, the better protected the child will be for any eventuality.

1. Some strenuous physical exercise daily. This may be had in either play or work, and it may have to come late in the day, after school.

2. An understanding of how strenuous physical exercise clears his system of excess energy and makes him feel better both physically and emotionally so that he will assume the responsibility for using this emotional catharsis himself.

3. The development of a sense of humor so that he can laugh even when he himself is involved. If he never needs to use this as a cathartic, it will not be wasted. It is a trait that contributes greatly to social acceptance.

4. An understanding that crying is not always a sign of being a baby. There are times and places when it can be used to clear the body of pent-up emotions. A good cry can be good for a child if he knows when and where to use it.

5. A close, affectional relationship with at least one family member, preferably a parent whose mature perspective can help him to develop a perspective on his own problems.

If the social distance between parent and child is too great a gap to close, then an older sibling, a grandparent, or some other relative who is *readily accessible* should be substituted.

6. An intimate friend in whom he can confide his troubles and to whom he can verbalize complaints he would hesitate to verbalize to an older person. One or two intimate friends are more valuable, from a mental-health point of view, than a large number of playmates, none of whom are close enough to the child emotionally for him to want to confide in them.

7. A willingness on the child's part to talk about his problems to a person he feels will be sympathetic. Far too many parents, grandparents, and teachers unwittingly build up a barrier between the child and themselves by refusing to answer his questions, by criticizing him for "tattling" when he is merely explaining what happened, or by showing a lack of interest in what he says. Unless discouraged from doing so, children will talk freely about everything, *including* their problems. When they are discouraged by a critical or uninterested attitude on the part of an important person in their lives, they develop a general reluctance to talk to anyone, keeping their problems as well as their interests and joys to themselves.

8. A respect on the part of others for a child's reasons for his emotions so that he will be willing to discuss them. When a child is afraid, for example, he has a reason for being afraid, even though this reason may seem completely unjustified to an adult. Similarly, a child does not become angry unless he feels that he has a reason to be angry. He may have misinterpreted what was said to him or failed to understand why he was not permitted to do something he wanted to do, but to him, his anger was justified. Laughing at a child; scolding or criticizing him; calling him by a derogatory name, such as "fraidycat"; or accusing him of being disrespectful will only intensify his emotion and drive it further underground. He should be encouraged to tell why he is frightened, angry, worried, jealous, or even happy and then be helped to understand why his emotion is unjustified or is a poor way of meeting the situation.

In conclusion, all the suggestions just given may be regarded as ways of encouraging the child to learn to use emotional catharsis at an early age, before he develops the habit of controlling his emotions in ways that will win social approval but take a heavy toll in terms of physical and mental health. The child who learns to use emotional catharsis early and well will be able to gain satisfaction both from his emotions and from the approval of the social group at minimum expense to his well-being.

BIBLIOGRAPHY

(1) ALBERT, R. S.: The role of mass media and the effect of aggressive film content upon children's aggressive responses and identification choices. *Genet. Psychol. Monogr.,* 1957, **55,** 221–285.

(2) ALDOUS, J., and L. KELL: Child-rearing values of mothers in relation to their children's perceptions of their mothers' control: an exploratory study. *Marriage fam. Liv.,* 1956, **18,** 72–74.

(3) ALEXANDER, I. E., and A. M. ADLERSTEIN: Affective responses to the concept of death in a population of children and early adolescents. *J. genet. Psychol.,* 1958, **93,** 167–177.

(4) ALEXANDER, T.: Certain characteristics of the self as related to affection. *Child Develpm.,* 1951, **22,** 285–290.

(5) ALLINSMITH, W.: Conscience and conflict: the moral force in personality. *Child Develpm.,* 1957, **28,** 469–476.

(6) AMES, L. B.: Development of interpersonal smiling responses in the preschool years. *J. genet. Psychol.,* 1949, **74,** 273–291.

(7) AMES, L. B.: The sense of self of nursery school children as manifested by their verbal behavior. *J. genet. Psychol.,* 1952, **81,** 193–232.

(8) AMMONS, C. H., and R. B. AMMONS: Aggression in doll-play: interviews of two- to six-year-old white males. *J. genet. Psychol.,* 1953, **82,** 205–213.

(9) ANGELINO, H., J. DOLLINS, and E. V. MECH: Trends in the "fears and worries" of school children as related to socioeconomic status and age. *J. genet. Psychol.,* 1956, **89,** 263–276.

(10) ANGELINO, H., and E. V. MECH: "Fears and worries" concerning physical changes: a preliminary survey of 32 females. *J. Psychol.,* 1955, **39,** 195–198.

(11) ANONYMOUS: Ambivalence in first reactions to a sibling. *J. abnorm. soc. Psychol.,* 1949, **44,** 541–548.

(12) AUSUBEL, D. P.: Relationships between shame and guilt in the socialization process. *Psychol. Rev.,* 1955, **62,** 378–399.

(13) BAKWIN, H.: Emotional deprivation in infants. *J. Pediat.,* 1949, **35,** 512–521.

(14) BANHAM, K. M.: Senescence and the emotions: a genetic theory. *J. genet. Psychol.,* 1951, **78,** 175–183.

(15) BANKSTON, H. S.: Gaining emotional maturity through group discussion. *Understanding the Child,* 1954, **23,** 25–26.

(16) BARKER, R. G., T. DEMBO, and K. LEWIN: Frustration and regression: an experiment with young children. *Univer. Iowa Stud. child Welf.,* 1941, **18,** No. 386.

(17) BARNARD, J. W., P. G. ZIMBARDO, and S. B. SARASON: Anxiety and verbal behavior in children. *Child Develpm.,* 1961, **32,** 379–392.

(18) BARSCHAK, E.: Happiness and unhappiness in childhood and adolescence of a group of women students: a comparative study of English and American girls. *Brit. J. Psychol.,* 1952, **43,** 129–140.

(19) BARTLETT, C. J., and J. E. HORROCKS: A study of the needs status of adolescents from broken homes. *J. genet. Psychol.,* 1958, **93,** 153–159.

(20) BATEMAN, M. M., and J. S. JENSEN: The effect of religious background on modes of handling anger. *J. soc. Psychol.,* 1958, **47,** 133–141.

(21) BAYLEY, N.: On the growth of intelligence. *Amer. Psychologist,* 1955, **10,** 805–818.

(22) BEELER, S.: Angry girls: behavior control by girls in latency. *Smith Coll. Stud. soc. Wk.,* 1953, **23,** 205–226.

(23) BELL, E. C.: Nutritional deficiency and emotional disturbances. *J. Psychol.,* 1958, **45,** 47–74.

(24) BENNETT, E. M., and D. E. JOHANNSEN: Psychodynamics of the diabetic child. *Psychol. Monogr.,* 1954, **68,** No. 11.

(25) BERKOWITZ, L.: The expression and reduction of hostility. *Psychol. Bull.,* 1958, **55,** 257–284.

(26) BERLYNE, D. E.: A theory of human curiosity. *Brit. J. Psychol.,* 1954, **45,** 180–191.

(27) BERLYNE, D. E.: An experimental study of human curiosity. *Brit. J. Psychol.,* 1954, **45,** 256–265.

(28) BLOCK, J., and B. MARTIN: Predicting the behavior of children under frustration. *J. abnorm. soc. Psychol.,* 1955, **51,** 281–285.

(29) BOLL, E. S.: The role of preschool playmates—a situational approach. *Child Develpm.,* 1957, **28,** 327–342.

(30) BONNEY, M. E.: Social behavior differences between second grade children of high and low sociometric status. *J. educ. Res.,* 1955, **48,** 481–495.

(31) BOSSARD, J. H. S.: *Parent and child.* Philadelphia: University of Pennsylvania Press, 1953.

(32) BOSSARD, J. H. S., and E. S. BOLL: Child behavior and the empathic complex. *Child Develpm.,* 1957, **28,** 31–42.

(33) BOUSFIELD, W. A., and W. D. ORBISON: Ontogenesis of emotional behavior. *Psychol. Rev.,* 1952, **59,** 1–7.

(34) BOWERMAN, C. E., and J. W. KINCH: Changes in family and peer orientation of children between the fourth and tenth grades. *Soc. Forces,* 1959, **37,** 206–211.

(35) BOWLBY, J.: Some pathological processes set in train by early mother-child separation. *J. ment. Sci.,* 1953, **99,** 265–272.

(36) BOWLBY, J., M. AINSWORTH, M. BOSTON, and D. ROSENBLUTH: The effects of mother-child separation: a follow-up study. *Brit. J. med. Psychol.,* 1956, **29,** 211–247.

(37) BOYD, N. A., and G. MANDLER: Children's responses to human and animal stories and pictures. *J. consult. Psychol.,* 1955, **19,** 367–371.

(38) BRANSON, B. D.: Anxiety, discrimination, and self-ideal discrepancy. *Personnel Guid. J.,* 1960, **38,** 373–377.

(39) BRECKENRIDGE, M. E., and E. L. VINCENT: *Child development,* 4th ed. Philadelphia: Saunders, 1960.

(40) BROIDA, D. C., and G. G. THOMPSON: The relationship between certain Rorschach "insecurity" hypotheses and children's reactions to psychological stress. *J. Pers.,* 1954, **23,** 167–181.

(41) BROWN, D. C.: Masculinity-femininity development in children. *J. consult. Psychol.,* 1957, **21,** 197–202.

(42) BRUCH, H.: Developmental obesity and schizophrenia. *Psychiatry,* 1958, **21,** 65–70.

(43) BÜHLER, C.: School as a phase of human life. *Education,* 1952, **73,** 219–222.

(44) BURCH, N. R., and T. H. GREINER: Drugs and human fatigue: GSR parameters. *J. Psychol.,* 1958, **45,** 3–10.

(45) CASLER, L.: Maternal deprivation: a critical review of the literature. *Monogr. Soc. Res. Child Develpm.,* 1961, **26,** No. 2.

(46) CASTANEDA, A., D. S. PALERMO, and B. R. MC CANDLESS: Complex learning and performance as a function of anxiety in children and task difficulty. *Child Develpm.,* 1956, **27,** 327–332.

(47) CATTELL, R. B., and W. R. COAN: Personality factors in middle childhood as revealed by parents' ratings. *Child Develpm.,* 1957, **28,** 439–458.

(48) CLARKE, T. W.: Allergy and the "problem child." *Nerv. Child,* 1952, **9,** 278–281.

(49) CLIFFORD, E.: Discipline in the home: a controlled observational study of parental practices. *J. genet. Psychol.,* 1959, **95,** 45–82.

(50) COLE, L.: *Psychology of adolescence,* 5th ed. New York: Holt, 1959.

(51) COLE, N. J., O. M. SHAW, J. STENECK, and L. H. TABOROFF: A survey assessment of current parental attitudes and practices in child rearing. *Amer. J. Orthopsychiat.,* 1957, **27,** 815–822.

(52) COSER, R. L.: Some social functions of laughter. *Hum. Rel.,* 1959, **12,** 171–182.

(53) DAVIDSON, H. L., and L. S. GOTTLIEB: The emotional maturity of pre- and post-menarcheal girls. *J. genet. Psychol.,* 1955, **86,** 261–266.

(54) DAVIS, A., and R. J. HAVIGHURST: *Father of the man.* Boston: Houghton Mifflin, 1947.

(55) DAVIS, J. M.: A reinterpretation of the Barker, Dumbo, and Lewin study of frustration and aggression. *Child Develpm.,* 1958, **29,** 503–506.

(56) DAVITZ, J. R.: Contributions of research with children to a theory of maladjustment. *Child Develpm.,* 1958, **29,** 3–7.

(57) DENNIS, W., and P. NAJARIAN: Infant development under environmental handicap. *Psychol. Monogr.,* 1957, **71,** No. 7.

(58) DESPERT, J. L.: Suicides and depression in children. *Nerv. Child,* 1952, **9,** 378–389.

(59) DINGWALL, M.: Maintenance of mental health. III. Going to school the first five years. *Ment. Hlth, Lond.,* 1949, **9,** 31–33.

(60) DORIS, J.: Test-anxiety and blame-assignment in grade school children. *J. abnorm. soc. Psychol.,* 1959, **58,** 181–190.

(61) DRAGSOW, J.: Problems of progeny related to parental education. *J. educ. Psychol.,* 1957, **48,** 521–524.

(62) DUNBAR, F.: Homeostasis during puberty. *Amer. J. Psychiat.,* 1958, **114,** 673–682.

(63) DYER, W. G.: A comparison of families of high and low job satisfaction. *Marriage fam. Liv.,* 1956, **18,** 58–60.

(64) EARLE, A. M., and B. V. EARLE: Early maternal deprivation and later psychiatric ill-

ness. *Amer. J. Orthopsychiat.*, 1961, **31**, 181–186.

(65) ELKINS, D.: Some factors related to the choice status of ninety eighth-grade children in a school society. *Genet. Psychol. Monogr.*, 1958, **58**, 207–272.

(66) FAW, T.: Learning to deal with stress situations. *J. educ. Psychol.*, 1957, **48**, 135–144.

(67) FESHBACK, S.: The drive-reducing function of fantasy behavior. *J. abnorm. soc. Psychol.*, 1955, **50**, 3–11.

(68) FISHMAN, J. A.: Negative stereotypes concerning Americans and American-born children receiving various types of minority-group education. *Genet. Psychol. Monogr.*, 1955, **51**, 107–182.

(69) FITT, A. B.: An experimental study of children's attitudes toward school in Auckland, N.Z. *Brit. J. educ. Psychol.*, 1956, **26**, 25–30.

(70) FITZSIMONS, R.: Developmental, psychological, and educational factors in children with nonorganic articulation problems. *Child Develpm.*, 1958, **29**, 481–491.

(71) FOLKMAN, J. D.: Stressful and supportive interaction. *Marriage fam. Liv.*, 1956, **18**, 102–106.

(72) FRANK, L. K.: Play in personality development. *Amer. J. Orthopsychiat.*, 1955, **25**, 576–590.

(73) FRANK, L. K., and M. H. FRANK: Teachers' attitudes affect children's relationships. *Education*, 1954, **75**, 6–12.

(74) FRASER, D. C.: Environmental stress and its effect on performance. *Occup. Psychol.*, 1957, **31**, 248–255.

(75) GAIER, E. L.: Selected personality variables and the learning process. *Psychol. Monogr.*, 1952, **66**, No. 17.

(76) GARDNER, D. B., G. R. HAWKES, and L. G. BURCHINAL: Noncontinuous mothering in infancy and development in later childhood. *Child Develpm.*, 1961, **32**, 225–234.

(77) GARDNER, D. B., and M. K. SWIGER: Developmental status of two groups of infants released for adoption. *Child Develpm.*, 1958, **29**, 521–530.

(78) GARRISON, K. C.: *Growth and development*, 2d ed. New York: Longmans, 1959.

(79) GESELL, A.: Maturation and infant behavior pattern. *Psychol. Rev.*, 1929, **36**, 307–319.

(80) GESELL, A., F. L. ILG, and L. B. AMES: *Youth: the years from ten to sixteen.* New York: Harper & Row, 1956.

(81) GERWITZ, J. L.: A factor analysis of some attention-seeking behaviors of young children. *Child Develpm.*, 1956, **27**, 17–36.

(82) GLASER, K., and L. EISENBERG: Maternal deprivation. *Pediatrics*, 1956, **16**, 626–642.

(83) GOLD, M.: Suicide, homicide, and the socialization of aggression. *Amer. J. Sociol.*, 1958, **63**, 651–661.

(84) GOLDFARB, W.: Emotional and intellectual consequences of psychologic deprivation in infancy: a revaluation. In P. H. Hoch and J. Zubin, *Psychopathology of childhood.* New York: Grune & Stratton, 1955. Pp. 105–119.

(85) GOLDSTEIN, A.: Aggression and hostility in elementary school children in low socioeconomic areas. *Understanding the Child*, 1955, **24**, 20–21.

(86) GOODE, W. J.: The theoretical importance of love. *Amer. sociol. Rev.*, 1959, **24**, 38–47.

(87) GOUGH, H. G.: On making a good impression. *J. educ. Res.*, 1952, **46**, 33–42.

(88) GREGORY, I.: Studies of parental deprivation in psychiatric patients. *Amer. J. Psychiat.*, 1958, **115**, 432–442.

(89) GRONLUND, N. E.: Generality of sociometric status over criteria in measurement of social acceptability. *Elem. Sch. J.*, 1955, **55**, 173–176.

(90) HAMALAINEN, A. E.: Kindergarten-primary entrance age in relation to later school adjustment. *Elem. Sch. J.*, 1952, **52**, 406–411.

(91) HARLOW, H. F.: The nature of love. *Amer. Psychologist*, 1958, **13**, 673–685.

(92) HARLOW, H. F., and R. R. ZIMMERMAN: Affectional responses in the infant monkey. *Science*, 1959, **130**, 421–432.

(93) HARRIS, D. B., and S. C. TSENG: Children's attitudes toward peers and parents as revealed by sentence completions. *Child Develpm.*, 1957, **28**, 401–411.

(94) HARTLEY, R. E.: Some safety valves in play. *Child Study*, 1957, **34**, 12–14.

(95) HARTRUP, W. W.: Nurturance and nurturance-withdrawal in relation to the dependency behavior of preschool children. *Child Develpm.*, 1958, **29**, 191–201.

(96) HAVIGHURST, R. J.: *Human development and education.* New York: Longmans, 1953.

(97) HAWKES, G. R., L. G. BURCHINAL, and B. GARDNER: Pre-adolescents' views of some of their relationships with their parents. *Child Develpm.*, 1957, **28**, 393–399.

(98) HEATHERS, G.: Acquiring dependence and independence: a theoretical orientation. *J. genet. Psychol.*, 1955, **87**, 277–291.

(99) HEINICKE, C. H.: Some effects of separating two-year-old children from their parents. *Hum. Rel.*, 1956, **9**, 105–176.

(100) HENRY, A. F.: Sibling structure and perception of the disciplinary roles of parents. *Sociometry*, 1957, **20**, 67–74.

(101) HILGARD, E. R.: *Introduction to psychology*, 3d ed. New York: Harcourt, Brace & World, 1962.

(102) HOPPER, H. E., and S. R. PINNEAU: Frequency of regurgitation in infancy as related to the amount of stimulation received from the mother. *Child Develpm.*, 1957, **28**, 229–235.

(103) ILG, F. L., J. LEARNED, A. LOCKWOOD, and L. B. AMES: The three-and-a-half-year-old. *J. genet. Psychol.,* 1949, **75,** 21–31.

(104) INSELBERG, R. M.: The causation and manifestations of emotional behavior in Filipino children. *Child Develpm.,* 1958, **29,** 249–254.

(105) JERSILD, A. T.: *In search of self.* New York: Teachers College, Columbia University, 1952.

(106) JERSILD, A. T.: Emotional development. In L. Carmichael (Ed.), *Manual of child psychology,* 2d ed. New York: Wiley, 1954. Pp. 833–917.

(107) JERSILD, A. T.: *Child psychology,* 5th ed. Englewood Cliffs, N.Y.: Prentice-Hall, 1960.

(108) JERSILD, A. T., and R. J. TASCH: *Children's interests and what they suggest for education.* New York: Teachers College, Columbia University, 1949.

(109) JOHNSON, B. L.: Influence of puberal development on responses to motivated exercise. *Res. Quart. Amer. Ass. Hlth Phys. Educ. Recr.,* 1956, **27,** 182–193.

(110) JOURARD, S. M.: Self-disclosure and other-cathexis. *J. abnorm. soc. Psychol.,* 1954, **59,** 428–431.

(111) KAFFMAN, M.: Evaluation of emotional disturbance in 403 Israeli kibbutz children. *Amer. J. Psychiat.,* 1961, **117,** 732–738.

(112) KAGAN, J.: Socialization of aggression and the perception of parents in fantasy. *Child Develpm.,* 1958, **29,** 311–320.

(113) KEISLAR, E. R.: Experimental development of "likes" and "dislikes" of others among adolescent girls. *Child Develpm.,* 1961, **32,** 59–66.

(114) KEISTER, M. E.: Relation of mid-morning feeding to behavior of nursery school children. *J. Amer. Diet. Ass.,* 1950, **26,** 25–29.

(115) KING, E. B.: Effect of age on entrance into grade 1 upon achievement in elementary school. *Elem. Sch. J.,* 1955, **55,** 331–336.

(116) KIRKPATRICK, M. E.: The mental hygiene of adolescence in the Anglo-American culture. *Ment. Hyg., N.Y.,* 1952, **36,** 394–403.

(117) KLATSKIN, E. H., E. B. JACKSON, and L. C. WILKIN: The influence of degree of flexibility in maternal child care practices on early child behavior. *Amer. J. Orthopsychiat.,* 1956, **26,** 79–93.

(118) KNOWLES, R. C.: Psychogenic illness and delinquency in children. *Marriage fam. Liv.,* 1957, **19,** 172–177.

(119) KOCH, H. L.: The relation of certain formal attitudes of siblings to attitudes held toward each other and toward their parents. *Monogr. Soc. Res. Child Develpm.,* 1960, **25,** No. 4.

(120) KOPPITZ, E. M.: Relationships between some background factors and children's interpersonal attitudes. *J. genet. Psychol.,* 1957, **91,** 119–129.

(121) KRAUS, J. C.: *A longitudinal study of children.* New York: Board of Education, 1956.

(122) L'ABATE, L.: Personality correlates of manifest anxiety in children. *J. consult. Psychol.,* 1960, **24,** 342–348.

(123) LACEY, J., and R. VAN LEHN: Differential emphasis in somatic response to stress. An experimental study. *Psychosom. Med.,* 1952, **14,** 71–81.

(124) LAKIN, M.: Personality factors in mothers of excessively crying (colicky) infants. *Monogr. Soc. Res. Child Develpm.,* 1957, **22,** No. 1.

(125) LANDRETH, C.: *The psychology of early childhood.* New York: Knopf, 1958.

(126) LAPOUSE, R., and M. A. MONK: Fears and worries in a representative sample of children. *Amer. J. Orthopsychiat.,* 1959, **29,** 803–818.

(127) LAWSON, E. D., and R. STAGNER: Group pressure, attitude change and autonomic involvement. *J. soc. Psychol.,* 1957, **45,** 299–312.

(128) LAWSON, R., and M. H. MARX: Frustration: theory and experiment. *Genet. Psychol. Monogr.,* 1958, **57,** 393–464.

(129) LESSER, G. S.: The relationship between overt aggression and fantasy aggression as a function of maternal response to aggression. *J. abnorm. soc. Psychol.,* 1957, **55,** 218–221.

(130) LEVIN, H., and R. R. SEARS: Identification with parents as a determinant of doll play aggression. *Child Develpm.,* 1956, **27,** 135–153.

(131) LEVIN, H., and V. F. TURGEON: The influence of the mother's presence on children's doll play aggression. *J. abnorm. soc. Psychol.,* 1957, **55,** 304–308.

(132) LEVINSON, B. M.: The inner life of the extremely gifted child, as seen from the clinical setting. *J. genet. Psychol.,* 1961, **99,** 83–88.

(133) LEVY, D. M.: The infant's earliest memory of inoculation: a contribution to public health procedures. *J. genet. Psychol.,* 1960, **96,** 3–46.

(134) LEVY, E.: Children's behavior under stress and its relation to training by parents to respond to stress situations. *Child Develpm.,* 1959, **30,** 307–324.

(135) LEWIS, N. A., and J. A. TAYLOR: Anxiety and extreme response preference. *Educ. psychol. Measmt,* 1955, **15,** 11–116.

(136) LIPSITT, L. P.: A self-concept scale for children and its relationship to the children's form of the manifest anxiety scale. *Child Develpm.,* 1958, **29,** 463–472.

(137) LIVSON, N., and P. H. MUSSEN: The relation of ego control to overt aggression and

dependency. *J. abnorm. soc. Psychol.*, 1957, **55**, 66–71.

(138) LÖVAAS, O. I.: Effect of exposure to symbolic aggression on aggressive behavior. *Child Develpm.*, 1961, **32**, 37–44.

(139) LUND, F. H.: Biodynamics or Freudian psychodynamics. *Education*, 1957, **78**, 41–54.

(140) MACCOBY, E. E.: Children and working mothers. *Children*, 1958, **5**, 83–89.

(141) MACFARLANE, J., L. ALLEN, and M. P. HONZIK: *A developmental study of behavior problems of normal children between twenty-one months and fourteen years.* Berkeley, Calif.: The University of California Press, 1954.

(142) MAISON-NEUVE, J.: Contribution to the sociometry of mutual choices. *Sociometry*, 1954, **17**, 33–46.

(143) MALONE, A. J., and M. MASSLER: Index of nail-biting in children. *J. abnorm. soc. Psychol.*, 1952, **47**, 193–202.

(144) MANDLER, G., and S. B. SARASON: A study of anxiety and learning. *J. abnorm. soc. Psychol.*, 1952, **47**, 166–173.

(145) MARGOLESE, M. S.: Mental disorders in childhood due to endocrine disorders. *Nerv. Child.*, 1948, **7**, 55–77.

(146) MARTINSON, F. M.: Ego deficiency as a factor in marriage: a male sample. *Marriage fam. Liv.*, 1959, **21**, 48–52.

(147) MAW, W. H., and E. W. MAW: Information recognition by children with high and low curiosity. *Educ. Res. Bull.*, 1961, **40**, 197–201.

(148) MAW, W. H., and E. W. MAW: Nonhomeostasis experiences as stimuli of children with high curiosity. *Calif. J. educ. Res.*, 1961, **12**, 57–61.

(149) MAW, W. H., and E. W. MAW: Selection of unbalanced and unusual designs by children high in curiosity. *Child Develpm.*, 1962, **33**, 917–922.

(150) MC CANDLESS, B. R., A. CASTANEDA, and D. S. PALERMO: Anxiety in children and social status. *Child Develpm.*, 1956, **27**, 385–391.

(151) MC KEACHIE, W. J., D. POLLIE, and J. SPEISMAN: Relieving anxiety in classroom examinations. *J. abnorm. soc. Psychol.*, 1955, **50**, 93–98.

(152) MC NALLY, E.: The worries of the younger pupils in Scottish secondary schools. *Brit. J. educ. Psychol.*, 1951, **21**, 235–237.

(153) MC REYNOLDS, P., M. ACKER, and C. PIETILA: Relation of object curiosity to psychological adjustment in children. *Child Develpm.*, 1961, **32**, 393–400.

(154) MERRY, F. K., and R. V. MERRY: *The first two decades of life*, 2d ed. New York: Harper & Row, 1958.

(155) MILES, C. C.: Gifted Children. In L. Carmichael (Ed.), *Manual of child psychology*, 2d ed. New York: Wiley, 1954. Pp. 984–1063.

(156) MONTAGUE, J. B.: A study of anxiety among English and American boys. *Amer. sociol. Rev.*, 1955, **20**, 685-689.

(157) MOUSTAKAS, C. E.: Emotional adjustment and the play therapy process. *J. genet. Psychol.*, 1955, **86**, 79–99.

(158) MUNN, N. L.: *The evolution and growth of human behavior.* Boston: Houghton Mifflin, 1955.

(159) MUSSEN, P. H., and M. C. JONES: Self-conceptions, motivations, and interpersonal attitudes of late- and early-maturing boys. *Child Develpm.*, 1957, **28**, 243–256.

(160) NAGY, M. H.: Children's conceptions of some bodily functions. *J. genet. Psychol.*, 1953, **83**, 199–216.

(161) NAKAMURA, C. Y.: The relationship between children's expressions of hostility and methods of discipline exercised by dominant and overprotective parents. *Child Develpm.*, 1959, **30**, 109–117.

(162) NYE, F. I.: The rejected parent and delinquency. *Marriage fam. Liv.*, 1956, **18**, 291–300.

(163) O'CONNOR, N.: The evidence for the permanently disturbing effects of mother-child separation. *Acta Psychol.*, 1956, **12**, 174–197.

(164) OTIS, N. B., and B. R. MC CANDLESS: Response to repeated frustration of young children differentiated according to need area. *J. abnorm. soc. Psychol.*, 1955, **50**, 349–353.

(165) PALERMO, D. S.: Racial comparisons and additional normative data on the children's manifest anxiety scale. *Child Develpm.*, 1959, **30**, 53–57.

(166) PALERMO, D. S.: Relation between anxiety and two measures of speed in a reaction time test. *Child Develpm.*, 1961, **32**, 401–408.

(167) PEASE, S., and D. GARDNER: Research on the effects of noncontinuous mothering. *Child Develpm.*, 1958, **29**, 141–148.

(168) PHILLIPS, B. N., E. HINDSMAN, and E. JENNINGS: Influence of intelligence on anxiety and perception of self and others. *Child Develpm.*, 1960, **31**, 41–46.

(169) PICKREL, E. W.: The differential effect of manifest anxiety on test performance. *J. educ. Psychol.*, 1958, **49**, 43–46.

(170) PORTER, B. M.: The relationship between marital adjustment and parental acceptance of children. *J. home Econ.*, 1955, **47**, 157–164.

(171) PRATT, K. C.: A study of the "fears" of rural children. *J. genet. Psychol.*, 1945, **67**, 179–194.

(172) PRATT, K. C.: The neonate. In L. Carmichael (Ed.), *Manual of Child psychology*, 2d ed. New York: Wiley, 1954. Pp. 215–291.

(173) PRESSEY, S. L., and A. W. JONES: 1923–

1953 and 20–60 age changes in moral codes, anxieties, and interests as shown by the "X-O Tests." *J. Psychol.*, 1955, **39**, 485–502.

(174) PRUGH, D. G., E. M. STAUB, H. H. SANDS, R. M. KIRSCHBAUM, and E. A. LONIHAN: A study of the emotional reactions of children and families to hospitalization and illness. *Amer. J. Orthopsychiat.*, 1953, **23**, 70–106.

(175) RATHBAN, C., L. DI VIRGILIO, and S. WALD-FOGEL: The restitutive process in children following radical separation from family and culture. *Amer. J. Orthopsychiat.*, 1958, **28**, 408–415.

(176) RHEINGOLD, H. L.: The modification of social responsiveness in institutional babies. *Monogr. Soc. Res. Child Develpm.*, 1956, **21**, No. 2.

(177) RHEINGOLD, H. L., and N. BAYLEY: The later effects of an experimental modification of mothering. *Child Develpm.*, 1959, 30, 363–372.

(178) RIBBLE, M. A.: *The personality of the young child.* New York: Columbia University Press, 1955.

(179) SARASON, I. G.: Test anxiety, general anxiety, and intellectual performance. *J. consult. Psychol.*, 1957, **21**, 485–490.

(180) SARASON, S. B., K. DAVIDSON, F. LIGHTHALL, and R. WAITE: Classroom observations of high and low anxious children. *Child Develpm.*, 1958, **29**, 287–295.

(181) SCHONFELD, W. A.: Deficient development of masculinity. *Amer. J. Dis. Children*, 1950, **79**, 17–29.

(182) SEARS, P. S.: Doll play aggression in normal young children: influence of sex, age, sibling status, father's absence. *Psychol. Monogr.*, 1951, **65**, No. 6.

(183) SEARS, R. R.: A theoretical framework for personality and social behavior. *Amer. Psychologist*, 1951, **6**, 476–483.

(184) SEARS, R. R., E. E. MACCOBY, and H. LEVIN: *Patterns of child rearing.* New York: Harper & Row, 1957.

(185) SHAFFER, L. F., and E. J. SHOBEN: *The psychology of adjustment,* 2d ed. Boston: Houghton Mifflin, 1956.

(186) SHAPIRO, D. S.: Perceptions of significant family and environmental relationships in aggressive and withdrawn children. *J. consult. Psychol.*, 1957, **21**, 381–385.

(187) SIEGEL, A. E.: The influence of violence in the mass media upon children's role expectations. *Child Develpm.*, 1958, **29**, 35–56.

(188) SIEGEL, A. E., and L. G. KOHN: Permissiveness, permission, and aggression: the effect of adult presence or absence on aggression in children's play. *Child Develpm.*, 1959, **30**, 131–141.

(189) SIEGEL, S. M.: The relationship of hostility to authoritarianism. *J. abnorm. soc. Psychol.*, 1956, **52**, 368–372.

(190) SKLAREW, B. H.: The relationship of early separation from parents to differences in adjustment in adolescent boys and girls. *Psychiatry*, 1959, **22**, 399–405.

(191) SMITH, W., E. K. POWELL, and S. ROSEN: Manifest anxiety and food aversions. *J. abnorm. soc. Psychol.*, 1955, **50**, 101–104.

(192) SMOCK, C. D.: Perceptual rigidity and closure phenomenon as a function of manifest anxiety in children. *Child Develpm.*, 1958, **29**, 237–247.

(193) SMOCK, C. D., and B. G. HOLT: Children's reactions to novelty: an experimental study of "curiosity motivation." *Child Develpm.*, 1962, **33**, 631–642.

(194) SONTAG, L. W., C. T. BAKER, and V. L. NELSON: Mental growth and personality development: a longitudinal study. *Monogr. Soc. Res. Child Develpm.*, 1958, **23**, No. 2.

(195) SPITZ, R. A.: Reply to Dr. Pinneau. *Psychol. Bull.*, 1955, **52**, 429–452.

(196) STAGNER, R.: *Psychology of personality,* 3d ed. New York: McGraw-Hill, 1960.

(197) STAUDT, V. M.: Character formation is the teacher's business. *Education*, 1957, **77**, 198–202.

(198) STOLZ, L. M., et al.: *Father relationships with war-born children.* Stanford, Calif.: Standford University Press, 1954.

(199) STRAUS, M. A., and J. H. STRAUS: Personal insecurity and Sinhalese social structure: Rorschach evidence for primary school children. *Child Develpm. Abstr.*, 1959, **33**, No. 246.

(200) SUTTON-SMITH, B., and B. G. ROSENBERG: Manifest anxiety and game preferences in children. *Child Develpm.*, 1960, **31**, 307–311.

(201) TASCH, R. J.: The role of the father in the family. *J. exp. Educ.*, 1952, **20**, 319–361.

(202) VOLLMER, H.: Jealousy in children. *Amer. J. Orthopsychiat.*, 1946, **16**, 660–671.

(203) WALLIS, R. S.: The overt fears of Dakota Indian children. *Child Develpm.*, 1954, **25**, 185–192.

(204) WALSH, A. M.: *Self-concepts of bright boys with learning difficulties.* New York: Teachers College, Columbia University, 1956.

(205) WALTER, L. M., and S. S. MARZOLF: The relation of sex, age, and school achievement to levels of aspiration. *J. educ. Psychol.*, 1951, **42**, 285–292.

(206) WALTERS, J., D. PEARCE, and L. DAHMS: Affectional and aggressive behavior of preschool children. *Child Develpm.*, 1957, **28**, 15–26.

(207) WALTERS, R. H., W. E. MARSHALL, and J. R. SHOOTER: Anxiety, isolation, and susceptibility to social influence. *J. Pers.*, 1960, **28**, 518–529.

(208) WATERHOUSE, I. K., and I. L. CHILD: Frustration and the quality of performance. *J. Pers.*, 1956, **21**, 298–311.

(209) WATSON, J. B., and R. R. RAYNOR: Conditioned emotional reactions. *J. exp. Psychol.*, 1920, **3**, 1–4.

(210) WHITING, J. W. M., and I. L. CHILD: *Child training and personality*. New Haven: Yale University Press, 1953.

(211) WIRT, R. D.: Ideational expression of hostile impulses. *J. consult. Psychol.*, 1956, **20**, 185–189.

(212) WORCHEL, P.: Catharsis and the relief of hostility. *J. abnorm. soc. Psychol.*, 1957, **55**, 238–243.

(213) YARROW, L. J.: Maternal deprivation: toward an empirical and conceptual re-evaluation. *Psychol. Bull.*, 1961, **58**, 459–490.

(214) YOUNG, F. M.: The incidence of nervous habits observed in college students. *J. Pers.*, 1947, **15**, 309–320.

(215) ZAIDA, S. M. H.: Reactions to stress as a function of the level of intelligence. *Genet. Psychol. Monogr.*, 1960, **62**, 41–104.

(216) ZANDER, A.: Group membership and individual security. *Hum. Rel.*, 1958, **11**, 99–111.

(217) ZELIGS, R.: Social factors annoying to children. *J. appl. Psychol.*, 1945, **29**, 75–82.

(218) ZUK, G. H.: The influence of social context on impulse and control tendencies in preadolescents. *Genet. Psychol. Monogr.*, 1956, **54**, 117–166.

(219) ZWEIBELSON, I.: Test anxiety and intelligence test performance. *J. consult. Psychol.*, 1956, **20**, 479–481.

8

SOCIAL
DEVELOPMENT

Social development means acquisition of the ability to behave in accordance with social expectations. It has been defined as the "process by which an individual, born with potentialities of enormously wide range, is led to develop actual behavior which is confined within a much narrower range— the range of what is customary and acceptable for him according to the standards of his group" (41). Becoming socialized involves three processes which, although they are separate and distinct, are so closely interrelated that failure in the development of one will result in a lower level of socialization than one might normally anticipate.

The three processes involved in socialization are (*1*) proper performance behavior, (*2*) the playing of approved social roles, and (*3*) the development of social attitudes. *Proper performance behavior* means that the child will behave in a manner approved by the social group. As every social group has its own standards of what is "proper" behavior, the child must know what that behavior is and pattern his own behavior along the approved lines. A *social role* is a pattern of customary behavior which is defined and expected by members of the social group. Every social group has its own recognized patterns of behavior for members of the two sexes as well as for different areas of behavior. There is, for example, a prescribed role for a parent and for a child, for a teacher and for a pupil, for a sibling and for a grandparent (131).

The third process involved in socialization, the development of *social attitudes,* is that of becoming "imbued with a sense of oneness, intercommunication, and cooperation" (74). A socialized person likes people and social activities; he is a "friendly" person who reflects his attitudes toward people in the quality of his behavior. In short, becoming socialized means that the child behaves in such a way that he will fit into the social group with which he wishes to be identified and will be accepted by the group as a member.

Socialization versus Conformity. On the surface, it may appear that "socialization" and "conformity" are synonymous—that a person must be slavishly conventional in his behavior and attitudes if he is to be an accepted member of the social group. Within limits, *this is correct in childhood*. While the child is learning how to become a social person, he must have a stable model to copy, and he must copy it with a minimum of variation. After learning what the social group expects of him, he may vary his behavior to fit his own needs and desires, provided he does not vary it too much or to the point where he disregards social expectations.

At no age is a "rugged individualist" an accepted person. If a person does not want to conform to the standards of the group, the group does not want to accept him as a member. A slight variation from the group, however, provided the group regards it as superior to the accepted pattern of behavior, not only will be acceptable but also will be imitated. The members of the group will make this deviant pattern their own pattern.

Sociability versus Nonsociability. A *social* person is one who conforms to the three criteria of social development. He behaves in an approved manner, plays the role society prescribes for him, and has favorable attitudes toward people and social activities. Relatively few people, either children or adults, conform to all three of these criteria. Most, however, willingly create the impression that they conform in order to win social approval and acceptance. They do so by learning to use "fronts" to cover up thoughts and feelings that might be considered socially unacceptable. They learn not to look bored, even though they may be bored; not to talk about tabooed subjects in the presence of those who disapprove; and not to look pleased when someone they dislike is hurt.

A *nonsocial* person fails to measure up in one or more of these criteria. He may behave as the social group expects but have unfavorable attitudes toward people and social activities; he may like people and social activities, but his behavior may not conform to standards essential to acceptance; or he may fail to measure up successfully in all

three criteria. A child may be nonsocial because he is ignorant of what the group expects, because he willfully disregards social expectations, or both (63).

A nonsocial person may, therefore, be either unsocial or antisocial. An *unsocial* child has not yet learned what society expects of him. An *antisocial* child, on the other hand, knows what others expect of him but intentionally does the opposite. He is disobedient, quarrelsome, and destructive; he bullies others and derives personal satisfaction from being unfair.

In contrast to the social person is the *gregarious* one, who craves the presence of others and is lonely when he is by himself but who is satisfied merely to be with others, regardless of the kind of contact he has with them. Gregarious behavior is characteristic of most animals of the lower level of development, whereas social behavior is characteristic of higher animals and human beings. Gregarious behavior is found in the early months of babyhood, before the baby has had an opportunity to learn how to interact socially with others. It is occasionally found among children and even among adolescents and adults who have developed fears of close social contacts as a result of some traumatic experience but whose craving for companionship is too strong for them to be satisfied without some contact with members of the human species.

In childhood, there is a strong drive to be with others. When this need is not met, the child will be unhappy; when it is met, he will be satisfied and happy. Some children can be satisfied with gregarious behavior, but most are satisfied only when they are accepted members of a social group. Anything, therefore, which interferes with their socialization and acts as a barrier to their acceptance by the group will lead to unhappiness.

LEARNING TO BE SOCIAL

No child is born social or antisocial. He is not even gregarious at first, though the drive to be with people develops early in the first year of life. What the child's attitudes to-

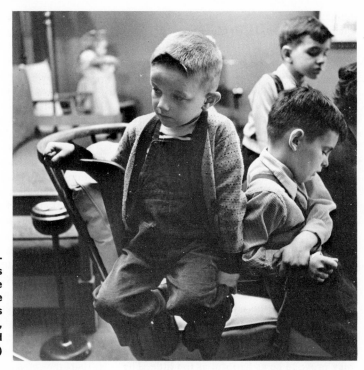

A child may be non-social because he is ignorant of what the group expects, because he willfully disregards social expectations, or both. (Standard Oil Co., N.J.)

ward people and social experiences will be and how he will get along with other people will depend largely upon learning experiences during the early, formative years of his life. These experiences will, in turn, depend upon the opportunities he has for socializing, upon his motivation to take advantage of these opportunities, and upon the direction and guidance he receives from parents, teachers, and older siblings in the best methods of making social contacts.

Should all these factors, which play so important a role in his learning, be favorable, the chances are that he will develop into a social person. Should they be unfavorable, all or in part, the chances are very great that he will be less social than other children of his age or that he will become unsocial, in the sense that he withdraws from the social group and spends as much time in solitude as possible, playing the role of a "lone wolf." He may become antisocial, developing an antagonistic attitude toward people and violating the established mores and customs of the social group—thus becoming a "rugged individualist."

Essentials of Socialization. If the child is to learn to live socially with others, he must, first, have ample *opportunities* to learn to do so. This is especially important during the years when socialization is a dominant phase of the child's development. As Harris has emphasized, "Socialization does not proceed in a vacuum" (94). Even before a child enters school, he benefits from social contacts with persons outside his immediate family and neighborhood. A nursery school or kindergarten, where there is direction and guidance in making social contacts successfully, provides a child excellent opportunities for learning to be social (113).

Each year, the child is normally given more opportunities for contacts, not only with children of his own age and level of ability, but also with adults of different ages and different backgrounds. As a result, there is a gradual increase in social participation and interaction with others. If opportunities for social participation are restricted, owing to geographic isolation, family regulations, or unfavorable social attitudes on the child's part, the limitations may "result not only in immediate unhappiness, but also in subsequent difficulties in interpersonal relationships" (161).

It has been found that children brought up in institutions where there are restrictions on social participation are less mature socially than those who are given normal opportunities for participation. This immaturity is shown in fewer contacts with others, even when there are other people available; less interest in social life; and less desire to participate in social activities. Children deprived of opportunities for social participation because of prejudice against them not only do not learn to be as social as their agemates but often develop antisocial attitudes which affect the quality of their social behavior. Being cut off from social contacts forces them to engage in play activities with little socializing value, such as watching television, going to the movies, listening to the radio, or reading the comics (216).

While social participation is essential to social development, *too much participation* may prove to be as harmful as too little. The child who is dissatisfied if he is not with others fails to develop resources within himself to be happy when circumstances force him to be alone. Indiscriminate sociability, or being with others just for the sake of companionship without taking into consideration congeniality of interests or other factors, does little to develop healthy social attitudes. Even worse, the child who craves companionship of any kind becomes unstable in his interests and values, changing them according to the type of child or adult he is with in the hope of winning acceptance. The child thus tends to be highly suggestible and easily influenced by anyone with whom he happens to come in contact (207, 218).

The second essential to becoming a social person is *motivation.* Whether the child will have the necessary motivation to learn to be social will depend, to a large extent, upon how much satisfaction he derives from social contacts. The *kind of social contacts* the child has is more important than the number. If he enjoys his contacts with people, he will want to repeat them. If he

does not, he will tend to shun people. He is thus likely to exaggerate unsatisfactory past experiences and to convince himself that he prefers to be alone (48). While the drive for social contacts appears, in the human infant, to be "species-specific and biologically inherent," whether it will lead to social behavior will depend upon the satisfaction the child derives from being with others.

Studies of social deprivation in young children have revealed that when this deprivation is of short duration, it increases the child's motivation to win the attention and affection of others. If the deprivation is strong and prolonged, however, anxiety may become so intense that the child will literally be afraid to establish social contacts. He will then attempt to satisfy the social drive by being an onlooker, thus becoming a passive rather than an active participant in social activities. This, of course, will not give him as great satisfaction as he would get from active participation (79, 96, 219).

The third essential in learning to be social is that the *method* used be adequate to achieve the desired results. Some forms of social behavior are learned indirectly, under conditions of minimal direct teaching; some are learned directly and under guidance. By *trial and error,* a child will learn some of the behavior patterns necessary for good social adjustments. He will discover, for example, that quarreling with his playmates wins fewer friends than being cooperative.

He may learn how to get along with others by *imitation*—by observing what others do and then by practicing it, pretending to be the other person. This is known as *role practice;* the learning comes through identification with the person the child is imitating (65, 184). Unless he is fortunate enough to have a good model for identification, however, he may find himself imitating behavior that leads to poor social adjustments. Furthermore, most children are unselective in what they imitate. They will imitate *anything,* good or bad, in the person they are with regardless of whether it will increase their social acceptance or hinder it (175).

Studies of speech defects, for example,

have revealed that young children quickly imitate the stuttering or lisping of a child with whom they associate (141). Similarly, studies have revealed how quickly young children imitate the fears, anxieties, and angers of other children and how closely their responses to these emotions resemble the responses of the people they are with (140). Learning to play appropriate social roles comes from imitation. If a boy is constantly associated with his mother and if his siblings are girls, he is likely to imitate them and act like a girl instead of learning *not* to act like a girl—an essential to good social adjustments for all boys (65).

In the long run, the child will learn more quickly how to be social, and the end results will be better, if his learning is guided and directed by persons more experienced than he. In short, he will learn best if he is *taught*. Marshall has pointed out the importance of guidance by stressing that "when children have too few experiences at home that provide the techniques and interests required for participation in play with peers, they will often fail in their attempts to play and, as a consequence, will show excessive dependence on teachers" (135).

Since the social group exerts so marked an influence on the personality of the child, it is obvious that the members of the social group should be selected because of the desirable influence they can exert. This guidance must come from adults. A child does not recognize the harmful effects that will come from associating closely with children who are highly prejudiced or have moral standards that differ widely from those of his parents. As long as he enjoys playing with such children, he will not be concerned about the far-reaching influence they have on his attitudes.

Time Needed to Become Social. Learning to be a social person does not come overnight. Furthermore, the child learns in cycles, with rapid improvement followed by little or no improvement or even by regression to lower levels of behavior. The periods in which little gain is seen may be discouraging for the child and for his parents or

teachers. Whether he eventually recovers lost ground or rises from the plateau in which he appears to be standing still will depend largely upon the strength of his motivation.

Although social development is normally rapid in childhood, most children feel far from satisfied with the results achieved when childhood comes to an end. Studies of the sources of unhappiness reported by adolescent boys and girls put great emphasis on social problems. Adolescents feel, for example, that they are far from the goal of learning how to get along with people; that they do not know how to treat their friends to avoid quarrels and the breakup of their friendships; that they do not know how to be at ease in social situations; and that they do not know how to develop the qualities that will make them potential leaders.

IMPORTANCE OF EARLY SOCIAL EXPERIENCES

Happy social experiences encourage the child to want to repeat the experiences. By contrast, too many unhappy social experiences tend to encourage unwholesome attitudes toward all social experiences and toward people. Because children can be made social, unsocial, or antisocial more easily during the early, formative years of their lives than later, their early social experiences are important in determining what sort of adults they will become.

It is commonly said that a person is a "born introvert" or a "born extrovert." There is little evidence to substantiate this belief. On the contrary, evidence points to the fact that the person was *made* an introvert or an extrovert by the type of early social experiences he had. Because his early associations are almost exclusively with family members, the individual's attitudes and behavior in social situations are, in the strictest sense, homegrown.

While it is true that unfavorable attitudes and behavior patterns may be modified and changed as the child grows older and discovers what a handicap they are, it is questionable whether they can ever become as favorable as they might have been, had his early social experiences given him a better start.

Family Influences. No one specific member of the family nor any one specific aspect of family life is responsible for socializing the child. If the total character of the home environment is favorable, the chances are that favorable social attitudes will develop; if the home atmosphere is marked by constant friction and tension, the chances are equally great that unfavorable social attitudes will be generated. Furthermore, the size of the family in which the child grows up will affect his early social experiences (28).

Studies of social adjustments have revealed that specific early influences in the child's home life are highly important. Children who come from a *socioeconomic background* that provides opportunities for healthy physical and psychological development make better social adjustments than children who come from poorer socioeconomic backgrounds (132). The *type of relationships* that exist between the child's parents, between him and his siblings, and between him and his parents and the position of the child within the family—whether he is the oldest, the middle, the youngest, or an only child—are contributing factors to his social adjustments (28). Only children, for example, or those with siblings widely separated in age or of a different sex tend to be more withdrawn when they are with children outside the home than children with siblings nearer to them in age or of the same sex do. When children have siblings of the same sex as they, they find it difficult to make associations with children of the other sex outside the home but easy to make associations with those of the same sex (24, 121).

The social behavior and attitudes of a child reflect the *treatment* he receives in the home. The child who is rejected, for instance, may carry the resulting attitude of martyrdom outside the home and even into adult life. He will go around with a "chip on his shoulder," interpreting everything people say or do as an indication of their rejection of him. Another example may be seen in the effect parental expectations have on the child's socialization. Each year, the child becomes increasingly aware that he is expected to overcome his aggressiveness and antisocial behavior if he wishes to win parental approval (85, 184). Children from middle-class families are under greater pressure to conform than those from lower-class or even upper-class families.

Of all the home factors in the early years of life which influence the child's social behavior and attitudes, perhaps the most important is the type of *child-rearing methods* used by his parents. Young children who are raised democratically are active and socially outgoing. In the democratic home, there is not only freedom but also a high level of interaction between parent and child through the parents' spontaneous expression of warmth. The child is encouraged to engage in activities demanding intellectual curiosity, originality, and constructiveness.

Children who are indulged, on the other hand, show physical apprehension and lack of skill in muscular activities. They become inactive and withdrawn in their social relationships. Children who are subjected to authoritarian child-rearing methods are quiet, nonresistant, well behaved, and unaggressive. Curiosity, originality, and fancifulness are restricted by parental pressures. Children from democratic homes usually make the best social adjustments (136).

In summary, then, it is apparent that the home may be regarded as the "seat of learning" for the development of social skills and of the desire to participate in activities with other people. Only when children have satisfactory social relationships with members of their family can they enjoy social relationships with people outside the home, have healthy attitudes toward people, and learn to function successfully in groups of their peers (140).

Outside Influences. Early social experiences outside the home are likewise important determinants of what the child's social attitudes and behavior patterns will be (48). If his relationships with peers and adults outside the home are favorable, he will enjoy social contacts and want to repeat them. If they are unpleasant or frightening, he will want to avoid such contacts in the future, he will develop unfavorable attitudes toward outsiders, and he will fall back on the companionship of family members. If family relationships have been no more pleasurable than contacts with outsiders, however, he will shut himself away from people whenever he can and will become a social isolate (62).

When a child enjoys social contacts with outsiders, he will want to behave in a manner that will win their approval and acceptance. Even preschool children imitate the patterns of social behavior of their peers in their attempts to gain social acceptance. Among older children, the influence of the peer group is greater because the desire for social acceptance is stronger (5).

If a child's playmates are older than he, he strives to keep up with them and, as a result, develops more mature patterns of behavior. If the older children are bossy, he may not find his contacts with them pleasant; he will then choose younger children as his playmates, bossing them as the older children have tried to boss him. When his playmates or siblings are all of his own sex, he often has difficulty in making good social adjustments with playmates of the opposite sex. Although early social contacts outside the home are often characterized by fighting, preschool children usually show more affectionate than aggressive responses to their playmates. The satisfaction the child derives from his early social experiences encourages him to seek further contacts outside the home (24, 121, 217).

The child's basic social attitudes—attitudes toward people in general, toward certain people or certain social groups, and toward social life as an experience—are greatly influenced by the peer group. These attitudes are learned, to some extent, at home but they can be changed as a result of the child's experiences with the peer group. Each year, his desire for status in the group grows, and his attitudes are increasingly influenced by pressures from the group.

Consistency of Behavior and Attitudes.

Established patterns of social behavior and social attitudes tend to remain consistent. While any change is likely to be slight, attitudes are less subject to change than behavior patterns (74). To determine how consistent the social behavior established in early childhood is, attempts have been made to discover whether the child's adjustments improve with age. A follow-up study of a group of 21 kindergarten children revealed that, 10 years after the original study, 10 had improved their social adjustment, 10 had remained the same, and 1 had declined slightly (178).

Studies of adolescents and adults have revealed how consistent early childhood patterns of social participation remain. Children whose early social experiences were unfavorable tend to participate less in group activities than those who had favorable early experiences. Because there is a close relationship between a child's liking for social activities and how much other children like and accept him, those children who make good social adjustments from the start derive the most enjoyment from social participation. Popular children become more active participants in school and extracurricular affairs during their high-school and college years and in community affairs during adulthood than the unpopular (64).

By the end of childhood, the child has absorbed many social attitudes from his parents, teachers, and peer group; from his personal experiences; and from radio, television, books, and other media of mass communication. Unless he discovers that poor social attitudes will make him unpopular, he is not likely to consciously try to develop favorable attitudes or change unfavorable ones already established. The child who at an early age develops a fondness for another child, for example, will continue to cling to that child even when parents and teachers try to persuade him that the child is not a "good influence" (99). Prejudice—dislike for a group of people because of their race, religion, or socioeconomic status—is also persistent once it is established. Similarly, the child who voluntarily isolates himself from other children because of unsatisfying early experiences is not easily persuaded that he could "have more fun" if he played with other children. These points will be discussed in more detail later in this chapter and in the following chapter.

In summary, then, the importance of laying good foundations in the early years is apparent. As Bain has said, "When the child enters school, he begins to reap the rewards or suffer the ills which flow from the first six years of life" (12). If his home has done a good job, the child can adjust to others and to social patterns easily and adequately. He is not forced to learn the hard way. He knows what to expect, and he is prepared to evaluate the new social realities he will meet. The child who gets off to a bad start, on the other hand, acquires a reputation that follows him from class to class. The result is that he is likely to continue to make poor social adjustments unless he receives some help in improving the poor foundations established in his early childhood days in the home.

INFLUENCE OF THE SOCIAL GROUP

At all ages people are, to varying degrees, influenced by the social group with which they have constant associations. This influence is greatest during childhood, the time of greatest plasticity. Furthermore, there is a common predictable pattern of influence.

Pattern of Influence. During the preschool years, the family is the most influential socializing agency in the child's life. Even though the preschooler plays with children outside the home, he is still too young to be group-conscious; thus, his playmates have little influence on his behavior and attitudes. In addition, the members of the play group change frequently, and their influence over him is less than it would be if group membership were more constant. From seven years of age on, children have a greater dependence on the group; as a result, they are more susceptible to the influence of *group*

pressures than they were when they were younger or than they will be when they grow up (107).

When the child goes to school, his *teachers* begin to exert an influence over his socialization, though *peer* influence is usually greater than teacher influence. Peer influence likewise takes precedence over family influence (29, 142). As Pease and Swanson have pointed out, this time in the child's life is characterized by "rejection of adult or parental standards accompanied by an almost frantic acceptance of the standards dictated by 'the gang'" (169). The strong influence of the peer group over the child during the latter part of childhood comes partly from the child's desire to be acceptable to, and accepted by, the group and partly from the fact that he spends more time outside the home with the peer group in school and in play (15, 224). The relative amounts of time spent in the home and outside at different ages are shown in Figure 8–1.

Variations in Influence. Not all children are influenced in the same way by the social group, nor is a particular child always influenced in the same way. Of the many factors that determine how great the group's influence will be, the following are the most important:

1. Acceptability to the Group. Popular children are influenced more by the group and less by their families than children who do not get along well with their peers. When a child masters the skills that put him in a position of authority in the group, he not only achieves social acceptance but also has greater self-confidence and shows more ascendant behavior (98).

Should a child enjoy somewhat less than complete acceptance but see the possibility of gaining this acceptance, he will show a high degree of adherence to group standards, being motivated by a desire to improve his status in the group. The child who is unaccepted will go to any lengths to win the attention and approval of the group. If he sees little chance of being accepted, however, he has little motivation to conform to the standards of the group, and when he does conform, he does so only in public and only to forestall his complete rejection (58).

The child who is actively rejected by the group may become angry and vindictive, displacing his resentments against the group by hurting innocent victims or destroying property. He may, on the other hand, revert to earlier forms of social contact that he found satisfying—mainly contacts with family members—or he may be able to gain acceptance by another group, even though it is not the group he prefers. Whichever path he follows will markedly influence his attitudes and behavior (138, 140).

2. Security of Status. The closeness of the child's associations with the members of a group, either in the home or outside, will determine the amount of security he feels. This, in turn, will determine how much influence that group has over him and the manner in which he is influenced (181). The child who feels secure will be able to sway the behavior of others by both direct and indirect techniques. He will not blindly accept the commands and suggestions of others. Furthermore, he will feel free to express openly any disagreement he may have with the judgments of other members of the group. The child who feels less secure or who feels insecure will conform closely, both openly and privately, to the judgments of the group members. He will tend to follow the lead of others and will attempt to influence the behavior and judgments of the group members only by indirect means (58, 98, 147).

3. Type of Group. The influence of the group on the child comes not from the group itself so much as from the social distance or degree of affective relationship that exists between him and the other members of the group. Roughly, three types of social groups have been recognized: (1) the *primary* group, which has the strongest bonds of intergroup relations (family group or peer group); (2) the *secondary* group, which is characterized by more casual rela-

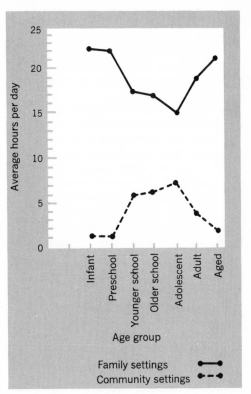

Figure 8–1. Time spent in family and community settings at different ages. (Adapted from H. F. Wright, Psychological development in Midwest, *Child Develpm.*, 1956, 27, 265–286. Used by permission.)

tionships (social club or organized play group); and (3) the *tertiary* group, which is marginal and transient in character (people the child comes in contact with on buses, on trains, or at the movies). Of these three, the primary group unquestionably has the greatest influence on the child (34).

The effect of social distance within groups has been illustrated in studies of children from urban, suburban, rural, and town environments. Comparisons of children from these backgrounds have suggested that children are more favorably influenced by suburban and urban than by town and rural groups. Children in rural districts have fewer opportunities for social contacts, and those living in towns are often cut off from close personal contacts because of the rigid class distinctions that divide one social class from another (36, 158).

4. Different Members of the Group.

Within a group, some members have more influence over the child than others. As a rule, the greatest influence comes from the leader and the least from the lowest-status members—those who are least popular with the rest of the group. The more solidly the group is formed and the more secure the child's status within that group, the greater its influence over him will be (98).

5. Child's Personality.

Children with authoritarian personality patterns have been found to be most influenced by the group. Such children have a constant fear of not being liked; as a result, they will submit blindly to power and authority. Furthermore, the feelings of insecurity which characterize the authoritarian personality tend to make them conventional and give them a great need for conformity (37). Any child who suffers from feelings of inadequacy or inferiority, however, regardless of what causes such feelings, will be more influenced by the group than the child who has greater self-confidence and self-acceptance (11).

6. Affiliation Motive.

The influence of the group also varies according to the strength of the child's *affiliation motive*—how anxious the child is to be accepted. The stronger the child's affiliation motive, the greater his susceptibility to influence from group members will be, especially those who hold high status in the group. His motivation to gain status is influenced, too, by his own status in the group. Children with high status have a stronger motivation to be popular than those with such a low status that they have no hope of winning acceptance (104).

That desire for social acceptance has a strong influence on the child's behavior may be seen from the fact that many children are willing to misbehave in order to win the attention and approval of the peer group, even when this is contrary to their own values and the standards of their homes (222). Similarly, many bright children who

crave acceptance from the peer group will work below their capacities to avoid being classed as "brains," a designation which is sure to bring rejection. The more attractive the group seems to the child, the more anxious he will be to be accepted, and the more willing, in turn, he will be to allow himself to be influenced by it (58, 68).

Areas of Influence. The group influences the child's pattern of development in a number of ways. The first is through his *willingness to conform* to the behavior, attitudes, and values of the group. Social conformity takes two forms: *acquiescence,* or agreement with group opinion through group pressures, and *conventionality,* or concurrence with the mores, attitudes, and values of the group. The more accepted the child is by the group, the more willing he is to conform; the more willing he is to conform, the better accepted he will be (18). Willingness to conform is especially strong in the latter part of childhood, when the desire for social acceptance reaches its peak.

By the time the child reaches adolescence,

. . . conformity may be the price one pays for safety. An early-acquired fear of making mistakes may create enough anxiety to prevent an adolescent from being different from the rest of the group. An early-acquired fear of losing the love of one's parents, which in childhood led to model behavior, may also be manifested in conformity to group standards; it may survive as a fear of losing group acceptance (206).

Conformity to the group is learned first from child-training methods used in the home. The child is punished for nonconformity and rewarded for conformity to parental wishes. The stronger the child's desire for acceptance, either by the home group or by the peer group, the more willing he is to conform. The child may and often does feel that "any status in the group is better than none." As a result, he will conform in the hope of winning the status he craves. Only the leader, whose status in the group is usually secure, can afford to deviate. The child who is unsure of his status or the one whose status is low has a strong motivation to conform: He fears social rejection (52, 91, 152).

How seriously conformity will influence the child's adjustments will depend upon the extent of the conformity. *Extreme* conformity results in loss of individuality, submission to others, and rejection of personal desires. It may even lead to unsocial behavior. Furthermore, it may cause the child to change his values—an act that will lead to strong feelings of guilt. These are the prices a child must pay for social acceptance and approval (105).

Reasonable conformity—as contrasted with unreasonable, or blind, conformity—is a socializing force that enables the child to learn the patterns of behavior that will guarantee social acceptance. As such, it will lead to good personal as well as good social adjustments.

Nonconformity, on the other hand, is just as detrimental to good personal and social adjustments as extreme conformity. The child who refuses to conform to the accepted patterns of behavior of the group, regardless of his reasons for not conforming, finds himself a social outcast. He is deprived of the satisfactions of group belonging and of the learning experiences which can come only from belonging (52).

The second important way the group influences the child is by helping him to achieve *independence* from his parents and become an individual in his own right. Through his associations with his peers, he learns to think independently, to make his own decisions, to accept points of view and values not shared by his family, and to learn forms of behavior approved by the group to which he belongs. This is a part of the weaning process "through which he changes from complete dependence on others into a person who can hold his own with his own age group and move with his age group into youth and adulthood as an equal" (113).

American children from middle-class cultural backgrounds learn independence sooner than children from many foreign countries because of the stress we place on group life

and social acceptance. As a result of the transfer from parental to group dependence, the child becomes less egocentric and less subjected to adult demands; he enjoys greater freedom of thought and judgment and thus becomes more autonomous (23). Because his achievements gain more recognition from the peer group than from the family group, the child is more willing to adhere to the values and mores of the peer group (191).

Finally, the influence of the group is felt in the development of the child's *concept of himself as a person.* Even before a child knows why people accept or reject him, he senses what their opinions are and what their reactions mean. If the opinions of others are favorable, he will think favorably of himself; if they are unfavorable, he will come to dislike himself. He may, if he has a strong desire to be accepted, try to alter the impression others have of him. If this does not win him the acceptance he craves, he may attach himself to any group that will accept him; he will then accept their standards of behavior and their values. The peer group in which the child finds acceptance and to which he conforms thus affects his concept of himself as a person and determines the values that will govern his life (116, 134).

PATTERN OF SOCIAL DEVELOPMENT

Social development follows a pattern. An orderly sequence is observable in social behavior, in attitudes toward social contacts, and in choice of companions. At first, the young child lacks group feeling. Then there is a phase of partial adjustment, when he begins to establish his role and to play in a somewhat coordinated fashion with other children. In late childhood, group relationships are established, and the child enjoys group life. The group invents its name and organizes its activities, free from adult supervision and interference. At this time, the size of the social-contact group and the frequency of the child's participation in group activities both increase (79).

The child's attitude toward social activities and his interest in them are likewise predictable. Studies of groups of children have revealed that, while the two-year-old is solitary in his play, he is nevertheless influenced by older children to the extent that he imitates their behavior both in his play activities and in his conduct. The 2½-year-old grabs toys from other children and refuses to share them; he ignores requests and refuses to comply. By three years, the child shows the rudiments of team play; by four, he shows the beginnings of group influences. The four-year-old is conscious of the opinions of others—either adults or members of the peer group—and tries to gain attention by showing off.

The true "socialization age" begins with formal entrance into school, either kindergarten or first grade. Not only is the child then conscious of the attitudes and opinions of others, but he is anxious to win their attention and approval. The child who has always acted upon his own impulses now tries to use adult criteria to evaluate things. By the time he is ten years old, he can modify some of his feelings in accordance with the demands of the social group, thus showing a more mature type of behavior (22).

Normally, all children pass through these stages of socialization at approximately the same age. As in other types of development, bright children are accelerated in their social development, while dull children are retarded. Lack of opportunities for social contacts and for learning how to get along successfully with others will likewise delay a child's normal progress.

Knowing what the pattern of social development is makes it possible to predict what the child's behavior in a social situation is likely to be at a given age. One can readily predict, for example, that at a certain age a child will be timid in the presence of strangers; at another age, he will crave the companionship of children of his own age and sex; while at still another age, his interests will be centered on members of the opposite sex. Even though there are individual variations in this pattern, or timetable, as far as age is concerned, variations in the pattern itself are slight. Within a cultural group, social pressures and social expectations lead to similar learning experiences for all children. When a child's social behavior varies markedly from that of other children of the same age, it generally means that the child has made poor social adjustments or has developed unfavorable social attitudes.

PRESOCIAL BEHAVIOR

At birth, the baby is nongregarious, as may be seen in his complete lack of interest in people. As long as his bodily needs are taken care of, he does not crave or even miss the companionship of others. He does not distinguish between people and inanimate objects; he merely responds to stimuli in his environment. Much of what is popularly regarded as social behavior is, in reality, uninfluenced by social contacts. The crying baby can, for example, be quieted by lifting up the bed on which he is lying without any personal interaction at all.

During the first two months of life, the baby's reactions to external stimuli come only when the stimuli are intense, as in the case of loud noises. He does not even distinguish between the human voice and other noises. Although at first he gives similar responses when touched by a person or an object, he soon learns to distinguish between them because of the prominent role people play in his life. From the beginning of the third month, *gregarious* behavior predominates. The baby is contented when in the presence of others but is discontented, unhappy, and "fussy" when by himself (30, 113).

BEGINNINGS OF SOCIAL BEHAVIOR

Social behavior begins when the baby first distinguishes between *persons* and *objects*. His first social responses are to *adults* because his first social contacts are with adults. By the end of the second month, the baby turns his head when he hears a human voice and smiles in response to a smile or clucking sound. He expresses pleasure in the presence of others by kicking, smiling, and waving his arms.

During the third month, babies stop crying when they are talked to or when their attention is diverted by a rattle or some other mechanical device. They also show a beginning of interest in people by crying when a person leaves them. Most babies, at this time, recognize their mothers and other familiar people. They show their fear of unfamiliar people in timid responses, such as turning their heads and crying (83, 124).

In the fourth month, the baby makes anticipatory adjustments to being lifted, shows selective attention to the human face, looks in the direction of the person who leaves him, smiles in response to the person who speaks to him, shows delight in personal attention, and laughs when being played with. From the fifth or sixth month, the baby reacts differently to smiling and scolding and distinguishes between friendly and angry voices. He recognizes familiar persons with a smile; laughs in peekaboo play; imitates simple acts, such as the clapping of hands and waving of arms; resents opposition or interference; and shows definite expressions of fear in the presence of strangers (225).

During the sixth month, the baby's social advances are more aggressive. He pulls the adult's hair; grabs his nose, eyeglasses, or clothes; and explores his different facial features. By the eighth or ninth month, the baby attempts to imitate speech sounds and simple acts and gestures observed in others. Between the tenth and twelfth months, he plays with his image in the mirror and even kisses it as if it were another person. At twelve months, he can refrain from doing things in response to "no-no," and he shows his fear and dislike of strangers by drawing away and crying when a stranger approaches.

From the fifteenth month on, the baby shows an increasing interest in adults and a strong desire to be with them and to imitate them. At two years, he can cooperate with adults in a number of routine activities. Thus, in a relatively short period of time, the baby has changed from a passive member of the family who receives much attention but gives little in return, to an active member who initiates social contacts and is a part of the social group that constitutes the family (78, 113).

Reactions to Other Babies. Social reactions to other babies lag behind social reactions to adults. The first indication that a baby perceives another occurs between the ages of four and five months, when the baby smiles at another baby or shows attentive interest in the cry of another. Friendly contacts between babies six to eight months old consist of looking, smiling, and reaching out and touching. Unfriendly contacts consist of blind attempts to grasp something held by another baby and often result in impersonal fights. Between nine and thirteen months, the baby explores other babies by pulling their hair or clothes, imitates the behavior and vocalization of others, and shows for the first time cooperation and social use of material. When a toy is taken away by another, the baby becomes angry, fights, and cries (30, 225).

Social reactions toward other children during the second year develop rapidly. From the thirteenth to the eighteenth month, the young child smiles and laughs in imitation of another child. Interest shifts from play materials to the playmate, and there is less fighting over toys and more cooperative play. During the last half of the second year, the child is definitely interested in play with children; he regards play materials as a means of establishing social relationships. The child cooperates with his playmate, modifies his behavior to adjust to his playmate's activity, and engages in games with other children (124, 201).

Behavior in Social Situations. As a result of the child's contacts with others, certain forms of social behavior begin to develop. In order to become a part of the social group, the baby *imitates* those about him, both adults and other babies. He first imitates facial expressions, such as laughing and crying, around the third month; then gestures and movements, such as waving bye-bye, shaking the head, or throwing a kiss, from the age of six months; and still later, around the twelfth month, sounds, such as "choo-choo," "tick-tock," "ding-dong," or simple speech sounds.

By the fifth month, the baby begins to distinguish familiar people from strangers. This results in *timidity* and *shyness* in the presence of strangers, appearing first around the sixth month and becoming most pronounced from the ninth to the twelfth month —the period commonly known as the "strange age." At this time, the baby reacts to strangers with a solemn stare, puckered lips, whimpering, and crying. He hides his head and clings to the person holding him. This is the age of "infantile fearfulness"—a time when the baby needs the security of familiar people (83).

Toward the end of the second year, there is another "strange age." How pronounced it will be depends largely upon the opportunities the baby has had to come in contact with different people and new environments. At this time, there is an ostrichlike desire to hide from strangers. The child buries his head in the mother's lap or hides behind a piece of furniture; he is shy about accepting things from strangers and sometimes refuses to speak. This self-conscious, shy behavior is especially pronounced between sixty-six and eighty-six weeks of age, but it is often seen among older children as well if they suffer from feelings of insecurity. This shyness often persists and reaches another peak as children approach adolescence (30, 133).

Rivalry, especially in play with other children and in the bid for attention from adults, appears during the second year. The baby tries to take the toys of others, not because he wants them, but because it gives him pleasure to assert his superiority.

Social cooperation appears first in the baby's play with adults. Because the adult is willing to do the lion's share of giving and taking, cooperation is successful, but with others of approximately the same age, co-operative play lasts for only a few minutes at a time (113).

Resistant behavior, as expressed by tensing the body, crying, and refusing to obey, becomes pronounced after the baby is eighteen months old and continues even after he has achieved a certain degree of independence. Whether this resistant behavior will develop into negativism as the child grows older will depend to a large extent upon the opportunity he is given to be independent. It will also be influenced by how realistic he is about his limitations and consequent need for help (14).

SOCIAL BEHAVIOR IN EARLY CHILDHOOD

From ages two to six years, the child develops into a distinctly socialized individual. He learns to adapt himself to others and to cooperate in group play activities. When his school days begin, he is prepared for active group participation. Most of the important types of social behavior necessary to adjustment to others begin to develop in early childhood.

These years are often called the "pregang age"—the time when the child is normally learning how to make social contacts and get along with people outside the home, especially children of his own age. Follow-up studies of groups of children have revealed that the social attitudes and behavior established during the preschool years persist with little change (178).

The number of contacts the child has with other children during the pregang period is an important factor in determining how far his social development will progress. Children of kindergarten age who have had nursery-school experience enter into a decidedly larger number of social contacts and make better adjustments than those who have not had this experience (26, 178).

As has been pointed out, however, the *kind* of social experiences the child has is more important than the number. If he has had pleasant contacts with other children or adults outside the home, even though they were only occasional, he usually wants to repeat them. If he has had primarily unpleasant contacts, he will shun further contacts, even when they are readily available. By doing so, he will be deprived of important learning experiences.

One of the many advantages of nursery school or kindergarten is that it provides social experiences under the guidance of trained teachers who promote enjoyable contacts and are on the alert to see that no child is subjected to treatment that might condition him to avoid social contacts. A busy mother who sends her child out to play with the neighborhood children cannot control the situation as a teacher can. Consequently, her child may be subjected to such unpleasant experiences that he will withdraw rather than face such experiences in the future. Furthermore, in a neighborhood group, the younger children are often teased and bullied and "bossed around" by the older children. The younger children will be conditioned unfavorably to future social contacts and will want to avoid them. The older children, too, are learning patterns of social behavior that will lead to serious social problems if they treat their peers as they treat younger children (26, 79, 201).

Relations with Adults. With each succeeding year, the young child spends less time with adults and derives less enjoyment from them. His interest in playmates of his own age constantly grows stronger. While the two-year-old passively relies on adults for attention and assistance, the three-year-old resists adult influence and wants to be independent. He becomes self-assertive and difficult to handle. The four- or five-year-old gradually becomes more friendly and cooperative, seeking the approval and trying to avoid the disapproval of adults (28, 79).

Despite his resistance to adult authority, the young child is, nevertheless, greatly influenced by adults in his behavior and in his social attitudes. Parents and teachers are primarily responsible for setting the pattern for the social attitudes the child will have— whether these will be attitudes of good will and friendly cooperation toward all or of intolerance and prejudice against those who are different (124, 225).

Relations with Other Children. Before the age of two years, young children engage in solitary or parallel play. Even though two or three children play in the same room and with similar toys, no social interaction takes place. Their only contacts consist of imitating or watching one another or of attempting to take one another's toys.

From the age of three or four years, children begin to play together, to talk to one another while they play, and to select from the children present those with whom they prefer to play. The size of the play group increases with age, from two members at three years to three or four members at six years. Even then, the group splits, and the children play in twos. The most common behavior of these groups consists of watching each other, holding conversations, and making verbal suggestions (108, 161).

A study of preschool children has revealed that as the children advance in age, there is an increase in friendly approaches to other children and a decrease in hostile interactions (see Figure 8–2). Among boys, for example, those 2½ to 3½ years of age made one association and one friendly approach interaction with other children every 2 minutes; those 5½ to 6½ years of age made two associations and two friendly approach interactions every 2 minutes. Girls, 2½ to 3½ years of age made one association with other children every 6 minutes and one friendly approach interaction every 3 to 4 minutes. In the older group, 5½ to 6½ years of age, girls made associations with other children every 2 minutes and one friendly approach interaction every 1½ minutes. Age for age, boys made more friendly as well as more hostile approaches to other children (135).

Throughout the years of early childhood, the child is self-centered in his social behavior. He likes to boast of his achievements and even of his family. He cooperates when it is convenient to him and when his own interests or activities are not interfered with. While this behavior shows a shift away from

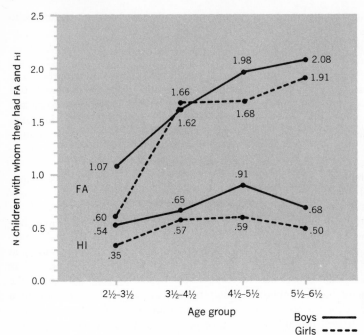

Figure 8–2. Friendly approaches (FA) increase and hostile interactions (HI) decrease when children have an opportunity to be with their peers. (Adapted from H. R. Marshall, Relations between home experiences and children's use of language in play interactions with peers, *Psychol. Monogr.,* **1961, 75, No. 5. Used by permission.)**

the egocentrism of the baby, the shift is far from complete. The child may, from time to time, revert to the simpler forms of social behavior, especially when he is thrown with a group of strange children. Under such circumstances, he may approach them in a sequence of behavior patterns that follow closely the general pattern of early social development, from solitary to parallel to co-operative play (108, 124).

Behavior in Social Situations. As a result of early social contacts with children and with adults, the child begins to develop types of social behavior that will prove to be invaluable to him. Because, as a baby, he was helpless and required constant care, every young child is self-centered. Play with other children soon teaches him to adjust himself to group life, to give and take, and to share his possessions with his playmates. Through imitation of the actions, words, and emotions of others, the child tries to conform to a pattern approved by the group to which he belongs.

Many forms of behavior appear to be unsocial or even antisocial, but, in reality,

each is important in the socializing process. The foundations laid in early childhood will determine how the child will adjust when his environment becomes broader and he does not have the protection and guidance of his parents.

Of the characteristic forms of behavior that appear in early childhood, those discussed in the following sections are most common.

NEGATIVISM

Negativism is a form of exaggerated resistive behavior, "replete with all the emotional concomitants of infantile self-assertion" (8). It is an "interesting combination of self-assertion, self-protection, and of resistance to excessive pressure" (133). When the child has a particularly difficult time making his wants fit in with those of other people, he becomes "cranky," stubborn, and downright rebellious (14). He is hard to manage and difficult to live with. Negativism is often aggravated by the fact that adults do not realize that a child may have wants that are important to him, that he is incapable of doing things as well or as quickly as an older child, and that he has been so accustomed to having things done for him that it is hard for him to adjust to doing things for others, how and when they wish them to be done.

Causes of Negativism. Negativism is a product of social situations. It occurs as a result of aggressive discipline or an intolerant attitude toward normal childish behavior. It generally appears in connection with the established home routine, when the child refuses to comply with the adult's requests that he carry out a certain activity at a scheduled time. It also appears in situations involving strangers.

The more the child is frustrated by adult interference, the more negativistic his behavior will be (79, 161). When child training is inconsistent, children learn that resistance is "their best defense in the face of erratic training." It often occurs when toilet training is begun before the child is ready or when "quick-tempoed persons push slow-tempoed persons too fast" (133).

Age of Negativism. Resistant behavior begins at about eighteen months of age and reaches a peak between three and six years, after which it recedes rapidly. Boys often experience a second peak between ten and eleven years of age (see Figure 8–3). Decline in negativism comes partly from social influences, partly from the child's realization that it is to his advantage to comply, and partly from the fact that adults learn to respect the child's wishes (1, 79).

Because negativism is so common, it may be regarded as "normal"; it is certainly almost inevitable. Even well-adjusted children are usually negativistic for a time, though their negativism is less frequent and less severe than that of poorly adjusted children. If a child does not show negativism at any time, there is reason to believe that he is lethargic and below par physically or that his environment is so artificially controlled to avoid all friction that he will be headed for difficulty later on (8, 14, 156).

Form of Expression. Among young children, negativism may take the form of physical tenseness, which is the opposite of "cuddliness"; of failure to carry out requests, even though they apparently understand; of pretending not to hear or understand; of stubbornness in connection with all routine activities, such as eating and toileting; and of many little acts of self-assertiveness, such as commanding, demanding, walking away, or hiding when called. Extremely negative children may hold their breath until they are literally blue in the

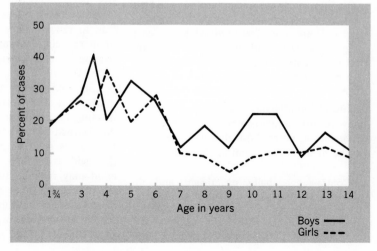

Figure 8–3. The pattern of negativistic behavior among boys and girls in childhood. (Adapted from J. Macfarlane, L. Allen, and M. P. Honzik, *A developmental study of the behavior problems of normal children between twenty-one months and fourteen years,* University of California Press, 1954. Used by permission.)

face, force themselves to vomit, or refuse to urinate or to swallow food.

Negativism is commonly associated with temper tantrums, destructiveness, moodiness, and somberness. The well-adjusted child generally expresses his negativism in direct forms, while the poorly adjusted child expresses his negativistic feelings in diffuse and generalized ways, the most common of which are temper outbursts (109, 133, 156).

Between the ages of four and six years, there is a decline in physical forms of resistance and an increase in verbal forms. There is a growing use of protective lying. The child uses "No" as an answer to all sorts of suggestions, questions, and amiable approaches. He subtly pretends not to hear or understand; he refuses to see the point, insists upon referring to a subject that has been closed, and is careless in carrying out requests or duties; and he annoys others and makes repeated complaints.

Variations in Negativism. Negativism varies in form, frequency, and intensity at different ages. No significant relationship has been found between *intelligence* and negativism. Children of all intellectual levels seem to be subject to negativism at approximately the same ages. In the higher *socioeconomic groups,* boys show slightly less negativism than girls. This difference has been explained by the fact that boys are more likely to be spoiled than girls. On the whole, children show more resistance to other children than to adults (9, 23). Persistently negativistic girls are often *first-born,* while the least negativistic are nonfirsts. Among boys, on the other hand, the persistently negativistic are nonfirsts (133).

Value of Negativism. Parents and teachers may regard negativism as a nuisance, but Bahnam has pointed out that it is important in the social development of the child:

Contra-suggestibility, negativism, and obstinacy in children may be taken as signs of potentiality for good social adjustment. They are forms of behavior that are unsatisfactory in themselves, but that at least show vitality, motivation, and the beginnings of selective sensitivity to a complex social situation. They indicate that the child is capable of developing social and emotional attachments and antagonisms. . . . Children become excessively obstinate when demands are made that are impossible for them to execute, when the demands are humiliating, unfair, or exceedingly disagreeable or painful. Obstinate contrariness is a compensatory adaptive reaction, only partially successful, in the interest of self-preservation, growth, and development. It is likely to change to cooperative behavior when the child finds something he can do that will bring satisfaction to him while complying with the wishes of those for whom he cares (14).

AGGRESSION

Aggression is an actual or threatened act of hostility, usually unprovoked by another person. Ordinarily, it reaches its peak between the ages of 4½ and 5½ years (135). It may be a form of displaced anger, arising when the child cannot express his anger directly toward the person or object that gave rise to it. Generally, it is a reaction to frustration which predisposes the child to attack a person or object that stands in the way of his doing what he wants to do. It is especially strong in a child who wants power and dominance or who is identified with an aggressive adult or aggressive children. The more frustrated a child is, the more aggressive he is likely to become. A child who learns from experience that aggression will lead to reward, either in attaining his goal or in reducing his anxiety, will continue to use aggression whenever he is frustrated (126, 167).

The child who is nonaggressive has generally had less fortunate experiences in meeting his needs in aggressive attacks; he has learned that withdrawal and renunciation of his goal are more effective ways to deal with frustration or to allay anxiety. A child may restrain his aggressiveness while his parents or other adults are around because of fear of punishment, but this restraint only serves to produce more frustrations which will lead to even greater aggressiveness when no adults are present (183, 188).

Causes of Aggressiveness.   Aggressiveness is aroused when something happens to keep the child from achieving a *goal that is important to him.* There are many causes of aggressiveness in young children; which will dominate will depend largely upon the child himself. Aggressiveness may come from the child's desire to have attention and to demonstrate his superiority. It may be a form of self-protection arising from the fact that he feels insecure and is on the defensive, or it may be an expression of jealousy. Sometimes aggressiveness comes from poor social relationships, while, at other times, it indicates an improved sociability. Younger children have fewer and briefer contacts with other children than older children do, and as a result they have fewer opportunities for aggressiveness. By the third year, however, there is a definite increase in aggressiveness as contacts with other children become more frequent.

Identifying with aggressive fantasy characters in movies, in cartoons, or on television tends to increase aggressiveness in children, though it sometimes acts as a form of catharsis and decreases aggressiveness in real-life situations if children get rid of their aggressive feelings by "taking it out" on the characters in the fantasy experiences. Any interference with the adult-child interaction becomes frustrating to the child and leads to aggressiveness. The longer the frustration continues, the more aggressive the child becomes (96, 164, 167).

Physical punishment is a common cause of aggressiveness; in turn, it is often the result of aggressiveness. Children who are punished a great deal for their aggressiveness or whose mothers are most permissive toward aggressive behavior show more aggression than children whose parents take a middle-of-the-road approach. Just being identified with an aggressive person, whether an adult or an older child, may make a child aggressive; it will certainly increase any aggressive tendency he may have (126, 130, 182).

Expressions of Aggressiveness.   Aggressiveness is expressed most commonly in *provoked physical aggression,* as when a child engages in a physical attack after provocation; in *outbursts of aggression,* or a display of uncontrolled temper-tantrum behavior; in *verbal aggression,* as when a child verbally attacks another with threats, scoldings, or lies; and in *indirect aggression,* which consists of an attack through another person or object, as when a child talks about another person or breaks things belonging to a person he would like to attack directly (125). With repetition, aggressive expressions develop into a pattern, and the child is labeled an "aggressive child" (4).

The young child generally expresses his aggressiveness by methods which range from mild physical attacks with the hands and feet or a bothersome or painful gadget to more serious attacks, in which the person attacked may be badly hurt. The younger the child, the more completely he expresses his aggression—he attacks more vigorously and cries more, thus "getting it out of his system." From the age of four or five years, there is a gradual decrease in direct expressions of aggressiveness and a progressive increase in indirect or deflected expressions of hostility, especially in verbal attacks—blaming others, tattling, and name calling (59, 69, 217).

Variations in Aggressiveness.   There are marked variations in the frequency and intensity of aggressiveness as well as in the form it takes in different children and in the same child at different times. Among young children, *boys* are usually more aggressive than girls. Boys use physical attacks most often, while girls tend to favor verbal forms. By the time they reach four or five years of age, however, boys have increased their use of verbal attacks (59, 135, 217). Sex differences in aggressiveness are shown in Figure 7–9, page 287.

Children with a strong *need for love* and affection quickly discover that aggressiveness will win disapproval. Therefore, to meet their need for love, they learn to be submissive, even in the presence of strong frustrations. *Maladjusted* children at every age are distinctly less able to control aggressive responses than well-adjusted children. Even in well-adjusted children, however, the intensity of aggressiveness will depend largely upon the degree of frustration experienced (69, 167, 177).

The *status* of the child *within the family* and *parental attitudes toward child training* are important factors in determining how aggressive the child will be (66). Older siblings, it has been found, tend to be less aggressive than younger children or only children (121). The mother who blames the child for his aggressiveness and feels that he should be punished for it or the one who blames herself because she is tired and cross is likely to increase aggressive behavior in her child (166). Aggressiveness is greater where parents are authoritarian and believe that corporal punishment is necessary in child training. It is also greater in children whose parents have a permissive attitude toward aggressiveness (130, 184).

Aggressiveness varies according to the *time of day,* the *setting* of the play, *familiarity* with other children in the setting, and whether or not *adults are present*. It is likely to be strongest during fatigue periods, just before eating and sleeping. The better the child knows the other children he is playing with, the more aggressive he is likely to be. In a study of preschool children, for example, it was found that the children who had attended school longer were more aggressive than the newcomers (167).

Children tend to be more aggressive when there is an adult around whose attention they want to attract or whose protection they can seek should their aggressiveness lead to a quarrel. Some young children, however, begin to be aggressive almost as soon as they are left alone with other children (96). Whether they will become more or less aggressive when adults are absent will depend upon the type of children they are playing with; if they are submissive, their playmates are more likely to "pick on" them than if they, too, are aggressive (190).

The *type of aggressive behavior* the child displays likewise varies. If the child has been trained in social conformity, he will be more likely to displace his aggressive behavior in a frustrating experience than to attack directly the person who has frustrated him. Should the child be frustrated by a parent, for example, he will displace his aggression to a sibling or a toy. The more anxious and guilty the child feels about his aggressiveness, the more likely he is to displace his aggressive responses (112). Popular children express their aggressions within the context of their play and have a definite single recipient of their aggression; they rarely displace it. By contrast, unpopular children more often displace their aggression, attacking anyone who happens to be around. Furthermore, the popular child uses verbal aggression less to attract attention to himself than the unpopular child; the unpopular child uses both physical and verbal aggression (61).

QUARRELING

Quarrels are angry disputes that generally start when a person makes an unprovoked attack on another. They are thus an outgrowth of aggression. Quarreling differs from aggression, however, in two major respects: (1) Quarreling involves two or more people, while aggression is an individual act; and (2) one of the people involved in a quarrel plays a defensive role, while, in aggression, the role is always "aggressive." Quarreling is like aggression in that both are highly charged with emotions, mainly anger; both involve attacks on another person; and in both, the attack may be physical or verbal. Because quarreling usually has its origin in aggression, the course of its development closely parallels that of aggression. It reaches its peak between the ages of three and four years and then begins to decline as the child learns how to make better social adjustments.

Causes of Quarreling. A child quarrels because he does not know how to make social contacts in a more mature way. Quarreling begins when one child attacks another's person or property. Among young children, a conflict over property is the usual starting point (159, 161).

Quarreling does *not* mean that children dislike each other. In fact, there are more quarrels among friends than among children who have little in common. Quarrels generally end by one child, usually the younger or the weaker of the two, yielding to the force of the other. Sometimes a parent or teacher interferes and puts an end to the quarrel. Only rarely is it ended by the interference of another child, by a compromise, or by one child yielding voluntarily. Once the quarrel is ended, regardless of *how* it was ended, the children involved are cheerful and friendly, taking up where they left off when the quarrel started. Rarely do they show resentment or break off the friendship.

Behavior in Quarreling. Quarreling may involve destroying another child's work, taking away his toys, screaming, crying, biting, kicking, hitting, name calling, and making derogatory statements. Most young children use physical attacks. If punished, they gradually substitute verbal for physical attacks. Quarrels among young children are short but intense; on the average, they last approximately 30 seconds and occur every 5 minutes while the children are together. As children grow older, quarrels occur less frequently but last longer, and the fighting is harder (79, 135).

Variations in Quarreling. The *type of activity* engaged in influences the frequency and intensity of quarreling. Constructive play of any type and meddlesome, destructive activities lead to most quarreling because they all involve comparisons with other children. The least quarreling occurs when the play is individual, quiet, and intellectual. *Boys* at every age quarrel more than girls; boys start more quarrels, they retaliate more, and their quarreling is more aggressive, dynamic, and outgoing. Girls will attack girls, but less violently than they attack boys. Girls tend to shift from physical to verbal attacks earlier than boys (181, 185).

Within the home, there is a great deal of quarreling among *siblings*. During early childhood, siblings of the same sex quarrel more than siblings of opposite sexes (121). Children of the lower *socioeconomic groups* are usually more aggressive and quarrel more, with both siblings and playmates, than children from the higher socioeconomic groups (146). The number of quarrels the child engages in is closely related to his *general activity*. The more the child "gets around," and the more contacts he has with other children, the more quarreling he is likely to do (113). Finally, quarreling is influenced by the amount and type of *guidance* the child receives from parents and teachers. Because middle-class parents put more emphasis on amicable play and show more disapproval of quarreling than lower-class parents, children from middle-class homes learn how to play together earlier than children from lower socioeconomic groups (17, 130).

Values of Quarreling. Unpleasant as quarreling may be for those who live and work with children, quarreling is an *educational experience* for the child. It teaches him, in a practical way, what other people will and will not tolerate. The child finds, for example, that if he grabs a toy from another child, the child will grab it back and start a quarrel. Furthermore, he discovers that "picking fights" makes him unpopular and can lead to physical discomfort and pain.

He also discovers that quarreling with a child who is bigger and stronger than he is likely to lead to defeat. Should he fight with a smaller child whom he can handle successfully, he will be shamed for his poor sportsmanship in "picking on" a little child. With guidance, a child learns that his ends can be reached more pleasantly by more social approaches, such as cooperation.

TEASING AND BULLYING

Teasing and bullying are aggressive forms of behavior that usually lead to quarreling. Teasing consists in a mental attack on another in an attempt to "get his goat" and thus arouse an angry response. It may involve calling someone by a nickname that arouses his anger or putting emphasis on his physical or mental weaknesses. In bullying, on the other hand, the attacker attempts to inflict physical pain on another because of the pleasure he derives from watching the victim's discomfort and attempts to retaliate. Bullying includes such things as pulling another's hair or clothes; pinching, poking, and pushing; and sticking another with a pin or putting a thumbtack in his chair.

Younger children in the home or in the school class are generally made the "butts" of the teasing and bullying of older children. Not all children, however, engage in these forms of aggressiveness. Boys tease and bully more, on the average, than girls, and children who show feelings of inferiority or insecurity engage in these activities more than better-adjusted children (79, 159).

RIVALRY

Rivalry is characterized by a desire to excel, or to outdo others; it is always stimulated by another person. Competition for prestige is not apparent before the age of four years (103). Children of two years of age show no signs of the competitive spirit, and when placed in a competitive situation, they merely look at each other occasionally. A year later, some competition appears, but it is eclipsed by other social attitudes, especially imitation. By four years of age, however, the child has a better idea of excelling and is then interested in excelling. By the age of six years, most children have a well-developed competitive spirit (79, 201).

Variations in Rivalry. Children from the lower *socioeconomic groups,* boys especially, are more competitive at every age than those of the higher socioeconomic groups (146). When competing with *strangers,* children are quieter than when competing with friends. With their *friends,* they become noisy and excited. Young children, as a rule, will persist in a task longer when *competing with others* than when working alone.

Rivalry, followed by quarreling, is more common in the presence of a third person, especially an adult for whose attention the children compete. One of the most common forms of competition among young children is *bragging* about being first in some activity or about owning superior material possessions (30, 124).

Up to the time the child begins to associate regularly with other children in the presence of an adult, as in a nursery school, kindergarten, or organized play group, he is more anxious for *adult* than for peer *attention* and uses any means he can to get it. Gradually, as his interest shifts to the peer group, he brags and shows off his skills in an attempt to assert his superiority and capture the spotlight from another child (80).

Rivalry is very common in the home, especially when jealousy exists between *siblings.* Rivalry between siblings of the two sexes or between male siblings is likely to be stronger and to lead to more quarreling than rivalry between female siblings. This is especially true when the mother shows a preference for a son or when the older son is treated in such a way that the other children regard him as "mother's pet" (28, 121).

COOPERATION

Since the child of two or three years of age is self-centered and quarrelsome, it is difficult to get him to play in a cooperative manner with other children. By the end of the third or fourth year, however, there is an increase in cooperative play. The more opportunity the little child has to be with other children, the sooner he will learn to cooperate with them. Cooperative group work is not understood much before the child is six or seven years old. The stronger the friendship of the group members, the more cooperative they will be (24).

Delay in developing cooperative behavior is often due to lack of opportunity to learn work skills in the home. The young child who wants to "help mother" is far too often denied the opportunity to do so because the mother feels that he will be more of a hindrance than a help or because she feels that childhood should be a "happy, carefree

Children brought up by democratic training methods enjoy being cooperative and are able to extend the habit of cooperation to their outside social relationships and activities. (Standard Oil Co., N.J.)

time." Only if he has frequent opportunities for contacts outside the home does he learn to be cooperative.

One of the most important characteristics of popular children is that they are regarded as cooperative by their peers; lack of cooperativeness contributes to social rejection (55, 86). Where authoritarian child-training methods are used in the home to *force* cooperation, children often develop negative attitudes and tend to be uncooperative when parental authority is absent. Children brought up by more democratic child-training methods, by contrast, enjoy being cooperative. As a result, they develop the habit of cooperation in the home and carry it into their out-of-the-home social relationships (101, 120).

ASCENDANT BEHAVIOR

Ascendant behavior is "any kind of behavior by which an individual attains or maintains mastery of a social situation, or attempts to do so, so he is in control of his own act and can carry out his purposes" (157). It is the tendency to dominate others, or "bossiness." This tendency is nearly universal among young children; it usually shows itself first in the child's relationships with adults. Beginning when the child is three years of age, ascendancy increases as opportunities for social contacts increase; it reaches a peak around the age of five years and then declines (204).

Variations in Ascendant Behavior. Among nursery-school children, *girls* are significantly more dominating than boys in play situations. In kindergarten children, the reverse is true. When children are paired with those of the opposite sex, the girls are bossier than the boys (4, 157).

It is commonly believed that Northern children are more assertive than Southern children, that they have more quarrels with their playmates, that they have less socially acceptable ways of getting along with others, and that they are less amenable to suggestions from others. The explanation given for this is that Southern children are encouraged by their Negro nurses to behave like "little ladies" or "little gentlemen." As Negro nursemaids are far less common today than in the past, however, this belief is fast becoming an old wives' tale. A recent study of nursery-school children in the North and in the South has revealed no evidence of such differences (157).

Children who are especially assertive toward their contemporaries derive this pattern of behavior from their *home environments*. Such children come from homes where there are friction over disciplinary policies, many restrictions on their behavior, general home discord, and many coercive suggestions from parents. Furthermore, if the parent's attitude toward the child is one of dissatisfaction; if there is little rapport between parent and child; and if the parent shows little understanding and is unready or unwilling to answer the child's natural questions, assertiveness toward others is likely to develop (121, 133).

Value of Ascendant Behavior. When properly directed, ascendant behavior can be of great value to a child. Whether it develops into leadership, bossiness, or undifferentiated ascendance will be influenced, to a large extent, by the child's environment and the people he associates with. He will be bossy, for example, if he is with an adult who tolerates bossiness or with a younger child who has no alternative but to accept such behavior. With other children, the child will use commands, threats, or force to try to gain his objective. He will attempt to secure the materials he wants from his playmates, to direct or influence their behavior, and to resist mastery by others (157).

GENEROSITY

Typically, the young child is egocentric. He demands what he wants, and if it is denied, he will protest by crying or displaying his anger in a temper tantrum. Only after he begins to play with others does he learn to submerge self-interest in the interests of the group. Selfishness usually reaches a peak between the ages of four and six years. It then declines as the child discovers that being selfish leads to lack of social acceptance. By the end of childhood, selfishness has almost completely disappeared in children who make good social adjustments, though it continues to be a common form of behavior among those who make poor social adjustments (90, 214).

Generosity, as shown in a willingness to share with others, increases as selfishness decreases. In one experiment to determine at what age generosity begins to replace selfishness, children were asked to divide an uneven number of nuts between themselves and another child. Between the ages of four and six, the children kept a greater share of the nuts for themselves. After six years of age, they became more generous; at first they gave the other child more than they kept for themselves, and then they divided the nuts equally, leaving one out when they found there was only one left over after the division had been made (214).

In a similar experiment, where children were asked to share an uneven number of pennies earned by performing a cooperative task, selfishness was strongest in the preschool years but declined when the children entered school. The most marked transition from selfishness to generosity came during the fourth and fifth grades, the ages when children are especially anxious to be well accepted by the peer group and when gangs play a dominant role in their social lives (90). The trend from selfishness to generosity is shown in Figure 8–4, which plots the frequency of generosity, equal sharing, and selfishness according to age.

Variations in Generosity. *Poor* children, on the whole, are less selfish than children from well-to-do homes. The most selfish children come from the richest homes—homes where egocentrism is permitted or even encouraged. On the other hand, children from middle-class homes—homes where there is only moderate wealth—are the most generous of all. This may be explained by the strong emphasis middle-class parents place on training for social acceptance and good social adjustments. Children at all ages, but especially during the preschool years, are likely to be most generous in the *presence of an adult. Family size,* likewise, has an influence on generosity. Children from large families are more generous than children from small families, while only children tend to be the most selfish.

Whether the child will be selfish or generous will depend not so much upon the size of his family as upon the *type of training* he receives in the home. Children do not become generous simply because they grow older. Only guidance and a deliberate effort on the part of parents, teachers, and others will foster the development of generosity. There are no marked *sex differences* in generosity or selfishness. Again, whether the child will be selfish or generous will depend primarily on his home training and on social pressures from the peer group (90, 213, 214).

DESIRE FOR SOCIAL APPROVAL

Even a young baby likes to be noticed. Long before he can talk, he "senses" that he is the center of admiration and attention. With each succeeding year, the child becomes increasingly anxious to win the approval of others, first of adults and later of individuals his own age. The desire to impress his companions as well as adults often brings the child into conflict with adult regulations and the codes of the social group.

Absence of social approval not only makes the child unhappy but often drives him to behave in a way that, he has discovered from experience, invariably gets attention. Because young children equate attention and social approval, they often seek attention in socially unacceptable ways. That is why, when they sense that they are being neglected, they "cut up" and noisily demand attention from anyone who happens to be present (133).

While "cutting up" is often used to get attention, the young child may resort to devices that are more socially acceptable. These are mainly verbal. Children's questions, for example, are often attention-getting devices (141). So are urgent requests for help and boasting. Because most of the young child's contacts are with women, both at home and in preschool and play groups, he seeks attention from women more than from men (see Figure 8–5).

When young children learn that all attention is not satisfying, they begin to regulate their behavior to win praise and avoid disapproval. Much of the anxiety young children experience results from their being unsure of the reaction they will get when they do the things they want to do. A sign of

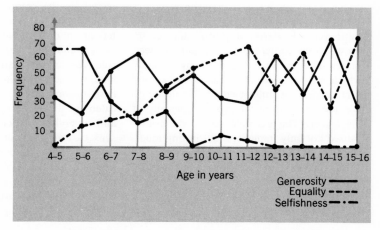

Figure 8–4. Frequency of generosity, equality, and selfishness, according to ages. (Adapted from R. Ugurel-Semin, Moral behavior and moral judgments of children, *J. abnorm. soc. Psychol.*, 1952, 47, 463–477. Used by permission.)

Frequency

80
70
60
50
40
30
20
10

4–5 5–6 6–7 7–8 8–9 9–10 10–11 11–12 12–13 13–14 14–15 15–16

Age in years

Generosity ———
Equality - - - -
Selfishness —·—

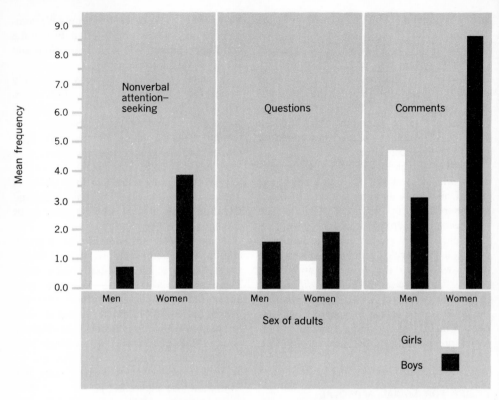

Figure 8–5. Attention seeking from male and female adults by young children of both sexes. (Adapted from J. L. Gewirtz, Three determinants of attention-seeking in young children, *Monogr. Soc. Res. Child Developm.*, 1954, 19, No. 2. Used by permission.)

approval, such as a smile or a nod, or a sign of disapproval, such as a frown or a harsh word, means more to a young child when it comes from an adult than when it comes from another child (140, 184). After the third year, however, approval and disapproval from contemporaries begin to mean more. This is well illustrated by a study which showed that the young child's food preferences are influenced by his desire to win the approval of the group, especially of the leader. The example set by the leader caused not only immediate but lasting modifications in the child's preferences (113). Much the same is true of clothes; the child will rebel against wearing a garment, even a favorite garment, if he finds that it leads to social disapproval (79).

SYMPATHY

Sympathy is behavior in which one is affected by the emotional states of another. In an extensive study of sympathetic behavior in nursery-school children, children of two and three years of age did not, as a rule, respond sympathetically to black-and-blue wounds, swellings, lumps, and minor flesh distortions; to Red Ridinghood being eaten by the wolf; to pictures of accidents and funerals; or to crippled persons or persons carrying crutches. The three-year-olds generally, though not universally, responded sympathetically to blind people and to people who wore bandages or whose injuries were colored with Mercurochrome or iodine or involved red swellings, scars, or scratches.

They were sympathetic to children deprived of their toys, food, or mothers or caught in physical dilemmas such as in a playpen or in a bicycle. They sympathized with a child who cried or had to stay in bed, who was frustrated in his activity, who was incapable of doing a job he had undertaken, or who was involved in an accident (159).

Responses in Sympathy. Young children respond sympathetically by helping others; by removing, attempting to remove, or punishing the cause of distress; by comforting others with pats, hugs, and kisses; by protecting and defending the person in distress; by telling an adult or child about an individual in distress; by asking questions to find out the cause of distress; and by suggesting or effecting solutions. Occasionally, unsympathetic responses are observed. These include laughing at the person in distress; using the situation to play his own role, usually a dominating one; attacking a child in distress; or merely staring (159). Some young children show sympathy by being kind to a newcomer in a group or by defending the rights of younger children or those who are unable to defend themselves (78, 214).

Variations in Sympathy. At two or three years of age, no *sex differences* in sympathetic behavior occur, though at later ages, girls are more sympathetic than boys. While sympathy increases with both mental age and chronological age, it is more dependent upon the *personality pattern* of the child. The child who is self-centered and absorbed in his own difficulties, who feels insecure as a result of unpleasant experiences in the past, or whose past experiences have been such that he cannot understand the suffering of another will show unsympathetic behavior.

Furthermore, children vary from *time to time* in the amount of sympathy they show. As the child gains more self-confidence, he is likely to be less sympathetic. When a child is *responsible,* either directly or indirectly, for the distress of another, he will be less sympathetic than if the distress were caused by another child. Sympathy, likewise, is dependent to a large extent upon the child's *ability to comprehend* the situation. This depends partly upon his mental and chronological age and partly upon his previous experiences (30, 159).

DEPENDENCY

The "independence-conscious" child, who constantly says, "I can do it," is still fundamentally dependent (108). At first, he is dependent mainly on his parents; later, he shifts some of his dependency to his siblings, especially older siblings who frequently play the role of parent substitutes (121). From 2½ to 4½ years, he shifts his dependency somewhat to the peer group (135, 138). Dependence on others for attention and affection, however, does not decrease as the child's need for help decreases. It may change in form, but it persists throughout the early years of childhood and often becomes stronger (80).

Dependent Behavior. Dependent behavior shows itself most commonly in seeking help when help is not needed, seeking attention and approval from others, and being highly suggestible. The more dependent the child is, the stronger and more highly developed these patterns of behavior will be. The dependent child welcomes *help* from anyone but is especially anxious to receive it from the person or persons on whom he is accustomed to rely, usually the mother or a teacher. An overdependent child, more from habit than from actual need, will seek help even when he is capable of being independent.

A habit of dependency, resulting from encouragement at home, leads the child to depend on his playmates as well as on adults. As a result, he is highly *suggestible* and easily *influenced.* In addition, he is unhappy when people pay little attention to him. He wants overt manifestations of their interest, and thus he seeks attention by asking for help when he does not need it, by asking questions, by doing things that are forbidden, and by reverting to infantile behavior. Because young children derive more satisfaction from their dependency on adults than on agemates, most of their attention-seeking behaviors are directed toward adults (80, 111). (See Figure 8–5, page 350.)

Variations in Dependency. Whether the child, as he grows older and acquires skills that normally lead to independence, will actually become independent will be greatly influenced by *child-training* methods and *learning opportunities* afforded by the home. Children who are trained to be dependent— who have too much done for them and who have too few responsibilities and too few opportunities to learn to do things for themselves—learn to be dependent. Dependency training is more characteristic of middle-class than of lower-class parents. Training for independence, by contrast, counteracts much of the dependency a child shows when he does not need help from others (92).

Overdependency, or a tendency to depend on others for more help, attention, and affection than is developmentally appropriate for the child's age and level of development, generally stems from *feelings of insecurity.* These feelings, in turn, are the effects of domination or rejection by the parent. In time, they lead to a generalized state of overdependency in which the young child depends on *anyone* who is available, whether an adult or another child. Overdependency is especially common among children who suffer from a *chronic illness,* such as asthma, and in first-born children whose *status in the family* is threatened by the arrival of siblings (133).

Overdependency can be lessened or increased according to the way it is *handled by parents or teachers.* If the child derives little satisfaction from being dependent on others, he is not motivated to continue to be dependent. The more parents and teachers encourage and reward independence in the child, the less dependent he will be (51). Isolating the child from adults when he wants to be with them, however, does *not* encourage the child to be more independent, as many adults believe it will. Because isola-

tion is frustrating for the child, it stifles any motivation he may have to be independent (96).

FRIENDLINESS

Young children show a friendly attitude toward both adults and other children. They crave social contacts and are unhappy when deprived of them. Much of the young child's behavior, such as his aggressiveness, his lack of sympathy, or his demands for attention, may suggest that he regards others as potential enemies and that he is self-bound. Such, however, is not the case. The child wants to be friends; in his childish, bungling way, he tries to let the other person know this. He simply *has not learned how to establish social contacts in a more favorable way.*

Studies of affectionate behavior in young children have revealed that affectionate approaches to other children are more frequent than aggressive approaches. While girls have a more friendly attitude toward their agemates than boys, both boys and girls *initiate* most of their social contacts by friendly overtures. Once a social contact has been initiated, it may develop into an unsocial one. A friendly approach may quickly turn into a quarrel, though, as has already been pointed out, the quarrel is short, and a friendly relationship is quickly reestablished (125, 130, 217). Were the young child not friendly, he would have little motivation to resume a friendly relationship after the quarrel ended. Like an older child, he would be more likely to break off the friendship and seek new friends (106).

Friendly Behavior. Young children express their friendliness by such overt acts as hugging, kissing, and stroking; by giving rapt attention to what the other person says or does; by trying to protect the person against aggressive acts of another; by helping in whatever way they can; by comforting the person in distress; and by wanting to be with the person constantly. As their ability to speak improves, they verbalize their friendliness by such remarks as "I love you," "You are my friend," or "I want to go with you."

There is a gradual increase in overt expressions of affection as children grow older. After the child's second or third birthday, parents tend to be more strict in their discipline; as a result, they show less approval and affection for the child than they did when he was young and helpless (13, 47). Receiving less affection gives the young child an incentive to express his own affection. The most common and most frequent expressions of friendliness are centered around wanting to be like another person and wanting to do things with and for him (80).

Importance of Early Social Behavior. If young children are to develop into social people, they must be encouraged to do so, rewarded for their efforts even when their behavior falls short of adult standards, and guided into methods of coping with social situations that will win the approval they crave. To achieve this goal, four important points must be kept in mind:

1. Young children's behavior in social situations is often not as unsocial as it appears to be. Because unsocial behavior has more attention value than social behavior, parents and teachers tend to overlook the social and concentrate on the unsocial. Also, because they often judge a child's behavior by adult standards, his behavior may *seem* worse than it actually is. Furthermore, since unsocial behavior in young children has considerable nuisance value, the child who behaves in an unsocial way is more of a problem for his parents and teachers than the one who conforms more closely to adult standards. Consequently, they often exaggerate the bad aspects of his behavior.

2. Adults must show the *right kind* of tolerance and understanding of the unsocial behavior of young children. Without question, much of the child's behavior would not be tolerated by the social group were he not "too young to know better." Adults showing the right kind of understanding and tolerance will recognize that a child cannot be expected to behave in a socially accept-

able manner unless he is taught how to do so. They will also recognize that a child cannot develop into a social person overnight. He can, however, be expected to show some improvement from month to month.

Tolerance and understanding can be dangerous if they lead to a hands-off policy, accompanied by the belief that the child will "outgrow" unsocial behavior patterns or will automatically "reform" when he discovers that they bring social disapproval and rejection. Children do not "outgrow" established patterns of behavior. Instead, the patterns become habitual. At no age do people automatically "reform"; they may *want* to reform, but they often do not know how to do so.

Even more serious is the fact that the child whose unsocial behavior is understood and tolerated *will assume that such behavior is socially acceptable.* Later, when he discovers that it is not, replacing it with more acceptable behavior will be a major task. Tolerance and understanding, when used in this negative way, are valueless as teaching devices. In fact, they are harmful because they suggest to the child that he is behaving in a socially approved manner and encourage him to repeat his unsocial acts.

3. The child needs guidance and help to learn how to act in a socially approved manner and to understand why social behavior is more satisfying than the behavior he is expected to abandon. If, for example, he is given a demonstration in real-life situations of how much easier it is to get what he wants by offering to share his possessions with another child than by grabbing, and if he sees how much more willing the other child is to play with him if he is generous than if he is aggressive, he will realize that it is to his personal advantage to behave as parents and teachers have told him.

4. When the child's behavior is guided into channels that will satisfy his need for attention and approval, his motivation to behave as parents, teachers, and society in general expect will increase. Should he, on the other hand, lack this guidance, he is likely to encounter social rejection. Because he gains little satisfaction from social contacts of a rejective sort, he will have little motivation to learn to behave in a socially approved manner.

Should his desire for social acceptance persist in spite of his rejection, he is likely to develop compensatory forms of behavior to satisfy it, inventing imaginary playmates to replace the real playmates he craves or displacing his angers by bullying and teasing younger children or those identified with a minority group. Whether he voluntarily withdraws from social contacts because of lack of satisfaction from them or whether he is forced out of such contacts by his unsocial behavior, the result is the same: He is deprived of the learning opportunities necessary to develop into a social person.

SOCIAL BEHAVIOR
IN LATE CHILDHOOD

After the child enters school and comes into contact with other children, family picnics and parties become a bore. At the same time, individual games give way to group games, and solitary play loses its charm. Since group games require a large number of playmates, the older child's circle of friends gradually widens. With changes in play interests comes an increasingly strong desire to be with, and to be accepted by, children outside the home. This is just as true of girls as of boys, though girls' play outside the home is frequently more restricted. Figure 8–1, page 333, shows the gradual increase in time spent outside the home with increasing age.

Upon beginning school, the child enters the "gang age"—an age when social consciousness develops rapidly and when becoming socialized is one of the major developmental tasks (99). Whether he is bold or shy, friendly or standoffish, the child must learn ways of approaching strangers. He must also learn how to treat his friends. He becomes a member of a peer group, and this group will gradually replace the family in its influence over his behavior and attitudes. The peer group is an "aggregation of people of approximately the same age who *feel* and *act together*" (99).

During this transition from the pregang age of early childhood to the gang age of late childhood, the child goes from one group to another or from group to individual activities. The "shifting-group" stage bridges the gap between the pregang and the gang ages. The informal play group of the early school days consists of only two or three children. It is formed to carry out a specific play activity and is thus transitory. At this time the activity itself, not friendship, is the basis for the organization of the group. Within the group, leadership shifts from one child to another, depending on which child takes the initiative in a specific activity. There are many brief quarrels, but these have no permanent effect on the makeup of the group (79).

Being suddenly thrown in with a large group of children in school does not bring about an abrupt change in social relationships. Instead, there is a gradual increase in group play from the sixth to the eighth year (25). With this change comes a gradual increase in socialization. The child becomes less selfish, self-centered, and aggressive and becomes more cooperative, outgoing, and group-conscious.

CHILDHOOD GANGS

The gang is a spontaneous local group having no authorization from outside and no socially approved aim. Although adults may know that it is being organized, it is formed by the children themselves, without support from parents, teachers, or youth leaders. It is an effort on the part of children to create a society adequate to meet their needs. As such, it is a substitute for what adult society fails to give. It offers relief from adult supervision, though it may not be hostile to the adults in authority. A gang does not need adult consent, nor is it subjected to outside control. The gang is not necessarily the product of a subnormal environment; it often develops where the environment is good.

There is a more definite pattern in the

gang makeup than in the informal group-ings of younger children. Gang members are selected because they are able to do things the others enjoy doing, not because they live near each other or because they can do what one or two members want to do at the moment. The gang exists inde-pendently of activities and then selects the various activities it will engage in. Contrary to popular opinion, the childhood gang is not necessarily composed of "hoodlums," though children's gangs in slum areas often are made up of children who are regarded as such by society. The typical child's gang is a *play group,* made up of children who have common play interests; its primary purpose is to have a good time, though, occasionally, having a good time may lead to mischief making (52, 86, 223).

From the age of six or seven years, boys and girls normally find increasing pleasure in being with small groups of their own sex. If restrained from being with their friends, for even a day, they become fretful, restless, and unhappy. Thus the gang begins to domi-nate the child's life. It sets the style in the clothing he wants to wear, determines the play activities he engages in, and gives him his ideas of right and wrong. Gangs develop their own systems of mores, which give them cohesiveness and protect their identity as ingroups (127). Belonging to a gang gives the child not only companionship and an opportunity to have fun but also a feel-ing of pride and status. As a result, he develops a strong loyalty to his gang. In the latter part of childhood, children lose interest in gang activities and often drop out (79). Figure 8–6 shows some of the ways in which the gang influences the child.

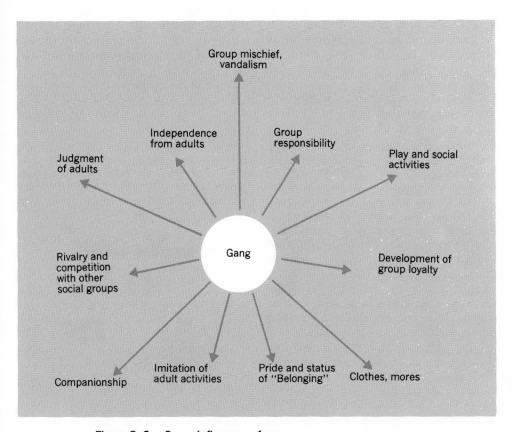

Figure 8–6.   Some influences of gangs.

To increase the feeling of group belonging among members, gangs use (*1*) *gang names,* many of which are taken from the street or neighborhood where the members of the gang live or from a popular book, movie, or comic; (*2*) *secret signals,* passwords, communication codes, or secret languages; (*3*) *insignia,* such as caps or armbands worn by all members of the gang; and (*4*) *initiation ceremonies* in which the skill or physical endurance of a child is tested before he is admitted to membership. Boys, more often than girls, use one or more of these devices to create loyalty within the gang and to make each member feel that he is important because he is accepted.

The *meeting place* of a gang of boys may be a street corner, garage, barn, shed, cellar, vacant lot, deserted house, school playground, or corner drugstore. Girls, whose activities are generally more closely supervised, usually meet at the home of one of the members, at the school playground, or at the corner drugstore or candy store. The ideal meeting place permits minimum adult interference and supervision but, at the same time, provides opportunities for the activities favored by the members.

The *activities* of the gang vary with the community. They include play of all types, such as sports, card games, and going to the movies or theater; mechanical and constructive activities, such as making a rendezvous; social activities, such as hikes, picnics, parties, and dramatic productions; reading; annoying other people, especially members of other groups, members of the opposite sex, and old people; fighting, stealing, gambling, drinking, and smoking, which are forbidden activities at this age; and exploring, which sometimes leads to wandering off for several days or which may be satisfied by camping trips under the supervision of an adult.

Gang activities often border on rowdyism. Boys are apt to be noisy, happy-go-lucky, careless, and trick-playing. In many groups, the activities are characterized by a mob spirit which leads individual members of the group to do things they would never do alone. The tendency toward hoodlumism, vandalism, or general annoyance to the community originates within the group; each member feels obligated because of loyalty to the group, to do what the group does, even though he knows it to be wrong. The excitement and reassurance that come from doing what others do tend to break down even the most rigidly established codes of behavior. Members of a gang often try to test the barriers imposed by adults; as a result, they may engage in behavior which, in adolescents, would be classed as "delinquent" (223).

Girls' gangs, by contrast, far less often engage in socially unacceptable behavior. Their worst offenses are occasional attempts to be grown-up and sophisticated by smoking and by engaging in scandalmongering. Because games and sports mean less to girls than to boys, the gang members spend much of their time talking about their parents, siblings, teachers, and other classmates, especially members of rival gangs; in making things to sell to raise money for charity; in putting on plays after making the costumes and scenery; in going to the movies together or watching television; in playing card games; in cooking food and eating; and in going out for picnics or exploring remote parts of the community together. A few girls' gangs go in for more strenuous activities, such as games and sports, and some, especially in poor neighborhoods, spend their time in mischief making or even in occasional fights with boys' gangs (52, 127).

SEX DIFFERENCES IN GANGS

Boys as a rule, start to form gangs earlier than girls. Both lose interest in gang life at puberty. Because girls mature earlier than boys, the girl's gang experience is shorter than that of the boy. Girls' gangs are usually smaller than boys'; they are much more closely organized and are surrounded with more secrecy. Their leaders are more autocratic, and they are less likely to welcome new members than boys' gangs are. To nongang members, girls sometimes are very unsocial in their behavior; they may even refuse to speak to girls in their classes who do not belong to their gang.

Boys are more likely than girls to include in their gangs children of slightly different ages, thus making a hierarchic social system possible. Leaders are chosen from the older, stronger, more ambitious, or more adventuresome boys. They exert a marked control as well as a marked influence over the other members. The leaders of girls' gangs are generally selected because they are more sophisticated and make a more attractive appearance than the other gang members (127).

BEHAVIOR IN SOCIAL SITUATIONS

A number of different types of behavior develop as a result of gang life. Some are outgrowths of behavior patterns developed during early childhood; others result from the broader social contacts the older child has. Some interfere with social adjustments, although, on the whole, with modifications and changes as the child grows older, they result in improved social adjustments. They are the foundations of social behavior normally found in the adults in our culture today. The most common forms of behavior in social situations during the gang age are discussed in the following sections.

Susceptibility to Social Approval and Disapproval. As soon as the child begins to crave the companionship of others, he also craves their approval of his dress, speech, and behavior. Should a conflict arise between the standards of the home and those of his playmates, the child will invariably side with the latter.

In discussing the older child's susceptibility to group approval and disapproval, Church and Stone have pointed out that "for a 7- or 8-year-old the worst 'sin' is to be in any way different from other children. . . . He apes the dress and mannerisms of older children and subscribes to the group code, even when it runs sharply counter to his own, his family's, and the school's" (44). Because the girl's peer culture conforms more closely to adult values than the boy's,

there is less need for a girl to run counter to these values. Like boys, however, girls at this age are highly susceptible to the approval and disapproval of the group.

Older children also crave attention from others, both adults and members of the peer group. Among girls, demands for attention begin to decline at the age of eight years. Among boys, demands for attention show a sharp rise between the ages of eight and ten but begin to decline at eleven. First-born boys "noisily demand attention" at the peak period, though this tendency is especially marked in children who are emotionally dependent. Craving for attention stems from insecurity and is associated with such traits as timidity, jealousy, moodiness, and overdependency. First-born girls also tend to be attention demanders, as do only children (133).

Oversensitivity. A common outgrowth of susceptibility to social approval and disapproval is *oversensitivity*—the tendency to be easily hurt and to interpret what others say and do to mean that they are hostile. This is almost universal in the latter part of childhood. As Macfarlane et al. have pointed out, in discussing the results of a study of older children, "Oversensitiveness was like the common cold—almost everybody had it" (133). In fact, it proved to be the most frequently reported form of problem behavior among normal children as they reached school age. For boys, oversensitiveness reaches a peak at eleven years and then drops abruptly; for girls, the rise continues until puberty. Boys discover that oversensitiveness is not "manly," and they learn to eliminate it or cover it up at an early age.

Oversensitiveness is, to some extent, due to the strong desire the older child has for social acceptance—a desire which makes him highly susceptible to the attitudes of both adults and members of the peer group. It is also an effective device for coping with parents. When frustrated in what he wants to do, the older child soon discovers that putting up a fight and being negativistic are poor weapons; they rarely bring the desired results. Hurt feelings, however, baffle parents and often make them feel guilty because they have "hurt" their child in an attempt to do the things they feel are best for him. As long as the child can use this device to get the upper hand in a conflict situation, oversensitiveness will persist. Because most children can see through this ruse, the older child generally reserves his oversensitiveness for the home (133).

Suggestibility. Perhaps at no other age is the normal individual so suggestible to those about him as during late childhood. Studies of school children have shown that the peak of misdemeanors usually comes between the ages of seven and eight years, when loyalty to the group renders the child highly suggestible to other members of the group, especially the leader (111). Joy in the wanton destruction of property, for example, reaches its peak during the gang age. While boys are more vigorous and bold and are less inhibited in their destructive escapades than girls, both are motivated by a desire to do what their friends are doing. Destructiveness almost always occurs when children are with their companions, in a group (46).

Contrasuggestibility. While accepting in a more or less unquestioning manner the suggestions of the group, the child begins to revolt against adults and to act in direct contradiction to them. This *contrasuggestibility* is usually strongest in those whose suggestibility to the group is very pronounced. In the presence of adults, they rebel against suggestions which, had they come from their own playmates, would doubtless have been accepted. They stubbornly do what they are warned not to do, such as stepping in deep snow or playing in the rain.

Contrasuggestibility is similar to negativism in the young child; the older child, like the younger, does just the opposite of what he is asked to do, or he refuses to do anything. While negativism normally reaches its peak between the ages of three and six years and then recedes as parents adjust their demands to the more mature capacities of their children and as children, in turn, become intellectually mature enough to under-stand why their parents place certain restrictions on their behavior, there is another peak just before puberty in boys. This is shown in Figure 8–3, page 341.

At this time, boys who are members of gangs are breaking away from adult authority as much as they can in order to assert themselves as individuals. Should parental discipline be too restrictive, they will react much as they did during the preschool years, refusing to comply with *any* parental wish. The more restrictive the home discipline, the more negativistic the child's attitude will be, and the more temper tantrums he will have. Because girls' gangs are never given as much freedom as boys' gangs, the older girl is more accustomed to being restricted; as a result, she is less likely to experience a period of contrasuggestibility as she approaches puberty (30, 108).

Rivalry and Competition. *Competition* with other individuals and *rivalry* between groups are equally stimulating to the child. Each of the three types of competition usually found during the gang age—rivalry among group members for recognition within the group itself, conflicts between the gang and rival gangs, and conflicts between the gang and organized agencies of society—has a different effect on the socialization of the child. The first is likely to lead to hostility and quarreling within the gang, thus serving to weaken the solidity of the group and the loyalty of each member. The second serves to build up solidity and feelings of loyalty, while the third, if kept from leading to destructiveness and defiance of adult authority, serves to develop independence (5, 34).

Competition among older children is likely to lead to much quarreling. It may be expressed in aggressive fighting or in more subtle ways, such as criticism of others, "ganging up" on a single child who may be disliked for his annoying behavior or because he belongs to a minority group, teasing and bullying others, ignoring a child or a group of children, or arguing without any real provocation and with the apparent desire to make the other person uncomfortable or annoyed (79, 113).

Good Sportsmanship. Good sportsmanship, or the ability to cooperate with the group to the extent of submerging individual personalities into the group patterns, is an outgrowth of group life. The child soon learns that he must "play the rules of the game"; any infringement upon these, such as cheating, tattling, lying, or using underhanded methods, will not be tolerated. When working together for a common reward, children show positive interactions, such as helping each other and sharing materials, while competing against one another results in negative interactions, such as appropriating materials, making unfriendly remarks, and trying to obstruct or dominate others (5, 196).

Good sportsmanship includes not only willingness to cooperate with others but also willingness to share with others. As was pointed out in the discussion of generosity among young children (pages 348 to 349), generosity develops rapidly after the child enters school but especially rapidly during the fourth and fifth grades, when the desire to be an acceptable member of a gang reaches its peak (90, 214). (Refer to Figure 8–4, page 349.) Not only must the child who wants to be considered a "good sport" be generous with his material possessions, but he must also be generous in his attitude toward losing to another, whether in school or in games. No matter how badly he wants to win, he must share the pleasure of victory with the winner instead of pouting, complaining, or accusing him of being unfair. Good sportsmanship is more important for boys than for girls; boys place a higher value on this attribute (86, 197).

Responsibility. Closely related to good sportsmanship and cooperation is *responsibility*—the willingness to assume one's share of the load. The young child, because of his helplessness, must depend on others to do many things for him. This dependency should decrease with increase in motor and speech development, but it cannot do so unless the child has opportunities to learn to assume responsibilities for his own affairs or to share in the responsibility for the group's affairs. Too many responsibilities, given to the child too suddenly, will undermine his confidence, especially if he meets with failure. For that reason, the development of responsibility must be gradual, starting with responsibility for simple tasks and increasing as the child gains confidence in his ability to carry them out successfully (92).

Studies of how responsibility is developed have revealed that it, like many other patterns of social behavior, is "homegrown"; it has its roots in the child's early training. Children from large families, through necessity, must develop responsibility for their own affairs and must assume responsibility for the care of younger siblings. Girls, on the whole, are expected to assume more responsibilities in the home than boys. Boys, however, often have some work experience outside the home as they approach the end of childhood, and this gives them the training in assuming responsibilities that girls get from the home environment (144).

An analysis of the logs of fifth-grade children's out-of-school activities revealed that girls mentioned household tasks much more frequently than boys. Children from the lower social classes were expected to assume more responsibilities in the home than were children from the upper-middle and upper classes (144). Because willingness and ability to carry one's share of the load are closely correlated with popularity and leadership, training in assuming responsibility is valuable in increasing a child's social acceptance and in preparing him to assume a leadership role.

Children who are not given opportunities to acquire the self-confidence needed to be independent tend to fall far short of what one would normally expect. Figure 8–7 shows the ideal trend in self-reliance as compared with the actual trend at different ages. While the actual trend may closely approximate the ideal by the time the child reaches legal maturity, it falls short of the ideal in the latter part of childhood.

Social Insight. Social insight is the ability to put oneself in the psychological shoes of another and to perceive a situation from his perspective. It is the ability to feel imagina-

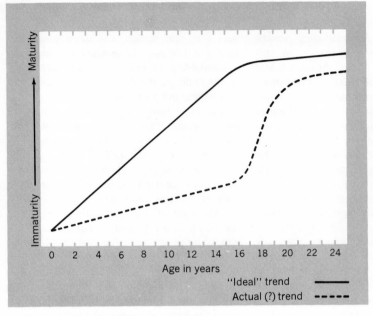

Figure 8–7. Schematic diagram showing how self-reliance ideally develops and how it actually develops in the American culture under conditions of parental resistance to independence. (Adapted from S. L. Pressey and R. G. Kuhlen, *Psychological development through the life span*, Harper & Row, 1957. Used by permission.)

tively and to think of oneself in the total mental-emotional attitude of another person (35). To make good social adjustments, one must be able to perceive and predict the behavior, thoughts, and feelings of others (11, 76). Prediction is based first on the individual's behavior, then on the meaning of the behavior, and lastly on the deeper attitudes or feelings. The ability to discriminate emotional reactions from facial expressions is one of the earliest forms of social insight (19, 70).

Social insight normally increases with age, owing partly to mental maturation and partly to learning from social experiences. Only in very late childhood, however, is it sufficiently developed for the child to be able to understand the behavior and feelings of other children (62, 209). Children whose social perception is superior to that of their peers usually make better social adjustments and receive greater social acceptance.

In the latter years of childhood, not only do children have a better understanding of the behavior, motives, and feelings of others, but also they begin to be aware of class distinctions, socioeconomic status, and the pres-

tige values associated with such status (40). This is, in part, responsible for the prejudice and social discrimination which appear at this age. There is also an increase in self-perception, or *self-discovery*. The child is not able to see himself as others see him until after he can perceive the meaning of the behavior of others. For successful social adjustments, however, self-insight is as important as social insight.

Variations in Social Insight. Even though social insight normally increases as children grow older, some children show mature insight, while others are very immature. There is a slight *sex difference* in social insight, with girls a bit more mature than boys. The higher the *intelligence* of the child, the more perceptive he is likely to be; this contributes to the popularity of bright children. There is a marked relationship between the child's *status in the group* and his insight. The more popular the child, the more social insight he develops. The unpopular child, because he lacks social acceptance, has limited opportunities to develop social insight. As a result, he often says and does things which antagonize his playmates and thus increase his lack of acceptance (11, 53, 67, 77).

The more *secure* the child feels about his status in the group, the better his social insight will be. Security enables him to judge without fear of loss of status and without an anxiety that colors his reactions (179). The child who is a *leader* has, as a rule, better social insight than children who are followers; the leader must understand the wishes and interests of the group members if his leadership is to be effective (43, 76).

Social insight varies according to the *personality* of the child; the better adjusted the child, the more interest he has in others. By contrast, the poorly adjusted child tends to be self-bound, and this deprives him of opportunities to learn about others. The child who does not like himself generally has better social insight than the child who is self-acceptant. The former is more perceptive to the feelings of others as a result of his heightened sensitivity to interpersonal relationships (170). Furthermore, he often projects the traits he dislikes in himself to others; this biases his judgment of others. If, on the other hand, he perceives other children as similar to himself, he generally can judge them better than if he perceives them as different (89, 128).

Sympathy. Until social insight is well developed, the older child, like the younger one, will behave in a cruel way. With the development of social insight, however, comes the ability to understand a situation, to be affected by the emotional states of another, and to develop a "fellow feeling." The child whose social insight is poorly developed behaves in a somewhat "hard-boiled," or "tough," way. Instead of wanting to help others or being able to understand and share their emotional experiences, he takes delight in teasing and bullying, getting great satisfaction from being able to make others angry, frightened, or nervous. A delay in the development of sympathy leads to poor social acceptance; the child who wants to improve his social acceptance must improve his social insight and, through it, his sympathy for others (159, 213).

Social Discrimination. Social discrimination appears early in childhood but is not well developed until the child becomes a member of a gang. Gang members develop the attitude that *any* member of their group is all right but that anyone who is not a member is inferior. This is a form of snobbishness, based on whether or not one belongs to the group. It soon becomes *generalized* to include anyone who is different because of religion, race, socioeconomic status, or sex.

The child who discriminates against others treats them as inferiors because they are different, not because of an inferiority per se. Those who deviate are regarded as belonging to an "outgroup" or a "minority group," not because of their numerical inferiority, but because their status is considered inferior. The child who belongs to a gang feels that his status is superior to that of a child who does not belong, and he feels that if his gang is recognized as superior, all other gangs are "outgroups" and hence inferior (95, 137).

Prejudice. Back of discrimination is prejudice—a tendency to classify *all* who belong to other groups, whether they are social, religious, racial, or sex groups, as inferior and to treat them accordingly. It is a set of attitudes which causes, supports, or justifies discrimination (7). In prejudice, there is a tendency to *prejudge* as inferior those who belong to a group against which there are unfavorable social attitudes, not because of what they are, but because of their identification.

In prejudice there are three elements, all of which influence the behavior associated with them. There are, first, widely accepted *beliefs* concerning those against whom prejudice is directed—beliefs rarely based on personal experiences but generally on stereotypes concerning the personal qualities of those who belong to a specific group. The second element of prejudice is the *emotional accompaniment,* which may range from cold indifference to bitter and violent hostility. Finally, there are definite beliefs concerning the appropriate *treatment* of those against whom the prejudice is directed—indifference, exclusion, or active persecution (50, 215).

Origin of Prejudice.   Prejudices are the product of social learning. Very early, a child becomes aware of differences between people, but awareness of differences, per se, does not mean that he will be prejudiced (154, 199). Only when he becomes aware of the social attitudes toward those who are different and only when pressure is placed on him to accept these social attitudes does prejudice develop (2). Studies have revealed that while children are aware of differences between people, there are no indications of prejudiced behavior before four years of age. Prejudiced *attitudes* generally appear between three and four years, while prejudiced *behavior* comes slightly later (198).

What is sometimes interpreted as prejudice may not actually be such. Children may *prefer* to be with children whose background is similar to theirs because they feel more "at home" with them. This does not mean that they dislike members of another group or feel superior to them. Prejudice involves hostility and discrimination. If the preference is for others of one's own kind, without any hostility toward members of another group, the cleavage between the child and members of another group may be due to a "comfort differential"—a feeling of greater "at homeness" with one group than with another (139).

In general, however, by the time the child enters school, the seeds of prejudice are already taking root. As Giles has pointed out, "Little children, on first coming to school, have the words, and sometimes the feelings, of prejudice" (82). In time, prejudiced attitudes may become so habitual that the child is not even aware of them until some stress situation arises, such as the entrance into school of children from a group against which there is prejudice or the infiltration into a neighborhood of members of an "out-group." Prejudiced attitudes are not always reflected in the child's behavior: They may appear only when social approval gives sanction to such behavior or when the stress situation is too great for the child to hide

his prejudiced feelings behind a cloak of socially approved behavior (2, 21).

Prejudice is *learned* in many different ways. Some prejudices are learned through unpleasant experiences with a person of a certain group. This conditions the child to dislike not only that person but all who are identified with him because of their group affiliation. Some prejudices come from an uncritical acceptance of the cultural values of the home and of the social group. When certain groups are segregated in school or in the community, for example, the child assumes that they are inferior because society treats them as if they were (49, 215). Most prejudices, however, come from imitating the attitudes and behavior of parents, teachers, peers, neighbors, or characters in mass media of communication (155). As Zeligs has aptly put it, "Children catch their prejudices from their social environment" (226).

Few parents actually teach their children to be prejudiced. However, their attitudes and behavior, their restrictions on the playmates of their children, and their tendency to stereotype all individuals of a given racial or religious group with certain physical, behavioral, and mental characteristics result in a pattern of prejudice which their children imitate. It is not the parents' attitudes alone, but the whole home influence, that is responsible for the development of prejudice (45, 73, 195, 227).

As children spend more and more time with the peer group, they "catch" some of their prejudices from the group members. In their desire to gain status in the group, older children accept the prejudices of other children because it is the "thing to do." In addition, prejudice gives the older child a feeling of self-importance, often serving as an outlet for his frustrations and thwarted aggressions (165). As Allport has said, prejudice may be a "psychological crutch" used by immature and psychologically crippled children, or it may come from a desire to conform to group expectations (2).

Even when prejudice conflicts with the child's concept of good sportsmanship or with his religious teachings, his desire to inflate his ego or to conform to group expectations may be strong enough to make him cling to his prejudices. He will then rationalize his doing so by saying that "everyone" does it or by saying that the people he knows in certain groups against which there is prejudice are "typical" of the group (7).

Variations in Prejudice. How prejudiced a child will be depends partly upon his *home environment,* partly upon the *neighborhood* and *community* in which he lives, and partly upon the degree of prejudice his *playmates* have. *Boys* are more prejudiced than girls; *Southern children,* more than Northern children; children from *professional families,* less than those from the lower socioeconomic groups; and those with *fewer contacts* with groups against which there is prejudice, more than those with more contacts (172, 212). Children brought up in homes where authoritarian *child-training* methods are used are generally more rigid and intolerant in their attitudes than children from more democratic homes (129, 155, 165).

The more anxious a child is to maintain his *status* in the peer group, the more willing he is to accept the prejudices of the group members. Thus, to be sure he will have friends, the child chooses his friends from his own group and discriminates against those from other groups, especially racial and religious groups against which prejudice is often strong in childhood (123). The child who comes from a home with a strong *religious* background tends to be more prejudiced than the child whose religious training is less rigid (186, 221).

Certain forms of *mass communication* have a strong influence on the development of prejudice. The stereotyped portrayal of Negroes in movies and on television, for example, tends to perpetuate and reinforce children's concepts of racial superiorities and inferiorities (189). The most important factor influencing the degree of prejudice of the child is his own *personality pattern.* Children who show a high degree of prejudice are rigid, illiberal, intolerant, and punitive in their attitudes. They usually suffer from marked feelings of inadequacy, inferiority, and insecurity. Frequently, they feel unloved and unwanted and come from broken or unhappy homes (10, 211).

Effects of Prejudice. Prejudice affects the child who is prejudiced just as it does the victim of his prejudice, though in a different way (7). The child who is prejudiced often becomes rigid, cruel, intolerant, and vindictive—a pattern which may and often does become so habitual that it affects his relationships with people against whom he has no prejudice (119). Children against whom there is prejudice come to believe that the social environment is hostile and that no one likes them. They are subjected to ridicule, teasing, bullying, and physical aggressions and are ignored and left out of things. Some react to this treatment by withdrawal from the social group; others react by excessive aggressions in the form of defensive reactions; still others turn their hostility against society in general and become potential delinquents. Relatively few children accept discrimination as a challenge to show others their worth (21, 160).

The more aware the child is of the prejudice people direct toward him, the more damaged he will be psychologically. Being called "nigger" or "kike" leaves no question in his mind about the group's attitude toward him (7). As a result, he begins to think unfavorably about himself and the group with which he is identified. Negro children, for example, learn to associate prestige with whites and to associate an inferior status with their own racial group (199). In time, the weight of prejudice cramps and distorts the personality development of the minority-group member. In describing the serious psychological damage to the child against whom prejudice is directed, Allport has said:

A child who finds himself rejected and attacked on all sides is not likely to develop dignity and poise as his outstanding traits. On the contrary, he develops defenses. Like a dwarf in a world of menacing giants, he cannot fight on equal terms. He is forced to listen to their derision and laughter and submit to their abuse. There are a great many things such a dwarf-like child may do, all of them serving as his ego defenses (2).

There are *individual differences* in the way prejudice affects children. A child who feels rejected and unloved at home is more affected by prejudice outside the home than the child whose home offers him security and love. A child who has gained some social acceptance in the peer group is less affected by prejudice than the child who has little or no acceptance. A member of a 4-H club, for example, attaches less significance to being called a "kike" than a child from a slum area who has no club affiliation. Girls smart more from the humiliating treatment of majority-group members than boys because they have been trained *not* to be aggressive; as a result, they do not fight back as boys do (10, 82). Figure 8–8 shows some of the ways in which prejudice is expressed among children.

The victim of prejudice, under *all* conditions, faces a difficult predicament. As Jersild has pointed out:

As a member of a minority group it is dangerous for him to use against others the weapons they use against him. If he is aggressive he invites attack. If he turns the other cheek the result may be further abuse. If, as he grows older, he becomes resigned to the fact that the doors of opportunity are closed he runs the risk of being called lazy and shiftless. If he tries to assert himself through the usual channels of competition for position, wealth, or power he runs the risk of being called "pushy" or unscrupulous (113).

Attempts to Curb Prejudice. Because prejudice is psychologically damaging to those who are prejudiced as well as to those against whom prejudice is directed, many attempts have been made to modify, if not to eliminate entirely, children's prejudices before they develop into habitual attitudes. This is usually very difficult, though the younger the child, the more hope there is that his prejudices can be eliminated. If prejudice fills a deep-seated need in the child's life, age alone is not an important factor. The child who uses his prejudices to displace thwarted aggressions, for example, will be less motivated to modify his prejudices than the child whose prejudices come from the belief that "everyone feels that way" (137, 165).

Prejudice places a barrier between people;

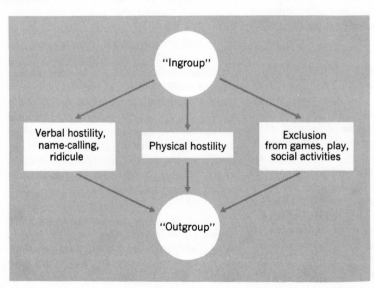

Figure 8–8. Some ways in which prejudice is expressed among children.

attempts have been made to break down this barrier and bring children together so that they can get to know one another better. If prejudice is based on stereotyped beliefs, personal contact might correct the stereotype and thus reduce the prejudice. If it is based on unfavorable personal experiences, however, or if the contact is involuntary, as in the case of desegregated schools, personal contacts will not necessarily reduce the prejudice. They may even intensify it (49). Helping the child to develop better social insight about people against whom he has prejudice, by explaining *why* they are different, may help to reduce prejudice (150, 151).

Because most prejudice in children comes not from personal contacts but from "social contagion," the most hopeful way of combating it is to make prejudice *unfashionable.* No child can be expected to have a tolerant attitude when the members of the peer group are intolerant. Even a child whose status in the group is secure will be influenced by peer-group attitudes to some extent. For a child whose status in the group is insecure, following the crowd is a method of improving social acceptance. For him, prejudice may win the social acceptance he craves, while tolerance may result in rejection. Under such conditions, he will not modify his prejudice until the rest of the group leads the way (84, 119).

Since peer-group prejudices are learned by social contagion from adult groups—mainly from the parents of the group members—children cannot be expected to modify their prejudices as long as they have a constant pattern of prejudice to imitate in their homes. Thus far, efforts to reduce prejudice have made little headway; the hopes of eliminating it are still very dim.

Sex Antagonism. In the early years of childhood, boys play with girls much as they did during babyhood; social harmony between the two is common (149). As late as the first, and sometimes the second, grade in elementary school, boys *may* be willing to play with girls, provided the girls can keep up the pace the boys set. At this time, a little boy may even show a marked interest in a girl in his class and prefer to associate with her rather than with a boy. Most children, however, during kindergarten or first grade, begin to prefer persons of their own sex. This tendency becomes more pronounced with each passing year until the sixth or seventh grade, when girls begin to show a preference for boys (31, 93).

A marked cleavage between members of the two sexes develops during this period of antagonism. Boys and girls belittle one another's interests, skills, and activities; they refuse to associate with one another even at parties; and they are constantly bickering, name calling, and quarreling. In giving her impression of boys at this age, Marshall said that they were "noisy, rough, slam bang 'shooters' and 'clubberers,' and that they were regarded as public enemies by the girls in the group. . . . The hostile behavior of these boys suggested that they were solving some life problem or were generally frustrated" (135).

For the most part, boys are the aggressors in this battle of the sexes. Girls retaliate by refusing to associate with boys and return in kind the treatment they receive from them. Should a boy show any interest in a girl, he is likely to be regarded as a "sissy" by his male contemporaries (31). Little boys, even in kindergarten or first grade, may show the typical sex antagonism of an older boy if they associate with older boys and imitate their attitudes as they do their behavior (33, 76, 79). Most children, however, do not show such strong sex antagonism until the fifth to the seventh grade—the time when the cleavage is at its peak (149).

Causes of Sex Antagonism. There is no evidence that sex antagonism comes from physical causes or from the maturation of any mental ability. Rather, all evidence points to *cultural influences*. There are cultural pressures on both boys and girls to develop interests appropriate to their sex, to engage in activities that are culturally sex-linked, and to regard one sex as superior and the other as inferior, instead of different

(62). Furthermore, boys and girls acquire certain *values* as part of their social learning. For older boys, even mothers seem to lose some of their former importance because they have no recognized status assigned to them as men do by their occupations (33, 202).

School textbooks also help to create the impression that males are superior to females. In an analysis of third-grade readers it was found that only 27 per cent of the central characters and only 37 per cent of the subordinate characters were female. This led to the comment that the "implication of this difference for a girl is that being female is a pretty bad thing, that the only people worth writing about are boys and men. If the content of these readers is typical of other social influences, small wonder that girls might develop for this reason alone an inferiority complex about their sex" (42).

That the cleavage between the sexes, with its accompaniment of antagonistic attitudes and behavior, is a product of cultural rather than inherent factors has been emphasized by Bonney:

Accepting inter-personal attitudes which exist between and within sex groups in any classroom is much more likely to be due to such factors as level of socioeconomic home background, the extent to which boys and girls have enjoyed pleasant associations in groups, the extent to which they have been separated in seating and eating situations, and the extent to which teachers and other adults have encouraged or minimized sex differences by direct and indirect teachings, rather than to constitutional differences or so-called natural stages of sex development (25).

Variations in Sex Antagonism. Not only does sex antagonism vary with the age of the child, but it also varies from child to child within one age group. Children with *low social status* who suffer from feelings of inadequacy or insecurity as a result, generally show greater antagonism toward members of the opposite sex than children whose social status is more secure (33).

Boys, because of their feeling of masculine superiority, are generally less antagonistic toward girls than girls are toward boys, in spite of the fact that boys are primarily responsible for arousing the antagonism. Girls' attitudes toward boys are emotionally toned, while boys' attitudes toward girls are more objective and neutral (93).

The unfavorable attitude of girls toward boys stems partly from the girls' resentment of the greater freedom parents and teachers grant to boys, partly from parental favoritism toward boys, and partly from the greater social maturity of girls. The earlier puberty of girls makes boys of the same age seem "immature" (79, 93). Attitudes of boys and girls toward peers of their own sex and of the opposite sex are shown in Figure 8–9. In small *urban* and *suburban* communities, where there is a breaking down of sharp differences in sex roles and where children are encouraged by parents to begin dating at an early age, sex antagonism is not so great nor does it last so long as in communities where the sex roles are more sharply differentiated and where early dating is less encouraged (31, 149).

Effects of Sex Antagonism. Sex antagonism affects the child who begins the belittling of members of the opposite sex just as it affects the child who is the victim of the belittling. This means that boys are unfavorably affected just as girls are. Boys develop unjustified feelings of masculine superiority. As they grow older, therefore, they often treat women in the home, in social life, and in business as their inferiors. Women who, as children, were subjected to the treatment that accompanies sex antagonism often develop resentments against men and against the fact that they were born women; they are dissatisfied with their culturally approved sex role and resent the preferred role society grants to men. These attitudes can and often do affect the lifetime adjustments, both personal and social, of both men and women (27, 33, 168).

Sex antagonism makes it difficult for boys and girls to become friends even if they should want to. Many girls prefer the games

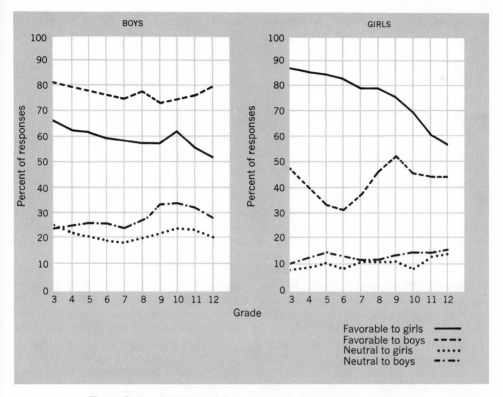

Figure 8–9.   Attitudes of boys and girls toward peers of their own sex and of the opposite sex at different ages during childhood. (Adapted from D. B. Harris and C. S. Tseng, Children's attitudes toward peers and parents as revealed by sentence completions, *Child Develpm.*, 1957, 28, 401–411. Used by permission.)

and sports of boys, and many boys would prefer to play with girls because they have neither the interest nor the physical capacities to play the games of boys. Any attempt to play with members of the opposite sex or to engage in play activities considered appropriate for the opposite sex, however, is likely to lead to amusement or ridicule on the part of parents and scorn on the part of contemporaries.

While parents today encourage children of the two sexes to associate in social activities at an earlier age than in the past, this encouragement does not come until the child is approaching puberty (31). By then segregation of the sexes has already persisted long enough to allow unfavorable attitudes to become well developed and to

allow children to learn only the activities considered appropriate for their own sex. As a result, they have little in common; they do not really want to become friends, and the adjustment problems of adolescence, especially in the area of heterosexual relationships, are greatly intensified.

Sex antagonism has far-reaching effects on the development of social skills, such as the ability to talk to people, to be at ease in social situations, to have good manners, and to know the socially correct things to say and do. These skills are important to good social adjustments not only in childhood but throughout life. Because boys regard all social skills as "sissified" and scorn all opportunities for social contacts where such skills may be learned, they are markedly inferior to girls in this area of their development. Boys have indicated, on a self-rating scale, that even as early as the fourth grade they feel inadequate in social relations as compared with girls (114).

SOCIALIZING INFLUENCES IN LATE CHILDHOOD

From the above description of different forms of social behavior, it is apparent that the older child's behavior is more social than that of the younger child. Whether this improvement is the result of increased intellectual and emotional maturity or of social pressures is difficult to say; certainly all play some role. There is no question, however, that the gang is of major importance in the socialization of the child. The gang age is a time of profound change—a time when the child starts out as an individual and ends as a member of a social whole.

Havighurst has stated that the gang can help the child in four ways: (1) in getting along with his agemates and knowing how to behave in a way that is socially acceptable to his peers; (2) in developing a rational conscience and a scale of values to replace the moral values of his parents which he accepted as an "authoritarian conscience"; (3) in learning appropriate social attitudes, such as how to like people and how to enjoy social life and group activities; and (4) in achieving personal independence by gaining emotional satisfaction from friendships with peers (99).

For the most part, gang life favors the development of good qualities. It teaches the child to be democratic, to fit his desires and actions into those of the group, to cooperate with the group, to develop skills which will enable him to do what his peers do, and to eliminate selfishness and individualism. At the same time, it develops self-control, fair play, courage, justice, forbearance, loyalty, fidelity, devotion to a cause, loyalty to a leader, insight into the nature of the social process, and sensitiveness to the motives and feelings of others. In his competition for status, the child tries to improve himself and to change his ego-

centric interests into group interests. As Brown has said, "Such learning matures children" (34).

On the other hand, gang life favors the development of such undesirable qualities as the use of slang and swearing, the telling of salacious stories and jokes, truancy, mischievousness, attitudes of contempt for rules and those in authority, the breaking of home ties and the shifting of loyalties from home to group activities, snobbishness, discrimination against members of minority groups, and the breaking down of ideals established in the home. Most of these undesirable effects of gang life are transitory. As the child grows older, many of them are eliminated (52, 223).

One of the most valuable things a child learns from being a member of a gang is how to evaluate himself *realistically*. In the home, where personal bias, stemming from parental affection, is strong, the child learns to think of himself as his parents think of him—as a "superior" person. In the gang, this personal bias does not exist. He is viewed realistically by members of the peer group and judged by what he says and does. As the child discovers from his daily contacts with gang members what other people think of him, he begins to reevaluate his concept of himself and to revise it to fit with reality. If his contemporaries like him, he thinks favorably of himself and becomes a self-acceptant person (117, 127).

The socializing influence of the gang makes the gang member a better-adjusted person. A child who has never belonged to a gang is deprived of many learning experiences. As a result, his behavior often falls short of social expectations. He is likely to develop a distorted, unrealistic concept of himself. If he does not belong to a gang because no gang will accept him, he thinks of himself as an inferior and unworthy person. Should his lack of membership be due to geographic isolation, he is likely to develop feelings of martyrdom and to envy those who are privileged to enjoy what he craves but has been denied through no fault of his own. If, on the other hand, his nonmembership in a gang is voluntary, he will learn to think of himself as "queer" and "different" because no one can understand why he scorns the pattern of life his age-mates favor.

In time, a child who has been rejected by a gang or who voluntarily withdraws from gang membership because he derives too little satisfaction from it is likely to have a *generalized negative attitude toward all social activities.* If he cannot be accepted by the gang he wants to join, he often feels that he does not want to belong to any gang, or if he withdrew from gang life because he did not enjoy it, he has little motivation to try it again. Consequently, he is often at a loss to know how to spend his leisure time and frequently resorts to reading, television watching, or daydreaming—all of which fit his needs because they give him enjoyment and, at the same time, can be carried out without playmates. They do not, however, provide the opportunities for socialization that contacts with people do. As a result, the child is likely to develop into an unsocial or antisocial adult.

SOCIAL BEHAVIOR AT PUBERTY

With the beginning of puberty comes a change in social attitudes, a decline in interest in activities with the group, and a tendency to prefer solitude. As puberty progresses and the rate of puberty changes speeds up, there is a speeding up of changes in social attitudes and behavior. In general, the changes parallel growth in height; the faster the growth, the more pronounced the changes. This period can justifiably be called the "antisocial stage."

Because of the antisocial behavior so characteristic of this age, puberty is sometimes called the "negative phase" and a "period of disequilibrium." (See pages 140 to 142 for an earlier discussion of the meaning of "negative phase.") These labels suggest that the child's attitude toward life is "anti," that he is negating some of the social characteristics developed so slowly and laboriously throughout the childhood years.

During this time, the pattern of social development is interrupted. The child is not, however, on a plateau in the curve of social learning; instead, he is skidding downward, often abruptly, from the point where he seemed to be close to the adult peak.

As growth in height begins to slow down, with the advent of sexual maturity, the worst of the negative phase has passed. The young adolescent then begins to climb upward, slowly at first but then at increasing speed, motivated by a strong desire to be socially acceptable to the peer groups of both sexes. Even though he begins the upward climb, whether the effects of the negative phase on his future socialization will be left behind or not depends on many factors. When puberty occurs, how long it lasts, how closely it conforms to the puberty periods of his agemates, and how parents, teachers, and peers treat him during this transitional period—all are important.

For most children, this step backward and downward in the socialization process is only an interlude, unpleasant while it lasts but leaving few if any permanent scars. When puberty occurs at approximately the same time that it occurs in his agemates, the child and his friends are all in the "same boat." All are experiencing the antisocializing effects of this physical upheaval simultaneously. By conforming to the prevailing group pattern of unsocial behavior the child will win the tolerance, if not the acceptance, of the group. His antisocial attitudes and behavior will be tolerated because everyone else is feeling and behaving the same way (200, 205).

Beginnings of Antisocial Behavior. It is impossible to give a specific age at which antisocial behavior and attitudes will begin because there are such marked individual differences in the age of sexual maturing. On the average, however, puberty starts about a year earlier in girls than in boys. (See pages 136 to 137 for a more complete discussion of the age of sexual maturing.) The average age for the beginning of puberty changes in girls is eleven years, and in boys, twelve years. The first signs of antisocial behavior, therefore, can be expected to appear at approximately these ages.

The worst aspects of antisocial behavior occur in the six- to twelve-month period preceding sexual maturity. This means, for girls, at some time between the twelfth and thirteenth birthdays, and for boys, between the thirteenth and fourteenth birthdays. After the peak has been reached, there is normally a rather rapid decline in antisocial behavior. Because girls, on the average, mature more rapidly than boys, the antisocial behavior characteristic of girls at this age is generally more pronounced than that of boys. There are such marked individual differences, however, that many boys experience as pronounced reversals in their patterns of social development as girls do (72).

Causes of Antisocial Behavior. Since the antisocial behavior of the prepubescent or pubescent child is not the result of ignorance of social expectations, it cannot be called "unsocial." Typically, the child knows what society expects of him and has, in later childhood, conformed to those expectations. There is ample evidence that during puberty the child *intentionally* does the opposite of what is expected of him. He knows, for example, that harassing little children is regarded as poor sportsmanship, and yet he teases and bullies younger siblings or neighborhood children. Similarly, he knows the rules of the home and school, but now he is disobedient, breaking the very rules he formerly obeyed.

Why, one may justifiably ask, does the child behave this way? Without question, antisocial behavior at this age is partly the result of rapid and far-reaching *physical* and *glandular changes*. A physical upheaval of the type that occurs during puberty could not occur without having some effect on behavior. In this case, the effect is bad, primarily because rapid growth is accompanied by a tendency to be tired, listless, and devoid of reserve energy (16, 39). Furthermore, changes in the size and position of the different organic systems upset body homeostasis; this upset is invariably accompanied by psychological upheavals resulting in a state of disequilibrium. The upset is further accentuated by changes in the functioning of the different glands of the endocrine system and temporary hormonal imbalances (193).

Antisocial behavior is by no means entirely the result of physical changes. *Environmental factors* play a very important, if not a major, role. Because the child is beginning to look more like an adult—not only in size but also in body contour—parents and teachers decide that the time has come for him to "put away childish things" and assume the responsibilities of maturity (56). The result is that new duties and responsibilities are assigned to him at a time when he is least able, physically, to assume them (38, 153). Furthermore, after the carefree days of childhood, the child resents the sudden imposition of new duties and responsibilities. He resents the fact that he is not asked but told to assume them, whether he likes it or not. This leads to feelings of martyrdom—feelings which, alone, would be enough to lead to antisocial attitudes and behavior. Whether a child feels martyred because of his religion or race, because he is expected to do things he feels too tired and listless to do, or because he has never been expected to do them before is of little consequence; he resents this treatment and expresses his resentment in antisocial behavior (56, 60).

Feelings of martyrdom are most likely to occur when the child's sexual maturing deviates markedly from that of his agemates, either in the time it occurs or in the time needed to complete it. The early-maturing child, for example, shows characteristic negative-phase behavior sooner than his friends. Such behavior is met with intolerance; friends, parents, and teachers tell the child that he is "too young to act that way." When the late maturer behaves in a manner characteristic of his level of development, he is told that he is "too old to act that way" (114, 115, 163).

Girls, on the whole, mature more rapidly than boys, and their negative-phase behavior is likely to be more pronounced. But because girls are expected to behave more maturely than boys, they are subjected to more criticism and social rejection for their antisocial behavior. Intolerance and lack of understanding give rise to feelings of martyrdom at any age, but at puberty, when feelings of martyrdom come from multiple causes, such feelings are intensified and lead to even more pronounced antisocial behavior (54, 173).

Physical changes, accompanied by unfavorable physiological states, lead to self-concern and anxiety. The child who is excessively worried about himself becomes excessively *self-bound*. A self-bound person is never social. Much of the self-concern a child experiences at puberty stems from ignorance of the causes of the physical changes taking place in his body and of their normal pattern of development. Furthermore, if the child has a preconceived idea of what he wants to look like when he is grown up and if his body changes are not coming up to his expectations, his anxiety will be increased. This, in turn, will increase his tendency to be self-bound (179, 180).

Anxiety always leads to unsocial behavior. When it is met with intolerance on the part of others, it gives rise to anger, and, together, anger and anxiety predispose the child to be antisocial. They make him feel that he is a martyr, mistreated and misunderstood by peers, parents, and teachers —all those on whom he has depended for understanding and affection.

Effects of Puberty Changes. Changes in attitudes and behavior are inevitable at puberty, and, understandably, they are changes for the worse rather than for the better. The following changes have been reported among boys and girls.

Changes in Self-concept. Social attitudes and behavior are, at every age, influenced by the individual's self-concept. The child with a favorable self-concept will accept himself and like himself as a person. He will be more likely to have favorable attitudes toward others, and this will lead to better socialization; the person who accepts himself usually accepts others. Poor self-concepts, by contrast, lead to self-rejection, and this, in turn, leads to unfavorable social attitudes and rejection of others (76).

Studies of changes in self-concept have revealed that children change their feelings about themselves as their bodies change and as the attitudes of significant people in their lives change. The deterioration in self-concept that occurs during early adolescence is gradually overcome as the individual becomes more satisfied with his newly developed body and as other people come to react more favorably toward him (194).

A study of the self-evaluations of boys and girls from nine to thirteen years—when puberty changes are most rapid and their effects on behavior are most pronounced— has shown that there is a downward trend in their evaluation of their intelligence, co-operativeness, generosity, sociability, popularity, and ability to be entertaining and amusing. The ratings are shown in Figure 8–10. Because these ratings are on the whole, unfavorable, they lead to unfavorable self-concepts which, in turn, are reflected in unfavorable attitudes toward others and toward social situations in general. Thus, a vicious circle is set into motion with the result that there is a heightening in the unfavorable social behavior of the child as puberty progresses (3).

Changes in Attitudes and Behavior. The effects of the radical physical changes that occur at puberty are, for the most part, devastating to the pattern of social development. Some of the changes in behavior are so pronounced that the child literally reverts to behavior characteristic of the preschool years; some are more suggestive of the patterns characteristically found in the juvenile delinquent; and some are new and different from any experienced before but are unsocial or antisocial. In many respects, these changes *seem* worse than they actually are, partly because they follow so closely the socialized behavior characteristic of the gang

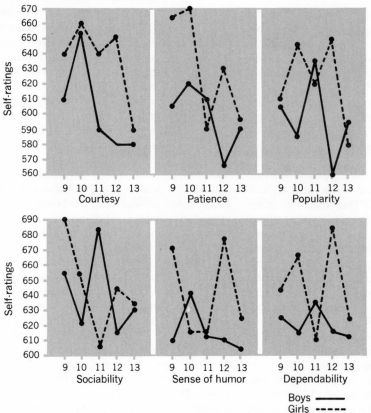

Figure 8–10. Self-evaluations of boys and girls in the latter years of childhood. (Adapted from Sister M. Amatora, Developmental trends in pre-adolesence and early adolescence in self-evaluation, *J. genet. Psychol.*, 1957, 91, 89–97. Used by permission.)

age and partly because the child, who now looks almost like an adult, is judged by standards more in keeping with his size and general appearance than with his level of development.

The most characteristic behavioral change is from social to antisocial behavior. The pubescent child has an *antagonistic attitude* toward everyone—parents, siblings, teachers, relatives, peers, and society in general. He is hostile and suspicious of their motives, and he feels that anything said or done to him is an act of aggression, thus justifying his retaliation. He goes around with a chip on his shoulder, a snarl on his face, and a readiness to fight.

Instead of being cooperative as he was before, he now goes out of his way to spoil other people's fun. He is not satisfied with letting them carry the load without his help; he wants to make things difficult for them

and block whatever they do. Not only does he refuse to help others, but he neglects his own duties and responsibilities, feeling martyred when he is criticized or punished. He seems to delight in being *uncooperative* (57, 171).

He is even more *aggressive* than a preschool child. He instigates fights with siblings or peers for no apparent reason. Younger siblings generally are the butt of his aggressions, and he tries to justify his behavior by claiming that his parents give them privileges he never enjoyed at their age or that someone must teach them that they "can't get away with murder." His aggressiveness toward his parents and relatives is verbal, mainly criticism, faultfinding, arguing about everything he is asked or told to do, and accusing them of treating him unfairly or of not "understanding" him.

If he does not show his aggressiveness

directly, he does so indirectly by trying to stir up trouble among siblings or between parents, by carrying tales, by going to one parent to complain about the unfair treatment he has received from the other, or by telling one parent how much more favorably the parent of a friend treats his spouse. The mother, who had formerly been his favorite parent, now becomes the usual butt of his criticism. He does not necessarily feel that she misunderstands or mistreats him more than the father, but she is readily available and more tolerant toward his aggressiveness than the father (56).

Aggressive patterns of behavior developed in the home are carried outside the home. The pubescent child quarrels over the most trivial matters and picks fights with members of his gang, is highly critical of whatever they do, and seems to delight in hurting their feelings. He also attacks them indirectly by saying they act "babyish" or "stupid," look like "kids," and have manners like "alley cats."

The *social insight* developed during the earlier years seems to disappear completely. Both at home and in the peer group, the child shows no understanding of how others feel; he is as unsympathetic when they are in trouble as he was when he first emerged from babyhood. The social traits he worked so hard to develop in the hope of increasing his popularity vanish, and his former friends now regard him as an "oddball" (79, 200). He acquires a *poor reputation* among the peer group, and many of his friendships—some of which date back to the first year in school—are broken up. His former friends claim they are "fed up with the way he behaves," talking down his nose to and about them and criticizing them and everything they do (153, 205).

This does not seem to bother the pubescent child; in fact, he claims that social activities "bore" him, that he prefers to be alone. *Isolation* now replaces social participation, often developing suddenly, sometimes over a weekend. The child no longer lingers after school to be with his friends; he comes straight home, goes to his room, shuts his door, and emerges only when it is

time to eat. He is equally "bored" with his family. He participates in holiday celebrations for as short a time as possible and shows by his actions, lack of willingness to talk, and the expression on his face how thoroughly uninterested he is. Reproof or teasing merely adds to his feelings of martyrdom and seems to substantiate his claim that no one loves or understands him.

If the pubescent child spent the time he is in isolation studying or engaging in some creative activity, it would not have such a bad effect. Usually, however, he spends this time *daydreaming*. In his daydreams he plays the role of a martyr suffering at the hands of an intolerant parent, teacher, or peer. The daydreams usually end with his becoming a hero—an ending which gives him great emotional satisfaction and which enables him to justify to himself his antisocial behavior. Enjoyable as such daydreams may be, they merely intensify the child's already existing belief that no one cares for him.

Time spent in social isolation is often devoted to thinking about sex, reading or studying pictures with a sex theme, or exploring the genital organs and engaging in masturbation. As is true of excessive daydreaming, *excessive preoccupation with sex* is unwholesome; it contributes nothing to good social adjustments and may even increase the child's antagonism toward members of the opposite sex (113, 223).

Sex antagonism normally reaches a peak during the early part of puberty (see Figure 8–9, page 367). At this time, both boys and girls go out of their way to show members of the opposite sex how much they dislike and resent them. This aversion may be expressed in teasing, bullying, and other forms of physical aggression, such as hitting, kicking, tripping, or bumping into another child. It may take the form of unprovoked verbal attacks, as in name calling, mimicking, criticizing, or making disparaging comments. Perhaps at no other age are members of either sex more sarcastic, more prone to make biting comments, or more critical. This unprovoked hostility is directed toward *all members* of the opposite sex, though it is generally more controlled when directed toward adults than toward the peer group. Girls, as a rule, show more sex aversion than boys; it also appears earlier in girls, owing to their earlier sexual maturing (79, 93).

A very common form of antisocial behavior of the pubescent child is *resistance to authority,* both at home and in school. This behavior starts during the gang age, but it is much stronger and more openly expressed during puberty. The gang-age child is far less likely to defy parents and teachers openly than the pubescent child is. He also is less likely openly to accuse people in authority of unfairness. While resistance to authority may occasionally lead to serious misdemeanors, it always has a "nuisance value."

Not only do teachers and parents feel that they must let the defiant child know that his defiance will not be tolerated, but they are also annoyed by his petty displays of rebellion—a pattern of behavior which suggests that he is testing their authority to see how far he can go without being punished. He will, for example, show his disdain for those in authority by being inattentive or rude; by whistling when he is told not to talk; by being late for meals, classes, or family functions; by doing assigned jobs so carelessly that they must be redone; or by whispering when others are trying to carry on a conversation. It is obvious that the child is going out of his way to "get under their skin" (205).

Communication with others is essential to becoming a socialized person. Even a baby tries, in his way, to communicate with others and to make himself a part of the social group. The antisocial pubescent child intentionally rejects this tool of socialization. He refuses to communicate with others except in cases of necessity. He will, for example, answer a question with a simple "Yes" or "No" and will put an end to further questioning by saying, "I can't remember" or "I don't know." Though once eager to join in conversations with adults as well as peers, he now shows an *excessive reserve,* a tendency to shut himself up within himself and to withdraw from the social group, implying by his actions, facial expressions, and impatience that the group "bores" him, not that he feels inadequate.

Excessive reserve is associated with the withdrawal syndrome. At puberty it reaches its peak and stems from rejection *of* the social group rather than rejection *by* the social group. Closely associated with excessive reserve is *shyness.* While a young baby usually goes through a "shy age" toward the end of the first year of life, his shyness is caused by strange people or strange objects and his resultant fear. At puberty, shyness occurs in the presence of *all* people, not only strangers. The puberty "shy age" reaches its peak for boys at twelve years, and for girls, from eleven to fourteen years (133). This is shown in Figure 8–11.

Fear is always at the basis of shyness. At puberty, the child is afraid of how people whose approval he formerly craved feel about his changing body and changed behavior. He is often embarrassed about his "new look," and he is even more embarrassed about behavior which he knows others regard as antisocial. His shyness thus comes from feelings of guilt and shame more than from fear of strange people or strange social situations (57, 200).

Persistence of Antisocial Behavior. While almost all children experience antisocial behavior to some extent, early and late maturers experience them most intensely. Furthermore, many antisocial behavior patterns wane and disappear as sexual maturity is completed and as the young adolescent's desire for social acceptance provides him with the necessary motivation to try to conform more closely to social expectations.

Even though the child may have antagonized friends and alienated the affection and respect of parents, teachers, and adults while he was in the negative phase, his later behavior is so improved that he is "forgiven" for his temporary lapse. If the time when he matures sexually coincides approximately with the time his friends mature, they are all behaving in much the same way as he. As a result, his antisocial behavior is actu-

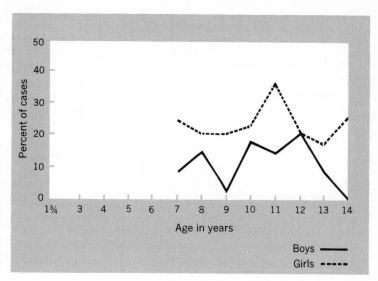

Figure 8–11. Shyness in childhood follows a different developmental pattern for boys and girls. (Adapted from J. Macfarlane, L. Allen, and M. P. Honzik, *A developmental study of the behavior problems of normal children between twenty-one months and fourteen years*, University of California Press, 1954. Used by permission.)

ally *in conformity with the group pattern* at that time. It is not likely to develop into a habit because it lasts for a relatively short time and is followed by a period in which, as a young adolescent, the child has a strong motivation to behave in a socially more acceptable manner (115, 153).

Deviant sexual development often results in individual variations that are difficult to overcome. The *early maturer* shows exaggerated forms of antisocial behavior earlier than the average child of his age primarily because he cannot convince his parents and teachers that he wants to be treated in accordance with his level of physical maturity, not in accordance with his chronological age. In his attempts to convince them, he becomes overly aggressive, demanding attention and privileges; he rebels against authority and is negativistic; he becomes argumentative and quarrelsome because he feels that no one tries to see his point of view; and his unfavorable concept of himself, arising from the way people treat him, makes him hypersensitive. This poor self-concept may be expressed in excessive shyness or in boasting and a cocky manner (115, 163).

If the early maturer's attempts to gain the status he feels he deserves are successful, he will generally abandon his antisocial

behavior and become a well-adjusted person. Having matured earlier than his agemates, he may be able to develop more mature behavior and greater self-confidence than they and to reinforce this by social learning. If he can do so, he becomes warmer, friendlier, emotionally more stable, and more forceful in group situations, and he makes a better appearance than his immature agemates. Because those early maturers who are not hampered by restraints owing to their age get a head start in developing poise and self-confidence, they are often selected as leaders in adolescence and adulthood; this further increases their poise and self-confidence (114). If the early maturer is thwarted in his attempts to gain status and this thwarting persists until his agemates catch up to him, however, he is very likely to develop the habit of being antisocial—a habit which may and often does persist into adult life.

This habit is even more likely to develop and persist in the *late maturer*. The child who lags behind his contemporaries in sexual maturing is usually treated by both agemates and adults in accordance with his physical appearance rather than in accordance with his chronological age and academic status. People treat him like a "kid" because he looks like a child. In his fight to gain the status he feels he deserves, he develops antisocial attitudes and patterns of behavior. The longer he lags behind his classmates in sexual maturing, the longer he reinforces his immature feelings and behavior patterns through repetition.

The late maturer is apt to gain the reputation of being "anti" everything for two reasons: First, his antisocial behavior persists long after his earlier-maturing contemporaries are well on the way to becoming socialized adults; and second, the contrast between his antisocial behavior and his contemporaries' more socialized behavior focuses attention on him. Once a reputation of this kind is built up, it is likely to persist long after the child has gained the status he was fighting for (153, 163).

Serious Aspects of Antisocial Behavior. Not only does the child lose ground in his social development during puberty, but he also injures his social adjustments, his self-concept, and his reputation among peers, family members and teachers by his negative-phase behavior.

Most children are able to counteract the harm they have done and resume the upward trend in the curve of socialization with no permanent damage. As with any setback, however, more effort and time are necessary than would be required had the setback not occurred.

Perhaps the most difficult aspect of the upward climb is the rebuilding of broken friendships. Most pubescent quarrels with peers are verbal. The psychological damage caused by the name calling, criticism, derogatory comments, and belittling that are characteristic of the negative phase is hard to repair and almost impossible to eradicate. A psychological hurt conditions a child to have an unfavorable attitude toward the person who inflicted the pain, even though he may forget the circumstances under which it was inflicted.

Another serious aspect of negative-phase behavior is that it gives the child an unfavorable reputation. If his social milieu could be changed after the negative phase

ended and if he could bury his unfavorable reputation by establishing new friendships, the matter would not be so serious. But most children continue to live in the same neighborhood, attend the same school, and associate with the same people as they did during the negative phase. The job of building a new reputation is especially difficult because the pubescent child has behaved antisocially in so many groups that his bad reputation is widely known.

The children for whom the upward climb is steepest and who, as a result, may never be able to make the grade are those whose sexual maturing comes earlier or later than that of their agemates. As was stressed earlier, the deviant maturer has a longer time to develop the habit of behaving in an antisocial way and to acquire an unfavorable reputation. Therefore, his task of undoing the damage done during puberty is greatly intensified.

Furthermore, because of the child's deviant development, the people with whom he is associated are less tolerant of his antisocial attitudes and behavior than they would have been had his development coincided with that of his peers. Consequently, the deviant child is subjected to greater criticism and disapproval from every social group than his agemates were. Social criticism and disapproval at any age lead to poor self-acceptance. Thus the deviant maturer must add to the other tasks of improving his social adjustments that of improving his self-concept. This task is never easy, especially when a poor reputation makes social acceptance difficult to achieve.

In conclusion, it must be recognized that the impact of age of sexual maturing on behavior and attitudes *need not be unfavorable* after sexual maturity has been achieved. Unfortunately, it more often is than not. How seriously and how persistently it will affect the child's behavior will depend to a large extent upon the type of early foundations that have been laid and upon the treatment the child receives from his parents, teachers, and peers as he passes through these difficult years.

BIBLIOGRAPHY

(1) ALLEN, R. M.: A longitudinal study of six Rorschach protocols of a three-year-old child. *Child Develpm.*, 1951, **22**, 61–69.

(2) ALLPORT, G. W.: *The nature of prejudice.* Cambridge, Mass.: Addison-Wesley, 1954.

(3) AMATORA, SISTER M.: Developmental trends in pre-adolescence and early adolescence in self-evaluation. *J. genet. Psychol.*, 1957, **91**, 89–97.

(4) AMMONS, C. H., and R. B. AMMONS: Aggression in doll play: interviews of two- to six-year-old white males. *J. genet. Psychol.*, 1953, **82**, 205–213.

(5) ANDERSON, H. H., and G. L. ANDERSON: Social development. In L. Carmichael (Ed.), *Manual of child psychology*, 2d ed. New York: Wiley, 1954. Pp. 1162–1215.

(6) ANGELINO, H., and E. V. MECH: "Fears and worries" concerning physical changes: a preliminary survey of 32 females. *J. Psychol.*, 1955, **39**, 195–198.

(7) ARTER, P. M.: The effects of prejudice on children. *Children*, 1959, **6**, 185–189.

(8) AUSUBEL, D. P.: Negativism as a phase of ego development. *Amer. J. Orthopsychiat.*, 1950, **20**, 796–805.

(9) AUSUBEL, D. P.: Prestige motivation of gifted children. *Genet. Psychol. Monogr.*, 1951, **43**, 53–117.

(10) AUSUBEL, D. P.: Ego development among segregated Negro children. *Ment. Hyg., N.Y.*, 1958, **42**, 362–369.

(11) AUSUBEL, D. P., and H. M. SCHIFF: Some intrapersonal and interpersonal determinants of individual differences in socioempathic ability among adolescents. *J. soc. Psychol.*, 1955, **41**, 39–56.

(12) BAIN, R.: Making normal people. *Marriage fam. Liv.*, 1954, **16**, 27–31.

(13) BALDWIN, A. L.: The effect of the home environment on nursery-school behavior. *Child Develpm.*, 1949, **20**, 49–61.

(14) BANHAM, K. M.: Obstinate children are adaptable. *Ment. Hyg., N.Y.*, 1952, **36**, 84–89.

(15) BARKER, R. G., and H. F. WRIGHT: *Midwest and its children.* New York: Harper & Row, 1954.

(16) BAYLEY, N.: Individual patterns of development. *Child Develpm.*, 1956, **27**, 45–74.

(17) BEHERS, M. L.: Child-rearing and the character structure of the mother. *Child Develpm.*, 1954, **25**, 225–238.

(18) BELOFF, H.: Two forms of social conformity: acquiescence and conventionality. *J. abnorm. soc. Psychol.*, 1958, **56**, 99–104.

(19) BENDER, I. E., and A. H. HASTORF: The perception of persons: forecasting another person's responses on three personality scales. *J. abnorm. soc. Psychol.*, 1950, **45**, 556–561.

(20) BERENDA, R. W.: *Influence of the group on the judgments of children: an experimental investigation.* New York: King's Crown, 1950.

(21) BIRD, C., E. D. MONACHESI, and H. BURDICK: Studies of group tensions. IV. The effect of parental discouragement of play activities upon the attitudes of white children toward Negroes. *Child Develpm.*, 1952, **23**, 295–306.

(22) BOBROFF, A.: The stages of maturation in socialized thinking and the ego development of two groups of children. *Child Develpm.*, 1960, **31**, 321–338.

(23) BOEHM, L.: The development of independence: a comparative study. *Child Develpm.*, 1957, **28**, 85–92.

(24) BOLL, E. S.: The role of preschool playmates: a situational approach. *Child Develpm.*, 1957, **28**, 327–342.

(25) BONNEY, M. E.: Social behavior differences between second grade children of high and low sociometric status. *J. educ. Res.*, 1955, **48**, 481–495.

(26) BONNEY, M. E., and E. L. NICHOLSON: Comparative school adjustments of elementary school pupils with and without preschool training. *Child Develpm.*, 1958, **29**, 125–133.

(27) BORING, E. G.: The woman problem. *Amer. Psychologist*, 1951, **6**, 679–692.

(28) BOSSARD, J. H. S., and E. S. BOLL: *The sociology of child development*, 3d ed. New York: Harper & Row, 1960.

(29) BOWERMAN, C. E., and J. W. KINCH: Changes in family and peer orientation of children between the fourth and tenth grades. *Soc. Forces*, 1959, **37**, 206–211.

(30) BRECKENRIDGE, M. E., and E. L. VINCENT: *Child development*, 4th ed. Philadelphia: Saunders, 1960.

(31) BRODERICK, C. B., and S. E. FOWLER: New patterns of relationships between the sexes among preadolescents. *Marriage fam. Liv.*, 1961, **23**, 27–30.

(32) BROWN, A. W., and R. G. HUNT: Relations between nursery school attendance and teachers' ratings of some aspects of children's adjustment in kindergarten. *Child Develpm.*, 1961, **32**, 585–596.

(33) BROWN, D. G.: Sex-role development in a changing culture. *Psychol. Bull.*, 1958, **55**, 232–242.

(34) BROWN, F. J.: *Educational sociology*, 2d

ed. Englewood Cliffs, N.J.: Prentice-Hall, 1954.

(35) BROWNFIELD, E. D.: Communication—key to dynamics of family interaction. *Marriage fam. Liv.*, 1953, **15**, 316–319.

(36) BURCHINAL, L. G., G. R. HAWKES, and B. GARDNER: Adjustment characteristics of rural and urban children. *Amer. sociol. Rev.*, 1957, **22**, 81–87.

(37) CANNING, R. R., and J. M. BAKER: Effect of the group on authoritarian and non-authoritarian persons. *Amer. J. Sociol.*, 1959, **64**, 579–581.

(38) CAPLAN, H.: The role of deviant maturation in the pathogenesis of anxiety. *Amer. J. Orthopsychiat.*, 1956, **26**, 94–107.

(39) CATTELL, R. B., and R. W. COAN: Personality factors in middle childhood as revealed by parents' ratings. *Child Develpm.*, 1957, **28**, 439–458.

(40) CENTERS, R.: Social-class identification of American youth. *J. Pers.*, 1950, **18**, 290–302.

(41) CHILD, I. L.: Socialization. In G. Lindzey (Ed.), *Handbook of social psychology.* Cambridge, Mass.: Addison-Wesley, 1954. Pp. 655–692.

(42) CHILD, I. L., E. H. POTTER, and E. M. DEVINE: Children's textbooks and personality development: an exploration in the social psychology of education. *Psychol. Monogr.*, 1946, **60**, No. 3.

(43) CHOWDHRY, K., and T. M. NEWCOMB: The relative abilities of leaders and non-leaders to estimate opinions of their own groups. *J. abnorm. soc. Psychol.*, 1952, **47**, 51–57.

(44) CHURCH, J., and L. J. STONE: The early school years. *Children*, 1960, **7**, 113–114.

(45) CLARK, K. B.: Race prejudice and children. *Child*, 1953, **17**, 113–115.

(46) CLARK, W. H.: Sex differences and motivation in the urge to destroy. *J. soc. Psychol.*, 1952, **36**, 167–177.

(47) COLEMAN, W. R., E. KRIS, and S. PROVENCE: The study of variations of early parental attitudes. *Psychoanal. Stud. Child.*, 1954, **8**, 20–47.

(48) COMMESS, H. H.: Some characteristics related to social isolation of second grade children. *J. educ. Psychol.*, 1962, **53**, 38–42.

(49) COOK, S. W.: Desegregation: a psychological analysis. *Amer. Psychologist*, 1957, **12**, 1–13.

(50) COOPER, J. B.: Emotion in prejudice. *Science*, 1959, **130**, 314–318.

(51) CRANDALL, V. J., A. PRESTON, and A. RABSON: Maternal reactions and the development of independence and achievement behavior in young children. *Child Develpm.*, 1960, **31**, 243–251.

(52) CRANE, A. R.: The development of moral values in children. IV. Pre-adolescent gangs and the development of children. *Brit. J. educ. Psychol.*, 1958, **28**, 201–208.

(53) CRONBACH, L. J.: Processes affecting scores on "understanding of others" and "assumed similarity." *Psychol. Bull.*, 1955, **52**, 177–193.

(54) CROW, A.: Parental attitudes toward boy-girl relations. *J. educ. Sociol.*, 1955, **29**, 126–133.

(55) DAHLKE, H. O.: Determinants of sociometric relations among children in the elementary school. *Sociometry*, 1953, **16**, 327–338.

(56) DALE, R. J.: A method for measuring developmental tasks: scales for selected tasks at the beginning of adolescence. *Child Develpm.*, 1955, **26**, 111–122.

(57) DAVIDSON, H. L., and L. S. GOTTLIEB: The emotional maturity of pre- and post-menarcheal girls. *J. genet. Psychol.*, 1955, **86**, 261–266.

(58) DITTES, J. E.: Attractiveness of group as function of self-esteem and acceptance by group. *J. abnorm. soc. Psychol.*, 1959, **59**, 77–82.

(59) DEBUS, R. L.: Aggressive behavior in young children. *Forum Educ.*, 1953, **11**, 95–105.

(60) DUNBAR, F.: Homeostasis during puberty. *Amer. J. Psychiat.*, 1958, **114**, 673–683.

(61) DUNNINGTON, M. J.: Behavioral differences of sociometric status groups in a nursery school. *Child Develpm.*, 1957, **28**, 103–111.

(62) DYMOND, R. F., A. S. HUGHES, and V. L. RAABE: Measurable changes in empathy with age. *J. consult. Psychol.*, 1952, **16**, 202–206.

(63) ELKIN, F.: Socialization and the presentation of self. *Marriage fam. Liv.*, 1958, **20**, 320–325.

(64) ELKINS, D.: Some factors related to the choice-status of ninety eighth-grade children in a school society. *Genet. Psychol. Monogr.*, 1958, **58**, 207–272.

(65) EMMERICH, W.: Parental identification in young children. *Genet. Psychol. Monogr.*, 1959, **60**, 257–308.

(66) ERON, L. D., T. J. BANTA, L. O. WALDER, and J. H. LAULICHT: Comparison of data obtained from mothers and fathers on child rearing practices and their relation to child aggression. *Child Develpm.*, 1961, **32**, 457–472.

(67) EXLINE, R. V.: Group climate as a factor in the relevance and accuracy of social perception. *J. abnorm. soc. Psychol.*, 1957, **55**, 382–388.

(68) FEINBERG, M. R.: Relation of background experience to social acceptance. *J. abnorm. soc. Psychol.*, 1953, **48**, 206–214.

(69) FERGUSON, R. G.: Some developmental factors in childhood aggression. *J. educ. Res.*, 1954, **48**, 105–117.

(70) FIELDS, S. J.: Discrimination of facial expression and its relation to personal adjustment. *J. soc. Psychol.*, 1953, **38**, 63–71.

(71) FISHMAN, J. A.: Negative stereotypes concerning Americans among American-born children receiving various types of minority-group education. *Genet. Psychol. Monogr.*, 1955, **51**, 107–182.

(72) FRANK, L. K., and M. H. FRANK: *Your adolescent, at home and in school.* New York: Viking, 1956.

(73) FRENKEL-BRUNSWICK, E., and G. HAVEL: Prejudice in the interviews of children. 1. Attitudes toward minority groups. *J. genet. Psychol.*, 1953, **82**, 91–136.

(74) FREEMAN, H. E., and M. SHOWELL: The role of the family in the socialization process. *J. soc. Psychol.*, 1953, **37**, 97–101.

(75) FRIEDMAN, A.: Observations in a play group of young children. *Ind. Psychol. Bull.*, 1951, **9**, 25–30.

(76) GAGE, N. L.: Accuracy of social perception and effectiveness in interpersonal relationships. *J. Pers.*, 1953, **22**, 128–141.

(77) GALLAGHER, J. J.: Social status of children related to intelligence, propinquity, and social perception. *Elem. Sch. J.*, 1958, **58**, 225–231.

(78) GARRISON, K. C.: *Growth and development,* 2d ed. New York: Longmans, 1959.

(79) GESELL, A., F. L. ILG, and L. B. AMES: *Youth: the years from ten to sixteen.* New York: Harper & Row, 1956.

(80) GEWIRTZ, J. L.: A factor analysis of some attention-seeking behaviors of young children. *Child Develpm.*, 1956, **27**, 17–36.

(81) GEWIRTZ, J. L.: A program of research on the dimensions and antecedents of emotional dependence. *Child Develpm.*, 1956, **27**, 205–211.

(82) GILES, H. H.: *The integrated classroom.* New York: Basic Books, Inc., Publishers, 1959.

(83) GRAY, P. H.: Theory and evidence of imprinting in human infants. *J. Psychol.*, 1958, **46**, 155–165.

(84) GREENBERG, H., J. PIERSON, and S. SHERMAN: The effects of single-session education techniques on prejudice attitudes. *J. educ. Sociol.*, 1957, **31**, 82–86.

(85) GRIFFITHS, W.: *Behavior difficulties of children as perceived and judged by parents, teachers, and children themselves.* Minneapolis: The University of Minnesota Press, 1952.

(86) GRONLUND, N. E.: Sociometric status and sociometric perception. *Sociometry*, 1955, **18**, 122–128.

(87) GUINOUARD, E. D., and J. F. RYCHLAK: Personality correlates of sociometric popularity in elementary school children. *Personnel Guid. J.*, 1962, **40**, 438–444.

(88) HALE, C. J.: Physiological maturity of Little League baseball players. *Res. Quart. Amer. Ass. Hlth Phys. Educ. Recr.*, 1956, **27**, 276–284.

(89) HALPERN, H. M.: Empathy, similarity, and self-satisfaction. *J. consult. Psychol.*, 1955, **19**, 449–452.

(90) HANDLON, B. J., and P. GROSS: The development of sharing behavior. *J. abnorm. soc. Psychol.*, 1959, **59**, 425–428.

(91) HARDY, K. R.: Determinants of conformity and attitude change. *J. abnorm. soc. Psychol.*, 1957, **54**, 289–294.

(92) HARRIS, D. B., A. M. ROSE, K. E. CLARKE, and F. VALASEK: Personality differences between responsible and less responsible children. *J. genet. Psychol.*, 1955, **87**, 103–106.

(93) HARRIS, D. B., and C. S. TSENG: Children's attitudes toward peers and parents as revealed by sentence completions. *Child Develpm.*, 1957, **28**, 401–411.

(94) HARRIS, E. K.: The responsiveness of kindergarten children to the behavior of their fellows. *Monogr. Soc. Res. Child Develpm.*, 1946, **11**, No. 2.

(95) HARRIS, M.: Caste, class, and minority. *Soc. Forces*, 1959, **37**, 248–254.

(96) HARTRUP, W. W., and Y. HIMENO: Social isolation vs. interaction with adults in relation to aggression in preschool children. *J. abnorm. soc. Psychol.*, 1959, **59**, 17–22.

(97) HARTRUP, W. W., and E. D. KELLER: Nurturance in preschool children and its relation to dependency. *Child Develpm.*, 1960, **31**, 681–689.

(98) HARVEY, O. J., and J. RUTHERFORD: Status in the informal group: influence and influencibility at differing age levels. *Child Develpm.*, 1960, **31**, 377–385.

(99) HAVIGHURST, R. J.: *Human development and education.* New York: Longmans, 1953.

(100) HEATHERS, G.: Acquiring dependence and independence: a theoretical orientation. *J. genet. Psychol.*, 1955, **87**, 277–291.

(101) HIGHBERGER, R.: Maternal behavior and attitudes related to behavior of the preschool child. *J. home Econ.*, 1956, **48**, 260–264.

(102) HILGARD, J. R.: Sibling rivalry and social heredity. *Psychiatry*, 1951, **14**, 375–385.

(103) HIROTA, K.: Experimental studies of competition. *Jap. J. Psychol.*, 1951, **21**, 70–81.

(104) HOCHBAM, G. M.: The relation between group members' self-confidence and their reaction to group pressures to conformity. *Amer. sociol. Rev.*, 1954, **19**, 678–687.

(105) HOFFMAN, M. L.: Conformity as a defense mechanism and a form of resistance to genuine group influence. *J. Pers.*, 1957, **25**, 412–424.

(106) HORROCKS, J. E., and M. E. BUKER: A study of the friendship fluctuations of preadolescents. *J. genet. Psychol.*, 1951, **78**, 131–144.

(107) HUNT, R. G., and V. SYNNERDAHL: Social influence among kindergarten children. *Sociol. soc. Res.*, 1958, **43**, 171–174.

(108) HYMES, J. L.: Early childhood. *Children,* 1960, **7**, 111–113.

(109) ILG, F. L., J. LEARNED, A. LOCKWOOD, and L. B. AMES: The three-and-a-half-year-old. *J. genet. Psychol.,* 1949, **75**, 21–31.

(110) JACK, L. M.: An experimental study of ascendant behavior in preschool children. *Univer. Iowa Stud. Child Welf.,* 1934, **9**, No. 3.

(111) JAKUBCZAK, L. F., and R. H. WALTERS: Suggestibility as dependency behavior. *J. abnorm. soc. Psychol.,* 1959, **59**, 102–107.

(112) JERARD, S., and R. H. WALTERS: A study of some determinants of aggression in young children. *Child Develpm.,* 1960, **31**, 739–747.

(113) JERSILD, A. T.: *Child psychology,* 5th ed. Englewood Cliffs, N.J.: Prentice-Hall, 1960.

(114) JONES, M. C.: The later careers of boys who were early- or late-maturers. *Child Develpm.,* 1957, **28**, 113–128.

(115) JONES, M. C., and P. H. MUSSEN: Self-conceptions, motivations, and interpersonal attitudes of early- and late-maturing girls. *Child Develpm.,* 1958, **29**, 491–501.

(116) JOSSELYN, I. M.: Psychological changes in adolescence. *Children,* 1959, **6**, 43–47.

(117) JOURARD, S. M., and R. M. REMY: Perceived parental attitude, the self and security. *J. consult. Psychol.,* 1955, **19**, 364–366.

(118) KANOUS, L. E., R. A. DAUGHERTY, and T. S. COHN: Relation between heterosexual friendship choices and socioeconomic level. *Child Develpm.,* 1962, **33**, 251–255.

(119) KATZ, D., I. SARNOFF, and C. MC CLINTOCK: Ego-defense and attitude change. *Hum. Rel.,* 1956, **9**, 27–45.

(120) KLATSKIN, E. H., E. B. JACKSON, and L. C. WILKIN: The influence of degree of flexibility in maternal child practices on early child behavior. *Amer. J. Orthopsychiat.,* 1956, **26**, 79–93.

(121) KOCH, H. L.: The relation of certain formal attributes of siblings to attitudes held toward each other and toward their parents. *Monogr. Soc. Res. Child Develpm.,* 1960, **25**, No. 4.

(122) KUTNER, B.: Patterns of mental functioning associated with prejudice in children. *Psychol. Monogr.,* 1958, **72**, No. 7.

(123) LAMBERT, W. E., and Y. TAGUCHI: Ethnic cleavage among young children. *J. abnorm. soc. Psychol.,* 1956, **53**, 380–382.

(124) LANDRETH, C.: *The psychology of early childhood.* New York: Knopf, 1958.

(125) LESSER, G. S.: The relationship between various forms of aggression and popularity among lower-class children. *J. educ. Psychol.,* 1959, **50**, 20–25.

(126) LEVIN, H., and R. R. SEARS: Identification with parents as a determinant of doll play aggression. *Child Develpm.,* 1956, **27**, 135–153.

(127) LEWIS, E.: The function of group play during middle childhood in developing the ego complex. *Brit. J. med. Psychol.,* 1954, **27**, 15–29.

(128) LUNDY, R. M.: Self-perceptions and descriptions of opposite sex sociometric choices. *Sociometry,* 1956, **19**, 272–277.

(129) LYLE, W. H., and E. E. LEVITT: Punitiveness, authoritarianism, and parental discipline of grade school children. *J. abnorm. soc. Psychol.,* 1955, **51**, 42–46.

(130) LYNN, R.: Personality characteristics of the mothers of aggressive and unaggressive children. *J. genet. Psychol.,* 1961, **99**, 159–164.

(131) MACCOBY, E. E.: Role-taking in children and its consequences for social learning. *Child Develpm.,* 1959, **30**, 239–252.

(132) MAC DONALD, M., C. MC GUIRE, and R. J. HAVIGHURST: Leisure activities and the socioeconomic status of children. *Amer. J. Sociol.,* 1949, **54**, 505–519.

(133) MACFARLANE, J., L. ALLEN, and M. P. HONZIK: *A developmental study of the behavior problems of normal children between twenty-one months and fourteen years.* Berkeley, Calif.: University of California Press, 1954.

(134) MANIS, M.: Social interaction and the self-concept. *J. abnorm. soc. Psychol.,* 1955, **51**, 362–370.

(135) MARSHALL, H. R.: Relations between home experiences and children's use of language in play interaction with peers. *Psychol. Monogr.,* 1961, **75**, No. 5.

(136) MARSHALL, H. R., and B. R. MC CANDLESS: Relationships between dependence on adults and social acceptance by peers. *Child Develpm.,* 1957, **28**, 413–419.

(137) MARTIN, J. G., and F. R. WESTIE: The tolerant personality. *Amer. sociol. Rev.,* 1959, **24**, 521–528.

(138) MC CANDLESS, B. R., C. B. BILOUS, and H. L. BENNETT: Peer popularity and dependence on adults in preschool-age socialization. *Child Develpm.,* 1961, **32**, 511–518.

(139) MC CANDLESS, B. R., and J. M. HOYT: Sex, ethnicity, and play preferences of preschool children. *J. abnorm. soc. Psychol.,* 1961, **62**, 683–685.

(140) MC CANDLESS, B. R., and H. R. MARSHALL: Sex differences in social acceptance and participation of preschool children. *Child Develpm.,* 1957, **28**, 421–425.

(141) MC CARTHY, D.: Language development. In L. Carmichael (Ed.), *Manual of child psychology,* 2d ed. New York: Wiley, 1954. Pp. 492–630.

(142) MC CLUSKY, H. Y.: The status of youth in our culture. *Education,* 1955, **76**, 206–209.

(143) MC CONNELL, G.: Questions about you. *Education,* 1959, **80**, 112–114.

(144) MC CULLOUGH, C. S.: A log of children's out-of-school activities. *Elem. Sch. J.,* 1957, **58,** 157–165.

(145) MC GUIRE, C., and G. D. WHITE: Social-class influences on discipline at school. *Educ. Leadership,* 1957, **14,** 229–231, 234–236.

(146) MC KEE, J. P., and F. B. LEADER: The relationship of socioeconomic status and aggression to the competitive behavior of preschool children. *Child Develpm.,* 1955, **26,** 135–142.

(147) MENZEL, H.: Public and private conformity under different conditions of acceptance in the group. *J. abnorm. soc. Psychol.,* 1957, **55,** 398–402.

(148) MERRY, F. K., and R. V. MERRY: *The first two decades of life,* 2d ed. New York: Harper & Row, 1958.

(149) MEYER, W. J.: Relationships between social need strivings and the development of heterosexual affiliation. *J. abnorm. soc. Psychol.,* 1959, **59,** 51–57.

(150) MILLER, K. M., and J. B. BIGGS: Attitude change through undirected group discussion. *J. educ. Psychol.,* 1958, **49,** 224–228.

(151) MITNICK, L. L., and E. MC GINNIES: Influencing ethnocentrism in small discussion groups through a film communication. *J. abnorm. soc. Psychol.,* 1958, **56,** 82–90.

(152) MOELLER, G., and M. H. APPLEZWEIG: A motivational factor in conformity. *J. abnorm. soc. Psychol.,* 1957, **55,** 114–120.

(153) MORE, D. M.: Developmental concordance and discordance during puberty and early adolescence. *Monogr. Soc. Res. Child Develpm.,* 1953, **18,** 1–128.

(154) MORLAND, J. K.: Racial recognition by nursery school children in Lynchburg, Va. *Soc. Forces,* 1958, **37,** 132–137.

(155) MOSHER, D. L., and A. SCODEL: Relationships between ethnocentrism in children and the ethnocentrism and authoritarian rearing practices of their mothers. *Child Develpm.,* 1960, **31,** 369–376.

(156) MOUSTAKAS, C. E.: The frequency and intensity of negative attitudes expressed in play therapy: a comparison of well-adjusted and disturbed young children. *J. genet. Psychol.,* 1955, **86,** 309–325.

(157) MUMMERY, D. V.: Family backgrounds of assertive and nonassertive children. *Child Develpm.,* 1954, **25,** 63–80.

(158) MUNSON, B. E.: Personality differentials among urban, suburban, town, and rural children. *Rur. Sociol.,* 1959, **24,** 257–264.

(159) MURPHY, L. B.: *Personality in young children.* New York: Basic Books, Inc., Publishers, 1957.

(160) MUSSEN, P. H.: Differences between the TAT responses of Negro and white boys. *J. consult. Psychol.,* 1953, **17,** 373–376.

(161) MUSSEN, P. H., J. J. CONGER, and J.

KAGAN: *Child development and personality,* 2d ed. New York: Harper & Row, 1963.

(162) MUSSEN, P. H., and L. DISTLER: Child-rearing antecedents of masculine identification in kindergarten boys. *Child Develpm.,* 1960, **31,** 89–100.

(163) MUSSEN, P. H., and M. C. JONES: Self-conceptions, motivations, and interpersonal attitudes of late- and early-maturing boys. *Child Develpm.,* 1957, **28,** 243–256.

(164) MUSSEN, P. H., and E. RUTHERFORD: Effects of aggressive cartoons on children's aggressive play. *J. abnorm. soc. Psychol.,* 1961, **62,** 461–464.

(165) MUUS, R., and C. B. STENDLER: Intergroup education in the public schools. *Educ. Forum.,* 1956, **20,** 151–164.

(166) NOWLIS, V.: A search for significant concepts in a study of parent-child relationships. *Amer. J. Orthopsychiat.,* 1952, **22,** 286–299.

(167) OTIS, N. B., and B. R. MC CANDLESS: Responses to repeated frustration of young children differentiated according to need area. *J. abnorm. soc. Psychol.,* 1955, **50,** 249–253.

(168) OVESEY, L.: Masculine aspirations in women. *Psychiatry,* 1956, **19,** 341–351.

(169) PEASE, D., and L. V. SWANSON: Middle childhood and preadolescence deserve study too. *J. home Econ.,* 1958, **50,** 33–35.

(170) PERKINS, H. V.: Teachers' and peers' perceptions of children's self-concepts. *Child Develpm.,* 1958, **29,** 203–220.

(171) POWELL, M.: Age and sex differences in degree of conflict within certain areas of psychological adjustment. *Psychol. Monogr.,* 1955, **69,** No. 2.

(172) PROTHRO, E. T.: Ethnocentrism and anti-Negro attitudes in the deep South. *J. abnorm. soc. Psychol.,* 1952, **47,** 105–108.

(173) RAFFERTY, F. T., and E. S. STEIN: A study of the relationship of early menarche to ego development. *Amer. J. Orthopsychiat.,* 1958, **28,** 170–179.

(174) REISSMAN, L.: Class, leisure, and social participation. *Amer. sociol. Rev.,* 1954, **19,** 76–84.

(175) ROSENBLITH, J. F.: Learning by imitation in kindergarten children. *Child Develpm.,* 1959, **30,** 69–80.

(176) ROSENBLITH, J. F.: Imitative color choices in kindergarten children. *Child Develpm.,* 1961, **32,** 211–223.

(177) ROSENZWEIG, S., and L. ROSENZWEIG: Aggression in problem children and normals as evaluated by the Rosenzweig Picture-Frustration Study. *J. abnorm. soc. Psychol.,* 1952, **47,** 683–688.

(178) RYAN, M. E.: Social adjustment of kindergarten children ten years later. *Smith Coll. Stud. soc. Wk,* 1949, **19,** 138–139.

(179) SCHNEIDERMAN, L.: Social perception as a

function of identification. *J. Psychol.*, 1954, **37**, 155–162.

(180) SCHNEIDERMAN, L.: The estimation of one's own body traits. *J. soc. Psychol.*, 1956, **44**, 89–99.

(181) SEARS, P. S.: Doll play aggression in normal young children: influence of sex, age, sibling status, father's absence. *Psychol. Monogr.*, 1951, **65**, No. 6.

(182) SEARS, P. S., and H. LEVIN: Levels of aspiration in preschool children. *Child Develpm.*, 1957, **28**, 317–326.

(183) SEARS, R. R.: Effects of frustration and anxiety on fantasy aggression. *Amer. J. Orthopsychiat.*, 1951, **51**, 498–505.

(184) SEARS, R. R., E. E. MACCOBY, and H. LEVIN: *Patterns of child rearing.* New York: Harper & Row, 1957.

(185) SEARS R. R., J. W. M. WHITING, V. NOWLIN, and P. S. SEARS: Some child-rearing antecedents of aggression and dependency in young children. *Genet. Psychol. Monogr.*, 1953, **47**, 135–234.

(186) SECORD, P. F., and E. SAUMER: Identifying Jewish names: does prejudice increase accuracy? *J. abnorm. soc. Psychol.*, 1960, **61**, 144–145.

(187) SEIDLER, M. B., and M. J. RAVITZ: A Jewish peer group. *Amer. J. Sociol.*, 1955, **61**, 11–15.

(188) SHAPIRO, D. S.: Perceptions of significant family and environmental relationships in aggressive and withdrawn children. *J. consult. Psychol.*, 1957, **21**, 381–385.

(189) SIEGEL, A. E.: The influence of violence in the mass media upon children's role expectations. *Child Develpm.*, 1958, **29**, 35–56.

(190) SIEGEL, A. E., and L. G. KOHN: Permissiveness, permission, and aggression: the effect of adult presence or absence on aggression in children's play. *Child Develpm.*, 1959, **30**, 131–141.

(191) SIMPSON, R. L., and I. H. SIMPSON: The school, the peer groups, and adolescent development. *J. educ. Sociol.*, 1958, **32**, 37–41.

(192) SMITH, M. E.: Childhood memories compared with those of adult life. *J. genet. Psychol.*, 1952, **80**, 151–182.

(193) SMITH, W. D., and D. LEBO: Some changing aspects of the self concept of pubescent males. *J. genet. Psychol.*, 1956, **88**, 61–75.

(194) SPIVACK, S. S.: A study of a method of appraising self-acceptance and self-rejection. *J. genet. Psychol.*, 1956, **88**, 183–202.

(195) SPRINGER, D. V.: National-racial preferences of fifth-grade children in Hawaii. *J. genet. Psychol.*, 1953, **83**, 121–136.

(196) STENDLER, C. B., D. DAMRIN, and A. C. HAINES: Studies in cooperation and competition: 1. The effects of working for group and individual rewards on the social climate of children's group. *J. genet. Psychol.*, 1951, **79**, 173–197.

(197) STENDLER, C. B., and N. YOUNG: Impact of first grade entrance upon the socialization of the child: changes after eight months of school. *Child Develpm.*, 1951, **22**, 113–122.

(198) STEVENSON, H. W., and N. G. STEVENSON: Social interaction in an integrated nursery school. *Genet. Psychol. Monogr.*, 1960, **61**, 37–75.

(199) STEVENSON, H. W., and E. C. STEWART: A developmental study of racial awareness in young children. *Child Develpm.*, 1958, **29**, 399–409.

(200) STOLZ, H. R., and L. M. STOLZ: *Somatic development of adolescent boys.* New York: Macmillan, 1951.

(201) STONE, L. J., and J. CHURCH: *Childhood and adolescence.* New York: Random House, 1957.

(202) STOODLEY, B. H.: Mother role as focus of some family problems. *Marriage fam. Liv.*, 1952, **14**, 13–16.

(203) STOTLAND, E., S. THORLEY, E. THOMAS, A. R. COHEN, and A. ZANDER: The effects of group expectations and self-esteem upon self-evaluation. *J. abnorm. soc. Psychol.*, 1957, **54**, 55–63.

(204) STOTT, L. H., and R. S. BALL: Consistency and change in ascendance-submission in the social interaction of children. *Child Develpm.*, 1957, **28**, 259–272.

(205) STOUFFER, G. A. W., and J. OWENS: Behavior problems identified by today's teachers and compared with those of E. K. Wichman. *J. educ. Res.*, 1955, **48**, 321–331.

(206) STRANG, R. M.: *An introduction to child study*, 4th ed. New York: Macmillan, 1959.

(207) STRAUSS, A. L.: The learning of roles and of concepts as twin processes. *J. genet. Psychol.*, 1956, **88**, 211–217.

(208) TAFT, R.: The ability to judge people. *Psychol. Bull.*, 1955, **52**, 1–23.

(209) TARWATER, J. W.: Self-understanding and the ability to predict another's response. *Marriage fam. Liv.*, 1953, **15**, 126–128.

(210) THOMPSON, G. G., and S. L. WITRYOL: Adult recall of unpleasant experiences during three periods of childhood. *J. genet. Psychol.*, 1948, **72**, 111–123.

(211) TRENT, R. D.: The relation between expressed self-acceptance and expressed attitudes toward Negroes and whites among Negro children. *J. genet. Psychol.*, 1957, **91**, 25–31.

(212) TRIANDIS, H. C., and L. M. TRIANDIS: Race, social class, religion, and nationality as determinants of social distance. *J. abnorm. soc. Psychol.*, 1960, **61**, 110–118.

(213) TURNER, W. D.: Altruism and its measurement in children. *J. abnorm. soc. Psychol.*, 1948, **43**, 502–516.

(214) UGUREL-SEMIN, R.: Moral behavior and moral judgments of children. *J. abnorm. soc. Psychol.,* 1952, **47,** 463–474.

(215) VOSK, M.: Correlates of prejudice. *Rev. educ. Res.,* 1953, **23,** 353–361.

(216) WALLACE, E. H.: Selected out-of-school factors that affect Negro elementary school children. *J. educ. Res.,* 1960, **54,** 118–120, 137–140.

(217) WALTER, J., D. PEARCE, and L. DAHMS: Affectional and aggressive behavior of pre-school children. *Child Develpm.,* 1957, **28,** 15–26.

(218) WALTERS, R. H., and P. KARAL: Social deprivation and verbal behavior. *J. Pers.,* 1960, **28,** 89–107.

(219) WALTERS, R. H., W. E. MARSHALL, and J. R. SHOOTER: Anxiety, isolation, and susceptibility to social influence. *J. Pers.,* 1960, **28,** 518–529.

(220) WEISS, W.: An examination of attitudes toward Negroes. *J. soc. Psychol.,* 1961, **55,** 3–21.

(221) WILSON, W. C.: Extrinsic religious values and prejudice. *J. abnorm. soc. Psychol.,* 1960, **60,** 286–288.

(222) WITTENBERG, R. M., and J. BERG: The stranger in the group. *Amer. J. Orthopsychiat.,* 1952, **22,** 89–97.

(223) WOLMAN, B.: Spontaneous groups of children and adolescents in Israel. *J. soc. Psychol.,* 1951, **34,** 171–182.

(224) WRIGHT, H. F.: Psychological development in Midwest. *Child Develpm.,* 1956, **27,** 265–286.

(225) YARROW, L. J.: Infancy. *Children.* 1960, **7,** 110–111.

(226) ZELIGS, R.: Your child's good-will depends on you. *J. Negro Educ.,* 1951, **20,** 32–38.

(227) ZELIGS, R.: Children's concepts and stereotypes of American, Greek, English, German, and Japanese. *J. educ. Sociol.,* 1955, **28,** 360–368.

SOCIAL
ADJUSTMENTS

Social adjustment means the success with which a person adjusts to people in general and to the group with which he is identified in particular. A well-adjusted person has learned such social skills as the ability to deal diplomatically with people— both friends and strangers—so that their attitudes toward him will be favorable and they will want to accept him. He has developed good social attitudes, such as a willingness to help others, even if he is personally inconvenienced. He is not self-bound.

Children are *expected* to become better adjusted to social life each year and to conform to social expectations for their age. No one expects a baby to be a well-adjusted person; he is too self-bound to consider others and too ignorant of social expectations to know how to conform to socially approved patterns of behavior. The older child, however, is judged more critically.

The socialization process begins in the home. The young child applies the type of social adjustments he learns at home to the social situations he encounters in the school, the neighborhood, and the community. As his interest in the home and his dependency on family members are gradually replaced by interest in, and dependency on, peers, however, the socialization process shifts from the home to the school and playground. Which group ultimately plays the greater role in his socialization will be determined by the child's emotional ties with, and his dependency on, that group—the family or the peer group (45, 200).

IMPORTANCE OF
SOCIAL ADJUSTMENTS

In a culture that puts a high value on social adjustments, as in the American culture of today, parents and teachers provide the child with opportunities to learn to make good adjustments. They motivate him to do so by rewarding him with approval when he comes up to their expectations.

Mothers, for example, realize that their

384

daughters will be happier if they are popular with both girls and boys, and they begin to provide social experiences involving members of both sexes even before childhood ends (49). Fathers recognize that success in business depends as much on making good social adjustments as on ability, and they urge their sons to belong to gangs and to learn to be "regular boys" (51). Today's teachers are more concerned about behavior that leads to poor adjustment than about behavior that disrupts the smooth running of the classroom (240).

All parents realize that there is a close relationship between a child's social adjustments and his happiness. Middle-class parents are especially concerned because they are "future-oriented." They feel that good social adjustments for their daughters will lead to successful marriage, while good social adjustments for their sons are a necessary stepping-stone to success in business and upward social mobility (3, 38). Because most teachers have middle-class backgrounds, they hold similar values and consider social adjustment in childhood to be as important as academic success (136).

That these concerns are justified is readily apparent in evidence that points to the persistence of the type of social adjustment the child makes. The reason for this persistence is that any behavior that is rewarded by social approval gives satisfaction to the child and is thus repeated until, in time, it becomes habitual. In a study of adolescent boys who later became schizophrenic, for example, it was revealed that, as children, they were the quiet, withdrawn type who caused no trouble for their teachers but who did poor school work and made poor adjustments to the peer group. By adolescence, they were definitely maladjusted in social situations, and by adulthood, many of them were institutionalized (44). Similarly, in a follow-up study of children from kindergarten into adulthood, it was found that those who were dependent as children were also dependent as adults. Those who strove for social recognition and achievement by competition with their peers showed the same strong striving for achievement as adults (200).

The type of social adjustment the child makes leaves its mark on his self-concept. This likewise contributes to its persistence. A child who makes good social adjustments develops a favorable self-concept; if other people like him, he likes himself. By contrast, children who make poor social adjustments are unhappy and dislike themselves. As a result, they usually develop into self-centered, introverted, unsocial or antisocial people whose adult happiness and success are seriously jeopardized.

Difficulties in Making Good Social Adjustments. If poor foundations are laid in the *home,* the child will find it difficult to make good social adjustments outside the home even though he may be strongly motivated to do so. The child brought up by authoritarian methods, for example, frequently develops attitudes of resentment toward all in authority. Constant criticisms and punishments reduce his self-concept to zero. With too permissive training in the home, the child comes to disregard the wishes of others, feeling that he can be a law unto himself (75, 178).

Having a poor *model to imitate* in the home also has serious effects on the child's social adjustment. In a study of the effects of the parental role model on the development of criminality, it was found that children whose parents reject them or who engage in deviant behavior frequently develop into juvenile delinquents or adult criminals. Such children develop unstable, aggressive personalities which push them into revengeful acts, often leading to criminality. When parents show acceptant attitudes and provide a home environment characterized by emotional warmth, children develop more wholesome personalities; as a result, they are less likely to imitate the deviant patterns of their parents (189).

Poor adjustment in early social experiences is likely to lead to unfavorable attitudes which decrease the child's motivation to learn to get along with people or to participate in social activities. Social participation provides opportunities for learning how to behave in a socially acceptable way and for learning the meanings and values that constitute the culture of the group with which the child is identified. For this reason, the more he withdraws, the less socialized he will become (18, 97).

CRITERIA OF SOCIAL ADJUSTMENT

To determine how well adjusted the child is socially, four criteria must be applied; one alone is inadequate. The first criterion is the child's *overt performance* as judged against standards of the group with which he is identified. Only if his performance comes up to group expectations for his age and level of development will he be accepted by the group.

The second criterion is the success with which he can adjust to *any group* with which he comes in contact. A child may, for example, adjust successfully to the family group but be so timid, shy, and withdrawn with people outside the home that he is overlooked or rejected. Similarly, the child may make good adjustments to the teacher but very poor adjustments to the peer group, or the reverse. If the child were identified with only one group or with several groups so similar in makeup that the patterns of adjustment learned for one could be transferred to the other, he would have less difficulty becoming a socialized person. In real life, however, a child must adjust to multiple group memberships, each with its own expectations and demands.

The third criterion is the child's *attitude* toward people, toward social participation, and toward his role in the social group. At every age, attitudes are reflected in the quality of a person's behavior. The child who develops an unfavorable attitude toward some racial or religious group, for example, will treat any member of that group in accordance with his prejudice. He will not judge the individual as a person but will prejudge him on the basis of his group identification. A favorable attitude toward

social participation is an indication that a child has made good social adjustments.

The fourth criterion, closely related to the third, is the degree of *personal satisfaction* the child derives from social contacts. The child whose social contacts are pleasurable will want to repeat them. How much satisfaction the child gets from the role he plays in the social group will likewise give a clue to the type of social adjustment he has made. If he prefers to be a follower, he will be satisfied when he is in the follower role but uneasy and inadequate in the leader role (205, 239).

Difficulties in Applying Criteria.   It is far from easy to apply these criteria and to be sure that the results obtained are true indications of the type of social adjustment the child has made. Because social acceptance is an indication of how closely the child's behavior conforms to social expectations, it is possible to determine the degree of the child's social adjustment by finding out what others think of him, how well he is accepted by the peer group, what evaluations are made of him by teachers, and whether he plays the role of leader, follower, or rejectee in the peer group.

The first two criteria can be applied fairly successfully. Objective techniques of assessing attitudes and satisfactions, however, are more difficult. One must ask the child what his attitudes are, how much he likes social activities, and how people treat him, or one must try to *infer* his attitudes and satisfactions from what he says about himself, about other people, and about group activities. When a child says that he does not want to go out to play with other children, for example, that their play "bores" him, or that he would rather read or watch television, it is obvious that he derives less satisfaction from social than from solitary activities.

Similarly, if he constantly makes critical, derogatory comments about peers, teachers, or other adults, or if he complains that other children tease him, take his toys away, or won't let him play with them, it is apparent that he enjoys little social acceptance and is actively disliked by some or many members of the peer group. The child who is family-oriented at an age when other children are peer-oriented is so because he derives more satisfaction from companionship with members of the family group than with members of the peer group. On the other hand, the child who wants to be with the peer group at all times and who scorns activities with the family is showing that he is well adjusted socially.

A word of caution about inferring too much about a child's social adjustments from what he says or does is essential. Many children, when they are annoyed or angry, say things that they actually do not mean or that they mean only at that time. When their anger passes, they may even claim they never said such things. Studies of children's quarrels have shown that at the peak of the quarrel they may say things to and about the child with whom they are quarreling that suggest that they are bitter enemies and that their relationship is marked by extreme hostility. However, this is not the case, as is shown by the speedy resumption of their former friendly relationship.

Studies of prejudice have revealed that many children, especially those who feel insecure in their social relationships, behave in a discriminatory way. When it is the "thing to do" to treat minority-group children as inferiors, they will follow the crowd in the hope of increasing their acceptance (7) (see pages 362 to 363).

Only when there is a *consistent* pattern of behavior is it safe to predict that this is a true indication of the child's attitudes. The child who claims, day after day, that he does not want to play with other children but prefers to do things at home has unquestionably developed an unfavorable attitude. Similarly, the child who consistently claims that he is never selected to be the leader in school activities or that he "doesn't think it is fair for certain children always to be leaders and give no one else a chance" is literally saying that he wants very much to play the leader role and is dissatisfied with the follower's role that has been forced upon him.

SOCIAL EXPECTATIONS

The social group expects certain patterns of social behavior of every person who belongs or wants to belong to the group. It judges the person in accordance with his ability or willingness to come up to these expectations and accepts or rejects him on this basis.

With each passing year, the child is expected to accomplish certain *developmental tasks*. Before he enters school, for example, he is expected to relate himself emotionally, by showing affection for, and interest in, his parents, his siblings, and other people; he is expected to distinguish right from wrong in simple situations and act according to the socially approved pattern in these situations. During his elementary-school years, the child is expected to learn to get along with his agemates, to play an appropriate sex role, and to conform to more complex standards of right and wrong (136).

Social expectations are defined in terms of *social roles,* or patterns of customary behavior established by the social group (179). The child's behavior is judged in terms of these expectations. Should his behavior be considered "inappropriate" because it does not conform to group expectations, he will encounter social rejection, the degree of which will vary according to the amount of his deviation (242).

Variations in Social Expectations. One of the major difficulties the child encounters in learning approved social roles is that each of the various subsocieties of our culture has its own definition of what constitutes "acceptable" behavior. For example, aggressiveness is approved by some subsocieties and disapproved by others. As a result, whether an aggressive child will be considered "well adjusted" will depend upon the group with which he is identified and by whose standards he is judged (136). Furthermore, in different subsocieties, approved standards for children of different ages vary, and within the same age group, there are different standards for members of the two sexes.

A survey of some of the social expectations for different cultural groups and subsocieties within cultures will show how different they are and how confusing this might be for a child.

Cultural Expectations. Each cultural group has its own values, based on what will contribute to successful adjustment to the pattern of life established by the group. The group then expects all its members to conform to these values (15, 93, 179). As Stendler has pointed out, "As cultures differ, so do the personalities embedded in these cultures" (238).

Even when cultures are similar in their major aspects, they differ in the emphasis they place on commonly held values. For example, the French put a higher value on thrift and on individuality than Americans (238). Germans value work and discipline more highly than Americans (210). The English believe that a "well-brought-up child" must be reserved and must control his antisocial impulses, whereas Americans value a "market personality" that will enable the child to get ahead (100).

A few illustrations will serve to show how great the differences in cultural values can be, even when the cultures have similar backgrounds. Americans encourage upward social mobility, though it usually leads to anxiety; the English encourage stability and self-satisfaction, which result in less emotional tension. American children learn to be more concerned with conduct of a personal or individualistic nature, while the English are more concerned with their obligations to others (198). A comparison of American students with Arab, Armenian, and Jewish students in Lebanon showed that the Americans put less value on academic performance and achievement than the others (87). American Indians put more value on reserve, generosity, autonomy, bravery, and ability to withstand pain and hardships than white Americans (236).

A comparison of values of Negro and East Indian groups living in Trinidad revealed that the Negroes, motivated by the "pleasure principle," are impulsive, self-indulgent, and desirous of immediate satisfaction. As a result, they tend to be immature, maladjusted, and even prone to criminality. The East Indians, by contrast, put a higher value on future rewards; they are willing to deprive themselves of present pleasures in the hope of gaining greater rewards in the future. Consequently, they are more stable, better adjusted, more successful, happier, and far less prone to criminality than the Negroes (197).

Going further afield, we find that differences in values are even greater in cultures which are dominated by vastly different political and social philosophies (186). The present-day cultural standard of the "ideal person" in the Soviet Union includes such qualities as courage, endurance, unselfishness, the capacity to overcome obstacles, and the ability to "swim upstream" no matter how strong the current may be. All these qualities fit into the cultural ideal of the person whose service is to and for the state rather than for individual gain (8).

The Israeli, likewise, value service to the state. In the kibbutzim (collective farms), parental functions are transferred to adults trained to mold children according to the Israeli ideals. The peer group, from early babyhood, plays an important role in the socialization process (152). Concepts of the "ideal person" in countries dominated by a political philosophy which emphasizes the state rather than the individual differ greatly from the American ideal, which puts high value on such qualities as energy, competitiveness, ability to adjust, fair play, prestige, efficiency, and social mobility—qualities which lead to individuality (8).

When a cultural group is composed of people of different cultural backgrounds, each with its own values, confusion about which values to adopt is greatly increased for the child. For example, even when Sioux Indian children live side by side with American children and attend the same schools, their behavior reflects the cultural values of their ancestors. For the Sioux, competition is not considered desirable, and therefore Sioux children do not try to outshine their peers in sports or school work. The American children show a strong desire to win, and they work hard to achieve success in both sports and school work. To each group, the values of the other seem strange (99, 231).

Subsociety Expectations. Within every cultural group, each subsociety has its own values. In our country, there are *regional differences* in values, with greater emphasis placed on the general American values in some parts of the country than in others. There are also differences in values between *urban* and *rural* people within the same regions (57, 58, 198, 204). If the child is a member of a *minority* group, he will learn values that differ, in many respects, from those of the child who has a majority-group status in the same community. In the United States, for example, happiness, security, family love, and happiness are high in the value systems of white people, while justice, opportunity for advancement, and acceptance in the community are rated highest in the value systems of Negroes (145).

A child reared in a *large family* develops different values from those of a child reared in a small family in the same cultural group. In a large family, conformity is essential to successful living and is highly valued. In a small family, individuality is more highly valued (43). When a family is dissatisfied with its status in the community and wants to get ahead, it will put high value on vocational and social upward mobility. Reared in such a family, a child learns to be competitive (54).

Social-class Expectations. Within every subsociety, there are social classes, each with its own values and its own standards of socially acceptable behavior (115). Because there are no external or recognized ranks in the American culture, the status of the child is determined by the occupation of the male head of the family, by the source of the family income, by the house the family lives in, and by the area in which the house is located (266).

In each social class, the "fabric of daily living" is permeated by the expectations the class sets up for its members. The social class determines what the attitudes and patterns of behavior for the different members will be. The upper class, for example, stresses family background and leisure pursuits. The upper-middle class, whose values are oriented toward the upper class, puts emphasis on the importance of money and position in the community. The working, or lower-middle, class rejects the idea of advancement through individual achievement in favor of the idea of collective action for social gain. The lowest class does not expect to advance through either individual or collective efforts; it therefore stresses the importance of enjoying what one has (115).

Parents try to train their children to conform to the values of their social class in the hope of making them into well-adjusted, happy people. Working-class parents put emphasis on honesty and neatness, idealizing the "poor but honest" person who is *respectable* even if not respected by the social group as a whole. Middle-class parents put more emphasis on responsibility and inner controls, both of which are essential if the child is to get ahead in life. Middle-class parents are more punitive about aggressiveness than lower-class parents, more restrictive about home duties, and less permissive about sex (161, 168).

Indirectly, membership in a social class influences the child's socialization by restricting his learning to a *particular social pattern* of behaving and believing. Conformity is achieved by social pressures—first from the family and later from the peer group, the school, and the people in the community. Conformity to the social pattern produces a personality constellation typical for children of that social class (215, 229).

Davis and Havighurst have described the differences in social-class values and their effects on the social behavior of children in different areas of adjustment thus:

Whereas the middle-class child learns a socially adaptive fear of receiving poor grades in school, of being aggressive toward the teacher, of fighting, of cursing, and of having early sex relations, the slum child learns to fear quite different social acts. His gang teaches him to fear being taken in by the teacher, of being a softie with her. To study homework seriously is literally a disgrace. Instead of boasting of good marks in school, one conceals them, if he ever receives any. The lower-class individual fears not to be thought a street-fighter: it is a suspicious and dangerous social trait. He fears not to curse. If he cannot claim early sex relations his virility is seriously questioned (83).

Sex-role Expectations. Within every social class, there are approved patterns of behavior for members of the two sexes. These patterns differ for different cultural groups, and they vary from time to time. Once a stereotyped pattern of approved "masculine" and "feminine" behavior is learned, the child can be assured of social acceptance. Lack of conformity to the socially approved sex role, on the other hand, leads to criticism, ridicule, and social ostracism (33, 120, 231).

Girls, for example, may be "tomboys" during the preschool years and find that social reactions to them are colored only by amusement and tolerance. They discover long before childhood is over, however, that they must learn to be "girls" in appearance and behavior if they want to avoid scorn, disapproval and the social stigma of being "crowing hens that come to no good end"— as the old nursery rhyme claims (120, 254).

Social attitudes toward boys are not so tolerant. At no time in his life can a boy act like a girl and avoid social disapproval or even rejection (90). As Koch has pointed out, "There is evidence that it is more serious in our culture for the boy to deviate from the male type than for the girl to deviate from the female type. In other words, a sissy is more frowned upon than is a tomboy. Since a 'man is known by the company he keeps,' it will be viewed by the culture as important that a boy's companions be predominantly male" (160). While the social group may tolerate a girl's deviations from the approved pattern, *toleration does not mean social approval;* it means merely the absence of social rejection (123).

Although "proper" behavior varies somewhat from group to group, there are certain fairly universal *stereotypes of what is appropriate for boys and girls in the American culture.* Boys, on the whole, are aware of this earlier because sex-inappropriateness is less accepted in boys than in girls. A boy who is sympathetic, kind, and thoughtful of others may be admired by adults, but he soon discovers that members of the peer group think he is a "sissy" (133, 168). Similarly, parents may regard aggressiveness in a girl as a sign of initiative and look upon her as a potential leader because she has a lot of "spunk," but the peer group will dislike her because she is too "bossy." On the other hand, aggressiveness in a boy is usually admired by other boys; they regard him as "daring" and often choose him as a leader (217). By the time children enter school, they are well aware of what their peers expect for members of each sex, and their concepts of sex-appropriate behavior are almost photostats of adult concepts (33). Figure 9–1 shows the adult-approved qualities for members of the two sexes.

There are likewise culturally approved *interests* for members of the two sexes. Boys learn, long before they enter school, that only certain toys and games are considered appropriate for boys (72, 256). While girls may play boys' games with only slight social disapproval, this tolerance decreases each year (143, 202). There are also sex-appropriate interests in books, comics, television or radio programs, and movies. Children are *expected* to like the ones considered appropriate for their sex (62, 63). Socially approved interests in school subjects and in vocational choices for members of the two sexes will be discussed in detail in later chapters (241).

While children of middle- and lower-class groups are expected to adhere to the culturally approved patterns of behavior for their sex groups, the emphasis placed on certain patterns of behavior varies from one *social class* to another. For example, in boys, competitiveness and aggressiveness are more highly valued in the lower classes, while manners and politeness are more highly valued in the middle and upper classes.

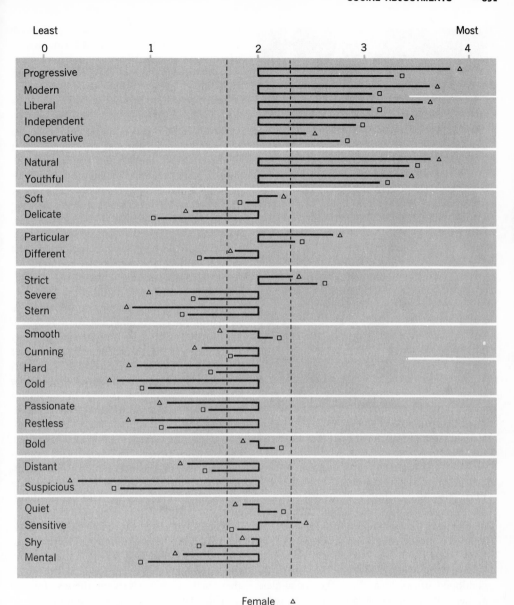

Female △
Male □

Figure 9–1. Adult-approved sex-appropriate qualities showing those more valued by men and those more valued by women. (Adapted from E. M. Bennett and L. R. Cohen, Men and women: personality patterns and contrasts, *Genet. Psychol. Monogr.*, 1959, 59, 101–155. Used by permission.)

others, no deviation is approved. By control of the environment and a uniform method of training in the home, school, and community, an attempt is made to mold every child into a carefully prescribed pattern.

The child who grows up in a culture which tolerates some individuality will be accepted by the group even though his behavior is not a photostat of that of other children of his age. In the regimented culture, a nonconformist of any degree will be punished by social rejection. The more clearly defined the cultural group's concept is of the "ideal person"—the person who will fit best into the pattern of life prescribed for the members of that group—the greater will be the conformity required for social acceptance. This is true of the present-day Soviet and Israeli cultures (8, 152).

Several specific examples of variations in demands for conformity will show how cultural groups differ. In a cross-societal study of cultures, it has been found that societies that believe in the malevolence of the supernatural world are punitive in their child rearing; parents who believe in aggressive supernatural powers reward their children for self-reliance and independence but punish them for absence of these behaviors; those who believe in benevolent supernatural powers are nurturant in their treatment of their children and put less pressure on them to conform to rigid social standards.

These different attitudes exist because parents want their children to be trained to live successfully in a world influenced by the supernatural powers they believe in. If they believe in malevolent dieties, for example, they demand great conformity to social standards and punish their children for lack of conformity (163).

A cultural group that places high value on education as a stepping-stone to upward social mobility, as is true of many Jewish families, expects great conformity to school standards as a means to the desired end. Members of such a group develop this conformity in their children by using more authoritarian child-training methods than are used in families where less emphasis is

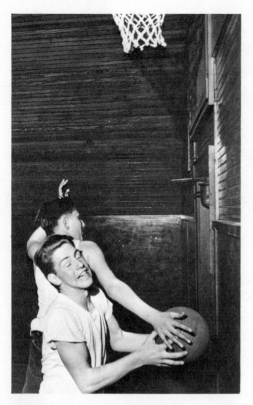

Boys learn that only certain games are considered appropriate for boys. (Standard Oil Co., N.J.)

Little girls of the lower social-class groups are expected to be "little ladies." Little girls of the middle and upper groups may be tomboys, though this value changes as they grow older, and they, too, are expected to behave like "little ladies" (26, 142). As childhood draws to a close, the social-class values of sex-appropriateness are more clearly spelled out than before.

CONFORMITY TO SOCIAL EXPECTATIONS

How much conformity the social group expects and demands of its members before it will accept them varies markedly. In some cultures, a person may retain some individual qualities and still be acceptable. In placed on social mobility (87). Because of the value they place on social mobility, middle-class American families expect greater conformity to socially approved standards of behavior on the part of their children than middle-class English families, whose values are less oriented toward upward mobility. In addition, the indifference to outside criticism by the English results in less pressure for conformity on the part of children than is true of middle-class American families, who, on the whole, are anxious to avoid all criticism of themselves and of their children (198). White children, as a rule, are expected to conform more closely to social expectations than Negro children (142).

Within a cultural group, the demands for conformity differ often in regard to *different forms of behavior,* with greater demands for conformity in sex-appropriate behavior than in other areas. In lower-class families, not only is sex-appropriate behavior more clearly defined than in middle-class families, but more pressure is placed on children to learn what is sex-appropriate. This is done by rewarding the child for behaving according to these concepts and punishing him when he does not come up to expected standards. Middle-class parents, by contrast, are more permissive in their attitudes, especially toward girls. The result is that they are more tolerant toward masculine behavior in girls and feminine behavior in boys than lower-class parents are (33, 217).

Difficulties in Conformity. A child may have some *inherent tendency* that makes conformity to social expectations difficult, if not impossible. A boy with small stature and weak musculature is incapable of conformity in a culture where the ideal for males centers around physical strength and motor skills; a girl who lacks musical or artistic ability cannot acquire the skills which are regarded as an essential part of the social competency of a "lady." Children who have been *molded* to fit into one cultural group's expectations are ill prepared for conforming if they are shifted to another cultural group (32, 238). This is one of the major prob-

lems a socially mobile child must face, as will be stressed later in the chapter.

Still other children may find it difficult to conform to the ideals of the group with which they are identified because they *do not approve* of the ideals of that group. For example, a child may not approve of his own group's discrimination against people of a minority group. As a result, he will find it hard to conform, even though lack of conformity may lead to his rejection (7).

The young child who has learned to conform to the socially approved pattern of behavior for his age may find it difficult to change his pattern of behavior to conform to the approved pattern for an older age. A girl who was trained not to be aggressive may discover, as she grows older, that those who get anywhere, whether in school or in social activities, do not sit back and let other girls take the lead. If she wants to be a leader rather than a follower, she must develop more aggressiveness than her early training permitted. It is difficult for the girl to throw off the influences of this training and play a role which she formerly learned was inappropriate for a girl—that of an aggressive, dominant, and forceful person (118, 123).

One of the most common and most serious causes of difficulty in conforming to the approved social role is *confusion* about what is approved. The child often discovers that there is not one approved pattern, but several. He is then confused about which is the right pattern. Lower-class children, for example, may learn from their parents the approved patterns of behavior for their social-class group, but when they go to school they may discover that the teacher and many members of the class have different values and expectations. If the child adheres to the patterns of his family, he is likely to be rejected in school; if he adheres to those of the school, he is likely to earn the reputation of being a "softy" or a "sissy" in the home and in the neighborhood (43, 134).

In no area of behavior is the confusion about socially approved patterns more common and more serious than in social expectations regarding sex-appropriateness. As was pointed out earlier, not only are there social-class differences in what is considered sex-appropriate, but also there are different standards within these groups for older and younger children. Furthermore, confusion is accentuated by the model the child has available to imitate.

In appearance, for example, there is no clear-cut model for boys and girls. Mothers often wear slacks and have short haircuts; men wear brightly colored playclothes that, to the child, are similar to the mother's slacks and shirts. It is hard for a child to know which is male and which female. There is confusion in the child's mind also about sex-appropriateness of work for adults. If the mother works outside the home and the father helps with the dishes, the baby, and the family wash, the child has hardly any way of knowing what society expects of the two (229).

As in all learning, the child must have an *opportunity to learn* socially approved patterns of behavior, either by direct teaching or by having a model to imitate. Children brought up in homes where authoritarian child-training methods are used generally learn socially approved behavior earlier than those whose parents permit or encourage individuality. Because lower-class parents favor authoritarian child training, lower-class children learn socially approved patterns of behavior for *their group* sooner than middle-class children learn middle-class values (225). Furthermore, in middle-class families, where the father's work frequently takes him away from home, opportunities for learning sex-appropriate behavior are limited because of the absence of a masculine model (26, 217).

A child may know what is socially approved behavior but have little *motivation* to follow the approved pattern. If he is anxious to be accepted by others, his motivation will be greater than if he does not care about acceptance or feels that there is little or no chance for it. If a child is treated favorably by his teachers and is popular with his classmates, he will readily

accept their values and try to learn to conform to their expectations (251). Otherwise, he will conform to the values of the group that will accept him. When lower-class children deliberately violate middle-class standards of behavior and conform to the standards of behavior approved by the lower-class group, they do so to gain social acceptance in the only group where acceptance is possible for them. Most children who become delinquents have rejected the values of the group that rejected them in favor of the values of the group that accepted them (69).

In no case is motivation to conform to socially approved patterns more clearly illustrated than in the case of sex-appropriateness. When boys find their relationships with their fathers warm, affectionate, and rewarding, they want to imitate them and become "masculine"; if they feel that their fathers have little interest in them, they, in turn, have little motivation to imitate the role model of their fathers (162). A girl's lack of motivation to learn sex-appropriate behavior may come from her realization that the female sex role is less rewarding than the male role (151, 173).

Confusion, lack of learning opportunities, and lack of motivation prevent many capable and intelligent children from learning to behave in a socially approved manner. As a result, these children lack the social acceptance they crave and deserve, and they make poorer adjustments in every area than they would be capable of making were they not hindered by these obstacles.

Consequences of Nonconformity. Living up to social expectations is essential not only to social acceptance but also to self-acceptance. It is difficult or impossible for a child to have a favorable opinion of himself when he knows that he has failed to live up to what others expect of him and has,' as a result, lost their esteem. As children grow older, they become increasingly aware of the type of social adjustments they make. They know whether other people like them, dislike them, or ignore them.

Because it is often difficult for lower-class children to conform to social expectations in school, they feel that they are less successful than other children in meeting society's and their own expectations (239). As a result, they participate less in group activities than they would like, partly because they feel they are not acceptable and partly because they feel inadequate. By the time they reach adolescence, their social adjustments fall so far short of social expectations that they are literally social misfits in school and in community affairs. They often drop out of school. Many of them join groups of other social misfits who, motivated by a desire to compensate for feelings of resentment engendered by social rejection, turn to behavior that may lead to juvenile delinquency (73).

While some children become social misfits through no fault of their own, others could make better social adjustments than they do. They have little motivation to do so, either because they derive too little satisfaction from social activities or because they find other activities more satisfying. If they reject conformity to social expectations and do as they please, they must face criticism, scorn, and rejection. This is especially true in a culture like that of America, which puts marked emphasis on conformity and punishes the nonconformist by rejection. By contrast, an English child can be more of an individualist because there is less cultural pressure to conform to a rigidly established pattern of socially approved behavior in England and because criticism is less bothersome and less ego-deflating to the English than to Americans. In our culture, there is no place for the "rugged individualist."

The only way a nonconformist can improve his status in the group is to sacrifice some of his individualism and learn to conform, whether he approves of these expectations or not. If being an individualist means more to him than social acceptance, he must be prepared to pay the price for his individuality; if being accepted by the group means more to him than individuality, he must be willing to pay the price demanded by the social group for its acceptance of him. This is a matter in which it is impossible for a child to "have his cake and eat it too."

Being willing to conform to group expectations is not enough. The child must know what these expectations are and how to behave in order to fulfill them. A child whose training in the home stresses conformity, emphasizes the meaning of group expectations, and provides a model to imitate—either parents or older siblings—will not find it difficult to learn to conform. The greatest difficulty is found among those who have a foreign-culture background, those whose parents are socially mobile, and those who have marginal social acceptance or few opportunities for social contacts.

Children with a foreign-culture background are often bilingual; as a result, they find communication with the peer group difficult and are often discriminated against because they are "different." Socially mobile children, as will be discussed later in the chapter, bring to the new cultural group the attitudes, values, and patterns of behavior learned in their former group. Because they, too, usually lack social acceptance, they are deprived of opportunities to know what the expectations of the new social group are.

COMPANIONS AND FRIENDS

Every child wants the companionship of people. Furthermore, he *needs* it to develop into a personally and socially well-adjusted individual. Need for companionship is shown early in life when the baby cries until someone comes to be with him. As the child grows older, this need increases in intensity, and the type of people who are able to satisfy it changes. At first, the child merely wants to *do* things with others. Those who satisfy this desire are his playmates, or "companions." Later, he wants more than companions; he wants "friends"—people who will play with him and with whom he can *communicate* besides. He wants to be able to exchange ideas with them, to ask their advice, to confide his troubles in them, or to criticize them if he feels they are wrong.

Meeting Friendship Needs. At every age, the child's need for companionship is best met by those he feels are interested in him, who understand him, and who will comfort him in times of trouble and rejoice with him in times of success—in short, those who *love* him. At some ages, parents satisfy this need best, but at other ages, teachers and other adults outside the home or peers are best able to do so. Furthermore, the form of expression of interest and love will also have to change to meet the child's needs. The baby or young child wants overt expressions of love from his companions, while the older child finds such expressions embarrassing and annoying. He wants their interest and love to be shown in more subtle ways, such as a willingness to listen to what he has to say, to answer his questions, and to help him to solve a problem he is unable to solve alone (75, 135, 258).

The child's need for companionship is likewise best met by those who are *similar* to him in the major areas of his interests, attitudes, and values: Because they and he have much in common, they literally "speak the same language." The tradition that companionship needs are best met by those who are different and can thus complement each other has little supporting evidence. On the contrary, much evidence shows that congeniality is based on similarities.

A child has greater respect for, and more congeniality with, children who view life as he does than with children who view life differently. Furthermore, similarity facilitates expressions of affection and gives the child the comfortable feeling of being "at home" with the other person (2, 149). When there is antagonism between the sexes, for example, the child feels more comfortable with members of his own sex; when there is no antagonism, he feels at home with members of both sexes (49, 153).

This is true also with respect to racial background. In a study of Oriental and Caucasian children in Hawaii, it was found that the children preferred as their companions children of their own race and sex, not because of prejudice, but rather because they had the comfortable feeling of being "at home" with those whose background was similar to theirs (188). Similarly, "success-oriented" people—those who put high value on ability and skill, whether in play, social contacts, or academic activities—are more at home with other success-oriented people; and "goodness-oriented" people—those who put high value on love, sympathy, compassion, and faith—find others with a similar orientation more congenial (184).

In general, the *number of companions* a child needs will increase as he grows older. The preschool child is usually happy with one or two playmates; the "gang-age" child, on the other hand, needs three or four to eight or ten. Even within an age group, children differ in the number of children needed to satisfy their companionship requirements. As Barclay has pointed out:

Some children prefer the company of one or two close friends because they share a deep and genuine understanding, a real mutuality of interests. Others may team-up with an easygoing pal because the bigger group is too demanding, too rough on their illusions or self-deceptions, too unpredictable to be borne with comfort. . . . There are those who thrive on the variety and stimulation a big group offers. And there are others, unsure of themselves and their opinions, who shrink from close relationships . . . and seek comfort and safety in doing what the crowd dictates (21).

Types of Companions. From experience, the child discovers what types of companions he likes best, and he selects, from those who are available, the ones he finds most congenial. Adults and older children prove to be the most desirable companions for the baby during the first year or two of life because they satisfy his desire for playmates and, at the same time, satisfy his physical needs. They will play with him when he wants to be played with and in the way he wants to play. A child his own age or slightly older will not cater to the egocentric needs of the one- or two-year-old. At this age, the baby is definitely family-oriented in his choice of companions (45).

In the preschool days, the child's companions are usually adults of the family, brothers and sisters, or a few children from the immediate neighborhood. By 3½ years, friends are very important to a child. He selects one or two from a group whom he wants to sit beside or play with. They may be of the same sex or of the opposite sex. With each passing year, the child spends more time with his friends and develops more friendships with different children (35, 45).

Compared with the baby, who willingly accepts any companions who will do things for him, the young child becomes selective in choosing his friends. Such factors as age, intelligence, and good sportsmanship become very important. By the age of four years, children show a definite preference for playmates of their own sex, and unisexual friendships increase each year. Race cleavages also appear at this time, and children begin to show a decided preference for friends from their own racial groups (80, 188).

When the child enters school and begins to be interested in group play, new criteria, combined with old ones, are used in the selection of playmates. He must select his friends from the immediate neighborhood in which he lives, but within this neighborhood, he selects as companions those of the same size, sex, chronological age, mental age, social maturity, and interests. As children grow older, personality traits play an important role (132, 149). Traits that rank high in value for the older child include cheerfulness, generosity, friendliness, co-operativeness, honesty, even-temperedness, sense of humor, and good sportsmanship (41, 84).

The older child shows a definite preference for playmates of his own racial group. By the fifth grade, children also take socio-economic status into consideration. While children of the lower social classes have more freedom of choice in the selection of their friends than children of the middle classes, whose parents put pressure on them to choose the "right" type of friends, the lower-class child nevertheless often finds himself barred from participation in social activities with children of the middle class. He is thus forced to select his friends mainly from his own social class (49, 84).

Substitute Companions. Owing to geographic isolation, lack of acceptance, or some other cause, many children find themselves deprived of companionship. As a result, they experience the detrimental effects that come with social deprivation (259). A very bright child, for example, will find little in common with children of average intelligence, even though there may be many available for him to play with. If he belittles their "stupidities and inanities," he will arouse their hostility and their parents' resentment. As a result, they will reject him, and he will be lonely, friendless, and an "island within" (169).

When the need for companionship is strong, the child deprived of friends will find a substitute. An older child who does not win the acceptance of the peer group may fall back on the companionship of family members (15). If this does not provide him with adequate satisfaction, he will seek other substitutes. The substitutes he chooses will depend partly upon his age and partly upon what is available. Young children generally find imaginary playmates a satisfactory substitute for real playmates. Older children, who have outgrown, mentally, the ability to endow imaginary friends with the life qualities of real friends, are more likely to turn to a pet animal.

Imaginary Companions. To the young child, imaginary companions are lifelike, possessing names, physical characteristics, and abilities to do things which one normally associates with real children. The child derives keen pleasure from playing with his imaginary playmates; they fill a gap in his social life. Imaginary playmates are more common among girls than boys, and to girls they are more realistic. They are more prevalent among children of superior intelligence and among only children or siblings where there is a large age difference (11, 234).

Imaginary companions in most instances are little boys or girls. Sometimes they are of the child's own sex and sometimes of the opposite sex. The child plays with his imaginary playmate as if it were a real person. He talks to it and in many instances takes it with him wherever he goes. No matter what the activity may be, the real child is the boss, and the imaginary playmate is a submissive follower. The usual age for imaginary companions is between three and four years, with 3½ years the high point. By the time the child enters school and has playmates of his own, he usually abandons the imaginary companion, though he may occasionally play with it (47, 148).

As so many children have imaginary companions during the preschool years, the practice may be regarded as "normal." It is more common and more persistent among children who have unsatisfactory emotional relationships with their parents or who find little congeniality in their relationships with siblings or other children.

No one type of personality predisposes children to have imaginary companions. Children who are happy and well adjusted have them during the preschool years just as other children do. They are more common, however, among children who have such personality difficulties as timidity in the presence of other children, a domineering manner with other children, fear of physical activities, sensitivity, an undemonstrative manner, evasiveness, irresponsibility, eagerness to be in the limelight, and fear of being outdone by others (264).

Having an imaginary companion is a far from satisfactory solution to the lonely child's problem. Although the child may gain personal satisfaction from his imaginary companion, it does not help him to make good adjustments to others. With his imaginary companion, the young child plays the role of "boss"; this does not help him learn to be cooperative—an essential in relationships with real people.

Furthermore, in his relationships with his imaginary friend, the young child becomes egocentric; he has everything just as he wants it, he does not have to consider others, and he can be as selfish as he wishes. When he discovers that the techniques he has used in his social adjustments with his imaginary companion do not work so successfully with real children, he is likely to withdraw from them and seek some other substitute better suited to his more mature intellectual development. If he does not withdraw, he must learn new techniques of making social adjustments.

If the child chooses the latter course, there is no reason to believe that playing with imaginary companions will do permanent damage to his later social adjustments. Guidance and help in making social adjustments to real children will undoubtedly help him. A study of college freshmen compared students who had never had imaginary companions with those who had had such substitutes. The latter lacked self-sufficiency, disliked solitude, and sought advice and encouragement more often than the former. In addition, those who had had imaginary playmates were less neurotic, less introverted, and more dominating in face-to-face situations; they were wholesomely self-confident, well adjusted to their environment, sociable, and gregarious. Although they did make a different type of social adjustment, it is apparent that those who played with imaginary companions were not permanently damaged (264).

Pets.   While young children like pets of all types—hamsters, mice, rabbits, turtles, chameleons, or birds—the older child gains little satisfaction from pets that do nothing to show their affection or hold the child's interest. All children like to play with pets, and even little toddlers enjoy romping with a kitten or puppy. As the child grows old enough to want playmates to share his playtime, he finds a dog or cat a satisfactory substitute when no human playmates are available. Interest in dogs and cats increases rapidly from seven to fourteen years, with a peak around the twelfth year. Both boys and girls prefer dogs to cats, and their interest in playing with cats culminates sooner than their interest in dogs. The cat's repertoire of activities is great enough to make it an interesting companion, but it is an egocentric animal who shows little affection for anyone, even the person who takes care of it. Dogs, on the other hand, show great affection for their masters, which is why they usually make the best substitute companions (9).

A child gains many things from a pet besides companionship. In the dog, the child finds an outlet for his affection. It serves as a source of ego-satisfaction and ego-gratification; it satisfies the child's desire for power; and, most important of all, it serves as an effective social aid. It helps the child who is timid or shy to make many contacts with children and with adults that he would hesitate to initiate if he were alone. Furthermore, the give-and-take relationship that the child has with a pet does not foster the development of the unsocial traits so often found among children who have substituted imaginary playmates for real playmates (43).

Treatment of Companions. In spite of the child's desire for companions, he often treats siblings, members of the peer group, and his pet animals badly. It is not uncommon for a child who is angry at a parent, sibling, or peer to displace his anger on his pet, fighting with him or calling him names (40, 258). As was stressed in the preceding chapter, young children quarrel very often and very aggressively with their companions. If the child does not learn how to treat his playmates in a more mature manner, he quickly discovers that other children will not play with him, especially at the time of puberty. Antisocial behavior on the part of a pubescent child frequently leads to the breakup of friendships that have persisted for a number of years (112).

The tendency to be callous and cruel is usually strongest toward children of minority groups or toward newcomers in the neighborhood who are attempting to estab-

In a pet, the child finds an outlet for affection, a source of ego satisfaction, and often an effective social aid. (Standard Oil Co., N.J.)

lish friendships (214). When with members of their gang, children are more cruel to outsiders than when they are alone (76, 132).

Persistence of Friendships. Until the child learns how to get along with others with a minimum of quarreling, his friendships are likely to be short-lived. Quarreling is not, however, the only reason for the shifting pattern of friendships. In the early years of childhood, when companions are selected mainly because they are available and willing to play, the child shifts his playmates frequently when they no longer want to play the games he wants to play. If the number of children available is limited, the child soon discovers that if he wants to have playmates he must play as they want to play.

Shifts in friendship during the preschool years occur often when children begin to prefer playmates of their own sex. At about the age of five years, boys drop their girl playmates in favor of boy playmates. Because the girl is then left without a playmate, she must find a new one, and generally she must choose a member of her own sex. This shift in playmates results in large part from pressure on the boy, frequently from his father, to play with boys in order to avoid being called a "sissy." By the time children enter the first grade, most of their playmates will be members of their own sex (133, 235).

Among older children, fluctuations in friendship are common, even among friends of the same sex. A child shifts from best friend to enemy, or from casual acquaintanceship to close friendship, quickly and often for little reason. When there are plenty of children available to choose from, as when a child enters school, he can afford to break off a friendship and not find himself friendless. Consequently, when his interests change or when he no longer derives satisfaction from his old friends, he breaks off his friendships and establishes new ones. From five years of age up to puberty, fluctuations in friendships are common; they become less pronounced, however, with each passing year (144). As may be seen in Figure 9–2, stability in friendship occurs somewhat earlier for girls than for boys.

There is little relationship between social acceptance and friendship fluctuation. Children who are popular change their friends almost as much as those who are less well accepted (41). When a group of elementary-school children were asked their reasons for changing their friends, the most common reasons given were lack of recent contact, a recent quarrel, the fact that one friend was replaced by another, incompatibility, conceitedness, bossiness, disloyalty, and underhandedness (14). With broader social experience, the child normally increases his social insight and his ability to make better social adjustments. As a result, he is more careful in the selection of his friends, choos-

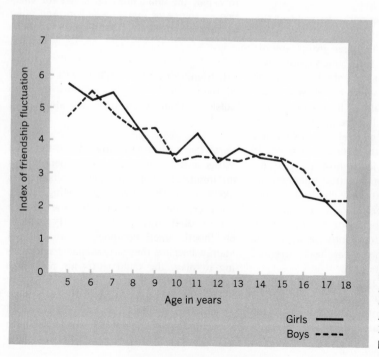

Figure 9–2. Friendship fluctuations of boys and girls at different age levels. (Adapted from J. E. Horrocks and M. E. Buker, A study of friendship fluctuations of preadolescents, *J. genet. Psychol.*, 1951, 78, 131–144. Used by permission.)

ing them because of similar interests and values rather than just because they like to play the same games. As a result, there is greater stability in friendship (15).

Friendship fluctuations in childhood do not necessarily result in the breaking off of friendships. Instead, friendships wax and wane, often to wax again. The child may shift from one child to another, for example, and then return to the first. This is true even in friendships between children of the two sexes. While a friendship between a boy and girl during kindergarten days is likely to end when the boy discovers that other boys regard him as a "sissy," he often resumes this friendship during adolescence. As long as friendships end because of changes of interests, there is always the possibility that they will be resumed when interest patterns change again.

Two things are likely to put a permanent end to a friendship: a *quarrel* which has caused hurt feelings and a *change in values* that is so pronounced that old friends no longer have anything in common. During puberty, many friendships end permanently because the pubescent child has hurt the feelings of his former friends by his derogatory comments. Friendships between children of different racial, religious, or socioeconomic groups often end when family pressures force the children to accept the values of their own groups.

Socializing Influence of Friends.   Friends are valuable to a child for two reasons. First, they give him satisfaction by *fulfilling his need for companionship* with the type of companion he enjoys, and second, they contribute heavily to the *socialization process* begun in the home. If the child has friends who fulfill the criteria of good socialization —personal satisfaction and learning to behave in a socially approved manner—he will live up to society's expectations. How much friends contribute to the child's happiness and his socialization has been stressed thus by Barclay:

Good friends—either in one's or two's or by the group—offer companionship in pleas-

ure and comfort in pain. They broaden or sharpen one another's interests; enhance one another's fun. They provide sounding boards for the exploration of ideas too personal (or too fantastic) to discuss with adults; mirrors in which to evaluate the effectiveness of new approaches; measuring sticks by which to judge the value of new attitudes. They represent standards of comparison against which youngsters can gauge personal progress and growth. They act as allies, supporting one another as they test their ability to resist adults—a difficult but necessary part of developing independence. They understand. They appreciate (21).

Some children are satisfied with one close friend; others need a large group. The important aspect of the problem of making good social adjustments is not how many friends children need but that their friends be of the *right type* as far as socialization is concerned. Several friends can generally contribute more to the child's socialization than one can because each can contribute something different. One friend, for example, may help a child to see how important it is to act in a sex-appropriate way; another may show him the importance of being cooperative instead of aggressive; while still another may help him to develop social insight and learn to be sympathetic. A single child, no matter how desirable a friend he may be, is too young and inexperienced in matters of social expectation to be able to do the entire job of socializing his friend; a group, made up of children of different interests and backgrounds, can do the job better.

As for the more important aspect of the matter—the *type of child* who supplies satisfaction for the social needs of his friend— some children are "good influences," whereas others, equally "nice" children with equally good family backgrounds, can have a detrimental influence. They can cause the child to make poor social adjustments and may even make him antisocial. As Barclay has pointed out, "Some relationships, individual and group, are—like it or not—'poison.' Through the mysterious action of group dynamics even 'thoroughly nice' youngsters can bring out the worst in each other. When reasonable efforts at guidance fail the only answer may be to break it up" (21).

Some children, if they feel inadequate, seek out companions whose behavior they admire because it contains the elements their own behavior lacks. The quiet, self-effacing child, for example, may try to win the friendship of one who is as daring and reckless as he is timid. Should such a child accept the admiration of the quiet child, the influence he will have on the quiet friend may lead to good or to poor social adjustments. If he tries to "reform" the quiet child by daring him to do things he would hesitate to do on his own, he may either increase the quiet child's feeling of inadequacy or convince him that he is more worthy than he thought.

Similarly, a child brought up in an authoritarian home where he has learned to be dependent may acquire the self-confidence needed to achieve greater independence by associating with a child whose home environment has been more democratic. Or he may be persuaded by his friend to reject not only parental authority but all adult authority, which will lead him into trouble and result in poor social adjustments (19, 265). Thus it becomes apparent that if the child is to learn to make good social adjustments and derive pleasure from his social relationships, his playmates and friends must be the *right type for him*.

What is true of human friendships is equally true when the child has substitute companions; they must be the right type for him. An *imaginary playmate* may give the child satisfaction, but, as was pointed out earlier, this playmate can do nothing to further the child's social adjustments. In fact, having an imaginary playmate is likely to lead to poor social adjustments with real playmates.

The socializing influence of a *pet* is more negative than positive. A pet dog or cat, for example, will let the child know how much teasing or bullying he will tolerate by snapping, biting, or scratching the child, but the animal cannot supply the positive training in social adjustments that a human companion can. A pet, for example, cannot provide the child with a model of socially approved behavior and then use pressures to see that he accepts this model. No dog or cat knows what is considered sex-appropriate behavior for a boy, nor will the animal ridicule the boy if he fails to act in a sex-appropriate manner.

SOCIAL ACCEPTANCE

Friendship is a two-way experience. To have friends, the child must want friends and must be accepted as a friend by those whose friendship he craves. Social acceptance—or "popularity"—is an index of the success with which a child has taken his place in the social group and the extent to which his associates like to work or play with him. More specifically, *popularity* means the general admiration in which a person is held even by those who do not associate with him. A popular child may have few friends but many admirers; he is liked for exhibiting qualities admired but not necessarily envied. Because many admire him, he is in line for selection for a leadership role, especially if his popularity is based on respect from the group.

Respect is earned through demonstrated or imputed abilities and is associated with the qualities of accomplishment. As Naegele has remarked, the respected "are chosen for office rather than invited to parties" (206). Among children, neither the popular nor the respected have the closeness of real friendships. *Acceptance,* by contrast, means being chosen as an associate for a realistic activity in a group of which one is a member (209). An active member of a group is not necessarily popular or respected or accepted. Sometimes a child who is literally in everything and pushes himself into the different groups in his school class is thoroughly disliked by his classmates.

There is no direct relationship between social acceptance and the child's desire for social contacts. Furthermore, there is no indication that any child is completely lacking in the desire to relate himself to his peers. Some children, however, prefer close, personal contacts with others; they are "sociable," "companionable," or "chummy." Others prefer to keep their distance and are considered "aloof" (267). The child may form friendships easily, or he may be aloof and form them slowly. Children and adolescents, as a rule, form friendships more easily and are less discriminating in the choice of friends than adults, though there are marked variations in every age group.

A child may be accepted by few and accept many, or he may be accepted by many and show an accepting attitude toward few. The most popular children, those whom the sociologists label "stars," fall into the second category. Stars are those who, in spite of the fact that they are liked and accepted by almost everyone, do not reciprocate many of the friendship choices either because they find little interest in some of the children who want to be their friends or because they are afraid of alienating others by showing an interest in those who are less well liked by the group (66).

Conditions Affecting Acceptance. Whether a child will be accepted in a given group depends not upon the child himself but also upon the *tastes* and *interests* of the group or groups available for him to associate with. The child's status in a group—whether he will be accepted, rejected, or ignored— seems to "depend not so much on one's role-taking ability per se but also on social techniques which vary with the structure and function of the particular group" (96). As Barclay has commented, in discussing the problem of a child who craves social acceptance but enjoys little, "Sometimes such a youngster is simply the victim of the peculiar chemistry of a particular group that passes adult understanding. Sometimes the qualities in him that those in his immediate circle resent would be major assets in another setting." Because children's friendships fluctuate so markedly, even as childhood comes to a close, "today's outcast may be tomorrow's leader" (22).

Within a group, not all children agree either upon those whom they will accept or reject or upon the degree to which they will accept or reject them. There is generally more agreement on those they dislike than on those they like. This means that *unpopular* children are more or less universally disliked by their agemates, though they are disliked for different reasons and in different degrees. Furthermore, children show a tendency to dislike many of their agemates and to like only a few.

When there is high agreement among children regarding likes or dislikes for their agemates, the group tends to split into cliques, with little of the "stick-together" quality that makes for group loyalty (203). Figure 9–3 shows the relationships between those who are liked and those who are disliked by their classmates. If the social climate or morale of a school class is to be good, the majority of the children must enjoy the acceptance of their classmates. One of the responsibilities of a leader, whether it is a teacher or camp counselor, is to try to draw together the subdivisions of the group that have split apart because the members of one clique dislike the members of another (66, 105).

Degree of Acceptance. Social acceptance ranges from the star to the social isolate. The *star* is at the center of an admiring group whose members claim him as their most intimate friend even though he does not, as was pointed out earlier, reciprocate many of these friendship choices (66). He may be admired by the group for his athletic skills, his scholastic successes, his poise and social know-how, his good sportsmanship, or his ability to influence his agemates.

At the other extreme is the *social isolate,* who either withdraws voluntarily from the social group because of lack of interest in the children with whom circumstances place him or is rejected by them. The first type of social isolate is known as the "voluntary" social isolate, and the second as the "involuntary." The involuntary isolate may *think* he is unwanted, whether this is true or not, and isolate himself from the group. He may thus be a "subjective" isolate rather than an actual or "objective" isolate (206).

Few children fall in either of the extreme categories of stars and isolates. Rarely is any child either accepted by everyone or rejected by everyone. In speaking of stars, Jersild has said, "No one, in other words, has a corner on the market of social acceptability" (150). The same can be said about the "market" of social isolation.

Most children fall between the two extremes, enjoying varying degrees of social acceptance. Some are just on the line of acceptance. They are the *fringers* and are in a precarious position; they may lose what acceptance they have simply by doing or saying something that might turn others against them. Then there is the *climber,* who has gained acceptance in one group but wants to gain acceptance in a socially more favored group. Like the fringer, he is in an uncertain position. He can easily lose his acceptance in the original group and not gain acceptance in the other if he does or says things that antagonize members of either. Children in the *above-average* category enjoy varying degrees of social acceptance; in no case is their acceptance as great as that of the star.

In the *below-average* category, there are varying degrees of isolation, either voluntary or involuntary. All children in this category have some friends, even though the number falls below that of the average for their age groups. In addition to those who are rejected or who voluntarily withdraw from the group, there are those whom the group overlooks, the *neglected.* They are not disliked, nor are they liked; because they are shy, withdrawn, and nondescript in behavior, they have so little to offer the group that no one wants to associate with them (58, 108, 209). The different degrees of social acceptance are illustrated in Figure 9–4.

Awareness of Acceptance. Ability to recognize one's status in the group—*socioempathic ability*—is essential to good social adjustments. It determines how the individual will behave in a social situation. A child who does not recognize his lack of social acceptance will behave as if he were liked. This is apt to increase his lack of acceptance because it will make other children think he is "pushy." On the other hand, a child who recognizes his acceptance will have self-confidence, which will be reflected in good social adjustments. A child who is unsure of his status will try to "play safe"; in doing so, he will create the impression that he is vacillating or is suffering from feelings of personal inadequacy. The more accurately

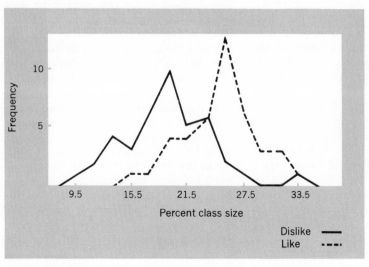

Figure 9–3. Percentages of children who are liked and disliked by their classmates. (Adapted from J. F. Muldoon, The concentration of liked and disliked members in groups and the relationship of concentration to group cohesiveness, *Sociometry,* 1955, 18, 73–81. Used by permission.)

Isolated (unpopular)

Climber (seeking acceptance)

Average (general acceptance)

Above average (popular)

Superior degree of acceptance (popular, sought-after, preferred)

Figure 9–4.   Varying degrees of a child's social acceptance.

a child can determine what his status in the group is, the better able he is to know how to behave (15, 146).

Up to the age of four or five years, most children are unaware of how others feel about them. Gradually, their awareness grows as their social horizons broaden and as their contacts with other people of all ages increase. Even before they enter school, they have enough awareness of how others feel to verbalize this awareness in such comments as "He doesn't like me" or "No one wants to play with me." Gradually, the child recognizes *levels of preference;* he recognizes that some children are liked better than others and that some people like him, some dislike him, and some ignore him (95, 195).

Variations in Awareness.   While normally there is an increase in accuracy of socioempathic ability with age, there are marked variations at every age level. Furthermore, the ability to perceive one's status in the group generally develops more slowly than the ability to perceive the status of others.

A person can be more objective about a matter that affects others than about one that affects him. There is a close relationship between *intelligence* and socioempathic ability, with bright children showing greater accuracy than those who are less bright (263). *Girls,* age for age, are generally superior to boys in this ability (15, 35) (see Figure 9–5). The more *anxious* a child is to be accepted, the more aware he is of how others feel about him; the less anxious he is for acceptance, the less accurate his judgments of his popularity are (107, 248).

Finally, accuracy of perception of popularity varies according to *how popular* the child is. Very unpopular children tend to underestimate their unpopularity mainly because their lack of social acceptance has deprived them of the opportunity to learn how people feel about others. Very popular children tend to underestimate their popularity; the social distance between themselves and the majority of the group members is so great that they are unable to realize how much they are liked. The ability to recognize *indifferent attitudes* is generally

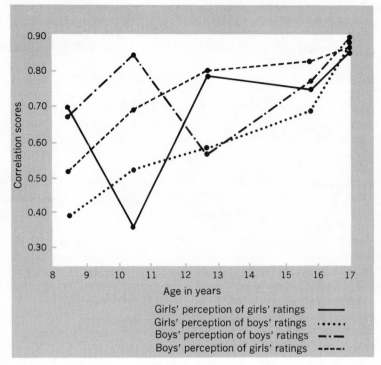

Figure 9–5. Sex differences in perception of sociometric status. (Adapted from D. P. Ausubel, H. M. Schiff, and E. B. Glasser, A preliminary study of developmental trends in socioempathy: accuracy of perception of own and others sociometric status, *Child Develpm.*, 1952, 23, 111–128. Used by permission.)

Girls' perception of girls' ratings ——
Girls' perception of boys' ratings ·····
Boys' perception of boys' ratings —·—
Boys' perception of girls' ratings ----·

poorer than the ability to recognize acceptance or rejection. In spite of these variations, most children are well aware of how others feel about them by the time they reach the fifth grade (15, 46, 250).

Sources of Awareness. The child's awareness of the degree of acceptance others grant him comes from many sources. Even before he can comprehend words, the young child can tell by the *tone of voice* and by the *facial expression* how a person feels about him (10, 53). From the *treatment* he receives from others, he gets a good clue to what their opinion of him is. If they fight with him, grab his toys, and refuse to allow him to play with them, he can be fairly sure that they do not like him, especially if they do not treat other children this way. If others are willing to *do what he wants them to do* or if they voluntarily imitate his behavior, speech, or clothes, the child can be sure that he is liked. And if he has a *number of friends,* he knows he is more popular

than the child who has only a few (47, 112, 243).

Perhaps the most objective and most accurate clue to his level of acceptance is what *others call him.* If they call him by his given name, this suggests that he is not on intimate terms with them. If they call him by an affectionate nickname, this suggests a close relationship. If the nickname is derogatory, however—"Stink-pot" or "Fatso"—this means lack of social acceptance (89).

Knowing the category in which the child is grouped by his peers is another clue. Levels of acceptance are designated by such names as "wheels" (the top crowd, or the ones who run everything); "brains" (those who take little interest in anything but studies); "mice" (the quiet ones who are inoffensive and ineffectual); "drips" (would-be wheels who make others uncomfortable); and "dopes" (would-be brains who arouse antagonism) (190). A child who is called a "crybaby," a "pest," a "nut," a "big showoff," or a "sourpuss" or who is accused of "blowing his top," "griping about everything," or "being tied to his mother's apron strings" should have no difficulty knowing in what category he has been pigeonholed (112, 243).

Traits Leading to Acceptance or Rejection.
There is no such thing as a "popular" or "unpopular" type of personality pattern. Even those children who are most highly accepted have some traits that are disliked. The child who is not popular, on the other hand, may have some traits that are liked. In the accepted child, the disliked traits are compensated for by socially approved traits; in the rejected or neglected child, the desirable traits are overshadowed by the undesirable ones (41). No child needs to be a "paragon of perfection" to be accepted. Because social acceptance comes from the reactions of others to the child's *total personality* rather than to specific traits, the dominant traits will determine whether he will be accepted or rejected. As Bonney has pointed out, "A socially good personality is a positive achievement: it is not simply the result of avoiding the bad" (41). Popular children are, on the whole, well-adjusted children because their dominant traits are those which conform to social expectations (125).

That certain traits contribute to social acceptance does not mean that the more highly developed those traits are, the greater the child's acceptance will be. Having *any trait in excess* is likely to lead to poor acceptance, even when the trait per se is a highly admired one. For example, a child will have a better chance for social acceptance if he is generous than if he is stingy, but if he is so generous that he is literally willing to give the shirt off his back to anyone who asks for it, he is likely to create the impression that he is trying to "buy" social acceptance.

Similarly, although being active in social life at every age contributes to social acceptance, a hyperactive child can readily create the impression that he is pushy. He may make others nervous by his constant movements. Truthfulness is always an admired trait, but one can be too truthful. The too truthful child appears to lack social insight and is regarded as tactless because some of the things he says hurt others (150).

Traits Leading to Popularity.
There are certain characteristics which distinguish socially acceptable children of different ages and in different groups. For the most part, these characteristics remain fairly constant through the childhood years and then change, to a certain extent, as the individual emerges into adolescence. *No one single trait distinguishes the popular from the unpopular child.* Instead, the distinguishing quality is the *degree and direction of outgoing energy.*

The child is popular because what he is and what he does win the admiration of others. He makes himself felt and admired in the group by doing things that make him stand out rather than by refraining from things the group would dislike. Social acceptance is thus closely related to the child's ability to distinguish himself from his associates (125, 128).

"Popularity Syndromes."
There are two *personality syndromes* characteristic of popular people. While both contain socially admired traits, they differ in the degree of outgoing energy the individual expends. In the first, there is more aggressiveness, as shown in social activity and contributing one's share to this activity. In the second, there is less aggressiveness, and less energy is expended in trying to attract and win the admiration of the group. The first syndrome is characteristic of those who are "success-oriented"—who want to achieve status and advancement; the second is characteristic of those who are "goodness-oriented"—who put high value on friendship traits, such as love, sympathy, and faith, in their interpersonal relationships. As a rule, children who have a personality syndrome of the first type are more popular (81, 125, 129).

The *direction* of the child's outgoing energy is just as important as the degree. When a child is aggressive, there is always the danger that the aggressiveness will be too strong or that it will be expressed in socially unacceptable patterns of behavior. If a child has a strong sense of humor, for example, he may be so carried away by the satisfaction he gets from being able to make others laugh that he will gain the spotlight of attention by hurting other people's feelings. Before he realizes what he is doing, he may win their disapproval. A sarcastic child may have the power to influence other children, but he is rarely popular with them. A child who clowns may gain temporary acceptance, but unless he can fortify his status with more desirable traits, he is likely to be considered a "fool" or a "nitwit." Similarly, the child who talks is more likely to win social acceptance than the quiet child, but if he constantly turns his conversation in the direction of himself, he will be considered stuck-up and boastful or a "bore who always talks about himself" (77, 117, 209).

Specific Traits. Almost universally, children who are well accepted are friendly and cooperative. They adjust without making a disturbance, comply with requests, accept gracefully what happens, and make good adjustments to adults as well as to children. They are kind to others, share what they have, are willing to take turns in any game the group plays, and show impartiality toward other members of the group. They assume responsibilities, participate in and enjoy social activities, feel secure in their status, and compare themselves favorably with their peers.

Highly accepted children are expansive, dynamic, objective, and free from fears and anxieties. They have strong self-regarding attitudes—attitudes that are expressed in willingness to assert themselves without being overly anxious to please. They are optimistic, happy, cheerful, and good-natured and have a healthy sense of humor. The popular child is primarily "group-centered" rather than "ego-centered"; he thinks first of others, building up their egos

instead of tearing them down to inflate his own (24, 81, 84, 125).

The child who is well accepted has learned to turn his energies into socially approved patterns of behavior which show that he has a sense of his proper place and role as a member of a group; this is especially true of his sex role. Instead of being slavishly conventional, the well-accepted child is original and yet conforms to the broad pattern of the group, observing its rules, regulations, and mores. Furthermore, he is flexible in the sense that he can and will adapt his way of doing things to conform to social expectations.

He is mature, emotionally, intellectually, and socially. He shows his social maturity by accepting people as they are—by not criticizing them or trying to change them to suit his own whims—and by social insight, which enables him to size up and adjust quickly and successfully to different people in different social situations. His emotional maturity is apparent in well-controlled, even-tempered behavior, free from anxiety, temper outbursts, or displays of jealousy. He is intelligent and alert, but not so intelligent that he is a misfit in the group. Furthermore, he is usually a good student, not so much because of greater intelligence but because he is conscientious in his studies (20, 52, 98, 101).

Variations in Acceptance Traits. Traits that make a child popular and accepted vary according to *age* and *group*. Among first-grade children, the quiet, inconspicuous children are more popular than the active, talkative, and aggressive ones. By the third grade, on the other hand, the quiet children are likely to be overlooked, while those often mentioned by their teachers for undesirable behavior are the ones most often mentioned by their peers for desirable behavior (254, 258).

Acceptance values differ according to the *socioeconomic* status of the group. Boys of the lower socioeconomic groups are more admired by their peers if they do not conorm too closely to adult standards of behavior, while those of the upper socioeconomic groups are admired when they do. Upper-class children enjoy greater social acceptance if they have verbal fluency, are good students, and are active participants in group affairs, while middle- and lower-class children are more admired if they are quiet, mind their own business, and are "good company" (101, 215). There are likewise *sex differences* in traits that lead to social acceptance. Boys admire "real boys," those who are adventuresome, assertive, and competitive in sports; girls, at least up to the fifth grade, admire the "little lady" who is quiet, reserved, and well mannered (254).

Traits Militating against Social Acceptance. Whether or not a child will be popular in a given group depends partly upon his own qualities and partly upon the group. A child who is too different from the other members of the group in appearance, intelligence, personality, family background, interests, or any one of a number of different traits is likely to be regarded as "queer" or "different" and therefore will not be an acceptable member of that group. Should he be placed in a group with children whose interests and abilities are more nearly like his, however, his chances of social acceptance will be greatly increased. The social group expects more of a very bright child, for example, than of children of average intelligence; it also assigns different roles to him and treats him differently. As a result, he is often lonely and has few friends. Thus the behavior deviations of a child who lacks social acceptance may be the result of lack of acceptance, not the cause of it (52, 169).

"Alienation Syndromes." There are three types of alienation syndromes. The first is the *recessive syndrome,* characterized by listlessness, quietness, reserve, social uninterest, and a tendency to withdraw from group activities. Children with the recessive syndrome are usually not "smart" in their school work but are rarely troublesome to their teachers. They are likely to be overlooked by other children or to be rejected by them because they do not fit into the pattern of activities of the group or are not good at games. Classmates may consider such children "OK" but they generally say, "They are not my friends" (113).

The second alienation syndrome—the *socially uninterested syndrome*—is characterized by most of the traits found in the recessive type, but also by a cluster of traits that cause the child to be self-bound and selfish. Like the recessive syndrome, the socially uninterested syndrome is likely to cause the child to be neglected rather than rejected.

The third pattern—the *socially ineffective syndrome*—is characteristic of children who may be energetic but who turn their energies into channels that make other children dislike them. They try to win attention and acceptance by annoying others with such aggressive behavior as shouting, bullying, showing off, insisting on having their own way, and refusing to comply with the rules and regulations that other children accept. In a less aggressive manner, they annoy others by dawdling, doing things their own way, failing to carry out assigned tasks, and being silly, thus keeping other children from concentrating on what they are trying to do. They often complain and bid for sympathy and help from adults (113, 125, 166).

Children of this type like to pick fights with others, stir up trouble, swear and use other "shocking" words, tattle, and make sarcastic comments to hurt others; they think they should be first and have the best of everything (117, 168). They are poor sports, poor losers, and "pests." They make nuisances of themselves. Because of their antisocial behavior and their tendency to spoil the fun of others, they are more likely to be rejected than neglected. Also, they are regarded as potential traitors who might run and tattle on the group if they do not get what they want (98, 170, 246).

The personality pattern of *every* unpopular child is that of the ingrown, self-bound, self-centered person. He is restless, suffers from feelings of insecurity and inferiority, and lacks a feeling of belonging. He is more likely to have personality disturbances of greater or lesser severity than the popular child. Frequently, he feels so frustrated that he becomes aggressively antagonistic to others, especially to adults in authority or to other children who assume leadership roles. No matter how hard he tries, he invariably feels that he has made a failure of what he has undertaken. Such unfavorable self-concepts lead to poor adjustments, and these, in turn, result in greater unpopularity as the child grows older. In addition, unfavorable self-concepts undermine the child's self-confidence and self-respect. The result is that children who are unpopular are not very effective in working with others (74, 129).

Factors Influencing Social Acceptance. Analyses of well-accepted children have revealed that certain factors contribute to their popularity, while others militate against it.

1. First Impression. The first impression the child makes on others goes a long way toward determining their attitudes toward him and their willingness to accept him as a playmate or friend (121). If, for example, his shyness creates the impression that he is uninterested in social activities, he is likely to be neglected. As a result, the members of the group will have no opportunity to know what kind of person he is or whether they would find him an enjoyable playmate. Should a child be so anxious to have friends that he literally "pushes" himself upon them, he will create the impression that he is aggressive; this will militate against their acceptance of him (168, 170). If he makes them laugh by being silly, they may on more sober reflection decide that, while he is "funny," he is really a "nut." Or they may consider his sarcasm cruel and decide to reject him (117). The first impressions made by a newcomer are especially important. If he impresses the group members favorably,

they will accept him; if he impresses them unfavorably, his chances of acceptance are slim (214).

2. Looks. While young children are not so "looks-conscious" as adolescents, they do take looks into consideration in the selection of friends and leaders (61, 256). For a newcomer, looks are more important than for children who are already established (214).

Among elementary-school children, looks are rated high in importance in choice of friends. In one study, two-thirds of the popular children were rated as having an attractive appearance, while less than one-fifth of the unpopular children were so described. No child who was called "ugly" was among the popular, and no child who was described as "very attractive" was among the unpopular. Girls at all ages rate personal attractiveness as more important in the choice of friends than boys do. The most popular children at all ages are those who are in complete accord with the group norms in dress, grooming, and manners (98, 254). A child who is "different" in looks, because of size or clothing, is likely to run into problems of acceptance.

3. Physical Condition. The most popular children are generally vigorously healthy and in a better all-around condition than their classmates. Furthermore, good health improves the child's appearance and contributes to happiness and superiority in the skills needed for group play. The happy child is a cheerful child; everyone likes to be with cheerful people. Children whose health is poor are likely to be socially maladjusted. Physically handicapped children, it has been found, are usually either withdrawn or overly active, either of which will militate against social acceptance. Children with hearing problems, for example, often fight to become group members or leaders. If they are challenged by the group, they usually withdraw and play alone (86).

4. Intelligence. *Bright* children and those who are successful in their school work are

better liked than those who are less bright. Very bright children, on the other hand, tend to be inconsiderate of the rights of others or so indifferent to them that they make no real attempt to adjust (169, 171). Such behavior does not lead to social acceptance, though it may lead to admiration. In schools where there are many bright children, the bright are more popular than in schools where the bright child is rare and thus "different" or "queer."

In an attempt to gain group acceptance, many bright children do not demonstrate their superior abilities or let others know how bright they actually are. This kind of behavior is likely to be the beginning of underachievement, which is so characteristic of bright children (109, 122). Social acceptance, on the other hand, is generally lower for those who are *dull* than for those who are very bright. Dull children are less companionable, and they generally feel inferior and inadequate. As a result, they tend to make poor social adjustments (20).

Children who are *academically competent,* especially those who read well, are more popular than those whose academic work falls below par (249, 257). An exception to this is the very bright child who does so well academically that he gains the reputation of being a "brain" or a "curve-raiser" —one whose work is so good that it raises the class standard. Poor academic work, on the other hand, whether due to low intelligence or poor study habits, generally leads to poor social acceptance (70, 157). Children who read or speak well tend to be better liked than those whose language is inferior in quality and social usefulness. The child who speaks well has a meaningful type of communication, which contributes to his social acceptance (222).

5. Social Insight.   Age for age, the bright child generally has better social insight and self-insight than the child who is less bright. Because the ability to make good social adjustments is greatly influenced by how accurately a person can size up a social situation and perceive how he fits into it, the child whose social insight is equal or superior to that of his agemates will make better social adjustments than the child whose social insight is below expectations for his age (84). How social insight develops and the role it plays in social adjustments were discussed in detail on pages 259 to 261.

Children who are unpopular or who are "fringe" members of a group may not be lacking in insight, but rather in social skills. Because children under eight or nine years of age are rarely able to perceive the attitudes of others toward them, good social adjustments to a group are not possible much before that age. With each passing year, the child's social insight and self-insight increase. Those who are superior in these characteristics are usually more acceptable than those who lag behind (15).

6. Sex.   While it is true that there are popular boys just as there are popular girls, indications are that girls, as a group, enjoy greater popularity than boys. Among older children, girls are, at every age, more highly socialized than boys; as a result, girls make better social adjustments (254).

As girls approach adolescence, however, they often develop feminine "inferiority complexes." Because of being teased and bullied by boys during the period of "sex antagonism," they often have a poor opinion of themselves and make less favorable social adjustments than their superior social maturity would justify (132). The effect of sex antagonism on social adjustments was discussed in detail on pages 366 to 368. Girls with older brothers generally make better social adjustments and are more popular than girls with older sisters or girls who have only sisters. Boys with older sisters or with sisters only, by contrast, make poorer social adjustments and are less popular than boys with older brothers or brothers near them in age (43, 160).

7. Proximity to Group.   The more contacts a child can have with other children, the greater his chances will be to form friendships and become an accepted member of

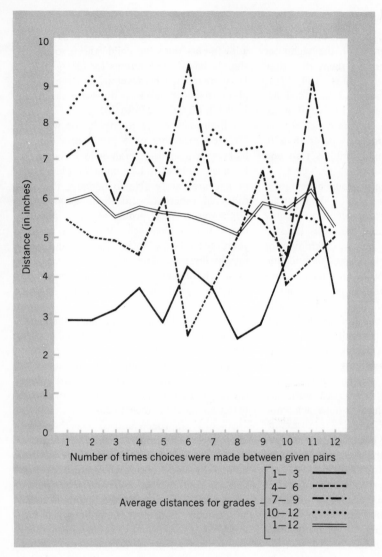

Figure 9–6. Comparison of the on-the-map distances in inches between the homes of pairs of children with high sociometric choices. (Adapted from M. V. Devault, Classroom sociometric mutual pairs and residential proximity, *J. educ. Res.*, 1957, 50, 605–610. Used by permission.)

the group. If his personality pattern is such that others dislike him, however, close proximity can just as readily increase social rejection. Propinquity thus may be a facilitator, but it is not a sufficient condition for the development of positive attraction.

Studies have revealed that children who are transported to school by bus have fewer friends and are less popular than those who live within the neighborhood of the school (41). Among adolescents who can use the family car for transportation to school activities, distance from school is far less important than among younger children (88, 109). The relationship between friendship selection and geographic proximity at different ages is illustrated in Figure 9–6.

8. Family Relationships. The child from a happy home will be more popular than the child from a home marked by friction and tension. The one who learns how to get

along harmoniously with others at home carries this pattern of social adjustments into his relationships with people outside the home.

Child-training practices that are strict and authoritarian, that encourage dependence, or that tend to make the child family-oriented when his peer group has become group-oriented will in general foster poor social adjustments and lack of popularity in the child (45, 154, 229).

Although a home that requires the child to assume some responsibility better prepares him for social adjustments than the home that does not, dependency is not always as detrimental to social adjustments as is believed. Its seriousness is related to the *type* of dependency. Children who are emotionally dependent on their parents for comfort, affection, and support make poorer social adjustments than children who depend on parents for help—"instrumental dependency." In fact, instrumental dependency has been found to have no relationship to popularity (137, 187). Overprotective parents who set up blocks against the child's participation in activities with his peers are likely to deprive him of the social learning necessary for popularity (131, 190).

While some investigations report that children from small families are more popular than those from large families, others report just the opposite. In-between children are generally more popular than the oldest or youngest of the family. Only children, if they come from a superior socioeconomic group, may make good social adjustments, but generally they are less popular than children with siblings. The explanation given for the popularity of children from large families is that they have learned to make social adjustments in the home and have developed a pattern of behavior which helps them to be popular outside the home. On the other hand, children from small families are generally subjected to more democratic home training, and this helps them to develop qualities that contribute to good social adjustments and to success in leadership roles (101, 253).

Perhaps the most important aspect of family relationships is how the child feels about his family and how his family feels about him. Children who have warm, friendly feelings about their families, who enjoy participating in activities with different family members, and who are encouraged by their families to participate in social activities outside the home make the best social adjustments with the peer group. Good family relationships include favorable relationships not only with parents but also with siblings; popular children are on more friendly terms with their siblings than those who are less popular (98, 101). The relationship between family relations and social acceptance outside the home is shown in Figure 9–7.

When a child is not popular with his peers and when his family relationships offer him little satisfaction, he is deprived of two of the most important sources of emotional security. He lacks a sense of belonging. Some children who are unpopular with their peers find satisfaction at home, while others who do not find satisfaction at home find it among their peers. To be well adjusted and to make good social adjustments, a child should be on friendly terms with *both* his family and the peer group (98).

9. Socioeconomic Status. Most popular children come from homes that provide superior cultural, social, and economic conditions. Because the socioeconomic status of the family is largely determined by the father's occupation, there is a close correlation between the child's social acceptance and the father's occupation, especially during adolescence, when "status-consciousness" reaches its peak (91, 230).

This does not mean that a child from a low socioeconomic group will *always* lack social acceptance in his school class. He *can* enjoy high peer acceptance, but only when he takes over the values and behavior patterns of his higher-status classmates. This will be discussed in more detail in the section of this chapter dealing with social mobility. Among every age group, socioeco-

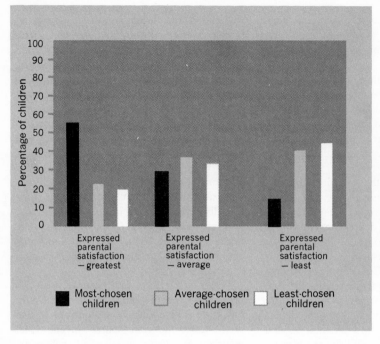

Figure 9–7. Relationships between children's social acceptance and parental satisfactions with the child. (Adapted from D. Elkins, Some factors related to the choice-status of ninety eighth-grade children in a school society, *Genet. Psychol. Monogr.*, 1958, 58, 207–272. Used by permission.)

nomic status is more important as a determinant of social acceptance for girls than for boys (52).

There are a number of reasons for the relationship between social acceptance and socioeconomic status. The most important is that the values and patterns of behavior of the upper social classes conform more closely to *cultural expectations* and *standards* than those of the lower classes. For example, the excessive aggressiveness of boys of the lower social classes does not conform to cultural standards (168). Also, children of the lower social classes are less well *dressed, groomed,* and *mannered* than children of the upper classes—all of which help to determine social acceptance.

Children of the middle and upper classes are taught *conformity* as a means of achieving status; they learn what to do and how to do it; they are taught to inhibit their emotional expressions. In addition, they are made to feel loved and wanted in their homes. Such an environment contributes to a feeling of security and to good personal adjustment (57). Finally, there is a tendency among people of all ages to *attribute*

more favorable characteristics to members of the upper social groups than to those of the lower. This suggests that "in our society, personality, like other commodities, has a price associated with it" (176).

Children who are poorly accepted generally come from homes where the fathers have low-status occupations. Lower-class children are self-conscious about family status and about the way classmates rate them and their families. As a result, not only are they deprived of the social and cultural advantages of middle- and upper-class children, but they also develop an inferiority complex about their status. In discussing the reasons why lower-class children frequently lack social acceptance, Mussen et al. have pointed out:

Economic factors may partially account for the relatively poor social standing of lower-class children. Poverty may mean poor health, poor clothes, and little participation in social activity. Any of these factors may reduce the child's opportunities for establishing stable peer relationships, and may thus handicap him in learning good social techniques. Moreover, the lower-class child's awareness of his lack of social know-how may produce feelings of inferiority and inadequacy and hence withdrawal from social interactions (205).

10. Degree of Adjustment.

A child who shows the social maturity the group expects by "acting his age" and conforming to the group's expectations in interests and values is more acceptable than the child who acts "babyish" or who fails to conform. Similar interests and values lead to similar ways of expressing and receiving affection and to favorable feelings about others. They lessen the social distance between the child and others, thus making friendships possible.

When a child is different from his age-mates, because of his religion, race, or socio-economic status, he tends to interpret this to mean that he is "inferior" (80, 175, 211). In a large consolidated school, for example, a rural child gains less acceptance, as a rule, than an urban child because his interests, values, and clothes are different from those of his urban classmates; they tend to regard him as a "country hick" (212). The child with foreign-born parents whose home reflects the culture of his parents' native country feels "different," and this leads to feelings of inadequacy. When a person is identified with two cultural groups having conflicting values, interests, and patterns of behavior, he does not feel that he belongs to either. He is less accepted in both groups than he would be if he were identified solely with one or the other (156).

Good adjustment comes only when the child is willing and able to accept himself. As long as he is dissatisfied with himself, he cannot make good personal adjustments or good social adjustments. Lower-class children find it difficult to accept themselves; they would like to "better themselves," and often their parents encourage them to try to gain social mobility. Furthermore, good adjustment comes only when the child accepts his sex role, as prescribed by his social group. If he dislikes the prescribed sex role or cannot easily conform to it, he will have unfavorable attitudes toward himself. This, in time, will lead to self-rejection and will thus predispose him toward poor personal and social adjustments (15, 64, 192).

11. "Halo" Effect of Popularity.

A *psychological "halo"* is an extension of a person's reputation which provides others a basis for making judgments about the person. The psychological halo of a person with a good reputation predisposes others to judge him favorably. If two children get into a fight, for example, the child who is known as a "good sport" will be judged far more favorably than the child who is known as a "sourpuss," a "crybaby," or a "bad sport." Consequently, a favorable reputation contributes to social acceptance just as an unfavorable reputation detracts from it.

According to the popular belief that "nothing succeeds like success," a child who wants to be socially successful tries to create the impression that he has many friends, that he is a good sport, that he has all the qualities the group admires, and that others are happy to have him as a member of their group. He boasts about his friends, associates with the group as much as possible, and identifies himself with the group members by his dress, speech, and actions. If he successfully creates the impression that he is popular, he will have a distinct advantage over the child who is known to be unpopular (22, 121, 126).

While the child's reputation and status in the group are determined partly by his actual behavior, they are more influenced by the picture other children carry in their minds of him and of the group with which he is identified. There is a tendency to believe that "birds of a feather flock together," that a person can best be judged "by the company he keeps." This means that once a child has built up an identity or reputation, it is hard to change. The result is that the accepted remain accepted, the outcasts usually remain outcasts, and the neglected continue to remain on the fringe of things. Older children, as a rule, give more consideration to reputation in selecting their friends than younger children (254).

Popularity among children is highly concentrated in a few; those who are most popular in the classroom are generally most popular on the playground as well. The child who has a close personal relationship with another child is generally well accepted by other children. The child without a close personal friend, on the other hand, may not be rejected by other children, but he is not generally sought out as a companion. To remedy this situation, he may choose to identify himself with the "stars," although he has little, if any, contact with them. He is thus protected from rebuff and can rationalize his contact with the stars, just as one might rationalize one's attraction to a motion-picture celebrity. Many quiet children who are overlooked and neglected by their peers choose friends who have won the spotlight of attention, even though they may not have won peer acceptance. By identifying themselves with such children, they too hope to win the attention of the peer group (21). If they can win the reputation of "belonging" to a group that is accepted, the halo from the group will be expanded to include them.

Persistence of Social Acceptance. In a newly organized group of children, there is likely to be considerable trial and error before friendship preference patterns crystallize (40, 95, 266). But, in general, persistence in sociometric status begins at the pre-school level; children consistently choose the same friends day after day. From then on, there is less and less shifting from one group to another, though social acceptance varies somewhat with the activity engaged in.

Even when there is a large turnover in the class—as shifts occur in the population or as children go from elementary to junior high school—constancy of social status within the group remains. Social-acceptance scores have been found to be almost as constant as intelligence- and achievement-test scores. The child's acceptance score in one group, therefore, is a reliably accurate index of what his acceptance score in any similar group will be (125, 166, 249). This means that "chance events . . . windfall successes

and failures, have little influence on the acceptance scores of children" (209). Fluctuations occur mainly in the middle of the group of socially accepted children—those who are already partially accepted. It is most unusual for those who are popular to "fall from grace" or for those who are quiet, withdrawn, and neglected to gain wholehearted acceptance. Those who are rejected because they are disliked tend to be more disliked the more often they come in contact with others; they do not acquire new friends to compensate for their growing number of enemies (77). The stability of a child's social acceptance, however, will depend partly upon the stability of the group and the extent to which there is a turnover of children who are able to attain a high degree of social acceptance (125, 266).

Reasons for Persistence. There are definite reasons for the persistence of a child's popularity or unpopularity. The *personality characteristics* that lead to acceptance, rejection, or neglect tend to remain stable or to intensify as children grow older. The *fundamental values* by which people judge others likewise remain stable. Within a group, the child acquires a *reputation,* and even if he changes, his reputation generally does not. People who are unpopular make little headway in gaining popularity even after receiving professional help to change the traits that led to their social rejection (233).

Persistence of sociometric status is due also to the number and closeness of *contacts* with group members. The more contacts the child has and the closer they are, the more likely he is to retain a stable status in the group. A favorable *background,* in terms of the socioeconomic status of the family, contributes to stability of social acceptance, while an unfavorable background contributes to stability of social rejection. In commenting on the persistence of sociometric status, Jersild has emphasized:

When we consider the forces that, in a sense, render acceptance or rejection a self-perpetuating condition it appears that there is a kind of fatalism in a child's life as a member of his peer group. The child's fortunes (or misfortunes) with his age-mates often seem to follow the rule that to him that hath shall be given and from him that hath not shall be taken away even that which he has. We might ask, is the wheel of fate, after its first few rounds, destined to move in the same course, to high ground for some and into a deeper rut of misfortune for others? . . . We might take the view that when a child leaves the confines of the home and is thrown upon the mercies of his peers and teachers his fate is already pretty well determined by the combined forces of his heredity and the kind of upbringing he has received (150).

Improving Social Acceptance. Because the sociometric status of children tends to persist or to become less favorable, it is important that every possible attempt be made to improve the child's social acceptance before the group gets into the habit of neglecting or rejecting him and before he gets into the habit of withdrawing from the group or of using socially unacceptable behavior patterns in his attempt to win acceptance. While it is true that some boys and girls become more popular as they grow older and as the values of the group change, it is too great a risk to sit back and hope that this will happen to every unpopular child. Improving social acceptance is difficult at any age. The older the person and the longer he has been unpopular, the harder it is to increase his popularity. On the other hand, if poor social adjustments are recognized early and remedial steps are taken to correct them, the chances of improving the child's social acceptance are better (140).

Two major obstacles stand in the way of improving the child's sociometric status. The first is the failure of parents and teachers to *recognize* the child's poor social adjustments until he has become a social isolate. Parents have a tendency to overestimate their child's social acceptance and to blame other children when their child is not accepted. Teachers often regard a child as well adjusted if he does good school work and causes little or no trouble in the classroom.

They frequently fail to recognize in a child the traits that will make him unacceptable to other children (164, 182).

The second major obstacle to improving a child's social acceptance is his *reputation* in the peer group. If the child has developed the habit of withdrawing from social activities, he will acquire the reputation of being "queer" or "different," both of which are synonymous with "inferior" in children's minds. If he has developed patterns of socially unacceptable behavior, he is likely to be thought of as a "dope" or a "drip"—a reputation that will make later acceptance almost impossible (190, 266).

Aids to Improving Social Acceptance. If the child is to learn to behave in such a way that others will want to accept him, he needs guidance. He must be shown how to behave and how to replace socially undesirable behavior patterns with more desirable ones. In addition, he must be motivated to want to improve his behavior. As Barclay has stated, "If a youngster is genuinely interested in getting along better with others he can often be helped with sympathetic guidance to change his unfortunate ways" (22). But he must be *helped by persons more experienced than he.* When adults withdraw from children's social activities completely and let children make and run their own groups, "devastating things can happen," such as teasing, bullying, and extreme and harmful competition both socially and academically (106).

Once isolation is started, it becomes a circular reaction (52, 59). But attempts to increase a child's social acceptance often meet with considerable success. A child who is shy and withdrawn can be given an opportunity to work and play with other children in the group through seating arrangements in the classroom, through group projects, and by rotating leadership for different group projects. A child who lacks the skills needed to keep pace with the activities of his peers can be given help in acquiring these skills (181). Class discussions of popularity and the effect of lack of popularity help to make children more understanding and tolerant of others. When a child is an isolate because of his minority-group status, the group can learn to be more tolerant of him through either direct or vicarious experiences with individuals of minority groups (158).

If a teacher has prestige in the eyes of the group and if she praises a child for outstanding activity in the group, this will focus the group's attention on him, and it *may* increase his acceptance. Whether it will or not will depend mainly on how the praise is given. If the praise is for the child's contribution to the group, it will have a favorable influence on the group's reaction to him; if it is for his personal achievement, it is likely to increase his rejection because the group will think of him as "teacher's pet" (104).

Equally important as changing the group's attitude toward the child is changing the child's attitude toward himself, toward the group, and toward social activity with his peers. The unpopular child compares himself unfavorably with others; this makes him feel inadequate. He then wants to avoid the group and its activities. Often he depends upon the parent or teacher for his social contacts. Only when the child learns to understand himself and accept himself can he learn to make satisfactory adjustments to others. Children who have been helped to acquire competence in certain performances gain greater self-confidence; they are more willing to enter into situations where there are other children, and, as a result, they make better social adjustments (22, 74, 223).

The child who does not know how to go about making friends can be shown how to do so, while the child who has annoying mannerisms can be helped to correct them. A child can be encouraged to display any talent or skill he may have which will place him in the limelight and thus win the favorable attention of other children. Because most of a child's social contacts are in play, a child who can be helped, at home or in school, to improve his play skills will almost certainly increase his social acceptance (181).

Figure 9–8 shows the changes which occurred in one group of children from October to January. During this time, attempts were made to increase the social acceptance of the isolates. While the "stars" remained the "stars," the number of isolates was reduced from seven to three in this short period of time. Even when children are rejected or neglected by their peers, however, there is no guarantee that any improvement in acceptance will be permanent. Lasting improvement will depend mainly on whether the child changes his attitudes and behavior enough to make him more socially acceptable than he previously was (233).

Limitations to Improving Social Acceptance. No adult, whether parent or teacher, can *dictate* to children whom they will like or be willing to accept as a member of their play group (104). This is the prerogative of the group. All the adult can do is to create situations which will enable the group to see the child in a more favorable role. For example, when social cleavages develop in a classroom, they tend to persist. Even by seating children side by side, the teacher cannot force them to be friendly if they do not want to be (91). As Elkins has stated, it is "easier to adjust the academic requirements to the needs of the youngster than it is to adjust the social needs of the child to the group in which he is a misfit or to attempt to adjust the social responses of the group to such a child" (98). While marked gains in social acceptance are often made by children who have been helped to improve their social behavior, the chances of making such gains are much greater when the group is small (158).

Because there are limits to what can be done to improve a child's social acceptance, the important thing is to help the child gain enough self-confidence to make an effort to become a member of the group before he becomes resigned to playing the role of an isolate or before he develops forms of compensation which will militate against later acceptance. This should be done before the group gets so accustomed to thinking of him as a "fringer" that they overlook any po-

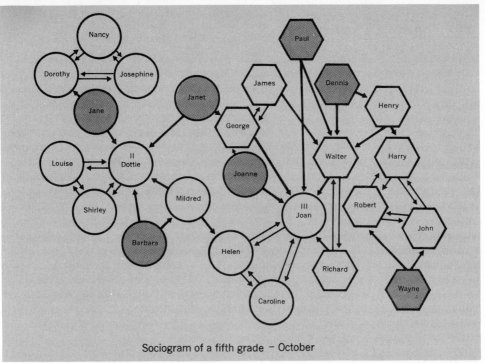

Sociogram of a fifth grade – October

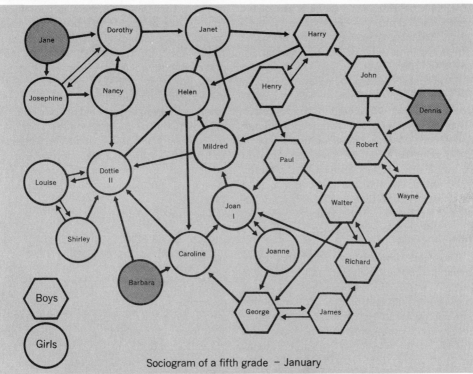

Boys

Girls

Sociogram of a fifth grade – January

Figure 9–8. Improvement in social acceptance from October to January. Note that "Dottie" and "Joan" are still the "stars," while the number of social isolates has been reduced from seven to three. (Adapted from F. J. Brown, *Educational sociology*, 2d ed., Prentice-Hall, 1954. Used by permission.)

tential abilities he may have. Gaining the reputation of being an isolate or a "fringer" may result in a persistence of that status. As Jersild has pointed out, "A youngster who, for one reason or another, has received a bad reputation in the elementary grades may still be plagued by it in junior high school, for even though many of the children there are new to him, one first-class gossip from the former grade may be able to stir up doubts and suspicions against him" (150).

Importance of Social Acceptance. The type of social adjustment the child makes is greatly influenced by the degree to which his contemporaries find him acceptable (70). The child who is popular is happy and secure; he develops a favorable concept of himself because others have put their stamp of approval on him. He learns to get along well with others and develops socially acceptable behavior because he is one of the group. In addition, he develops social skills which facilitate ease and poise in social situations, thus increasing his acceptance (58, 111, 170).

The popular child is mentally free to turn his attention outward and to become interested in people and things outside himself. With popularity comes the self-confidence and security which enable a person to be creative and original. He feels supported in his originality by the approval of the group. In addition, he has the self-confidence to make suggestions that will lead to the increased enjoyment of the group; as a result, he is often selected for leadership roles (209).

The more popular the child, the more colorful, outgoing, original, and creative he is likely to be. He becomes more involved with people than with things, is more flexible and willing to adjust, and does not stick as closely to a stereotyped role as those who feel less secure. On the other hand, a popular child, even if he is a "star," does not flaunt tradition. He knows what the social group expects of him, and, within broad limits, he conforms to these expectations. A child whom everyone seems to like and

wants to claim as a friend often becomes indifferent toward others and develops a feeling of superiority. Unless this is reflected in behavior that will antagonize others, however, it merely adds to his self-confidence; this, in turn, leads to an aloofness that is characteristic of all who are very popular (66, 157).

The unpopular child finds himself an outsider: He is unhappy and insecure. He feels that he is "different" and, as a result, becomes timid or resentful. If he attempts to force himself into a group that has rejected him, he develops many socially unacceptable forms of behavior which add to his unpopularity and push him further out of the group (71). In addition, he becomes self-bound, thinking more about himself than about others. This sets up barriers to interaction and makes later acceptance difficult, if not impossible. Children who are "fringers"—neither totally accepted nor totally rejected—live in a state of uncertainty which makes them anxious and insecure. As a result, they are hypersensitive about what others say or do, they are insecure in any social situation, and they conform slavishly in the hope of improving their status. As Frank and Frank have said, "The results of being left out of a group, or the price paid for staying 'in' with a small few, involves self-doubt, mean, harmful tactics toward others and, in most cases, a personal philosophy of life that may be self-destructive" (106).

The way a child treats others is greatly influenced by the amount of acceptance he believes he has from them; this, in turn, influences the way others treat him. Children with low peer acceptance are considerate toward those with high peer acceptance, but inconsiderate toward those who, like themselves, enjoy low acceptance. Children with high peer acceptance, on the other hand, are considerate toward those with high peer acceptance but inconsiderate toward all others.

There seems to be a "kind of 'peck order' in the social hierarchy" of childhood. The child who is on the fringe of acceptance tends to treat members of the peer group with whom he wants to be associated with great consideration and often shows marked deference toward them. In this way, he hopes to gain their favor and, with it, their acceptance. Only when a child is so completely rejected that he has few friends does he lack motivation to win friends. If he feels the situation is hopeless, he often behaves in an antisocial way toward others, as if he had contempt for them and their opinions (111, 250).

Popularity is used by many parents, teachers, and peers as an index of a child's success in making social adjustments. Therefore, a child learns to think of himself as a success or a failure in terms of how many friends he has and how secure his status in the group is. Many a child who literally buries himself in a group does so, not because he gets great satisfaction from being a member of the group or from its activities, but rather because this is an escape from a feeling of worthlessness (21).

Because there is a tendency for more children to be unpopular than popular and because the number of unpopular children increases rather than decreases with advancing age, many more children develop unfavorable self-concepts and make poor adjustments than is healthy for any social group (140). Children who are constantly confronted with the cultural value of social acceptance cannot fail to develop unfavorable self-concepts when they realize that their lack of acceptance is interpreted by others as lack of success. In commenting on the damaging effects of lack of social acceptance on the child's developing personality, Barclay has stated:

Not every child can be a social lion. "Being liked by all" is neither a realistic goal nor an especially constructive one. Most children are liked by some, disliked by some others, and of merely neutral interest to the great majority. Being actively disliked, however, can be painful and at times destructive. Children in such a spot should be spared harsh criticism and exhortations and helped instead to feel better about themselves, to see how their assets can be put to use and their liabilities corrected in the interest of achieving the kind of companionship for a happier, livelier life (22).

Persistent social acceptance from year to year does not necessarily guarantee a wholesome adjustment on the child's part, nor does it necessarily mean that the child's social development is progressing in a manner that will guarantee wholesome adjustments in adult life. If the child is accepted by his peers because they admire and respect him, well and good. If he is accepted because he is willing to do as he is told by the group, to sacrifice personal values and standards of behavior to buy his popularity, and to play a role imposed upon him by the group, even if that role is contrary to his own standards of behavior, then the price of acceptance is too high. The temporary satisfaction the child derives from this acceptance will be outweighed by the permanent damage it may do to his personality and his moral values. *Only when social acceptance and wholesome social and personal development go hand in hand is social acceptance an ideal to be striven for by every child* (267).

SOCIAL MOBILITY

One of the major obstacles many children encounter in achieving social acceptance or in feeling secure in the social acceptance they have achieved is social mobility. *Social mobility* is the process of changing one's status in the social structure; it also involves changes in social relationships (1). Social mobility may be vertical or horizontal. In *horizontal* mobility, there is a transition from one group to another on the same level; in *vertical* mobility, there is a transition from one social stratum to another. Vertical mobility may be ascending or descending—"upward" or "downward." In ascending social mobility, the individual is known as a "climber"; in descending mobility, he is known as a "slider," a "decliner," or a "skidder," depending on how rapidly he goes down the social ladder (82, 262).

Between the climber and the slider are those whose status is less well defined and less secure. They are trying to move upward but are not sure of their success. They are usually called "strainers" and "clingers." A *strainer* is a person who is only tentatively accepted; as a result, his status gives him little satisfaction and security, and his social adjustments are poor. The *clinger* is peripheral to the group because he has not completely adopted the approved patterns of the group. While he is not rejected, his status is precarious, and, at any time, should he say or do something the group disapproves of, he may forfeit what status he has (12, 190).

Not all children, of course, encounter the problems that social mobility brings. Some belong to families that are static; they remain year after year in the same community, the same neighborhood, or even the same house. This is more common in small towns and rural areas than in cities or suburban areas. Since the Second World War, however, social mobility has become an increasingly serious problem for children as

well as for their families. More children than adolescents face the problem, for it is during the early years of marriage, when the children are small, that the breadwinner of the family is more likely to change jobs or be promoted from the lower to the higher strata of the organization in which he works (213). The common pattern of geographic mobility and its relationship to social mobility are shown in Figure 9–9.

In horizontal mobility, the move is generally for *personal* reasons on the part of parents. In vertical mobility, by contrast, the move is more often for *advancement,* if it is upward, or is due to some family *misfortune,* such as death of the breadwinner or parental divorce, if it is downward. Children from lower-class families encounter fewer problems from social mobility than those from middle- or upper-class families because workers from the lower-class groups do not move around so much even when they change jobs. When they do move, they generally go from rural to urban areas (167, 220).

When mobility is vertical, the child encounters all the difficulties associated with horizontal mobility *plus* the necessity of conforming to new ideas, new beliefs, new

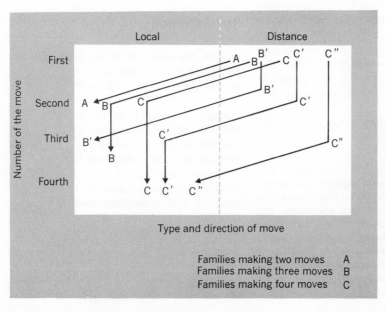

Figure 9–9. Common patterns of geographic isolation. (Adapted from V. H. Whitney and C. M. Grigg, Patterns of mobility among a group of families of college students, *Amer. sociol. Rev.,* 1958, 23, 643–652. Used by permission.)

values, and new behavior patterns of the group with which he must now try to identify himself (12). Adjusting to a new group is *never* easy for a child, even when the group is composed of children of similar backgrounds, similar interests, and similar values.

Because upward mobility means an improvement in standards of living and more prestigeful social contacts, parents are anxious to help their children make successful adjustments to their new social groups. They stress the importance of learning behavior patterns that will meet with the approval of the new group. Children, themselves, may have a strong drive to achieve upward social mobility. They may hope to "better" themselves by being identified with a social group that is superior to the group their family is identified with; in fact, they often want to "show others" that they are not "like their families" (1, 27).

By contrast, no one—adult or child—likes to skid downhill socially. It is always an ego-deflating experience because it implies failure. Furthermore, the person resents having to associate with people of a lower class; he considers their values, interests, and behavior patterns inferior to those he has been accustomed to. Because downward social mobility means living in a less desirable neighborhood, having a house that is inferior to the old one, and having fewer material possessions, the child will be unhappy about his new status. All this, added to the belief that the new group is "inferior," weakens his motivation to try to identify himself with it. To make the situation worse, the child is likely to find that his old social group will not accept him since he has changed his status and, with it, his neighborhood, his school, and his ability to have the status symbols they consider important (38).

Achieving Acceptance in New Groups.
In spite of the strong motivation of the upwardly mobile child and his parents to gain social acceptance in the new group and in spite of the desire of the downwardly mobile to retain status in the old group, the achievement of these goals is extremely difficult. To gain social acceptance in a new group, regardless of the child's age, there are two essentials: making a favorable impression on the group and showing enough aggressiveness to attract the attention of the group members without, at the same time, antagonizing them.

The importance of *making a favorable impression* was well illustrated in a study of assimilation of newcomers into groups. The study found that there is a high correlation between popularity on the first day in the classroom and 11 weeks later. Older children tend to be more "choosy" about the acceptance of newcomers than younger children. The difficulty of gaining acceptance, however, varies according to the *type* of group as well as according to the *age* of the members (214, 269).

Groups that are well organized, self-sufficient, and self-contained look upon *any* newcomer as a possible disruptive influence. They are satisfied with things as they are and are not anxious to make changes. If the newcomer creates the impression that he is aggressive, he is rejected as a potential troublemaker. Less successful groups, by comparison, are more willing to take in newcomers in the hope that they will contribute new ideas or new abilities to the group's plans. A group that has few successful ballplayers, for example, will give a better welcome to a good player than to a mediocre player. The less successful the group, the more eager it is to bring in "new blood" (269).

The second essential in winning social acceptance in a new group is well-controlled and well-camouflaged *aggressiveness* on the part of the newcomer. Rarely do already established groups take the initiative in making contacts with a new child. Only when he creates a favorable first impression will the group members go out of their way to contact him. Under most conditions, therefore, it is up to the new child to make the contacts by trying to talk or play with some of the members of the group, by trying to attract their attention, or by observing and imitating their play.

At first, he is likely to be ignored or rebuffed. If he is anxious to have friends, he will continue trying; if he is timid or suffers from feelings of personal inadequacy, he will give up and remain an isolate, ignored if not actually rejected. A child may succeed, in time, in gaining acceptance to the group if he wins the attention and favor of a member who will persuade the others to accept him (214).

Because aggressiveness can be and often is interpreted as "pushiness," a newcomer seldom knows just how much he must do to win the group's attention and acceptance. This is an especially difficult problem for the child who is trying to identify himself with a group composed of children of a higher socioeconomic status. Being unfamiliar with their values and accepted patterns of behavior, he may use methods that arouse antagonism and win rejection.

As boys tend to be aggressive, especially those from a lower-class background, a boy finds social acceptance more difficult to achieve in childhood if his family is upwardly mobile. In adolescence, a girl finds it more difficult, not because she becomes more aggressive as she gets older, but because socioeconomic status plays a more important role in social acceptance then than in childhood (1, 28). The only type of aggressiveness that a socially mobile person can use successfully, without running the risk of social rejection on the grounds that he is a "pusher," is aggression of a "congenial and disarming" type (82). Few children have the social sophistication to know when pushiness replaces "congenial and disarming" aggression.

Because of the difficulties encountered in gaining acceptance, most children have to be satisfied with making friends with those who are least popular and have the fewest ties with the group. They are often left with the choice of having no friends at all or of being friends with those whom others do not want. Once a child gains some acceptance, he can observe the approved patterns of behavior and the values of the members of the group. He can then model his behavior along the approved lines in the hope that, in time, the group will accept him.

If the child does gain acceptance—and this is more likely to occur in horizontal than in vertical mobility—his status need not necessarily be less secure than that of children whose families are static. In a study of elementary-school children, it was found that those who had moved once or twice or had been in a school system for a period of only 1 to 3 years had greater acceptance among their classmates than those who had been in one school throughout their entire academic life or who had moved around a lot and had been in one school system for less than 1 year (92).

Regardless of what status the newcomer is able to achieve, it is often far from satisfactory. This is more true of older than of younger children. During the preschool years and even during the first year or two of elementary school, the social life of the child is unstable. A newcomer can be assimilated into a group more quickly and more easily then than later, after the social life of the group becomes more stable and after the group begins to break up into gangs (22).

Children from the higher socioeconomic groups generally find it easier to be accepted in a new group than children from the lower. The latter find it especially difficult when they are trying to gain acceptance in a group of a higher status than theirs (269).

Effects of Mobility. Whether social adjustment is judged by objective or subjective standards, the effects of mobility are more often unfavorable than favorable. A family may improve its standard of living, but the effect on the social adjustment of the child is rarely favorable. In time, the child may improve his adjustments and be happy, but there is likely to be a period following the move when emotional stress, feelings of insecurity and loneliness, and a longing to return to the old and familiar predominate (12, 243). As Bossard has said, "Mobility has its advantages, but I wouldn't wish them on anyone" (43). That the effects are more serious in vertical mobility, whether upward or downward, than in horizontal is well illustrated in a study of upwardly mobile families in which it was found that the children were constantly driven by their fathers to achieve a higher-status position in their peer groups. The children were closely supervised by their parents to prevent behavior that might reflect unfavorably on the family and thus militate against its acceptance by members of the group with which it wanted to be identified. In addition, parents put strong pressures on the children to develop patterns of behavior that would lead to the family's higher-class acceptance. They were expected to excel in both school and social affairs. As a result of this constant driving, the home atmosphere was highly emotionally toned, and the relationships with the parents were anything but favorable (57).

Lack of acceptance is difficult for any child. It is especially difficult for one who enjoyed social acceptance in the neighborhood from which he moved. Furthermore, it is hard for him to understand why he is not accepted in his new neighborhood or school. The more popular he was in his former group, the less satisfied he will be to have to form friendships with "fringers" or social isolates in the new group (247).

A child who has not enjoyed much social acceptance in the old setting may be promised by parents that "things will be different" when the family moves. If they are not different, the child's dissatisfaction will be intensified.

Sources of Dissatisfaction.   The dissatisfaction experienced by the socially mobile child comes from many sources, not from lack of social acceptance alone. The child may find that there are *gaps in his school work;* he may even have to go back a grade in the new school. If he is not as well prepared as his new classmates, he may do work far below his former standards. This is a source of concern for him and is likely to lead to friction in the home, especially when parents put a high value on academic achievement (57, 243).

Because every group has *different values* and *different social expectations* for its members, a child may be confused and disturbed when he discovers that behavior judged acceptable in the old group is frowned upon or ridiculed in the new group. A child from a rural background is likely to experience adjustment difficulties in an urban or suburban setting. Until the child learns and accepts the cultural values of his new group, he not only will be deprived of social acceptance but may even be the object of ridicule and scorn (30, 207, 262).

The most common and most serious source of dissatisfaction the socially mobile child experiences comes from *lack of a sense of identity.* He feels that he does not belong anywhere, either in the old group with which he no longer has contacts or in the new group which has not accepted him as a recognized member. Because every child wants to have friends and because most parents stress the importance of social acceptance, being unidentified with any group becomes a source of constant distress and dissatisfaction to the child. He may begin to doubt his adequacy and to feel bitter resentments toward those who refuse to accept him (27, 57, 247).

Lack of identity has three serious consequences for the mobile child. The first of these is *lack of opportunity to learn* what the group expects so that he can develop values and patterns of behavior that will lead to social acceptance. The child who is *in* a group but not *of* the group has no real way of knowing what group expectations are. As Davis and Havighurst have stated, "If a child associates intimately with no one but slum adults and children, he will learn only slum culture" (83).

The second serious consequence of lack of identity is a *feeling of insecurity.* While all people at all ages, even those who are static, suffer from feelings of insecurity at times, these feelings are generally related to situations in which they have met with failure in the past or for which they feel unprepared. For the socially mobile person, feelings of insecurity may become *generalized* and affect every aspect of his life, especially his social relationships. Lacking firm ties with either the old or the new group, the child who is socially mobile feels insecure with everyone.

To compensate for their insecurity, many mobile children overconform in appearance, speech, beliefs, and actions; they are afraid that differences will be judged as signs of social inadequacy (38, 255). Being unsure of their status, they become status-conscious and want every possible status symbol— money to spend, a big home, and as many cars as the other children's families have. As parents of socially mobile children are anxious to have their children accepted by the "right children," they are only too willing to supply the necessary status symbols, even if it means going in debt to "keep up with the Joneses" (37).

Closely related to status consciousness and motivated by the feeling of insecurity for which the child is trying to compensate is the tendency to be *hostile* toward all who are socially inferior, even family members whom the child judges as inferior to the new social group. Much of the prejudice children have against minority-group members comes from feelings of insecurity, one common cause of which is social mobility (232). The causes of prejudice and the effects on a child's behavior were discussed in detail on page 362 to 364.

The third important effect of lack of identity is the feeling of *social isolation*—of being friendless. Because social mobility involves partial or complete severance of emotional ties with former friends without compensatory ties with new friends, the child lacks what every child craves—playmates who want to play with him and who accept him as a member of the group. This means that the child is cut off from the companionship of the peer group at the very time when he must make other major adjustments in the pattern of his life (79, 226).

The downwardly mobile child experiences all these effects of social mobility in more intense forms. Added to the effects of mobility per se is the feeling of shame at losing status in the eyes of others (38). In conclusion, there is evidence that Bossard summed up the serious effects of social mobility on the child's social adjustments correctly, from both the objective and the subjective point of view, when he said that "mobility has its advantages, but I wouldn't wish them on anyone" (43).

LEADERS AND FOLLOWERS

No matter what their ages, children in any group seldom have a relationship of complete equality. One child usually stands out as the recognized leader, even when the group is made up of only two or three children. Shakespeare said, "As two men ride of a horse, one must ride behind." So it is with children. Because of the prestige associated with leadership, every child at some time or other wants to be a leader. He is encouraged in this desire by his parents. Not only do they believe that leadership is a sure indication that their child has made superior social adjustments, but they also derive vicarious pleasure from the child's status. Few children, however, achieve the status of a leader; most are followers (39).

A *leader* is a member of a group whom others are willing to follow because he has demonstrated his mastery of social relationships, is able to elicit positive reactions toward himself from the group members, and can contribute better than the other group members to satisfying the needs of the group as a whole. A leader is not just a person in authority; he is one who can arouse *emotional reactions* from members of the group. Because of this, he has the ability to get others to act in a certain way (85, 114, 268).

Leadership status may be *formal,* in that the leader is appointed or elected to play the role, or it may be *informal,* in that the leader is regarded as such by at least one-third of the group (184). The child who is a leader differs from the children who are considered the "big wheels" in the class be-cause he has followers; the group crystallizes about him. The "big wheels" have prestige in the eyes of the group but do not neces-sarily have followers (103).

Leaders can be divided, roughly, into two categories. The first is the *authoritarian* leader—one who is a bully and despot and who can lead by power alone. The authori-tarian leader may win the respect of the group, but he rarely wins its affection. The second is the *democratic* leader—one who shows great concern for the feelings and interests of the group members. Such a leader leads by making suggestions rather than by giving orders. In contrast to the authoritarian leader, he wins both the re-spect and the affection of the group members.

The larger the group, the more leadership skill is needed and the more likely it is to be authoritarian in nature (130, 159). Young children, accustomed to being told what to do in the home, will accept authori-tarian leadership more readily than older children. In lower-class groups, where chil-dren are accustomed to authoritarian con-trol in the home, the group leaders tend to be more authoritarian than in middle- and upper-class groups, where the members have learned, in the home, to expect more demo-cratic methods of control (165, 268).

Followers, like leaders, are accepted members of the social group with which they are identified; they retain this status as long as they are willing to do what the majority of the group members want to do and as long as they are willing to follow the leader. Just as there are different types of leaders, so are there different types of fol-lowers. Some follow because following is easier than leading; others lack the qualities to be leaders. Some followers contribute little to the group and are content to go along with the crowd; others carry a heavy load for the leaders and are satisfied to do work while the leaders get the credit.

Some followers are constructive members of the group; others are destructive—the "tear-downers," who constantly criticize the leader and his policies. These are usually the children who wanted to be leaders but were not chosen; as a result, they are bitter and vindictive toward those who were chosen. A large group is likely to have followers of all types, whereas a small group is likely to be much more homogeneous in interests, at-titudes, and values. A small group is also likely to contain few if any troublemakers. Consequently, the leader needs less leader-ship skill in a small group than in a large one (130).

Whether a child will play the role of a leader or a follower does not depend so much upon the qualities he has as upon the relationship of his attributes to those of the group. *He may be a leader in one group and a follower in another.* As long as he is able to meet the needs of the group, he will be accepted as their leader. When he is no longer able to do so, he will be forced to relinquish his leadership role. It will then be taken over by another child who is better able to meet the group's needs (28, 85, 155).

Leadership techniques vary from group to group. As Jersild has pointed out, "One child may be a leader partly because he is very voluble, mobile, and able to cover much ground. Another child may select and dominate the play activities of a group by virtue of aggressive methods and coercion. Still another child leads because he is re-sourceful in seeing new and original possi-bilities and in establishing friendly relations with other children" (150).

CHARACTERISTICS OF LEADERS AND FOLLOWERS

All leaders, at all ages, have certain charac-teristics that distinguish them from follow-ers. The qualities that distinguish the two, however, differ in *degree* rather than in kind. That is why a child may be a leader in one group and not in another. If a child has athletic skills superior to those of the other group members, for example, he will have a good chance of being their leader. In another group, his skills may be inferior to those of one or more of the group members; consequently, he will have little chance of being selected as the leader.

Differences between Leaders and Followers. While the traits that distinguish leaders also appear in followers, they are less well developed in the followers. The most important of these traits are:

1. Popularity.   A leader is always popular, but a popular child is not always a leader. Popularity is thus one factor that determines whether the group will select the child as a leader, and it is a very important factor. Many children who are followers are as popular as, or perhaps even more popular than, the leaders. They are liked because they are easygoing, cheerful, and good fun and are able to adapt themselves readily to different social situations. However, they lack some of the essential qualities of leadership, or they lack the motivation to be leaders (34, 110, 141).

2. Conformity to Group Ideal.   To be a leader, the child not only must be popular but must represent the group's ideal more nearly than other group members. He must conform to the norms and values of the group in appearance, behavior, and attitudes. The more closely the child conforms to the group's ideal, the more secure his leadership status will be. *Esteem* from the group and from others outside the group enhances his popularity within the group. To be the leader of a boys' gang, for example, the boy must be a good athlete, a good sport, and an all-around person. By contrast, the follower does not have the esteem enjoyed by the leader because he does not come up to the group ideal in many respects, though he conforms closely enough to be accepted.

3. Personal and Social Adjustment.   If a child has made good *personal* adjustments, he will accept himself and be confident that he has something to contribute to others; if he has made good *social* adjustments, he will be democratic and diplomatic in his relationships with others, showing interest in them, but not to the point where he tries to be his "brother's keeper." A leader is expected to be superior to the group in these areas. He will conform to group expectations, but not as slavishly as followers; he will thus have something new to contribute to the group. A well-adjusted child is *socially more active* than a poorly adjusted one; as a result, he learns how to deal successfully with people (17, 65, 184).

4. Degree of Maturity.   A child who is well adjusted creates the impression of being more *mature* than his agemates. He is able to control his emotions in social situations, showing superior frustration tolerance and an ability to express hostility tactfully. Even when he is enthusiastic, the mature child expresses his feelings with control. He is not impulsive in his actions when excited and enthusiastic; instead, he shows good judgment and deliberation (251).

Perhaps the most evident indication of his maturity is his realistic approach to everything. He seems to "use his head" when decisions are made and points out to his peers the advantages and disadvantages of the acts they want to carry out. This realism is likewise apparent in his assessment of himself. He suffers neither from delusions of grandeur nor from delusions of inferiority or persecution. Rather, he sees himself as he is and his relationships with others as they are, not in a distorted way (85). Followers, as a rule, are either younger or *seem* younger than those who are chosen for leadership roles. In both attitudes and behavior, they seem to be relatively immature.

5. Motivation.   Unquestionably, one of the most outstanding differences between a leader and a follower is the leader's motivation to be a leader and his willingness to make the *sacrifices* of time, effort, and personal desires required to play this role. Most young children, as was pointed out before, want to be leaders, but when they discover what it takes to be a leader, they are often unwilling or unable to perform the tasks required. If they have been brought up in

authoritarian homes, with little opportunity to develop leadership qualities, they may not be able to initiate acts that will bring satisfaction to the group, nor will they be capable of assuming responsibility without adult guidance and supervision. By contrast, the leader is willing to accept responsibility not only for success but also for failure. In addition, he is willing and able to do the work needed to reach the group's goal and to initiate actions that will bring satisfaction to the group (93).

If the desire to be a leader is motivated by a desire for recognition and prestige or by a desire to compensate for a feeling of inadequacy, the motivation is strong enough to enable the child to make any personal sacrifices necessary to reach his goal. Perhaps the greatest sacrifice a leader must make is to adapt his personal interests to those of the group; he must be group-centered rather than self-centered. The child who cannot or will not sacrifice his personal interests for those of the group causes friction, poor morale, and discord within the ranks. As Jersild has pointed out, the "most warmly accepted leader is the one who makes it pleasant to be a follower" (150). To be "warmly accepted" requires many sacrifices on the child's part.

6. Extroversion.   If a child wants to be a leader, he must *express,* not hide, the qualities needed for leadership. In all leaders, extraversion is more marked than introversion. The larger the group, the more important it is for the group to be aware of the leadership potentials a child has. If the child does not express his abilities when he is young, his chances of being selected as a leader grow slimmer with each passing year, as the play group increases in size (55, 130).

Similarities between Leaders and Followers. Among the traits often found in both leaders and followers are superior *intelligence,* proficiency in *motor skills* that are important to the group, *physical attractiveness, sociability,* favorable *socioeconomic status, efficiency,* and *verbal facility* (4, 114, 251).

Many of these characteristics are more highly developed in followers than in leaders. They may make the child a potential leader—a potentiality which may or may not be realized, depending on the group he is in and on what other traits needed for leadership he possesses. The child with very high intelligence, for example, is less likely to be a leader than the child whose intelligence is high but not so high that he has little in common with the group (169). Similarly, a child from a very high socioeconomic background is less likely to be a leader than a child whose socioeconomic background is only slightly more favorable than that of the rest of the group. In the former, there is too much difference between the child and the group for the members to feel "comfortable" with him. They may feel that his favorable status has given him a false sense of his importance.

DEVELOPMENT OF LEADERSHIP

According to tradition, some people are "born leaders," while others who do not "have what it takes" are "born followers." As has just been pointed out, however, many children who are followers have the same traits as the leaders, perhaps even in a more highly developed form. The *use* the child makes of his abilities determines whether he will be a leader or follower; this, in turn, is determined largely by the type of training he has during the early years of life.

Studies of leadership have revealed that leadership is not an inborn trait but is one which develops over a relatively long period of time and with considerable effort on the child's part. The child must learn the skills and habits which contribute to social effectiveness, and he must learn to play the roles essential for a leader. If leadership comes by chance, to fill a void left by another, it is not likely to persist.

The roots of leadership are found in childhood experiences. Of these experiences, the most important are the treatment the child receives in the home and parental attitudes regarding child-training methods. Within a family, some children seem more predisposed to play leadership roles than others. This is not so much a difference in inherent abilities as a difference in the *treatment* the child receives from his parents and what they expect of him. Only children and oldest children are more likely to develop leadership abilities than younger children. The oldest children in a family are given many responsibilities, while only children become mature for their age because of their constant association with their parents (6, 160).

Democratic child training during the early, formative years is far more likely to provide an environment conducive to the development of leadership qualities than strict authoritarian training is. As Miles has stated:

> Parents of successful leaders show outstandingly different attitudes from the parents of other groups of children. . . . In general, parents of successful children are less inclined to protect children from the normal risks of life, to shield them from the normal responsibilities of life, and to prevent them from developing an adequate degree of independence which is so necessary for good mental health and normal functioning in the social group. . . . Much more leeway is allowed children in making decisions, using judgment and experimenting with new situations. Also, the individual personality is given far more respect—his rights and his opinions are given consideration in the family group (193).

Under democratic child training, family relationships are generally good, and the child develops good patterns of social adjustment in the home. He carries these outside the home and is thus able to make satisfying peer adjustments. The child who makes good peer adjustments has many opportunities to learn to be a leader (25, 184). It thus becomes apparent, as Allen has said, that "some of the strongest roots of leadership seem to lie in childhood experiences" and that leaders are not born but made (6).

Pattern of Leadership Development. The pattern of development of leadership is pre-

dictable and is similar for all leaders. Leadership ability shows itself as soon as two children are placed together. The dominant child takes the toys that appeal to him. Should the toy be in the possession of the other child, he will push, pull, kick, and do everything within his power to get it. By the age of ten months, the baby is usually conscious of his triumphs, and a smile of self-satisfaction lights up his face. The baby who has been forced into a position of submission looks sorrowful, whimpers, or cries.

The leader in preschool years is characteristically superior to the other members of the group in size, intelligence, and generally in age. Because of his superior age and intelligence, he has more suggestions to offer for play, and thus the other children are willing to follow his lead. Sex is an unimportant factor in leadership at this age. Girls often assume the role of leadership over boys as well as over other girls. Likewise, social status, nationality, and physical attractiveness are not so important now as they will be later. Fairness and social responsibility to the group, on the other hand, are important characteristics of the child leader (47, 150). The child leader shows marked self-confidence.

There is, during the early childhood years, a marked tendency for the leader to be the tyrannical boss of the group. He expects others to follow his wishes and becomes angry or sullen if they rebel. Should his techniques become too tyrannical, he will find himself displaced and another child recognized as the new leader by the group. In contrast to the "bully," who tries to lead by brute force, the "diplomat" leads by artful and indirect suggestions, bargains, or even bribes and threats. The diplomat is generally able to hold a following longer than the bully.

During late childhood, the leader represents the group's ideal. He must be a good athlete and an all-around good sport. Should he fall short of the group's expectations, and should he display traits his peers dislike, he soon loses prestige and is replaced by another who, at the moment, more closely approximates the group's standards.

As childhood progresses, leaders are needed for different activities—school and class offices, sports, gangs, and community groups, like the Boy Scouts and Girl Scouts. The same child will not necessarily have the leadership qualifications needed for all such groups. Thus there is a tendency among older children to select leaders for *specific group activities*. There is no question, however, that the prestige and experience gained from leading one group activity will carry over to other activities and give the child who has been a leader an advantage over another who may be equally suited for leadership but who lacks experience (29, 119, 268).

The *technique of leadership* among older children differs from that which proves successful among younger children. The leader can be authoritarian and despotic only when the group is very large and is unanimous in its admiration and respect for him. For the most part, however, the leader must give the rest of the group some choice; they, in turn, must agree to his suggestions and be willing to follow them. In a large group, there is likely to be less agreement among the members than in a small group. The larger the group, then, the more leadership skill the leader will need. The child who has had little or no previous experience as a leader is not likely to possess this skill.

Persistence of Leadership. According to tradition, "Once a leader, always a leader." This does not necessarily follow, especially during the early years of childhood. The young child who becomes the leader of his nursery school or kindergarten group will not necessarily be the top executive in an important corporation when he is an adult, nor will he necessarily be a leader in his high-school or college days. While leaders may come and go at all ages, leadership tends to become more persistent as childhood progresses. Furthermore, it tends to be more persistent in boys than in girls.

Factors Encouraging Persistence. Three factors influence the persistence of leadership: the stability of the group, the adapt-

ability of the leader, and the motivation of the leader. It is much easier for a child to be a leader in *stable groups* than in those whose members change and in which new interests and values appear. For boys, great prestige is associated with outstanding athletic ability. Consequently, a boy who shows marked athletic promise during the gang age is likely to continue to be a leader through his adolescence. Athletic participation and honors in high school, in turn, are more predictive of future leadership than nonathletic participation and honors. Similarly, as greater value is placed on socioeconomic status as children grow older, leadership is more likely to be persistent among those whose socioeconomic status is superior to that of the other group members (184).

A child who is *adaptable* can use the skills acquired in handling one group to handle another group. As children grow older, however, their needs change. Therefore, the leader will have to change his methods of meeting their needs, or the group members will no longer find him a satisfactory leader. Generally, democratic homes foster adaptability, while authoritarian homes foster rigidity. As groups tend to become larger in later childhood, it becomes increasingly important for a child to be adaptable if he wants to continue to be a leader (154).

Finally, persistence of leadership is dependent upon the *persistence of motivation* to be a leader. Most children discover that leadership requires more sacrifices than they are willing to make. Furthermore, girls discover that being a leader is regarded as less sex-appropriate than being a follower; girls who are leaders are often suspected of being "bossy"—a characteristic that is not admired in girls. Boys, on the other hand, are regarded as the "natural" leaders. Consequently, greater prestige is associated with leadership among boys than among girls. These social attitudes have a strong influence on the child's motivation (60, 90, 208).

Factors Militating against Persistence. Under three conditions, leadership is unlikely to be persistent: when the leader is forced on the group, when the leader selected is a "stopgap" leader, and when the leader fails to meet the needs of the group. When a leader is *selected* by a teacher, camp counselor, or some other *adult,* the group members usually resent interference in what they consider their own rights. Even though they may have to accept the child who has been appointed, the chances are slim that he will be able to retain his position when the group is allowed to make its own choice *unless* he demonstrates that he is able to fill their needs. A leader selected to *fill a gap* created by the withdrawal of a chosen leader will not retain his leadership status or be selected for leadership roles again unless he proves to be a satisfactory leader; he will be regarded merely as a "stopgap" until the right leader can be found.

The most important condition determining the retention of leadership is whether the leader *fills the needs* of the group to their satisfaction. A "bossy" leader, for example, does not fill the needs of the followers for independence and self-expression. Similarly, a leader from the "wrong side of the tracks" will not fill the needs of the group, even though he did when the group members were younger and socioeconomic status was not so highly valued as it is later (125).

Reasons for Persistence.   In spite of the factors militating against the persistence of leadership, the normal pattern is for leadership to become increasingly persistent as childhood progresses. As a result, a few children in a group stand out as recognized leaders. There are a number of reasons for this. First, the *qualities* that are liked by others and which were responsible for the child's choice for a leadership role tend to be persistent because they become a part of the child's personality pattern. If there is a change, it is generally because of a conscious desire on the part of the child to strengthen the favorable characteristics and inhibit the unfavorable ones. The child who

wants to be a leader makes it his business to see that the qualities that favor his leadership are strong (65).

Second, the leader has certain *learning opportunities* that the follower does not have. They enable him to develop better social insight, superior social skills, and greater self-confidence than the follower. The more experience in leadership the child has when he is young, the better his chances will be of being selected as a leader when he grows older.

Third, leadership persists because of the *halo effect.* All halos tend to attribute to the wearer qualities which the group admires and to "build him up" into a more important person than he actually is. If the child is strongly motivated toward leadership, and if he comes close to the group's ideal, his halo will be enhanced, his prestige increased, and his chances of future leadership roles intensified (42, 114).

Finally, persistence in leadership occurs because a leader is *adaptable;* he is able to channel the group members into activities with which they will be satisfied, and he will be competent as their leader. This requires skillful tactics and may sometimes be a matter of considerable concern for the leader. Should the group want to engage in activities in which the leader is unqualified to lead, he must improve his qualifications or try to change the interests of the group (155). A girl, for example, may be a successful leader as long as the group is interested in neighborhood games and sports. When the group members become interested in social activities, however, her chances of retaining leadership are slim if she has nothing to offer but athletic skills. She must either acquire superior social skills or try to persuade the group to retain its interest in sports. If she fails, she will be forced to relinquish her leadership status.

Satisfactions and Dissatisfactions from Leadership.   When judged by *objective* criteria, leadership is regarded as a certain index of good social adjustments. The larger the group and the more often a child is selected for leadership roles, the better adjusted the child is thought to be. To judge a child's social adjustments fairly, however, one must also take into consideration the *subjective* criteria—how the child feels about being a leader. Most children enjoy the prestige of leadership and are willing to pay the price in terms of extra work and sacrifice of personal desires. They are even willing to give up close, personal friendships in order to be friendly with all who want to be their friends.

As a result of the favorable attitudes of the social group—peers and adults—toward the child who is a leader, the child leader develops a characteristic leader personality, often labeled a "dynamic" personality. This personality pattern is characterized by self-confidence, assertiveness, and an aloofness toward others that is shown in lack of slavish conventionality and lack of close, warm friendships with a few members of the peer group.

Frequently, the child develops feelings of personal superiority, though he soon discovers that these feelings must be well guarded or he will acquire the reputation of having a "swelled head"—a reputation that could quickly lead to the loss of his leadership status. His feeling of superiority is expressed, however, whenever he has to play the role of follower. He finds it difficult to play this role and often tries to tell the leader how to do things (119, 251).

Because every child leader has seen leaders come and go, he is aware of the possibility that this can happen to him too. If he hears grumblings of discontent, if his suggestions are challenged, or if there is outright criticism of him as a person or of the way he is playing the leadership role, much of his satisfaction is counteracted by feelings of anxiety and resentment. Should he be replaced by another leader, his resentments against the group will be greatly increased, and in time he will come to doubt his own leadership ability. Psychological damage is especially likely to occur among children of low socioeconomic backgrounds who find that the leadership roles they once played are later taken over by children of better socioeconomic backgrounds, even though they may not be more competent leaders (224).

Satisfactions and Dissatisfactions from Followership. In the eyes of others, a follower is one who has made poor social adjustments. Every child, sooner or later, becomes aware of this objective judgment. The more emphasis parents and teachers place on "trying to be a leader," the more inadequate and the more resentful the child who is a follower becomes. In time, this leads to a personality pattern that will militate against his being *able* to be a leader, even though he should be selected for such a role. If, for example, a child who has never been selected as leader by the peer group is appointed to a leadership role by a teacher, the chances are that he will not play this role to the satisfaction of the group, even though he has the inherent potentials of a leader. His attitude toward his ability lacks the self-confidence needed for leadership, and his resentments make him behave in an antisocial way toward those who are his followers (138, 225).

This is one of the reasons why adults find it so difficult to develop leadership in children who, according to adult standards, have the potentials of leadership but are not selected by the peer group for this role. Even though the children may like the child and accept him as a member of the peer group, they resent having their prerogative of selecting their leader usurped. This makes them judge the leadership performance of the child more critically than they would have, had they selected him themselves. Furthermore, when they verbalize their criticisms of his leadership and rebel against his suggestions, the child finds the role of leader less satisfying than he had anticipated, and the critical attitude of the group increases his doubts about his leadership abilities.

As a result of such experiences, a child soon develops a "follower complex"—a firmly established belief that he can be nothing but a follower. This often affects his attitude toward accepting a leadership role later, should one be offered him. Studies of adolescent and adult women, for example, have revealed that they shy away from semi-executive or executive roles in business and industry, not because they lack the ability or training for such roles, but because they have developed "follower complexes" during the years when the leadership roles in their classes were held mainly by boys and when they learned that leadership was not sex-appropriate for a girl (132).

How a follower will feel about his role will depend not only on how much he wants to be a leader but also on how he is treated by the leader. If he *wants* to be a leader but is not selected, he will feel more inadequate about his social adjustments than the child who is content to be a follower. He cannot be satisfied with the follower role, however, unless he is satisfied with the way the leader *treats him.*

Young children show their resentment over being "bossed" in their negativism toward the suggestions of adults and in their quarrels with their playmates. A child may not want to be a leader, but, at the same time, he does not want to be bossed by a leader. If the leader is democratic in his techniques, the follower is generally content to let someone else do the work and assume the responsibilities while he reaps the benefits. This will not lead to

feelings of inadequacy, especially if he is popular and gains satisfaction from group acceptance (29, 93).

Unquestionably, a child who enjoys his leadership role and who leads to the satisfaction of the group has made superior social adjustments. If it is a case of "uneasy rests the head that wears the crown," however, and if the child leader is anxious about his ability to hold the group together or retain his status, the success of his social adjustment as judged by *subjective* criteria is inferior to that of the happy, contented follower.

The child who makes the poorest social adjustments of all is the one who is forced to be a follower when he wants to be the leader. Even if he does not show his resentments openly, they will color his attitudes toward the group and toward his participation in the activities the group as a whole enjoys. If, on the other hand, he shows his resentments openly by being a "tearer-downer" who tries to persuade other followers to join his rebellion against the leader and who undermines the morale of the group by his hypercritical, negativistic attitude, he will soon discover that the important members of the group resent him. In time, this will lead to his rejection by the group. Thus, judged both objectively and subjectively, such a child makes the poorest social adjustments.

BIBLIOGRAPHY

(1) ABEGGLEN, J. C.: Personality factors in social mobility: a study of occupationally mobile businessmen. *Genet. Psychol. Monogr.,* 1958, **58**, 101–159.

(2) ABEL, H., and R. SAHINKAYA: Emergence of sex and race friendship preferences. *Child Develpm.,* 1962, **33**, 939–943.

(3) ABERLE, D. F., and K. D. NAEGELE: Middle-class fathers' occupational roles and attitudes toward children. *Amer. J. Orthopsychiat.,* 1952, **22**, 366–378.

(4) ABRAHAMSON, S.: Our status system and scholastic rewards. *J. educ. Sociol.,* 1952, **25**, 441–450.

(5) ALDOUS, K., and L. KELL: A partial list of some theories of identification. *Marriage fam. Liv.,* 1961, **23**, 15–19.

(6) ALLEN, P. J.: The leadership pattern. *Amer. sociol. Rev.,* 1952, **17**, 93–96.

(7) ALLPORT, G. W.: *The nature of prejudice.* Cambridge, Mass.: Addison-Wesley, 1954.

(8) ALT, H.: Basic principles of child rearing in the Soviet Union: first-hand impressions of an American observer. *Amer. J. Orthopsychiat.,* 1958, **28**, 223–240.

(9) AMATORA, SISTER M.: Interests of preadolescent boys and girls. *Genet. Psychol. Monogr.,* 1960, **61**, 77–113.

(10) AMES, L. B.: The sense of self of nursery school children as manifested by their verbal behavior. *J. genet. Psychol.*, 1952, **81**, 193–232.

(11) AMES, L. B., and J. LEARNED: Imaginary companions and related phenomena. *J. genet. Psychol.*, 1946, **69**, 147–167.

(12) ANDERSON, C. A.: A skeptical note on the relation of vertical mobility to education. *Amer. J. Sociol.*, 1961, **66**, 560–570.

(13) ARTER, P. M.: The effects of prejudice on children. *Children*, 1959, **6**, 185–189.

(14) AUSTIN, M. C., and G. G. THOMPSON: Children's friendships: a study of the bases on which children select and reject their best friends. *J. educ. Psychol.*, 1948, **39**, 101–116.

(15) AUSUBEL, D. P., and H. M. SCHIFF: Some intrapersonal and interpersonal determinants of individual differences in socioempathic ability among adolescents. *J. soc. Psychol.*, 1955, **41**, 39–56.

(16) BAGBY, P. H.: Culture and the causes of culture. *Amer. Anthropologist*, 1953, **55**, 535–554.

(17) BAILARD, V.: Developing leadership. *Personnel Guid. J.*, 1953, **32**, 135–138.

(18) BAKER, J. W., and A. HOGWORTH: Social histories of successful and unsuccessful children. *Child Develpm.*, 1961, **32**, 135–149.

(19) BAKWIN, H.: Juvenile delinquency. *J. Pediat.*, 1953, **42**, 387–391; 1954, **44**, 338–342.

(20) BARBE, W. E.: Peer relationships of children of different intelligence levels. *Sch. Soc.*, 1954, **80**, 60–62.

(21) BARCLAY, D.: Friendship's many faces. *The New York Times*, Aug. 13, 1961.

(22) BARCLAY, D.: "No one will play with me." *The New York Times*, Oct. 29, 1961.

(23) BARCLAY, D.: Leads to developing leadership. *The New York Times*, Feb. 4, 1962.

(24) BARON, D.: Personal-social characteristics and classroom social status: a sociometric study of fifth and sixth grade girls. *Sociometry*, 1951, **14**, 32–43.

(25) BARR, J. A., and K. H. HOOVER: Home conditions and influences associated with the development of high school leaders. *Educ. Admin. Superv.*, 1957, **43**, 271–279.

(26) BARRY, H., K. M. BACON, and I. L. CHILD: Cross-cultural survey of some sex differences in socialization. *J. abnorm. soc. Psychol.*, 1957, **55**, 327–332.

(27) BEILIN, H.: The pattern of postponability and its relation to social class mobility. *J. soc. Psychol.*, 1956, **44**, 33–48.

(28) BEILIN, H., and K. V. BERGIN: The social mobility of a limited urban group and some implications for counseling. *Personnel Guid. J.*, 1956, **34**, 544–552.

(29) BELL, G. B., and H. E. HALL: The relationship between leadership and latency. *J. abnorm. soc. Psychol.*, 1954, **49**, 156–157.

(30) BENDIX, R., and F. W. HOWTON: Social mobility and the American business elite. *Brit. J. Sociol.*, 1957, **8**, 357–369; 1958, **9**, 1–14.

(31) BENE, E.: Suppression of heterosexual interest and of aggression by middle class and working class grammar school boys. *Brit. J. educ. Psychol.*, 1958, **28**, 226–231.

(32) BENEDICT, R.: Child rearing in certain European countries. *Amer. J. Orthopsychiat.*, 1949, **19**, 342–350.

(33) BENNETT, E. M., and L. R. COHEN: Men and women: personality patterns and contrasts. *Genet. Psychol. Monogr.*, 1959, **59**, 101–155.

(34) BERKOWITZ, L.: Social desirability and frequency of influence attempts as factors in leadership choice. *J. Pers.*, 1956, **24**, 424–435.

(35) BIEHLER, R. F.: Companion choice in the kindergarten. *Child Develpm.*, 1954, **25**, 45–51.

(36) BJERSTEDT, A.: The interpretation of sociometric status scores in the classroom. *Acta psychologica*, 1956, **12**, 1–14.

(37) BLALOCK, H. M.: Status consciousness: a dimensional analysis. *Soc. Forces*, 1959, **37**, 243–248.

(38) BLAU, P. M.: Occupational bias and mobility. *Amer. sociol. Rev.*, 1957, **22**, 392–399.

(39) BOGEN, I.: Pupil-teacher rapport and teachers' awareness of status structure within the group. *J. educ. Sociol.*, 1954, **28**, 104–114.

(40) BOLL, E. S.: The role of preschool playmates: a situational approach. *Child Develpm.*, 1957, **28**, 327–342.

(41) BONNEY, M. E.: Choosing between the sexes on a sociometric measurement. *J. soc. Psychol.*, 1954, **39**, 99–114.

(42) BORGATTA, E. F., R. F. BALES, and A. S. COUCH: Some findings relevant to the great man theory of leadership. *Amer. sociol. Rev.*, 1954, **19**, 755–759.

(43) BOSSARD, J. H. S., and E. S. BOLL: *The sociology of child development*, 3d ed. New York: Harper & Row, 1960.

(44) BOWER, E. M., T. A. SHELLHAMER, and J. M. DAILEY: School characteristics of male adolescents who later became schizophrenic. *Amer. J. Orthopsychiat.*, 1960, **30**, 712–729.

(45) BOWERMAN, C. E., and J. W. KINCH: Changes in family and peer orientation of children between the fourth and tenth grades. *Soc. Forces*, 1959, **37**, 206–211.

(46) BRANDT, R. M.: The accuracy of self estimate: a measure of concept reality. *Genet. Psychol. Monogr.*, 1958, **58**, 55–59.

(47) BRECKENRIDGE, M. E., and E. L. VINCENT: *Child development*, 4th ed. Philadelphia: Saunders, 1960.

(48) BRIELAND, D.: A variation of the "guess who" technique for the study of the adjustment of children. *J. educ. Res.*, 1952, **45,** 385–390.

(49) BRODERICK, C. B., and S. E. FOWLER: New patterns of relationships between the sexes among preadolescents. *Marriage fam. Liv.*, 1961, **23,** 27–30.

(50) BROWN, A. W., and R. G. HUNT: Relations between nursery school attendance and teachers' ratings of some aspects of children's adjustment in kindergarten. *Child Develpm.*, 1961, **32,** 585–596.

(51) BROWN, D. G.: Masculinity-femininity development in children. *J. consult. Psychol.*, 1957, **21,** 197–202.

(52) BROWN, W. H., and L. B. BOND: Social stratification in a sixth grade class. *J. educ. Res.*, 1955, **8,** 539–543.

(53) BROWNFIELD, E. D.: Communication—key to dynamics of family interaction. *Marriage fam. Liv.*, 1953, **15,** 316–319.

(54) BUCHER, C. A.: The atomic age strikes youth. *Education*, 1955, **76,** 203–205.

(55) BUGENTAL, D. E., and G. F. J. LEHNER: Accuracy of self-perception and group-perception as related to two leadership roles. *J. abnorm. soc. Psychol.*, 1958, **56,** 396–398.

(56) BÜHLER, C.: School as a phase of human life. *Education*, 1952, **73,** 219–222.

(57) BURCHINAL, L., B. GARDNER, and G. R. HAWKES: Children's personality adjustment and the socio-economic status of their families. *J. genet. Psychol.*, 1958, **92,** 149–159.

(58) BURGESS, E. W.: Social relations, activities, and personal adjustment. *Amer. J. Sociol.*, 1954, **59,** 352–360.

(59) BUSWELL, M. M.: The relationship between the social structure of the classroom and the academic success of pupils. *J. exp. Educ.*, 1953, **22,** 37–52.

(60) CAMPBELL, W. J.: Preferences of children for others of the same or opposite sex. *Aust. J. Psychol.*, 1955, **7,** 45–51.

(61) CANNON, K. L., R. STAPLES, and I. CARLSON: Personal appearance as a factor in social acceptance. *J. home Econ.*, 1952, **44,** 710–713.

(62) CAPPE, D.: Types of story books enjoyed by kindergarten children. *J. educ. Res.*, 1956, **49,** 555–557.

(63) CARSLEY, J. D.: The interests of children (ages 10–11) in books. *Brit. J. educ. Psychol.*, 1957, **27,** 13–23.

(64) CASSEL, R. N., and R. G. SAUGSTAD: Level of aspiration and sociometric distance. *Sociometry*, 1952, **15,** 318–325.

(65) CATTELL, R. B., and G. F. STICE: Four formulae for selecting leaders on the basis of personality. *Hum. Rel.*, 1954, **7,** 493–507.

(66) CHAPIN, P. S.: Sociometric stars as isolates. *Amer. J. Sociol.*, 1950, **56,** 263–267.

(67) CHILD, I. L.: Socialization. In G. Lindzey (Ed.), *Handbook of social psychology*. Cam-

bridge, Mass.: Addison-Wesley, 1954. Pp. 655–692.

(68) CHRISTIANSON, H. M., M. L. ROGERS, and B. A. LUDLUM: *The nursery school: adventure in living and learning*. Boston: Houghton Mifflin, 1961.

(69) CHWAST, J.: Value conflicts in treating delinquents. *Children*, 1959, **6,** 95–100.

(70) CLARK, R. A., and C. MC GUIRE: Sociographic analysis of sociometric valuations. *Child Develpm.*, 1952, **23,** 129–140.

(71) COMMOSS, H. H.: Some characteristics related to social isolation of second grade children. *J. educ. Psychol.*, 1962, **53,** 38–42.

(72) CONN, J. H.: Children's awareness of sex differences. II. Play attitudes and game preferences. *J. child Psychiat.*, 1951, **2,** 82–99.

(73) COOK, E. S.: An analysis of factors related to withdrawal from high school prior to graduation. *J. educ. Res.*, 1956, **50,** 191–196.

(74) COX, F. N.: Sociometric status and individual adjustment before and after play therapy. *J. abnorm. soc. Psychol.*, 1953, **48,** 354–356.

(75) CRANDALL, V. J., A. PRESTON, and A. RABSON: Maternal reactions and the development of independence and achievement behavior in young children. *Child Develpm.*, 1960, **31,** 243–251.

(76) CRANE, A. R.: Pre-adolescent gangs: a sociopsychological interpretation. *J. genet. Psychol.*, 1955, **86,** 275–279.

(77) CROFT, I. J., and T. G. GRYGIER: Social relationships of truants and juvenile delinquents. *Hum. Rel.*, 1956, **9,** 439–466.

(78) CUNNINGHAM, R.: *Group behavior of boys and girls*. New York: Teachers College, Columbia University, 1951.

(79) CURTIS, R. F.: Occupational mobility and urban social life. *Amer. J. Sociol.*, 1959, **65,** 296–298.

(80) DAHLKE, H. O.: Determinants of sociometric relations among children in the elementary school. *Sociometry*, 1953, **16,** 327–338.

(81) DAVIDS, A., and A. N. PARENTI: Personality, social choice, and adults' perception of these factors in groups of disturbed and normal children. *Sociometry*, 1958, **21,** 212–224.

(82) DAVIS, A.: Personality and social mobility. *Sch. Rev.*, 1957, **65,** 134–143.

(83) DAVIS, A., and R. J. HAVIGHURST: *Father of the man*. Boston: Houghton Mifflin, 1947.

(84) DAVITZ, J. R.: Social perception and sociometric choice of children. *J. abnorm. soc. Psychol.*, 1955, **50,** 173–176.

(85) DE HAAN, R. F.: Social leadership. In *57th Yearb. Nat. Soc. Stud. Educ.*, 1958, Pt. 2. Pp. 127–243.

(86) DENHOFF, E.: The physically handicapped child in the nursery school. *Except. Children*, 1954, **20,** 202–208.

(87) DENNIS, W.: A cross-cultural study of the

reinforcement of child behavior. *Child Develpm.*, 1957, **28**, 431–438.

(88) DEVAULT, M. V.: Classroom sociometric mutual pairs and residential proximity. *J. educ. Res.*, 1957, **50**, 605–610.

(89) DEXTER, E. S.: Three items related to personality: popularity, nicknames, and homesickness. *J. soc. Psychol.*, 1949, **30**, 155–158.

(90) DIAMOND, S.: Sex stereotypes and acceptance of sex roles. *J. Psychol.*, 1955, **39**, 385–388.

(91) DINEEN, M. A., and R. GARRY: Effect of sociometric seating on a classroom cleavage. *Elem. Sch. J.*, 1956, **56**, 358–362.

(92) DOWNIE, N. M.: A comparison between children who have moved with those who have been in continuous residence on various factors of adjustment. *J. educ. Psychol.*, 1953, **44**, 50–53.

(93) DUFF, J. C.: Quest for leaders. *J. educ. Sociol.*, 1958, **32**, 91–95.

(94) DUKES, W. F.: Psychological studies of values. *Psychol. Bull.*, 1955, **52**, 24–50.

(95) DUNNINGTON, M. J.: Behavioral differences of sociometric status groups in a nursery school. *Child Develpm.*, 1957, **28**, 103–111.

(96) DYMOND, R. F., A. S. HUGHES, and V. L. RAABE: Measurable changes in empathy with age. *J. consult. Psychol.*, 1952, **16**, 202–206.

(97) ELKIN, F.: Socialization and the presentation of self. *Marriage fam. Liv.*, 1958, **20**, 320–325.

(98) ELKINS, D.: Some factors related to the choice-status of ninety eighth-grade children in a school society. *Genet. Psychol. Monogr.*, 1958, **58**, 207–272.

(99) ERIKSON, E.: *Childhood and society.* New York: Norton, 1950.

(100) FARBER, M. L.: English and Americans: values in the socialization process. *J. Psychol.*, 1953, **36**, 243–250.

(101) FEINBERG, M. R., M. SMITH, and R. SCHMIDT: An analysis of expressions used by adolescents at varying economic levels to describe accepted and rejected peers. *J. genet. Psychol.*, 1958, **93**, 133–148.

(102) FEY, W. F.: Acceptance by others and its relation to acceptance of self and others: a revaluation. *J. abnorm. soc. Psychol.*, 1955, **50**, 274–276.

(103) FIELDER, F. E.: A note on leadership theory: the effect of social barriers between leaders and followers. *Sociometry*, 1957, **20**, 87–94.

(104) FLANDERS, N. A., and S. HAVUMAKI: The effect of teacher-pupil contacts involving praise on the sociometric choices of students. *J. educ. Psychol.*, 1960, **51**, 65–68.

(105) FORLANO, G., and J. W. WRIGHTSTONE: Measuring the quality of social acceptability within a class. *Educ. psychol. Measmt*, 1955, **15**, 127–136.

(106) FRANK, L. K., and M. H. FRANK: Teachers' attitudes affect children's relationships. *Education*, 1954, **75**, 6–12.

(107) FRENCH, E. G., and I. CHADWICK: Some characteristics of the affiliation motivation. *J. abnorm. soc. Psychol.*, 1956, **52**, 296–300.

(108) FROMM-REICHMANN, F.: Loneliness. *Psychiatry*, 1959, **22**, 1–15.

(109) GALLAGHER, J. J.: Peer acceptance of highly gifted children in elementary school. *Elem. Sch. J.*, 1958, **58**, 465–470.

(110) GARDNER, G.: Functional leadership and popularity in small groups. *Hum. Rel.*, 1956, **9**, 491–509.

(111) GERARD, H. B.: Some effects of status, role clarity and group goal clarity upon the individual's relations to group process. *J. Pers.*, 1957, **25**, 475–488.

(112) GESELL, A., F. L. ILG, and L. B. AMES: *Youth: the years from ten to sixteen.* New York: Harper & Row, 1956.

(113) GOERTZEN, S. M.: Factors relating to opinions of seventh grade children regarding the acceptability of certain behaviors in the peer group. *J. genet. Psychol.*, 1959, **94**, 29–34.

(114) GOLD, M.: Power in the classroom. *Sociometry*, 1958, **21**, 50–60.

(115) GOLDSCHMIDT, W.: Social class in America: a critical review. *Amer. Anthropologist*, 1950, **52**, 483–498.

(116) GOLDSTEIN, A.: Aggression and hostility in the elementary school in low socioeconomic areas. *Understanding the Child*, 1955, **24**, 20–21.

(117) GOODCHILDS, J. D.: Effects of being witty on position in the social structure of a small group. *Sociometry*, 1959, **22**, 261–272.

(118) GOODENOUGH, E. W.: Interest in persons as an aspect of sex differences in the early years. *Genet. Psychol. Monogr.*, 1957, **55**, 287–323.

(119) GORDON, L. V.: Personal factors in leadership. *J. soc. Psychol.*, 1952, **36**, 245–248.

(120) GOUGH, H. G.: Identifying psychological femininity. *Educ. psychol. Measmt*, 1952, **12**, 427–439.

(121) GOUGH, H. G.: On making a good impression. *J. educ. Res.*, 1952, **16**, 33–42.

(122) GRACE, H. A., and N. L. BOOTH: Is the "gifted" child a social isolate? *Peabody J. Educ.*, 1958, **35**, 195–196.

(123) GRAY, S. W.: Masculinity and femininity in relation to anxiety and social acceptance. *Child Develpm.*, 1957, **28**, 203–214.

(124) GREEN, T. L.: The cultural determination of personality in Ceylon. *Sch. Soc.*, 1952, **75**, 164–166.

(125) GRONLUND, N. E., and L. ANDERSON: Personality characteristics of socially accepted, socially neglected, and socially rejected junior high school pupils. *Educ. Admin. Superv.*, 1957, **43**, 329–338.

(126) GRONLUND, N. E., and W. S. HOLMLUND: The value of elementary school sociometric status scores for predicting pupils' adjustment in high school. *Educ. Admin. Superv.*, 1958, **44**, 255–260.

(127) GRONLUND, N. E., and A. P. WHITNEY: Relation between pupils' social acceptability in the classroom, in the school, and in the neighborhood. *Sch. Rev.*, 1956, **64**, 267–271.

(128) GROSSMAN, B., and J. WRIGHTER: The relation between selection-rejection and intelligence, social status and personality amongst sixth grade children. *Sociometry*, 1948, **11**, 346–355.

(129) GUINOUARD, D. E., and J. F. RYCHLAK: Personality correlates of sociometric popularity in elementary school children. *Personnel Guid. J.*, 1962, **40**, 438–444.

(130) HARE, A.: Situational differences in leader behavior. *J. abnorm. soc. Psychol.*, 1957, **55**, 132–135.

(131) HARRIS, D. B., A. M. ROSE, K. E. CLARK, and F. VALASEK: Personality differences between responsible and less responsible children. *J. genet. Psychol.*, 1955, **87**, 103–106.

(132) HARRIS, D. B., and S. C. TSENG: Children's attitudes toward peers and parents as revealed by sentence completions. *Child Develpm.*, 1957, **28**, 401–411.

(133) HARTLEY, R. E.: Sex role pressures and the socialization of the male child. *Psychol. Rep.*, 1959, **5**, 457–468.

(134) HARTLEY, R. E., and S. A. KLEIN: Sex-role concepts among elementary-school-age girls. *Marriage fam. Liv.*, 1959, **21**, 59–64.

(135) HARTUP, W. W., and E. D. KELLER: Nurturance in preschool children and its relation to dependency. *Child Develpm.*, 1960, **31**, 681–689.

(136) HAVIGHURST, R. J.: *Human development and education.* New York: Longmans, 1953.

(137) HEATHERS, G.: Acquiring dependence and independence: a theoretical orientation. *J. genet. Psychol.*, 1955, **87**, 277–291.

(138) HIGGIN, G.: The effect of reference group functions on social status ratings. *Brit. J. Psychol.*, 1954, **45**, 88–93.

(139) HILGARD, E. R.: *Introduction to psychology,* 3d ed. New York: Harcourt, Brace & World, 1962.

(140) HILLIARD, P.: *Improving social learnings in the elementary school.* New York: Teachers College, Columbia University, 1954.

(141) HOLLANDER, E. P., and W. B. WEBB: Leadership, fellowship, and friendship: an analysis of peer nominations. *J. abnorm. soc. Psychol.*, 1955, **50**, 163–167.

(142) HONIGMANN, J. J.: *Culture and personality.* New York: Harper & Row, 1954.

(143) HONZIK, M. P.: Sex differences in the occurrence of materials in the play constructions of preadolescents. *Child Develpm.*, 1951, **22**, 15–35.

(144) HORROCKS, J. E., and M. E. BUKER: A study of the friendship fluctuations of preadolescents. *J. genet. Psychol.*, 1951, **78**, 131–144.

(145) HUGHES, J. H., and G. G. THOMPSON: A comparison of the value systems of Southern Negro and Northern white youth. *J. educ. Psychol.*, 1954, **45**, 300–309.

(146) HUNT, R. G., and V. SYNNERDAHL: Social influence among children. *Sociol. soc. Res.*, 1959, **43**, 171–174.

(147) HUREWITZ, P.: The neutral isolate: some personality, behavioral, and role perception dynamics compared with a group of sociometric leaders. *Dissert. Abstr.*, 1961, **22**, Pt. 1, 6630.

(148) ILG, F. L., J. LEARNED, A. LOCKWOOD, and L. B. AMES: The three-and-a-half-year-old. *J. genet. Psychol.*, 1949, **75**, 21–31.

(149) IZARD, C. E.: Personality similarity and friendship. *J. abnorm. soc. Psychol.*, 1960, **61**, 47–51.

(150) JERSILD, A. T.: *Child psychology,* 5th ed. Englewood Cliffs, N.J.: Prentice-Hall, 1960.

(151) JOSSELYN, I. M.: Cultural forces, motherliness and fatherliness. *Amer. J. Orthopsychiat.*, 1956, **26**, 264–271.

(152) KAFFMAN, M.: Evaluation of emotional disturbance in 403 Israeli kibbutz children. *Amer. J. Psychiat.*, 1961, **117**, 732–738.

(153) KANOUS, L. E., R. A. DAUGHERTY, and T. S. COHN: Relation between heterosexual friendship choices and socioeconomic level. *Child Develpm.*, 1962, **33**, 251–255.

(154) KATES, S. L., and L. N. DIAB: Authoritarian ideology and attitudes on parent-child relationships. *J. abnorm. soc. Psychol.*, 1955, **51**, 13–16.

(155) KATZ, E., P. M. BLAU, M. L. BROWN, and F. L. STRODBECK: Leadership stability and social change: an experiment with small groups. *Sociometry*, 1957, **20**, 36–50.

(156) KEISLAR, E. R.: Girls' social groups rate each other. *Calif. J. educ. Res.*, 1953, **4**, 227–232.

(157) KERCKHOFF, A. C., and T. C. MC CORMICK: Marginal status and marginal personality. *Soc. Forces*, 1955, **34**, 48–55.

(158) KINNEY, E. E.: A study of peer group acceptability at the fifth grade level in a public school. *J. educ. Res.*, 1953, **47**, 57–64.

(159) KIPNIS, D.: The effects of leadership style and leadership power upon the inducement of an attitude change. *J. abnorm. soc. Psychol.*, 1958, **57**, 173–180.

(160) KOCH, H. L.: The relation of certain formal attributes of siblings to attitudes held toward each other and toward their parents. *Monogr. Soc. Res. Child Develpm.*, 1960, **25**, No. 4.

(161) KOHN, M. L.: Social class and parental values. *Amer. J. Sociol.*, 1959, **64**, 337–351.

(162) KORNER, I. N.: Of values, value lag, and

mental health. *Amer. Psychologist*, 1956, **11**, 543–546.

(163) LAMBERT, W. W., L. M. TRIANDIS, and M. WOLF: Some correlates of beliefs in the malevolence and benevolence of supernatural beings: a cross-societal study. *J. abnorm. soc. Psychol.*, 1959, **58**, 162–169.

(164) LANGFORD, L. M., and O. W. ALM: A comparison of parent judgments and child feelings concerning the self adjustment and social adjustment of twelve-year-old children. *J. genet. Psychol.*, 1954, **85**, 39–46.

(165) LATHAM, A. J.: The relationship between pubertal status and leadership in junior-high-school boys. *J. genet. Psychol.*, 1951, **78**, 185–194.

(166) LAUGHLIN, F.: *A study of the peer status of sixth and seventh grade children.* New York: Teachers College, Columbia University, 1953.

(167) LENSKI, G. E.: Trends in inter-generational occupational mobility in the United States. *Amer. sociol. Rev.*, 1958, **23**, 514–523.

(168) LESSER, G.: The relationship between various forms of aggression and popularity among lower-class children. *J. educ. Psychol.*, 1959, **50**, 20–25.

(169) LEVINSON, B. M.: The inner life of the extremely gifted child, as seen from the clinical setting. *J. genet. Psychol.*, 1961, **99**, 83–88.

(170) LEWIS, E.: The function of group play during middle childhood in developing the ego complex. *Brit. J. med. Psychol.*, 1954, **27**, 15–29.

(171) LIDDLE, G.: Overlap among desirable and undesirable characteristics in gifted children. *J. educ. Psychol.*, 1958, **49**, 219–228.

(172) LITWAK, E.: Occupational mobility and extended family cohesion. *Amer. sociol. Rev.*, 1960, **25**, 9–21.

(173) LLOYD-JONES, E.: Women today and their education. *Teach. Coll. Rec.*, 1955, **57**, 1–7.

(174) LOTT, B. E., and A. J. LOTT: The formation of positive attitudes toward group members. *J. abnorm. soc. Psychol.*, 1960, **61**, 297–300.

(175) LUCK, J. M.: A study of peer relationships. *Group*, 1955, **17**, 13–20.

(176) LUFT, J.: Monetary value and the perception of persons. *J. soc. Psychol.*, 1957, **46**, 245–257.

(177) LUNDY, R. M., W. KATKOVSKY, R. L. CROMWELL, and D. J. SCHOEMAKER: Self acceptability and descriptions of sociometric choices. *J. abnorm. soc. Psychol.*, 1955, **51**, 260–262.

(178) LYNN, R.: Personality characteristics of the mothers of aggressive and unaggressive children. *J. genet. Psychol.*, 1961, **99**, 159–164.

(179) MACCOBY, E. E.: Role-taking in children and its consequences for social learning. *Child Develpm.*, 1959, **30**, 239–252.

(180) MACFARLANE, J., L. ALLEN, and M. P. HONZIK: *A developmental study of the behavior problems of normal children between twenty-one months and fourteen years.* Berkeley, Calif.: University of California Press, 1954.

(181) MARSHALL, H. R.: Relations between home experiences and children's use of language in play interaction with peers. *Psychol. Monogr.*, 1961, **75**, No. 5.

(182) MARSHALL, H. R.: Training adults to judge children's social acceptance. *J. educ. Psychol.*, 1962, **53**, 27–31.

(183) MARTIN, W. E.: Learning theory and identification. **III.** The development of values in children. *J. genet. Psychol.*, 1954, **84**, 211–217.

(184) MARTIN, W. E., N. GROSS, and J. G. DARLEY: Studies of group behavior: leaders, followers, and isolates in small organized groups. *J. abnorm. soc. Psychol.*, 1952, **47**, 838–842.

(185) MASON, B. D.: Leadership in the fourth grade. *Sociol. soc. Res.*, 1952, **36**, 239–245.

(186) MATSUMATO, M., and H. T. SMITH: Japanese and American children's perception of parents. *J. genet. Psychol.*, 1961, **98**, 83–88.

(187) MC CANDLESS, B. R., C. B. BILOUS, and H. L. BENNETT: Peer popularity and dependence on adults in preschool age socialization. *Child Develpm.*, 1961, **32**, 511–518.

(188) MC CANDLESS, B. R., and J. M. HOYT: Sex, ethnicity, and play preferences of preschool children. *J. abnorm. soc. Psychol.*, 1961, **62**, 683–685.

(189) MC CORD, J., and W. MC CORD: The effects of parental role model on criminality. *J. soc. Issues*, 1958, **14**, No. 3, 66–74.

(190) MC GUIRE, C.: Family and age-mates in personality formation. *Marriage fam. Liv.*, 1953, **15**, 17–23.

(191) MC GUIRE, C., and G. D. WHITE: Social-class influences on discipline at school. *Educ. Leadership*, 1957, **14**, 229–231, 234–236.

(192) MEDINNUS, G. R.: An examination of several correlates of sociometric status in a first grade group. *J. genet. Psychol.*, 1962, **101**, 3–13.

(193) MILES, K. A.: Relationship between certain factors in the home background and the quality of leadership shown by children. Reported by J. E. Anderson, Parents' attitudes on child behavior: a report of three studies. *Child Develpm.*, 1946, **17**, 91–97.

(194) MC KEE, J. P., and F. B. LEADER: The relationship of socioeconomic status and aggression to the competitive behavior of preschool children. *Child Develpm.*, 1955, **26**, 135–142.

(195) MILLER, R. V.: Social status and socio-empathic differences. *Except. Children*, 1956, **23**, 114–119.

(196) MILLER, W. B.: Lower class culture as a

generating milieu in gang delinquency. *J. soc. Issues,* 1958, **14,** No. 3, 5–19.

(197) MISCHEL, M.: Preference for delayed reinforcement: an experimental study of a cultural observation. *J. abnorm. soc. Psychol.,* 1958, **56,** 57–61.

(198) MONTAGUE, J. B.: A study of anxiety among English and American boys. *Amer. sociol. Rev.,* 1955, **20,** 685–689.

(199) MOSHER, D. L., and A. SCODEL: Relationships between ethnocentrism in children and ethnocentrism and authoritarian rearing practices of their mothers. *Child Develpm.,* 1960, **31,** 369–376.

(200) MOSS, H. A., and J. KAGAN: Stability of achievement and recognition seeking behaviors from early childhood through adulthood. *J. abnorm. soc. Psychol.,* 1961, **62,** 504–513.

(201) MOUSTAKAS, C. E.: The frequency and intensity of negative attitudes expressed in play therapy: a comparison of well-adjusted and disturbed young children. *J. genet. Psychol.,* 1955, **86,** 309–325.

(202) MOYER, K. E., and B. VON H. GILMER: Experimental study of children's preferences and use of blocks in play. *J. genet. Psychol.,* 1958, **89,** 3–10.

(203) MULDOON, J. F.: The concentration of liked and disliked members in groups and the relationship of concentration to group cohesiveness. *Sociometry,* 1955, **18,** 73–81.

(204) MUNSON, B. E.: Personality differentials among urban, suburban, town, and rural children. *Rur. Sociol.,* 1959, **24,** 257–264.

(205) MUSSEN, P. H., J. J. CONGER, and J. KAGAN: *Child development and personality,* 2d ed. New York: Harper & Row, 1963.

(206) NAEGELE, K. N.: Friendship and acquaintances: an exploration of some social distinctions. *Harv. educ. Rev.,* 1958, **28,** 232–252.

(207) NAM, C. B.: Nationality groups and social stratification in America. *Soc. Forces,* 1959, **37,** 328–333.

(208) NEIMAN, L. J.: The influence of peer group upon attitude toward the feminine role. *Soc. Probl.,* 1954, **2,** 104–111.

(209) NORTHWAY, M. E., and M. MC C. ROOKS: Creativity and sociometric status in children. *Sociometry,* 1955, **18,** 450–456.

(210) OPLER, M. L.: The influence of ethnic and class subcultures on child care. *Soc. Probl.,* 1955, **3,** 12–21.

(211) OPPENHEIM, A. N.: Social status and clique formation among grammar school boys. *Brit. J. Sociol.,* 1955, **6,** 228–245.

(212) ORZACK, L. H.: Preference and prejudice patterns among rural and urban schoolmates. *Rur. Sociol.,* 1956, **21,** 29–33.

(213) PHILLIPS, B. E.: Impact of pupil mobility on the schools. *Educ. Admin. Superv.,* 1957, **43,** 101–107.

(214) PHILLIPS, E. L., S. SHENKER, and P. REVITZ: The assimilation of the new child into the group. *Psychiatry,* 1951, **14,** 319–325.

(215) POPE, B.: Socio-economic contrasts in children's peer culture values. *Genet. Psychol. Monogr.,* 1953, **48,** 157–220.

(216) PROTHRO, E. T.: Arab students' choices of ways to live. *J. soc. Psychol.,* 1958, **47,** 3–7.

(217) RABBAN, M.: Sex-role identification in young children in two diverse social groups. *Genet. Psychol. Monogr.,* 1950, **42,** 81–158.

(218) REEVES, J. M., and L. GOLDMAN: Social class perceptions and school maladjustment. *Personnel Guid. J.,* 1957, **35,** 414–419.

(219) REISMAN, D.: Permissiveness and sex roles. *Marriage fam. Liv.,* 1959, **21,** 211–217.

(220) ROSE, A. M.: Distance of migration and socioeconomic status of migrants. *Amer. sociol. Rev.,* 1958, **23,** 420–423.

(221) ROSENBERG, B. G., and B. SUTTON: A revised conception of masculine-feminine differences in play activities. *J. genet. Psychol.,* 1960, **96,** 165–170.

(222) ROSENTHAL, F.: Some relationships between sociometric position and language structure of young children. *J. educ. Res.,* 1957, **48,** 483–497.

(223) ROSENTHAL, S.: A fifth grade classroom experiment in fostering mental health. *J. child Psychiat.,* 1952, **2,** 302–329.

(224) SATTERLEE, R. L.: Sociometric analysis and personality adjustment. *Calif. J. educ. Res.,* 1955, **6,** 181–184.

(225) SCHIFF, H.: Judgmental response sets in the perception of sociometric status. *Sociometry,* 1954, **17,** 207–227.

(226) SCHORR, A. L.: Mobile family living. *Soc. Casewk,* 1956, **37,** 175–180.

(227) SCHMUCK, R. A.: Upward mobility and I.Q. performance. *J. educ. Res.,* 1961, **55,** 123–127.

(228) SEARS, P. S.: Child-rearing factors related to playing of sex-typed roles. *Amer. Psychologist,* 1953, **8,** 431.

(229) SEARS, R. R., E. E. MACCOBY, and H. LEVIN: *Patterns of child rearing.* New York: Harper & Row, 1957.

(230) SEWELL, W. H., and A. O. HALLER: Social status and the personality adjustment of the child. *Sociometry,* 1956, **19,** 114–125.

(231) SHERRIFFS, A. C., and R. F. JARRETT: Sex differences in attitudes about sex differences. *J. Psychol.,* 1953, **35,** 161–168.

(232) SILBERSTEIN, F. B., and M. SEEMAN: Social mobility and prejudice. *Amer. J. Sociol.,* 1959, **65,** 258–264.

(233) SINGER, A.: Certain aspects of personality and their relations to certain group modes and constancy of friendship choice. *J. educ. Res.,* 1951, **45,** 33–42.

(234) SPERLING, O. E.: An imaginary playmate representing a pre-stage of the super-ego. *Psychoanal. Stud. Child.,* 1954, **9,** 252–258.

(235) SPEROFF, B. J.: The stability of sociometric choice among kindergarten children. *Sociometry*, 1955, **10**, 129–131.

(236) SPINDLER, D. G., and L. S. SPINDLER: American Indian personality types and their socio-cultural roots. *Ann. Amer. Acad. Pol. Soc. Sci.*, 1957, **311**, 147–157.

(237) STENDLER, C. B.: Social class differences in parental attitude toward school at grade 1 level. *Child Develpm.*, 1951, **22**, 37–46.

(238) STENDLER, C. B.: The learning of certain secondary drives by Parisian and American children. *Marriage fam. Liv.*, 1954, **16**, 195–200.

(239) STOTLAND, E., S. THORNLEY, E. THOMAS, A. R. COHEN, and A. ZANDER: The effects of group expectations and self-esteem upon self-evaluation. *J. abnorm. soc. Psychol.*, 1957, **54**, 55–63.

(240) STOUFFER, G. A. W., and J. OWENS: Behavior problems identified by today's teachers and compared with E. K. Wickman. *J. educ. Res.*, 1955, **48**, 321–331.

(241) STRANG, R.: How children and adolescents view their world. *Ment. Hyg., N.Y.*, 1954, **38**, 28–33.

(242) STRAUSS, A. L.: The learning of roles and of concepts as twin processes. *J. genet. Psychol.*, 1956, **88**, 211–217.

(243) STUBBEFIELD, R. L.: Children's emotional problems aggravated by family moves. *Amer. J. Orthopsychiat.*, 1955, **25**, 120–126.

(244) SULLENGER, T. E., L. H. PARKS, and W. K. WALLIN: The leisure time activities of elementary school children. *J. educ. Res.*, 1953, **46**, 551–554.

(245) SUTTON-SMITH, B., and P. GUMP: Games and status experience. *Recreation*, 1955, **48**, 172–174.

(246) SUTTON-SMITH, B., and B. G. ROSENBERG: Peer perceptions of impulsive behavior. *Merrill-Palmer Quart.*, 1961, **7**, 233–238.

(247) SWITZER, R. E., J. C. HIRSCHBERG, L. MYERS, E. GRAY, N. H. EVERS, and R. FORMAN: The effect of family moves on children. *Ment. Hyg., N.Y.*, 1961, **45**, 528–536.

(248) TAFT, R.: The ability to judge people. *Psychol. Bull.*, 1955, **52**, 1–23.

(249) TAYLOR, E. A.: Some factors relating to social acceptance in eighth grade classrooms. *J. educ. Psychol.*, 1952, **43**, 257–272.

(250) TAYLOR, F. K.: Awareness of one's social appeal. *Hum. Rel.*, 1956, **9**, 47–56.

(251) TERRELL, G., and J. SHREFFLER: A developmental study of leadership. *J. educ. Res.*, 1958, **52**, 69–72.

(252) THOMPSON, G. G., and R. NISHIMURA: Some determinants of friendship. *Amer. Psychologist*, 1950, **5**, 309–310.

(253) THORPE, J. G.: An investigation into some correlates of sociometric status within school classes. *Sociometry*, 1955, **18**, 49–53.

(254) TUDDENHAM, R. D.: Studies in reputation. III. Correlates of popularity among elementary school children. *J. educ. Psychol.*, 1951, **42**, 257–276.

(255) TUMIN, M. M.: Some unapplauded consequences of social mobility in a mass society. *Soc. Forces*, 1957, **36**, 32–37.

(256) TYLER, L. E.: The relationship of interests to abilities and reputation among first-grade children. *Educ. psychol. Measmt*, 1951, **11**, 255–264.

(257) WALL, H. R.: A differential analysis of some intellective and affective characteristics of peer accepted and peer rejected preadolescent children. *Dissertation Abstr.*, 1961, **21**, 2790.

(258) WALTERS, J., D. PEARCE, and L. DAHMS: Affectional and aggressive behavior of preschool children. *Child Develpm.*, 1957, **28**, 15–26.

(259) WALTERS, R. H., W. E. MARSHALL, and J. R. SHOOTER: Anxiety, isolation and susceptibility to social influence. *J. Pers.*, 1960, **28**, 518–529.

(260) WEISS, W.: An examination of attitude toward Negroes. *J. soc. Psychol.*, 1961, **55**, 3–21.

(261) WEST, S. S.: Sibling configuration of scientists. *Amer. J. Sociol.*, 1960, **66**, 268–274.

(262) WESTOFF, C. F., M. BRESSLER, and P. C. SAGI: The concept of social mobility: an empirical inquiry. *Amer. sociol. Rev.*, 1960, **25**, 375–385.

(263) WILLIAMS, M. F.: Acceptance and performance among gifted and elementary school children. *Educ. Res. Bull.*, 1958, **37**, 216–220, 224.

(264) WINGFIELD, R. C.: Bernreuter personality ratings of college students who recall having had imaginary playmates during childhood. *J. child Psychiat.*, 1948, **1**, 90–94.

(265) WITRYOL, S. L., and J. E. CALKINS: Marginal social values of rural school children. *J. genet. Psychol.*, 1958, **92**, 81–93.

(266) WITRYOL, S. L., and G. G. THOMPSON: A critical review of the stability of social acceptability scores obtained with the partial-rank-order and the paired-comparison scales. *Genet. Psychol. Monogr.*, 1953, **48**, 221–260.

(267) WITTENBERG, R. M., and J. BERG: The stranger in the group. *Amer. J. Orthopsychiat.*, 1952, **22**, 89–97.

(268) WOLMAN, B.: Leadership and group dynamics. *J. soc. Psychol.*, 1956, **42**, 11–25.

(269) ZILLER, R. C., and R. D. BEHRINGER: A longitudinal study of the assimilation of the new child in the group. *Hum. Rel.*, 1961, **14**, 121–133.

PLAY

Play is a term so loosely used that its real significance is apt to be lost. It is any activity engaged in for the enjoyment it gives, without consideration of the end result. It is entered into voluntarily and is lacking in external force or compulsion. *Work* is an activity toward an end; the individual carries out the activity, not necessarily because he enjoys it, but because he wants the end result. Work may be done voluntarily or involuntarily. *Drudgery*—work that is imposed on the individual by others—has no element in common with play; it is not engaged in voluntarily, nor is its end result important to the person.

Play versus Work. Although many people try to make a distinction between work and play activities, there are no activities that may be classed exclusively as either. Whether an activity belongs in one category or the other depends not upon the activity itself but upon the individual's *attitude* toward it (157). Collecting, for example, is a form of play for a child or an adult who makes it a hobby, but it is work for the person who collects articles to sell for a profit. Similarly, drawing may be a pleasant pastime, but if the motive is to enter one's drawings in a contest or to earn a living as an artist, drawing becomes a form of work.

Any activity that is directed toward an end other than enjoyment cannot rightly be called "play." Games and sports are "play" to young children because the thought of winning or competing with others does not enter in; the only aim is to have fun. As children grow older, however, competition between gangs becomes important, and games or sports then become highly competitive. As a result, these activities become more like work than play. Beating the rival gang is more important than the enjoyment derived from the activity. Likewise, in junior and senior high school, competition with other schools or with other classes emphasizes the end result—winning—rather than the fun of playing.

Children distinguish between work and play on the basis of *exterior conditions.* Work is class activity or chores done around the house, while play is everything else. To them, play means doing what *they want to do,* while work means doing things *they have to do.* Bright children emphasize that work is useful activity, while play is useless; work is a serious activity requiring application and attention, while play is a restful and easy activity (37, 108). Bright children thus come closer to the adult distinction between work and play than children of average intelligence.

Adults regard play as a means of gaining pleasure; they look upon leisure activities as a change from their usual work activities. Much of the pleasure they gain from leisure-time activities comes from being able to do what they want to do rather than what they must do. They may want to be creative—to achieve something that will give them satisfaction—or they may merely want to be with their friends. Thus, what they do in their leisure time is regarded as "play," but how they play will depend upon what gives them enjoyment (44, 72). Figure 10–1 shows that an activity may be "play," "work," or "drudgery."

Relative Time Spent in Work and Play. Although adults from the upper social classes may have an unusual amount of free time, they do not always spend it in play; much of the community and charity work is car-ried on by volunteer workers from the upper social classes who feel these activities make some contribution to persons less fortunate than they. Adults of the lower social classes, owing to the short workweek and the many laborsaving devices of today, have more time to spend as they wish than is used for work. Because relatively few people from the lower social classes engage in community activities, they have proportionally more playtime than members of the upper or middle social classes (1, 12, 72).

The same is true for children. Much of the free time of upper-class children is devoted to activities their parents believe will prepare them for successful social adjustments, such as music, dancing, or skating lessons (38). In the home, they are expected to assume only small responsibilities, such as caring for their rooms and clothing and occasionally helping with the meals.

Children of the lower social classes, by contrast, have no formal social training outside of school, nor are they expected to assume many home duties while they are young. As a result, they have proportionally more time free for play. As they reach the fourth or fifth grade in school, girls from the lower classes are expected to devote more time to home responsibilities, such as care of the younger children, laundry work, cleaning, and preparation of meals, while

"Work"   "Play"   "Drudgery"

Figure 10–1.—An activity can be "work," "play," or "drudgery" for the child.

boys spend much of their after-school time in jobs to earn money (108). Because parents of the lower classes do not place a high value on education, their children spend less out-of-school time on studies in late childhood than children of the middle and upper classes (12, 26).

VALUE OF PLAY

Play is such an accepted part of child life that few people stop to consider how important its role is. Far too often, parents and teachers regard play as a "waste of time." They do not realize that too little play deprives the child of many of the learning opportunities essential to wholesome development. As Millichamp has pointed out, play "helps the child to develop as a person" (111). To achieve this goal, the child must have a *balance* of work and play—not too much or too little of either. When a child begins to be bored with play and asks, "What shall I do now?" it is evident that the scale has been too heavily tipped on the play side. If, on the other hand, he shows boredom with his studies or home duties, or if he begins to work below his capacity, it means that the work side of the scale has been overloaded; he then needs more time and opportunity for play.

Play makes many contributions to the development of a child, most of which cannot be made through other channels.

Physical Value. Active play is essential if the child is to develop his muscles properly and exercise all parts of his body. It also serves as an outlet for surplus energy which, if pent up, makes the child tense, nervous, and irritable. True, the physical benefits of play could be achieved by engaging in "setting-up" exercises several times daily, but because the child does not appreciate the importance of exercise, he would probably rebel against these exercises and do them in such a halfhearted way that any benefit he might derive from them would be counteracted by the emotional tension aroused.

As childhood progresses, many children find sedentary play, such as reading, watching television, or going to the movies, more pleasurable than active play. Their attitude toward different types of play is greatly influenced by the attitudes of significant people in their lives, especially parents and peers. In discussing the influence of parental attitudes toward active play, Martin and Vincent stated:

The *attitude of parents* toward physical play and exercise has much to do with the child's attitude. If the parents are enthusiastic about games and sports, or about walks in the open, they will participate in these, sometimes sharing the activity with the child, sometimes teaching the child basic skills in the various sports, but all the time setting an example and passing on their enthusiasm. If, on the other hand, the parents consider intellectual activities to be the only desirable way to spend time, and if they regard sports and games as something for the unintelligent only, they may discourage activities involving physical play. And the child, consequently, may be retarded in his progress in general body control (105).

Therapeutic Value. Play is therapeutic. It acts as a catharsis for the elimination of pent-up energy. In everyday life, the child needs some release from the tensions that the restrictions imposed on him by his environment give rise to. Play helps him to express his emotions in a socially acceptable way and allows him to get rid of pent-up energy in a manner that will meet social expectations and win social approval (111).

These purposes may be served by active physical play—in games and sports—or they may be achieved by indirect methods, such as identification with a character in a book, in a movie, or on the television screen. As the child reads a story or watches a play unfold on the screen, he can express his fears, resentments, anxieties, or even his joys to his satisfaction and thus clear his system of them. Fantasy or make-believe play also serves as an outlet for anxieties and for the tensions anxiety brings (4). Similarly, mass media, such as comics, movies, and television, serve as outlets for aggressions which

Often, play serves as a catharsis for the elimination of pent-up energy, the release of tensions, and the expression of emotions in a socially acceptable way. (Standard Oil Co., N.J.)

the child cannot express directly (2, 116, 141).

Not only does play provide a therapeutic release for emotional tensions, but it provides an *outlet for needs and desires* which cannot be otherwise met. If they are met satisfactorily in play—whether in dramatic play or through identification with fictional characters—the frustrations of daily life will then be lessened. The child who wants to play the role of a leader, for example, may not be able to achieve this status in real life, but in dramatic play, he can be the father, the teacher, or the general of his army of toy soldiers.

Furthermore, in his play, the child is often able to formulate and carry out plans which

help him to solve problems that are of great importance in his private life. The child who has problems with handwriting in school, for example, can acquire skills needed for writing with some success through drawing and painting. Or, through his dramatic play, he may find a method of dealing successfully with the domination of an older sibling (56, 69, 70).

The therapeutic value of play has been employed in dealing with children's behavior problems in the form of *play therapy*. As Axline has pointed out, "Play therapy is based upon the fact that play is the child's natural medium of self-expression. It is an opportunity which is given to the child to 'play out' his feelings and problems, just as in certain types of adult therapy, an individual 'talks out' his difficulties" (7). When a child plays house with dolls that represent different family members, for example, it is possible for the therapist to get a clue to how he feels about the different members of his family. Should he hit a doll that represents a baby or younger sibling, or should he have the mother doll slap a doll representing an older sibling, it is possible to conclude what his attitudes toward the members of his own family are.

In either free or controlled situations, an observer can learn about a child's problems, and a child can learn about his own problems and how to face them (8). As Conn has said, the child "not only learns what he has contributed to the total situation [i.e., his problems] but for the first time finds himself secure in a personal relationship. He can therefore begin to develop the courage that comes from self-criticism, a sense of freedom arising out of self-expression and be helped in the direction of happy, healthy living" (34).

Educational Value. Through his play with toys of all types, the young child learns to know the shapes, colors, sizes, and textures of objects as well as their significance. As he grows older, he develops many skills in games and sports. Exploring, collecting, and other favored forms of play in late childhood furnish the child with information that cannot be obtained from school books.

Reading, plays, concerts, and well-selected movies broaden the child's information and at the same time give him enjoyment. Because material in books and movies and on television is often presented with vivid imagery and in exciting forms, it captures and holds the child's attention, thus increasing his motivation to learn (130). Play helps the child to comprehend and control the world in which he lives and to distinguish between reality and fantasy (111).

In play, the child *learns about himself* and others and about his relationships with them. He learns about his abilities and how they compare with the abilities of others, and he is thus enabled to establish a clearer

and more realistic concept of himself (8). Play permits him to experiment and to test his abilities without taking full responsibility for his actions, as he would have to in activities of a more serious nature (80). In drawing, for example, he can experiment as much as he pleases and know that he will not be graded on the basis of what he has drawn. In play, the child assumes many different roles and thus learns which roles give him the greatest satisfaction and at the same time enable him to establish the most satisfying relationships with others. Furthermore, he learns to play the sex role society expects him to play by pretending, in his play, to be the people who embody the socially approved patterns of behavior for his sex group (83).

Social Value. By playing with other children, the child learns how to establish social relationships with strangers and how to meet and solve the problems such relationships bring. Through cooperative games, even with adults, he learns to give and take (8, 102). Because adults tend to be tolerant of a child's aggressive tendencies in play, however, cooperation is more readily learned from play with other children. Within the family, make-believe play helps to reduce hostilities between parents and children and between older and younger siblings, thus resulting in better social adjustments in the home and a better home climate (28, 142).

It is true that the child might learn to *behave in a social manner* through his contacts with children in school, but the typical school environment, unlike free play, offers little opportunity for social behavior. Rarely does the home or the school give the child sufficient outlet for the desire for *social contacts.*

Moral Value. Play is one of the most important factors in the moral training of the child. Although he learns what the group considers right and wrong in the home or in the school, the enforcement of the acceptance of moral standards is never so rigid there as in the play group. The child knows that he must be fair, honest, truthful, self-controlled, a good sport, and a good loser if he is to be an acceptable member of the play group. He also knows that his playmates are far less tolerant of his lapses from the accepted codes of behavior than the adults of his home and school environments. He therefore learns to toe the mark more quickly and more completely in play than in any other situation (45).

CHARACTERISTICS OF CHILDREN'S PLAY

Certain characteristics of child play, which may be found in whatever group of children one studies, serve to show how different it is from adult play.

Play Follows a Pattern of Development. From early babyhood to maturity, definite play activities are popular at one age and not at another, no matter what the individual's environment, nationality, or economic status may be.

During the first two or three months of life, when the baby is gaining control of the muscles in the head and arm regions, his play consists mainly of looking at people and objects and of making random movements in an attempt to grab objects held before him. From then on, his arms and hands will have come under enough voluntary control to enable him to grasp, hold, and examine small objects and toys; his play is then exploratory in nature. After he can walk, he plays by pushing or pulling wheel toys. How a child plays thus depends upon the development of motor and intellectual functions (85).

In this predictable pattern, toy play begins in the first years of life and reaches a peak between seven and eight years of age. During the "toy age," the child's play is largely determined by the type of toys he has to play with. Interest in toy play comes chiefly from the fact that the child imagines his toys have life qualities—that they are capable of talking, acting, and feeling as he does. How the child plays with his toys, how long he plays with them, and how much enjoy-

ment he derives from toy play will depend partly upon his intellectual and motor development, partly upon the toy, and partly upon the conditions under which he plays— whether alone, with an adult, or with another child. When the right toy is used for the right age and right level of development, the child will derive more pleasure from toy play and will persevere longer in it (114, 168). As intellectual development progresses, the child begins to lose interest in toys because he is no longer able to endow them with life qualities. This occurs earlier in bright children (89).

After the child enters school, his play interests change, partly because of his increased mental maturity and partly because of peer pressures to stop playing with toys that, in the eyes of the group, are characteristic of "babies." During the first and second grades of school, however, there is an overlapping of the play activities characteristic of early and late childhood. A child will often continue to play with his favorite toys when away from the peer group but will play in a more mature way when with the group. At first, the child is interested in running games; after that, sports with strict rules and regulations become the favorite pastimes.

Patterns in Specific Play Activities. Studies of childhood play have revealed that the various kinds of play occur in a more or less regular order and at predictable times in the child's pattern of development. *Block building,* for example, passes through four distinct stages. In the first stage, the child merely handles and carries blocks and piles them in irregular masses; in the second, he constructs rows and towers; in the third, he develops patterns and techniques for building more complicated designs; and in the fourth, he dramatizes and reproduces actual structures (82, 102). At three years of age —in the first stage—the child is primarily concerned with problems of balance and size and methods of combining blocks; by four, he begins to make crude and sprawling structures, loosely hung together; at five, he can build highly integrated, carefully balanced structures; and at six, he uses these intricate structures as settings for dramatic play (145). Definite patterns appear likewise in *drawing,* starting with scratching and dotting with a crayon in the one-year-old and developing into drawing pictures against backgrounds by the time the child is eight (13). Similarly, *reading* interests and interest in *movies, collecting, television, radio,* and *singing* all occur in a more or less regular order and at predictable times.

Play Is Influenced by Tradition. Many of the play activities of young children are imitations of adult activities. Because the activities in any culture are more or less stereotyped, the play of little children in a particular culture changes little from generation to generation, regardless of the specific neighborhood environment. Young children imitate the play of older children, who have imitated the play of the generation of children preceding them. Thus, in every culture, one generation passes down to

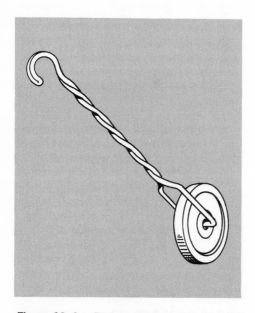

Figure 10–2. Early walking toy represented on Greek vases. (Adapted from C. Landreth, *The psychology of early childhood,* Knopf, 1958. Used by permission.)

the next the forms of play which it finds most satisfactory.

The type of play that becomes traditional within a culture, however, depends upon the values of that culture. A comparative study of the play of children in America and in Japan has revealed that the Japanese engage in informal group activities, while the Americans emphasize team play and competitive games. American children put strong emphasis on dramatic play only during early childhood, while Japanese children show an interest in dramatic play much longer. Furthermore, there is a greater variety in the traditional play patterns of American children than in those of Japanese children (138).

Studies of art have revealed that pictures of children in different cultures and at different times in history show them playing with balls and other toys not unlike those used by American children today. For example, when babies are just beginning to walk, a walking toy, used as a prop to help them maintain their balance, has been recognized for centuries as a favorite toy. Figure 10–2 shows a walking toy represented on a Greek vase.

The influence of tradition has also been observed in the *drawings* of children of different cultures. These drawings are influenced by the handwriting conventions of the cultural group with which the child is identified. In a comparative study of Arab and American children, it was found that Arab children place their drawings at the top right of the page far more often than at the left, while for the American children, the reverse is true: Arabic writing is from right to left, and American writing is from left to right (42). Comparison has revealed that the drawings of Bedouin children are, by tradition, small compared with those of American children of the same age. Bedouin drawings average approximately 2 inches, while those of Americans average approximately 6. Traditionally, drawings of Bedouin children show rectangular human trunks and an absence of clothing; those of American children show clothed and rounded trunks (43). Characteristic drawings of the human figure by Bedouin children are shown in Figure 10–3. Compare these drawings with those made by American children, shown in Figure 10–5, page 459.

The influence of tradition is also apparent in the fact that there are *seasonal patterns* in children's play. Roller skates, jumping ropes, jacks, and bicycles come out with the first warm days of spring. Summer brings a shift of interest to wading, swimming, and boating; then the cool days of fall renew the child's interest in the more active play enjoyed during the spring months. With the approach of winter, the child looks forward to snow for sledding, snowball fighting, ice skating, and—in rural districts—sleigh riding.

Games and sports are likewise influenced by the seasonal factor. As a general rule, the more active games are reserved for the cooler months of the year, and those that require less exertion for the warmer months. Baseball, for example, is regarded as a spring and summer sport, while football and hockey are reserved for fall and early winter (147).

In spite of the cultural variations in traditional play, the differences are mainly variations in emphasis. Certain aspects of the play are emphasized to conform to the values of the particular culture. Children in all cultures draw, but what they draw and how they draw vary from one culture to another. Blindman's buff, in different forms, is played in many countries in Europe. Tag, in different forms, is played in Burma, Iraq, and the Sahara Desert, as well as in most European countries (158).

Tradition determines what is *sex-appropriate* play, regardless of children's preferences. Among the lower-income groups, tradition plays a more important role than among the higher-income groups. In the latter, more money can be spent for new and different toys, and travel and social mobility bring the child in contact with more children of different cultural groups.

Play Activities Decrease in Number with Age. Studies have shown that the number of activities pursued gradually decreases as

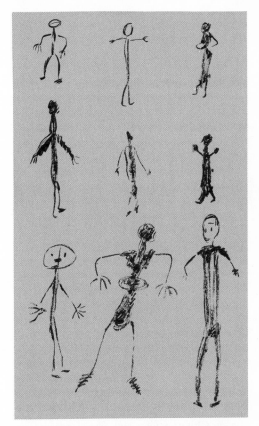

Figure 10–3. Human-figure drawings by Bedouin children. (Adapted from W. Dennis, The human figure drawings of Bedouins, *J. soc Psychol.*, 1960, 52, 209–219. Used by permission.)

children grow older. Around the age of twelve years, there is not only a decrease in number of play activities engaged in but also a change in type of activity enjoyed. At this time, the favorite activities include highly organized games and sports and more solitary pursuits, such as going to the movies, watching television, watching sports, and reading (174).

Comparisons of the number of different activities at different ages showed that, among eight-year-olds, an average of 40.11 different play activities were engaged in during 1 week, while among persons twenty-two years old and older, the average was

17.71. Play activities involving play with other children likewise decrease with age. At 7½ years, an average of 27 are engaged in, as compared with 21 at 11½ years and 13 at 16½ years (170).

Causes of Decrease. The number of play activities decreases because older children have less *time* available for play; they have a greater *understanding of their interests and abilities* and, in addition, a longer *attention span.*

Children abandon some activities because they have become *boring* or are regarded as babyish. For example, kindergarten children begin to show a decreasing interest in blocks because other materials, such as paints, clay, crayons, and chalk, offer a greater variety of interesting activities (101). Dramatic play loses its appeal when the child is no longer able to imagine that he is the person he impersonates. Similarly, toys lose their appeal when the child no longer can endow them with life qualities and when doing so is regarded by the peer group as babyish (102, 126).

The narrowing of the number of play activities may be the result of *lack of playmates.* Children who lack social acceptance in the peer group find themselves limited to solitary forms of play. This is especially true for boys because most of the play of older boys centers in gang activities. Racial or religious prejudice against the child may deprive him of playmates. In a study of the out-of-school activities of Negro elementary-school children, it was found that proportionally more time was spent watching television, listening to the radio, going to the movies, and reading comics than was spent on club and group activities. Children who are not accepted by the peer group must limit their play activities to those they can enjoy alone (91, 161).

Time Spent in Play Decreases with Age. As leisure time decreases because of new duties and because of the time spent in school, the child must select from the available play activities those which please him most and concentrate on them. This becomes increasingly true as the child grows older (108).

The amount of time a child has for play will be influenced, to some extent, by the socioeconomic status of the family. Among upper-class children, less and less time is available for play as they grow older and devote more time to school and out-of-school lessons; in the lower-class group, more time is devoted to home duties or after-school jobs.

Time Spent in Specific Activities Increases with Age. Because of poor concentration, little children go from one toy to another or from one play activity to another. A two-year-old, for example, can attend to a play activity for 6.9 minutes, on the average, as compared with 12.6 minutes for a five-year-old. When play materials are interesting to them, nursery-school children will persevere in a play situation even when the activity is difficult (168). This is apparent also in reading, radio listening, and television watching.

As children grow older and intellectually more mature, they can comprehend more. As a result, their interest does not wane so quickly, and they can attend to what they are doing for longer periods of time (172). When interest in an activity wanes, children spend less time on that activity. Kindergarten children, for example, begin to find block building less interesting than formerly and therefore devote less time to it (102).

Childhood Play Is Informal. The play of little children is spontaneous and informal. The child plays when and with what toys he wishes, regardless of time or place. He does not need special play equipment or special playclothes.

Gradually, play becomes more and more formal; much of the spontaneity of play disappears during adolescence. Even during the gang age, the child feels that special clothing, special equipment, and a special place for play are essential. Appointments are made to meet and play at a definite time, and each player is expected to appear promptly.

Perhaps in no respect is the trend toward formality more apparent than in the child's attitude toward his playmates. As a pre-schooler, the child is willing to play with anyone available, but as a member of a gang, he will play only with gangmates; if they are not available, he will play alone, listening to the radio, watching television, or reading the comics. Similarly, at around the age of six, a boy feels that he must play only with boys, and a girl that she must play only with girls (68, 91).

Play Is Less Physically Active as the Child Grows Older. During the first three grades in school, children care little about sedentary play until late in the day, when they are tired. Then they like to watch television or be read to. From grade four on, however, there is a gradual increase in time spent in reading, going to the movies, watching television, listening to the radio, listening to music, and watching sports events (81, 147). Interest in active play reaches its lowest point during early puberty. At that time, children not only withdraw from active play but also spend little time reading, playing indoor games, or even watching television. Most of their playtime is devoted to day-dreaming—a form of play that requires a minimum of effort and expenditure of energy.

TYPES OF PLAY

How and what the child plays will depend largely upon his age and level of development. The favorite types of play during the childhood years are discussed in the following section.

FREE, SPONTANEOUS PLAY

The child's earliest play is free and spontaneous. It has no rules and regulations and is, for the most part, solitary. The child plays as he wishes to play and stops when he is no longer interested. Play of this type loses popularity late in childhood, when competitive games are more favored (70, 145).

Free, spontaneous play is mostly exploratory. The baby derives keen enjoyment from stimulating the sense organs and experiencing different sensations. By the time he is three months old, he explores his toys by sucking, banging, and pulling at them and investigates any object within his reach (85).

Owing to poor motor coordination, the little child is apt to be very destructive. He breaks his toys because they are not strong enough to withstand the strain of his exploratory behavior. By the end of the second year, the child turns his attention to more advanced and complicated forms of play that tax his developing mentality (80).

DRAMATIC PLAY

In dramatic, or make-believe, play, the child, through language or overt behavior, deals with materials or situations as if they had attributes other than those they actually have; it is a "game of illusion" for the child (65). Dramatic play is a common and popular form of play during the preschool years but loses much of its appeal after children enter school. The school-age child begins to view life more realistically, and his ability to attribute living qualities to things decreases as his ability to reason increases.

Dramatic impersonations usually begin between the ages of 1½ and 2 years and reach their peak during the kindergarten age (104). Very bright children, particularly, enjoy dramatic play of a creative and constructive type. They usually lose interest in this play quite early, however, because they become realistic relatively early (4).

Young children learn much of their make-believe play from older children, especially siblings. Older children, in turn, add to their acquired repertoire of dramatic play episodes by using ideas they get from television, movies, personal experiences, and

Children acquire a repertoire of dramatic play episodes from movies and television. (Adapted from Children's Play, a McGraw-Hill Text-Film.)

talks with their parents and older siblings. Books and stories provide little basis for dramatic play because young children understand what they see better than what they hear and because so many of the stories written for children today do not lend themselves well to dramatization.

Boys, for two reasons, have more ideas for dramatic themes than girls; first, the themes of movies and television stories are more suitable for boys than for girls, and second, parents talk to their sons about cowboys, guns, fighting, and other topics that can be used in dramatizations more than they talk to their daughters about topics that are considered sex-appropriate for girls (104).

Functions of Dramatic Play. Dramatic play adds to the child's ability to *transcend his actual limitations* and go beyond the restrictions imposed by reality; it enables him to *realize his wishes vicariously;* and it provides opportunities for him to rid himself of irritations, to remove or overcome conditions which annoy or thwart him in real life. The more strongly the child is *frustrated,* the more make-believe play he will engage in.

The *poorly adjusted* child engages in more make-believe play than the well-adjusted child (65). Observations of nursery-school children at play revealed that those who spent the most time in manipulative play had the lowest anxiety scores, while those with higher anxiety scores devoted more time to make-believe play (120).

In dramatic play, a child pretends to be someone he loves and admires and whom he would like to resemble. By assigning a role to a doll, a toy animal, or some other toy, he changes his own status; this gives him a feeling of self-importance and *compensates for his dissatisfaction with his real self* (120).

One of the important advantages of dramatic play is that it *encourages the young child to speak.* To be able to play dramatically with others, the child not only must make suggestions for the roles to be played but also must speak in the role he is playing. This helps him to increase his vocabulary. Even more important, it acts as a *socializing force,* encouraging him to make contacts with other children (104). Figure 10–4 shows the mean frequencies of use of dramatic play suggestions by boys and girls.

Pattern of Dramatic Play. Children under three years of age show a predominant interest in (*1*) *personification*—talking to dolls or inanimate objects or playing games involving imagined creatures, such as a "bogeyman"; (*2*) *make-believe use of materials,* including the imaginative naming of objects—calling a slide a train—or simple, overt, imaginative behavior, such as drinking from an empty cup; and (*3*) *make-believe situations* involving the complicated use of materials, such as playing house. In most instances, their play is related to the materials before them. After three years of age, *make-believe use of materials* proves to be the most typical imaginative activity. As children grow older, the materials are used in increasingly more complicated ways, such as using sand to build a tunnel instead of merely digging into it with a shovel. In addition to this, children after three years of age engage in play involving *make-believe situations, constructive activities* with raw materials, and *dramatic play* of a more or less complicated type (103).

Stone and Church, describing the typical pattern of children's dramatizations, have shown that definite stages are reflected in play:

> For a three-year-old, a block can be a doll, a train, a building, a cow. For the five-year-old, a block is a building material, and he wants some approximation of a real train to run in and out of the railroad station he makes with his blocks. The three-year-old can people a universe with sticks and stones and paper and rags—which, however, he does not try to shape in representational images. The four-year-old, to be a successful cowboy, wants some outstanding prop—a broad-brimmed hat, a cap pistol, or a neckerchief. For him, one element can stand for the whole configuration "cowboy." The five-year-old, though, is likely to feel dissatisfied in his role-playing unless he can wear the full regalia of his part (145).

Themes of Dramatic Play. The dramatic play of children is a mirror of the culture which surrounds them; it dramatizes events of their everyday lives. Everything the child

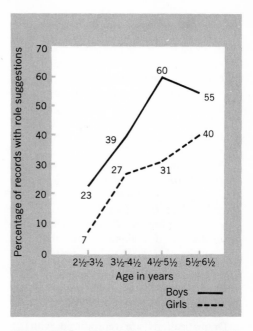

Figure 10–4. Suggestions for roles in dramatic play by boys and girls at different ages. (Adapted from H. R. Marshall, Relations between home experiences and children's use of language in play interactions with peers, *Psychol. Monogr.,* 1961, 75, No. 5. Used by permission.)

hears or sees is repeated in imitative form. Dramatic play also reflects the spirit of the particular period in which the child is growing up. For example, during the Second World War, both boys and girls played war games in which they were soldiers and their toys were tanks, guns, and airplanes. With the advent of the "air age," children's dramatizations have been concentrating more on reaching the moon than on fighting an enemy (60).

The usual themes of imaginative play of young children are (*1*) *domestic patterns,* including playing house, furnishing a house, cooking, eating, taking care of babies, and being fathers and mothers; (*2*) *imitating animals* that crawl and growl; (*3*) *taking care of the sick* by imitating a doctor or nurse; (*4*) *playing store;* (*5*) traveling and other activities connected with *transporta-*

tion, such as riding in automobiles, trains, or buses; putting gas or air in a car; riding in an airplane; and sailing a boat; (6) *punishing,* playing policeman, and gun play in general; (7) *burning* and playing fireman; (8) *killing* and *dying;* (9) giving *parties* and having *weddings;* and (10) playing the part of *legendary characters* such as Santa Claus, Cinderella, the Big Bad Wolf, or George Washington (104, 115).

Playing house is a universal favorite with children of the preschool years. The younger children passively allow themselves to be led around, while the older ones assume the roles of "mommy" or "daddy." Older children, instead of making believe that they are people of everyday life, pretend that they are fairies, Indians, "G" men, or bandits. Western scenes resemble television westerns, in which people, not animals, are shot (104).

Dramatizations are reproduced with astonishing fidelity; even the tone of voice of the person imitated is copied so well that one could almost believe the real person was speaking. Few stage properties as such are needed. A hat, a cane, a long skirt, or some article usually associated with the person imitated is all the child needs to imagine that he is that person. A rug placed across two overturned chairs serves as a tent, a den, or a cave.

DAYDREAMING

Daydreaming is a form of mental play. The role the child plays in his daydreams is more dramatic, more heroic, more fanciful, and more remote from daily life than the role played in make-believe play. In make-believe play, the child may play the role of an aviator by donning an aviator's cap and pretending to ride through space as he runs across the playroom with a toy airplane held above his head. In a daydream, however, he will see himself as a real aviator, garbed in the clothing of an aviator and riding through space in a real airplane.

While the young child generally centers his make-believe play around the mundane experiences of daily life, such as playing house or playing Sunday school, the daydream has more glamour, romance, and excitement in both setting and action. Many of the ideas for daydreams come from books, comics, movies, and television programs that have an element of the fanciful or of unreality.

About the time the child enters school, make-believe play begins to lose its appeal, and daydreaming takes its place (65). While daydreaming may begin earlier— and it does in bright children—it reaches a peak during puberty. It is popular among older children when they are bored or restricted in other play, as when they must sit through a long, drawn-out family meal. A *well-adjusted child* usually daydreams only when he cannot engage in other forms of play. The *poorly adjusted child,* by contrast, *substitutes* daydreaming for play with other children or for constructive play (121).

Most children are too full of energy to be satisfied with such inactive play as daydreaming. With the rapid growth and physical changes that accompany puberty, however, the child's energy is depleted. As a result, he substitutes mental for physical play. As has already been pointed out, many children engage in only the most inactive forms of play at puberty—listening to the radio, playing records, or watching television. Often they prefer to daydream because it takes less energy and is more satisfying. Girls at every age daydream more than boys. Furthermore, at puberty, girls develop more rapidly than boys and, consequently, have less energy for active play.

Pattern of Development. Enjoyment of daydreaming parallels the development of intelligence in children who are *well adjusted.* Because imagination develops more rapidly than reasoning ability, the older child can imagine himself in any role he wishes and not realize how incongruous this is. Gradually, as his reasoning ability develops, he begins to see the incongruity. He then approaches his daydreams with the same critical attitude that he uses in assessing his constructions, whether they are drawings, paintings, or wood models.

Jersild has given a graphic description of the effect reasoning has on the enjoyment a child derives from daydreaming:

An eight-year-old boy rides, in his fancies, jauntily over the western range on a fine horse, ready for combat with horse thieves, coyotes, or Indians. As the plot unfolds, his activities become increasingly complex. He has a trusty rifle and a belt of ammunition at the start; but when he stops to camp, he needs materials for making a fire, cooking utensils, and what not, so he finds it necessary to pretend that he had an extra pack horse with him from the beginning. As the drama goes on, he may find himself so burdened with equipment, horses, and other paraphernalia that the job of planning and ordering things in the daydream becomes somewhat arduous. This tendency for a daydream to bog down under its own weight as it calls for more and more ingenuity and "thinking" frequently occurs in adults, spoiling what might otherwise have been a fine time (80).

Many children, as their reasoning ability develops, find it difficult to reconcile what they imagine with reality, and, as Jersild pointed out, what might have been a fine time is spoiled. In a *poorly adjusted child,* however, self-insight is not well developed. As a result, he does not recognize incongruities between reality and products of the imagination. Furthermore, because of his poor social adjustments, he spends much time alone; this encourages him to become self-bound—a tendency which fosters unrealistic thinking about himself. Consequently, he derives enjoyment from daydreaming much longer than a better-adjusted child of equal intellectual ability.

Themes of Daydreams. Although children's daydreams may have any imaginable setting and may relate to any activity, two major varieties are most popular—the "conquering-hero" and the "suffering-hero" types. In the former, the child sees himself as he would like to be in real life. Whether he is a cowboy, an athletic hero, or an aviator who is the first person to reach the moon will depend upon his interests and wishes. The important aspect of the dream is that it centers around him, and every other character pays homage to him.

In the "suffering-hero" daydream, the dream centers around a child who is a martyr, misunderstood and mistreated by parents, teachers, siblings, peers, or society in general. The satisfaction comes from the happy ending, in which the martyr turns out to be a hero. Furthermore, those who have misunderstood or mistreated the hero not only are penitent but want to do all within their power to compensate for the physical or mental pain they have inflicted on him. Consequently, the suffering hero is treated even more favorably than the conquering hero; to the adulation of others is added penitence for their wrongdoing.

The child who is poorly adjusted derives keen satisfaction from such daydreams because they show him that he is right and others are wrong. He thus frees himself from any feelings of guilt or inadequacy for not having gained the social acceptance he craves. As children approach puberty and begin to develop antisocial attitudes, "suffering-hero" daydreams predominate. They are almost universal during puberty. However pleasurable such daydreams may be, and however much they free the child from self-doubts and feelings of inadequacy, they are an unhealthy form of play. They tend to exaggerate an already existing belief that "nobody loves me" and to build up antisocial attitudes that intensify the child's poor social adjustments (20, 71). The child is still faced with a series of problems: He has not learned how to assess himself realistically, he is unwilling to accept himself as he is, and he continues to have unhealthy attitudes toward people and social situations.

Effects of Daydreaming. For too many children, daydreaming becomes a favorite pastime. It can be engaged in at any time, and it requires no equipment, playmates, or even physical exertion. In no other play is ego-satisfaction so complete. In no other way can one so thoroughly get away from the commonplace experiences of daily life and relieve the boredom life often brings.

Daydreaming is especially satisfying when one's daily life at school or home is monotonous and ego-threatening. For the child who is *unhappy* and *dissatisfied* with himself and his role in life, escape into his daydream world is the bright spot of the day. In this private world everything goes as he wants it to go; he is complete master of the situation. Although reading, listening to the radio, and watching television may provide escape from boredom and general dissatisfaction, they do not give the child this ego-inflating experience.

The child who finds satisfaction in daydreams learns to avoid being critical about them. He must make a choice between seeing the daydream as an impossible experience and seeing himself as he would like to be. For a dissatisfied and unhappy child, this choice is an easy one; he chooses the path that leads to the greatest satisfaction. For the happy, well-adjusted child, the need to escape reality is not so great; therefore, he engages in daydreams only when he is bored or has had an experience that, temporarily, makes him feel inadequate.

In spite of the pleasure a child derives from daydreaming, it is unquestionably one of the most dangerous forms of play, if not the most dangerous. *Physically,* it is harmful to the well-being of a child to sit around and daydream instead of engaging in play which requires exercise of the body. Also, daydreams often give rise to a strong emotional state. Emotional disturbances are more likely to happen in "suffering-hero" daydreams than in the "conquering-hero" variety.

The *psychological* damage of daydreaming is far more serious than the physiological. The child who derives enough satisfaction from his daydreams to prefer them to other play soon develops a romanticized concept of himself which is far removed from reality. The more he dislikes his real self, the more he lives in his world of daydreams, where he can see himself as he would like to be. This contributes to the poor adjustment that led him into excessive daydreaming; a vicious circle is then set in motion.

Just as excessive daydreaming leads to poor personal adjustments, so does it lead to poor *social adjustments*. The daydreamer rarely has good self-insight. Not seeing himself as he is, he cannot understand why people do not treat him in accordance with what he believes to be his superiority, and he shows this resentment in his treatment of them. Trapped by these unfavorable attitudes, the child makes poorer and poorer social adjustments as time goes on. The result is that he finds himself with fewer and fewer friends and more and more enemies.

Just as too much daydreaming is unhealthy, so is *too little*. The child who lacks the ability to imagine himself as he would like to be must be content to see himself as he is. This image is rarely to his liking. Some daydreams may inspire the child to duplicate in real life what has happened in his daydream world. A child who sees himself as an athletic hero, for example, may work hard to develop the skills needed to make him a hero in real life. Likewise, every child needs some morale booster when he is discouraged and when his attempts to achieve success have failed or have gone unrecognized. Seeing himself as a conquering hero can increase his motivation to continue trying until he finally reaches his goal. Without such a morale booster, the child might let his anxieties and frustrations get so strong a hold on him that they would dominate his life.

If a child does not daydream, he will be deprived of the pleasure daydreaming can bring to a life that is not entirely to one's satisfaction. Children who daydream too little—and they are in the minority—may not have the intellectual capacity to imagine things that are not actually happening, or they may not have the knowledge from which daydreams can be fashioned. A child who lacks opportunities to read, to watch television, or to see movies, for example, must fashion his daydreams on the building materials he has—information about everyday experiences in his own life. These materials are inadequate to make daydreams that will be satisfying.

Children who are kept so busy from the time they waken in the morning until they go to bed at night, with "extras" imposed by ambitious parents or by parents who need their help, will have little free time for mental play. Often, what free time they have will not be used for daydreaming because they will be too tired, both physically and mentally, to engage in play which requires the mental effort that daydreaming does.

Finally, too little daydreaming may result from feelings of guilt on the child's part. If a child has been reproved or punished for "white lies"—imaginary experiences that are so realistic they are believed to be real and are reported as such—his desire to engage in *any* imaginative thinking will be curbed for fear of reproof or punishment. He will be conditioned to regard *all* use of the imagination as wrong because he has learned to associate it with social disapproval.

CONSTRUCTIVE PLAY

Up to the age of five or six years, the child puts objects together without a preconceived plan or pattern. If, by chance, they should resemble a familiar object, he is delighted with his achievement. From the age of six years, he uses materials specifically and appropriately for building and construction.

The child who is too realistic or too much of a dreamer does not play creatively. The too realistic child is unable to imagine things that he does not see in his daily life, and merely reproducing what he is surrounded with gives him little satisfaction. The child who dreams too much spends his energies in daydreaming; he never gets around to reproducing his creations because he satisfies himself with their imaginary forms. As children grow older and are better able to distinguish between fantasy and reality, they lose interest in make-believe play and turn their attention to constructive play (20, 171).

Some children derive great satisfaction from creative achievements, while others do not. Some have their creative abilities developed by guidance and by encouragement to use the materials provided by parents and teachers. Others, with equal creative abilities, are deprived of these essentials to the development of their potentials. As a result, they do not discover the satisfaction that can be derived from such play and are not motivated to train their capacities. Even when a child is provided with encouragement and materials, his motivation may be weakened by criticism.

The most common forms of constructive play for different ages and levels of development are described in the following paragraph.

Making Things. Early constructive play consists of making mud pies, constructing mountains or tunnels from sand, and playing with blocks, beads, scissors, clay, paint, crayons, and paste. Although young children make things that have a definite meaning and can be recognized, the object's practical use is of secondary importance. In block building, for example, children call their structures "houses" or "boats," but not until after the third year is block construction coordinated with dramatic play (69, 114). By the time they reach kindergarten, most children shift their interest from block building to painting, clay modeling, finger painting, crayoning with colored chalk, playing with puzzles, and making collages (102).

In late childhood, children build tents, playhouses, huts, snowmen, and dams. Boys produce large, crude structures in connection with their outdoor play. Girls, on the other hand, construct finer and more delicate objects; they make doll clothes, paper dolls, and drawings; they paint and make models out of clay.

At first, the child is pleased with whatever he makes and proudly displays it to anyone who happens to be present. Later, he becomes more critical of his workmanship, especially in painting and drawing. He not only ceases to boast about his work but often covers it up or even destroys it if others come to look at it. Between the fourth and eighth grades, both girls and boys lose interest in handicrafts. They still like to cook, however, and if they have a definite talent for a specific form of creative work, such as painting, drawing, or clay modeling, it becomes a hobby—the favorite solitary play activity (13, 147).

Drawing.   One of the most frequent outlets for the creative fervor is drawing. Owing to poor muscle coordination, the young child cannot actually draw, but he takes keen delight in scribbling, making crude and often totally aimless movements with pencil or crayon. To him, drawing is a means of expression rather than a means of creating beauty. The finished product is far less important than the creation of it (63).

Pattern of Development.   Drawing is an expression of what is uppermost in the

To the young child, painting or drawing is a vehicle for self-expression. His drawings are often only a symbolic representation of what he sees. (Adapted from **Children's Play**, a McGraw-Hill Text-Film.)

child's mind at the moment. His first drawings are symbolic, not direct copies of objects. The child draws things as he remembers them, but he is not interested in perspective, proportions, or relationships. He puts in details that interest him, such as buttons on a coat, while omitting essentials, such as a man's legs. From about the sixth year, the child tries to reproduce what he sees and begins to show regard for size, perspective, and correctness of detail.

By the time the child is eight years old, perspective is well developed. Transparency, or drawing a person or object as it would be viewed in an X-ray picture, is quite rare after eight years of age. Except when a child is truly gifted, originality in drawings disappears very soon. Young children show great interest in color, while older children show a major interest in form. The young child draws mainly with a crayon, while the older child draws with a pencil (30, 88). From the time the child is six years old, the major change in the pattern of development of his drawing consists in elaboration of the ground against which the objects are drawn.

When a design is too difficult for a young child to reproduce, he tends to simplify the drawing according to certain principles. The tendencies are to substitute something meaningful for a meaningless design; to unify and "close" the design; and to introduce rhythm, symmetry, or conventional proportions when these are lacking. There is a tendency to shorten a rectangle, to "square" anything with angles, to substitute a circle for any design that suggests roundness, to widen angles, and to simplify designs by omitting details. At no time is there any indication that the young child is attempting to build up a whole from isolated parts. His drawings are always wholes, even when many parts are missing. Young children scatter drawings randomly over the paper; the older child combines the separate drawings into a unit (74, 101).

Because the child draws mainly from memory, his drawings are usually inaccurate and incomplete. There is a marked lack of proportions, as may be seen in pictures of people whose heads are larger than their bodies. The faces are rigid and expressionless, and all people, all houses, or all animals tend to follow a stereotyped pattern. Ornamentation appeals to the child; he therefore concentrates more attention on it than on other parts of the drawings. Animals are frequently drawn with human heads but with animallike bodies and four legs.

By the time the child is six or seven years old, his drawings become compositions, with a relationship between the different parts. In spontaneous drawing, children seldom draw anything bizarre or eccentric, though many of their drawings may, to an adult, appear to be caricatures (64, 110).

Subjects of Children's Drawings. The drawings of young children usually represent familiar objects, rarely designs. The human form is most popular, with the adult form slightly more popular than the child's (see Figure 10–5). Animals are less frequently drawn than houses and trees. Among older children, more emphasis is placed on the drawing of machines, designs, animals, houses, flowers, and trees, and less on the human form. Older children frequently draw cartoons of the comic-strip type; subject matter is varied, but favorite characters are teachers and peers whom they dislike (48, 79).

Sex differences in the subjects of drawings appear early. Boys draw the human figure less often than girls, but boys are better at representing the body proportions correctly. Girls are more interested in ornamenting their drawings of the human figure. Between the ages of five and eleven years, children usually draw people of their own sex, but by eleven or twelve, girls begin to draw more figures of the opposite sex than of their own.

The six-year-old indicates sex awareness in his drawings by varying the hair, clothes, and facial features of his figures. Girls usually draw full-faced figures, while boys draw profiles as often as the full face. Boys often draw machines, airplanes, tanks, and battle scenes, while girls rarely do. Age for age, children of higher *socioeconomic groups* draw more details than those of lower socio-

Figure 10–5. Typical drawings of a man by first-grade children. (Adapted from M. A. Hughes and L. Stockdale, The young child and graphic expression, *Childh. Educ.*, 1940, 16, 307–314. Used by permission.)

economic status. Also, the *intellectual level* of the child influences the quality and subject matter of his drawings (64, 84, 164).

Crayoning and Painting. Creative activities involving the use of crayons and paint are popular during childhood and follow much the same pattern of development as drawing. At two years of age, the child begins to experiment with crayons; by three, he can control the use of his crayon; at four, he uses imagination; by five, he begins to be self-conscious about his work. Shortly after the child learns to use crayons, watercolors become an equally popular medium of self-expression. The young child derives keen enjoyment from covering pages of paper with bright colors. In recent years, finger painting, a glorified form of mud-pie play, in which the paints are the consistency of mud and are put on the paper with the finger or hand, has become popular (62, 153).

MUSIC

Whether they have musical talent or not, little children like to sing. The baby engages in this form of self-expression when he introduces rhythm into his babbling. It gives him great pleasure, and he laughs heartily at himself. Children give a bodily response to music while they are still in the crib. Later, they spontaneously walk, hop, and clap to the accompaniment of music. By the age of four or five years, most children can sing simple melodies, can beat good rhythm, and can recognize simple tunes. When a child does not know all the words of a song, he will supply his own (80).

Young children like to listen to music produced by others. Among preschool children, it has been found that the mean number of minutes spent listening to records is 20.20 daily. There is no appreciable increase in this time as children grow older, but in the latter part of childhood, listening to music on the radio becomes a favorite pastime. Children derive the greatest enjoyment from listening to music produced by themselves, even though it may be vastly inferior to that produced by others.

The child's interest in music *follows a developmental pattern*. At two years, the child dances to radio or phonograph music; at three, he likes to watch and listen to a phonograph, he can recognize several melodies, and he may have his favorites. A year later, he can run the phonograph himself, he likes to experiment with the piano, and he can sing songs correctly and likes to dramatize them. At five years, the child may pick out tunes on the piano and learn to play a few familiar, simple melodies; he likes to sing or dance to music on the radio or phonograph. At six years, he enjoys his own phonograph records. At seven, he has a

craving for piano or dancing lessons and likes to use various percussion instruments; at eight, he shows less desire to practice but likes to have an audience when he plays; he like to play duets, and he may even improvise passages of his own. At nine years, the child really applies himself to practice; he is beginning to be interested in composers, and he enjoys executing staccato or legato notes (62).

Singing is the most frequent form of musical expression because it requires no technical training. Children's favorite songs vary according to their major current interests. During the first four grades in elementary school, school songs are the most popular. As the child grows older, there is an increased interest in classical, folk, and patriotic songs and less interest in religious and holiday songs. Interest in popular and dance music increases with age.

Study of specific songs in these classifications showed that children prefer songs of easily perceived tonal values and slow cadence. Such songs are "singable" and can thus be enjoyed by all, whether they have musical ability or not. Also, these songs can be learned without too much effort and thus are not regarded as part of a singing lesson. Children's reactions to classical music are influenced mainly by familiarity with the music, not by socioeconomic status (53, 119).

COLLECTING

From the age of three years, every normal child collects things. In early childhood, the things are usually valueless and trivial. Once they are collected, they are generally forgotten or given little attention. From six years to adolescence, collecting things that interest them especially at the moment is one of the most popular forms of play for both boys and girls. Girls, as a rule, collect more things than boys do. At every age they collect different types of things (20, 63). The peak age for collecting comes at ten years for boys and a year later for girls. Older children keep their collections in a place where they will not be disturbed—in attics, cellars, desks, old trunks, jars, boxes, or baskets.

GAMES AND SPORTS

Games and sports are contests with set rules, undertaken for amusement or for a stake. *Sports* are always physical contests, while *games* may be either physical or mental. Sports usually, though not always, involve either greater physical exertion or more rigid rules than games. The term "sport" is usually reserved for contests of highly organized teams, such as baseball, football, or basketball, though it can apply to individual outdoor contests, such as track, tennis, or hunting. Children's contests fall largely in the category of games. The following description of contests is therefore mainly a description of games rather than sports.

Types of Games.   Simple games, generally referred to as "mother games" because they are usually played with the mother, begin to appeal to the baby during the second half of his first year. Finger play, pat-a-cake, peekaboo, hide-and-seek (behind furniture, a piece of cloth, or merely a hand), pigs-to-market, mirror play, and similar games, passed down from one generation to another, seem to have an appeal that is universal.

Around the fourth or fifth year, the child becomes interested in *neighborhood games*. These are of the *undefined-group* type, in which any number of children can take part. The games are organized by one child or by an older child or an adult. They are simple and brief, with few rules, and they are often invented on the spot. Frequently, they are modified as play goes on. Typical games of this sort are tag, hide-and-seek, puss-in-the-corner, dodging, run-sheep-run, advancing statues, and cops-and-robbers (70, 123).

By the age of five, the child plays games that test his skills; he walks on street curbs or on a crack in the pavement, jumps down steps, hops on one foot, skips, jumps rope, bounces balls, or plays jacks. These are of a lower social organization than neighborhood games because they are individual rather than group and because their competitive element is of relatively little importance. The child's interest in particular games of this type will depend largely upon his motor and intellectual development (70).

Between the ages of eight and twelve years, when children congregate in gangs, games become largely competitive in spirit; they are more highly organized and have more rigid rules than the games of younger children. The typical neighborhood games give way to *team, pair,* or *double-pair games*. At this age, children, especially boys, want to learn to play the sports of the junior and senior high-school students; they lose interest in "kid games." Instead of playing cops-and-robbers, for example, they play baseball or football. Instead of playing games, such as running tag, they race, as at a track meet (91, 123).

With the change to *sports* comes an interest in acquiring skill. At first, play is largely individual, and the child concentrates on playing a better game than any of the other players. Because of this egocentric interest, the child is not a good team player. He wants to dominate the play instead of limiting his efforts to his own role; he would play the whole game if the other players would allow it. Gradually, however, as he learns to cooperate with the other players, he derives more enjoyment from sports and is more likely to retain his status as a member of the team. By the time he reaches adolescence, the typical child is a good team player. He can cooperate with the other players and adhere strictly to the rules of the game, although he may not be a skillful player in the sense that he has acquired proficiency in the sport (63).

In addition to strenuous outdoor games and sports, most children like to play *indoor games*. At first, these games are played with parents or older siblings. After the child begins to establish friendships in the neighborhood, however, he plays them with his friends. Because parents often disapprove of the type of game the gang members play, especially when they play for stakes, children often play "indoor games" outdoors. The most popular games of this type are card games, ranging from the simple "old maid" to a modified form of bridge, Parcheesi, jacks, and craps. Boys much more often play for stakes than girls do, though this is more common among boys of the lower than of the middle or upper social-class groups (178).

Values of Games and Sports. Games and sports not only are pleasant forms of play but also have great value as socializing agents. From them the child learns how to get along with other children, to cooperate in different activities, to play the role of a leader as well as a follower, and to evaluate himself and his abilities realistically by comparing himself with his playmates.

A high-status position in games gives the child prestige and power among his peers. Such a position may be achieved through popularity, though it is far more likely to come from the child's competence in the game. A very popular child, for example, may be selected captain of the gang's baseball team, but it is far more likely that the child who is the best player will be selected, though he may not be as well liked as some of the other children. The child who has demonstrated his playing skill gains the reputation of being a "good player." This not only guarantees him a role on the team but also supports his selection for a high-status role in activities where sport competence is not involved (148).

The child who lacks social acceptance in a peer group must play games with family members if he wants to enjoy this form of play. While it is true that adults can teach him how to play a game, they usually fail to teach him how to be a "good sport." Adults are inclined to allow a child advantages in playing, while his contemporaries will yield no point. In discussing the importance of peer play, DuBois has said:

This challenges the child to develop skill, and in due course he is stimulated by victory and makes even greater effort. . . . When young people do not participate in sports, the scales are heavily weighted against their successful social and emotional adjustment; they frequently are headed for trouble, because

they have not had the opportunity to learn to win humbly, to lose gracefully, and to endure physical discomfort to attain a goal. In short, they have not had the privilege of learning the discipline of good sportsmanship, so necessary for a happy adult life (45).

READING

At around the age of two, little children like to look at books containing large bright pictures of people, animals, and familiar household objects. While looking at the pictures, they enjoy being told simple stories about them. Even if the young child cannot understand the words, he enjoys the flow of sounds and the vocal inflections and facial expressions of the reader.

Preschool children, it has been found, listen to stories about ½ hour daily, with a mean of 23.14 minutes for one group studied (107). Such early experiences have a marked influence on the child's later reading interest. They influence not only how much he will read but also what he will read (31, 49).

Early Reading Interests. The young child likes small books that he can handle easily; he likes attractive pictures and short stories. Because he does not always understand the meaning of the words in the stories, he enjoys listening to stories in jingles and rhymes. Young children prefer stories about things that "could happen" to those that "actually happened." They most enjoy stories that are sprinkled with a *bit* of unreality, but they dislike those which are so far removed from their experiences that they cannot understand them. The more facts of life the young child has, the more antagonistic he is to fantasy in stories (29, 121). The attitude of the mother toward fantasy, however, has an important influence on the young child's attitude. The mother who feels that fantasy is superfluous or that it encourages flight from reality influences the child to prefer realism in his stories. Most young children enjoy fantasy, and they like to identify themselves with the characters of the stories they hear (177).

Because stories read to young children influence their attitudes and behavior, there is a great deal of concern about what books are suitable for young children. Stories recommended for young children today emphasize the importance of realistic content. Of those most highly recommended, about one-third have children as characters, one-third have animals, and the others have mainly adults, especially females. Few of the stories considered suitable for the young child are about fairies or supernatural creatures. There is also more emphasis on social behavior and regard for other people in today's stories than in those popular with children in past generations (23).

Most young children prefer stories about familiar people and animals. They like the children's classics, such as *The Three Bears, Mother Goose,* and *Cinderella,* and modern books, such as *Little Black Sambo* and *Mary Poppins.* By kindergarten age, they like humorous stories, dramas about Western life, and the comics. Their favorite characters are animals, boys, and girls. They like these characters for their personal qualities or their humor. Because of the child's belief in animism, animals that behave like human beings are very popular. Furthermore, because the child is able to identify himself with the animals, he derives great enjoyment from hearing about what they do (19, 49, 57).

Reading Interests of Late Childhood. Although he may read well, the older child is limited in what he can read by what his parents provide or by what he can borrow from his friends or from the school or public library. Certain cultural pressures also influence his reading interests. He learns to read what he is supposed to read and what is considered appropriate for his sex (33, 58, 139). Furthermore, how much he reads and what he reads are greatly influenced by class values, with children of the middle and upper classes reading what parents and teachers think appropriate and children from the lower classes reading what they wish, with little or no supervision (71).

As the child grows older, his reading tastes change. He calls what he does not

like "babyish." With intellectual growth and school experiences, he becomes more realistic and regards everything related to fantasy as "phony." The child who enjoyed stories dealing with animals several years earlier now begins to lose interest in animal stories because he can no longer identify with the animals (19, 57).

As for the three major interest patterns in reading—adventure and violence, love and glamour, and educational materials—preferences vary according to the *child's age* and reading ability.

Book format and illustrations appeal more to some children than to others. Furthermore, what appeals to children is usually different from what appeals to adults. Too much emphasis on description, whimsy, and scenes and customs that are foreign to the child's experience will make a child dislike a book, even though it may be rated high by adults. With few exceptions, children prefer their stories to have happy endings and to be as free from anxiety-producing elements as possible (19, 58).

At six and seven years of age, children prefer stories about nature, the wind, birds, trees, and flowers. For the eight-year-old, the most favored reading is fairy tales. The appeal of these stories lies in their fantastic, imaginative element. Rather closely related to the interest in fairy stories is the interest in stories of other lands, especially when they center around children. By the age of nine, the child begins to lose interest in fairy tales. Boys shift to stories of the boy-scout type; stories of adventure; comedies; and horror, or "spooky," stories (152).

As children reach puberty, their reading interests become more "sophisticated." The eleven-year-old is interested mainly in tales of adventure and mystery. Science and invention are popular reading topics for boys, while homelife and school life are more popular with girls. Because of the twelve-year-old's tendency to worship heroes, he prefers books about legendary or historical heroes as well as biographies of great men and women. Books about invention, athletics, and adventure are very popular with boys, while girls show a preference for books relating to homelife, boarding-school or college life, adventure stories written for boys, nature stories, and Bible stories. These reading interests become intensified among thirteen-year-olds, but few new interests develop. After the child becomes sexually mature, stories dealing with romance and love become popular, especially with girls (57, 92). Changes in interest patterns are shown in Figure 10–6.

Individual Differences.   While there are fairly well-marked age differences in reading preferences, differences within each age group are even greater. These differences depend primarily upon the sex and intelligence of the readers. *Boys* like reading matter that concentrates on adventure, vio-

lence, mystery, sports, travel, science, and war; *girls* prefer stories of real life, with everyday characters and a flavor of romance. These sex differences become more pronounced as children grow older (154, 156).

Age for age, girls read more than boys; boys tend to prefer the pictorial media—comics, movies, and television (9). While children of different levels of *intelligence* have similar reading interests at the same ages, bright children read more and select books of higher caliber than average or dull children (162). *Negro* children and children of the lower socioeconomic groups read comics more than books. Their preference may be due to the fact that they receive little encouragement to read from their parents and have few books available in their homes rather than to differences in intellectual level (108, 161).

Magazines and Newspapers.   From the fifth grade on, children have an increased interest in newspapers and magazines; the older child spends more time on these than on books. Boys show a greater interest in newspapers, and girls in magazines. Bright children show a preference for the "better" type of newspaper and magazine, while those who are not so bright or who come from poorer homes prefer the tabloids and children's magazines or, as they grow older, the more sensational magazines. When children first begin to read newspapers, their main interest is in the comic strips. Gradually, as a result of their studies and their discussions of current events in school, they begin to read the news of the day, foreign news, political news, and editorials (92, 131).

Comics.   Comics are cartoon stories in which the story element is less important than the pictures. Most of the comics published today relate to adventure rather than to comedy, and their appeal is principally emotional. Comics are "skewed toward reality." When the situation is real, the people are unreal; when the situation is unreal, the people are real.

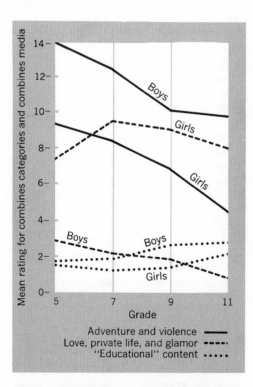

Figure 10–6. Patterns of interest in different types of mass communication. (Adapted from P. I. Lyness, Patterns in the mass communications tastes of the young audience, *J. educ. Psychol.*, 1951, 42, 449–467. Used by permission.)

The characters are occasionally humorous, but for the most part they are "serious fellows, intent on dangerous adventure and noble deeds." To accomplish these ends, they use methods ranging from magic to "just plain violent means." Good always triumphs in the end. About 50 per cent of the comics today have animal characters; many of these comics are humorous (143, 172).

The comics present a vivid and realistic picture of contemporary American life. Characters coming from every walk of life reflect the cultural patterns of acceptance and rejection regarding ethnic groups. There are comics to appeal to all ages and all tastes. They appear in newspapers as "comic strips" and in magazine form as "comic books." The subject matter of the comics includes all types of adventure, humor, romance and sex, animal antics, and detective stories. Some are based on literary classics or even on stories from the Bible. Approximately equal space is devoted to humor and crime. The child of today is literally surrounded with comics. Most children buy some of the comics they read and obtain others by swapping with their classmates and friends. Great prestige is associated with owning a large number of comics for swapping purposes (27, 100).

As early as three or four years of age, before the child can read or understand many of the words he hears, he asks to have the comics read to him. From then on, interest in the comics increases rapidly, reaching a peak during the sixth or seventh grade and then declining. Even among high-school students, however, approximately two-thirds claim that they read the comics regularly. Studies of elementary-school children have revealed that the mean number of comic books read in the fourth through the sixth grades ranges from 12 to 14 a week (27, 140, 172). In a study of children six to eleven years of age, it was found that 96 per cent of the boys and 91 per cent of the girls read the comics regularly (179).

The child's first interest in reading the newspaper, as was pointed out earlier, is centered around his interest in the comics. Long before he is interested in the news of the world, he has become a daily reader of the comic strips, and this interest persists even after he begins to read other parts of the newspaper. Boys and girls have different tastes in comics, and boys, at every age, read more comics than girls (9). The slow learner reads more comics and fewer books than the rapid learner, and he concentrates on different types of comics (156, 162).

Favorite Comics. Children's interests in comics, books, and magazines follow the same general pattern (92). Among preschool children, the favorite comics are those in which animals, such as Bugs Bunny and Mickey Mouse, dress and talk like human beings. In the early grades of elementary school, sex differences in interest begin to be apparent. Boys like excitement and adventure and have little interest in realism. Comics with fast action, plenty of conversation, lots of danger, and a hero who wins by the narrowest margin have the greatest appeal. The boy who is beginning to be interested in science likes comics centered around impossible scientific devices, and these rarely seem incredible to him (170, 172).

Late childhood is the beginning of the hero-worshiping age. Since boys like comic-book heroes they can identify with, boys from the sixth grade on are "attracted to those magazines whose contents, action, and stories are predominantly masculine and are written from a masculine standpoint, whose central characters find adventure through the mastery of danger, whose stories feature a good deal of crime and violence, whose main theme is sports and athletics, and whose chief appeal is humor" (27).

Girls in the early grades of school like comics featuring women, children, and animals. They prefer women who can perform marvelous feats or who have athletic superiority. They are less interested in adventure, mystery, and thrills than boys, and they show a greater interest in animal comics. The older girl prefers romance to adventure. She wants her comics to be "feminine," although some girls at this age like the typically "masculine" comic also (172). Commenting on the favorite comics of girls from

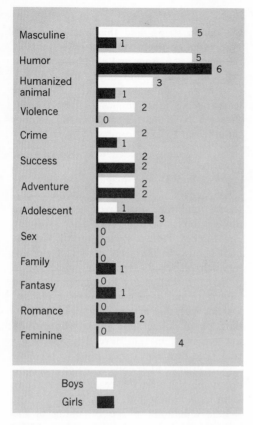

Masculine — 5 / 1

Humor — 5 / 6

Humanized animal — 3 / 1

Violence — 2 / 0

Crime — 2 / 1

Success — 2 / 2

Adventure — 2 / 2

Adolescent — 1 / 3

Sex — 0 / 0

Family — 0 / 1

Fantasy — 0 / 1

Romance — 0 / 2

Feminine — 0 / 4

Boys ☐
Girls ■

Figure 10–7. Frequency with which characteristic "appeals" appear in the 10 most popular comic books for boys and girls. (Adapted from R. F. Butterworth and G. G. Thompson, Factors related to age-grade trends and sex differences in children's preferences for comic books, *J. genet. Psychol.*, 1951, 78, 71–96. Used by permission.)

the fifth grade on, Butterworth and Thompson state, "Girls show a preference for comic books that feature feminine characters and pursuits, typical adolescents, a certain element of romance, dating, etc., and all varieties of humor" (27). Figure 10–7 shows the types of comics that appeal to boys and girls at different ages.

Reasons for Interest. Not all children read the comics for the same reasons, but certain reasons are almost universal.

Through *identification* with characters in

the comics, children have an excellent opportunity to solve many of their emotional and personal problems. As Podolsky has stressed, "The current crop of comics appeals to the child's love for the supernatural and the imaginative. They deal with mystery, bloodshed, crime, and murder. They pass the bounds of the physical, leave the intellectual, and play heavily in the emotional field" (122).

Comics offer the child *escape* from the humdrum reality of the daily routine. They are *easy to read;* they are *cheap;* they are exciting, mysterious, thrilling, and sometimes humorous; they are often in *serial form* and thus give the reader something to look forward to; and they often give good *moral lessons.* The *characters* do things the child himself would like to do, and they are brave, strong, and beautiful, with an unfailing ability to master difficulties. Also, the *art* of the comics is easy to understand and colorful (10, 16, 166).

Evaluation of Comics. Without question, comics will be an important part of children's reading for many years to come. It is impossible—and undesirable—to keep a child from reading comics once he goes to school and associates with other children. A child who is not permitted to read comics when his friends are permitted to do so is "different." A child who cannot talk about the comics when his friends are discussing them, who has no comics to swap with his friends, and who is forced to admit he is "not allowed" to read comics will get the reputation of being a "goody-goody" and of being "tied to mother's apron strings"—a reputation that may lead to lack of acceptance among his agemates.

Some of the many arguments given *in favor* of the comics are:

1. The comics constitute a kind of modern folklore, corresponding to the Greek and Norse myths.

2. The comics supply to children of limited reading ability a reading experience which is thoroughly enjoyable. They may be used to motivate the child in the development of his reading skill. They stimulate the child to read further and may break down his resistance to reading if the material is presented as entertainment.

3. The educational attainment of children who read comics frequently is almost identical with that of children who read them infrequently.

4. If children actually read the text of the comics, they will be introduced to a wide vocabulary, including many words which they repeatedly encounter in other reading.

5. The comics offer an excellent technique for propaganda, especially antiprejudice propaganda.

6. They serve as effective methods of simplified teaching.

7. They meet children's needs for overcoming, in imagination, some of the limitations of their age and ability and for obtaining a sense of adventure denied them in real life.

8. To normal children, the comics offer the mental catharsis which Aristotle claimed for the drama. Thus the readers are released from feelings of inadequacy and insecurity and from fear of aggression toward or from others.

9. They are cheap, and therefore the child can freely choose and buy those he prefers.

10. They give the child pleasure by offering him a chance for identification.

11. There are no more behavior problems among children who read comics frequently than among those who do not. Those with the best critical understanding are best adjusted, even when they read comics frequently and have the greatest interest in them.

12. Normal aggressive reactions find release in fantasies stimulated by comic books. Through identification with the characters in the comics, the child is able to adjust himself better to life (10, 14, 16, 27, 32, 90, 143, 172).

The arguments *against* reading the comics are:

1. The comics tend to crowd out reading of a more desirable sort. They distract the child from more worthwhile literature.

2. Many poor readers merely get the story from the pictures without making an effort to read the text.

3. The adventures portrayed in the comics are so far removed from reality that children do not acquire an understanding of the world as it is, such as they can obtain from reading material that is closer to real life.

4. There is little or no progression of reading experience within the area of the comics.

5. The art, stories, and language of most comic strips are inferior in quality. Because the comics make use of both "respectable" and "vulgar" slang, they put the stamp of approval on the use of slang in everyday speech and encourage the child to use slang when parents and teachers are trying to discourage its use.

6. Comics tend to overstimulate the child with material relating to sex, frightening experiences, and violence.

7. They keep children from other activities and interests.

8. Opposition of parents to the reading of comics may lead to disagreements, arguments, secretiveness, and feelings of guilt on the child's part.

9. Comics lead to juvenile delinquency. There is no evidence, however, that comics entice youth into crime. Rather, those who are responsive to crime portrayals on occasion use the ideas and techniques seen in the comics. Comics are thus often used as "scapegoats." While delinquents read many more "harmful" and "questionable" comics than nondelinquents, this may not be a cause-and-effect relationship. On the other hand, the reading of comics may keep the spiral of delinquency alive among delinquents.

10. The child who finds it necessary to bury himself in the comics usually does so because his real world is uninteresting or intolerable.

11. Comics have an unfavorable effect on the child's attitudes. According to Podolsky:

The attitude fostered by the comic books pervades the child's daily life both in school and at home. At school he becomes a daydreamer or an idler in the belief that some miracle will intervene to save him from his just deserts; he acquires the idea that no academic preparation for life is necessary, that just a bit of brawn and foxiness will see him through. At home the child is prone to become a "dead weight." The household is managed to care for him, yet he is interested neither in how things are managed nor in any participation therein. He is making a very poor preparation for the democratic life which predicates and necessitates the cooperative effort of all citizens (122).

12. Comics counteract the efforts of parents and teachers to help the child learn to make better social adjustments. Through identification with aggressive characters in the comics, children are encouraged to become more aggressive at the time when attempts are being made to discourage their aggressiveness. Furthermore, comics encourage the child to stereotype people, thus increasing the tendency to be prejudiced against certain groups—a tendency which parents and teachers try to counteract by helping children to develop better social insight (9, 10, 78, 116, 155).

In summary, it is apparent that there is no agreement regarding the effect of comics. Instead, it is very obvious that they have their good and bad features as far as the child's mental health and personality development are concerned. As long as reading the comics is a favorite form of play among American children, no child can be expected to be deprived of comics without running the risk of far more serious psychological damage than he would receive from reading them. On the other hand, devoting an *unreasonable* portion of playtime to comics not only is unwise but is the source of potential psychological harm. If the child *wants* to devote more time to comics than his agemates do, this may be regarded as a "danger signal" of poor personal or social adjustment.

The child who reads comics with discrimination and who does not allow them to become his dominant play interest has been found to be an avid reader of library books. There is no evidence that his reading of comics affects his school achievement, especially in the areas of spelling and reading, which, according to many critics of comics reading, are most likely to be adversely affected. In conclusion, it appears that there is "no justification for curtailing children's access to comic books" (16).

MOVIES

Few five- or six-year-olds understand enough of what is shown on the movie screen to be able to concentrate on it for an entire performance. They become restless from boredom. Not realizing that the noise and shooting are only make-believe, they often shut their eyes and cry in fear. By the time the child is seven years old, he can concentrate for a longer time. He has a better understanding of what the picture is about; he knows that what he sees on the screen is only make-believe, and he is less frightened by it than the young child.

At this age, some children attend the movies once a week regularly, and others only occasionally. As going to the movies on Saturday afternoon is one of the favorite gang activities of both boys and girls, the child who belongs to a gang is likely to be a more frequent and more regular attendant than the child who has no one to go with. To an older child, going to the movies with parents or siblings or going alone merely advertises to his agemates that he is unpopular (92, 161, 170).

Movie Preferences. The major motive for attending movies is to get a "thrill." Anything that involves adventure or mystery offers excitement which children do not get from everyday life (47). Many children, as they grow older, prefer movies to books or games because movies offer more thrills.

Little children, whether boys or girls, like comics and animated films, especially those with animals as the main characters (92, 170). *Sex differences* in movie preferences begin around the age of six years and become more pronounced as children reach adolescence. These differences parallel the differences in reading interests. Boys are especially interested in movies dealing with adventure, war, cowboys, and Indians, while girls prefer movies in which there are dancing, singing, and animals. Both boys and girls like comedies and cartoons; they want the heroes to be active and the heroines pretty. Throughout childhood, both boys and girls dislike love stories, though girls begin to be interested in such films slightly earlier than boys.

Children who are *unhappy,* because of unfavorable conditions in the home or elsewhere, are quite likely to become addicted to crime movies. They use this type of escape in much the same way that adults use alcohol. They "drown their unhappiness in artificial excitement, thus obtaining a slight measure of relief" (122).

Influence of Movies. Three major factors determine how great the influence of movies on children will be. These are discussed in the following paragraphs:

1. Type of Child. What a child "gets" from the movies depends on his background and his needs. He takes from a movie what he can use or what will function in his life (52). The child who is aggressive, for example, is likely to be less aggressive after seeing a film with an aggressive theme. The less aggressive child, on the other hand, is usually more aggressive after viewing such a film because, in his mind, seeing such action on the screen gives aggression the stamp of approval and tends to release the aggressiveness he has inhibited (2). What the child thinks others expect of him; what he thinks his rights, his obligations, and the appropriate behavior for him are; and what he expects from others will also influence how he reacts to a film and what effect it will have on his behavior. A child who fears a policeman because of the stereotype of policemen he has seen in the comics will be more intimidated by a policeman on the screen than the child who has a more favorable concept (141, 170).

2. What Is Understood and Remembered. The young child understands and hence re-

members little of what he sees on the movie screen. Older children, it has been reported, retain about 70 per cent as much as adults, and their memories persist over a period of 3 to 4 months. Even among young children, pictures that present a new world or that present the familiar in a new and fascinating way will be remembered longer than pictures that absorb the attention less.

The more exciting the picture, the less critical the child's attitude and the more influenced he will be by what he remembers. Young children are, on the whole, less critical of, and more influenced by, what they see on the screen than older children, in spite of the fact that young children remember less of what they see. Likewise, children with lower IQ's retain less but are less critical and more influenced than children with higher IQ's (2, 52, 141).

3. Identification with Characters. Most important of all, the influence of movies varies according to whether or not the child identifies with a character on the screen (47). When the child identifies closely with one of the characters, he shares, vicariously, the experiences of that character. If the character is aggressive, for example, this will tend to increase the child's aggressiveness. If he does not identify closely with the character, watching the film may act as a cathartic for pent-up aggressions and thus decrease his aggressiveness (116).

Children tend to identify with characters whose actions are most relevant to their needs and who are most similar to them in age, sex, and race. The child also tends to identify with a character whose social class is related to his aspired social class rather than to his present social class. The more the child identifies with a character on the screen, the more he remembers of the picture and, in turn, the greater its influence on his attitudes and behavior will be (96, 97).

Specific Effects. Movies give the child *pleasure* and provide him with *excitement* he does not get from his everyday life. For young children, the movies provide ideas to be used in *play,* such as games of cowboys or Indians. The older child gets ideas about *how to behave* and about the *world* in which he lives. The ideas he gets about *people* of different types may lead to tolerance or intolerance, depending on how the characters are shown and the situations in which they are placed. When the characters portray unfamiliar people, he is likely to stereotype groups with which the characters are identified (47). Whether this will lead to *prejudice* or *tolerance* in real life will depend on how they are presented on the screen (9, 167).

Movies may have a pronounced *emotional effect* on a child. They often frighten him, causing nightmares or daytime fears that are difficult for an adult to understand unless he knows the circumstances that have given rise to them. *Eating disturbances,* caused by emotional tension, may cause the child to lose weight or become ill. Nail biting and other *nervous mannerisms* are likewise frequent aftermaths of too much movie attendance. Many children suffer from *eyestrain* and *general fatigue* as a result of attending movies in the late afternoon or evening following a busy day in school or at play. All these effects are intensified if the movies contain horror elements (122, 170).

RADIO

The baby enjoys hearing music or simple jingles over the air, but not until three years of age does the child show any real interest in radio listening. By five, he listens to scattered radio programs; at six, he listens several hours weekly; and at seven, he likes to hear certain programs daily and is annoyed when he misses one of them. Each year, interest in listening to the radio increases (109, 170).

The school child spends from 1 to 3 hours daily listening to the radio. This, for the average child, is more than the time devoted to leisure reading or attendance at the movies. In many cases, it is more than the time spent in play with other children. While boys prefer the pictorial media, such as comics, movies, and television, to reading and radio listening, there is no marked sex difference at any age in the amount of time boys and girls devote to radio listening. Children with high IQ's listen less than those with lower IQ's, and better students listen less than poorer students. Rural children, who have fewer opportunities for a variety of play activities, spend more time listening to the radio than urban children. Better-adjusted children listen to the radio less than the poorly adjusted, and their program preferences are different (9).

For the major part of childhood, the radio is not so popular as television. A child can listen to the radio at times, however, when it would be impossible for him to watch television—when he is doing household chores, for example. Many children keep their radios tuned to musical programs while they are studying or reading.

Because radios cost much less than television sets, many children have their own radios in their rooms. In most families, there is only one television set, and the child often finds that other family members want to view a program he has no interest in. Because the family television set is generally in the living room, the child cannot use it while he is in his room studying or reading; parents would not permit this, but they usually do not know that he is listening to his radio if he has it turned low. Consequently, radio fills a play need in his life which television cannot always fill (170).

In the latter part of childhood, radio is generally preferred to television, especially among bright children. Older children no longer enjoy the programs designed for young children, and other television programs cater mainly to the interests of adults, with emphasis on news, romance, and special events. The musical programs on the radio appeal especially to the older child. In addition, the older child is often bored or impatient with the commercials used on television; he is thus more critical than he might otherwise be. While he becomes increasingly critical of radio programs as he grows older, he still finds more interest in them than in television. The result is that older children listen to the radio less than they did when they were younger, but they generally prefer radio to television. In early childhood, the reverse is true (172).

Program Preferences. In general, the child's program preferences at different ages follow his preferences in reading and movies (93). The preschool child listens to children's programs which deal mainly with animals and familiar people doing familiar things. He also likes simple music, whether vocal or instrumental. By the age of six years, he begins to lose interest in children's programs; now he wants programs that are entertaining rather than educational. He likes plays dealing with adventure, mystery, crime, and comedy, and he likes popular dance music. Quiz shows appeal to the older child, as do dramas of domestic life, slapstick comedies, sports reports, and occasionally the news of the day.

For the most part, the older child dislikes programs of a serious nature, such as classical music and educational, religious, or historical talks. Boys have a narrower range of program preferences than girls. They prefer programs emphasizing adventure, mystery, comedy, and crime, while girls like popular music and comedy shows (109, 125, 170). Figure 10–8 shows the program preferences of boys and girls at different ages.

Effects of Radio. There is a tendency to overestimate the undesirable effects of radio listening and to underemphasize the educational and other advantages. Some writers hold that radio listening gives the child an outlet for his aggressive tendencies, while others maintain that it cultivates the child's appetite for violence. The fact that a high percentage of children listen to radio programs in which violence and crime are stressed would suggest that children need the tension-releasing experience such programs offer (109, 125). There is no question, however, that the effect of radio listening will be influenced by the amount of time spent listening and the type of program habitually listened to.

The favorable influences of radio listening have been listed as follows: It offers the child a form of entertainment within the home and thus acts as an incentive to keep the child at home and with the family; it increases the child's knowledge about history, current events, geography, literature, and many other subjects, and it supplements what he learns in school; it improves his speech by increasing his vocabulary, improving his grammar, and giving him a good model of diction; it encourages him to read to supplement his knowledge of subjects he has heard about over the air; and it offers him models with whom he can identify, thus acting as an incentive to self-improvement (170).

Critics of radio listening emphasize its harmful effects. These are most pronounced when the child concentrates on programs of violence, crime, and mystery. Terrifying programs affect the general physical condition of the child by producing nervous tension. Nightmares, loss of sleep, poor appetite, and loss of weight are the results. Then, too, children rebel against going to bed at suitable times if there are programs they are anxious to hear. This means that they get less sleep than they need or that they go to bed angry and emotionally upset (122).

The child who spends much of his time listening to the radio gets too little exercise for his normal development and for a healthy condition. His school work suffers partly because he does not give enough time to his studies and partly because he does not concentrate when he is studying. As Podolsky has pointed out, "Children cannot be expected to pay attention or concentrate on dull school subjects when their nervous systems are overwrought, their minds still weary from lack of sleep, their digestion disturbed" (122).

Many children claim that they can study better when listening to the radio than when in a quiet room. In a test of the reading of sixth-graders during the playing of the radio, it was found that reading was adversely affected by variety but not by musical programs. There was less effect on those with

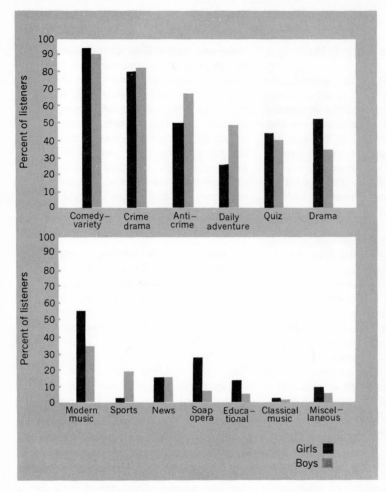

Figure 10–8. Percentages of habitual listeners among boys and girls to different radio programs. (Adapted from E. A. Ricciuti, Children and radio: a study of listeners and nonlisteners to various types of radio programs in terms of selected ability, attitudes, and behavior measures, *Genet. Psychol. Monogr.*, 1951, 44, 69–143. Used by permission.)

high IQ's than on those with lower IQ's (112). The avid radio listener often picks up a vocabulary of slang and other undesirable forms of speech (107).

TELEVISION

As television combines the appealing features of the movies and radio, it is most attractive to children. The time spent on television watching is out of all proportion to the amount of time devoted to other forms of play for far too many children (137). As Witty has described it, television is "children's most time-consuming activity" (174). The appeal of television, like that of

other forms of amusement, varies markedly from child to child and from age to age in the same child. Many babies are introduced to television while they are still in their cribs; for them, television is a "built-in babysitter" (128). For the preschool child, television watching is an *added* play activity, not a substitute activity.

Variations in *interest* in television exist within each age group. Although children of all levels of intelligence find it one of their most pleasurable forms of amusement, bright children begin to lose interest in it sooner than dull children, and good students enjoy it less than poor students (9, 136). Television appeals more to children who are poorly adjusted, both personally and socially, than to those who are well adjusted. As a result, the former usually watch television more than the latter (46). Television watching is more time-consuming among children of the lower socioeconomic groups than among those of the higher groups, especially as childhood progresses (17, 136).

Time Spent on Television. The amount of time a child spends watching television is not foolproof evidence of his interest in it. The time may be regulated by family rules, by the amount of school work or homework the child has, or by whether the family owns a television set. It has been estimated that from the age of three years on, the child spends from one-sixth to one-seventh of his waking hours on television (128). At the time of peak interest, around six years, the average child devotes 4 hours daily to television. After he enters school, the time declines to 2 or 3 hours during the school week, with more time over the weekends and during vacation periods (117, 133, 175).

As children grow older and are permitted to stay up later at night, the time spent on television during school days increases. After the age of twelve, however, children are given more and more homework, and television watching declines (11, 132, 172). School-age children usually watch television in the late afternoon and early evening, though many also manage to do so before they go to school and during or after their noon meal. Children watch television more in winter than in summer, and urban children watch more than rural children. Boys, on the whole, spend more time on television than girls (9, 17, 104, 163). Figure 10–9 shows the mean daily minutes spent watching television at different ages.

The time spent on television is markedly influenced by whether or not the family owns a television set, by how many watchers there are in the family, by how much the family members can agree upon the programs to be viewed, and by how long the family has owned a set. In a large family with children of different ages and of both

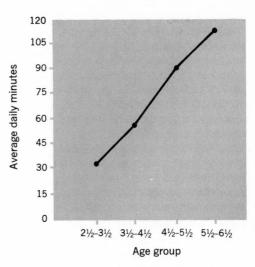

Figure 10–9. Time spent daily watching television by children of different ages. (Adapted from H. R. Marshall, Relations between home experiences and children's use of language in play interactions with peers, _Psychol. Monogr.,_ 1961, 75, No. 5. Used by permission.)

sexes, no one child has as much time to view his favorite programs as is possible in a smaller family. Children whose families own television sets watch more, and more regularly, than children who must rely on friends or neighbors to share theirs. If the family has owned a set for a long time, the time spent watching television will be influenced by individual interests. If the set is a "new toy," however, the child will watch any and every program available, regardless of his interests, until the novelty has worn off. In areas of the country where reception is poor, the amount of time a child spends watching television is not dependent so much on his interests as on how many programs are available and when they are available (11, 75, 133).

Program Preferences. Preschool children like simple stories about animals and familiar people, music, cartoons, and simple comedy. First- and second-grade children like puppet shows, cowboy presentations, harmless mysteries, humor, family-life situations, and prize-presenting programs. By the third and fourth grades, children are interested in imaginative programs, such as those about rockets and spaceships, and in variety shows, mystery and detective stories, dramatic plays, and music. Fifth- and sixth-grade children continue to like these programs, but they also like presentations dealing with science and feats of skill. Stories, comedy, cartoons, and music are popular at every age, while educational programs tend to be unpopular, especially among children with lower IQ's (136, 137, 161). Boys like the hero to be aggressive and to defend himself and others, whereas girls care little for aggressive heroes (9, 95).

When children first start to watch television, they will watch any program available. After 6 months, however, they learn to be more discriminating. They develop well-balanced program preferences and want variety as well as quality. Teachers often help them to select programs that tie in with their school work (54). On the whole, children today prefer to watch the kinds of programs their parents and teachers would choose for them (134, 171). As Schramm has pointed out:

We have discovered a very interesting, although hardly surprising, thing about young children's media habits. Up to about the age of ten, they are very closely related to their parents' media habits. In fact, if you can tell me one fact—the father's education—I can predict with some confidence what kind of media patterns his children would have; and if you tell me what kind of television the parents watch, what music they hear, and so on, then I could predict with almost complete confidence what use their children will make of the media. After the age of ten . . . the influence of the parents tends to be diluted by the influence of the peer group (128).

Effects of Television. Ever since the arrival of television as a popular form of children's amusement, parents, educators, law-enforcing officers, and the clergy have shown a great concern about its effect on the child. Concern has ranged from the effect television has on reading and other leisure-time activities to its effect on moral behavior and its relationship to the serious increase in juvenile delinquency.

This concern is not new; every time a new medium of mass communication is introduced, members of the older generation have blamed the new medium for all the defects they see in the young. Movies, radio, and comics have all been blamed for the rise in juvenile delinquency; now it is television's turn to take the blame. In each case, the concern has given rise to research studies to discover just how great an influence that particular mass medium had on children's attitudes and behavior. Some of the studies of the effects of television maintain that television is more harmful than helpful; others take the opposite view; and still others maintain that the effects are too slight to be considered seriously (75, 95, 128, 133).

Without question, when a child spends one-sixth or more of his waking time in one activity, it is bound to have some influence over his actions and his attitudes. Furthermore, it is bound to contribute to the shaping of his personal and moral values. Whether the influence is immediate or long-term or both, however, will depend not so much upon the programs the child sees as upon the child himself. Schramm, from his study of the influence of television on over six thousand children, has stressed this point as an important determinant of the effect of television:

More important than what television brings to the child is what the child brings to television. And this is our responsibility. What kind of child are we sending to television? . . . If we use television as a baby sitter, at the cost of other human contacts, we are obviously remiss. If we do not introduce our children to books, simply because television is so easily available, then we are being foolish. If we do not help our children to build up healthy contacts with other humans their own age, simply because television "keeps them at home," then we are truly doing them an unkindness (128).

Variations in Effects. The effect of television on a child, like that of movies, is greatly influenced by what he remembers, how much he understands, and whether or not he identifies with characters on the television screen. If he identifies with a desirable character, identification will be more helpful than harmful, but if he identifies with a character who embodies disapproved moral standards or extreme aggressiveness, he is likely to be harmed (9, 175).

When a child's needs are not met in real life and he uses television as an escape mechanism, it will have a greater influence on his attitudes and behavior than if he had no need to escape into a substitute world. Because many of the programs a child watches, especially during the evening hours, are not meant for children, he does not always understand what he sees. Partial understanding and distortion of the meaning of a program can be more damaging than no understanding.

A word of caution in assessing the effects of television is in order. One must consider whether the physical or psychological damage that has been claimed to result from television is actually the result of television watching per se or whether avid television watching is the result of physical or psychological damage already present in the child. A child who has poor eyesight, for example, may not be able to see well enough to play the games of the peer group, or his parents may not permit him to play games in which his glasses might be broken. Under such conditions, the child may turn to television watching as a substitute for play. How much this will affect the already poor vision of the child is still an unanswered question among doctors (75).

Similarly, a child who lacks social acceptance may become an avid television watcher. He then becomes more unsocial and makes poorer social adjustments with each passing year because he is deprived of the learning experiences his agemates have. Consequently, he *appears* to have been psychologically damaged by too much television watching. This cause-and-effect solution is not acceptable, however; it is too simple. While there is no doubt that excessive television watching may contribute to poor

social adjustment, the fact that the child has been deprived of learning opportunities cannot be overlooked. Which is more important is still an open question (75, 128, 133).

Specific Effects. The many reported effects of television watching are worth a critical analysis. Until further information is available, however, it is impossible to conclude how helpful or how damaging television is and whether the effects—good or bad—are temporary or permanent. Until the present generation of television watchers has lived through the major part of its life-span, no one can tell what the long-term effects will be. There is almost unanimous agreement, however, on one point: The well-adjusted child is less likely to be adversely affected, either temporarily or permanently, than the poorly adjusted child, and the healthy child less than the unhealthy (175).

Of the many effects of television watching that have been reported, the following have received the most attention:

1. Physical Effects. The arguments against television claim that it interferes with a regular schedule of eating and sleeping. A child is likely to delay his meal to watch a program he wants to see or to eat while watching the program, with the result that he does not chew his food properly (150). Furthermore, eating snacks while watching television, which is common among people of all ages but especially among children, takes the edge off the appetite and results in a diet too heavily weighted with starches and sweets. Many obese children are avid television watchers because they are unable to engage in the strenuous play of their agemates; eating snacks while watching television merely increases the problem (24).

Interference with sleep is even more serious than interference with eating. Children who stay up beyond their usual bedtime to watch television get too little sleep (94, 163). Young children often dream or have nightmares about the programs they have seen (51, 122). Too much television can make children nervous and high-strung, especially if they concentrate on terror programs (133, 172). As Podolsky has pointed out:

There is a natural tendency of the child's mind to continue turning over throughout the night what he has seen or heard before going to sleep. There is a deepening of impressions the next day by retelling and re-enacting these things during play-time. There is a potent tendency in children to vicarious participation in plots seen or heard, so that in recollection or dreams, the child substitutes himself and family for the victim or victims, thus intensifying unwholesome emotional reactions, often to a state of fearful struggle against a terrifying threat to the safety or existence of himself as well as members of his family (122).

2. Effects on Other Forms of Play. Television watching always cuts into the time available for other activities, especially out-of-door play and play with other children. As a result, the child is deprived of the healthful exercise and emotional release that out-of-door play provides (175). Furthermore, he is deprived of the learning experiences needed for good *social adjustments* (75, 133).

Too much time devoted to television results in an unbalanced play program, with little time devoted to creative play, movie attendance, or listening to the radio. When television is added to a child's activities, the child usually reads less, even devoting less time to comics than formerly. The reading of books is affected more than the reading of newspapers and magazines because the latter continue to appeal through their pictorial sections and comic strips (137, 175). What the child does read, however, is likely to be of better caliber and to be motivated by what he has seen on television. Moreover, watching television often opens up new interests and encourages the child to increase his knowledge by reading (41, 66, 113).

3. Effects on School Work. Many students spend more time on television than on their studies. This is certain to have some effect on the child, even though the time spent on television might not have been spent on studies, especially if the child is not interested in them and has little motivation to do good work (73, 161). The more serious aspect of this problem is that television gives children material in such an exciting and vivid way that it is hard for school books to compete with it for the child's interest and attention. Far too many avid television watchers become so addicted to this excitement that they find lessons and school books boring (129, 130, 132).

Some children are motivated to "follow up" what they have seen on the television screen and thus fill gaps in their school curriculum. They read material they might not otherwise have read. The better student, after the novelty of television wears off, does not allow it to interfere with his school work. This is not true of the poorer student (11, 59, 67, 132). Teachers often blame poor school work on television. Their attitudes, however, are often influenced by whether they own a set or not; nonowners are less tolerant than owners (170).

4. Effects on Family Activities. In the family, television watching produces closer physical proximity but restricts social interaction. It prevents the family members from reading, conversing, and playing. On the other hand, it stimulates new family interests and widens the circle of family friends. There are more visitors in the home, less visiting outside the home, less driving for pleasure, and less attendance at movies (6, 94, 150). Unquestionably the most serious and unfavorable effect of television on family life is that many parents use television as a "pacifier" for their children in place of discipline (94).

5. Effects on Attitudes. What a child sees on the television screen is so real that attitudes established after viewing different programs are likely to be transferred to real-life situations. In a study of the effects of television programs on children's concepts of, and attitudes toward, law enforcement, it was found that children tended to believe that sheriffs are dishonest, that criminals are treated "mean," that it is all right to "beat up" criminals, that it is all right for police to be dishonest in order to catch criminals, and that criminals are "smart" (135).

A constant television diet of crime, terror, and cruelty will, in time, blunt the child's sensitivities; he will consider antisocial and destructive behavior almost "normal." Furthermore, repeated exposure to crime and violence will eventually "blunt the child's sensitivity to human suffering" (175). As Podolsky has pointed out:

Seeing constant brutality, viciousness, and unsocial acts results in hardness, intense selfishness, even in mercilessness, proportionate to the amount of exposure and its play on the native temperament of the child. Some cease to show resentment to insults, to indignities, and even cruelty toward helpless old people, to women, and to other children. Altruistic impulses not followed by appropriate actions soon become sterile and non-existent. . . . The effects of habituation in the form of callousness to the suffering of others, begins as early as the seventh year and it mounts year by year, leading to an ever-increasing amount of over-exciting horrors. Crime and horror are found to be uppermost in the minds of the addicts much of the time, day and night (122).

6. Effects on Beliefs. Many children believe that anything said on the air is true and that the television announcer knows more about everything than parents, teachers, or doctors. If this attitude becomes habitual, it will have a profound influence on the child's buying habits as he grows older, just as it influences his behavior patterns during childhood (175). In addition, it is likely to lead to a generalized gullibility. Many a child, for example, will urge his mother to buy a certain cereal because he believes it will make him into the type of person he wants to be. The child will insist upon eating the cereal, regardless of its nutritional value, because the claims on television were so convincing.

Minimizing the Harmful Effects of Television. This brief summary of arguments for and against television watching shows that the consensus is that television contributes less that is beneficial and more that is harmful to the child's wholesome development than other forms of play. Until there is evidence to the contrary, it is obvious that a child needs more direction and control in this area of his play than in any other, even in the reading of comics. Figure 10–10 shows the beneficial effects of television weighed against the harmful.

Because the themes and pictures in many comics are harmful, parents and teachers try to keep this type of comic out of the child's reach. In addition, social pressure has forced merchants in many communities to remove these harmful comics from their shelves. Far too many parents show less concern about television than about comics. In fact, many parents actually *encourage* their children to watch television; it is a "built-in baby-sitter" when children are tired and fretful. Furthermore, parents permit children greater freedom in the choice of television programs than in the choice of comics or movies.

To avoid much of the harm that can come from television watching, Abraham Ribicoff, former Secretary of the Department of Health, Education, and Welfare, has offered the following suggestion: "As a child watches what he is permitted to watch and listens to what he is permitted to listen to, parents must learn to get tough with themselves and their children, as well as with the television industry. . . . If he [the youngster] is permitted to sit like a vegetable, pursuing moronic murders and ceaseless crimes, he suffers, and his parents do too—in the end" (118).

This, of course, does not mean that children should be deprived of the enjoyment and benefit that can come from this form of play. It does mean that direction and guidance are vitally important if the child is to develop wholesome concepts about himself, about people, and about life in general and if he is to learn a moral code that will be in keeping with the moral code approved by society. Long before television was dreamed of, Plato stressed the importance of guid-

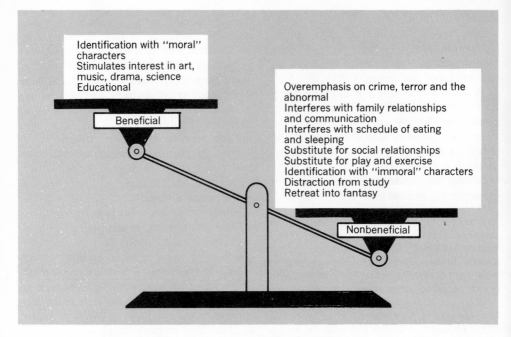

Figure 10–10. Scale of generally beneficial and detrimental television watching.

ance in what the child hears when he said, "And shall we just carelessly allow children to hear any casual tales which may be devised by casual persons, and to receive in their minds ideas for the most part the very opposite of those which we should wish them to have when they are grown up?"

VARIATIONS IN PLAY

Not all children play alike. Although the play interests of the child conform more or less closely to a pattern, variations may be traced to one or more of the following factors.

Health. Healthy children play more than sickly ones. The healthier the child, the more surplus energy he has, over and above the requirements for living, and hence the greater his energy for play. Children who lack energy prefer sedentary play. They would rather read, watch television, or go to a movie than engage in games and sports (70). This preference is most apparent during the physical growth spurt of the closing years of childhood. The child is then so tired and listless most of the time that he cannot possibly derive pleasure from any activity that requires the expenditure of energy. As a result, the favorite play of the pubescent child is daydreaming—the type of play that requires a minimum of energy but gives maximum satisfaction (40, 63).

Motor Development. The child's level of motor development plays an important role in determining what his play will be. When he is incapable of throwing and catching balls, for example, he cannot take part in the many ball games that his agemates enjoy. Similarly, a young child with poor motor coordination cannot cut, crayon, paint, or do many of the things from which other young children derive keen enjoyment.

As children's play involves motor coordination at every age, a child who lags behind in this area of development is likely to find himself a social misfit; as a result, he is forced into play activities which involve a minimum of motor coordination. Many awkward children become avid readers or television addicts, not because they get greater enjoyment from such play, but because their inferior motor development prevents them from playing as they would like to (63, 70).

Intelligence. Compared with dull babies, bright babies are more active and playful, and their play shows greater ingenuity. During the second year, the bright child rapidly advances from sensory to imitative and imaginative play. This is not true of the dull child. Month after month, his play shows little change, and it is soon obvious that he is lagging behind other children of his age. The gap becomes more and more apparent as he gets older (39).

In comparison with mentally defective children, children with normal or above-normal intelligence show a marked preference for play materials that lead to constructive activity. Children of normal intelligence also show a greater stability in the duration of their interest in each play material chosen. During the preschool years, children with high IQ's show an interest in equipment for dramatic play and creative activities, such as clay, scissors, and paint. In their constructions, not only do they make more complicated designs with blocks, paints, or crayons, but they show greater originality and derive greater satisfaction from their play than less bright children (13, 114). Bright children also derive more enjoyment from being read to, and they like more advanced books, especially those that give information instead of merely telling a story (106).

Among older children, differences in the play of those with high and low IQ's become even more marked. Bright children are more solitary and less social in their play interests, and they participate in fewer activities that involve vigorous physical play than children of average intelligence. Bright children show far less interest in games and sports than those of average intelligence, but they show more interest in intellectual games, such as card and guessing games. They prefer a balance of play interests, including both distinctly physical and distinctly intellectual pursuits. They get their greatest enjoyment from play that demands the use of their intelligence or some basic skills. They find such simple games as tag, hide-and-seek, and drop-the-handkerchief boring, while the dull child prefers these (162). Bright children enjoy collecting and putting what they collect into systematic arrangements. They also have more hobbies than the less bright children (39, 70). Very bright children at every age spend more time reading than children of average intelligence, and they have a wider range of reading interests. The type of reading they prefer also differs from that of the average child. Gifted children enjoy reading dictionaries; atlases; encyclopedias; books on science, history, and travel; biographies; folk tales; informational fiction; poetry; and dramatic works. They dislike fairy tales and show relatively little interest in emotional fiction. They prefer detective stories to crude adventure and mystery and show an interest in romance even before the age of ten (31, 89, 106).

These differences in interests are also seen in the choice of comics, movies, and radio and television programs. Here the patterns of interest are even more marked than in reading; these types of play appeal more to children with lower IQ's than to those with high IQ's (75, 97). Very bright children, who get little satisfaction from play with their peers, often find daydreaming pleasurable. Because of their intellectual superiority, they can produce daydreams with such vivid and exciting themes that they are tempted to devote more time to such play than is psychologically healthy (20, 80).

Sex. Given the same environment and the same toys, boys and girls display no really significant differences in their play activities until the gang age. But inasmuch as there are, in most homes, different environments and different toys for members of the two sexes, children become aware at an early age that certain types of play are considered appropriate for boys and others for girls.

The sex role for girls today is less clearly defined than the sex role for boys. Therefore, many games formerly played only by boys, such as Ping-Pong, hide-and-seek, and even baseball, are now played by both sexes. The reverse is not true, however. Girls' games are still girls' games.

In toy play, girls favor dolls, doll furniture, beads, and blocks, while boys prefer trains, cars, horses, airplanes, and tools. Boys play more strenuously than girls and prefer such games as baseball, football, and marbles, while girls like jumping rope and playing hide-and-go-seek and house or school. Girls prefer games which are quieter and more aesthetic in nature. In dramatizations, boys pretend to be fathers, soldiers, doctors, aviators, or truck drivers, while girls play feminine roles, such as mothers, nurses, or teachers. Even when playing with the same toys, boys and girls play differently. In block play, for example, boys construct more masculine objects than girls (76, 83, 162).

In early childhood, boys show a greater range of play interests than girls. In later childhood, the reverse is true because boys no longer engage in play that is considered "feminine," while girls add to their own repertoire some of the games of boys. In spite of this shift, however, sex differences in the range of play interests are more marked in late childhood than earlier. Boys soon lose interest in some of the play that is appropriate for them and narrow down their play to activities that girls have not appropriated (21, 35).

Environment. Young children from poor environments play less than children from better environments. This is due, in part, to a difference in health, but, to a large extent, it may be traced to the fact that children from poor environments have fewer toys,

less time, and less space in which to play. While there are often more play companions available in the poorer environments, this factor alone is inadequate to compensate for the other factors mentioned.

Rural children, because of their geographic isolation, play few organized games. They have less equipment for play and usually less free time because they are expected to help with the work on the farm or in the home. Urban children can usually count on more playmates, and they usually have more play equipment (70, 147, 161).

Socioeconomic Status. The play activities of children of different social-class backgrounds are different both quantitatively and qualitatively. Moreover, the differences increase as children grow older. Children of the higher socioeconomic groups increasingly prefer play activities that cost money, such as tennis, swimming, or watching athletic contests, while children of the lower socioeconomic classes engage in play activities involving little expenditure of money, such as jacks, ball games, or tag.

The social class to which the child belongs influences the kind of books he reads, the movies he sees, and the type of organized recreational clubs he belongs to. Children of economically privileged families engage in more cultural activities, such as dancing, music, and art lessons; dramatics; choir; and organized activities, such as Girl Scouts and Boy Scouts, than children from less privileged homes (38, 98, 160, 161).

Amount of Leisure Time. The child with limited playtime engages in activities that can be completed in the time available. When household or other duties take up most of the child's time, he is apt to be tired when playtime comes and to engage in play activities that require only a small expenditure of energy. The amount of leisure time the child has for play depends primarily upon the economic status of the family. Among children living in a residential suburban community, it was found that those of the higher economic level had few home duties and little or no work outside the home, while children from the poorer homes had less time for leisure activities and more duties (70, 108).

Play Equipment. If a child is given certain types of toys, he will use them, and his play activities will thus be influenced by them. Should the play equipment favor constructive play, as in the case of blocks, sand, or hammer and nails, the play will of course be primarily constructive. Predominance of dolls, household equipment, or soldiers puts emphasis on imaginative, make-believe play (106, 123).

Because young children spend relatively short periods of time in any one type of play, they need a wide variety of toys and materials. Too much equipment, however, is just as bad as too little. A limited amount of well-selected equipment encourages the child to be resourceful and social (85, 86).

Many adults make the mistake of assuming that a child will automatically know how to use the equipment they provide for him. This assumption seems to them to be borne out when the child shows an immediate interest in a new toy and begins to explore it and try to use it in different ways. The fact that a child plays for only a short time with his toys, however, going from one to another, is due to two things: (1) His attention span is short, and (2) he cannot think of anything else to do with a particular toy and is bored with it.

Loss of interest in block play during the kindergarten age, for example, is unquestionably due in part to lack of guidance in how to play with blocks. Because blocks are considered more sex-appropriate for boys than for girls, little boys get more encouragement and help in block play than girls (102).

On the other hand, even though dramatic play is considered more sex-appropriate for girls, boys receive more help in dramatic play than girls. Parents talk to their sons more about the roles the boys want to play and give them more suggestions on how to play the roles (104). Furthermore, as so

many of the television programs and movies for children are based on themes more appropriate for boys' than for girls' play—cowboys, westerns, and shooting—boys get more help from this source than girls.

SATISFACTIONS AND DISSATISFACTIONS FROM PLAY

Not all children can be expected to derive satisfaction from the same play, nor can children derive satisfaction from the same play at different periods. Because of differences in intelligence, interest, and many other factors, a child needs the type of play that will fit his needs. Whether a particular play activity gives him enjoyment and, at the same time, is socially approved will depend partly upon the child and partly upon what is available to him.

A child might derive more satisfaction from playing as a member of a team than from watching television or from reading a book, but if he is not acceptable to the team members, he will be deprived of the opportunity to engage in team play. Under such conditions, he must then substitute a form of play that is available and derive what satisfaction he can from it. If it fails to meet his needs, he will then search for another substitute, and another, until he finds the one that gives him the most satisfaction.

This is well illustrated in the case of children who deviate markedly from the average in intelligence, on either the plus or the minus side. If a bright child derives little satisfaction from the play activities of his classmates, he soon discovers that older children, whose play could meet his needs better, will not play with him because he is identified with a lower grade. Consequently, he has no alternative but to find a substitute for the play he would prefer. It may be a long search, and he may never find a substitute completely to his liking.

Much the same is true of play that is considered sex-appropriate. A girl might prefer football to dolls, but if the boys will not accept her as a member of their team, she must play the games that are available to her or not play at all. A boy is faced with the same dilemma. He either plays the way the social group expects him to play or faces the choice of winning social disapproval for engaging in play that is scorned by the group but which he enjoys or of playing in a way that wins group approval but which gives him little satisfaction.

The important point to keep in mind when analyzing differences in play is not that children play differently and that their play varies from one age to another, but rather that *many of their play activities are substitutes for the types of play they would prefer* but are prevented from enjoying. Many children never find substitutes that give them as much satisfaction as they could have derived from the play they would have preferred. Furthermore, the substitutes may be harmful to them, either physically or psychologically, or harmful to the social group. The child who satisfies his need for excitement by watching television or reading comics, for example, would be better off if he could satisfy it as he would like to in competitive sports with the peer group.

On the positive side, this suggests that even our present-day emphasis on providing play space and play equipment for children is not enough. If the use of this space and equipment is to bring the desired results, positive steps must be taken to provide every child the opportunity to *play in a way that will meet his personal needs* and thus eliminate his having to find substitute forms which give him less satisfaction or which will be socially disapproved.

This problem becomes especially serious in the latter part of childhood, when delinquent behavior begins to appear. Many children who later become juvenile delinquents do so because their forms of play are not acceptable to the social group. The child who makes *good social adjustments* finds play activities which meet his needs and also win the approval of the social group. By contrast, the child who makes *poor social adjustments* plays in a way that gives him little satisfaction, though it may win social approval, or in a way which is harmful to him or to the social group but which gives him satisfaction. *The crux of the play problem is thus closely related to the problem of social adjustments; if the latter can be solved, the former will solve itself.*

BIBLIOGRAPHY

(1) ABEGGLEN, J. C.: Personality factors in social mobility: a study of occupationally mobile businessmen. *Genet. Psychol. Monogr.,* 1958, **58**, 101–159.

(2) ALBERT, R. S.: The role of mass media and the effect of aggressive film content upon children's aggressive responses and identification choices. *Genet. Psychol. Monogr.,* 1957, **55**, 221–285.

(3) ALMY, M. C.: *Child development.* New York: Holt, 1955.

(4) AMEN, E. W., and N. RENISON: A study of the relationship between play patterns and anxiety in young children. *Genet. Psychol. Monogr.,* 1954, **50**, 3–41.

(5) AMES, L. B.: Free drawing and completion drawing: a comparative study of preschool children. *J. genet. Psychol.,* 1945, **66**, 161–165.

(6) APPELL, C. T.: Television's impact upon middle-class family life. *Teach. Coll. Rec.,* 1960, **61**, 265–274.

(7) AXLINE, V. M.: *Play therapy.* Boston: Houghton Mifflin, 1947.

(8) AXLINE, V. M.: Observing children at play. *Teach. Coll. Rec.,* 1951, **52**, 358–363.

(9) BAILYN, L.: Mass media and children: a study of exposure habits and cognitive effects. *Psychol. Monogr.,* 1959, **73**, No. 1.

(10) BAKWIN, R. M.: The comics. *J. Pediat.,* 1953, **42**, 633–635.

(11) BATTIN, T. C.: The use of the diary and survey method involving the questionnaire technique to determine the impact of television on school children in regard to viewing habits and formal and informal education. *Speech Monogr.,* 1953, **20**, 135–136.

(12) BEILIN, H.: The pattern of postponability

and its relation to social class mobility. *J. soc. Psychol.,* 1956, **44,** 33–48.

(13) BELL, J. E.: Perceptual development and the drawings of children. *Amer. J. Orthopsychiat.,* 1952, **22,** 386–393.

(14) BENDER, L.: The psychology of children's reading and the comics. *J. educ. Sociol.,* 1944, **18,** 223–231.

(15) BERNHART, E. N.: Developmental stages in compositional construction of children's drawings. *J. exp. Educ.,* 1942, **11,** 156–184.

(16) BLAKELY, W. P.: A study of seventh grade children's reading of comic books as related to certain other variables. *J. genet. Psychol.,* 1958, **93,** 291–301.

(17) BLOOD, R. O.: Social class and family control of television viewing. *Merrill-Palmer Quart.,* 1961, **7,** 205–222.

(18) BLYLER, D.: The song choices of children in the elementary grades. *J. Res. music Educ.,* 1960, **8,** 9–15.

(19) BOYD, N. A., and G. MANDLER: Children's responses to human and animal stories and pictures. *J. consult. Psychol.,* 1955, **19,** 367–371.

(20) BRECKENRIDGE, M. E., and E. L. VINCENT: *Child development,* 4th ed. Philadelphia: Saunders, 1960.

(21) BROWN, D. G.: Sex-role development in a changing culture. *Psychol. Bull.,* 1958, **55,** 232–242.

(22) BROWN, F. J.: *Educational sociology,* 2d ed. Englewood Cliffs, N.J.: Prentice-Hall, 1954.

(23) BROWNMAN, M. T., and M. C. TEMPLIN: Stories for younger children in 1927–1929 and in 1952–1955. *Elem. Sch. J.,* 1959, **59,** 324–327.

(24) BRUCH, H.: Developmental obesity and schizophrenia. *Psychiatry,* 1958, **21,** 65–70.

(25) BÜHLER, K.: *The mental development of the child.* New York: Harcourt, Brace & World, 1930.

(26) BURCHINAL, L., B. GARDNER, and G. R. HAWKES: Children's personality adjustment and the socioeconomics status of their families. *J. genet. Psychol.,* 1958, **92,** 149–159.

(27) BUTTERWORTH, R. F., and G. G. THOMPSON: Factors related to age-grade trends and sex differences in children's preferences for comic books. *J. genet. Psychol.,* 1951, **78,** 71–96.

(28) CAHN, P.: The role of play in the development of fraternal relationships of an older brother. *Sauvegarde,* 1949, **4,** 40–52.

(29) CAPPA, D.: Types of story books enjoyed by kindergarten children. *J. educ. Res.,* 1956, **49,** 555–557.

(30) CAPPA, J.: Les manifestations artistiques chez l'enfant. *Nouv. Rev. pedag.,* 1947, **3,** 89–93.

(31) CARSLEY, J. D.: The interests of children

(ages 10–11) in books. *Brit. J. educ. Psychol.,* 1957, **27,** 13–23.

(32) CAVENAUGH, J. R.: The comics war. *J. crim. Law Criminol.,* 1949, **40,** 28–35.

(33) CHILD, I. L., E. H. POTTER, and E. M. LEVINE: Children's textbooks and personality development. *Psychol. Monogr.,* 1946, **60,** No. 3.

(34) CONN, J. H.: The play interview as an investigative and therapeutic procedure. *Nerv. Child,* 1948, **7,** 257–286.

(35) CONN, J. H.: Children's awareness of sex differences. II. Play attitudes and game preferences. *J. child Psychiat.,* 1951, **2,** 82–99.

(36) CORNELIUS, R.: Games minus competition. *Childh. Educ.,* 1949, **26,** 77–79.

(37) COUSINET, R.: Investigation of what students think of play and work. *J. psychol. norm. Path.,* 1951, **44,** 556–568.

(38) CRAMER, M. W.: Leisure time activities of economically privileged children. *Sociol. soc. Res.,* 1950, **34,** 444–450.

(39) CRUICKSHANK, W. M., and G. O. JOHNSON: *Education of exceptional children and youth.* Englewood Cliffs, N.J.: Prentice-Hall, 1958.

(40) DAVIDSON, H. L., and L. S. GOTTLIEB: The emotional maturity of pre- and post-menarcheal girls. *J. genet. Psychol.,* 1955, **86,** 261–266.

(41) DEMPSEY, D.: And after TV fades, there still remains the magic of a book. *The New York Times,* Nov. 14, 1954.

(42) DENNIS, W.: Handwriting conventions as determinants of human figure drawings. *J. consult. Psychol.,* 1958, **22,** 293–295.

(43) DENNIS, W.: The human figure drawings of Bedouins. *J. soc. Psychol.,* 1960, **52,** 209–219.

(44) DONALD, M. N., and R. J. HAVIGHURST: The meaning of leisure. *Soc. Forces,* 1959, **37,** 355–360.

(45) DU BOIS, F. S.: The security of discipline. *Ment. Hyg., N.Y.,* 1952, **36,** 353–372.

(46) DUVALL, E. M.: *The effect of TV on the family and child life.* Nashville, Tenn.: Report of the Second National Conference on Family Life of the Methodist Church, 1954.

(47) ELKIN, F.: The psychological appeal of the Hollywood western. *J. educ. Sociol.,* 1950, **24,** 72–86.

(48) ELKISH, P.: Significant relationships between the human figure and the machine in the drawings of boys. *Amer. J. Orthopsychiat.,* 1952, **22,** 79–85.

(49) EPHRON, B. K.: *Emotional difficulties in reading.* New York: Julian Press, 1953.

(50) ERIKSON, E. H.: Sex differences in the play configurations of preadolescents. *Amer. J. Orthopsychiat.,* 1951, **21,** 667–692.

(51) EVRY, H.: TV murder causes bad dreams. *Film World,* 1952, **8,** 247.

(52) FEARING, F.: Influence of the movies on

attitudes and behavior. *Ann. Amer. Acad. Pol. Soc. Sci.*, 1947, **254**, 70–79.

(53) FISHER, R. L.: Preferences of different age and socioeconomic groups in instrumental musical situations. *J. soc. Psychol.*, 1951, **33**, 147–152.

(54) FOGLER, S.: Progress report on TV. *Elem. Sch. J.*, 1953, **53**, 513–516.

(55) FRANK, L. K., and M. H. FRANK: *Your adolescent, at home and in school.* New York: Viking, 1956.

(56) FRANK, L. K., and R. E. HARTLEY: Play and personality formation in preschool groups. *Personality*, 1951, **1**, 149–161.

(57) FREIDSON, E.: Adult discontent: an aspect of children's changing taste. *Child Develpm.*, 1953, **24**, 39–49.

(58) GAIER, E. L., and M. J. COLLIER: The latency-stage story preferences of American and Finnish children. *Child Develpm.*, 1960, **31**, 431–451.

(59) GAMBLE, M. A.: The viewers' views on classroom TV. *Educ. Screen*, 1951, **30**, 226–227.

(60) GARRISON, K.C.: *Growth and development,* 2d ed. New York: Longmans, 1959.

(61) GESELL, A., and L. B. AMES: The development of directionality in drawing. *J. genet. Psychol.*, 1946, **68**, 45–61.

(62) GESELL, A., and F. L. ILG: *Child development.* New York: Harper & Row, 1949.

(63) GESELL, A., F. L. ILG, and L. B. AMES: *Youth: the years from ten to sixteen.* New York: Harper & Row, 1956.

(64) GOODENOUGH, F. L., and D. B. HARRIS: Studies in the psychology of children's drawings. II. 1928–1949. *Psychol. Bull.*, 1950, **47**, 369–433.

(65) GREENACRE, P.: Play in relation to creative imagination. *Psychoanal. Stud. Child*, 1959, **14**, 61–80.

(66) GREENAWAY, E.: Reading standards raised by television. *The New York Times*, Nov. 4, 1954.

(67) GREENSTEIN, J.: Effect of television upon elementary school grades. *J. educ. Res.*, 1954, **48**, 161–176.

(68) HARRIS, D. B., and S. C. TSENG: Children's attitudes toward peers and parents as revealed by sentence completions. *Child Develpm.*, 1957, **28**, 401–411.

(69) HARTLEY, R. E.: *Growing through play: experiences of Teddy and Bud.* New York: Columbia, 1952.

(70) HARTLEY, R. E., L. K. FRANK, and R. M. GOLDENSEN: *Understanding children's play.* New York: Columbia, 1952.

(71) HAVIGHURST, R. J.: *Human development and education.* New York: Longmans, 1953.

(72) HAVIGHURST, R. J.: The leisure activities of the middle-aged. *Amer. J. Sociol.*, 1957, **63**, 152–162.

(73) HEMMERLING, R. L., and H. HURST: The effects of leisure activities on scholastic achievement. *Calif. J. educ. Res.*, 1961, **12**, 86–90.

(74) HILDRETH, G.: The simplification tendency in reproducing designs. *J. genet. Psychol.*, 1944, **64**, 329–333.

(75) HIMMELWEIT, H. T., A. N. OPPENHEIM, and P. VANCE: *Television and the child: an empirical study of the effect of television on the young.* Fair Lawn, N.J.: Oxford University Press, 1958.

(76) HONZIG, M. P.: Sex differences in the occurrence of materials in the play constructions of preadolescents. *Child Develpm.*, 1951, **22**, 15–35.

(77) HORNE, B. M., and C. C. PHILLES: A comparative study of the spontaneous play activities of normal and mentally defective children. *J. genet. Psychol.*, 1942, **61**, 33–46.

(78) HOULT, T. F.: Comic books and juvenile delinquency. *Sociol. soc. Res.*, 1949, **33**, 279–284.

(79) HUGHES, M. A., and L. STOCKDALE: The young child and graphic expression. *Childh. Educ.*, 1940, **16**, 307–314.

(80) JERSILD, A. T.: *Child psychology*, 5th ed. Englewood Cliffs, N.J.: Prentice-Hall, 1960.

(81) JERSILD, A. T., and R. J. TASCH: *Children's interests and what they suggest for education.* New York: Teachers College, Columbia University, 1949.

(82) JOHNSON, H. M.: *The art of block building.* New York: John Day, 1933.

(83) JOHNSON, R. C., C. JOHNSON, and L. MARTIN: Authoritarianism, occupation, and sex role differentiation of children. *Child Develpm.*, 1961, **32**, 271–276.

(84) JOLLES, I.: A study of the validity of some hypotheses for the qualitative interpretation of the H-T-P for children of elementary school age. 1. Sexual identification. *J. clin. Psychol.*, 1952, **8**, 113–118.

(85) LANDRETH, C.: *The psychology of early childhood.* New York: Knopf, 1958.

(86) LEONARD, A.: Toys for toddlers. *Today's Hlth*, 1952, Dec., 42–43, 60.

(87) LEROY, A.: Dessins en transparence et niveau de développement. *Enfance*, 1950, **3**, 276–287.

(88) LEROY, A.: Representation of perspective in the drawings of children. *Enfance*, 1951, **4**, 286–307.

(89) LEVINSON, B. M.: The inner life of the extremely gifted child, as seen from the clinical setting. *J. genet. Psychol.*, 1961, **99**, 83–88.

(90) LEWIN, H. S.: Factions and fears about the comics. *Nation's Schools*, 1953, **52**, 46–48.

(91) LEWIS, E.: The function of group play during middle childhood in developing the ego complex. *Brit. J. med. Psychol.*, 1954, **27**, 15–29.

(92) LYNESS, P. I.: Patterns in mass communications tastes of the young audience. *J. educ. Psychol.*, 1951, **42**, 449–467.

(93) LYNESS, P. I.: The place of the mass media in the lives of boys and girls. *Journalism Quart.*, 1952, **29**, 43–54.

(94) MACCOBY, E. E.: Television: its impact on school children. *Publ. Opin. Quart.*, 1951, **15**, 421–444.

(95) MACCOBY, E. E.: Why do children watch television? *Publ. Opin. Quart.*, 1954, **18**, 239–244.

(96) MACCOBY, E. E., and W. C. WILSON: Identification and observational learning from films. *J. abnorm. soc. Psychol.*, 1957, **55**, 76–87.

(97) MACCOBY, E. E., W. C. WILSON, and R. V. BARTON: Differential movie-viewing behavior of male and female viewers. *J. Pers.*, 1958, **26**, 259–267.

(98) MAC DONALD, M., C. MC GUIRE, and R. J. HAVIGHURST: Leisure activities and socioeconomic status of children. *Amer. J. Sociol.*, 1949, **54**, 505–519.

(99) MACHOVER, K.: *Personality projection in the drawing of the human figure.* Springfield, Ill.: Charles C Thomas, 1949.

(100) MALTER, M. S.: The content of current comic magazines. *Elem. Sch. J.*, 1952, **52**, 505–510.

(101) MALRIEU, P.: Comments on some free drawings by children. *J. Psychol. norm. path.*, 1950, **43**, 239–244.

(102) MARGOLIN, E. B., and D. A. LETON: Interest of kindergarten pupils in block play. *J. educ. Res.*, 1961, **55**, 13–18.

(103) MARKEY, F. V.: Imaginative behavior of preschool children. *Child Develpm. Monogr.*, 1935, No. 18.

(104) MARSHALL, H. R.: Relations between home experiences and children's use of language in play interactions with peers. *Psychol. Monogr.*, 1961, **75**, No. 5.

(105) MARTIN, P. C., and E. L. VINCENT: *Human development.* New York: Ronald, 1960.

(106) MAYBURY, M. W.: Selection of materials by nursery school children of superior mental intelligence. *J. educ. Res.*, 1952, **46**, 17–31.

(107) MC CARTHY, D. L.: Language development. *Monogr. Soc. Res. Child Develpm.*, 1960, **25**, No. 3, 5–14.

(108) MC CULLOUGH, C. M.: A log of children's out-of-school activities. *Elem. Sch. J.*, 1957, **58**, 157–165.

(109) MC KELLAR, P., and R. HARRIS: Radio preferences of adolescents and children. *Brit. J. educ. Psychol.*, 1952, **22**, 101–113.

(110) MERRY, F. K., and R. V. MERRY: *The first two decades of life,* 2d ed. New York: Harper & Row, 1958.

(111) MILLICHAMP, D. A.: Another look at play. *Instit. Child Study Bull.*, Toronto, 1953, **15**, No. 4, 1–13.

(112) MITCHELL, M. A.: The relationship of reading to social acceptability of sixth grade children. *Teach. Coll. Contr. Educ.*, 1949, No. 953.

(113) MORGAN, D.: Television versus reading. *Wilson Libr. Bull.*, 1955, **26**, 327.

(114) MOYER, K. E., and B. VON H. GILMER: Experimental study of children's preferences and use of blocks in play. *J. genet. Psychol.*, 1956, **89**, 3–10.

(115) MURPHY, L. B.: *Personality in young children.* New York: Basic Books, Inc., Publishers, 1957.

(116) MUSSEN, P. H., and E. RUTHERFORD: Effects of aggressive cartoons on children's aggressive play. *J. abnorm. soc. Psychol.*, 1961, **62**, 461–464.

(117) New York Times Report: TV-watching habits of students studied. *The New York Times,* Jan. 2, 1954.

(118) New York Times Report: Parents advised to curb TV fare. *The New York Times,* July 28, 1961.

(119) O'BRIEN, C. C.: The role of music in guiding the child. *Education,* 1953, **73**, 1–6.

(120) PELLER, L. E.: Models of children's play. *Ment. Hyg., N.Y.,* 1952, **36**, 66–83.

(121) PELLER, L. E.: Daydreams and children's favorite books. *Psychoanal. Stud. Child.,* 1959, **14**, 414–433.

(122) PODOLSKY, E.: Horrors. *Calif. P-T Jour.,* 1952, Dec., 23.

(123) REECE, L. H.: The play needs of children aged 6 to 12. *Marriage fam. Liv.,* 1954, **16**, 131–134.

(124) REICHENBERG-HACKETT, W.: The geo sign test: a semistructural drawing situation utilized as a screening test for adjustment. *Amer. J. Orthopsychiat.,* 1950, **20**, 578–594.

(125) RICCIUTI, E. A.: Children and radio: a study of listeners and non-listeners to various types of radio programs in terms of selected ability, attitudes, and behavior measures. *Genet. Psychol. Monogr.,* 1951, **44**, 69–143.

(126) ROSENBERG, B. G., and B. SUTTON-SMITH: A revised conception of masculine-feminine in play activities. *J. genet. Psychol.,* 1960, **96**, 165–170.

(127) RUSSELL, D. H.: The development of thinking processes. *Rev. educ. Res.,* 1953, **23**, 137–145.

(128) SCHRAMM, W.: *Children and television.* Washington, D.C.: Television Information Office, 1959.

(129) SCHRAMM, W.: *The impact of educational television.* Urbana, Ill.: The University of Illinois Press, 1960.

(130) SCHRAMM, W.: Mass media and educational policy. *60th Yearb. Nat. Soc. Stud. Educ.,* 1961, Pt. 2, 203–229.

(131) SCHRAMM, W., J. LYLE, and E. B. PARKER: Patterns in children's reading of newspapers. *Journalism Quart.*, 1960, **37**, 35–40.

(132) SCHRAMM, W., J. LYLE, and E. B. PARKER: Children's learning from television. *Stud. publ. Commun.*, 1961, No. 3, 86–98.

(133) SCHRAMM, W., J. LYLE, and E. B. PARKER: *Television in the lives of our children.* Stanford, Calif.: Stanford, 1961.

(134) SCOTT, L. F.: A study of children's TV interests. *Calif. J. educ. Res.*, 1953, **4**, 162–164.

(135) SCOTT, L. F.: Social attitudes of children revealed by responses to television programs. *Calif. J. second. Educ.*, 1954, **22**, 176–179.

(136) SCOTT, L. F.: Relationships between elementary school children and television. *J. educ. Res.*, 1958, **52**, 134–137.

(137) SEAGOE, M. V.: Some current research in television for children. *Calif. J. educ. Res.*, 1952, **3**, 151–153.

(138) SEAGOE, M. V., and K. MURAKAMI: A comparative study of children's play in America and Japan. *Calif. J. educ. Res.*, 1961, **12**, 124–130.

(139) SEWARD, B., and D. B. HARRIS: The reading ease, human interest value, and thematic content of *St. Nicholas* magazine. *J. educ. Psychol.*, 1951, **42**, 153–165.

(140) SHALTER, A.: A survey of student reading. *Eng. J.*, 1951, **40**, 271–273.

(141) SIEGEL, A. E.: The influence of violence in the mass media upon children's role expectations. *Child Develpm.*, 1958, **29**, 35–56.

(142) SOLOMON, J. C.: Play technique as a differential therapeutic medium. *Nerv. Child*, 1948, **7**, 296–300.

(143) SPIEGELMAN, M., C. TERWILLIGER, and F. FEARING: The content of the comic strips: a study of a mass medium of communication. *J. soc. Psychol.*, 1952, **35**, 37–57.

(144) STOLZ, H. R., and L. M. STOLZ: *Somatic development of adolescent boys.* New York: Macmillan, 1951.

(145) STONE, L. J., and J. CHURCH: *Childhood and adolescence.* New York: Random House, 1957.

(146) STRANG, R. M.: *An introduction to child study,* 4th ed. New York: Macmillan, 1959.

(147) SULLENGER, T. E., L. H. PARKE, and W. K. WALLIN: The leisure time activities of elementary school children. *J. educ. Res.*, 1953, **46**, 551–554.

(148) SUTTON-SMITH, B., and P. GUMP: Games and status experience. *Recreation*, 1955, **48**, 172–174.

(149) SUTTON-SMITH, B., and B. G. ROSENBERG: Manifest anxiety and game preferences in children. *Child Develpm.*, 1960, **31**, 307–311.

(150) SWANSON, C. F., and R. L. JONES: Television owning and its correlates. *J. appl. Psychol.*, 1951, **35**, 352–357.

(151) SYMONDS, P. M.: *The dynamics of human adjustment.* New York: Appleton-Century-Crofts, 1946.

(152) THAYER, L. O., and N. H. PRONKO: Some psychological factors in the reading of fiction. *J. genet. Psychol.*, 1958, **93**, 113–117.

(153) THOMAS, R. M.: Effects of frustration on children's paintings. *Child Develpm.*, 1951, **22**, 123–132.

(154) THORNDIKE, R. L.: *Comparative study of children's reading interests.* New York: Teachers College, Columbia University, 1941.

(155) THORNDIKE, R. L.: Words and the comics. *J. exp. Educ.*, 1942, **10**, 110–113.

(156) THORNDIKE, R. L., and F. HENRY: Differences in reading interests related to differences in sex and intelligence level. *Elem. Sch. J.*, 1940, **40**, 751–763.

(157) TYLER, L. E.: The relationship of interests to abilities and reputation among first grade children. *Educ. psychol. Measmt*, 1951, **11**, 255–264.

(158) United Nations Report: Games of childhood same around world. *The New York Times*, May 24, 1953.

(159) VERNON, M. D.: The development of imaginative construction in children. *Brit. J. Psychol.*, 1948, **39**, 102–111.

(160) VOLBERDING, E.: Out-of-school behavior of eleven-year-olds. *Elem. Sch. J.*, 1948, **48**, 432–441.

(161) WALLACE, E. H.: Selected out-of-school factors that affect Negro elementary school children. *J. educ. Res.*, 1960, **54**, 118–120, 137–140.

(162) WANG, J. D.: The relationship between children's play interests and their mental ability. *J. genet. Psychol.*, 1958, **93**, 119–131.

(163) WEATHERS, G. R.: Children up late for TV, a study shows. *The New York Times*, Dec. 3, 1954.

(164) WEIDER, A., and P. A. NOLLER: Objective studies of children's drawings of the human figure. 1. Sex awareness and socioeconomic level. *J. clin. Psychol.*, 1950, **6**, 319–325.

(165) WELLS, C. A., and T. J. LYNCH: The amount of free reading engaged in by intermediate grade pupils who have viewed television for one year or more. *J. educ. Res.*, 1954, **47**, 473–477.

(166) WERTHAM, F.: The curse of the comic books. *Relig. Educ.*, 1954, **49**, 394–406.

(167) WIESE, M. J., and S. G. COLE: A study of children's attitudes and the influence of a commercial motion picture. *J. Psychol.*, 1946, **21**, 151–171.

(168) WILSON, L. A.: The influence of a child purpose on the perseverance of young children. *J. exp. Educ.*, 1955, **23**, 353–358.

(169) WINSTEL, B.: The use of a controlled play situation in determining certain effects of

maternal attitudes on children. *Child De-velpm.*, 1951, **22**, 299–311.

(170) WITTY, P. A.: Children's interest in comics, radio, motion picture, and TV. *Educ. Admin. Superv.*, 1952, **38**, 138–147.

(171) WITTY, P. A.: Comparative studies of interest in TV. *Educ. Admin. Superv.*, 1954, **40**, 321–335.

(172) WITTY, P. A.: Comics, television, and our children. *Today's Hlth*, 1955, Feb., 18–21.

(173) WITTY, P. A., A. COOMER, and D. MC BEAN: Children's choices of favorite books: a study conducted in ten elementary schools. *J. educ. Psychol.*, 1946, **37**, 266–278.

(174) WITTY, P. A., *et al.:* Studies of children's interests: a brief summary. *Elem. Eng.*, 1960, **37**, 469–475.

(175) WITTY, P. A., and P. KINSELLA: Children and the electronic Pied Piper. *Education*, 1959, **80**, 48–56.

(176) WITTY, P. A., and D. MOORE: Interest in reading the comics among Negro children. *J. educ. Psychol.*, 1945, **36**, 303–308.

(177) WOLFENSTEIN, M.: The impact of a child's story on mothers and children. *Monogr. Soc. Res. Child Develpm.*, 1946, **11**, No. 1.

(178) WOLMAN, B.: Spontaneous groups of children and adolescents in Israel. *J. soc. Psychol.*, 1951, **34**, 171–182.

(179) ZORBAUGH, H.: The comics and where they stand. *J. educ. Sociol.*, 1944, **18**, 196–203.

(180) ZORBAUGH, H.: What adults think of the comics as reading for children. *J. educ. Sociol.*, 1949, **23**, 225–235.

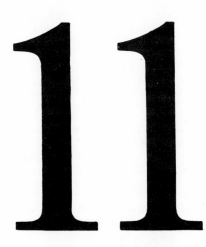

11

DEVELOPMENT
OF
UNDERSTANDING

As James pointed out many years ago, the newborn infant experiences the world as a "big, blooming, buzzing confusion" (116). He has no understanding of his environment or of where the source of discomfort lies when he cries for help. All he knows is that he is uncomfortable; he then uses the only means at his disposal—crying—to try to gain relief. As a result of maturation and learning, the child gradually begins to understand what he sees, hears, smells, tastes, and feels. His environment begins to be meaningful to him, and he begins to understand why he feels as he does on different occasions.

Maturation provides a state of readiness to understand. Before understanding can develop, the child's brain and nervous system must develop, and the sense organs—used for perceiving—must become functionally mature. Understanding parallels mental growth. When mental growth is rapid, as in a very bright child, understanding is above the norm for the child's age level; in a dull child, understanding lags behind the norm (182). Similarly, a hierarchy of information-processing abilities, essential to understanding complex situations and behavior patterns, parallels the development of the brain's reasoning ability (154).

Learning, too, is essential to understanding. The child must learn how to perceive differences in things he sees, hears, smells, tastes, and feels as soon as the sensory and neural structures of his body are ready for use. Understanding begins when the child develops the ability to discriminate. At two weeks of age, a baby will give momentary heed to a dangling ring, indicating that he notices something different in his environment. From then on, his behavior indicates that he can discriminate differences in people and things. He will smile at the sight of people who are familiar or object and cry when they are unfamiliar. His understanding increases as his ability to perceive relationships between new and old situations increases. The more readily a child can associate new meanings with old experiences, the more meaningful the old experiences become and the more integrated they are in a system of interrelated ideas (42, 143).

Value of Understanding. The type of adjustment the child makes to life is greatly influenced by his understanding of his environment, of people, and of himself. The child who understands the danger of automobiles, high places, and animals, for example, will be cautious; the child who lacks this understanding will not take proper precautions in a potentially dangerous situation and may consequently be handicapped for life by some resulting physical disability.

If a child does not understand his limitations, whether they are physical or mental, he will not understand why people treat him as they do, and he will misinterpret their actions. A boy who does not recognize his physical limitations may feel that his lack of acceptance in a play group is due to discrimination, whereas it is actually due to his lack of play skills. He will build up resentments that will make later acceptance difficult, and at the same time he will make himself unhappy. Furthermore, if he continues to misunderstand the reason for his rejection, he will have little motivation to cultivate qualities that might increase his chances of acceptance.

Attitudes toward other people, toward things, and toward what is important in life are likewise dependent upon understanding. The child who does not understand that much of what he sees in a movie or on television is merely make-believe is likely to develop unrealistic or false attitudes toward life (183). Similarly, if he does not understand the value of repetition in learning, he may develop a resentful attitude toward a teacher who requires him to write and rewrite the misspelled word in a composition. He may regard this assignment as a punishment rather than as a proved way of learning (76).

Unquestionably, one of the greatest values of understanding is that it enables a child to adapt to changes, both personal and environmental. Changes in body form at puberty, with their accompanying changes in behavior and interest, provide a good illustration. The child who understands that these changes occur in a predictable pattern and who knows *why* they are taking place will react with less fear, anxiety, or resentment than the child who does not understand.

CHILDREN'S CONCEPTS

Understanding is based on concepts. *Concepts* are not direct sensory data; instead, they result from the elaboration and combination—the tying together, or linking—of discrete sensory experiences. The common elements in diverse objects or situations serve to unite objects or situations into a common concept (238). Vinacke has defined concepts as

. . . cognitive organizing systems which serve to bring pertinent features of past experience to bear upon a present stimulus-object. . . . They are selective systems which, in conjunction with attitudes, operate in the control of response. They represent the organization of experience and determine the meaning of objects. . . . They develop during the learning process, becoming more complex and, in general, more differentiated and efficient with increase in age (239).

Concepts are symbolic in that they depend upon the properties of absent situations and objects as well as upon the properties of situations and objects present at the time the response is made. Frequently concepts have an affective quality—an "emotional weighting"—which becomes a part of the concept and which determines how the individual feels about the person, object, or situation of which the concept is a symbol. This emotional weighting determines, to a large extent, the type of response the person will make (76, 252). Concepts are thus complex affairs which are continuously changing with experience and with the accumulation of new knowledge. How complex they are may be illustrated by a simple

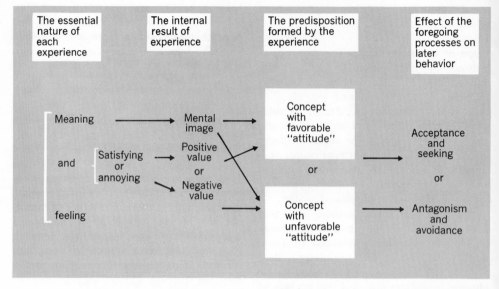

Figure 11–1.   The composite nature of a concept. (Adapted from A. D. Woodruff, *Basic concepts of teaching,* Chandler, 1961. Used by permission.)

drawing that shows the composite nature of a concept (see Figure 11–1).

Concepts may relate to *objects;* to *people;* to *qualities,* such as "good" and "dishonest"; or to *relationships,* such as "above" and "when" (197). They may be *definite* ("one-half teaspoon of salt") or *indefinite* (a "generous helping of salt") (117, 161). Concepts are not always *conscious,* nor are they always verbalized (169). Some concepts are well developed, some only partially developed, and some very inaccurately developed. Some concepts will develop more fully and be corrected with time, and some will never develop beyond the foundation stages laid in childhood (238).

As Russell has pointed out, children often "show clear understanding of a concept but inability to verbalize it" (197). A child may, for example, have a clear and accurate concept of what "generosity" means but not know the word that describes this quality. He may know, from his play, that when you mix red paint with blue, you get one shade if you allow the red to predominate and another if you allow the blue to predominate. He does not know the names for these shades, however, and as a result cannot at-tach the label "magenta" to the first and "violet" to the second.

The child's concepts are important be-cause they determine what the child knows, what he believes, and, to a large extent, what he does. Furthermore, the accuracy or inaccuracy of his concepts affects his under-standing. The more concepts a child has, the better developed they are, and the more accurate they are, the greater his under-standing will be. Simple reading material, for example, employing meaningful words and illustrated with relevant pictures, can be better understood by a young child than material containing many different words on a page, many different ideas, involved sen-tences, and abstract or unfamiliar words (53). Even the mechanical devices of capi-talization and punctuation may give the child a hint of the relationship a strange word has to the words surrounding it (117).

Concepts develop rapidly because of the child's curiosity about the world in which he lives. It has been estimated that before chil-dren enter school they have a store of sev-eral hundred concepts. These are simple, for the most part, including such concepts as roundness, redness, dog, animal, food, and love, and many are partially or totally inaccurate. By adolescence, the child has built up a store of several thousand concepts. Furthermore, he has added new meanings to old concepts and corrected many of his inaccuracies.

HOW CONCEPTS DEVELOP

Because of their limited knowledge and experience, children cannot perceive an object or situation in the same way that an adult can, even though their sense organs are equally well developed. As Russell has stated, this means that children's concepts are often developed slowly "out of percepts, memories, and images, and their development is aided greatly by language or other symbols" (197).

Russell has further explained that some concepts help the child to develop other concepts: "Concepts of time help explain concepts of social custom. . . . Esthetic and humorous concepts grow in relation to social concepts" (197). For example, a child learns to perceive an older person's slipping and falling on a banana peel as funny because this act violates an already learned social concept about the dignity and respect accompanying adulthood. Similarly, when children learn concepts of historic time, they have a basis on which to explain why people used to live, dress, and behave differently from the way they do today. This is especially apparent in the understanding of religious concepts. The child who develops concepts of appropriate behavior and appearance for members of the two sexes can transfer this knowledge to help him to develop concepts of masculine or feminine beauty; he learns to think of beauty not as an abstract concept but in relation to his concept of what is sex-appropriate (76, 161).

Essentials in Concept Development. Concept development is a long and difficult process. If concepts are to be accurate and if the child is to develop enough concepts to meet his needs for understanding his world,

the following essential conditions must be satisfactorily met:

1. Ability to See Relationships. The child, like the adult, interprets new experiences in relation to knowledge formerly acquired. This means that to be able to perceive meanings, the child must be able to see the relationships between new experiences and previous experiences. The greater the similarity between the new and the old, the more meanings the child should be able to perceive. If he is unable to see any relationship between the experiences, his understanding of the new situation will be limited. This was well illustrated in a study of the reactions of a group of six- to eight-year-olds to hospitalization. Children whose parents had trained them to respond to general stress situations reacted with stress to being hospitalized for tonsillectomy because they did not see the relationship between this particular stress situation and general stress situations. Children who had been trained to react to a specific stress situation, such as hospitalization, however, responded more favorably and were more comfortable in their hospital experience because they understood it and knew what to expect (145).

Observation has shown that even before a baby is a year old, he is able to interpret new happenings in terms of what he has already learned. For example, he begins to have less fear of strangers because he has learned that a strange person often brings him new and pleasurable experiences. Similarly, he has learned that his mother does not always look the same; sometimes she wears a hat and coat, and sometimes she wears a dress with no hat or coat. The fear that characterizes the "strange age" then disappears (30).

By the age of two, the child is capable of making simple generalizations. From then on, there is a steady increase in his ability to group things together that belong together and to give abstract, conceptual explanations of the groupings. The ability of the three-year-old to interpret new experiences in terms of old experiences accounts, to a large extent, for his marked increase in knowledge. The ability to see relationships, however, and to see them accurately is always easier when the material is in line with past experiences (197).

2. Ability to Comprehend Underlying Meanings. Children perceive things at their face value, missing any meaning that is not apparent at first glance. Young children, it has been found, interpret pictures first in terms of static form and later in terms of activity. Not until they are more mature do they interpret the picture in terms of the thoughts and feelings expressed by the artist. When meanings are subtle, even older children usually miss the underlying thought. The abstract meanings of *cartoons,* for example, are not grasped by a child much before adolescence (195, 207).

The same is true of *proverbs.* When a child is asked the meaning of the proverb "He is too old a dog to learn new tricks," he answers that it means that it is hard to teach a dog a trick. Similarly, the child usually fails to get the meaning of the proverb "All that glitters is not gold." He thinks only in terms of "gold" and how it "glitters." In the latter part of childhood, with increased comprehension, children are capable of getting some of the metaphorical meaning of proverbs (191).

3. Ability to Reason. To be able to understand accurately what he sees or hears, the child must use inductive thinking and sometimes even deductive and creative thinking. Because these mental abilities develop slowly, a child often misinterprets what he observes. In the process of discovering meaning, the child must recognize common elements in objects or situations and set aside unrelated items. For example, if a child has known only "short-haired dogs, he must mentally give a shaggy dog a haircut before he can see the generalization 'dog'; but, at the same time, he must be ready to add shagginess to his original concept of what a dog can be" (161). This requires a reasoning ability that many children do not have until they reach the end of childhood.

Sources of Meaning. Development of ability to comprehend meaning progresses rapidly during the early years of life. At first, the baby discovers the meaning of the objects in his immediate environment through *sensory exploration.* He looks and listens, and he smells, tastes, and touches everything within his grasp. As a result, he observes meanings which, when fused with meanings previously observed, cause strange and unfamiliar objects to become familiar. The more often he can observe an object, with short time intervals between the observations, the more quickly it will become meaningful to him (195, 252).

When motor coordination is sufficiently developed that the child can handle things at will, *motor manipulation* supplements the information gained through sensory exploration. The child discovers qualities such as smoothness, softness, and warmth. Too often, the "hands-off" policy, which many adults enforce, deprives the child of one of his most valuable sources of information (237).

As soon as the child is old enough to put words together, he begins to *ask questions* about things which arouse his curiosity. The "questioning age" begins around the third year and reaches its peak at approximately the sixth year, but the individual will continue to use this method of gaining information throughout the rest of his life. How useful it is to him will depend upon the satisfaction he derives from it during the early years of childhood (159, 238).

The young child is motivated to ask questions primarily because of genuine curiosity, but he may also want to check upon or supplement information he has gained through his own experimentation. Questioning is motivated at times by a desire for attention. Then the child shows little interest in the answers given to his questions, often asking the same question several times.

What the child sees in *pictorial mass media,* especially comics, movies, and television, forms the basis for many of his concepts. If teachers or policemen are constantly depicted in a particular way, the child will come to think that *all* teachers or *all* policemen have the characteristics he has observed in the pictures. This, as will be pointed out later, is one of the common ways in which stereotypes develop.

Because most pictorial mass media have elements of unreality, even though they may be "skewed toward reality," the child is likely to develop concepts that are unrealistic. An illustration of this may be found in the unrealistic concepts of parents that children derive from movies, television programs, or comics. If parents are usually depicted as far more glamourous and exciting than anything the child has ever experienced at firsthand, he will tend to develop a critical, unrealistic attitude toward his own parents (46, 249).

Educational films and educational television serve to develop concepts of a more realistic type. A child whose concept of "elephant" is based only on a far-off view of an elephant in a zoo or on pictures of elephants in a book, for example, gets a more accurate concept if he sees a travel picture of an elephant in its natural habitat (190).

Before the child is capable of *reading,* he learns many meanings from looking at pictures, from being read to, or from having stories told to him. Even the simplest storybooks introduce new meanings into the child's life, and through careful observation of pictures, details of objects and persons which he formerly had not noticed become apparent to him. Each year, the child relies more and more heavily on reading to increase his understanding. When what he reads is supplemented by discussions with adults or by educational films in school, his understanding is greatly increased (24, 117, 190, 198).

Evaluation of Sources of Information. While children use new sources of information as they grow older, they never completely abandon the old ones. They may use the older sources less and less, not necessarily because they find the new ones more accurate and more complete, but because

circumstances make it difficult or impossible to use the old sources. This is especially true of motor manipulation. When the child is confronted with a "hands-off" policy, he has no alternative but to use another source, even though motor manipulation might give him more information. If he wants to know how the fur coat of a stranger feels but his mother will not permit him to touch it, he may get some information by looking closely at the coat and from the mother's explanation that it "feels just like your stuffed rabbit." His understanding would be greater, however, if he were permitted to explore the coat directly. Similarly, he may discover that his questions are not always answered or that they are not always answered correctly.

When the child is able to read without having to pay too much attention to the mechanics of reading, he will turn to books as a source of information. This does not mean that he will stop asking questions, however. If he is permitted to ask questions and if he feels that the information he is receiving is accurate, he will prefer this source over the more laborious, time-consuming source of reading. One of the arguments given in favor of pictorial mass media is that these media often arouse the child's curiosity and motivate him to explore further, thus increasing his understanding of new objects and situations.

FACTORS INFLUENCING CONCEPT DEVELOPMENT

Because children are subjected to different influences, all children of the same age and level of development will not have the same concepts. Of the many factors that influence concept development, the following are the most important:

1. Condition of the Sense Organs.   The sense organs are the channels through which sensory experiences pass in their path to the brain; therefore, the condition of the sense organs is vitally important to concept devel-

opment. The child who is color-blind, for example, will perceive objects in his environment differently from the child with normal vision. The parable of the "blind man's idea of the sun" points out what an important role vision plays in the development of concepts. A child who is totally or partially deaf will build up concepts in which sound plays little or no role. Because children differ in the efficiency of their sensory apparatus, no two children receive exactly the same primary data of the world in which they live. The foundations on which their concepts are built differ, and therefore their concepts will differ (76).

2. Intelligence.

With maturation of intelligence, especially in the areas of memory and reasoning, the child's ability to develop concepts increases. Intelligence makes it possible for the child to benefit from experience, to observe, to remember, to discriminate, to generalize, to deduct, and to hold images in mind.

Intelligence plays a far less important role in the *affective* element of concepts, however, than in the *cognitive* aspects. A very bright child, for example, will see and understand elements in a situation that a child of less intelligence would not recognize (197, 239). This does not affect the feeling tone or the "emotional weighting" of the concept because knowing and feeling are not necessarily related. That the bright child likes or dislikes a certain object or situation is not the result of his intellectual ability but of some past experience in which he associated pleasant or unpleasant feelings with the object or experience. A bright child's concept of "dog" will contain greater cognitive elements than a dull child's concept if both have had the same learning opportunities. The *type of association* each child has had with dogs in the past, however, will influence his emotional weighting of the concept.

3. Opportunities for Learning.

Because concepts are a product of learning, opportunity for learning is even more important than intelligence in the development of con-

cepts. But if learning opportunities are equal for all children, the child with a higher IQ will develop superior concepts. The correlation between concept development and experience is greater than that between concept development and intelligence.

The older the child is, the more learning opportunities he has had; therefore, chronological age plays as important a role in the conceptual ability of the child as mental age (238, 239). A study designed to determine what children's concepts of justice are at different ages revealed that older children are aware of many more relevant factors than younger children. The older child, for example, takes into consideration the person's *reason* for his misbehavior, while the younger child views the misbehavior at its face value and decides on that basis alone what a just punishment would be (71).

Because age and experience go hand in hand, the older child will have different and more complete concepts than the younger child. Furthermore, concepts often change as a result of experience, especially concepts of self and of others. In fact, concepts continue to develop and change as long as a person lives and has new experiences (76, 142, 252).

The influence of learning opportunities has been shown in a number of studies of the development of children's concepts. In a study of children's concepts of different internal organs, such as the lungs and stomach, and their functions, it was found that there was little relationship between a child's mental or chronological age and his concepts. On the other hand, there was a marked correlation between the child's concepts and his parents' knowledge. There was also a high correlation with what the child had learned in school about bodily functions (174).

Similarly, the child's concepts of birth were found to be closely correlated with the amount and type of sex instruction he had received at home and in school. For example, Hungarian children, who are taught less about sex than American or British children, tended to have more fantasy than truth in their concepts of birth. Children who attended schools high in sex prejudice were found to have fewer and less accurate concepts of birth than those who attended schools low in sex prejudice (173).

The influence of opportunity to learn on the development of the child's concepts is shown also in *social-class* differences in concepts. Some concepts are general in a culture, such as concepts of time, space, and numbers. Others are specific to a social class, such as the concepts of "nurse," "maid," and "travel." In the latter, the child's concepts will be determined to a large extent by the socioeconomic group to which his family belongs (110).

In addition, because names as *symbols* play an important part in the child's concepts, the larger the vocabulary and the more accurately the child perceives the meaning of words, the more complete and accurate his concepts will be. Since children from lower socioeconomic groups have, on the whole, more limited and less accurate vocabularies than children from the higher socioeconomic groups, the concepts developed by these children will be different. Children from *rural* environments have different, and often fewer, opportunities for learning than those from *urban* environments; thus variations in their experiences are mainly responsible for variations in their concepts (210, 231).

4. Type of Experience.

Early concept development is based on *concrete experiences*. The more direct and concrete the experience, the better the concept is likely to be. Later, many concepts are gained through vicarious experiences, especially those presented by factual material in books, in movies, and on radio and television (98, 110, 161, 208).

Concepts related to familiar objects or to the child's experiences, such as concepts of clouds, of the flying of airplanes, or of the rising of bubbles in water, are acquired earlier than concepts relating to less familiar objects or situations, such as the functions of the heart and muscles, the meaning of gravitation, or the geological origin of hills and lakes (179).

5. Amount of Guidance.

Concepts vary according to the amount of guidance and training the child receives. While it is true that anything new or interesting arouses the child's curiosity, there are nevertheless many things that he would not notice unless his attention were directed specifically to them. The more he is encouraged to observe details, the more meaningful the objects in his environment become. Toys, if properly selected, help to develop the child's perception of space and color, just as well-selected books and pictures help him to develop an ability to perceive the beautiful or the comic. Strict adherence to a definite time schedule enables the child to judge time better than a haphazard schedule would. Music in the home, as a part of the play life of the child, builds up not only an appreciation of music but also a genuine fondness for it.

In commenting on the importance of guidance in the development of understanding, Woodruff has pointed out:

> In a very simple world one can learn what he needs to know through natural daily experience. In a complex world there is so much we have to learn that we cannot learn it through the slow process of personal discovery. A person's chances for success in life are greatly enhanced by learning those things that are most important in his search for satisfaction, as early and efficiently as possible, and as accurately and validly as possible (252).

6. Type of Mass Media.

Not only does the child learn new meanings from books, movies, television, and radio, but he also learns to associate certain labels or names with the concepts he is developing (198, 237). What kind of concepts the child will develop, how meaningful they will be, and what type of emotional weighting they will have will depend largely upon what he reads, sees, and hears. Material that is not right for his age or level of development can contribute to the development of confused or faulty concepts. This is more closely related to vocabulary development than to other factors; the better the child's understanding of words, the better his understanding of concepts for which the words act as symbols will be (240, 246).

7. Sex. How the child views a person, an object, or a situation is influenced by whether he belongs to the male or the female sex. Because children are trained, from earliest childhood, to think and act in a manner considered appropriate for members of their sex, this is bound to be reflected in the meanings they associate with different experiences and objects. To a girl, for example, clothing may be something that improves one's looks and wins admiration; to a boy, clothing is something which protects one from cold and which is worn because society dictates it. To a boy, the study of mathematics may be a stepping-stone to a future job; to a girl, it may be a "waste of time."

Not only do the cognitive elements of concepts differ for boys and girls, but the emotional weighting often differs greatly also. Boys' concepts of poverty, for example, are likely to be realistic and factual, while girls' concepts are more heavily weighted with pity and emotional concern (76). Because sex differences increase with age as training in playing socially approved sex roles increases, the concepts of boys and girls become more divergent as they grow older.

8. Personality. On the whole, the well-adjusted child will have more accurate, more realistic, and less emotionally weighted concepts than the poorly adjusted child. Because every child views life from a frame of reference in which he plays the central role, what the child thinks of himself and his relationships with other people will determine what his frame of reference is. If he is *well adjusted,* for example, he will view himself, his abilities, and his relationships with others realistically; he will see himself as he is and as others see him. As a result, his concept of himself will be very similar to that held by other people.

The *poorly adjusted* child, on the other hand, may build up so unrealistic a concept

of himself that even his parents would not recognize it as a concept of their child. Because this concept is so remote from the concepts others hold of him, it will lead to behavior that will increase his poor adjustments. Either he will think of himself as a martyr and act in accordance with this belief, or he will think of himself as inferior and unworthy and will withdraw from others so as not to impose his unworthiness on them.

CHARACTERISTICS OF CHILDREN'S CONCEPTS

Children's concepts differ from those of adults more in degree than in kind. Concepts which may seem "illogical" to an adult are not so from the point of view of a child, whose experiences are different and whose knowledge is more limited (197, 238).

To understand children's concepts and to know how children view their world and their relationship to it, one must know some of the outstanding characteristics of children's concepts.

Concepts Are Individualized. Children's concepts are personalized. Because no two children have the same intellectual abilities or the same learning experiences, no two will have the same understanding of an object or situation. Their concepts do, however, contain meanings which are similar to those of all other children. In addition, when children have similar training and learn similar values, there will be similar elements in their concepts. This means, in short, that while *every concept is unique for every child, it is not totally different* (239).

Children who are poor view a picture of a poor family very differently from those who have never experienced poverty and who, as a result, do not understand what it means to be poor. While the picture is the same for both, their understanding of what is depicted in the scene will be very different. Furthermore, the emotional weighting of children's concepts of poverty will depend upon their personal experiences (76).

Concept Development Follows a Pattern. Studies of children's concepts have revealed that there is a pattern of development similar for all children, though the time needed to develop concepts and the level of development attained will depend upon the child's intelligence and opportunities for learning.

Children's concepts change with age, but instead of moving in definite stages, they seem to move, as Russell has pointed out, "along a continuum from simple to complex, from concrete to abstract, from undifferentiated to differentiated, from discrete to organized, from egocentric to more social" as new meanings are associated with old to become part of a system of ideas (197).

One example, at this point, will be sufficient to show how predictable the pattern of concept development is. In a study of the development of the concept of "flag" and sense of national identity, it was found that the pattern of development followed a fairly stable order for all the children studied. At first, when concepts are vague and generalized, the child merely names the flag; to him, it belongs in a class of objects with common characteristics, such as stars. By the time the child is six or seven years old, he can differentiate between flags as representative of different countries. A year later, his concept of countries broadens, and he regards the flag as a symbol of a country.

The eight-year-old has a vague concept of states and governments; he regards the flag as a conventional symbol of identification with a particular country. By the time the child is ten years old, he has developed a concept of abstract loyalty to a country, and a flag is a symbol of that loyalty. Between eleven and twelve years, the child understands the meaning of the ritual connected with the flag (244).

Concepts Are Hierarchical. In the pattern of development, concepts become hierarchical, and names are attached to objects and classes of objects. This hierarchy develops as concepts go from the simple to the more complex levels. At about twenty-six months of age, children pass from the preabstract period into a period in which they are able to grasp *first-hierarchy* concepts; they are able to understand, for example, that "men" and "women" are "people." At about the middle of the fourth year, they enter the *second-hierarchy* period, when they are able to grasp such concepts as "potatoes" are "vegetables," "apples" are "fruit," and both "vegetables" and "fruit" are "food." With advancing age, the child is able to grasp increasingly complex concepts of still higher hierarchies (239). The hierarchical structure of concepts is illustrated in Figure 11–2.

Concepts Develop from Undefined to

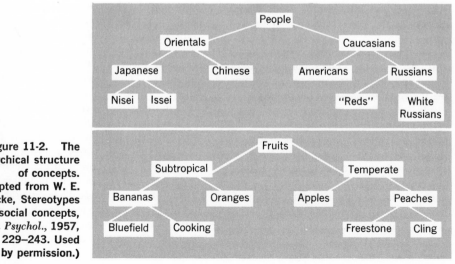

Figure 11-2. The hierarchical structure of concepts. (Adapted from W. E. Vinacke, Stereotypes as social concepts, *J. soc. Psychol.*, 1957, 46, 229–243. Used by permission.)

Specific. The vague, undefined concepts of the young child are gradually replaced by more specific ones. The young child first responds to the total situation rather than to any one part of it. He does not notice details as quickly as he observes whole objects. The result is that he responds to objects or situations that have common elements as if they were the same. Because of this, he develops concepts in which meanings are vague and unformulated.

In a qualitative analysis of children's responses to words in the Stanford-Binet vocabulary test, it was found that the responses given by younger children differ markedly from those given by older children. The younger child usually employs description and inferior explanation, while the older child stresses the class features of word meanings. In defining "gown," for example, the younger child says "you wear it," while the older child defines it as "an evening dress" (78). In illustrating how vague and undifferentiated concepts gradually develop into specific and differentiated concepts, McCullough has stated:

Facets of a concept can be numerous. Take the word *paws.* As a spoken word, of course, it must first be untangled from *pause.* Position makes a difference (front or back), kind (racoon or dog), shape (long, broad), size (big, little), composition (three-toed, bare, furry), feeling (cold, rough), sound (thumping, stealthy), time (old, young), number (many, few) (161).

Concepts Develop from Specific to General. At first, the child's concepts are too vague and undifferentiated to enable him to see their relationship to other concepts. As a result, he cannot put them into categories. With experience, he is able to distinguish partial elements of objects and to group together those which have features in common. In this early type of classification, the object's structure and function play a dominant role in the child's understanding of its meaning (10). The child notices, for example, that there are common elements in the concepts of "rain," "snow," and "sunshine." As he discovers that they are all known as "weather," he categorizes them into the general concept—"weather" (252). How specific concepts develop into general concepts is illustrated in Figure 11–3.

Stereotypes are one form of general concepts. As Vinacke has explained, stereotyping is a "tendency to attribute generalized and simplified characteristics to groups of people in the form of verbal labels" (239). In stereotypes, the psychological or physical characteristics attributed to groups of people are usually uncomplimentary; they therefore lead to prejudice. When the stereotyped characteristics are psychological, they are more likely to lead to prejudice than when they are physical.

In stereotyping, it is assumed that the unfavorable characteristics attributed to a certain group of people are not found in other groups, while traits that are desirable and found in other groups are not found in the stereotyped group. The stereotype, like other concepts, has a verbal symbol or name, such as "nurse," "oldster," "spinster," or "Negro." When the verbal symbol is spoken, it tends to arouse in the hearer a generalized concept of the person who is a member of that group and to whom is attributed the characteristics associated with that group (68, 180, 205).

Stereotypes also include favorable or unfavorable responses toward the person or group with which the stereotype is identified. The form the response will take depends on the meanings included in the stereotype.

In a study of adjectives used to describe Negroes, it was found that a wide variety was used, including "flashy," "superstitious," "musical," "God-fearing," and "happy-go-lucky." Those adjectives that the person feels describe the Negro best will determine his attitude toward the Negro, and this, in turn, will affect his treatment of the Negro.

Furthermore, a person's attitude toward the qualities he attributes to the Negro is an important determinant of his behavior. If his attitude toward "musical" is favorable, for example, it will lead to more favorable behavior than if he feels a musical person is likely to be shiftless and a "loafer." Similarly, if he considers Negroes flashy and his

THE CONCEPTUAL LEARNING

THE SYMBOLIC LEARNING

"Now the sun is shining, Buster"

"That's rain, Billy"

"It's snowing, son"

"All this is weather, my boy"

"It's cold and icy, now"

A specific concept of RAIN + A specific concept of SNOW + A specific concept of SUNSHINE and HEAT + A specific concept of ICE and COLD = A general concept of WEATHER

Figure 11–3. How specific concepts accumulate and make general concepts. (Adapted from A. D. Woodruff, *Basic concepts of teaching*, Chandler, 1961. Used by permission.)

attitude toward "flashy" is unfavorable, his whole concept of the Negro will be unfavorable and will lead to an unfavorable stereotype of all Negroes (245).

Concepts Are Cumulative. In developing concepts, the child builds new meanings on old. Only when an old concept has been found to be erroneous does the child discard it and build a completely new one. Development of the concept of "orange" comes from the association of new meanings with the original meaning of orange as a fruit. As the child learns that a specific color is called "orange," that a type of tree is called "orange," that a drink is called "orange juice," and that a certain flower is called "orange blossom," he gradually comes to understand that "orange" means more than a fruit.

In the building of concepts, the child may make new associations or new relationships between meanings acquired earlier but not

perceived as related. This is apparent in some school studies. In social studies, for example, the child does not always immediately see the relationship of the material he is studying to the material learned in some other course or acquired from reading, movies, or television (221, 252). Each year, new experiences provide the child with new meanings, thus enriching and broadening the concepts already established. The cumulative process is never completed; it continues over a lifetime (76).

Concepts Are Emotionally Weighted. All concepts contain some emotional weighting. As Woodruff has said, "There is no such thing as a feeling which is not connected with some concept and there is no such thing as a concept which does not have some element of feeling associated with it and part of it." Woodruff goes on to explain why this is so: "While concepts are forming through experience, the individual is also learning what value each of the objects and forces has for him through his impressions of how each of them affects him. This sense of value becomes a part of each concept and determines how he feels about it. This tends to influence his behavior toward that thing" (252).

In general, concepts that are *subjective*—concerned with self or with objects, people, or situations related to oneself—are more heavily weighted with feeling tones than concepts of a more *objective* nature. A child who is forced to drink milk will have a different concept of milk than of a drink he has had no contact with, such as a cocktail. School subjects the child is studying have a heavier emotional weighting than school subjects he has not yet studied.

The emotional weighting of concepts may develop slowly or rapidly. It will develop more rapidly if it is conditioned. The child may be conditioned to like something very quickly, for example, if it is associated with some pleasant emotion. Just as concepts change, so does the emotional weighting of the concept. The child who enters school with a concept of school as a pleasant, "grown-up" experience often changes his concept to the point where, before he has completed the second grade, he dislikes school and regards everything connected with it as an unpleasant experience (121).

Values are concepts heavily weighted with emotions. They are concepts of the desirable which influence the child's selection from available modes, means, and ends of action. Because they are primarily subjective, they are stronger predispositions of behavior than concepts with less heavy emotional weighting are. While every child develops his own concepts of what is *desirable to him,* pressures put on him at home and later in the peer group help him to develop values that are approved in the social group with which he is identified (157).

A child who grows up in a large family, for example, develops different concepts of what is important from those of the child who grows up in a small family. In a large family, conformity is highly valued; the child who conforms is treated better by parents than the nonconformist. By contrast, in the small family, where more value is placed on individuality, the child learns that he gets more satisfaction from originality than from conformity (29).

Values learned at home often change when children discover that their concepts are not shared by persons outside. Children of the middle class often discover that honesty is a handicap to popularity; their attitudes then change, and the original emotional weighting is weakened (134).

Concepts Are Sometimes Resistant to Change. The emotional weighting of a concept provides a source of satisfaction for the child which may make change difficult. Moreover, a concept, once formed, does not "vanish when it is contradicted by fact or authority" (138). Instead, it is maintained until it can be replaced by an alternative concept that is equally satisfying or until the child is no longer able to accept it because of social pressures or because of his greater intellectual maturity.

If children's beliefs about Christmas have been built up on the Santa Claus myth, it is often difficult for them to replace these beliefs with beliefs based on the religious significance of Christmas. They frequently rationalize their belief in Santa Claus by saying that he "always eats the food I put out for him." When they can no longer defend this belief, they often react unfavorably toward their parents or even toward the idea that Christmas is an important event. Many a child, disillusioned about Santa Claus, will claim that "Christmas doesn't mean anything now," or he will mistrust his parents, saying that "next they'll tell me there is no God." In time, most children reorganize their concept of Christmas along culturally accepted lines. When this is done, Santa Claus can still have a "place in the child's world" (138).

Concepts Influence Behavior. The final important characteristic of concepts is that they influence the behavior of the child and the type of adjustments, both personal and social, he makes to life. The child who has a realistic concept of himself, for example, will make better personal and social adjustments than the child whose self-concept is unrealistic. Similarly, the child who has a favorable concept of a person belonging to a minority group will treat the person more favorably than the child who shows prejudice based on a stereotype of the group with which the person is identified (239).

The child who develops a concept of "mother" from reading; from movies, television, or comics; or from association with mothers of his friends builds up a stereotype of "mother." He then uses this as a frame of reference for judging his own mother. Much of the friction between mother and child may be traced to the fact that both have concepts of what the other should be like, and neither comes up to the other's expectations (204).

Values, which are based on concepts of what is important, have a marked influence on behavior. If the child places high value on popularity, he will do all within his power to win the acceptance of the social group. If he places high value on school work and grades, he not only will work up to his capacity but may even be tempted to cheat to be able to get high grades.

The important thing to note is that in a given culture where values and knowledge of a similar kind exist, children acquire, in the process of growing up, concepts that are similar to those of other children. This makes it possible for people to understand each other and to predict, with reasonable accuracy, how different people will behave in different situations (67).

MISCONCEPTIONS

Children's concepts are often erroneous. The child frequently misinterprets what he hears or what he observes. He may see, hear, smell, taste, or feel correctly but associate faulty meanings with what he has observed; or he may misinterpret the label associated with the concept. This is especially likely to happen when the label is verbal rather than written (42, 195). If a person refers to "pause" in his work, for example, the child may think this refers to an animal's "paws,"

or reference to having "read" a book may be confused with a "red book." The most common errors occur in the area of *stereotypes*. Because stereotypes are generalized or average pictures that are common to a group of people, they do not take individual differences into account. As a result, a child comes to think that *all* people of a particular group are alike and acts in accordance with this concept (239).

In the early stages of concept learning, the child makes many errors. At first, concepts are so vague that the child cannot see the relationship between those which have elements in common; as a result, he cannot classify them into categories. With learning and experience, he makes fewer errors in concepts as well as in classification. For example, he shows less tendency to classify the living with the nonliving or animals with plants (10). Decrease in errors of classification of concepts is illustrated in Figure 11–4.

Increasing the accuracy of what is learned requires guidance. This is well illustrated in the case of stereotypes. Parents and teachers are far less likely to correct wrong concepts of people belonging to certain groups, such as "teacher," "Jew," or "English," than to correct errors in concepts relating to everyday objects or situations, such as "house," "school," "table," or "family" (239). Unless errors in concepts are corrected soon after they occur, however, the association becomes so firmly established through repetition that their later correction will be very difficult, if not impossible.

While the *cognitive* aspects of a faulty concept can be corrected with the learning of correct information, the *emotional* aspect of the concept is likely to be persistent. If a child is conditioned by an older sibling to think of arithmetic as a "hard" or "boring" subject, for example, he may readily change this concept when he finds it not so difficult as he had expected. But if he is conditioned to dislike arithmetic, it is far less likely that the emotional weighting of the concept can be so radically changed that he will like the subject, though he may adopt an attitude of indifference.

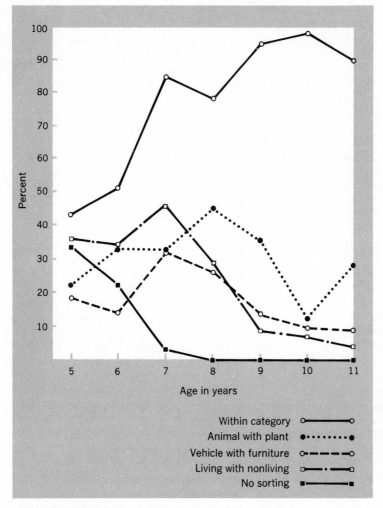

Figure 11–4.
Classification of concepts into categories contributes to decrease in errors in concepts. (Adapted from M. Annett, The classification of instances of four common class concepts by children and adults, *Brit. J. educ. Psychol.*, 1959, 29, 223–236. Used by permission.)

Within category   o———o
Animal with plant   ●·········●
Vehicle with furniture   o– – – –o
Living with nonliving   □–·–·–□
No sorting   ■———■

Causes of Misconceptions. Errors in perception, resulting from the association of faulty meanings, may be traced to a number of causes, the most important of which are the following:

1. The child may have received *incorrect information* about the subject. When parents are not certain about the correct answer to a child's question, they may "make up" an answer merely to satisfy his curiosity or to keep him quiet. On the other hand, they may give him information which they *sincerely believe* is correct but which is not. Sometimes they are preoccupied with other interests and do not hear the child's question

correctly; they then answer it as they *thought* the child asked it. They give correct information about the question they *thought* the child asked but incorrect information about the question he actually asked.

If the child seeks information from siblings or peers, he has an even greater chance of getting incorrect or partially correct information. His information may also be faulty if he reads unauthoritative or out-of-date sources, such as old textbooks (39).

2. Superstitious beliefs frequently give rise to misconceptions. When superstitions are passed on to the child by a parent, teacher, or someone else in authority, he is less likely to question them than if they are told to him by a member of the peer group. If a parent tells a child that a black cat running across his path is an omen of trouble, for example, he will build up a concept of black cats as evil influences. The child who is told that red hair is a sign of temper will build up a stereotype of red-haired people as hot-tempered. Children from homes of inferior socioeconomic status are likely to learn more superstitious beliefs than children from higher socioeconomic backgrounds (197, 238).

3. *Limited experience* makes it impossible for the child to judge things accurately. This has been demonstrated in laboratory experiments of weight illusion. When a pound of cotton is placed side by side with a pound of lead, the child invariably says the pound of cotton is heavier because he judges weight in terms of size. If he is asked to pick them up and weigh them in his hands, he usually gets the opposite illusion because he does not realize that the *total* feel of the cotton must be balanced against the *concentrated* feel of the lead. What is true of laboratory experiments is equally true outside the laboratory. Because of lack of critical attitude, resulting from limited experience and undeveloped intelligence, the child may readily associate completely wrong meanings with what he observes without realizing how incongruous the association is (197).

4. *Gullibility* is the basis of many misconceptions. Children who have been brought up in authoritarian homes learn to believe that "mother knows best." This quickly spreads to the belief that *anyone older* than they or *anyone in authority* knows more than they do; as a result, they accept what is said without question. Older children are capable of independent thinking, but they may have already developed the habit of depending on others to do their thinking for them. The more unsure children are of their social acceptance and the more anxious they are for group approval, the more gullible they will be (22, 241).

5. *Faulty reasoning* may cause misconceptions. In young children, reasoning ability has not yet developed enough to enable them to attack a problem in a critical manner. Furthermore, they have too little information on which to build accurate concepts about objects or conditions not present at the time. While normal reasoning ability increases with age, lack of training or opportunity to use his reasoning ability because of authoritarian training in the home or school will often cause the older child to reason inaccurately. As a result, when two objects or two situations are alike in one or more respects, he is apt to conclude that they are alike in every way (252). For example, if he has accepted the belief that *all* Scotsmen are "tight" about money and he knows that Mr. MacDougall has come from Scotland, he will conclude that Mr. MacDougall is "tight" (254). Faulty reasoning may lead to very amusing—but totally incorrect—conclusions, as the following story shows. After a teacher explained to his pupils the scientific principle of expansion and contraction, one of them answered a question about why the days in winter are shorter than those in summer thus: "During the winter months, the days get cold and contract. In the summertime, they get hot and expand" (178).

6. *Vivid imagination* may lead to conclusions not justified by the data available. In the growth of different intellectual abilities, imagination outstrips reasoning. As a result, the young child does not have the check on his imagination that he will have later; he believes that what he imagines has actually happened. After seeing an elephant in a parade on television, he may believe that he saw the elephant in a parade on the street near his home. Similarly, data of a purely imaginary sort in his dreams or daydreams may seem so realistic that they are incorporated into his developing concepts. Many of the "white lies" of early childhood can be traced to this source (48).

7. Closely related to vivid imagination, and dependent on it, is *unrealistic thinking*. The child is encouraged to think unrealistically about things, including himself, by the stories he hears and later reads, by the scenes and actions he sees on movie and

television screens, by the comics, and even by the home and school. Because most children prefer stories about things that *might* happen, books, comics, movies, and television programs often contain an element of unreality. The happenings are presented in such a way that the uncritical child believes they actually do happen, and he comes to believe that they could happen in real life just as they do in books or on the screen (16, 45, 202).

Furthermore, because children tend to identify themselves with fictional characters, they feel that the things that happen in stories can and do happen in real life also. Even as the child grows older, persistent exposure to unrealistic thinking in mass media of communication motivates him to continue to think unrealistically about life (31, 152).

Because a democratic form of government seeks to provide everyone with opportunities to develop his innate abilities, the child is encouraged to believe that he, too, can become a rich, famous, and successful person if he is only willing to make use of his talents. This unrealistic thinking is strengthened by the "rags-to-riches" stories which children are encouraged to read and by the implications of parents and teachers that any child can be a Horatio Alger if he wants to badly enough (253). This constant exposure to unrealism is bound to influence the child's thinking, especially when it has the stamp of approval of parents and teachers.

8. Every concept sooner or later acquires a verbal label, and many misconceptions result from a *misunderstanding of words.* Even though a child's comprehension vocabulary at every age is larger than his use vocabulary, there are always gaps as well as errors in his understanding of words. Many children, for example, claim they know the meaning of such common words as "gown," "butterfly," "purple," or "dime," but when asked to tell specifically what these words mean, they show that they have misconceptions or only partially correct concepts of the meaning of the things for which these words serve as verbal labels.

Since a limited or incorrect vocabulary leads to misinterpretations, the child is likely to develop misconceptions about things he is seeking information about; the explanation may be correct, but his interpretation of it is erroneous. This is often true of explanations of scientific phenomena, of religion, and of sex. Even when the words are explained, the child may not comprehend the meaning completely unless the explanation is accompanied by pictures or a demonstration that he can see or feel (23, 106).

Variations in Errors. While it is true that all perception is subject to error and that the extent of the error is closely related to the age of the individual, there are nevertheless common errors within each age group. As a general rule, the more *subjective* the perception, the more influenced it is by personal bias or prejudice, which, in turn, results in faulty concepts. *Objective* facts, on the other hand, may be observed incorrectly because of insufficient knowledge on the subject's part to enable him to perceive them correctly (76, 252). Such common misconceptions as "telephone wires are hollow," "flowers have no function for the plant," "the heart beats only when we are sick or frightened," and "water is lighter than air" are caused by faulty or inadequate information which the child has acquired from his contact with others or by misinterpreting what he has read (179).

Faulty concepts about self are not caused by faulty information but rather by *personal bias.* The child, like the adult, prefers to think of himself as *he would like to be,* with traits and characteristics that are approved by the social group. If asked, then, to judge himself, he will do so in terms of the ideal self. In an experiment in which children were asked to check one word in a pair that more nearly described them, it was found that children tended to overestimate the presence of socially desirable traits and to underestimate the presence of undesirable ones. This tendency was stronger in older children, who are more aware of the opinions of others than younger children (113).

Boys, at every age, tend to underrate

themselves, and this tendency becomes stronger as they grow older. Girls tend to overrate themselves—not because girls are, on the whole, better adjusted, but rather because they wish to compensate for feeling inferior to boys (102). As was pointed out in the discussion of social insight, the ability to perceive one's own status in the group is consistently inferior to the ability to perceive the status of others (15). This suggests that misconceptions are more common in subjective than in objective matters.

Seriousness of Misconceptions. It is generally assumed that if a child is given correct information he will build up correct concepts. This is not always so, however. One of the earliest and one of the most important investigations of the accuracy of children's concepts was made by G. Stanley Hall in 1891. According to his findings, children have more faulty information when they enter school than one would expect. Children from better neighborhoods have fewer faulty concepts than children from poorer neighborhoods. Likewise, there are fewer misconceptions regarding objects or experiences common in a neighborhood than about less common ones (99).

Other studies have revealed similar findings. Misconceptions at any one age are closely related to the characteristic concepts held by the child at that age. The errors are systematic, not accidental or uniquely individual, and they are fairly uniform among children of that level of development (197, 221). In numbers, for example, errors are related to the concepts of addition, subtraction, multiplication, or division that the child is currently learning (114). Jersild has pointed out, however, that in spite of these errors, a "child may possess vast stores of information that are meaningful and useful to him in his everyday life, even though he may be lacking on many items of knowledge that adults take more or less for granted" (120).

Misconceptions are serious, not only because they are difficult to revise if they are permitted to persist, but also because they affect the child's adjustments. In his school work, the child is handicapped by misconceptions regarding words used by the teacher or in textbooks. If his concepts are limited or faulty, he may not be able to understand the teacher's explanations (42). Likewise, when reading for pleasure or watching movies or television, he will misinterpret what he hears or sees if his concepts of certain words are faulty or if he habitually views life in an unrealistic way (16, 86).

The major source of difficulty arising from misconceptions is to be found in the area of social relationships. The child who misinterprets what others say or do or who does not perceive his own status in the group accurately will be handicapped in his social adjustments. To make good adjustments, the child must be able to perceive accurately not only his status in the group but the status of others as well (15).

Serious misconceptions often result from stereotyping. The child who puts all people in a category because they have a common physical or personal characteristic will react to them as if they were all alike; as a result, he will often behave in such a way as to lead to poor social adjustments (239).

SOME COMMON CONCEPTS OF CHILDREN

Whatever concepts a child has, they are a reflection of his own personal and unique development. Some concepts, however, are so common among children in a given culture that one can accept them as "typical." Of these, the following types are most common.

CONCEPTS OF LIFE

Because of the young child's limited experience and knowledge, he does not distinguish between living and inanimate objects. On the contrary, he believes, as primitive peoples do, that all objects have the same life qualities that one finds in the human being and are therefore animate (238). *Animism,* or the tendency to ascribe consciousness to inert objects, is one of the outstanding characteristics of the young child's perception.

Unquestionably, adults encourage children to maintain and develop their animistic beliefs. Children's stories tell about toys and animals that are able to think and feel as people do (31, 39, 202). Many *movies* and *television* programs for children show animated toys, trees, houses, and other objects. Although an older child or adult realizes that such films are pure fantasy, the young child does not (16, 24). The more the child identifies with these objects or characters, the easier it is for him to imagine that they have the same qualities that he has (152, 153). Furthermore, *parents* or other *adults* imply that inanimate objects are animate. When an angry child kicks a chair, his mother is likely to say, "Poor chair, you hurt him. Go and tell him you are sorry." Under such conditions, it is not surprising that the child is animistic in his thinking.

A number of studies have been concerned with finding out when children begin to endow inanimate objects with life qualities and how long they persist in doing so. In one of the most comprehensive studies, Piaget concluded that there were four successive stages in the animistic concepts of young children. In the first stage, when children are four to six years old, everything that is in any way active is regarded as conscious, even though it is stationary. In the second stage, between the ages of six and seven years, consciousness is attributed only to things that can move. The sun and a bicycle are regarded as conscious, while a table and a stone are not. Between the ages of eight and ten, in the third stage, the child makes an essential distinction between movement that is due to the object itself and movement that is introduced by an outside agent. Bodies that can move of their own accord, such as the sun or the wind, are looked upon as conscious, while objects that receive their movement from without, such as bicycles, are regarded as devoid of consciousness. In the fourth and final stage, which begins at the age of eleven years,

consciousness is restricted to plants and animals, or to animals alone (181).

More recent studies have revealed that there are no definite stages through which children pass in the development of these concepts, but rather a gradual transition from one phase to another. Furthermore, children of the same age differ markedly; some adolescents may have concepts similar to those of children (66).

Children distinguish between "living" and "having life." "Living" is more often applied to inanimate objects than "having life." When they say an object is "alive," they usually do not attribute sensory or functional characteristics to it. Thus the child's definition of "alive" differs from that of an adult. To a child, "alive" usually means "active"; this is not "animism" in the correct sense of the word.

From kindergarten on, there is a progressive decrease in the number of children who attribute life to inanimate objects (131, 220). In a study of seven- and eight-year-olds, most of the children said a dog, a tree, or the moon was living; fewer claimed that a river, a watch, or an automobile had life qualities; and very few said that a bicycle, a pencil, or a stone had (130). When asked "What makes the engine go?" even young children recognize that the presence of a human being is necessary for the guidance of the engine. In a study in which children were asked if all things that move are living, approximately one-third said "No" at six years of age; all said "No" by eleven years. This is illustrated in Figure 11–5. As children reach school age, they become increasingly aware of the fact that movement is not the sole criterion of life (128).

CONCEPTS OF DEATH

Closely related to concepts of life are concepts of death. Children's concepts of death, which depend largely upon their religious instruction, range from brutal destruction to liberation (23, 176). In one study of large groups of children, it was found that children between the ages of three and five years look upon death as a departure or change of abode. They deny that death is a regular and final process because, at this level of development, they look upon everything as alive, including the dead and lifeless (171). They cannot comprehend the finality of death; instead, they believe that the dead person or pet will return (1).

Between the ages of five and nine years, children personify death. They regard it as inevitable but do not try to explain why it occurs because they do not recognize it as a process which results from certain conditions and in certain circumstances. At this age they are not likely to worry about death unless they feel anxious and insecure in their family relationships. Then they will worry about the death of a parent or some other family member, not about themselves. Few children, unless they have experienced long or severe illness, think of death in relation to themselves. To the great majority, death is associated with old age, not with youth (1, 171, 176).

Influence of Mass Media. In spite of the parental desire to spare the child firsthand contact with death—even when a member of the family or a pet animal dies—he sooner or later has secondhand experiences with it through mass media. He then develops his concept of what death really means. In discussing the influence of mass media on children's concepts of death, Barclay has commented:

The way that life is lived today children are exposed continually to ersatz examples of death on television which are either cold, bloodless and unmourned or violently reacted to in the most melodramatic manner possible. At the same time, news programs, newspapers and picture magazines show them graphic evidences of real death and of real reactions to it—some stricken, some apparently emotionless, a few smirkingly self-conscious. The adults close to a child rarely comment on such things. If the child is upset by death in a movie or television show, his parents reassure him that the upsetting incident was just "make believe." But he knows

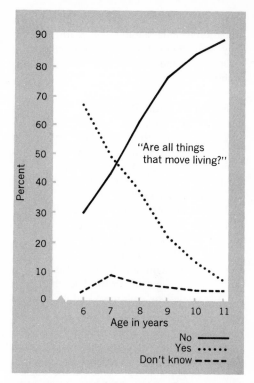

Figure 11–5. Increased realization with age that movement alone does not mean "living." (Adapted from W. H. King, The development of scientific concepts in children, *Brit. J. educ. Psychol.*, 1961, 31, 1–20. Used by permission.)

that at other times and other places it is surely real. What is the mystery? Why are adults reluctant to speak of this obviously important matter? (20)

The more mystery there is surrounding death in the child's home, school, or neighborhood, the more he is forced to form his concepts of death from the information he has been able to get from mass media. What his concept will be will depend to a large extent upon the types of mass media he enjoys and the programs or movies he prefers. If he looks at the pictures in newspapers or news magazines, he will often be limited to information about death from accident or murder. Concepts formed from such sources will certainly not give him a wholesome understanding of death; in fact, they will often lead to heavy emotional weighting of the concept, with fear predominating.

Influence of Adult Reactions. The child's concepts of death are also influenced by adults' reactions to it. In their attempt to shield the child from the grief they themselves experience when a member of the family or a close friend dies, parents often are so absorbed in their own grief that the child goes unnoticed. He is often frightened and upset by the parents' reaction and resentful over their neglect. As Barclay has explained, these circumstances not only affect the child emotionally but also help to color his concepts of death. The child who is "surrounded by gaunt-eyed adults who do not see you or hear a word that you say can magnify the idea of death's enormity almost beyond belief" (20).

A child may get the idea that he is personally responsible for some of the neglect his parents show him. Unless they take time to explain the reason for their grief or preoccupation with practical matters related to death, the child can readily interpret their behavior as a form of rejection. As Barclay has pointed out, to avoid the development of unhealthy concepts, the child "needs reassurance that the total preoccupation of those he loves best does not represent a rejection of him but an upset that will pass with time; that they will recover from their stricken manner and smile and be his again" (20).

Concepts of Life after Death. Children are not very much concerned about what happens after death. Many are told that after death a person goes to Heaven, where he has everything he ever wanted but did not have when he was alive. Unless religious instruction emphasizes Hell as a place of eternal punishment, the child learns to think of life after death as a pleasant experience. Because he has little personal interest in the matter, however, the concept formed in early childhood is likely to persist with few modifications until he reaches adolescence (1).

If the child receives little or no religious instruction about life after death, he seldom wonders about it or builds up any concept of it. If the child does have religious instruction on the subject, he is likely to develop such an unrealistic concept that he will have to revise it radically when he reaches adolescence and becomes aware of how unrealistic it is (215, 219).

CONCEPTS OF CAUSALITY

The ability to see cause-and-effect relationships develops gradually, not in stages, as was formerly believed (181). This ability is more closely related to the child's experiences and to the type of learning experiences he has than to either his chronological or mental age. If the child has learned a number of superstitious beliefs to explain natural phenomena or accidental happenings, he will have many more faulty concepts of causality than he would if his learning experiences had been more realistic (252).

Similarly, a child who reads books and comics or who sees movies and television programs with a fairy-tale slant will come to think that *magic* causes anything whose cause is not immediately apparent. Children often learn, in their religious instruction, that *God* is responsible for everything; they think of God as the cause of everything they wonder about (152, 234).

Faulty instruction is likewise responsible for some faulty concepts of causality. Parents either do not know the answers to the child's questions or do not want to give him the correct answers. When a child asks questions about birth, for example, any plausible answer that will put an end to his questioning seems justified to the embarrassed parent, who does not realize that misinformation may lead to a faulty concept (173).

As a result of differences in learning experiences, children's concepts of causality cover a wide range at every age. Even in the same child, some concepts will be immature and others mature; some will be completely faulty, some partially faulty, and some correct. Those related to the child's personal experiences will be the best developed and the most accurate. School work that emphasizes scientific studies, especially if it is supplemented by demonstrations and educational films, fosters the development of accurate concepts of causality and helps children correct inaccurate concepts. Educational movies or television programs and factual, realistic books and comics also help children to develop accurate concepts of causality (179, 208).

Pattern of Development. In spite of the differences attributable to individual learning experiences, there is a general pattern in the development of concepts of causality. Young children's concepts are usually illogical, inaccurate, and magical in content; there is little indication that children under seven or eight years of age understand cause and effect (128, 237). By the time children of normal intelligence reach eight or nine, however, they can, without special instruction, understand cause-and-effect relationships in simple situations. Furthermore, there seems to be no difference in the difficulty of learning concepts of causality relating to the body and those relating to natural phenomena. Both are dependent upon the development of reasoning ability and personal experiences (238, 252).

The relationship between development of reasoning ability, learning experiences, and development of concepts of causality has been demonstrated in simple experiments with children of different ages. In one experiment, the water level in a container was raised by inserting an object into the water; in the other, a shadow was produced by turning a flashlight on an unlighted candle. It was found that children under seven years of age could see the cause-and-effect relationship if they were given an explanation; with repeated observation, some of them could observe the relationship without explanation. After seven, most of the children could observe the relationship without explanation; as their verbal skill increased, they could explain their understanding of the relationship better (166).

Some Specific Concepts. A number of studies have been made of the pattern of development of concepts of causality in different areas. A study of concepts of *birth*, for example, has revealed that the child first believes that a baby originates simply from the baby itself. At the age of eight years, he usually takes into consideration the role played by the mother, and sometimes that played by the father. Many young children think babies come from God, the stork, or a store (173).

The child's concepts of *bodily functions* are largely dependent upon the opportunities he has had to learn about them. Few children, even when very young, attribute mystical qualities to the body. In one study, not a single child, for example, referred to the soul and its role in controlling the body. They did, however, say that the most important parts of the body are the heart and the brain, suggesting that they saw a cause-and-effect relationship between these organs and the functioning of the body. Not until children are ten years of age and older do they begin to see a cause-and-effect relationship between the different organs of the body and its functioning (87). Up until then, most children describe body organs but not the different systems and their functioning. The only system that they report as important is the skeletomuscular system (228).

Most young children think of the functioning of the body in terms of specific organs. Their concept of the brain, up to the age of seven years, is that it is in the head and that it is round and composed of bone, blood, and skin. Only after the fifth or sixth grade do they include flesh and cells in their brain concept. As a rule, they think of the brain as mostly bone, indicating a confusion between it and the skull. Until children are eight years old, they attribute to the brain intellectual activities mainly, especially thinking. Even after eight, there is little indication that they understand the functions of the brain.

Nerves are thought of as threads composed mainly of bone, blood, and flesh and covering all or part of the head, with the major function being "feeling." Many confuse "nerves" with "nervousness" (87, 174).

Concepts of *breathing* are as erroneous as those of the brain and nerves. The child sees little relationship between breathing and life. To him, breathing takes place mostly in the nose, mouth, and throat, and the air circulates somewhere in the head region. Not until children are nine years old do they recognize breathing as a process of taking in and expelling air. They do not think of it in terms of the interchange of oxygen or its effects on the body. Only toward the end of childhood do children recognize that the lungs are the organs of breathing and that breathing is essential to life. To older children, lungs are represented as round bags, made of bone, skin, blood, and flesh. Some children locate the lungs in the head or neck; few locate them in the chest (87, 174). Figure 11–6 shows two examples of children's placement of the important organs of the body at different age levels. Even at the sixth-grade level, children fail to include the sex organs in their placement of the different body organs (228).

In the child's concept of the *digestive process,* digestion takes place in the mouth and stomach. The stomach, which is meant for storing or eating food, is usually located in the upper part of the trunk and is believed to be composed of skin, bone, flesh,

and blood. The purpose of eating is vague to children. If they say anything about its purpose, they generally say that "you eat to make you grow," but they have only nebulous ideas of how eating and growing are related.

Likewise, they have little understanding of the relationship between eating, digestion, and elimination. Young children often believe that food goes from the mouth to the stomach and then to the arms and legs. The older child is more likely to include the intestines in the route that food takes through the body, though he may be confused about the roles played by the kidneys and the intestines. Figure 11–7 shows the paths taken by food in the digestive process as conceived by a child eight years and seven months of age and by one nine years and eleven months. It is thus apparent that even older children have poor concepts of the cause-and-effect relationship between eating and living (87, 172).

Children are inclined to attribute all diseases to *germs.* Young children draw a germ as a dot or as some abstract figure. Children eight years of age and older think of germs as abstract figures or animals—a fly or worm (see Figure 11–8). They believe that germs enter the body through the mouth, nose, or skin and that they make the person ill, damage the body, or live in the body.

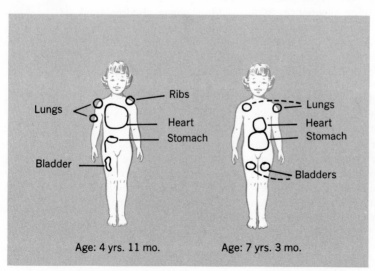

Age: 4 yrs. 11 mo.   Age: 7 yrs. 3 mo.

Figure 11–6. Examples of children's placement of some bodily organs at different ages. (Adapted from E. Gellert, Children's conceptions of the content and function of the human body, *Genet. Psychol. Monogr.,* 1962, 65, 293–405. Used by permission.)

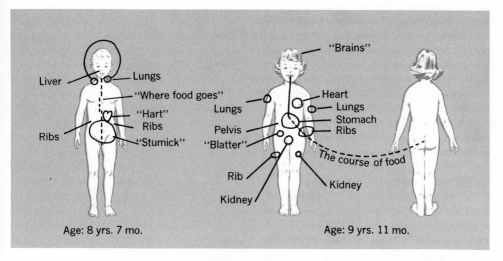

Figure 11–7.   Some examples of children's concepts of the digestive process. (Adapted from E. Gellert, Children's conceptions of the content and function of the human body, *Genet. Psychol. Monogr.*, 1962, 65, 293–405. Used by permission.)

Germs can leave the body, they believe, through the mouth, nose, skin, or anus and can be ejected by coughing, sneezing, or anal evacuation. When the doctor gives medicine, that pushes the germs out of the body (172, 175).

CONCEPTS OF SPACE

To judge space accurately, the child must learn to compare the space to be perceived with familiar objects whose size or distance from him is known. He must learn to regard the degree of clearness of outline and color and the amount of detail visible as clues, and he must learn that different sensations in the eyes, resulting from convergence or strain, help him to interpret what he observes. The distance of the object from the child plays an important role in determining how accurately he will judge its size. He tends to judge close objects larger than they actually are and distant objects smaller than they are. In relation to his own size, they often seem this way to him (56).

Little babies rarely reach for objects more than 20 inches away from them; this shows that they have some estimate of distance even before they are a year old. As soon as they begin to creep and crawl, they have more opportunity to learn to evaluate distance and size (33, 88).

By playing with blocks, carts, tricycles, and other play equipment, the child soon learns the common cues which enable him to perceive short distances accurately. Longer distances, because they are unrelated to his own body—for example, the distance between two trees or the length of a street block—are extremely difficult for him to perceive. Not until adolescence can he perceive long distances correctly, and even then his judgments are often erroneous (197).

Perceptions of distance, direction, and size are all improved by training. Toys and kindergarten equipment—beads for stringing, blocks, cylinders, form boards, puzzles, nests of cubes, tricycles, sleds, and coasters—give the child an opportunity to measure in terms of "long" and "short." In school, he learns the meaning of inches, feet, yards, pounds, and the different standard measures of space and weight, even though the concepts may be so formalized that he has difficulty applying them to his everyday experiences (184).

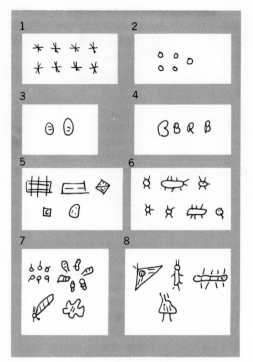

Figure 11–8. Children's concepts of "germs." (Adapted from M. H. Nagy, The representation of "germs" by children, *J. genet. Psychol.*, 1953, 83, 227–240. Used by permission.)

Varieties of Concepts. As early as six months of age, the baby can discriminate between *simple geometric forms* (circle, square, cross, triangle, and oval) and can use this discrimination as a learning cue. Between fifteen months and two years of age, children develop concepts of triangularity and other forms. Terman and Merrill find that a two-year-old of average intelligence should be able to insert a circle, a square, and a triangle into a three-hole form board. In the three-year-old, concepts of roundness are well enough developed to enable the child to distinguish cylindrical and two-dimensional roundness (232, 238). The ability to perceive differences in form continues to improve gradually.

In a study to determine whether form or color played a more important role in per-

ception, children were presented objects in such a way that they had to match the objects on the basis of form or color, but never on both bases simultaneously. Children under three years of age matched the objects on the basis of form rather than color; children from three to six matched on the basis of color; while those over six matched on the basis of form. Baley has formulated the principle that "with the progress of the child's development, formal elements in his perception take more and more predominance over the material elements, such as color" (18). In figure-ground discrimination, the preschool child's perception of ground is nearer the adult level than his perception of figures (162).

While young children can judge the size of similar-shaped objects as well as adults can, they have difficulty when the figures are different in form; in comparing the size of a triangle with that of a square, for example, they find it hard to get cues for their judgments. Between the ages of three and four years, children are more influenced by the effect of illusion when judging the relative size of different geometric figures than when they are younger. The figures that spread out over greater space, such as stars, appear to the child to be larger than the more compact figures, such as squares and rectangles (74).

Concepts of *relative size* appear first between the ages of three and four years, when the child realizes that he must regard himself as one object among other objects in space. At this time, a child can select the largest and smallest objects from a group placed before him, and by the time he is five years old, he can select middle-sized objects. The extent of the difference in size somewhat influences the child's response. Not much before nine years of age, however, can he judge "middleness" as accurately as he can "bigness" and "smallness" (238). If the difference in size is very small, the perception of relative difference becomes increasingly inaccurate (195).

In an experiment in which children were asked to judge the relative sizes of the blackboard and the length of the school building, it was found that their ability to judge the size of the blackboard correctly improved with age but that their tendency to underestimate the length of the school building persisted (128).

Nursery-school children can perceive realistically their own body sizes and those of their parents. They perceive the father as the larger parent and themselves as smaller than both parents. They have a tendency, however, to perceive members of the opposite sex as larger than members of their own sex (126).

The ability to distinguish between *right* and *left* begins to develop at about five years of age and improves fairly rapidly between six and seven (225). In the *first stage* of the pattern, up to seven or eight years of age, the child has a nondifferentiated conception of right and left; he applies the concept to his arms and legs but not to objects. In the *second stage,* from seven or eight to ten or eleven years, he develops a concrete differentiation of right and left; he relates the concept to himself as well as to objects, but, in the case of objects, he can differentiate correctly only when some perceptual prop, such as another person or object, is given. In the *third stage,* from ten or eleven years of age on, the child has an abstract concept of right and left; he can differentiate the two in an adult manner without the need for perceptual props (72).

Elementary-school children do not have a well-generalized notion of the cardinal *directions.* While they may be able to identify south and east, they are likely to fail to identify southeast. Furthermore, they have difficulty using directions correctly in describing locations of places, though they can fairly accurately locate cities, especially nearby cities (82, 146).

The ability to judge *distance* develops fairly rapidly. From his experience with standard objects in the distance, such as an automobile or a one-story house, the child learns that objects appear to be smaller when they are far away than when they are close at hand. Furthermore, he learns that

he can tell how far away they are by how clearly he can see details (56). By the time he is four years old, his perception of distance is similar to that of adults. On the other hand, perception of *depth* is slow in developing. Even at five or six years of age, the child is not usually able to see three dimensions in objects. In comparing the *speed* of two moving objects, the five-year-old is fairly accurate (82).

CONCEPTS OF WEIGHT

Judgments of weight depend partly upon judgments of size and partly upon knowledge of the weight of different materials. The child judges mainly by size; as a result, when he picks up objects, he does not make the necessary muscular adjustments to han-

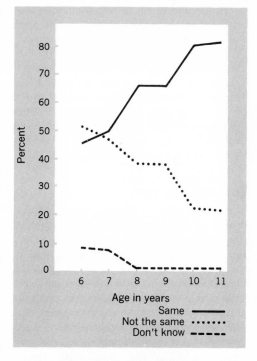

Figure 11–9. Improvement with age in ability to estimate correctly the weights of two equal objects of different shapes. (Adapted from W. H. King, The development of scientific concepts in children, *Brit. J. educ. Psychol.,* 1961, 31, 1–20. Used by permission.)

dle them without breakage. A small toy or household object, for instance, may slip through the child's fingers and break because he did not expect it to be as heavy as it is.

Gradually the child learns from experience that certain things are "heavy," while others are "light." Of even greater importance, he learns that he must consider what the object is made of as well as its size. In time, he discovers that if he wants to determine just what the weight of an object is, he must pick it up, hold it with his fingers or place it in the palm of his hand, and then move his hand up and down (34, 88). In this manner, a five-year-old child can tell the difference between a 3- and a 15-gram weight when they are the same size. With practice, he can tell the difference when the weights vary only 3 or 4 grams (232).

In an experiment in which children were asked to estimate the weight of a milk bottle when filled and when empty, young children tended to underestimate both. With age, however, they gradually improved their estimates. In estimating the weight of two lumps of Plasticine, equal in size and in weight but different in shape, children showed a gradual increase in accuracy with age (128). The results of the experiment are shown in Figure 11–9, page 513.

NUMBER CONCEPTS

Words relating to numbers are used soon after the child starts to speak. This early use of number words, however, is merely a form of "parrot speech." What a number really means to a child and when he can use it in a meaningful way are difficult to determine. The development of number concepts appears to be a function of age and of educational development (250). Terman and Merrill found that the average child of four can count two objects; the average child of five can count four; and the average child of six can count twelve (232). Young children who go to nursery school or kindergarten generally learn the meaning of numbers sooner than those who do not go. Young children's concepts of numbers above

10, however, are generally vague and confused; they think of 100 and 1,000 as similar (156).

The developmental pattern of number concepts has revealed no distinct stages but rather a gradual improvement (250). The developmental pattern indicates that understanding increases as the child grows older and as his experiences broaden:

1 year	"One-by-one" pattern of manipulating objects (rudiment of counting).
18 months	Can build a tower of three to four cubes. Uses the word "more."
2 years	Distinguishes between one and many. Says "two balls" when handed a second ball.
2½ years	Counts by rote, 1, 2, "lots." Can give "just one" cube on request.
3 years	Can count two objects. Can give "just two" cubes on request.
4 years	Counts with correct pointing to three objects. Verbal counting without pointing exceeds counting of objects.
5 years	Most children can count 13 pennies. One-third can count to 30 or more. Most mistakes come after the number 9.
6 years	Can count to 100. Can count by tens to 100. Can count by fives to 50. Can add correctly within 10. Can subtract correctly within 5.
7 years	Can count by fives and tens to 100. Can add within 20. Can subtract within 10.
8 years	Can count by twos to 20. Can count by threes to 30. Can count by fours to 50. Can add within 25. Can subtract within 25. Can deal with simple fractions, multiplication and division.
9 years	Number concepts to 1,000 or beyond (114).

From grades 2 to 11, there is a gradual increase in understanding of indeterminate number concepts, such as "few," "several," and "some" (38). Because so much emphasis is placed on *quantitative* concepts—number concepts relating to increase or decrease in amount—in school textbooks, especially in arithmetic and social studies books, children gradually develop more definite and more accurate concepts of what numbers mean. References to "$15 a ton," a "500-mile trip," or a "trip of 20 days" may be relatively meaningless until the child has had instruction in their use and opportunities for comparison. At every age, girls have more accurate number concepts than boys, although boys often, as a result of their greater interest in social studies, develop clearer concepts of quantity. Children of the higher socioeconomic groups have more number concepts and more accurate concepts than those of the lower groups (117, 156). The pattern of development of number concepts for boys and girls is shown in Figure 11–10.

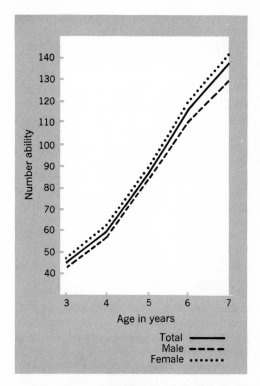

Figure 11–10. Development of number concepts in young children. (Adapted from W. E. Martin, Quantitative expressions in young children, *Genet. Psychol. Monogr.*, 1951, 44, 147–219. Used by permission.)

MONEY CONCEPTS

Money becomes meaningful to a child only when he has an opportunity to use it. True, he may be able to identify different coins, but the names of the coins are relatively meaningless until he learns their value or knows what they can buy. Because few children in our culture have much opportunity to spend money until they reach the school years, the development of money concepts during the preschool years lags behind that of many other concepts (155).

At five years of age, the average child can name pennies only. A year later, he can name pennies, nickels, and dimes, and some children know how many pennies there are in a nickel or dime (232). The seven-year-old knows what a quarter is, and many children can tell how many pennies there are in a quarter (114). At that time, the child can ask for correct change in a store. The child at 8½ years can match equivalent amounts with different coins, even when the money combinations are complex (201).

By five years of age, children begin to understand that money has to do with buying, though they do not understand that specific coins must be used for buying different things. By the age of 6½ years, children realize that a nickel will buy more than a penny but less than a dime. They also realize that money can buy services as well as objects and that change is sometimes given when money is used to make a purchase. By the age of seven, average children know exactly how much each coin is worth in comparison with every other coin (221, 222).

Variations in Concepts. Marked variations in children's concepts of money stem from differences in learning experiences. The child

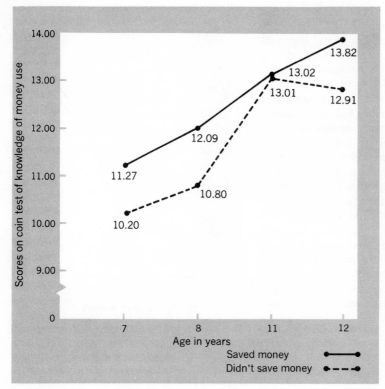

Figure 11–11. Relation of saving and not saving to an understanding of the meaning of money. (Adapted from H. R. Marshall and L. Magruder, Relations between parent money education practices and children's knowledge and use of money, *Child Develpm.*, 1960, 31, 253–284. Used by permission.)

who *earns money* by jobs at home or outside the home learns more about what money means in terms of time and effort than the child who receives his money as an allowance or dole from his parents (89). In general, experience with money decreases with a rise in number of siblings in the family; the more siblings there are, the less money each child has to spend.

The child has more experience in the handling of money if his *mother works* because he has more home responsibilities involving the use of money. The amount of money the child spends, however, is not as important in the development of concepts as the way he uses the money. Children who *save* their money have a better understanding of its meaning than those who *spend* it. This is illustrated in Figure 11–11. Children who *spend foolishly* learn more about the value of money than children who *spend wisely* or children whose spending is closely supervised (155).

Boys, as a rule, have more accurate concepts of what money will buy than girls. This is because boys are given greater freedom in the use of their money and are, in general, given money for more of their personal needs. Furthermore, older boys earn more money outside the home and therefore develop a "money sense" earlier than girls. Giving money as a reward for good behavior or achievements and taking it away as a punishment do little to teach the child the value of money and how to use it wisely (155).

American children, as a whole, show little interest in family budgeting and spending. Because of this, they deprive themselves of valuable learning experiences in finding out how money can be spent wisely; how much money is needed for essentials, such as food and clothing; how important it is to have a reserve for the proverbial "rainy day"; and how much a person can expect to earn in different vocations.

This lack of interest in money is not always the child's fault. In authoritarian homes, the parents handle money matters without consulting the child. In homes where child training is more democratic, parents often feel that children should not be concerned about financial problems and, consequently, do not discuss such matters with the child or in his presence. Frequently, they do not tell him of personal sacrifices they have made to give him the material possessions he craves or the opportunities they want him to have. As a result, the child has little motivation to learn about money. Consequently, even when he enters adolescence, his money concepts are on a low level of development and are mainly egocentric.

Related Meanings. The child's concepts of money often contain meanings that have little direct relationship to the use of money for spending or saving or to how much the various denominations of money can buy. In learning these extraneous meanings and practices, the child uses parental attitudes as a model; the parents' attitudes and practices are, in turn, a product of their social class. As the child comes in contact with other adults, with mass media, and with members of the peer group, he not only associates new meanings with money but also adds an emotional weighting to his developing money concept (177, 186).

The young child learns that money is often used to *buy love* because his parents shower him with toys and gifts and say that this is because they "love him so much." In time, he thinks that money can be used to *buy friendship,* and he wants a big allowance so that he can treat his peers and thus win their acceptance. The "dole system" of giving money encourages the child to become "adept at managing his parents." He may associate this behavior with money throughout his life, using money to get what he wants by *bribing people.* When the child is paid at home for doing household chores, he comes to regard everything as having a "price tag"; this colors his *attitude toward work* in school and, later, in his job (177). Even before he enters school, the child discovers that money is needed for material possessions and that material possessions have *prestige value.* If he has more toys than his playmates, they envy him; if they have more, he envies them. After he goes to school, he discovers that social acceptance is greatly influenced by the socioeconomic status of the family; that the socioeconomic status is judged by such symbols as size of house, number of cars, and kind of clothing; and that money is the determining factor in the possession of these status symbols. Money is thus considered a necessary tool in achieving friendship and *status in the group* (55, 135, 200).

Older children associate *independence* with money. Because every child wants more independence than parents and teachers are willing to grant, he thinks in terms of getting a job to earn money to do as he pleases; most children who work outside the home do so for this reason. Furthermore, the association of money with independence colors the child's attitude toward *schooling* and plays an important role in his *vocational choice* (70, 77). If education will train him for a job that will pay well, he will study; if he can get more money without advanced training, he will want to leave school as soon as the law permits, get a job, and be independent. Any job that pays well at the time appeals to him more than a job that will pay well only after a long period of training. The child's attitude toward *people* and toward *material things* is likewise colored by his concept of money. He comes to believe that the more a thing costs, the better it is, and that the more money a person makes, the more successful he is: Human worth and material worth are judged by a monetary yardstick (64, 150, 177). If the child has been associated with elderly relatives who are dependent on their married children for support, he comes to think of money as a source of *personal security* and learns the value of saving. If his elderly relatives are financially independent, and if his parents put more value on buying status symbols than on saving, he will feel that one should spend what he has and let the future take care of itself (186, 221).

TIME CONCEPTS

Time perception in adults is none too accurate, but it is even worse in children. This explains the apparent disobedience of young children when they fail to come home at the appointed time. Time seems to pass quickly when they are active or interested in play, but slowly when they are idle.

By the time the child is ready for kindergarten, he has only the merest rudiments of conventional time knowledge; when he enters the first grade, his concepts are still incomplete and often faulty. Concepts of time develop very slowly because they are abstract and involve subjective appreciation and more reasoning than the young child is capable of. He may understand numbers on a clock or the time of some specific daily occurrence, but the understanding of dates in historical time, of the word "generation," and of chronological order is beyond him (56, 85). Furthermore, because time has varying meanings and is not connected with the present alone, it is very confusing to a child. For example, "now" will be "yesterday" when tomorrow comes (238).

Many time concepts, especially those relating to conventional time, are dependent upon the growth of number concepts. A child cannot understand completely the meaning of "month" until he has a correct concept of 30 or 31 and its relationship to 7 days.

Learning of Time Concepts. The child first learns those time concepts which have a personal reference, and later those which are more remote from his experience. By the age of six years, for example, he has a good comprehension of conventional time, but not until he is nine or ten can he comprehend long periods of time in the past.

Direct training is of less value than impressions that accumulate in the process of growing older. The child must build up a foundation of related concepts, mainly concepts of numbers, before training can be of much value. He must then learn to associate meanings from his personal or school experiences and from what he learns in books

and from movies, television, and other forms of mass communication with his developing time concepts. These meanings are often too remote for him to see the relationship at once (32, 252).

Understanding the meaning of time depends upon the *use of cues,* such as the time of meals or other regular activities. If the daily routine is haphazard, children will find it difficult to develop time concepts. Because young children do not have a crowded schedule and because most of their time is free for play, they have very few cues to aid in the development of their concepts. Furthermore, they have very few cues to tell them how much time different activities require. Dallying over dressing or eating, for example, does not help them to get a correct estimate of how much time these activities require (214).

After the child enters school and his schedule becomes more crowded, he has a motivation to work up to his capacity in many activities where he formerly dallied; as a result, he gets a better estimate of how much time he needs to accomplish them. Furthermore, the rigid schedule of the school day, with the ringing of a bell at the end of a given period of time, not only helps him to estimate how much he can accomplish in that amount of time but also enables him to associate more accurate meanings with "morning" or "afternoon." If cues are to be of value, however, they must be within the framework of the child's experience; any extraneous cue will confuse him and thus delay the development of time concepts or lead to faulty ones (238, 252).

Errors occur mainly when *indefinite cues* are used. The young child, for example, has no idea of the length of time; he usually judges it in terms of what he is doing. Until he learns that time passes quickly when he is involved in one activity and slowly when he is involved in another, he cannot judge it correctly. Much of the dallying over dressing and eating, which occurs between the ages of three and five years, may be traced to faulty time perception rather than to lack of motor skills (120).

Errors in the estimation of the *duration*

of time may also be traced to lapse of time, another factor which the child rarely takes into consideration. Recent time is judged more correctly than distant time because the estimates are related to the person's retention of memories of events connected with the activity or occurring during the ensuing interval. Retention diminishes with time; therefore, there is a corresponding contraction of the judgments of the intervals. This is especially true for periods of time up to 6 months (56).

Indefinite cues are also responsible for errors in the estimation of the relative ages of people or in the estimation of relative lengths of time. If the child is asked who he thinks has lived longer—his mother or his grandmother—he finds it hard to estimate because he has little factual information to use as cues. Similarly, unless stress has been placed on the relative lengths of a week and a month or of the summer vacation and the Christmas vacation, he may be at a loss to tell which is longer. If he does a greater variety of things during the Christmas holidays than during the summer, he is likely to estimate the former as longer (158).

Perception of the time of day, day of the week, or season of the year is more accurate because the specific activities associated with these periods act as a cue. Day is distinguished from night because the former is light and the latter dark and because day is the time when the child can be up and night is the time when he must sleep. Morning is perceived as different from afternoon because morning is playtime and afternoon is nap time. The days of the week are likewise known through the activities associated with them. Sundays are usually known first because the father is at home and the routine of the day is often interrupted for family trips (195).

Genetic Sequence. In spite of the marked individual differences that appear in the child's orientation in time, time concepts come into use in a relatively uniform sequence in the life of every child. Ames found that words indicating the present come first, then words relating to the

future, and finally words indicating the past. The use of "today," for example, appears at twenty-four months; "tomorrow," at thirty months; and "yesterday," at thirty-six months. This suggests that time in relation to the ending of things is understood before time in relation to beginnings.

The ability to tell at what time a thing happens in terms of another activity appears before the ability to give an actual clock time. Children know morning or afternoon at four years; what day it is, at five years; the names of the days of the week, at five; and what time it is, at seven. At seven, they also know what month it is and what season. When they are eight, they know what year and what day of the month it is, and they can name the month correctly.

By the time they are five years old, children can tell what time they go to bed; by six, when they have supper, when they get up, when they go to school, and when afternoon begins. Most children can tell their ages when they are three years old; when their next birthday will be, at four; and how old they will be on the next birthday, by the time they are five (5). While this pattern is similar for all children, just when a particular child will reach a certain stage in the pattern will depend largely upon intelligence and learning opportunities (147).

In learning to tell time by the clock, all children follow a similar genetic sequence. They can first tell time and set the clock by the hour, then by the half hour, and later by the quarter hour. They must learn the meaning of the difference in the lengths of the hands, however, before they can do either. Most children learn to tell time when they are six years old (32, 214).

Concepts of Duration of Time. The ability to estimate time intervals correctly develops only after the child has learned to relate time to different activities. Longer intervals are usually underestimated, while shorter ones are exaggerated; the best evaluation has been found in intervals from 30 seconds to 1 minute in duration. Up to the age of eight years, children have difficulty judging the length of a second. When they use cues,

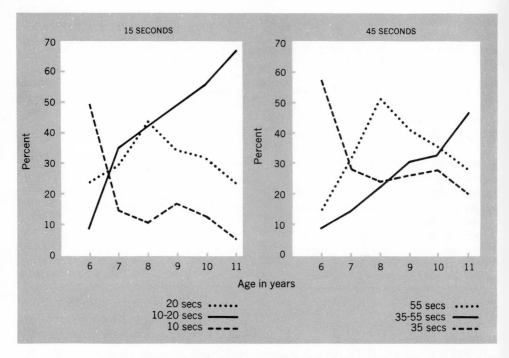

Figure 11–12.   Improvement in estimation of time units with age. (Adapted from W. H. King, The development of scientific concepts in children, *Brit. J. educ. Psychol.*, 1961, 31, 1–20. Used by permission.)

such as counting aloud, they are able to increase their accuracy (91).

In a comparison of the ability of fifth-grade children and college students to estimate intervals of time, it was found that the college students were only 15 to 18 per cent superior to the children. The children's degree of accuracy suggests that they had already developed certain cues for estimating time (90). Unlike the younger child, the school-age child has discovered that judgments of time are not influenced by the activity alone but also by one's frame of reference. One's attitude toward the activity serves as a cue (92). Figure 11–12 shows the improvement in estimation of two time lengths, 15 seconds and 45 seconds, as children grow older. While six-year-olds tend to underestimate both, eight-year-olds show a steady increase in correct estimates, especially for the shorter time (128).

Concepts of Historical Time.   The ability to think of the past as different from the present passes through two stages. In the first, or "negative," stage the child learns that the past differs from the present because in the past, for example, people wore skins or worshiped idols. In the second stage, the child not only distinguishes historical periods but also forms a picture of successive epochs not unlike that formed by the adult. It is easier for children to understand periods of time in the past if the periods are pivoted around events rather than around people or places. Concepts of historical time and of the continuity of time are often vague and confused because they have been taught in terms that are abstract and remote from the child's experiences (32, 120, 158).

Children of today learn about historical time earlier than their grandparents or parents did. When a child sees movies or television programs or reads "historical" comic books about King Arthur and the knights of his Round Table, for example, medieval Britain, with its life and customs, becomes far more meaningful than if he merely read stories about King Arthur. Similarly, if the child sees Biblical movies or movies based on events in ancient Rome or Egypt, the past becomes very meaningful to him. One of the good features of mass communication is that it helps to increase the child's comprehension of events, people, and places not related to his immediate experiences (208).

CONCEPTS OF BEAUTY

Nothing is beautiful or ugly in and of itself. What the young child perceives as beautiful is *what he likes*. People he likes are regarded as beautiful, no matter how they may be judged by objective standards. When the child goes out of the home into the neighborhood and school, he discovers that other people have different ideas of beauty. No longer, then, are things beautiful or ugly simply because he likes or dislikes them; his concepts of the beauty and ugliness of color, of nature, and of the human face and form are conditioned by group standards rather than by individual reactions (14, 212).

In addition, the older child is subjected to *mass-communication influences*. Even before he starts school, he has begun to think of beauty and ugliness in terms of what he sees in pictures, books, magazines, and comics and on the moving-picture or television screen. Heroes and heroines, their homes, and all their material possessions are regarded as beautiful, while villains or "underdogs" and their possessions are regarded as ugly. Each year, the influence of mass media on the child's comprehension of beauty increases. Because he and most of his friends see the same movies or television programs and read the same books and comics, the influence of mass communication is increased by peer influences. The more the child identifies with the characters in books or on the screen, the greater their influence on his concepts of beauty will be (16, 45, 153, 249).

Specific Aesthetic Concepts. The influence of cultural pressures has been reported in a number of studies relating to the child's concepts of beauty. In a study of facial features, it has been found that there are developmental trends in aesthetic preferences for thickness of lips, width of mouth, distance between eyes, and length of nose. As the child grows older, his preferences are increasingly similar to those of adults (230). Cultural pressures are likewise important in influencing the child's growing preference for certain geometric figures—for rectangles having the "golden-section" ratio and for isosceles triangles, for example (11).

Studies of what children consider beautiful have revealed that they like pictures of *familiar* people and animals doing familiar things. They like commonplace objects such as houses, boats, trees, and airplanes (14). Oriental children prefer pictures of Orientals, while non-Orientals prefer Caucasians. Boys prefer pictures of boys, while girls prefer pictures of girls (213). Children like any action theme containing human interest or dealing with exciting events. Landscapes have little appeal for the young child, though the older child likes them if they contain familiar objects (247).

Realistic pictures appeal to children much more than those which are highly stylized (28). Colored pictures are preferred only when the colors are realistic. Children also like *simplicity* in pictures; the popularity of the comics is due partly to this factor. As children mature, they begin to like more complexity in drawings (84, 194, 247).

At all ages, children like *color*. The young child likes colors that are bright and gaudy; he perceives pastel shades and subdued hues as ugly. With increasing age, however, his attitude changes. By adolescence, both boys and girls show a marked preference for duller shades and less saturated hues; they regard the saturated colors as "loud" or "hideous." Most children like blue, red, and green best, and black, white, yellow, and orange least. Boys prefer red, while girls prefer blue and violet (27, 28, 216).

Preferences for certain *color combinations* are very indefinite in young children. Red-blue and red-green are the favorite combinations of older children, while orange-green is the least favored combination. At every age, there are more pronounced individual differences for preferred color combinations than for preferred single colors. This is due, to a large extent, to the different associations individuals make with various color combinations (194).

Children display a liking for *music* even before they are a year old. Because the songs and music a young child first hears have a definite tune or rhythm, the child learns to prefer that kind of music. By the time he is three, the young child has definite preferences for certain types of music and has his favorites within each type. The more often he hears his favorites, the more beautiful they are to him. With each succeeding year, his affection for the old and familiar increases; this is an important factor in determining his standard of what is beautiful.

In addition to the role played by association in aesthetic perception in music, understanding of meaning is also important. By kindergarten age, the child can discriminate pitch and intensity with a fair degree of accuracy; he can pitch his voice when a model pitch is given and can march in time to a rhythm. From then on, he shows preferences for certain tone intervals or harmonies. There are marked individual differences in children's preferences, depending partly upon training and partly upon their musical aptitude. Even in classical music, differences in preference depend largely upon musical knowledge and the familiarity of the music (80, 127).

CONCEPTS OF THE COMIC

Nothing is comic of its own accord. Whether a person perceives something to be comic or not depends to a large extent upon the meanings he associates with it. There are two types of comic perception: objective and subjective. In the *objective* type, the person sees humor in a situation in which others are involved; in the *subjective* type, he sees humor in a situation involving himself and his acts. The more intelligent a person is, the better able he is to see himself in perspective and to be amused by his own "pomposity and pretensions." Those of lesser intellectual ability, on the other hand, lack the insight to appraise themselves realistically or to perceive the incongruities in their behavior. As a result, subjective humor is more likely to be found in those of the higher intellectual levels (2, 36).

Britt has pointed out that *situations which are perceived as comic* fall, roughly, into three categories, each of which gives rise to a type of comic perception distinctive from the others: (*1*) "Derisive humor" has a sting to it and provides the person with a feeling of superiority at another's expense; (*2*) "sympathetic humor" provides the person amusement at the misfortune of another; and (*3*) "whimsical humor" is based on the perception of subtle incongruities in a set of circumstances (36).

In all three categories, the person's attention is focused on someone or something outside himself. The humor is therefore *objective* rather than subjective. For the most part, children's perception of the comic falls into the derisive and sympathetic categories. Children derive pleasure from feeling superior to others or from being able to ridicule those whom they regard as inferior. Not until the latter part of childhood can the child understand the subtle incongruities which give rise to whimsical humor. For that reason, most children's jokes make jibes or deal with tabooed subjects such as sex and religion (34, 164, 165).

Variations in Perception of the Comic. The child's perception of the comic depends to a large extent upon *past experiences* and how the *memories* of these experiences are associated with new experiences. Reactions to comic situations depend upon the *mood* and *emotional reaction* at the time the comic situation appears. During a temper tantrum, a child can see nothing funny in a situation which, under normal conditions, he would regard as very funny. His *physical state* also influences his reaction; when he is tired, things seem less funny than when he is rested. In addition, the *attitude of other people* toward the source of the comic affects his attitude. A joke that is amusing in one situation may seem meaningless or even repugnant in another if the attitude of the group toward it is unfavorable (164).

What the child perceives as comic is likewise influenced by his intelligence and personality. The more *intelligent* the child, the more meaning he can perceive; the less intelligent he is, the more difficulty he will have understanding what other children find amusing. How the child reacts to jokes and other humorous situations is greatly influenced by his *personality* pattern. If he has a tendency to be rebellious and resistant to authority, he will find much more humor in a situation where a person in authority is in a predicament than the less rebellious child will. The child who feels insecure can rarely see the humor in a situation in which he himself is involved. He prefers humor which bolsters his ego—humor of the objective type, where he can laugh at others (47, 51, 144).

Perception of the comic is also influenced by how much a person can *empathize* with, or imagine himself in the place of, a character in a humorous situation. In a study of children's reactions to cartoons, it was found that those who could most readily imagine themselves in the humorous situation could enjoy the situation most (192). *Social pressures,* too, play a part. The child discovers even before he starts to play with other children that only certain forms of humor are socially approved. Later, he finds that the peer group likewise approves only certain forms. Consequently, he tries to avoid those forms which are likely to lead to social disapproval (94).

Development of Perception of the Comic. Until a child has developed concepts of size, money, time, and so on, he is unable to see

incongruities. Similarly, until he has developed concepts of different social roles, he is unable to see the humor in a situation in which a person in authority finds himself in a predicament. Because much humor is based on language, the child must know the meaning of words before he can appreciate jokes or even simple puns. As the child's language comprehension increases, he is better able to understand more complex and abstract jokes.

The close relationship between intelligence and the ability to perceive the comic means that with intellectual development the child's perception of the comic becomes more subtle and abstract; he understands witty dialogue as well as slapstick comedy (6, 100, 251). Because most cartoons contain elements of hostility, very intelligent or older children can detect the hidden hostility more readily than the younger and less intelligent (36, 47).

Concepts of the comic follow a *developmental pattern* that is influenced to some extent by age, intelligence, and interests. Many similar elements are found in the comic concepts of young children, older children, and adolescents. The younger the child, however, the more obvious and concrete the humor must be to be appreciated, and the more closely it must be related to familiar objects and situations (96, 164, 251).

Comic Concepts in Young Children. While vocal play is one of the earliest forms of humor, babies also perceive comedy in annoying people, dropping things, and blowing bubbles in water. After the first year, children enjoy making faces, doing stunts, and hiding from people and then laughing. Among preschool children, humor is called forth mainly by slapstick situations involving physical incongruities, by noises and grimaces made by the child himself or by others, by word play, by the funny antics of animals, by comic drawings, and by simple jokes. Surprise and suspense are fundamental elements in the perception of the comic at this age.

Comic Concepts in Older Children. The

As the child's understanding develops, his ability to comprehend a joke or to "get the point" of a funny story is recognized as an indication of intelligence by the child, by his peers, and by adults. (Standard Oil Co., N.J.)

school child will join in with others to laugh at anything whether he thinks it funny or not. Like the younger child, he sees humor mainly in incongruities or in the unusual; in the abasement of dignity; in people who defy authority—as he would like to do but fears doing because of punishment; and in the misfortunes and predicaments of others, especially those whom he looks up to and respects. He will laugh heartily, for example, if he sees his father fall or stumble. Clown acts in the circus or comedy situations in the movies or on the television screen also appeal to the older child because they contain one or more of these elements of humor.

Because of his greater understanding of words, the older child enjoys puns, riddles, and jokes. Practical jokes and jokes relating to forbidden subjects, such as sex, have a strong appeal. Practical jokes are usually aimed at a person in authority or someone against whom the child has some prejudice. The child enjoys them because he feels that he is "getting even" with that person by

making him appear ridiculous, by putting him in a predicament, or by embarrassing him (36, 110). As Gesell has pointed out, even ten-year-old children are "not very skilled at high-class humor"; they still enjoy "corny" jokes, jokes related to sex, smutty stories, and some slapstick when they are eleven (89).

Value of Perception of the Comic. The child who can perceive the comic is more *acceptable to the peer group* than the child who cannot. Because the ability to perceive the comic is regarded as a sign of intelligence, and because brightness leads to social acceptance, every child likes to create the impression that he "gets the point" of a joke. If the other children laugh, he laughs too, whether he understands the joke or not. The louder and longer his laugh, the more sense of humor his peers attribute to him; this, he believes, means that they regard him as "bright."

Furthermore, laughing at jokes or other comic situations is a compliment to the person who is responsible for them. If the child does not laugh, he is likely to make others think he disapproves of the joke or of the person. As Coser has said, "Humor invites laughter, as a mark of its acceptance. If some group members refuse to respond, they indicate their rejection of the humorist, as well as of those who understand and feel with him" (60). Thus the child who disapproves of humor directed at a minority group will hesitate to show his disapproval if the rest of the peer group reacts favorably. He is just as anxious to avoid being considered a "goody-goody" as he is to avoid being considered "dumb" (164, 165).

As the child's social contacts increase, he discovers that having a sense of humor is a highly valued characteristic and that children who are popular almost always have this quality (73, 144). Consequently, in his desire to win social acceptance, he has a strong motivation to increase his ability to perceive the comic or to create the impression that he is able to do so. In order to create the impression that they have a good sense of humor, children will "spend much time and go to great pains in their efforts to discover what makes people laugh, and how to gauge timing and emphasis to bring out the comic in what they do or say" (120).

Being able to laugh at a comic situation also aids the child's *self-acceptance;* it increases his feeling of self-importance and superiority. One of the sources of pleasure of the comics or of movie or television comedies is that the child identifies himself with the character who puts another person in a predicament. He thus vicariously enjoys the feeling of superiority that comes from such humor. His enjoyment is intensified if the character in a predicament is a person in authority; if the hero with whom the child identifies breaks every law and does so with immunity, this gives the child a feeling of superiority without involving personal risk (17, 46).

In addition, being able to laugh at another person serves as a form of *emotional catharsis* for the child, ridding him of pent-up emotional energy. The more he can make others laugh, or the more other children will laugh with him at a comic situation, the greater the cathartic effect and the more enjoyable the experience for the child. Thus it is apparent that perception of the comic plays an important role in the child's development, a role far greater than most adults recognize (189).

CONCEPTS OF SELF

Concepts of self develop earlier and are subject to greater change and modification than social concepts. Sometime during the first year of life, the baby discovers himself as an individual. He does not, however, distinguish between himself and his environment as early as he distinguishes other people from his environment. He is, for example, aware of his mother's hand before he is aware of his own hand; he identifies his mother's voice before he identifies his own vocalizations. He is able to recognize others in a mirror or in pictures before he recognizes himself.

Because a baby is primarily egocentric, he forms concepts about himself before he forms concepts about others; what he thinks of himself thus colors what he thinks of others. Concepts of self are used as a standard by which to judge others and interpret their behavior (6, 195).

The child's self-concept includes physical and psychological self-images. The *physical* self-images are generally formed first; they relate to the child's general appearance— its attractiveness or unattractiveness, its sex-appropriateness or sex-inappropriateness— and to the importance of the different parts of his body to his behavior and the prestige they give him in the eyes of the world. The child's *psychological* self-images are based on his thoughts, feelings, and emotions; they consist of the qualities and abilities that play a role of importance in his adjustment to life, qualities such as courage, honesty, independence, self-confidence, and aspirations and abilities of different types.

Coordinating his physical and psychological self-images is often difficult for the child; consequently, he is apt to think of himself as a dual personality, with a specific appearance and a specific personality make-up. As he grows older, these self-concepts gradually fuse, and he perceives himself as a unified individual (8, 119, 199).

"Mirror Images." The child's concepts of, and feelings about, himself are based on what he thinks significant people in his life —his parents, siblings, peers, and teachers— think of him; they thus become "mirror images" (124). As Frank has stated, "The child learns to think and feel about himself as defined by others. He develops an image of self as the chief actor in his 'private world.' This image develops primarily from the way parents, teachers, and other significant persons describe, punish, praise, or love him" (83).

Mirror images may be faulty. They are based on the child's interpretation of how people treat him, and because the child is incapable of perceiving below the surface of the speech and behavior of others, he often fails to grasp the true meaning of the motivations behind their speech and behavior. Thus he may base his self-image on a *misinterpretation*. Should his parents, for example, call him a "naughty boy" when he misbehaves but fail to call him a "good boy" when he does what they want him to do, he will build up a concept of himself as "naughty" and come to believe that he is inferior (50, 123, 137). Should the teacher give more time to a slow learner than to him, he may readily misinterpret this to mean that the teacher likes the slow learner better.

Similarly, the child who belongs to a minority group against which there are prejudices may readily accept the cultural stereotype ascribed to his group by his peers and think of himself as inferior. This then results in a discrepancy between the favorable concept of himself held by members of his own group and the unfavorable concept held by members of other groups. When children recognize the unfavorable concepts members of other racial, religious, or social-class groups hold of members of their group, they tend to shun other groups and identify themselves with their own group. This helps

them to achieve more favorable mirror images—images that are more compatible with those they have formed in the family group (37, 129, 188).

Favorable versus Unfavorable Self-concepts. Few adults are aware that a child builds up unfavorable self-concepts through misinterpreting the speech and behavior of others. Consequently, such concepts get a strong hold on the child before they are corrected. What is even more serious is the fact that few adults, either parents or teachers, *try to control* the development of the child's self-concepts to ensure that they will be both realistic and favorable. The result is that self-concepts develop haphazardly and contain many misconceptions. Even though the child develops better social insight and makes more accurate appraisals of his abilities, appearance, achievements, and roles as he grows older, his self-concepts are likely to be colored by mirror images formed earlier.

To achieve *realistic self-concepts,* the child must be able to be psychologically independent of those on whom he has depended for security; he must be able to think of himself as an individual, free from the influence of the attitudes of others. If his concept of self is unrealistically favorable, however, he "sets up defenses to preserve his present idea of himself. He rationalizes. He resists the impact of thoughts that would make it necessary for him to reexamine his self-concept" (219).

Elementary-school children lack the ability to evaluate themselves accurately. They tend to overestimate their good qualities and to underestimate those which are socially disapproved; they give themselves a "self-halo." Even in adolescence, children still tend to see themselves in terms of mirror images of significant people in their lives (15, 196). The reason for this is that the child is dependent on others for security and status. By "satellizing," or identifying himself with others, he gains security and status. His dependence, however, prevents him from evaluating himself accurately. He constantly sees himself through the eyes of those with whom he has identified. Only when he can "desatellize" himself—and this rarely comes until after the gang age of late childhood is over—can he assess his abilities realistically without interference from social pressures or fear of social disapproval (12, 219).

Pattern of Development. Self-concepts, like other concepts, develop in a predictable way. In this pattern, development of awareness of self is not a unitary process, nor does it take place all at one time. Instead, the child perceives different aspects of himself at different times (199). He distinguishes between himself and others before he forms concepts of his appearance and of his abilities. As he grows older, as his experiences broaden, and as his intellectual capacities mature, his concepts of himself grow through the discovery of new qualities and new potentialities. In the development of a healthy personality pattern, it is essential that the concepts of self change as new self-discoveries are made; the unrealistic and biased elements of early concepts must be replaced by more realistic and unprejudiced ones.

Hierarchy of Self-concepts. Concepts of self are hierarchical in nature; the most basic—the *primary* self-concept—is acquired first. It is formed by the experiences the child has in the home and is made up of many individual concepts, each resulting from experiences with different members of the family group. The young child's concept of himself as a person is most influenced by his relationships with his mother. The frequency and quality of his relationships with other members of the family will determine how important a role they play in the formation of his primary self-concept (33, 62).

The primary self-concept includes both physical and psychological self-images, though the former are more frequent in the early years of childhood than the latter. The psychological self-images are formed first from the child's social contacts with his siblings and his comparison of himself with them. Similarly, his concepts of his roles in

life, of his aspirations, and of his responsibilities to others are first formed from parental teachings and pressures (157, 211).

As the child's social horizons broaden and his contacts outside the home increase, he acquires other concepts of himself. These are the *secondary* concepts in the hierarchy and relate to how he sees himself through the eyes of others. The primary self-concept frequently determines the selection of situations in which the secondary self-concepts will be formed. A child who has developed a self-concept characterized by beliefs in his own importance, for example, will select playmates who regard him much as his parents do. In this secondary self-concept will be physical as well as psychological self-images. The child will think of his physical structure as people outside the home do, and he will evaluate his psychological self-images, formed at home, by comparisons with what peers, teachers, and other adults outside the home think.

It is not uncommon for the child to discover a discrepancy between his primary and secondary self-concepts. Generally, though not always, the primary self-concepts are more favorable than the secondary. When a discrepancy exists, the child must close the gap between the two if he is to be a happy, well-adjusted person. He may do this by trying to force others to change their unfavorable concepts of him so that they will correspond to the favorable concepts he has of himself. This rarely works; usually the child must revise his unrealistic self-concepts so that they will more closely approach reality. Because the primary self-concepts are generally the older and the more favorable, however, the child resists changing them. Consequently, he makes poor social adjustments and avoids social situations where others hold unfavorable concepts of him and where he is not treated in accordance with expectations based on his primary self-concept (33, 62).

Important Elements in Pattern of Development. All children add to their self-concepts meanings that their cultural group regards as important. These elements are

Figure 11–13. Differentiation in male and female figures in children's drawings by the age of eight years. (Adapted from I. J. Knopf and T. W. Richards, The child's differentiation in sex as reflected in drawings of the human figure, *J. genet. Psychol.,* **1952, 81, 99–112. Used by permission.)**

added at predictable times, and they are similar for all children, although variations in subsocieties affect them somewhat. The following are most universally found:

1. Meanings Related to Sex Differences.

By progressive comparisons of his own body with those of other children and adults, the child becomes aware of sex differences. By the time he is three or four years old, he is aware of his own sex and also of the clothing and hairstyles associated with members of the two sexes. Not only do children at an early age become aware of physical sex differences, but they also notice differences in the urination posture of the two sexes. As a

general rule, children in our culture identify sex differences sooner by genital organs than by clothing because males and females sometimes dress so nearly alike that it is difficult for young children to distinguish between them. When the body is clothed, hair is a more accurate clue to the sex of the individual than clothing (9, 58, 109, 122, 187).

By four or five years of age, most children can identify the sex of children by their genitals, and a year later they can identify the sex of adults by theirs. Girls, on the whole, are able to identify physical sex differences sooner than boys, and children with two parents, sooner than children with one parent (35, 125). By the end of childhood, however, boys have usually caught up with girls in their ability to identify physical sex differences (226).

By the age of eight years, there are striking differences in children's drawings of male and female figures. These differences are illustrated in Figure 11–13. By the time they reach adolescence, boys put more emphasis on secondary sex characteristics in their drawings than girls. This suggests a greater awareness of sex differences among boys (132). Children of the higher socioeconomic groups include more sex characteristics in their drawings than children of the lower groups (69).

Awareness of *mental differences* between the sexes, as shown in differences in interests, aptitudes, or achievements, comes much later than awareness of physical differences. Many children, in fact, are not aware of such mental differences until the school requires that boys take certain courses and girls take others or until parents and peers emphasize that certain play activities are "better" for boys and others "better" for girls. Soon after entering school, children discover that boys and girls have different subject-matter preferences in books, movies, and radio programs (193). They also notice that their mothers and fathers and other women and men have different interests and engage in different activities (233). Awareness of sex differences, both physical and psychological, generally reaches a peak in the latter part of childhood, when puberty changes focus the child's attention on his changing body and interests.

As children come to include more and more concepts relating to sex differences in their self-concepts, they also add *emotional weighting*. When the child discovers the meaning of sex differences, he learns that different social attitudes are associated with the labels "male" and "female." Thus his attitude toward his sex, as well as his attitude toward other aspects of self, is a mirror image of the attitudes of significant people in his life (107). With his increasing contacts with people, he begins to perceive how people feel about his sex; he sees that people treat boys and girls differently, that parents are more lenient in the disciplining of boys, and that teachers give boys greater freedom and a wider choice of play and school activities. Even school books portray boys and men more favorably than girls and women (54, 209).

That children are aware of the more favorable social attitude shown boys may be seen in the free drawings of boys and girls. Among young children, both boys and girls show a preference for drawing members of their own sex. As childhood progresses, however, girls show a greater and greater preference for drawing figures of the male; no such shift is found in the case of boys (25). Awareness of social attitudes toward sex is also apparent in the fact that girls, far more often than boys, wish they could change their sex (40, 107). When girls realize that such a change is impossible, they are likely to develop an unfavorable self-concept; boys develop an increasingly more favorable self-concept as they come to realize the social prestige associated with being a boy (41).

2. Meanings Related to Sex Roles.

Shortly after children become aware of physical sex differences, but before they realize that there are psychological sex differences, they become aware of differences in appropriate sex-role behavior. They first learn what the appropriate behavior for their sex is by identifying themselves with parents of their

sex and by parental training and pressures. Later, they learn the appropriate sex role by identifying with the cultural ideal and stereotype for their sex, though this is more true of boys than of girls (105, 106, 151). Most girls are aware of the approved sex role for their sex by the time they are four or five years old; boys become aware of their approved sex role a trifle earlier because of the greater pressures put on boys to be "manly." This occurs even though little boys live in a world peopled mainly by females (255). By the time boys are four years old, they begin to take on a "tough masculine role" and to scorn any play or behavior that is associated with girls. With each passing year, the tendency to conform to the approved masculine role increases (109, 236).

At every age in childhood, boys are more clearly aware of what it means to be "manly" than girls are of what it means to be "feminine." Also, both boys and girls of the working class are earlier and more clearly aware of their sex-role patterns than children of the middle and upper classes are. For children of the working class, this awareness comes between four and five years of age; for children of the higher classes, it comes at approximately six (9, 41, 122). The reason for this social-class difference is that boys and girls in the upper classes are treated alike; they are even dressed alike for play, the time when they have the most contact with one another. Furthermore, there is less demand for girls in the upper classes to do housework—"woman's work"—and there is greater tolerance of the "tomboy" pattern. Perhaps most important of all, mothers of the upper social classes tend to be more dissatisfied with their sex role than mothers of the working class; hence they have less motivation to train their daughters for the approved feminine role than mothers of the lower classes (187, 255).

The unfavorable *emotional weighting* of the developing sex concepts of girls is intensified as they discover that the role they are expected to play in life is regarded as inferior (107). This coincides with their discovery of what it means to live in a masculine-oriented culture. As Lynn has pointed out,

The superior position and privileged status of the male permeates nearly every aspect, minor and major of our social life. The gadgets and prizes in boxes of breakfast cereal, for example, commonly have a strong masculine rather than feminine appeal. And the most basic social institutions perpetuate this pattern of masculine aggrandizement. Thus the Judeo-Christian faiths involve worshipping God, a "Father," rather than a "Mother," and Christ, a "Son" rather than a "Daughter" (151).

As both girls' and boys' attitudes toward the girl's sex role deteriorate, their attitudes toward the male role become progressively more favorable (102, 109). In spite of this, girls, by the time they are eleven or twelve years old, do not want to do the things boys do; they realize that to be socially acceptable, they must be "feminine" (108).

3. Meanings Related to Racial Differences. While many children at three years of age find it difficult to distinguish their racial identification, most can do so by the time they are four. They make this identification on the basis of skin color and other physical characteristics at first, and later on the basis of name and conformity to a social stereotype. White children generally learn to identify themselves with a racial group sooner than Negro children, especially when Negroes and whites live in segregated sections of the community (167, 205, 217). Under such conditions, white children come in contact with members of the Negro race who work as servants in their homes or the homes of their friends, but Negro children have no similar learning experience (170). Girls, as a rule, become aware of racial differences sooner than boys because personal appearance—the cue used first to identify racial differences—is stressed more for girls than for boys (95). Since children identify themselves first with members of a certain race on the basis of physical features, they have difficulty identifying persons of mixed races, such as members of different Oriental groups (213).

By the time children are four or five years old, they know that certain labels are applied to members of different races. When asked, "What are you?" they use ethnic designations, such as "American," "colored," "Jewish," or "Italian" (104). As their social experiences increase, they learn that certain surnames are identified with certain racial groups and that their own names serve as labels of racial-group membership. They also discover that there are social stereotypes about members of their racial group and that other people judge them in terms of these stereotypes (13, 205, 239).

How children are treated affects the emotional weighting of their racial awareness and colors their concepts of themselves (245). Negro children have less favorable attitudes toward themselves than toward members of the white race for this reason. In play, they discover that white children usurp the more desirable roles; as they come in contact with mass media of communication, they learn to associate prestige with members of the white race because most of the mass media are "white-oriented" (95, 217).

4. Meanings Related to Social-class Differences. Even before the child enters school, he discovers that there are differences in the way people live and that these differences are responsible for putting people into various categories, such as "rich" and "poor" (76). He likewise discovers that differences in social status are related to the occupation of the father. Not until he has the broader social contacts that come with entrance into school, however, does he develop definite concepts of his own status in the social structure. Then he clarifies his concepts of social-class differences, using such cues as father's occupation, size of house, number of cars in the family, and type and amount of clothing of each family member. On the basis of these cues he identifies himself with a particular social class and includes social-class membership in his concept of self

(112, 115). Girls, as a rule, tend to identify themselves consistently higher in the social-class structure than boys (15). Some of the cues children use in identifying social-class differences are shown in Figure 11–14.

In the young child, socioeconomic status of the family plays a minor role in the developing self-concept. His first realization of its significance comes when he recognizes that some children have more toys and other material possessions than others. If he has fewer and smaller toys than his play-mates, he is likely to be envious and to want what they have; if he has more and bigger toys—toys which they envy—he will feel superior. Later, when social acceptance by the peer group becomes important to him, he will discover that those who have more in the way of material possessions are, other factors being equal, the better-accepted members of the group and are generally among the ones selected for leadership roles.

Among girls, even more than among boys, socioeconomic status plays an increas-

M=Middle class cues   W=Working class cues

Figure 11–14. Some cues used by children to identify social-class differences. (Adapted from G. Jahoda, Development of the perception of social differences in children from 6 to 10, Brit. J. Psychol., 1959, 50, 159–175. Used by permission.)

ingly important role as childhood progresses. That is why girls tend to identify themselves with a higher socioeconomic group than their family status justifies. Belonging to a higher group or gaining acceptance in a gang composed of girls from a higher group is ego-satisfying to them. It is this realization of how people judge socioeconomic status that contributes to the emotional weighting of the developing self-concept (252).

Influence of Concepts of Self. The child's concept of himself as an individual is a prime determinant of his behavior. Either lack of self-acceptance or overconfident, unrealistic self-acceptance often results in behavior that leads to poor social adjustments. Only when the self-concept is in harmony with the concept held by others can the child make good social adjustments (15, 119, 219).

Favorable self-judgments decline, and favorable judgments of others increase as the child advances in social learning. At every age, the child is able to judge the degree of social acceptance of others more accurately than he can judge his own. He tends to exaggerate any bad qualities he might have, and this leads to feelings of inadequacy, shyness, and self-consciousness (12, 236).

The effects of unfavorable self-judgments are well illustrated in boys who do not conform to the cultural stereotype of sex-appropriateness. As Hartley has pointed out, the cultural picture of sex-appropriateness is "oversimplified and overemphasized. It is a picture drawn in black and white, with little or no modification, and it is incomplete, including only a few of the many elements that go to make up the role of the mature male" (105). There is, for example, an overemphasis on physical strength and athletic skills. A boy whose physique or learning opportunities deprive him of acquiring sex-appropriate behavior will, as a result, develop an unfavorable self-concept. The important role the self-concept plays in determining the quality of the child's behavior will be discussed in detail in the chapter on personality development.

SOCIAL CONCEPTS

Social concepts, or concepts relating to people and social situations, are developed from social perceptions. *Social perception* is the ability to understand, from observing the facial expressions and behavior of others, what their thoughts and emotional reactions are. It includes the ability to "size up" the personality of others quickly and accurately on the basis of available cues. If the individual is to make satisfactory social adjustments and get along with all types of people with success, he must develop social perception. He can then modify his own behavior to fit into the accepted social pattern. He thus becomes *socialized* to the extent that he is a welcome member of the social group to which he belongs.

The baby differentiates the voice from other sounds by the time he is one month old, and at the age of two months he shows an interest in people by smiling and laughing when he comes in contact with them. By the third month, he can differentiate between strangers and familiar persons, and at six months he is greatly influenced by facial expressions. Not until he is eight months old, however, does he respond to the emotional behavior of others in a way which signifies that he has an understanding of the facial expressions. An angry face causes the baby to turn away, while a smiling face leads to aggressive movements, such as coming toward the person, holding out his arms, or handing him a toy. There is no evidence that the baby understands the underlying meaning in what he observes in others; he merely judges their reactions to him on the basis of surface values (79).

The older child includes in his developing social concepts not only an understanding of the feelings and emotions of others as expressed in their overt behavior but also an understanding of their meanings (93). Thus the child's social perceptions are colored by his past experiences, by what he has heard others say or has observed in their behavior, and by social pressures from the group. The more heavily weighted the concepts are with emotionally toned attitudes, the more impact they have on the child's judgment of a present social situation (44, 65, 76).

How markedly the child's social concepts are influenced by adult and peer values has been illustrated in a study in which Negro and white children were asked to predict teachers' attitudes toward Negro children. The results of the study showed that Negro children estimated the teachers' attitudes to be more prejudiced than white children, reflecting the influence of ego-involvement (13). Similarly, children of the lower socioeconomic groups were influenced more by the factor of ego-involvement than children of the higher socioeconomic groups (6). In other studies, it has been found that when a teacher shows a preference for certain pupils, the peer group tends to estimate the sociometric status of those pupils to be higher than it is, while the popularity of the pupils she least prefers is likely to be underestimated (97).

Development of Social Concepts. Because the child's social concepts are influenced by his own experiences as well as by his awareness of the cultural values of the people with whom he is associated, he learns to perceive differences in the appearance and actions of others. In addition, he learns to like or dislike what he perceives and to respond to others accordingly.

The older child is better able to discriminate in social-behavior values and to evaluate what adults will approve or disapprove. Girls are slightly more discriminating in this respect than boys. Older children size up both adults and their contemporaries fairly accurately and develop specific concepts of them in terms of socially approved behavior (3, 15, 248). Even within the family, children develop specific concepts of the approved social role for the mother, the father, the child, and the other family members (103, 107). This topic will be discussed in detail in the chapter on family relationships.

Prejudice against certain *racial* groups plays an important role in the development of the child's concepts of members of those groups (139). Prejudice against a member of a minority group, as was stressed earlier, is usually not based on the personal experience of the child but is a reflection of the cultural patterns and stereotypes of the environment (81, 168). The preschool child can distinguish people of different races on the basis of skin and hair color and other physical features, but the degree of difference between the child's physical appearance and that of people of other racial groups determines the age at which he becomes aware of the difference (7, 140, 188, 217). In the case of the Negro, for example, the white child can identify the Negro with dark pigmentation of the skin earlier than the one whose skin coloring is lighter (13). Children of mixed Oriental races cannot be identified as early as those of one specific Oriental group (213). Because children of minority groups are sensitized to racial differences earlier than those of majority groups, social concepts of minority-group children contain meanings of racial differences earlier (81, 95). The child's concepts of race include not only the appearance of people of different racial groups but also their occupations, clothing, living quarters, personalities, and abilities. These associations become stronger as children grow older (188).

In the development of social concepts, the child adds meanings related to *sex differences* and approved *sex roles*. While learning how he differs from members of the opposite sex and what the approved sex role for members of his sex is, he learns to judge others—parents, siblings, peers, and adults outside the home—in terms of these meanings. Social concepts also include meanings related to *social-class* identification. Even in the preschool years, some children make vague social distinctions on the basis of crude and concrete cues which enable them to compare their social milieu with that of others. Figure 11–15 shows the pattern of increase in perception of social differences with age.

For most children, perception of social-class differences develops rapidly during the childhood years, reaching the adult level during early adolescence (52). Estvan found that among elementary-school children, the ability to understand and appreciate high

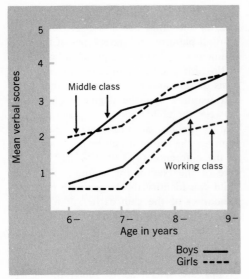

Figure 11–15. Increase in perception of social-class differences with age. (Adapted from G. Jahoda, Development of the perception of social differences in children from 6 to 10, *Brit. J. Psychol.*, 1959, 50, 159–175. Used by permission.)

socioeconomic status, as represented by a picture of a mansion, was more closely related to development of social maturity than to differences in children's social backgrounds. At the age of six years, for example, only 30 per cent of the children studied were able to discriminate between the mansion and any other home situation; by twelve, the percentage had risen to 68. With this increasing sensitivity to social-class differences came a higher regard for what the mansion symbolizes in our culture.

Similarly, it was found that children take time to perceive the meaning of poverty. Very few children, when they first entered school, were able to interpret the meaning of a picture showing a poor house; by twelve, however, more than half the group knew not only what the house meant but also what poverty meant. By the time childhood is over, most children are aware of status differentials and of the value people place on "better" ways of living (76).

Influence of Social Concepts. Social concepts, like concepts of self, play a role of major importance in determining how children will behave. Much of the tactlessness or cruelty of young children is due to poor social perception. As a result of their constant contact with parents, with siblings, and later with members of the peer group and adults outside the home, they learn to "size up" familiar people with a fair degree of accuracy. Because their contacts with strangers are limited, however, they tend to appraise strangers incorrectly.

In the absence of adult supervision, an older child is likely to comment with brutal frankness about the qualities he dislikes in some of his peers and even in his teachers. While this is unkind and untactful, it is a way of learning to appraise others. The child is learning to see, through the eyes of others, which characteristics are socially acceptable and which are unacceptable. One of the important advantages of gang membership is that it gives the child an opportunity for social-concept learning. This, in turn, helps him to learn how to respond to others —an essential to good social adjustment (65, 227, 229).

No concepts are static. They change as new meanings are learned and as new attitudes, included in the concepts, are acquired. This is especially true of social concepts. Because of a young child's limited social experiences, he must often form his social concepts on the basis of what others say about certain people or certain groups of people. Even when he has opportunities for personal contact with them, his limited understanding restricts his ability to evaluate them and their behavior accurately. With the broadening of his social experiences and the increase in his understanding, he sees familiar people in a new light and often changes his concept of them. This is perhaps most obvious in the child's concept of his mother. While the child is young and his contacts with other people are limited, his mother is a near-perfect person in his eyes. Later, as a result of contact with the mothers of his friends and with the stereotype of "mother" portrayed in different mass media, he begins to evaluate his own mother in terms of a new concept (111). How seriously this can affect parent-child relationships will be discussed in detail in the chapter on family relationships.

All social concepts include socially conditioned elements which are subject to change when new values are substituted for old. Mass media of communication have played an important role in changing children's concepts about people of other countries or other periods in history. By pointing out and correcting somewhat the stereotyped and often grotesque ideas children frequently have about people of different races, the mass media have helped to lessen prejudice and to improve children's behavior toward people of other races (81, 254).

The emotional weighting of a concept determines to a large extent the ease or difficulty of changing the concept. As was stressed in the discussion of prejudice on pages 362 to 363, if prejudice is built upon an unpleasant experience with a person or group of a particular racial or religious background, it will be much more difficult to modify than if it is based on peer-group pressures, for emotional weighting plays a more important role in the former.

Estvan and Estvan found that, with age, children move in the direction of socially accepted attitudes; their attitudes toward life situations change from negative to positive and from egocentric to social (76). As they learn what is to be avoided and what sought for in their cultural setting, they change their attitudes toward what is desirable in people and social situations to conform to the approved cultural patterns (134).

Only when the emotional weighting of social concepts is changed can there be any real or permanent change in the concept itself. And unless this occurs, there can be no change in the pattern of behavior associated with the concept. Just changing the cognitive aspect of a concept alone is not enough; the effective aspect must likewise be changed if there is to be any change in behavior. If a child develops an unfavorable attitude toward school, parents and teachers can explain to the child until they are "blue in the face" why education is important to him. The child may understand and agree with all they say, but unless something can be done to improve his attitude toward school or toward a teacher who has conditioned him to dislike school, his concept of school will remain unfavorable. Because attitudes are so difficult to change, unfavorable attitudes should not be allowed to become habitual.

BIBLIOGRAPHY

(1) ALEXANDER, I. E., and A. M. ADLERSTEIN: Affective responses to the concept of death in a population of children and early adolescents. *J. genet. Psychol.,* 1958, **93,** 167–177.

(2) ALLPORT, G. W.: *Personality: a psychological interpretation.* New York: Holt, 1937.

(3) AMATORA, SISTER M.: Can elementary school children discriminate certain traits in their teachers? *Child Develpm.,* 1952, **23,** 75–80.

(4) AMEN, E. W.: Individual differences in apperceptive reactions: a study of the response of preschool children to pictures. *Genet. Psychol. Monogr.,* 1941, 23, 319–385.

(5) AMES, L. B.: The development of the sense of time in the young child. *J. genet. Psychol.,* 1946, **68,** 97–125.

(6) AMES, L. B.: The sense of self of nursery school children as manifested by their verbal behavior. *J. genet. Psychol.,* 1952, **81,** 193–232.

(7) AMMONS, R. B.: Reactions in projective doll-play interviews of males two to six years of age to differences in skin color and facial features. *J. genet. Psychol.,* 1950, **76,** 323–341.

(8) ANDERSON, J. E.: Personality organization in children. *Amer. Psychologist,* 1948, **3,** 409–416.

(9) ANGRILLI, A. F.: The psychosexual identifi-

cation of pre-school boys. *J. genet. Psychol.,* 1960, **97,** 329–340.

(10) ANNETT, M.: The classification of instances of four common class concepts by children and adults. *Brit. J. educ. Psychol.,* 1959, **29,** 223–236.

(11) AUSTIN, T. R., and R. B. SLEIGHT: Aesthetic preference for isosceles triangles. *J. app. Psychol.,* 1951, **35,** 340–341.

(12) AUSUBEL, D. P.: *Ego development and the personality disorders.* New York: Grune & Stratton, 1952.

(13) AUSUBEL, D. P.: Ego development among segregated Negro children. *Ment. Hyg., N.Y.,* 1958, **42,** 362–369.

(14) AUSUBEL, D. P., F. DEWITT, B. GOLDEN, and S. H. SCHPOONT: Prestige suggestion in children's art preferences. *J. genet. Psychol.,* 1956, **89,** 85–93.

(15) AUSUBEL, D. P., H. M. SCHIFF, and E. B. GASSER: A preliminary study of developmental trends in sociopathy: accuracy of perception of own and others' sociometric status. *Child Develpm.,* 1952, **23,** 111–128.

(16) BAILYN, L.: Mass media and children: a study of exposure habits and cognitive effects. *Psychol. Monogr.,* 1959, **73,** No. 1.

(17) BAKWIN, R. M.: The comics. *J. Pediat.,* 1953, **42,** 633–635.

(18) BALEY, S.: Color, form, and size perception in the preschool child. *Psychol. Abstr.,* 1948, **22,** No. 248.

(19) BANHAM, K. M.: Obstinate children are adaptable. *Ment. Hyg., N.Y.,* 1952, **36,** 84–89.

(20) BARCLAY, D.: Questions of life and death. *The New York Times,* July 15, 1962.

(21) BAYLEY, N.: On the growth of intelligence. *Amer. Psychologist,* 1955, **10,** 805–818.

(22) BEHRENS, M. L.: Child-rearing and the character structure of the mother. *Child Develpm.,* 1954, **25,** 225–238.

(23) BERNARDA, M.: Wat den Kenjonge mensen over den Dood. *Opvoedk. Fijdschr.,* 1949, **30,** 32–40.

(24) BERNSTEIN, M. R.: Relationship between interest and reading comprehension. *J. educ. Res.,* 1955, **49,** 283–288.

(25) BIELIANSKAS, V. J.: Sexual identification in children's drawings of human figure. *J. clin. Psychol.,* 1960, **16,** 42–44.

(26) BLAKELY, W. P.: A study of seventh grade children's reading of comic books as related to certain other variables. *J. genet. Psychol.,* 1958, **93,** 291–301.

(27) BLUM, L. H., and A. DRAGOSITZ: Finger painting: the developmental aspect. *Child Develpm.,* 1947, **18,** 88–105.

(28) BON, I. R., and D. C. LOPEZ: Preferences in colors and illustrations of elementary school children in Puerto Rico. *J. educ. Psychol.,* 1953, **44,** 490–496.

(29) BOSSARD, J. H. S., and E. S. BOLL: *The sociology of child development,* 3d ed. New York: Harper & Row, 1960.

(30) BOUSFIELD, W. A., and W. D. ORBISON: Ontogenesis of emotional behavior. *Psychol. Rev.,* 1952, **59,** 1–7.

(31) BOYD, N. A., and G. MANDLER: Children's responses to human and animal stories and pictures. *J. consult. Psychol.,* 1955, **19,** 367–371.

(32) BRADLEY, N. C.: The growth of the knowledge of time in children of school age. *Brit. J. Psychol.,* 1947, **38,** 67–78.

(33) BRANDT, R. M.: Self: missing link for understanding behavior. *Ment. Hyg., N.Y.,* 1957, **41,** 24–33.

(34) BRECKENRIDGE, M. E., and E. L. VINCENT: *Child development,* 4th ed. Philadelphia: Saunders, 1960.

(35) BRIELAND, D., and L. NELSON: Age trends in sex identification as determined by a picture test. *Amer. Psychologist,* 1951, **6,** 309.

(36) BRITT, S. H.: *Social psychology of modern life,* rev. ed. New York: Holt, 1949.

(37) BRODBECK, A. J., and H. V. PERLMUTTER: Self-dislike as a determinant of marked ingroup, out-group preferences. *J. Psychol.,* 1954, **38,** 271–280.

(38) BROTHERTON, D. A., J. M. READ, and K. C. PRATT: Indeterminate number concepts. II. Application by children to determinate number groups. *J. genet. Psychol.,* 1948, **73,** 209–236.

(39) BROWMAN, M. T., and M. C. TEMPLIN: Stories for younger children in 1927–29 and 1952–55. *Elem. Sch. J.,* 1959, **59,** 324–327.

(40) BROWN, D. G.: Sex role preferences in young children. *Psychol. Monogr.,* 1956, **71,** No. 14.

(41) BROWN, D. G.: Sex-role development in a changing culture. *Psychol. Bull.,* 1958, **55,** 232–242.

(42) BROWNELL, W. A., and G. HENDRICKSON: How children learn information, conceptions and generalizations. *49th Yearb. Nat. Soc. Stud. Educ.,* 1950, Pt. 1, 92–128.

(43) BROWNFIELD, E. D.: Communication: key to dynamics of family interaction. *Marriage fam. Liv.,* 1953, **15,** 316–319.

(44) BRUNER, J. S., and R. TAGIURI: The perception of people. In G. Lindzey (Ed.), *Handbook of social psychology.* Cambridge, Mass.: Addison-Wesley, 1954. Vol. II. Pp. 634–654.

(45) BURTON, D. L.: Comic books: a teacher's analysis. *Elem. Sch. J.,* 1955, **56,** 73–77.

(46) BUTTERWORTH, R. F., and G. G. THOMPSON: Factors related to age-grade trends and sex differences in children's preferences for comic books. *J. genet. Psychol.,* 1951, **78,** 71–96.

(47) BYRNE, D.: The relationship between humor and the expression of hostility. *J. abnorm. soc. Psychol.*, 1956, **53**, 84–89.

(48) CALOGERAS, R. C.: Some relationships between fantasy and self-report behavior. *Genet. Psychol. Monogr.*, 1958, **58**, 273–325.

(49) CAPPA, D.: Types of story books enjoyed by kindergarten children. *J. educ. Res.*, 1956, **49**, 555–557.

(50) CARTER, D. C.: The influence of family relationships and family experience on personality. *Marriage fam. Liv.*, 1954, **16**, 212–215.

(51) CATTELL, R. B., and L. B. LUBORSKY: Personality factors in response to humor. *J. abnorm. soc. Psychol.*, 1947, **42**, 402–421.

(52) CENTERS, R.: Social-class identification of American youth. *J. Pers.*, 1950, **18**, 290–302.

(53) CHALL, J. S.: *Readability: an appraisal of research and application.* Columbus, Ohio: Ohio State Univer., Bur. Educ. Res. Monogr., 1958, No. 34.

(54) CHILD, I. L., E. H. POTTER, and E. M. LEVINE: Children's textbooks and personality development: an exploration in the social psychology of education. *Psychol. Monogr.*, 1946, **60**, No. 3.

(55) COBB, H. V.: Role-wishes and general wishes of children and adolescents. *Child Develpm.*, 1954, **25**, 161–171.

(56) COHEN, J., C. E. M. HANSEL, and J. SYLVESTER: An experimental study of comparative judgments of time. *Brit. J. Psychol.*, 1954, **45**, 108–114.

(57) COLLIER, M. J., and E. L. GAIER: Adult reactions to preferred childhood stories. *Child Develpm.*, 1958, **29**, 97–103.

(58) CONN, J. H.: Children's awareness of sex differences. II. Play attitudes and game preferences. *J. child Psychiat.*, 1951, **2**, 82–99.

(59) CORDEAU, R.: The "golden section" in the drawings of children. *Enfance*, 1953, **6**, 147–151.

(60) COSER, R. L.: Laughter among colleagues. *Psychiatry*, 1960, **23**, 81–95.

(61) CRANE, A. R.: The development of moral values in children. IV. Pre-adolescent gangs and the moral development of children. *Brit. J. educ. Psychol.*, 1958, **58**, 201–208.

(62) DAI, B.: A socio-psychiatric approach to personality organization. *Amer. sociol. Rev.*, 1952, **17**, 44–49.

(63) DAMERON, L. E.: Mother-child interaction in the development of self-restraint. *J. genet. Psychol.*, 1955, **86**, 289–308.

(64) DAVIS, J. A.: Status symbols and the measurement of status perception. *Sociometry*, 1956, **19**, 154–165.

(65) DAVITZ, J. R.: Social perception and sociometric choice of children. *J. abnorm. soc. Psychol.*, 1955, **50**, 173–176.

(66) DENNIS, W.: Animistic thinking among college and high school students in the Near East. *J. educ. Psychol.*, 1957, **48**, 193–198.

(67) DENNIS, W.: Arab and United States children: some psychological comparisons. *Trans. N.Y. Acad. Sci.*, 1960, Ser. II, Vol. 22, 589–605.

(68) DEUTSCHER, I.: The stereotype as a research tool. *Soc. Forces*, 1958, **37**, 55–60.

(69) DIXON, J. C.: Development of self recognition. *J. genet. Psychol.*, 1957, **91**, 251–256.

(70) DUNSING, M.: Spending money of adolescents. *J. home Econ.*, 1956, **48**, 405–408.

(71) DURKIN, D.: Children's concept of justice: a further comparison with the Piaget data. *J. educ. Res.*, 1959, **52**, 252–257.

(72) ELKIND, D.: Children's conceptions of right and left: Piaget replication study, IV. *J. genet. Psychol.*, 1961, **99**, 269–276.

(73) ELKINS, D.: Some factors related to the choice-status of ninety eighth-grade children in a school society. *Genet. Psychol. Monogr.*, 1958, **58**, 207–272.

(74) ESTES, B. W.: Judgment of size in relation to geometric shape. *Child Develpm.*, 1961, **32**, 277–286.

(75) ESTVAN, F. J.: The relationship of social status, intelligence, and sex of ten- and eleven-year-old children to an awareness of poverty. *Genet. Psychol. Monogr.*, 1952, **46**, 3–60.

(76) ESTVAN, F. J., and E. W. ESTVAN: *The child's world: his social perception.* New York: Putnam, 1959.

(77) EWENS, W. P.: Experience patterns as related to vocational preferences. *Educ. psychol. Measmt*, 1956, **16**, 223–231.

(78) FEIFEL, H., and I. LORGE: Quantitative differences in the vocabulary responses of children. *J. educ. Psychol.*, 1950, **41**, 1–18.

(79) FIELDS, S. G.: Discrimination of facial expression and its relation to personal adjustment. *J. soc. Psychol.*, 1953, **38**, 63–71.

(80) FISHER, R. L.: Preference of different age and socioeconomic groups in instrumental musical situations. *J. soc. Psychol.*, 1951, **33**, 147–152.

(81) FISHMAN, J. A.: Negative stereotypes concerning Americans among American-born children receiving various types of minority-group education. *Genet. Psychol. Monogr.*, 1955, **51**, 107–182.

(82) FRAISSE, P., and P. VAUTREY: Perception of space, of speed, and of time in the five-year-old child. *Enfance*, 1952, **5**, 1–20.

(83) FRANK, L. K., and M. H. FRANK: *Your adolescent, at home and in school.* New York: Viking, 1956.

(84) FRENCH, J. E.: Children's preferences for pictures of varied complexity of pictorial pattern. *Elem. Sch. J.*, 1952, **52**, 90–95.

(85) FRIEDMAN, K. C.: Time concepts of elementary-school children. *Elem. Sch. J.*, 1944, **44**, 337–342.

(86) GAIER, E. L., and M. J. COLLIER: The latency-stage story preferences of American and Finnish children. *Child Develpm.*, 1960, **31**, 431–451.

(87) GELLERT, E.: Children's conceptions of the content and function of the human body. *Genet. Psychol. Monogr.*, 1962, **65**, 293–405.

(88) GESELL, A., and F. L. ILG: *Child development*. New York: Harper & Row, 1949.

(89) GESELL, A., F. L. ILG, and L. B. AMES: *Youth: the years from ten to sixteen*. New York: Harper & Row, 1956.

(90) GILLILAND, A. R., and D. W. HUMPHREYS: Age, sex, method, and interval as variables in times estimation. *J. genet. Psychol.*, 1943, **63**, 123–130.

(91) GOLDSTONE, S., W. K. BOARDMAN, and W. T. LHAMON: Kinesthetic cues in the development of time concepts. *J. genet. Psychol.*, 1958, **93**, 185–190.

(92) GOLDSTONE, S., W. T. LHAMON, and W. K. BOARDMAN: The time sense: anchor effects and apparent duration. *J. Psychol.*, 1957, **44**, 145–153.

(93) GOLEIN, E. S.: Forming impressions of personality. *J. Pers.*, 1954, **23**, 65–67.

(94) GOODCHILDS, J. D.: Effect of being witty on position in the social structure of a small group. *Sociometry*, 1959, **22**, 261–272.

(95) GOODMAN, M. E.: *Race awareness in young children*. Cambridge, Mass.: Addison-Wesley, 1952.

(96) GRAHAM, L. R.: The maturational factor in humor. *J. clin. Psychol.*, 1958, **14**, 326–328.

(97) GRONLUND, M. E.: The accuracy of teachers' judgments concerning the sociometric status of sixth grade pupils. *Sociometry*, 1950, **13**, 197–225, 329–357.

(98) GUNDERSON, A. G.: What seven-year-olds like in books. *J. educ. Res.*, 1957, **50**, 509–520.

(99) HALL, G. S.: The contents of children's minds on entering school. *Ped. Sem.*, 1891, **1**, 139–173.

(100) HARMS, E.: The development of humor. *J. abnorm. soc. Psychol.*, 1943, **38**, 351–369.

(101) HARRIS, D. B., H. G. GOUGH, and W. E. MARTIN: Children's ethnic attitudes. **II.** Relationship to parental beliefs concerning child training. *Child Develpm.*, 1950, **21**, 169–181.

(102) HARRIS, D. B., and S. C. TSENG: Children's attitudes toward peers and parents as revealed by sentence completions. *Child Develpm.*, 1957, **28**, 401–411.

(103) HARTLEY, E. L., and D. C. KRUGMAN: Note on children's social role perception. *J. Psychol.*, 1948, **26**, 399–405.

(104) HARTLEY, E. L., M. ROSENBAUM, and S. SCHWARTZ: Children's use of ethnic frames of reference. *J. Psychol.*, 1948, **26**, 367–386.

(105) HARTLEY, R. E.: Sex-role pressures and the socialization of the male child. *Psychol. Rep.*, 1959, **5**, 457–468.

(106) HARTLEY, R. E.: Some implications of current changes in sex role patterns. *Merrill-Palmer Quart.*, 1960, **6**, 153–164.

(107) HARTLEY, R. E., F. P. HARDESTY, and D. S. GORFEIN: Children's perceptions and expressions of sex preference. *Child Develpm.*, 1962, **33**, 221–227.

(108) HARTLEY, R. E., and A. KLEIN: Sex-role concepts among elementary-school-age girls. *Marriage fam. Liv.*, 1959, **21**, 59–64.

(109) HARTRUP, W. W., and E. A. ZOOK: Sex-role preferences in three- and four-year-old children. *J. consult. Psychol.*, 1960, **24**, 420–426.

(110) HAVIGHURST, R. J.: *Human development and education*. New York: Longmans, 1953.

(111) HAWKES, G. R., L. G. BURCHINAL, and B. GARDNER: Preadolescents' views of some of their relationships with their parents. *Child Develpm.*, 1957, **28**, 393–399.

(112) HOLLINGSHEAD, A. DE B.: *Elmtown's youth*. New York: Wiley, 1949.

(113) HURLOCK, E. B.: A study of self-ratings by children. *J. appl. Psychol.*, 1927, **11**, 490–502.

(114) ILG, F. L., and L. B. AMES: Developmental trends in arithmetic. *J. genet. Psychol.*, 1951, **79**, 3–28.

(115) JAHODA, G.: Development of the perception of social differences in children from 6 to 10. *Brit. J. Psychol.*, 1959, **50**, 159–175.

(116) JAMES, W.: *The principles of psychology*. New York: Holt, 1890.

(117) JAROLIMEK, J., and C. D. FOSTER: Quantitative concepts in fifth-grade social studies text books. *Elem. Sch. J.*, 1959, **59**, 437–442.

(118) JERSILD, A. T.: Self-understanding in childhood and adolescence. *Amer. Psychologist*, 1951, **6**, 122–126.

(119) JERSILD, A. T.: *In search of self*. New York: Teachers College, Columbia University, 1952.

(120) JERSILD, A. T.: *Child psychology*, 5th ed. Englewood Cliffs, N.J.: Prentice-Hall, 1960.

(121) JERSILD, A. T., and R. J. TASCH: *Children's interests and what they suggest for education*. New York: Teachers College, 1949.

(122) JOHNSON, R. C., C. JOHNSON, and L. MARTIN: Authoritarianism, occupation, and sex role differentiation of children. *Child Develpm.*, 1961, **32**, 271–276.

(123) JOSSELYN, I. M.: The family as a psychological unit. *Soc. Casewk*, 1953, **34**, 336–344.

(124) JOURARD, S. M., and R. M. REMY: Perceived parental attitude, the self, and security. *J. consult. Psychol.*, 1955, **19**, 364–366.

(125) KATCHER, A.: The discrimination of sex differences by young children. *J. genet. Psychol.*, 1955, **87**, 131–143.

(126) KATCHER, A., and M. M. LEVIN: Children's conceptions of body size. *Child Develpm.*, 1955, **26**, 103–110.

(127) KESTON, M. J., and I. M. PINTO: Possible

factors influencing musical preferences. *J. genet. Psychol.,* 1955, **86**, 101–113.

(128) KING, W. H.: The development of scientific concepts in children. *Brit. J. educ. Psychol.,* 1961, **31**, 1–20.

(129) KLAUSNER, S. Z.: Social class and self concept. *J. soc. Psychol.,* 1953, **38**, 201–205.

(130) KLINGBERG, G.: The distinction between living and not living among 7–10-year-old children, with some remarks concerning the so-called animism controversy. *J. genet. Psychol.,* 1957, **90**, 227–238.

(131) KLINGENSMITH, S. W.: Child animism: what the child means by "alive." *Child Develpm.,* 1953, **24**, 51–61.

(132) KNOPF, I. J., and T. W. RICHARDS: The child's differentiation in sex as reflected in drawings of the human figure. *J. genet. Psychol.,* 1952, **81**, 99–112.

(133) KOCH, H. L.: The relation in young children between characteristics of their playmates and certain attributes of their siblings. *Child Develpm.,* 1957, **28**, 175–202.

(134) KOHN, M. L.: Social class and parental values. *Amer. J. Sociol.,* 1959, **64**, 337–351.

(135) KOLKO, G.: Economic mobility and social stratification. *Amer. J. Sociol.,* 1957, **63**, 30–38.

(136) KOMAROVSKY, M.: Functional analysis of sex roles. *Amer. sociol. Rev.,* 1950, **15**, 508–516.

(137) KOPPITZ, E. M.: Relationship between some background factors and children's interpersonal attitudes. *J. genet. Psychol.,* 1957, **91**, 119–129.

(138) KOWITZ, G. T., and E. J. TIGNER: Tell me about Santa Claus: a study of concept change. *Elem. Sch. J.,* 1961, **62**, 130–133.

(139) LAMBERT, W. E., and TAGUCHI, Y.: Ethnic cleavage among young children. *J. abnorm. soc. Psychol.,* 1956, **53**, 380–382.

(140) LANDRETH, C., and B. C. JOHNSON: Young children's responses to a picture and inset test designed to reveal reactions to persons of different skin color. *Child Develpm.,* 1953, **24**, 63–80.

(141) LARK-HOROVITZ, B., and J. NORTON: Children's art abilities: the interrelation and factorial structure of ten characteristics. *Child Develpm.,* 1960, **31**, 453–462.

(142) LEHMANN, I. J.: Learning. III. Attitudes and values. *Rev. educ. Res.,* 1958, **28**, 468–474.

(143) LEUBA, C.: Relation of stimulation intensities to learning and development. *Psychol. Rep.,* 1962, **11**, 55–65.

(144) LEVINE, J., and F. C. REDLICH: Failure to understand humor. *Psychoanal. Quart.,* 1955, **24**, 560–572.

(145) LEVY, E.: Children's behavior under stress and its relation to training by parents to respond to stress situations. *Child Develpm.,* 1959, **30**, 301–324.

(146) LORD, E. E.: A study of spatial orientation of children. *J. educ. Res.,* 1941, **34**, 481–505.

(147) LOVELL, K., and A. SLATER: The growth of the concept of time: a comparative study. *J. child Psychol. Psychiat.,* 1960, **1**, 179–190.

(148) LUCHINS, A. S.: On the theories and problems of adolescence. *J. genet. Psychol.,* 1954, **85**, 47–63.

(149) LUCIO, W. H., and C. D. MEAD: An investigation of children's preferences for modern pictures. *Elem. Sch. J.,* 1939, **39**, 678–689.

(150) LUFT, J.: Monetary value and the perception of persons. *J. soc. Psychol.,* 1957, **46**, 245–251.

(151) LYNN, D. B.: A note on sex differences in the development of masculine and feminine identification. *Psychol. Rev.,* 1959, **66**, 126–135.

(152) MACCOBY, E. E., and W. C. WILSON: Identification and observational learning from films. *J. abnorm. soc. Psychol.,* 1957, **55**, 76–87.

(153) MACCOBY, E. E., W. C. WILSON, and R. V. BURTON: Differential movie-viewing behavior of male and female viewers. *J. Pers.,* 1958, **26**, 259–267.

(154) MARK, H. J.: Elementary thinking and the classification of behavior. *Science,* 1962, **135**, 75–87.

(155) MARSHALL, H. R., and L. MAGRUDER: Relations between parent money education practices and children's knowledge and use of money. *Child Develpm.,* 1960, **31**, 253–284.

(156) MARTIN, W. E.: Qualitative expressions in young children. *Genet. Psychol. Monogr.,* 1951, **44**, 147–219.

(157) MARTIN, W. E.: Learning theory and identification. III. The development of values in children. *J. genet. Psychol.,* 1954, **84**, 211–217.

(158) MC AULAY, J. D.: What understandings do second grade children have of time relationships? *J. educ. Res.,* 1961, **54**, 312–314.

(159) MC CARTHY, D.: Language development. *Monogr. Soc. Res. Child Develpm.,* 1960, **25**, No. 3, 5–14.

(160) MC CULLOUGH, C. M.: A log of children's out-of-school activities. *Elem. Sch. J.,* 1957, **58**, 157–165.

(161) MC CULLOUGH, C. M.: Implications of research on children's concepts. *Read. Teacher,* 1959, **13**, 100–107.

(162) MEISTER, D.: A comparative study of figure-ground discrimination in preschool children and adults. *J. genet. Psychol.,* 1949, **74**, 311–323.

(163) MERRY, F. K., and R. V. MERRY: *The first two decades of life,* 2d ed. New York: Harper & Row, 1958.

(164) MIDDLETON, R.: Negro and white reactions to racial humor. *Sociometry*, 1959, **22**, 175–183.

(165) MIDDLETON, R., and J. MOLAND: Humor in Negro and white subcultures: a study of jokes among university students. *Amer. sociol. Rev.*, 1959, **24**, 61–69.

(166) MOGAR, M.: Children's causal reasoning about natural phenomena. *Child Develpm.*, 1960, **31**, 59–65.

(167) MORLAND, J. K.: Racial recognition by nursery school children in Lynchburg, Virginia. *Soc. Forces*, 1958, **37**, 132–137.

(168) MOSHER, D. L., and A. SCODEL: Relationships between ethnocentrism in children and the ethnocentrism and authoritarian rearing practices of their mothers. *Child Develpm.*, 1960, **31**, 369–376.

(169) MUNN, N. L.: *The evolution and growth of human behavior.* Boston: Houghton Mifflin, 1955.

(170) MUUS, R., and C. B. STENDLER: Intergroup education in the public schools. *Educ. Forum*, 1956, **20**, 151–164.

(171) NAGY, M. H.: The child's theories concerning death. *J. genet. Psychol.*, 1948, **73**, 3–27.

(172) NAGY, M. H.: Children's ideas on the origin of illness. *Hlth educ. J.*, 1951, **9**, 6–12.

(173) NAGY, M. H.: Children's birth theories. *J. genet. Psychol.*, 1953, **83**, 217–226.

(174) NAGY, M. H.: Children's conceptions of some bodily functions. *J. genet. Psychol.*, 1953, **83**, 199–216.

(175) NAGY, M. H.: The representation of "germs" by children. *J. genet. Psychol.*, 1953, **83**, 227–240.

(176) NATTERSON, J. M., and A. G. KUNDSON: Observations concerning fear of death in fatally ill children and their mothers. *Psychosom. Med.*, 1960, **22**, 456–465.

(177) NEISSER, E. G.: Emotional and social values attached to money. *Marriage fam. Liv.*, 1960, **22**, 132–139.

(178) New York Times Report: Long and short days simplified by pupil. *The New York Times*, Feb. 11, 1962.

(179) OAKES, M. E.: Children's explanations of natural phenomena. *Teach. Coll. Contr. Educ.*, 1947, No. 926.

(180) PERLMUTTER, H. V., and D. SHAPIRO: Stereotypes about Americans and Europeans who make specific statements. *Psychol. Rep.*, 1957, **3**, 131–137.

(181) PIAGET, J.: *The origins of intelligence in children.* New York: International Universities Press, Inc., 1952.

(182) PINNEAU, S. R., and H. E. JONES: Development of mental abilities. *Rev. educ. Res.*, 1958, **28**, 392–400.

(183) PODOLSKY, E.: Horrors. *Calif. Parent-Teacher J.*, 1952, Dec., p. 23.

(184) PRATT, K. C., W. E. HARTMANN, and J. C. MEAD: Interdeterminate number concepts. III. Representation by children through selection of appropriate aggregations. *J. genet. Psychol.*, 1954, **87**, 39–63.

(185) PRESSEY, S. L., and A. W. JONES: 1923–1953 and 20–60 age changes in moral codes, anxieties, and interests, as shown by the "X-O Tests." *J. Psychol.*, 1955, **39**, 485–502.

(186) PREVEY, E. E.: Developing good habits in the use of money. *J. home Econ.*, 1948, **38**, 79–81.

(187) RABBAN, M.: Sex-role identification in young children in two diverse social groups. *Genet. Psychol. Monogr.*, 1950, **42**, 81–158.

(188) RADKE-YARROW, M. J., and B. LANDE: Personality correlates of differential reactions to minority group belonging. *J. soc. Psychol.*, 1953, **38**, 253–272.

(189) RAPP, A.: A phylogenetic theory of wit and humor. *J. soc. Psychol.*, 1949, **30**, 81–96.

(190) REID, F.: Films provide a rich source of vocabulary study. *J. educ. Res.*, 1958, **51**, 617–623.

(191) RICHARDSON, C., and J. CHURCH: A developmental analysis of proverb interpretations. *J. genet. Psychol.*, 1959, **94**, 169–179.

(192) ROBERTS, A. F., and D. M. JOHNSON: Some factors related to the perception of funniness in the humor situation. *J. soc. Psychol.*, 1957, **46**, 57–63.

(193) ROSENBERG, B. G., and B. SUTTON-SMITH: A revised conception of masculine-feminine differences in play activities. *J. genet. Psychol.*, 1960, **96**, 165–170.

(194) RUDISILL, M.: Children's preferences for color versus other qualities in illustrations. *Elem. Sch. J.*, 1952, **52**, 444–451.

(195) RUSSELL, D. H.: The development of thinking processes. *Rev. educ. Res.*, 1953, **23**, 137–145.

(196) RUSSELL, D. H.: What does research say about self-evaluation? *J. educ. Res.*, 1953, **46**, 561–573.

(197) RUSSELL, D. H.: *Children's thinking.* Boston: Ginn, 1956.

(198) RUSSELL, D. H.: Contributions of reading to personal development. *Teach. Coll. Rec.*, 1960, **61**, 435–442.

(199) SARBIN, T. R.: A preface to a psychological analysis of the self. *Psychol. Rev.*, 1952, **59**, 11–22.

(200) SCHIFF, H.: Judgmental response sets in the perception of sociometric status. *Sociometry*, 1954, **17**, 207–227.

(201) SCHUESSLER, K., and A. L. STRAUSS: A study of concept learning by scale analysis. *Amer. sociol. Rev.*, 1950, **15**, 752–762.

(202) SCHWARTZ, E. K.: A psychoanalytic study of the fairy tale. *Amer. J. Psychother.*, 1956, **10**, 740–762.

(203) SEARS, R. R., E. E. MACCOBY, and H. LEVIN: *Patterns of child rearing.* New York: Harper & Row, 1957.

(204) SECORD, P. F., and S. M. JOURARD: Mother-concepts and judgments of young women's faces. *J. abnorm. soc. Psychol.,* 1956, **52,** 246–250.

(205) SECORD, P. F., and E. SAUMER: Identifying Jewish names: does prejudice increase accuracy? *J. abnorm. soc. Psychol.,* 1960, **61,** 144–145.

(206) SEWELL, W. H., and A. O. HALLER: Social status and the personality adjustment of the child. *Sociometry,* 1956, **19,** 114–125.

(207) SHAFFER, L. F.: *Children's interpretation of cartoons.* New York: Teachers College, Columbia University, 1930.

(208) SHANE, H. G.: Children's interests. *NEA J.,* 1957, **46,** 237–239.

(209) SHERRIFFS, A. C., and R. F. JARRETT: Sex differences in attitudes about sex differences. *J. Psychol.,* 1953, **35,** 161–168.

(210) SILLER, J.: Socioeconomic status and conceptual thinking. *J. abnorm. soc. Psychol.,* 1957, **55,** 365–371.

(211) SMITH, W. D., and D. LEBO: Some changing aspects of the self-concept of pubescent males. *J. genet. Psychol.,* 1956, **88,** 61–75.

(212) SPIEGEL, L. A.: The child's concept of beauty: a study in concept formation. *J. genet. Psychol.,* 1950, **77,** 11–23.

(213) SPRINGER, D. V.: Awareness of racial differences of preschool children in Hawaii. *Genet. Psychol. Monogr.,* 1950, **41,** 215–270.

(214) SPRINGER, D. V.: Development in young children of an understanding of time and the clock. *J. genet. Psychol.,* 1952, **80,** 83–96.

(215) STACEY, L. L., and M. L. REICHEN: Attitudes toward death and future life among normal and subnormal adolescent girls. *Except. Children,* 1954, **20,** 259–262.

(216) STAPLES, R., and H. CONLEY: The use of color in the finger painting of young children. *Child Develpm.,* 1949, **20,** 201–212.

(217) STEVENSON, H. W., and E. C. STEWART: A developmental study of racial awareness in young children. *Child Develpm.,* 1958, **29,** 399–409.

(218) STILES, F. S.: Developing an understanding of human behavior at the elementary school level. *J. educ. Res.,* 1950, **43,** 516–524.

(219) STRANG, R.: How children and adolescents view their world. *Ment. Hyg., N.Y.,* 1954, **38,** 28–33.

(220) STRAUSS, A. L.: The animism controversy: Reexamination of Huang-Lee data. *J. genet. Psychol.,* 1951, **78,** 105–113.

(221) STRAUSS, A. L.: The development and transformation of monetary meanings in the child. *Amer. sociol. Rev.,* 1952, **17,** 275–286.

(222) STRAUSS, A. L., and K. SCHUESSLER: Socialization, logical reasoning, and concept development in the child. *Amer. sociol. Rev.,* 1951, **16,** 514–523.

(223) SUTTON, R. S.: The effect of vocabulary building on reading skills. *Elem. Sch. J.,* 1953, **54,** 94–97.

(224) SUTTON, R. S.: Behavior in the attainment of economic concepts. *J. Psychol.,* 1962, **53,** 37–46.

(225) SWANSON, R., and A. L. BENTON: Some aspects of the genetic development of right-left discrimination. *Child Develpm.,* 1955, **26,** 123–133.

(226) SWENSEN, C. H., and K. R. NEWTON: The development of sexual differentiation on the draw-a-person test. *J. clin. Psychol.,* 1955, **11,** 417–418.

(227) TAFT, R.: The ability to judge people. *Psychol. Bull.,* 1955, **52,** 1–23.

(228) TAIT, C. D., and R. C. ASCHER: Inside-of-the-body test. *Psychosom. Med.,* 1955, **17,** 139–148.

(229) TARWATER, J. W.: Self-understanding and the ability to predict another's response. *Marriage fam. Liv.,* 1953, **15,** 126–128.

(230) TAYLOR, C., and G. G. THOMPSON: Age trends in preferences for certain facial proportions. *Child Develpm.,* 1955, **26,** 97–102.

(231) TEMPLIN, M.: *Certain language skills in children.* Minneapolis: The University of Minnesota Press, 1957.

(232) TERMAN, L. M., and M. A. MERRILL: *Stanford-Binet Intelligence Scale,* 3rd rev. Boston: Houghton Mifflin, 1960.

(233) TERMAN, L. M., and L. E. TYLER: Psychological sex differences. In L. Carmichael (Ed.), *Manual of child psychology,* 2d ed. New York: Wiley, 1954. Pp. 1064–1114.

(234) THAYER, L. O., and N. H. PRONKO: Some psychological factors in the reading of fiction. *J. genet. Psychol.,* 1958, **93,** 113–117.

(235) TUCKMAN, J., I. LORGE, and G. A. SPOONER: The effect of family environment on attitudes toward old people and the older worker. *J. soc. Psychol.,* 1953, **38,** 207–218.

(236) TUDDENHAM, R. D.: Studies in reputation. I. Sex and grade differences in school children's evaluations of their peers. II. The diagnosis of social adjustment. *Psychol. Monogr.,* 1952, **66,** No. 1.

(237) VERNON, M. D.: The development of perception in children. *Educ. Res.,* 1960, **3,** 2–11.

(238) VINACKE, W. E.: Concept formation in children of school age. *Education,* 1954, **74,** 527–534.

(239) VINACKE, W. E.: Stereotypes as social concepts. *J. soc. Psychol.,* 1957, **46,** 229–243.

(240) VINEYARD, E. E., and H. W. MASSEY: The interrelationship of certain linguistic skills and their relationship with scholastic achieve-

ment when intelligence is ruled constant. *J. educ. Psychol.*, 1957, **48**, 279–286.

(241) WALTERS, R. H., W. E. MARSHALL, and J. R. SHOOTER: Anxiety, isolation, and susceptibility to social influence. *J. Pers.*, 1960, **28**, 518–529.

(242) WATERS, J., F. I. STROMBERG, and G. LONIAN: Perceptions concerning development of responsibility in young children. *Elem. Sch. J.*, 1957, **57**, 209–216.

(243) WEIDER, A., and P. A. NOLLER: Objective studies of children's drawings of the human figure. I. Sex awareness and socioeconomic level. *J. clin. Psychol.*, 1950, **6**, 319–325.

(244) WEINSTEIN, E. A.: Development of the concept of flag and the sense of national identity. *Child Develpm.*, 1957, **28**, 167–174.

(245) WEISS, W.: An examination of attitude toward Negroes. *J. soc. Psychol.*, 1961, **55**, 3–21.

(246) WERNER, H.: Change of meaning: a study of semantic processes through the experimental method. *J. gen. Psychol.*, 1954, **50**, 181–208.

(247) WHIPPLE, G.: Appraisal of the interest appeal of illustration. *Elem. Sch. J.*, 1953, **53**, 262–269.

(248) WITRYOL, S. L.: Age trends in children's evaluation of teacher-approved and teacher-disapproved behavior. *Genet. Psychol. Monogr.*, 1950, **41**, 271–326.

(249) WITTY, P. A.: Children's interest in comics, radio, motion pictures, and TV. *Educ. Admin. Superv.*, 1952, **38**, 138–147.

(250) WOHLWILL, J. F.: A study of the development of the number concept by scalogram analysis. *J. genet. Psychol.*, 1960, **97**, 345–377.

(251) WOLFENSTEIN, M.: Children's understanding of jokes. *Psychoanal. Stud. Child.*, 1954, **8**, 162–176.

(252) WOODRUFF, A. D.: *Basic concepts of teaching.* San Francisco: Chandler, 1961.

(253) YOUMANS, E. G.: Occupational expectations of twelfth grade Michigan boys. *J. exp. Educ.*, 1956, **24**, 259–271.

(254) ZELIGS, R.: Children's concepts and stereotypes of Norwegian, Jew, Scotch, Canadian, Swedish, and American Indian. *J. educ. Res.*, 1952, **45**, 349–360.

(255) ZUK, G. H.: Sex-appropriate behavior in adolescence. *J. genet. Psychol.*, 1958, **93**, 15–32.

12

MORAL
DEVELOPMENT

Morality is conformity to the moral code of the social group. The term comes from the Latin word *mores,* meaning "manners, customs, or folkways." Moral concepts are the rules to which the members of a given culture have become accustomed over a period of time. They determine the expected behavior patterns of all members of that culture. *To act in a moral way thus means to act in conformity to group standards of conduct.* A person whose behavior conforms to group expectations wins social approval and, with it, the acceptance of the group.

Ethical behavior, which is often confused with moral behavior, is a more inclusive concept. It applies to human conduct generally, rather than to that of any particular cultural group. An ethical person is usually moral, but a moral one may not always be ethical. A moral person may conform to the standards of *his particular group,* but these standards may not be the accepted standards of people in other groups. A thief, for example, may be considered "moral" by the gang with which he is identified because he behaves in accordance with the mores of the gang. As judged by society in general, however, his behavior would not be ethical (203).

Immorality is failure to conform to the expectations of the group; it consists of behavior directed against the interests and welfare of the group. A person who is immoral is not so because of ignorance but rather because he does not approve of the behavioral standards of the group with which he is identified or because he feels no obligation to conform to group expectations. In most cases, his unwillingness to conform stems from his belief that he owes the group nothing because the group has treated him in a manner which he resents. Juvenile delinquents and adult criminals may be considered "immoral" because they know what is expected of them but *intentionally* violate the group's expectations.

Unmoral, or nonmoral, behavior, on the other hand, is behavior which—even when unfavorable to the group—is so not because the individual *intends* harm but rather because he does not know what is socially approved. Much of the misbehavior of young children is unmoral rather than immoral. By the time the child reaches school age, he has ordinarily had the necessary opportunities to learn what society expects of him. A child is expected to know that taking things that belong to others without their permission is wrong and is labeled "stealing." If he steals, his act is not condoned by the group; he is regarded as "too old" for such behavior.

No child can be expected to learn all the mores of the group before childhood is over. When a child does things that the group regards as wrong, it is often assumed that his parents are to blame, that they have not fulfilled their parental duty to teach him what the group expects. By the time the child reaches adolescence, society expects him to behave in accordance with the mores of the group; when he fails to do so, it is generally because he does not want to rather than because he is ignorant of society's expectations.

Laws and Customs. In every social group, certain acts are considered either "right" or "wrong" because they further or hinder the welfare of the members of the group. The most important mores are incorporated into *laws*, with specific penalties for breaking them. Others, which are just as binding as the laws themselves, persist as *customs*, without specific penalties for breaking them (112).

Taking the material possessions of others is considered serious enough to hinder the welfare of the group. It is therefore a legal offense and has prescribed penalties attached to it. "Borrowing" the material possessions of others, without gaining their consent or without their knowledge, is not considered as serious as stealing, though it is against the mores of the group. Customs prohibiting "borrowing" are enforced by social disapproval. Similarly, it is customary not to handle the possessions of another without his knowledge and consent. While violation of this custom will incur no legal action, social disapproval will be the penalty should there be any damage.

Moral standards may vary from group to group, depending on what has been accepted by the groups as socially approved behavior. Within a community, different social classes and different religious groups often have their own individual codes of behavior even though there is uniformity in the more important mores. There are differences in standards of sex behavior, for example, for people of different social classes and for members of the two sexes, although the more important standards of sex behavior, such as those relating to rape or polygamy, are embodied in laws that are binding for both sexes and for all social classes (105).

Conformity to Mores. Most children learn that it is to their personal advantage to conform to group mores, even though they may not always agree with them. As Wiggam has stated:

Intelligent individuals know that right conduct is simply intelligent conduct—the conduct that gets the best results. . . . They tend to choose the right conduct simply because they see it is the course of action that promises the best consequences. An intelligent child or adult discovers he can get what he wants in life more easily and surely by honesty than by deception, by kindness than by cruelty, by accepting social duties than by dodging them (211).

Some children, by contrast, are "socially stupid"; they violate the mores of the group either because they disapprove of them or because they feel that they have the right to do as they please—that they are "above the law." Unfortunately, society does not condone violations of its mores. Such children pay the penalty in the form of social rejection—a penalty that is far more harmful to their egos than the temporary pleasure they receive from disregarding the social mores.

TRUE MORALITY

True morality is behavior which conforms to social standards and which is also carried out voluntarily by the individual. It comes with the transition from *external* to *internal authority* and consists of conduct regulated from within. It is accompanied by a feeling of personal responsibility for one's acts. In addition, it involves giving primary consideration to the welfare of the group while relegating personal desires or gains to a position of secondary importance. True morality is rarely found in children, but it should appear during the adolescent years (74).

Moral development of the highest type has an *intellectual* aspect and an *impulsive* aspect. The child must learn what is right and what is wrong, and as soon as he is old enough he must understand why it is so. He must have plenty of opportunities to take part in group activities so that he can learn what the group expects. In addition, he must develop the desire to do what is right, to act for the common good, and to avoid wrong. This can be accomplished most successfully by associating pleasant reactions with what is right and unpleasant reactions with what is wrong. To ensure his willingness to act in a socially desirable way, the child must receive the approval of the group (28, 77).

Role of "Conscience."   According to tradition, children are born with a "conscience," or the ability to *know* what is right or wrong. In keeping with this tradition is the belief that misbehavior is the result of some inherited weakness, the origin of which is ascribed to either the mother's or the father's side of the family. Those who hold to such beliefs maintain that the child cannot be reformed; as a result, they see little need of devoting time and effort to his moral training. The justification for corporal punishment was founded on the belief that such punishment would "drive out the devil" and thus make the "naturally bad" child into a good one (74).

Today, it is widely accepted that the child is not born with a "conscience" but that "right" and "wrong" are learned (178). As Eysenck has pointed out, "conscience" is a conditioned anxiety response to certain types of situations and actions built up by pairing aggressive acts with punishment, which leads to fear and anxiety responses on the child's

part. It is an "internalized policeman" which is called by such names as "superego" and "inner light." He further explains that conscience is "usually conceived as some kind of *deus ex machina* implanted in the human being in some mysterious way, which ceaselessly keeps an eye on his activities, and gives him a sharp tweak whenever he deviates from the straight and narrow path of duty" (55).

The "voice of conscience" is thus the internalized standard which controls the individual's behavior. True morality is found only when a person's behavior is guided by conscience, the "internalized policeman." This is too complex for a young child to acquire; therefore, his behavior is controlled mainly by environmental restrictions (6, 55). There is a gradual shift, however, from environmental to internalized controls (25, 26, 27). By the time the child approaches adolescence, the "internalized policeman" should have taken over much of the control of his behavior. By the time he reaches legal maturity, the transition should be complete; the individual will then have reached the level of "true morality" (139).

Role of Guilt and Shame.   When the child develops the "warning and punishing voice of conscience," he carries it with him wherever he goes and uses it as a guide to his behavior. If his behavior does not come up to standard, he feels guilty, ashamed, or both. As Ausubel has said, *guilt* is a "special kind of negative self-evaluation which occurs when an individual acknowledges that his behavior is at variance with a given moral value to which he feels obligated to conform" (11). Before guilt can develop, however, a person must *first* accept certain standards of right and wrong and of good and bad as his own; *second,* he must accept the obligation of regulating his behavior to conform to whatever standards he has thus adopted and must feel accountable for lapses from these standards; and *third,* he must possess sufficient self-critical ability to recognize that a discrepancy between his behavior and his internalized values has occurred (11).

Shame, by contrast, is an "unpleasant emotional reaction of an individual to an actual or presumed negative judgment of himself by others resulting in self-depreciation vis-a-vis the group." It can be nonmoral, as when a person commits a breach of propriety and is embarrassed, or moral, as when a person is unfavorably judged by others because his behavior has fallen below their moral standards. *Shame relies on external sanctions alone, though it may be accompanied by guilt. Guilt relies on both internal and external sanctions* (11, 55).

In true morality, guilt must be present. The person must conform to the mores of the group through inner-directed standards rather than outer-directed standards (6). As Ausubel has explained, "Guilt is one of the most important psychological mechanisms through which an individual becomes socialized in the ways of his culture. It is also an important instrument for cultural survival since it constitutes a most efficient watchdog within each individual, serving to keep his behavior compatible with the moral values of the society in which he lives" (11). If a child felt no guilt, he would have little motivation to conform to social expectations.

One cannot watch a child constantly to shame him into conformity, nor can one force a child to conform except through threats of severe punishment. In true morality, guilt serves the important role of an "internalized watchdog" (11). How much emotional stress the child will experience and whether it will take the form of guilt or shame or both will be determined largely by the type of moral code the child learns and the way in which he learns it (6). If training is very authoritarian, the child's conscience is likely to become too rigid. Intense feelings of guilt and anxiety will then militate against good adjustments and lead to unhappiness. To forestall this, the child should be encouraged to develop tolerance for minor weaknesses in himself and in others. Undeveloped feelings of guilt, by contrast, will deter the development of conscience (94, 100).

Variations in Internal and Environmental Controls. At every age, there are marked individual differences in the degree to which a person's acts are controlled by conscience or by environmental pressures. This is not entirely due to differences in opportunity to develop internal controls, as is shown by the fact that some people from the best environments lack the "inner guiding light," while some from the poorest environments have well-developed consciences and behave in a manner that suggests that they are "insulated" from the pressures of their environment to behave in an immoral fashion.

When a conflict occurs between social codes and a person's impulses, the *morally mature* person knows how to handle the conflict to his satisfaction and to the satisfaction of the group. The *immature person,* by contrast, allows his impulses to control his behavior unless he is intimidated by the social pressures of the group (4). The person who develops a morally mature approach to conflict situations has been conditioned to feel anxious and guilty if he allows his impulses to dominate. As a rule, people with *extroverted personality* patterns are more susceptible to social approval and are therefore more easily conditioned to anxiety in conflict situations than those who are introverted (11).

In a study of "good boys" in a delinquency area, it was found that those who were "insulated" from the mores of their social group had developed internalized law-abiding norms because of favorable home training and the satisfaction they derived from their parents' affection. Those who were not "insulated" and whose behavior was regulated by environmental pressures rather than by internalized standards came mainly from homes where moral training was meager and where parent-child relationships were poor. As a result, they had little motivation to learn to control their behavior to satisfy group standards unless there was a threat of punishment (167).

In general, children from *middle-class* homes develop stronger consciences and develop them at earlier ages than children from the lower classes. What constellation of concepts and values the child's conscience will contain, however, and how strong or weak it will be will depend upon the type of *moral training* the child has had. This varies greatly within a social-class group, just as it does between social-class groups (25, 27, 77).

MORALITY IS LEARNED

At birth, the child has no conscience and no scale of values. Thus he is nonmoral, or unmoral. Before he can behave in a moral way, he must learn what the group to which he belongs believes to be right or wrong. He learns this primarily from the parent-child relationship, for the foundations of moral development are laid before the child comes in contact with the peer group (10, 31). What he learns at home will have a marked influence on the type of children he will select as playmates (38, 98, 100).

No child can be expected to develop a moral code alone. He must be taught the group's standards of right and wrong and must build up a desire to do what the group considers right because of anticipated social approval or reward (11, 77). Through contacts with others, especially with children and adults outside the home, he has an opportunity to see how they evaluate his behavior.

The lawmakers set the pattern for the moral behavior of the child. Parents and others who are responsible for guidance must then help him to learn to conform to this pattern. If the socially acceptable pattern of behavior is accompanied by satisfaction, it will be repeated and in time will become habitual (31).

Learning to behave in a socially approved manner is a long, slow process which extends into adolescence. It is one of the important developmental tasks of childhood. Before the child enters school, he is expected to distinguish right from wrong in simple situations and to lay the foundations for the development of a conscience; before

childhood is over, he is expected to develop a scale of values and a conscience to guide him when he must make a moral choice (74, 139).

With age, the child becomes increasingly aware that he is expected to conform to rules and regulations and to overcome his antisocial behavior. Middle-class children, as a rule, learn to conform earlier than lower- or upper-class children. Variations in moral codes, however, slow down learning. If there is a conflict between the home code and that of his peers, the child may substitute the code of his peers for that learned in the home (37, 39, 69).

Phases of Moral Development. If true morality is to be attained, moral development must take place in two separate and distinct phases: (*1*) *the development of moral behavior,* and (*2*) *the development of moral concepts.* Moral knowledge does not guarantee moral conduct because the child's behavior is motivated by factors other than knowledge. Social pressures, how the child feels about himself and the way he is treated by his family and peers, his desires at the moment, and many other factors influence how he will behave when a choice must be made. Studies of honesty have revealed correlations of approximately .25 between moral knowledge and conduct (98).

DEVELOPMENT OF MORAL BEHAVIOR

The child can learn to behave in a socially approved manner through trial and error, through direct teaching, or through identification. Of the three, the last two—direct teaching and identification—are not only the best methods but also the most widely used. Trial-and-error learning in any area is time- and energy-consuming, and the end results are often far from satisfactory.

Direct Teaching. The whole purpose of discipline is to teach the child what is right and to pressure him to act as society expects. If a positive kind of discipline is used and if it is used consistently, ethical conduct sooner or later becomes habitual. When praise, social approval and reward are associated with socially desirable behavior, ethical conduct is learned more quickly than it otherwise would be (55, 83).

Studies have revealed that learning to behave in a socially acceptable manner follows the same laws as all other forms of learning. The child must *first learn to make correct specific responses in specific situations.* Should the standards learned in the home, the school, and the play group all agree, it will be easy for the child to see the similarity and thus, in time, to *develop abstract concepts* of right and wrong. If they differ from one situation to another, the child is confused and wonders why he is punished for an act which in another situation was ignored or looked upon as socially acceptable (166, 202).

Of even more serious consequence, a condition of this sort makes it impossible for the child to develop moral concepts that will hold for the same act in different situations. If the child is permitted to sneak cake from the cake box which he has been told not to touch, is it surprising that he is confused when he is punished for taking pencils from other children's desks at school? Stealing should be regarded as wrong in every situation and should be punished consistently if the child is to learn to behave in accordance with the codes of adult society.

Transfer-of-training experiments have shown that transfer comes when the objective aspects of situations are similar. When they are different, it is questionable whether transfer will take place. Will the child who learns not to take money from a pocketbook, for example, transfer this learning and know that he must not take money from cash registers? The objective features of the two situations are different, and consequently the child may not see the common features of the two, which are so obvious to an adult.

Moral training should therefore involve teaching the child to look for *common features of apparently different situations.* By eight or ten years of age, the child can be taught that it is wrong to take money belonging to other people, whether it comes from their pocketbooks, from their desks or bureau drawers, or from a cash register. In this way moral training can lead to the development of moral concepts of a general rather than of a specific sort (149, 214).

Identification. In identification, the child takes over the values of another and models his behavior after the behavior of that person. Identification may accompany learning through direct teaching—discipline. The child learns to do what the adult does as well as what the adult tells him to do. When a child identifies with a person he admires, without any pressure or direct teaching involved, the child will voluntarily imitate the patterns of behavior he observes in that person (116, 187).

Discipline without some identification is less effective than discipline with identification, especially for young children; their limited understanding makes it difficult for them to know why they are expected to do certain things, and, as a result, they may lack motivation to do them (119). As Landreth has pointed out, "Where there is no identification, parental admonitions are probably sounding brass and tinkling cymbals" (113).

Because the child gives his emotional allegiance to different people at different ages, there are shifts in the patterns of moral behavior he imitates. In the preschool years, his identification is with a parent or an older sibling, usually of the same sex as he; later, it is with a teacher or a recreational leader; and still later, with a member of the peer group. Children frequently identify with a character in a book, in a movie, on the television screen, or even in the comics. Identification with fictional characters can be detrimental to the child's development of healthy moral behavior. From such identification, the child can develop an "exalted belief in his own capacity to destroy tradition, flout morals, and reject qualities of discipline that have been historically established and have through the ages withstood the test of application. Clearly the youngster can develop out of the experiences the point of view that he is a law unto himself, that his wishes are superior to the demands of society" (122).

Identification as a source of learning moral behavior becomes increasingly important as children grow older and rebel against discipline in the home and school. Having someone with whom to identify fills the gap and provides the anchorage necessary to the development of wholesome moral behavior (66, 107). If the child identifies with gang members whose moral behavior conforms to social expectations, his desire for social acceptance will motivate him to pattern his behavior along the lines dictated by the group. Studies of the effects of parental role models on criminality have revealed that parental rejection and deviant parental models both lead to criminality. Parental rejection, however, plays the stronger role because it deprives the child of a stable source of identification (39, 136).

The type of person with whom the child identifies will have a marked influence on the type of moral behavior he learns, especially during the early, formative years. At that time, the parent and teacher are generally the sources of identification. Consequently, if they behave in a morally approved manner, the child will lay a healthy foundation of morality which will not be easily shaken later, should he identify with fictional characters who seem "romantic" but whose behavior does not always coincide with the moral principles he learned earlier. As Havighurst has stressed, from studying the influences of identification, "The inference is clear that schools, churches, and youth-serving agencies influence the ideals of youth as much or more through the presence and behavior of teachers, clergy and youth-group leaders as through their verbal teachings" (74).

DEVELOPMENT OF MORAL CONCEPTS

The second phase of moral development consists of the learning of moral concepts, or the principles of right and wrong, in an abstract, verbal form. This, of course, is too advanced for a young child. It is therefore

Through training and example the child becomes increasingly aware that there is a distinct code of appropriate behavior, even in sports and games. (Standard Oil Co., N.J.)

necessary to wait until the child has the mental capacity to generalize and transfer a principle of conduct from one situation to another. Language skills make this easier because concepts are *derived from concrete cases*. Nevertheless, the child must be mentally mature enough to see the relationship between an abstract principle and concrete cases and to associate these with memory images of specific situations. The ability to relate sets of rules systematically to different situations develops gradually as the child's experiences increase (194).

Learning what concepts the group approves is relatively easy if the child has good discipline and a good model to identify with. Learning to control his behavior to conform to these concepts is harder because he is expected to assume the responsibility himself instead of relying on others. If he is not strongly motivated to do so, there will be a discrepancy between his moral knowledge and his behavior; he will *know* what he is expected to do, but he will not always do it.

Pattern of Concept Development. It has been found that a relationship exists between the development of moral concepts and the child's mental, social, emotional, and cultural development. In the development of unselfishness, for example, a six-stage pattern has been noted. These stages are egocentrism, characterized by a purely selfish attitude; sociocentrism, or obedience to moral and religious rules and customs; awareness of social reactions, or fear of social disapproval; superficial reciprocity, based on feelings of guilt if sharing is not equal; deeper and enlarged reciprocity, based on the desire to maintain good relations with one's friends; altruism, or desire to make sacrifices for others; and, finally, a sense of justice, based on the belief that it is right to be unselfish and wrong to be selfish (201).

Similarly, a pattern has been found in the development of concepts of justice regarding one's person. When asked, "What should be done if someone punches you?" young children said they would appeal to a person in authority such as a parent or teacher, while older children said they would return the aggressive act. Toward the close of childhood, children perceive justice in terms of the motivation for the act and want to know the circumstances that gave rise to it. The older child's moral judgments are thus characterized by equity, while the young child judges an act on its surface value (50).

Specific to General Concepts. Concepts are at first specific and relate to the specific situations in which they were learned. As the child's capacity for comprehending relationships increases, his concepts of right and wrong in different though related situations merge. As a result, general concepts are gradually learned because the child is able to recognize a common element in a variety of situations. In order to do this, the child must have personal experiences with real situations. General concepts have little meaning if they are not associated with real experiences (74, 98).

The preschool child is incapable of abstract thinking. He defines "good behavior" in terms of specific acts, such as "obeying mother" or "helping mother," and "bad behavior" in terms of not doing what the mother wants or of saying "bad words." Up to the age of six or seven years, the child guides his behavior by specific moral concepts taught by the parents. By the time he is eight or nine, his concepts become more generalized. For example, "stealing is wrong" rather than it is "wrong to steal a ball" (194). At this age, he shows signs of trying to conform to the concepts approved by the group, and by the time he is ten years old, he considers the group's concepts a guide to his behavior, even when they conflict with those taught in the home (24).

Generalized moral concepts which reflect social values are known as *moral values.* The child's moral values change as he associates with more people and with people whose values differ from those of his parents. By the time a child is twelve years old, however, his moral values should begin to show some stability. His concepts of goodness and of "good behavior," for example, are no longer related simply to gratification, but to postponement of gratification and future rewards. As the child grows older and peer recognition becomes more valuable to him than adult recognition, he measures "goodness" in terms of what his peers believe it to be (48, 118, 144).

In spite of variations in moral values between adults and children and between different individuals within the same age groups, the child gradually accepts adult moral values and coordinates them with his moral concepts (213). By adolescence, his moral code is fairly well formed, though it is still open to change if subjected to strong environmental pressures. Changes usually involve a shift in emphasis, and shift is generally in the *direction of conventional morality,* to conform to the moral code of adult society (157).

Difficulties in Learning Moral Concepts.
Learning the moral values of the social group takes time, just as learning specific moral concepts does, and it is made difficult for the child by a number of factors, the most important of which are discussed below:

1. The Child's Intellectual Development.
A low level of intelligence makes it difficult for the child to understand the teaching of moral concepts and to perceive the situations in which they apply. A short attention span, which is characteristic of children of lower levels of intelligence, is related to impulsiveness and restless behavior. Poor reasoning, likewise characteristic of such children, results in lack of foresight and planning, which, if combined with impulsiveness, is likely to lead to behavior that violates the mores of the group.

This does not mean that a low level of intelligence is *always* the cause of immoral behavior. It does mean, however, that those whose intellectual capacities are limited find it difficult to learn the moral concepts of the group and to apply them to specific situations without constant guidance and control. As a result, the less intelligent child is more likely to meet his problems with methods that do not conform to the mores of the group than the more intelligent child. In a difficult classroom assignment, cheating offers the less able student a means of solving a difficulty which a brighter student may not have. But even though the brighter student may not feel a need to cheat, he may find it easier to cheat than to be honest, especially if cheating has the stamp of approval of the peer group (22, 147).

2. Type of Teaching. In the teaching of moral concepts, adults often tell the child what is "wrong" and what he should not do rather than what is "right" and what he should do. As a result, children are more certain of what they should not do than of what they should do in a situation where a moral decision must be made. Because too much emphasis is placed on the negative aspect of moral codes and too little on the positive, the "path to goodness is left highly undefined for the child" (50). In their concepts of justice, for example, children are often perplexed about what is socially acceptable behavior when a person attacks them because they have been taught not to be aggressive but have not been taught to put up a rightful self-defense (50).

3. Changes in Social Values. Because the child's moral values reflect social values, they change if the social values change. If parents teach a young child that smoking is wrong, he will probably change his concept about smoking when he grows older and discovers that his friends do not hold this concept. On the other hand, if parents bribe a child to eat, to go to bed, or to behave when there is company, he will learn to think that bribery is all right. In his contacts with people outside the home, however, he will discover that bribery is considered wrong, and he will revise his concept accordingly (157, 162). Changes in concepts of right and wrong are shown in Figure 12–1.

4. Different Moral Codes. In learning moral concepts, the child is confused by the fact that there is not one moral code accepted by all people. Even though all may accept certain general moral concepts, he learns that they place more emphasis on some than on others. People who come from the lower socioeconomic groups tend to be arbitrary and authoritarian in their interpretation of moral concepts, while those from upper-middle- and upper-class backgrounds distinguish between degrees of seriousness of an act, such as cheating (109). When the child perceives inconsistencies between what parents and teachers tell him he should do and what they themselves do, it adds still further to his confusion about what is "right" and what is "wrong."

5. Variation with Different Situations. One of the greatest difficulties the child meets in learning moral concepts comes from the fact that what is right in one situation may be

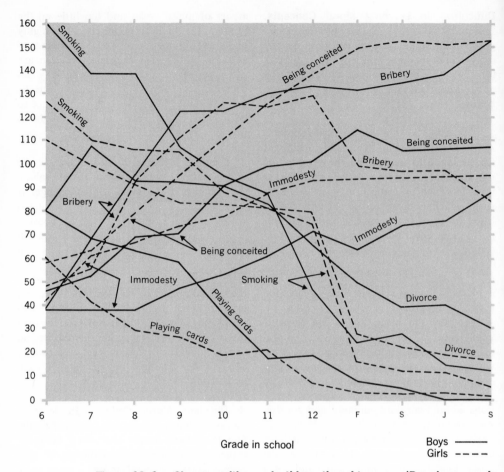

Figure 12–1. Changes with age in things thought wrong. (Based on unpublished data of S. L. Pressey. Adapted from S. L. Pressey and R. G. Kuhlen, *Psychological development through the life span*, Harper & Row, 1957. Used by permission.)

wrong in another (147, 201). These subtle differences are very difficult for him to comprehend. For instance, why is it wrong for him to take a cookie from a box in a store when he is permitted to help himself at the cookie jar at home? Likewise, why is it wrong to take money that has been put in his bank when it is all right to use money from his pocketbook? If his classmates ask for help on homework or a test, he finds it difficult to understand how this can be interpreted as "cheating" when he has been taught to share what he has with others. If

it is right to share his toys, for example, why is it wrong to share his school work?

6. Conflict with Social Pressures. Another source of confusion is the conflict that sometimes arises between concepts and social pressures. If a child learns that it is "wrong" to fight and he also learns that he will be considered a "sissy" if he does not fight back when someone attacks him, either he will follow the moral code and be labeled a "sissy," or he will violate the code and be considered a "regular boy" (108).

Effects of Confusion. Regardless of what has given rise to it, confusion in moral concepts has three serious effects. First, confusion *slows down the learning process.* When there is a conflict between the code of the home and that of the peer group, the child must decide which to follow. If his decision is in favor of the code of the peer group, he will have to relearn at least part of the code he learned at home; if it is in favor of the home code, he will try to reconcile the two by modifying each (37, 97).

The second effect of confusion is that it leads the child to *question the fairness* of the concepts. A very young child sees no conflict between the rules his parents establish and those that govern the lives of other children; he may try to evade the home rules and rebel against adult authority, but he does not question the justice of this authority. As his social horizons broaden and he discovers that his friends are sometimes governed by moral concepts that differ from his, however, he will question the fairness of the concepts he is expected to follow. Rebellion against moral concepts on the basis of their fairness generally reaches its peak during the gang age and extends into adolescence (39, 193).

The third and most serious effect of confusion in moral concepts is its *impact on moral decisions.* It is difficult for a child or anyone else to know what decision to make when there is confusion about what is right and what the group expects of him. As long as the child is young and the decision is made for him by parents, teachers, or other adults in authority, this is not a serious problem. But, as he grows older and is expected to have an internalized code of morality, he must make the decision without adult help. The decision he makes will then be influenced partly by the value the group places on different types of behavior and partly by what is more important to him personally. If the group values honesty more highly than cheating, the child will act in accordance with this guideline. By doing so, he will hope to win group approval. On the other hand, if the peer group regards neatness as a characteristic of a "sissy" while parents regard it as an essential of good training, the boy who prefers peer approval to adult approval will conform to group expectations even though his parents may punish him for violating their code.

Not only is the child expected to choose between conflicting behavioral potentials those which will win group approval, but he also is expected to learn to "say 'No' and 'Don't' to himself and to refrain from prohibited acts" (59). This should not imply that the child can become a law unto himself and base his decisions solely on his own personal wishes. It means that his decisions must be guided by knowledge of what is best for the group and what the group expects of him. In addition, he is expected to "learn to regulate his personal desires and compulsions so that, when a situational conflict arises, he does what he ought to do rather than what he wants to do" (80).

When a conflict arises between the moral values of one social group and another, the child must decide which moral code he prefers to follow and then be prepared to accept the punishment and rejection of the other social group whose moral code he has violated (144). The more anxious a child is for group acceptance, the more "group-linked" he will be in his moral decisions when he is with the group. He may, however, act differently when he is away from the group or when he feels that the group will not learn of his behavior. Many children do things with their gangs that they would not do if they were alone in order to maintain their status in the group (34, 39).

FACTORS INFLUENCING MORAL DEVELOPMENT

The moral development of children is determined to a large extent by their environment. Of the many environmental factors affecting morality, the following are most important:

The Family. Parents and other family members influence the child in four distinct ways: (*1*) The family's behavior serves as a model for the child to imitate. (2) By the use of approval or disapproval, reward or punishment, the family teaches the child to behave in a socially desirable manner. (3) By planning the punishment to fit the misdeed, the family teaches the child to recognize the severity of his wrongdoing. (4) The family does much to motivate the child to do right (49, 100, 118, 145).

Under normal conditions a child looks up to and admires his parents, relatives, and older brothers and sisters. If the conduct of these individuals is desirable, the child will accept it as standard and behave in a manner approved of by the members of his social group. When discipline is reasonable and consistent, the child will develop moral competence in the form of self-control and self-direction. Even a poor parental model, however, can be compensated for if the child has a warm and close relationship with his parents, especially with the mother (136).

If family relationships are good, the child will be more influenced by his parents than by anyone else. Nonetheless, a healthy parent-child relationship may not be adequate to foster good moral development if the parents are unable to communicate successfully with the child. Clear communication ensures that the child will know what he is expected to do and encourages him to want to do it. Poor communication between parent and child, characteristic of the latter years of childhood, has the opposite effect. At this time, communication is not influenced by lack of verbal understanding on the child's part but by lack of emotional warmth between parent and child (99, 129).

When parent-child relationships are unfavorable or when the child's home is broken by divorce, separation, or death, the quality of the child's moral behavior deteriorates, and his attitude toward misbehavior changes. Unfavorable parent-child relationships, often dating from the child's early days, are frequently reflected in such misdemeanors as truancy, dishonesty, destructiveness, and— as the child grows older—juvenile delinquency (65, 190).

The *socioeconomic status* of the family plays an important role in the moral devel-

opment of the child. This is illustrated in the case of honesty in Figure 12–2. While it is true that children from all socioeconomic levels steal, lie, and become truants, such behavior is more common among children of the lower socioeconomic groups (147). Because the socioeconomic status of the family establishes the developmental background of the child, it determines what moral values he will learn and what patterns of moral behavior will be available for him to imitate (179). Middle-class parents punish children mainly for "swiping," using "ugly" language, losing their tempers, fighting with siblings, and being disobedient; lower-class parents punish more for aggressiveness which might lead to harm to others, use of tabooed language, and defiance (109, 160).

Playmates. Even among nursery-school children, the influence of companions is powerful enough to cause the children to deviate from parental attitudes toward aggression. With the development of "group feeling" comes an increasing independence of adult rules, accompanied by an increase in the influence of group authority. The influence of the child's companions is greatest when they are actually with him and in a position to influence his behavior by example, suggestion, and favorable or unfavorable reaction to his attitudes and behavior (39). Group influence is greatest when the group is small and tightly knit.

If the child is to be an accepted member of the peer group, he must accept the moral values of the group and pattern his behavior along the lines it approves, even though they may be different from the standards set by the home. If a child refuses to help a friend with his homework or in an examination, he may find that the peer group will reject him because of his "disloyalty" to the gang (77).

School. The relationship the child has with his teacher and his classmates has a marked influence on his behavior. If he causes trouble in the classroom, the pupil-teacher relationship will be affected adversely (88, 192). Similarly, if the teacher does not like the pupil, or if his behavior falls below her moral standards, she may have such an unfavorable effect on him that he will have little motivation to try to conform to teacher-approved standards (146).

Because most teachers come from middle-class homes, there is a tendency to emphasize middle-class moral values in the school. For middle-class pupils, the school thus serves to reinforce home training. Children from the lower classes, on the other hand, sometimes find school and home values in conflict. While some accept the new values learned at school, others are likely to be confused. If the child fails to win peer acceptance at school, he is likely to turn against the school and reject the moral concepts it teaches (98).

An authoritarian teacher may put such fear into a child that he comes to fear not only the teacher but school work and grades as well. In time, this feeling may develop into a generalized fear and dislike of school —an unfavorable attitude which militates against good behavior. Once such an atti-

tude has developed, it is not likely to change until the child is placed under the influence of a more democratic teacher (8, 117).

In determining the degree of classroom dishonesty, the pupil-teacher relationship is more influential than the formal educational philosophy of the school (10). The personality of the teacher and the way she handles the classroom situation have more impact than the emphasis placed on character and citizenship training. If moral training in the school is to be effective, there must be not only good pupil-teacher relationships but also opportunities to discuss moral concepts and put them into practice in actual situations (98, 146).

A good relationship with classmates whose moral values are similar to those the child learned at home will help to reinforce these values; a good relationship with children whose moral values differ from those he learned at home will motivate him to reject family values in favor of peer values. When children from lower-class homes are rejected by their middle-class classmates, they

Figure 12–2. Contrasting trends of honest behavior and consistently honest behavior. Children from the superior economic group (Y) become more honest and more consistently honest with age; children from the underprivileged group become more deceptive and more consistently deceptive with age. (Based on data from H. Hartshorne, M. A. May, and F. K. Shuttleworth, *Studies in the organization of character*, Macmillan, 1930. From F. K. Shuttleworth, The adolescent period: a graphic atlas, *Monogr. Soc. Res. Child Develpm.*, 1949, 14, No. 1. Used by permission.)

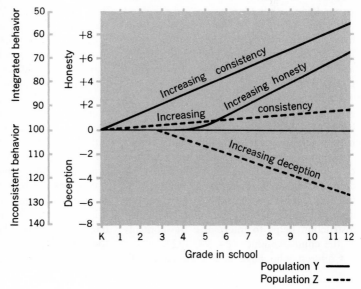

often turn to misbehavior as a way of gaining status. Affiliating with other children who refuse to act according to approved school standards not only gives them the companionship they crave but also enables them to retaliate against the school, their teacher, and their classmates (39).

Religious Instruction. Religious instruction influences the child's moral development, first, by shaping his ideas about the importance of specific values and ideals and, second, by reinforcing the moral code he has learned by "divine sanctions"—the will of God and the role of Heaven and Hell. From home, Sunday school, or church instruction, the child learns to connect certain ideas of good and bad, right and wrong, with the concept of God: God lays down certain rules and then punishes those who break the rules. The child believes that wrongdoing will be punished in this life as well as in the life after death. He is often taught that God is "watching him" and "keeping a record" of his misdeeds. Some children are threatened with eternal punishment in Hell if they misbehave and are given graphic descriptions of what this punishment will consist of. While many religions emphasize God's reward for good behavior —a happy life in Heaven after death—the emphasis is usually on punishment for wrongdoing rather than on reward for good behavior. The use of religion to enforce moral codes differs from social enforcement in that religion stresses God's disapproval and future punishment rather than present punishment (84).

Children who have been subjected to religious instruction of this type generally begin to doubt some of the religious teachings at adolescence. With this doubt comes rejection of some of the beliefs and rejection of some of the religious sanctions. Such children, for example, continue to believe that religion *teaches* people how to be good but does not *make* them good. Good religious instruction helps to internalize the controls of the child's conduct (84, 98, 132).

Children who have had wholesome religious experiences, without too much emphasis on punishment after death, have moral values and standards of behavior more in keeping with those approved by the social group than children whose religious instruction has been more limited or of an unwholesome type. Children who attend Sunday school or church, for example, cheat less and are more honest in other respects than children whose attendance is limited (98, 132). Delinquents, on the other hand, have generally been found to have a limited religious education or a religious education with excessive emphasis on punishment after death (65, 182, 206).

Recreational Activities. From contact with other children, the child learns how to play fairly, to cooperate, and to do things that will help, not harm, others (24). He discovers that the childish method of revenge —"an eye for an eye" or its mathematical equivalent—does not win social approval. He learns to judge the deeds of others objectively, trying to discover the underlying reasons for them, in place of accepting reciprocity as a justice principle (50).

Competitive athletics, which are so popular in late childhood, offer splendid opportunities for moral training. Any behavior that does not measure up to the moral code of good sportsmanship will not be tolerated. Too much emphasis on winning, however, encourages the player to cheat because if he plays fairly and loses, he feels inferior (39).

On the assumption that a child's moral standards are influenced by his reading, parents and teachers encourage children to read books that will contribute to the establishment of desirable moral concepts and acceptable patterns of behavior. The good influence of books, however, is often counteracted by the child's reading of comics, especially those stressing crime and horror (see pages 466 to 468 for a discussion of the influence of comics). Concentration on the crime reports in newspapers can be as damaging to the child's moral concepts as too much comic-book reading (118, 145).

Because children attend movies more and

more frequently as they grow older and because they tend to accept uncritically what they see on the screen, movies have a marked effect on the child's moral values. They help to mold his outlook on life, to create a desire for riches and luxury, and to suggest the ease of crime. Movies can have a detrimental effect on the child's moral behavior, but this is not so likely to happen among well-adjusted children as among those who are less well adjusted.

Intelligence. The relationship between intelligence and morality is not so important as was previously believed. It is true that the child must be able to distinguish between right and wrong and to foresee the consequences of his acts, but this does not necessarily require intelligence of a superior level. It has been found that the correlation between honesty scores and intelligence among school children is .50. This would suggest that there was little more than a chance relationship between intelligence and honesty in the group studied (98).

Studies of very bright children have revealed that they are superior to children of average intelligence in honesty, truthfulness, and similar moral traits. They are much less likely to cheat in school than the less bright, mainly because they have no need to do so to be at the top of the class. Were they to be placed in a threat situation, as their less bright classmates are, they might be tempted to cheat, but such situations are unlikely to occur for them.

Occasionally, very bright children have weak moral characteristics, and some even develop into juvenile delinquents. The number of juvenile delinquents with very high IQ's, however, is very small in comparison with the number with lower intelligence. Both in the school and in the home, very bright children often misbehave, intentionally breaking rules and defying authority. This kind of behavior is not due to ignorance but rather to boredom and resentment against rules which they regard as unfair (36, 120). In spite of occasional exceptions, intelligent children know that "right conduct is simply intelligent conduct" and that it is to their personal advantage to act as the group expects them to act (211).

Sex. There is no evidence that boys and girls differ in morality as a result of native factors, nor is there evidence that they differ if they receive similar moral training (50). On the other hand, as Jones has pointed out, "Our culture does not expect the same behavior patterns of girls that it expects of boys, and the training that it gives them is different" (98).

Because social acceptance and avoidance of social disapproval mean more to girls and are often harder for them to achieve, they tell more lies of a social type than boys. Furthermore, girls tend to lie to win the favor of others more than boys do. Dishonesty in social situations, as in cheating in a "party test," has also been found to be greater among girls. In other situations, cheating is no more common among girls than among boys. At every age, but especially in late childhood and adolescence, boys are more rebellious against discipline than girls and are less willing to conform to rules, regardless of whether or not they consider them fair (81, 200). This is illustrated in Figure 12–3.

Because of their rebellious attitudes, boys misbehave more in school and at home than girls do (53). As has already been stressed, mothers tend to be lenient in the discipline of their sons, and as mothers do most of the disciplining of children, boys discover early that they can defy rules and avoid punishment more easily than girls (35, 42). They likewise discover that their teachers, most of whom are women, are lenient toward them and punish them less than they punish girls for the same misbehavior (117, 138).

Furthermore, in the peer group, defiance of authority is more highly valued by boys. The boy who dares to break rules is regarded as "masculine." Many boys misbehave in order to win peer approval and acceptance. As they grow older, boys are more likely to become delinquent than girls; once again, this often stems from desire to

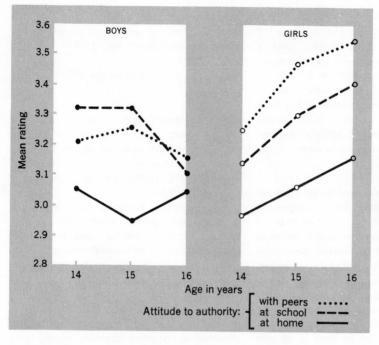

Figure 12–3. Sex differences in conformity to rules as the child approaches adolescence. (Adapted from E. Tuma and N. Livson, Family socioeconomic status and adolescent attitudes to authority, *Child Develpm.*, 1960, 31, 386–399. Used by permission.)

win peer approval. It is not, of course, the only reason for greater delinquency among boys, but it is an important factor (212).

Methods of Learning Moral Values. How the child develops his moral concepts will have a very important influence on his motivation to act in accordance with them. Like all concepts, moral concepts have a strong emotional weighting. If this weighting is favorable, it will serve as a positive motivation, and vice versa. Because the methods used to teach moral concepts and the effect these methods have on the child's attitudes are closely related to discipline, these matters will be discussed in detail in the following section.

DISCIPLINE

Discipline is a "process of training and learning that fosters growth and development." It comes from the same word as "disciple"—one who learns or voluntarily follows a leader. The parents and teachers are the leaders, and the child is the disciple who learns from them the ways of life that lead to usefulness and happiness. Discipline is thus society's way of teaching the child the moral concepts and the moral behavior approved by the group (48).

The goal of all discipline is to mold the child so that he will be able to adjust to the traditional roles prescribed by the cultural group with which he is identified. Because there is no single cultural pattern, however, there is no overall philosophy of child training to influence the disciplinary methods used. Thus there are wide variations in the specific methods used within one cultural group, even though all aim to produce the same end result (176, 213).

SOCIAL ATTITUDES TOWARD DISCIPLINE

As DuBois has pointed out:

[From] time immemorial, discipline has been regarded as an essential ingredient of man's life. Experience has demonstrated that objectives can be achieved and individuals can be happy only if human energies are directed in an orderly fashion. Since a person's desires often conflict with the desires of others, society has set up regulations for the common good to which each member of the group must adhere or suffer a penalty (48).

The methods of discipline used to achieve the common good, however, will depend upon the socially accepted philosophies of the nature of man and the beliefs of the group relating to supernatural powers. Where people believe that sinfulness is innate, society sanctions cruel and punitive methods of discipline (48). Where they believe in the malevolence of the supernatural world, cruel punishment is also used, and emphasis is placed on rigid training. By contrast, groups believing in the benevolence of the supernatural world favor more relaxed forms of discipline with less emphasis on punishment (45, 111).

In recent years, there has been a general relaxing of punitive methods of discipline. In addition, there has been a growing belief that wrong behavior is the result of the child's training rather than of innate sinfulness. This transition has led to the development of two conflicting concepts of discipline, the "negative" and the "positive" concepts. According to the negative concept, discipline means control by *external* authority, usually arbitrarily applied. It is a form of restraint through distasteful or painful means. This is synonymous with punishment. Punishment does not, however, always weaken the individual's tendencies to act in a socially disapproved manner, nor does it give assurance that the abandoned activity will be replaced by more acceptable behavior.

The positive concept of discipline is synonymous with education and counseling in that it emphasizes *inner* growth—self-discipline and self-control. This, in turn, leads to motivation from within. Negative discipline forces immaturity on the individual, while positive discipline encourages maturity. Since the principal function of discipline is to teach the easy acceptance of needful restraint and to help direct the child's energies into useful and socially acceptable channels, positive discipline will achieve this end more successfully than negative discipline (16, 60).

NEED FOR DISCIPLINE

There has never been a time when it was believed that a child did not need discipline, but there have been changes in attitudes toward the *reasons for needing discipline*. In the past, it was believed that a child needed discipline because society required him to behave in a certain way and would tolerate no deviations from the approved pattern. Now it is recognized that the child needs discipline if he is to be a happy, well-adjusted person. As Vincent and Martin have said, "Everyone needs discipline (rules of conduct) in order to adjust his needs and desires to those of others, and in order to keep the affection and approval of people around him" (203).

The child needs the steadying influence of discipline to counterbalance the feeling of insecurity that his constantly changing values give him. Furthermore, discipline helps him to direct his energies into approved channels and to behave in an approved manner (125, 175).

As Geisel has pointed out:

The infant comes among us as a little savage, and the first fifteen years of his life are in a very real sense the disciplinary years, for his growing-up is really a process of learning to do right things at the right time, in the right place, and meaningfully. . . . Children do not characteristically yearn to become civilized. They do not wish to be ordered, trained, disciplined. . . . As a rule, they do not yearn to live orderly lives. They want to be free to make their own decisions. . . . But they are generally reluctant to make their decisions on the basis of the greatest good to the greatest number. In short, they are reluctant to discipline themselves (62).

Discipline fills certain needs for a child and thus adds to his happiness and adjustments:

1. Discipline gives the child a feeling of security by telling him how far he can go and what he may or may not do.

2. By living according to certain standards, the child is able to avoid frequent feelings of guilt. From time to time, he is bound to do something wrong and feel guilty, but frequent feelings of guilt lead to unhappiness and poor adjustments.

3. When a child does the right thing, it is possible for adults to praise him. Praise is interpreted as love, while scolding and disapproval are interpreted as rejection. The child needs love to develop successfully.

4. Discipline serves as an ego-bolstering motivation; it encourages the child to accomplish what is required of him.

5. Discipline helps the child to develop a conscience—the "internalized voice" that guides him in making choices of his own (62, 203).

Because discipline is a developmental need of every child, the child who is subjected to irregular and sporadic discipline cannot develop into a happy, well-adjusted person. No child is experienced enough to know how to discipline himself, but with adult help, he can learn to behave in a socially approved manner and eventually learn self-discipline. Adults can set an example of willing acceptance of discipline. They can time discipline properly; it is a waste of time to try to teach a child to do something before he is capable of understanding the reason for it. By explaining rules to the child and by praising him for following them, adults can help the child to understand the purpose and benefits of discipline (35, 176).

Variations in Need for Discipline. Because children differ in their *hereditary makeup* and in their *rate of maturation,* discipline that is developmentally appropriate for one child may not be appropriate for another of the same age. A few kind words, for example, may teach one child not to play with matches, while another of the same age may not understand the words used in the prohibition and may need a tap on the fingers to make him understand (203). Older chil-

dren need a different kind of discipline. Instead of being told what to do and what not to do, they need to have an explanation of why certain forms of behavior are acceptable and others are not. This helps the child to broaden his moral concepts and motivates him to do what is expected (83).

The need for discipline also varies according to the *time of day.* For three-year-olds, the peak periods for discipline usually come at 8 A.M., noon, and 6 P.M.; for six-year-olds, the peak period is 4 P.M.; and for nine-year-olds, noon. Discipline is most likely to be needed in connection with routine activities, such as eating, going to bed, or preparing for school; it is least needed when the child is free to play as he chooses (35). Times of the day when discipline is most often needed are shown in Figure 12–4.

Variations in the need for discipline are greatly influenced by such factors as loss of sleep, poor health, and special events that interfere with a child's usual routine. When the child is tired, for example, his behavior is likely to deteriorate. The activity in which the child is engaged likewise affects the need for discipline; if the child dawdles over a meal or resists going to sleep, there is more need for discipline than if he is playing with his toys.

Finally, the need for discipline varies on *different days* of the week, with weekends and Mondays the usual times for increased discipline. Normally, older children need discipline less often than younger children. It has been reported that three-year-olds are involved in disciplinary incidents, on the average, approximately once a day; six-year-olds, every other day; and nine-year-olds, every fourth day. The reason for this decline is that as the child grows older, he can communicate better and understand what is expected of him (35).

ESSENTIALS IN DISCIPLINE

Discipline consists primarily of habit formation and involves four essential principles: (*1*) The child must act in a desirable manner and eliminate undesirable behavior. He must

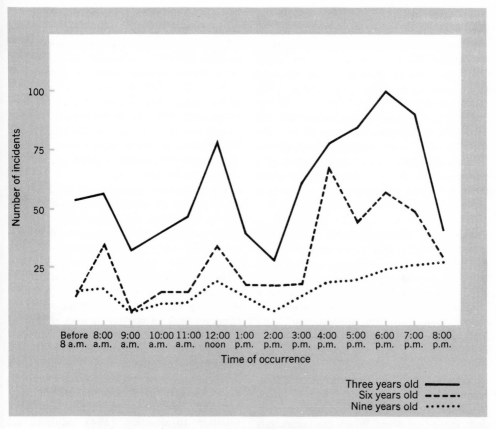

Figure 12–4. Frequency of discipline by the hour of occurrence and age of the child. (Adapted from E. Clifford, Discipline in the home: a controlled observational study of parental practices, *J. genet. Psychol.*, 1959, 95, 45–82. Used by permission.)

learn what is considered desirable and undesirable by the social group. (*2*) He must associate satisfaction with desirable acts and dissatisfaction with undesirable acts if he is to have the necessary motivation to repeat the desirable and refrain from the undesirable. (*3*) He must make the desirable act so automatic that he will, in time, repeat it without need of supervision. (*4*) He must learn to substitute desirable for undesirable behavior so that his needs will be as well met by the desirable as they previously were by the undesirable.

Every disciplinary method contains certain elements that help to fulfill these principles. The following elements are essential in any method of discipline.

Rules and Laws. Rules and laws serve two useful purposes in discipline. In the first place, they act as an *educational agency* to acquaint the child with the standards of conduct that are acceptable to the group. As Settlage has pointed out, "In setting limits for the child we foster the development of personality strength and in our decision as to what the limits shall be we communicate our personal and cultural value system" (175). The second purpose of rules is to *restrain undesirable behavior.* How many rules there will be will depend to some extent upon the size of the family and the disciplinary technique used. The more authoritarian the discipline, the more rules there will be. The number of rules likewise varies according to the activity. In most families there are more rules for play outdoors, for example, than for television watching (15).

If there were no rules, the child would do as he pleased; he would then find that the social group would not tolerate him. By the end of childhood, rules and laws should not be needed if discipline has been of the right sort. But since many children as well as adolescents and adults would quickly lapse into undesirable behavior without rules to guide them, rules and laws continue to serve as a preventative to antisocial behavior.

Consistency. Unless discipline is consistent, the child is at a loss to know what to do and whom to obey. In discussing the importance of consistency, Settlage has emphasized: "To set a limit is to act on a value judgment; and if one is not sure of what he values, then confusion, inconsistency, and ambivalence result" (175). Inconsistency in training slows down the learning process, while consistency speeds it up (1). In an experiment with nursery-school children, commands were given in pairs by two adults. When the commands were identical, the children tended to obey. When the commands were different and incompatible, the children sometimes vacillated between the activities, obeying one adult or the other or both in turn; more frequently, however, they obeyed neither adult (141). Among older children, the effects of inconsistency are even more serious. Either the children are confused and do not know what to do, or they lose respect for the disciplinarian and refuse to obey him (35, 164).

Severity or laxity of discipline, per se, is not as damaging as inconsistency. Studies have revealed, for example, that children who later became criminals had inconsistent discipline, while children who were subjected to severe discipline, if this was consistent, rarely developed into criminals (136).

The more consistent the discipline, the better adjusted and happier the child will be. This is shown in better integration of behavior and a more realistic approach to

life (134, 143). Inconsistent discipline, by contrast, leads to friction between child and adult. Not knowing exactly what is expected of him, the child does much as he pleases. As a result, he often develops patterns of behavior that fail to measure up to social expectations (16). Figure 12–5 shows how inconsistent behavior on the part of an adult affects the child. First-born children, it has been found, are more likely to be subjected to inconsistent discipline than second- or later-born children (115).

Far too often, parents and teachers are either unsure of what they want the child to do or unsure of what they should do to achieve the behavior they expect. Most parents—and many teachers as well—do not have a single pervasive philosophy about child training, nor are they consistent in the application of the method they generally use. They vary from leniency bordering on complete lack of control to such rigid control that the child is given little freedom of action (176). Those who are most restrictive or most permissive tend to be more consistent than those between these extremes; even the very strict and the very lenient, however, vary from time to time and from situation to situation (184). Middle-class mothers tend to be the least consistent disciplinarians; they are often strict about rules but then fail to follow through on their requirements (208).

Mothers tend to vacillate more in their discipline than fathers. There are many reasons for this; mothers must live with the child twenty-four hours a day, and they want to avoid unfavorable parent-child relationships; they are more understanding of the reasons for the child's behavior than fathers are; they judge the child by child standards, while fathers are more likely to judge him by adult standards; and, finally, severity is not included in the stereotype of the "loving and kind" mother, while it is a part of the cultural stereotype of the "good father." For all these reasons, mothers vacillate between doing what they want to do and what society expects them to do (93).

Studies of inconsistent mothers have shown that they usually have certain characteristics in common. They show ambivalent attitudes toward their children, fluctuating between hostility and concern about the children's welfare. Their behavior toward the child is inconsistent in that they threaten but fail to impose effective restrictions; they impose restrictions and then apologize, as if admitting they were wrong; or they impose restrictions on one occasion but not on another. They complain of their inability to get their children to obey them, and they rationalize their poor control over their children. These characteristics, for the most part, stem from feelings of guilt for having to restrict their children. The children soon sense this; they try to outwit their mothers, or they engage in antisocial behavior, feeling sure that they will not be punished if they handle the matter in such a way as to increase the mother's feelings of guilt. Should they provoke the mother's anger, she is likely to use punishment as a means of retaliation—not as a way of showing the child what he may not do. Thus, it is not real discipline but a way of expressing maternal anger (164).

Not only do parents vacillate between lenient and strict discipline, but they often use a trial-and-error approach to see what method works best. Within one disciplinary incident, it has been found that parents of three- and six-year-olds often use as many as seven different methods of control; they try emotional appeals, humor, appeals to the child's self-esteem, bribes and coaxing, ignoring the child's behavior, punishing him, and diverting his attention. Furthermore, most parents have no one consistent method of punishment. As Jackson has pointed out, "They do not threaten or scold or spank: rather, they are more likely to threaten *and* scold *and* spank" (93).

There are many *causes of inconsistency* in disciplining children. Fluctuation in the warmth of the parent-child relationship due to changes in the child's attitude toward his parents and his parents' attitudes toward him is one cause. When the relationship between parent and child is warm, discipline will be lenient, but when the relationship is strained, discipline will be severe (143).

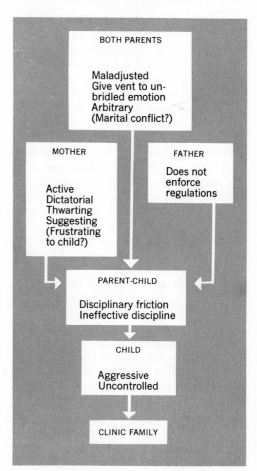

Figure 12–5. **Effects of inconsistent parental behavior on the child. (Adapted from W. C. Becker, D. R. Peterson, L. A. Hellmer, B. J. Shoemaker, and H. C. Quary, Factors in parental behavior and personality as related to problem behavior in children,** *J. consult. Psychol.,* **1959, 23, 107–118. Used by permission.)**

When the child tries to live up to parental expectations, parents are more lenient than when he makes little effort to do so (2, 204).

The satisfaction parents derive from their parental role likewise influences the consistency of discipline (195). Family conflicts about the best methods of discipline tend to undermine the disciplinarian's feeling of adequacy and lead to inconsistency in applying discipline. Many middle-class mothers today are confused by the conflicts they find between the recommendations made in parent-oriented literature and those made by members of their families (29, 106, 196).

Perhaps the most common cause of inconsistency comes from differences in concepts of discipline held by fathers and mothers. As Vincent and Martin have pointed out, "The most destructive pattern is the one in which two parents operate in the same home, one at one extreme, the other at the opposite extreme in discipline" (203). When there is disagreement between parents, they tend to settle upon a strict rather than a permissive position. Two reasons have been suggested for this: First, each parent feels that he should be stricter than he is; second, each fears that the other will be jealous or resentful if he seems to be more lenient toward the children (158).

While it is not essential that parents agree entirely about discipline, it is essential that they support one another in specific instances, such as giving permission to do something or withholding permission. Otherwise, the child will quickly learn to play one parent against the other and thus be able to do much as he pleases. Criticism of one parent by the other regarding the method of discipline used is even more serious than inconsistency.

If the criticism is not made in front of the child, it hurts the child indirectly by making the criticized parent feel insecure in his disciplinary role (142, 173). When made in front of the child, it hurts the child directly by weakening his respect for the disciplinarian. In time, this attitude may spread to all in authority. Husbands tend to be more critical than wives of the disciplinary methods used by their spouses. Middle-class husbands, however, are less critical than lower-class husbands (128, 196, 210).

Punishment. In disciplining a child, both punishment and reward play important roles. Punishment serves to inhibit undesirable acts, while reward serves to reinforce desirable acts. If they are to fulfill their roles adequately and contribute to healthy mental and emotional growth, however,

. . . both rewards and punishment need to be deserved and understood by the child. If either reward or punishment is given when not deserved, the child is confused and misled. A question may arise here as to what is meant by "deserved." Generally speaking, reward or punishment is deserved if the child, who has had the opportunity to learn from previous experience what is desirable behavior, has either performed that behavior better than might have been reasonably expected, or has failed to perform it as well as might be expected (203).

Even though positive motivation, in the form of reward, brings better results than negative motivation, in the form of punishment, punishment should not be eliminated. Recognition of the possible consequences of an act is essential to all moral behavior. Because recognition of the possible consequences necessitates an evaluation of the act, every child must learn to weigh alternative acts and the consequences associated with each. He thus learns to decide for himself whether the act is worth its "price" (175).

Punishment serves two major functions in discipline: (1) It deters the repetition of socially undesirable acts, and (2) it shows the child what the social group regards as right or wrong. As the child's criterion of the seriousness of his offense is the severity of the punishment, the desirability of consistent punishment is apparent. Unfortunately, because most parents and other adults punish in anger, this criterion loses its value. If the child learns that inevitably a wrong act will result in a given punishment, he will think twice before carrying out the act.

Types of Punishment. Certain forms of punishment are widely used in our culture. Figure 12-6 shows the kinds of punishment parents reported using at the time the child entered nursery school and a year or so later. The comparison shows the perma-

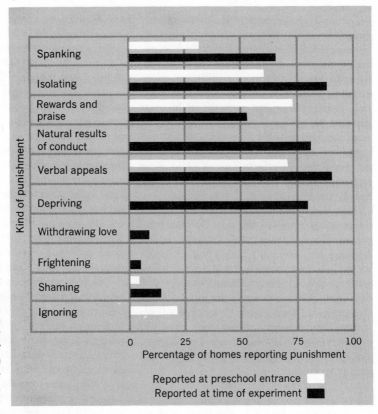

Figure 12–6. Kinds of punishment reported by parents. (Adapted from M. J. Radke, The relation of parental authority to children's behavior and attitudes, The University of Minnesota Press, 1946. Used by permission.)

nency of the kinds of punishment used, and it also indicates that more punishments are used as children grow older. Analysis of the punishments reported from the point of view of the influence they are presumed to have on behavior reveals that most are aimed at undermining the child's power or restricting his freedom—spanking, depriving, isolating, frightening, shaming, and withdrawing love. Similar forms of punishment are also used for older children (35).

Most parents think of *corporal punishment,* especially slapping and spanking, as the most effective way of dealing with the wrongdoings of a child. This attitude may come from the acceptance of the traditional belief that by sparing the rod you spoil the child, or it may come from the fact that parents have not discovered better ways of handling the child. While corporal punishment is generally limited to relatively mild slaps and spanks, it may be so severe that the child will be permanently damaged or even killed (see page 70). Some children deliberately invite corporal punishment in order to get the attention of the parent, but most children resent it.

Contrary to popular opinion, corporal punishment is one of the least satisfactory types of punishment because the child seldom associates it with the act for which he is being punished. Since the anger of the adult is a more dominant factor in the situation than the act itself, the child tends to associate the whipper with pain rather than the wrong deed with pain.

If corporal punishment is used, it should be administered while the prohibited act is going on. When punishment is delayed, the child does not associate the act and the punishment; consequently, the whole value of the punishment is lost.

Corporal punishment, if used at all, should be used only up to about two or three years of age—when the child is capable of comprehending what is said to him. After that time, a form of punishment more definitely related to the act should be used. If it is used after that age, the child must feel that his parents love him, in spite of his misdeeds. As Kanner has pointed out, an occasional spanking or slapping will leave no permanent ill effects on the child if he feels that his parents "like him, and think he's all right" (102).

The most effective punishment has a direct relationship to the act. For that reason, scolding, depriving the child of pleasure, isolating him from his playmates when the wrong act had nothing to do with them, putting him to bed without supper, and other "stock" punishments are not as effective as the adults who use them expect them to be. They are easy to use, it is true, and require little if any ingenuity, but they do not serve the purpose as well as individualized punishment.

Variations in Punishment.   Since demands for conformity to adult standards increase with *age,* older children are likely to be punished more, and punished more severely, than younger children. Parents tend to disagree more about the punishment that should be used for older children, with the result that their discipline of them is less consistent than that of younger children (35, 173).

There is no real difference in the punishment given to children of the two *sexes* when they are young, but as they grow older, there are differences in the amount and type of punishment used and in the reason for punishment. Among older children, girls, on the whole, are punished less than boys because girls conform more to adult expectations (101). Boys are punished more severely, and they receive more corporal punishment. Girls are more often punished for defiance of authority than boys; the desire for independence, which defiance of authority suggests, is more highly valued

and is given more freedom of expression in boys than in girls (109).

Punishment varies somewhat according to the *socioeconomic status* of the family. Middle-class parents usually want their children to internalize standards of behavior; this they attempt to achieve by showing disapproval, by depriving the child of privileges or of the company of others, by stimulating guilt or feelings of shame in the child, or by threatening loss of parental love. Lower-class parents, by contrast, believe that desired standards of behavior can best be achieved by external force; as a result, they use physical punishment—often of a severe type—shame and ridicule to "toughen the child up," and rejection, showing the child they do not want to be "bothered with him."

Lower-class parents think mainly of the immediate consequences of the child's misbehavior, and they therefore focus their attention on the act. By contrast, middle-class parents focus their attention on the child's intent. Better-educated middle-class parents, especially those who have had some training in child care, are more critical of the use of corporal punishment than middle-class parents with less education (29, 76, 109, 160).

Among young children, mothers do most of the punishing, but as children grow older, punishment comes from both parents. Fathers tend to punish their sons more often and more severely than their daughters, while the reverse is true for mothers. Although fathers do less punishing than mothers in middle-class homes, the fathers use more corporal punishment.

Mothers tend to think of the child's intent before punishing for misbehavior, whereas fathers emphasize the act itself. While there is disagreement between parents in every social class about what is the best form of punishment to use, parents of the lower classes generally favor corporal punishment over all other forms; in the upper classes, fathers favor corporal punishment more than mothers do. As a result, children of the lower classes are less often subjected to confusion about right and wrong stemming from parental disagreement (35, 109).

According to Havighurst, there are only two kinds of people who may safely allow the punishment of the child to serve as a release for their aggressions. *Parents* may do this safely within narrow limits because they are so close to the child emotionally that the child can accept occasional punishment from them without doubting their affection for him. Total *strangers* may likewise punish a child for inflicting damage on their property or taking their possessions. By doing so, they teach the child that he will be punished for infringing on the rights of others. On the other hand, people who have frequent relationships with the child but are not very close to him emotionally, such as teachers, club leaders, and neighbors, should not punish a child aggressively. They will usually find that reward is a more effective way to achieve their purposes (73).

Cautions in Use of Punishment. Adults generally use punishment to correct faults in behavior, without taking into consideration the child's motive. This obviously is unfair to the child. The adult who administers the punishment should make a definite effort to analyze the child's behavior in order to discover what motivated the wrongdoing. Telling the child why the punishment is given not only emphasizes its educational value but also makes the child realize that it was not due to mere anger or personal annoyance.

Obedience can be won through punishment or fear of punishment, but the effects on the child are often bad, especially if the parents try to modify too quickly and at too early an age the child's natural drives. Unless punishment is suited to the act, it is not educational. To a child, punishment means pain inflicted by an older, bigger, and stronger person because a rule, made arbitrarily by an adult, was broken. Furthermore, punishment is likely to create resentment and hostility and to inhibit thought and action. As a result, it rarely fosters learning and thus defeats its purpose. If punishment is to be successful, emphasis should be placed on what the punishment is supposed to teach the child; it should never be humiliating, as is so often true of corporal punishment (48).

Rewards. The authoritarian adult who depends too much on the use of punishment is likely to lose sight of the value of using rewards in the discipline of the child. If the child is to learn to act in a socially desirable way, it must be worth his while to do so. Therefore, rewards must be used to build up pleasant associations with the desired act. In emphasizing the importance of counterbalancing punishment with reward, Vincent and Martin have stated:

Severity does not, as a rule, teach a child to do a task as well as he would do it with encouragement. No child, for example, can be taught to use the toilet, or any other activity involving muscle control, as effectively under strict and grim disciplinary methods as he can by encouragement and gentle persuasion. Scolding a child who stutters only makes him stutter more. Beating a child physically may fail to stop his undesirable behavior, and even if it does succeed in changing the offending behavior it may, as we say, "break his will" by shattering his self-esteem. . . . Praise for accomplishment is effective in helping children to want to improve behavior and skills. Parental approval is a potent instrument in discipline (203).

In spite of the fact that parental approval is a "potent instrument," however, parents tend to use less approval and more punishment as children grow older. This is illustrated in Figure 12–6, page 565.

Although there is no question about the value of building up pleasant associations with the behavior one wants the child to repeat, this does not mean that artificial rewards or "bribes" that have no relationship to the act should be used. Like punishments, rewards should have a *direct* relationship to the act so that they will motivate the child to repeat it. Perhaps the simplest and yet most effective reward is social recognition in the form of praise. A comment such as, "You cleaned up your room very well, Johnnie," can always be tied in with the act. At the same time, it satisfies the child's normal desire for social recognition. Vincent and Martin have stressed, however, that "praise needs to be used judiciously, not just when the parent happens to feel in a pleasant mood, but when the child has done something really well. Otherwise the child can establish no reasonable standard by which he can measure his achievements" (203).

Gifts are sometimes given as rewards for good behavior. As Jersild and Tasch have pointed out, the "child's gratitude often seems to go quite beyond the material value or even the practical usefulness of what is given" (95). A gift may be a token of affection, it may represent a respect for the child's abilities and achievements, it may serve as a form of encouragement, or it may be a token of confidence. In any instance, it adds to the child's feeling of self-importance. Under no conditions should the gift be a bribe for good behavior or a form of payment for learning to behave in a socially approved way (98).

It is commonly believed that praising or rewarding a child for good behavior will make him conceited, but it has been found that when positive techniques, in the form of praise, encouragement, or balanced criticism, are used in school, desirable responses outweigh the undesirable in the ratio of 46:1. Consistently desirable responses are reported, regardless of the kind of positive technique used. Even children who at first show undesirable responses later show desirable responses (98).

As children grow older and receive less and less recognition for their efforts to do what is expected of them, rewards serve as a powerful source of motivation for them to continue to try to live up to expectations. If their efforts go unnoticed or unappreciated, they have little motivation, and what motivation they may have is often dampened by constant criticism and nagging about what they have done wrong.

DISCIPLINARY METHODS

Most parents and teachers regard discipline as a means of controlling the child's actions *at the moment*. While this, unquestionably, is one of the primary functions of discipline, the *long-term influence* should not be overlooked. In addition to controlling specific acts, discipline must establish standards of behavior which will become an integral part of the child and which will therefore modify his overall behavioral pattern (203). Two types of restrictive practices are used in discipline. The first sets limits to the child's behavior but, at the same time, encourages the child to engage in acceptable behavior. The second uses "blanket warnings," which leave the child insecure and afraid to engage in any new activity, though they do prevent him from doing what society does not want him to do (121).

The type of discipline used in training the child to conform to the mores of the group depends partly upon the training and education of parents and teachers and partly upon the environment in which the child lives (12). Disciplinary techniques that lead to unfavorable attitudes in one situation may bring favorable results at another time and with another child. In general, disciplinary techniques can be divided into three broad categories: authoritarian, democratic, and permissive.

Authoritarian Disciplinary Techniques. Strict rules and regulations to enforce the desired behavior characterize all kinds of authoritarian discipline. Techniques include severe punishment for failure to come up to expected standards and little or no recognition, praise, or other signs of approval when the child meets the expected standards. Authoritarian discipline may range from reasonable restraints in the child's behavior to *rigid* restraints that permit him no freedom of action except that which conforms to prescribed standards. Authoritarian discipline always means control through *external* force in the form of punishment, especially corporal punishment. Even as the child grows older, parents who use rigid authoritarian methods rarely relax their control or abandon corporal punishment. Furthermore, they do not encourage the child to make decisions regarding his acts; they tell him how to act. Thus he is deprived of the opportunity to learn to control his own behavior.

In families where authoritarian discipline is more reasonable, the child is still restricted in what he may do, and the decision for his acts is made for him. His wishes are not completely disregarded, however, and there are fewer irrational restrictions, such as forbidding the child to do what his peers do (42, 83, 203).

Democratic Disciplinary Techniques. Democratic methods of discipline employ explanation, discussion, and reasoning to help the child understand why he is expected to behave in a certain way. They emphasize the educational aspect of discipline rather than the punitive. Punishment is never harsh; it is used only when there is evidence that the child *willfully* refused to do what he was expected to do.

When the child's behavior comes up to expected standards, the democratic disciplinarian rewards him with praise or some other expression of approval. Democratic discipline tries to develop *internal* controls by educating the child to behave in the approved manner and by showing him the rewards for doing so. Democratic methods may range from extreme leniency and little control to careful planning of the child's activities so that his energies are directed into prescribed channels and prevented from going into activities frowned on by the social group (106, 176, 203).

Permissive Disciplinary Techniques. Permissive discipline is really little or no discipline. It does not seek to guide the child into socially approved patterns of behavior and does not employ punishment. Some parents and teachers, mistaking permissiveness for *laissez faire,* allow the child to grope through situations too difficult for him to cope with alone with no guidance or control (106).

For many parents, permissive discipline is a protest against the rigid and harsh discipline under which they were brought up. In such cases, the child has no limits or boundaries set on what he may do; he is permitted to make his own decisions and act on them in any way he wishes (35, 82, 175).

Mothers are far more likely to use permissive discipline than fathers. Mothers often feel guilty about restricting their children, and they often give in to the child's demands when he accuses them of being "mean" (164). Most parents and teachers who use permissive discipline, however, believe that it is the best way to train the child to conform to social expectations and, at the same time, avoid the psychological damage that has been reported by the psychoanalytic school to be a direct outcome of authoritarian methods (82).

In discussing parental reasons for using permissive discipline, Vincent and Martin have pointed out:

Some parents see in their relationships with their children only the necessity to make them happy as each day goes by, not recognizing that this treatment may deprive the children of the strength that comes from wise restriction, and that it is likely to give them a false idea of what to expect from life outside the home. Such parents permit the child to select his activities as nearly as they can make it possible for him to do so. They give him a minimum of guidance, and may even consider guidance as domination of the child's personality. They lean over backwards to get the child to express his ideas, to say what he wants to say, in order to encourage his "self-expression." They state their own ideas as little as possible in order not to "indoctrinate" him. They praise his every effort in order to give him "self-confidence." They avoid correcting him or calling his errors to his attention so as not to give him an "inferiority complex." Parents who behave this way fail to realize that children need help in knowing what is good for them, and that only when children are sure that their parents will protect them and will see that they do what is good for them, can they feel genuinely secure (203).

Factors Influencing Choice of Method.

Parents and teachers usually have reasons for using the method of discipline they choose. There is a strong tendency to use discipline *similar to that their parents used.* They may, however, swing to the opposite extreme if they feel that the method their parents used was wrong (215). For example, when parents feel that their unhappy childhood resulted from authoritarian discipline, they often use permissive discipline in their own homes; parents brought up with permissive training, on the other hand, often become authoritarian, especially if they feel that lack of guidance was a great handicap to them (33, 91).

In choosing their method of discipline, parents of today are guided less by their own consciences about what is right than by conformity to group-approved methods. As Brodbeck et al. have said, "It appears that internal standards have presumably lost some of the power to influence social conduct which they once possessed: a 'social radar set' has been substituted for the 'voice of conscience' " (30). *Young parents* tend to be more democratic and permissive than older parents. Also, young parents exercise more control when children are young than when they approach adolescence (106).

Training for parenthood, either by preparental courses or through advice from child-care experts, encourages the use of democratic discipline. In general, the better the parent understands the child and his needs, the less authoritarian his discipline will be (174, 188). Because *mothers* generally have a better understanding of the child and his needs, they tend to be less authoritarian than fathers (173).

Parents from *rural* areas are, as a rule, more authoritarian than urban parents (207). Regardless of social class, *Negro* parents tend to be more permissive than white parents (171). On the whole, parents of the middle *socioeconomic* class are stricter, more coercive, and less tolerant than parents of the lowest classes. Middle-class parents, however, are more consistent; those from the lower classes often swing back and forth between authoritarian and permissive methods (123, 128, 208). Within the middle-class group, parents who are better educated use more democratic discipline than those who are less well educated (42). Finally, *foreign-born* parents are more authoritarian than native-born parents (161).

The *religious* background of the family has a decided influence on the type of disciplinary method used. Jewish parents have been reported to be less authoritarian, to demand less adherence to absolute authority, to be more democratic and flexible, and to be less overprotective of their children than Baptist parents. Because Catholic parents are often concerned about outside influences on their children, they tend to be dogmatic and authoritarian in their discipline (209). Within a family, parents are generally stricter with their *daughters* than with their *sons.* They believe that "boys will be boys"; furthermore, they do not want their boys to be regarded as "sissies" (104).

Disciplinary methods vary according to the *age of the child.* In a study of children three to nine years of age, it was found that the most common forms of discipline used for the three-year-olds included reasoning, scolding, coaxing, spanking, diverting their attention, ignoring them, or forcibly isolating them; for the six-year-olds, the most common forms were reasoning, scolding, coaxing, threatening, isolating, spanking, taking away privileges, and ordering them to do what they were told to do; for the nine-year-olds, the most frequently used disciplinary methods were reasoning, scolding, appealing to self-esteem, threatening, ignoring, and using humor, isolation, and social disapproval (35).

The type of discipline used also varies according to the *situation.* Fears and anxieties, for example, are usually handled nonpunitively, while defiance of parental authority and negativistic or aggressive behavior (disobeying, breaking toys, spitting on others, or hitting a sibling) call for punishment. Likewise, dependency problems, such as refusal to eat, are usually treated punitively (30). Parents who use permissive discipline are not necessarily consistent in its use. For example, they are less permissive about toilet training, dependence, aggressiveness, and sex behavior than about other forms of behavior (156).

The adult's *concept of his role* has a marked influence on his disciplinary approach to the child. Parents who hold to the traditional concept of the parental role tend to be more authoritarian than parents who have accepted the more modern concept (3, 18, 177). Teachers who believe that there should be a rigid routine in the classroom use more authoritarian discipline than those who have a more democratic concept of teaching. Finally, the *occupation* of the parent has a marked influence on the type of discipline he will use. Mothers whose professions take them outside the home tend to be more authoritarian than mothers who remain at home, while fathers who hold executive positions tend to be more authoritarian than fathers whose occupations carry less authority (23, 204).

EVALUATION OF DISCIPLINE

Discipline should not be evaluated in terms of its immediate results. Children can be forced into a pattern of behavior approved by adults and can quickly be made into "perfect little ladies or gentlemen." The long-term harm done to their personalities, however, may outweigh any temporary advantages. As DuBois has pointed out:

Parents must think in terms not only of the immediate behavior at two, six, or sixteen years . . . but also of the ultimate results of discipline at twenty, forty, and sixty, when parental control is no longer in force. Then the individual must be constructively self-directed or else suffer remorse because of violation of his personal code or be punished by society when his conduct is contrary to its laws (48).

There are certain wholesome and unwholesome functions of discipline which must be kept in mind when disciplinary techniques are evaluated.

THE MAJOR WHOLESOME FUNCTIONS OF DISCIPLINE ARE:

1. To teach the child that the world responds in orderly fashion to his actions and that certain behaviors will always be followed by punishment, while others will be followed by praise. Consistent discipline helps the child to learn that there is a moral orderliness in the world.
2. To teach the child a *reasonable* degree of conformity, but not too much conformity.
3. To help the child develop self-control and self-direction. Then he can make wise decisions on his own responsibility and develop a "conscience."

THE UNWHOLESOME FUNCTIONS OF DISCIPLINE ARE:

1. To intimidate the child.
2. To release the disciplinarian's aggression (73).

Wholesome discipline is always *consistent*. The severity of discipline has been found to bear no relationship to the moral character of the child, but consistency of discipline is very closely related to moral competence. The child who is consistently disciplined is better adjusted than the child whose discipline is inconsistent. Children who are well adjusted have a sense of freedom; their behavior is well integrated, and they have a realistic approach to life situations (73, 134, 143, 208).

Because lower-class parents tend to be inconsistent in their discipline, swinging from permissiveness to extreme authoritarianism and often administering harsh and drastic punishment, lower-class children develop feelings of inadequacy and loss of self-confidence. These increase with age. Even more serious, they learn to be secretive, sly, and dishonest to avoid punishment which they fear will be the inevitable consequence of nonconformity to parental demands. By contrast, upper-class children, who are more consistently disciplined, develop feelings of adequacy and self-confidence, which result in better personal and social adjustments (135, 160).

The *timing* of discipline is as important as its consistency. Because the child is most vulnerable to outside influences during the early years of life, the type of discipline used and the attitude of the disciplinarian strongly influence the child's subsequent behavior and personality. In discussing the serious consequences of discipline during these "vulnerable" years, Spock has pointed out that if the child is "regularly shamed for his accidents, accidents in the general and in the sanitary sense, he acquires a sense of shame and unworthiness. If he is excessively dominated he becomes defiant or submissive. If he is constantly warned that the parent will no longer love him unless he behaves differently, his whole personality will be poisoned with uneasiness and antagonism" (181).

When the child is in the process of learning to be independent, authoritarian discipline is far more damaging than earlier, when he is too immature to be anything but dependent, or later, when adult attitudes are far less important than peer attitudes (5). In the same way, overpermissiveness at the time when the child is just learning to make adjustments outside the home may give the child the feeling that his parents do not care enough about him to help him make the adjustments; as a result, he may develop attitudes of bitter resentment toward them if he fails in his attempts. After the child has learned to make adjustments outside the home he will interpret permissiveness to mean that his parents believe he is capable of managing his own affairs; this will bolster his self-confidence.

Stone has shown that, in discipline, timing and the attitude of the disciplinarian follow the same principle as timing of unfavorable influences in prenatal life: When a structure is in the process of forming, unfavorable environmental factors lead to developmental irregularities (189).

In the light of this statement, an attempt can be made to evaluate the most commonly used disciplinary techniques.

Overly Strict Discipline. Even though overly strict discipline is more damaging to a child at certain times during the developmental pattern than at others, there is *no* time when it does not leave an unfavorable mark on his behavior or personality. Overly strict parents who use harsh and punitive methods to achieve their ends may make the child conform to their standards and be a "good" child. But while there is surface goodness, there is apt to be smoldering resentment which will break out sooner or later. Such parents may, on the other hand, push the child into asserting his independence prematurely. Expecting absolute and immediate obedience may, then, lead to disciplinary problems; the child may assert his independence by doing many things he otherwise would not have done (17, 37, 205).

The overdisciplined child feels that the world is hostile, and he acts accordingly. As Frank has said, "The stricter the parents, the stronger may be the revolt and the more outrageous the 'hell-raising' or the more submissive conformity to parents and priggish self-justification" (58). Too much rebellion against too strict discipline may eventually lead to delinquency. The overly disciplined child often develops a generalized feeling of martyrdom, which may lead to apathy and resignation but is more likely to lead to extremes of behavior. The child must prove to himself and to others that he will not allow himself to be dominated. He believes that if the world is hostile to him, he can be hostile to the world—a belief that is at the root of much juvenile delinquency (1, 131).

If the child's resentments against overly strict discipline and harsh punishment lead to even harsher punishment, they may be "driven underground" and then find new channels of expression. They may be expressed in aggressiveness toward other children—especially younger siblings and members of minority groups—a hypercritical attitude toward all in authority, or fantasy in which the child wins out in his battle against the person whose restrictions he resents (2).

Among young children, the most common indirect expressions of resentment are aggressive attacks on younger and weaker children; among older children, verbal attacks in the form of criticism are most common. At all ages, children who discover that rebellion will lead to harsher and more punitive discipline learn to turn their aggressions inward and gain expression for them in fantasy (17, 51, 86, 126). This is illustrated in Figure 12–7.

If children feel a strong sense of obligation toward their parents or learn that it is not to their best advantage to criticize the teacher to her face, they criticize the resented person behind his back. A young child may criticize one parent to the other, or he may complain about his teacher to his parents. An older child is more likely to carry his complaints to members of the peer group (151).

How the child will react to overly strict discipline will vary according to his past experiences. If he discovers that he gains more favor from his parents when he is submissively obedient, even though inwardly rebellious, and if he needs their love to be happy, he will repress his resentments and be a "good" child. An older child who satis-fies his need for attention and approval in the peer group may openly defy parental authority, knowing that this makes him a hero in the eyes of the peer group—or a martyr, if he is too severely punished for his rebellion. If the child perceives the mother as the stricter disciplinarian, he is likely to turn his resentments inward because he prefers his mother to his father and does not want to jeopardize his status with her. If, on the other hand, he perceives his father as the stricter disciplinarian, he is more likely to turn his anger outward. He will either attack the father directly or displace his anger by attacking an innocent victim (44, 81).

Some children are more sensitive to threat of loss of affection than others, and some children fear punishment more than others. Consequently, what a child does in a disciplinary situation will be greatly influenced by these factors. But whatever he does, it is more likely to lead to maladjustive than to adjustive behavior. As Davitz has pointed out, "Punishment and rejection give rise to

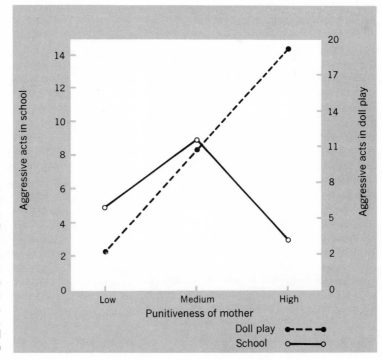

Figure 12–7. Relation of interpersonal and fantasy aggression to punitiveness of the mother. (Adapted from R. R. Sears, Relation of aggressiveness to punitiveness in the home, *Amer. Psychologist,* 1953, 6, 476–483. Used by permission.)

fear; fear promotes defensive reactions; and the defensive reactions elicit further punishment. This is the vicious circle of maladjustment. The child lives in an interpersonal world of constant threat. The consequence is unhappiness and fear" (44). The "vicious circle" of punishment, which leads to maladjustive behavior, is illustrated in Figure 12–8.

Personality is likewise unfavorably affected by overly strict discipline. There is a tendency for the strictly disciplined child to become sullen, obstinate, and negativistic in his attitudes toward anyone in authority. While the child may be outwardly quiet, well behaved, and nonresistant, he often harbors deep resentments which make him unhappy and insecure and which restrict his curiosity, originality, and fancifulness and lead to lack of self-confidence.

In the older child, lack of confidence leads to feelings of guilt about independent thoughts and actions and thus impedes social and emotional development. Furthermore, lack of confidence will cause the child to think of himself as "worthless" and will lead to poor personal and social adjustment, accompanied by lack of success in whatever he undertakes (6, 12, 184). Overly strict discipline during the early, formative years may lead to the development of an "authoritarian personality" characterized by rigidity and inability to change attitudes and patterns of behavior to meet new demands in life. When this occurs, the child becomes so submissive that he is less competitive and socially successful than other children while, at the same time, becoming compulsively obedient and defiant (21, 129).

Many children, subjected to too much and too severe punishment, learn to be sly, secretive, and dishonest in order to avoid punishment when they defy authority (150, 193). A study of the effects of child-training methods on the personality patterns of Chinese children, who, traditionally, are subjected to strict authoritarian discipline, has revealed that they become withdrawn, shy, suspicious, sensitive, and introverted (170).

Because the child who is strictly disciplined is uncertain about his ability to conform to adult expectations, he develops into an anxious, insecure person. Even as early as nursery-school years, this personality damage is apparent. In a study of nursery-school children's play with paints and crayons, it was found that those who had been subjected to overly strict discipline in the home showed a lower tolerance for being dirty and messy than children from homes where discipline was less strict. The training received in the home carried over into their play; those from strict homes were afraid to be free in their play because of their anxiety about parental disapproval and punishment (7).

When parents inhibit their desire to use corporal punishment, they usually substitute "psychological punishment," such as withdrawal of love. This kind of punishment is extremely harsh and, if repeated too often, can have a devastating influence on the child's personality. Studies of psychiatric patients, for example, have revealed that they experienced more psychological than physical punishment during their childhood days (68).

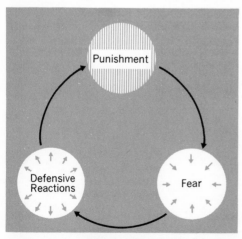

Figure 12–8. The "vicious circle" of punishment. (Adapted from M. E. Breckenridge and E. L. Vincent, *Child development*, 4th ed., Saunders, 1960. Used by permission.)

Permissive Discipline. When discipline is too lenient, a child is confused and insecure. He does not know just what he should or should not do, and he becomes fearful, anxious, and often excessively aggressive. Furthermore, he is likely to become resentful because he feels that his parents care too little about him to take the trouble to guide him and thus help him to avoid mistakes.

When parents never make any demands on their children, the children take advantage of parental uncertainty and assert themselves. Furthermore, when they make mistakes because of lack of parental guidance, they feel cheated out of the pride of achievement and develop a feeling of contempt for their parents' "softness." The disciplinary problems that result from complete lack of discipline can be as serious as those engendered by overly strict discipline (37, 82, 203).

The most serious effect of too lenient discipline comes from the reactions of people outside the home. In the school or neighborhood, the undisciplined child is soon labeled a "spoiled brat" or a "little monster"— neither label contributing to social acceptance (205). As Jersild has pointed out:

If children have not been disciplined in a manner that would put a curb on their expectations from others, they are due for some hard jolts as they move on in the years. Without being aware of it, they may have illusions concerning their own rights and a vague notion of omnipotence which will clash sooner or later with the realities of life. The overindulgent parent, likewise, may be so forebearing and so patient that the child demands from others a degree of patience and forebearance which they will not be able to give him (94).

When the child, suffering from lack of guidance, discovers that people outside the home reject him and punish him for the behavior he has been permitted to engage in at home, he turns against his parents and blames them for his social rejection (82).

Democratic Discipline.   The child is best disciplined if his parents feel secure in their position of "authority." In their parental role, they attempt to teach the child what society expects, and they motivate him to live up to these expectations. The fundamental principle of *democratic* discipline, the form of discipline which embodies the good points of authoritarian and permissive discipline but which avoids the harmful features of both, is that the child is brought up permissively, but with guidance and motivation from adults and with internalized controls over his behavior. In its best form, discipline of this type leads to good personal and social adjustments. It results in independence in thinking, initiative in action, and a healthy, positive, confident self-concept which is reflected in active, outgoing, and spontaneous behavior (62, 150).

Greater freedom in the home, characteristic of democratic discipline, shows itself in better cooperation, greater persistence in the face of obstacles, better self-control, greater creativity, and a friendlier approach to people (185). In the school, teachers who have a warm, friendly, cooperative relationship with their pupils find that their pupils make better personal and social adjustments, are less troublesome, and do better school work. Democratic discipline in the school, as in the home, thus leads to more favorable results than either authoritarian or permissive discipline (150).

In summarizing the findings of a study to determine the effects on behavior and personality of authoritarian versus democratic discipline, Watson stated, "It is impressive . . . to find no clear personality advantage associated in general with strict discipline in a good home. Where differences [in personality] do emerge, they are consistently to the credit of the more permissive upbringing" (205). By "permissive" Watson does not mean the overly permissive discipline evaluated above; he means the more democratic form, in which the child is respected as an individual and is permitted to guide his own behavior when he is able to do so.

Children's Reactions to Discipline.   If discipline is to teach the child to behave in a socially acceptable manner, the child must have a healthy attitude toward the disciplinary methods used and toward the disciplinarian. How the child *perceives* discipline and how he reacts are more important than the method used.

A study of children's perceptions of their parents showed that older children perceived their mothers as less dominant, punitive, and threatening and more friendly and understanding than their fathers. As children approached adolescence, however, they perceived parents of their own sex as less benevolent and more frustrating than parents of the opposite sex. Girls are well aware that their mothers are stricter with them than with their brothers, and they often interpret this, rightly or wrongly, to mean that their mothers prefer their brothers (101, 172).

Young children are sensitive to fairness on the part of both parents and teachers, and they become increasingly so as they grow older. If they consider the treatment they receive "unfair," they become resentful and feel that they have been abused. Whether the treatment is actually unfair or not is less important than the way the child interprets it. His grievances are important for two reasons: They affect his attitude toward people in authority and his willingness to try to conform to social expectations, and they also affect his concept of himself. If he believes that he has been the victim of unfair treatment, serious personality disturbances may result.

Unfavorable repercussions are most likely when children are kept from doing what members of the peer group are permitted to do. As Klineberg has pointed out, "The meaning to an individual of a certain amount of frustration will surely vary in relation to the amount of frustration to which he sees other individuals subjected" (107). On the other hand, the child who feels that the discipline he receives is fair and that the restrictions on his behavior are for his own good will have a far more favorable attitude toward the restrictions and toward his parents than the child who feels that his parents are being "mean" or revengeful (67, 92).

Because of their limited knowledge and experience, young children tend to misinterpret discipline and the attitude of the disciplinarian toward them. A frown on the mother's face when she asks the child to stop doing something, for example, may be interpreted by the child to mean that the mother is *angry with him*. In reality, the frown may be totally unrelated to the child and what he is doing; it may come from a headache or from some previously annoying experience. Many children believe that the mother is unfair when she blames them for things. This leads not only to resentments but also to feelings of martyrdom (144).

Even older children sometimes misinterpret the behavior and attitudes of others. This may result from making judgments on the basis of too few cues, or it may be a reflection of their own attitudes. In school, for example, the child may feel that the teacher's criticism of his behavior means that she dislikes him when, in reality, she wants to help him. If he has been accustomed to being criticized at home, he feels that *any* criticism from *any* source reflects an unfavorable attitude toward him. He does not look under the surface to see whether there was another motive behind the criticism (32). If a teacher has an authoritarian attitude toward her pupils and disbelieves what they say, they not only resent this but also feel that the teacher is unfair (8). Once a teacher or parent has created the impression of being unfair, children tend to interpret everything he does as unfair.

Most children feel that their parents should be firm or strict, that they should require obedience, and that they should not spoil them. Many feel, however, that their parents should criticize constructively and reason with them instead of punishing them. When a group of nursery-school children were asked what their mothers or fathers should do when their children were naughty, most of them recommended spankings. A few suggested isolation, and even fewer suggested scolding and talking crossly. Most children prefer to have the mother administer the punishment because they feel that she is more lenient than the father (79).

The assumption is that effective disciplinary techniques will prevent recurrence of undesirable behavior. When children were asked how they felt after they were punished, most of them reported that they felt unhappy and had memories of physical pain. Very few, on the other hand, reported feeling penitent or making resolutions for better behavior in the future. Studies of adolescents and adults have revealed that the effects of discipline persist and affect both the personality and the behavior of the individual as he grows older. Very strict discipline is often associated with personality maladjustments, unhappiness, and delinquency (77, 205).

Variations in Attitude.   Children's attitudes toward discipline are influenced by a number of factors, *age* especially. When children are young, they feel secure in the belief that "mother knows best." When they come in contact with other children who *report* that different disciplinary methods and different forms of punishment are used in their homes, however, they begin to rebel against their parents and their parents' standards.

Whether the reports a child receives from the peer group are accurate or not is of minor concern; the fact that he accepts them means that they will have a profound effect on his own attitudes. They may incite open rebellion, in which the child misbehaves in order to prove his independence (39, 63).

That attitudes toward discipline change with age is apparent in the way children react to punishment. Among three-year-olds, for example, the most frequent reaction to discipline is crying. Children may cry because they are angry at not being permitted to do what they want to do, but more often their crying comes from fear of losing the love of the mother or father.

Children at the six- to nine-year level, by contrast, most often react to discipline by being angry. While both crying and anger are responses to the frustrations caused by discipline, the older child has learned that it is considered "babyish" to cry. Furthermore, the angry response of the older child implies that he has less fear of losing his parents' love than the younger child, but a stronger feeling that the discipline is unfair. The young child's crying usually lasts for a shorter time than the older child's anger, though the modal time for both has been found to be only 5 minutes. Although the older child may not show his anger overtly, he may suppress it into a resentment which will unfavorably affect his later attitudes toward discipline of all types and toward all in authority (35).

At all ages, *boys* resent unfair discipline and rebel against corporal punishment more than girls. Both in the home and in the school, boys and girls have different attitudes toward rules. Boys regard rules as a method of restricting their socially unacceptable behavior and of keeping them out of trouble. Girls, by contrast, perceive rules as a way of teaching them how to behave, of giving them standards of conduct approved by the social group, and of channeling their energies into socially approved behavior. Girls' attitudes are mainly *positive,* while boys' attitudes are mainly *negative* (47).

Attitudes are influenced by the *socioeconomic* and *cultural* groups to which the child belongs. Children from poorer groups favor an appeal to authority to meet disciplinary problems. They tend to hold the individual child responsible for any violation of rules of conduct, and they advocate punishment more often than children from better social backgrounds. The latter seem to perceive an environmental basis for misconduct, and they suggest that the circumstances which produced the misbehavior be changed (50, 194).

In the case of truancy, for example, children of low socioeconomic status suggest that the truant officer punish the child; children of better socioeconomic status suggest that the truant might be unhappy in school and that a change of school might solve the problem. Underprivileged children tend to evaluate parental disciplinary methods as too strict, while children of average socioeconomic status think their parents are too easy. Fathers are considered "too easy" more frequently than mothers (46, 175, 205).

Children who are *bright* are likely to be bored by too many rules. Lack of definite limits on their behavior, however, tends to make them insecure and unhappy. They are very sensitive to fairness, especially on the part of teachers.

The child who is not so bright is likely to become resentful when disciplined; he does not always understand rules and therefore feels that he is being treated unjustly. In general, children who are subjected to *democratic forms of discipline* report that they feel happy and secure, free from the anxieties and resentments experienced by children whose discipline has been too strict or too lenient (41, 120, 193).

DISCREPANCIES BETWEEN MORAL CONCEPTS AND BEHAVIOR

There is no such thing as *absolute consistency;* among adults as well as among children, there are many discrepancies between a person's moral code and his behavior. Abstract knowledge that it is wrong to cheat does not keep children from cheating when a situation arises in which they are tempted to cheat or when they find it to their personal advantage to do so (98, 147). Similarly, children who say it is "wrong" to fight with their classmates are not always consistent in their behavior. As Pressey and Kuhlen have pointed out, "There are no separate groups of saints and sinners. Most people are sometimes honest, sometimes not, sometimes helpful, sometimes not—average in virtue as in other traits" (157). Most people, however, are consistent in relating their moral beliefs to their behavior. It becomes a matter of honor to live up to their standards. If they do not, they feel guilty, and if caught, they feel ashamed (11, 55).

Causes of Discrepancies. Delinquent children are rarely ignorant of the wrongs they do; in fact, their moral knowledge is very similar to that of nondelinquents (36, 65). As Eysenck has stated, "The delinquent child as well as the criminal adult is usually only too well aware of the *fact* that his conduct is contrary to moral precept; his evil-doing is not by and large due to ignorance" (55). Even among young children,

misbehavior is often due to causes other than ignorance of what is expected of them.

Discrepancies between moral knowledge and moral behavior in childhood frequently result from *confusion* in the child's mind about the meaning of the rules he is expected to follow. Sometimes a child is confused when abstract concepts must be applied to situations that have little in common with situations he has previously met. He may, for example, know that it is wrong to steal from a person but be confused about whether taking something from a public park falls in this category (22).

Children from the higher socioeconomic groups, on the whole, have better moral teaching at home than those from the lower groups. As a result, children from poorer homes tend to experience more confusion about what is right and wrong and to do more things that are contrary to social expectations (75, 198). Confusion may also arise when the child sees a discrepancy between what his parents say and what they do. If it is all right for them to preach one thing and practice another, he feels that it is all right for him to do the same (163).

Confusion often arises from the way the different forms of mass media, especially movies and television, present certain behavior. As Barclay has said:

Television makes plain that The Law is clear and inexorable on such matters as premeditated murder, horse-stealing, bank hold-ups and the robbing of stagecoaches. But just what this dramatic and powerful force has to do with what they consider the mere pranks and shenanigans of youth—prying off hubcaps, altering road signs, worming into empty houses, "borrowing" automobiles—is not so easily understood. In fact, books and movies and TV shows may even confuse their understanding by presenting such actions as harmless fun or high adventure (14).

Discrepancies between concepts and behavior are especially likely to occur when the moral concepts of the parents *differ from those of the child's peers.* When the child must decide between what his parents and what his friends think right, he will be influenced by what is more important to him personally. If, for example, honesty is more valued by the group than cheating, and if this coincides with his parents' concepts, he will be honest; if cheating is approved by the group because it shows loyalty to a friend in distress, it is more likely to be accepted as "right" by the child because it is more advantageous to him personally to win peer than parental approval. Boys are confronted with such discrepancies more than girls (10, 34).

Frequently confusion occurs because *moral concepts conflict with one another.* Truthfulness may conflict with loyalty to one's friends or with ideals of courtesy and sympathy. A child may knowingly tell a lie to spare the feelings of another, just as an adult may (98).

The discrepancy between moral knowledge and moral behavior is most often due to emotional and motivational factors. Studies of moral development have revealed that the cognitive and *emotional* aspects represent distinct processes, that they show different developmental trends, and that they are influenced in their development by different conditions (10). In anger, for example, a child may do something he knows is wrong to "get even" with the person who has angered him. If the child feels that the mother has blamed him for an incident for which she should have taken some of the blame herself, he becomes angry and does things he knows he should not do. In the latter part of childhood, when there is a generalized rebellion against adult authority, boys and girls often tend to value honesty less highly than before. Many of the acts of juvenile delinquents are motivated by the way their classmates treat them: They strike back at them or at anyone who happens to be available, and they do things they know are wrong (130, 138).

Motivational factors are the chief cause of discrepancies between moral knowledge and moral behavior: The child frequently finds it expedient to behave in a way that he knows is not right. Disobedience at home or in school is often motivated by a desire for attention. The child who feels that he is being ignored finds the satisfaction of being in the limelight far greater than the temporary discomfort of being punished (103, 192). Or the child may intentionally disobey rules and defy adult authority to prove to himself and to his peers that he is grown-up and independent (212). To do this, the child may have to sacrifice some of his abstract concepts of right and wrong, but the end result of winning approval is worth any price he may have to pay. Many children lie or blame others to avoid punishment, ridicule, or social disapproval. In games, a child may cheat because he lacks the motor skills needed to win fairly. In school, he may cheat because parental pressures have been used to force him to get better grades than he is capable of getting without cheating. Or he may cheat to avoid being left behind when his friends are promoted. He knows that to maintain his status in the peer group, he must maintain his status in school. If he is incapable of doing this, even by cheating, he is motivated to become a truant (148, 163, 183).

The emotional and motivational factors back of the discrepancy between moral knowledge and moral behavior are especially strong when authoritarian discipline prevails. In a study of honesty among children in different cultures, including the United States, England, Mexico, Germany, Finland, and Sweden, it was found that children from societies with democratic backgrounds were more honest and less defensive than children from countries where more authoritarian training prevailed. Furthermore, children from authoritarian countries tended to show less sense of fair play and responsibility than those from countries which put more emphasis on democratic training (153).

Effects of Discrepancy on Children. Few children fail to recognize the discrepancy between their behavior and their moral knowledge. The child who is caught cheating, for example, may try to justify his act by claiming that everyone does it, but he still knows that it is wrong, and he feels guilty (163). The child who intentionally destroys the property of others may justify it because of the way they have treated him, but even when trying to justify his act he knows that it is wrong, and if he is caught and punished he feels ashamed (34).

Children who have a selfish attitude feel justified in their selfish behavior, even when they know selfishness is disapproved of. On the other hand, children who have a disapproving attitude toward selfishness have vague feelings of guilt when they act selfishly and sometimes show it by such gestures as hesitancy before acting (201).

The temporary satisfaction the child gets from social approval from the peer group when he defies adult authority is not great enough to compensate for the feelings of guilt he experiences. He therefore tries to compensate by claiming he was ignorant of the wrong, by saying that everyone else does it, or by projecting the blame to a parent, teacher, or member of the peer group. If he can convince himself as well as others that there was no discrepancy between his moral knowledge and behavior or that the discrepancy was not his fault, he then frees himself of feelings of guilt and shame (11, 55).

MISDEMEANORS

A misdemeanor is mischievousness, disobedience, or willful badness of a minor sort. Most little children learn, unfortunately, that they get more attention when they are naughty than when they are good. They therefore are often *intentionally* naughty when they feel that they are being ignored. Even though they are punished, the pleasure they derive from being in the spotlight far outweighs the temporary discomfort of the punishment. Much of the destructiveness of young children is caused not by clumsiness or lack of motor control but by a willful attempt to attract attention to themselves.

Groups of older children delight in willful misbehavior because it gives each member a sense of personal importance. Misbehavior that annoys others, such as ringing doorbells, letting air out of automobile tires, or drawing pictures on pavements, houses, or fences, gives the group members special pleasure because it makes them feel that they are masters of the situation.

Even though misbehavior in school—whispering, passing notes, or tormenting other pupils—is sure to result in punishment, the child feels that it is well worthwhile because all eyes in the classroom are focused on him and all pupils listen attentively while the teacher scolds or administers punishment. While most older children know that their mischievous behavior is considered wrong, they often act impulsively; attention, social approval, or some other motive seems more important than doing what adults expect (152).

That most children are aware of their misbehavior has been shown by a study in which children were asked to name the worst acts they had committed and to give their reasons for the acts. First- and second-graders emphasized acts which inconvenienced others, such as talking out of turn, assaulting other children in school, breaking objects, playing with fire, or disobeying parents. Third-graders, by contrast, put more emphasis on acts that are morally wrong, thus indicating their awareness that they were doing things they were not supposed to do. While younger children attempted to justify their misbehavior, the older children showed feelings of guilt by referring to the inconvenience or harm their misbehavior brought to others. At no time was there an indication that their misbehavior stemmed from ignorance of what was expected (72).

Variations in Misdemeanors. The frequency and seriousness of misdemeanors vary markedly at different ages, among different children of the same age level, and under different conditions. Normally, misdemeanors increase throughout childhood. The peak comes shortly before adolescence, when the child is making a transition from parental to group authority; at this time there is often a relaxation of external controls over his behavior without the necessary development of internalized controls (11, 37). Furthermore, this is the time when the child is striving for peer acceptance. To win the group's admiration and to prove that he is worthy of acceptance, he may feel that it is necessary to commit bold, daring, or mischievous acts. Boys, especially, place great value on independence and admire defiance of adult authority (199).

Increase in misdemeanors with age has been illustrated in a study of "dares" in which the child flaunts a generally accepted social value by means of unorthodox behavior. In accepting dares to do such things as challenging parental authority, engaging in socially aggressive behavior (by ridiculing peers to their faces, pulling a girl's hair, or putting snow down a classmate's back), or risking danger or exposure to mysterious elements (by walking over thin ice, picking up a snake, jumping over fire, or riding through a cemetery at night), boys try to prove to themselves and to their peers that they are "regular boys" with all the admired characteristics of members of the male sex.

As childhood progresses, the tendency to challenge authority figures in the home and school and to engage in conflict with legal authority increases. Regardless of what form the dare takes, the attraction to "dare situations appears to reflect strivings for social esteem" (212). If the dare leads to adult disapproval or punishment, the price is not too great for the child who craves social acceptance from the peer group.

At every age, both at home and in school, boys are more disobedient, boisterous, disruptive, attention-seeking, negativistic, impertinent, and destructive than girls. The tendency to be troublesome shows a consistent sex difference from kindergarten through the sixth grade (see Figure 12–9). As a result, more boys become delinquent at adolescence, and their offenses are, on the whole, more serious. Sex differences in troublesome behavior exist because boys at every age are given more freedom to do as they please and because there is greater social tolerance for boys' misbehavior (154). Furthermore, boys feel that to win group approval, they must be willing to flaunt adult authority (74).

Among children of the *lower social*

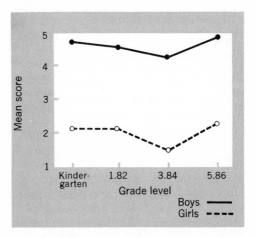

Figure 12–9. Sex differences in conduct problems in school for children of different ages. (Adapted from D. R. Peterson, Behavior problems of middle childhood, *J. consult. Psychol.*, 1961, 25, 205–209. Used by permission.)

classes, where discipline is inconsistent, where little emphasis is placed on training the child to recognize right from wrong, and where harsh corporal punishment is used even for minor misdemeanors, repeated misbehavior is common. Furthermore, as such children become older, their misbehavior becomes increasingly serious and more likely to lead to trouble with law-enforcing authorities. This is true also of children of better socioeconomic status if they are unaccepted by their peer group or if they feel unloved and unwanted in the home (39).

In the process of growing up, most children pass through what Gesell has called "periods of disequilibrium"—times when they are difficult to manage and when misbehavior is quite common. (See pages 29 to 30 for a discussion of the times when disequilibrium most often occurs.) As has already been stressed, children tend to be most troublesome when they are tired—late in the day, just before the evening meal, and at bedtime (35). They are also troublesome when they are not feeling up to par physically, as when they are recovering from an illness, or when they have difficult adjustments to make in the patterns of their lives, as when starting school, going to a new school, adjusting to a stepparent, or being taken care of by someone else when the mother is ill or away from home (63).

Home misdemeanors are often markedly different from misdemeanors occurring in other situations. The common misdemeanors in the *home* at different ages depend largely on what the child is expected to learn. If the parents expect the young child to take care of his bodily needs and personal possessions and to play with his siblings without fighting, he will be considered naughty if he fails to do so and will be punished. He is also expected to learn simple home rules. If he is unable or unwilling to learn them, his parents will interpret this as willful disobedience.

Studies of the common home misdemeanors of children of preschool age have emphasized capriciousness, bed wetting, temper tantrums, dawdling, aggressive approaches to peers and playmates, demanding attention, breaking toys and family possessions, being rude to relatives or family friends, and defying parental authority. All these, it may be seen, are related to the immaturity of the child and are often provoked by the way in which discipline has been applied in the home. Children from *authoritarian* homes commit more misdemeanors than children from more permissive homes (30, 48).

Home misdemeanors commonly associated with late childhood include willful disobedience and defiance of adult authority, aggressive verbal attacks on siblings, dawdling over routine activities, temper outbursts, shirking responsibilities, lying, minor pilfering, sneakiness, breaking and spilling things, and rudeness to relatives or family friends (63).

Because teachers are concerned about good classroom behavior and pupil achievement, they disapprove of anything that interferes with school routine, disregarding the long-term effects of the child's behavior on his personality and on his adjustments to life. If the child is "good" in class, in the sense that he does his work, makes no trouble for the teacher, and does not get into arguments or fights with his classmates, the teacher rates him high in conduct. Children who make trouble for the teacher and fail to work up to their capacities, on the other hand, are rated low in conduct and are regarded by the teacher as "troublesome" (146, 192).

While *school misdemeanors* vary greatly, according to the backgrounds of the children, the types of teachers they have, and many other factors, there is a tendency for inattentiveness, "cutting up," vandalism, lying, and carelessness in work to decrease from the first to the sixth grades and for smoking, unexcused absences, stealing, swearing, drinking, and illicit sex acts to make their appearance. The older child intentionally violates school rules much more than the younger child (53).

The child's behavior in school likewise varies according to the *subject matter* being studied; the less interested the child, the more troublesome he is likely to be. It has been found, for example, that children are more troublesome in mathematics classes than in social studies classes. If the child is talented in mathematics, he will be bored by the slow pace of the class and will resort to mischievous behavior; similarly, if he lacks interest and ability in mathematics, he will become bored and mischievous. During discussion periods, the child who lacks self-confidence does not participate; instead, he spends his time drawing, writing notes, whispering, and being generally troublesome (110).

When school discipline is *authoritarian* rather than democratic, children show greater resentment against the teacher and against school in general. This leads to more misdemeanors of both minor and major importance (8, 88, 117). How the child *perceives* his teacher's attitude toward him is just as important to his behavior as how the teacher actually treats him (146). Children who have a favorable concept of themselves generally feel that the teacher has a favorable concept of them. Such children do better work in school and are less troublesome (43). Girls perceive teachers' attitudes as more favorable than boys do, and children of the upper and middle social classes perceive them as more favorable than children of the lower social classes do. The *better accepted* the child is by the peer group, the better his behavior in school; well-accepted children do not have to try to win peer favor by doing things that are annoying and disruptive in the classroom (212).

Common Childhood Misdemeanors. While children do countless things that adults regard as "naughty" or "bad," certain misdemeanors are almost universal. These may vary in frequency and seriousness from child to child and in the same child from one age to another. Of the many childhood misdemeanors, the following are most frequently reported:

1. Dishonesty. Sometimes dishonesty is unintentional; most often, however, it is intentional. Children who have been subjected to strict discipline in which corporal punishment was freely applied try to escape the inevitable punishment by using a form of dishonesty which they have discovered, from past experience, brings them the immunity they desire. Similarly, children who have been subjected to psychological punishment, especially threats of loss of parental love, scoldings, or unfavorable comparisons with siblings, are motivated to be dishonest to escape these ego-deflating and anxiety-producing punishments. By contrast, children who are subjected to more democratic discipline in the home and school have less motivation to be dishonest (143, 176).

Dishonesty appears in the preschool years but is more pronounced late in childhood. Boys and girls learn, from their own experiences or from those of their friends, ways and means of deceiving others, especially parents and teachers. They may pretend to be ill to avoid an unpleasant task; they may hide broken objects or pretend that someone else did the damage; they may feign ignorance of a rule which they have broken; they may cheat in school work or athletics; or they may steal.

2. Lying. One of the most common forms of dishonesty is lying. Children's lies have been classified under seven categories: (*a*) the playful lie, which results from make-believe play or imaginary incidents; (*b*) the lie of confusion, which grows out of the child's inability to report details accurately or the beclouding of the issue by suggestions of another; (*c*) the lie of vanity, designed to draw attention to oneself; (*d*) the lie of malevolence or revenge, motivated by hate; (*e*) the excusive lie, resulting from fear of rigid discipline or corporal punishment; (*f*) the selfish lie, calculated to deceive others so that the child may get what he wants; and (*g*) the loyal, or conventional, lie, to safeguard a friend (98).

Among young children, most untrue statements are not meant to deceive others but are due primarily to fantasy. Some are due to exaggerations, inaccuracies, and imitation of dishonesty in adults. Pressure to say the proper thing often encourages young children to lie. In addition, many young children learn to lie to protect themselves from punishment or threat of punishment (129, 183).

Older children sometimes lie or blame others to avoid punishment they know they deserve. A small percentage, usually boys, consider it "smart" to try to "get away with" wrongdoing without being punished. This attitude is encouraged when adolescents or adults boast about their success in escaping punishment for wrongdoing or when the child is actually taught to believe that it is all right to break rules if one is clever enough to get away with it. Most lies, however, are due to fear of punishment, disapproval, or ridicule (129, 208). The frequency of lying at different ages for boys and girls is shown in Figure 12–10.

Children under eight years of age think it is wrong to lie because it is forbidden by adults. If they are not punished, they have no feeling of guilt or shame for lying; if they are punished, they feel guilty and often ashamed of themselves. After eight years of age, the child regards lying as wrong because it is in conflict with mutual trust and affection. The older child also recognizes

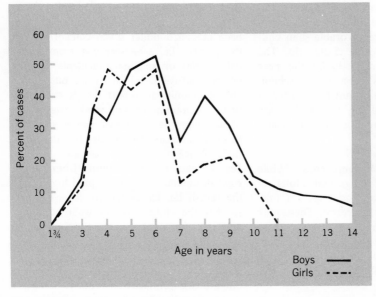

Figure 12–10. Sex differences in lying at different ages in childhood. (Adapted from J. Macfarlane, L. Allen, and M. P. Honzik, *A developmental study of the behavior problems of normal children between twenty-one months and fourteen years,* **University of California Press, 1954. Used by permission.)**

that if he is caught in his lies, unpleasant consequences will usually follow. This shift in attitude toward lying shows the development from morality involving objective responsibility to morality involving subjective responsibility—a shift from control by rules to control by conscience (139).

3. Cheating.   Many older children cheat in school because so much emphasis is put on grades. There is a tendency for boys to cheat more than girls, for children of low-grade intelligence to cheat more than those who are brighter, and for poorer children to cheat more than those from better socio-economic backgrounds. Children who do good school work are less tempted to cheat than those whose school work is poor (147).

Bright children, who do not need to cheat to come out at the top of the class, may be tempted to cheat by helping a less able friend. In this way, they hope to increase their social acceptance and counteract the impression that they are "brains" (39, 212). In commenting on the overemphasis on grades and its influence on cheating, Rogosin has pointed out:

We cannot continue to tell children that "Honesty pays" and then hammer at them

"Don't be a failure." Something is bound to crack. . . . Putting a premium on acquiring high marks, and then assuming that resistance to temptation will automatically take place because of a generalized trait of honesty, is to fly in the face of all the available scientific information and evidence. Honor systems of one kind or another cannot be said to exist in a social vacuum (163).

4. Stealing.   The child learns at a young age that it is wrong to steal or use the possessions of others without their knowledge and consent. The seriousness of stealing, however, is interpreted differently at different ages (77). When boys in grades 1 to 12 were asked to rate 20 offenses relating to honesty in order of seriousness, it was found that their attitudes toward different offenses changed as they grew older (54).

OFFENSES CONSIDERED MORE SERIOUS IN UPPER GRADES:

To snitch fruit from a peddler's stand
To swipe flowers from a park
To take a wheel from a wagon you find in the alley
To swipe your mother's wrist watch and pawn it
To lift $1 from your father's pants pocket when taking the pants to the tailor

To swipe $1 from your boss's desk
To take a wagon from a boy's back yard
To sneak a rubber ball from a dime-store counter

OFFENSES CONSIDERED LESS SERIOUS
IN UPPER GRADES:

To keep $1 you find on the street without trying to find the owner
To keep a candy package you find after it has fallen from a truck
To help yourself to chocolates from a box in your sister's room
To borrow your brother's baseball without asking
To ride on the streetcar for half fare when you should pay full fare
To sneak by an "L" cashier without paying

OFFENSES CONSIDERED EQUALLY SERIOUS
IN UPPER AND LOWER GRADES:

To swipe $1 from your brother's bank at home
To keep $1 you see a man drop from his pocket
To keep a ball and glove you find in the school yard
To snitch three tickets from a movie cashier
To steal candy and cigarettes from a boxcar
To swipe and sell lead pipes from an old warehouse

All the offenses against honesty that increased in seriousness involved actual stealing in one form or another. Those which seemed to become less serious related to hoodwinking persons in authority, keeping found property, and using the belongings of siblings. When asked the reasons for their judgments, the younger boys reported fear of punishment more frequently than the older boys. By contrast, the older boys gave as their most frequent reason the unwillingness to injure others (54).

5. Destructiveness. Destructiveness is usually unintentional in young children. When the young child is angry, however, he frequently destroys his possessions and those of others as a form of retaliation. When a group of college students were asked to recall their motives for destructiveness when they were children, the men said they were influenced by the crowd situation, the enjoyment of excitement, and their hostility toward the individual whose property was destroyed. Girls claimed that they were motivated more by the enjoyment and excitement than by hostility.

After the age of ten, children usually resist the urge to destroy because they fear breaking the law and being punished (34). Sometimes older children persist in destructiveness, not because of anger alone, as is true in many acts of juvenile delinquents, but because they want to prove to themselves and to the peer group that they are unafraid to flaunt the law and defy those in authority (36, 212). Sex differences in destructiveness are shown in Figure 12–11.

6. Truancy. Truancy becomes an increasingly common misdemeanor as children grow older. Many truants come from broken homes where parents or siblings are delinquent. Often they have changed schools frequently and have repeated grades. They are frequently disciplinary problems because of their antisocial behavior, their use of attention-getting devices, their aggressive behavior, and their poor work habits. Many truants have poor health records, are sickly and pampered at home, and are only children or the only boy or girl of the family (88, 146, 148). Truancy may come from school phobia, a fear of school caused by unfavorable home conditions rather than by conditions within the school. This will be discussed in more detail in relation to school interests in the following chapter.

Psychological Damage from Misdemeanors.
All children misbehave at some time or other, and they should. Even those who have been subjected to such harsh and punitive discipline that they are afraid to misbehave will sooner or later seek an outlet for the fear and resentment engendered by such child-training methods. Because these emotions have been bottled up within the child and have accumulated strength, they may lead to serious crimes, not necessarily against those who have been responsible for them but often against innocent victims. The

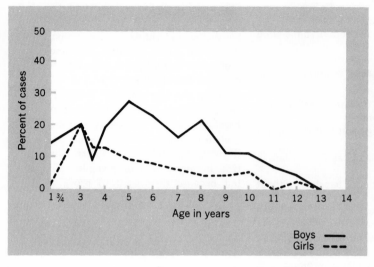

Figure 12–11. Sex differences in destructiveness at different ages in childhood. (Adapted from J. Macfarlane, L. Allen, and M. P. Honzik, *A developmental study of the behavior problems of normal children between twenty-one months and fourteen years,* University of California Press, 1954. Used by permission.)

"good" child can be *too good for his own good* and for that of society. The child who is "no trouble" to his parents or teachers is hiding something behind his facade of model conduct; he may be hiding a desire for revenge which will strike when it is least expected.

Although a certain amount of misbehavior in childhood is normal, the child can be expected to be less troublesome as he grows older. Because the social group expects "boys to be boys," it tolerates more misdemeanors in boys than in girls. Only when the number and seriousness of the child's misdemeanors deviate either above or below the norm for his age and sex group is there any reason for serious concern.

The child who is more troublesome, *both* in the home and in the school, than appears to be "normal" for his age is showing a danger signal of potential future trouble. He may improve to some extent if democratic training is substituted for authoritarian, but that alone will not be adequate. It is essential to get at the root of the trouble to find out why he misbehaves more than his agemates. If the child is more troublesome than is normal for his age *either* in school *or* at home, it suggests that the trouble lies not with the poor adjustment of the child but with the environment in which

he is more troublesome. A child whose teacher reports that he is as "good as gold" at school, for example, may be the product of authoritarian training in the home and democratic training in the school. Under such conditions, if the misdemeanors in the home are to be reduced, the home discipline should duplicate that of the school; obviously the school discipline "works" better than the home discipline. The child who is "good as gold" *both* at home and at school is headed for trouble. All one has to do is to read the newspaper to find out how often such children "pick up a shotgun and blast away at their innocently sleeping families"!

Perhaps the most serious aspect of misdemeanors in childhood is that they tend to give the child feelings of satisfaction, which motivate him to repeat the behavior. Keeping the level of satisfaction constant, however, usually requires an increase in the strength of the stimulus. A child who derives satisfaction from taking a quarter from his mother's pocketbook when he is a first-grader, for example, may have to steal a dollar to gain the same satisfaction when he is a fifth- or sixth-grader. Similarly, the child who gains satisfaction from peer approval when he flaunts adult authority will soon discover that he must flaunt it more openly and more brazenly as time passes if he is to continue to win approval. Like the alcoholic or drug addict, the child who inflates his ego by misbehaving must have stronger and stronger doses to maintain a constant level of satisfaction.

Equally serious, misdemeanors deprive the child of opportunities to learn how to gain satisfaction from socially acceptable behavior. If he can get satisfaction from being naughty, why would he want to be good, especially if he receives little attention and even less admiration from the peer group when he is good? If peer values remained constant and the peer group continued to admire the daring and naughty child, the problem would not be so serious. One of the areas of greatest change, however, relates to moral values. The child who was admired because he was naughty will later be scorned unless he mends his ways. If the satisfaction received from misdemeanors in childhood takes away the child's motivation to mend his ways, he will continue to try to win social approval by the tried and proved method of childhood and will increase the

seriousness of his misdemeanors when he discovers that in their milder form they no longer work.

As long as misdemeanors win social approval from the peer group, the child will not develop serious and lasting feelings of guilt or shame. Even before childhood is over, however, he discovers that many of his peers disapprove of lying, cheating, stealing, truancy, willful disobedience, and other misdemeanors which they formerly envied, admired, or applauded. When this change in peer attitudes reinforces the disapproval of the adult group, the child begins to suffer from the effects of shame and guilt. Gradually he builds up the belief that since his acts are considered unworthy of social approval, he too is unworthy of social approval. In time, this will develop into a generalized feeling of inadequacy and inferiority, which will warp his mental health. It will then lead to poor personal and social adjustments as well as to unhappiness and general discontent.

BIBLIOGRAPHY

(1) ABBE, A. E.: Maternal attitudes toward child behavior and their relationship to the diagnostic category of the child. *J. genet. Psychol.*, 1958, **92**, 167–173.

(2) ABERLE, D. F., and K. D. NAEGELE: Middle-class fathers' occupational roles and attitudes toward children. *Amer. J. Orthopsychiat.*, 1952, **22**, 366–378.

(3) ALDOUS, J., and L. KELL: Child-rearing values of mothers in relation to their children's perceptions of their mothers' control: an exploratory study. *Marriage fam. Liv.*, 1956, **18**, 72–74.

(4) ALDRICH, C. A.: On the subject of orderly and lawful behavior. *Pediatrics,* 1948, **1**, 725–732.

(5) ALLEN, F. H.: Special problems of infancy and childhood. *Ann. Amer. Acad. Pol. Soc. Sci.*, 1953, **286**, 65–73.

(6) ALLINSMITH, W.: Conscience and conflict: the moral force in personality. *Child Develpm.*, 1957, **28**, 469–476.

(7) ALPER, T. G., H. T. PLANE, and B. I. ABRAMS: Reactions of middle and lower class children

to finger paints as a function of class differences in child-training practices. *J. abnorm. soc. Psychol.*, 1955, **51**, 439–448.

(8) ANDERSON, H. H., G. L. ANDERSON, I. H. COHEN, and F. D. NUTT: Image of the teacher by adolescent children in four countries: Germany, England, Mexico, United States. *J. soc. Psychol.*, 1959, **50**, 47–55.

(9) ARIAMOV, E. A.: Fantasy and lying in childhood. *Semia i Shkola,* 1948, **11**, 16–19.

(10) AUSUBEL, D. P.: Prestige motivation of gifted children. *Genet. Psychol. Monogr.*, 1951, **43**, 53–117.

(11) AUSUBEL, D. P.: Relationship between shame and guilt in the socializing process. *Psychol. Rev.*, 1955, **62**, 378–390.

(12) BAKWIN, H., and R. M. BAKWIN: Discipline in children. *J. Pediat.*, 1951, **39**, 623–634.

(13) BALDWIN, A. L.: Socialization and the parent-child relationship. *Child Develpm.*, 1948, **19**, 127–136.

(14) BARCLAY, D.: "Law course" for the young. *The New York Times,* April 16, 1961.

(15) BARTOW, J. A. R.: Family size as related

to child-rearing practices. *Dissertation Abstr.,* 1961, **22**, 558.

(16) BECKER, W. C., D. R. PETERSON, L. A. HELLMER, B. J. SHOEMAKER, and H. C. QUARY: Factors in parental behavior and personality as related to problem behavior in children. *J. consult. Psychol.,* 1959, **23**, 107–118.

(17) BECKER, W. C., D. R. PETERSON, Z. LURIA, B. J. SHOEMAKER, and L. A. HELLMER: Relations of factors derived from parent-interview ratings to behavior problems of five-year-olds. *Child Develpm.,* 1962, **33**, 509–535.

(18) BEHERS, M. L.: Child rearing and the character structure of the mother. *Child Develpm.,* 1954, **25**, 225–238.

(19) BELLER, E. K.: Two attitude components in younger boys. *J. soc. Psychol.,* 1949, **29**, 139–151.

(20) BELLINGER, G., and E. B. WARING: *How do children feel toward younger brothers and sisters?* Ithaca, N.Y., Cornell Ext. Bull., 1953, No. 881.

(21) BISHOP, B. M.: Mother-child interaction and the social behavior of children. *Psychol. Monogr.,* 1951, **65**, No. 11.

(22) BLANK, L.: The intellectual functioning of delinquents. *J. soc. Psychol.,* 1958, **47**, 9–14.

(23) BLOCK, J.: Personality characteristics associated with the fathers' attitudes toward child rearing. *Child Develpm.,* 1955, **26**, 41–48.

(24) BOBROFF, A.: The stages of maturation in socialized thinking and in the ego development of two groups of children. *Child Develpm.,* 1960, **31**, 321–330.

(25) BOEHM, L.: The development of conscience: a comparison of American children of different mental and socioeconomic levels. *Child Develpm.,* 1962, **33**, 575–590.

(26) BOEHM, L.: The development of conscience: a comparison of students in Catholic parochial schools and in public schools. *Child Develpm.,* 1962, **33**, 591–602.

(27) BOEHM, L., and M. L. NASS: Social class differences in conscience development. *Child Develpm.,* 1962, **33**, 565–574.

(28) BRECKENRIDGE, M. E., and E. L. VINCENT: *Child development,* 4th ed. Philadelphia: Saunders, 1960.

(29) BRIM, O. C.: The acceptance of new behavior in child-rearing. *Hum. Rel.,* 1954, **7**, 473–491.

(30) BRODBECK, A. J., P. NOGEE, and A. DI MARCIO: Two kinds of conformity: a study of the Riesman typology applied to standards of parental discipline. *J. Psychol.,* 1956, **41**, 23–45.

(31) BURTON, R. V., E. E. MACCOBY, and W. ALLINSMITH: Antecedents of resistance to temptation in four-year-old children. *Child Develpm.,* 1961, **32**, 689–710.

(32) CHANSKY, N. M.: The attitudes students assign to their teachers. *J. educ. Psychol.,* 1958, **49**, 13–16.

(33) CLARK, E. J.: Teacher reactions toward objectionable pupil behavior. *Elem. Sch. J.,* 1951, **51**, 446–449.

(34) CLARK, W. H.: Sex differences and motivation in the urge to destroy. *J. soc. Psychol.,* 1952, **36**, 167–177.

(35) CLIFFORD, E.: Discipline in the home: a controlled observational study of parental practices. *J. genet. Psychol.,* 1959, **95**, 45–82.

(36) COHEN, A. K.: *Delinquent boys.* New York: Free Press, 1955.

(37) COLM, H.: Help and guidance as discipline for preadolescents. *Nerv. Child,* 1951, **9**, 131–138.

(38) COOPER, W. M.: Parental delinquency. *Phylon,* 1950, **11**, 269–273.

(39) CRANE, A. R.: The development of moral values in children. IV. Preadolescent gangs and the moral development of children. *Brit. J. educ. Psychol.,* 1958, **28**, 201–208.

(40) CRIST, J. R.: High-school dating as a behavior system. *Marriage fam. Liv.,* 1953, **15**, 23–28.

(41) CRUICKSHANK, W. M., and G. O. JOHNSON: *Education of exceptional children and youth.* Englewood Cliffs, N.J.: Prentice-Hall, 1958.

(42) DAMERON, L. E.: Mother-child interaction in the development of self-restraint. *J. genet. Psychol.,* 1955, **86**, 289–308.

(43) DAVIDSON, H. H., and G. LANG: Children's perceptions of their teachers' feeling toward them related to self-perception, school achievement, and behavior. *J. exp. Educ.,* 1960, **29**, 107–118.

(44) DAVITZ, J. R.: Contributions of research with children to a theory of maladjustment. *Child Develpm.,* 1958, **29**, 3–7.

(45) DICKENSON, J. R., and H. S. LEVIN: The role of discipline in modern education. *Nerv. Child,* 1951, **9**, 122–124.

(46) DOLGER, L., and J. GINANDES: Children's attitude toward discipline as related to socioeconomic status. *J. exp. Educ.,* 1946, **15**, 161–165.

(47) DOUVAN, E.: Independence and identity in adolescence. *Children,* 1957, **4**, 186–190.

(48) DU BOIS, F. S.: The security of discipline. *Ment. Hyg., N.Y.,* 1952, **36**, 353–372.

(49) DUKES, W. F.: Psychological studies of values. *Psychol. Bull.,* 1955, **52**, 24–50.

(50) DURKIN, D.: Children's concepts of justice: a comparison with the Piaget data. *Child Develpm.,* 1959, **30**, 59–67.

(51) DURRETT, M. E.: The relationship of early infant regulation and later behavior in play interviews. *Child Develpm.,* 1959, **30**, 211–216.

(52) DUVALT, E. M., and A. B. MOTZ: Age and education as factors in school experience and personal-family adjustments. *Sch. Rev.,* 1945, **53,** 413–421.

(53) EATON, M. T., L. A. D'AMICO, and B. N. PHILLIPS: Problem behavior in school. *J. educ. Psychol.,* 1956, **47,** 350–357.

(54) EBERHART, H. C.: Attitude toward property: a genetic study by the paired comparison rating of offenses. *J. genet. Psychol.,* 1942, **60,** 3–35.

(55) EYSENCK, H. J.: The development of moral values in children. VII. The contribution of learning theory. *Brit. J. educ. Psychol.,* 1960, **30,** 11–21.

(56) FINNEY, J. C.: Some maternal influences on children's personality and character. *Genet. Psychol. Monogr.,* 1961, **63,** 199–278.

(57) FITE, M. D.: Aggressive behavior in young children and children's attitudes toward aggression. *Genet. Psychol. Monogr.,* 1940, **22,** 151–319.

(58) FRANK, L. K.: The concept of maturity. *Child Develpm.,* 1950, **21,** 21–24.

(59) FRANK, L. K.: Play in personality development. *Amer. J. Orthopsychiat.,* 1955, **25,** 576–590.

(60) FROE, O. D.: The negative concept in discipline and its relation to rapport in counseling. *Educ. Admin. Superv.,* 1953, **39,** 470–477.

(61) GARDNER, L. P.: An analysis of children's attitudes toward fathers. *J. genet. Psychol.,* 1947, **70,** 3–28.

(62) GEISEL, G. B.: Discipline viewed as a developmental need of the child. *Nerv. Child,* 1951, **9,** 115–121.

(63) GESELL, A., F. L. ILG, and L. B. AMES: *Youth: the years from ten to sixteen.* New York: Harper & Row, 1956.

(64) GEWIRTZ, J. L.: A factor analysis of some attention-seeking behaviors of young children. *Child Develpm.,* 1956, **27,** 17–36.

(65) GLUECK, S., and E. H. GLUECK: *Unravelling juvenile delinquency.* New York: Commonwealth Fund, 1950.

(66) GOUGH, H. G., and D. R. PETERSON: The identification and measurement of predispositional factors in crime and delinquency. *J. consult. Psychol.,* 1952, **16,** 207–212.

(67) GRAY, S. W., and R. KLAUS: The assessment of parental identification. *Genet. Psychol. Monogr.,* 1956, **54,** 87–114.

(68) GREENFIELD, N. S.: The relationship between recalled forms of childhood discipline and psychopathology. *J. consult. Psychol.,* 1959, **23,** 139–142.

(69) GRIFFITHS, W.: *Behavior difficulties of children as perceived and judged by parents, teachers, and children themselves.* Minneapolis: The University of Minnesota Press, 1952.

(70) GRINDER, R. E.: New techniques for research in children's temptation behavior. *Child Develpm.,* 1961, **32,** 679–688.

(71) GRINDER, R. E.: Parental child rearing practices, conscience, and resistance to temptation of sixth-grade children. *Child Develpm.,* 1962, **33,** 803–820.

(72) GUMP, P. V., and J. S. KOUNIN: Milieu influences in children's concepts of misconduct. *Child Develpm.,* 1961, **32,** 711–720.

(73) HAVIGHURST, R. J.: The function of successful discipline. *Understanding the Child,* 1952, **21,** 35–38.

(74) HAVIGHURST, R. J.: *Human development and education.* New York: Longmans, 1953.

(75) HAVIGHURST, R. J.: Moral character and religious education. *Relig. Educ.,* 1956, **51,** 163–169.

(76) HAVIGHURST, R. J., and A. DAVIS: A comparison of the Chicago and Harvard studies of social class differences in child rearing. *Amer. sociol. Rev.,* 1955, **20,** 438–442.

(77) HAVIGHURST, R. J., and H. TABA: *Adolescent character and personality.* New York: Wiley, 1949.

(78) HAWKES, G. R.: A study of personal values of elementary school children. *Educ. psychol. Measmt.,* 1952, **12,** 654–663.

(79) HAWKES, G. R., L. G. BURCHINAL, and B. GARDNER: Measurement of pre-adolescents' views of family control of behavior. *Child Develpm.,* 1957, **28,** 387–392.

(80) HEMMING, J.: The development of children's moral values. *Brit. J. educ. Psychol.,* 1957, **27,** 77–88.

(81) HENRY, A. F.: Sibling structure and perception of disciplinary roles of parents. *Sociometry,* 1957, **20,** 67–74.

(82) HENRY, J.: Permissiveness and morality. *Ment. Hyg., N.Y.,* 1961, **45,** 282–287.

(83) HENRY, J., and J. W. BOGGS: Child-rearing, culture, and the natural world. *Psychiatry,* 1952, **15,** 261–271.

(84) HILLIARD, F. H.: The influence of religious education upon the development of children's moral ideas. *Brit. J. educ. Psychol.,* 1959, **29,** 50–59.

(85) HOEFLIN, R.: Child rearing practices and child care resources used by Ohio farm families with preschool children. *J. genet. Psychol.,* 1954, **84,** 271–297.

(86) HOFFMAN, M. L.: Power assertion by the parent and its impact on the child. *Child Develpm.,* 1960, **31,** 129–143.

(87) HOLLINGWORTH, L. S.: *Children above 180 IQ: origin and development.* New York: Harcourt, Brace & World, 1950.

(88) HYMES, J. L.: *Behavior and misbehavior: a teacher's guide to action.* Englewood Cliffs, N.J.: Prentice-Hall, 1957.

(89) ILG, F. L., and L. B. AMES: *Child behavior.* New York: Harper & Row, 1955.

(90) ILG, F. L., J. LEARNED, A. LOCKWOOD, and L. B. AMES: The two-and-a-half-year-old. *J. genet. Psychol.,* 1949, **75,** 21–31.

(91) INGERSOLL, H. L.: A study of the transmission of authority patterns in the family. *Genet. Psychol. Monogr.*, 1948, **38**, 225–302.

(92) ITKIN, W.: Relationships between attitudes toward parents and parents' attitudes toward children. *J. genet. Psychol.*, 1955, **86**, 339–352.

(93) JACKSON, P. W.: Verbal solution to parent-child problems. *Child Develpm.*, 1956, **27**, 339–349.

(94) JERSILD, A. T.: *Child psychology*, 5th ed. Englewood Cliffs, N.J.: Prentice-Hall, 1960.

(95) JERSILD, A. T., and R. J. TASCH: *Children's interests and what they suggest for education.* New York: Teachers College, Columbia University, 1949.

(96) JOHNSON, R. C.: Early studies of children's moral judgments. *Child Develpm.*, 1962, **33**, 603–605.

(97) JONES, L. V., and C. MORRIS: Relations of temperament to the choice of values. *J. abnorm. soc. Psychol.*, 1956, **53**, 345–349.

(98) JONES, V.: Character development in children: an objective approach. In L. Carmichael (Ed.), *Manual of child psychology,* rev. ed. New York: Wiley, 1954. Pp. 781–832.

(99) JOSSELYN, I. M.: Psychological changes in adolescence. *Children*, 1959, **6**, 43–47.

(100) JUSTIN, F.: Home training in human values. *J. home Econ.*, 1950, **47**, 722.

(101) KAGAN, J.: The child's perception of the parent. *J. abnorm. soc. Psychol.*, 1955, **53**, 257–258.

(102) KANNER, L.: *A word to parents about mental hygiene.* Madison, Wis.: The University of Wisconsin Press, 1957.

(103) KAPLAN, L.: The annoyances of elementary school teachers. *J. educ. Res.*, 1952, **45**, 649–665.

(104) KELL, L., and J. ALDOUS: The relation between mothers' child-rearing ideologies and their children's perceptions of maternal control. *Child Develpm.*, 1960, **31**, 145–156.

(105) KINSEY, A. C., W. B. POMEROY, C. E. MARTIN, and P. H. GEBHARD: *Sexual behavior in the human female.* Philadelphia: Saunders, 1953.

(106) KLATSKIN, E. H.: Shifts in child care practices in three classes under an infant care program of flexible methodology. *Amer. J. Orthopsychiat.*, 1952, **22**, 201–205.

(107) KLINEBERG, O.: Cultural factors in personality adjustment of children. *Amer. J. Orthopsychiat.*, 1953, **33**, 465–471.

(108) KOCH, H. L.: The relation of certain formal attributes of siblings to attitudes held toward each other and toward their parents. *Monogr. Soc. Res. Child Develpm.*, 1960, **25**, No. 4.

(109) KOHN, M. L.: Social class and parental values. *Amer. J. Sociol.*, 1959, **64**, 337–351.

(110) KOWATRAKUL, S.: Some behaviors of elementary school children related to class room activities and subject areas. *J. educ. Psychol.*, 1959, **50**, 121–128.

(111) LAMBERT, W. W., L. M. TRIANDIS, and M. WOLF: Some correlates of beliefs in the malevolence and benevolence of supernatural beings: a cross societal study. *J. abnorm. soc. Psychol.*, 1959, **58**, 162–169.

(112) LANDIS, P. H.: *Adolescence and youth: the process of maturing.* New York: McGraw-Hill, 1952.

(113) LANDRETH, C.: *The psychology of early childhood.* New York: Knopf, 1958.

(114) LANGSTON, R. D.: Children's overt and fantasy aggression toward peers as a function of perceived severity of parental punishment. *Dissert. Abstr.*, 1961, **21**, 2367.

(115) LASKO, J. K.: Parent behavior toward first and second children. *Genet. Psychol. Monogr.* 1954, **49**, 97–137.

(116) LAZOWICK, L. M.: On the nature of identification. *J. abnorm. soc. Psychol.*, 1955, **51**, 175–183.

(117) LEAVITT, J.: Teacher-pupil relationships. *J. educ. Res.*, 1959, **29**, 210–217.

(118) LEHMANN, I. J.: Learning. III. Attitudes and values. *Rev. educ. Res.*, 1958, **28**, 468–474.

(119) LEVIN, H., and R. R. SEARS: Identification with parents as a determinant of doll play aggression. *Child Develpm.*, 1956, **27**, 135–153.

(120) LEVINSON, B. M.: The inner life of the extremely gifted child, as seen from the clinical setting. *J. genet. Psychol.*, 1961, **99**, 83–88.

(121) LEWIN, K.: Time perspective and morale. In G. Watson, *Civilian morale.* Boston: Houghton Mifflin, 1952.

(122) LINDEN, M. E.: The older person in the family. *Soc. Casewk*, 1956, **37**, 75–81.

(123) LITTMAN, R. A., R. C. A. MOORE, and J. PIERCE-JONES: Social class differences in child rearing: a third community for comparison with Chicago and Newton. *Amer. sociol. Rev.*, 1957, **22**, 694–704.

(124) LIU, C. H.: *The influence of cultural background on the moral judgments of children.* Ph.D. thesis, Columbia University, 1950.

(125) LOURIE, N. V.: Discipline: a consistent, non-punitive concept. *Child Welf.*, 1951, **30**, 3–6.

(126) LYLE, W. H., and E. E. LEVITT: Punitiveness, authoritarianism, and parental discipline in grade school children. *J. abnorm. soc. Psychol.*, 1955, **51**, 42–46.

(127) LYNN, D. B.: Sex-role and parental iden-

tification. *Child Develpm.*, 1962, **33**, 555–564.

(128) MACCOBY, E. E., and P. K. GIBBS: Methods of child rearing in two social classes. In W. E. Martin and C. B. Stendler (Eds.), *Readings in child development.* New York: Harcourt, Brace & World, 1954. Pp. 380–396.

(129) MACFARLANE, J., L. ALLEN, and M. P. HONZIK: *A developmental study of the behavior problems of normal children between twenty-one months and fourteen years.* Berkeley, Calif.: University of California Press, 1954.

(130) MAC RAE, D.: A test of Piaget's theories of moral development. *J. abnorm. soc. Psychol.*, 1954, **49**, 14–18.

(131) MADOFF, J. M.: The attitudes of mothers of juvenile delinquents toward child rearing. *J. consult. Psychol.*, 1959, **23**, 518–523.

(132) MANWELL, E. M., and S. L. FAHS: *Consider the children—how they grow,* rev. ed. Boston: Beacon Press, 1951.

(133) MARSTEN, B. H., and J. C. COLEMAN: Specificity of attitudes toward parental and non-parental authority figures. *J. indiv. Psychol.*, 1961, **17**, 96–101.

(134) MARTIN, M. H.: Some reactions of preschool children to discipline. *Nerv. Child,* 1951, **9**, 125–130.

(135) MC ARTHUR, C.: Personality differences between middle and upper classes. *J. abnorm. soc. Psychol.*, 1955, **50**, 247–254.

(136) MC CORD, J., and W. MC CORD: The effects of parental role model on criminality. *J. soc. Issues,* 1958, **14**, No. 3, 66–74.

(137) MC GUIRE, C.: Family life in lower and middle class homes. *Marriage fam. Liv.,* 1952, **17**, 1–6.

(138) MC GUIRE, C., and G. D. WHITE: Social-class influences on discipline at school. *Educ. Leadership,* 1957, **14**, 29–31, 234–236.

(139) MEDINNUS, G. R.: Objective responsibility in children: a comparison with Piaget data. *J. genet. Psychol.*, 1962, **101**, 127–133.

(140) MERRY, F. K., and R. V. MERRY: *The first two decades of life,* 2d ed. New York: Harper & Row, 1958.

(141) MEYERS, C. E.: The effect of conflicting authority on the child. *Univer. Iowa Stud. child Welf.,* 1944, **20**, 31–98.

(142) MILLER, D. R., and G. E. SWANSON: *The changing American parent.* New York: Wiley, 1958.

(143) MILTON, G. A.: A factor analytic study of child-rearing behaviors. *Child Develpm.,* 1958, **29**, 381–392.

(144) MORGAN, P. K., and E. L. GAIER: The direction of aggression in the mother-child punishment situation. *Child Develpm.,* 1956, **27**, 647–657.

(145) MORRIS, C., and L. V. JONES: Value scales and dimensions. *J. soc. Psychol.*, 1955, **51**, 523–535.

(146) MOUSTAKAS, C. E.: *The teacher and the child: personal interaction in the classroom.* New York: McGraw-Hill, 1956.

(147) MUELLER, K. H.: Can cheating be killed? *Personnel Guid. J.,* 1953, **31**, 465–468.

(148) MULLEN, F. A.: Truancy and classroom disorders as symptoms of personality problems. *J. educ. Psychol.*, 1950, **41**, 97–109.

(149) MUNN, N. L.: *The evolution and growth of human behavior.* Boston: Houghton Mifflin, 1955.

(150) MUSSEN, P. H., and J. KAGAN: Group conformity and perceptions of parents. *Child Develpm.*, 1958, **29**, 57–67.

(151) NAKAMURA, C. Y.: The relationship between children's expressions of hostility and methods of discipline exercised by dominant, overprotective parents. *Child Develpm.*, 1959, **30**, 109–117.

(152) New York Times Report: Pupils told how to avoid crimes. *The New York Times,* Feb. 20, 1961.

(153) New York Times Report: U.S. children top list for honesty. *The New York Times,* Sept. 3, 1961.

(154) PETERSON, D. R.: Behavior problems of middle childhood. *J. consult. Psychol.*, 1961, **25**, 205–209.

(155) PIKAS, A.: Children's attitudes toward rational versus inhibiting parental authority. *J. abnorm. soc. Psychol.*, 1961, **62**, 315–321.

(156) PROTHRO, E. T.: Patterns of permissiveness among preliterate peoples. *J. abnorm. soc. Psychol.*, 1960, **61**, 151–154.

(157) PRESSEY, S. L., and R. G. KUHLEN: *Psychological development through the life span.* New York: Harper & Row, 1957.

(158) PUTNEY, S., and R. MIDDLETON: Effect of husband-wife interaction on the strictness of attitudes toward child rearing. *Marriage fam. Liv.,* 1960, **22**, 171–173.

(159) RADKE, M. J.: *The relation of parental authority to children's behavior and attitudes.* Minneapolis: The University of Minnesota Press, 1946.

(160) RAINWATER, L.: A study of personality differences between middle and lower class adolescents: the Szondi test in culture-personality research. *Genet. Psychol. Monogr.,* 1956, **54**, 3–86.

(161) RAPP, D. W.: Child rearing attitudes of mothers in Germany and the United States. *Child Develpm.,* 1961, **32**, 669–678.

(162) RETTIG, S., and B. PASAMANICK: Changes in moral values among college students: a factorial study. *Amer. sociol. Rev.,* 1959, **24**, 856–863.

(163) ROGOSIN, H.: What about "cheating" on

examinations and honesty? *Sch. Soc.*, 1951, **74**, 402–403.

(164) ROSENTHAL, M. J.: The syndrome of the inconsistent mother. *Amer. J. Orthopsychiat.*, 1962, **32**, 637–644.

(165) ROY, K.: Parents' attitudes toward their children. *J. home Econ.*, 1950, **42**, 652–653.

(166) RUSSELL, D. H.: *Children's thinking.* Boston: Ginn, 1956.

(167) SCARPITTI, F. R., E. MURRAY, S. DINITZ, and W. C. RECKLESS: The "good" boy in a high delinquency area: four years later. *Amer. sociol. Rev.*, 1960, **25**, 555–558.

(168) SCHAEFER, E. S., and R. Q. BELL: Development of a parental attitude research instrument. *Child Develpm.*, 1958, **29**, 339–361.

(169) SCHOEPPE, A.: Sex differences in adolescent socialization. *J. soc. Psychol.*, 1953, **38**, 175–185.

(170) SCOFIELD, R. W., and C.-W. SUN: A comparative study of the differential effect upon personality of Chinese and American child training practices. *J. soc. Psychol.*, 1960, **52**, 221–224.

(171) SCOTT, R. B., A. D. FERGUSON, M. E. JENKINS, and F. F. CUTLER: Growth and development in Negro infants. V. Neuromuscular patterns of behavior during the first year of life. *Pediatrics*, 1955, **16**, 24–29.

(172) SEARS, R. R.: A theoretical framework for personality and social behavior. *Amer. Psychologist*, 1951, **6**, 476–483.

(173) SEARS, R. R., E. E. MACCOBY, and H. LEVIN: *Patterns of child rearing.* New York: Harper & Row, 1957.

(174) SEARS, R. R., J. W. M. WHITING, V. NOWLIS, and P. S. SEARS: Some child-rearing antecedents of aggression and dependency in young children. *Genet. Psychol. Monogr.*, 1953, **47**, 135–234.

(175) SETTLAGE, C. F.: The values of limits in child rearing. *Children*, 1958, **5**, 175–178.

(176) SEWELL, W. H., P. H. MUSSEN, and C. W. HARRIS: Relationships among child training practices. *Amer. sociol. Rev.*, 1955, **20**, 137–148.

(177) SHAPIRO, M. B.: Some correlates of opinion on the upbringing of children. *Brit. J. Psychol.*, 1952, **43**, 141–149.

(178) SHERIF, M.: *An outline of social psychology.* New York: Harper & Row, 1948.

(179) SILLER, J.: Socioeconomic status and conceptual thinking. *J. abnorm. soc. Psychol.*, 1957, **55**, 365–371.

(180) SLAVSON, S. R.: Authority, restraint, and discipline in group therapy with children. *Nerv. Child*, 1951, **9**, 187–195.

(181) SPOCK, B.: What we know about the development of healthy personality in children. *Understanding the Child*, 1951, **20**, 2–9.

(182) STACEY, L. L., and M. L. REICHEN: Attitudes toward death and future life among normal and subnormal adolescent girls. *Except., Children*, 1954, **20**, 259–262.

(183) STAINS, K. B.: The beginnings of dishonesty. *Understanding the Child*, 1954, **22**, 55.

(184) STAPLES, R., and G. W. SMITH: Attitudes of grandmothers and mothers toward child-rearing practices. *Child Develpm.*, 1954, **25**, 91–97.

(185) STENDLER, C. B.: A study of some sociomoral judgments of junior high school children. *Child Develpm.*, 1949, **20**, 15–28.

(186) STENDLER, C. B., and N. YOUNG: Impact of first grade entrance upon the socialization of the child: changes after eight months of school. *Child Develpm.*, 1951, **22**, 113–122.

(187) STOKE, S. M.: An inquiry into the concept of identification. In W. E. Martin and C. B. Stendler (Eds.), *Readings in child development.* New York: Harcourt, Brace & World, 1954. Pp. 227–239.

(188) STOLZ, L. M., et al.: *Father relations of war born children.* Stanford, Calif.: Stanford, 1954.

(189) STONE, L. J.: A critique of studies of infant isolation. *Child Develpm.*, 1954, **25**, 9–20.

(190) STOTT, D. H.: *Delinquency and human nature.* Fife, Scotland: Carnegie United Kingdom Trust, 1950.

(191) STOUFFER, G. A. W.: Behavior problems of children as viewed by teachers and mental hygienists. *Ment. Hyg., N.Y.*, 1952, **36**, 271–283.

(192) STOUFFER, G. A. W., and J. OWENS: Behavior problems identified by today's teachers and compared with those reported by E. K. Wickman. *J. educ. Res.*, 1955, **48**, 321–331.

(193) STRANG, R.: How children and adolescents view their world. *Ment. Hyg., N.Y.*, 1954, **38**, 28–33.

(194) STRAUSS, A. L.: The development of conceptions of rules in children. *Child Develpm.*, 1954, **25**, 193–208.

(195) STROUP, A. L.: Marital adjustment of the mother and the personality of the child. *Marriage fam. Liv.*, 1956, **18**, 109–113.

(196) TASCH, R. J.: Interpersonal perceptions of fathers and mothers. *J. genet. Psychol.*, 1955, **87**, 59–65.

(197) THOMPSON, G. G.: *Child psychology*, 2d ed. Boston: Houghton Mifflin, 1962.

(198) TRENT, R. D.: The expressed values of institutionalized delinquent boys. *J. genet. Psychol.*, 1958, **92**, 133–148.

(199) TUDDENHAM, R. D.: Studies in reputation. I. Sex and grade differences in school children's evaluations of their peers. II. The diagnosis of social adjustment. *Psychol. Monogr.*, 1952, **66**, No. 1.

(200) TUMA, E., and N. LIVSON: Family socioeconomic status and adolescent attitudes to

authority. *Child Develpm.*, 1960, **31**, 386–399.

(201) UGUREL-SEMIN, R.: Moral behavior and moral judgments of children. *J. abnorm. soc. Psychol.*, 1952, **47**, 463–474.

(202) VINACKE, W. E.: Concept formation in children of school age. *Education*, 1954, **74**, 527–534.

(203) VINCENT, E. L., and P. C. MARTIN: *Human psychological development.* New York: Ronald, 1961.

(204) VON MERING, F. H.: Professional and nonprofessional women as mothers. *J. soc. Psychol.*, 1955, **42**, 21–34.

(205) WATSON, G.: Some personality differences in children related to strict or permissive parental discipline. *J. Psychol.*, 1957, **44**, 227–249.

(206) WATTERBERG, W. W.: Church attendance and juvenile misconduct. *Sociol. soc. Res.*, 1954, **34**, 195–202.

(207) WERNER, E.: Milieu differences in social competence. *J. genet. Psychol.*, 1957, **91**, 239–249.

(208) WHITE, M. S.: Social class in child rearing practices and child behavior. *Amer. sociol. Rev.*, 1957, **22**, 704–712.

(209) WHITEMAN, P. H.: The relation of religious affiliation to parents' opinions concerning child rearing and children's problems, and parents' evaluations of their own personalities. *Dissert. Abstr.*, 1959, **20**, 2149–2150.

(210) WHITING, J. W. M., and I. L. CHILD: *Child training and personality: a cross cultural study.* New Haven: Yale, 1953.

(211) WIGGAM, E. A.: Do brains and character go together? *Sch. Soc.*, 1941, **54**, 261–265.

(212) WITRYOL, S. L., and J. E. CALKINS: Marginal social values of rural school children. *J. genet. Psychol.*, 1958, **92**, 81–93.

(213) WOLFENSTEIN, M. T.: A developmental study of children's fantasies about moral problems. II. Conceptions of "goodness." *Amer. Psychologist*, 1950, **5**, 304–305.

(214) WOODRUFF, A. D.: *Basic concepts of teaching.* San Francisco: Chandler, 1961.

(215) WOODS, P. J., K. B. GLAVIN, and C. M. KETTLE: A mother-daughter comparison on selected aspects of child rearing in a high socioeconomic group. *Child Develpm.*, 1960, **31**, 121–128.

13

SOME CHILDHOOD INTERESTS

Interests play an important role in the child's life because they determine, to a large extent, what he will do and how well he will do it. An *interest* is a learned motive which drives the person to preoccupy himself with an activity when he is free to choose what he will do. An interest is "something with which the child identifies his personal well-being" (255). When a child sees that something will benefit him, he becomes interested in it; this motivates learning. As long as the child finds something satisfying, he continues to be interested in it. When satisfaction wanes, so does interest (280).

A *whim* is a temporary interest; while it lasts, it may be as strong as, or even stronger than, an interest, but because it gives only temporary satisfaction, it wanes in strength very rapidly. True interests are more persistent because they satisfy a need in the individual's life.

Many adults fail to recognize that what appears to be an interest may be, in reality, only a whim. As a result, they make the mistake of expecting a child to continue a task or activity which no longer brings him satisfaction. A child may, for example, want to learn to play the piano because an older sibling or a playmate is taking music lessons. In the belief that this desire is based on an interest and that the interest, in turn, means that the child has musical talent, parents make arrangements for music lessons; they buy a piano and then force the child to practice. If playing the piano gives the child little satisfaction, his interest will rapidly wane, and he will rebel against the lessons and the practice.

Because every interest satisfies some need in the child's life, even though the need may not be readily apparent to an adult, the stronger the need, the stronger and more lasting the interest. The child who has a strong need for companionship will direct his energies into activities that will bring him into contact with others. If these contacts fail to satisfy his need, either because he is unacceptable to the children who are available or because he has little in common with them, his interest will not wane but will be turned into other channels that satisfy his need better (184, 280). He may, for example, play with imaginary playmates, or he may identify with people in books, in comics, in the movies, or on the television screen (186, 268).

The more frequently the child expresses his interest in an activity, the stronger it will become. On the other hand, interests are subject to extinction through disuse (125, 255). Should the child's environment limit his opportunities to play with other children, his interest in playmates will wane, and a substitute interest will take its place. If he can find a thoroughly satisfying substitute, a time will come when he will have little interest in people; he may even claim that people "bore him." Similarly, when a child cannot see how the abstract facts he learns in arithmetic will benefit him, his interest in arithmetic will wane, even though it may have been very strong before he started school.

An activity that fails to satisfy, stimulate, or challenge the individual is boring. Such an activity is the opposite of an interest. When children are bored, they are likely to get into mischief and cause trouble for others in the hope of stirring up some excitement, thus turning a boring situation into an interesting one. For the most part, children experience *boredom* when they are forced to do things that do not fit their needs or give them satisfaction. Boredom is especially likely to occur in school, where the curriculum and method of teaching must be planned for the group rather than for the individual.

DEVELOPMENT OF INTERESTS

The child is not born with any ready-made interests; rather, he develops them as a result of learning experiences. The following fundamental facts are essential to an understanding of how, why, and when interests develop:

1. There Are Individual Differences in Interests. The development of interests closely parallels the child's physical and mental development. The child who is devel-

oping more rapidly or more slowly than the average will be out of step with his age-mates. This is why a very bright child has little in common with children whose intelligence ranges around the norm (184). It is also one of the reasons why the late-maturing child encounters certain social problems; his social interests are still those of a child, while the interests of his age-mates are those of an adolescent (156, 211).

2. Interests Depend upon Readiness to Learn. Because interests are closely correlated with physical and mental development, a child cannot acquire interests before he is physically and mentally ready to do so. A child cannot, for example, have a real interest in ball games until he has the strength and muscle coordination necessary for ball play. Similarly, a child cannot be interested in history until his intelligence has developed to the point where he can comprehend the meaning of historical facts.

One of the major problems in religious or sex instruction is that of satisfying the child's curiosity about these matters with material that is not too abstract for him to comprehend. Explanations must often be so oversimplified that the child builds up concepts which must later be radically revised.

3. Interests Depend upon Opportunities to Learn. Regardless of the child's readiness to learn, he cannot develop interests unless he has an opportunity to do so. This, in turn, is dependent upon his environment and the interests of the people, both children and adults, with whom he is most closely associated. The type of environment a child has throughout the years of his childhood determines what interests he will develop and how strong they will be.

The young child's environment is limited largely to the home; consequently, his interests are "homegrown." The first-born child, it has been found, usually has a wider range of interests than later-born siblings because he has more contacts with adults. Second- and later-born siblings, by contrast, have more contacts with siblings than with adults; as a result, they imitate the interests of their older siblings. If the older sibling is of the same sex, the child develops more interests because he imitates a sibling of the same sex more than a sibling of the opposite sex (166). Children brought up in large families develop more interests than children from small families because of the greater variety of interests of different family members (7).

As the environment of the child broadens to include the school, the neighborhood, and the community, opportunities are opened up for the acquisition of new interests. From school, he learns to be interested in areas unknown to him before he entered school, such as history, geography, and foreign languages. From contacts with members of the peer group, he acquires interests in play that would have been impossible to develop in the home.

When the satisfaction from peer contacts is greater than from family contacts, the child who must choose between peer and family interests will choose the former. If gangmates show a contempt for anything but the simplest and plainest clothes, for example, he will have little or no interest in either his clothes or his appearance, regardless of how much pressure his parents exert. Since the child of today comes in contact with mass media at an extremely early age, he acquires many interests sooner than would have been possible a generation or so ago.

4. Interests Change with Age. Along with physical and mental changes come changes in interests. This is well illustrated in the child's play interests. While he is very young, his physical and mental development makes it possible for him to be interested only in games with few rules and regulations. Gradually he "outgrows" these simple play activities and wants to take part in games and sports which involve highly skilled movements of the body and which have rules and regulations to govern these movements. At puberty the child literally puts away his childish interests and develops new interests that are more closely related to his mature body and mind. See pages 140 to 141 for a more complete discussion of changed interests at puberty.)

As new interests develop, many of the interests acquired in early childhood change or are abandoned. A child's interest in money, for example, changes as he grows older. As a small child, his interest centers on filling his piggy bank. In later childhood, he discovers that money can provide him with material possessions that give him satisfaction; his interest in money then shifts from saving to spending (214).

Because interests will continue to change as long as physical and mental changes are taking place, one should not expect children's interests to be stable. Changes in interests reflect growth in understanding and

As he develops physically and mentally, the child progresses from interest in simple, disorganized play to more skillful games, and onward toward even more mature activities. (Standard Oil Co., N.J.)

the acquisition of new knowledge. Interests that satisfied needs when the child was young cannot continue to satisfy his needs when he becomes more mature (82). When growth slows down and a mature level of development is reached, interests normally become more stable (280).

5. *Cultural Influences Determine Interests.* Cultural influences in the child's environment play an important role in the development of his interests by controlling his learning opportunities. From parents, teachers, and other adults, the child is given opportunities to learn what the cultural group considers appropriate interests and is deprived of opportunities to develop interests which the social group considers inappropriate. For example, the amount of interest he shows in different school subjects and in school in general is greatly influenced by the attitudes of significant people in his environment (259).

A comparison of the amount of interest English and American students showed in different school subjects revealed that the two groups were similar in many respects. It was found, however, that English boys showed a greater interest in drawing than American boys. The difference was explained by the fact that drawing is considered more sex-appropriate for boys in England than in America (259). It was further found that American boys showed a greater interest in arithmetic than English boys because of the high value Americans place on this "practical" subject as the basis for later success in business (291).

In general, girls are encouraged to become interested in indoor play, while boys are encouraged to develop outdoor play interests; the cultural group considers the former "feminine" and the latter "masculine" (292).

6. *Interests Are Emotionally Weighted.* In the development of interests, interpersonal relationships are more important than specific teaching. The child who dislikes his teacher may learn to dislike not only tne subject she teaches but school in general. By contrast, liking the teacher may result in an interest in a school subject that is strong enough to become a generalized interest in school itself. Thus it is apparent that interests are markedly influenced by likes and dislikes.

Studies of interests have shown that patterns of likes and dislikes are established early and remain relatively stable over the years. When the child enters school, he likes most things, although his likes and dislikes are general rather than specific. For example, he will like anything that falls in the category of "play" and dislike anything that might be considered "work." By the time

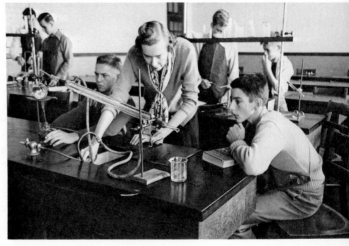

they are ten years old, children whose initial attitude toward everything was favorable develop patterns of interest through the acquisition of *dislikes*. The boy will dislike anything that might be classed as "sissy." Boys, more than girls, develop a dislike for anything that is "work" and, as a result, acquire antiwork and anti-intellectual attitudes which markedly affect their interests (292).

7. Development of Interests May Be Limited. Limitations in the child's physical and mental capacities or in his experiences will set limits on his interests. A physically handicapped child, for example, cannot acquire the same interest in sports as a child whose physical development is normal. In the same way, mental handicaps limit a child's interest in academic studies to the point where he does not have enough interest to be able to keep up with his agemates; as a result, he is put into special classes where emphasis is placed on nonacademic subjects (65).

While the type of environment the child has during his childhood years determines what interests he will develop, it may also cut him off from developing interests that might be very satisfying to him. Children who are discriminated against because of their race or religion often cannot satisfy their need for play involving companionship with the peer group; they are forced to develop interests in play activities where companionship is unessential (295).

Interests sometimes develop as a result of frustration and are closely related to the child's level of aspiration. It is not unusual for a child to develop an interest in something beyond his reach; for example, a boy with a small, puny body may develop a strong interest in sports. By identifying himself with players, he derives, vicariously, the enjoyment that other boys derive from the activity itself. Similarly, Negroes often develop a strong interest in recreations and vocations which whites enjoy but which are closed to Negroes because of their race (280).

Importance of Interests. Interests are important because they serve as a source of strong motivation to learn. A child who is interested in an activity, whether it is a form of play or work, will put forth more effort to learn than the child who is less interested or actually bored. If learning experiences are to tap the child's full resources, they must be timed to coincide with his interests. This is the "teachable moment,"—the time when the child is ready to learn because he is interested in what learning will bring him in the way of personal advantage (129).

Furthermore, interests add enjoyment to a child's life. If he is interested in carrying out a required activity, the experience will be far more enjoyable than if he is forced to carry it out in spite of lack of interest. If he lacks interest, his achievements will fall far short of his capacities. One of the reasons for underachievement among bright children is that they have too little interest in a subject to work up to their capacities, and, as a result, they are bored (76, 184).

Because interests are closely related to likes and dislikes and are markedly influenced by them, a child may be conditioned by unfavorable experiences to dislike a situation or an activity early in life. He is then cut off from later opportunities to develop interests in similar situations or activities. A boy who feels that helping with work in the home is not masculine will be conditioned to dislike all housework. As a result, he will show little or no interest in the home and how it is run. This will cut him off from many activities that might prove to be enjoyable to him or contribute to the happiness of his family life (291).

There are many indications that the range of interests a child acquires is too narrow to enable him to become acquainted with many interests that might serve his needs and fulfill his varied potentialities. Development of interests is greatly influenced by opportunities provided by the environment, and for this reason the home, the school, and the community should try to expose the growing child to as many activities as possible to enable him to discover which meet his needs and which do not. Given opportunities to try out many different activities, he can determine from his own experiences which give him satisfaction and which bore him.

When one fails to acquire certain interests in childhood, he may be penalized throughout life. Many adults report that they regret not acquiring more interests in childhood (288). While interests can be acquired at any age, the child has more time and more opportunity to learn new interests than the adult. This is well illustrated in the case of recreational interests. In the home, the school, and the neighborhood, the child is provided with time, equipment, space, and guidance in learning different play interests; the adult must provide these for himself (72, 131).

The most important fact to remember is that, because interests are learned, the child can be guided in the development of interests that will contribute to his happiness and success. A child can learn to be interested in reading worthwhile books if he is encouraged to do so and if he sees a model of reading enjoyment in his parents. If he is permitted to spend his leisure time as he pleases, however, he will often develop such strong interests in reading comics or watching television—because they require less effort and because "everyone else" does it— that he will never discover the satisfaction that reading interests can bring.

Then, too, because interests are learned, undesirable interests can be eliminated and replaced by more desirable ones. The sooner this is done, the better. Once an interest is well learned, it provides a source of satisfaction that may be difficult to replace; this will militate against the development of more wholesome interests. The child whose interest in Christmas centers around Santa Claus and his pack of toys may find it difficult to substitute the satisfaction of the religious observance of Christmas for the gifts Santa Claus has brought him. Had less emphasis been placed on Santa Claus in the first place, and more on the religious observances, the child's interest in Christmas would persist long after he no longer believed in Santa Claus.

METHODS OF DISCOVERING CHILDREN'S INTERESTS

Through *observation* of what objects a child plays with, buys, collects, or uses when it is apparent that there is an element of spontaneity in his activity, it is possible to get a clue to his interests. The degree of his interest may be determined by the length of time he spends with the activity in a given period of time or by what he says he enjoys doing or says he engages in frequently (125, 255). Many activities that occupy much of the child's free time, however, such as listening to the radio or watching television, do not seem to represent strong interests on the child's part but a lack of something better to do.

Other clues to the child's interests are the *questions* he asks, *what he talks about* when he is with his contemporaries, *what he reads about* when he is free to select his books, and *what he draws* and paints spontaneously. One of the most satisfactory ways of determining a child's interests at a given age is to study his *wishes*. When asked what they would like to have if they could have anything they wanted, most children state very frankly wishes for things that interest them most (152). Numerous studies of children's interests have been made using this approach.

The young child's wishes emphasize material possessions, such as toys, money, clothes, and material improvements in the home. The elementary-school child concentrates his wishes on personal achievement, personal improvement, skills to earn money and gain independence, and greater popularity and social acceptance. He wishes he had better living quarters, could travel and see the world, and be morally better. By the sixth grade, the child's wishes become less egocentric and more social; he wishes for things that will help others as well as things which interest him. Girls put more emphasis on personal attractiveness and popularity, while boys emphasize skills, personal achievement, and independence. In their expressed wishes, Negro children put more emphasis on material possessions than white children of the same age (54, 152).

A similar but perhaps more realistic approach to the study of interests consists in asking the child to tell or to write down the three *things that interest him most*. This approach emphasizes the interests the child *already* has, rather than things he would like to have. When asked to tell his "three greatest interests in school" or in some other area of life, the child must know specifically what the word "interest" means if the information he reveals is to be of value. When used with older children, this approach gives a clue to their already formed interests and can be of great value in determining where their satisfactions come from (7, 8, 9).

SOME CHARACTERISTIC INTERESTS

In spite of marked individual differences, certain interests are commonly found among American children and are fostered by environmental influences that are fairly universal in our culture. These interests will be discussed in the following pages.

RELIGIOUS INTEREST

Religion is, according to Webster's dictionary, "the outward act or form by which men indicate recognition of a god or gods to whom obedience and honor are due." It involves a desire for help, security, and consolation not given by the world; a dependence on a power outside of oneself; a feeling of confidence in the power appealed to; and an emotional reaction of a reverential sort.

Religion includes two elements: belief and *practice*. Both are important throughout life, but at different ages the relative importance of each varies. The younger the child, the greater his interest in religious practices.

Interest in religious beliefs is slower in developing because it depends upon the intellectual development of the child; the younger the child, the less able he is to comprehend the meaning of religious beliefs (193).

The child's interest in religion is fostered by the training he receives in the home, Sunday school, or church and by the emphasis placed on religious observances in his daily life. The child who has a home environment in which grace is said before every meal, who is expected to say his prayers before going to bed, and who has parents who read or tell him stories from the Bible will have a greater interest in religion than the child whose main contact with religion is his weekly visit to Sunday school. Every young child, however, regardless of the religious instruction he receives, is curious about the heavens above him, which produce the rain, snow, and sunshine, as well as about the everyday world. Between the ages of three and four years, the child's questions often relate to religion. "Who is God?" "Where is Heaven?" "How do you get there?" Mysteries about birth, death, growth, and the elements are often explained in religious terms. The child accepts almost any answers he gets, but they satisfy him only temporarily and, in many cases, lead to doubt and skepticism during the adolescent years.

Factors Affecting Religious Interest. Of the many factors that determine how great the child's interest in religion will be, the following have been found to be the most important:

1. Religious Training. Many parents try to forestall the religious skepticism that is so common in adolescence by providing *rigid religious training* in childhood. It has been found, however, that the more rigid and dogmatic the training in childhood, the more likely the adolescent is to have doubts about the religious concepts he had formerly accepted.

A religion that is suited to an adult is no more suited to a child than an adult novel is. If religion is to mean anything to a child, not only should it be concrete in form and presented in language that the child can understand, but it should also be presented in a less dogmatic fashion than is usually the case. The child wants to satisfy his curiosity by asking questions. Religious instruction must provide for this if it is to fulfill its purpose. Most Sunday schools emphasize formal rote learning and dogmatic instruction rather than interpretation of religious doctrines. When instruction is authoritarian, the child has no opportunity to question what he is taught. Instead, he is expected to accept passively what he has learned and let faith supplant reason (4, 182).

When a child's religious training in childhood is neglected, inadequate, or unsuited to his level of development, he is likely to become atheistic or agnostic as he becomes older and to take little or no part in church activities. The more religious training the child has, the more likely he is to feel the need for religion as he grows older (4, 150, 293).

2. Religious Beliefs.

What the child learns to believe and how interesting his beliefs are to him will determine how great his interest in religion will be. The child's religious beliefs are based on the concepts he develops as a result of his religious training. As Landis has pointed out, "Young children form their ideas regarding religion with frail capacity and slight experience, and they gradually approximate the concepts of their elders" (174). At first, the child's religious experiences are marked by "fantasies and egocentrism" (4). Because such experiences meet important needs in his life, he will have a strong but purely egocentric interest in religion.

A child's beliefs will depend largely on the teaching he receives. If a child is taught to think of God as a person who will become angry when people do something wrong and to believe that He will punish people for their sins, his beliefs about religion will be very different from those of a child who has had God presented to him in another manner. Furthermore, if teaching involves the use of everyday language and experiences, the child develops definite and concrete concepts. Because these concepts have a personal meaning for him, he is likely to accept them uncritically (21, 43).

The religious beliefs of a young child are based on realistic concepts. He thinks of God, Heaven, Hell, angels, and the Devil in terms of the pictures he has seen of them or the stories he has been told about them. How pictures of people and scenes foreign to the child's everyday experience can distort his religious concepts has been well illustrated by Murphy's statement that children are apt to learn of Jesus,

. . . not as an ideal grown-up who helped people, but as a little baby whose mother put him in a straw thing in a barn instead of a crib, and to whom queer-looking men in striped gowns brought presents no baby could use. They learn, too, that there was a bad king, with a ferocious face, of whom the baby's mother was afraid, so that she had to take him a long way from home, riding on an animal that is not seen in the city, nor even in the zoo (209).

Later, as the child's comprehension increases and as his experiences become more varied, his concepts will change. His concept of God as a father will be influenced by his experiences with his own father and with the fathers of his friends. Likewise, his concepts of sin and forgiveness will reflect the ways he has been treated when he misbehaved (170, 193).

Because the child tends to regard everything in his environment as *animate,* he interprets religion in that way (248). He endows the sun, moon, stars, and all the elements with the same life qualities that human beings have. Distortions of religious concepts, due to misunderstanding of the words used to describe or explain them, are common among young children. Jersild gives as an example a young child who told his mother about Jesus' 12 bicycles (disciples) and who was puzzled about the "consecrated cross-eyed bear" (consecrated cross I'd bear) (151).

Because the child builds up concepts

about unknown people, places, and situations in terms of those he knows, it is not surprising that his concepts about the unknown become confused with already developed concepts. Vagueness and confusion of meaning in concepts relating to spiritual experiences, such as "conversion," "cross," "rosary," "Savior," and "Christian," are greater than in concepts relating to special religious days or places, such as "Christmas," "Sunday," and "church" (157). As Estvan and Estvan have pointed out, children "find religion difficult to understand. Many of the concepts are abstract, the language often difficult, and much that happens is based on the far away and long ago" (90).

Studies of *specific religious concepts* have revealed that they vary in detail according to the pictures the child has seen and the teachings he has had. Most children have a concept of *God* as a person, made of flesh and blood. He is very large, has a kindly or stern face, is old, wears long white flowing garments, and has a white beard or whiskers. Some children think of God as wearing a crown and having wings. God's role is that of a creator, a provider, and a controller of natural phenomena. He can see everything everywhere, and He spends his time watching people to see how they behave. If they are bad, He punishes them, though He can be supplicated through prayer. While all children think of God as all-powerful, some think of Him as kind, and others regard Him as terrifying and awe-inspiring. Most children think of God's abode as in the heavens or in the clouds (170, 193).

The child conceives of *Heaven* as a place where people have everything they want, especially the things they have not had in daily life, and where there is eternal happiness and peace. The people who go to Heaven become winged *angels* and wear long flowing white garments. It is ruled over by God just as the earth is. *Hell*, by contrast, is a place where there is eternal unhappiness and punishment, ranging from fire to deprivation of all pleasures. It is ruled over by the *Devil*, who is in the form of a man with horns and tail and who carries a pitchfork. He is red all over, as is Hell (4).

Most children believe in *miracles* and accept the fact that God can do anything. *Church* is a place where people are made good, while *Sunday* is a day of fairly strict religious observance. Good people say their *prayers* daily and can expect to have them answered. The *Bible* was written by God; every word of it is true, and to doubt it is sinful. What happens to a person *after death* depends on what sort of life he lived on earth. These concepts, in general, are very similar for all children of the Christian faith (3, 109, 239).

Closely related to the child's religious concepts is his concept of *Santa Claus*. Children under four years of age accept every detail of the Santa Claus myth. The five-year-old accepts the realism of Santa's clothes, his hearty laugh, and his reindeer. By the time the child is six, he knows that many children doubt the existence of Santa Claus, but he tries to repel all suspicion. A year later, in spite of moments of skepticism, he clings to his belief because of the enjoyment he derives from it. By the time the child is nine, the Santa Claus myth has been abandoned; at that age, "Santa Claus as a real being passes from the child's life" (168).

Concepts of *religious denominations* are very confusing for a child. In a study of the development of Jewish children's concepts about their religious denomination, it was found that these concepts develop in stages at predictable ages. In the first stage, beginning around the age of five or six years, most Jewish children know that they are "Jewish"; this concept is undifferentiated, however, except that it implies that Jews are different from Catholics or Protestants. In the second stage, from seven to nine years, they develop a concrete concept of a Jew as a person who behaves in a certain way; he goes to the Jewish synagogue, celebrates Jewish holidays, and wears a Jewish star.

In the third stage, from ten to eleven years, children develop an abstract concept of a Jew as a person who believes in one God and worships in a different way from people with other religious affiliations. As is true of all concepts, religious concepts depend on the child's level of conceptual development. Since this varies from child to child, each reaches a specific stage in the developmental pattern at a slightly different age. A similar pattern has been found in children's concepts of Catholicism (87, 88).

3. Religious Attitudes.

As was pointed out earlier, the child is interested in anything that will benefit him personally. His attitude toward religion is egocentric and self-seeking. To a young child, prayers and worship are means of attaining some childish desire; if he is good, his prayers will be answered and his wishes fulfilled. This attitude is in keeping with the child's personality. Just as he is accustomed to having things done for him by adults, so he visualizes God as a person who will do things for him (182, 193). To the young child, for example, Christmas is a time to receive toys and gifts; giving presents to others does not mean much to him.

The religion of the older child is also *egocentric*. This is well illustrated in the study made by Freeman of first-grade pupils' concepts of Christmas. They believed Christmas to be an occasion to appease their acquisitive tendencies to a pitch of greediness. As Freeman pointed out, all were "strong on getting," with very little thought of "giving." Typical reactions were as follows: "Last Christmas I got a tricycle and the next year I got a mamma doll." "I like Christmas because Santa has brought me a wagon and a new brown suit" (100, 168). Most children whose religious instruction has emphasized the "fatherly" nature of God have a very personal relationship with a very personal God. They feel that God is "their father" and that His interest in them is so great that they can turn to Him in times of trouble (191, 193).

Aside from this interest in God as a person who will help him in times of trouble, the child's religion is an impersonal experience. For most children, religion is a means of self-improvement, of getting what they want in life, and of avoiding sin and its

consequences. Typically, the child's attitude, unlike that of the adolescent or adult, is not affected by emotionality. Even the thought of sin or punishment is impersonal and unemotional (4, 185, 230).

Expressions of Interest.

Interests are always expressed in action. When the child's interest in religion is strong, he will devote considerable time to religious activities. How long his interest will persist will be determined, to a large extent, by how long he continues to believe what he has been taught. Religious beliefs are often weakened when the child discovers that they conflict with the beliefs of his friends or with what he learns at school or from his reading.

The most common ways in which children express their interest in religion are discussed in the following paragraphs:

1. Interest in Religious Stories.

The stories in the Bible appeal to the child in much the same way as fairy stories (157). Both relate to people, countries, and situations so different from those of the child's everyday environment that he enjoys hearing them over and over. At different ages children show preferences for different parts of the Bible. Children under eight years of age prefer stories relating to the birth and childhood of Jesus and the childhood of such characters as Samuel, Moses, Joseph, and David, while older children show a greater interest in the historical books of the Old Testament. Most children are interested primarily in persons and happenings rather than in doctrines (108).

2. Interest in Prayer.

While most young children say prayers in a somewhat parrot-like fashion, the older child often makes up his own prayers. Children under eight years of age feel that prayer is a way of talking to God; they believe that God answers their prayers by telling them how to be good or what to do or not to do. They put a strong emphasis on requests for material things and for help in doing things they feel incapable of doing alone. The older child puts more emphasis on asking for help, on seeking forgiveness for wrongdoing, and for thanking God for His help (170). On the whole, however, children's prayers are a "begging ritual," with emphasis on "pennies from heaven" (151, 191, 303).

An analysis of children's prayers has revealed that they fall into three major categories, each of which relates to specific things children seek through prayer. These three categories are:

1. Prayers concerning the variety and abundance of the good things of life, for which little children are encouraged to thank God. These blessings range from "the morning light" to "the clothes we wear." This idea is expressed in grace said at the table. An example of this type of prayer is:

For my big ball and kiddie car
On which I ride so fast and far
Thank you, Father, thank you.

2. Direct petitions for special privileges, such as protection and care, especially during the night, and for guidance. This is illustrated by the child's favorite prayer:

Now I lay me down to sleep,
I pray thee, Lord, my soul to keep.
If I should die before I wake,
I pray thee, Lord, my soul to take.
If I should live for other days,
I pray thee, Lord, to guide my ways.

3. Prayers for personal help in doing things which the children are led to believe they cannot achieve by themselves, such as:

Father lead me day by day
Ever in thine own sweet way.
If I'm tempted to do wrong
Make me steadfast, wise, and strong.
Show me what I ought to do,
Teach me to be pure and true (191).

While the child uses prayer as a means of requesting many things from God, as in the case of the awkward boy who, finding himself inferior in sports, prayed, "O God, help me to run fast," the child is often disappointed when his requests are not granted (191). In time, then, he is likely to become

skeptical of the value of prayer. True, he may continue to pray from force of habit or because it is expected of him, but he has little confidence that it will bring any results. Thus prayer in the older child and the adolescent is likely to degenerate into a ritual (29, 43, 239). Figure 13–1 shows the typical transition in a child's reaction to prayer as he grows older.

3. Interest in Religious Observances. Religious services in Sunday school or church may appeal to the child because of their colorful pageantry. He usually likes to sing, and the ritual of the church service intrigues him. He enjoys looking around at people at worship, to see what they are doing. His attitude is a strange mixture of awed reverence and curiosity (38, 111).

When the novelty of the service wears off, the child begins to rebel against church attendance. He enjoys going to Sunday school only as long as his friends go too. He likes young people's organizations, such as gymnasiums in the cities and "sociables" in small communities, picnics, holiday celebrations, and outings. His interest is thus primarily social rather than religious (86). A small percentage of older boys and girls attend Sunday school, and an even smaller percentage go to church. In addition to finding it difficult to understand the meaning of the church service, especially the sermon, children dislike the "generally restrictive nature and length of religious services planned more for adults than children. Yet, many young people like going to church because the whole family goes. For them, social values outweigh the moral and religious. If nothing else, going to church gives them an opportunity to 'dress up' and 'meet friends' " (90).

As a general rule, the percentage of children who attend church becomes smaller as the community becomes larger. Children as well as adults living in suburban areas attend more than those in urban areas because it is "the thing to do." Attendance is greater among upper- than among lower-social-status groups, and upper-status people are more active in church organizations than

Figure 13–1.   Typical transition in a child's reaction to prayer.

lower. Children learn, long before childhood is over, that membership in certain churches has more status value than membership in others. Belonging to the "right church" and being active in it becomes a status symbol for the child, just as it does for his parents (177, 193, 218, 313).

When parents attend church or observe religious rites in the home infrequently, the child is less active than when parents are active participants. Children whose parents are Catholic or Jewish, it has been found, put more emphasis on religious observances in the home than those whose parents are of the Protestant faiths (12, 86, 111). Families split by death or divorce are less active participants than families that are not split. When parents have different religious affiliations, they are less active in church affairs than when split by divorce (38). If one parent has no church affiliation, there is little religious participation.

Girls, at every age, are more active in religious observances and have more favorable attitudes toward these observances than boys. Girls tend to conform closely to the socially approved ways of viewing religion, while boys are more neutral or negative in their attitudes (90). Toward the end of childhood, both boys and girls, but especially boys, attend Sunday school and church less and less and participate less actively in organizations connected with the church.

Religious Doubt.   Although most young children accept religious teachings implicitly, almost all express some doubts. This is apt to occur when prayers are not answered and is more frequent among very bright children. When the young child does question his religious teachings, his reactions are unemotional and objective. When the episode that gave rise to the doubt passes, his doubt likewise passes and is quickly forgotten (170).

The older child is often confused about denominational differences and expresses concern about which doctrines are right. Likewise, he may become critical of some of the religious concepts he learned when he was a little child. This may be due to the inadequacies and inconsistencies in his religious teaching, but it is more likely to result from his studies in school, especially his study of science. By the time the child reaches adolescence, his greater mental maturity and his increased knowledge lead to serious religious doubts (185).

Very often a child assumes a critical attitude because he enjoys asking questions to put the Sunday-school teacher "on the spot." What appears to be religious doubt is, in reality, little more than a form of childish "smartness." How superficial the critical attitude of the child is may be seen from the fact that he is not really worried or distressed; he forgets the whole matter after Sunday school is over. This contrasts markedly with the adolescent, who ponders over religious concepts and becomes emotionally disturbed when they conflict with scientific or pseudoscientific ones (108, 109).

As long as the child can believe without question what has been taught at home or in school, his interest in religion will persist. When he begins to doubt the teachings, his interest wanes; the greater the doubting, the greater the waning in interest. Typically, as children approach adolescence, their interest in religion and religious activities starts to wane because of their growing doubt. Doubt is often intensified by peer pressures. When a child's friends say they doubt the religious beliefs of their parents, doubting becomes the popular thing to do.

INTEREST IN THE HUMAN BODY

One of the earliest forms of exploratory behavior is the young baby's watching and investigating of his own body. Later, when the young child discovers a mirror, he enjoys observing himself in it. He is very much interested in seeing what his face looks like when he "makes faces" at himself, and he laughs with glee at his image (40, 107).

By the time the child is 3½ years old, he is interested in how his body functions and what the different parts of the body are used for. He makes comments and asks questions about the various parts of the body; examines his navel, eyes, hair, breast, and anus; and looks at himself in the mirror and calls

the attention of other children to different parts of their bodies. Like many other interests of the child, the interest in his body is objective and impersonal. The behavior of a child during elimination, for example, is just as matter-of-fact as in brushing the hair (146, 201).

The young child's interest in bodily differences between boys and girls is also devoid of emotional tone. Most children react to genital differences with tranquil, unperturbed acceptance. Even children who are unprepared for these differences are not upset when they first notice them. Some young children refer to the genitals as "funny" (meaning "strange") because they are surprised at seeing genitals different from their own. Relatively few young children regard genital differences as a source of concern or interest. Before children attain school age, however, their interest in sex differences begins to grow, and in the latter part of childhood it reaches a peak. The growth of the genitals and the development of the secondary sex characteristics focus the child's attention on these sex differences and heighten his interest in them (60, 163).

The younger child's interest is centered mainly on the exterior of his body. He explores the different parts of his body thoroughly to see what sensations they produce. The older child shifts his interest to the interior of his body. He wants to know what is inside his head, his trunk, and his limbs; he wants to know what the names of the different parts are, what they do, and what they look like. This interest motivates him to ask innumerable questions, to look at pictures in magazines and books which show the location and shape of the different organs, and to give rapt attention when adults discuss physical ailments.

In spite of this interest, most children develop very faulty concepts of the body and how it functions because of faulty instruction in the home or inaccurate answers to questions. In some cases, the errors arise because the child misinterprets the meanings of technical terms. It is not unusual, for example, for the child to confuse the terms "brain," and "skull" and to think that breathing involves "taking in" air only (106, 212, 213). (Refer to pages 509 to 510 for a more complete discussion of the child's concepts of the body and how it functions.)

The child's interest in his body does not, as a rule, include interest in health unless his health is so poor that it prevents him from doing what other children do (8, 9). If a child is handicapped by a chronic illness, such as asthma or diabetes, he often becomes so health-conscious that he thinks and talks too much about it. The well-adjusted child is not health-conscious; the poorly adjusted child, by contrast, not only is preoccupied with his ailments but frequently uses them to explain academic or social inadequacies or to avoid doing things he does not want to do. By the time the child reaches adolescence, he appreciates the relationship between health, appearance, and the activities he wants to engage in. As a result, his interest in health often becomes an obsession (16, 165, 176).

SEX INTEREST

The American child of today grows up in an environment where sex is everywhere. He soon discovers that he must show an interest in it if he is to fit into the social life of his peers. The comic books he reads and the movies and television shows he sees often have a sex theme; they show him what is sex-appropriate in appearance and behavior and thus help to focus his attention on sex and arouse an interest in it. Newspaper and magazine advertisements, especially those which make veiled suggestions about female hygiene or ways of increasing male potency, help to keep the child's interest in sex alive.

Comics classed as "objectionable" by adults because of their emphasis on sex appeal more to poorly adjusted children than to the well adjusted. Even the best-adjusted children, however, like sex comics, partly because everyone else does and partly because they are forbidden fruit. By reading these comics, children not only do what the peer group expects them to do but also assert their independence of adult authority (23). Talking about sex or telling off-color

jokes with a sex theme is likewise the thing to do when with the peer group, especially for boys. Away from the watchful eyes and alert ears of adults, children like to talk about sex and to show one another pictures or books relating to sex (78).

Areas of Sex Interest. A brief analysis of areas of interest will serve to show how widespread the child's preoccupation with sex is and how this interest increases with age, reaching a peak as childhood draws to a close.

Love Object. The young baby's first love is for himself. In this *autoerotic* stage, which lasts for the first five or six months of life, the baby shows no attachment to others. The first object of attachment is the *mother, nurse,* or *person who takes care of the baby.* Gradually, during the babyhood years, love attachments are extended to other members of the home environment. The strongest attachments are to those who make the baby's associations especially happy. Often, the baby's attachment to a pet or toy and his affection for it are stronger than his love for persons.

When the child begins to play with *other children,* he singles out one or two children and develops a strong emotional attachment to them. At first, the affection is directed toward an older child who, like the adult, makes the child the center of attention. Because associations of this sort are pleasant to the child, he builds up an affectionate attitude toward his playmate.

As childhood draws to a close, the affection formerly concentrated on an adult member of the family is often shifted to an adult outside the home—a teacher, camp counselor, or playground instructor. As they approach adolescence, many children begin to "hero-worship" a movie actor or actress, always of the same sex as they, or some national or sports hero. While hero worshiping reaches its peak in the early years of adolescence, it begins before childhood is over.

During childhood, a *romance* occasionally develops between a boy and girl in which the boy displays an attitude of affection and respect toward the girl and a desire to serve her by carrying her books to and from school and protecting her from teasing. Childhood romances differ markedly from adolescent romances in that there is no physical expression of affection between the children other than perhaps an occasional shy holding of hands. The girl may likewise show deep affection for the boy, but she has no desire for physical demonstrations of this affection.

Children's *expressions of affection* change with age. In the young child, affection is expressed by patting, fondling, or kissing and a desire for close, personal contact. The child may go to extremes, following the loved one wherever she goes and raising stormy protests if she leaves the house without taking him along. Pets and favorite toys are caressed, hugged, kissed, and carried around wherever the young child goes.

In young children, concentration of affection on one person is often of brief duration. A child may show great fondness for a person, but as soon as the person leaves, the child will be diverted to someone else, provided the other person gives the child attention and affection.

The older child's affection is shown by wanting to be with the person he loves and admires, by doing things for that person, and by trying to imitate him in any way possible. Whether the object of affection is a friend of the same sex, a friend of the opposite sex, a parent, a teacher, or a "hero," the expression of affection is the same. Showing affection by physical contact is regarded as "babyish" and is embarrassing if seen by a member of the peer group; the older child is afraid such behavior will be considered "mushy" or a sign that he is "tied to some adult's apron strings." To avoid all such problems, he maintains a surface reserve, though his interest in that person remains strong.

Sex Antagonism. According to the old saying, "Where there is hate, there is love." A child may not *hate* members of the opposite sex, and he may not *love* them; he may merely feel superior to them. Regardless of what his reaction may be, *antagonism between the sexes indicates that there is an interest in members of the opposite sex,* not a complete indifference to them. In spite of the fact that boys generally develop an attitude of masculine superiority and express their feelings of superiority by refusing to play with girls, they are less antagonistic toward girls than girls are toward boys (126).

Antagonism on the part of girls generally reaches its peak during the early part of puberty; it is then replaced by an active interest in winning the attention and favor of members of the opposite sex. While some of the sex antagonism of girls undoubtedly stems from resentment, some of it also stems from interest, even though they cannot express this interest directly (5). (See pages 365 to 368 for more details about sex antagonism.)

Curiosity about Sex. Interest in sex is shown most clearly in the child's curiosity about all matters pertaining to sex. This interest increases as the child grows older and is capable of seeing and understanding things that were incomprehensible to him when he was younger. Should a pet, for example, have young, the little child's interest will be concentrated mainly on playing with the young. The older child, by contrast, will be curious to know the whys and wherefores of their arrival. Similarly, the matter-of-fact acceptance of genital differences on the part of the young child will be replaced by a strong curiosity about these differences. From his own experiences, the child learns that there are reasons for everything, and he wants to know the reason for these differences.

In the process of exploring his body, the baby sooner or later touches his sex organs and discovers that this results in a pleasurable sensation. By chance, he discovers his navel and derives fun from putting his fingers in the "hole." Other than that, sex arouses no curiosity in the child until approximately the end of the third year, when the boy notices that his body differs from that of the little girl; that he stands up when he goes to the toilet, while she sits down; and that adults have certain physical features, such as "bumps" and hair on the body, which little children do not have. The genitals are the focus of interest in the young child. His attitude is completely impersonal and objective, however, with none of the morbid interest one associates with adolescent curiosity (60, 163, 238).

Six-year-olds show an active and frank curiosity about sex matters, more far-reaching than that of preschool children. They are definitely aware of differences in the body structure of boys and girls and seek an explanation for these differences. This curiosity is not purely intellectual but has a strong emotional drive. As children grow older, sexual curiosity becomes disguised. It is there, nevertheless, and is merely suppressed because children have learned that they may be punished if they express it too aggressively. Like any strong interest that is suppressed, interest in sex will find indirect outlets. Children express their interest in sex by reading books or comics with sex themes, by talking about sex to members of the peer group, by telling and enjoying off-color jokes and stories, or by exploring the sex organs (17, 108).

With the radical changes that take place on the surface of the body at puberty and with the accompanying new sensations of the sex organs, interest in sex becomes almost an obsession. This interest becomes subjective and personal. It is not, for example, concentrated on the origin of babies or on genital differences, but rather on how the changes that are taking place in the child's body affect him personally. As the rate of puberty changes increases, interest in sex heightens until it occupies much of the child's time and thought (98, 309).

A common source of interest in sex is the arrival of a new baby or the appearance of kittens or puppies. The young child is naturally curious to know where they came from, and any logical explanation will satisfy his curiosity for the time. Preschool children generally think babies come from God or are bought from stores.

By the time children are seven or eight years old, they know that doctors bring babies, and they are aware that mothers have some role in the coming of babies. Children from nine to eleven have heard their playmates discuss various conceptions of the origin of babies, and some know about genital contact. Very intelligent children are generally precocious in their knowledge of reproduction (60, 238).

Of the many methods used by children to satisfy their curiosity about sex, the most common are (1) asking questions, (2) exploring the sex organs, (3) engaging in homosexual play, and (4) masturbating.

Every child asks *questions* about a variety of subjects. The more intelligent the child, the more questions he is likely to ask (60). When the topic of sex is raised, however, parents become embarrassed, and many try to avoid the subject because they want to "prevent calamities." The result is that the child must go elsewhere for information.

Among preschool children, the most common questions relate to the origin of babies, the coming of another baby, the sex organs and their functions, and physical sex differences. Among older children, emphasis is on the origin of babies, the process of birth, and the relation of the father to reproduction. Typical questions asked by three- to twelve-year-olds are: "Will she have baby birds some day?" "Do the baby deer come out of an egg like the chickens do?" "Does it hurt the baby deer when it comes out of the mother deer?" "Does the baby calf come out of the mother?" "Do they look like little seeds?" (238).

One of the difficulties children have in obtaining information about sex through questioning is lack of an adequate sex vocabulary. Most children, however, acquire names for the genital organs, such as "thing" for both the male and the female genital organ; "puss," "hole," "susie," and "pocketbook" for the female organ; and "teapot," "piece of rope," or "hose" for the male (60). Unquestionably, some of the misinformation children acquire and then pass on to their friends comes not from faulty teaching but from *misinterpretation of good teaching* which is too advanced for the child to comprehend.

Sex curiosity often expresses itself in *exploration of the sex organs*. At the age of six years, children commonly engage in *mutual* exploration. The search to discover what the sex organs are and how they function is often carried to dangerous extremes, such as the insertion of short, unclean, or rusty objects into body orifices. "Doctor games" give the child an excuse to examine the sex organs of his playmates. Among eight-year-olds, sex behavior consists in comparing masculine prowess in the toilet, peeping, telling smutty jokes, provocative giggling, some masturbation, using obscene language, and having "secrets" about "boy-girl" favorites. From nine years of age until puberty, there is progressively more provocative behavior, such as insertion of the penis into the girl's vagina, manual exploration associated with direct observation of the reproductive anatomy, exhibitionism, and oral contacts (163, 238).

Children from the lower social classes are generally not taught that sex play is wrong, nor are they punished for it; therefore, they have little feeling of guilt or shame, even if caught in such play. By contrast, children from the middle and upper social classes learn that any form of sex play is considered "wrong," and they are almost always punished if caught. This does not stop them from satisfying their curiosity; it merely encourages them to engage in sex play in secret (254).

Sex play with members of the same sex—*homosexual play*—is a form of sex exploration. It is more common than *heterosexual* play—play with members of the opposite sex. Homosexual play usually consists in exhibition of the genitals, manual manipulation of the genitals, mutual manipulation of the genitals, and anal or oral contacts with genitals. The child generally engages in such play with companions close to his own age, though the initial experience is often with an older child or an adult. Most sex play ends with the onset of adolescence among normal, well-adjusted children. If it continues after that age, it may be regarded as a danger signal of poor adjustments (163).

For the young child, *masturbation* is a form of sex exploration carried out primarily to satisfy the child's curiosity about the genital organs and the sensations he receives when stroking, fondling, or playing with them. He discovers by chance that touching the genitals gives more pleasurable sensations than touching any other part of his body. It is not surprising, therefore, that he repeats the act, especially when he is alone and has little to engage his attention and interest. Masturbation also serves to release tension in the young child. Sometimes manipulation of the sex organs is caused by local irritations or pressure from tight clothing (163, 238).

The young child makes no attempt to be secretive about playing with his sex organs, nor does he show shame or guilt when caught in the act. The school child who has learned from scoldings or punishment that it is considered naughty practices masturbation when alone. If he has not discovered the pleasurable sensations that come from playing with the sex organs through his own exploration, he generally learns to do so from watching other children or from the suggestions of older children.

Boys are generally introduced to the "new sport" of masturbation by older boys or adults; most girls learn from their own exploration or from watching other girls. Masturbation is more common among boys than among girls, and among children who are poorly adjusted than among those who are well adjusted. Most children, however, masturbate to some extent (163, 164, 198, 238).

While no known physical harm comes from masturbation, its psychological damage may be serious. Many children who are poorly adjusted and unhappy turn to masturbation as a source of compensation for their feelings of inadequacy. The more they masturbate, the more inadequate they feel; this is reflected in poorer and poorer adjustments, accompanied by greater unhappiness. While all social classes regard masturbation at all ages with disfavor, members of the middle and upper classes are less tolerant

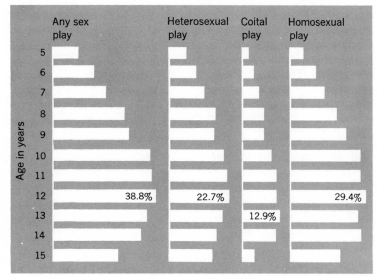

Figure 13–2. Types of sex play among children. (Adapted from A. C. Kinsey, W. B. Pomeroy, and C. E. Martin, *Sexual behavior in the human male*, Saunders, 1948. Used by permission.)

than members of the lower classes (254). In the lower classes, however, this tolerance changes with the sexual maturing of the child. The adolescent boy who masturbates is regarded as "degenerate" and "effeminate"; the manly boy is expected to satisfy his sex drive by petting and sexual intercourse (163, 164). The common forms of sexual behavior in childhood and early adolescence are shown in Figure 13–2.

Attitudes toward Sex. As the child satisfies his curiosity about sex, he acquires attitudes which determine the quality of his behavior. The child learns to regard sex as the significant people in his life do. As these significant people change from parents, to teachers, to peers of the same sex—and, in adolescence, to peers of the opposite sex—the child's attitudes will change also. The basic attitude established in the home in the early years of the child's life, however, dominates later attitudes (155). As Mussen et al. have pointed out:

No amount of information or reassurance in preadolescence or adolescence will enable the child to adopt a healthy attitude toward sexuality if in the preceding years he has been taught to fear sexual responses. . . . Clinicians have found that when unfavorable

sexual attitudes have been built up . . . it is extremely difficult, and sometimes impossible, to shift them through the use of rational advice given in adolescence. Even extensive psychotherapy may fail to change attitudes which have become too deeply ingrained (210).

The serious consequences of unfavorable attitudes are not limited to sexual behavior. If the child learns to think of the sex organs and their functions as something to talk about only in a whisper; if he has learned to think of touching his sex organs as wicked and depraved; and if he has learned to think of the marital relationship as something to be "endured" only for the sake of having children, he will endow his own feelings with these beliefs. While this may not be serious when he is a child, it will become extremely serious when he is an adult.

The amount and accuracy of the information the child receives are not as important in the shaping of his attitudes as the way in which the information is given. A child may forget most or all of the answer to his question, "Where do babies come from?" but he is not likely to forget the *way* in which it was answered, the expression on the face of the person who answered it, or the ease or difficulty the person had in talking to him about it. These behavior symbols convey to the child how that person feels about sex.

If the symbols suggest to the child that the person regards sex as a natural phenomenon, related to love and a happy marriage, he will learn to think of it that way too; if the symbols suggest that sex is something to be talked about in whispers, that it is embarrassing and not entirely "nice," he will adopt a similar attitude. As Mussen et al. have emphasized, "The important part of sex education depends not on biological instruction *per se,* but upon the demonstration of healthy attitudes on the part of parents, teachers, and other influential adults" (210).

While it is generally agreed that the child should get his first information about sex from his parents—preferably a parent of the same sex—some parents are incapable of giving this information accurately because of their limited knowledge. Other parents have such an unfavorable attitude toward sex that any information they give, no matter how accurate it may be, will be unintentionally misleading or biased. Parents who surround sex with mystery and taboos or who establish a "conspiracy of silence" not only encourage the development of unfavorable attitudes but also whet the child's curiosity to learn more. The greater this conspiracy of silence, the greater the child's curiosity (71, 175).

On the whole, children who get their first information about sex from their parents or from school have more favorable attitudes than those who receive most of their information from other sources (80, 175). The education and socioeconomic status of parents also play a part in forming children's attitudes toward sex; children from better backgrounds have more favorable attitudes (180, 254).

Far too many children get their information about sex from a friend or classmate. It is often given in whispers, with demands for promises "never to tell" where it came from, and is usually accompanied by embarrassed giggles and sneers. Under such circumstances it would be hard for children to develop wholesome attitudes toward sex (17, 108). Furthermore, because many children do not get the point of dirty stories and suggestive pictures, they are likely to be confronted with roars of laughter and taunts of "lily-white," "innocent," or "pure" if they ask their friends for explanations. While such remarks may be only the friends' way of covering up their own ignorance, they suggest to less experienced children that their peers consider them too young to understand these matters. This adds to the confused information they already have.

Books written in a matter-of-fact way to give a child the "facts of life" generally encourage a wholesome attitude on his part. There is no guarantee, however, that they always will. A child who has been brought up to believe that babies come from the stork or from the doctor's satchel, for example, may find hearing the coldly stated facts and seeing the unadorned drawings of pregnancy and childbirth a traumatic experience. Unless the child has someone to interpret such a book to him in a sympathetic way, he is likely to develop feelings of fear and revulsion, neither of which will be easy to overcome later.

Importance of Sex Instruction. Because sex plays such an important role in a person's life, the foundations laid in early childhood are of vital importance. Whether the child's attitude toward sex will be healthy or not will depend largely on the source from which he gets his information. Perhaps in no other area of development is guidance more vital. If the child could remain in ignorance about sex until he reached the junior or senior high school, he could be expected to get accurate and adequate information from courses specially designed for this purpose. But this is impossible. Even before he enters the first grade, the child has gathered some information, or misinformation, and has an already developed attitude (155).

If the child is to have correct and adequate information about sex, and if he is to have healthy attitudes, he needs well-planned and carefully guided sex education. This education should be of two types: *constructive* and *preventive*. Constructive education should build up healthy attitudes about sex and marriage, while preventive education should teach the child what to avoid in his sexual relationships but should not terrify him by emphasizing the ill effects of sexual promiscuity.

Today, more and more children are getting sex instruction earlier than in the past, and more and more are getting their information from parents and relatives (175). These trends are illustrated in Figure 13–3. If the child's curiosity about sex is not satisfied in the home, however, he will seek satisfaction elsewhere. Much of the information the child gets from outside the home comes from suggestive pictures in comics, from books or magazines his friends buy "under cover," from dirty stories and jokes, and from the school grapevine. While some schools do have special courses in sex education or combine information about sex with a course in hygiene, biology, or general science, most children have a large fund of information about sex before they take these courses (17, 108).

VOCATIONAL INTERESTS

The child's interest in his future vocation develops early, not because he must begin to prepare for his life work then, but rather because his attention is focused on the future by people constantly asking him what he is going to do when he grows up. As he reads books, sees movies and television shows, looks at the comics, and hears people talk about their jobs, he develops an interest in what his future will be like.

The child's vocational interests are greatly influenced by identification with someone he admires. He decides he wants to do what his ideal does, whether this ideal is a parent, a relative, a teacher, or the policeman who patrols the crossing to his school. During the elementary-school years, the child's concepts of his future are vague, poorly defined, and unrealistic. To him, the future is a time when he will be independent of parental and adult authority. To achieve this independence, he knows that he must have money and that this will necessitate getting a job. His vocation therefore becomes a means to an end; he thinks little about the enjoyment or prestige he will get from working, but much about the freedom he will have. Rarely does he think about his abilities or his aptitude for the kind of work he aspires to do (91, 214, 266).

Age of Choosing. Owing to environmental forces which compel an individual to come to some decision about his future, most

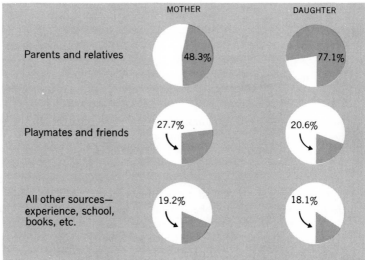

Figure 13–3. Proportion of two generations receiving first sex information from specified sources. The percentages total more than 100 because several subjects mentioned more than one source. (Adapted from P. H. Landis, Marriage preparation in two generations, *Marriage fam. Liv.*, 1951, 13, 155–156. Used by permission.)

MOTHER   DAUGHTER

Parents and relatives   48.3%   77.1%

Playmates and friends   27.7%   20.6%

All other sources— experience, school, books, etc.   19.2%   18.1%

children make their vocational choices between the ages of nine and eighteen years. Because girls are expected to marry and devote their time to homemaking, they are not pressured to think about and plan their vocations as early as boys (27, 41, 217).

Children of the lower classes, unlike children from the middle and upper classes, give so little thought to their vocational preparation and plans for the future that if they are asked what they plan to do when they grow up, they are likely to say, "Go to work"; they rarely state what that work will be. In general, people from the lower-class groups are *present-oriented* in the sense that they think only in terms of the present; the future can take care of itself. By contrast, people of the middle- and upper-class groups are *future-oriented,* putting more emphasis on the future and being willing to make sacrifices at the present to reap greater rewards in the future (30, 230).

The pattern of vocational choice followed by the majority of children is as follows:

1. Period of fantasy choices, when the child's occupational aspirations are indiscriminate and "unreal." Instead of being governed by such occupational realities as abilities and training, the child makes fantasy attempts to play adult roles. This period lasts up to the eleventh year.

2. Period of tentative choices, from eleven to seventeen years, when occupational preferences are based first on likes and dislikes or interests, but later on aptitudes and capacities and, still later, on personal values and ideals.

3. Period of realistic choices, which occurs after the age of seventeen years, when there is consideration of occupational opportunities and other realities (110).

That the major part of childhood is spent in the "fantasy-choice" period is important because the attitudes the child will have toward different types of work and the interest he will have in them are determined then. These attitudes will lead to personal satisfaction, and it will then be difficult to change his interest from a chosen vocation for which he is unfitted to one for which he is fitted. The third period normally begins in the latter part of adolescence, but many children never reach this stage.

Factors Influencing Vocational Choice. The child's choice of his future vocation is rarely a whim. It may be based on a whim, but it is more likely an interest that will persist until the child's physical and mental development enables him to assess it more realistically and to see other possibilities open to him. Of the many factors that influence the child's interest in a particular vocation, the following are the most important:

1. Parental Wishes. The young child usually accepts his parents' plans for his future. The influence of the parents is twofold: they (*a*) emphasize jobs they think desirable, and (*b*) advise the child to avoid other types of work (148). If the father dislikes his work, or if his job has little prestige, he not only discourages the child from entering his field but often projects his own thwarted aspirations onto his child and encourages him to go into a line of work with greater prestige. As a result of these parental attitudes, the range of vocational choice may be greatly limited for the child, and he may develop negative attitudes toward the type of work for which he is best qualified.

2. Family Relationships. The relationship the child has with his parents and his early experiences in the home have an important influence on his vocational choice. Overprotective and overdemanding parents, for example, weaken the child's self-confidence (244).

3. Family Status. The child, while still in elementary school, becomes aware of the fact that the "adult world is stratified along some principle of differentially evaluating occupations" and that people are stratified on the basis of the jobs they hold (288). He becomes aware of the meaning of different status symbols, such as houses, cars, and neighborhoods, and judges different occupations in terms of the prestige symbols they can provide for the worker. He learns that in this hierarchy of occupations professional and semiprofessional occupations are at the top of the prestige scale, while jobs for the semiskilled and menial jobs are at the bottom. He further discovers that many prestige occupations have titles; he then wants an occupation with an important-sounding title. He accepts adult attitudes and values associated with different occupations, and these have a profound influence on his choice (34, 274, 288, 301).

4. Prestige Value of Occupation.
Knowing that certain occupations carry prestige, the child is encouraged to aspire to these occupations—to the "right" jobs—regardless of his interest or ability. Parents who consider social status and prestige more important than interest often support the child in his aspirations, making personal sacrifices to enable him to get the necessary education and steering him away from menial, overall, or blue-collar jobs (103, 113, 171, 265). Among Negro families, teaching is a favored vocational choice for children; not only does teaching have high prestige value, but it is a less competitive field than many others (14, 127).

White parents, on the whole, have higher achievement values for their children than Negro parents. Italian parents put little pressure on their children; they say they will be "satisfied" with lower occupational achievement but are "pleased" when achievement is higher than their expectations. Jewish parents, by contrast, put strong pressure on their children to strive for high-status occupations. Furthermore, they are willing to make many personal sacrifices so that their children can come up to their expectations. Although most children expect to get ahead of their fathers, they are realistic enough to understand that they may not be able to reach the vocational goals their parents set for them (89, 246, 272, 279).

5. Admired People.
Important as parents are in determining what the child's vocational interests and aspirations will be, his interests are also greatly influenced by *anyone he admires*—a teacher, a relative, a neighbor, or a popular hero from the mili-tary, sports, or entertainment world. A child who belongs to a gang wants to do what his friends want to do; a child who hero-worships an older sibling wants to do what the sibling does (166, 308).

6. The Child's Abilities and Interests.
The child's physical and intellectual abilities, his personality, and his interests all play some role in determining his vocational choice. If the child has a strong interest in some school subject or in an outside activity, such as sports, he will want to incorporate this interest into the choice of his adult vocation (51). Children with high IQ scores usually choose the higher occupations or professions, while those with lower intellectual ratings are more likely to choose trades, skilled labor, and clerical work (184, 223). The child's personality is just as important as his intelligence in determining his vocational interest. Unadventuresome children, it has been found, want "safe jobs," while those who are more aggressive and daring want "exciting jobs" (51). The influence of personality on vocational choice is shown in Figure 13–4.

In choosing their future vocations, children do not ordinarily take into consideration their abilities for a given occupation or the market for it. This is by no means the child's fault alone. He has little opportunity to know what his abilities are, nor has he any way of knowing what types of jobs are available.

Furthermore, since he is often encouraged in his unrealistic aspirations by parents, relatives, or teachers, he assumes that he is qualified for the type of work he aspires to do (266). Unrealistic vocational aspirations are most common among children who do poor academic work and among those of the lower classes. Children who have had some work experience are more realistic than those who have never worked outside the home (120, 148, 278).

7. Sex-appropriateness.
At an early age, children discover that certain lines of work are considered appropriate for men and others for women. They also learn that boys

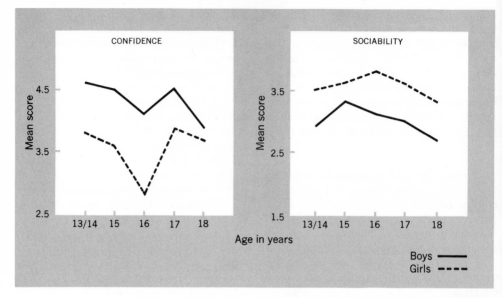

Figure 13–4. Influence of personality factors on vocational selection. (Adapted from S. M. Chown, Personality factors in the formation of occupational choice, *Brit. J. educ. Psychol.*, 1959, 29, 23–33. Used by permission.)

are expected to look upon their work as a lifetime career, while girls regard it as a stop-gap between school and marriage.

Among the sex-labeled jobs are law, medicine, and engineering for men, and teaching, nursing, and clerical work for women. A few girls aspire to masculine jobs—often because of a strong fondness for a father or some male relative who is in such a job—but most think in traditional terms. Boys rarely aspire to feminine vocations; not only do they want to go into the traditional masculine fields, but they put great stress on a "good job." For them, work means not just an income but a chance for upward mobility. Since girls accept the culturally approved attitude toward working, they generally choose vocations requiring little preparation beyond high school or college. Furthermore, since they want their brief working careers to be pleasant, they choose occupations that provide easy hours, an opportunity for companionship, and safety from job loss (75, 133, 240, 284).

8. Desire for Independence. Each year the

child becomes more frustrated by adult restrictions and more anxious for independence. His resentments against adult domination make him want to "do as he pleases" and not be "bossed" (287). He thinks mainly in terms of economics, believing that when he can earn enough money to support himself he will be independent. Under such conditions, the desire for independence plays an important role in his vocational thinking. A "good job" does not mean satisfaction in work, but rather money to spend (8). He therefore aspires to a job that will pay well from the start.

9. Cultural Stereotypes. In the development of vocational interests, many children are influenced by cultural stereotypes. The unfavorable stereotype of the teacher makes many girls decide against a career in teaching (253). The stereotype of a scientist as a "queer" and "unsocial" person causes many boys and girls to steer away from a scientific career, even though their interests and abilities may fit them admirably for such a career (199).

Changes in Vocational Interests. Although some children know as early as the sixth grade what their vocational ambitions are, most children shift from one vocational choice to another. Those who choose to enter a profession usually make their decisions earlier than those who decide to go into factory work or some other line of work that requires less ability and a shorter period of training (27, 217). Among adolescents, vocational interests shift frequently, partly because earlier choices now seem unrealistic and partly because marked changes in interest characteristically occur in adolescence.

Importance of Vocational Choice. It is important to a person's success and happiness that he do the kind of work he can do well and enjoys doing. Emphasis on "what are you going to do when you grow up?" is likely to force a decision on a child before he is able to make a wise choice. Early choice also puts a ceiling on the individual's aspirations and limits the range of his interests (233).

Equally serious as making a vocational decision too soon is making one that is out of line with one's capacities. The child who aspires beyond his capacities feels frustrated when he cannot reach the goal he set for himself and guilty when he realizes that his parents' sacrifices will not be repaid by his vocational success. Furthermore, the chances are that he will never be really satisfied with the kind of work he is able to do; he will always remember what he or his parents wanted. Much job dissatisfaction can be traced to the worker's belief that his job does not carry as much prestige as he would like. He may be able to compensate to some extent by going into work closely related to his chosen vocation and thus vicariously get some of the satisfaction he had hoped for (264).

Going into a line of work below one's capacity is also serious. The child who is bright but whose friends lack the capacity for the kind of work he is capable of doing may be swayed in his vocational choice by peer pressure. If they put high value on getting a job as soon as they complete high school, he may decide to go to work instead of going to college. The temporary satisfaction he derives from earning money—and therefore gaining independence—will soon be overshadowed by the realization that the only work he can do with his limited education bores him. Popular children are most in danger of making this mistake; to retain their popularity, they must do what everyone else does.

One of the most serious aspects of early vocational choice is the strong positive attitudes children develop toward certain lines of work and the equally strong negative attitudes they develop toward other lines. If the child constantly hears his father complain about his work and if he is constantly warned against it and told the advantages of other lines, he will develop such strong likes and dislikes that his decisions about his own future will be too biased to guide him into the type of work he is capable of doing.

SCHOOL INTERESTS

To a young child, going to school means "growing up"; he looks forward eagerly to the time when he will have the status of a "school child." The life of a scholar appeals to the young child, and he is challenged by what there is to learn. He likes things that are distinctly a part of school more than things that are common to both school and life outside of school, such as games and outdoor play. First- and second-graders usually like and often idealize the teacher.

As the child progresses through the grades, however, his interest in things that are distinctly a part of school and scholarship declines, and his interest in things that go along with life outside of school, such as recess, play, and sports, increases. By the end of elementary school, the child often dislikes his teacher, the school program, the rules and regulations of the school, and the school's physical appointments. He rebels against doing his homework and longs for the time when he can leave school (152).

By the sixth or seventh grade, approximately one out of every five children is distinctly dissatisfied with school. This unfavorable attitude may be a reflection of the growing child's need for freedom and independence. It is influenced by the fact that the child has only casual contacts with the teacher and is thus deprived of the emotional warmth that is generally associated with interests. Furthermore, as the child grows older, he is more influenced by peer attitudes. If his friends like school, he will, and vice versa (125, 259). Then, too, this change in attitude toward school with age may not be so great as it appears to be; the older child may *verbalize* his dislike more openly than the younger child (70).

In discussing the change in attitudes toward school, Estvan and Estvan have pointed out:

A general notion about school seems to be acquired early in life and for first graders the institution has undoubtedly a high place in their scale of values. As children grow older, they develop more extensive and refined concepts which enable them to discriminate in their perception of the objective features of school and, particularly, of the educational processes. This development is marked by a greater sensitivity to the social aspects of school life, and by a devaluation of the worth of the institution as a whole. Why does the school lose out in the value system of many sixth grade pupils? The answer may lie in the changes which accompany adolescence. Vacillating between child and adult roles, there is both a resistance to symbols of authority as represented in the school, and a negation of childish things associated with "grade" schools. Furthermore, their quest for new experiences and expanding interests may come in direct competition with school concerns which have lost much of their novelty by this time. This lessening of enthusiasm for school may also be an outcome of the kinds of experiences the child has had in school some of which, apparently, have not kept the original flame burning as brightly as before (90).

The child's interest in school not only changes as he grows older but becomes more *selective.* He likes certain things better than he did at first, but most things he likes less. While most children agree that learning is "good" in the sense that it prepares one for life, that learning new things can be "fun," and that one should appreciate the opportunities school affords, their negative attitudes, as shown in their constant criticism of school, mitigate their interests. They have mixed feelings about school. If their negative feelings outweigh the positive, their interest will be weak; the stronger their positive feelings, the stronger their interest (90).

Areas of Interest in School. Some children are interested primarily in academic activities, and others in extracurricular activities. Since the major part of the school day is devoted to academic activities, the child who fails to find them interesting will have an unfavorable attitude toward school (8, 10).

Interest in *school subjects* changes as the child progresses through the grades. Children in the early grades show an interest in mathematics, art, and English, but little in nature study, natural science, geography, and local or world news. Girls show less interest in mathematics as they progress in school, but a relatively stable interest in English usage, writing, and reading. Boys, on the other hand, show a stable interest in mathematics but a decline of interest in English. There is an increase in interest in nature study and natural science as children reach junior high school. Students lack interest in certain subjects because they fail to see the need for a subject, because they find the subject matter uninteresting or too difficult and the instructional methods monotonous, or because they feel that the teacher fails to "put the subject across." The child tends to evaluate learning experiences on the basis of their ability to excite or interest him rather than their usefulness in preparing him for the future (90, 152, 167).

When a school subject has the reputation of being "hard," students are likely to approach it with an unfavorable attitude. If they make poor grades in a subject or fail it, they inevitably dislike it. If a school subject ties in with daily interests, children are apt to like it; that is why they become more interested in science as they grow older. It also explains their growing interest in history, especially in the case of boys (10, 94).

Extracurricular activities gain in popularity as the child goes through school. There is a growing interest in clubs, sports, games, and physical education, and recess periods become increasingly popular. Social relationships play an important role in the child's interest in extracurricular activities. When children form groups and exclude others from their activities or when certain pupils run everything in the school, the situation is likely to make the child who is left out dislike school. The child's attitude toward school is more influenced by his relationships with his peers than by his relationships with his teachers (162, 205).

Summing up the child's interest in school, one is justified in saying that it

... appears that children are not as fond of school as adults *would* like them to be. The fault does not lie in their disregard for learning as such. Rather, it seems to be based on the kinds of things pupils do in school, the way they get along with others, and the evaluation made of their efforts. If we may judge from their comments, many children do not find school activities very interesting. Compared with a steadily increasing diet of movies, television, and travel experiences, school is "work" and not very stimulating at that (90).

Where the blame lies is still an open question. Dislike for school may be a cultural attitude that the child has assimilated from others. It is the "thing to do" not to like school and to regard most if not all school subjects as a "bore." Unquestionably, part of the blame can be traced to the ever-increasing number of exciting forms of entertainment available to children; by comparison, school work seems both dull and hard. If the child spends as much time watching television as he does on his studies, his studies will undoubtedly seem uninteresting, if not actually boring (134).

Dislike for School. While most children who are not interested in school regard it as

a "necessary evil," a few actively dislike it; some have an obsessive fear of it. Children who dislike school often engage in misdemeanors to annoy the teacher and to upset the children who want to study. The lessons they find most boring elicit the most troublesome behavior (85, 124, 167). School misdemeanors are discussed in more detail on pages 582 to 583.

Children show their dislike for school in many ways, the two most extreme of which are truancy and school phobia. In both, children try to escape from a situation which holds little interest for them. Because boys are more aggressive in the expression of their dislikes and are less afraid of being punished if caught, they are more likely to defy authority and "play hooky" than girls are (136).

The *truant* is a child who absents himself from school without a lawful cause and without the permission of his parents or the school authorities. He goes where he can do as he pleases without being seen by parents, neighbors, or law-enforcing officers. He may leave school in the middle of the day, complaining to the teacher that he "doesn't feel well" or that his parents want him to come home early. As there is always the chance that the parents will be notified in such circumstances, however, the truant usually skips school for the entire day (203, 290).

In back of the child's dislike for school lies failure, often both academic and social failure. The child who does poor academic work and who is constantly criticized by his teacher finds school an ego-deflating experience. If he is not promoted with his classmates, he finds it embarrassing to be with younger children, and he is bored with going over the same material he covered the previous year. Because overage children generally lack social acceptance in the class, the repeater finds few friends; this adds to his dislike for school (205).

Frequently, the truant feels that the teacher dislikes him or has treated him unfairly. All in all, he feels that school is such a humiliating and boring experience that he can no longer tolerate it. As Tyerman has said, "To be unable to do the work of the class and to be disliked by the other children is bound to discourage and depress a child" (290).

Children who are truants with their parents' knowledge and consent have adopted their parents' attitudes toward school and learned to place a low value on education. This is especially true of children of the lower socioeconomic groups, whose parents often want them to help at home or get jobs as soon as they look old enough to obtain working papers (136).

Unfavorable attitudes toward school due to *school phobia*—an abnormal and obsessive fear of school—are most common in kindergarten and the first four grades, though they occasionally develop among older children (203, 205). School phobia is a total or partial aversion to school and is expressed in such physical symptoms as nausea, anorexia, and a slight fever. The child may go to school and then complain of some somatic problem, such as upset stomach or headache. On the surface, the child's fear of school appears to stem from some aspect of the school situation, as shown by heightened anxiety when it is time for him to go to school (50, 159). There is little evidence, however, that such is the case. Instead, the fear is part of a generalized anxiety resulting from fear of being away from the mother, a strong dependency on the mother or a mother substitute, and inability to establish autonomy.

When the child discovers that fear is considered "babyish" or that he may be forced to go to school in spite of his dislike for it, he generally projects the blame to someone or something in the school situation. He maintains that the teacher does not like him and that he is afraid of her; he claims that he is unfairly treated by the teacher; he blames his classmates, saying that they are "always teasing him" or "won't play with him"; or he maintains that he is afraid of failing a test. Not recognizing that school phobias are "homegrown," some parents and schools try putting the child into another class or even another school, hoping in that way to change the child's attitude. This rarely works, however, because the fault does not lie in the school but in the child and his relationship with his parents (159, 243, 294).

Factors Influencing Interest. Just as attitudes toward school may range from positive to negative and from strong to weak, so does the accompanying interest in school vary. On the whole, there are more unfavorable attitudes and less interest than one would hope for. In general, girls are more interested in school than boys, and children from the middle and upper social classes more than those from the lower classes.

Unfavorable attitudes tend to increase as children grow older; the result is that many children drop out of school when they reach the age at which it is legally possible to do so (10, 61, 90).

Obviously, there are reasons for the steady decline in interest in school. To discover what these reasons are, one must examine the factors that influence the child's attitudes toward school. Studies indicate that of the many contributing factors, the following are the most influential:

1. Parental Influences. The influence of parents is unquestionably one of the strongest and most persistent factors determining what the child's interests in school will be. Not only do parents influence his attitude toward school in general, but they have a profound influence on his attitude toward the importance of education, toward studying, toward different school subjects, and toward his teachers. When parents show an interest in the child's schooling and pride in his achievements, he usually lives up to his capacities; when they are indifferent, he is likely to be indifferent also (79, 124, 271, 300). As Parker has stated, "Boys and girls are not delivered as raw materials at the school door. They are already products—products of five or six years of processing in their homes. More and more we realize that what the school can do to develop a child's potential is limited by what the home has already done, and is doing, to him and for him" (219).

While most parents, even if their own education has been limited, feel that their children should have a good education, they unfortunately foster—often unconsciously—unfavorable attitudes in their children. Many parents, for example, have unfavorable attitudes toward teaching as a profession and toward teachers as a group. These will be reflected in their attitude toward the child's teacher; their attitude, in turn, will influence the child's (18). As Stone and Church have pointed out:

Some of our negative feelings about education are early communicated to our children, making it difficult for them to approach school with the enthusiasm that is developmentally so timely. Quite early, adults (especially men) convey to children (especially boys) that school is to be spoken of disparagingly, that it is something of a penal institution, that it is less an opportunity than a forced drudgery, and that real life ends at the schoolhouse door (275).

Parents have a very strong influence on the child's attitude toward different school subjects (114). Most parents feel that boys should do well in mathematics and should like the subject; for girls, however, they can see little practical value to be gained from mathematics. In addition, they think it "odd" for a girl to be interested in a subject so sex-inappropriate. As a result, "Self-concepts in regard to mathematical ability are well established in the early school years and it is very difficult for even the best teacher to change them in spite of the fact that potentiality is much in evidence" (227). When the child develops an unfavorable attitude toward any school subject, he will have little interest in it and little motivation to do as well as he might. Consequently, he comes to believe that he has little ability in this subject; this attitude puts a damper on any interest he otherwise might have had.

What parental attitudes toward school will be depends on many factors. The *social class* with which the parents are identified is one factor. Middle-class parents put great emphasis on the importance of school, on homework, on academic achievement, and

on conforming behavior in the classroom because they know that vocational and social mobility can be achieved only through education. Furthermore, middle-class mothers prepare their children for school by helping them learn to read and write so that adjustment will be easier when children enter the first grade (32, 35). While parents of the upper-lower class regard education as necessary for vocational success, they are not great believers in education per se. To most lower-class parents, success in school is unimportant; such parents reject school and what it stands for, showing little or no interest in their children's studies or homework, in school activities, in the PTA, or in their children's grades (70, 74, 271).

Parental attitudes vary according to *religion* and *racial background*. Jewish parents as a group put more value on education and expect more from their children than Catholic or Protestant parents (246). Negro, Italian, and Mexican parents, it has been found, have less favorable attitudes toward education than American-born white parents (19, 70). The parents' *aspirations* for their child also influence their attitude toward school. If they feel that their child must "get ahead" in life, their attitude toward education will be very different from that of parents whose aspirations are lower (33, 114). Unrealistically high aspirations may discourage the child; as a result, he not only will do poor work but will also develop an unfavorable attitude toward school. Middle-class parents want their children to go to college or beyond, whereas lower-class parents are satisfied if their children complete high school (141, 246, 311).

Parental attitudes toward education vary according to the *sex of the child*. Because parents know that a boy's success in adult life will be greatly influenced by his education, they want him to do well in school. They constantly press him to high achievement, often disregarding his interests and abilities. Because parents believe a daughter's success in life will depend upon the kind of marriage she makes, they put a great deal of emphasis on the girl's success in extracurricular activities (1). Furthermore, a boy is expected to show an interest in subjects that will be of practical value, such as mathematics and science, while girls are expected to show a greater interest in cultural subjects, such as English, art, music, and foreign languages (199, 227).

The *parent-child relationship* has a marked influence on the child's attitude toward school, his teacher, and his desire to achieve academic success. If the child has developed a hostile attitude toward his parents, he may transfer this attitude to his teacher and to all in authority in the school. If he has learned to be timid in the home because of authoritarian child-training methods, he will be timid in the presence of his teacher and classmates (286). When parents show little interest in the child or when he feels that another sibling is the parental favorite, he has little motivation to try to please his parents; his school work then suffers. Overprotectiveness, overindulgence, rejection, domination—all tend to "cripple the child's chances of adjusting successfully to the school situation, either socially or scholastically" (118, 210, 260, 267).

Parent-child relationships likewise influence the child's attitude toward different school subjects. If a boy has a strong emotional attachment to his mother, for example, and if she has a negative attitude toward mathematics, he is likely to develop a similar attitude. If, on the other hand, the boy has a strong emotional attachment to the father, who believes that mathematics is important to success in life, he will have a strong motivation to do good work in mathematics to please his father (227). When parents read little themselves, they cannot expect the child to develop a positive attitude toward reading (154).

2. Sibling Influences. Because young children try to identify with and imitate their older siblings, the young child's attitude toward school will be greatly influenced by the older siblings' attitudes. Since boys tend to have less favorable attitudes toward school than girls, the boy with an older male sibling is more likely to have an unfavorable attitude toward school than he would have if the older sibling had been female. Furthermore, boys tend to have less favorable attitudes toward women teachers than girls do. As most of the teachers in the early grades are women, boys with older male siblings often develop, even before they go to school, an unfavorable attitude toward teachers. This is less likely to happen if the older sibling is a girl (166).

Emotional stress among siblings affects the child's attitude toward school, his relationships with his classmates, and his achievement, just as emotional stress coming from poor parent-child relationships does (139). Only children, spared most of these sibling-relationship problems, generally make better adjustments to school, teachers, and classmates. In addition, they usually have better relationships with their parents than children with siblings (38, 305).

3. Early School Experiences. If the child makes good adjustments to school, his attitude will be far more favorable than if he makes poor adjustments. While these adjustments are influenced, in part, by the attitudes he brings to school from the home, they are also influenced by his *readiness,* both physical and psychological, for school.

Readiness, to a large extent, is dependent on age. Because schools in America are planned for school entrance at the age of six years, underage and overage children are more likely to have social- or emotional-adjustment problems than children who enter at six (22, 122, 162). (Refer to pages 129 to 130 for a discussion of physical readiness for school.)

Psychological readiness means more than readiness to learn what is taught in school. It means that the child is physically able to be independent of adult aid and direction, that he can adjust socially to strangers, that he is emotionally mature enough to accept the restrictions school demands without becoming disturbed, and that he is able to accept the fact that there are prestige hierarchies among his classmates in which he may not have the high status he would like to have. Whether the child will be psychologically ready for school will depend mainly on his training at home and his previous social experiences, both in the home and with the peer group. Children who have attended nursery school or kindergarten generally make better adjustments to school than those who have not (20, 42).

Because reading plays such an important role in the curriculum of elementary school, the child who is not ready to learn to read when he enters the first grade will be handicapped in his adjustments. Reading readiness is not dependent upon intelligence alone but is markedly influenced by parent-child relationships, the cultural environment of the home, and many other factors (263). Children who are emotionally disturbed because of poor parent-child or sibling relationships encounter reading difficulties unrelated to their levels of intelligence. Most children adjust to school in a relatively short time, but the child who is not ready shows his continuing adjustment difficulties by crying, being overdependent on the teacher, or becoming quiet and withdrawn. Furthermore, if the teacher and his classmates react unfavorably to his immaturity, he will come to dislike school intensely and may develop school phobia (2, 187, 243).

By contrast, the child who adjusts quickly not only will enjoy school but also will find the attitudes of his teacher and classmates more favorable. After the original glamour of school has worn off, a favorable attitude toward school may be somewhat tarnished by unpleasant personal experiences in school or by pressures from the peer group; an unfavorable attitude generally becomes increasingly unfavorable because it militates against good adjustments. Poor adjustments, in turn, lead to unfavorable attitudes with their accompaniment of decreasing interest (152).

4. Peer Attitudes.   To ensure his acceptance by the peer group, the child learns that he must accept the group's interests and values. One such value relates to school. Part of the child's unfavorable attitude toward school is unquestionably peer-instigated. He must verbalize his dislike for school or run the risk of being called a "brain" or "teacher's pet." If his friends "gripe," he will "gripe"; he cannot afford to be different because this will jeopardize his status in the group. The child's unfavorable attitude toward school often "reflects no more than the widespread and thoroughly American characteristic of unfavorable criticism of his institutions" (125).

Once the child accepts the values of the peer group and develops attitudes similar to theirs, he becomes critical of school. The more critical he is, even though his criticism is mainly to win peer approval, the poorer his adjustment to school. In time, the child who criticized school because it was the "thing to do" convinces himself that he does not like school or anything connected with it.

Peer attitudes toward school vary according to the sex and the socioeconomic status of the child. In elementary school, girls are expected to be interested in their studies and to do good work, while boys may appropriately assume an antiwork attitude. By junior or certainly by senior high school, attitudes of the peer group change. Older girls are not supposed to be as interested in their studies as boys, who *must* study to prepare for their future vocations. It has been found that lower-class boys who belong to a peer group of middle-class boys show an interest in school as a means to a better vocational future; some want to go to college. By contrast, middle-class boys in a predominantly lower-class school group accept the lower-class values and attitudes, developing an unfavorable attitude toward school and education in general (95, 160, 292).

5. Acceptance by Peer Group.   No child can be expected to like school if he is unpopular. Good relationships with the teacher and good marks do not compensate for lack of acceptance by the peer group. Children who belong to minority religious or racial groups or whose families are identified with lower-level vocations generally experience poor peer acceptance. Furthermore, they discover that the "rewards" school has to offer—grades, prizes, school offices, and

teacher approval—generally go to those of the majority racial and religious groups or to those of the middle and upper socioeconomic groups. This conditions them even further to dislike school (90, 113, 216).

Physically handicapped children find themselves left out of many activities their classmates enjoy; the few extracurricular activities they can participate in generally have a low prestige value. Children who deviate markedly from the norm in mental ability likewise enjoy poor social acceptance. Furthermore, very bright children tend to be hypercritical of school in general and of their lessons and teachers in particular; this attitude does not increase their liking for school or their acceptance by their less critical classmates (84, 142). Dull children generally dislike school because of peer rejection and because they are made to feel inadequate both in the classroom and in play (24, 216). If parents are ashamed of their children's academic situation or show little sympathy toward the child, blaming him for not "trying" to do his work, this further intensifies the child's dislike for school (116, 153, 312).

6. Academic Success. Academic success contributes to good social and school adjustment, both of which contribute to a favorable attitude toward, and interest in, school. Popular children are, for the most part, those who do well—but not too well—in school; unpopular children are often scholastic failures (47, 149). In our culture, academic success is measured by grades and awards. These tell the child how he rates in relation to his classmates, and they have a marked influence on his attitude toward school. In fact, it has been found that there is a high correlation between a child's grades and his perception of school. There is also a high correlation between a child's grade in a particular school subject and his attitude toward that subject. A poor grade stifles his motivation to try to do better. This results in an even poorer grade, with an increasingly unfavorable attitude toward school (39, 189, 195, 285).

Many children who receive poor grades are afraid to take their report cards home, fearing parental scoldings or punishment. Other children feel that their poor grades show that they have not been fairly treated (249). Children who find learning difficult often try to convince themselves that grades are unimportant, although most children know that *grades are considered important* in our culture. Middle-class children, especially, know that their prestige in the eyes of their teachers and classmates and the approval of their parents are greatly influenced by the academic success they achieve (195, 251). Unless children can get good grades without anxiety or cheating, they are unlikely to enjoy school work (49, 73, 283, 314).

When a child is faced with academic failure, he is apt to develop compensatory defense mechanisms. Poor readers, for example, are often aggressive, cocky, and hostile toward authority. These unfavorable personality characteristics decrease their chances of social acceptance. Lack of acceptance, in turn, decreases their liking for school. Good readers, by contrast, have no reason to feel inadequate; they have pride in their achievement, make better social adjustments, and consequently develop a favorable attitude toward school (229).

7. Attitude toward Work. The child's interest in school is markedly affected by his attitude toward *work*. Even before children enter school, they make a distinction between things that are considered "work" and things that are labeled "play." Furthermore, they have definite feelings about activities belonging to these two categories. It has been found that by the time children reach the age of ten, they have developed a dislike for *anything* that might be considered work. This antiwork attitude shows itself indiscriminately in all activities connected with the school as well as with the home.

Boys, even more than girls, have unfavorable attitudes toward work; this accounts, in part, for boys' more unfavorable attitude toward school. The only time when boys have a really favorable attitude toward work is when it relates to a long-range goal, such as acquiring a car or preparing for a better job. If they feel that their work in school will eventually be rewarded, they are willing to work to achieve their goal. But their attitude toward school—the situation that requires this work—is not appreciably improved (134, 292).

8. Teacher-Pupil Relationships.

While some children like their teachers, those who do not are apt to criticize school mainly because of their dislike for the teacher (84, 181). The preschool child is more dependent than the elementary-school child; as a result, he generally has a more friendly attitude toward the teacher. If his attitude is hostile at first, it gradually becomes more favorable (see Figure 13–5). The older child shifts his interest from teacher to peers, and his interaction with the teacher becomes more formal (see Figure 13–6, page 627).

Factors that influence the teacher-pupil relationship include (a) the child's concept of the teacher, (b) the child's personal experiences, (c) the child's concept of a "good teacher," (d) the child's sex, and (e) the teacher's attitudes toward her pupils.

Even before the child enters school, he has a *concept of what a teacher is* (179). He has learned something about teachers from his parents, siblings, and playmates, as well as from the stereotypes of teachers in storybooks, in movies, in comics, and on television. Younger siblings, it has been found, base their concepts of the teacher on an older sibling's attitude. As boys generally dislike teachers more than girls, a boy with an older male sibling often enters school with a well-established unfavorable concept of the teacher (166).

Studies of the portrayal of teachers in literature and in the movies have revealed that the stereotype of both male and female teachers that is presented to children is unfavorable. In literature, for example, the female teacher is usually unattractive, middle-aged, and dowdy in appearance. When young, she is portrayed as masculine; when middle-aged, "shrill and witchlike." The male teacher is portrayed as "stooped, gaunt, and grey with weariness. His suit has

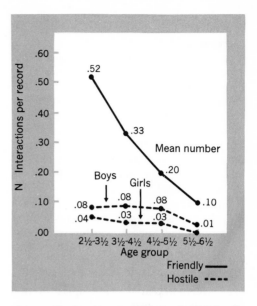

Figure 13–5. Mean number of all friendly interactions and mean number of hostile interactions between children and teachers per 2-minute observation record for each age group. (Adapted from H. R. Marshall, Relations between home experiences and children's use of language in play interactions with peers, *Psychol. Monogr.*, 1961, 75, No. 5. Used by permission.)

the shine of shabby gentility and hangs loosely from his undernourished frame." In the movies, teachers generally play comedy roles, though occasionally they appear as self-sacrificing, weak people who have devoted their lives to their pupils at the expense of their own happiness (253).

The child's concept of the teacher is likewise affected by his interpretation of his own *personal experiences*. If the child perceives the teacher as weak and hostile or unfriendly, he will dislike her and cause many disciplinary problems; if he perceives her as weak but friendly, he will try to take advantage of her, but he will not show the respect that good classroom discipline requires. If he perceives her as strong and hostile, he may not be a disciplinary problem, but he will be rebellious and will dislike her as well as school. By contrast, if he feels that she is strong and friendly, he will like and respect her and make an effort to be cooperative (310).

A child often interprets a teacher's disapproval of his behavior as disapproval of himself as a person. If this happens he will dislike her and regard her as an "unfair" or "mean" person (162). Because girls have more favorable concepts of teachers, they like school more than boys; for the same reason, upper- and middle-class children like school more than those from the lower classes (67, 173).

The child's concept of a "good" teacher is based on his personal experiences and on stereotypes and is used as a measuring rod to assess his own teacher. If a teacher measures up favorably, he likes her, and this increases his interest in school. Children dislike teachers who are (or who appear to be) unfair, who have pets, who show dislike for certain students, and who give unfair examinations. They dislike teachers who scold a lot, who are unduly cross or bossy, who become angry when a child fails to understand, who give too much homework, who punish or embarrass a child in front of the class, and who are not interested in their pupils (13, 278).

Children like a teacher who treats her pupils as her equals and who is friendly, kind, patient, interested in children, and understanding. They like a teacher who knows how to teach and who is strict though fair. In elementary school, children generally prefer male teachers; they find men less authoritarian and more friendly than women. It is a fact that male teachers go into elementary teaching because of a love for children and a sensitivity to the thoughts and feelings of others, while women teachers are more likely to do so for status reasons. Children quickly sense the teacher's attitude toward them and react accordingly (196, 277).

The *sex of the child* often affects the pupil-teacher relationship. Even in nursery school and kindergarten, boys show more hostility to their teachers than girls do, and teachers, as a rule, show more hostility to boys than to girls. This is illustrated in Figure 13–6. In elementary school, teachers find girls easier to handle than boys, and they tend to favor girls (302). Men teachers, on the other hand, find that girls like to take advantage of them, that boys are better sports than girls about correction, and that girls tend to carry a grudge when they get mad at the teacher (48).

Unquestionably, some of the difficulty women teachers have with boys stems from the fact that they do not understand boys very well and that they try to make boys conform to standards of behavior more appropriate for girls. In their study of teachers' attitudes toward boys and girls, Meyer and Thompson stated:

We feel that the consistent trends in our findings imply that teachers' negative attitudes toward their male pupils arise from a lack of appreciation for the term "normal" male child. In our culture, aggressive, outgoing behavior is as normal in the male as quiescent, nonassertive behavior is in the female. The teacher who attempts to thwart this behavior by means of threats and punishment can only meet with frustration since the boy is confronted with a conflicting social code (202).

Because boys are sensitive to fairness; because they are aware of the disapproval of their teachers; and because they are punished more than girls in school, they build up a dislike for their teacher, work below their capacities, and cause disturbances in the classroom. In general, their attitudes toward school grow less and less favorable. For all these reasons, many more boys than girls want to leave school as soon as they can legally do so.

As has already been pointed out, boys are the chief truancy problem; their dislike for school causes them to shun it if possible. Much of this dislike stems from poor pupil-teacher relationships. In the junior and senior high schools, when children come in contact with more male teachers, boys feel that they are more fairly treated. Their relationship with their teachers improves, and, in turn, their attitude toward school improves (48, 202).

Because the *attitudes of most teachers*

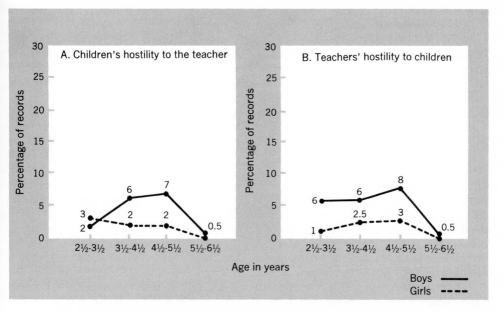

Figure 13–6. There is greater hostility between boys and their teachers than between girls and their teachers. (Adapted from H. R. Marshall, Relations between home experiences and children's use of language in play interactions with peers, *Psychol. Monogr.*, 1961, 75, No. 5. Used by permission.)

are molded by their own middle-class backgrounds and values, they often do not understand or approve the behavior of children from lower-class backgrounds (57). Middle-class children try to conform to teacher expectations; as a result, they are usually liked by their teachers and enjoy a more favorable teacher-pupil relationship.

Teachers do not actually show favoritism toward their middle- and upper-class pupils. Rather, they have more conflicts with their lower-class pupils because of a clash of values. This is especially true of lower-class boys whose background has encouraged them to be aggressive and whose parents put a low value on academic achievement (135, 140, 202).

Teachers tend to have better relationships with popular children than with isolates or neglectees. Obviously, the behavior that makes a child liked by his peers also makes him liked by his teacher. Because bright children tend to be critical of their teachers and of the school, teachers sense this critical attitude and have a less friendly relationship with bright children than with those who are less gifted (84).

9. Emotional Climate of the School.

Even though the emotional climate of the school may vary slightly from day to day, a teacher creates an atmosphere that is generally consistent. Teachers who are well-adjusted people create a more wholesome emotional climate in their classrooms than those who are less well adjusted (282, 306).

Teachers who are poorly adjusted have trouble with classroom discipline and make the pupils dislike them and school. The effect of the teacher's poor personality adjustment is shown not only in poor discipline but also in the emotional reactions of the pupils. As Laycock has pointed out, " 'Dithery' teachers have 'dithery' pupils while bossy teachers have meek and resentful pupils and tense teachers have tense pupils" (178).

Teachers who have a rejective attitude

toward themselves and toward others create a poor emotional atmosphere in the classroom; they reject the pupils they dislike, showing suspicions about the pupils' honesty and making them feel ashamed of their inadequacies in academic work. Teachers who have an indifferent or negative attitude toward teaching or toward their roles as teachers bring out the same attitude in their pupils (52, 66, 183).

By contrast, teachers who have a favorable concept of the teacher's role and who like their work and are friendly with their pupils motivate the pupils to work up to their capacities; they have relatively few disciplinary problems. A relaxed, friendly atmosphere in the classroom promotes a favorable attitude on the part of the pupils both toward the teacher and toward school.

A teacher who is primarily interested in the subject matter she teaches will have a less harmonious relationship with her pupils than the teacher whose main concern is with her pupils' welfare. The former will show an acceptant attitude toward pupils only when they do good work. This will lead to poor pupil morale and a tense atmosphere in the classroom (252).

Because many teachers have a middle- or lower-class background and have moved up the social ladder by their academic achievements, they urge their students to do the same. This encourages students to work primarily for grades. When this occurs, as has already been stressed, children's attitudes toward school become unfavorable, and their interest in school declines (130).

Underachievers and Overachievers. It is commonly believed that interest is primarily responsible for the quality of work the child does in school. This means that an interested pupil will do not only better work than his less interested classmates but also better work than one would normally expect from a child of his abilities. It is also widely assumed that when a child works below what one would normally expect, the cause is lack of interest. The teacher is often blamed for not stimulating the child's interest, and the child himself is frequently

scolded or punished by parents and teachers because he is "lazy."

In recent years, with the widespread use of intelligence and achievement tests, it has become apparent that many more children work below their capacities than was formerly recognized. It has also become apparent that there is an increase in cheating and in parental and other outside help. Furthermore, with the growing desire on the part of parents to have their children go to college and with the increased competition in getting into college, scientific interest has been focused on overachieving and underachieving children. For the most part, studies have emphasized that the assumed cause—interest in school work—plays a far less important role than was formerly believed.

An *underachiever* is a student who does not "appear to be functioning academically up to his assessed ability as determined by an individual intelligence test" (96). There is a distinct disparity between his performance on an individual intelligence test and on an achievement test. Such a student may be considered an "intellectual delinquent." More specifically, a student is considered an underachiever when his performance places him 30 or more percentiles below his ability standing in the group. In other words, the underachiever works at about two-thirds of his capacity. In the case of the gifted student, the underachiever falls in the middle third of the school rank instead of in the upper third (117).

There are two types of underachievers: the *long-term* underachiever, who shows over a period of time that he is working below his capacity, and the *situational* underachiever, who works below capacity because of some traumatic experience, such as a transfer to another school, a death in the family, or an emotion-producing experience. The situational underachiever may become a long-term underachiever, or his underachievement may last only until he adjusts to the situation which has given rise to his underachievement. Some students are *general* underachievers, working below their capacities in all school subjects, while others are *specific* underachievers, working below their capacities in certain subjects only (117, 121).

An *overachiever* is a student whose academic achievement is above his tested ability: He does better work than one would expect. The child may be a long-time overachiever, or his overachievement may develop as a result of some traumatic experience, such as threat of failure. Like underachievement, overachievement may be general or specific. There is evidence that there are more underachievers than overachievers at all educational levels.

Causes of Underachievement and Overachievement. There is much evidence that underachievement and overachievement are caused by conditions unrelated to school or school work. Furthermore, there is evidence that many children do not know why they work below their capacities, even though they have been told repeatedly by parents and teachers that they could "do better." In spite of the fact that they get poorer grades than they should get, many underachievers actually like school, though their interest is likely to be concentrated on the nonacademic aspects (76, 121).

Underachievement and overachievement are symbolic of a variety of basic personal and social problems. Very rarely are they the result of poor teaching or lack of educational opportunity; rather, *the cause lies within the child himself* (81, 220). Furthermore, the environments of the home and school, per se, are not directly to blame, though they are, indirectly, at the basis of the trouble because they promote emotional and personality problems which lead to hostility. The child may direct his hostile attitude toward school and toward those who are in charge of his education (137, 256, 257). Figure 13–7 shows how personality factors, fostered by the home and school environments, contribute to the child's underachievement.

The emotional and personality problems that lead to dislike for school usually begin at home, though they are often fostered by the school environment. If the child comes

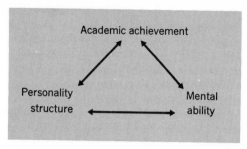

Figure 13–7. **Personality and mental ability contribute to the child's school achievement. (Adapted from A. D'Heule, J. C. Mellinger, and E. A. Haggard, Personality, intellectual, and achievement patterns in gifted children,** *Psychol. Monogr.,* **1959, 73, No. 13. Used by permission.)**

from an authoritarian home where pressures are placed on him to achieve success in school; if he has been so overprotected at home that he feels inadequate to cope with the school situation; or if his parents' attitudes are negative or indifferent toward education, he is likely to develop an unfavorable attitude toward school. Should his homelife be disturbed by parental quarrels and strife or broken by death or divorce, or should he feel rejected by one or both parents, he will develop a hostility which will affect his outlook on life and be projected to the school situation (26, 96, 117).

Certain conditions in the school intensify the child's already hostile attitude. The teacher's attitude and the emotional climate that she creates in the classroom are of great importance. When the curriculum is inappropriate for the child's level of development or when a transfer from one school to another gives rise to social and academic adjustment problems, the child is likely to show increased hostility toward school.

Underachievement and overachievement may result from conditions in the school which develop a hostile attitude on the part of the child. When they originate in the school, they are usually specific rather than general. They seldom begin in the school, however, if the child is well adjusted (298).

Poor social acceptance often encourages

overachievement or underachievement. The not-too-bright child may hope to improve his social status by good academic work, especially in schools where high academic achievement is admired by the peer group. The very bright child, by contrast, tries to improve his social status by doing only average work. The stronger his desire for social acceptance, the more he will tend to work below capacity, especially in schools where low prestige is associated with high academic success.

Whether a hostile attitude will lead the child to overachieve or underachieve will depend largely upon his personality and his needs. A child who has a strong need for attention, approval, and affection and who has learned that these will be satisfied only when he lives up to parental expectations tends to show his hostility by driving himself to do more than he is capable of doing; he feels valued only in proportion to his ability to bring home high grades. An equally hostile child who has found that nothing seems to be adequate to win approval and affection will develop a "what's the use?" attitude and become an underachiever. When parents put little value on education, the child knows that academic success will bring little approval and affection; he slips into the habit of underachievement because he has no real motivation to do otherwise (93, 137).

If academic success is highly valued by parents, by teachers, or by the peer group, however, the child who feels inadequate or who is hostile because he has not won acceptance may become an overachiever in the hope of winning acceptance. He accepts the values of those whose approval he craves and tries to gain a secure status by his accomplishments. Thus, it is apparent that *underachievement and overachievement stem from much the same cause, a feeling of insecurity and inadequacy accompanied by hostility;* they are relatively uninfluenced by interest in school work or in the school as an institution (26, 234).

Beginnings of Underachievement and Overachievement.
Underachievement and over-

achievement can start at any time during the child's school life, although they usually begin during the second or third grade and are well developed by the time the child reaches junior or senior high school (93, 256). The underachiever or overachiever in college generally has a history of such behavior tracing back to his early elementary-school days. In discussing the high-school underachiever, Shaw and Grubb have pointed out that the hostility which leads to underachievement is not caused by the school but is a "problem which the underachiever brings with him, at least in embryo form, when he enters high school" (257).

As a rule, underachievement and overachievement begin about the time that school grades are substituted for "progress reports." Since parents can assess their children's achievements better by the traditional marking system, they either begin to demand better work or adopt an attitude of indifference (258). Figure 13–8, which shows the patterns of underachievement for boys and girls, indicates that the predisposition to underachievement is present in a readily recognizable form by the time children enter high school.

Most underachievers are unaware that they are not working up to their capacities. Like any act repeated over a period of time, underachieving becomes habitual. When children are accused of not doing their best, they usually give their parents "unrealistic, superficial, and largely implausible" excuses (76). They may use such protective defense mechanisms as negativism, stubbornness, withdrawal, or daydreaming. Ordinarily, however, they project the blame to others, claiming that teachers are being unfair, that those who do better are guilty of cheating, or that they have been forced to take subjects which do not interest them and for which they have no ability (99, 296).

Similarly, overachievement can become a habit. The overachiever, like the underachiever, is usually unaware of the underlying causes of his overachievement. He generally attributes it to a strong interest in school work or to a burning ambition to "get ahead" in life. Because doing good

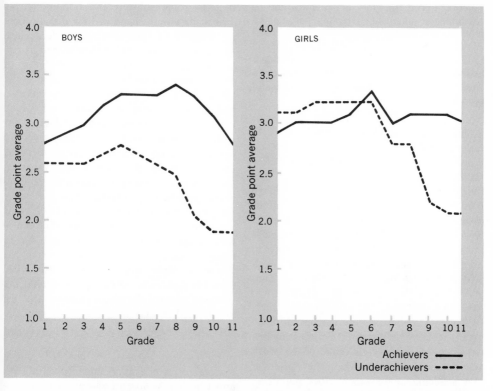

Figure 13–8. The onset of underachievement in boys and girls. (Adapted from M. C. Shaw and J. T. McCuen, The onset of academic underachievement in bright children, *J. educ. Psychol.*, 1960, 51, 103–105. Used by permission.)

work is socially approved, the overachiever has little motivation to change and little desire to know just why he is working above his capacity (206).

Variations in Underachievement and Overachievement. In general boys tend to underachieve, and girls tend to overachieve. The most important reason for this *sex difference* is that girls are more responsive to family pressures and are more anxious to conform to adult expectations than boys. Boys, by contrast, become rebellious when pressure is put on them. They consciously or unconsciously work below their capacities in order to assert their independence (117, 298). Furthermore, good academic work has more prestige in the eyes of the peer group for girls; to increase their peer accept-

ance, they work above their capacities. Boys concentrate on athletic achievement and shy away from the feminine "taint" of intellectual achievement (96).

Underachievement is most common among *very bright* children, while overachievement occurs most frequently among students of average and below-average ability (26, 96). When parents realize that their children are bright, they put pressures on them to excel. As Rothney and Koopman have stated:

Education is a means of raising one's social status in America. A child or youth who can do well in school, win a scholarship, or enter a college, can raise the status and inflate the egos of members of his family. Doing well in school can reflect glory on the parents. And if the glory is supplemented by the financial gain of a scholarship, parents and relatives are doubly pleased. In view of these social and financial rewards it is not unusual to find the gifted child pushed, prodded, coaxed, and bribed to get good marks or to show other evidence that he is a successful student (247).

This coaxing, prodding, bribing, and pushing may make the child so hostile and rebellious that he will intentionally work below his capacity in revolt against parental authority. It may, on the other hand, make him try to live up to parental expectations as a way of winning love and affection. If he finds that satisfying his parents' expectations by academic achievement does not win *peer acceptance,* however, he is faced with a dilemma: Which means more to him, parental or peer approval? If he fails to win either parental approval or peer acceptance, he becomes so hostile that he loses all motivation to achieve success. In discussing the tendency of very bright children to work below their capacities when they discover that academic achievement does not bring peer prestige and acceptance, Gowan has said:

> The gifted underachiever . . . appears to be a kind of intellectual delinquent who withdraws from goals, activities, and active social participation generally. As a child, his initial attempt at creative accomplishment may not have been seen by others as "worthwhile," but only as "queer" or "different." The blocking of this avenue of rewarding behavior by others . . . may blunt his work libido, stifle his creativity, and consign him to a routine of withdrawal and escape as the most tolerable method of insulating his ego from hurt in an alien and disinterested world (117).

When children are expected to do *equally well in all school subjects,* just because they do well in one or two, they come to dislike the subjects in which they are unable to come up to parental expectations. If they are constantly pressured to do good work, they may devote too much of their study time to some subjects and not enough to others; they may cheat; or they may become so antagonistic that they will underachieve as a protest against what they regard as unfair expectations. Thus, some children of average ability may become overachievers in subjects for which they have an aptitude, and underachievers in subjects for which their aptitude is limited (187, 258).

Middle-class children, particularly, are likely to become overachievers. Because middle-class parents place a high value on achievement—especially academic achievement, which they regard as a necessary stepping-stone to the fulfillment of their vocational aspirations for their children—they press their children to work up to capacity and beyond. The more they press, the more hostile and antagonistic the children become. Since children know what the ultimate reward for high achievement is, however, they may be willing to accept the challenge and live up to parental expectations.

Lower-class parents, by contrast, put a low value on education and show little interest in their children's educational achievements. They provide children with little motivation to live up to their capacities. Even in school, such children receive little encouragement because teachers are often hostile to children of lower-class backgrounds. Consequently, there are more underachievers than overachievers among lower-class children (57, 68).

Underachievers are likewise more numerous among *upper-class* children. According to upper-class values, high achievement in school is not necessary to vocational or social success; in fact, "gentlemen's grades" are more highly valued than "grinds' grades." The child, therefore, is not pressed to be at the top of his class; his parents are satisfied if he does passable work or shows adequate ability to get into a good college. Teachers tend to favor upper-class children; as a result, they often grade such children higher than they deserve. The attitudes of parents and teachers provide upper-class children little motivation to work beyond their capacities (68, 96).

Effects of Underachievement and Overachievement. One might logically expect overachievers to show a strong interest in school, and underachievers to have a strong dislike for it. Studies, however, have shown that *both* have unfavorable attitudes toward school, though of different types; *neither* likes school. Studies have also revealed that while behavior problems in the classroom usually stem from underachievers, truancy is more common among overachievers (137, 290).

For neither underachievers nor overachievers is school a happy, relaxed, ego-satisfying experience; it is, instead, accompanied by anxiety and feelings of guilt or shame. The *overachiever* may win parental and teacher approval, but this is overshadowed by a constant fear of failure; by an anxiety that is ever present, though especially strong at the time of tests and examinations; and by the feelings of inadequacy that come from the child's recognition of his intellectual limitations. Furthermore, the overachiever feels guilty if he takes time out to enjoy himself. He feels that he must drive himself to study while his classmates play. In his desire to live up to adult expectations, he must usually sacrifice the acceptance of the peer group, and this leads to a dislike for school.

Overachievers are usually the least popular members of a class, not only because of their high marks but also because achievement of high marks is possible only when the child develops a powerful drive to succeed, which makes him nervous, tense, anxious, and highly sensitive to social approval and disapproval—characteristics that militate against peer acceptance. Furthermore, to achieve success, the overachiever must be highly competitive, often playing up to the teacher to win favor or refusing to help a classmate with a school assignment. Peer acceptance will reach the zero point if the overachiever gains the reputation of trying to be at the top of the class by siding with the teacher against his classmates (121, 137, 298).

When the underachiever knows he is working below his potential, he feels guilty and ashamed. His parents and teachers are constantly prodding or punishing him for not doing what he is capable of, and he is made to feel that he is a "slacker" (79). He inevitably develops a dislike for school and everything connected with it. These unfavorable attitudes not only militate against the child's desire to study but also lead to an "I don't care" attitude, which results in his withdrawal from competition with other students who are more eager than he to achieve academic success. One of the effects of withdrawal from academic competition is withdrawal from the social group. Many underachievers become unsociable and self-sufficient, developing into voluntary isolates (76, 117).

Because guilt and shame are unpleasant emotional experiences and are inevitably accompanied by feelings of inadequacy and helplessness, the underachieving child often develops an elaborate system of *defense mechanisms* to free himself from some of the guilt and shame he would otherwise experience. As Walsh has pointed out, the underachieving child may "simulate indifference or bravado, he may fight blindly and hopelessly, dig in his heels stubbornly, or withdraw into daydreams or unreachable passivity. While he may see himself as threatened and helpless, in the one area of academic achievement he can be the winner. No one can make him learn anything" (296).

The serious thing about underachievement is that it is not a "surface phenomenon easily modifiable but rather is related to the basic personality matrix of the individual" (256). It is difficult to correct without major corrections in the personality structure. Furthermore, because the underachiever is usually a bright and able child, much valuable potential talent is lost through his lack of interest in school and his disinclination to study.

Underachievers are also a "morale problem" for schools. When a few children develop an unfavorable attitude toward school and work below their capacities, other children are easily influenced to imitate them. Children who dislike school usually verbalize their dislike to their classmates. The underachievers' attitudes toward school are heavily weighted with hostility against those who press them to do better work and with guilt and shame because they are falling below expectations, and their highly emotional attacks on the school, the teachers, and the different courses of study can strongly influence their classmates' morale. As has already been pointed out, bright students tend to be highly critical of school, and they are more often underachievers than dull children are.

The bright child may win the respect of his agemates because of his good academic work, even though it is far below his capacity. Because of their respect for him, the less bright children are swayed by his attitudes and his verbal attacks on the school and thus develop similarly unfavorable attitudes. If it is the thing to do to criticize, and if the brightest members of the class are the most vocal critics, the peer group will follow in the footsteps of the bright underachievers (130, 135, 277, 302).

INTEREST IN CLOTHES

Long before the child recognizes the importance of his physical appearance, he has gradually become aware that certain of his needs are met by his clothes. With this awareness comes interest. An aspect of clothing that has great influence on the judgments others make of a child at one age may later wane in importance and be replaced by another aspect that has greater symbolic value. When this happens, the child's interest also changes and centers on that aspect of his clothing which, at that time, has greater symbolic value.

In all cultures, clothes have at least three functions: utilitarian, aesthetic, and symbolic of the wearer's status. Each cultural group emphasizes the function of clothing that meets the needs of its members best. In very cold climates, for example, the utilitarian function of clothing is dominant; in very warm climates, where the utilitarian function is less important, emphasis is placed on the aesthetic value. Since members of

the upper social classes do not have to identify their status by their clothing, they can concentrate their interest on aesthetic values. Among members of the lower social classes, by contrast, clothing is used mainly to symbolize the status the wearers *would like* to be identified with; by wearing clothing like members of the upper classes, they can create the impression that they are identified with them (25, 218, 262).

The child learns the cultural values associated with clothing as he learns other cultural values—through identification with parents and other members of the social group and through imitation of their expressed values. If his parents and members of the peer group regard clothing as an important status symbol, so will he; if they consider clothing important because of its aesthetic or utilitarian value, he will also. Furthermore, when he learns that physical attractiveness is an asset to social acceptance, he discovers that clothing is an even greater asset. Jersild has emphasized the role clothing plays in the judgments of others thus:

Clothing and grooming may reveal many nuances of attitude toward self. Sometimes directly, sometimes more subtly, a person's clothes and grooming are a projection of himself—his "real" or an idealized self which he is striving to live up to. We may suspect that a person does not accept himself wholeheartedly as he is if he feels a need to falsify his appearance to a considerable degree. . . . There are many ways of trying to look like the person one is not. One may strive to appear conspicuously older or younger. The young girl who disapproves of herself as she is attempts by make-up and hair-do to play up to an older part, and the older person who cannot accept his years tries to dress younger than his years. . . . The fact is that an article of clothing which seems thoroughly objective in character may have tremendous subjective meaning. It may be an important projection of self, a means of self-defiance, of self-vindication, or it may be a means of communicating with others (150).

Focal Points of Interest. The many need-satisfying aspects of clothes give rise to an interest in them. The most important needs met by the child's clothing are discussed below:

1. Autonomy. Every child wants to be independent of adult or sibling domination, often before he is ready to handle his affairs himself. The more restrictive the environment, the greater the child's desire to become independent. The baby's only interest in clothes is that they not restrict his movements. Clothes that do so irritate him because he wants to be as independent as his helpless, dependent state will permit. Much of the crying that accompanies being dressed is simply the child's protest over an interference with his freedom. He is still not aware that clothes improve his looks (236, 273).

Before the baby reaches the end of the first year of life, he discovers that he can remove his cap, socks, booties, or mittens, and still later he learns that he can remove all his clothes. This is a source of real satisfaction to him; it is a symbol of his growing autonomy. The young child is eager to dress himself and rebels when he is not permitted to do so. His interest in clothes comes from the sense of independence and achievement that he gets from being able to manipulate them, rather than from the clothes themselves (236).

Once the child has acquired the skills necessary to dress himself, he turns his interest toward deciding what he wants to wear and how he wants to wear it. If the mother feels that a particular garment is more suitable than another, the child who wants to be independent will rebel against wearing it, not because of the garment, but because he wants to make his own decisions. During the negativistic age (see pages 340 to 342), the child will be particularly rebellious against wearing clothing chosen by another and will be happy when he is permitted to choose his own. In authoritarian homes, where "mother knows best," a constant source of conflict between parent and child comes from deprivation of independence in clothing selection. In democratic homes, where the child is given some independence—with suggestions but not demands from parents—much of this friction is eliminated (15, 108).

How the child wears his clothes also becomes a symbol of autonomy. If his parents insist that he be neat, clean, and tidy, he will rebel and make himself look sloppy. When he discovers that the peer group considers tidiness the sign of a "sissy," a boy will go out of his way to look unkempt, thus showing his autonomy from parental domination. Girls discover that making a good appearance is vital to social acceptance. Consequently, they are willing to conform to parental values because these are the same as peer values. They assert their independence by demanding the right to wear what they consider appropriate, regardless of parental values (15, 250, 289).

2. "Growing Up." Closely related to the child's interest in achieving independence is his interest in "growing up"—in reaching a status where he will have the rights and privileges enjoyed by older siblings or adults. To a child, age and autonomy go hand in hand. If he is to be independent, he must create the impression that he is older than he is. If he looks his age or younger, he soon discovers that the rights and privileges he craves are denied him. This is one of the major problems faced by the slow-maturing child. If he retains a childish body longer than his agemates, parents and teachers are likely to withhold from him the privileges his more mature-looking agemates enjoy (69).

The child soon discovers that clothes can make one look older; his interest, as a result, is focused on the clothes which will make him look older and which will be the "key" to the autonomy he craves (143). That is why the first clothes of a particular kind, especially if they are like the clothes of an older child, are worn with such pride. To a boy, the first long trousers signify that he is no longer a "little boy"; he is now approaching manhood. Similarly, to a girl, the first nylon stockings or the first white gloves are insignia of growing up. An older girl wants to use lipstick, above all other forms of makeup, because lipstick symbolizes the passage from childhood into adolescence (46, 215).

3. Attention. When a very young baby's physical needs are met, he is satisfied. Before he is three or four months old, however, this is not enough; he wants attention from others and will demand it by crying. Very early in life, the child discovers that his clothes attract attention. When he begins to play with other children, he finds that they notice, admire, comment on, and openly envy his clothes. Even three-year-olds, it has been reported, notice one another's clothes and refer to their newness, color, or any feature that is different. It is not, therefore, surprising, that the little child learns of the powerful effect that clothing has on others and the gratification that it gives the wearer (209).

New clothes have a peculiar charm for the child. He wants to wear a new garment as soon as it is bought, whether or not it is appropriate for the occasion. He is ridiculously proud of it, and if it is not noticed, he calls attention to it by such remarks as "See my new shoes!" A garment loses much of its charm if it is ignored or if unfavorable comments are made about it.

Children at all ages are especially interested in the *colors* of their clothes. If the garment is of a favorite color, they will like it, regardless of whether it is becoming or appropriate. Most young children like light and bright colors, primarily because they have great attention value. No red is too red, and no green too green to appeal to a young child (144).

Children also discover that *ornamentation* in their clothing has great attention value. Because girls' clothes can be ornamented more than boys', girls are greatly interested in ruffles, bows, and costume jewelry. These not only attract attention but also are symbols of grown-up sophistication. Many little girls literally put on every kind of ornament they own at one time in the hope of winning the attention and arousing the envy that add to their feelings of self-importance (198, 218).

While the young child wants attention at any price, the *older child* discovers that attention is not always favorable. Being noticed and being admired are ego-satisfying; being noticed and being scorned or ridiculed are ego-deflating. Consequently, the older child becomes interested in what is "right" and "appropriate." He wants to win the approval of others as much as he wants to win their attention. He discovers that bright colors are considered "bad taste"; as a result, he shows a preference for darker and less highly saturated hues (144).

Similarly, the child learns to be more selective in ornamentation, using not only less ornamentation but only that which is suitable to the occasion. As childhood draws to a close, much of the overdressing that young children enjoy is replaced by an interest in "correct" dressing (200, 221, 250, 261).

Beginning around the eighth or ninth year, many children become self-conscious and want to *avoid attention.* One way to be inconspicuous, they discover, is to look like everyone else. Children then become *slavishly conventional* in their clothing. If they are forced to wear clothing that is different from that of their friends, they feel embarrassed and ashamed. They are afraid to go out of the house for fear of being laughed at or teased. The desire to avoid attention becomes as strong as the previous desire to attract attention (198, 250).

4. Individuality. No child likes to think of himself as "just another person"; he wants to be recognized as an individual (11). Clothing, the young child learns, not only has attention value but also helps to identify him as a person. He is himself, not like a sibling or another child.

The young child may not object to being dressed like a sibling; this, he discovers, has greater attention value than being dressed differently. As was pointed out in the discussion of twins, triplets, and other forms of multiple birth (see pages 52 to 53), however, the child soon discovers that the satisfaction of being noticed because he looks like a sibling is overshadowed by the fact that he *feels* that he is only a part of a whole—not an individual in his own right. It is then that he wants his clothing to be individualized (207, 269).

Much of the satisfaction the younger child derived from wearing "hand-me-downs" is lost when he discovers that these garments are recognized by others as having belonged to an older sibling. This tends to counteract his individuality. Only if the "hand-me-downs" can be individualized by some ornamentation to make them distinctly his will he want to wear them.

When the child reaches the self-conscious stage, in the latter part of childhood, he still wants to retain some individuality in his appearance. He can conform and yet be different by wearing his favorite colors in garments cut exactly like those of the peer group. The more popular the child, the less anxious he is to hide his identity. By contrast, the less popular child hopes to gain acceptance by hiding his individuality (55, 143, 250).

5. Identification with the Social Group. The desire for individuality is replaced by a desire for identification with the social group as the child grows older and wants to be a member of a gang. Therefore, the child develops a strong interest in clothing that serves as a *status symbol*—a symbol of identification with the gang. It makes little difference whether the clothes other children wear are becoming to him, whether they are approved by parents and other adults, or whether they conform to the prevailing styles. If his friends wear them, he wants to wear them too.

He may want to choose different colors, but aside from that, the more closely his clothing resembles that of his friends, the better he likes it. This holds true not only for the clothes themselves but also for the way he wears them. If his friends want to be sloppy in appearance, he will too, just as he will want to imitate their neatness in dress (112, 147, 276, 297).

6. Sex-appropriateness. Every child learns, when he begins to play with members of the peer group, that social acceptance is facilitated if he is able to create the impression that he is sex-appropriate. As the desire to belong to a gang increases and as the child becomes increasingly aware of the role sex-appropriateness plays in social acceptance, interest in sex-appropriate clothes increases. To differentiate themselves from girls, boys become interested in typically masculine clothes, with emphasis on blue jeans and sport shirts. Furthermore, they affect "roughness" in their appearance, which is in direct contrast to the neatness identified with the female appearance (144, 198).

The older girl, anxious to be identified as feminine, shows a preference for feminine clothes. She wants to make a neat, tidy appearance, and she derives keen enjoyment from dressing up in her best clothes whenever possible (250). One of the reasons for the older girl's interest in using cosmetics, as Wax has pointed out, is that they "help to identify a person as feminine in our culture. . . . The girl who wears cosmetics is insisting on her right to be treated as a woman rather than a child" (299).

7. Camouflage. The young child has little interest in his body, nor is he concerned about his physique, his freckles, his teeth, or the color or texture of his skin and hair. As long as he is not so homely that other children ridicule him, he accepts his appearance as it is.

As children reach the end of childhood, however, they begin to take more interest in their appearance. If they are conspicuously different from their agemates in size—taller or shorter, thinner or fatter—they are self-conscious about it.

Because many children have a definite concept of what they want to look like when they grow up, they become seriously concerned about their bodies at puberty. The girl who always wanted to be tall and slender, for example, will be disturbed by the accumulation of fat over her hips and abdomen. Similarly, a boy who is a late maturer may fear that he will always be short and slender.

The child discovers, from his own experience and from what others say, that certain types of clothes camouflage or minimize the aspects of his appearance that he dislikes. Because girls' clothes are less standardized than boys', girls become more interested in clothes that camouflage their appearance than boys, and they become interested at an earlier age.

Girls generally use certain beauty aids to improve their looks before they discover that clothes can make them more attractive. For example, the girl discovers that having a permanent wave or putting her hair up in curlers makes her so much prettier that even her most critical friends comment on it. In her dramatic play, she learns that grown-up clothes and fancy costumes do wonders for her appearance. It is not surprising, then, that girls show a preference for clothes that "do something" for them (143, 150, 215, 261).

Boys have far less interest in the camouflage aspect of clothing because attractive appearance is not so highly valued among boys. In fact, a boy who is attractive, who is

neatly groomed, and who makes a good appearance is likely to be labeled a "sissy." Boys use camouflage in their clothing only to create the impression that they conform to the popular stereotype of the "regular boy"; they use their oldest, most tattered, and least becoming clothes to create this impression (218).

Thus it is apparent that what is generally regarded as a "sophisticated" interest in clothes appears long before childhood is over. The child may not know *how to achieve* his desired goal as an adolescent or adult does; he may have to discover this by trial and error. The boy may discover, for example, that checks or stripes in his shirts make him look more like the "he-men" on the screen than plain-colored shirts do.

Similarly, from dressing up in dramatic play, the little girl may discover that ruffles make her look more feminine than straight lines and that dark colors make her look more grown-up than light colors. Once these discoveries are made, they influence the child's interest in clothes. The better clothes can meet the child's need for looking the way he wants to look, the more interested he will be in them and the more he will like them (128). Figure 13–9 shows the seven needs filled by clothes in the child's life.

Value of Clothes to the Child. Every child learns that the cultural group places high value on clothes. His parents' emphasis on the right clothes for the occasion, on improving his appearance, on being clean and neat, and on taking care of his clothes all convey to him the idea that clothes are important. Because they are important to the significant people in his life, they become important to him also. The aspects of his clothes that are important to him, however, may not be the same as those which have high value for his parents. When it is important for him to win social acceptance, his interest in clothes will be in proportion to the role they play in winning this acceptance. When, on the other hand, it is important for him to be like his agemates, his interest in clothes will be in proportion to their ability to make him look like them.

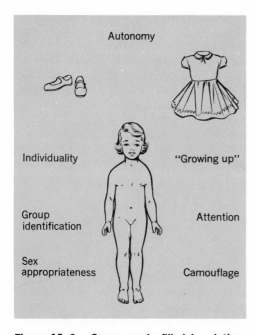

Autonomy

Individuality

"Growing up"

Group identification

Attention

Sex appropriateness

Camouflage

Figure 13–9. Seven needs filled by clothes in the child's life.

In a culture which places high value on appearance—and most cultures, no matter how primitive they may be, do place high value on appearance—it is normal for a child to be interested in his clothes. An *undue obsession* with clothes, however, suggests some sort of weakness or distortion in the structure of the self; it suggests a personality problem in which clothes are being used as a form of compensation. The child whose interest in neatness and cleanliness, for example, is obsessional is showing an interest that is far from normal. This interest may be a reflection of fear of adult disapproval and punishment associated with the high value the child's parents have placed on his clothes and on maintaining an attractive appearance.

Similarly, the child who refuses to go to school because his mother insists that he wear leggings to ward off the possibility of getting a cold is showing a personality characterized by feelings of inadequacy and inferiority. He is afraid to be different because he lacks assurance of his status in the group. When an obese girl insists upon wearing petticoats and ruffles, one cannot assume that she is ignorant of the fact that they make her look even fatter. She knows that being different is usually interpreted to mean "inferior"; therefore, she wants to dress like her agemates to counteract any belief they might have that she is inferior to them.

When a child is *deliberately* unkempt and when he wears anything that happens to be readily available because it is "easier" than selecting the right garment, there is probably something the matter with his personality. If he were unaware of the social values associated with clothes, this disregard might be understandable. No child brought up in our culture, however, can reach school age without being aware of the high value placed on appearance and clothing. Therefore, disregard is not due to ignorance but to defiance of authority and to hostility toward the social group.

The more important clothing is to parents, the more the child who feels unloved and unappreciated will defy his parents by refusing to accept their values. Similarly, the child who feels that people outside the home are hostile to him will show his resentments by ignoring their values. A well-adjusted child, by contrast, who must be poorly dressed, out of style, or inappropriately dressed for the occasion or who must wear clothing unsuited to him because of economic necessity feels uncomfortable, ashamed, and inadequate. He wants to conform to social expectations; when economic inadequacy makes this impossible, he becomes emotionally disturbed (128, 261).

In conclusion, then, it is apparent that the child's clothes not only are a source of much pleasure to him but also add tremendously to his attitude of self-confidence. A well-dressed child is more self-confident, better mannered, and less rowdy than a poorly dressed one. This is increasingly true as the child grows older. The attitude of the social group must also be taken into consideration when evaluating the influence of clothing on the child's behavior and attitudes. What the group thinks is quickly sensed by the child and is then reflected in his attitude toward himself. As Read has pointed out:

Children do like clothes and find real satisfaction in them. Bright colors or gay materials, the feel of different textures in clothing, the comfortable, familiar garment as well as the new one—these are all things that bring pleasure to the child. Clothes make a contribution to the process of growing up when they are right from his standpoint. They can help to make the man (236)!

BIBLIOGRAPHY

(1) ABERLE, D. F., and K. D. NAEGELE: Middle-class fathers' occupational roles and attitudes toward children. *Amer. J. Orthopsychiat.*, 1952, **22**, 366–378.

(2) AGRAS, S.: The relationship of school phobia to childhood depression. *Amer. J. Psychiat.*, 1959, **16**, 533–536.

(3) ALEXANDER, I. E., and A. M. ADLERSTEIN: Affective responses to the concept of death in a population of children and early adolescents. *J. genet. Psychol.*, 1958, **93**, 167–177.

(4) ALLPORT, G. W.: *The individual and his religion.* New York: Macmillan, 1950.

(5) ALLPORT, G. W., J. M. GILLESPIE, and J. YOUNG: Religion of the freshman college student. *J. Psychol.*, 1948, **25**, 3–33.

(6) AMATORA, SISTER M.: Contrasts in boys' and girls' judgments in personality. *Child Develpm.*, 1954, **25**, 51–61.

(7) AMATORA, SISTER M.: Analyses of certain recreational interests and activities and other variables in the large family. *J. soc. Psychol.*, 1959, **50**, 225–231.

(8) AMATORA, SISTER M.: Expressed interests in later childhood. *J. genet. Psychol.*, 1960, **96**, 327–342.

(9) AMATORA, SISTER M.: Interests of preadolescent boys and girls. *Genet. Psychol. Monogr.*, 1960, **61**, 77–113.

(10) AMATORA, SISTER M.: School interests in later childhood. *Education*, 1960, **81**, 32–37.

(11) AMES, L. B.: The sense of self of nursery school children as manifested by their verbal behavior. *J. genet. Psychol.*, 1952, **81**, 193–232.

(12) ANDERS, S. F.: Religious behavior in church families. *Marriage fam. Liv.*, 1955, **17**, 54–57.

(13) ANDERSON, H. H., G. L. ANDERSON, I. H. COHEN, and F. D. NUTT: Image of the teacher by adolescent children in four countries: Germany, England, Mexico, United States. *J. soc. Psychol.*, 1959, **50**, 47–55.

(14) ANDERSON, W. F.: Attitudes of parents of differing socio-economic status toward the teaching profession. *J. educ. Psychol.*, 1954, **45**, 345–352.

(15) ANGELINO, H., L. A. BARNES, and C. L. SHEDD: Attitudes of mothers and adolescent daughters concerning clothing and grooming. *J. home Econ.*, 1956, **48**, 779–782.

(16) ANGELINO, H., and E. V. MECH: "Fears and worries" concerning physical changes: a preliminary survey of 32 females. *J. Psychol.*, 1955, **39**, 195–198.

(17) ANGELINO, H., and E. V. MECH: Some "first" sources of sex information as reported by sixty-seven college women. *J. Psychol.*, 1955, **39**, 321–324.

(18) AUSTER, D., and J. MOLDSTAD: A survey of parents' reactions and opinions concerning certain aspects of education. *J. educ. Sociol.*, 1957, **31**, 64–74.

(19) AUSUBEL, D. P.: Ego development among segregated Negro children. *Ment. Hyg., N.Y.*, 1958, **42**, 362–369.

(20) AXTELL, J. B., and M. W. EDMUNDS: The effect of preschool experience on fathers, mothers, and children. *Calif. J. educ. Res.*, 1960, **11**, 195–203.

(21) AYAD, J. M., and P. R. FARNSWORTH: Shifts in the values of opinion items: further data. *J. Psychol.*, 1953, **36**, 295–298.

(22) BAER, C. J.: The school progress and adjustment of underage and overage students. *J. educ. Psychol.*, 1958, **49**, 17–19.

(23) BAILYN, L.: Mass media and children: a study of exposure habits and cognitive effects. *Psychol. Monogr.*, 1959, **73**, No. 1.

(24) BALDWIN, W. K.: The social position of the educable mentally retarded child in the regular grades in the public schools. *Except. Children*, 1958, **25**, 106–108, 112.

(25) BARBER, B., and L. S. LOBEL: "Fashion" in women's clothes and the American social system. *Soc. Forces*, 1952, **31**, 124–131.

(26) BARRETT, H. O.: An intensive study of 32 gifted children. *Personnel Guid. J.*, 1957, **36**, 192–194.

(27) BAXTER, L. C.: Vocational guidance for elementary school pupils. *Elem. Sch. J.*, 1951, **51**, 343–345.

(28) BEDOIAN, V. H.: Social acceptability and rejection of the underage, at-age and overage pupils in the sixth grade. *J. educ. Res.*, 1954, **47**, 513–520.

(29) BEEKMAN, E.: What high-school seniors think of religion. *Relig. Educ.*, 1947, **42**, 333–337.

(30) BEILIN, H.: The pattern of postponability and its relation to social class mobility. *J. soc. Psychol.*, 1956, **44**, 33–48.

(31) BENDER, I. E.: Changes in religious interest: a retest after 15 years. *J. abnorm. soc. Psychol.*, 1958, **57**, 41–46.

(32) BENE, E.: Some differences between middle-class children and working-class grammar school boys in their attitudes toward education. *Brit. J. Sociol.*, 1959, **10**, 148–152.

(33) BERDIE, R. F.: Why don't they go to college? *Personnel Guid. J.*, 1953, **31**, 352–356.

(34) BETTELHEIM, B., and E. SYLVESTER: Notes on the impact of parental occupations; some cultural determinants of symptom choice in emotionally disturbed children. *Amer. J. Orthopsychiat.*, 1950, **20**, 785–795.

(35) BLAKELY, W. P.: A study of seventh grade children's reading of comic books as related to certain other variables. *J. genet. Psychol.*, 1958, **93**, 291–301.

(36) BOGEN, I.: Pupil-teacher rapport and the teacher's awareness of status structure within the group. *J. educ. Sociol.*, 1954, **28**, 104–114.

(37) BOND, J. A.: Analysis of factors affecting scholarship of high school pupils. *J. educ. Res.*, 1952, **46**, 1–16.

(38) BOSSARD, J. H. S., and E. S. BOLL: *The sociology of child development*, 3d ed. New York: Harper & Row, 1960.

(39) BOWER, E. M., and J. A. HOLMES: Emotional factors and academic achievement. *Rev. educ. Res.*, 1959, **29**, 529–544.

(40) BRECKENRIDGE, M. E., and E. L. VINCENT: *Child development*, 4th ed. Philadelphia: Saunders, 1960.

(41) BRIM, O. G., and R. FORER: A note on the relation of values and social structure in life planning. *Sociometry*, 1956, **19**, 54–60.

(42) BROWN, A. W., and R. G. HUNT: Relations between nursery school attendance and teachers' ratings of some aspects of children's adjustment in kindergarten. *Child Develpm.*, 1961, **32**, 585–596.

(43) BROWN, D. G., and W. L. LOWE: Religious beliefs and personality characteristics of college students. *J. soc. Psychol.*, 1951, **33**, 103–129.

(44) BROWN, F. J.: *Educational sociology*, 2d ed. Englewood Cliffs, N.J.: Prentice-Hall, 1954.

(45) BÜHLER, C.: School as a phase of human life. *Education*, 1952, **73**, 219–222.

(46) BUSH, G., and P. LONDON: On the disappearance of knickers: hypotheses for the functional analysis of the psychology of clothing. *J. soc. Psychol.*, 1960, **51**, 359–366.

(47) BUSWELL, M. M.: The relationship between the social structure of the classroom and the academic success of the pupils. *J. exp. Educ.*, 1953, **22**, 37–52.

(48) CALLENDER, W. P.: Who likes whom? *Clearing House*, 1955, **29**, 490–492.

(49) CHANSKY, N. M.: Threat, anxiety, and reading behavior. *J. educ. Res.*, 1958, **51**, 333–340.

(50) CHOI, E. H.: Father-daughter relationships in school phobia. *Smith Coll. Stud. soc. Wk*, 1961, **31**, 152–178.

(51) CHOWN, S. M.: Personality factors in the formation of occupational choice. *Brit. J. educ. Psychol.*, 1959, **29**, 23–33.

(52) CHRISTENSEN, C. M.: Relationships between pupil achievement, pupil affect-need, teacher warmth, and teacher permissiveness. *J. educ. Psychol.*, 1960, **51**, 169–174.

(53) CLARK, W. H., and C. M. WARNER: The relation of church attendance to honesty and kindness in a small community. *Relig. Educ.*, 1955, **50**, 340–342.

(54) COBB, H. V.: Role-wishes and general wishes of children and adolescents. *Child Develpm.*, 1954, **25**, 161–171.

(55) COBLINER, W. J.: Feminine fashion as an aspect of group psychology: analysis of written replies received by means of a questionnaire. *J. soc. Psychol.*, 1950, **31**, 283–289.

(56) COFFIN, T. E.: Television's impact on society. *Amer. Psychologist*, 1955, **10**, 630–641.

(57) COHN, W.: On the language of lower-class children. *Sch. Rev.*, 1959, **67**, 435–440.

(58) CONDON, M. E.: Extracurricular activities of physically handicapped students. *Personnel Guid. J.*, 1958, **37**, 53–54.

(59) CONN, J. H.: Children's awareness of the origin of babies. *J. child Psychiat.*, 1948, **1**, 140–178.

(60) CONN, J. H.: Children's awareness of sex differences. II. Play attitudes and game preferences. *J. child Psychiat.*, 1951, **2**, 82–99.

(61) COOK, E. S.: An analysis of factors related to withdrawal from high school prior to graduation. *J. educ. Res.*, 1956, **50**, 191–196.

(62) CRANDALL, V. J., A. PRESTON, and A. RABSON: Maternal reactions and the development of independence and achievement behavior in young children. *Child Develpm.*, 1960, **31**, 243–251.

(63) CRANE, A. R.: The development of moral values in children. IV. Pre-adolescent gangs and the moral development of children. *Brit. J. educ. Psychol.*, 1958, **28**, 201–208.

(64) CROW, A.: Parental attitudes toward boy-girl relations. *J. educ. Sociol.*, 1955, **29**, 126–133.

(65) CRUICKSHANK, W. M., and G. O. JOHNSON: *Education of exceptional children and youth*. Englewood Cliffs, N.J.: Prentice-Hall, 1958.

(66) CUMMINS, R. E.: Research insights into the relationship between teachers' acceptance attitudes, their role concepts, and students' acceptance attitudes. *J. educ. Res.*, 1960, **53**, 197–198.

(67) DAVIDSON, H. H., and G. LANG: Children's perceptions of their teachers' feelings toward them related to self-perception, school achievement, and behavior. *J. exp. Educ.*, 1960, **29**, 107–118.

(68) DAVIS, A.: Socio-economic influences upon children's learning. *Understanding the Child*, 1951, **20**, 10–16.

(69) DAVIS, A., and R. J. HAVIGHURST: *Father of the man*. Boston: Houghton Mifflin, 1947.

(70) DEMOS, G. M.: Attitudes of student ethnic

groups on issues related to education. *Calif. J. educ. Res.*, 1960, **11**, 204–206.

(71) DESENBERG, B. M.: Home sex education and monogamy. *Marriage fam. Liv.*, 1947, **9**, 89–92.

(72) DONALD, M. N., and R. J. HAVIGHURST: The meaning of leisure. *Soc. Forces*, 1959, **37**, 355–360.

(73) DORIS, J.: Test-anxiety and blame assignment in grade school children. *J. abnorm. soc. Psychol.*, 1959, **58**, 181–190.

(74) DOUVAN, E.: Social status and success strivings. *J. abnorm. soc. Psychol.*, 1956, **52**, 219–223.

(75) DOUVAN, E.: Independence and identity in children. *Children*, 1957, **4**, 186–190.

(76) DRASGOW, J.: Underachievers. *J. counsel. Psychol.*, 1957, **4**, 210–211.

(77) DREGER, R. M.: Some personality correlates of religious attitudes, as determined by projective techniques. *Psychol. Monogr.*, 1952, **66**, No. 3.

(78) DREGER, R. M.: Spontaneous conversation and story-telling of children in a naturalistic setting. *J. Psychol.*, 1955, **40**, 163–180.

(79) DREWS, E. M., and J. E. TEAHAM: Parental attitudes and academic achievement. *J. clin. Psychol.*, 1957, **13**, 328–332.

(80) DRUCKER, A. J., H. T. CHRISTENSEN, and H. H. REMMERS: Some background factors in sociosexual modernism. *Marriage fam. Liv.*, 1952, **14**, 334–337.

(81) DULLES, R. J.: The myth of underachievement. *J. educ. Sociol.*, 1961, **35**, 121–122.

(82) DUNKELBERGER, C. J., and L. E. TYLER: Interest stability and personality traits. *J. counsel. Psychol.*, 1961, **8**, 70–74.

(83) DUVALL, E. M., and A. B. MOTZ: Age and education as factors in school experience and personal-family adjustments. *Sch. Rev.*, 1945, **53**, 413–421.

(84) DYE, M. G.: Attitudes of gifted children toward school. *Educ. Admin. Superv.*, 1956, **42**, 301–308.

(85) EATON, M. T., L. A. D'AMICO, and B. N. PHILLIPS: Problem behavior in school. *J. educ. Psychol.*, 1956, **47**, 350–357.

(86) EISTER, A. W.: Some aspects of institutional behavior with reference to churches. *Amer. sociol. Rev.*, 1952, **17**, 64–69.

(87) ELKIND, D.: The child's conception of his religious denomination: I. The Jewish child. *J. genet. Psychol.*, 1961, **99**, 209–225.

(88) ELKIND, D.: The child's conception of his religious denomination. II. The Catholic child. *J. genet. Psychol.*, 1962, **101**, 185–193.

(89) EMPEY, L. T.: Social class and occupational aspiration: a comparison of absolute and relative measurement. *Amer. sociol. Rev.*, 1956, **21**, 703–709.

(90) ESTVAN, F. J., and E. W. ESTVAN: *The child's world: his social perception.* New York: Putnam, 1959.

(91) FAGIN, B.: Guiding the vocational interests of the child. *Education*, 1953, **74**, 171–179.

(92) FAHS, S. L.: The beginnings of mysticism in children's growth. *Relig. Educ.*, 1950, **45**, 139–147.

(93) FEINBERG, H., and E. MOSCOVITCH: Achievement on the Stanford Achievement Test of children in difficult own home situations compared with children placed out of the home. *J. exp. Educ.*, 1957, **26**, 67–80.

(94) FINE, B.: Children most interested in science. *The New York Times*, July 10, 1955.

(95) FITT, A. B.: An experimental study of children's attitudes toward school in Auckland, N.Z. *Brit. J. educ. Psychol.*, 1956, **26**, 25–30.

(96) FLIEGLER, L. A.: Understanding the underachieving gifted child. *Psychol. Rep.*, 1957, **3**, 533–536.

(97) FORD, T. R.: Social factors affecting academic performance: further evidence. *Sch. Rev.*, 1957, **65**, 415–422.

(98) FRANK, L. K., and M. H. FRANK: *Your adolescent, at home and in school.* New York: Viking, 1956.

(99) FRANKEL, E.: A comparative study of achieving and underachieving high school boys of high intellectual ability. *J. educ. Res.*, 1960, **53**, 172–180.

(100) FREEMAN, H. A.: First graders' religious ideas. *Sch. Soc.*, 1931, **34**, 733–735.

(101) FREUD, S.: *The standard edition of the complete works of Sigmund Freud.* London: Hogarth, 1953–1962.

(102) GALLAGHER, J. J.: Peer acceptance of highly gifted children in elementary school. *Elem. Sch. J.*, 1958, **58**, 465–470.

(103) GALLER, E. H.: Influence of social class on children's choice of occupations. *Elem. Sch. J.*, 1951, **51**, 439–445.

(104) GARDNER, G. E.: A factor in the sex education of children. *Ment. Hyg., N.Y.*, 1944, **28**, 55–63.

(105) GARRISON, K. C.: *Growth and development*, 2d ed. New York: Longmans, 1959.

(106) GELLERT, E.: Children's conceptions of the content and function of the human body. *Genet. Psychol. Monogr.*, 1962, **65**, 293–405.

(107) GESELL, A., and F. L. ILG: *Child development.* New York: Harper & Row, 1949.

(108) GESELL, A., F. L. ILG, and L. B. AMES: *Youth: the years from ten to sixteen.* New York: Harper & Row, 1956.

(109) GILLILAND, A. R.: Changes in religious beliefs of college students. *J. soc. Psychol.*, 1953, **37**, 113–116.

(110) GINZBERG, E., J. W. GINZBERG, S. AXELROD, and J. C. HERMA: *Occupational choice.* New York: Columbia, 1951.

(111) GLASNER, RABBI S.: Family religion as a matrix of personal growth. *Marriage fam. Liv.,* 1961, **23,** 291–293.

(112) GLICKMAN, A. S.: Clothing leadership among boys. *Dissertation Abstr.,* 1958, **18,** Pt. 1, 682–684.

(113) GOFF, R. G.: Some educational implications of the influence of rejection on aspiration levels of minority group children. *J. exp. Educ.,* 1954, **23,** 179–184.

(114) GOLDBERG, M. L.: Motivation of the gifted. *57th Yearb. Nat. Soc. Stud. Educ.,* 1958, Pt. 2, 87–109.

(115) GOLDWORTH, M.: The effects of an elementary-school fast-learning program on children's social relationships. *Except. Children,* 1959, **26,** 59–63.

(116) GOODLAD, J. I.: Some effects of promotion and non-promotion upon the social and personal adjustment of children. *J. exp. Educ.,* 1953, **22,** 301–328.

(117) GOWAN, J. C.: Dynamics of the underachievement of gifted children. *Except. Children,* 1957, **24,** 98–101, 122.

(118) GROFF, P. J.: Children's attitudes toward reading and their critical reading abilities in four content-type materials. *J. educ. Res.,* 1962, **55,** 313–317.

(119) GRONLUND, N. E.: Relationship between sociometric status of pupils and teachers' preferences for having them in class. *Sociometry,* 1953, **16,** 142–150.

(120) GRUNES, W. F.: On perception of occupations. *Personnel Guid. J.,* 1956, **34,** 276–279.

(121) HAGGARD, E. A.: Socialization, personality, and academic achievement in gifted children. *Sch. Rev.,* 1957, **65,** 388–414.

(122) HAMALAINEN, A. E.: Kindergarten-primary entrance age in relation to later school adjustment. *Elem. Sch. J.,* 1952, **52,** 406–411.

(123) HARMS, E.: The development of religious experience in children. *Amer. J. Sociol.,* 1944, **50,** 112–122.

(124) HARPER, L. E., and B. WRIGHT: Dealing with emotional problems in the classroom. *Elem. Sch. J.,* 1958, **58,** 316–325.

(125) HARRIS, D. B.: How children learn interests. *49th Yearb. Nat. Soc. Stud. Educ.,* 1950, Pt. 1, 129–135.

(126) HARRIS, D. B., and S. C. TSENG: Children's attitudes toward peers and parents as revealed by sentence completions. *Child Develpm.,* 1957, **28,** 401–411.

(127) HARRISON, E. C.: A study of vocational attitudes. *J. Negro Educ.,* 1953, **22,** 471–475.

(128) HARTMANN, G. W.: Clothing: personal problem and social issue. *J. home Econ.,* 1949, **41,** 295–298.

(129) HAVIGHURST, R. J.: *Human development and education.* New York: Longmans, 1953.

(130) HAVIGHURST, R. J.: Social-class influences on American education. *60th Yearb. Nat. Soc. Stud. Educ.,* 1961, Pt. 2, 120–143.

(131) HAVIGHURST, R. J., and K. FEIGENBAUM: Leisure and life style. *Amer. J. Sociol.,* 1959, **64,** 396–404.

(132) HEIL, L. M., and C. WASHBURNE: Characteristics of teachers related to children's progress. *J. teacher Educ.,* 1961, **12,** 401–406.

(133) HEISLER, F.: An elementary-school background for vocational guidance. *Elem. Sch. J.,* 1955, **55,** 513–516.

(134) HEMMERLING, R. L., and H. HURST: The effects of leisure time activities on scholastic achievement. *Calif. J. educ. Res.,* 1961, **12,** 86–90.

(135) HENRY, J.: Docility or giving teacher what she wants. *J. soc. Issues,* 1955, **11,** No. 2, 33–41.

(136) HERSOV, L. A.: Persistent non-attendance at school. *J. child Psychol. Psychiat.,* 1960, **1,** 130–136.

(137) D'HEULE, A., J. C. MELLINGER, and E. A. HAGGARD: Personality, intellectual, and achievement patterns in gifted children. *Psychol. Monogr.,* 1959, **73,** No. 13.

(138) HOCH, P. H., and J. ZUBIN: *Psychosexual development.* New York: Grune & Stratton, 1949.

(139) HODGES, A., and B. BALOW: Learning disability in relation to family constellation. *J. educ. Res.,* 1961, **55,** 41–42.

(140) HOEHN, A. J.: A study of social status differentiation in the classroom behavior of nineteen third grade teachers. *J. soc. Psychol.,* 1954, **39,** 269–292.

(141) HOFFMAN, L. W., S. ROSEN, and R. LIPPITT: Parental coerciveness, child autonomy, and child's role at school. *Sociometry,* 1960, **23,** 15–22.

(142) HOLLINGWORTH, L. S.: *Children above 180 IQ: origin and development.* New York: Harcourt, Brace & World, 1950.

(143) HOULT, T. F.: Experimental measurement of clothing as a factor in some social ratings of selected American men. *Amer. sociol. Rev.,* 1954, **19,** 324–328.

(144) HUNT, L. A.: A developmental study of factors related to children's clothing preferences. *Monogr. Soc. Res. Child Develpm.,* 1959, **24,** No. 1.

(145) HUTT, M. L., and R. G. GIBBY: *The child: development and adjustment.* Boston: Allyn and Bacon, 1959.

(146) ILG, F. L., and L. B. AMES: *Child behavior.* New York: Harper & Row, 1955.

(147) JACOBI, J. E., and S. G. WALTERS: Social status and consumer choice. *Soc. Forces,* 1958, **36,** 209–214.

(148) JAHODA, G.: Social class attitudes and levels of occupational aspiration in secondary modern school leavers. *Brit. J. Psychol.,* 1953, **44,** 95–107.

(149) JENSEN, V. H.: Influence of personality traits on academic success. *Personnel Guid. J.*, 1958, **36**, 497–500.

(150) JERSILD, A. T.: *In search of self.* New York: Teachers College, Columbia University, 1952.

(151) JERSILD, A. T.: *Child psychology*, 5th ed. Englewood Cliffs, N.J.: Prentice-Hall, 1960.

(152) JERSILD, A. T., and R. J. TASCH: *Children's interests and what they suggest for education.* New York: Teachers College, Columbia University, 1949.

(153) JOHNSON, C. J., and J. R. FERREIRA: School attitudes of children in special classes for mentally retarded. *Calif. J. educ. Res.*, 1958, **9**, 33–37.

(154) JOHNSON, M. S.: Factors related to disability in reading. *J. exp. Educ.*, 1957, **26**, 1–26.

(155) JONES, A.: Sexual symbolic response in prepubescent and pubescent children. *J. consult. Psychol.*, 1961, **25**, 383–387.

(156) JONES, M. C., and P. H. MUSSEN: Self-conceptions, motivations, and interpersonal attitudes of early- and late-maturing girls. *Child Develpm.*, 1958, **29**, 491–501.

(157) JOSEPHINA, SISTER: A study of some common religious terms for six-year-old children. *Relig. Educ.*, 1961, **56**, 24–25.

(158) JOSSELYN, I. M.: Psychological changes in adolescence. *Children*, 1959, **6**, 43–47.

(159) KAHN, J. H., and J. P. NURSTEN: School refusal: a comprehensive view of school phobias and other failures of school attendance. *Amer. J. Orthopsychiat.*, 1962, **32**, 707–718.

(160) KEISLAR, E. R.: Peer group ratings of high school pupils with high and low school marks. *J. exp. Educ.*, 1955, **23**, 375–378.

(161) KEY, C. B., M. R. WHITE, W. P. HONZIK, A. B. HEINEY, and D. ERWIN: The process of learning to dress among nursery school children. *Genet. Psychol. Monogr.*, 1936, **18**, 67–163.

(162) KING, E. B.: Effect of age on entrance into grade 1 upon achievement in elementary school. *Elem. Sch. J.*, 1955, **55**, 331–336.

(163) KINSEY, A. C., W. B. POMEROY, C. E. MARTIN, and P. H. GEBHARD: *Sexual behavior in the human female.* Philadelphia: Saunders, 1953.

(164) KIRKENDALL, L. A.: Toward a clarification of the concept of male sex drive. *Marriage fam. Liv.*, 1958, **30**, 367–372.

(165) KLEIN, W. C.: Development of health knowledge and understanding test for fifth grade pupils. *Res. Quart. Amer. Ass. Hlth Phys. Educ. Recr.*, 1961, **32**, 530–533.

(166) KOCH, H. L.: The relation of certain formal attributes of siblings and attitudes held toward each other and toward their parents. *Monogr. Soc. Res. Child Develpm.*, 1960, **25**, No. 4.

(167) KOWATRAKUL, S.: Some behaviors of elementary school children related to classroom activities and subject areas. *J. educ. Psychol.*, 1959, **50**, 121–128.

(168) KOWITZ, G. T., and E. J. TIGNER: Tell me about Santa Claus: a study of concept change. *Elem. Sch. J.*, 1961, **62**, 130–133.

(169) KRAUS, P. E.: *A longitudinal study of children.* New York: Board of Education, 1956.

(170) KUHLEN, R. G., and M. ARNOLD: Age differences in religious beliefs and problems during adolescence. *J. genet. Psychol.*, 1944, **65**, 291–300.

(171) KUNDE, T. A., and R. V. DAVIS: Comparative study of occupational prestige in three western cultures. *Personnel Guid. J.*, 1959, **27**, 350–352.

(172) KURTZ, J. J., and E. J. SWENSON: Factors related to overachievement and underachievement in school. *Sch. Rev.*, 1951, **59**, 472–480.

(173) LAIRD, D. C. S.: How eleven-year-old boys see their teachers. *Prog. Educ.*, 1956, **33**, 115–118.

(174) LANDIS, B. Y.: Religion and youth. In E. Ginzberg, *The nation's children.* Vol. 2. *Development and education.* New York: Columbia, 1960. Pp. 186–206.

(175) LANDIS, P. H.: Marriage preparation in two generations. *Marriage fam. Liv.*, 1951, **13**, 155–156.

(176) LANTAGNE, J. E.: An analysis of the health interests of 3,000 secondary school children. *Res. Quart. Amer. Ass. Hlth Phys. Educ. Recr.*, 1950, **21**, 34–39.

(177) LANTZ, H.: Religious participation and social orientation of 1,000 university students. *Sociol. soc. Res.*, 1949, **33**, 285–291.

(178) LAYCOCK, S. R.: Effects of the teacher's personality on the behavior of pupils. *Understanding the Child*, 1950, **19**, 50–55.

(179) LEAVITT, J.: Teacher-pupil relationships. *J. educ. Res.*, 1959, **29**, 210–217.

(180) LEE, M. R.: Background factors related to sex information and attitudes. *J. educ. Psychol.*, 1952, **43**, 467–485.

(181) LEEDS, C. H.: Teacher behavior liked and disliked by pupils. *Education*, 1954, **75**, 29–37.

(182) LENSKI, G. E.: Social correlates of religious interest. *Amer. sociol. Rev.*, 1953, **18**, 533–544.

(183) LEVIN, H., T. L. HILTON, and G. F. LEIDERMAN: Studies of teacher behavior. *J. exp. Educ.*, 1957, **26**, 81–91.

(184) LEVINSON, B. M.: The inner life of the extremely gifted child, as seen from the clinical setting. *J. genet. Psychol.*, 1961, **99**, 83–88.

(185) LOWE, W. L.: Religious beliefs and religious delusions. *Amer. J. Psychother.,* 1955, **9,** 54–61.

(186) MACCOBY, E. E., W. C. WILSON, and R. V. BURTON: Differential movie-viewing behavior of male and female viewers. *J. Pers.,* 1958, **26,** 259–267.

(187) MACFARLANE, J., L. ALLEN, and M. P. HONZIK: *A developmental study of the behavior problems of normal children between twenty-one months and fourteen years.* Berkeley, Calif.: University of California Press, 1954.

(188) MALLINSON, G. G., and W. M. CRUMRINE: An investigation of the stability of interests of high-school students. *J. educ. Res.,* 1952, **45,** 369–383.

(189) MALPASS, L. F.: Some relationships between students' perceptions of school and their achievement. *J. educ. Psychol.,* 1953, **44,** 475–482.

(190) MANN, H.: How real are friendships of gifted and typical children in a program of partial segregation? *Except. Children,* 1957, **23,** 199–201, 206.

(191) MANWELL, E. M., and S. L. FAHS: *Consider the children—how they grow,* rev. ed. Boston: Beacon Press, 1951.

(192) MARSHALL, H. R.: Relations between home experiences and children's use of language in play interactions with peers. *Psychol. Monogr.,* 1961, **75,** No. 5.

(193) MC CANN, R. V.: Developmental factors in the growth of a mature faith. *Relig. Educ.,* 1955, **50,** 147–155.

(194) MC CARTHY, D.: Language development. In L. Carmichael (Ed.), *Manual of child psychology,* 2d ed. New York: Wiley, 1954. Pp. 492–630.

(195) MC DAVID, J.: Some relationships between social reinforcement and scholastic achievement. *J. consult. Psychol.,* 1959, **23,** 151–154.

(196) MC GEE, H. M.: Measurement of authoritarianism and its relation to classroom behavior. *Genet. Psychol. Monogr.,* 1955, **52,** 89–146.

(197) MC GUIRE, C., and G. D. WHITE: Social-class influences on discipline at school. *Educ. Leadership,* 1957, **14,** 229–231, 234–236.

(198) MEAD, M.: *Male and female.* New York: Morrow, 1952.

(199) MEAD, M., and R. MÉTRAUX: Image of the scientist among high school students. *Science,* 1957, **126,** 384–390.

(200) MENDELSOHN, H., and I. CRESPI: The effect of autistic pressure and institutional structure on preferences in a choice situation. *J. soc. Psychol.,* 1952, **36,** 109–123.

(201) MERRY, F. K., and R. V. MERRY: *The first two decades of life,* 2d ed. New York: Harper & Row, 1958.

(202) MEYER, W. J., and G. G. THOMPSON: Sex differences in the distribution of teacher approval and disapproval among sixth-grade children. *J. educ. Psychol.,* 1956, **47,** 385–396.

(203) MILLER, T. P.: The child who refuses to attend school. *Amer. J. Psychiat.,* 1961, **118,** 398–404.

(204) MILNER, E.: A study of the relationship between readiness in grade one school children and patterns of parent-child interaction. *Child Develpm.,* 1951, **22,** 95–112.

(205) MORRISON, I. E., and I. F. PERRY: Acceptance of overage children by their classmates. *Elem. Sch. J.,* 1956, **56,** 217–220.

(206) MOTTO, J. J.: A reply to Drasgow on underachievers. *J. counsel. Psychol.,* 1959, **6,** 245–247.

(207) MOWRER, E. R.: Some factors in the affectional adjustment of twins. *Amer. sociol. Rev.,* 1954, **19,** 468–471.

(208) MUELLER, K. H.: Can cheating be killed? *Personnel Guid. J.,* 1953, **31,** 465–468.

(209) MURPHY, L. B.: *Personality in young children.* New York: Basic Books, Inc., Publishers, 1957.

(210) MUSSEN, P. H., J. J. CONGER, and J. KAGAN: *Child development and personality,* 2d ed. New York: Harper & Row, 1963.

(211) MUSSEN, P. H., and M. C. JONES: Self-conceptions, motivations, and interpersonal attitudes of late- and early-maturing boys. *Child Develpm.,* 1957, **28,** 243–256.

(212) NAGY, M. H.: Children's conceptions of some bodily functions. *J. genet. Psychol.,* 1953, **83,** 199–216.

(213) NAGY, M. H.: The representation of "germs" by children. *J. genet. Psychol.,* 1953, **83,** 227–240.

(214) NEISSER, E. G.: Emotional and social values attached to money. *Marriage fam. Liv.,* 1960, **22,** 132–139.

(215) New York Times Report: Lipstick charts youth maturity. *The New York Times,* Mar. 20, 1959.

(216) NORMAN, R. D., and M. F. DALEY: The comparative personality adjustment of superior and inferior readers. *J. educ. Psychol.,* 1959, **50,** 31–36.

(217) NORTON, J. L.: Patterns of vocational interest development and actual job choice. *J. genet. Psychol.,* 1953, **82,** 235–262, 263–278.

(218) PACKARD, V.: *The status seekers.* New York: Pocket Books, 1961.

(219) PARKER, J. C.: Comment on children. *Children,* 1960, **7,** 116.

(220) PASSOW, A. H.: Study of underachieving gifted. *Educ. Leaders,* 1958, **16,** 121–125.

(221) PEARSON, L. H.: Teen-agers' preferences in clothes. *J. home Econ.,* 1950, **42,** 801–802.

(222) PERKINS, H. V.: Teachers' and peers' perceptions of children's self concepts. *Child Develpm.*, 1958, **29**, 203–220.

(223) PHILBAD, C. T., and G. L. GREGORY: The role of test intelligence and occupational background as factors in occupational choice. *Sociometry*, 1956, **19**, 192–199.

(224) PHILLIPS, B. N., F. J. KING, and C. MC GUIRE: Studies on anxiety: I. Anxiety and performance on psychometric tests varying in complexity. *Child Develpm.*, 1959, **30**, 253–259.

(225) PHIPPS, M. J.: Some factors influencing what children know about human growth. *Amer. Psychologist*, 1949, **4**, 79–81.

(226) PITJE, G. M.: Sex education among the Pedi. *Intern. J. Sexol.*, 1951, **4**, 212–216.

(227) POFFENBERGER, T., and D. NORTON: Factors in the formation of attitudes toward mathematics. *J. educ. Res.*, 1959, **52**, 171–176.

(228) POPE, B.: Socio-economic contrasts in children's peer culture prestige values. *Genet. Psychol. Monogr.*, 1953, **48**, 157–220.

(229) PORTERFIELD, O. V., and H. F. SCHLICHTING: Peer status and reading achievement. *J. educ. Res.*, 1961, **54**, 291–297.

(230) POWELL, M.: Age and sex differences in degree of conflict within certain areas of psychological adjustment. *Psychol. Monogr.*, 1955, **69**, No. 2.

(231) PRESSEY, S. L., and A. W. JONES: 1923–1953 and 20–60 age changes in moral codes, anxieties, and interests, as shown by the "X-O Tests." *J. Psychol.*, 1955, **39**, 485–502.

(232) PSATHAS, G.: Ethnicity, social class, and adolescent independence from parental controls. *Amer. sociol. Rev.*, 1957, **22**, 415–423.

(233) PUSEY, N. M.: Stress on job choice decried by Dr. Pusey in education panel. *The New York Times*, Jan. 21, 1954.

(234) RABINOWITZ, R.: Attributes of pupils achieving beyond their level of expectancy. *J. Pers.*, 1956, **24**, 308–317.

(235) RAINWATER, L.: A study of personality differences between middle and lower class adolescents: the Szondi Test in culture-personality research. *Genet. Psychol. Monogr.*, 1956, **54**, 3–86.

(236) READ, K. H.: Clothes help build personality. *J. home Econ.*, 1950, **42**, 348–350.

(237) Recreation Survey: Recreational interests and needs of high-school youth. *Recreation*, 1954, **47**, 43–46.

(238) REEVY, W. R.: Child sexuality. In *The encyclopedia of sexual behavior*. Englewood Cliffs, N.J.: Hawthorn Books, 1961. Pp. 258–267.

(239) REMMERS, H. H., and D. H. RADLER: *The American teenager*. Indianapolis: Bobbs-Merrill, 1957.

(240) RENNE, R. R.: Woman power and the American economy. *J. home Econ.*, 1957, **49**, 83–86.

(241) REUSS, C. F.: Research findings on the effects of modern-day religion on family life. *Marriage fam. Liv.*, 1954, **16**, 221–225.

(242) RIESMAN, D.: Permissiveness and sex roles. *Marriage fam. Liv.*, 1959, **21**, 211–217.

(243) RODRIQUEZ, A., M. RODRIQUEZ, and L. EISENBERG: The outcome of school phobia: a follow-up study based on 41 cases. *Amer. J. Psychiat.*, 1959, **116**, 540–544.

(244) ROE, A.: Early determinants of vocational choice. *J. counsel. Psychol.*, 1957, **4**, 212–217.

(245) ROGOSIN, H.: What about "cheating" on examinations and honesty? *Sch. Soc.*, 1951, **74**, 402–403.

(246) ROSEN, B. C.: Race, ethnicity, and the achievement syndrome. *Amer. sociol. Rev.*, 1959, **24**, 47–60.

(247) ROTHNEY, J. W. M., and N. E. KOOPMAN: Guidance of the gifted. *57th Yearb. Nat. Soc. Stud. Educ.*, 1958, Pt. 2, 347–361.

(248) RUSSELL, D. H.: The development of thinking processes. *Rev. educ. Res.*, 1953, **23**, 137–145.

(249) RUSSELL, I. L., and W. A. THALMAN: Personality: does it influence teachers' marks? *J. educ. Res.*, 1955, **48**, 561–564.

(250) RYAN, M. S.: *Psychological effects of clothing*. Ithaca, N.Y.: Cornell Univer. Agr. Exp. Sta. Bull., 1952, No. 882; 1953, No. 900.

(251) SARNOFF, I., F. LIGHTHALL, B. WAITE, K. DAVIDSON, and S. SARASON: A cross-cultural study of anxiety among American and English school children. *J. educ. Psychol.*, 1958, **49**, 129–136.

(252) SCATES, D. E.: Significant factors in teachers' classroom attitudes. *J. teacher Educ.*, 1956, **7**, 274–279.

(253) SCHWARTZ, J.: The portrayal of educators in motion pictures, 1950–1958. *J. educ. Sociol.*, 1960, **34**, 82–90.

(254) SEARS, R. R., E. E. MACCOBY, and H. LEVIN: *Patterns of child rearing*. New York: Harper & Row, 1957.

(255) SHANE, H. G.: Children's interests. *NEA J.*, 1957, **46**, 237–239.

(256) SHAW, M. C., and D. J. BROWN: Scholastic underachievement of bright college students. *Personnel Guid. J.*, 1957, **36**, 195–199.

(257) SHAW, M. C., and J. GRUBB: Hostility and able high school underachievers. *J. counsel. Psychol.*, 1958, **5**, 263–266.

(258) SHAW, M. C., and J. T. MC CUEN: The onset of academic underachievement in bright children. *J. educ. Psychol.*, 1960, **51**, 103–105.

(259) SILLER, J.: Socioeconomic status and conceptual thinking. *J. abnorm. soc. Psychol.*, 1957, **55**, 365–371.

(260) SILVERMAN, J. S., M. W. FITE, and M. M. MOSHER: Clinical findings in reading disability children: special cases of intellectual inhibition. *Amer. J. Orthopsychiat.*, 1959, **29**, 298–314.

(261) SILVERMAN, S. S.: Clothing and appearance: their psychological implications for teen-age girls. *Teach. Coll. Contr. Educ.*, 1945, No. 912.

(262) SIMMEL, G.: Fashion. *Amer. J. Sociol.*, 1957, **62**, 541–558.

(263) SIMON, M. D.: Body configuration and school readiness. *Child Develpm.*, 1959, **30**, 493–512.

(264) SIMPSON, R. L., and I. H. SIMPSON: The psychiatric attendant: development of an occupational self-image in a low-status occupation. *Amer. sociol. Rev.*, 1959, **24**, 389–392.

(265) SINGER, S. L., and S. STEFFLRE: Age differences in job values and desires. *J. counsel. Psychol.*, 1954, **1**, 89–91.

(266) SINNET, E. R.: Some determinants of agreement between measured and expressed interests. *Educ. psychol. Measmt*, 1956, **16**, 110–118.

(267) SPACHE, G.: Personality patterns of retarded readers. *J. educ. Res.*, 1957, **50**, 461–469.

(268) SPERLING, O. E.: An imaginary companion representing a pre-stage of the super ego. *Psychoanal. Stud. Child.*, 1954, **9**, 252–258.

(269) STAINS, K. B.: Developing independence in children. *Understanding the Child*, 1951, **20**, 49.

(270) STAUDT, V. M.: Character formation is the teacher's business. *Education*, 1957, **77**, 198–202.

(271) STENDLER, C. B.: Social class differences in parental attitude toward school at grade 1 level. *Child Develpm.*, 1951, **22**, 37–46.

(272) STEPHENSON, R. M.: Mobility orientation and stratification of 1,000 ninth graders. *Amer. sociol. Rev.*, 1957, **22**, 204–212.

(273) STEWART, A. H., I. H. WEILAND, A. R. LEIDER, C. A. MAUGHAN, T. R. HOLMES, and H. S. RIPLEY: Excessive infant crying (colic) in relation to parent behavior. *Amer. J. Psychiat.*, 1954, **110**, 687–694.

(274) STEWART, L. H.: Relationship of socioeconomic status to children's occupational attitudes and interests. *J. genet. Psychol.*, 1959, **95**, 111–136.

(275) STONE, L. J., and J. CHURCH: *Childhood and adolescence.* New York: Random House, 1957.

(276) STOUT, D. R., and A. LATZKE: Values college women consider in clothing selection. *J. home Econ.*, 1958, **50**, 43–44.

(277) STRANG, R.: Characteristics of a classroom which promotes mental health. *Nerv. Child*, 1954, **10**, 363–367.

(278) STRANG, R.: How children and adolescents view their world. *Ment. Hyg., N.Y.*, 1954, **38**, 29–33.

(279) STRODBECK, F. L., M. R. MC DONALD, and B. C. ROSEN: Evaluation of occupations: a reflection of Jewish and Italian mobility differences. *Amer. sociol. Rev.*, 1957, **22**, 546–553.

(280) STRONG, E. K.: Satisfactions and interests. *Amer. Psychologist*, 1958, **13**, 449–456.

(281) SWEETSER, F. S.: *Grade-school families meet television.* Boston, Boston University Press, 1953.

(282) SYMONDS, P. M.: Characteristics of the effective teacher based on pupil evaluations. *J. exp. Educ.*, 1955, **23**, 289–310.

(283) SYMONDS, P. M.: What education has to learn from psychology. VI. Emotion and learning. *Teachers Coll. Rec.*, 1958, **60**, 9–22.

(284) TERMAN, L. M., and L. E. TYLER: Psychological sex differences. In L. Carmichael (Ed.), *Manual of child psychology*, 2d ed. New York: Wiley, 1954. Pp. 1064–1114.

(285) THISTLEWAITE, D. L.: Effects of social recognition upon the educational motivation of talented youth. *J. educ. Psychol.*, 1959, **50**, 111–116.

(286) TOBY, J.: Orientation to education as a factor in the school maladjustment of lower-class children. *Soc. Forces*, 1957, **35**, 259–266.

(287) TROW, D. B.: Autonomy and job satisfaction in task-oriented groups. *J. abnorm. soc. Psychol.*, 1957, **54**, 204–209.

(288) TUCKMAN, J.: Rigidity of social status rankings of occupations. *Personnel Guid. J.*, 1958, **36**, 534–537.

(289) TUDDENHAM, R. D.: Studies in reputation: I. Sex and grade differences in school children's evaluation of their peers. II. The diagnosis of social adjustment. *Psychol. Monogr.*, 1952, **66**, No. 1.

(290) TYERMAN, M. J.: A research into truancy. *Brit. J. educ. Psychol.*, 1958, **28**, 217–225.

(291) TYLER, L. E.: The relationship of interests to abilities and reputation among first-grade children. *Educ. psychol. Measmt*, 1951, **11**, 255–264.

(292) TYLER, L. E.: The development of "vocational interests": I. The organization of likes and dislikes in ten-year-old children. *J. genet. Psychol.*, 1955, **86**, 33–34.

(293) VAN DORN, V., and F. MAYFARTH: Religious nurture and childhood education. *Relig. Educ.*, 1949, **44**, 141–148.

(294) WALDFOGEL, S., E. TESSMAN, and P. B. HAHN: A program for early intervention in school phobia. *Amer. J. Orthopsychiat.*, 1959, **29**, 324–332.

(295) WALLACE, E. H.: Selected out-of-school factors that affect Negro elementary school children. *J. educ. Res.*, 1960, **54,** 118–120, 137–140.

(296) WALSH, A. M.: *Self-concepts of bright boys with learning difficulties.* New York: Teachers College, Columbia University, 1956.

(297) WARDEN, J. A.: Some desires or goals for clothing of college women. *J. home Econ.*, 1957, **49,** 795.

(298) WATSON, G. W.: Emotional problems of gifted students. *Personnel Guid. J.*, 1960, **39,** 98–105.

(299) WAX, M.: Themes in cosmetics and grooming. *Amer. J. Sociol.*, 1957, **62,** 588–593.

(300) WEIGAND, G.: Adaptiveness and the role of parents in academic success. *Personnel Guid. J.*, 1957, **35,** 518–522.

(301) WEINSTEIN, E. A.: Children's conceptions of occupational stratification. *Sociol. soc. Res.*, 1958, **42,** 278–284.

(302) WEINSTEIN, E. A., and P. N. GEISEL: An analysis of sex differences in adjustment. *Child Develpm.*, 1960, **31,** 721–728.

(303) WELFORD, A. T.: An attempt at an experimental approach to the psychology of religion. *Brit. J. Psychol.*, 1946, **36,** 55–73.

(304) WHEELER, L. R., and V. D. WHEELER: Differences in religious ideas and attitudes of children who go to church and those who never attend. *Relig. Educ.*, 1945, **40,** 149–161.

(305) WINKLEY, R., K. JACKSON, O. A. FAUST, M. F. MURRAY, and E. G. CERMAK: Emotional reactions and behavior of children in the home. *J. Pediat.*, 1951, **38,** 476–481.

(306) WITHALL, J.: Assessment of the social emotional climate experienced by a group of seventh graders as they move from class to class. *Educ. psychol. Measmt*, 1952, **12,** 440–451.

(307) WITHEY, R. A.: The role of religion in higher education. *Sch. Soc.*, 1952, **76,** 257–261.

(308) WITTY, P. A., and T. F. GUSTAFSON: Studies of TV: an eighth yearly report. *Elem. Eng.*, 1957, **34,** 536–542.

(309) WOLMAN, B.: Sexual development in Israeli adolescents. *Amer. J. Psychother.*, 1951, **5,** 531–559.

(310) WOLMAN, B. B.: Education and leadership. *Teach. Coll. Rec.*, 1958, **59,** 465–473.

(311) WORELL, L.: Level of aspiration and academic success. *J. educ. Psychol.*, 1959, **50,** 47–54.

(312) WORTH, W. H.: Promotion or not promotion? *Educ. Admin. Superv.*, 1960, **46,** 16–26.

(313) ZIMMER, B. G., and A. H. HAWLEY: Suburbanization and church participation. *Soc. Forces,* 1959, **37,** 338–345.

(314) ZWEIBELSON, I.: Test anxiety and intelligence test performance. *J. consult. Psychol.*, 1956, **20,** 479–481.

14

FAMILY RELATIONSHIPS

The dynamics of the American culture have brought about many changes in our patterns of family living and have fundamentally affected the status of women and the relationships between men and women, husbands and wives, and parents and children (177).

Of the many changes that have occurred, the following are the most important:

Families are smaller.

Ties with relatives are weaker. The family unit living under one roof usually consists of the immediate family group only, not of a larger kinship group.

Less work is done in the home.

More wives and mothers work outside the home.

Divorce and family separations are more common.

Child-training methods are more democratic.

More training is done in the school.

Recreation has shifted out of the home.

Social mobility and vocational mobility have increased.

The material milieu of the home has become more important (33, 308, 310).

Figure 8–1, page 333, shows the increase in the amount of time children spend outside the home as they grow older.

Changes in the pattern of family living are primarily the result of the cultural influence of the many different groups which make up our population. As Burgess has pointed out:

Never before in human history has any society been composed of so many divergent types of families. Families differ by sections of the country, by ethnic and religious groups, by economic and social classes, and by vocations. They are different according to the family life-cycle and by number and role of family members. They vary by the locus of authority within the family and by widely different styles of life (42).

Because of the many different cultural influences in America, variations in the pattern of family life are great. The family is a very closely knit unit among Jews, for example, and because of this, the family has a greater influence on the Jewish child than on children from many other religious groups (99, 150, 214).

Changes in the pattern of family living inevitably cause changes in the relationships of different family members. The rapid rate of change in America means that today's children have many experiences which their parents never had and which their parents are often unable or unwilling to understand. The widespread use of television in the home enables the child of today to know much more about many subjects than his parents could possibly have known at the same age. The child learns, from television, how other people live, and this often makes him critical of his parents and the pattern of life in his own home. Many children from homes where the parents' education has been limited become critical of the way their parents behave and feel ashamed of them (239, 247). Children whose parents are foreign-born or newly urbanized encounter more difficulties in this respect than children whose parents feel at home in their present environment (205, 218). Young parents, as a rule, understand their children better than older parents because the smaller the age gap between parent and child, the less change there will have been in cultural values and patterns of living (33, 101).

Child-training methods in America have undergone an almost revolutionary change; as a result, there has been much confusion about the proper way to bring up children. This is in direct contrast to most primitive and many civilized cultures today, in which there is a set pattern for family life and a prescribed, rigid program for child training. It is also in direct contrast to the *continuous* patterns of child training of cultures which prepare the child for his adult roles by starting with simple learning experiences and progressing to more complex learning experiences of a similar nature (24, 38).

Our training of the child is characterized by *discontinuities* in the sense that the training in childhood has little or no relationship to the pattern of life in adulthood. This adds to the difficulties the child encounters in his adjustments and increases tension in the family. The child brought up by continuous training has fewer conflicts; he gains a sense of security and experiences relatively little tension in family relationships. Continuities in training also give parents a greater sense of security in their parental role (24, 187).

That many American parents feel inadequate for their role is apparent in the frequency with which they seek advice from relatives, friends, or child-guidance experts (21, 264, 277). When parents feel inadequate, the tensions they build up are reflected in the parent-child relationship. Conflicts between parents about the best way to train the child increase family friction and intensify the feeling of inadequacy the mother has about her parental role (280). In a study of the concerns mothers had about their babies during the early months of babyhood, it was found that the mean number of worries reported was 4.1, with many mothers reporting a far higher number. Maternal worries are bound to be reflected in the relationship of the mother with her baby (229). Figure 14–1 shows the different sources of concern young mothers reported. Crying was the most common.

INFLUENCE OF FAMILY RELATIONSHIPS ON THE CHILD

In spite of radical changes in the American pattern of family life, the family is still the "most significant part of the child's 'social network'" (48). Bossard and Boll have emphasized what the home means to the child:

Home is the place the child comes back to, with his experiences. It is the lair to which he retreats to lick his wounds: the stage to which he returns to parade the glory of his achievements: the refuge he finds in which to brood over his ill treatment, real or fancied. Home, in other words, is the place to which one brings the everyday run of social experience, to sift, to evaluate, to appraise, to understand, or to be twisted, to

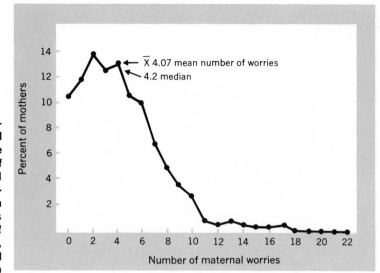

X̄ 4.07 mean number of worries
4.2 median

Number of maternal worries

Percent of mothers

Figure 14-1. Frequency of maternal worries during the early months of babyhood. (Adapted from W. O. Robertson, An investigation of maternal concerns by mail survey, *Child Developm.*, 1961, 32, 423–436. Used by permission.)

fester, to be magnified, or ignored, as the case may be (33).

For many years, psychoanalysts have stressed the importance of early family experiences on the child's behavior and attitudes. According to Freud, neuropathic parents who overprotect the child and smother him in affection awaken in him "a disposition for neurotic diseases" (91). Flügel points out that too severe or too careful parents make the child rebellious, not only toward his parents, but toward all adult authority (89). The emphasis on "momism" since the Second World War has stressed the psychological damage caused by maternal dominance and maternal overprotection (274).

More recently, studies of maternal deprivation—where the babies were separated from their mothers and institutionalized—have revealed how important a role early family relationships play in the child's development. While some of the detrimental effects of maternal deprivation may be counteracted if a satisfactory mother substitute is provided, there is evidence that this is often not adequate, principally because finding a satisfactory substitute is not always easy or even possible (36, 94, 226, 228). Figure 14–2 shows the effects of the loss of mother or father during early childhood as reflected in depressive states as the child reaches adulthood.

Because the home is the child's first environment, it sets the pattern for his attitudes toward people, things, and life in general. Furthermore, because the child identifies with the family members he loves, he imitates their patterns of behavior and learns to adjust to life as they adjust (152, 158). While the pattern established in the home will be changed and modified as the child grows older, it will never be completely eradicated (211).

Areas of Influence. A quick survey of the areas of the child's life on which family relationships leave their mark will show how widespread their influence is.

1. The Child's Personality. In a home where parents are overanxious and overconcerned about their children, where discipline is inconsistent, and where there is worry, anxiety, and lack of a sense of

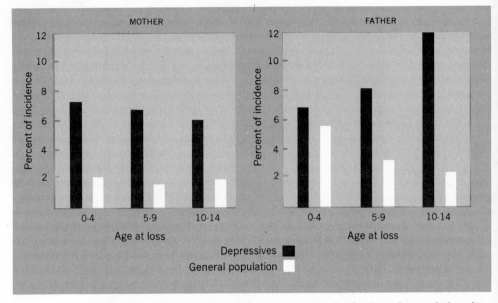

Figure 14-2. The long-term effects of loss by death of mother or father during the childhood years. (Adapted from J. Bowlby, Childhood mourning and its implications for psychiatry, *Amer. J. Psychiat.,* **1961, 118, 481–498. Used by permission.)**

humor, children are likely to be highly emotional and subject to frequent outbursts of temper (164, 175). Children who have nonorganic speech disorders often come from homes where there are disturbed family relationships which make the child emotionally insecure and maladjusted (182, 226).

Maladjusted children are usually the product of maladjusted parents. As Teagarden has pointed out, "All manner of behavior deviations can be, and often are, accounted for by the subtleties of home relationships" (281). Children whose mothers are poorly adjusted to marriage are likely to have more, and more serious, behavior problems than children whose mothers are better adjusted to their marital roles. Eating problems, nervous mannerisms, enuresis, and a host of similar problems are characteristically found in children whose family situations involve domestic discord (32, 161).

Children from broken homes or homes where parents are "emotionally divorced" develop personality patterns that interfere

with good adjustments to people outside the home (19, 64, 167). Prolonged and repeated absence of one or both parents from the home also adversely affects the child's adjustments. Children who have been deprived of a normal homelife by wars, natural disasters, industrial dislocation, and "social and psychosocial factors" are affected physically, intellectually, and emotionally (289). When parents ignore their children and devote little time to them as they grow older, their poor adjustments frequently lead to delinquency (50, 299). If family relationships are seriously disturbed, children are likely to become neurotic or delinquent. Even though children do not fully comprehend the meaning of their parents' behavior, they "sense" intuitively the psychological climate of the home—whether or not all is well and how their parents feel about them (29, 53, 158, 225, 245).

Favorable family relationships, by contrast, lead to a healthy self-concept and good personal and social adjustments. It has been found that children's motivations are similar to those of their parents, especially during the preschool years. Even after the peer-group influence begins to dominate the child, it does not overshadow the importance of family relationships to the child's developing personality (287).

2. Adjustments outside the Home. No one procedure, practice, technique, or way of doing things in the home makes for good or bad adjustment outside the home. Rather, the attitude toward the child—love and affection and being wanted, appreciated, trusted, and accepted as a person—determines how well he will adjust (129, 272).

When parental attitudes toward the child are unfavorable, as in the case of the dominant, the possessive, or the ignoring parent, the child's adjustments to school and to members of the peer group are likely to be poor. The child who is made dependent on his mother by her overprotectiveness either becomes aggressive or continues to be dependent on people outside the home, neither of which will lead to good social adjustments (11, 59). The child who does not experience affection in the home finds it difficult to establish affectional relationships with people outside; as a result, he appears to be cold and uninterested in people, a condition which will not foster good social relationships (35, 121).

The child learns through family relationships, especially relationships with the parents, to conform to group standards, mores, and traditions and to cooperate with others. He develops patterns of social behavior similar to those of his parents. How aggressive the child will be will depend largely upon the way he is treated in the home. Homes where the atmosphere is democratic and where there is a happy relationship with the members of the family foster the development of socially acceptable assertiveness, while those marked by discord, severe punishment, and autocratic rule promote socially unacceptable modes of aggression (90, 168, 183, 200). A definite relationship exists between the child's *status in the group* and his parents' opinions regarding child-training methods. In families where the mother dominates the home, boys tend to dislike girls, and girls tend to dislike boys. When fathers are strict disciplinarians, their sons tend to displace their aggressiveness, to develop problem behavior in school, and to achieve little popularity. If the father-son relationship is warm and friendly, boys make much better peer adjustments. How the child feels about adults in general is influenced by his relationships with his parents. The nearer the child is in age to a sibling, the less friendly he is to adults. This may be explained mainly in terms of the child's jealousy (133, 152).

3. School Success. The child's performance in school is adversely affected by poor relationships between him and his parents or other family members (133, 196). Overprotection makes the child overly dependent, and this interferes with his early school adjustments. Rejection at home makes the child feel insecure, and this likewise leads to poor adjustments to school work (189). Disturbances in the family relationships have an especially serious effect on school work which requires thinking (137, 293). Likewise, a low parental regard for education and for cultural pursuits has a retarding influence on the child's progress in school (85, 234, 256).

4. Success in Adult Life. The position of the child in the family and his relationship with the members of his family have a great deal to do with his success in later life (5). Marital happiness of parents influences not only their child's attitudes toward marriage but also his adjustment to marriage in adult years (169, 295). Because parents influence the child's attitudes toward different types of *vocations,* whether the individual will be a vocational success is determined largely by the attitudes toward work established in the home when he was a child (230, 288).

Variations in Family Influence. Not all members of the family exert the same influence on the child; how much influence a family member will have will depend largely upon the emotional relationship which exists between him and the child. Because the *mother* spends more time with the child than the father, and because she shows her affection for the child more openly, she exerts a greater influence than the father (214). In a study of child-behavior problems related to parental attitudes toward the child, it was found that conduct problems more often resulted when the children had maladjusted mothers, while personality problems generally resulted from unwholesome attitudes on the part of fathers (209).

Even though the *father's* influence is less than the mother's, it cannot be ignored. An autocratic father can cause maladjustive development in the child as readily as a permissive father whose discipline is ineffectual (208). In *sibling* relationships, a child is influenced more by an older sibling of his own sex than by one of the opposite sex because he tends to identify with a member of his own sex (152). When grandparents or other relatives live in the home, their influence on the child is far greater than when they see him only occasionally. The influence they exert will also be determined by the closeness of the emotional relationship between them and the child (33, 101).

How the child will react to different influences in the home and how his relationships with the various members of the family will develop will depend to a large extent upon what *type of individual* he is. The quiet child will react differently from the aggressive child, just as the introvert will react differently from the extrovert. Furthermore, the influence of family relationships varies according to the child's age; the younger the child, the more influence the family has. Unfavorable family relationships in the early years may be offset by favorable relationships with peers or adults outside the home as the child grows older.

On the other hand, favorable family relationships during early childhood may not be strong enough to offset later unfavorable relationships outside the home. Thus the events of late childhood and adolescence have a great influence on the character structure tentatively formed during the child's early years (206).

CHANGES IN FAMILY RELATIONSHIPS

Relationships with people rarely remain static; as people change, their relationships with one another also change. Family relationships tend to change for the worse. This deterioration generally begins during the latter part of the first year of life and is readily apparent early in the second year. It is shown by a decrease in parental warmth toward the child and an increase in restrictiveness and punitiveness (14, 33, 242).

While relationships among family members may improve somewhat when the child first goes to school—whether it is nursery school, kindergarten, or the first grade—they usually do not. Adjusting to school is always accompanied by emotional tension of greater or lesser severity, which is expressed in an increase in the number of behavior problems or in the intensity and frequency of those that already exist.

If the child makes satisfactory adjustments to school, home problems normally subside, only to flare up again later and lead to further deterioration in family relationships. As the child spends more and more time with people outside the home, new interests and values give rise to increasing friction with family members. In the closing years of childhood, family relationships steadily decline, and friction becomes the dominant aspect of the relationship pattern. The child whose adjustments to the academic and social aspects of school are poor or below his expectations will experience more family friction than the child who makes better adjustments (33, 53, 74, 152).

CAUSES OF DETERIORATION

Deterioration in family relationships is caused by conditions which, to some extent, are controllable. As people change, there must be an adjustment in their relationships, or deterioration will set in. Because children change more than parents, most of the adjustment must be made by parents. When growth and development are most rapid, adjustments to the child and his changed needs are especially important if harmonious relationships are to exist.

Deterioration may occur in *any* family relationship, not only that between parent and child. A survey of the different types of relationships within the family will illustrate that deterioration in each has its own cause or causes.

Changes in Parent-Child Relationships. In no area of a child's development is change more pronounced than in his decreasing dependence on others and his increasing *need for independence* and opportunity for achievement. Many parents fail to recognize how rapidly the child outgrows his infantile dependency. Even if they do recognize it, some mothers, for selfish reasons, refuse to adjust to it and thus thwart the child's natural strivings. Whenever a strong need is thwarted—and need for independence is one of the strongest needs of childhood—it will lead to friction (53, 59, 184). And because the times when the desire for independence is strongest are during periods of rapid growth and development in babyhood and again at the end of childhood, these will be the most stressful times in the family. In commenting on the failure of many parents to recognize and adjust to the changed needs of their children, Bowerman and Kinch have pointed out:

There would appear to be something like a law of perseveration in human relations, according to which we tend to react to another person in the same manner until there is some force operating, such as a status change imposed on the relationship which modifies our perception of the other and the way in which we shall react to them. We would expect, for this reason, that parents tend to hold the same demands and expectations of their children until a change in external circumstances forces them to look at

their children from a new perspective. These changes are increase in growth and puberty changes and starting high school or junior high school (34).

Deterioration in parent-child relationships also comes when children fail to adjust to changed *needs in their parents*. As long as children are small and helpless, parents derive satisfaction from doing things for them and from the reward they receive in the form of childish love and dependency. When children no longer need to depend so much on their parents and are no longer as demonstrative in their affection, consideration, and respect, they often treat their parents in such a way that the parents feel rejected. Even when children are less critical and rebellious than is typical in the American culture of today, their changed behavior cannot fail to contribute to a deterioration in parent-child relationships (33, 97, 204).

Changes in the Family Pattern. Whenever there is a change in the accustomed pattern of family life, adjustments must be made by *all* family members. Otherwise, the homeostasis of the family will be upset, and trouble will ensue. The arrival of a new baby in the home usually upsets every member of the family. Similarly, the arrival of an elderly relative as a permanent member of the household is always upsetting (3, 92, 152).

When the pattern of family life is upset by upward or downward social mobility or by the mother going to work outside the home, the children who are only indirectly involved in these changes often develop strong feelings of insecurity and anxiety. These feelings contribute to an unhealthy emotional climate in the home and to a deterioration of all family relationships.

High value placed on socialization and peer acceptance has encouraged children to learn to accept the interests and values of their peers and to spend more and more time outside the home as they grow older. Furthermore, the trend toward suburban living has meant that the father spends more time commuting to and from work and less time at home. In addition, mechanization of the home has made it less necessary for the mother to call on children for help in household chores. All this adds to the tendency for the family unit to disintegrate, with each family member going his own way and developing his own individual interests and values (34, 262).

Each year, children grow further and further away from the family and closer and closer to people outside the home. Consequently, their contacts with family members are fewer and less influential and less meaningful than their contacts with people unrelated to the family unit (214, 245).

Changes in Sibling Relationships. Deterioration in family relationships often spreads to sibling relationships. The older sister who regarded her younger sibling as an "adorable doll" when he was a baby later comes to consider him a "brat" when she is expected to be his unpaid baby-sitter. Similarly, the younger sibling who formerly regarded an older sibling as an idol finds that the idol loses its glamour when he treats him as a nuisance and refuses to play with him (141, 152).

Changes in Relationships with Relatives. As children grow older, their relationships with their relatives, especially their grandparents, usually change. The doting grandmother who "spoiled" the child when he was a baby may turn into a strict disciplinarian, and the grandfather, who beamed with pride at the sight of his new grandson, may now terrify the young child by his scowls, his threats of a spanking, or his tales about what happens to naughty children after they die (3, 92, 284). The relationship of the child with his grandparents will be discussed in more detail later in the chapter.

Effects of Changes in Family Relationships. Changes in family relationships sometimes result in more harmony. Unfortunately, this is the exception rather than the rule. Once poor relationships are established, they tend to persist and grow worse, partly because people develop the *habit of reacting to one*

another in a particular way and partly because there is less and less communication between them and thus less understanding (178, 245).

Studies of mothers' treatment of their babies have revealed that the way they treat them during infancy is significantly related to the way they treat them as they grow older. Changes occur in *quantity* rather than in *quality* of treatment; indulgent parents tend to become more indulgent, and rejective parents more rejective. Consequently, small frictions in early childhood are likely to become major disruptions in late childhood (238).

Family relationships reach their low point, and communication is likely to become almost nonexistent, during puberty. The pubescent child who feels that his parents do not understand him does not give them an opportunity to do so; he keeps his thoughts, feelings, and emotions to himself (33, 69). Without communication, understanding is impossible. The parent whose only explanation for a rule is that "mother knows best" has a poorer relationship with her child than the one who believes that a child is entitled to know the reason for a rule (49).

If a child misinterprets his parents' behavior to mean that they reject him or love him less, he will become anxious, insecure, and rebellious. The parents, in turn, not understanding what is behind the child's behavior, feel unappreciated and rejected. In time, they will reject him because of the mutual hostility that is generated. This vicious cycle may begin at any time, but it is most likely to begin early in childhood, when the child finds it difficult to understand the behavior of others unless the reasons for their behavior are spelled out for him in words he can comprehend. Once it begins, it is likely to gain momentum (108). The "vicious cycle" of parent-child relationships is shown in Figure 14–3.

If one of the people involved in a poor relationship can change his attitude, the relationship may readily improve. This is most likely to occur if there is a period of separation to enable all involved to get a better perspective on the problem. Few children are away from home and parents long enough to gain the therapeutic effect of separation, however; even summer camping is not usually enough to allow parents to change the pattern of their behavior toward the child (106, 140, 238).

RESPONSIBILITY FOR DETERIORATION IN FAMILY RELATIONSHIPS

According to traditional belief, it "takes two to make a quarrel"; so does it take two to bring about a deterioration in an affectional relationship. Furthermore, in a quarrel, one person plays the aggressive role, while the other plays the defensive; it is thus the aggressor who starts the quarrel and the defendant who keeps it alive. Similarly, in family relationships, one person is more to blame than the other because one plays a more aggressive role. All evidence seems to point to the parents as the aggressors—the ones who are primarily responsible for the deterioration. Parents are the prime instigators even when the poor relationship is between siblings or between children and elderly relatives.

If parents showed no favoritism; if they did not expect older children to assume responsibility for younger siblings without sufficient compensation or reward for their personal sacrifices; if they did not make comparisons between siblings as a method of motivating each to greater effort; and if they did not grant privileges to younger siblings which they did not grant to older siblings, hostilities and rivalries would be kept to a minimum, and sibling relationships would then be more harmonious. Similarly, if parents showed a greater respect for elderly relatives, children would follow their example and have a better relationship with them.

If the child is constantly criticized by parents, he naturally believes that criticism is a permissible form of social relationship. When parents are dissatisfied with themselves and with the parental role, they are likely to be critical of the child and everything he does. By contrast, parents who

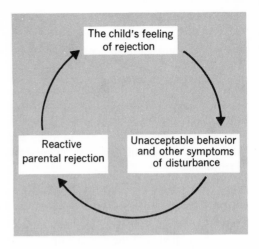

Figure 14-3. The "vicious cycle" of parent-child relationships. (Adapted from D. Hallowitz, and B. Stulberg, The vicious cycle of parent-child relationship breakdown, *Soc. Casewk*, 1959, 40, 268–275. Used by permission.)

accept themselves are more acceptant of their children; they have little motivation to find fault with them or to try to change them.

As was stressed in the chapter on social development, the child must learn how to make social adjustments that will lead to social acceptance. As was further stressed, guidance should play an important role in this learning. The same is true of family relationships. The young and inexperienced child does not know how to establish satisfactory relationships with others. He must be taught, or he must have a good model to identify with and imitate. If parents show him how to get along well with others and if they set a good model of interfamily relationships, the child will make good adjustments too.

FACTORS INFLUENCING FAMILY RELATIONSHIPS

In recent years, numerous studies have been aimed at evaluating the various home factors that influence the child's attitudes and behavior. Results have shown that the influence of home situations and family relationships is far greater than was originally believed. While no attempt will be made here to discuss the factors in the order of their importance, as complete a survey as possible will be made. It will become apparent that the deterioration of family relationships is not due to one factor alone but to many and that most, if not all, of these factors are controllable.

PARENTAL ATTITUDES

Parental attitudes influence the way parents treat their child, and their treatment of him, in turn, influences his attitude toward them. Fundamentally, therefore, the parent-child relationship is dependent upon the parents' attitudes. And as was stressed earlier (pages 66 to 70), many parental attitudes are formed before the child is born. Many are *romanticized;* they are based on what parents would *like* their children to be.

Parental attitudes are influenced partly by *cultural values,* partly by the *personality patterns* of the parents, and partly by their *concepts* of the *role of parents.*

Cultural Values.   Around the turn of the century, Freud contended that too much "parental tenderness" accelerates sexual maturity, "spoils" the child, and makes him unable to be satisfied with a smaller amount of love in later life (91). This theory was echoed by many American psychologists. The one who sounded the loudest warnings was J. B. Watson, who, during the twenties, advised parents to beware of too much mother love because of the harmful effects it has on the personality development of the child as he grows older (298).

Now the pendulum has swung to the opposite extreme. It is agreed that mother love and affection are needed for good mental health. Too much, rather than too little, affection should be shown the child, especially during early childhood. One of the strongest exponents of the importance of love in the child's life is Ribble. According to her:

Poor relationship with the parents leads to reactions in the infant which tend to become the basis of adult personality disorders. The most important asset of the baby as he begins life is two emotionally healthy parents. His deepest need by far is the understanding care of one consistent individual, his mother. Perhaps in time we shall recognize the danger of the emotionally unhealthy personality and shall see that emotional disturbance in the parents is as dangerous as is tuberculosis or syphilis (228).

This emphasis on the importance of "mothering," on understanding the child and his needs, means that children today receive more affection from their parents than was formerly believed good for them. When this attitude is carried to extremes and is prolonged into adolescence, it is likely to result in a socially and emotionally immature individual who is unfitted to make adjustments to the demands of adult life (274).

Personality of Parents.   Even when a general cultural attitude toward children exists, the attitude of parents toward their children is markedly influenced by their own personality patterns. Attitudes vary from adult to adult and from time to time in the same adult. This inconsistency, or "ambivalence," does not necessarily depend upon the child's behavior, but upon the momentary mood of the parent, his memories of the way he was treated as a child, changes in the pattern of family living brought about by the child, and the value placed upon parenthood by the cultural group (175, 242, 292).

The parents' attitude toward the child may be a reflection of their own *adjustment* to life and to marriage. Family happiness and unity are markedly affected by such factors as husband-wife relationships, in-law interference, money problems, and the health and personality characteristics of the parents. The attitude of the parents toward one another has more impact on preschoolers than on older children (82, 161, 210).

Concept of Parental Role.   The attitude of the mother toward motherhood plays an important role in her relationships with her child. When a woman does not want to have a child and tries unsuccessfully to force an abortion, she develops feelings of guilt and resentment toward the child. When a woman is unhappy about her pregnancy, she is likely to experience more emotional tension and nausea than is normal. This tension reaction often persists for many months after the infant is born (44, 55, 202, 313).

Very often there is a resentment toward the second child, especially if the interval between the arrival of the first and second is short. Most mothers feel guilty about their unfavorable attitudes toward their babies and attempt to compensate by being over-indulgent. Frequently, however, the joys of parenthood are enough to bring about a change in maternal attitudes.

Parental attitudes are more favorable when the child is *wanted*. Most adults have a preference for a family of a given size, but they may increase the size of the family in the hope of having a child of a preferred sex. The child thus added may turn out to be unwanted if it is not of the desired sex. The child most likely to be unwanted is the child of an unwed mother (47, 83, 291).

The *age of the parents* is influential in determining their attitudes toward the child. Young parents are likely to take their parental responsibilities lightly, while overage parents are apt to be more nervous and less energetic and thus overprotective and demanding. Should one parent be overage, there may be a clash in interests and values between the parents regarding the child's behavior. The *educational level* of parents is more important than age. Parents of higher educational levels give their children more freedom than those of lower educational levels (21, 235).

The age and educational level of parents also affect their *feeling of adequacy* for the parental role. Parents who are older and better educated generally feel more adequate; this is reflected in a more relaxed, acceptant attitude toward the child. Some parents feel adequate to meet the needs of a child of a given age only. These "age-specific" parents have an inflexibility which prevents them from growing along with their children (229, 242, 292). A mother who "loves" little babies, for example, may have a good relationship with her child during his first years of life, but unless she develops some flexibility, she will be unable to meet his needs as he grows older. The child senses the parent's feeling of inadequacy and reacts unfavorably to it (22).

Typical Parental Attitudes.   Certain fairly universal parental attitudes in the American culture are the products of tradition, of parental teachings, and of experiences in living with children. While parental attitudes are more liberal today than in the past, marked differences are found in different social groups (4, 22, 242).

Overprotectiveness.   Parental overprotection consists in *excessive physical contact* of the parent and child, *prolongation of infantile care, prevention of the development of self-reliance,* and *lack or excess of parental control.*

Overprotective parents allow no competing interest to interfere with their parental duties; they reduce their other interests to a minimum. Overprotection is more common among the more favored socioeconomic groups (43, 57, 165).

The most common causes of overprotection are a *long period of anticipation and frustration* during which the woman's desire for a child is thwarted by sterility, miscarriages, or the death of infants; *conditions in the child,* such as physical handicaps and illnesses that frighten the parents; *sexual incompatibility* between husband and wife which causes the mother to transfer her love to the child; *social isolation; emotional impoverishment* in early life and an unhappy childhood; *development of dominating characteristics* resulting from undue responsibility in childhood and continuance of this role in marriage; and *thwarted ambitions.* Sometimes mothers overprotect their children to compensate for guilt stemming from a hostile or rejecting attitude toward them (11, 59, 184).

One of the most serious effects of overprotectiveness is that it fosters *overdependency* in the child. The child *is* dependent, and his needs must be met, but *how* the parents handle his dependency will determine whether or not he will become overdependent (4, 260). Inconsistent handling will encourage dependence, whereas consistent handling and recognition of changing needs and abilities will foster independence (11, 233, 261).

When a child is overdependent, he wants excessive help, attention, approval, and physical contact and proximity with others. By contrast, the child who is independent initiates his own activities, completes the activities he starts, performs routine tasks, gains satisfaction from work, and strives to overcome obstacles. The child who is successful in his adjustments develops independence because he has friends and sources of satisfaction outside the home; he does not have to rely on his parents for love and security to the same extent as the child who lacks these outside sources of satisfaction (23, 34, 146).

Nervous tendencies, such as excitability, restlessness, and lack of concentration, are common among overprotected children. Such children often are obese and have an immature look. Their characteristic *personality pattern* is manifested by a low level of ego strength, of aspiration, and of frustration tolerance. They show many withdrawing reactions, lack emotional control, and openly refuse responsibility. They seem to be afraid to grow up; they have no confidence in their abilities; they are easily influenced by, and dependent upon, the group; and they are excessively sensitive to criticism (59, 260).

In *school,* the overprotected child often has difficulties. He will want extra attention from the teacher, and his work will be unsystematic and careless. When he gets along poorly in school, his parents become more attentive; in turn, the child does even worse work. In his *social* adjustments, the over-

protected child may be a troublemaker. He is socially immature in behavior, he has no sense of responsibility, he bids for attention, he is selfish and spoiled, and he is often quarrelsome (168, 233).

Permissiveness. Permissiveness is the opposite of overprotectiveness; the permissive parent is "giving" instead of "taking." He gives time, thought, and effort instead of material things; he accepts the child's early ideas and ambitions instead of foisting his own upon him; he encourages the child to play with other children; he makes the child feel accepted and strong; and he shows a tolerance for, and understanding of, the child's weaknesses. Permissiveness may go too far and result in indulgence. Even when casually indulgent, the parent is tolerant but rather haphazard in his treatment of the child (122, 278).

Permissiveness affects parents as well as children. Permissive parents report that their lives are disrupted by their children's noisiness, that their privacy is often ignored, and that their attempts to limit or control their children's activities are resisted. In addition, furniture receives more than normal wear and tear, and the house is usually cluttered. Permissive parents often have to expend more energy and money on their children than they would like. Parents who tend to hold traditional views about the role of the child should not try to be permissive because it will lead to too much friction with the child and too many parental frustrations. If permissiveness is not carried to the extreme of indulgence, however, it will lead to better parent-child relationships and a healthy family life (11, 13, 30).

Children from homes which encourage reasonable freedom have been found to be resourceful, cooperative, self-reliant, and well adjusted in social situations. They show perseverance and can assume responsibilities. When the mother is more permissive than the father, children show more favorable behavior than when the father is more permissive.

If parents are indulgent, the child has

difficulty making social adjustments. He is selfish, demanding, and tyrannical and expects constant attention, affection, and service. He responds to denials of his wishes or to discipline with impatience, outbursts of temper, or assaults. He will use every device, whether coaxing, bullying, or wheedling, to get his own way; when alone, he will be restless and unhappy (33, 175).

Rejection.   Parental rejection need not necessarily mean overt rejection; it may be characterized either by nonchalance, inertness, and a general atmosphere of unconcern for the child's welfare or by active dominance and conspicuous hostility. Frequently, in rejection, the impression is created that the parent is overprotective. The parent's attitude is covered with a "coating of ostensible affection and pleasant relations" (278).

Many rejecting mothers have an unsatisfactory sexual life or are dissatisfied with their marriages because of the responsibilities or the clash of personalities entailed. Rejecting fathers, on the other hand, have been found to come from homes where they were somewhat spoiled by dominating mothers. Their parents were poorly mated and quarreled frequently, and the discipline of the children was harsh and inconsistent (158, 215).

Parental rejection jeopardizes normal security feelings, undermines the child's self-esteem, and induces feelings of helplessness and frustration, which can permanently disable the child in his adjustment to life. Among young children who feel rejected, enuresis, feeding difficulties, nail biting, and other nervous mannerisms are common. As children grow older, antisocial behavior— aggression; cruelty; lying; stealing; swearing; seeking attention, praise, and unnecessary help; and showing off—is common (24, 175).

In spite of its bad features, parental rejection has some constructive value. Rejected children are likely to develop independence and to become capable of amusing themselves and of developing special inter-ests. They are alert, shrewd, cunning, realistic, and in a hurry to grow up and leave school. Socially, they are early maturers (40, 187).

Acceptance.   Parental acceptance is characterized by a keen interest in, and love for, the child. The accepting parent not only wanted the child—and in many cases planned for him—but also did not find child care a trying or difficult job. The accepting parent puts the child in a position of importance in the home and develops a warm emotional relationship with him (255, 292).

There are different types of parental acceptance, depending upon the emotional maturity of the parents. Emotionally mature parents aim at the development of an independent individual and do all they can to achieve this goal. Emotionally immature parents are neurotically attached to their child and try to mold him to suit their own standards. When acceptance is accompanied by indulgence, parents tend to identify themselves so completely with the child that they try to live their own lives over in his. Acceptance accompanied by a democratic attitude, by contrast, leads to the participation of the child in family discussions and the independence of the child as a person (8, 20).

The accepted child is generally socialized, cooperative, friendly, loyal, emotionally stable, and cheerful. He accepts responsibilities and cares for his own property as well as for that of others. As a rule, he is honest, straightforward, and dependable; he faces life confidently and has a clear idea about his plans and ambitions for the future. He can see himself realistically and can appraise his strengths and weaknesses objectively. As Symonds has pointed out, "good citizens, good scholars, good workers, good husbands and wives, and good parents come from homes in which the children are wanted and accepted" (278).

Domination.   In every home, one parent is likely to dominate the whole family. A dominating parent usually comes from a family in which one or both parents were dominating. As a child, this parent was forced into submissiveness. As a parent, he dominates his own children in much the same way as he himself was dominated.

The child who is dominated by one or both parents shows better-socialized behavior than the child who is given more freedom. He is honest, polite, and careful, but he is also likely to be shy, docile, self-conscious, submissive, and sensitive. He feels inadequate, inferior, confused, bewildered, and inhibited. He is easily led and dominated by his family but not by his peers. As he grows older, he is likely to feel cheated, to be afraid that others will cheat him, and to develop a "sucker complex" (242, 292).

Submission to Child.   Just the opposite of the dominating parents are the submissive parents, who permit their children to dominate the home. If possible, the child's every wish is gratified, even against the parents' better judgment. The child literally bosses his parents and treats them with little or no respect. In its active form, parental submission consists in willfully catering to a child's whims and wishes. In general, parents who submit to their children have inadequate personalities characterized by childishness and failure to accept responsibility. They themselves were children of submissive parents and imitate in their own behavior the pattern set for them by their parents (33).

When parents permit themselves to be dominated by the child, the child often becomes disobedient and irresponsible. He defies authority and is unmanageable, aggressive, stubborn, antagonistic, and careless. At the same time, he is independent and self-confident. Frequently he has an exaggerated opinion of himself and is uninhibited in his boasting. When a mother is oversubmissive, there is a tendency for the child to be infantile in his behavior and to have a rebellious, defiant, tyrannizing attitude toward her (242, 278).

Favoritism.   Parents react differently to different children, and they show it by their attitudes and actions. In spite of the typical parent's claim that he "loves all his children equally," his actions are not so convincing to his children. The child who perceives that he is the favorite learns that he can do and say things that the less favored siblings would probably be punished for (22). The child who is not the favorite likewise perceives his status and resents the privileges given to the favorite. Parental favoritism often increases as children grow older. The favored child shows a greater desire to please the parent, while his siblings become more hostile and rebellious (49, 233, 238).

Certain children are more likely to be parental favorites than others. The *sex* of the child influences the pattern of parental behavior from the moment of the child's birth. The father differentiates his behavior toward daughters and sons from their earliest childhood (49, 72, 242). He "plays up to his roughhousing little boy and pays mild courtship to his little girl, selecting gentler games" (187). Figure 14–4 shows the correlation between the socioeconomic status of mothers and the treatment they give their sons and daughters. While mothers of the higher socioeconomic groups are, on the whole, more warm and accepting than mothers of the lower socioeconomic groups, all mothers give preferential treatment to boys (20).

Boys, however, claim that their mothers side with their siblings more than girls do. The boys' attitude may be just a bid for greater attention and sympathy; it may also stem from the fact that boys are more aggressive than girls and voice their resentments at supposed favoritism more openly. *First-born* children, more often than later-born children, claim that their parents show favoritism toward a sibling. This is closely related to the tendency for first-born children to experience jealousy more often than later-born children (152, 313). (See pages 288 to 292 for a more complete discussion of jealousy.)

A child who is bright, who does good work in school, who is popular, and who is ambitious for future achievement is likely to become a parental favorite; the more *suc-*

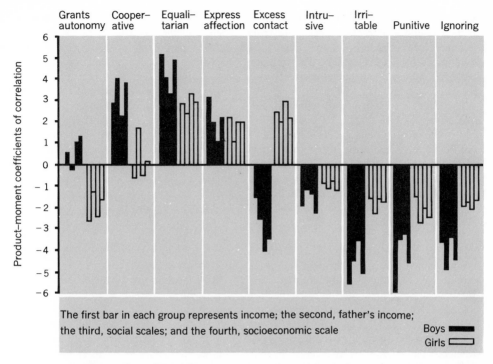

Figure 14-4.   The effect of the socioeconomic status of the mother on her treatment of her sons and daughters. (Adapted from N. Bayley and E. S. Schaefer, Relationships between socioeconomic variables and the behavior of mothers toward young children, *J. genet. Psychol.*, 1960, 96, 61–77. Used by permission.)

cessful the child, the more willing the parent is to make sacrifices for him, even if this entails slighting some of the other siblings. A very bright child, especially a son, is far more likely to be given a long and expensive education than a less bright son or an equally bright daughter (4, 232).

At the opposite extreme, children who are *handicapped*, either physically or mentally, usually receive more than their share of parental attention and affection, and their siblings conclude that they are the "pets." In a study of twins where one was normal and the other handicapped by cerebral palsy, it was found that the nonpalsied child felt he was unfairly treated because of the excessive attention his parents gave to his twin (251).

Parental Ambitions.   From the moment of a child's birth, and often earlier, parents are ambitious for their child. Often, without taking into consideration the child's abilities or interests, overambitious parents strive to have the child satisfy thwarted ambitions in their own lives. Almost all parents measure their child's achievements against some ideal (232).

Parental ambitions include educational, athletic, social, or financial success. The father is especially disturbed if his children lack initiative and responsibility; are disobedient, insufficiently aggressive, or excitable; do poor work in school or are inadequate in athletics; or display "childish behavior." The greatest concern centers around the sons, especially the first-born son, for whom ambitions are higher than for those born later (1, 137).

Mothers who have given up successful careers have a tendency to demand conformity and high standards of performance in their children. Parents expect more from "planned-for" children than from the "unplanned-for" (255, 292). The relation between ambition and social mobility was discussed on pages 421 to 426.

The child is well aware of what his parents expect of him. When he does not live up to their expectations, he feels inadequate and becomes quarrelsome, disobedient, irresponsible, and resentful. As a result of such attitudes, he frequently does poor work in school or engages in fantasy and daydreaming. As Rand et al. have pointed out, "Trouble arises when the parental wish becomes selfish. When the major wish is gratification of the parental ego or a desire to live again one's own life through the child, parents rob the child of individuality and force the development of interests that are not native or dwarf capacities that should be dominant" (223). The child who is "exploited" in order to fulfill parental ambitions often complains, whines, and feels cheated. He is precocious in dress and speech and has a compulsion to compete and a desire to excel. He is a "poor sport"; to avoid making a mistake, he avoids situations in which he is not certain of success. While pressures to live up to parental expectations may affect children differently as far as their achievements are concerned, few children have favorable attitudes toward parents who put strong pressure on them (164, 233).

Importance of Parental Attitudes. Parental attitudes play a role of major importance in determining the attitudes and behavior of the child. Children who become successful as they grow older almost always come from homes where parental attitudes toward them were favorable and where a wholesome relationship existed between parent and child. Such a relationship will produce a happy, friendly child who is relatively free from anxieties and who is a constructive, interdependent member of the group (53).

A good parent-child relationship is an affectional relationship. Such a relationship is indicated by the degree to which the child shows a feeling of trust and security in his parents by sharing confidences with them and by going to them for advice and help on perplexing problems; by the degree to which the child has an opportunity for self-expression and for recognition of his work and play activities; and by the degree to which the family possesses solidarity or mutual loyalty (11, 111, 172).

Unsuccessful children, by contrast, are usually the product of unfavorable parent-child relationships. The child who is deprived of attention and affection from his parents is hungry for affection; he wants to be everywhere and is afraid of missing out. Furthermore, he is *overwilling* to please and to do things for others. All this is a form of compensation and an attempt to buy affection at any cost (94).

As the child grows older, poor relationships with his parents are often expressed in parent-child conflicts. The most damaging effects come from a poor relationship with the mother because the child is with his mother more than with his father, and, as a result, her influence is greater (139, 158, 169).

Figure 14–5 shows some of the ways in which parental attitudes influence the child's personality. Parents who are perceived as inhibiting and demanding, for example, produce impulsive children. Warm, supportive, affective parents produce buoyant, spontaneous, gregarious children; and cold, indifferent parents produce gloomy, guilty, seclusive, socially withdrawn children. Most important of all is the degree of parental tolerance toward the child and his behavior. The more tolerant the parent, the greater the child's ego strength (254).

If parental attitudes changed for the better as children grew older, their effect on family relationships would be less serious. As has been stressed before, however, parental attitudes tend to be persistent and to change quantitatively rather than qualitatively.

CHILD-TRAINING METHODS

When both parents were brought up in homes that were similar in control, they are likely to reproduce in their own family the

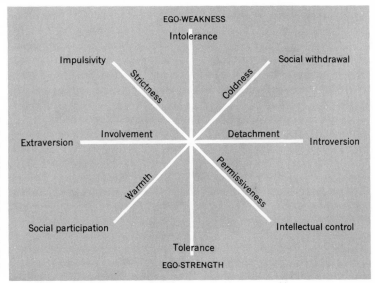

Figure 14-5. Relationship between perceived parental behavior and the child's personality. (Adapted from P. E. Slater, Parental behavior and the personality of the child, *J. genet. Psychol.*, 1962, 101, 53–68. Used by permission.)

methods used by their parents. If they were brought up by different methods, there is likely to be conflict about what method to use and a certain amount of modification of methods (21).

Because there have been marked shifts in attitudes regarding child rearing in recent years, there is likely to be conflict between parents and grandparents, which may create conflicts for the child. When grandmothers live in the home, the mother is likely to be stricter and the grandmother more permissive than when they live in separate homes (259).

Preparental education in child training leads to greater permissiveness, except in areas relating to discipline, sleep, toileting, and feeding. These are the areas where child care directly interferes with the adults' own work, pleasure, or rest (140, 305).

Variations in Methods. Variations in child-training methods are found within different *social groups*. Parents from *rural* districts are, on the whole, more authoritarian in their methods than *urban* parents. *Mothers* are usually less strict than fathers, and *younger* parents more democratic than older. *Foreign-born* parents are more authoritarian than native-born parents (224, 227).

Social-class differences in child training are marked. Middle-class parents are more exacting in their expectations; they begin training earlier, supervise their children's activities more closely, and put greater emphasis on individual achievement than parents from the lower classes (151, 168). Differences in child-training methods used by mothers of different social classes are illustrated in Figure 14–6.

The more *conservative* the parent, the more intolerant and rigid he is likely to be in his child-training methods. Fathers, on the whole, tend to be more inflexible than mothers, mainly because they have less understanding of the child and his needs (20, 22). In addition, men are more critical of the way their wives train the children than women are of their husbands. This not only leads to friction between the parents but causes the mother to feel inadequate in her parental role (280).

The *working mother* carries into the home the habits of efficiency and the expectations characteristic of the business world. A comparison of professional and nonprofessional women as mothers revealed that the professional women put more emphasis on discipline and the development of independence in their children, while the nonprofessional

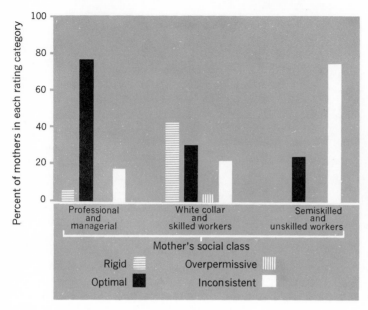

Figure 14-6. Relationship between mother's social-class membership and her predominant type of child care. (Adapted from E. H. Klatskin, E. B. Jackson, and L. C. Wilkin, The Influence of degree of flexibility in maternal child care practices on early child behavior, *Amer. J. Orthopsychiat.,* 1956, 26, 79–93. Used by permission.)

women emphasized the protective, empathic, and understanding functions of the maternal role. Professional women have more and stricter rules, they expect more from their children, and they require their children to assume more responsibilities in the home. They justify their method of child training on the grounds that it is good preparation for adult life. Nonprofessional women believe that childhood should be a time when the child enjoys himself and has little responsibility (292).

Children's Reactions to Child-training Methods. Children react far more favorably to training methods which they consider just and reasonable than to those they regard as unfair and unreasonable (see pages 575 to 578). The parent-child relationship is thus greatly influenced by the way children perceive the training they receive and the interpretation they place on the parents' motivation for punishment. If the child feels that he is unduly restricted in comparison with his agemates, he will displace his anger by aggressive attacks on siblings, thus incurring further punishment and developing more resentment toward his parents. The more authoritarian the child

training, the more resentful the child and the more likely he is to be defiant and willfully disobedient. Defiant behavior contributes heavily to the deterioration of parent-child relationships that characteristically occurs as the child grows older (57, 118, 172, 176).

Children who have learned to associate morality with religion and who think of God as a punishing agent develop strong feelings of guilt in connection with their resentment of parents who, as they perceive it, have usurped God's prerogative to punish them. If children feel that their parents do not agree on the proper method of training or disciplining them, they begin to lose respect for their parents. If, in addition, the mother is blamed by the father for not bringing up the children properly, children have less respect for the mother than for the father (48, 132, 280).

Because girls conform to parental expectations more than boys, girls' relationships with parents tend to be better. Girls may resent their parents' domination, however, and even though they do not verbalize their resentment it affects their relationships with their parents. In spite of the fact that sibling relationships are often strained, siblings generally rally to the defense of a sibling who they feel has been unfairly treated, and they put up a united front of defiance against the offending parent. This, too, threatens good parent-child relationships (66, 285).

FAMILY SIZE

The family is a complex of interactional systems made up of the different members of the family. The larger the family, the larger the number of interactional systems. To determine how many interactional systems there will be in a given family, the following formula has been suggested:

$$2^n - n - 1$$

Each interactional system has its own unique emotional quality which affects the personality and behavior of all the members of the family (124).

In discussing the influence of family size on family relationships, Bossard and Boll have pointed out that "with the addition of each person to a family or primary group, the number of persons increases in the simplest arithmetical progression in whole numbers, and the number of interpersonal relationships within the group increases in the order of triangular numbers" (33). A specific example will help to show how much more complex the interactional system becomes with the arrival of each new baby. At first, there are three family members—mother, father, and child; this means five interactions. With the arrival of a new sibling, there will be 11 interactions. Then, if another comes, the number of interactional systems will increase to 26. Should the grandmother come to live with the family, the number would jump to 57.

Furthermore, each family group is composed of individuals of different ages and of both sexes. The masculine sex may predominate, the two sexes may be equally represented, or the family may be dominantly feminine. These variations influence the behavior of each member.

Each family member has his own interests, needs, and aspirations; therefore, each makes different demands on every other family member. This often causes friction and results in an unhealthy emotional climate in the home. When the mother's demands on the child are different from those made by the father or when mother and father use conflicting disciplinary techniques, the child is at a loss to know which parent he should obey or give his allegiance to. If he obeys one parent, there will be friction with the other and friction between his parents. The larger the family, the greater the personality interaction and the greater the chances for friction (48).

In many families, relatives, roomers, or servants become a part of the enlarged family group. These outsiders, like the members of the immediate family, influence the behavior of each individual within the group. Even a deceased member of the family can have an influence. The role each individual plays and the influence he has are not determined by closeness of kinship but by the needs of the child and the satisfaction he derives from each. A parent, for example, may not play as important a role in the child's life as a grandparent, an older sibling, or a servant (33, 124). Figure 14–7 shows the pattern of an "elongated family" —in this case, members of four generations, with representatives from both sides—and illustrates the many possible sources of friction.

All evidence points to the fact that the "nuclear family"—parents and children only —plays a more important role in the child's development than the elongated family. Three characteristic nuclear families—the one-child family, the small family, and the large family—will serve to illustrate how various family patterns influence the child and affect family relationships.

One-child Families. According to tradition, only children fall into two types: (1) the spoiled, egocentric, antisocial, and therefore very unpopular children, commonly known as "brats"; and (2) the withdrawn, sensitive, nervous children who shrink from social contacts, are overdependent on their parents, and are often labeled "mice" (186). Neither type, it is obvious, is looked upon

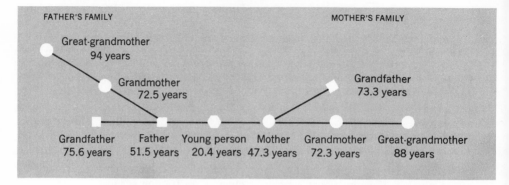

Figure 14-7. Pattern of an elongated family. (Adapted from R. Albrecht, Intergeneration parent patterns, *J. home Econ.*, 1954, 46, 29–32. Used by permission.)

as well adjusted or is likely to make a success in life.

Early studies of only children emphasized the inferiority of the only child. G. Stanley Hall said, "Being an only child is a disease in itself. The only child is greatly handicapped. He cannot be expected to go through life with the same capacity for adjustment that the child reared in the family with other children has" (107).

More recently, opinions about only children have changed markedly. Emphasis is now being placed on the importance of the home setting in determining whether or not being an only child is a handicap; "oneliness" per se is not the environmental specter it was so widely assumed to be. Whatever role the mere presence or absence of siblings may play in the development of personality, its importance certainly is not crucial (45, 271).

Whether the only child will develop into a mature, confident, and well-adjusted person or not will be largely determined by the type of parents he has, what their attitudes toward him are, and how they treat him. There is no such thing as a "typical" only child any more than there is a "typical" child with siblings (45).

An opportunity to learn to get along with others and to adapt oneself to the social group is one of the advantages most often stressed for children with siblings. If an only child has had no preschool experience, he must at school age adjust to a group whose behavior is already unlike his. This makes adjustment difficult but by no means impossible (271).

The only child uses his parents as models, and he associates primarily with adults; therefore, he tends to be more mature for his age than a child with siblings. Maturity of behavior, it has been found, contributes to good social adjustments and to leadership status within the group. (Refer to pages 428 and 430.) Furthermore, the only child is not so likely to be "spoiled" by sibling rivalry and jealousy as the child from the small family (120, 152).

The advantages of being an only child in a town or city environment compensate for the disadvantages. But in a rural environment the only child is isolated; his contacts with other children are rare and are likely to be limited to the school. As a result, his personal and social development is somewhat handicapped. Modern methods of transportation, the trend toward consolidated schools, and the widespread use of mass media of communication, especially movies and television, give the rural child of today many more opportunities for social contacts than were possible in the past.

Although only children develop a personality pattern distinctly different from that of children with siblings, there is no evidence that only children are more emotionally unstable, that they have more scholastic problems, or that they are more retarded academically than non-only children. The only child does not, however, participate voluntarily in extracurricular activities quite so much as the child with siblings (33, 194).

Because of the widespread belief that only children are pampered and spoiled, it has been generally accepted that there are more instances of problem behavior among them than among non-only children. For the most part, the forms of problem behavior that occur more frequently among only children than among non-only, such as nail biting, crying, restlessness, and overactivity, are traceable to home factors characteristic of the environment in which there is an only child. Outside of the home, they are less troublesome, and as they reach adolescence, they generally make better adjustments in the home than children plagued by sibling rivalries and jealousies (33, 304).

Small Families. A small family is one with two or three children. It is usually planned with regard to size, spacing, and child-rearing education; parenthood is intensive rather than extensive. The activities and roles of each family member are individualized; there is a democratic organization, with cooperation between parents and child. There are pressures on the child to live up to parental expectations, and the family is under stress to achieve and get ahead. Discipline of the child is mainly the responsibility of the mother.

In the small family, there are definite economic and social advantages for the child, but he must "pay a price for this, chiefly in the form of problem-creating circumstances" (33). A child from a small family is protected and made the center of attention in his early social experiences. He may thus get an exaggerated opinion of his own importance in group life. Crises within the small family make a great impact on the child because there are so few members to share them. The child often does poor school work because of emotional disturbances.

While the economic status of the small family may be superior, broken homes are more frequent, thus adding to the child's problems of adjustment. Furthermore, a child from a small family is more likely to be overprotected and hence dependent than a child from a larger family (59, 75, 265). In spite of the disadvantages associated with the small family, children from small families are generally superior in physical, emotional, and social adjustments to children from very large families. On the other hand, there is evidence that a medium-sized family, especially one with three, four, or even five children, is superior to either the very large or the very small family (33, 75).

Large Families. A large family is one with six or more children. If large families are not planned, all members learn to accept the ever-growing brood as a matter of fate; this attitude affects their reaction to crises, especially illness or death of one of the parents. Emphasis is on the group rather than on the individual.

With a large number of children, there is little opportunity for parental overprotection, nagging, or pressure. Discipline is often carried out by older siblings who are given the role of parent substitutes. There are few economic or social advantages, especially for the older children. On the other hand, children in a large family have a chance to live relatively independently from adults; this helps to foster independence and maturity of behavior (7, 8, 33, 266).

The large family is, through necessity, a working unit; each child is assigned a role according to the order of his birth and is expected to carry it out. The first-born girl, for example, becomes "mother's helper" and is regarded as the "dependable one" by the other family members. The first-born boy is generally expected to help his father with the masculine tasks of the household; should anything happen to the father, he is expected to become the father surrogate, playing the role the father played even to the extent of sacrificing his education to go to work to support the family. The child who shows special capabilities, whether domestic or otherwise, becomes known as the "capable one" and is expected to do things to help other family members. The "baby" of a large family, coming after all the important roles have been assigned, generally becomes the "spoiled one"—the child who is waited on by others and who contributes nothing of importance to the family welfare (33).

If the child likes the role assigned him, all will be well. The very fact that the role is assigned and not voluntarily selected, however, is likely to lead to friction. The oldest daughter may bitterly resent her role as "mother's helper" and feel that her younger sisters should share some of the responsibilities thrust upon her. This can lead to deterioration in parent-child as well as in sibling relationships.

As things are always happening in a large family, the child learns to adjust repeatedly to change in role, in status, and in responsibilities. Because the family lives on a close margin, all members must work together and must learn to organize and submit to authority. While this fosters cooperation, it also results in authoritarian living; the more authoritarian the pattern of living, the less healthy the emotional climate of the home (33).

Children from large families are more likely to do poor work and to be under-achievers in school than children from smaller families. This is not necessarily because they are less bright but rather because the demands made on them in the home prevent them from studying. Furthermore, the resentments fostered by authoritarian control often encourage underachievement as a form of rebellion against adult domination (see pages 628 to 632).

Children from large families are less likely to be emotionally disturbed or to exhibit as much problem behavior as children from small families. Although the large family may not provide economic security, it does provide the child with five conditions that make for emotional security: someone to turn to if he does not get enough attention and understanding from harried or indifferent parents; better understanding of his problems by siblings than he could get from

his parents; better teaching from siblings than from parents; little jealousy because there is little opportunity for emotional coddling; and little overdependency (33). Not all children from large families, however, experience feelings of security, nor are all well adjusted. Boys, on the whole, tend to be better adjusted than girls. The in-between children are better adjusted than the first- or last-born, with the fourth-born the best adjusted of all. The first-born is generally the least well adjusted.

When poor adjustment occurs among children from large families, it is generally traceable to specific conditions within the pattern of family life of that particular family. The parents may be autocratic and domineering; a child may feel exploited, as when the first-born girl is expected to take care of younger siblings; a younger child may be spoiled or overdominated by an older sibling; or health problems may result from inadequate food or lack of proper medical attention. Adjustment thus depends *not on the size of the family per se but on the kind* of family it is (33). If the financial status of the family is good, many of the adverse effects of the large family on family relationships are minimized or even eliminated. The financial factor plays an important role (33, 205).

SIBLING RELATIONSHIPS

Very early in life, the child becomes aware of his status in the family and of the role he is expected to play. Most children regard their roles as inferior to those of their siblings and wish they had been born sooner or later in the family constellation so that their roles would be different. While they can see all the advantages associated with other ordinal positions, they usually fail to see the disadvantages. As a result, their resentments act as further contribution to sibling friction.

As Freud pointed out many years ago, the child's position in a sequence of brothers and sisters greatly affects the course of his later life (91). Of the many factors that contribute to the significance of the child's position in the family, the following are the most important.

Ordinal Position. Traditional beliefs about the "best position" in the family have been reinforced by fairy tales in which the oldest child is usually represented as uncertain, mistrustful, shrewd, stingy, or wealthy, and the youngest as secure, open, confiding, stupid, naïve, spontaneous, fond of animals, soft, good-natured, generous, humane, or poor. The youngest child is generally shown as the preferred sibling (110). Contrary to these popularly held beliefs, there is no "ideal position" within a family. In fact, there is "no position in the family circle which does not involve, as a consequence of its peculiar nature, certain special problems of adjustment" (103).

Studies to determine the relative merits of different family positions have revealed that the long-term effects are not so pronounced as popularly believed, though the effects on the older child tend to be the least persistent, and on the youngest the most persistent. While each position provides certain emotional satisfactions and dissatisfactions, the effects on the child will depend more on his sex and age than on his position per se. In addition, the effects will be greatly influenced by how he *perceives* his status (33, 241, 242).

The law of primogeniture, favoring the first-born in accession to title, property, and wealth, is based on the supposed superiority of the *first-born*. Studies of intelligence, however, show that there is a definite tendency for the intelligence quotient to increase progressively from the first-born to the later-born, at least as far as the eighth-born child. Genius, on the contrary, occurs more frequently among first-born than among later-born siblings (282).

Studies of personality and social adjustment have revealed that the oldest child is in a position which makes successful adjustment very difficult. His rather high-pitched relationship with his mother steadily lessens in intensity, especially when a second child arrives (133, 160, 241). As Montague has stated:

The first-born does seem to take rather a beating. For a year or more he is emperor of the universe. Everything exists to cater to his needs. . . . Then more or less abruptly the halcyon existence is terminated, or at least considerably changed, by the eruption into it of a brother or sister. . . . Really, can one wonder that the first-born is often what parents frankly call "a mess"! (194)

In addition to being overprotected, the first-born child is the victim of the comparative inexperience of his parents, and he is likely to be expected to assume responsibilities for the care of younger children. Because many parents are concerned about the effects the arrival of a second child will have on the first, they tend to encourage the continuation of the attitude of self-importance fostered when the first child was an only child. As a result, the older child lords it over the younger sibling, makes disparaging comments about the progress of the younger child, encourages the younger sibling to engage in competitive activities in which he is sure to emerge the loser, and uses various attention-getting devices to claim the mother's attention (87, 152, 242).

Parental overprotectiveness is likely to make the older child more conservative and less dominant and aggressive than the younger siblings. He usually lacks self-confidence and leadership qualities, is easily influenced by suggestion, and is very gullible. He is more dependent and more excitable, has his feelings hurt more easily, and is less demonstratively affectionate than later-born siblings. Because of parental idealism, the older child often suffers from feelings of failure; being worried and anxious to escape blame, he develops feelings of insecurity (4, 22, 133).

The oldest child often becomes selfish and spoiled. As Strauss has said, "He will walk constantly as if with a chip on his shoulder. This he will do because he must constantly be on his guard. He has learned from bitter experience that he may be displaced. In line

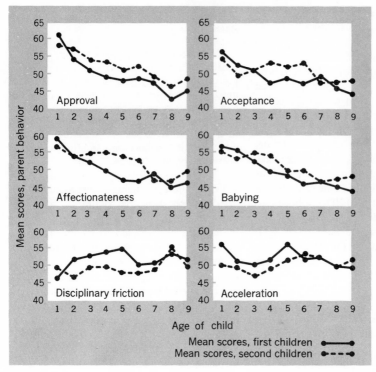

Figure 14-8. Age trends in parental behavior toward first- and second-born children. (Adapted from J. K. Lasko, Parent behavior toward first and second children, *Genet. Psychol. Monogr.*, 1954, 49, 97–137. Used by permission.)

with this, a general attitude of pessimism is common among first-born" (273).

The *second-born* child is spared much of the parental anxiety, emotional tension, and overprotectiveness experienced by the first-born. As a result, the second-born is usually less dependent than the first. Because the mother is less strained by anxiety and less ambivalent about her loss of freedom when the second child is born, the mother-child relationship will be warmer and more relaxed (98, 160, 241) (see Figure 14–8).

Between the ages of one and two years, the second child uses the first as a pacemaker. He rarely can keep up with the first, however, and often the first child's superior attitude and overlording behavior add to the younger's feelings of inadequacy (87, 160).

In spite of the fact that mothers give less instruction to second-borns, they excel first-borns on mental tests. Those with a male sibling do better than those with a female older sibling. The male sibling "keeps the sib on his toes. It isn't that the male has greater

skill or knowledge but rather that he, by the challenge he presents, stimulates or alerts his sib more than does a girl. Jealousy of him because he tends to be favored by his mother may also spark the alerting" (152). As a rule, second-born children are less neurotic and introverted and more fun-loving and humorous than first-borns (6, 51).

The *middle child* in a family of three or more children is apt to be somewhat neglected. He, too, tends to lack aggressiveness, but he is more aggressive than the oldest child. The middle child is rather easily influenced by suggestion; he is frequently flighty; his attention is easily distracted from the thing at hand; he shows more than the usual craving for physical demonstrations of affection; and he is generally gregarious in his social attitudes. It has been found that there are more extremely unpopular children among the middle children of families than among those of any other ordinal position (74, 304).

The *youngest child* of a family is likely to

be pampered and spoiled; other members of the family often continue to do things for him long after he is capable of doing them for himself. Sometimes, because he seems so much younger and less mature than the other children, the family tends to leave him out of things and to treat him as if he did not actually fit into the family pattern of living. These two extremes of behavior—indulgence and disregard—are bound to influence his outlook on life and, in turn, his behavior (6).

Older siblings often assume the role generally held by parents in the discipline of the youngest child. The "baby" resents being "bossed"; furthermore, he complains that he never has new clothes or toys, that he is the object of criticism and buck-passing, and that he is pushed into the background. As a result, he frequently becomes defiant and irritable. He develops a "chip-on-the-shoulder" attitude which affects relationships not only with members of the family but also with people outside the home (33, 205, 242).

According to Adler, the youngest children in families "bear unmistakable signs of the fact that they have been the youngest." Adler also believes that they have the greatest incentive to strive to surpass their siblings. Youngest children expect help from other members of the family and assume that things will always come out the way they want them to because other people will always be there to help (2). Because their self-confidence has never been jolted by competition with a newly arrived sibling, they have an advantage over other siblings. This may result in an optimistic outlook on life (273).

Age Differences.   If the age difference between siblings is small, the greatest impact is on sibling relationships; if the age difference is large, parent-child relationships receive the greatest impact. A two- to four-year spacing is especially stressful for sibling relationships, but more so for boy-boy combinations. A first-born child with a close sibling becomes reserved; he controls his anger and other emotional upsets better than the

second-born child. This is not because he has a deep affection for the younger sibling, but rather because he is afraid he will be punished if he reacts to the younger sibling in an aggressive manner (152).

The first-born, having been the center of attention until the arrival of the sibling, has a status to defend, but he is handicapped in his struggle with his sibling by parental restraints. By contrast, second-borns are encouraged by parents to defend themselves; as a result, they are less hesitant to express their anger and attack directly. If the spacing between siblings is larger, they are thrown together less in play and thus have fewer areas of friction. When an older sibling is expected to take care of a younger sibling, however, there is likely to be friction (33, 152, 242).

The age difference between children is an important factor in determining how the mother treats them. When they are closely spaced, she treats them more rationally, more democratically, and with more understanding, although any difference in treatment becomes less pronounced as the second child reaches school age (160).

If the age difference between siblings is large, there is an entirely different parent-child relationship with each child. Parents tend to expect the older child to set a good example for the younger, and they criticize him when he fails to do so. The younger child, in turn, is expected to imitate the older and to obey him. These parental expectations contribute to poor sibling relationships (33, 242).

Sex of Siblings.   Sibling relationships are markedly influenced by the sex of the siblings. Both boys and girls react very differently to brothers and to sisters. Sex alone, however, is not the determining factor: age differences, ordinal position, and attitudes of parents have a marked influence.

In a girl-girl combination, there is more jealousy than in a boy-girl or boy-boy combination. An older sister is likely to play a more aggressive role in her relationships with a younger sister than with a younger brother. Should the younger sister try to give directions to the older, the older girl will put up a fight to retain her position. Similarly, boys fight more with their brothers than with their sisters, partly because parents will not permit as much overaggression against sisters as against brothers. When the age difference between siblings, whether they are of the same sex or of opposite sexes, is large, a more affectionate, friendly, and cooperative relationship exists (175).

Among young children, siblings of opposite sexes are stimulating and security-taxing, especially for the first-born child. This leads to self-confidence and poise. Girls who have brothers, especially older brothers, become less sensitive than girls with sisters; they learn to take the teasing boys engage in without having their feelings hurt. A girl with only male siblings will either become a tomboy or develop the feeling that all members of the male sex should pay her homage and treat her as a little princess, just as her brothers did when she was a little child (273).

Boys with older sisters, it has been found, become more withdrawn and dependent than boys whose older siblings are brothers. A boy with an older sister who is resentful and jealous of him just because he is a boy is likely to become nervous and to underachieve in school. If he develops feminine characteristics and becomes known as a "sissy" among his male peers, the emotional stress that interferes with his school achievement will be increased (133, 152).

Throughout the gang age, the antagonism that exists between the sexes outside the home is carried into the home and leads to new conflicts between brothers and sisters. The relationship between siblings of the two sexes generally reaches a low point at the time of puberty (97, 113). Parents tend to speed up the emancipation of their sons and to retard that of their daughters. Sometimes older girls rebel against the inferior status assigned to girls and demand rights and privileges equal to those enjoyed by their brothers (111, 303).

In spite of the fact that the father is more anxious than the mother that the first-born be a boy or that the majority of the children in the family be boys, the father generally shows favoritism toward his daughters and acts as a strict disciplinarian toward his sons. The mother generally favors the boys; her obvious preference for her sons, especially the first-born, leads to much of the sibling rivalry that exists in homes where there are siblings of both sexes (113, 242).

Typical Sibling Relationships. In spite of variations, there is a more or less universal pattern of sibling relationships; this pattern shows a steady increase in frictional relationships as childhood progresses. Among older children, the acquisition of interests and values from their association with the peer groups leads to clashes not only with their parents but also with their siblings.

Older brothers and sisters, especially if they are adolescents, constantly criticize and find fault with their younger siblings, "picking on" them and nagging them about everything and anything. The younger sibling, in turn, tries to retaliate by making fun of the older sibling or by tattling to a parent. He may even project his aggressions on a still younger sibling (33, 97).

Sibling stress and quarreling come from many causes, the most common of which are sibling crossness, lack of proper respect for another's property, and demands by parents that an older sibling be responsible for the care of a younger child. Young siblings like to associate with older siblings, but the older children consider this "tagging along" or "getting in the way." This leads to quarreling, in which the older child is generally able to get the better of the younger. Younger siblings often wish they could change places with older siblings, especially when an older sibling is a boy (33, 160, 245).

As siblings learn to socialize and as they develop peer contacts, they usually get along more amicably in the home. This does not mean that quarreling comes to an end; it means, rather, that conflicts normally become less frequent and less intense, only to flare up again during the early part of puberty. Furthermore, as we are an age-graded society, children feel "less comfortable with vertical relationships than with horizontal ones." They feel more at home and on a par with their agemates, whether they are members of the peer group or siblings, than with parents, teachers, or other adults. This further contributes to a better sibling relationship. In time, the sibling bond, especially the sister-sister relationship, becomes second in strength to the parent-child bond (62).

Significance of Sibling Relationships. The frictional relationship between siblings is undoubtedly one of the major causes of deterioration in family harmony. Sibling rivalries and jealousies may be kept from overt expression by threat of punishment, but like any thwarted emotional experience, they will sooner or later erupt and cause trouble. The home environment governed by more democratic practices is likely to be more tempestuous but psychologically healthier because resentments are expressed and the atmosphere cleared (152).

The serious aspect of sibling friction is that it becomes a pattern of social relationships which the child is likely to carry outside the home and apply to his relationships with the peer group. Habitual quarreling, name calling, bullying, and teasing will not contribute to his chances of acceptance in the peer group. Also, sibling friction weakens the child's motivation to form social relationships with people outside the home. When his relationships with his siblings are not pleasant, he has little motivation to expand his social contacts further.

If poor sibling relationships affected only the children of the family, the situation would not be so unpleasant nor the home atmosphere so unhealthy. It is almost impossible, however, for parents to stand on the sidelines and watch their children fight, call names, or tattle; they feel that they must step in and put a stop to the quarreling. By doing so, they usually make matters worse. They are accused of taking sides, of showing favoritism, or of being unfair.

Who is to blame for the deterioration of sibling relationships as childhood progresses? Most husbands blame their wives, maintaining that they have not been good disciplinarians. Wives, in turn, are apt to blame husbands for neglecting their parental duties, for giving too little time to the training of the children, and for expecting adult behavior from children. Pointing the finger of accusation at anyone leads to resentments and makes a bad situation worse. If family relationships are to be kept from deteriorating, it seems apparent that the two serious causes of deterioration—poor sibling and parent-child relationships—must be attacked. Children must learn, from a good example on the part of their parents and from direct teaching and guidance, how to get along well with people, whether they are siblings, peers, or adults; parents must learn to accept every child as an individual, even though he does not measure up to parental expectation, so that there will be no evidence of favoritism.

Perhaps the most constructive approach is to apply the old maxim, "Busy hands are kept out of mischief." A return to the old-fashioned philosophy of child training, in which every child was expected to make his contribution to the family welfare according to his abilities, might readily lead to better sibling relationships and, in turn, to better family relationships.

HOME SETTING

The kind of home the child has will have a marked influence on his outlook on life and on his relationships with parents, siblings, and other individuals who live permanently or temporarily in the home. Of the many factors in the home setting that influence the attitudes and behavior of the child, the following are the most important.

Socioeconomic Status. The pattern of family life differs in the various socioeconomic groups. There are differences in home management and table manners; in husband-wife relations; in concepts of the roles of parents, children, and relatives; in family values; in the use of money; in social conformity; in child training and attitudes toward discipline; and in attitudes toward family life (25, 173, 185). Middle-class parents, as a rule, regard their children with "possessive pride and hope." They emphasize social conformity to achieve status, supervise their children closely, and expect their children to avoid any behavior that might bring criticism on the family. Because the middle-class child is wanted by his parents and is regarded as a fulfillment of their marriage, he is treated in a kindly manner, is usually brought up in a democratic home atmosphere, and is given as many advantages as his parents can afford. In spite of all the parental attention the middle-class child receives, the constant pressure to maintain the family status often leads to behavior problems and neurosis (20, 33, 242, 292).

Far too often, the attitude of lower-class parents is that a child is the "inevitable payment for sex relations" (33). This attitude does not produce warm parent-child relationships. Parental control is usually authoritarian, but discipline is inconsistent. The lower-class child often feels unloved, unwanted, and rejected at home; to compensate for this, he seeks companionship outside the home (4, 175).

The socioeconomic status of the family influences the *type* of home and the *location of the home* in the community. This determines to a large extent what kind of associates the child will have. Because the social structure of our country is characterized by potential *social mobility,* there is always the possibility of shifting to another socioeconomic group (185). Shifting of social classes tends to disrupt family relationships. Should one parent be mobile and the other static, the child is likely to identify himself with the parent having the higher status; this will lead to family friction resulting from different ideals and values (28, 101, 162).

Economic Status. The economic status of the family frequently determines what the family social status will be. As Teagarden has pointed out, "The parental anxiety that is engendered by poverty, together with possible malnutrition and overcrowding, will in many cases cause psychic wounds" (281). A home setting of great wealth in which children are neglected by their parents and

brought up by ignorant or uninterested servants may produce even more harmful effects on the child's attitudes than those suffered in homes where poverty predominates (83, 116).

Economic insecurity makes for emotional insecurity, but economic security does not necessarily imply emotional security. The greatest emotional security occurs among children from the middle-income group. Economically favored parents generally handle their children intelligently and thus create fewer behavior problems. Furthermore, parents in a favorable economic position have more time and money for recreational activities in which the whole family can participate (119, 302).

Parental Occupations. The *father's* occupation is important to a young child only insofar as it has a direct bearing on the child's welfare. For the older child, however, the father's occupation has a cultural significance in that it affects the child's social prestige (72). Elementary-school children stratify people on the basis of jobs and accept the adult attitudes and values concerning different jobs (302). When a child is ashamed of his father's occupation, either because of the level of work done or because of the type of clothes demanded by the work, the child's attitude toward his father, his home, and himself will be adversely affected (26, 33, 212).

The father's occupation affects the child indirectly in that it influences the father's standards for the child. From his experiences in work, the father knows what attitudes, skills, and qualities are essential to success. He then tries to foster them in the child. Thus, standards of the occupational world "infect" the home and influence the father's role (1). If the father's job takes him away from home, there will be a temporary break in the family and a change in the home environment. Many occupations require shifts of residence. As long as the child is young, the major effect of moving will be a break in the continuity of family life, but as he grows older, the effects will be more far-reaching. The child will have to adjust to a new school, to new friends, and to the mores of a new community. In addition, his parents will be preoccupied with problems arising in connection with the change and will be able to give him less time and attention than usual. During a period of adjustment, tension and friction in the home will increase (276). See pages 423 to 424 for a more complete discussion of the adjustment problems encountered by a newcomer in the school peer group.

Today more *mothers* work outside the home than ever before. How this affects children depends partly upon their age and partly upon the provision made for their care. The young child usually feels lonely and unhappy when the mother is away for a major part of the day. Also, he is confused by the different forms of discipline used by the mother and the mother substitute. In homes where the mother works, home duties are neglected, meals are irregular, there are few opportunities for social life and recreation with the family, and each child must assume more home duties than he would otherwise (174, 207, 221). Children of working mothers often come to school late; they are not so well groomed as children whose mothers do not work; they are often inadequately fed, owing to the necessity of getting their own meals or eating at irregular times; and they are often nervous, which makes it difficult for them to concentrate and do good work at school. Young children are more affected by the mother's employment than older children, though older girls usually resent the additional home responsibilities they are expected to assume (234).

The mother's *reason for working* has a marked effect on her attitude toward her role as a mother; this, in turn, affects her relationship with the children. If she must work to maintain the family's financial status, the effects will be better than if she works merely to get away from the family and to escape home responsibilities. Because employment does not fit into the cultural stereotype of "mother," she may feel guilty about being away from home, especially if working is not motivated by economic necessity (100, 221, 248).

When the mother goes out of her way to avoid imposing extra home duties on her husband and children, the children perceive her as kind, positive, and nonassertive and thus tend to become nonassertive and somewhat ineffective themselves. When the mother does not like her work or when she feels guilty about liking it, her relationships with the family are poor, and the children tend to become assertive and hostile.

Furthermore, the mother who dislikes her work often imposes domestic tasks on her children and thus increases their hostility toward her. A mother who enjoys her work and who feels positive toward it provides a model for her children to imitate; they usually develop a strong drive for achievement and do good work in school (135, 216, 268).

When the mother starts to work has an important effect on mother-child relationships. If the mother starts to work before the child becomes accustomed to spending all his time with her—before any definite relationship has been established—the effects will be minimal. If strong attachments have been formed, however, the child will suffer from maternal deprivation unless a satisfactory mother substitute is provided—a substitute whom the child likes and whose methods of child training will not cause confusion or resentments on the child's part (174, 207). (See pages 262 to 265 for a discussion of the effects of maternal deprivation.)

When mothers work sporadically—to get extra money for Christmas gifts or a summer vacation, for example—the effect on parent-child relationships is more serious than when the mother works continuously. In the former case, adequate provision is usually not made for the children, and they may face complicated adjustment problems. Mothers who work sporadically often fail to provide any substitute care for older children, with the result that the children may get into trouble in the neighborhood (104, 204).

How the child feels about his mother's working depends partly upon how seriously her work interferes with his life, partly upon what his friends' mothers do, and partly on the stereotype he has built up of "mother." If he has the culturally accepted stereotype of "mother" as a homemaker, he will not be able to understand why his mother is different. Most children object to having their mothers work because they are lonely and feel that there is no homelife when the mother is away. Furthermore, when the mother comes home from work, she is often tired and irritable; this affects her relationships with the children (135, 216, 221).

If the mother is engaged in work that has prestige in the eyes of the child's friends, the child will be proud of her; if her job does not keep her away from home too long or interfere too much with his life, a child may be proud of his mother simply because she is earning money. If everything in the home must be run like clockwork and if the child is constantly pressed to do things in a businesslike way, his reactions to his mother and her work will be very different from what they would be if she left her principles of efficiency behind in the office (292).

The type of adjustment the child makes to his mother's work may range from quiet submission to bitter resentment. As Siegel et al. have pointed out, "Maternal employment *per se* is not the overwhelmingly influential factor in children's lives that some have thought it to be" (253). When mother-child relationships are poor and when the child is psychologically damaged by the mother's working, the trouble often comes from *factors other than her employment.* If she works because she has a rejective attitude toward her role of homemaker and mother; because of economic necessity due to divorce, separation, or desertion; because of high aspirations for her child's future; or because her marital relationships are unsatisfactory, her unfavorable attitudes rather than her work are at the basis of poor mother-child relationships (253, 268, 300). As Maccoby has stressed, "Clearly no single way of organizing family life is best for all. Some mothers should work while others should not" (174).

Outsiders in the Home. Although the *ideal* American family is a nuclear family, the *typical* American family is often an extended or elongated one (62). The presence of grandparents or other elderly relatives in the home is certain to influence the child's behavior.

Should the child's parents be living in the home of grandparents, they must frequently defer to the wishes of the grandparents to ensure harmony in the home. Today, as a result of the dependency of old people, many elderly parents live with their children. The three-generation household is a "hazardous type of living in which the combined virtues of a diplomat, statesman, and saint are needed" (157). Refer to Figure 14–7, page 668, for the characteristic pattern of the elongated family. Note, especially, the predominance of female members in this family.

How "hazardous" a family of three generations is will depend partly upon the parents' attitudes toward the elderly parents and the necessity of caring for them, partly upon the child's attitudes, and partly upon whether the elderly relatives are male or female. Unquestionably the most hazardous type of three-generation household, as far as children and parents are concerned, is the one in which the elderly relatives are female (3, 71, 222, 275).

When there is a maternal grandmother in the home, making demands on the mother, the situation is unsatisfactory for the father as well as for the children. Generally, it leads to a withdrawal of the father from family activities and throws extra burdens on the mother. In addition, it leads to friction between husband and wife which is damaging to the emotional climate of the home. Children suffer because of the contradictory demands made on them by the mother and the grandmother (48). The serious effects on the child are shown in maladjustive behavior in the home and at school. Figure 14–9 shows the effect of a family-living pattern of this type. Because a grandfather would come in contact with the children less, he would be a less disruptive influence than the grandmother (92, 151).

In spite of the fact that children are encouraged to have feelings of loyalty to-

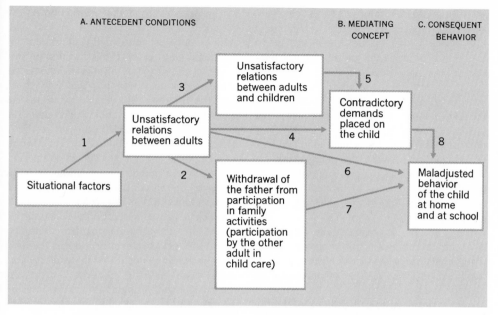

A. ANTECEDENT CONDITIONS

B. MEDIATING
CONCEPT

C. CONSEQUENT
BEHAVIOR

Figure 14-9. The effects of unfavorable family conditions on the child's adjustive behavior at home and at school. (Adapted from A. W. Clark and P. Van Sommers, Contradictory demands in family relations and adjustments to school and home, _Hum. Relat._, 1961, 14, 97–111. Used by permission.)

ward their kinfolk, there is likely to be friction when relatives criticize the child or his parents or when they try to exert authority over the child. Friction is increased when relatives from the two sides of the family come from different socioeconomic groups. There is a tendency for the child, as he becomes aware of social-class differences, to identify himself with the relatives of the higher-class parent and to feel ashamed of the relatives of the lower-class parent (33). Where the child's family has been socially mobile and has acquired a pattern of life that differs markedly from that of the relatives, he is especially likely to be ashamed of his relatives (28, 128, 191).

Guests in the home have a marked influence on the child. The child gets new social perspectives for measuring his parents, the family status, and the pattern of family living; he learns new social roles and skills; and he acquires new interests and new information from listening to what the guests say. He may resent the presence of guests,

however, because it means extra work for every member of the family, it disrupts his own plans for play, and it often creates tensions with his parents, who want him to make a "good impression." Being a guest, on the other hand, has most of the advantages and few of the disadvantages of having guests (33).

One source of trouble in many families is the _mother surrogate_. While relatively few families with young children today have full-time, live-in domestic servants, many employ a baby-sitter occasionally. If the baby-sitter is more lenient than the mother, the child may be confused and may become resentful of his mother's strict control. On the other hand, having help with domestic duties gives the mother more free time to devote to the child and eliminates some of the tension and friction which come when the mother is overworked (174, 207).

Broken Homes. If the home is broken, because of death, separation, or divorce, the whole pattern of family life is changed. When the break is due to death, the family may have to give up the home and go to live with a grandparent or some other relative. There are usually financial problems when the remaining parent is the mother, and problems of child care when the remaining parent is the father. Should the break be caused by separation, divorce, or desertion, there are the added complications of antagonism between the parents and the shifting of the child from one parent to another. Thus the *type* of broken home will determine what influence it will have on the child (234, 236).

When the break comes in the child's life is as important as, if not more important than, what caused the break. In early childhood, when the child's environment is limited almost exclusively to the home, a break in the accustomed pattern of family life is likely to be especially traumatic for him; he becomes insecure and feels as if his whole world were falling apart. Furthermore, a break in the home deprives the young child of a source of satisfaction for his psychological needs, especially when the missing parent is the mother. To compensate

for the loss of emotional satisfaction he experiences when his home is broken, the child usually becomes highly dependent on the remaining parent; this results in immaturity of behavior. Should the home be broken after the child has reached school age, his interests will have shifted to the peer group and his school work, and thus some of the damaging effects will be eliminated. Even in older children, a break in the home causes enough emotional strain and damage to the parent-child relationship to be expressed in misconduct in the school and in the home (18, 94, 194, 263).

When a break in the home is caused by *death* and the child recognizes that the parent will never return, he mourns the loss. This mourning begins with protest and passes from despair into detachment. In adolescents and young adults, many cases of mental illness, especially of the manic-depressive type, have been traced to the loss of a beloved parent through death during the early, vulnerable years of childhood. To some extent, the effects of the parent's death will depend on the kind of relationship the child had with the parent. The effects are more serious in early life when the mother dies, and later, when the father dies (36, 131, 236). The long-term effects on the pattern of the child's life are illustrated in Figure 14–10.

Should the child lose both parents, the effects are doubly serious. Besides having to accept radical changes in the pattern of his life, the child will have to adjust to the care of another person, often a person unknown to him. To reduce his feelings of insecurity, of inadequacy, and of being unwanted, the child may try to conform to the wishes of the substitute parents; by so doing, he often develops a personality pattern that leads to poor adjustments (234, 290).

A home broken by divorce can be more damaging to the child than a home broken by death. Bossard has suggested seven possible effects a home broken by divorce can have on the child:

Conflict is created when the child is attached to both parents; the child carries

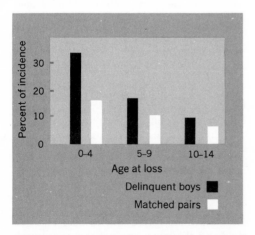

Figure 14-10. Relation between death of parent and later delinquency of the child. (Adapted from J. Bowlby, Childhood mourning and its implications for psychiatry, *Amer. J. Psychiat.*, 1961, 118, 481–498. Used by permission.)

within himself the continuing awareness of the problem; the child may find restraints placed upon him which were not present when the parents were together; the child must often face the transition from a broken home to a stepchild status; the child may have to shift between two homes and adjust to two home climates; the child may compare his home life with that of children from unbroken homes; and the child may develop new and disturbed points of view toward both parents (33).

One of the most serious effects is that divorce makes the child "different" in the eyes of the peer group. If he is asked where the missing parent is, he will be embarrassed and ashamed. Furthermore, he may feel guilty if he enjoys the time he spends with the missing parent or if he would prefer to live with the missing parent instead of with the parent who is taking care of him (95, 102).

Homes that are *temporarily broken* by the father's absence produce stress situations for the child as well as for the parents when the father returns. A study of war-born children whose fathers were away from home when they were born and during the early part of their lives indicated that the children had more behavior problems, had more contacts with close relatives and fewer with other children, made poorer social adjustments outside the home, were more dependent on adults, and had greater feelings of anxiety than children who had grown up in a home where both parents were present (269).

A study of the children of Norwegian fishermen, who, through necessity, are away from home for long periods of time, has revealed that these children become dependent on the mother, are overprotected, and tend to idealize the father. Boys have no male source of identification and hence become somewhat effeminate. Furthermore, when the father does not measure up, in real life, to the child's ideal, friction will develop between them. If a strong bond exists between mother and son, the boy may resent the father's return and be antagonistic and resentful (309).

Temporary absence of the mother affects young children of both sexes seriously because it deprives them of the stable source of care they have been accustomed to. In the case of older children, the temporary absence of the father is more serious for boys than for girls because it deprives the boy of the stable source of identification he needs to learn the appropriate male role and because he has a feeling of being different from other boys (201, 234).

Remarriage is often considered a solution to the problems of the broken home. It brings with it its own problems, however, and necessitates difficult adjustments for all, especially the child. While remarriage may eliminate some of the financial problems of the broken home and thus prevent radical changes in the standard of living of the family, the interpersonal problems created are often so difficult to solve that they counteract the favorable effects (95, 102, 131, 159).

For the child, the major problem will be adjusting to the *stepparent*. How he will adjust to the new parent and the new pattern of life created by the stepparent will be influenced by many factors. His age at the time of the remarriage is one such factor. The younger the child, the better he will adjust to the stepparent, especially when the stepparent is the father. The young, dependent child who has few memories of the missing parent will generally adjust better than an older child because the stepparent provides the young child with a sense of security. Among older children, both boys and girls tend to resent the stepparent, whether it is a mother or a father (33, 147, 234). If children are introduced to a stepparent without any warning of the change, resentments are built up from the start (213, 256).

Then there is the stereotype of the stepparent, especially that of the "wicked stepmother," which the child learns from fairy tales, movies, or friends. He has a mental picture of the stepmother by which he judges her every act, tending to misinterpret everything she says or does. This "hangs a millstone around the neck of the stepmother and makes her role an exceedingly difficult one" (256).

The personality traits of the stepparent, especially his feelings regarding his adequacy for the role, and the personality of the child, which may have been damaged during the period of the broken home, are likewise important factors in determining the effects the stepparent will have on the child. The stepmother comes in contact with the child more than the stepfather; therefore her influence over the child is greater (147, 256).

The attitude of the peer group affects the relationship older children will have with stepparents. If the child feels that having a stepparent makes him "different" and if his friends feel sorry for him, his attitude toward the stepparent will be far less favorable than if his friends accept the situation (147, 256, 290). Poor stepparent-child relationships will inevitably affect the relationship of the parents.

CONCEPTS OF FAMILY ROLES

In primitive cultures and in most civilized cultures, the role of each member of the family has historically been rigidly prescribed by custom, convention, and law. As a result, the child learns the roles he is expected to play at different periods in his life and accepts these roles without question. In the Japanese family, for example, the roles of the mother and father are distinct, with the approved role for the father more authoritarian than that for the mother. Each child learns, at an early age, that these are the roles he will be expected to play when he reaches adulthood (180, 279).

In the American culture today, urban life and the growing tendency for mothers to work outside the home are bringing about changes in the roles of all the family members (39, 46). Because of the changes that have taken place in our concepts of the approved roles for different family members, there is less psychological distance between parent and child in America than in cultures, such as the Japanese, where the roles of parents and children are based on the belief in the authority of parents over child and of males over females (180). *As psychological distance decreases, friction is likely to increase.* As a result, one of the contributing causes to the increase in deterioration of family relationships in America as children grow older can be traced to changed concepts of family roles.

Concepts of family roles are learned from personal experiences in the child's home and in the homes of relatives and friends; from observations of the roles played by other family members; and from books, movies, television, radio, comics, and other media of mass communication. Most of the books and media of mass communication which deal with family life present a picture of democratic family living which may be quite different from the pattern followed in the child's home (16, 88). Furthermore, every child and every adult has different learning experiences; therefore, it is not surprising to find different concepts of each family role within one family (73). This would not happen in a culture where the roles were rigidly prescribed by tradition and where few changes occurred from one generation to another (37, 39, 180).

Not only does the child develop a concept of "mother" or of "father," but he also adds to his concept a liking or disliking for the person represented by the verbal label "mother" or "father." This *emotional weighting* may vary from strong to weak. Similarly, when mothers have a romanticized or unrealistic concept of "child," they associate love with this concept and disappointment or even anger with any other. Much of the ambivalence mothers experience in their relations with their children can be traced to the discrepancy between their ideal concept and reality (238).

As the child's environment shifts from the home to the neighborhood and school, changes take place in his concepts of family members. Furthermore, the child's increasing ability to perceive meanings in situations makes him realize that the mother plays a less powerful role in decision making, in the earning of money, and in the management of the home and children than he had

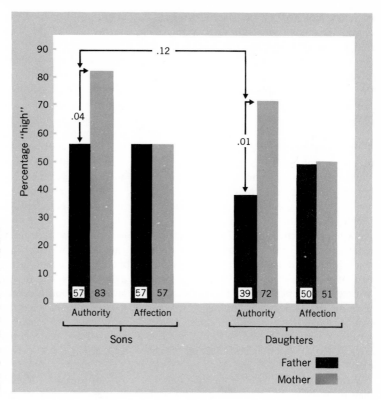

Figure 14-11. Children's perceptions of parental roles. (Adapted from W. C. Bronson, E. S. Katten, and N. Livson, Patterns of authority and affection in two generations, *J. abnorm. soc. Psychol.*, 1959, 58, 143–152. Used by permission.)

thought. There is then a shift in his concept of the roles played by the mother and father. This shift is shown in Figure 14-11. In addition, the child's concept of "child" changes from "one who can dominate the parents"—as he did when he was younger— to "one whom the parents, as disciplinarians, control and dominate" (79).

Parents also change their concepts of the roles the other parent and the child play. When the woman conceives the role of "father" to be equal to that of "mother," she may be forced to change this concept when she discovers how unrealistic it is to expect the father to play an equal role when his work requires him to be away from home many hours a day (46, 185).

The father, on the other hand, may change his concept of the role of "father" when he discovers that his wife is unable to manage the home and children without his aid; he then assumes some of the responsibilities formerly associated with his concept

of "mother." Similarly, many of the mother's unrealistic concepts of children built up during her own childhood or youth are changed when she assumes the role of motherhood and discovers that children do not conform to her earlier concept (55, 109, 280, 311).

Changes in concepts often lead to conflicts and tension *unless the concepts of all family members change in the same direction and to the same extent.* If the changes mean that the concepts will be more alike, friction and tension will be reduced; if they become more disparate, tension and friction will be increased. Even though changes in concepts generally lead to a deterioration in family relationships, lack of rigidity does permit greater individuality and flexibility in the face of changing circumstances (39, 294).

Specific Concepts. Certain concepts of different family roles are widely held by both adults and children in the American culture of today and may be considered typical. A careful examination of these concepts will reveal how different, in some respects, the child's concept and the adult's concept of a given role are. It will also help to explain the role these concepts play in the deterioration of family relationships as children grow older.

1. Concept of Parents. To an *adult,* a parent is not just a person who brings a child into the world and cares for him during the helpless years of childhood. "Good parents," from the adult point of view, are people who want the child to be equipped for a happy, useful life (278). As Bain has pointed out, "Good parents are thoroughly committed to the idea that the primary business of parents is to make their children as completely independent of the parents at as early an age as possible. Parents who accept this Golden Rule will produce normal people. They will help construct a good society without which normal people cannot exist" (12).

While all parents want to be good parents, they have different beliefs about the way to achieve this goal. In general, parents' concepts of their roles fall into two categories: traditional and developmental. The *traditional* concept emphasizes the authoritarian role of the parent, which stresses "making" the child conform to a pattern by instilling in his mind the culturally approved moral and religious values. The *developmental* concept, by contrast, emphasizes respect for the person and a permissive, growth-promoting type of guidance (70, 122, 156, 295).

The child frequently perceives the parent as a frustrating individual, while the parent sees himself as a facilitating being (30, 79, 144). To most children, parents are people who do things for them and on whom they can depend. Their concepts of parents are more often based on parental activities than on the physical appearance or the personality makeup of the parents. To children, a "good parent" is permissive or giving; he takes an interest in the home, the children, and the children's interests; he respects the children's individuality; and he inspires love, not fear (4, 56, 86, 144).

Not only do children have definite concepts of what a mother and father should be, but they are also aware of weaknesses in parents. There are certain things they disapprove of or dislike in parents. The things that most commonly annoy children are punishment, interference with their pleasures, and parent-child conflicts. Most children, in addition, have individual "peeves" about their parents (15, 105).

Children not only know what they dislike in their parents but also have fairly definite ideas of what they would like their parents to be and what traits they would like their parents to possess. They would like them to set a good example and to be companionable, understanding, kind, loving, affectionate, and good-natured. The characteristics they regard as most important are personality traits that make their parents more interested in, and sympathetic toward, them (33, 126).

2. Concept of "Mother." The *traditional* concept of the mother's role, which is more commonly held by members of the lower than of the middle and upper classes today, is that of the authoritarian person, who disciplines, teaches, and takes care of the children and the house with little help from the father. She may even be the provider for the family. The concept of the role of the mother in middle-class families is more *developmental* and stresses fostering the development of the child, having interests outside the home, having assistance from the father in the care of the children, and sometimes having outside help so she can do more for and with the children. Men, as a rule, cling to the traditional concept, while women more often accept the developmental concept (242, 280).

The young child thinks of the mother as the person who does things for him, takes care of his physical needs with understanding, relates herself lovingly to him, can tolerate a great deal of childish mischief, and comes to his aid in time of trouble. While

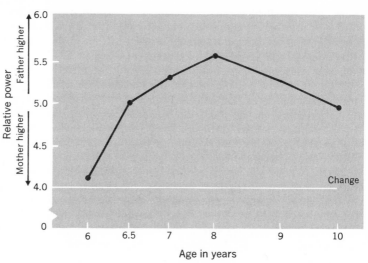

Figure 14-12. Shifts in the child's discrimination of the relative importance of the mother's and the father's role in the home. (Adapted from W. Emmerich, Family role concepts of children ages six to ten, *Child Develpm.,* **1961, 32, 609–624. Used by permission.)**

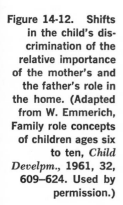

they are young, both boys and girls perceive the mother as exercising stronger authority than the father (see Figure 14–12). When the mother is perceived as very high in authority, she is not perceived as affectionate; children do not perceive authority and affection as going hand in hand (79, 105, 199).

As children grow older, their concepts of "mother" change to some extent. While they still think of the mother primarily in terms of what she does for them, they recognize that she has less authority and prestige in the eyes of the world than they had thought when they were younger (see Figure 14–12) (80). Furthermore, they are more influenced by the stereotype of "mother" presented in mass media, especially in movies and on television. In recent years, many popular movies have portrayed "mother" as "a boy's (or a girl's) worst friend." They show her as silly, meddling, stifling, "thoroughly rancid," selfish, snobbish, or meek and maudlin; she is often such an autocrat that the child sides with the father, whom she dominates. These portrayals do not help to form a favorable image of the mother in the child's mind (60). The influence of social pressures on the older child's concept of the mother has been described thus by Stoodley:

As children grow up they naturally pick up ideas as to who is the "big wheel" in their family. More often than not it isn't Mother. Perhaps they go to a school where the teachers are women, but the principal is a man. Perhaps they see that the jobs they consider important are occupied mostly by men. Or perhaps they absorb the sentiment of their social milieu which associates prestige with some specific kind of expertness, whether it be that of the certified public accountant, the skilled mechanic, or the physician. Society does not associate this expertness with the mother's role. . . . Faithful to the trend of social influence, as the child orients to a competitive environment in which the prize goes to specific expertness, the mother's influence is more than likely to go into a partial and sometimes a total eclipse (270).

It is not surprising that as children's concepts of the role the mother plays in the home and in society change, their attitudes toward the mother change also. As a result of these changes, children make a more critical assessment of their mother as a person and of her role in the home, especially when her interests and activities interfere with their pleasures or when the impression she makes on the peer group is not as favorable as they would like (15, 97, 181).

Boys tend to idealize their mothers as they

grow older, and they are less critical of them than girls are. In late childhood and adolescence, boys often develop a stereotype of an ideal mother who possesses such traits as kindness, sincerity, conscientiousness, high morals, refinement, and femininity; she is a good mixer and lacks such traits as conceit. This stereotype of an ideal mother (the "modal mother," shown in Figure 14–13) is used not only to judge their own mothers but also to evaluate girls and other women (243).

3. Concept of "Father."

Traditionally, the father is the provider and the head of the house. If the father teaches the child, he does so unconsciously, by example rather than by precept. This concept is held mainly by fathers of the lower socioeconomic classes. By contrast, fathers of the middle and upper classes hold more to the *developmental* concept of the father's role, which emphasizes understanding the children, being "pals" or companions, consciously teaching the children, guiding their development, and doing things for and with them.

The father who holds to the developmental concept of his role uses democratic forms of control over the child, tries to avoid severe punishment, and is interested in helping the child prepare for a future in keeping with his abilities. Lower-class parents disagree more on the role the father should play in the home than middle- and upper-class parents (54, 142, 156).

The concept of the role of the father has been subject to greater change in recent years than that of the mother. Many men, especially those who are foreign-born or whose parents are foreign-born, find it difficult to accept the developmental concept. Because the father is traditionally authoritarian in his attitudes toward the child, the man who loves his sons is often considered "soft and unmasculine." Therefore, to conform to social ideals, the father becomes strict and harsh in his treatment of his sons; by so doing, he is likely to make bullies out of them (17, 280).

Many men feel that they are inadequate as fathers, especially in such areas as discipline, companionship, and the teaching of character traits. Fathers who have been separated from their children for a relatively long period of time during the early, formative years feel particularly inadequate in these respects (269).

Most *children* have a fairly definite concept of "father," which differs markedly from their concept of "mother." According to this concept, the father is away from home more than the mother; he punishes more and harder than the mother; he knows more and is, in general, more important than the mother because he earns the money, owns more, and is the head of the family, the "boss" (181, 270). The tendency to perceive the father's role as a more powerful one in the family increases with age. This is shown in Figure 14–12, page 685. Because the father is perceived as the more powerful parent, he is more feared and is regarded as more dominating and less nurturant; the younger child links aggressiveness with the father and nurturance with the mother. Both boys and girls think of the father as "stronger, larger, darker, more dirty, more angular and more dangerous" than the mother (144).

As children grow older, they develop a concept of an "ideal" father, based on books and mass media of communication as well as on their observations of the fathers of their friends. According to this ideal, the father is just, loving, controlled, lots of fun, clean, mild, industrious, and demanding of high standards of himself and others. Because fathers rarely come up to this ideal, the child becomes critical of the father's shortcomings; this critical attitude soon becomes general, spreading to everything the father says or does (67, 144, 279).

As fathers are with their children less than mothers, children can build up an ideal concept of the father more easily. For the same reason, fathers have more difficulty counteracting the unpleasant traits or behavior their children associate with them. As a result, the relationship between the father and child is more damaged by concepts of an ideal parent than the mother-child relationship (58, 144).

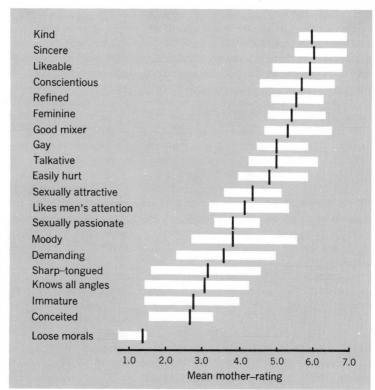

Kind
Sincere
Likeable
Conscientious
Refined
Feminine
Good mixer
Gay
Talkative
Easily hurt
Sexually attractive
Likes men's attention
Sexually passionate
Moody
Demanding
Sharp–tongued
Knows all angles
Immature
Conceited
Loose morals

1.0   2.0   3.0   4.0   5.0   6.0   7.0

Mean mother–rating

Figure 14-13. The "modal-mother profile." (Adapted from P. F. Secord and S. M. Jourard, Mother-concepts and judgments of young women's faces, *J. abnorm. soc. Psychol.*, 1956, 52, 246–250. Used by permission.)

4. Concept of "Child." The *traditional* adult concept of a "good" child is one who respects his parents, obeys, pleases adults, shares and cooperates in the duties of the home, and is healthy and eager to learn. He honors his parents for their unselfish devotion to him. The daughter is supposed to help in the household; the son is expected to achieve independence early and to contribute to his support in the home. This traditional concept is more commonly held by lower-class than by middle- and upper-class parents, and more by fathers than by mothers (54, 279).

According to the *developmental* concept, which is more widely held by middle- and upper-class parents, the child is guided into a pattern of development suited to his innate makeup, rather than forced to conform to socially approved ideals. The daughter is a learner, with few responsibilities, and the family serves her. The son, like the daughter, is dependent on the family (111, 129, 261).

The *child's* concept of his role is markedly influenced by his parents' concepts. If they think of him as a dependent, he will learn to believe that this is the child's role; if they wait on him, he will believe that a child should be waited on. Regardless of social class, most children hold the concept, based on their moral and religious training in the home, the school, and Sunday school, that a "good" child honors and respects his parents, is obedient, and is cooperative but never a troublemaker in the home (33, 54).

No matter how much the child may resent parental authority, he perceives himself as having less power in the home than his parents (79). This holds true even in the child-centered home, where a permissiveness in child training prevails and where parents exert little authority or control. While he may perceive himself as nearly independent, the child also perceives his parents as assuming the responsibility for the management of the home and for taking care of his physical and psychological needs (122).

5. Concept of Relatives. Because relatives play a less important role in the life of the child than members of the immediate family, his concepts of them are built on fewer personal experiences and are likely to include meanings he has acquired from his peers' comments and from stories, movies, television, and comics. A child whose most intimate friend has a grandmother living in his home may hear things about her that will influence his developing concept of "grandmother." If grandparents are depicted favorably in stories or on the screen, the child will be likely to develop a favorable concept of "grandmother" or "grandfather."

In the American culture of today, elderly people are stereotyped as unattractive in appearance, rigid and punitive in their attitudes, quarrelsome and hard to live with, and old-fashioned in their dress, in their manner of doing things, and in their values (117, 154, 155). The child learns much of this from his parents indirectly by the way they talk about elderly people (283). It is not surprising, therefore, that he incorporates this stereotype into his own concept of "elderly people" and transfers it to his concept of grandparents.

The child's concept of grandparents, however, will be greatly influenced by the closeness of his associations with his own grandparents. If he has many personal contacts with them, his concept will be based more on personal experiences than on stereotypes or on what others say; if his contacts are limited, the reverse will be true.

A study of how adults remember their grandparents shows how persistent childhood concepts are. On the whole, the adults reported that they remember their grandmothers as stronger in authority than their grandfathers. Men remember their grandmothers as more affectionate than their grandfathers, while women remember their grandfathers as more affectionate. Furthermore, because the concept of "grandmother" emphasizes her authority in the home, there is a tendency to have greater respect for the grandmother than for the grandfather (39). Concepts of grandparents are shown in Figure 14–14.

As has already been stressed (pages 681

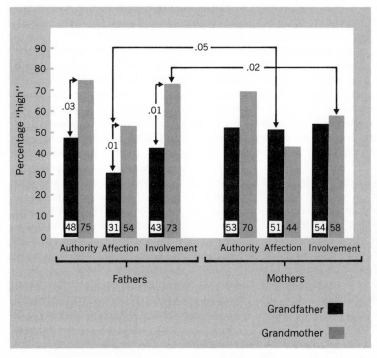

Figure 14-14. Children's concepts of grandparents as reported by adults. (Adapted from W. C. Bronson, E. S. Katten, and N. Livson, Patterns of authority and affection in two generations, *J. abnorm. soc. Psychol.*, 1959, 58, 143–152. Used by permission.)

to 682), the child's reactions to a stepparent will be greatly influenced by his concept of "stepmother" or "stepfather." The young child has not had an opportunity to learn the cultural stereotype of the "wicked stepmother" from fairy tales, stories, movies, or comments by peers; therefore, he reacts to a stepmother on the basis of the way she treats him. Since a stepmother is usually kind and loving to her stepchildren, the young child makes good adjustments to her (256).

As children grow older, their concept of "stepmother" becomes unfavorable. They build up a stereotype of the "wicked stepmother," and this is often reinforced by what members of the peer group say about their stepmothers and by what they have read. Stepfathers do not appear in fairy tales, though they do appear in modern fiction and on the modern screen. In general, they are depicted so favorably that any stereotype the child may develop of a stepfather is likely to be more favorable than his stereotype of a stepmother. His concept may be further reinforced by what his friends say about their stepfathers (213, 240, 256).

Effects of Concepts. Concepts of the roles of different family members will have an important bearing on family relationships. If a parent thinks he is a "good parent" but his child thinks he is not, there will be a poor parent-child relationship (245). A mother who believes that doing things for her children makes her a "good mother" may discover that her children regard her as cold, uninterested, and even rejecting. If their concepts of a "good mother" include demonstrations of affection and permissiveness, they will perceive her far less favorably than she perceives herself, and this will lead to poor mother-child relationships (4). *It is not the relationship of the parent and child, per se, that is important, but how the child and parent perceive it* (245).

Far too often, concepts of family roles are so romanticized that they fail to coincide with reality. The result is that few family members, whether they are parents, children, grandparents, or siblings can hope to come up to the expectations of other family members. Few parents, for example, can approach the romanticized concept of the "ideal" parent presented in the stereotypes of parents in books, in comics, or on the screen. The child who judges his parents by such stereotypes is likely to become highly critical of them and to feel that his parents are inferior to the parents of his friends (16, 181).

Similarly, few husbands or wives can come up to their spouses' romanticized concepts of the role of "mother" and "father." A man may feel that he is a "good father" if he provides well for his children and gives them advantages he never had. His wife, on the other hand, may feel that he is a "neglectful father" because he devotes little time to his children and leaves the major responsibility for their care to her (156). The woman whose concept of "good mother" includes giving children advantages from money she earns by outside work may find that her husband's concept differs radically; this leads to friction about her job (248). Men are more critical of their wives' roles as mothers than women are of their husbands' roles as fathers, primarily because men have a greater tendency to romanticize the role of motherhood (37, 280).

Unrealistic concepts may become more realistic with time and with direct contacts with family members. A husband whose concept of the mother's role did not include work outside the home may change his attitude toward his wife's working when he realizes that the children are not neglected, that they are proud of the work their mother does, that the home atmosphere is more relaxed because each member has outside interests, and that there is not the financial strain that formerly gave rise to friction (248).

The child who formerly thought that his mother's undemonstrativeness meant rejection may come to realize that she shows her affection in ways he did not understand before. Furthermore, as he grows older, he is glad that she does not embarrass him by demonstrations of affection. With personal contacts with older people, especially relatives, the child will revise and may even abandon the former concept he held about old people and grandparents. Should these changes in concepts of family roles occur, there will be an improvement in family relationships (4, 155, 283). As has been said before, however, changes do not always—or even usually—lead to improved relationships.

Because patterns of behavior in social relationships tend to be persistent, unfavorable concepts about any family member can be the source of deterioration in the relationships with those members and, in turn, can lead to a deterioration in the relationships with other family members. A child who gets along badly with a grandmother because he has a poor concept of "grandmother," for example, often stirs up enough trouble in the family to lead to general family friction. The child who dislikes a stepmother because he has a concept of her based on fairy tales can cause enough trouble in the home to precipitate a separation or divorce.

PREFERENCE FOR ONE PARENT

In any human relationship, there is a tendency to like, dislike, or be neutral toward the person involved. A child, as was pointed out earlier, shows a preference for one sibling over another; he also prefers one parent to another. The preference may be so slight as to be barely recognizable by the child or by his parents, or it may be so marked that no one can fail to recognize it.

A slight preference for one parent may be accepted with good humor, or it may lead to hurt feelings and friction. On the other hand, it takes a very mature adult to accept outright rejection from a child without resentment. The close bond that develops between the child and the preferred parent will cause the other parent to feel that he is the third member of the situation in which "three makes a crowd."

Psychoanalysts explain the child's preference for one parent in terms of the Oedipus theory—that there is an innate, unconscious sexual desire among sons for their mothers and among daughters for their fathers. If this were true, it would mean that the child's preference would *always* be for the parent of the opposite sex. To date, studies have not revealed this to be true. Instead, the child's attitude toward the parent is determined by the child's age, his position in the family, the way he is treated by his parents and their attitude toward him, the child's personality, cultural attitudes toward the relative importance of the mother and father, and many other factors. Thus it becomes apparent that parental preferences are learned; there is no evidence of a congenital preference for either parent (33).

That there is no such congenital preference is further evident in the fact that preferences are not persistent; rather, they change from one age to another and from one circumstance to another. In general, however, there is a tendency for children of both sexes to prefer the mother to the father when they are very young. Among older children, there is an increase in affection for the father, but the mother remains the favorite. With the approach of puberty, girls show a less favorable attitude toward both parents, but the tendency is still to favor the mother. Boys have a more favorable attitude toward both parents as they approach puberty, but, as a rule, they too prefer the mother (113, 148). Preferences for parents during childhood are shown in Figure 14–15).

Reasons for Preference. In the child's mind, the preferred parent has an advantage over the other parent, and that advantage is generally in favor of the child. Of the many factors that determine how the child perceives his parents and interprets what each means to him, the following are the most important:

1. Time Spent with the Child. Traditionally, the mother is the parent who spends more time with the child. Furthermore, she generally plays with children more and thus provides them with more happy experiences than the father (66).

As children grow older, the father plays

with them less and tends to become more intolerant of their noisiness and normal childish behavior. Mothers, by contrast, are more tolerant and show more affection toward the child (11, 33, 34). Because mothers are more understanding than fathers, children claim that mothers are easier to get along with (96).

The longer a parent is separated from the child, the greater the child's preference for the remaining parent will be. Children born while their fathers were in the war, for example, responded to the fathers on their return with shy, withdrawing, and unresponsive behavior. The fathers, in turn, became critical of the children and their behavior. The children then turned even more than before to the mothers for attention and affection (269).

Should the mother be separated from the child for a period of time, the child may shift his affection to the father and prefer him to the mother, even after the mother's return. If the child is institutionalized or placed in the care of a stranger, he is likely to suffer from emotional deprivation (94). (See pages 261 to 265.)

2. Care of the Child. When children are very young, the mother is unquestionably the preferred parent; she is the one who supplies most of their material wants (11, 9, 96, 227). When they can express a preference, however, young children prefer the mother for some activity such as cooking, holding hands, having a bath, and reading, and the father for others, especially for playing games. Girls prefer to have their mothers dress them; they prefer to sit beside their mothers, to sleep with them, and to do things to help them. Boys prefer their fathers in these situations. When services are required of parents, the father is preferred in case of broken toys and need of money, and the mother for help in case of illness, trouble in school, loss of something, or hurt feelings 9).

3. Expression of Affection. Fathers may have as great affection for their children as mothers, but they often fail to show it in

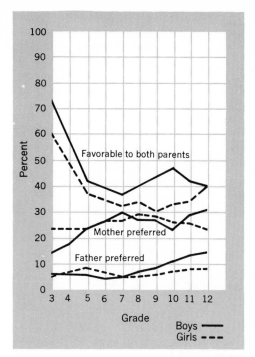

Figure 14-15. Boys' and girls' preferences for mothers and fathers at different ages in childhood. (Adapted from D. B. Harris and S. C. Tseng, Children's attitudes toward peers and parents as revealed by sentence completions, *Child Develpm.*, 1957, 28, 401–411. Used by permission.)

ways the child can understand. Males in our culture learn, from childhood, that any overt expression of affection is regarded as "feminine" and that a masculine man must keep emotional expressions under control. As a result, many fathers *seem* to a young child to be harsh, threatening, and frightening (144, 209). Mothers, on the other hand, are not held back by such restrictions; as a result, they are perceived by the child as warm and are favored for this reason (20, 22, 59, 204).

4. Discipline. The parent who restricts the child most and punishes most is less preferred. The mother is usually more tolerant and uses corporal punishment less than the father, and this contributes to the child's preference for the mother. Both boys and

girls, however, definitely prefer the father when the mother punishes them, and the mother when the father punishes them. It is difficult for children to understand how a person who loves them can be punitive; they therefore interpret punishment as lack of affection and prefer the parent who *appears* at the time to like them better (57, 144).

In lower-class families, especially, children perceive the father as more punitive than the mother. Boys, under conditions of harsh corporal punishment from the father, turn to the mother for help and learn to fear and dislike the father (156, 224).

As Henry has stated, "children often tend to turn more to the parent who 'lets me' and away from the parent who 'won't let me'" (122). Furthermore, if a parent resents the child's preference for the other parent, he may vie with that parent for the child's affection by being more permissive. This is likely to lead to friction between the parents, with each accusing the other of being too lenient (280).

5. Parental Expectations. The parent who expects too much of the child and who is critical when he does not live up to these expectations is less favored than the parent whose expectations are more within the child's capacities. Mothers of "planned-for" children and mothers who are professional women tend to expect too much of their children. They set goals that are unrealistically high and expect the child to be efficient and businesslike (58, 255, 292).

Many fathers, likewise, expect their children, especially their sons, to measure up to the standards of the business world. Socially mobile parents are most likely to set unrealistically high aims for their children; the more the parents have moved up the vocational and social ladder through their own efforts, the more likely they are to have high aspirations for their children. Girls are expected to achieve social success, while boys are pressured to win school and vocational success (1, 4, 232, 242).

When a parent is away from home for a period of time, he tends to be more demanding than the parent who is with the child constantly and who is, as a result, more aware of what one can normally expect of a child. Because the more demanding parent is then critical of the child when he is with him, the child turns to the other parent for affection and approval (269).

The mother who works outside the home tends to have higher expectations for her child than the person who takes care of him during her absence does. The result is that the surrogate mother is often preferred to the real mother. One of the counteracting effects of the unfavorable attitude the child is likely to develop toward a grandparent because of the prevailing stereotype of "old person" is that the grandparent is often more understanding and tolerant of the child than the parent (3, 92).

6. Parental Favoritism. The youngest child in the family—or the first-born, should the child be a boy—is usually the mother's favorite. When there are boys and girls in the same family, the mother's preference is usually for the boys. Thus it is not surprising that at an early age, a boy begins to show a greater preference for his mother, while a girl tends to prefer the father. This tendency grows stronger as children get older and become more clearly aware of parental differences.

As girls approach puberty, they often develop a generalized attitude of antagonism toward all members of the male sex, including their fathers. Consequently, they show a less favorable attitude toward their fathers than they did earlier. Girls also show a less favorable attitude toward their mothers at this time, owing primarily to their resentment of their mothers' preference for boys (9, 40, 113). See Figure 14–15, page 691, for the typical pattern of attitudes toward both parents.

7. Status of Parents. While the mother is the "boss" when the children are very young and their care is primarily her responsibility, the child discovers, as he grows older, that the father likes to be the "big boss." It is the father who makes many decisions about family matters, who gives the children their allowances, who dictates what the family will do or not do, who earns the money for the family, and who holds any position in the community that may be held by a family member. After the child is six years old, he perceives the father's role as more powerful than the mother's role (see Figure 14–12, page 685); this makes the father a more important person than the mother. In lower-class and lower-middle-class families, the father's role is distinctly superior to that of the mother as far as control over the family is concerned (79, 156, 242).

Furthermore, as children learn that "woman's work" is less highly valued by the cultural group than the work of men, they accept this evaluation and put a lower value on the mother. Much of the change in children's attitudes toward their parents can be traced to the child's acceptance of the cultural belief that men contribute more to society than women and that therefore men are more important. Just as children show a preference for prestigeful members of the peer group, so they show a preference for the parent whose status in the family is superior (31, 270).

8. Idealism of Parents. Every child has ideals for his parents and for his relationships with them. The parent who more closely approaches his ideal will be the one he prefers and shows the greatest respect for. A father may not come up to the son's ideal in appearance, but if he holds a job that has prestige in the community and in the eyes of members of the peer group, the son will show a greater preference for him than he would if the father's job lacked prestige. Similarly, when the mother comes close to the stereotype of an "ideal mother," the son will have a more favorable attitude toward her than he would if she fell short of the stereotype. Appearance plays a less important role in the boy's values than in the girl's; therefore, the son is less concerned than the daughter if the mother falls short of the stereotyped mother in looks (148, 270).

Girls have highly unrealistic ideals of parents. This is one of the reasons for the less favorable attitudes older girls develop toward both parents. Furthermore, because favoritism toward a sibling, especially a male sibling, does not fit into the girl's romanticized concept of a mother, the girl tends to have a less favorable attitude toward her mother than toward her father. By contrast, the boy who is the mother's favorite finds his mother close to his idealized concept and shows a preference for her. As the child's ideals change, so do his preferences. The parent who more closely approaches his ideal at the time, other factors being equal, is usually the favorite parent (113, 270).

Parental Reactions to Childish Preferences. Just as a child resents parental favoritism toward one sibling, so does a parent resent a child's preference for the other parent. The father who discovers that the child prefers to be with his mother and to have his mother do things for him has a less warm and affectionate feeling toward the child than the father who is preferred. It is flattering to an adult to feel that he is an important person in the eyes of his child, and it is ego-deflating to feel that he is unimportant.

The more sacrifices the father makes for the child, the more he resents the child's preference for the mother. Because children lack what is known as "tact," a parent usually knows how he stands in the child's affections. The child who says he would rather have "mommy do it" is telling his father very plainly that he prefers his mother, at least for that particular activity.

It is difficult for a person, whether a child or an adult, to react in a friendly way to a person who obviously prefers another. The child's preference for the mother can often be attributed to the father's behavior toward the child. The father who is perceived as punitive, harsh, threatening, or uninterested cannot expect the child to perceive him entirely favorably. Much of the preference the child shows for the mother can be traced to the fact that he perceives her as warm, understanding, and less punitive than the father.

Once a preference has been established, it is difficult to break down. This is equally true of a parent's preference for one child and of a child's preference for one parent. This persistence can be traced to the effect of preference on an individual's behavior and the reaction his behavior elicits from the other person. The parent who is first favored—the mother—because of her care of the child, literally gets the "inside track" on the child's affection. He reacts to her favorably, and this reinforces her favorable reaction to him. A circular reaction results which is difficult or impossible to break.

While factors other than care of the child contribute to his preference for the mother, most children remain dependent and need some parental care until they reach adolescence. Consequently, the factors that might put the father in the position of preference as the child grows older, such as his greater power in the home, his prestige in the community, or his vocational success, may not be strong enough to counteract the initial advantage the mother has. The father's position in the preference ratio may improve as the child grows older, but the mother usually remains the favorite throughout the childhood years.

Children at all ages try to imitate those whom they admire. The child who loves his mother wants to be just like her; he imitates her actions, her speech, her values, and her interests. Were it not for cultural pressures, most boys would grow up to be "sissies" because they would pattern their behavior on the mother's behavior (77, 170, 201).

Also, as boys reach school age, they learn that the status of the male is superior to that of the female. The father then has greater prestige than he had earlier, and this facilitates the boy's identification with him. It is flattering to anyone to be imitated; it is especially flattering to a father who has resented his son's earlier preference for the mother. As a result of this ego-inflation, the father's attitude toward his son may so change that his rating with the son will shoot up; it is unlikely, however, to reach a position above that of the mother. In any event, this change goes a long way toward improving father-son relationships.

Many mothers, while claiming that they want their sons to be "masculine" boys and encouraging them to try to be "just like daddy," secretly resent the shift of their son's affection to the father. This is reflected in a less warm mother-son relationship; it often supplies the motivation for the mother to turn her attention to her daughter, thus improving the mother-daughter relationship. In many families, as children approach adolescence there is a split between the sexes. The father and sons are on one side, and the mother and daughters are on the other. Any split in family relationships, no matter how slight it may be, is likely to lead to friction. Thus, as preferences for one parent may shift to the other parent, they continue to play a role of importance in the deterioration of family relationships. Were there no other causes of deterioration, the shifting of preferences alone would be enough to bring it about.

BIBLIOGRAPHY

(1) ABERLE, D. F., and K. D. NAEGELE: Middle-class fathers' occupational roles and attitudes toward children. *Amer. J. Orthopsychiat.,* 1952, **22,** 366–378.

(2) ADLER, A.: *The education of children.* New York: Greenberg, 1930.

(3) ALBRECHT, R.: Intergeneration parent patterns. *J. home Econ.,* 1954, **46,** 29–32.

(4) ALDOUS, J., and L. KELL: Child-rearing values of mothers in relation to their children's perceptions of their mothers' control: an exploratory study. *Marriage fam. Liv.,* 1956, **18,** 72–74.

(5) ALLEN, P. J.: Childhood backgrounds of success in a profession. *Amer. sociol. Rev.,* 1955, **26,** 186–190.

(6) ALTUS, W. D.: Birth order, intelligence, and adjustment. *Psychol. Rep.,* 1959, **5,** 502.

(7) AMATORA, SISTER M.: Analyses of certain recreational interests and activities and other variables in the large family. *J. soc. Psychol.,* 1959, **50,** 225–231.

(8) AMATORA, SISTER M.: An investigation of certain economic factors in large families. *J. soc. Psychol.,* 1959, **49,** 207–214.

(9) AMMONS, R. B., and H. S. AMMONS: Parent preferences in young children's doll-play interviews. *J. abnorm. soc. Psychol.,* 1949, **44,** 490–505.

(10) Anonymous: Ambivalence in first reactions to a sibling. *J. abnorm. soc. Psychol.,* 1949, **44,** 541–548.

(11) ANTONVSKY, H. F.: A contribution to research in the area of the mother-child relationship. *Child Develpm.,* 1959, **30,** 37–51.

(12) BAIN, R.: Making normal people. *Marriage fam. Liv.,* 1954, **16,** 27–31.

(13) BAKWIN, H.: "Pure mother" overprotection. *J. Pediat.,* 1948, **33,** 788–794.

(14) BALDWIN, A. L.: Changes in parent behavior during childhood. *Amer. Psychologist,* 1947, **2,** 425–426.

(15) BARCLAY, D.: How girls judge mother's role. *The New York Times,* June 21, 1953.

(16) BARCLAY, D.: Family business in brief. *The New York Times,* Feb. 18, 1962.

(17) BARTEMEIER, L.: The contribution of the father to the mental health of the family. *Amer. J. Psychiat.,* 1953, **111,** 277–280.

(18) BARTLETT, C. J., and J. E. HORROCKS: A study of the needs status of adolescents from broken homes. *J. genet. Psychol.,* 1958, **93,** 153–159.

(19) BATCHELOR, I. R. C., and M. NAPIER: Broken homes and attempted suicide. *Brit. J. Delinq.,* 1953, **4,** 99–108.

(20) BAYLEY, N., and E. S. SCHAEFER: Relationships between socioeconomic variables and the behavior of mothers toward young children. *J. genet. Psychol.,* 1960, **96,** 61–77.

(21) BEHRENS, M. L.: Child-rearing and the character structure of the mother. *Child Develpm.,* 1954, **25,** 225–238.

(22) BELL, R. Q.: Retrospective attitude studies of parent-child relations. *Child Develpm.,* 1958, **29,** 323–338.

(23) BELLER, E. K.: Dependency and independence in young children. *Amer. Psychologist,* 1950, **5,** 293.

(24) BENEDICT, R.: Continuities and discontinuities in cultural conditioning. *Psychiatry,* 1938, **1,** 161–167.

(25) BENEDICT, R.: Child rearing in certain European countries. *Amer. J. Orthopsychiat.,* 1949, **19,** 342–350.

(26) BETTELHEIM, B., and E. SYLVESTER: Notes on the impact of parental occupation: some cultural determinants of symptom choice in emotionally disturbed children. *Amer. J. Orthopsychiat.,* 1950, **20,** 785–795.

(27) BISHOP, B. M.: Mother-child interaction and the social behavior of children. *Psychol. Monogr.,* 1951, **65,** No. 11.

(28) BLAU, P. M.: Occupational bias and mobility. *Amer. sociol. Rev.,* 1957, **22,** 392–399.

(29) BLOCK, J.: Personality characteristics associated with fathers' attitudes toward childrearing. *Child Develpm.,* 1955, **26,** 41–48.

(30) BLOOD, R. O.: Consequences of permissiveness for parents of young children. *Marriage fam. Liv.,* 1953, **15,** 209–212.

(31) BORING, E. G.: The woman problem. *Amer. Psychologist,* 1951, **6,** 679–692.

(32) BOSSARD, J. H. S., and E. S. BOLL: Marital unhappiness in the life cycle. *Marriage fam. Liv.,* 1955, **17,** 10–14.

(33) BOSSARD, J. H. S., and E. S. BOLL: *The sociology of child development,* 3d ed. New York: Harper & Row, 1960.

(34) BOWERMAN, C. E., and J. W. KINCH: Changes in family and peer orientation of children between the fourth and tenth grades. *Soc. Forces,* 1959, **37,** 206–211.

(35) BOWLBY, J.: Some pathological processes set in train by early mother-child separation. *J. ment. Sci.,* 1953, **99,** 265–272.

(36) BOWLBY, J.: Childhood mourning and its implications for psychiatry. *Amer. J. Psychiat.,* 1961, **118,** 481–498.

(37) BRIM, O. G., R. W. FAIRCHILD, and E. F. BORGATTA: Relations between family problems. *Marriage fam. Liv.,* 1961, **23,** 219–226.

(38) BRONFENBRENNER, U.: Soviet methods of character education: some implications for research. *Amer. Psychologist,* 1962, **17,** 550–564.

(39) BRONSON, W. C., E. S. KATTEN, and N. LIVSON: Patterns of authority and affection in two generations. *J. abnorm. soc. Psychol.,* 1959, **58,** 143–152.

(40) BROWN, D. G.: Sex-role development in a changing culture. *Psychol. Bull.,* 1958, **55,** 232–242.

(41) BURCHINAL, L. G., and J. E. ROSSMAN: Relations among maternal employment indices and developmental characteristics of children. *Marriage fam. Liv.,* 1961, **23,** 334–339.

(42) BURGESS, E. W.: The family in a changing society. *Amer. J. Sociol.,* 1948, **53,** 417–422.

(43) BURLINGHAM, D. T.: Precursors of some psychoanalytic ideas about children in the sixteenth and seventeenth centuries. In R. S. Eissler, A. Freud, H. Hartmann, and E. Kries, *The psychoanalytic study of the child.* New York: International Universities Press, Inc., 1951. Pp. 244–254.

(44) CAPLAN, G.: The disturbance of the mother-child relationship by unsuccessful attempts at abortion. *Ment. Hyg., N.Y.,* 1954, **38,** 67–80.

(45) CATTELL, R. B., and R. W. COAN: Person-

ality factors in middle childhood as revealed by parents' ratings. *Child Develpm.*, 1957, **28,** 439–458.

(46) CAVAN, R. S.: *The American family.* New York: Crowell, 1953.

(47) CENTERS, R., and G. H. BLUMBERG: Social and psychological factors in human procreation: a survey approach. *J. soc. Psychol.,* 1954, **40,** 245–257.

(48) CLARK, A. W., and P. VAN SOMMERS: Contradictory demands in family relations and adjustments to school and home. *Hum. Relat.,* 1961, **14,** 97–111.

(49) CLIFFORD, E.: Discipline in the home: a controlled observational study of parental practices, *J. genet. Psychol.,* 1959, **95,** 45–82.

(50) COHEN, A. K.: *Delinquent boys.* New York: Free Press, 1955.

(51) COHEN, F.: Psychological characteristics of the second child as compared with the first. *Indian J. Psychol.,* 1951, **26,** 79–84.

(52) COLE, L.: *Psychology of adolescence,* 5th ed. New York: Holt, 1959.

(53) COLE, N. J., O. M. SHAW, J. STENECK, and L. H. TABOROFF: A survey assessment of current parental attitudes and practices in child rearing. *Amer. J. Orthopsychiat.,* 1957, **27,** 815–822.

(54) CONNOR, R. T., B. J. JOHANNIS, and J. WATERS: Parent-adolescent relationships. *J. home Econ.,* 1954, **46,** 183–191.

(55) COOPER, L.: Predisposition toward parenthood: a comparison of male and female students. *Sociol. soc. Res.,* 1957, **42,** 31–36.

(56) COX, F. N.: An assessment of children's attitudes toward parent figures. *Child Develpm.,* 1962, **33,** 821–830.

(57) COX, F. N., and P. M. LEAPER: Assessing some aspects of the parent-child relationship. *Child Develpm.,* 1961, **32,** 637–649.

(58) CRANDALL, V. J., and A. PRESTON: Verbally expressed needs and overt maternal behavior. *Child Develpm.,* 1961, **32,** 261–270.

(59) CRANDALL, V. J., A. PRESTON, and A. RABSON: Maternal reactions and the development of independence and achievement behavior in young children. *Child Develpm.,* 1960, **31,** 243–251.

(60) CROWTHERS, B.: Poor Mom. *The New York Times,* Apr. 22, 1962.

(61) CRUICKSHANK, W. M., and G. O. JOHNSON: *Education of exceptional children and youth.* Englewood Cliffs, N.J.: Prentice-Hall, 1958.

(62) CUMMING, E., and D. M. SCHNEIDER: Sibling solidarity: a property of American kinship. *Amer. Anthropologist,* 1961, **63,** 498–507.

(63) DAVIDS, A., and M. J. LAWTON: Self-concept, mother concept, and food aversions in emotionally disturbed and normal children. *J. abnorm. soc. Psychol.,* 1961, **62,** 309–314.

(64) DESPERT, J. L.: *Children of divorce.* Garden City, N.Y.: Doubleday, 1953.

(65) DINITZ, S., R. R. DYNES, and A. C. CLARKE: Preferences for male or female children: traditional or affectional? *Marriage fam. Liv.,* 1954, **16,** 128–134.

(66) DOUVAN, E.: Independence and identity in adolescence. *Children,* 1957, **4,** 186–190.

(67) DREGER, R. M., and A. SWEETLAND: Traits of fatherhood as revealed by the factor analysis of a parent attitude scale. *J. genet. Psychol.,* 1960, **96,** 115–122.

(68) DU BOIS, F. S.: The security of discipline. *Ment. Hyg., N.Y.,* 1952, **36,** 353–372.

(69) DUNBAR, F.: Homeostasis during puberty. *Amer. J. Psychiat.,* 1958, **114,** 673–682.

(70) DUVALL, E. M.: Conceptions of parenthood. *Amer. J. Sociol.,* 1946, **52,** 193–203.

(71) DUVALL, E. M.: *In-laws: pro and con.* New York: Association Press, 1954.

(72) ECKHOFF, E., J. GAUSLAR, and A. L. BALDWIN: Parental behavior toward boys and girls. *Acta psychol.,* 1961, **18,** 85–99.

(73) ELKIND, D.: Children's conceptions of brother and sister: Piaget replication study. *J. genet. Psychol.,* 1962, **100,** 129–136.

(74) ELKINS, D.: Some factors related to the choice-status of ninety eighth grade children in a school society. *Genet. Psychol. Monogr.,* 1958, **58,** 207–272.

(75) ELLIS, A., and R. M. BEECHLEY: A comparison of child guidance clinic patients coming from large, medium, and small families. *J. genet. Psychol.,* 1951, **79,** 131–144.

(76) ELLIS, E.: Social psychological correlates of upward social mobility among unmarried career women. *Amer. sociol. Rev.,* 1952, **17,** 558–563.

(77) EMMERICH, W.: Parental identification in young children. *Genet. Psychol. Monogr.,* 1959, **60,** 257–268.

(78) EMMERICH, W.: Young children's discrimination of parent and child roles. *Child Develpm.,* 1959, **30,** 403–419.

(79) EMMERICH, W.: Family role concepts of children ages six to ten. *Child Develpm.,* 1961, **32,** 609–624.

(80) EMMERICH, W.: Variations in the parent role as a function of the parent's sex and the child's sex and age. *Merrill-Palmer Quart.,* 1962, **8,** 3–11.

(81) ESTVAN, F. J., and E. W. ESTVAN: *The child's world: his social perception.* New York: Putnam, 1959.

(82) FARBER, B.: Marital integration as a factor in parent-child relations. *Child Develpm.,* 1962, **33,** 1–14.

(83) FARBER, B., and L. S. BLACKMAN: Marital role tensions and number and sex of children. *Amer. sociol. Rev.,* 1956, **21,** 596–601.

(84) FARRAR, M. S.: Mother-daughter conflicts

extended into later life. *Soc. Casewk,* 1955, **36**, 202–207.

(85) FEINBERG, H., and E. MOSCOVITCH: Achievement on the Stanford Achievement Test of children in different home situations compared with children placed out of the home. *J. exp. Educ.,* 1957, **26**, 67–80.

(86) FINCH, H. M.: Young children's concepts of parent roles. *J. home Econ.,* 1955, **47**, 99–103.

(87) FISCHER, A. E.: Sibling relationships with special reference to the problems of the second-born. *J. Pediat.,* 1952, **40**, 254–259.

(88) FISHER, H. H.: Family life in children's literature. *Elem. Sch. J.,* 1950, **50**, 516–520.

(89) FLÜGEL, J. C.: *The psychoanalytic study of the family.* London: International Psychoanalytical Library, 1929, No. 3.

(90) FREEMAN, H. E., and M. SHOWELL: The role of the family in the socialization process. *J. soc. Psychol.,* 1953, **37**, 97–101.

(91) FREUD, S.: *The standard edition of the complete psychological works of Sigmund Freud.* London: Hogarth, 1953–1962.

(92) FRIED, E. G., and K. STERN: The situation of the aged within the family. *Amer. J. Orthopsychiat.,* 1948, **18**, 31–54.

(93) FRUMKIN, R. M.: Marital status and mental health. *Sociol. soc. Res.,* 1953, **39**, 237–239.

(94) GARDNER, D. B., G. R. HAWKES, and L. G. BURCHINAL: Noncontinuous mothering in infancy and development in later childhood. *Child Develpm.,* 1961, **32**, 225–234.

(95) GARDNER, G. E.: Separation of the parents and the emotional life of the child. *Ment. Hyg., N.Y.,* 1956, **40**, 55–64.

(96) GARDNER, L. P.: An analysis of children's attitudes toward fathers. *J. genet. Psychol.,* 1947, **70**, 3–28.

(97) GESELL, A., F. L. ILG, and L. B. AMES: *Youth: the years from ten to sixteen.* New York: Harper & Row, 1956.

(98) GEWIRTZ, J. L.: A factor analysis of some attention-seeking behaviors of young children. *Child Develpm.,* 1956, **27**, 17–36.

(99) GLASNER, RABBI S.: Family religion as a matrix of personal growth. *Marriage fam. Liv.,* 1961, **23**, 291–293.

(100) GLENN, H. M.: Attitudes of women regarding gainful employment of married women. *J. home Econ.,* 1959, **51**, 247–252.

(101) GLICK, P. C.: The life cycle of the family. *Marriage fam. Liv.,* 1955, **17**, 3–9.

(102) GOODE, W. J.: *After divorce.* New York: Free Press, 1956.

(103) GOODENOUGH, F. L., and A. M. LEAHY: The effect of certain family relationships upon the development of personality. *J. genet. Psychol.,* 1927, **34**, 45–71.

(104) GLUECK, S., and E. T. GLUECK: *Unravelling juvenile delinquency.* New York: Commonwealth Fund, 1950.

(105) GRACE, H. A., and J. J. LOHMANN: Children's reactions to stories depicting parent-child conflict situations. *Child Develpm.,* 1952, **23**, 61–74.

(106) GRAY, S. W., and K. KLAUS: The assessment of parental identification. *Genet. Psychol. Monogr.,* 1956, **54**, 87–114.

(107) HALL, G. S.: *Aspects of child life and education.* Boston: Ginn, 1907.

(108) HALLOWITZ, D., and B. STULBERG: The vicious cycle of parent-child relationship breakdown. *Soc. Casewk,* 1959, **40**, 268–275.

(109) HANDEL, G., and R. D. HESS: The family as an emotional organization. *Marriage fam. Liv.,* 1956, **18**, 99–101.

(110) HANDSCHIN-NINCK, M.: Aeltester und Jüngster in Marchen. *Prax. Kinderpsychol. Kinderpsychiat.,* 1956, **7**, 167–173.

(111) HARRIS, D. B.: Parental judgment of responsibility in children and children's adjustment. *J. genet. Psychol.,* 1958, **92**, 161–166.

(112) HARRIS, D. B., and W. E. MARTIN: Mothers' child-training preferences and children's ethnic attitudes. *Amer. Psychologist,* 1950, **5**, 467.

(113) HARRIS, D. B., and S. C. TSENG: Children's attitudes toward peers and parents as revealed by sentence completions. *Child Develpm.,* 1957, **28**, 401–411.

(114) HARTLEY, R. E., F. P. HARDESTY, and D. S. GORFEIN: Children's perceptions and expressions of sex preference. *Child Develpm.,* 1962, **33**, 221–227.

(115) HAVIGHURST, R. J.: Social class differences and family life education at the secondary level. *Marriage fam. Liv.,* 1950, **12**, 133–135.

(116) HAVIGHURST, R. J.: *Human development and education.* New York: Longmans, 1953.

(117) HAVIGHURST, R. J., and R. ALBRECHT: *Older people.* New York: Longmans, 1953.

(118) HAWKES, G. R., L. G. BURCHINAL, and B. GARDNER: Measurement of preadolescents' views of family control of behavior. *Child Develpm.,* 1957, **28**, 387–392.

(119) HAWKINS, H., and J. WALTERS: Family recreation activities. *J. home Econ.,* 1952, **44**, 623–626.

(120) HAYES, D. T.: Freedom and fears in the family today. *Understanding the Child,* 1952, **21**, 39–44.

(121) HEATHERS, G.: Acquiring dependence and independence: a theoretical orientation. *J. genet. Psychol.,* 1955, **87**, 277–291.

(122) HENRY, J.: Permissiveness and morality. *Ment. Hyg., N.Y.,* 1961, **45**, 282–287.

(123) HENRY, J., and J. W. BOGGS: Child-rearing, culture, and the natural world. *Psychiatry,* 1952, **15**, 261–271.

(124) HENRY, J., and S. WARSON: Family structure and psychic development. *Amer. J. Orthopsychiat.,* 1951, **21**, 59–73.

(125) HERBST, P. G.: The measurement of family relationships. *Hum. Relat.*, 1952, **5**, 3–35.

(126) HERTZ, R. F.: 100,000 children tell how children should behave. *This Week Mag.*, July 24, 1955.

(127) HESS, R. D., and J. V. TORNEY: Religion, age, and sex in children's perceptions of family authority. *Child Develpm.*, 1962, **33**, 781–789.

(128) HIGGIN, G.: The effect of reference group functions on social status ratings. *Brit. J. Psychol.*, 1954, **45**, 88–93.

(129) HIGHBERGER, R.: Maternal behavior and attitudes related to behavior of the preschool child. *J. home Econ.*, 1956, **48**, 260–264.

(130) HILGARD, J. R.: Sibling rivalry and social heredity. *Psychiatry*, 1951, **14**, 375–385.

(131) HILGARD, J. R., M. F. NEWMAN, and F. FISK: Strength of adult ego following childhood bereavement. *Amer. J. Orthopsychiat.*, 1960, **30**, 788–798.

(132) HILLIARD, F. H.: The influence of religious education upon the development of children's moral ideas. *Brit. J. educ. Psychol.*, 1959, **29**, 50–59.

(133) HODGES, A., and B. BALOW: Learning disability in relation to family constellation. *J. educ. Res.*, 1961, **55**, 41–42.

(134) HOEFLIN, R.: Child-rearing practices and child care resources used by Ohio farm families with preschool children. *J. genet. Psychol.*, 1954, **84**, 271–297.

(135) HOFFMAN, L. W.: Effects of maternal employment on the child. *Child Develpm.*, 1961, **32**, 187–197.

(136) HOFFMAN, L. W.: The father's role in the family and the child's peer-group adjustment. *Merrill-Palmer Quart.*, 1961, **7**, 97–105.

(137) HOFFMAN, L. W., S. ROSEN, and R. LIPPITT: Parental coerciveness, child autonomy, and child's role at school. *Sociometry*, 1960, **23**, 15–22.

(138) ILG, F. L., J. LEARNED, A. LOCKWOOD, and L. B. AMES: The three-and-a-half-year-old. *J. genet. Psychol.*, 1949, **75**, 21–31.

(139) ISCH, M. J.: Fantasied mother-child interaction in doll play. *J. genet. Psychol.*, 1952, **81**, 233–258.

(140) ITKIN, W.: Relationships between attitudes toward parents and parents' attitudes toward children. *J. genet. Psychol.*, 1955, **86**, 339–352.

(141) JERSILD, A. T.: *Child psychology*, 5th ed. Englewood Cliffs, N.J.: Prentice-Hall, 1960.

(142) JOHNSON, P. P.: Conceptions of parenthood held by adolescents. *J. abnorm. soc. Psychol.*, 1952, **47**, 783–789.

(143) JOSSELYN, I. M.: Psychological changes in adolescence. *Children*, 1959, **6**, 43–47.

(144) KAGAN, J., B. HOSKEN, and S. WATSON: Child's symbolic conceptualization of parents. *Child Develpm.*, 1961, **32**, 625–636.

(145) KAGAN, J., and J. LEMKIN: The child's differential perception of parental attributes. *J. abnorm. soc. Psychol.*, 1960, **61**, 440–447.

(146) KATES, S. L.: Suggestibility, submission to parents and peers, and extrapunitiveness and impunitiveness in children. *J. Psychol.*, 1951, **31**, 233–241.

(147) KAVANAGH, G.: The influence of a stepmother's motivation in marriage upon her stepchild's symptom formation. *Smith Coll. Stud. soc. Wk*, 1961, **32**, 65–66.

(148) KENT, D. P.: Subjective factors in mate selection—an exploratory study. *Sociol. soc. Res.*, 1951, **35**, 391–398.

(149) KINSEY, A. C., W. B. POMEROY, C. E. MARTIN, and P. H. GEBHARD: *Sexual behavior in the human female*. Philadelphia: Saunders, 1953.

(150) KLAPP, O. E.: Ritual and family solidarity. *Soc. Forces*, 1959, **37**, 212–214.

(151) KLATSKIN, E. H., E. B. JACKSON, and L. C. WILKIN: The influence of degree of flexibility in maternal child care practices on early child behavior. *Amer. J. Orthopsychiat.*, 1956, **26**, 79–93.

(152) KOCH, H. L.: The relation of certain formal attributes of siblings to attitudes held toward each other and toward their parents. *Monogr. Soc. Res. Child Develpm.*, 1960, **25**, No. 4.

(153) KOCH, M. B.: Anxiety in preschool children from broken homes. *Merrill-Palmer Quart.*, 1961, **7**, 225–231.

(154) KOGAN, N., and F. C. SHELTON: Images of "old people" and "people in general" in an older sample. *J. genet. Psychol.*, 1962, **100**, 3–21.

(155) KOGAN, N., and F. C. SHELTON: Beliefs about "old people": a comparative study of older and younger samples. *J. genet. Psychol.*, 1962, **100**, 93–111.

(156) KOHN, M. L., and E. E. CARROLL: Social class and the allocation of parental responsibilities. *Sociometry*, 1960, **23**, 372–392.

(157) KOLLER, M. R.: Studies of three-generation households. *Marriage fam. Liv.*, 1954, **16**, 203–206.

(158) KOPPITZ, E. M.: Relationships between some background factors and children's interpersonal attitudes. *J. genet. Psychol.*, 1957, **91**, 119–129.

(159) LANDIS, P. H.: Sequential marriage. *J. home Econ.*, 1950, **42**, 625–627.

(160) LASKO, J. K.: Parent behavior toward first and second children. *Genet. Psychol. Monogr.*, 1954, **49**, 97–137.

(161) LAW, S.: The mother of the happy child. *Smith Coll. Stud. soc. Wk*, 1954, **25**, 1–27.

(162) LEMASTERS, E. E.: Social class mobility

and family integration. *Marriage fam. Liv.*, 1954, **16**, 226–232.

(163) LEVIN, H., and V. F. TURGEON: The influence of the mother's presence on children's doll play aggression. *J. abnorm. soc. Psychol.*, 1957, **55**, 304–308.

(164) LEVINSON, B. M.: Parental achievement drives for preschool children: the Vineland Social Maturity Scale and the Social Deviation Quotient. *J. genet. Psychol.*, 1961, **99**, 113–128.

(165) LEVY, D. M.: *Maternal overprotectiveness.* New York: Columbia, 1943.

(166) LEVY, D. M., and A. HESS: Problems in determining maternal attitudes toward newborn infants. *Psychiatry*, 1952, **15**, 273–286.

(167) LIVERANT, S.: MMPI differences between parents of disturbed and nondisturbed children. *J. consult. Psychol.*, 1959, **23**, 256–260.

(168) LIVSON, N., and P. H. MUSSEN: The relation of ego control to overt aggression and dependency. *J. abnorm. soc. Psychol.*, 1957, **55**, 66–71.

(169) LU, Y. C.: Parent-child relationships and marital roles. *Amer. sociol. Rev.*, 1952, **17**, 357–361.

(170) LYNN, D. B.: The husband-father role in the family. *Marriage fam. Liv.*, 1961, **23**, 295–296.

(171) LYNN, D. B., and W. L. SAWREY: The effects of father-absence on Norwegian boys and girls. *J. abnorm. soc. Psychol.*, 1959, **59**, 258–262.

(172) LYNN, R.: Personality characteristics of the mothers of aggressive and unaggressive children. *J. genet. Psychol.*, 1961, **99**, 159–164.

(173) MAAS, H. S.: Some social class differences in the family systems and group relations of pre- and early adolescents. *Child Develpm.*, 1951, **22**, 145–152.

(174) MACCOBY, E. E.: Children and working mothers. *Children*, 1958, **5**, 83–89.

(175) MACFARLANE, J., L. ALLEN, and M. P. HONZIK: *A developmental study of the behavior problems of normal children between twenty-one months and fourteen years.* Berkeley, Calif.: University of California Press, 1954.

(176) MADOFF, J. M.: The attitudes of mothers of juvenile delinquents toward child rearing. *J. consult. Psychol.*, 1959, **23**, 518–523.

(177) MARMOR, J.: Psychological trends in American family relationships. *Marriage fam. Liv.*, 1951, **13**, 145–147.

(178) MARSHALL, H. R.: Relations between home experiences and children's use of language in play interactions with peers. *Psychol. Monogr.*, 1961, **75**, No. 5.

(179) MARSHALL, J.: Children in the present world situation. *Amer. J. Orthopsychiat.*, 1953, **23**, 454–464.

(180) MATSUMOTO, M., and H. T. SMITH: Japanese and American children's perceptions of parents. *J. genet. Psychol.*, 1961, **98**, 83–88.

(181) MAXWELL, P. H., R. CONNOR, and J. WALTER: Family member perceptions of parent role performance. *Merrill-Palmer Quart.*, 1961, **7**, 31–37.

(182) MC CARTHY, D.: Language disorders and parent-child relationships. *J. speech hear. Disord.*, 1954, **19**, 514–523.

(183) MC CORD, W., J. MC CORD, and A. HOWARD: Familial correlates of aggression in nondelinquent male children. *J. abnorm. soc. Psychol.*, 1961, **62**, 79–93.

(184) MC FARLAND, M. B., and J. B. REINHART: The development of motherliness. *Children*, 1959, **6**, 48–52.

(185) MC GUIRE, C.: Conforming, mobile, and divergent families. *Marriage fam. Liv.*, 1954, **14**, 109–115.

(186) MC GUIRE, C., and G. D. WHITE: Social-class influences on discipline at school. *Educ. Leadership*, 1957, **14**, 229–231, 234–236.

(187) MEAD, M.: *Male and female.* New York: Morrow, 1952.

(188) MEAD, M.: Some theoretical considerations on the problem of mother-child separation. *Amer. J. Orthopsychiat.*, 1954, **24**, 471–483.

(189) MEDINNUS, G. R.: The relation between several parent measures and the child's early adjustment to school. *J. educ. Psychol.*, 1961, **52**, 153–156.

(190) MERRY, F. K., and R. V. MERRY: *The first two decades of life*, 2d ed. New York: Harper & Row, 1958.

(191) MOGEY, J. B.: Changes in family life experienced by English workers moving from slums to housing estates. *Marriage fam. Liv.*, 1955, **17**, 123–128.

(192) MONAHAN, T. P.: Broken homes by age of delinquent children. *J. soc. Psychol.*, 1956, **51**, 387–397.

(193) MONCUR, J. P.: Symptoms of maladjustment differentiating young stutterers from non-stutterers. *Child Develpm.*, 1955, **26**, 91–96.

(194) MONTAGUE, A.: Sex, order of birth and personality. *Amer. J. Orthopsychiat.*, 1948, **18**, 351–353.

(195) MORRIS, W. W., and A. L. NICHOLAS: Intra-family personality configurations among children with primary behavior disorders and their parents: a Rorschach investigation. *J. clin. Psychol.*, 1950, **6**, 309–319.

(196) MORROW, W. R., and R. C. WILSON: Family relations of bright high-achieving and under-achieving high school boys. *Child Develpm.*, 1961, **32**, 501–510.

(197) MOSHER, D. L., and A. SCODEL: Relationships between ethnocentrism in children and the ethnocentrism and authoritarian rearing practices of their mothers. *Child Develpm.,* 1960, **31,** 369–376.

(198) MOSS, H. A., and J. KOGAN: Stability of achievement and recognition seeking behaviors from early childhood through adulthood. *J. abnorm. soc. Psychol.,* 1961, **62,** 504–513.

(199) MOTT, S. M.: Concept of mother: study of four- and five-year-old children. *Child Develpm.,* 1954, **25,** 99–106.

(200) MUMMERY, D. V.: Family backgrounds of assertive and non-assertive children. *Child Develpm.,* 1954, **25,** 63–80.

(201) MUSSEN, P. H., and L. DISTLER: Child-rearing antecedents of masculine identification in kindergarten boys. *Child Develpm.,* 1960, **31,** 89–100.

(202) NEWTON, N.: *Maternal emotions.* New York: Hoeber-Harper, 1955.

(203) NICHOLS, R. C.: A factor analysis of parental attitudes of fathers. *Child Develpm.,* 1962, **33,** 791–802.

(204) NYE, F. I.: The rejected parent and delinquency. *Marriage fam. Liv.,* 1956, **18,** 291–300.

(205) NYE, I.: Adolescent-parent adjustment: age, sex, sibling number, broken homes, and employed mothers as variables. *Marriage fam. Liv.,* 1952, **14,** 327–332.

(206) O'CONNOR, N.: The evidence for the permanently disturbing effects of mother-child separation. *Acta psychol.,* 1956, **12,** 174–197.

(207) PERRY, J. B.: The mother substitutes of employed mothers: an exploratory inquiry. *Marriage fam. Liv.,* 1961, **23,** 362–367.

(208) PETERSON, D. R., W. C. BECKER, L. A. HELLMER, D. J. SHOEMAKER, and H. C. QUAY: Parental attitudes and child adjustment. *Child Develpm.,* 1959, **30,** 119–130.

(209) PETERSON, D. R., W. C. BECKER, D. J. SHOEMAKER, Z. LURIA, and L. A. HELLMER: Child behavior problems and parental attitudes. *Child Develpm.,* 1961, **32,** 151–162.

(210) PFEIFFER, M. S., and D. D. SCOTT: Factors in family happiness and unity. *J. home Econ.,* 1952, **44,** 413–414.

(211) PHILLIPS, E. L.: Parent-child similarities in personality disturbances. *J. clin. Psychol.,* 1951, **7,** 188–190.

(212) PODOLSKY, E.: The father's occupation and the child's emotions. *Understanding the Child,* 1954, **23,** 22–25.

(213) PODOLSKY, E.: The emotional problems of the stepchild. *Ment. Hyg., N.Y.,* 1955, **39,** 49–53.

(214) POFFENBERGER, T.: A research note on father-child relations and father viewed as a negative figure. *Child Develpm.,* 1959, **30,** 489–492.

(215) PORTER, B. M.: The relationship between marital adjustment and parental acceptance of children. *J. home Econ.,* 1955, **47,** 157–164.

(216) POWELL, K. S.: Maternal employment in relation to family life. *Marriage fam. Liv.,* 1961, **23,** 350–355.

(217) POWELL, M.: Age and sex differences in degree of conflict within certain areas of psychological adjustment. *Psychol. Monogr.,* 1955, **69,** No. 2.

(218) PRESSEY, S. L., and A. W. JONES: 1923–1953 and 20–60 age changes in moral codes, anxieties, and interests, as shown by the "X-O Tests." *J. Psychol.,* 1955, **39,** 485–502.

(219) PURCELL, K.: A method of assessing aspects of parent-child relationships. *Child Develpm.,* 1962, **33,** 537–553.

(220) RADKE, M. J.: *The relation of parental authority to children's behavior and attitudes.* Minneapolis: The University of Minnesota Press, 1946.

(221) RADKE-YARROW, M., P. SCOTT, L. DE LEEUW, and C. HEINIG: Child-rearing in families of working and nonworking mothers. *Sociometry,* 1962, **25,** 122–140.

(222) RAMSEY, C. E., and L. NELSON: Changes in values and attitudes toward the family. *Amer. sociol. Rev.,* 1956, **21,** 605–609.

(223) RAND, W., M. E. SWEENEY, and E. L. VINCENT: *Growth and development of the young child,* 6th ed. Philadelphia: Saunders, 1958.

(224) RAPP, D. W.: Child-rearing attitudes of mothers in Germany and the United States. *Child Develpm.,* 1961, **32,** 669–678.

(225) REXFORD, E. N., and S. T. VAN AMEROGNEN: The influence of unsolved maternal oral conflicts upon impulsive acting out in young children. *Amer. J. Orthopsychiat.,* 1957, **27,** 75–87.

(226) RHEINGOLD, H. L.: The modification of social responsiveness in institutional babies. *Monogr. Soc. Res. Child Develpm.,* 1956, **21,** No. 2.

(227) RHEINGOLD, H. L.: The measurement of maternal care. *Child Develpm.,* 1960, **31,** 565–575.

(228) RIBBLE, M. A.: *The personality of the young child.* New York: Columbia, 1955.

(229) ROBERTSON, W. O.: An investigation of maternal concerns by mail survey. *Child Develpm.,* 1961, **32,** 423–436.

(230) ROE, A.: Early determinants of vocational choice. *J. counsel. Psychol.,* 1957, **4,** 212–217.

(231) ROSE, A. A.: The homes of homesick girls. *J. child Psychiat.* 1948, **1,** 181–189.

(232) ROSEN, B. C.: Race, ethnicity, and achievement syndrome. *Amer. sociol. Rev.,* 1959, **24,** 47–60.

(233) ROSENTHAL, M. J., M. FINKELSTEIN, E. NI, and R. E. ROBERTSON: A study of mother-child relationships in the emotional disorders of children. *Genet. Psychol. Monogr.,* 1959, **60,** 65–116.

(234) ROUMAN, J.: School children's problems as related to parental factors. *J. educ. Res.,* 1956, **50,** 105–112.

(235) ROY, K.: Parents' attitudes toward their children. *J. home Econ.,* 1950, **42,** 652–653.

(236) RUSSELL, I. C.: Behavior problems of children from broken and intact homes. *J. educ. Sociol.,* 1957, **31,** 124–129.

(237) RYERSON, A. J.: Medical advice on child rearing, 1550–1900. *Harv. educ. Rev.,* 1961, **31,** 302–323.

(238) SCHAEFER, E. S., and N. BAYLEY: Consistency of maternal behavior from infancy to preadolescence. *J. abnorm. soc. Psychol.,* 1960, **61,** 1–6.

(239) SCHRAMM, W., J. LYLE, and E. B. PARKER: *Television in the lives of our children.* Stanford, Calif.: Stanford University Press, 1961.

(240) SCHWARTZ, E. K.: A psychoanalytic study of the fairy tale. *Amer. J. Psychother.,* 1956, **10,** 740–762.

(241) SEARS, R. R.: Ordinal position in the family as a psychological variable. *Amer. sociol. Rev.,* 1950, **15,** 397–401.

(242) SEARS, R. R., E. E. MACCOBY, and H. LEVIN: *Patterns of child rearing.* New York: Harper & Row, 1957.

(243) SECORD, P. F., and S. M. JOURARD: Mother-concepts and judgments of young women's faces. *J. abnorm. soc. Psychol.,* 1956, **52,** 246–250.

(244) SENN, M. J. E.: A relook at the effects of maternal deprivation. *Children,* 1962, **9,** 237–239.

(245) SEROT, N. M., and R. C. TEEVAN: Perception of the parent-child relationship and its relation to child adjustment. *Child Develpm.,* 1961, **32,** 373–378.

(246) SEWELL, W. H., P. H. MUSSEN, and C. M. HARRIS: Relationships among child training practices. *Amer. sociol. Rev.,* 1955, **20,** 137–148.

(247) SHANE, H. G.: Children's interests. *NEA J.,* 1957, **46,** 237–239.

(248) SHARP, L. J.: Employment status of mothers and some aspects of mental illness. *Amer. sociol. Rev.,* 960, **25,** 714–717.

(249) SHELDON, W. D., and L. CARRILLO: Relation of parents, home, and certain developmental characteristics to children's reading ability. *Elem. Sch. J.,* 1952, **52,** 262–270.

(250) SHELDON, W. D., and W. C. CUTTS: Relation of parents, home, and certain developmental characteristics to children's reading ability. II. *Elem. Sch. J.,* 1953, **53,** 517–521.

(251) SHERE, M. O.: Socio-emotional factors in families of the twin with cerebral palsy. *Except. Children,* 1956, **22,** 197–199.

(252) SHOBEN, E. J.: The assessment of parental attitudes in relation to child adjustment. *Genet. Psychol. Monogr.,* 1949, **39,** 101–148.

(253) SIEGEL, A. E., L. M. STOLZ, E. A. HITCHCOCK, and J. ADAMSON: Dependence and independence in the children of working mothers. *Child Develpm.,* 1959, **30,** 533–546.

(254) SLATER, P. E.: Parental behavior and the personality of the child. *J. genet. Psychol.,* 1962, **101,** 53–68.

(255) SLOMAN, S. S.: Emotional problems in "planned for" children. *Amer. J. Orthopsychiat.,* 1948, **18,** 523–528.

(256) SMITH, W. C.: Remarriage and the stepchild. In M. Fishbein and R. J. R. Kennedy (Eds.), *Modern marriage and family living.* Fair Lawn, N.J.: Oxford University Press, 1957. Pp. 457–475.

(257) SOFMAN, A.: Clinical manifestations of poor mother-child relationships. *Smith Coll. Stud. soc. Wk,* 1949, **19,** 107–108.

(258) STAPLES, F. R., and R. H. WALTERS: Anxiety, birth order, and susceptibility to social influence. *J. abnorm. soc. Psychol.,* 1961, **62,** 716–719.

(259) STAPLES, R., and G. W. SMITH: Attitudes of grandmothers and mothers toward child-rearing practices. *Child Develpm.,* 1954, **25,** 91–97.

(260) STENDLER, C. B.: Critical periods in socialization and overdependency. *Child Develpm.,* 1952, **23,** 3–12.

(261) STENDLER, C. B.: Possible causes of overdependency in young children. *Child Develpm.,* 1954, **25,** 127–146.

(262) STENDLER, C. B.: The learning of certain secondary drives by Parisian and American children. *Marriage fam. Liv.,* 1954, **16,** 195–200.

(263) STEPHENS, W. N.: Judgments by social workers on boys and mothers in fatherless families. *J. genet. Psychol.,* 1961, **99,** 59–64.

(264) STERNBERG, H.: Fathers who apply for child guidance. *Smith Coll. Stud. soc. Wk,* 1951, **22,** 53–68.

(265) STITH, M., and R. CONNOR: Dependency and helpfulness in young children. *Child Develpm.,* 1962, **33,** 15–20.

(266) STÖCKLE, O.: The family with many children and its significance for social education. *Heilpädag. Werkbl.,* 1954, **23,** 144–149.

(267) STOLZ, H. R., and L. M. STOLZ: *Somatic development of adolescent boys.* New York: Macmillan, 1951.

(268) STOLZ, L. M.: Effects of maternal employment on children: evidence from research. *Child Develpm.,* 1960, **31,** 749–782.

(269) STOLZ, L. M., et al.: *Father relations with war-born children.* Standford, Calif.: Stanford University Press, 1954.

(270) STOODLEY, B. H.: Mother role as focus of

some family problems. *Marriage fam. Liv.*, 1952, **14**, 13–16.

(271) STOTT, L. H., and M. P. BERSON: Some changes in attitudes resulting from a preparental education program. *J. soc. Psychol.*, 1951, **34**, 191–202.

(272) STOUT, I. W., and G. LANGDON: A report on follow-up interviews with parents of well-adjusted children. *J. educ. Sociol.*, 1953, **26**, 434–442.

(273) STRAUSS, B. V.: The dynamics of ordinal position effects. *Quart. J. child Behav.*, 1951, **3**, 133–145.

(274) STRECKER, E. A.: *Their mothers' sons.* Philadelphia: Lippincott, 1946.

(275) STRYKER, S.: Relationships of married offspring and parent. *Amer. J. Sociol.*, 1956, **62**, 308–319.

(276) STUBBEFIELD, R. L.: Children's emotional problems aggravated by family moves. *Amer. J. Orthopsychiat.*, 1955, **25**, 120–126.

(277) SUSSMAN, M. B.: Family continuity: selective factors which affect relationship between families at generational levels. *Marriage fam. Liv.*, 1954, **16**, 112–120.

(278) SYMONDS, P. M.: *The dynamics of parent-child relationship.* New York: Teachers College, Columbia University, 1949.

(279) TASCH, R. J.: The role of the father in the family. *J. exp. Educ.*, 1952, **20**, 319–361.

(280) TASCH, R. J.: Interpersonal perceptions of fathers and mothers. *J. genet. Psychol.*, 1957, **87**, 59–65.

(281) TEAGARDEN, F. M.: *Child psychology for professional workers,* rev. ed. Englewood Cliffs, N.J.: Prentice-Hall, 1946.

(282) TERMAN, L. M., and M. H. ODEN: *The gifted child grows up.* Stanford, Calif.: Stanford University Press, 1947.

(283) TUCKMAN, J., and I. LORGE: Attitude toward aging of individuals with experience with the aged. *J. genet. Psychol.*, 1958, **92**, 199–204.

(284) TUCKMAN, J., I. LORGE, and G. A. SPOONER: The effect of family environment on attitudes toward old people and the older worker. *J. soc. Psychol.*, 1953, **38**, 207–218.

(285) TUMA, E., and N. LIVSON: Family socio-economic status and adolescent attitudes to authority. *Child Develpm.*, 1960, **31**, 387–399.

(286) TURNER, R. H.: Children and women's work. *Sociol. soc. Res.*, 1952, **36**, 377–381.

(287) TYLER, F. B., J. E. RAFFERTY, and B. B. TYLER: Relationships among motivations of parents and their children. *J. genet. Psychol.*, 1962, **101**, 69–81.

(288) TYLER, L. E.: The development of "vocational interests": I. The organization of likes and dislikes in ten-year-old children. *J. genet. Psychol.*, 1955, **86**, 33–34.

(289) U.N. Report: *Children deprived of normal home life.* New York: United Nations, 1952.

(290) VINCENT, C. E.: The loss of parents and psychosomatic illness. *Social. soc. Res.*, 1955, **39**, 404–408.

(291) VINCENT, C. E.: The adoption market and the unwed mother's baby. *Marriage fam. Liv.*, 1956, **18**, 124–127.

(292) VON MERING, F. H.: Professional and non-professional women as mothers. *J. soc. Psychol.*, 1955, **42**, 21–34.

(293) WALLACH, M. A., D. N. ULRICH, and M. B. GRUNEBAUM: Relationship of family disturbance to cognitive difficulties in a learning-problem child. *J. consult. Psychol.*, 1960, **24**, 355–360.

(294) WALLER, W., and R. HILL: *The family: a dynamic interpretation.* New York: Holt, 1951.

(295) WALLIN, P.: Marital happiness of parents and their children's attitudes to marriage. *Amer. sociol. Rev.*, 1954, **19**, 20–23.

(296) WALLIN, P., and R. P. RILEY: Reactions of mothers to pregnancy and adjustment of offspring in infancy. *Amer. J. Orthopsychiat.*, 1950, **20**, 616–622.

(297) WALSH, A. M.: *Self-concepts of bright boys with learning difficulties.* New York: Teachers College, Columbia University, 1956.

(298) WATSON, J. B.: *Psychological care of infant and child.* New York: Norton, 1928.

(299) WATTENBERG, W. W.: *The adolescent years.* New York: Harcourt, Brace & World, 1955.

(300) WEIL, M. W.: An analysis of the factors influencing married women's actual or planned work participation. *Amer. sociol. Rev.*, 1961, **26**, 91–96.

(301) WEINSTEIN, E. A.: Children's conceptions of occupational stratification. *Sociol. soc. Res.*, 1958, **42**, 278–284.

(302) WILLIAMSON, R. C.: Socio-economic factors and marital adjustment in an urban setting. *Amer. sociol. Rev.*, 1954, **19**, 213–216.

(303) WINCH, R. F.: Further data and observations on the Oedipus hypothesis: the consequences of an inadequate hypothesis. *Amer. sociol. Rev.*, 1951, **16**, 784–795.

(304) WINKELEY, R., K. JACKSON, O. A. FAUST, M. F. MURRAY, and E. G. CERMACK: Emotional reactions and behavior of children in the home. *J. Pediat.*, 1951, **38**, 476–481.

(305) WOLFENSTEIN, M.: Trends in infant care. *Amer. J. Orthopsychiat.*, 1953, **33**, 120–130.

(306) WOLFLE, H. M.: The import of the caress in modern child psychology. *Amer. Psychologist*, 1949, **4**, 249.

(307) WOODRUFF, A. D.: *Basic concepts of teaching.* San Francisco: Chandler, 1961.

(308) WRIGHT, H. F.: Psychological development in Midwest. *Child Develpm.*, 1956, **27**, 265–286.

(309) WYLIE, H. L., and R. A. DELGADO: A pattern of mother-son relationship involving the absence of the father. *Amer. J. Orthopsychiat.*, 1959, **29**, 644–649.

(310) YOUNG, K.: What strong family ties mean to our society. *Soc. Casewk*, 1953, **34**, 323–329.

(311) ZEMLICK, M. J., and R. I. WATSON: Maternal attitudes of acceptance and rejection during and after pregnancy. *Amer. J. Orthopsychiat.*, 1953, **23**, 570–584.

(312) ZUK, G. H., R. M. MILLER, J. B. BARTRAM, and F. KLING: Maternal acceptance of retarded children: a questionnaire study of attitudes and religious backgrounds. *Child Develpm.*, 1961, **32**, 525–540.

(313) ZUNICH, M.: Relationship between maternal behavior and attitudes toward children. *J. genet. Psychol.*, 1962, **100**, 155–165.

15

PERSONALITY

According to tradition, the child is a "chip off the old block." The implication behind this traditional belief is that personality is inherited and not subject to change. This belief was widely accepted for centuries. Few people recognized the possibility that the child was like the parent because he had identified himself with the parent and *imitated* him. Thus the role of learning in personality development was either ignored or given little attention.

Since the turn of the present century, with the growth of the testing movement, the spotlight of scientific attention has been turned on personality. The traditional belief about the dominant role of heredity has been largely abandoned; in its place has come evidence to show that learning plays a large and vital role. While it is true that even the most ardent environmentalists do not go so far as to deny the role of heredity completely, there is growing evidence that in personality, as in intelligence, physique, and other characteristics, the hereditary endowment is subject to change and modification.

There is also growing evidence that changes and modifications can best be made during the early, formative years of life. While there is no deadline after which learning cannot bring about modifications in hereditary trait, there is evidence that the sooner they are made, the easier it will be for the child and the more lasting the effects will be.

Popular recognition of the important role personality plays in successful adjustments to modern life has given strong impetus to the scientific study of personality. In simpler cultures, personality is of secondary importance in social relationships, but in higher cultures, where social life is more complex, personality has a "marketable value." As a result, it is highly prized and eagerly sought after by all who want to make a success in life. Today's parents and teachers put great emphasis on developing personality patterns in children which will help them to make satisfactory adjustments both to the present and to the future.

MEANING OF PERSONALITY

What, one may ask, is this highly valued quality that is labeled "personality"? The term *personality* comes from the Latin word *persona,* meaning "mask." Among the ancient Greeks, the actors wore masks to hide their identity and to enable them to represent the characters they were depicting in the play. This dramatic technique was later adopted by the Romans, and from them we get our modern term *personality.*

To the Romans, *persona* meant "as one appears to others," not as one actually is. The actor was creating, in the minds of the audience, an impression of the character he was depicting on the stage, not an impression of what he himself was. From this connotation of the word *persona,* our popular idea of personality as the effect one has on others has been derived. What a person is, how he thinks and feels, and what is included in his whole psychological makeup are, to a great extent, revealed through his behavior. Personality, then, is not one definite, specific attribute; rather, it is the "quality of the individual's total behavior" (349).

This popular concept of personality has two serious defects: First, it emphasizes only one aspect of the intricate pattern of personality—the *expressiveness* of the individual; and second, it emphasizes only the *objective* aspect of personality—its effect on other people—not the subjective or interior organization which is responsible for the expressive aspect (11, 293).

In judging the personality of another person, one judges on the basis of the way the person expresses his thoughts, feelings, and emotions in speech and actions. These may reveal his true personality, but, on the other hand, they may not. A young child, for example, may reveal his real self through what he says and does, but even before he reaches school age, he learns to cloak motives, thoughts, and feelings that are socially unacceptable and to act according to social expectations.

A child who suffers from feelings of inadequacy may learn that inadequacy is not highly valued, while self-confidence is. He therefore becomes self-confident, often to the point of being bombastic. Likewise, showing off by clowning is more often a cloak for feelings of inadequacy than an expression of feelings of adequacy or superiority.

Thus it is apparent that judgments based on what is manifest or observable may not be a true indication of the child's real personality. The "quality of his total behavior" may not tell the true story of what the child's concept of himself is and what his real motives are—motives that have been cloaked in socially acceptable speech and actions.

Emphasis on the *objective* aspect of personality is a serious defect in defining personality because it fails to explain *why* the person speaks and acts as he does. It implies that there is a cause-and-effect relationship, *but the cause must be found through implication*—an implication that can readily be faulty if the individual has cloaked his actions to conform to social expectations. Inferring that a child is not afraid of a large dog may be correct, or it may not. Just because the child does not cry, run away and hide, or show any of the characteristic actions associated with fear is not positive proof that he is not afraid. He may have learned that it is regarded as babyish to show fear of dogs and that if he does so, he will be labeled a "fraidycat" by members of the peer group. Therefore, he stands his ground and tries to hide his fear in the hope that he will be judged as fearless—a quality highly valued by his peer group. *Only when attempts are made to discover the subjective or interior organization of his acts can one get a true picture of the child's real personality.*

Allport's Definition. Of the many proposed definitions of "personality," as it is viewed scientifically today, perhaps the most inclusive is that of Allport, who has defined personality as the *dynamic organization within* *the individual of those psychophysical systems that determine his unique adjustments to his environment* (11). The term "dynamic" points up the changing nature of personality; it emphasizes that changes can and do occur in the quality of a person's behavior. "Organization" implies that personality is not made up of a number of different traits, one added to the other, but that they are interrelated. This interrelationship changes, with some traits becoming more dominant and others less so with changes in the child and in his environment.

The "psychophysical systems" are the habits, attitudes, values, beliefs, emotional states, sentiments, and motives which are psychological in nature but which have a physical basis in the child's neural, glandular, and general bodily states. These systems are not the product of heredity, though they are based on hereditary foundations; they have been developed through learning as a result of the child's experiences.

The psychophysical systems are the *motivating forces* which determine what type of adjustment the child will make. Because each child has different learning experiences, the type of adjustment he will make is "unique" in the sense that no other child, even an identical twin, will react in exactly the same manner. Furthermore, because the psychophysical systems are the product of learning, the traditional belief that personality traits are inherited is refuted.

THE PERSONALITY PATTERN

Personality is made up of many components, some of which are *objective*—observable and measurable—and others of which are *subjective* and therefore less easily studied and measured. Among the objective components of personality are physical characteristics, such as body size and physique and factors in the mechanics and chemistry of the body which influence the speed and strength of movements; aptitudes and talents, both physical and intellectual; and traits, habits, behavior patterns, and modes of action. The subjective components of personality include motives, aspirations, feelings, ideas, and attitudes regarding self, convictions, commitments, and purposes that give direction to the individual's way of thinking, feeling, and acting (146).

The personality pattern is made up of *traits,* or specific qualities of behavior organized and integrated into a whole. These consist of reactions to frustrations, ways of meeting problems, aggressive and defensive behavior, and outgoing or withdrawing attitudes toward other people (166). The "core," or "center of gravity," of this pattern is the *concept of self*—the picture the individual holds of himself, his abilities, his characteristics, his worth, and his relations to the world about him.

The distinction between the normal and the abnormal personality pattern is to be found in the degree of organization that exists. The normal, healthy personality is a highly correlative, structured pattern; the abnormal personality shows disorganization in varying degrees. The severity of the abnormality is directly related to the degree of disorganization (59, 271, 293).

DEVELOPMENT OF THE PERSONALITY PATTERN

Three factors are responsible for the development of the personality pattern: the hereditary endowment, early experiences within the family, and events in later life. The pattern is inwardly determined and closely associated with the maturation of the physical and mental characteristics which constitute the individual's *hereditary endowment.* While environmental factors determine the form the personality pattern takes, it is not controlled from without but evolves from the potentials within the individual (6, 22). The importance of the hereditary foundations in determining the form the personality pattern will take has been stressed thus by Rainwater:

Personality is formed from the interaction of significant figures (first the mother, later the father and siblings, later extra familiar figures) in his environment with the child.

The child brings to this interaction a certain biological constitution, certain needs and drives, and certain intellectual capacities which determine his reactions to the way in which he is acted upon by these significant figures (236).

Learning plays an important role in the development of the personality pattern. Attitudes toward self and characteristic methods of responding to people and situations—the traits of personality—are learned through repetition and the satisfaction they bring. Gradually, the pattern forms around the self-concept. The traits, like the spokes of a wheel, are integrated with the "core" of this pattern—the self-concept. Because of this interrelationship, the self-concept has a strong influence on the behavior the child uses in his attempts to adjust to people and situations in his environment.

Social pressures from the home, the school, and the peer group have a marked influence on the form the traits will take. When aggressiveness is encouraged, for example, because it is considered a sex-appropriate trait for boys, the boy will try to learn to behave in an aggressive manner. If attempts to learn to react aggressively fail, either because the child is punished or because he does not have the strength to compete with others, he is likely to learn to react by using defense mechanisms, such as a "conquering-hero" daydream or a verbal attack.

COMPONENTS OF THE PERSONALITY PATTERN

The two major components of the personality pattern are the "core," or concept of self, and the "spokes of the wheel"—the traits, which are held together and influenced by the core. The role each plays in the child's personality will be discussed briefly.

The Self-concept. Of the components of the personality pattern, the self-concept is unquestionably the more important because it is the "core" of the pattern and influences the form the different traits will take. The self-concept, which is a "composite of thoughts and feelings which constitutes a person's awareness of his individual existence, his conception of who and what he is," contains an image or picture that the individual holds of himself. This self-image has two aspects: the *physical* and the *psychological*. The physical self-image consists of the individual's concepts of his physical appearance and his concepts of the importance of all parts of his body in relation to his behavior and to the prestige they give him in the eyes of others. The psychological self-image consists of traits such as honesty, independence, and helplessness (85, 145).

The self-image is a "mirror image," determined largely by the nature of the individual's relations with others. The role or status the individual occupies in a group or in society thus influences the concept he holds of himself (150, 164). Figure 15–1 shows that the child's concept of himself as a person is a "mirror image" of what he *believes* significant people think of him.

Development of Concept of Self. The personality is organized around the various concepts of self, each of which has a definite sociocultural reference station or has resulted from the interaction of the individual and a specific sociocultural environment. The organization of these concepts of self is *hierarchical*. The first and most basic concept of self (the primary concept) is, as Glasner has pointed out, formed "within the womb of family relationships" (111). Other concepts of self (secondary concepts) are acquired in other group environments outside the home. These concepts may be favorable or unfavorable, and they have varying degrees of importance in the general concept of self (50, 75).

The primary self-concept usually influences the selection of situations in which secondary concepts of self are formed. How well integrated the primary and secondary concepts will be will depend upon the degree of continuity between the primary and secondary sociocultural environments. A child brought up in a home environment where he is the center of attention, for example, will have to change his concept of self in

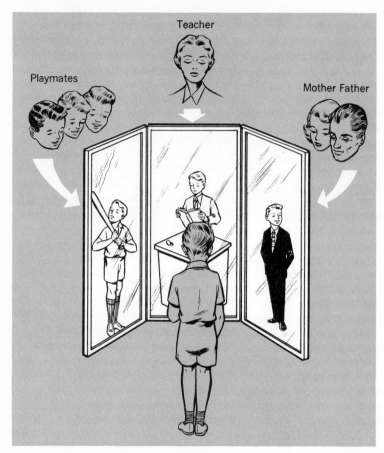

Figure 15-1. The child's concept of himself as a person is a mirror image of what he *believes* significant people in his life think of him.

environments outside the home, where his status will be markedly different. The degree of integration of primary and secondary selves will, in turn, affect the degree of adjustment the individual achieves (164).

The home environment is important in maintaining ego strength. Any break in the family may have serious effects on the child's concept of self. Not the parents alone but every member of the family group contributes to the child's developing concept of self (149, 187, 287). The relationships the child has with his parents and other family members are more influential than the experiences he shares with them.

Statements made by his parents—their praise or blame—contribute to the development of a concept of self. From this basic concept, the child develops further concepts of self. How people outside the home treat him, what they say about him, and what status he achieves in the group strengthen or modify the self-concept learned in the home environment (50, 57).

The child's relationships with people outside the home are more important than the experiences he shares with those in the home. Figure 15–2 shows the various influences that affect the child's concept of self. By the time the child reaches adolescence, the self-image is firmly established, though it may be revised later as the individual undergoes new social experiences (51, 293).

Concept of "Ideal Self." Every child has an *ideal self*, which is generally a concept built up from contacts with people, from reading, and from movies or television

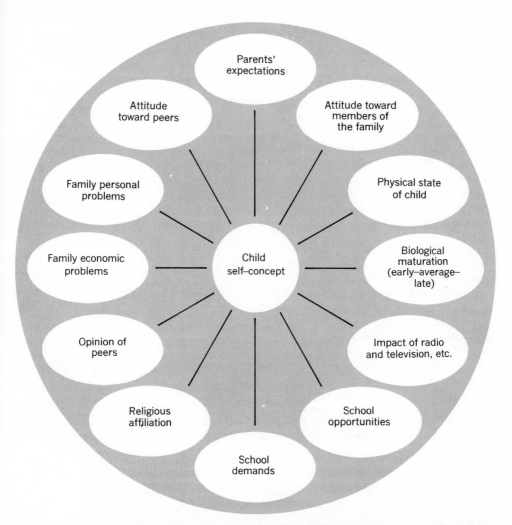

Figure 15-2. The impact of environmental influences on the developing self-concept in childhood. (Adapted from L. D. Crow and A. Crow, *Child development and adjustment*, Macmillan, 1962. Used by permission.)

shows. Very few children are satisfied with themselves as they are. The ideal self thus fills a need and acts as a guide to behavior (54, 258, 308).

Studies have shown that the child's ideal changes as he grows older and that his experiences outside the home influence the direction of change. For the most part, the ideal comes from the child's immediate environment and is derived from his contacts,

either directly or indirectly, with people he admires and would like to resemble.

The young child first selects as his ideal a parent or some member of the family. By the time he reaches the second grade and his contacts have broadened, his ideal is his teacher or some acquaintance outside the home or school. Many of these early ideals are used in the child's dramatic play. From then on, there is an increasing interest in ideals from remote sources, such as history, contemporary affairs, movies, television, or even the comics (18, 112, 127, 222, 339).

As the child approaches adolescence, his ideal is likely to be a young adult whom he admires, such as an athlete, a movie actor or actress, or a politician. Very few ideals are taken from literature, fiction, or religion; they are far more likely to come from television, movies, or the world of sports, and they are almost always American (127, 306).

Boys choose more ideals from remote environments at every age than girls; they idealize those who have important roles and status in society, especially athletes, scientists, and politicians. Girls, by contrast, generally idealize people who have made a success in social life or who are attractive in appearance, such as movie stars or members of foreign royalty. As the child grows older, association with people in positions of prestige has a marked influence on his choice of ideal (112, 129).

Boys who come from the higher socioeconomic groups more often idealize their fathers than boys from the lower groups, while girls from both groups usually select an ideal from outside the home. Not until adolescence does class-consciousness play an important role in the child's selection of his ideal (54, 266).

The child combines the qualities of his parents with those of outsiders and builds up a *composite* picture of the ideal self. Older children and adolescents have very specific ideas about what they would like to be and how they would like to change themselves (56, 346).

The child's ideal represents the values in his culture that appeal most to him. In his attempt to imitate his ideal, the child accepts these values as his own; they serve as models for his behavior. While the child's values change as he grows older, certain values remain constant from age to age (54, 187). Figure 15–3 shows changes in values from the fourth to the sixth grades. The child's sex likewise plays an important part in determining the values and the ideal he will select. Children almost always select ideals of their own sex (56, 196).

Influence of the Self-concept. Because the self-concept is the core of the personality pattern and, as such, influences the quality of the child's behavior, it plays a role of major significance in determining the type of adjustments the child will make. A *stable* self-concept, in which there is integration of

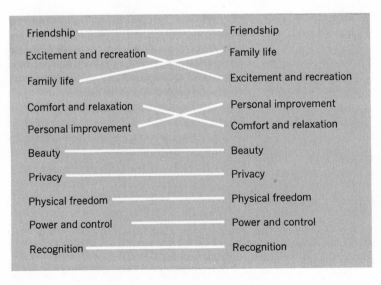

Friendship ——————— Friendship

Excitement and recreation ⤬ Family life

Family life ⤬ Excitement and recreation

Comfort and relaxation ⤬ Personal improvement

Personal improvement ⤬ Comfort and relaxation

Beauty ——————— Beauty

Privacy ——————— Privacy

Physical freedom ——————— Physical freedom

Power and control ——————— Power and control

Recognition ——————— Recognition

Figure 15-3.
Changes in values with increasing age. (Adapted from G. R. Hawkes, A study of personal values of elementary-school children, *Educ. psychol. Measmt,* 1952, 12, 654–663. Used by permission.)

the primary selves formed early in life and the secondary selves formed later, will lead to far better adjustment than an unstable self-concept. As was pointed out earlier, consistency of treatment in the home and continuity between the home and the outside environments are necessary for the development of a stable self-concept. Stability likewise requires that the child's real self and his ideal self be quite similar (50, 72, 75).

A stable self-concept may be composed mainly of positive or negative concepts, depending on the type of treatment the child has received from others in the home, where the primary self-concepts are formed. If the self-concept is composed mainly of positive concepts, the child will develop self-confidence, a high level of self-esteem, few feelings of inferiority and inadequacy, the ability to see himself realistically, and little compensatory behavior of a defensive sort, such as shyness and withdrawal. As a result, the child will make better social adjustments, will enjoy greater social acceptance, and will be more active in social groups, all of which will lead to more positive secondary self-concepts, which will reinforce the positive primary self-concepts.

If the self-concept is composed mainly of negative concepts, on the other hand, the child will make poor social adjustments; will experience feelings of uncertainty, inadequacy, and inferiority; and will use many defense mechanisms, all of which will reinforce the unfavorable primary self-concept developed in the home. At times of stress, such as adjustment to school or to death or divorce of the parents, the child with an unstable self-concept or a stable self-concept composed mainly of negative concepts will experience greater emotional reactions and make poorer adjustments than the child whose self-concept is more stable or whose self-concept is composed mainly of positive concepts (53, 59).

Instability of the self-concept is frequently caused by a marked discrepancy between the child's ideal self-concept and his real self-concept (221). Because of inexperience, the child tends to overestimate his capacities;

he is often encouraged by his parents to believe that he can do anything he wishes, as long as he tries hard enough. For the most part, the child's ideal is more an index of his "wishful estimate of his ability than of his real ability." As Jersild has pointed out, "The idealized image of the self clashes with reality for there is something false about it—it is out of gear with the 'real self' that might have developed; it is burdensome for a person to live up to this assumed role, to keep the pose, to live as if he were or had to be something he is not cut out to be" (146).

If a child clings to a glamourized ideal for too long, he is in for trouble. Not only will he fall short of his ideal and thus feel frustrated and inadequate, but he may find himself out of step with his contemporaries. As ideals change frequently during the childhood years, a child who keeps an ideal self based on a parent or teacher may find that his friends regard him as immature (54). As Sherif and Cantril have said, "If the idol is a person out of the reference group, then the individual becomes a social misfit in his or her immediate surroundings" (272). Each year, the child should be able to appraise himself—his abilities and his disabilities—with greater accuracy. If he can accept this realistically appraised self, he will make good social adjustments. The poorly adjusted child, by comparison, either overestimates himself and finds in the group no opportunity for assuming the status he believes he deserves or feels inadequate and rebels against accepting the concept of himself which he realizes falls short of his ideal. When this happens, "the individual sets up defenses to preserve his present idea of himself. He rationalizes. He resists the impact of thoughts that would make it necessary for him to reexamine his self-concept" (308).

Most children cannot evaluate themselves accurately; they use a "self-halo" or tend to emphasize favorable traits and deemphasize unfavorable ones. Not until adolescence can self-evaluation be expected to become more accurate and less biased (29, 251).

Parents and teachers are seldom aware of

the kind of self-concept a child is developing, and few try to make sure that it will be both realistic and favorable enough that the child will be willing to accept himself. The seriousness of the haphazard, uncontrolled development of the self-concept in childhood has been pointed out by Jersild:

From an early age, without being deliberate about it, he (the child) acquires ideas and attitudes about himself and others. These are woven into the pattern of his life. They may be true or false, healthy or morbid. Their development is left largely to chance. . . . A large proportion of children will move into adulthood troubled and unhappy about many things. Many will be afflicted by irrational fears which do not represent dangers in the external environment but unresolved problems within themselves. Many, as adults, will suffer from attitudes of hostility, vindictiveness, and defensiveness which are not a response to hostile forces in the outside world but represent attitudes carried over from unresolved childhood struggles. Many persons similarly will acquire persisting feelings of inferiority or other unhealthy attitudes regarding their personal worth which represent either an irrational estimate of themselves or a failure to accept themselves realistically as they are. In numerous ways there is a vast carry-over of unhealthy attitudes regarding self and others from childhood and adolescence into adult life (144).

Traits. The second important component of the personality pattern is the personality traits. A *trait* may be described as an aspect or dimension of personality which consists of a group of related and consistent reactions characteristic of a person's typical adjustment. It is a learned tendency to evaluate situations in a predictable manner and to react in a manner in which the individual has reacted more or less successfully in the past to similar situations in which he was similarly motivated. Because traits are not added, one to another, but are integrated into the pattern in which the self-concept is the "core," they are influenced by the self-concept. A child who thinks of himself as inferior, for example, will develop characteristic methods of adjusting that will differ

markedly from those developed by the child whose concept of self is more favorable (11, 51, 271, 293).

Traits have two outstanding characteristics: individuality and consistency. *Individuality* refers not to the fact that each individual has certain traits that are peculiarly his own, but rather to the fact that he has his own individual "quantity" of a particular trait. As Woodworth has put it, "Traits are 'dimensions' of behavior in which individuals differ" (349). No child has a corner on generosity, bravery, or any other desirable personality trait; every child has these traits, but in varying degrees. Most people cluster around the average in different traits (293). This means that most children are about average in generosity, bravery, and sociability; the very generous, very brave, or very sociable child is as infrequently found as the very stingy, the very cowardly, or the very unsocial.

The second characteristic of all traits, *consistency,* means that a person behaves in approximately the same way in similar situations and under similar conditions. A child may be self-confident in a situation in which he has learned the necessary skills to make good adjustments, but in a situation in which he has had no previous experience, he may lack self-confidence or even show fear. Similarly, a child may be fretful, irritable, and unsocial at a family gathering if he is tired, but quite the opposite if he is rested. There is an underlying pattern of consistency in a person's characteristic adjustments to life, however, although it is, like individuality, a matter of degree (11, 293).

Development of Traits. Traits are a product of learning; at the same time, they are based on a hereditary foundation. They are molded mainly by child training in the home and school and by imitation of the person with whom the child identifies himself. If the child identifies himself with the father, he will imitate the father's characteristic methods of reacting to people and situations to the point where it appears that he inherited these characteristics. Later, he will imitate the traits of members of the peer group, developing the characteristic methods of adjustment accepted and approved by the group (48, 54, 178, 329).

Some personality traits are learned by trial and error. If a child discovers, more by chance than by imitation or direct teaching, that aggressiveness wins approval from the peer group or satisfies a need, he will repeat the aggressive behavior whenever a similar situation arises. In time, this will develop into his characteristic method of adjusting to frustrations, and he will be known as an "aggressive child" (106, 110). Similarly, if a child discovers that he makes better adjustments by being rigid and inflexible, he will in time develop a "rigid personality pattern"—a characteristic method of adjustment in which the child is emotionally disturbed unless things go the way he has become accustomed to having them go (3, 261).

Admired Personality Traits.   Every cultural group has its own values regarding traits that are considered desirable or undesirable.

Sooner or later, every child learns which traits fall in each category. He discovers that people who have the admired traits win social approval and acceptance, while those who have the undesirable traits are criticized, scorned, and rejected.

Furthermore, the child discovers as he grows older that not all people value traits in the same way. Parents, teachers, and other adults value certain traits more highly than members of the peer group do, and vice versa. He also discovers that there are sex-approved and social-class-approved traits. In spite of these variations, he learns, certain basic traits are honored by all cultural groups. Honesty, respect for others as people, respect for authority, and a sense of appreciation are universally approved (15, 295).

In his desire to win the approval of important people in his life, the child tries to develop personality traits that will conform to the standards of the group with which he wants to be identified. Young children, in the preschool years, are more anxious to

Young children are often more anxious to have the approval of adults than of their peers. (Standard Oil Co., N.J.)

have the approval of adults than of their peers. For that reason, they strive to develop personality traits that will win for them the adult recognition and approval that they crave. But, as they enter school and become group-conscious, they are far more interested in winning the approval of their peers. As a result, the standards of socially approved personality traits change; the child now attempts to develop those traits which his playmates will respect.

As children grow older, personality traits which were admired in little children are regarded as "babyish," and new traits take their place in the favor of the group. The submissive, quiet, docile child must develop more aggressive traits. If he wants the approval of his playmates, the child often feels that he must develop personality traits which are not admired or even condoned by adults. With the onset of puberty and the psychological changes which accompany it, new standards of admired personality traits arise (209, 329). Traits that are greatly admired in a boy are not admired in a girl. A boy who is sympathetic, kind, and thoughtful is admired by adults, but both boys and girls look upon him as a "sissy." The very traits that are condemned in a boy, however, are admired in girls, not only by other girls but

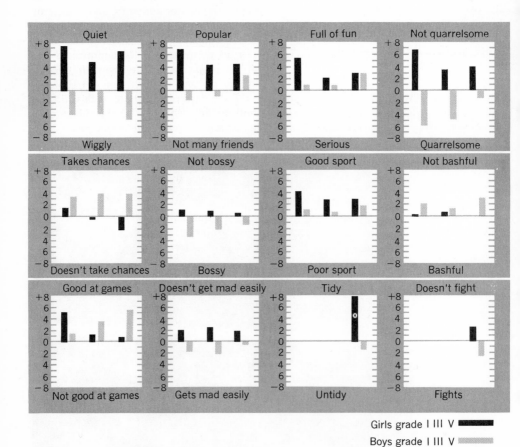

Figure 15-4. Children's concepts of "masculine" and "feminine" personality traits. (Adapted from R. D. Tuddenham, Studies in reputation. I. Sex and grade differences in school children's evaluation of their peers. II. The diagnosis of social adjustment, *Psychol. Monogr.*, 1952, 66, No. 1. Used by permission.)

also by boys. Similarly, an aggressive girl is labeled "bossy" by other children, but an aggressive boy is admired and is likely to assume the role of leadership.

By the time children enter school, concepts of "masculine" and "feminine" personalities are well established. The *typical girl* is judged to be quiet, popular, full of fun, a good sport, a "little lady," tidy, feminine, and modest. The *typical boy,* by contrast, is wiggly, quarrelsome, bossy, and a show-off. He takes chances, is not bashful, is good at games, and is a real boy. Thus, even in the primary grades, the pictures of a typical boy and a typical girl are almost photostats of adult concepts. These concepts are illustrated in Figure 15–4. Some revolutionary changes take place in the "most-admired-traits" lists of children, especially those of girls, between the ages of twelve and fifteen (56, 233, 282).

Various cultures value traits differently. A comparison of French and American children revealed that while children in both cultures develop personality patterns that are similar in major aspects, differences result because of the differences in values held by parents in the two cultures. For example, American children are encouraged to become independent sooner than French children; American children are encouraged to assume responsibility earlier; and sociability is not regarded as an important goal by the French, who stress individualism, while Americans emphasize conformity as essential to social acceptance (298).

The values held by members of a cultural group are used by adults as models in child-training methods. When American and English adults were asked to state what they thought constituted a properly brought-up child, the English adults stressed suppression of impulses which are socially disturbing, self-control, kindness to others, good manners, obedience, suppression of antisocial impulses, and self-reliance so that the individual will not be a burden to others.

The American pattern aimed at a smoothly functioning individual, equipped to get ahead with a varied armament of social skills, intelligence, geniality, good-natured-

For the emotionally secure child, going out into the world to encounter new experiences is an adventure, not a fear-provoking experience. (Standard Oil Co., N.J.)

ness, neatness, cleanliness, honesty, trustworthiness, straightforwardness, and sociability. In the American values, stress is on adjustment to other children, while in the English values, stress is on adjustment to adults (95).

PERSISTENCE AND CHANGE IN PERSONALITY

According to popular beliefs, based on the assumption that personality is a hereditary characteristic, personality persists in a relatively unchanged form throughout life. If any change occurs, it is likely to be a change for the better in young people and for the worse as people reach middle or old age. Changes in personality are attributed to physical changes. At puberty, for example, there is the change from the childish to the adult body; as this physical change is regarded as an improvement, the traditional belief holds that there will be an improvement in personality also. By contrast, the physical changes occurring at the time of the climacteric and with advancing age are regarded as forms of deterioration. The personality changes that are believed to accompany them are likewise believed to be changes for the worse. This point of view is shared by scientists to some extent. True, while they do not attribute these personality changes entirely to physical changes, they tend to regard periods when radical physical changes occur as "critical" periods in personality development (158, 328).

From a practical as well as from a theoretical angle, it is important to know just how persistent personality is, how much change one can expect, and when changes can best be made, should it become apparent that changes are essential to improve the child's adjustments. The practical aspects of this problem have been stressed by Roberts and Fleming:

To accept the idea that an individual is "born that way" and can do little about his personality characteristics breeds a defeatist attitude. On the other hand, to believe that an individual can make of himself what he will may hold out false hopes of rebirth. Educators and psychologists need, therefore, to know what the possibilities for modification are and at what stages in development modification is most possible. All people working in the field of guidance, whether they be teachers, parents, psychologists, ministers, or counsellors, need to be discriminating about what changes it is sound to work for in helping people solve their personality problems (244).

Meaning of Persistence. The term *persistence* means "enduring" and "constantly recurring"; *it does not mean that no change occurs.* It does mean, however, that there is a tendency for certain traits to remain in an unchanged, or relatively unchanged, form, even when training and social pressure have been operative. As Allport has stressed,

the "important fact about personality is its relatively enduring and unique organization" (11).

A child who, as an infant, showed irritability would show the same trait as he grew older, even though his irritability were somewhat modified and toned down as a result of environmental pressures. Likewise, a happy, good-natured child would remain cheerful, even in the face of adversity, if persistence were characteristic of different traits. As Landis has pointed out, however, "The evidence is convincing that personality is not fixed at three months, three years, ten years, or fifty years. Personality grows and changes throughout life" (166).

While certain personality traits change as the child passes through certain kinds of experiences, "each personality preserves a central stability, a central core or focus or 'center of gravity' which does not change. Some personalities are far more flexible than others, and change radically under radical changes in environment; others have a 'granite-like' quality which withstands the impact even of the most radical changes of environment" (51). The center of gravity leads to stability in the personality in that it preserves a balance of traits within that personality pattern. Once this center of gravity is fixed, it does not change unless radical steps are taken to produce such a change.

In young children, the "core" of personality is not well established. It can therefore be changed without disturbing the total personality balance. But the personality becomes less flexible as the individual grows older, because of the larger and more fixed "core" of habits and attitudes, and any change will require a great deal of effort and pressure. Also, care will have to be taken to avoid disturbing the personality balance. That persistence has not been well established in the young child is stressed by Davis and Havighurst thus:

We do not believe, in short, that the early personality is as irrevocable as the crack of doom. There certainly is no reason for a fatalistic view concerning man's ability to break the mold of his childhood learning.

Admittedly, this learning often sets the pattern for many later responses toward people; even for one's lifelong estimate of oneself. But new situations and new stimuli will change not only a man's behavior—they will change his belief in himself. Men have been saved from despair, and vice, and from even the deep shadows of insanity by a change in their opportunities, by a chance to work, or to gain social distinction; by finding someone who loved them, and had faith in their ability and courage; by the birth of a son or daughter, and the new responsibility and hope which it brought (77).

"Critical Period" in Personality Development. As far back as the sixteenth century, St. Ignatius claimed that if he could control the teaching of the child during the first six years of his life, nothing then could undo his teaching. Freud and many of his adherents had a similar point of view. Today, scientists are asking, "When does personality development reach a point where there will be little change, and does this ever happen?" There is agreement, however, that the early years are the "critical" years in personality development; with each passing year, the changes grow less and are more difficult to make (164). There is also evidence that many mild to severe personality disorders have their origin in the early years and that the basic personality patterns are laid at this time (23, 131, 235). As Bain has stated:

This is the period when mother love is perverted into "smother love," when paternal guidance swings drunkenly between anarchic gratification and tyrannical denial. This is when parents first begin to violate that fundamental principle that children are also people and hence have a right both to privacy and social interaction. The parents often want to show off the child and thus make the child into a "show-off." They expect things from him beyond his capacity and insult his intelligence because they think he doesn't know anything. They cheat and lie in his presence and then whip him for cheating and lying. They do not discipline him at all, or they discipline him too excessively. Very often they do both. The child is confused and made insecure (30).

Personality in the early years of life is preindicative of the sort of individual the child will grow up to be. Between the second and third years, the child learns to become autonomous, or self-directive; or he remains dependent. If his demands for independence are not handled wisely, he will become overdependent or hostile and willful (91, 299).

In the early years of life, the *affective index*—or pleasantly toned reactions which affect the child's outlook on life—are set. These likes and dislikes are not the result of chance attachment to an immediate experience but are the outcome of experiences with specific and closely related stimuli in the past which have become generalized attitudes. Tryon and Henry have emphasized the meaning of early-learned attitudes:

The importance of these early learning experiences is the fact that basic attitudes toward human relationships in later life are begun at this time and are patterned after the feelings and attitudes which develop from these experiences. . . . The modes of adjustment learned earliest seem to be those learned most thoroughly. Henceforth, there is a strong tendency for the individual to react to subsequent experiences and to make his adolescent social adjustment much in the same manner as he has made his childhood adjustment. . . . Thus it is that the early relationships of the child with the parents mold the basic desires and purposes of adjustment and the techniques of adjustment. This basic personality serves as the groundwork and gives the basic direction to the modes of social and personal adjustment in later life (326).

Evidence of Persistence. Mention of persistence of personality traits was made in some of the early baby biographies (274, 350). In recent years, genetic studies of groups of children over a period of time have emphasized the persistence of personality patterns and have shown under what conditions changes occur. They have shown that while traits vary from year to year within a narrow range, they remain fairly consistent over a period of time.

This finding makes possible a prognosis of

the child's future personality even as early as the first year of life. As the child grows older, predominant modes of behavior become less conspicuous. *No child remains absolutely consistent with respect to predominant forms of behavior, nor are there any revolutionary changes.* Shifts are always in the direction of behavior that has been evident at an earlier age, though not in a pronounced form (51, 205).

One of the most interesting and most extensive studies of persistence in personality traits was made on a group of 25 babies, first by Shirley and later by Neilon. During the 2-year period when the babies were under constant observation and study, Shirley noted a good deal of consistency. For example, the babies showed a decrease in irritability as they grew older. Modifications in their behavior likewise were noted. A baby who was fearful and who screamed at one year was fearful at two, but the screaming was replaced by running away (275).

Fifteen and a half years after Shirley made her study, Neilon matched objective measurements of personality and new personality sketches for 15 of the original 25 "Shirley babies" with the original sketches written by Shirley. There was definite evidence that personality similarities had persisted over this period of time and that some of the individuals were readily identifiable because of the uniqueness of their personality patterns (212).

With puberty changes, changes also occur in the individual's personality. It is important, therefore, to determine whether patterns of personality, established during the childhood years, change as the individual emerges into adolescence or whether the personality pattern remains much the same as it was. Even in late adolescence, some fluctuation in traits may appear, but for the most part, early patterns are maintained. In general, undesirable traits tend to be less undesirable because of the adolescent's strong desire to conform to socially approved patterns (253, 293).

Studies have shown a persistence of dependent behavior from the early school years into adulthood. They have also shown a persistence of striving for achievement and social recognition through competence in intellectual or athletic attainments or through improved economic and cultural milieus. Dependent behavior, as shown in seeking help from others when under stress, was more persistent among girls and women than among men. On the other hand, persistence in striving for achievement and social recognition was greater among boys and men. The reason for these sex differences can be found in the differences in social pressures on the two sexes (153, 202).

After a person reaches adulthood, constancy of personality traits is greater than before among both the well adjusted and the poorly adjusted. A study of six individuals, rated on 35 personality traits 50 years after their mother had recorded judgments about them in her diary, revealed that there was a 70 per cent persistence in the traits after this long interval of time. There was a general trend toward improvement, with both favorable and unfavorable traits showing improvement (284).

A study of early- and late-maturing boys showed that the personality patterns, influenced by the treatment they received from adults and peers because of their physical status at puberty, persisted into the early thirties. Those who matured early were, as young men, responsible, enterprising, sociable, warm, persistent in working toward a goal, self-controlled, responsible, dominant, and able to create confidence in others. These characteristics were similar to those they had shown in adolescence. By contrast, the men who had matured late were touchy, rebellious, impulsive, self-indulgent, and assertive; they sought encouragement and help until a fuss was made over them whenever they were hurt. In general, their behavior was a carryover of the "little-boy behavior" of their adolescent years (19, 148, 209).

Studies of maladjusted people have revealed that unusual behavior in childhood often leads to personality disturbances in adulthood. Records of patients in mental hospitals have shown that the personality characteristics of psychotic patients have been stable since childhood. Those who are excitable as adults have been excitable since childhood, and those who are schizophrenic have been apathetic since they were young children (104, 168, 323). In short, childhood schizophrenics tend to grow up to be adult schizophrenics, even though the clinical manifestations and their intensity may change. Children who are problem children often grow up to be juvenile delinquents and adult criminals. Those who are so poorly adjusted that they are problems in school and in the home have been found to contribute a disproportionate share to such serious social problems as crime, homicide, and suicide (31, 105, 246).

Variation in Persistence. Some individuals show more constancy in personality patterns than others, and some traits are more constant than others. The *traits* that have been found to be most persistent are those associated with intelligence, physical development, and temperament; those showing the least persistence are related to social situations, such as introversion, extroversion, attitudes, and values. Among the traits that have been found to be the most stable and consistent are affection, ambition, conscientiousness, sympathy, bossiness, contrariness, carelessness, irritability, nervousness, spunkiness, quarrelsomeness, and strength of will; among the less persistent are self-confidence, bravery, exactness, perseverance, shyness, and quick temper (11, 158, 284).

There are *sex differences* in stability of personality traits. Among boys and men, aggression and the drive for achievement have been found to be more persistent, and in girls and women, dependency and the desire for social prestige. There is evidence that persistence is greater in behavior characteristics that are traditionally sex-appropriate for members of the two sexes than in those which are appropriate for both sexes (154). Figure 15–5 shows the correlations between behavior ratings for the same males and females in childhood and in adulthood.

In the personality pattern, there is greater persistence in the *self-concept* than in the specific personality traits, although the self-concept may be modified by the individual's experience (60, 202, 315, 329). As Breckenridge and Vincent have stated, "The greater inflexibility of the older personality is probably due to a larger and more fixed core of personal habits and attitudes which, like any habit, no matter how fixed, can be changed if sufficient emotional shock and continuous and strong enough pressure is brought to bear upon it." The "center of gravity" of the personality pattern preserves a balance of traits within this pattern and thus lends stability to it (51).

Explanation of Persistence. *Heredity* plays an important role in determining how persistent the personality pattern will be. Any trait that is related, either directly or indirectly, to the child's hereditary endowment will remain more stable over the years than a trait that has little relationship to hereditary endowment. Inherent differences result in individual responses to the same people and the same situations during the early months of babyhood and become increasingly more pronounced as children grow older (220, 275).

While the *method of child training* used influences the personality development of the child in the early years of his life, there is little evidence that the method, per se, has as permanent an effect on personality as the attitudes of the parents. The attitudes of parents and the method of child training are relatively persistent; thus the child's learning is reinforced, his patterns of behavior are well established, and his concept of self is firmly developed (42, 188, 260).

Parental values play an important role in determining what parents will expect their children to learn and what behavior they will reward and punish. If intellectual achievement is highly valued by parents, it will be rewarded. Striving-for-achievement behavior will be reinforced and will thus tend to be persistent. If it is not rewarded, it will be extinguished (153, 202).

The *social environment,* both in and out of the home, contributes greatly to the persistence of the personality pattern. Because of the child's dependency during the early years of life, his environment will re-

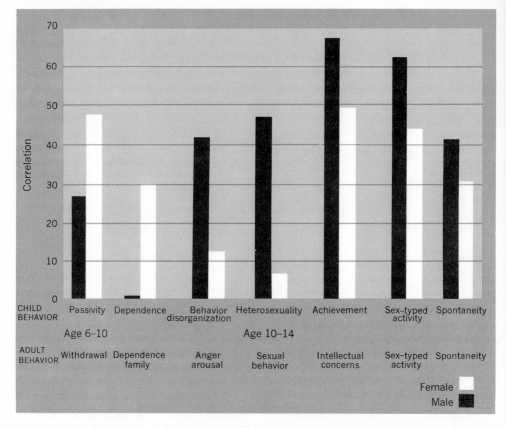

Figure 15-5. Some personality traits which show persistence from childhood into early adulthood. (Adapted from J. Kagan and H. A. Moss, *Birth to maturity: a study in psychological development,* Wiley, 1962. Used by permission.)

main that of the home or a substitute for the home. Furthermore, as was emphasized in the chapter on family relationships, the relationship of the child with the different family members is relatively stable. Therefore, during the early, formative years of the child's life, he learns to see himself as the members of the family see him and to adjust to life as they expect him to adjust. By the time his environment expands to include people outside the home, his concept of self will be well developed, and his personality traits will be well learned. In the family, every child is assigned a certain role which he is expected to play. This role is usually persistent, and the child learns to think of himself in terms of the role (47, 164, 299). Social pressures from the peer group rein-

force the learning that has taken place in the home, especially in relation to traits which are considered sex-appropriate. As a result, "for some children, the first four years of contact with the school and peer environments (i.e., during ages 6 to 10) crystallize behavioral tendencies which are maintained through young adulthood" (154).

The child's *personality pattern,* or some dominant trait in that pattern, tends to influence the behavior of the child and to determine what type of environment he will select when he is free to choose. A child who is friendly will select environments in which there are others; this constant association with others helps to increase and preserve his friendly attitude. The shy child, by contrast, will seek an environment of solitude; this increases his shyness (146).

Personality maladjustments, as was stressed earlier, are often the result of "circular behavior." When a child is punished and rejected, he learns to fear his parents. This fear is expressed in hostile behavior toward the parents; his hostility elicits counterpunishment and further rejection. Thus punishment gives rise to fear, fear promotes defensive reactions, and defensive reactions elicit further punishment and rejection—the "vicious circle of maladjustment." This circular behavior is seen in other forms of behavior also. Domination tends to elicit domination, and aggression is met with aggression. As a result, behavior patterns are reinforced and become so firmly established that they will be persistent unless steps are taken to break the "vicious circle" (79).

Should the child remain for a period of time in an environment which fosters the development of certain personality traits, especially during the early years of life, a change in environment at a later time may not be adequate to change the personality pattern. This has been illustrated in the case of adolescents who spent the early years of their lives in institutions where group routines fostered apathy, lack of ambition, restlessness, and uncontrolled emotionality. Even when placed in homes at a later age, these traits persisted (107, 214).

Studies of late maturers have revealed that an environment in which there are constant frustrations on the pubescent child's impulses fosters rebelliousness and sensitivity to threats of rejection by the peer group. As was pointed out earlier, men in their early thirties who had been late maturers still showed the psychological scars of the treatment they had received in childhood (19, 148, 209).

Meaning of Change. In spite of the traditional belief that personality is hereditary, there is a contradictory popular belief that the child will change his personality as he grows older. Parents often tell themselves that a child who is selfish, for example, will "outgrow" his selfishness; consequently, they do little or nothing to help him to realize what a serious handicap to social adjustments it is. The child may discover this stumbling block by trial and error, or it may be pointed out to him by a teacher or members of the peer group. Then, if his desire for social acceptance is strong enough, he will try to correct it. He does not "outgrow" selfishness; he tries, instead, to replace it with a more socially approved trait, generosity; this he does *by learning, not by maturation.*

Scientific evidence has shown that *changes* can and do occur in personality patterns. To "change" means to "alter" or to "vary": it does not necessarily mean that the alteration or change will be complete. *Thus the personality pattern is both persistent and subject to change.* As Cole has pointed out, "One's personality is not fixed by heredity; it grows, sheds some traits, acquires others, is sometimes supported by environmental pressures and sometimes warped by them, and is quickly affected by illness, disease, or unusual emotional strain" (71). While change is characteristic of physique and intelligence, personality is more "fluid, or subject to change through influence of the environment. . . . " (51). Changes in personality are more frequent and more pronounced in young children than in older children and adolescents, and very much more frequent than in adults (166, 299).

Changes in the child's characteristic method of adjusting to people and to situations may suggest that a greater change in his personality pattern has occurred than is actually the case. The "core" of the pattern, the child's self-concept, is relatively stable and changes only when the child perceives changes in the attitudes of significant people in his life toward him. He may modify his behavior in response to social pressures, however, in the hope of winning greater social approval or of avoiding social disapproval (50). An egocentric child, for example, may discover that stinginess leads to social rejection. He may, as a result, feel that it is a good policy to be generous when generosity counts—at times when it will win the approval and favor of the peer group.

With his siblings, parents, and relatives, he may continue to be selfish and stingy because he can count on their acceptance and does not have to buy it with generosity. Under stress, he will revert to his real pattern of adjustment, showing his stinginess even with members of the peer group. Thus the change was not a real change but only an apparent one (310).

Areas of Change. The part of the personality pattern least likely to change is the "core," the concept of self. The self-concept tends to become more fixed with age, though it may express itself in different ways as environmental conditions discourage one form of expression and encourage another. The child who suffers from feelings of personal inferiority and inadequacy may express these feelings about himself in excessive shyness and timidity when he is very young. As he grows older, he may realize that shyness is a social handicap and force himself to be more extroverted. While outwardly he may give the impression of self-confidence, even of cockiness, inwardly he is likely to remain as timid and as frightened of people and social situations as he ever was. He has merely put up a "front" as a cloak for his true self-concept (71, 315).

Similarly, a child may show little aggressiveness in his mother's presence, but in doll play, he may show his true self, attacking a sibling or even a mother doll as he would do in real life were he not held back by fear of punishment (267). Obviously, his concept of himself as a person who has been unfairly treated is still present, though his characteristic method of adjustment, stemming from this self-concept, has been changed by social pressures.

Changes in the personality pattern are far more likely to occur in specific *traits* than in the self-concept. A change may be *quantitative,* in that there is a weakening or strengthening of a trait already present, or it may be *qualitative,* in that a socially undesirable trait is eliminated and replaced by a more desirable one. Thus *change* does not necessarily mean change to an entirely different trait, nor does it mean a completely new personality pattern.

For the most part, changes consist in building upon characteristics already present, instead of developing something new and different. The most variable traits tend to be those which involve social relationships; the least variable are those which are based on some hereditary tendency. It is never possible, however, to tell which traits in a given child will be persistent and which will change; change depends partly upon the life experiences of the child and partly upon his hereditary endowment (166, 244, 307).

As the child becomes increasingly aware of what is socially approved or disapproved, he tries to conform to a pattern that will win greater acceptance. One study has shown that boys tend to make greater improvements in their personalities than girls; this was explained on the basis of greater social pressures on boys to improve (284).

Causes of Personality Changes. Changes in personality do not occur of their own accord. Furthermore, when changes do occur, they do so gradually. Sudden changes in personality are one of the criteria used to diagnose mental illness; they are not characteristically found among normal people (271, 293). Where there are structural disturbances in the brain, as in the case of a brain tumor, changed personality can generally be traced to one factor. But usually a change is brought about by the interaction of two or more causes.

Of the many causes of personality change identified to date, physical changes, environmental changes, social pressures, and change of self-concept are the most common and most important.

Physical changes may result from maturation or from illness, organic disorders, injuries, food, or drugs. During the early months of life, growth and development bring about personality changes in the baby. Environmental influences are less important than they will be later.

This point of view is stressed by Aldrich, who holds that "under normal conditions the forces of growth cause a most radical and gratifying change in personality to occur during the first 3 months of life. The compulsion and fear characteristic of the automatic, newborn stage gradually melt away until, during the third month, the baby blossoms into a smiling, cooing, pleasantly responsive individual" (5).

As the baby grows older, his muscular development makes more complex voluntary activity possible. Should the environment obstruct the normal use of his emerging ability, the baby will become antagonistic and rebellious. An environment which fosters the development of his personality will make him cooperative and responsive (153).

Physical changes such as those caused by illness, accident, or malnutrition bring about changes in the child's personality, mainly through their unfavorable effect on the self-concept. Such changes are especially common in a child who has learned to think of himself as a normal, healthy person, able to do what the members of the peer group do. If the handicap occurs early in the child's life, before the self-concept has been well formed, psychological damage will not be so serious (43, 74, 228, 342).

Changes in the physical or social *environment* may bring about changes in personality. The child who has been accustomed to living in a warm climate, where it is easy to have constant contacts with people outside the home, will probably develop into an expansive, extroverted person. Should he move to an extremely cold area where he must remain indoors for months at a time, limiting his social contacts to family members, he is likely to become introverted and shy in the presence of strangers.

The child whose neighborhood group is composed of children older and stronger than he will develop feelings of personal inadequacy. A change to a neighborhood where the play group is composed mainly of children of his age or younger may make him more assertive and aggressive; he may even achieve leadership status. Similarly, children who are troublesome at home because of authoritarian, permissive, or incon-sistent methods of discipline may become "good as gold" at school, where discipline is more consistent and more democratic (73, 254).

Whether changes in the environment will bring about improvement in the child's personality will depend partly on whether the changes improve his status and partly on whether his personality moves toward equilibrium with the environment. The child who is literally "out of focus" with his environment or who feels that his status in it is unfavorable will be more damaged than helped by the change (313, 319).

The rebelliousness and feelings of martyrdom of a child who has grown accustomed to being told what to do by adults, for example, are likely to change to self-confidence, self-assertiveness, or even "bossiness" when he begins to play with members of the peer group. Not only will his status change from that of an inferior to that of an equal, but the environment will be less restrictive and will offer more opportunities for the satisfaction of his needs. The change will move him toward an equilibrium with his environment and will bring about an improvement in the pattern of his behavior.

Children become increasingly aware that certain personality traits are admired and others disliked. *Social pressures* to conform to an approved personality pattern thus play an important role in bringing about changes in the personality. Social pressures become more important as the child grows older, and their influence on personality becomes stronger. The stronger the child's drive for social acceptance, the more he will try to develop acceptable personality traits (284, 319).

Psychotherapy is based on the assumption that a poorly adjusted person can be helped to make better adjustments, if he can develop a more favorable *self-concept*. Changing the self-concept, however, is far from easy; it can best be changed before the "core" of the personality is well developed, and the change must be made slowly to avoid upsetting the personality pattern (235).

To develop a more favorable self-concept, the child must gain insight into the causes that have led to his unfavorable self-concept, causes which are sometimes unknown to him or forgotten. He will need guidance to help him to recognize how irrational or harmful his unfavorable self-concept is and how adversely it affects his behavior; he must be motivated to want to change his self-concept; and he must be shown how or helped to make this change by guidance, change of environment, or both (144).

In an attempt to demonstrate experimentally how a socially desirable personality trait may be strengthened through training, Jack mapped out a program of training young children in such a way as to increase their self-confidence. Nonascendant, or easily dominated, children, Jack found, differed primarily from ascendant children in the degree of self-confidence they felt. The nonascendant children were trained to do things that the ascendant children could not do—assembling a mosaic of blocks and learning to know a storybook.

After a period of training sufficient to give the nonascendant children a feeling of self-confidence in their newly acquired skills, children from the two groups were paired together. Jack found not only that there were marked increases in the ascendancy scores of children in the trained group but also that they attempted to dominate the ascendant children. The experiment showed that ascendancy behavior can be increased by training and that the effects of training are *cumulative* (142). By increasing his self-confidence in one or more skills, the child can be encouraged to try others and thus develop more ascendant behavior (194, 218).

Socially undesirable traits can also be weakened or eliminated by training. Studies of children who showed immature reactions to failure, such as "giving up," asking for help, destructiveness, and rationalization, were given tasks graded in difficulty so that it was possible for them to see their progress and to achieve success most of the time. After a period of such training, there was marked improvement; the children showed

greater interest and effort in the tasks, they depended less on adults, and the sulking, crying, and violent emotional behavior characteristic of children who have experienced too many failures disappeared (332).

When children are helped to gain insight into themselves and others, they change their concepts about themselves and their relationships with others and thus improve their personal and social adjustments. Older children can generally be helped to change their self-concepts best by putting them in a new environment, away from home, as in a summer camp. There, through guidance and constructive group experiences, the child's view of the world and his relationship to it—his "internal frame of reference"—can be changed so that his characteristic manner of adjusting to life can be improved (120, 281).

Cautions in Personality Changes. In spite of the experimentally demonstrated changes that can be produced in personality traits, it is most important to bear in mind that the changes were brought about only in very young children, before the personality patterns had become well established. Furthermore, how permanent these changes were and whether they carried over to everyday life situations have not been reported. Only when the child's environment remains favorable will the changes be likely to become a permanent part of his personality pattern.

The child who lacks self-confidence, for example, cannot be expected to change to a self-confident person if his environment encourages repeated failures; such an environment is inevitable if parents and teachers expect the child to perform beyond his capacities. The cumulative effect of repeated failures leaves a scar on his personality by reinforcing an already present belief in his inferiority. Only if social expectations are lowered to the child's potentials can he be expected to increase his self-confidence.

In every personality, there is a "point of fixity beyond which change cannot be effected" (319). This means that while the pattern can be changed, it cannot be changed beyond certain limits without upsetting the balance of the entire pattern (244). While these limits of change may vary from one person to another and from one age to another in the same person, the limit exists and must be recognized if disturbance to the entire pattern is to be avoided. Furthermore, some areas of the pattern are more easily changed than others, and some may be so rigid that change is impossible.

These differences in flexibility come partly as a result of increasing age and partly as a result of life experiences. In every personality pattern there is a rigid portion which has developed in response to intense threat of anxiety. It includes defenses against impulses or drives found to be unacceptable to the significant people in the child's life. Any attempt to change this portion of the child's personality pattern will produce great anxiety and will be rigidly resisted (319).

Guidance and help may be ineffective because of the child's predispositions to certain forms of behavior, the effects of early training, or conflicts with home influences. Some children are more susceptible to guidance and more responsive to efforts to change their personality patterns than others. A child who is a voluntary isolate, for example, may prefer to be so because he has not found congeniality in the children available for him to associate with. Resistance to being changed into a social person does not necessarily mean that he will develop into a maladjusted adult; independence will not, per se, make one an unsocial outcast.

Changing one or two personality traits that are proving to be a distinct social handicap to the child is one thing, but trying to revamp the entire personality pattern is an entirely different story. As Breckenridge and Vincent have warned:

The very stability of a central core of personality around which habits and attitudes achieve a working balance in any given personality proves to be the reason we cannot, or should not try to make over basic traits in any personality unless we have the help of highly trained specialists. To change any basic trait without due regard to the other traits, habits, and attitudes which balance this trait may be to invite disaster through a serious disturbance in the total personality balance. . . . Apparently, while the core of stability of "the integration center" is still in the early stages of formation, much in the way of change or moulding is possible without disturbance to the general balance. Even so, it is not wise to force any child into a preconceived pattern. Even very young children seem to have a certain physiologic and psychologic constitution which can be forced only so far from its original pattern without producing stresses and strains which shatter the mechanism (51).

Significance of Persistence. Difficult as it may be to determine how persistent the personality pattern is and when, how, and how much it can be changed, the problems must be tackled—for several practical reasons:

1. If the personality pattern is persistent, good foundations which can guarantee reasonably good adjustment throughout life must be laid early. This can best be achieved by guidance to ensure that a favorable self-concept will be developed and that socially acceptable methods of adjusting to people and situations will be learned and reinforced through repeated experiences. If there were evidence that changes could be made easily as the child grew older or that he would automatically outgrow undesirable traits, then this would not be so important. Evidence to date, however, suggests that the early pattern is likely to persist.

2. Symptoms of maladjustment should be recognized and the maladjustments corrected as soon as they appear. Because there is little evidence that changes occur of their own accord or that they will be changes for the better, the sooner they are made, the easier they are and the more likely they are to persist. The same is true of changes in an undesirable concept of self. Unless changes are made in the direction of a more favorable concept of self, an undesirable self-concept will become so fixed that any attempt to change it later can upset the whole personality structure.

3. The personality pattern of the child influences the type of adjustment he makes, rather than vice versa. There is substantial evidence that the children who make good adjustments to life are those who have well-integrated personality patterns in which the "core" is a stable, realistic self-concept, while those who make poor adjustments have poorly integrated personalities with unstable and unrealistic self-concepts as the centers of gravity. Only through guidance is there a good chance that a favorable development will take place.

4. The personality pattern of the child becomes increasingly stable as he grows older; therefore, it is possible to predict, early in his childhood, what sort of person he will be as he grows older and what sort of adjustments he will make to life. Radical changes will not occur unless the child suffers from some form of mental illness as he approaches adulthood. That persistence is great enough and universal enough to allow prediction for the future is not a new idea; it traces its origin back to ancient Greek and Roman times. Plato, in writing of old age, pointed out that "he who is of a calm and happy nature will hardly feel the pressure of old age, but to him who is of the opposite disposition, youth and old age are equally a burden." Cicero, among the Romans, emphasized the possibility of predicting the future adjustments of a person from his present adjustments when he said, "Those with simple desires and good dispositions find old age easy to take. Those who do not show wisdom and virtue in their youth are prone to attribute to old age those infirmities which are actually produced by former irregularities."

Kelly explains why people expect personality to remain constant and, thus, why they believe they can predict a person's future adjustments from his present pattern of adjustments:

Because of the need to believe in consistency of one's self from moment to moment and from year to year, we tend to infer an unwarranted degree of consistency in others. Some consistency is indeed necessary for social intercourse. . . . While assuming that other adults are not likely to change, each of us, I suspect, wants to keep his

theory sufficiently flexible to permit the possibility of change in himself—especially changes in the direction of his ego ideal! Even though in retrospect few of these desired changes may have occurred, it's comforting to think that one *can* change if one tries hard enough (158).

Because change is not likely to occur unless "one tries hard enough," there is every justification for making changes, or for helping another person to make them, before it is too late to "try hard."

INDIVIDUALITY

Each personality pattern is *unique* in that it varies in the combination and organization of the traits that constitute the pattern, in the strength of the different traits, and in the "core" of the pattern, the self-concept. Even at birth there is a clearly discernible individuality in the infant's characteristic adjustment to his new environment. While the personality of the child is not developed at that time, the potential qualities are there. From these variations is built up a pattern from which the individual never completely escapes (205, 293). A month or two after birth, the baby begins to respond to other individuals, and his behavior is modified accordingly.

Because no two individuals have the same social environments, even if they have the same physical environments, they tend to exhibit increasingly different personality patterns as they grow older. Among first-graders, various personality "types" can be distinguished. Some children are helpers who can look out for other children; some are leaders who have sufficient initiative to make suggestions and attract followers; some are maternal; some are despotic; some like to joke and make fun of others; some are inveterate show-offs; some are much-loved favorites; and some are solitary and withdrawn (293).

Meaning of Individuality. Allport has referred to individuality as a "never-repeated phenomenon" and has emphasized that the "outstanding characteristic of man is his individuality" (11). Individuality in personality means differences in *kind,* rather than differences in amount. Within the personality pattern are not only differences in the "core" but also differences in traits. Some traits may be *common* to large groups of people, such as truthfulness, generosity, and sociability, because they have been developed by similar child-training methods and similar environmental influences. Others are *unique* in that they are not to be found in others because they have developed from unusual combinations of hereditary qualities, personal experiences, and social environments (164).

Even common traits contain a unique element; *no two people have exactly the same trait in exactly the same degree.* A child may be generous because generosity is a highly valued trait in the culture in which he grows up; he has been trained to be generous with his toys, his food, his money, his material possessions, his time, his praise of others, and his gratitude for what others have done for him. Nevertheless, he will express his generosity in his own individual way, and his expression of it will be influenced by his uniquely developed self-concept. To one child, generosity may be "good business"— a way to "buy popularity"—while to another it may be motivated by a feeling that he owes society something and is repaying his debt by helping those less fortunate than he. This point of view has been emphasized by Allport:

No two persons ever have precisely the same trait. Though each of two men may be aggressive (or esthetic), the style and range of the aggression (or estheticism) in each case is noticeably different. What else could be expected in view of the unique hereditary endowment, the different developmental history, the never-repeated external influences that determine each personality? The end product of unique determination can never be anything but unique (11).

Early Recognition of Individuality. The recognition of uniqueness—individual differences in personality—goes back at least as far as the ancient Greeks. Hippocrates referred to four different personality "types": The *sanguine,* or quick, active persons; the *choleric,* or strong and easily aroused persons; the *phlegmatic,* or slow and stolid type; and the *melancholic,* or sad and pessimistic individuals. Today there is fairly wide acceptance of the belief that individuals cannot be classified into "types" because the makeup of different personality patterns results in too many variations. Increasing emphasis is being placed on the importance of individual differences in personality.

Furthermore, it is recognized that one cannot accurately judge the personality of a child in terms of a stereotype of a given "personality type." To say that a child is a "typical" boy, a "typical" brat, or a "typical" grind is common, but these judgments are usually first impressions, based on the child's behavior or appearance (26, 192).

Studies of personality have revealed that there is no syndrome or combination of traits characteristically found in all people who are identified as artists, scientists, businessmen, teachers, or members of certain occupational, racial, or religious groups. Just as there is no "typical" stepmother, "typical" scientist, or "typical" teacher, so there is no "typical" American or "typical" Jew. While each may have traits in common with other members of his particular group, there are differences in the strength of the traits, in the self-concepts that are related to the traits and which influence them, and in the other traits which constitute the personality patterns (24, 46, 137, 197).

It is now rather generally believed that the foundation of personality comes from the maturation of hereditary traits but that these are influenced partly by learning in connection with direct social contacts and partly by conditioning. This point of view is expressed by Landis:

Personality is dynamic, a growing entity. Psychologically, it is vested with the capacity for maturation. Except as mutilated by environment, physical traits follow their predestined course from childhood to maturity. Psychologically, it is plastic, capable of an infinite number of modifications by external stimuli. Sociologically, it is dependent on the group to provide the patterns of development, for human nature is a group project (166).

While change is unquestionably brought about by environmental factors, the change is modified by the limitations of the original personality nucleus. Strong personality characteristics, which are based on hereditary traits, are not ironed out by training. Again, this suggests that heredity is responsible for the difference in resistance to change.

Once a trait has been developed, through environmental influences, it affects not only the individual's behavior but also his interests and attitudes. The trait is thus strengthened and made more resistant to change. In spite of environmental influences, each personality pattern has a tough core, or nucleus of traits. When this tough core is "coupled with the dynamic forces of growth, it prevents the individual from ever becoming a complete puppet of the forces that play upon him" (275). Because of this inner resistance, the child will react in his own individual manner to the people and things in his environment and will thus increase his individuality.

DETERMINANTS OF PERSONALITY

Individuality, the product of both hereditary and environment, can best be understood by an analysis of the many different determinants of personality. As no two children react in the same way to the same environmental influences, it will soon become apparent, from a study of the determinants of personality, that individuality can be expected to increase rather than decrease as children grow older.

Furthermore, as no two children are affected in the same manner by the same factor, it is impossible to rank the determinants of personality in the order of their importance. A child whose parents place high value on education, for example, will be more influenced by grades than a child whose parents put so low a value on education that poor grades do not disturb them. The former, reflecting in his self-concept the attitudes of the significant people in his life, will develop feelings of inadequacy if his grades are poor and feelings of superiority if they are high.

Some of the determinants of personality have their greatest effect on the "core" of the personality pattern, and some on the traits related to the "core." No determinant, however, affects just one part of the personality pattern. For example, a physical defect affects not only the child's characteristic pattern of adjustment to life but also the "core" of his personality pattern; it influences the child's concept of himself as a person in comparison with other members of the peer group.

How much or how little influence different factors will have on the personality development of the child will depend to a large extent upon the child's *ability to understand the significance of the factors in relation to himself.* His concept of self is influence by his comprehension of the attitude of the social group toward him. If his appearance is such that he is admired by others for it, appearance will be a favorable factor in his personality development. But if he is aware that his peers do not admire his looks, appearance will prove to be a liability in the personality pattern.

The following pages contain a hasty analysis of the determinants of personality that have been found to have the greatest influence on the type of personality pattern the child develops.

PHYSIQUE

Physique influences personality both directly and indirectly. *Directly* physique determines what the child can or cannot do. This is important at any age when physical activities have high prestige value in the peer group. The child with a small, delicate body or the obese child will be handicapped in many games and sports which form the basis for social acceptance in childhood (12, 278).

Indirectly, physique influences personality

by determining how the child feels about his body. This, in turn, is influenced by how significant people in his life feel about it. The child who is markedly overweight, for example, will not be affected by his obesity until he becomes aware that people regard it as ugly (151, 348). As Shaffer and Shoben have pointed out:

A puny boy is likely to develop different preferred mechanisms than a strong, healthy child, because he has different experiences. Anxiety provoked by threatening diseases or disabling symptoms may lead to defensive or nonadjustive behavior. In such cases, a person's structure or physiology frustrates his motives, creates conflicts, and shapes the experiences through which he learns his adjustments. The precipitating events are physiological but the adjustive process is psychological (271).

While there is some evidence that certain personality patterns are associated with certain types of body build, there is no evidence that this relationship is due to heredity. On the other hand there is evidence that awareness of cultural attitudes toward certain body builds is responsible for the personality patterns the individuals with these body builds develop (271, 293).

Every cultural group has its own standards of what is "right" or appropriate for boys and girls. In our culture, the "right" height is average for the sex to slightly above, and the "right" weight is average or in standard proportion to height. Extremes are regarded as "wrong." If the child is in a group of children of his own size, however, size will have no effect on his concept of self. Only when the variation from the *norm of his own group* is great enough to be noticed by others will it affect him.

At an early age, children become aware of any deviation from the group norm because of the effect it has on their social relationships. Nicknames that imply physical difference, such as "Fatty" or "Skinny," show how other children feel about these differences. Because being different makes the child feel inadequate, it affects his personality. Boys with well-proportioned bodies have been found to have well-adjusted personality patterns; by contrast, boys with physically inferior bodies develop some compensatory form of behavior which interferes with good social adjustments (65, 211).

Even though fat may be only temporary, the fat child becomes self-conscious, timid, retiring, slow, awkward, and incapable of holding a secure status among his peers. He is often at the mercy of more active children who tease and bully him. And because he is unable to engage in active play with other children, he becomes increasingly unsocial. He becomes more dependent on the mother and develops a tendency to be immature for his age (100, 167, 348).

PHYSICAL CONDITION

Alterations in the physical condition of the child will be reflected in behavioral changes, which may be slight or major, temporary or permanent, depending on how great or how permanent the physical changes are. A child who is tired becomes irritable and thus adjusts and reacts differently from the way he does when he is rested. Any condition that disturbs the homeostasis of the body will be likely to affect the quality of the child's adjustments. Upsets in homeostasis are most frequent during periods of rapid growth, but they also occur when growth is uneven. Uneven growth is likely to be accompanied by immaturity of behavior (82, 86, 134, 280).

Not only does good health enable the child to engage in all the normal activities of his age group, but it also has a favorable influence on personality. The attitude of the family and the social group in general is so much more favorable toward a healthy child than toward a sickly one that it is certain to have an effect on his behavior.

The child who is delicate and sickly comes to expect the consideration from others that he has been used to at home. He withdraws from the activities of other children and becomes overdependent on his parents.

Children with low energy levels resulting from a chronic illness or malnutrition often become shy, reserved, irritable, depressed, and unsocial. Those suffering from an irritating physical condition, such as hives or eczema, develop tempers and overactive responses (121, 229). The emotional instability of allergic children is shown in ebb and flow which may "alternate with almost incredible swiftness and vehemence" (241). Their personalities improve markedly when the allergy is brought under control. Children with diabetes seldom escape personality damage. The older the child when he develops the disease, the better able he is to control his negative emotions. The more severe the case, the more dependent and emotionally unstable the child will be (41, 68).

The effect of *physical defects* on personality will depend upon how much the child realizes that he is different. Children who suffer from polio are affected less by their handicaps if their environment limits them to other children with similar handicaps. Children who are deaf or blind develop a rigidity of personality when they are with children of normal hearing and sight. At first, children with cerebral palsy realize in a vague way that they are different. Later they may try to deny the handicap, or they may feel ashamed and guilty (43, 74).

The condition of the *endocrine glands,* or the glands of internal secretion, affects the personality development of the child. A hyperthyroid condition, for example, makes the child nervous, excited, jumpy, restless, and overactive. The opposite, a hypothyroid state, in which there is a deficiency of secretion from the thyroid glands, causes the child to be lethargic, unresponsive, depressed, dissatisfied, and distrustful. While there is not a large amount of evidence at the present time regarding the specific effects of the different glands of the endocrine system on the personality of the child, there is a strong belief that these glands are of no small importance in the personality makeup (86, 185).

INTELLIGENCE

Intelligence provides the child with the capacity for adjusting to life, for meeting and solving the problems adjustment requires.

Average intelligence makes it possible for the child to adjust with reasonable success if other conditions are favorable. But very low or very high IQ's frequently prove to be a disadvantage to social adjustment. The child who is very bright or very dull is generally damaged psychologically because he develops a concept of self that militates against good adjustment and because he acquires patterns of behavior that fall below the socially approved standards. Recognition of the social disapproval of his behavior lowers his self-concept even further, and this, in turn, leads to poorer social behavior (21, 155, 291, 352).

Except when there is a marked deviation from the norm, young children are not aware of what their intellectual level is; the bright do not realize how bright they are, the dull are unaware of their dullness, and the average take their intelligence for granted. After they enter school, however, children have a measuring rod against which to compare their intellectual capacities, and they measure their level of intellectual development by the type of adjustment they make to school work (335).

Effects of Deviant Intelligence. How a child feels about being intellectually different is greatly influenced by social attitudes, especially the attitudes of parents, teachers, and members of the peer group. Attitudes toward *brightness,* for example, differ from one school to another and, within a school, according to whether the bright children are popular or unpopular. They also vary according to the social-class backgrounds of the children, with those from the lower social classes putting less value on brightness than those from the middle or upper classes (87, 172, 243, 352).

The more superior the intelligence of the child, the less favorable the social attitude. A very bright child is often regarded as a "threat" by his peers; he may raise the standard of work in the class and make the teacher expect more of all the students. In addition, children of average intelligence feel uncomfortable when with a very bright child because they seem "stupid" by comparison. And as the cultural stereotype maintains that very bright people are "queer," there is a tendency to be hypercritical or suspicious of everything the very bright child says or does (97, 309).

Awareness of the fact that they are considered "queer" makes very bright children uneasy in the presence of the peer group (96). This, in turn, makes them inadequate in their social relationships and reinforces the popular idea that they are "queer." Furthermore, having little in common with their classmates, many bright children concentrate their energies on their studies or hobbies and thus increase their social isolation. Even though their preoccupation with intellectual pursuits may result in parent and teacher approval, their self-concept is not favorable (87).

An unfavorable self-concept, once formed, is likely to be so persistent that, as adults, those who are regarded as "intellectuals" often develop a superiority complex which causes them to be "intellectual snobs." This reaction is more often than not a compensation for feelings of inadequacy resulting from lack of social acceptance. Many of the personality problems of very bright children are caused by psychological isolation; when they have opportunities to associate with other children of similar intellectual capacities, their personality problems are minimized or eliminated (138, 174, 269, 317).

While children who are *mentally retarded* may hear their parents and neighbors refer to them as "not very bright," they are not usually aware of what this means until they go to school. Then, unless their retardation is so marked that they are segregated in special classes, dull children soon discover how dull they are. They also discover that the social attitude toward dullness is unfavorable (255). As the child grows older, his dullness becomes increasingly apparent to himself as well as to others. Many children who become truants do so in order to avoid the unbearable social reactions to their dullness (97, 330, 335).

A child whose intelligence is definitely below that of other children of the same age in school or in the neighborhood group finds himself an outsider. His interests are different from theirs, and he soon develops feelings of inadequacy which force him to leave the group. The brighter the peer group, the more unpopular the dull child is (132, 184, 257, 337).

Because of his narrow social experiences, the dull child has poor social insight as well as poor self-insight; thus this limitation makes social adjustments worse and adds to the social rejection he already experiences. In school, dull children are considered "pests" because they hold back the class and are often troublesome disciplinary problems. Out of school they are disliked because they are unaware of how unpopular they are. The psychological damage of dullness to personality is not so great as one might anticipate because dull children lack the social insight to recognize how unfavorable the social attitudes toward them are (33, 34, 199, 243).

EMOTIONS

Even a mild emotion causes sufficient physical imbalance to affect the child's behavior. When emotions are strong and persistent, damaging effects multiply. How a child perceives an emotion-provoking stimulus depends upon his past experiences and affects his characteristic method of adjustment.

If he has learned to perceive all people in authority as a threat to his independence, he will respond to such people with angry resentments. Some children develop the habit of expressing their emotions on the spot, some learn to inhibit the expression and release the pent-up emotional energy at a more opportune moment, while still others learn to release inhibited emotions by directing the emotional energy to some scapegoat. Thus it is apparent that the way in which the child learns to respond emotionally not only will affect the quality of his behavior but will influence the judgments of other people and their attitudes toward him (271, 293).

Too frequent, too intense, and apparently unjustified emotional outbursts on the child's part lead others to judge him as "immature."

Suppression of emotional expressions results in moodiness, which makes the child rude, snappy, gruff, uncooperative, and preoccupied with self. Heightened emotionality, even when the expressions are controlled, tends to make the child nervous, edgy, and ill at ease; it is often accompanied by specific mannerisms, such as nail biting or giggling, which create the impression that the child is "silly" or immature (181, 203, 204).

The *dominant* type of emotion the child experiences has an even more pronounced effect on his personality than general emotional tension. A child who has learned to fear people acts in a defensive way, showing timidity, anxiety, and lack of self-confidence. Others will react to this type of behavior by ridiculing or ignoring him; he will come to be known as a "timid" person. Similarly, a child who reacts aggressively when frustrated learns to be hostile to others. Because they resent his hostility, they react to him unfavorably; this increases his hostility, leading to a "chip-on-the-shoulder" type of adjustment to life (291, 354).

Unfortunately, the environment usually encourages the development of unfavorable emotional patterns (see pages 271 to 272). Too many and too frequent worries, for example, tend to weaken self-confidence; this, in time, leads to a feeling of personal inadequacy and inferiority. As time goes on, a generalized feeling of inadequacy so undermines the child's self-confidence that he is literally "licked before he starts" in any new situation (32, 176, 291, 312).

Similarly, repeated frustrations may cause the child to develop feelings of martyrdom because he convinces himself that the whole world is against him. Children differ greatly in their *frustration thresholds*—the level of tension below which a person can think rationally and behave effectively—but if circumstances lead to emotional tension that is too strong or too persistent, every child will reach a limit beyond which he will no longer be able to think rationally or behave effectively (170). He will then react in an aggressive manner, showing hostility which, to observers, seems out of proportion to the

frustrating stimulus. Other children may regress to infantile forms of behavior, thus creating the impression that they are immature or "babyish." Still others gain satisfaction by displacing their aggression on innocent victims; satisfaction of this type is usually short-lived because children are accused of being "poor sports" (210, 217).

People tend to judge a child favorably when he keeps his emotions under control. They also judge some forms of emotional expression more favorably than others. "Picking on others," for example, is judged less favorably than moodiness, just as generalized jitteriness is less readily tolerated than a nervous mannerism.

How the child's emotions will affect his concept of self will thus be greatly influenced by how they affect other people. The direct effect of emotions on personality, though often less serious than the effect they have on other people, should not be overlooked. When emotions are so strong or so persistent that they disorganize the child's behavior, they will have a serious effect on his characteristic patterns of adjustment to life.

EARLY EXPERIENCES

Childhood experiences and the memory of these experiences as the years go by leave an indelible impression on the individual's personality. Bartemeier maintains that "whatever emotional damage is inflicted on a child during the period of infancy has far greater effects upon the future character development than a similar damage inflicted at a later period when the personality has become more fully organized" (37).

The importance of early experiences to future personality development was first stressed by Freud, who found that many of his adult patients had had unhappy childhood experiences. Many students of personality now claim that persons subjected to undue thwartings during the early years of life regress to infantile modes of behavior, turn their interests from outer to inner spheres, and become self-centered and reflective rather than expressive. The adverse effects of early experiences can often be corrected, however, especially by psychoanalytic therapy.

Lack of "mothering" during the early years and emotional deprivation influence the personality development of the child, but if the deprivation is for only a short time, the effects will be fewer and less permanent. Refer to pages 262 to 265 for a more complete discussion of the effects of emotional deprivation.

There is lack of convincing evidence to prove that the individual's personality reflects the type of care he had during the early years of life; that is, there is no definite evidence that breast feeding or late toilet training is better than bottle feeding or early toilet training so far as the personality pattern is concerned. Nor is there any definite evidence that the effects of these early experiences carry into the adult years. On the other hand, there is ample evidence that the attitude and emotional reactions of the mother, the total cultural context of the environment in which the child grows up, and other factors in the child's total experience are of much importance in determining the pattern of his personality. Only when the mother's attitudes make the child feel anxious and guilty in relation to training or eating will there be any real effect on his personality (240, 288, 303).

FAMILY INFLUENCES

The effect of family relationships on the child will depend to a certain extent upon the child himself. A child who is nervous and tense will be more upset by the attention given to a new baby than a child of a more phlegmatic disposition. Similarly, a healthy child will react very differently to the attention and pampering he receives as the "baby" of the family than a delicate, sickly child will (47, 64).

The *type of homelife* the child has is largely determined by the parents. Homes characterized by friction and discord, lack of affectional relations, lack of parental interest in the child, and breaks due to separation, death, or divorce lead to emotional instability and poor adjustments on the child's part (252, 338, 355).

A pattern of homelife in which family members are companionable, where cooperative and democratic relations exist, and where attempts are made to meet the needs of the child produces a well-adjusted personality in the child. This type of home provides the affectional relationships every child needs with his parents and siblings.

How the child *perceives* his parents' attitudes is more important than the attitudes themselves. A child who perceives himself as accepted shows greater ego aspirations, tenacity, and independence from parents than one who feels rejected. As a rule, girls perceive themselves as more accepted by their parents than boys (226).

Parental attitudes that are favorable to the development of the child's personality are characterized by understanding, love, and interest in the child as an individual. Parental attitudes that have been found to be unfavorable to the child's personality development are characterized by lack of emotional warmth, rejection in such subtle forms as criticism and hostility submerged under a cloak of insincere care and affection, favoritism toward a sibling, and a high degree of behavioral control. Mothers who are not nurturant, it has been found, cause children to be hostile, dependent, lacking in conscience, and pessimistic; the children have a generalized expectation of failure, accompanied by lack of self-confidence (99). The parents' personalities and their attitudes toward the child are far more influential in the child's personality development than the external factors of the home environment are (94, 267). This point of view is stressed by Shirley:

A secure and wholesomely loved child goes forth to meet a new experience in a spirit of adventure, and comes out triumphant in his encounters with new places, new materials, and new friends, old and young. A child that is oversheltered or underloved goes forth from his home with misgivings and doubts, and gives an impression of inadequacy and immaturity in his encounter with new experiences that makes him unwelcome either in the society of adults or children (275).

The child's personality is also influenced indirectly by his parents through his tendency to imitate them and to identify himself with them. That children imitate their parents is seen in the fact that the personality pattern of both boys and girls in early childhood more closely resembles that of the mother than of the father, owing to the more constant contacts with the mother (54).

There are also indications of imitation in the personality disturbances of children which closely resemble those of the mother (208, 247). Because the child's personality is so strongly influenced by his parents, Symonds has justifiably claimed, "If an individual possesses a healthy, stable, courageous, and loving father and mother, the chances are that he will be a good student, a good worker, a good husband or wife, a good leader, and a good citizen" (311).

The type of *relationship that exists among siblings* has much the same influence on the child's personality development as his relationship with his parents. *Size of family* also plays an important role. The child from a small family develops not only a different personality pattern from that of a child from a large family but, on the whole, a better one (47, 162).

Compared with children from urban areas, *rural* children have been reported to be superior in both self-adjustment and social adjustments. In general, rural children are more self-reliant, have a greater sense of personal worth and of belonging, and have greater freedom from nervous symptoms and withdrawing tendencies. On the whole, they receive better ratings from their teachers and fewer unfavorable ratings from their peers than urban children (183, 267).

The *socioeconomic status of the family* affects the child's developing personality both directly and indirectly: *directly* because it determines what social-class standards the parents will accept and what child-training methods they will use, and *indirectly* because it determines where and how the family will live. The physical environment of the home, including such factors as size, neighborhood, and general condition of the furnishings, has little influence, per se, on the child's personality. The type of home and the neighborhood in which it is located do influence parental attitudes, however, and thus affect the child (193).

Even before a child from a *minority group* enters school, his personality is affected by the treatment he receives from other children. He develops feelings of inadequacy and inferiority, resentful attitudes toward society, and many forms of compensatory behavior that further increase the discrimination against him. The memory of unhappy childhood experiences, when other children were "mean" to him, leaves an indelible impression on the child—one which will alter his whole outlook on life and leave a permanent scar on his personality (271, 293).

Children from different minority groups seem to be affected in slightly different ways by discrimination. The Negro child, whose skin color is the darkest, makes the poorest adjustments because he is aware of the unfavorable stereotype associated with dark skin color; he often becomes quarrelsome and vindictive (116, 219).

The Jewish child is well aware of his minority-group status, and the effects are increasingly serious with each passing year. By adolescence, he may develop a personality pattern characterized by aggressiveness, destructiveness, submissiveness, or strong rebellion; also, he may develop a derogatory attitude toward other groups. Children of the Amish faith have been found to make poor social adjustments because they feel they do not "belong," that other children are mean to them, and that they do not have as much fun as other children (234).

CULTURAL INFLUENCES

It has been said that you can take a child away from his culture but that you cannot take the culture away from the child. Without question, custom and tradition are important in personality development. In every culture, children are subjected to pressures to develop a personality pattern that will conform as closely as possible to the standards set by the culture (39, 169).

In America, there are three types of cultural systems: the *general American* culture, *social-class* cultures, and *ethnic-group* cultures. Each of these has its own approved personality pattern. As a result, every social class and every cultural group produces a different basic personality. The *basic personality* is the organization of the drives and emotions of the individual, the deeper-lying parts of mental behavior.

The basic personality includes inner feelings toward parents and toward members of the same or of the opposite sex, guilt, emotional reactivity, and hostility. Many of these feelings may be unconscious. The cultural group to which the child's parents belong sets the pattern for this basic personality, and because of his early training, the child is disposed to adopt this pattern. The way the child is brought up is thus responsible for the type of personality he develops (119, 128, 189).

Since the basic personality pattern is dependent not so much upon biological inheritance as upon cultural pressures, the type of personality required for successful living in a culture can be consciously shaped and developed. The impact of culture is mediated chiefly through the family during the early years of life. Later, pressures from the school and the peer group supplement family pressures. From these pressures, the child learns to behave in a socially approved way in that culture and to have attitudes that are sex-appropriate.

Cultural values are reflected in the training of the child, and through this medium they leave their mark on his personality (66, 249). Japanese children are trained to be family-oriented; consequently, they develop a personality pattern characterized by loyalty, cooperation, self-sacrifice, and often an unrealistic concept of themselves and of their roles in life. By contrast, American children become egocentric, more realistic, concerned about their independence and rights, and more anxious to help themselves

than others (117). Thus it is apparent that "as cultures differ, so do the personalities embedded in those cultures" (298).

In a rapidly changing culture, parents may feel that it is unrealistic to guide their children's development by standards that were approved in their own youth. The problem is further complicated by *social mobility*. As parents improve their status in society, they must accept the patterns of the new social group with which they identify themselves and mold their own and their children's behavior according to these standards. Such changes often lead to feelings of insecurity and anxiety on the part of the child (191, 216, 232). Refer to pages 424 to 426 for a more complete discussion of the problems social mobility produces for a child and the effects of social mobility on his behavior and personality.

PLAYMATES AND FRIENDS

The young child is anxious to have the approval of his parents, but after he enters school, the approval of his peers becomes so important that he turns his attention to the development of personality traits which his playmates admire, even though they may not be the ones admired by his parents. In addition, he attempts to eliminate—or at least to minimize—the undesirable personality traits which the group disapproves of and which may put him in the position of a social isolate (48).

The popularity of the child plays a considerable part in the development of his personality. Children who are accepted in the social group or who find themselves from time to time in positions of leadership develop a self-confidence and poise which are lacking in children who are social isolates. The child who is friendly and self-confident, in turn, wins more friends; as his popularity increases, his poise, self-assurance, and leadership qualities also grow stronger. The popular child has a freer, lighter attitude; is more relaxed; and is less influenced by the opinions of others than the unpopular child. Unpopular children feel inferior; they are envious of their more popular associates; they resent being ignored by their peers; and they are sullen and irritable and ready to "fly off the handle" at the slightest provocation. This, naturally, does not help them to develop the personality traits which will make them popular.

Unpopular children show a degree of tension and often seem awed. They acquiesce to the popular children, try to impress them by showing off, or agree impetuously with whatever they suggest. How popularity, lack of popularity, and social neglect affect the characteristic patterns of the child's adjustment to others has been discussed in detail on pages 420 to 421.

SCHOOL INFLUENCES

The influence of the school in the personality development of the child is very great because the school becomes a substitute for the home, and the teacher a substitute for the mother. As Solomon has pointed out, "The schoolroom must be looked upon as a force secondary in importance only to the home in the development of human personality" (289). Not only does the school take up about one-half of the child's waking time, but it "presents the first encounter with a reality that sets definite demands at certain age levels, demands which are patterned by our competitive society" (134). Like the home, the school acts as a transmitter of cultural values and, with greater force than is exercised in the home, sees to it that the child accepts these values as a price for social acceptance (61, 295).

In emphasizing how the school influences the personality development of the child, Jersild has written:

The role of the school . . . is not only incidental but direct. It dispenses praise and reproof, acceptance and rejection, on a colossal scale. Even when the school situation is about as perfect as a human institution can be, children are likely again and again to be reminded of their failings, shortcomings, and limitations. In a good school setting such reminders are wholesome, for they help the child to face and deal with the realities of life. In the best of schools children are likely to suffer now and then from hurt pride. . . . Much of the failure at school is contrived. Much of the depreciation children encounter there is based upon false evaluation. Some of it rests upon a punitive approach to education which in some schools has a savage intensity (145).

In the early grades, the *teacher* is the most important single factor in the total school influence on the child's personality. The type of relationship the child has with his teacher at that time is more important than later, just as parent-child relationships are more important to the personality development of the child in the early years than they are as he approaches adolescence.

Directly, the teacher affects the way the child feels about himself by the way she corrects his behavior, ignores him or his social behavior, or interprets his school work. A child sees himself through the teacher's eyes as a "pest," a "bully," a "clown," or a "pet." *Indirectly,* the teacher influences the child and his personality by helping him to adjust to the group and by helping the group to adjust to him; she thus influences the degree of social acceptance he achieves (103, 289).

The personality pattern of the teacher influences the child's personality, *never the opposite.* The authoritarian teacher has much the same influence on the child's personality as the authoritarian parent. The overdependent teacher overvalues authority and status, while the overly independent teacher is lacking in sympathy and understanding and is likely to be harsh on passive pupils. A teacher who is warm and accepting in her attitude toward her pupils helps to motivate them to do good work; a teacher who is negative or indifferent robs her pupils of any motivation they may have and makes them feel rejected (67, 353). As Sister Mary Amatora has pointed out, it is of "vital importance to the development of wholesome personality in the children that they have teachers who possess well-adjusted personalities" (14).

The attitude of the teacher toward her work and toward children is very important.

The teacher who likes her work, who likes and understands children, and who is enthusiastic about what she is teaching creates a far better school climate than the teacher who has little interest in teaching or in children or who regards teaching as a stopgap between the completion of her education and marriage. A teacher who gets along well with children has fewer disciplinary problems and less friction and tension in the classroom than the teacher who feels inadequate in her role or who does not like her role (344).

When the teacher is fair, showing no favoritism toward any pupil and punishing only when she is sure that the wrong act was intentional, she creates a school climate in which tension and anxiety are kept at a minimum. Many children from lower-income families feel that the teacher favors children from more affluent homes. This, added to their feelings of inadequacy in school and rejection by the peer group, leads to a feeling of inferiority which, as time goes on, often increases to the point where they become truants (63, 198, 276, 330).

Maladjusted teachers do not always cause maladjustments in their pupils. Sometimes a teacher who has experienced maladjustments can understand and sympathize better with pupils who are having difficulties than well-adjusted teachers can. Any undesirable personality trait in the child that has originated in the home, however, can be crystallized or fortified in the school if the teacher shows maladjustive patterns of behavior. That is why a child with "both stable parents and stable teachers is fortunate. Conversely, emotional problems are aggravated when a child with unstable parents is exposed to unstable teachers" (289).

How much influence the teacher will have on the child depends to some extent upon the amount of interaction there is between teacher and pupil. When the school is organized on the "homeroom plan," with a special teacher in charge, the child comes into fairly close contact with this teacher. When there are different teachers for different subjects, his contact with all teachers is limited and impersonal. As children grow older, they tend to become critical of their teachers; this critical attitude influences them, indirectly, as much as if they admired and imitated their teachers. The critical child picks out flaws in the teacher's personality, appearance, and behavior and tries to avoid developing similar traits. Sometimes a disliked teacher exerts an unfavorable influence on her pupils by increasing emotional tension and thus leading to quarrelsome behavior outside of school (198, 276).

Grade placement and *school grades* indicate to a child how he compares with his classmates. If he is in a "slow" section, he discovers that he is considered less bright than children in the "fast" section. The markedly retarded child develops feelings of inadequacy not only because he is forced to repeat grades but also because his poor social insight leads to poor social acceptance. The child who is able to do the work of the school but who fails because of feelings of inadequacy engendered in the home comes to feel even more inadequate and to experience more failures (33, 335).

The very bright child, who meets the school standards successfully without too much effort, is likely to develop negative attitudes toward authority and an intolerance toward those who are less bright than he, whether they are his teachers or his classmates. Such children, even though they are promoted to a class of older children, often develop concepts of personal superiority which lead to behavior that makes them unpopular with their classmates and disliked by their teachers (138).

Grades and report cards tend to increase a child's feeling of inadequacy, anxiety, and emotional tension. Furthermore, grades lead to competition with other children and thus to increased anxiety. On the whole, pupils who make good grades or who receive social recognition through awards or teacher approval are likely to be better adjusted than those who make poor grades. The former are happier in school and have more favorable concepts of self (133, 182, 318).

Symonds has made the following comment on the effect of grades on the child's concept of himself as a person and on his relationships with children whose grades are better than his:

Marks make a tremendous difference to a pupil. They influence his estimate of himself; they serve as a sign to him that he is liked or disliked; they determine whether he is to remain with classmates or instead to become (what he considers) an outcast and forced to join a group of strange pupils in another class. They indicate success or failure; they determine promotion; they indicate the probability of future success; they influence his parents' attitude toward him. Marks help to determine whether a pupil thinks of himself as successful, smart, or as a failure, an outcast, stupid, a nitwit (312).

LEVEL OF ASPIRATION

The child's concept of self is greatly influenced by whether he regards himself as a success or as a failure. He may be a "success" in the eyes of others but a "failure" in his own eyes. *A person who is objectively a success can be, subjectively, a failure.* And it is how the child *feels about his achievements,* not his achievements themselves, that affects his self-concept.

By the time the child is three or four years old, he begins to establish standards for himself. With each passing year, pressures from parents, teachers, and peers make these standards more definite and specific. Often, in the hope of winning approval and recognition, the child sets his standards above his capacities. The standards become *levels of aspiration,* or the "level of future performance in a familiar task which an individual explicitly undertakes to reach" (312).

In establishing his levels of aspiration, the child is influenced by many people and many circumstances in his life. Most children, especially when they are young, are so ignorant of their capacities that they can easily be persuaded to set goals beyond their reach. This is justified by their parents on the ground that they can reach these goals if they will only try hard enough. Furthermore, parents set goals beyond their children's present capacities in the belief that high goals motivate children to make the most of their capacities and of the opportunities parents provide. Parents want their children to "get ahead," so they encourage them to think unrealistically about what they can do (156).

The more highly achievement is valued by a cultural group, the more parents encourage children to set goals beyond their reach in the hope that the goals will serve as driving forces to bring out the child's latent abilities—abilities they believe would otherwise lie dormant. Furthermore, many parents believe that expressing an aspiration level will increase the child's motivational level; they then encourage the child to say what he hopes to do in the belief that this will "put him on record." They believe that he will try to come up to what others expect of him because of what he has said he expected of himself (66, 157, 249).

In establishing his levels of aspiration, the child is also influenced by his ideal at the moment, the person with whom he has identified himself and whom he would like to resemble. Most children select as their ideals people who have made outstanding successes; therefore, children can readily set their aspirations way beyond their present, and perhaps even their future, capacities (129).

Every child discovers that a high aspiration level, when verbalized, raises his prestige in the eyes of everyone, including himself. A child who has a poor concept of self or who believes that others have a poor concept of him will often set a level of aspiration unrealistically high in the hope of increasing his prestige. Boys generally feel a greater need for achievement than girls, and thus they more often set goals beyond their capacities (56, 157, 336).

The child whose level of aspiration is too high for his abilities becomes an "impractical idealist" who sees himself constantly as a failure; the child who sets his aspirations below his abilities lacks "ambition" and "gets nowhere" in life; while the child who "has his feet on the ground" checks his aspirations with his achievements and constantly revises his aspirations to fit more realistically into his abilities. Most children, unfortunately, fall into either of the first two categories (51, 339).

The habit of aspiring to do too much or too little is set early in life and has a marked influence on the individual's concept of self. By adolescence, the relationship between level of aspiration and the individual's effort to achieve this aspiration is well set. Thus if the child is to be happy, successful, and well adjusted, he must learn early in life to assess his abilities realistically and to set his level of aspiration accordingly.

The child who measures up to his own expectations feels proud and satisfied with himself and with his achievements. This is more characteristic of the intelligent and well-adjusted child who has learned to judge himself and others realistically than of the less intelligent and less well-adjusted child. A child who has been accustomed to too much or too easy success often needs an occasional failure to keep him from becoming overconfident and to prepare him to meet stiff competition. Repeated success may lead a child to raise his levels of aspiration unrealistically high; a failure now and then helps him to bring them down to a more realistic level (114, 213).

Repeated failure causes the child to be unsure of himself and to lower his level of aspiration, perhaps to an unrealistically low point. The child is then variable and unpredictable in performance; he is anxious and worried and suffers from feelings of inadequacy; and he is submissive in his attitude toward others. All these conditions contribute to poor self-concepts, poor adjustment, and unhappiness (323, 351).

Many parents and teachers believe that threat of failure is a good incentive, that it will keep the child on his toes and motivate him to live up to his potential. If the child has realistic levels of aspiration, threat of failure may be just what he needs. But if his levels of aspiration are unrealistically high, threat of failure will increase his anxiety, lower his morale, and further weaken his already unfavorable self-concept.

Symonds has pointed out that the child who "has experienced failure probably never overcomes the weakness that results from these experiences, and is ever after liable to succumb to stress that he may encounter. This means that it is extremely important to arrange that a child experience success from the beginning if he is to have good learning potentiality in later years" (312). When a child is learning to think of himself as a person, guidance is of critical importance in helping him to see himself as a success, at least most of the time. This is possible only when his levels of aspiration are realistic.

THE CHILD'S NAME

A child is known to many people only by his name; his name, then, serves as a symbol by which people judge him. Unquestionably, his name plays an important role in the first judgments made by others. If it has pleasant associations for them, he will benefit. Furthermore, a child's name influences his conduct in subtle ways which he may not even recognize (101). The most important of these "subtle ways" is the effect the name has on his self-concept. If his name calls forth favorable associations in the minds of others, they will treat him favorably, and this will have a good effect on his self-concept; if others treat him unfavorably, he cannot fail to develop an unfavorable self-concept. Thus a child's name can be either a psychological asset or a psychological liability (207). Allen has said that the "choice of a given name to be bestowed upon the child is a matter of no little amount to him in his relations with other individuals, for an unfortunate selection may doom him to recurring embarrassment or even unhappiness" (10). Teagarden further emphasizes the point by saying, "The name that is given to a child at birth or shortly thereafter may constitute a psychological hazard" (316). The child's name may be a source of "exaggerated pride or exaggerated shame," or it may be the "core of a severe neurosis" (207). Not only the child's real name but also any nickname or name of endearment that his parents or relatives use will have serious effects on the development of his personality.

A name, per se, will have little or no influence on the child's self-concept. Its influence will be felt only when the child becomes aware of the attitudes of significant people in his life toward his name. When the child is old enough to play with other children, around the third year, he begins to realize the importance of his name. Names that lend themselves to distortions, names which are difficult to pronounce and which are therefore frequently mispronounced, names that other children criticize or make fun of, names that confuse the sexes, or names that result in queer initials (Charles Oliver Watson—C.O.W.) or meanings (Ima Virginia Bird) are certain to give the bearer uncomfortable feelings (55, 89).

Furthermore, the child discovers that names mean different things to different people. To a child, being called "mamma's little boy" means that his mother loves him, but to members of the peer group, it means that he is "tied to mamma's apron strings," and to a sibling, it means that he is "mamma's pet" (263).

A little girl who is pleased to have a name "like daddy's" may discover, as she grows older, that her name means that her sex was a disappointment to her parents—that they had hoped she would be a boy. Similarly, a little boy is proud to be called "Junior" at first because it identifies him with his father. Later, when members of the peer group call him "Junior" in a derisive way, he will decide that he hates it (101).

Few children accept their names unemotionally. Whether they like or dislike them depends not on their sound, but on the associations made with them. Given names and nicknames are more important than surnames to young children, but as childhood draws to a close, the surname is used more often, and social reactions to it begin to have an effect on the child's self-concept (101). A given name that annoys or embarrasses a child can be dropped and a nickname substituted for it, but nothing can be done about a family name that is a psychological hazard to the child unless the family as a whole is willing to change its name legally. Changing his surname alone is of little value as long as the other members of the family retain it (2, 55). For both given and family names, the child likes names that are easy to pronounce and spell and that lend themselves to unembarrassing nicknames. Only as the child grows older does he begin to prefer a name that is slightly distinctive (2, 25, 89).

If the child's name is liked by others, it makes him feel self-important; this reacts favorably on his concept of self. "Jack," for example, is liked by most boys because it is associated with a "regular boy," while "Percy" or "Albert" is often regarded as a "sissy" name. A surname like "Short," "Small," or "Little" is embarrassing to a boy because he knows that boys and men are most admired when they are large.

If a child dislikes his name, he may become shy, retiring, and easily embarrassed. The more he dislikes his name, the less self-accepting he is and the more damaging the effect of the name will be to his personality. Boys with peculiar names or names that draw unfavorable peer reactions are more affected by their names than girls. The reason for this is that boys tend to have more conventional names than girls; as a result, there is less "social spotlighting" for girls with unusual or peculiar names (90, 227).

Children of minority groups sometimes discover that their names awaken prejudice every time they are used. They therefore adopt nicknames or try to "improve" their names by dropping the last syllable or changing them completely. Foreign names associated with countries against which there is prejudice are often changed or Americanized (140, 207, 259, 341).

Nicknames. A nickname may have unfavorable or favorable effects, depending on how it originated, what associations it implies, and even how it is spoken. Many nicknames are verbal caricatures in the sense that they emphasize physical or psychological traits that are a source of embarrassment. As such, they are often expressive of the underlying emotional attitude of the peer group toward the child (290).

Studies of nicknames given to children have revealed that they fall into a number of categories, including "pet" names, or names of endearment; nationality or place-of-birth nicknames; names of animals; distortions of the real name; nicknames from the individual's initials; nicknames from physical defects; and nicknames based on personality defects. The effect of nicknames on the child's personality, as is true of his real name, will depend not so much on the nicknames themselves but on how the child interprets them (215).

Most children dislike their nicknames and build up a feeling of resentment against those who use them, especially when they know that the nicknames are a way of making fun of them. Widespread use of an embarrassing nickname may readily result in such strong feelings of inferiority and resentment that the child will withdraw from the group. Problem behavior often results from the child's attempts to compensate for a nickname that makes him feel inferior (301).

Not all children, of course, dislike their nicknames. As they grow older, they learn to distinguish between nicknames that imply ridicule and rejection and those that imply acceptance and affection (84). The possible unfavorable effects of a nickname are so great, however, that one must conclude that "Fortunate is the boy whose name and/or personal characteristics do not suggest humorous, bizarre nicknames to the imaginative minds of his peers" (123).

STATUS SYMBOLS

Even before his first birthday, the baby wants to be recognized as an individual. If he has siblings with whom he must compete for parental attention, anything that gives him a more favorable status than the siblings makes him feel that he is more important. The desire for a position of status becomes stronger as the child grows older. One way to increase his position in the group, he soon discovers, is to have status symbols. A *status symbol* is a "prestige" symbol in the sense that it tells others that the person has

a higher status than those with whom he is identified (78, 139).

Status symbols for various age groups and social groups differ. Going to a "name" school, for example, is a status symbol for an adolescent, but not for a child because the child does not realize how society rates different schools. Toys and playthings are status symbols for a child, but they have little value for an adolescent and, therefore, give him no prestige in the eyes of the peer group. Before status symbols can affect a child's personality, he must become aware of the meaning of the symbols to the social group and must realize that he is judged in terms of the status symbols he or his family possesses.

Some Status Symbols in Childhood. At all ages, *material possessions* are the most universal status symbols because they can be observed by all. Even before he enters school, the young child discovers the prestige value of his toys, clothes, and other possessions. He boasts and brags about what he has and claims that his possessions are superior. When he visits the homes of his playmates, he compares their possessions with his. If he thinks theirs are better than his, he becomes dissatisfied and envious (193, 270). His wishes and daydreams then begin to center around material possessions which have prestige value in the eyes of his playmates, and his dissatisfaction and envy grow (70). Studies have revealed that such "status symbols" as toys, bicycles, athletic equipment, a family car, clothes, television sets, radios, and pianos stand at the top of the list. Each year, children become increasingly aware of the role status symbols play in social acceptance, and their interest in material possessions increases (17).

Children notice deviations from the "average" in standards of living in terms of material possessions and are more aware of those that are qualitatively inferior than of those that are superior. They are far more attracted to upper-status patterns of living than to lower-status patterns. They often express sympathy for persons who cannot have better possessions (93).

By the fourth or fifth grade, most children can identify the symbols of social status and relate them quite accurately to economic status. Then the child comes to judge others and himself in terms of his *father's occupation*. If it is a prestigeful occupation that enables the family to have the status symbols that win prestige in the eyes of the peer group, it will have a favorable effect on the child's self-concept. An occupation that lacks prestige, even though it may be adequate to provide the status symbols that are important to social acceptance, will cause the child embarrassment and will thus damage his self-concept. Status symbols play a more important role in the social acceptance of girls than of boys; girls are therefore more harmed psychologically by inferior status symbols (93, 143, 300, 340).

Clothes are an ever-present manifestation of the status of the child. Not only do they tell, indirectly, the socioeconomic status of his family, but they tell, directly, his status in the peer group. For that reason, clothes are an important factor in personality development. The child is keenly aware of the attitude of others, primarily of his peers, toward his clothes. Compliance with the particular style accepted by the group to which he belongs becomes critical, even though the group may not conform to the prevailing styles in the community.

Having clothes that other children admire, envy, and imitate gives the child a feeling of importance. On the other hand, being dressed in clothes that other children make fun of gives the child feelings of inferiority. Being poorly dressed over a period of time is likely to lead to marked feelings of inadequacy (141, 279).

The influence of clothes on the individual's concept of self has been emphasized by Morton:

For the vast majority of the human race, clothing plays a large part in making for happiness and success. . . . Clothes help to make us self-confident, self-respecting, jolly, free or they make us self-conscious, shy, sensitive, restrained. . . . Clothes then make or mar us. They may enhance our personality or be so conspicuous as to subordinate us to

them, or they may be just ordinary, nondescript, characterless (201).

Growing up is difficult for the child because of the many adjustments he must make to the adult world. "Clothes may make growing up easier or harder. They may be a symbol of security, an extension of self, a way of identifying with someone, a means of real satisfaction" (237).

Effects of Status Symbols. The child whose parents have enough money to provide the clothes and material possessions that give him prestige in the eyes of the peer group will develop a better self-concept and thus a more wholesome personality than the child whose parents either cannot or will not make such provisions for him. If a child lacks social acceptance, he is likely to blame his father for not providing him with the status symbols his classmates have. He develops feelings of martyrdom, complaining about his lot, envying the lot of others, or telling others how "lucky" they are. Such self-pity makes the child unhappy and makes others uncomfortable (177, 262).

Some children, as a defense against feelings of inferiority, criticize or ridicule what others have. They assume a "sour-grapes" attitude; if they cannot have the "grapes," they claim they are not worth having. No child likes to have his material possessions criticized or ridiculed, so the child who uses this defense mechanism damages his personality directly by developing an unwholesome self-concept, and indirectly by behaving in a manner that will guarantee poor social acceptance (271).

LEVEL OF ADJUSTMENT

Adjustment is the extent to which an individual's personality functions efficiently in a world of other people. As Thompson has pointed out:

Normal adjustment is a relative thing. Every child suffers some anxiety, displays some behavior that is unacceptable to others, fails to reach some goals that are extremely important to him, and experiences some periods of what he calls unhappiness. However, the child whose psychological adjustment can be considered within normal range "bounces back" from these disappointments and depressions. He continues to orient his behavior toward goals that promise to satisfy his needs, and he adjusts his goal-setting to the social demands of his culture (320).

This means that a well-adjusted child, regardless of occasional setbacks and disappointments, will continue to hold to the goals he has set for himself and will strive to reach them. He does so because his goals have been set to meet needs in his life, not because they have been imposed on him by someone else or set to match those of the crowd. A well-adjusted child will modify his goals when it becomes apparent to him that they are unrealistically high. In making these modifications, however, he will not select substitutes unless they meet his needs satisfactorily.

Role of Self-acceptance. If the child's self-concept is to his liking, he will accept himself; if it is not, he will dislike and reject himself. Few children, however, are 100 per cent self-acceptant or self-rejectant. They usually want to become more like their ideal selves, and each year they become more personality-conscious. If a child is to have a healthy personality that he can accept, he must have an image of himself that he "can accept and live with, without feeling too guilty, anxious, or hostile, without being self-defeated or destructive of others" (102).

As a child compares himself with other children, he is often dissatisfied with the comparison and finds it difficult to accept himself as he is. He wants to improve his personality so that he can conform more closely to his ideal or to the patterns set by the children who are admired and liked. Under such conditions, having a "self-accepting attitude" is difficult, if not impossible (308). A self-accepting attitude consists of being able to live fairly comfortably with one's emotions; of having confidence in one's abilities to cope with life; of being willing to assume responsibilities and the

challenge of one's abilities without reaching for the impossible; and of having a healthy regard for one's rights and for oneself as a worthy person, even if not perfect. Self-acceptance does not mean smug self-satisfaction, but rather the willingness to face facts and conditions of life, whether favorable or unfavorable, as candidly and as fully as possible (146).

Aids to Self-acceptance. Self-acceptance is aided by a number of factors, each of which helps the child to develop a satisfactory concept of self. *First,* the child's hopes for, and demands upon, himself must be kept within the limits of his achievement; he must be realistic about himself and not aim for the impossible. This, of course, does not mean that he should lack ambition or set his goals below his capacities. It does mean, however, that he must set goals within his potentials, even though these potentials are lower than he would like them to be. Only when the gap between the real and the ideal self-concepts can be narrowed down to the point where the ideal may possibly be attained can the child accept himself and make good personal and social adjustments (173).

Second, self-understanding helps to close the gap between the real and the ideal. The child who understands himself does not merely recognize facts about himself; he also perceives the significance of these facts. To be self-accepting, for example, the child who is physically handicapped must not only realize that his handicap cuts him off from many activities but also realize that it does not cut him off from *everything;* there are some activities that he can enjoy with his peers, and he can make his contribution to the enjoyment of the group through them. Self-understanding and self-acceptance go hand in hand. The better the child understands himself, the more realistic he is and the smaller the gap between his real and his ideal self-concepts will be.

A *third* factor that influences the degree of self-acceptance the child achieves is the discrepancy between his concept of himself and the concepts others have of him. The child who lacks social insight and self-insight, as has been stressed earlier, makes poorer adjustments and is less acceptable to the peer group than the child whose perception of self is close to the percept others have of him. By being able to see himself as others see him, he can guide his behavior to conform to social expectations and thus increase his social acceptance. By contrast, a marked discrepancy between the opinions others have of him and the opinion the child has of himself will lead to behavior that antagonizes others and thus lowers their opinion of him. The less accepted he is by others, the harder it is for him to accept himself.

Finally, self-acceptance is greatly influenced by the stability of the self-concept. The child who sees himself one way at one time and another way at another time—sometimes favorably and sometimes unfavorably—is ambivalent about himself. In order for the child to be self-acceptant, his self-concept must be *both stable and favorable.* A stable self-concept composed mainly of negative concepts will lead to self-rejection.

Self-acceptance and Adjustment. No child can make good personal or social adjustments if he dislikes himself. On the other hand, when a person likes himself reasonably well, he will behave in a manner that will lead to social acceptance. The more others like and accept him, the better he will like himself and the more self-acceptant he will become. That is why the personality pattern tends to be persistent, with changes mainly of a quantitative type (see pages 716 to 717).

The longer self-acceptance persists, the stronger and more deeply rooted it will be. This is true likewise for self-rejection. In time, the characteristic pattern of adjustment the individual makes to life will be motivated by the degree of acceptance or rejection he has for himself. Thus, *both self-acceptance and self-rejection become self-perpetuating.*

No one, at any age, is consistently self-acceptant or self-rejectant. A child may be self-acceptant in his play because he plays as well as, or better than, the other children.

On the other hand, he may be self-rejectant in school because his marks fall far below theirs. Similarly, if a child's teacher has an acceptant attitude toward him, praising him for his achievements and helping him with his difficulties without being critical or punitive, he will be self-acceptant as long as he remains in the school. If he is subjected to criticism, punishment, teasing, and bullying when he goes home, he will perceive the home environment as rejective and will become self-rejectant.

Because self-acceptance is so greatly influenced by the environment and by the attitudes of significant people, it is logical that the degree of self-acceptance the child experiences will vary from time to time. The important point, however, is that *there must be a degree of consistency in his self-acceptance if he is to make good adjustments.*

Furthermore, this consistency must be in the direction of positive rather than negative self-concepts. In speaking of adolescents—and this holds true of children also—Jersild has pointed out that "self-acceptance denotes a predominant trend or direction in a person's life rather than a state in which everything is rosy. An adolescent who is wholehearted in accepting some aspects of his life may be in doubt or difficulty with respect to others. The prevailing bent, however, is in the direction of self-acceptance" (144).

There are certain times in life when self-acceptance is easy for a child, and others when it is almost impossible. Often, it depends on the attitudes of other people toward the child and his behavior *at that age.* It is easy, for example, for a baby to be self-acceptant; everyone accepts him or at least behaves in such a manner that he assumes they do. As he grows older, however, he discovers that he is less well accepted than before. In place of demonstrations of love come punishments and harsh, critical words and frowns. Interpreting them to mean rejection, he begins to have a less and less favorable opinion of himself. He accepts himself less and rejects himself more. The low point in family and social relationships for the child generally comes at puberty.

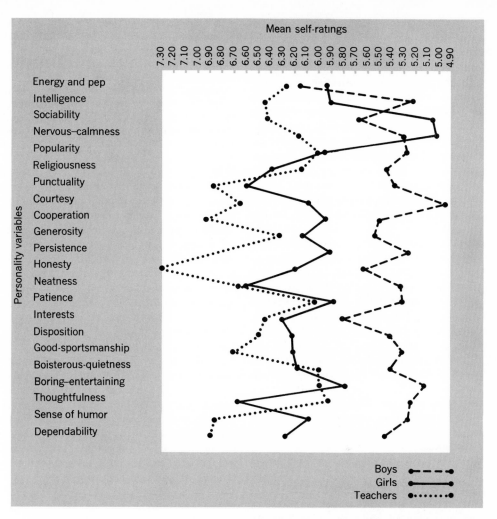

Figure 15-6. Self-ratings of elementary-school boys and girls and of their teachers. Note the tendency for boys to rate themselves less favorably than girls do, and for children of both sexes to have poorer opinions of themselves than teachers do. (Adapted from Sister M. Amatora, Comparisons in self-evaluation in personality, *J. soc. Psychol.*, 1955, 42, 315–321. Used by permission.)

Self-acceptance likewise reaches its low point then. Whether there will be an improvement as time goes on will depend largely on the type of social adjustments the young adolescent makes in the home, in school, and with members of the peer group (86, 147, 323).

Self-evaluations of children as they grow older have revealed that they rate themselves less favorably than they are rated by their teachers and by members of the peer group. This is illustrated in Figure 15–6. Girls, on the whole, rate themselves more favorably than boys. The poor opinion older children have of themselves unquestionably stems from the way they are treated by the different social groups with which they come in contact in their daily lives. It likewise is greatly influenced by the discrepancy between what they would like to be and what they perceive to be the opinions others have of them (15, 16).

Boys, especially, are sensitive to the low opinions others hold of them. Growing up in a world peopled by women, with female standards and values and with few opportunities for adult male contacts, the typical American boy of today learns to think of himself as inferior. He is constantly criticized and punished for behaving in a manner which is approved by peers but not by adult women. Furthermore, because doing good work in school is not considered sex-appropriate by the peer group, boys are constantly subjected to the humiliation of poor grades and the feelings of guilt which come when they realize that they are working below their capacities and below parental expectations. This further adds to their difficulties in liking and accepting themselves (223, 224, 312, 335).

Studies of well-adjusted and poorly adjusted children have revealed that certain patterns of behavior are characteristically associated with the two. A brief survey of these patterns of adjustment will show how important a reasonable amount of self-acceptance is.

WELL-ADJUSTED PERSONALITIES

The well-adjusted child enjoys a kind of "inner harmony"; he is at peace with himself, just as he is at peace with others (171). Bain has described the well-adjusted child thus:

He thinks, acts, and feels according to what is expected and tolerated within his society. . . . He is both satisfied and stimulated by the life he leads. He has the habit of happiness and the habit of making and breaking habits effectively. He is neither unduly frightened by the future nor wedded to the past. . . . He has no sense of sin but he profits by experience. He has a sturdy sense of humor which laughs *with* people, not *at* them. He knows his limitations and capacities

and acts accordingly. He has a fairly accurate judgment of others and of what others think of him. . . . He makes his goals and ideals consistent with his knowledge of what is possible, and he is open-minded about the "possible." He respects himself because he respects others. . . . He wants an opportunity to realize his own potentials so long as it does not prevent others from doing the same (30).

Well-adjusted children, like well-adjusted adults, make good social adjustments and have harmonious relationships with the people with whom they are associated, whether in the home, at school, in business, or in play. Because they accept themselves, they do not need to build up defenses or project the blame for the discrepancy between what they are and what they would like to be on others (96).

The degree to which a child adjusts to others, then, is indicative of how well adjusted he is as a person. In describing the type of child who makes the best adjustments to others, Barrett-Lennard has pointed out that he "genuinely appreciates and values others as he does himself. He is comfortable and open with them because he is comfortable and open with himself. He is not guarded in a personal sense because he has nothing to hide. He does not distort himself to please others, nor does he use them as scapegoats for self-dissatisfaction" (35).

PERSONALITY MALADJUSTMENTS

A child who becomes self-rejectant makes poor personal as well as social adjustments; he becomes a *maladjusted person*—one who, in childhood, is frequently referred to as a "problem child" (98). There are two major types of personality maladjustment: The *first* involves behavior which is satisfying to the child but which is socially unacceptable, while the *second* involves behavior which is socially acceptable but which is a source of continuous, excessive, and disturbing conflict to the child. Whether the child will engage in behavior which is satisfying to him and socially acceptable or whether he will behave in a socially acceptable manner, in spite of the psychological strain on him, will be characteristic of his own personality pattern and the level of adjustment he has attained (35, 271, 323).

There are a number of personality traits of an undesirable sort that appear in a mild form in children. At first, they appear to be harmless and are frequently allowed to persist, without any real effort being made to overcome them. No single pattern is serious when viewed by itself. When several patterns are observable in the same child, however, and when they seem to fit into a "personality picture," they are significant and may be regarded as "danger signals" of future trouble. Of the many such behavior patterns, the following are regarded as most serious:

Flying into fits of rage on the slightest provocation.

Showing signs of excessive "worriedness" and anxiety.

Frequently appearing depressed and rarely smiling or joking with others.

Repeated stealing of small articles, despite severe punishment.

Frequently appearing to be lost in daydreams.

Showing very sensitive reactions to real or imagined slights.

Excessive cruelty to younger or smaller children or animals.

Abnormal anxiety about achieving perfection in any task.

Frequent expression of the idea that he is being singled out for punishment more than others.

Inability to avoid misbehavior even when repeatedly warned and punished.

Excessive concern with physical appearance.

Habit of lying on any occasion to suit some purpose.

High degree of indecisiveness when relatively minor choices must be made.

Hostility toward any kind of authority.

Accident-proneness.

Repeated acts of destruction of material things.

Teasing and bullying others when feeling rejected.

Homesickness when away from familiar people and places.

"Clowning" as a means of attracting attention to himself.

Projecting blame on others and rationalizing acts when criticized.

Tattling on other children to win adult attention and approval.

"Sour-grapes" attitude—covering up disappointment by minimizing the value of unattainable things (52, 136, 206, 323).

Below the age of twelve years, children rarely succumb to a definite mental illness. But at that time, ineffective adjustments to everyday life situations are manifested in symptoms, such as crying, attention seeking, and daydreaming, which, if permitted to go unchecked, may result in serious mental illness as the child reaches maturity. No normal child is completely free from what is labeled "problem behavior." The average number of different forms varies from four to six per child, with the frequency varying according to the age of the child. A child may be quite disturbed and yet make good adjustments in school (179). Some children may be considered well adjusted by their teachers and yet be considered "problems" by their parents and seriously disturbed by clinical workers (38, 331).

Boys, as a rule, suffer more from personality disturbances than girls. Figure 15–7 shows the mean number of personality problems of children, such as feelings of inferiority, lack of self-confidence, hypersensitivity, anxiety, and shyness, from kindergarten through the sixth grade. From this, it is apparent that boys begin school with more personality problems than girls, but by the time girls are seven or eight years old, their personality problems increase, while those of boys decrease. The explanation offered for the increase among girls is the "early agitation" of adolescence, which begins sooner in girls than in boys, and the

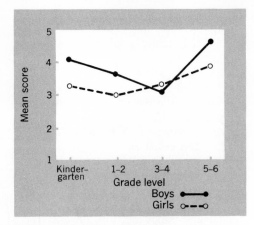

Figure 15-7. Sex differences in personality problems of children of different ages. (Adapted from D. R. Peterson, Behavior problems in middle childhood, *J. consult. Psychol.*, 1961, 25, 205–209. Used by permission.)

greater pressure on girls for sex-type conformity (225).

Once a pattern of maladjustive behavior appears, it is likely to persist. As Bennett has stated:

Maladjustive behavior shows a tenacious tendency to remain maladjustive. Forms of activity that succeed in doing the individual far more harm than good remain in operation even in the face of the strongest psychotherapeutic efforts. Minor forms of maladjustive behavior become permanent fixtures in the totality of an individual's behavior and often remain throughout his lifetime. Small things, insignificant in themselves, pile up and add burdens to the day-to-day existence and drain efficiency (40).

Unless minor disturbances are discovered and remedial measures taken to correct them, they are likely to develop into handicapping disorders. Personality maladjustments are seldom outgrown; instead, they become more serious and lead to more pronounced maladjustive behavior. While children can be helped to improve their adjustments by gaining better insight into themselves and a more realistic concept of their abilities, improvement is far from easy as

long as they remain in the environment that has been responsible for the development of the unrealistic self-concepts (246, 281).

Since most personality maladjustments have their origin in the home, the only way to eliminate the cause of the trouble would be for parents to remove the stresses built up by their unrealistic demands on the children or, as Jersild facetiously suggested, to "transport the children to another world" (146).

HAPPINESS IN CHILDHOOD

Most adults think of childhood as a happy, carefree period of life. As Rosenzweig and Rosenzweig have pointed out, "The golden days of childhood, as they appear in the conventional reminiscence of adults, are more consistent with fantasy than with fact. The myths of all races similarly portray the childhood of man as a paradise" (250). As a matter of fact, the child is probably no happier than the adult. While the adult is looking back longingly at his childhood and wishing he could return to it, the child is looking forward to the day when he will be "grown up" and free from the controls which constantly frustrate him.

The belief that the child can best be happy if he is carefree stems from the assumption that responsibilities and achievement can lead only to anxiety and frustration. Because money and the status symbols money can buy, such as clothes, houses, cars, entertainment, membership in exclusive clubs, and leisure to do what one wishes, are so highly valued by adults, they assume that material possessions are the source of happiness in childhood. The fairy tales of early childhood and the mass media of communication enjoyed by older children, adolescents, and adults all reinforce the belief that one cannot be happy if he is poor. It is not surprising, then, that parents shower their children with material possessions and give them every advantage that money can buy, often at great personal sacrifice, in the belief that this will guarantee a happy childhood.

Finally, there is a widespread popular belief that if a person has a happy childhood, he will *always* be happy and well adjusted. There are enough exceptions to this popular belief to justify rewording it to say: Happiness in childhood is not a foolproof guarantee of happiness in adulthood or even in adolescence. Conditions within the individual, such as an accident which handicaps him in the activities he has enjoyed and which deprives him of the social contacts that added greatly to his earlier happiness, can readily turn a happy child into an unhappy, neurotic, maladjusted adolescent or adult. Similarly, conditions in the environment that led to happiness at one age may not lead to happiness at other ages. The child who is accepted because of his skills in play, regardless of his race or religion, may find, as he reaches adolescence, that race and religion are more important to an adolescent's acceptance than to a child's. Consequently, the acceptance he formerly enjoyed may be replaced by rejection.

Retrospective Reports of Happiness. As adults look back upon their childhood days, they see it from a perspective of time that enables them to compare the happiness they experienced in childhood with the happiness they experienced at other ages. For the most part, retrospective studies show that childhood is remembered as a *relatively* happy age, though not free from memories of unhappy experiences. As the babyhood years are years of dependency, the feeling of being all-powerful and the center of attention is very satisfying to the baby and makes him happy. Only physical discomforts and pain, from illness or injury and occasional corporal punishment, make him unhappy (321).

After the child is four years old, there are many unfulfilled wishes, unsolved problems, and unpleasant incidents of being forced to do things he does not want to do and of being punished for things he does not consider wrong. No longer is the child omnipotent, as he was in babyhood. He now meets new environmental obstacles as well as new demands (36, 69, 285).

When the child goes to school, he meets more environmental obstacles and more demands from adults; he also comes into competition with other children. How well he can meet these demands and this competition will determine how happy he will be. Family and home are less important to the child's happiness than earlier, though friction with family members and feelings of guilt when parental expectations are not met contribute to his unhappiness (61, 346).

Reading between the lines of the retrospective reports, it becomes apparent that happiness does not depend on being carefree or on having material possessions, nor is unhappiness the result of not having these advantages. Fundamentally, the key to happiness, as reported in retrospective studies, is the *degree of adjustment* the child makes at different times during his childhood years.

Children who are well adjusted come from homes that are happy places, where discipline is used for more far-reaching purposes than merely deterring wrongdoing, where responsibility is a part of the routine of life, where there is religion, where the family enjoys recreations together, and where family relationships and attitudes toward children are wholesome. In such homes, children learn to take responsibilities on their own level, to be independent and take care of their own needs, to solve their own problems, and to be happy when alone (124, 202, 307).

If children are to be well adjusted, not only must adults know how to *create* a good environment for them, but once it is created, they must know how to *maintain* it. If the child learns to be secure in his intimate relationships with his family, he can tolerate the insecurity that comes when he tries to adjust to the world outside the home, and he can make satisfactory adjustments there, as he has in the home (187, 294).

Happiness and Adjustment. Happiness in childhood comes mostly from human relationships, not from material possessions or from freedom from responsibility. While it is true that material possessions that have prestige in the eyes of the peer group add to happiness by increasing the child's chances of gaining social acceptance, and while freedom from home and other responsibilities gives him time to be with the peer group, these factors by themselves are of little consequence in providing happiness in the childhood years. A child can be happy *only* when he feels that he is accepted by others; he will be accepted by others *only* if he is a reasonably well-adjusted person; and he can be a reasonably well-adjusted person *only* if he has a self-acceptant attitude. Because of the high value placed on social acceptance, no child in the American culture of today can hope to be happy if he is friendless (152, 238).

Even though social acceptance and happiness go hand in hand, the acceptance must be by the *people who are important in the child's life at that time.* As a young child, parents are the important people in his life, especially the mother. As he grows older, he must be accepted not only by his family but *also* by the members of the peer group whom he finds congenial and wants to have as friends (36, 48, 238).

The child soon discovers that pleasant relationships with others depend more upon his adjustment to them than upon their adjustment to him. He must fit into the socially approved pattern of the group if he is to be an accepted member of it. The child whose personality pattern has been developed along lines approved by the group has, therefore, a far better chance for successful social adjustments than the child whose personality is atypical for the group. While he might make good adjustments in a cultural group where certain of his outstanding traits were admired, he will not make good adjustments to the group with which he is associated unless he conforms to the pattern of that group (109, 329).

To be able to make good social adjustments, the child must first make good self-adjustments. No child, at any age, who is dissatisfied with himself can hope that others will want him as a friend. As long as a child has an unrealistic concept of himself, he will constantly fall below his ideal; this will make him dissatisfied and unhappy. To counteract this self-dissatisfaction, he will start to develop defense mechanisms, often thrusting the blame for his shortcomings on others. Long before children enter school they develop a repertoire of defense mechanisms to cope with people and situations that make them uncomfortable or lead to feelings of inadequacy.

The child who is flexible in his reactions, using the defense mechanisms that will make him more self-acceptant and more acceptable to others, will be far happier than the child who uses defense mechanisms which make him more comfortable about his own behavior but which antagonize others. A child can be comfortable about himself if he thrusts the blame on someone else, but when he discovers that this is regarded as poor sportsmanship and that it wins social disapproval, his self-acceptance will turn into self-rejection (206).

A realistic self-concept, on the other hand, eliminates much of the temptation to use defense mechanisms. If the child is realistic about himself, he will not expect more than he is capable of; consequently, he will not have to justify behavior that falls short of perfection. In this he can be aided by parents and teachers who recognize that a child is a child, not a miniature adult. As long as the child's adjustments to life compare favorably with the norm for his age, he can be satisfied with himself if the significant people in his life are likewise satisfied.

This suggests that *childhood happiness is not in the child's hands alone;* parents and teachers play a major role in determining how happy or unhappy a child will be by encouraging realistic self-concepts in the former case and unrealistic self-concepts in the latter. Expecting a child to be a child with the characteristic behavior of a child of his age instead of a paragon of perfection will go a long way toward guaranteeing a happy childhood.

BIBLIOGRAPHY

(1) ABBE, M.: Ideal personalities of pupils and teachers judged by pupils. *Jap. J. Psychol.,* 1950, **20,** 37–43.

(2) ADELSON, D.: Attitudes toward first names: an investigation of the relation between self-acceptance, self-identity, and group and individual attitudes toward first names. *Dissert. Abstr.,* 1957, **17,** 1831.

(3) AINSWORTH, L. H.: Rigidity, insecurity, and stress. *J. abnorm. soc. Psychol.,* 1958, **56,** 67–74.

(4) ALBERT, R. S.: The role of mass media and the effect of aggressive film content upon children's aggressive responses and identification choices. *Genet. Psychol. Monogr.,* 1957, **55,** 221–285.

(5) ALDRICH, C. A.: The pediatrician looks at personality. *Amer. J. Orthopsychiat.,* 1947, **17,** 571–574.

(6) ALEXANDER, F.: The dynamics of personality development. *Soc. Casewk,* 1951, **32,** 139–143.

(7) ALEXANDER, I. E., and A. M. ADLERSTEIN: Affective responses to the concept of death in a population of children and early adolescents. *J. genet. Psychol.,* 1958, **93,** 167–177.

(8) ALEXANDER, T.: Certain characteristics of the self as related to affection. *Child Developm.,* 1951, **22,** 285–290.

(9) ALEXANDER, T., and M. ALEXANDER: A study of personality and social status. *Child Developm.,* 1952, **23,** 207–213.

(10) ALLEN, L., L. BROWN, L. DICKINSON, and K. C. PRATT: The relation of first name preferences to the frequency in the culture. *J. soc. Psychol.,* 1941, **14,** 279–293.

(11) ALLPORT, G. W.: *Pattern and growth in personality.* New York: Holt, 1961.

(12) ALT, P. M.: Relationship of physique and temperament. *Sch. Rev.,* 1953, **61,** 267–276.

(13) AMATORA, SISTER M.: Guiding the child's personality potential to fruitful fulfillment. *Education,* 1952, **74,** 156–163.

(14) AMATORA, SISTER M.: Similarity in teacher and pupil personality. *J. Psychol.,* 1954, **37,** 45–50.

(15) AMATORA, SISTER M.: Validity in self-evaluation. *Educ. psychol. Measmt,* 1956, **16,** 119–126.

(16) AMATORA, SISTER M.: Developmental trends in pre-adolescence and early adolescence in self-evaluation. *J. genet. Psychol.,* 1957, **91,** 89–97.

(17) AMATORA, SISTER M.: Expressed interests in later childhood. *J. genet. Psychol.,* 1960, **96,** 327–342.

(18) AMEN, E. M., and N. RENISON: A study of the relationship between play patterns and anxiety in young children. *Genet. Psychol. Monogr.,* 1954, **50,** 3–41.

(19) AMES, R.: Physical maturing among boys as related to adult social behavior. *Calif. J. educ. Res.,* 1957, **8,** 69–75.

(20) AMIDON, E.: The isolate in children's groups. *J. teacher Educ.,* 1961, **12,** 412–416.

(21) ANASTASI, A.: Heredity, environment, and the question "how?" *Psychol. Rev.,* 1958, **65,** 197–208.

(22) ANDERSON, C. M.: The self-image: a theory of the dynamics of behavior. *Ment. Hyg., N.Y.,* 1952, **36,** 227–244.

(23) ANDERSON, J. E.: The relation of attitude to adjustment. *Education,* 1952, **73,** 210–218.

(24) ARMSTRONG, J. D.: The search for the alcoholic personality. *Ann. Amer. Acad. Pol. Soc. Sci.,* 1958, **315,** 40–47.

(25) ARTHAUD, R. L., A. N. HOHNECK, C. H. RAMSEY, and K. C. PRATT: The relation of family name preferences to their frequency in the culture. *J. soc. Psychol.,* 1948, **28,** 19–37.

(26) ASCH, S. E.: Forming impressions of personality. *J. abnorm. soc. Psychol.,* 1946, **41,** 258–290.

(27) AUSUBEL, D. P.: *Ego development and the personality disorders.* New York: Grune & Stratton, 1952.

(28) AUSUBEL, D. P., E. E. BALTHAZAR, I. ROSENTHAL, L. S. BLACKMAN, S. H. SCHPOONT, and J. WELKOWITZ: Perceived parent attitudes as determinants of children's ego structure. *Child. Developm.,* 1954, **25,** 173–183.

(29) AUSUBEL, D. P., H. M. SCHIFF, and E. B. GASSER: A preliminary study of developmental trends in sociopathy: accuracy of perception of own and others' sociometric status. *Child Developm.,* 1952, **23,** 111–128.

(30) BAIN, R.: Making normal people. *Marriage fam. Liv.,* 1954, **16,** 27–31.

(31) BAKER, J. W., and A. HOLZWORTH: Social histories of successful and unsuccessful children. *Child Developm.,* 1961, **32,** 135–149.

(32) BALDWIN, A. L., and H. LEVIN: Effects of public and private success or failure on children's repetitive motor behavior. *Child Developm.,* 1958, **29,** 363–372.

(33) BALDWIN, W. K.: The social position of the educable mentally retarded child in the regular grades in the public schools. *Except. Children,* 1958, **25,** 106–108, 112.

(34) BARBE, W. E.: Peer relationships of children of different intelligence levels. *Sch. Soc.*, 1954, **80**, 60–62.

(35) BARRETT-LENNARD, G. T.: The mature person. *Ment. Hyg., N.Y.*, 1962, **46**, 98–102.

(36) BARSCHAK, E.: A study of happiness and unhappiness in the childhood and adolescence of girls in different cultures. *J. Psychol.*, 1951, **32**, 173–215.

(37) BARTEMEIER, L.: The contribution of the father to the mental health of the family. *Amer. J. Psychiat.*, 1953, **110**, 277–280.

(38) BEILIN, H.: Teachers' and clinicians' attitudes toward the behavior problems of children: a reappraisal. *Child Develpm.*, 1959, **30**, 9–25.

(39) BENEDICT, R.: Child rearing in certain European countries. *Amer. J. Orthopsychiat.*, 1949, **19**, 342–350.

(40) BENNETT, E. M.: A socio-cultural interpretation of maladjustive behavior. *J. soc. Psychol.*, 1953, **37**, 19–26.

(41) BENNETT, E. M., and D. E. JOHANNSEN: Psychodynamics of the diabetic child. *Psychol. Monogr.*, 1954, **68**, No. 11.

(42) BETTELHEIM, B.: Mental health and current mores. *Amer. J. Orthopsychiat.*, 1952, **22**, 76–78.

(43) BICE, H. V.: Some factors that contribute to the concept of self in the child with cerebral palsy. *Ment. Hyg., N.Y.*, 1954, **38**, 120–131.

(44) BLOCK, J.: Personality characteristics associated with fathers' attitudes toward child-rearing. *Child Develpm.*, 1955, **26**, 41–48.

(45) BONNEY, M. E.: Choosing between the sexes on a sociometric measurement. *J. soc. Psychol.*, 1954, **39**, 99–114.

(46) BORG, W. R.: The effect of personality and contact upon a personality stereotype. *J. educ. Res.*, 1955, **49**, 289–294.

(47) BOSSARD, J. H. S., and E. S. BOLL: *The sociology of child development*, 3d ed. New York: Harper & Row, 1960.

(48) BOWERMAN, C. E., and J. W. KINCH: Changes in family and peer orientation of children between the fourth and tenth grades. *Soc. Forces*, 1959, **37**, 206–211.

(49) BOYD, G. F.: The levels of aspiration of white and Negro children in a nonsegregated elementary school. *J. soc. Psychol.*, 1952, **36**, 191–196.

(50) BRANDT, R. M.: Self: missing link for understanding behavior. *Ment. Hyg., N.Y.*, 1957, **41**, 24–33.

(51) BRECKENRIDGE, M. E., and E. L. VINCENT: *Child development*, 4th ed. Philadelphia: Saunders, 1960.

(52) BRENMAN, M.: On teasing and being teased: the problem of "moral masochism." *Psychoanal. Stud. Child.*, 1952, **7**, 264–285.

(53) BRODBECK, A. J., and H. V. PERLMUTTER: Self-dislike as a determinant of marked in group–out group preferences. *J. Psychol.*, 1954, **38**, 271–280.

(54) BRONSON, W. C.: Dimensions of ego and infantile identification. *J. Pers.*, 1959, **27**, 532–545.

(55) BROOM, L., H. P. BEEM, and V. HARRIS: Characteristics of 1,107 petitioners for change of name. *Amer. sociol. Rev.*, 1955, **20**, 33–39.

(56) BROWN, D. G.: Sex-role development in a changing culture. *Psychol. Bull.*, 1958, **55**, 232–242.

(57) BROWN, F. J.: *Educational sociology*, 2d ed. Englewood Cliffs, N.J.: Prentice-Hall, 1954.

(58) BROWN, L. P., H. D. GATES, E. L. NOLDER, and B. VAN FLEET: Personality characteristics of exceptional children and their mothers. *Elem. Sch. J.*, 1952, **52**, 286–290.

(59) BROWNFAIN, J. J.: Stability of the self-concept as a dimension of personality. *J. abnorm. soc. Psychol.*, 1952, **47**, 597–606.

(60) BUGENTAL, J. F. T., and E. C. GUNNING: Investigations into self-concept. III. Stability of reported self-identifications. *J. clin. Psychol.*, 1955, **11**, 41–46.

(61) BÜHLER, C.: School as a phase of human life. *Education*, 1952, **73**, 219–222.

(62) BUTTERWORTH, R. F., and G. G. THOMPSON: Factors related to age-grade trends and sex differences in children's preferences for comic books. *J. genet. Psychol.*, 1951, **78**, 71–96.

(63) CARLSON, R. O.: Variation and myth in the social status of teachers. *J. educ. Sociol.*, 1961, **35**, 104–118.

(64) CARTER, D. C.: The influence of family relationships and family experience on personality. *Marriage fam. Liv.*, 1954, **16**, 212–215.

(65) CATTELL, R. B., and R. W. COAN: Personality factors in middle childhood as revealed by parents' ratings. *Child Develpm.*, 1957, **28**, 439–458.

(66) CHILD, I. L., and M. K. BACON: Cultural pressures and achievement motivation. In P. H. Hoch and J. Zubin (Eds.), *Psychopathology of childhood*. New York: Grune & Stratton, 1955. Pp. 166–176.

(67) CHRISTENSEN, C. M.: Relationships between pupil achievement, pupil affect-need, teacher warmth, and teacher permissiveness. *J. educ. Psychol.*, 1960, **51**, 169–174.

(68) CLARKE, T. W.: Allergy and the "problem child." *Nerv. Child.* 1952, **9**, 278–281.

(69) CLIFFORD, E.: Discipline in the home: a controlled observational study of parental practices. *J. genet. Psychol.*, 1959, **95**, 45–82.

(70) COBB, H. V.: Role-wishes and general wishes of children and adolescents. *Child Develpm.*, 1954, **25**, 161–171.

(71) COLE, L.: *Psychology of adolescence*, 5th ed. New York: Holt, 1959.

(72) COWAN, E. L.: The "negative self concept" as a personality measure. *J. consult. Psychol.*, 1954, **18**, 138–142.

(73) CRANE, A. R.: The development of moral values in children. IV. Pre-adolescent gangs and the moral development of children. *Brit. J. educ. Psychol.*, 1958, **28**, 201–208.

(74) CRUICKSHANK, W. M., and G. O. JOHNSON: *Education of exceptional children and youth.* Englewood Cliffs, N.J.: Prentice-Hall, 1958.

(75) DAI, B.: A socio-psychiatric approach to personality organization. *Amer. sociol. Rev.*, 1952, **17**, 44–49.

(76) DANZINGER, K.: Parental demands and social class in Java, Indonesia. *J. soc. Psychol.*, 1960, **51**, 75–86.

(77) DAVIS, A., and R. J. HAVIGHURST: *Father of the man.* Boston: Houghton Mifflin, 1947.

(78) DAVIS, J. A.: Status symbols and the measurement of status perception. *Sociometry*, 1956, **19**, 154–165.

(79) DAVITZ, J. R.: Contributions of research with children to a theory of maladjustment. *Child Develpm.*, 1958, **29**, 3–7.

(80) DE GROAT, A. F., and G. G. THOMPSON: A study of the distribution of teacher approval and teacher disapproval among sixth-grade pupils. *J. exp. Educ.*, 1949, **18**, 57–75.

(81) DEMOS, G. M.: Attitudes of student ethnic groups on issues related to education. *Calif. J. educ. Res.*, 1960, **11**, 204–206.

(82) DEMPSEY, E. W.: Homeostasis. In S. S. Stevens (Ed.), *Handbook of experimental psychology.* New York: Wiley, 1951. Pp. 209–235.

(83) DESCOMBEY, J., and G. ROQUEBRUNE: Childhood personality and sibling relationships. *Enfance*, 1953, **6**, 329–368.

(84) DEXTER, E. S.: Three items related to personality: popularity, nicknames, and homesickness. *J. soc. Psychol.*, 1949, **30**, 155–158.

(85) DIXON, J. C.: Development of self recognition. *J. genet. Psychol.*, 1957, **91**, 251–256.

(86) DUNBAR, F.: Homeostasis during puberty. *Amer. J. Psychiat.*, 1958, **114**, 673–682.

(87) DURR, W. K.: Characteristics of gifted children: ten years of research. *Gifted Child Quart.*, 1960, **4**, 75–80.

(88) DYMOND, R. F.: Personality and empathy. *J. consult. Psychol.*, 1950, **14**, 343–350.

(89) EAGELSON, O. W.: Students' reactions to their given names. *J. soc. Psychol.*, 1946, **23**, 187–195.

(90) ELLIS, A., and R. M. BEECHLEY: Emotional disturbance in children with peculiar given names. *J. genet. Psychol.*, 1954, **85**, 337–339.

(91) ESCALONA, S. K., and M. LEITCH: Early phases of personality development. *Monogr. Soc. Res. Child Develpm.*, 1952, **17**, No. 1.

(92) ESTVAN, F. J.: The relationship of social status, intelligence, and sex of ten- and eleven-year-old children to an awareness of poverty. *Genet. Psychol. Monogr.*, 1952, **46**, 3–60.

(93) ESTVAN, F. J., and E. W. ESTVAN: *The child's world: his social perception.* New York: Putnam, 1959.

(94) FARBER, B.: Marital integration as a factor in parent-child relations. *Child Develpm.*, 1962, **33**, 1–14.

(95) FARBER, M. L.: English and Americans: values in the socialization process. *J. Psychol.*, 1953, **36**, 243–250.

(96) FEINBERG, M. R.: Relation of background experience to social acceptance. *J. abnorm. soc. Psychol.*, 1953, **48**, 206–214.

(97) FEINBERG, M. R., M. SMITH, and R. SCHMIDT: An analysis of expressions used by adolescents at varying economic levels to describe accepted and rejected peers. *J. genet. Psychol.*, 1958, **93**, 133–148.

(98) FEY, W. F.: Acceptance by others and its relation to acceptance of self and others: a revaluation. *J. abnorm. soc. Psychol.*, 1955, **50**, 274–276.

(99) FINNEY, J. C.: Some maternal influences on children's personality and character. *Genet. Psychol. Monogr.*, 1961, **63**, 199–278.

(100) FISHER, S., and S. E. CLEVELAND: The role of body image in psychosomatic symptom choice. *Psychol. Monogr.*, 1955, **69**, No. 17.

(101) FLUGEL, I.: On the significance of names. *Brit. J. med. Psychol.*, 1930, **10**, 208–213.

(102) FRANK, L. K.: Genetic psychology and its prospects. *Amer. J. Orthopsychiat.*, 1951, **21**, 506–522.

(103) FRANK, L. K., and M. H. FRANK: Teachers' attitudes affect children's relationships. *Education*, 1954, **75**, 6–12.

(104) FRAZEE, H. E.: Children who later became schizophrenic. *Smith Coll. Stud. soc. Wk*, 1953, **23**, 125–149.

(105) FREEDMAN, A. M., and L. BENDER: When childhood schizophrenic grows up. *Amer. J. Orthospychiat.*, 1957, **27**, 553–565.

(106) FRIED, E.: Ego functions and techniques of ego strengthening. *Amer. J. Psychother.*, 1955, **9**, 407–429.

(107) GARDNER, D. B., G. R. HAWKES, and L. G. BURCHINAL: Noncontinuous mothering in infancy and development in later childhood. *Child Develpm.*, 1961, **32**, 225–234.

(108) GARRISON, K. C.: *Growth and development*, 2d ed. New York: Longmans, 1959.

(109) GESELL, A., F. L. ILG, and L. B. AMES: *Youth: the years from ten to sixteen.* New York: Harper & Row, 1956.

(110) GEWIRTZ, J. L.: A factor analysis of some attention-seeking behaviors of young children. *Child Develpm.*, 1956, **27**, 17–36.

(111) GLASNER, RABBI S.: Family religion as a matrix of personal growth. *Marriage fam. Liv.*, 1961, **23**, 291–293.

(112) GLÖCKEL, H.: A comparative study of the

self-ideal in youth. *Child Develpm. Abstr.,* 1960, **34,** No. 649.

(113) GOFF, R. M.: Some educational implications of the influence of rejection on minority group children. *J. exper. Educ.,* 1954, **23,** 179–183.

(114) GOLDBERG, M. L.: Motivation of the gifted. *57th Yearb. Nat. Soc. Stud. Educ.,* 1958, Pt. 2, 87–109.

(115) GOLDSTEIN, A.: Aggression and hostility in the elementary school child in low socioeconomic areas. *Understanding the Child,* 1955, **24,** 20–21.

(116) GOODMAN, M. E.: *Race awareness in young children.* Cambridge, Mass.: Addison-Wesley, 1952.

(117) GOODMAN, M. E.: Japanese and American children: a comparative study of social concepts and attitudes. *Marriage fam. Liv.,* 1958, **20,** 316–319.

(118) GOUGH, H. G., and D. R. PETERSON: The identification and measurement of predispositional factors in crime and delinquency. *J. consult. Psychol.,* 1952, **16,** 207–212.

(119) GREEN, H. B.: Comparison of nurturance and independence in Jamaica and Puerto Rico, with consideration of the resulting personality structure and transplanted social patterns. *J. soc. Psychol.,* 1960, **51,** 27–63.

(120) GREENBERG, H., and D. FARE: An investigation of several variables as determinants of authoritarianism. *J. soc. Psychol.,* 1959, **49,** 105–111.

(121) GREENBERG, P., and A. R. GILLILAND: The relationship between basal metabolism and personality. *J. soc. Psychol.,* 1952, **35,** 3–7.

(122) GUSTAD, J. W.: Factors associated with social behavior and adjustment: a review of the literature. *Educ. psychol. Measmt,* 1952, **12,** 3–10.

(123) HABBE, S.: Nicknames of adolescent boys. *Amer. J. Orthopsychiat.,* 1937, **7,** 371–377.

(124) HARRIS, D. B., A. M. ROSE, K. E. CLARKE, and F. VALASEK: Personality differences between responsible and less responsible children. *J. genet. Psychol.,* 1955, **87,** 103–106.

(125) HARRIS, D. B., and S. C. TSENG: Children's attitudes toward peers and parents as revealed by sentence completions. *Child Develpm.,* 1957, **28,** 401–411.

(126) HAVIGHURST, R. J.: Social class and basic personality structure. *Sociol. soc. Res.,* 1952, **36,** 355–363.

(127) HAVIGHURST, R. J.: *Human development and education.* New York: Longmans, 1953.

(128) HAVIGHURST, R. J.: Social-class influences on American education. *60th Yearb. Nat. Soc. Stud. Educ.,* 1961, Pt. 2, 120–143.

(129) HAVIGHURST, R. J., and D. V. MAC DONALD: Development of the ideal self in New Zealand and American children. *J. educ. Res.,* 1955, **49,** 263–273.

(130) HAWKES, G. R.: A study of personal values of elementary school children. *Educ. psychol. Measmt,* 1952, **12,** 654–663.

(131) HAY-SHAW, C.: Maintenance of mental health. II. The first five years. *Ment. Hlth, London,* 1949, **9,** 3–6.

(132) HEBER, R. F.: The relation of intelligence and physical maturity to social status of children, *J. educ. Psychol.,* 1956, **47,** 158–162.

(133) HEFFERNAN, H.: The organization of the elementary school and the development of a healthy personality. *J. elem. Educ.,* 1952, **20,** 129–153.

(134) HELLERSBERG, E. F.: Unevenness of growth and its relation to vulnerability, anxiety, ego weakness, and the schizophrenic pattern. *Amer. J. Orthopsychiat.,* 1957, **27,** 577–586.

(135) HELPER, M. M.: Learning theory and the self-concept. *J. abnorm. soc. Psychol.,* 1955, **51,** 184–194.

(136) HILLSON, J. S., and P. WORCHEL: Self-concept and defensive behavior in the maladjusted. *J. consult. Psychol.,* 1957, **21,** 83–88.

(137) HIRSCH, W.: The image of the scientist in science fiction: a content analysis. *Amer. J. Sociol.,* 1958, **63,** 506–512.

(138) HOLLINGWORTH, L. S.: Personality and adjustment as determiners and correlates of intelligence. *39th Yearb. Nat. Soc. Stud. Educ.,* 1940, 271–275.

(139) HOULT, T. F.: Experimental measurement of clothing as a factor in some social ratings of selected American men. *Amer. sociol. Rev.,* 1954, **19,** 324–328.

(140) HOUSTON, T. J., and F. C. SUMNER: Measurements of neurotic tendency in women with uncommon given names. *J. genet. Psychol.,* 1948, **39,** 289–292.

(141) HUNT, L. A.: A developmental study of factors related to children's clothing preferences. *Monogr. Soc. Res. Child Develpm.,* 1959, **24,** No. 1, 3–47.

(142) JACK, L. M.: An experimental study of ascendant behavior in preschool children. *Univ. Iowa Stud. child Welf.,* 1934, **9,** No. 3.

(143) JAHODA, G.: Development of the perception of social differences in children from six to ten. *Brit. J. Psychol.,* 1959, **50,** 159–175.

(144) JERSILD, A. T.: Self-understanding in childhood and adolescence. *Amer. Psychologist,* 1951, **6,** 122–126.

(145) JERSILD, A. T.: *In search of self.* New York: Teachers College, Columbia University, 1952.

(146) JERSILD, A. T.: *Child psychology,* 5th ed. Englewood Cliffs, N.J.: Prentice-Hall, 1960.

(147) JONES, H.: Maintenance of mental health. *Ment. Hlth, London,* 1951, **10,** 40–42.

(148) JONES, M. C.: The later careers of boys

who were early- or late-maturing. *Child Develpm.*, 1957, **28**, 113–128.

(149) JOSSELYN, I. M.: The family as a psychological unit. *Soc. Casewk*, 1953, **34**, 336–344.

(150) JOURARD, S. M., and R. M. REMY: Perceived parental attitude, the self, and security. *J. consult. Psychol.*, 1955, **19**, 364–366.

(151) JOURARD, S. M., and P. F. SECORD: Body-cathexis and the ideal female figure. *J. abnorm. soc. Psychol.*, 1955, **50**, 243–246.

(152) JUSTIN, F.: Home training in human values. *J. home Econ.*, 1950, **47**, 722.

(153) KAGAN, J., and H. A. MOSS: The stability of passive and dependent behavior from childhood through adolescence. *Child Develpm.*, 1960, **31**, 577–591.

(154) KAGAN, J., and H. A. MOSS: *Birth to maturity: a study in psychological development.* New York: Wiley, 1962.

(155) KAGAN, J., L. M. SONTAG, C. T. BAKER, and V. L. NELSON: Personality and IQ change. *J. abnorm. soc. Psychol.*, 1958, **56**, 261–266.

(156) KAHL, J. A.: Educational and occupational aspirations of "common man" boys. *Harv. educ. Rev.*, 1953, **23**, 186–203.

(157) KAUSLAR, D. H.: Aspiration level as a determinant of performance. *J. Pers.*, 1959, **27**, 346–351.

(158) KELLY, E. L.: Consistency of the adult personality. *Amer. Psychologist*, 1955, **10**, 659–681.

(159) KLATSKIN, E. H., E. B. JACKSON, and L. C. WILKIN: The influence of degree of flexibility in maternal child care practices on early child behavior. *Amer. J. Orthopsychiat.*, 1956, **26**, 79–93.

(160) KLAUSNER, S. Z.: Social class and self-concept. *J. soc. Psychol.*, 1953, **38**, 201–205.

(161) KLINEBERG, O.: Cultural factors in personality adjustment of children. *Amer. J. Orthopsychiat.*, 1953, **33**, 465–471.

(162) KOCH, H. L.: The relation of certain formal attributes of siblings to attitudes held toward each other and toward their parents. *Monogr. Soc. Res. Child Develpm.*, 1960, **25**, No. 4.

(163) KOHN, M. L.: Social class and parental values. *Amer. J. Sociol.*, 1959, **64**, 337–351.

(164) KOPPITZ, E. M.: Relationships between some background factors and children's interpersonal attitudes. *J. genet. Psychol.*, 1957, **91**, 119–129.

(165) LAIRD, D. C.: How eleven-year-old boys see their teachers. *Prog. Educ.*, 1956, **33**, 115–118.

(166) LANDIS, J. T.: Personality: a 1954 view. *J. home Econ.*, 1954, **46**, 459–462.

(167) LANTZ, B.: Children's learning, personality, and physiological interactions. *Calif. J. educ. Res.*, 1956, **7**, 153–158.

(168) LANTZ, H. R.: Number of childhood friends as reported in the life histories of a psychiatrically diagnosed group of 1,000. *Marriage fam. Liv.*, 1956, **18**, 107–109.

(169) LASSWELL, T. E.: Social class and stereotyping. *Sociol. soc. Res.*, 1958, **42**, 256–262.

(170) LAWSON, R., and M. H. MARX: Frustration: theory and experiment. *Genet. Psychol. Monogr.*, 1958, **57**, 393–464.

(171) LAWTON, G.: *Aging successfully.* New York: Columbia, 1951.

(172) LAYCOCK, S. R.: Counseling parents of gifted children. *Except. Children*, 1956, **23**, 108–110, 134.

(173) LECKY, P.: *Self-consistency.* New York: Island Press, 1951.

(174) LIDDLE, G.: Overlap among desirable and undesirable characteristics in gifted children. *J. educ. Psychol.*, 1958, **49**, 219–223.

(175) LIPSET, S. M.: Constant values in American society. *Children*, 1959, **6**, 219–224.

(176) LIPSITT, L. P.: A self-concept scale for children and its relationship to the children's form of the manifest anxiety scale. *Child Develpm.*, 1958, **29**, 463–472.

(177) LUFT, J.: Monetary value and the perception of persons. *J. soc. Psychol.*, 1957, **46**, 245–251.

(178) LUND, F. H.: Biodynamics as Freudian psychodynamics. *Education*, 1957, **78**, 41–54.

(179) MACFARLANE, J., L. ALLEN, and M. P. HONZIK: *A developmental study of the behavior problems of normal children between twenty-one months and fourteen years.* Berkeley, Calif.: University of California Press, 1954.

(180) MACY, I. G., and H. J. KELLY: Body composition in childhood. *Hum. Biol.*, 1956, **28**, 283–308.

(181) MALONE, A. J., and M. MASSLER: Index of nail-biting in children. *J. abnorm. soc. Psychol.*, 1952, **47**, 193–202.

(182) MALPASS, L. F.: Some relationships between students' perceptions of school and their achievement. *J. educ. Psychol.*, 1953, **44**, 475–482.

(183) MANGUS, A. R.: Personality adjustments of rural and urban children. *Amer. sociol. Rev.*, 1948, **13**, 566–575.

(184) MANN, H.: How *real* are friendships of gifted and typical children in a program of partial segregation? *Except. Children*, 1957, **23**, 199–201, 206.

(185) MARGOLES, M. S.: Mental disorders in childhood due to endocrine disorders. *Nerv. Child*, 1948, **7**, 55–77.

(186) MARKS, R. W.: The effect of probability, desirability, and "privilege" on the stated expectations of children. *J. Pers.*, 1951, **19**, 332–351.

(187) MARTIN, W. E.: Learning theory and identification. III. The development of values in children. *J. genet. Psychol.*, 1954, **84**, 211–217.

(188) MARTIN, W. E.: Effects of early training on personality. *Marriage fam. Liv.*, 1957, **19**, 39–45.

(189) MC ARTHUR, C.: Personality differences between middle and upper classes. *J. abnorm. soc. Psychol.*, 1955, **50**, 247–254.

(190) MC GUIRE, C.: Family life in lower and middle class homes. *Marriage fam. Liv.*, 1952, **14**, 1–6.

(191) MC GUIRE, C., and G. D. WHITE, Social-class influences on discipline at school. *Educ. Leadership*, 1957, **14**, 229–231, 234–236.

(192) MC KEACHIE, W. J.: Lipstick as a determiner of first impressions of personality: an experiment for the general psychology course. *J. soc. Psychol.*, 1952, **36**, 241–244.

(193) MC KEE, J. P., and F. B. LEADER: The relationship of sociometric status and aggression to the competitive behavior of pre-school children. *Child Develpm.*, 1955, **26**, 135–142.

(194) MC KINNON, J. K. M.: Consistency and change in behavior manifestations. *Child Develpm. Monogr.*, 1942, No. 30.

(195) MC QUITTY, L. L.: A measure of personality integration in relation to the concept of self. *J. Pers.*, 1950, **18**, 461–462.

(196) MEAD, M.: *Male and female.* New York: Morrow, 1952.

(197) MEAD, M., and R. MÉTRAUX: Image of the scientist among high-school students. *Science*, 1957, **126**, 384–390.

(198) MEDLEY, D. M.: Teacher personality and teacher-pupil rapport. *J. Teach. Educ.*, 1961, **12**, 152–156.

(199) MITCHELL, A. C.: A study of the social competence of a group of institutionalized retarded children. *Amer. J. ment. Defic.*, 1955, **60**, 354–361.

(200) MORE, D. M.: Developmental concordance and discordance during puberty and early adolescence. *Monogr. Soc. Res. Child Develpm.*, 1953, **18**, 1–128.

(201) MORTON, G. M.: Psychology of dress. *J. home Econ.*, 1926, **18**, 584–586.

(202) MOSS, H. A., and J. KAGAN: Stability of achievement and recognition seeking behaviors from early childhood through adulthood. *J. abnorm. soc. Psychol.*, 1961, **62**, 504–513.

(203) MOULTON, R.: Oral and dental manifestations of anxiety. *Psychiatry*, 1955, **18**, 261–273.

(204) MOUSTAKAS, C. E.: Emotional adjustment and the play therapy process. *J. genet. Psychol.*, 1955, **86**, 79–99.

(205) MUNN, N. L.: *The evolution and growth of human behavior.* Boston: Houghton Mifflin, 1955.

(206) MURPHY, L. B.: Coping devices and defense mechanisms in relation to autonomous ego functions. *Bull. Menninger Clinic*, 1960, **24**, 144–153.

(207) MURPHY, W. F.: A note on the significance of names. *Psychoanal. Quart.*, 1957, **26**, 91–106.

(208) MUSSEN, P. H., and L. DISTLER: Child-rearing antecedents of masculine identification in kindergarten boys. *Child Develpm.*, 1960, **31**, 89–100.

(209) MUSSEN, P. H., and M. C. JONES: Self-conceptions, motivations, and interpersonal attitudes of late- and early-maturing boys. *Child Develpm.*, 1957, **28**, 243–256.

(210) NAKAMURA, C. Y.: The relationship between children's expressions of hostility and methods of discipline exercised by dominant overprotective parents. *Child Develpm.*, 1959, **30**, 109–117.

(211) NASH, H.: Assignment of gender to body regions. *J. genet. Psychol.*, 1958, **92**, 113–115.

(212) NEILON, P.: Shirley's babies after fifteen years: a personality study. *J. genet. Psychol.*, 1948, **73**, 175–186.

(213) NORMAN, R. D.: The interrelationships among acceptance-rejection, self-other identity, insight into self, and realistic perception of others. *J. soc. Psychol.*, 1953, **37**, 205–235.

(214) O'CONNOR, N.: The evidence for the permanently disturbing effects of mother-child separation. *Acta psychol.*, 1956, **12**, 174–191.

(215) ORGEL, S. Z., and J. TUCKMAN: Nicknames of institutionalized children. *Amer. J. Orthopsychiat.*, 1935, **5**, 276–285.

(216) ORT, R. S.: A study of role-conflicts as related to class level. *J. abnorm. soc. Psychol.*, 1952, **47**, 425–432.

(217) OTIS, N. B., and B. MC CANDLESS: Responses to repeated frustration of young children differentiated according to need area. *J. abnorm. soc. Psychol.*, 1955, **50**, 349–353.

(218) PAGE, M. L.: The modification of ascendant behavior in preschool children. *Univer. Iowa Stud. child Welf.*, 1936, **12**, No. 3.

(219) PARRISH, C. H.: Color names and color notions. *J. Negro Educ.*, 1946, **15**, 13–20.

(220) PAULSEN, A. A.: Personality development in the middle years of childhood: a ten-year longitudinal study of thirty public school children by means of Rorschach tests and social histories. *Amer. J. Orthopsychiat.*, 1954, **24**, 336–350.

(221) PEARL, D.: Ethnocentrism and the self-concept. *J. soc. Psychol.*, 1950, **40**, 137–147.

(222) PELLER, L. E.: Models of children's play. *Ment. Hyg., N. Y.*, 1952, **36**, 66–83.

(223) PERKINS, H. V.: Teachers' and peers' perceptions of children's self-concepts. *Child Develpm.*, 1958, **29**, 203–220.

(224) PERKINS, H. V.: Factors influencing

change in children's self-concepts. *Child Develpm.*, 1958, **29**, 221–230.

(225) PETERSON, D. R.: Behavior problems of middle childhood. *J. consult. Psychol.*, 1961, **25**, 205–209.

(226) PETERSON, D. R., W. C. BECKER, D. J. SHOEMAKER, Z. LURIA, and L. A. HELLMER: Child behavior problems and parental attitudes. *Child Develpm.*, 1961, **32**, 151–162.

(227) PLOTTKE, P.: The child and his name. *Indiv. psychol. Bull.*, 1950, **8**, 150–157.

(228) PODOLSKY, E.: How the child reacts to his physical defects. *Ment. Hyg., N.Y.*, 1953, **37**, 581–584.

(229) POLLOCK, G. H., and J. B. RICHMOND: Nutritional anemia in children. *Psychosom. Med.*, 1953, **15**, 477–484.

(230) POPE, B.: Socio-economic contrasts in children's peer culture values. *Genet. Psychol. Monogr.*, 1953, **48**, 157–220.

(231) PRESSEY, S. L., and R. G. KUHLEN: *Psychological development through the life span.* New York: Harper & Row, 1957.

(232) PROTHRO, E. T.: Cross-cultural patterns of national stereotypes. *J. soc. Psychol.*, 1954, **40**, 53–59.

(233) RABBAN, M.: Sex-role identification in young children in two diverse social groups. *Genet. Psychol. Monogr.*, 1950, **42**, 87–158.

(234) RADKE-YARROW, M., and B. LANDE: Personality correlates of differential reactions to minority group belonging. *J. soc. Psychol.*, 1953, **38**, 253–272.

(235) RAINES, G. N.: Adolescence: pattern for the future. *Geriatrics*, 1956, **11**, 159–162.

(236) RAINWATER, L.: A study of personality differences between middle and lower class adolescents: the Szondi Test in culture-personality research. *Genet. Psychol. Monogr.*, 1956, **54**, 3–86.

(237) READ, K. H.: Clothes help build personality. *J. home Econ.*, 1950, **42**, 348–350.

(238) REESE, H. W.: Relationships between self-acceptance and sociometric choice. *J. abnorm. soc. Psychol.*, 1961, **62**, 472–474.

(239) REISSMAN, L.: Levels of aspiration and social class. *Amer. sociol. Rev.*, 1953, **18**, 233–242.

(240) RHEINGOLD, H. L.: The measurement of maternal care. *Child Develpm.*, 1960, **31**, 565–576.

(241) RHODES, I. G.: Allergic causes of emotional disturbances in children. *Nerv. Child*, 1952, **9**, 369–377.

(242) RICH, G. G.: Childhood as a preparation for delinquency. *J. educ. Sociol.*, 1954, **27**, 404–413.

(243) RINGNESS, T. A.: Self-concepts of children of low, average, and high intelligence. *Amer. J. ment. Defic.*, 1961, **65**, 453–461.

(244) ROBERTS, K. E., and V. V. FLEMING: Persistence and change in personality patterns. *Monogr. Soc. Res. Child Develpm.*, 1944, **8**, No. 3.

(245) ROBINOWITZ, R.: Attitudes of pupils achieving beyond their level of expectancy. *J. Pers.*, 1956, **24**, 308–317.

(246) ROBINS, L. N., and P. O'NEAL: Mortality, mobility, and crime: problem children thirty years later. *Amer. sociol. Rev.*, 1958, **23**, 162–171.

(247) ROFF, M.: Intra-family resemblances in personality characteristics. *J. Psychol.*, 1950, **30**, 199–227.

(248) ROGERS, C. R.: Some observations on the organization of personality. *Amer. Psychologist*, 1947, **2**, 358–368.

(249) ROSEN, B. C.: Race, ethnicity, and the achievement syndrome. *Amer. sociol. Rev.*, 1959, **24**, 47–60.

(250) ROSENZWEIG, S., and L. ROSENZWEIG: Aggression in problem children and normals as evaluated by the Rosenzweig Picture-Frustration Study. *J. abnorm. soc. Psychol.*, 1952, **47**, 683–688.

(251) RUSSELL, D. H.: What does research say about self-evaluation? *J. educ. Res.*, 1953, **46**, 561–573.

(252) RUSSELL, I. L.: Behavior problems of children from broken and intact homes. *J. educ. Sociol.*, 1957, **31**, 127–129.

(253) RYAN, M. E.: Social adjustment of kindergarten children ten years later. *Smith Coll. Stud. soc. Wk*, 1949, **19**, 138–139.

(254) SANFORD, N., H. WEBSTER, and M. FREEDMAN: Impulse expression as a variable of personality. *Psychol. Monogr.*, 1957, **71**, No. 11.

(255) SARASON, S. B.: Mentally retarded and mentally defective children: major psychosocial problems. In W. M. Cruickshank, *Psychology of exceptional children and youth.* Englewood Cliffs, N.J.: Prentice-Hall, 1955. Pp. 438–474.

(256) SARASON, S. B., K. DAVIDSON, F. LIGHTHALL, and R. WAITE: Rorschach behavior and performance of high and low anxious children. *Child Develpm.*, 1958, **29**, 277–285.

(257) SARASON, S. B., and T. GLADWIN: Psychological and cultural problems in mental subnormality: a review of research. *Genet. Psychol. Monogr.*, 1957, **57**, 3–290.

(258) SARBIN, T. R.: A preface to a psychological analysis of the self. *Psychol. Rev.*, 1952, **59**, 11–22.

(259) SAVAGE, B. M., and F. L. WELLS: A note on singularity in given names. *J. soc. Psychol.*, 1948, **27**, 271–272.

(260) SCHAEFER, E. S., and R. G. BELL: Development of a parental attitude research instrument. *Child Develpm.*, 1958, **29**, 339–361.

(261) SCHAIE, K. W.: Differences in some characteristics of "rigid" and "flexible" individuals. *J. clin. Psychol.*, 1958, **14**, 11–14.

(262) SCHIFF, H.: Judgmental response sets in the perception of sociometric status. *Sociometry*, 1954, **17**, 207–227.

(263) SCHNEIDER, D. M., and G. C. HOMANS: Kinship terminology and the American kinship system. *Amer. Anthropologist*, 1955, **57**, 1194–1208.

(264) SCHNEIDERMAN, L.: The estimation of one's own body traits. *J. soc. Psychol.*, 1956, **44**, 89–99.

(265) SCHOEPPE, A.: Sex differences in adolescent socialization. *J. soc. Psychol.*, 1953, **38**, 175–185.

(266) SCHRAMM, W., J. LYLE, and E. B. PARKER: *Television in the lives of our children*. Stanford, Calif.: Stanford University Press, 1961.

(267) SEARS, R. R., E. E. MACCOBY, and H. LEVIN: *Patterns of child rearing*. New York: Harper & Row, 1957.

(268) SECORD, P. F., W. BEVAN, and W. F. DUKES: Occupational and physiognomic stereotyping in the perception of photographs. *J. soc. Psychol.*, 1953, **37**, 261–270.

(269) SEEMAN, M.: The intellectual and the language of minorities. *Amer. J. Sociol.*, 1958, **64**, 25–35.

(270) SEWELL, W. H., and A. O. HALLER: Social status and the personality adjustment of the child. *Sociometry*, 1956, **19**, 114–125.

(271) SHAFFER, L. F., and E. J. SHOBEN: *The psychology of adjustment*, 2d ed. Boston: Houghton Mifflin, 1956.

(272) SHERIF, M., and H. CANTRIL: *The psychology of ego-involvements*. New York: Wiley, 1947.

(273) SHERRIFFS, A. C., and R. F. JARRETT: Sex differences in attitudes about sex differences. *J. Psychol.*, 1953, **35**, 161–168.

(274) SHINN, M. W.: *Notes on the development of a child*. Berkeley, Calif.: University of California Press, 1909.

(275) SHIRLEY, M. M.: The impact of the mother's personality on the young child. *Smith Coll. Stud. soc. Wk*, 1941, **12**, 15–64.

(276) SHUMSKY, A., and W. I. MURRAY: Student teachers explore attitudes toward discipline. *J. teacher Educ.*, 1961, **12**, 453–457.

(277) SIEGEL, A. E.: The influence of violence in the mass media upon children's role expectations. *Child Develpm.*, 1958, **29**, 35–56.

(278) SILLS, F. D., and P. V. EVERETT: The relationship of extreme somatotypes to performance in motor and strength sets. *Res. Quart. Amer. Ass. Hlth Phys. Educ. Recr.*, 1953, **24**, 223–228.

(279) SILVERMAN, S. S.: Clothing and appearance: their psychological implications for teen-age girls. *Teach. Coll. Contr. Educ.*, 1945, No. 912.

(280) SIMPSON, S. L.: Hormones and behavior pattern. *Brit. med. J.*, 1957, **2**, 839–843.

(281) SLOBETZ, F., and A. LUND: Some effects of a personal developmental program at the fifth grade level. *J. educ. Res.*, 1955, **49**, 373–378.

(282) SMITH, A. J.: Similarity of values and its relation to acceptance and the projection of similarity. *J. Psychol.*, 1957, **43**, 251–260.

(283) SMITH, G. H.: Personality scores and the personal distance effect. *J. soc. Psychol.*, 1954, **39**, 57–62.

(284) SMITH, M. E.: A comparison of certain personality traits rated in the same individuals in childhood and fifty years later. *Child Develpm.*, 1952, **23**, 159–180.

(285) SMITH, M. E.: Childhood memories compared with those of adult life. *J. genet. Psychol.*, 1952, **80**, 151–182.

(286) SMITH, W. C.: Remarriage and the stepchild. In M. Fishbein and R. J. R. Kennedy (Eds.), *Modern marriage and family living*. Fair Lawn, N.J.: Oxford University Press, 1957. Pp. 457–475.

(287) SMITH, W. D., and D. LEBO: Some changing aspects of the self-concept of pubescent males. *J. genet. Psychol.*, 1956, **88**, 61–75.

(288) SMOCK, C. D., and G. G. THOMPSON: An inferred relationship between early childhood conflicts and anxiety responses in adult life. *J. Pers.*, 1954, **23**, 88–98.

(289) SOLOMON, J. C.: Neuroses of school teachers. *Ment. Hyg., N.Y.*, 1960, **44**, 79–90.

(290) SONTAG, L. W.: Some psychosomatic aspects of childhood. *Nerv. Child*, 1946, **5**, 296–304.

(291) SONTAG, L. W., C. T. BAKER, and V. L. NELSON: Mental growth and personality development: a longitudinal study. *Monogr. Soc. Res. Child Develpm.*, 1958, **23**, No. 2.

(292) SPOCK, B.: What we know about the development of healthy personalities in children. *Understanding the Child*, 1951, **20**, 2–9.

(293) STAGNER, R.: *Psychology of personality*, 3d ed. New York: McGraw-Hill, 1961.

(294) STAINS, K. B.: Developing independence in children. *Understanding the Child*, 1951, **20**, 49.

(295) STAUDT, V. M.: Character formation is the teacher's business. *Education*, 1957, **77**, 198–202.

(296) STEINER, I. D.: Some social values associated with objectively and subjectively defined social class membership. *Soc. Forces*, 1953, **31**, 327–332.

(297) STENDLER, C. B.: Social class differences in parental attitude toward school at grade 1 level. *Child Develpm.*, 1951, **22**, 37–46.

(298) STENDLER, C. B.: The learning of certain secondary drives by Parisian and American children. *Marriage fam. Liv.*, 1954, **16**, 195–200.

(299) STEVENSON, I.: Is the human personality more plastic in infancy and childhood? *Amer. J. Psychiat.,* 1957, **114,** 152–161.

(300) STEWART, L. H.: Relationship of sociometric status to children's occupational attitudes and interests. *J. genet. Psychol.,* 1959, **95,** 111–136.

(301) STOLZ, H. R.: Shorty comes to terms with himself. *Prog. Educ.,* 1940, **17,** 405–411.

(302) STOLZ, H. R., and L. M. STOLZ: *Somatic development of adolescent boys.* New York: Macmillan, 1951.

(303) STONE, L. J.: A critique of studies of infant isolation. *Child Develpm.,* 1954, **25,** 9–20.

(304) STOODLEY, B. H.: Mother role as focus of some family problems. *Marriage fam. Liv.,* 1952, **14,** 13–16.

(305) STOTT, L. H., and R. S. BALL: Consistency and change in ascendance-submission in the social interaction of children. *Child Develpm.,* 1957, **28,** 259–272.

(306) STOUGHTON, M. L., and A. M. RAY: A study of children's heroes and ideals. *J. exp. Educ.,* 1946, **15,** 156–160.

(307) STOUT, I. W., and G. LANGDON: A report on follow-up interviews with parents of well-adjusted children. *J. educ. Sociol.,* 1953, **26,** 434–442.

(308) STRANG, R.: How children and adolescents view their world. *Ment. Hyg., N.Y.,* 1954, **38,** 28–33.

(309) STRANG, R.: Psychology of gifted children and youth. In W. M. Cruickshank, *Psychology of exceptional children and youth.* Englewood Cliffs, N.J.: Prentice-Hall, 1955, Pp. 475–519.

(310) SULLIVAN, C., M. G. GRANT, and J. D. GRANT: The development of interpersonal maturity: applications to delinquency. *Psychiatry,* 1957, **20,** 373–385.

(311) SYMONDS, P. M.: Essentials of good parent-child relations. *Teach. Coll. Rec.,* 1949, **50,** 528–538.

(312) SYMONDS, P. M.: Pupil evaluation and self evaluation. *Teach. Coll. Rec.,* 1952, **54,** 138–149.

(313) TANNENBAUM, A. S.: Personality change as a result of an experimental change of environmental conditions. *J. abnorm. soc. Psychol.,* 1957, **55,** 404–406.

(314) TAYLOR, C., and A. W. COMBS: Self-acceptance and adjustment. *J. consult. Psychol.,* 1952, **16,** 89–91.

(315) TAYLOR, D. M.: Changes in the self concept without psychotherapy. *J. consult. Psychol.,* 1955, **19,** 205–209.

(316) TEAGARDEN, F. M.: *Child psychology for professional workers,* rev. ed. Englewood Cliffs, N.J.: Prentice-Hall, 1946.

(317) TERMAN, L. M.: The discovery and encouragement of exceptional talent. *Amer. Psychologist,* 1954, **9,** 221–230.

(318) THISTLEWAITE, D. L.: Effects of social recognition upon the educational motivation of talented youth. *J. educ. Psychol.,* 1959, **50,** 111–116.

(319) THOMPSON, C.: Concepts of the self in interpersonal theory. *Amer. J. Psychother.,* 1958, **12,** 5–17.

(320) THOMPSON, G. G.: *Child psychology,* 2d ed. Boston: Houghton Mifflin, 1962.

(321) THOMPSON, G. G., and S. L. WITRYOL: Adult recall of unpleasant experiences during three periods of childhood. *J. genet. Psychol.,* 1948, **72,** 111–123.

(322) THORPE, L. P.: *Child psychology and development,* 2d ed. New York: Ronald, 1955.

(323) TOPP, R. F.: Preadolescent behavior patterns suggestive of emotional malfunctioning. *Elem. Sch. J.,* 1952, **52,** 340–343.

(324) TORRANCE, E. P.: Some practical uses of a knowledge of self-concepts in counseling and guidance. *Educ. psychol. Measmt,* 1954, **14,** 120–127.

(325) TRIPPE, M. J.: The social psychology of exceptional children: factors in society. *Except. Children,* 1959, **26,** 171–175, 188.

(326) TRYON, C., and W. E. HENRY: How children learn personal and social adjustment. *49th Yearb. Nat. Soc. Stud. Educ.,* 1950, Pt. 1, 156–182.

(327) TUCKMAN, J., and I. LORGE: The best years of life: a study in ranking. *J. Psychol.,* 1952, **34,** 137–149.

(328) TUCKMAN, J., and I. LORGE: The projection of personal symptom into stereotype about aging. *J. Geront.,* 1958, **13,** 70–73.

(329) TUDDENHAM, R. D.: The constancy of personality ratings over two decades. *Genet. Psychol. Monogr.,* 1959, **60,** 3–29.

(330) TYERMAN, M. J.: A research into truancy. *Brit. J. educ. Psychol.,* 1958, **28,** 217–225.

(331) ULLMANN, C. A.: Identification of maladjusted school children. *Pub. Hlth Monogr.,* 1952, No. 7.

(332) UPDEGRAFF, R., and M. E. KEISTER: A study of children's reactions to failure and an experimental attempt to modify them. *Univer. Iowa Stud. Child Welf.,* 1937, **13,** No. 4.

(333) UGURAL-SEMIN, R.: Moral behavior and moral judgments of children. *J. abnorm. soc. Psychol.,* 1952, **47,** 463–474.

(334) WALDFOGEL, S.: The frequency and affective character of childhood memories. *Psychol. Monogr.,* 1948, **62,** No. 4.

(335) WALSH, A. M.: *Self-concepts of bright boys with learning difficulties.* New York: Teachers College, Columbia University, 1956.

(336) WALTER, L. M., and S. S. MARZOLF: The relation of sex, age, and school achievement

to levels of aspiration. *J. educ. Psychol.,* 1951, **42,** 285–292.

(337) WANG, J. D.: The relationship between children's play interests and their mental ability. *J. genet. Psychol.,* 1958, **93,** 119–131.

(338) WATSON, G.: Some personality differences in children related to strict or permissive parental discipline. *J. Psychol.,* 1957, **44,** 227–249.

(339) WEINGARTEN, S.: Reading as a source of the ideal self. *Read. Teacher,* 1955, **8,** 159–164.

(340) WEINSTEIN, E. A.: Children's conceptions of occupational stratification. *Sociol. soc. Res.,* 1958, **42,** 278–284.

(341) WELLS, F. L., and H. R. PALWICK: Note on usage of male personal names. *J. soc. Psychol.,* 1950, **31,** 291–294.

(342) WENAR, C.: The effects of a motor handicap on personality. II. The effects on integrative ability. *Child Develpm.,* 1954, **25,** 287–294.

(343) WHITING, J. W. M., and I. L. CHILD: *Child training and personality: a cross cultural study.* New Haven, Conn.: Yale, 1953.

(334) WHITLEY, H. E.: Mental health problems in the classroom. *Understanding the Child,* 1954, **23,** 98–103.

(345) WINGFIELD, R. C.: Bernreuter personality ratings of college students who recall having had imaginary playmates during childhood. *J. child Psychiat.,* 1948, **1,** 90–94.

(346) WINKER, J. B.: Age trends and sex differences in the wishes, identifications, activities, and fears of children. *Child Develpm.,* 1949, **20,** 191–200.

(347) WINKLEY, R., K. JACKSON, O. A. FAUST, M. F. MURRAY, and E. G. CERMAK: Emotional reactions and behavior of children in the home. *J. Pediat.,* 1951, **38,** 476–481.

(348) WOLFF, H.: Obesity in childhood: a study of the birth weight, the height, and the onset of puberty. *Quart. J. Med.,* 1955, **24,** 109–123.

(349) WOODWORTH, R. S., and D. G. MARQUIS: *Psychology,* 5th ed. New York: Holt, 1947.

(350) WOOLLEY, H. T.: Agnes: a dominant personality in the making. *J. genet. Psychol.,* 1925, **32,** 569–598.

(351) WORRELL, L.: Level of aspiration and academic success. *J. educ. Psychol.,* 1959, **50,** 47–54.

(352) ZANDER, A., and E. VAN EGMOND: Relationship of intelligence and social power to the interpersonal behavior of children. *J. educ. Psychol.,* 1958, **49,** 257–268.

(353) ZIMMERMAN, K. A., and E. LEWTON: Teacher personality in school relationships. *Educ. Leadership,* 1951, **8,** 422–428.

(354) ZUK, G. H.: The influence of social context on impulse and control tendencies in preadolescents. *Genet. Psychol. Monogr.,* 1956, **54,** 117–166.

(355) ZUNICH, M.: Relationship between maternal behavior and attitudes toward children. *J. genet. Psychol.,* 1962, **100,** 155–165.

Index